Sociology: A Down-to-Earth Approach

I took Sociology courses in high school and none have made as much sense as this text.

I found it extremely fascinating, well organized, easy to read, and most of all, interesting.

Thanks for your dedication to making the field of sociology more exciting to learn about.

It was a pleasure to read your work. I felt as though I became acquainted with you through your words.

Thank you again for your fine book. My college education would not have been complete without this course.

I have used this text in most of my subsequent classes.

"Dear Professor Henslin..."

The following are excerpts from letters and emails to Jim Henslin from students who have used various versions and editions of *Sociology: A Down-to-Earth Approach*.

Hi Mr. Henslin,
I hope this is still your email address. I am a student at Greenville Technical College in Greenville, South Carolina. I am currently taking Introduction to Sociology here at Tech and I must tell you, your book rocks!!!! It is the most fun I have ever had reading any textbook in my life!

Sincerely,
Kim B

Dear Professor Henslin,
I am a student at Stony Brook University in New York and I'm working toward a major in Sociology. I just completed an introductory summer course in Sociology that was taught with your textbook. I found your book to be incredibly interesting—so much that I am now reading the chapters we skipped over in class.

Thanks again,
Anna Maria Huertas Kormoski

Mr. Henslin,
I am a student at Texas Pan American University in Edinburg, Texas. I just want to take the time to write and say how much I have enjoyed your book. Not only is it very simple to understand, it is also very interesting. I was reluctant to take the class but through the text, I enjoy the class so much more.

Sincerely,
Julissa Rodriguez

Dear Mr. Henslin,
My name is Sydney Conley. I'm a student at Midlands Technical College in Columbia, South Carolina. I'm studying for a test that I have tomorrow in Sociology and I just thought you might like to know that I find your book Essentials of Sociology *very interesting. Thanks to your book, I'm considering continuing my study of Sociology.*

Thanks again
Sydney Conley

Hello Professor Henslin,
My name is Marta Holliday and I am a student at Marymount College in Tarrytown, NY. I am taking Introduction to Sociology at Nassau Community College to earn extra credits and your text was required reading for our class. I just wanted to tell you how much I enjoyed your book. I found the chapters fun and interesting—especially how you opened each with a sketch or a personal vignette.
    It was a pleasure to read your work. I felt as though I became acquainted with you through your words.

Sincerely,
Marta A. Holliday

I am currently a freshman at Dordt College, a liberal arts college in Sioux City, Iowa. I really enjoy your book so far. It is very easy to read and understand. I especially appreciate the "down-to-earthiness" of this book. I have found that I can apply the things I have learned [from your text] to my Psychology 201 class also. Thanks for your dedication to making the field of sociology more exciting to learn about.

Joya Gerritsma

My name is April and I live in West Virginia. I am currently reading the book that you wrote. I took Sociology classes in high school and none have made as much sense as this text. I just thought that I would write and let you know.

Sincerely,
April

Dear James,
Hey there, my name is Leo Chagolla. I attend the University of Toledo and I am a Pharmacy major.
When I registered for classes in the beginning of the fall semester, I was told I would either need to take
sociology or psychology as an elective. To tell you the truth, I only took sociology because I had to—and
it sounded easier than psychology. What I have discovered is that sociology has become one of the most
interesting subjects I have ever studied.

Your book, A Down-to-Earth Approach, *is marvelously well written and constructed. I seriously*
believe that reading your book has made me a better person. I am only one chapter away from completing
the book—my class was only supposed to read on to chapter 9—but I just cannot stop reading.

Leo Chagolla

Hello,
My name is Margaux Strawn and I have just signed up for Sociology 101. I had taken a course on
Sociology in high school many moons ago. I felt very overwhelmed when first reading your textbook,
but as I dug into the book, the reading became very easy and interesting. I would like to thank you
for helping to produce a book that already has me looking up more information on DuBois.

Sociology potential,
Margaux Strawn

Dear Mr. Henslin,
I would like to take a minute to write you a brief letter expressing my gratitude for your most interesting
and enlightening book. I have just begun my exploration into the world of sociology. With the help of
your book, and my college professor, you have helped to educate me in a discipline that was foreign to
me. I was unaware of the possibilities available to sociology majors, and after researching I have found
this is definitely the field for me!

Sincerely,
Katie Bailey

Dr. James Henslin,
I had acquired Essentials of Sociology: A Down-to-Earth Approach *as part of my required liberal arts*
core classes (Sociology 101) at Marquette University. I am now in the middle of my senior year and
would like to tell you that I have used this text in most of the subsequent classes that I enrolled in after
that class.

I want to thank you for helping the rest of my educational journey to be a pleasant one. It may also
interest you to know that I am an adult learner at age 41, who returned to college after 18 years of
factory work.

Doug Bulson
East Troy, WI
Marquette University

Dear Mr. Henslin,
I just finished a Sociology class using your text, the fourth edition of Sociology, A Down-to-Earth
Approach. *Tomorrow, I will take my final exam. I just wanted to commend you on this book. I*
found it extremely fascinating, well-organized, easy to read and most of all, interesting.

If you want a profile of some of your readers (students), I am 60 years old, a Catholic writer, author
of four books, and a late bloomer who is just now getting her college education. I will graduate in August
from Ottawa U. with a degree in Religion and a concentration on Psychology.

Thank you again for your fine book. My college education would not have been complete without
this course.

Sincerely,
Judy Esway
Mesa, AZ

Dear Mr. Henslin,
I just completed an Introduction to Sociology course at my local college (Lansing Community College
in Lansing, Michigan). It was great! I especially enjoyed reading your textbook. It is one of the best
textbooks I've come across yet! It was very engaging and easy to follow with current events which
I could relate to.

Sincerely,
Julie Markham

Sociology

Sociology A DOWN-TO-EARTH APPROACH

SIXTH EDITION

James M. Henslin Southern Illinois University, Edwardsville

Boston   New York   San Francisco
Mexico City   Montreal   Toronto   London   Madrid   Munich   Paris
Hong Kong   Singapore   Tokyo   Cape Town   Sydney

Editor-in-Chief, Social Sciences: Karen Hanson
Series Editor: Jeff Lasser
Editorial Assistant: Andrea Christie
Cover Administrator: Linda Knowles
Composition and Prepress Buyer: Linda Cox
Manufacturing Buyer: Megan Cochran
Marketing Manager: Judeth Hall
Signing Representative: Ward Moore
Photo Researcher: Myrna Engler
Fine Art Researcher: Laurie Frankenthaler
Editorial-Production Service: The Book Company
Text Designer: Deborah Schneck
Electronic Composition: Omegatype Typography, Inc.

For related titles and support materials, visit our online catalog at www.ablongman.com

Cataloging-in-Publication Data not available at time of publication
ISBN 0–205–35224–3

Printed in the United States of America
10 9 8 7 6 5 6 5 4 3 2   VHP   07 06 05 04 03

Chapter Opener Art Credits:

Chapter 1: *Second Circle Dance* by Phoebe Beasley, 1987. Collage, 36" × 36". © Phoebe Beasley/Omni-Photo Communications.

Chapter 2: *Robed Journey of the Rainbow Clan* by Helen Hardin, 1976. Acrylic. © Helen Hardin 1976. Photo © Cradoc Bagshaw 2003.

Chapter 3: *Story Teller* by Velino Shije Herrera, ca. 1925–1935. Gouache and pencil on paperboard, 10 1/16" × 15 1/16". Copyright Smithsonian Art Museum, Washington, DC, U.S.A./Art Resource, NY.

Chapter 4: *Eight Builders* by Jacob Lawrence, 1982. Gouache and tempura on paper, 40 × 52 in. Seattle Arts Commission, Seattle City Light One Percent for Art, Portable Works Collection. Artwork © 2002 Gwendolyn Knight Lawrence, courtesy of The Jacob and Gwendolyn Lawrence Foundation.

Chapter 5: *People* by Diana Ong, 1995. Computer graphics. © Diana Ong/SuperStock.

Chapter 6: *Group of People* by Bernard Bonhomme, 1999. Digital image. © Bernard Bonhomme/SIS.

Chapter 7: *Business City* by Jean-Pierre Stora, 1995. Oil on canvas, 81 × 116 cm. © The Grand Design/SuperStock.

Chapter 8: *Arrest in Washington D.C.* by Franklin McMahon, 1968. Acrylic on paper, 14 × 17 in. © Franklin McMahon/CORBIS.

Chapter 9: *Crossroads Housing Section, Capetown* by Franklin McMahon, 1985. Pen or pencil and acrylic on paper, 22 × 30 in. © Franklin McMahon/CORBIS.

Chapter 10: *Beg* by Graham Dean, 1991. Colored dyes, 71 cm. × 53 cm. © Graham Dean/CORBIS.

Chapter 11: *Women Conversing (Mujeres Conversando)* by Rufino Tamayo, ca. 1926. © Christie's Images/SuperStock. © State of the artist in support of Fundación Olga y Rufino Tamayo, A.C.

Chapter 12: *Many Mansions* by Kerry James Marshall (American, b. 1955), 1994. Acrylic and collage mounted on canvas, 290 × 343 cm. Max V. Kohnstamm Fund, 1995.147. Photo © The Art Institute of Chicago. All Rights Reserved.

Credits continue on page PC-1, which is a continuation of this copyright page.

To my fellow sociologists, who do such creative research on social life and who communicate the sociological imagination to generations of students.

With my sincere admiration and appreciation,

Jim Henslin

Brief Contents

Part I

The Sociological Perspective

Chapter 1   The Sociological Perspective   2

Chapter 2   Culture   37

Chapter 3   Socialization   65

Chapter 4   Social Structure and Social Interaction   97

Chapter 5   How Sociologists Do Research   129

Part II

Social Groups and Social Control

Chapter 6   Societies to Social Networks   155

Chapter 7   Bureaucracy and Formal Organizations   185

Chapter 8   Deviance and Social Control   211

Part III

Social Inequality

Chapter 9   Global Stratification   243

Chapter 10   Social Class in the United States   275

Chapter 11   Sex and Gender   307

Chapter 12   Race and Ethnicity   341

Chapter 13   The Elderly   379

Part IV

Social Institutions

Chapter 14   The Economy   409

Chapter 15   Politics   439

Chapter 16   The Family   467

Chapter 17   Education   503

Chapter 18   Religion   531

Chapter 19   Medicine   563

Part V

Social Change

Chapter 20   Population and Urbanization   597

Chapter 21   Collective Behavior and Social Movements   633

Chapter 22   Social Change and the Environment   665

Contents

To the Student from the Author   xxix
To the Instructor from the Author   xxx

Part I

The Sociological Perspective

1 The Sociological Perspective   1

The Sociological Perspective   2
Seeing the Broader Social Context   2
The Growing Global Context   4

Sociology and the Other Sciences   4
The Natural Sciences   4
The Social Sciences   4
The Goals of Science   6
■ *Down-to-Earth Sociology:* An Updated Version of the Old Elephant Story   6
■ *Down-to-Earth Sociology:* Enjoying a Sociology Quiz—Sociological Findings Versus Common Sense   7

Origins of Sociology   8
Tradition Versus Science   8
Auguste Comte and Positivism   9
Herbert Spencer and Social Darwinism   10
Karl Marx and Class Conflict   11
Emile Durkheim and Social Integration   11
Max Weber and the Protestant Ethic   13

The Role of Values in Social Research   14

Verstehen and Social Facts   15
Weber and *Verstehen*   15
Durkheim and Social Facts   15
How Social Facts and *Verstehen* Fit Together   16

Sexism in Early Sociology   17
Attitudes of the Time   17
Harriet Martineau   17

Sociology in North America   17
Early History: The Tension Between Social Reform and Sociological Analysis   17
Jane Addams and Social Reform   18
W.E.B. Du Bois and Race Relations   18
■ *Down-to-Earth Sociology:* Early North American Sociology: Du Bois and Race Relations   19
Talcott Parsons and C. Wright Mills: Theory Versus Reform   20
The Present: The Continuing Tension and the Rise of Applied Sociology   21
■ *Down-to-Earth Sociology:* Careers in Sociology: What Applied Sociologists Do   22
■ *Down-to-Earth Sociology:* Sociology or Social Work? Taking Back Children from the Night   23

Theoretical Perspectives in Sociology   23
Symbolic Interactionism   24
Functional Analysis   27
Conflict Theory   30
Levels of Analysis: Macro and Micro   31
Putting the Theoretical Perspectives Together   32

Trends Shaping the Future of Sociology   32

Summary and Review   34

2 Culture   37

What Is Culture?   39
Culture and Taken-for-Granted Orientations to Life   39
Practicing Cultural Relativism   41
■ *Cultural Diversity Around the World:* Do You Feel Sorry? Hire an Apology Specialist   42

Components of Symbolic Culture   43
Gestures   43
Language   44
■ *Down-to-Earth Sociology:* Emoticons: "Written Gestures" for Expressing Yourself Online   46
■ *Cultural Diversity in the United States:* Race and Language: Searching for Self Labels   47

■ *Cultural Diversity in the United States:* Miami—
    Language in a Changing City   48
    Values, Norms, and Sanctions   49
    Folkways and Mores   50

Many Cultural Worlds: Subcultures and Countercultures   50

Values in U.S. Society   52
    An Overview of U.S. Values   52
■ *Mass Media in Social Life:* Why Do Native Americans Like Westerns?   53
    Value Clusters   55
    Value Contradictions and Social Change   55
    Emerging Values   55
    Culture Wars: When Values Clash   56
    Values as Blinders   57
    "Ideal" Versus "Real" Culture   57

Cultural Universals   57
■ *Thinking Critically:* Are We Prisoners of Our Genes? Sociobiology and Human Behavior   58
    Animals and Language   59

Technology in the Global Village   60
    The New Technology   60
    Cultural Lag and Cultural Change   60
    Technology and Cultural Leveling   61

Summary and Review   62

3   Socialization   65

What Is Human Nature?   66
    Feral Children   66
    Isolated Children   66
■ *Down-to-Earth Sociology:* Heredity or Environment? The Case of Oskar and Jack, Identical Twins   67
    Institutionalized Children   68
    Deprived Animals   69

Socialization into the Self, Mind, and Emotions   70
    Cooley and the Looking-Glass Self   70
    Mead and Role Taking   71
    Piaget and the Development of Reasoning Skills   72
    Kohlberg and the Development of Morality   73
    Gilligan and Gender Differences in Morality   74
    Global Aspects of the Self, Reasoning, and Morality   74
    Freud and the Development of Personality   74
    Socialization into Emotions   75
■ *Down-to-Earth Sociology:* Signs of the Times: Are We Becoming Ik?   77
    The Self and Emotions as Social Control: Society Within Us   77

Socialization into Gender   78
    Gender Messages in the Family   78

    Gender Messages in the Mass Media   79
■ *Mass Media in Social Life:* From Xena, Warrior Princess, to Lara Croft, Tomb Raider: Changing Images of Women in the Mass Media   80

Agents of Socialization   81
    The Family   81
    The Neighborhood   82
    Religion   83
    Day Care   83
    The School   84
■ *Cultural Diversity in the United States:* Caught Between Two Worlds   84
    Peer Groups   85
    Sports   86
■ *Sociology and the New Technology:* Would Bionic Men and Women Be Fair in Sports? The Question of Genetic Engineering   87
    The Workplace   87

Resocialization   88
    Total Institutions   88
■ *Down-to-Earth Sociology:* Boot Camp as a Total Institution   89

Socialization through the Life Course   90
    Childhood   90
    Adolescence   91
    Young Adulthood   91
    The Middle Years   92
    The Older Years   92
    The Sociological Significance of the Life Course   93

Are We Prisoners of Socialization?   93

Summary and Review   94

4   Social Structure and Social Interaction   97

Levels of Sociological Analysis   98
    Macrosociology and Microsociology   98

The Macrosociological Perspective: Social Structure   99
    The Sociological Significance of Social Structure   99
    Culture   100
■ *Down-to-Earth Sociology:* College Football as Social Structure   101
    Social Class   101
    Social Status   101
    Roles   103
    Groups   104

Social Institutions   104
    The Sociological Significance of Social Institutions   106

The Mass Media as an Emerging
Social Institution   106
Comparing Functionalist and Conflict Perspectives   106
Changes in Social Structure   108
What Holds Society Together?   108
■ *Cultural Diversity in the United States:*
The Amish—*Gemeinschaft* Community
in a *Gesellschaft* Society   110

**The Microsociological Perspective: Social Interaction
in Everyday Life   111**
Symbolic Interaction   111
Dramaturgy: The Presentation of Self in Everyday
Life   115
■ *Mass Media in Social Life:* You Can't Be Thin Enough:
Body Images and the Mass Media   118
Ethnomethodology: Uncovering Background
Assumptions   120
The Social Construction of Reality   122

**The Need for Both Macrosociology and
Microsociology   124**

Summary and Review   125

4. Formulating a Hypothesis   132
5. Choosing a Research Method   132
6. Collecting the Data   132
7. Analyzing the Results   133
8. Sharing the Results   133

Research Methods   135
Surveys   135
■ *Down-to-Earth Sociology:* Loading the Dice: How *Not*
to Do Research   138
Participant Observation (Fieldwork)   139
Secondary Analysis   140
Documents   140
Unobtrusive Measures   141
Experiments   141
Deciding Which Method to Use   143
■ *Down-to-Earth Sociology:* The Hawthorne
Experiments   144
■ *Down-to-Earth Sociology:* Applied Sociology:
Marketing Research as a Blend of Quantitative
and Qualitative Methods   145
■ *Thinking Critically:* Doing Controversial Research—
Counting the Homeless   145

Gender in Sociological Research   147

Ethics in Sociological Research   148
Protecting the Subjects: The Brajuha Research   148
Misleading the Subjects: The Humphreys
Research   149

How Research and Theory Work Together   150
The Real World: When the Ideal Meets the
Real   150
■ *Thinking Critically:* Are Rapists Sick? A Close-Up View
of Research   150

Summary and Review   152

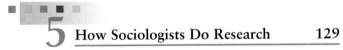

5 How Sociologists Do Research   129

What Is a Valid Sociological Topic?   130

**Common Sense and the Need for Sociological
Research   130**

A Research Model   131
1. Selecting a Topic   131
2. Defining the Problem   131
3. Reviewing the Literature   132

Part II

Social Groups and Social Control

6 Societies to Social Networks   155

Social Groups and Societies   156

The Transformation of Societies   157
Hunting and Gathering Societies   158
Pastoral and Horticultural Societies   159
Agricultural Societies   160
Industrial Societies   160
Postindustrial (Information) Societies   162

Bioeconomic Societies: An Emerging New Type
of Society?   162
■ *Sociology and the New Technology:* "So, You
Want to Be Yourself?" Cloning in the Coming
Bioeconomy   163

Groups Within Society   164
Primary Groups   164
Secondary Groups   165
In-Groups and Out-Groups   166
Reference Groups   168
Social Networks   169

Cultural Diversity in the United States: How Our Social Networks Perpetuate Social Inequality   171
A New Group: Electronic Communities   171
■ *Sociology and the New Technology:* Electronic Communities: Cybercommunications and Our Changing Culture   172

Group Dynamics   172
Effects of Group Size on Stability and Intimacy   173
Effects of Group Size on Attitudes and Behavior   175
Leadership   176
The Power of Peer Pressure: The Asch Experiment   178
■ *Thinking Critically:* If Hitler Asked You to Execute a Stranger, Would You? The Milgram Experiment   179
Global Consequences of Group Dynamics   181

Summary and Review   182

7 Bureaucracy and Formal Organizations   185

The Rationalization of Society   186
Why Did Society Change?   186
Marx: Capitalism Broke Tradition   188
Weber: Religion Broke Tradition   188

Formal Organizations and Bureaucracy   189
Formal Organizations   189
The Characteristics of Bureaucracies   190
■ *Down-to-Earth Sociology:* The McDonaldization of Society   193
"Ideal" Versus "Real" Bureaucracy   193
Dysfunctions of Bureaucracies   194
The Perpetuation of Bureaucracies   195
The Sociological Significance of Bureaucracies   196

Voluntary Associations   197
Functions of Voluntary Associations   197
Shared Interests   198
The Problem of Oligarchy   198

Working for the Corporation   200
The "Hidden" Corporate Culture   200
■ *Thinking Critically:* Managing Diversity in the Workplace   201

Humanizing the Corporate Culture   202
Attempts to Humanize the Work Setting   202
The Conflict Perspective   204
Technology and the Control of Workers   204
■ *Sociology and the New Technology:* Cyberslackers and Cybersleuths: Surfing at Work   205

U.S. and Japanese Corporations   206

How the Corporations Differ   206
The Myth Versus Reality   207
■ *Cultural Diversity Around the World:* Japanese and U.S. Corporations in an Age of Greed   208

Summary and Review   208

8 Deviance and Social Control   211

What Is Deviance?   212
■ *Cultural Diversity Around the World:* Human Sexuality in Cross-Cultural Perspective   213
How Norms Make Social Life Possible   213
Sanctions   214
Shaming and Degradation Ceremonies   214
■ *Thinking Critically:* Is It Rape, Or Is It Marriage? A Study in Culture Clash   215
Competing Explanations of Deviance: Sociology, Biology, and Psychology   216

The Symbolic Interactionist Perspective   217
Differential Association Theory   217
Control Theory   219
Labeling Theory   220
■ *Mass Media in Social Life:* Pornography on the Internet: Freedom Versus Censorship   223

The Functionalist Perspective   224
Can Deviance Really Be Functional for Society?   224
Strain Theory: How Social Values Produce Deviance   224
Illegitimate Opportunity Structures: Social Class and Crime   226
■ *Down-to-Earth Sociology:* Islands in the Street: Urban Gangs in the United States   227

The Conflict Perspective   229

Class, Crime, and the Criminal Justice System   229
Power and Inequality   230
The Law as an Instrument of Oppression   230

Reactions to Deviance   231
Street Crime and Prisons   231
■ *Thinking Critically:* "Three Strikes and You're Out!" Unintended Consequences of Well-Intended Laws   233
The Death Penalty   234
Legal Change   235
■ *Thinking Critically:* Changing Views: Making Hate a Crime   235
The Trouble with Official Statistics   236
The Medicalization of Deviance: Mental Illness   237
The Need for a More Humane Approach   239

Summary and Review   239

Part III
Social Inequality

9 Global Stratification 243

Systems of Social Stratification 245
Slavery 245
■ *Mass Media in Social Life:* What Price Freedom?
Slavery Today 248
Caste 249
Estate 250
Class 251
Global Stratification and the Status of Females 252

What Determines Social Class? 252
Karl Marx: The Means of Production 252
Max Weber: Property, Prestige, and Power 253

Why Is Social Stratification Universal? 254
The Functionalist Perspective: Motivating Qualified
People 254
The Conflict Perspective: Class Conflict and Scarce
Resources 255
Lenski's Synthesis 256

How Do Elites Maintain Stratification? 257
Ideology Versus Force 257

Comparative Social Stratification 258
Social Stratification in Great Britain 258
Social Stratification in the Former Soviet Union 259

Global Stratification: Three Worlds 260
The Most Industrialized Nations 261
The Industrializing Nations 261
■ *Thinking Critically:* Open Season: Children as Prey 264
The Least Industrialized Nations 265
Modifying the Model 265

How the World's Nations Became Stratified 266
Colonialism 266
World System Theory 267
■ *Thinking Critically:* When Globalization Comes Home:
Maquiladoras South of the Border 268
Culture of Poverty 270
Evaluating the Theories 270

Maintaining Global Stratification 270
Neocolonialism 270
Multinational Corporations 271
Technology and Global Domination 271

A Concluding Note 272

Summary and Review 272

10 Social Class in the United States 275

What Is Social Class? 276
Wealth 276
■ *Down-to-Earth Sociology:* How the Super-Rich Live 280
Power 280
Prestige 281
Status Inconsistency 283

Sociological Models of Social Class 284
Updating Marx 284
Updating Weber 285
Social Class in the Automobile Industry 288

Consequences of Social Class 288
Physical Health 289
Mental Health 290
Family Life 290
Education 290
■ *Down-to-Earth Sociology:* Can Money Buy
Happiness? 291
Religion 292
Politics 292
Crime and the Criminal Justice System 292
Social Class and the New Technology 292
■ *Sociology and the New Technology:* Closing the
Digital Divide: The Technology Gap Facing the Poor
and Minorities 293

Social Mobility 294
Three Types of Social Mobility 294
Women in Studies on Social Mobility 294
The Pain of Social Mobility 295

Poverty 295
Drawing the Poverty Line 296
■ *Down-to-Earth Sociology:* Exploring Myths
About the Poor 296
Who Are the Poor? 297
Children of Poverty 299
■ *Thinking Critically:* The Nation's Shame:
Children in Poverty 299
The Dynamics of Poverty 300
Why Are People Poor? 300
■ *Thinking Critically:* The Welfare Debate: The Deserving
and the Undeserving Poor 301
Welfare Reform 301
Deferred Gratification 302
Where Is Horatio Alger? The Social Functions
of a Myth 302

■ *Down-to-Earth Sociology:* Poverty: A Personal
Journey   303

Summary and Review   304

11   Sex and Gender   307

Issues of Sex and Gender   308

Gender Differences in Behavior: Biology or Culture?   309
■ *Thinking Critically:* Biology Versus Culture—Culture Is
the Answer   310
■ *Thinking Critically:* Biology Versus Culture—Biology Is
the Answer   311
The Dominant Position in Sociology   311
Opening the Door to Biology   312

Gender Inequality in Global Perspective   314

Sex Typing of Work   314
Prestige of Work   315
Other Areas of Global Discrimination   315
■ *Cultural Diversity Around the World:* Female
Circumcision   317

How Females Became a Minority Group   318

The Origins of Patriarchy   318
■ *Cultural Diversity Around the World:* "Pssst. You Wanna
Buy a Bride?" China in Transition   318

Gender Inequality in the United States   320

Fighting Back: The Rise of Feminism   320
■ *Down-to-Earth Sociology:* Making the Invisible Visible—
The Deadly Effects of Sexism   322
Gender Inequality in Education   322
Gender Inequality in Everyday Life   325

Gender Inequality in the Workplace   326

The Pay Gap   326
The Glass Ceiling and the Glass Escalator   330
The "Mommy Track"   331
Sexual Harassment   331
■ *Thinking Critically:* Sexual Harassment of Women in the
Military   332

Gender and Violence   333

Feminism and Gendered Violence   335
Solutions   335
■ *Mass Media in Social Life:* Beauty and Pain: How Much
Is an Ad Worth?   336

The Changing Face of Politics   336

Glimpsing the Future—With Hope   337

Summary and Review   338

12   Race and Ethnicity   341

Laying the Sociological Foundation   342

Race: Myth and Reality   342
■ *Cultural Diversity in the United States:* Tiger Woods and
the Emerging Multiracial Identity: Mapping New Ethnic
Terrain   343
■ *Down-to-Earth Sociology:* Common Sense and
Sociology: What Is Race?   344
Ethnic Groups   345
Minority Groups and Dominant Groups   346
How People Construct Their Racial-Ethnic Identity   347
Prejudice and Discrimination   347
■ *Thinking Critically:* Self-Segregation: Help or Hindrance
for Race Relations on Campus?   350
Individual and Institutional Discrimination   350

Theories of Prejudice   352

Psychological Perspectives   352
Sociological Perspectives   353
■ *Mass Media in Social Life:* Preaching Hatred: Crime
or Inalienable Right?   353
■ *Down-to-Earth Sociology:* The Racist Mind   356

Global Patterns of Intergroup Relations   356

Genocide   356
Population Transfer   357
Internal Colonialism   358
Segregation   358
Assimilation   358
Multiculturalism (Pluralism)   358
■ *Cultural Diversity in the United States and Around
the World:* "You Can Work for Us, But You Can't Live
Near Us"   359

Race and Ethnic Relations in the United States   360

White Europeans   361
Latinos   361
African Americans   365
■ *Down-to-Earth Sociology:* What You Reveal by Your
Voice: Racism in the Rental Market   368
■ *Thinking Critically:* Reparations for Slavery: Justice or
Foolishness?   369
Asian Americans   370
Native Americans   371

Looking Toward the Future   374

The Immigration Debate   374
Affirmative Action   374
■ *Cultural Diversity in the United States:* Glimpsing the
Future: The Shifting U.S. Racial-Ethnic Mix   375
Toward a True Multicultural Society   376

Summary and Review   376

13 The Elderly 379

Aging in Global Perspective 380

The Social Construction of Aging 380
Effects of Industrialization 381
The Graying of America 382

The Symbolic Interactionist Perspective 385

Deciding When You Are Old 385
What Does Old Age Mean? 386
Changing Perceptions of the Elderly 387
■ *Cultural Diversity Around the World:* China: Changing Sentiment about the Elderly 388
The Influence of the Mass Media 388
■ *Mass Media in Social Life:* Shaping Our Perceptions of the Elderly 389

The Functionalist Perspective 389

Disengagement Theory 389
Activity Theory 390
Continuity Theory 391

The Conflict Perspective 391

Social Security Legislation 391
Intergenerational Conflict 392

■ *Thinking Critically:* Exploding the Myth of U.S. Budget Surpluses: Can We Pay the Elderly's Social Security Out of Thin Air? 393
■ *Down-to-Earth Sociology:* Changing Sentiment About the U.S. Elderly 393
Fighting Back 396

Problems of Dependency 397

Isolation and Gender 397
Nursing Homes 397
■ *Cultural Diversity Around the World:* Alzheimer's Disease: Lessons from Sweden 399
Elder Abuse 400
The Elderly Poor 400

The Sociology of Death and Dying 402

Industrialization and the New Technology 402
Death as a Process 403
Hospices 403
Suicide and Age 404

Looking Toward the Future 405

■ *Thinking Critically:* How Long Do You Want to Live? Pushing Past the Limits of Biology 405

Summary and Review 406

Part IV

Social Institutions

14 The Economy 409

The Transformation of Economic Systems 410

Preindustrial Societies: The Birth of Inequality 410
Industrial Societies: The Birth of the Machine 411
Postindustrial Societies: The Birth of the Information Age 412
Bioeconomic Societies: The Merger of Biology and Economics 412
■ *Down-to-Earth Sociology:* "Your Name Is What? You Live Where? But You Sound Like You're Right Next Door." 412

The Transformation of the Medium of Exchange 413

Earliest Mediums of Exchange 413

Medium of Exchange in Agricultural Societies 413
Medium of Exchange in Industrial Societies 413
Medium of Exchange in Postindustrial Societies 414

World Economic Systems 415

Capitalism 415
Socialism 417
Ideologies of Capitalism and Socialism 418
■ *Mass Media in Social Life:* Greed Is Good—Selling the American Dream 418
Criticisms of Capitalism and Socialism 419
The Convergence of Capitalism and Socialism 419
■ *Cultural Diversity Around the World:* No Cash? No Problem! Barter in the Former Soviet Union 420

The Functionalist View of the Globalization of Capitalism 421

The New Global Division of Labor 421

■ *Cultural Diversity Around the World:* Doing Business
in the Global Village 422
Ownership and Management of
   Corporations 422
Functions on a Global Scale 423

**The Conflict View of the Globalization
of Capitalism 423**
The Inner Circle of Corporate Capitalism 423
Interlocking Directorates 425
Global Investing 426

Work in U.S. Society 428
The Decline of Agriculture and the Transition to
   Postindustrial Society 428
Women and Work 428
■ *Down-to-Earth Sociology:* Women in Business:
Maneuvering the Male Culture 430
The Underground Economy 430
Shrinking Paychecks 431
Patterns of Work and Leisure 431

**Facing the Future: Implications of Global
Capitalism 433**
Global Trade: Inequalities and Conflict 433
New Technologies and Downsizing: Utopia or
   Nightmare? 434
■ *Thinking Critically:* What Type of New Society? New
Technology and the Restructuring of
Work 434

Summary and Review 436

15   Politics   439

Micropolitics and Macropolitics 440

Power, Authority, and Violence 440

Authority and Legitimate Violence 441
Traditional Authority 442
Rational-Legal Authority 442
Charismatic Authority 442
Authority as Ideal Type 444
The Transfer of Authority 444

Types of Government 445
Monarchies: The Rise of the State 445
Democracies: Citizenship as a Revolutionary
   Idea 445
■ *Mass Media in Social Life:* Politics and Democracy
in a Technological Society 446
Dictatorships and Oligarchies: The Seizure of Power 447

The U.S. Political System 448
Political Parties and Elections 448
Democratic Systems in Europe 449
Voting Patterns 450
■ *Cultural Diversity in the United States:* The Politics
of Immigrants: Power, Ethnicity, and Social
Class 451
Lobbyists and Special-Interest Groups 452
PACs in U.S. Politics 453

Who Rules the United States? 454
The Functionalist Perspective: Pluralism 454
The Conflict Perspective: The Power Elite, or Ruling
   Class 455
Which View Is Right? 456

**War and Terrorism: A Means to Implement Political
Objectives 456**
Is War Universal? 456
How Common Is War? 456
Why Nations Go to War 457
Costs of War 457
Sowing the Seeds of Future Wars 458
Nuclear, Biological, and Chemical
   Terrorism 458

■ ■ ■ ■ EXPERIENCING SOCIOLOGY *September 11, 2001* ■ ■ ■ ■

9-11, the stunning day that changed the United States. We will only realize
its impact on society and our own lives as time goes on. These photos pick
up some of the highlights of this watershed event. (Page 459)

■ *Sociology and the New Technology:* Technology and
Terrorism 460
War and Dehumanization 460
■ *Down-to-Earth Sociology:* Biological Terrorism 461
A New World Order? 462

■ *Cultural Diversity Around the World:*
Roadblocks in the Path to the New World Order:
The Globalization of Capitalism Versus the
Resurgence of Nationalism 463
Summary and Review 464

16 The Family 467

Marriage and Family in Global Perspective 468
What Is a Family? 468
Common Cultural Themes 470
■ *Cultural Diversity Around the World:* Promoting Gender Equality: Family Life in Sweden 472

Marriage and Family in Theoretical Perspective 472
The Functionalist Perspective: Functions and Dysfunctions 472
The Conflict Perspective: Gender and Power 473
■ *Thinking Critically:* The Second Shift—Strains and Strategies 474
The Symbolic Interactionist Perspective: Gender and the Meanings of Marriage 475

The Family Life Cycle 476
Love and Courtship in Global Perspective 476
■ *Cultural Diversity Around the World:* East Is East and West Is West . . . Love and Arranged Marriage in India 477
Marriage 478
Childbirth 478
Child Rearing 479
The Family in Later Life 481

Diversity in U.S. Families 482
African American Families 482
Latino Families 483
Asian American Families 484
Native American Families 484
One-Parent Families 485
Families Without Children 485
Blended Families 486
Gay and Lesbian Families 486
■ *Sociology and the New Technology:* The Brave New World of High-Tech Reproduction: Where Technology Outpaces Law and Sometimes Common Sense 487

Trends in U.S. Families 488
Postponing Marriage 488
Cohabitation 489
■ *Down-to-Earth Sociology:* "What Do You Mean You Want Us to Live Together?" 490
Unmarried Mothers 491
The Sandwich Generation and Elder Care 491

Divorce and Remarriage 491
Problems in Measuring Divorce 491
Children of Divorce 493
■ *Down-to-Earth Sociology:* You Be the Sociologist: Curious Divorce Patterns 493

The Absent Father and Serial Fatherhood 495
The Ex-Spouses 495
Remarriage 495

Two Sides of Family Life 496
The Dark Side of Family Life: Battering, Child Abuse, Marital Rape, and Incest 496
■ *Down-to-Earth Sociology:* "Why Doesn't She Just Leave?" The Dilemma of Abused Women 497
The Bright Side of Family Life: Successful Marriages 498

The Future of Marriage and Family 499

Summary and Review 500

17 Education 503

The Development of Modern Education 504
Education in Earlier Societies 504
Industrialization and Universal Education 505

Education in Global Perspective 507
Education in the Most Industrialized Nations: Japan 507
Education in the Industrializing Nations: Russia 508
Education in the Least Industrialized Nations: Egypt 508

The Functionalist Perspective: Providing Social Benefits 509
Teaching Knowledge and Skills 509
Cultural Transmission of Values 509
Social Integration 510
Gatekeeping 511
Replacing Family Functions 511
■ *Down-to-Earth Sociology:* Home Schooling: The Search for Quality and Values 512
Other Functions 512
■ *Down-to-Earth Sociology:* How to Get More Out of College—and Still Enjoy It 514

The Conflict Perspective: Reproducing the Social Class Structure 515
The Hidden Curriculum 515
■ *Down-to-Earth Sociology:* Kindergarten as Boot Camp 516
Tilting the Tests: Discrimination by IQ 516
Stacking the Deck: Unequal Funding 517
The Correspondence Principle 518
The Bottom Line: Family Background and the Educational System 518

The Symbolic Interactionist Perspective: Fulfilling Teacher Expectations 520
  The Rist Research 520
  The Rosenthal-Jacobson Experiment 521
  How Do Teacher Expectations Work? 521
  ■ *Sociology and the New Technology:* Internet University: No Walls, No Ivy, No All Night Parties 522

Problems in U.S. Education—and Their Solutions 522
  Problems: Mediocrity and Violence 522
  Solutions: Retention, Safety, Standards, and Other Reforms 524
  ■ *Mass Media in Social Life:* School Shootings: When Myth Gives Way to Panic 525
  ■ *Thinking Critically:* Breaking Through the Barriers: Restructuring the Classroom 527

Summary and Review 528

18 Religion 531

What Is Religion? 532

The Functionalist Perspective 533
  Functions of Religion 533
  ■ *Down-to-Earth Sociology:* News Flash! Prayer Works! 534
  Functional Equivalents of Religion 536
  Dysfunctions of Religion 536

The Symbolic Interactionist Perspective 537
  Religious Symbols 537
  Rituals 538
  Beliefs 538
  Religious Experience 539
  Community 539

The Conflict Perspective 540
  Opium of the People 540
  A Reflection of Social Inequalities 540
  A Legitimation of Social Inequalities 540

Religion and the Spirit of Capitalism 541

The World's Major Religions 542
  Judaism 542
  Christianity 543
  Islam 544
  ■ *Cultural Diversity in the United States:* The New Neighbor: Islam in the United States 545
  Hinduism 546
  Buddhism 546
  Confucianism 547

Types of Religious Groups 547

  Cult 547
  Sect 548
  Church 549
  Ecclesia 549
  Variations in Patterns 549
  When Religion and Culture Conflict 550
  ■ *Thinking Critically:* How to Destroy a Cult: The U.S. Government Versus the Branch Davidians 550

Religion in the United States 552
  Characteristics of Members 552
  Characteristics of Religious Groups 553
  ■ *Down-to-Earth Sociology:* Bikers and Bibles 556
  Secularization of Religion and Culture 556

The Future of Religion 559
  ■ *Mass Media in Social Life:* God on the Net: The Online Marketing of Religion 560

Summary and Review 560

19 Medicine 563

Sociology and the Study of Medicine 564

The Symbolic Interactionist Perspective 564
  The Role of Culture in Defining Health and Illness 564
  ■ *Cultural Diversity Around the World:* "You Don't Know What *Empacho* Is? What Kind of Doctor Are You?" 565
  The Components of Health 566

The Functionalist Perspective 566
  The Sick Role 566

The Conflict Perspective 567
  Effects of Global Stratification on Health Care 567
  Establishing a Monopoly on U.S. Health Care 569
  ■ *Down-to-Earth Sociology:* To Establish a Monopoly, Eliminate Your Competition: How Physicians Defeated Midwives 571

Historical Patterns of Health 572
  Physical Health 572
  Mental Health 572

Issues in Health Care 573
  Medical Care: A Right or a Commodity? 573
  Social Inequality 573
  Malpractice Suits and Defensive Medicine 574
  Medical Incompetence 574
  Depersonalization: The Medical Cash Machine 575
  Conflict of Interest 576
  Medical Fraud 576
  Sexism in Medicine 577
  The Medicalization of Society 577
  ■ *Down-to-Earth Sociology:* The Doctor–Nurse Game 578

Medically Assisted Suicide 578

■ *Thinking Critically:* Should Doctors Be Allowed to Kill Patients? 579

Curbing Costs: Issues in Private and National Health Insurance 580

■ *Sociology and the New Technology:* Who Should Live, and Who Should Die? The Dilemma of Rationing Medical Care 582

Threats to Health 582

AIDS 582

The Globalization of Disease 586

Drugs: Alcohol and Nicotine 586

Disabling Environments 588

Misguided, Foolish, and Callous Experiments 588

The Search for Alternatives 590

Treatment or Prevention? 590

Health Care in Global Perspective 590

■ *Cultural Diversity Around the World:* Health Care in Sweden, Russia, and China 591

The Future of Medicine 592

■ *Sociology and the New Technology:* Genetic Profiling: Medicine in the Coming Bioeconomy 593

Summary and Review 594

Part V

Social Change

20 Population and Urbanization 597

POPULATION IN GLOBAL PERSPECTIVE 598

A Planet with No Space for Enjoying Life? 598

The New Malthusians 599

The Anti-Malthusians 600

Who Is Correct? 600

Why Are People Starving? 602

Population Growth 603

Why Do the Least Industrialized Nations Have So Many Children? 603

Implications of Different Rates of Growth 605

The Three Demographic Variables 606

Problems in Forecasting Population Growth 609

■ *Cultural Diversity Around the World:* Killing Little Girls: An Ancient and Thriving Practice 609

URBANIZATION 611

■ ■ ■ ■ **EXPERIENCING SOCIOLOGY** *Traveling with the Author* ■ ■ ■ ■

One of the most significant changes in the world is the global rush of poor, rural people to the cities of the Least Industrialized Nations. Some of these settlements are dangerous. I was fortunate to be escorted by an insider through this section of Medellin, Colombia. (Page 612)

The Development of Cities 614

The Process of Urbanization 615

U.S. Urban Patterns 616

■ *Down-to-Earth Sociology:* Reclaiming Harlem: "It Feeds My Soul" 618

Models of Urban Growth 618

The Concentric Zone Model 618

The Sector Model 620

The Multiple-Nuclei Model 620

The Peripheral Model 620

Critique of the Models 620

■ *Cultural Diversity Around the World:* Why City Slums Are Better than the Country: Urbanization in the Least Industrialized Nations 621

City Life: Alienation and Community 621

Who Lives in the City? 623

The Norm of Noninvolvement and the Diffusion of Responsibility 624

■ *Down-to-Earth Sociology:* Urban Fear and the Gated Fortress 625

Urban Problems and Social Policy 626

Suburbanization 626

Disinvestment and Deindustrialization 627

The Rural Rebound 628

The Potential of Urban Revitalization 628

Summary and Review 630

21 Collective Behavior and Social Movements 633

COLLECTIVE BEHAVIOR 634

Early Explanations: The Transformation of the Individual 634
Charles Mackay, Gustave LeBon, and Robert Park: How the Crowd Transforms the Individual 634

Herbert Blumer: The Acting Crowd 635

The Contemporary View: The Rationality of the Crowd 636
Richard Berk: The Minimax Strategy 637
Ralph Turner and Lewis Killian: Emergent Norms 637

Forms of Collective Behavior 638
Riots 638

■ ■ ■ ■ ■ **EXPERIENCING SOCIOLOGY** *Traveling with the Author* ■ ■ ■ ■ ■

With such a great focus in the national news—amidst concerns about a riot and perhaps even an insurrection—I couldn't resist going to Bloomington, Indiana, where Timothy McVeigh was to be executed. Here is my account of this media event, a study in collective behavior— "the riot that never was." (Page 640)

Panics 642
■ *Down-to-Earth Sociology:* Mass Hysteria 644
Moral Panics 644
Rumors 645
Fads and Fashions 646
Urban Legends 647

SOCIAL MOVEMENTS 648
■ *Cultural Diversity in the United States:* The Million-Man March: Another Step in an Unfinished Social Movement 649

Types and Tactics of Social Movements 650
Types of Social Movements 650
Tactics of Social Movements 651
Propaganda and the Mass Media 654
■ *Down-to-Earth Sociology:* "Tricks of the Trade"— The Fine Art of Propaganda 655

Why People Join Social Movements 656
Mass Society Theory 656
Deprivation Theory 665
Moral Issues and Ideological Commitment 657
A Special Case: The Agent Provocateur 658

On the Success and Failure of Social Movements 659
The Stages of Social Movements 659
The Rocky Road to Success 660
■ *Thinking Critically:* Which Side of the Barricades? Prochoice and Prolife as a Social Movement 660

Summary and Review 662

22 Social Change and the Environment 665

How Social Change Transforms Social Life 666
The Four Social Revolutions 666
From *Gemeinschaft* to *Gesellschaft* 666
Capitalism, Modernization, and Industrialization 667
Social Movements 669
Geopolitics and Ethnic Conflicts 669

Theories and Processes of Social Change 670
Cultural Evolution 670
Natural Cycles 671
Conflict Over Power 671
Ogburn's Theory 671
■ *Sociology and the New Technology:* From the Luddites to the Unabomber: Opposition to Technology 673

How Technology Changes Society 674
The Extent of the Transformation 674
The Cutting Edge of Change 676
Cyberspace and Social Inequality 679

The Growth Machine Versus the Earth 680
Environmental Problems in the Most Industrialized Nations 680
■ *Down-to-Earth Sociology:* Corporations and Big Welfare Bucks: How to Get Paid to Pollute 682

Environmental Problems in the Industrializing and Least
   Industrialized Nations   683
The Environmental Movement   683
▪ *Cultural Diversity Around the World:* The Rain Forests:
Lost Tribes, Lost Knowledge   684
▪ *Thinking Critically:* Ecosabotage   685
Environmental Sociology   686

Summary and Review   687

Glossary   GL-1

Suggested Readings   SR-1

References   R-1

Name Index   N-1

Subject Index   S-1

Boxed Features

■ ■ ■ ■ ■ Down-to-Earth Sociology

An Updated Version of the Old Elephant Story   6
Enjoying a Sociology Quiz—Sociological Findings Versus Common Sense   7
Early North American Sociology: Du Bois and Race Relations   19
Careers in Sociology: What Applied Sociologists Do   22
Sociology or Social Work? Taking Back Children from the Night   23
Emoticons: "Written Gestures" for Expressing Yourself Online   46
Heredity or Environment? The Case of Oskar and Jack, Identical Twins   67
Signs of the Times: Are We Becoming Ik?   77
Boot Camp as a Total Institution   89
College Football as Social Structure   101
Loading the Dice: How *Not* to Do Research   138
The Hawthorne Experiments   144
Applied Sociology: Marketing Research as a Blend of Quantitative and Qualitative Methods   145
The McDonaldization of Society   193
Islands in the Street: Urban Gangs in the United States   227
How the Super-Rich Live   280
Can Money Buy Happiness?   291
Exploring Myths About the Poor   296
Poverty: A Personal Journey   303
Making the Invisible Visible—The Deadly Effects of Sexism   322
Common Sense and Sociology: What Is Race?   344
The Racist Mind   356
What You Reveal by Your Voice: Racism in the Rental Market   368
Changing Sentiment About the U.S. Elderly   393
"Your Name is What? You Live Where? But You Sound Like You're Right Next Door."   412
Women in Business: Maneuvering the Male Culture   430
Biological Terrorism   461
"What Do You Mean You Want Us to Live Together?"   490
You Be the Sociologist: Curious Divorce Patterns   493
"Why Doesn't She Just Leave?" The Dilemma of Abused Women   497
Home Schooling: The Search for Quality and Values   512
How to Get More Out of College—and Still Enjoy It   514
Kindergarten as Boot Camp   516
News Flash! Prayer Works!   534
Bikers and Bibles   556

To Establish a Monopoly, Eliminate Your Competition: How Physicians Defeated Midwives   571
The Doctor–Nurse Game   578
Reclaiming Harlem: "It Feeds My Soul"   618
Urban Fear and the Gated Fortress   625
Mass Hysteria   644
"Tricks of the Trade"—The Fine Art of Propaganda   655
Corporations and Big Welfare Bucks: How to Get Paid to Pollute   682

■ ■ ■ ■ ■ Cultural Diversity Around the World

Do You Feel Sorry? Hire an Apology Specialist   42
Japanese and U.S. Corporations in an Age of Greed   208
Human Sexuality in Cross-Cultural Perspective   213
Female Circumcision   317
"Pssst. You Wanna Buy a Bride?" China in Transition   318
China: Changing Sentiment about the Elderly   388
Alzheimer's Disease: Lessons from Sweden   399
No Cash? No Problem! Barter in the Former Soviet Union   420
Doing Business in the Global Village   422
Roadblocks in the Path to the New World Order: The Globalization of Capitalism Versus the Resurgence of Nationalism   463
Promoting Gender Equality: Family Life in Sweden   472
East Is East and West Is West . . . Love and Arranged Marriage in India   477
"You Don't Know What *Empacho* Is? What Kind of a Doctor Are You?"   565
Health Care in Sweden, Russia, and China   591
Killing Little Girls: An Ancient and Thriving Practice   609
Why City Slums Are Better than the Country: Urbanization in the Least Industrialized Nations   621
The Rain Forests: Lost Tribes, Lost Knowledge   684

■ ■ ■ ■ ■ Cultural Diversity in the United States

Race and Language: Searching for Self Labels   47
Miami—Language in a Changing City   48
Caught Between Two Worlds   84
The Amish—*Gemeinschaft* Community in a *Gesellschaft* Society   110
How Our Social Networks Perpetuate Social Inequality   171
Tiger Woods and the Emerging Multiracial Identity: Mapping New Ethnic Terrain   343
"You Can Work for Us, But You Can't Live Near Us"   359

Glimpsing the Future: The Shifting U.S. Racial-Ethnic
Mix   375
The Politics of Immigrants: Power, Ethnicity, and Social
Class   451
The New Neighbor: Islam in the United States   545
"You Don't Know What *Empacho* Is? What Kind of Doctor
Are You?"   565
The Million-Man March: Another Step in an Unfinished
Social Movement   649

■ ■ ■ ■
Mass Media in Social Life

Why Do Native Americans Like Westerns?   53
From Xena, Warrior Princess, to Lara Croft, Tomb Raider:
Changing Images of Women in the Mass Media   80
You Can't Be Thin Enough: Body Images and the Mass
Media   118
Pornography on the Internet: Freedom Versus
Censorship   223
What Price Freedom? Slavery Today   248
Beauty and Pain: How Much Is an Ad Worth?   336
Preaching Hatred: Crime or Inalienable Right?   353
Shaping Our Perceptions of the Elderly   389
Greed Is Good—Selling the American Dream   418
Politics and Democracy in a Technological Society   446
School Shootings: When Myth Gives Way to Panic   525
God on the Net: The Online Marketing of Religion   560

■ ■ ■ ■
Sociology and the New Technology

Would Bionic Men and Women Be Fair in Sports? The
Question of Genetic Engineering   87
"So, You Want to Be Yourself?" Cloning in the Coming
Bioeconomy   163
Electronic Communities: Cybercommunications and Our
Changing Culture   172
Cyberslackers and Cybersleuths: Surfing at Work   205
Closing the Digital Divide: The Technology Gap   293
Technology and Terrorism   460
The Brave New World of High-Tech Reproduction: Where
Technology Outpaces Law and Sometimes Common
Sense   487
Internet University: No Walls, No Ivy, No All Night
Parties   522
Who Should Live, and Who Should Die? The Dilemma of
Rationing Medical Care   582

Genetic Profiling: Medicine in the Coming
Bioeconomy   593
From the Luddites to the Unabomber: Opposition
to Technology   673

■ ■ ■ ■
Thinking Critically

Are We Prisoners of Our Genes? Sociobiology and Human
Behavior   58
Doing Controversial Research—Counting the
Homeless   145
Are Rapists Sick? A Close-Up View of Research   150
If Hitler Asked You to Execute a Stranger, Would You?
The Milgram Experiment   179
Managing Diversity in the Workplace   201
Is It Rape, Or Is It Marriage? A Study in Culture Clash   215
"Three Strikes and You're Out!" Unintended Consequences
of Well-Intended Laws   233
Changing Views: Making Hate a Crime   235
Open Season: Children as Prey   264
When Globalization Comes Home: *Maquiladoras* South
of the Border   268
The Nation's Shame: Children in Poverty   299
The Welfare Debate: The Deserving and the Undeserving
Poor   301
Biology Versus Culture—Culture Is the Answer   310
Biology Versus Culture—Biology Is the Answer   311
Sexual Harassment of Women in the Military   332
Self-Segregation: Help or Hindrance for Race Relations on
Campus?   350
Reparations for Slavery: Justice or Foolishness?   369
Exploding the Myth of U.S. Budget Surpluses: Can We Pay
the Elderly's Social Security Out of Thin Air?   393
How Long Do You Want to Live? Pushing Past the Limits
of Biology   405
What Type of New Society? New Technology and the
Restructuring of Work   434
The Second Shift—Strains and Strategies   474
Breaking Through the Barriers: Restructuring the
Classroom   527
How to Destroy a Cult: The U.S. Government Versus the
Branch Davidians   550
Should Doctors Be Allowed to Kill Patients?   579
Which Side of the Barricades? Prochoice and Prolife as a
Social Movement   660
Ecosabotage   685

Guide to Social Maps

Figure 8.1   Some States Are Safer: Violent Crime in the United States   228

Figure 8.3   Executions in the United States   234

Figure 9.2   Global Stratification: Income of the Worlds' Nations   262–263

Figure 10.5   Patterns of Poverty   297

Figure 11.4   Percent of Women in the Work Force   327

Figure12.2   The Distribution of Dominant and Minority Groups in the
                  United States   348

Figure 13.1   The Graying of the Globe   382

Figure 13.4   As Florida Goes, So Goes the Nation: The Year 2025   384

Figure 14.2   The Globalization of Capitalism: U.S. Ownership in Other
                  Countries   426–427

Figure 14.3   The Globalization of Capitalism: Foreign Ownership of U.S.
                  Business   427

Figure 15.1   U.S. Political Parties   448

Figure 16.11   The "Where" of U.S. Divorce   492

Figure 17.2   Not Making It: Dropping Out of High School   507

Figure 17.4   The Unequal Funding of Education   517

Figure 18.2   Church Membership: Dominant Religion by County   544

Figure 19.6   Who Lacks Medical Insurance?   581

Figure 20.8   Net Migration Flows between Regions, 1999–2000   607

Figure 20.11   The Urban Giants: The Population of the World's Ten Largest
                  Megacities, in Millions   616

Figure 20.12   How Urban Is Your State? The Rural-Urban Makeup of the United
                  States   617

Figure 22.2   Hazardous Waste Sites: How Does Your State Rank?   681

To the Student from the Author

Welcome to sociology! I've loved sociology since I was in my teens, and I hope you enjoy it, too. Sociology is fascinating because it holds the key to so much understanding of social life.

If you like to watch people and try to figure out why they do what they do, you will like sociology. Sociology pries open the doors of society so you can see what goes on behind them. *Sociology: A Down-to-Earth Approach* stresses how profoundly our society and the groups to which we belong influence us. Social class, for example, sets us on a path in life. For some, the path leads to better health, more education, and higher income, but for others it leads to poverty, dropping out of school, and even a higher risk of illness and disease. These paths are so significant that they affect our chances of making it to our first birthday, as well as of getting in trouble with the police. They even influence how our marriage will work out, the number of children we will have—and whether or not we will read this book in the first place.

When I took my first course in sociology, I was "hooked." Seeing how marvelously my life had been affected by these larger social influences opened my eyes to a new world, one that has been fascinating to explore. I hope that this will be your experience also.

From how people become homeless to how they become presidents, from why people commit suicide to why women are discriminated against in every society around the world—all are part of sociology. This breadth, in fact, is what makes sociology so intriguing. We can place the sociological lens on broad features of society, such as social class, gender, and race-ethnicity, and then immediately turn our focus on the small-scale level. If we look at two people interacting—whether quarreling or kissing—we see how these broad features of society are being played out in their lives.

We aren't born with instincts. Nor do we come into this world with preconceived notions of what life should be like. At birth, we have no ideas of race-ethnicity, gender, age, or social class. We have no idea, for example, that people "ought" to act in certain ways because they are male or female. Yet we all learn such things as we grow up in our society. Uncovering the "hows" and the "whys" of this process is also part of sociology's fascination.

One of sociology's many pleasures is that as we study life in groups (which can be taken as a definition of sociology), whether those groups be in some far-off part of the world or in some nearby corner of our own society, we constantly gain insights into our own selves. As we see how *their* customs affect *them*, effects of our own society on us become more visible.

This book, then, can be part of an intellectual adventure, for it can lead you to a new way of looking at your social world—and in the process, help you to better understand both society and yourself.

I wish you the very best in college—and in your career afterward. It is my sincere hope that *Sociology: A Down-to-Earth Approach* will contribute to that success.

James M. Henslin, Professor Emeritus
Department of Sociology
Southern Illinois University, Edwardsville

P. S. I enjoy communicating with students, so feel free to comment on your experiences with this text. Because I travel a lot, it is best to reach me by e-mail: henslin@aol.com

Also, you may want to look at the Website for this text: *www.ablongman.com/henslin6e*

To the Instructor from the Author

Remember when you first got "hooked" on sociology, how the windows of perception opened as you began to see life-in-society through the sociological perspective? For most of us, this was an eye-opening experience. This text is designed to open those windows onto social life, so students can see clearly the vital effects of group membership on their lives. Although few students will get into what Peter Berger calls "the passion of sociology," we at least can provide them the opportunity.

Sociology is like a huge jigsaw puzzle. Only very gradually do the intricate pieces start to fit together. As they do so, our perspective changes as we shift our eyes from the many small, disjointed pieces onto the whole that is being formed. Although this analogy is imperfect, it indicates a fascinating process of sociological discovery. Of all the endeavors we could have entered, we chose sociology because of the ways in which it joins together the "pieces" of society and the challenges it poses to "ordinary" thinking. To share the sociological perspective with students is our privilege.

As instructors of sociology, we have set formidable tasks for ourselves—to teach both social structure and social interaction, and to introduce students to the main sociological literature, to both the classic theorists and contemporary research. And we would like to accomplish this in ways that enliven the classroom, encourage critical thinking, and stimulate our students' sociological imagination. Although formidable, these goals are attainable. This book, based on many years of frontline (classroom) experience, is designed to help you reach these goals. Its subtitle, *A Down-to-Earth Approach,* is not proposed lightly. My goal is to share the fascination of sociology with students, and thereby make your teaching more rewarding.

Over the years, I have found the introductory course especially enjoyable. It is singularly satisfying to see students' faces light up as they begin to see how separate pieces of their world fit together. It is a pleasure to watch them gain insight into how their social experiences give shape to even their innermost desires. This is precisely what this text is designed to do—to stimulate your students' sociological imagination so they can better perceive how the "pieces" of society fit together—and what this means for their own lives.

Filled with examples from around the world as well as from our own society, this text helps make today's multicultural, global society come alive for the student. From the international elite carving up global markets to the intimacy of friendship and marriage, the student can see how sociology is the key to explaining contemporary life—and his or her own place in it.

In short, this text is designed to make your teaching easier. There simply is no justification for students to have to wade through cumbersome approaches to sociology. I am firmly convinced that the introduction to sociology should be enjoyable, and that the introductory textbook can be an essential tool in sharing the discovery of sociology with students.

The Organization of this Text

The text is laid out in five parts. Part I focuses on the sociological perspective, which I introduce in the first chapter. We then look at how culture influences us in Chapter 2, examine socialization in Chapter 3, and compare macrosociology and microsociology in Chapter 4. In Chapter 5, we look at how sociologists do research. Placing research methods in the fifth chapter is not usual, but doing so allows students to first become immersed in the captivating findings of sociology—then, after whetting their interest, teaching them how sociologists gather their data. This works very well, but if you prefer the more traditional order, simply teach this chapter as the second chapter. No content will be affected.

Part II, which focuses on groups and social control, adds to the students' understanding of how significantly social groups influence our lives. Chapter 6 opens this part with an overview of groups—from society, which encompasses us, to the smaller networks in which we are immersed. In this chapter, we also look at the fascinating area of group dynamics. In Chapter 7, we examine the impact of bureaucracy and formal organizations. Then in Chapter 8, we focus on how groups "keep us in line" and sanction those who violate their norms.

In Part III, we examine how social inequality pervades society and how those inequalities have an impact on our own lives. Because social stratification is so significant, I have written two chapters on this topic. The first (Chapter 9), with its global focus, presents an overview of the principles of stratification. The second (Chapter 10), with its emphasis on variations in social class, focuses on stratification in U.S. society. After establishing this broader context, in Chapter 11 we examine gender, the most global of the social inequalities. Then in Chapter 12, we focus on inequalities of race and ethnicity, and in Chapter 13, those of age.

Part IV helps students become more aware of how social institutions encompass their lives. In Chapters 14 and 15, we look at how the economy and politics are our overarching social institutions. In Chapter 16, we examine the family, and in Chapter 17 we turn our focus on education. In Chapter 18, we look at the significance of religion, and, finally, in Chapter 19, that of medicine. Throughout, we look at how these social institutions are changing, and how their changes, in turn, influence our orientations and decisions.

With its focus on broad social change, Part V provides an appropriate conclusion for the book. Here we examine why our world is changing so rapidly, as well as catch a glimpse of what is yet to come. In Chapter 20, we analyze trends in population and urbanization, sweeping forces in our lives that ordinarily remain below our level of awareness. Our focus on collective behavior and social movements in Chapter 21, and social change and the environment in Chapter 22, takes us to the "cutting edge" of vital changes that engulf us all.

■ ■ ■ ■ ■

Themes and Features

Six central themes run throughout this text: globalization, cultural diversity, down-to-earth sociology, critical thinking, the new technology, and the growing influence of the mass media on our lives. Let's look at these six themes.

■ Globalization

The first theme, globalization, explores the impact of global issues. The new global economy, for example, which has intertwined the fates of nations, vitally affects our lives. The globalization of capitalism influences the kinds of skills and knowledge we need, types of work available to us, costs of the goods and services we consume, and even whether our country is at war or peace. In addition to the strong emphasis on global issues that runs throughout this text, I have written a separate chapter on global stratification. I have also featured global issues in the chapters on social institutions and the final chapters on social change: technology, population, urbanization, social movements, and the environment.

What occurs in Russia, Japan, and China, as well as in much smaller nations such as the various parts of the former Yugoslavia, has direct and far-reaching consequences on our own lives. Consequently, in addition to the global focus that runs throughout the text, the second theme, Cultural Diversity, also has a strong global emphasis.

■ Cultural Diversity in the United States and Around the World

The second theme, cultural diversity, has two primary emphases. The first is cultural diversity around the world. Gaining an understanding of how social life is "done" in other parts of the world often challenges our taken-for-granted assumptions of social life. At times, learning about other cultures gives us an appreciation for the life of other peoples; at other times, we may be shocked at some aspect of another group's way of life (such as female circumcision) and come away with a renewed appreciation of our own customs.

To highlight this sub-theme, I have written a series of boxes called *Cultural Diversity Around the World.* The boxed features, here and throughout the text, are one of my favorite features of the book. They are especially valuable for introducing the provocative and controversial materials that make sociology such a lively activity. Among the boxed features that stress this sub-theme of cultural diversity around the world are the appearance of apology specialists for hire in Japan (Chapter 3), an examination of human sexuality in Mexico and Kenya (Chapter 8), selling brides in China (Chapter 11), female circumcision in Africa (Chapter 11), love and arranged marriage in India (Chapter 16), infanticide in China (Chapter 20), and the destruction of the rain forests and indigenous people in Brazil (Chapter 22).

The second emphasis is cultural diversity in the United States. In this sub-theme, we examine groups that make up the fascinating array of people who compose the United States. Among the boxes I have written with this sub-theme *(Cultural Diversity in the United States),* are the significance of language—Spanish and English in Miami, and the terms people choose for their own racial-ethnic self-identification (both in Chapter 2), the resistance of social change by the Amish (Chapter 4), how Tiger Woods represents a significant change in racial-ethnic identification (Chapter 12), discrimination against immigrants (Chapter 12), Islam as the new religious neighbor (Chapter 18), cultural confusion in the health care of Mexican immigrants (Chapter 19), our shifting racial-ethnic mix (Chapter 20), and the Million-Man March (Chapter 21).

Looking at cultural diversity—whether it be in the United States or in other regions of the world—often challenges our own orientations to life. To see that there are so many varieties of "doing" social life is to highlight the arbitrariness of our own customs—and our taken-for-granted ways of thinking. These contrasts help students develop their sociological imagination. They are better able to see connections among key sociological concepts such as culture, socialization, norms, race-ethnicity, gender, and social class. As your students' sociological imagination grows, they can attain a new perspective on their own experiences—and a better understanding of the social structure of U.S. society.

◼ Down-to-Earth Sociology

As many years of teaching have shown me, all too often textbooks are written to appeal to the adopters of texts rather than to the students who must learn from them. Thus, a central concern in writing this book has

been to present sociology in a way that not only facilitates understanding but also shares its excitement. During the course of writing other texts, I often have been told that my explanations and writing style are "down-to-earth," or accessible and inviting to students—so much so that I have used this phrase as the book's subtitle. The term is also featured in my introductory reader, *Down to Earth Sociology,* 11th edition (New York: Free Press, 2001).

This third theme is highlighted by a series of boxed features that explore sociological processes that underlie everyday life. In these **Down-to-Earth Sociology** boxes, we consider such topics as the relationship between heredity and environment (Chapter 3), improper and fraudulent social research (Chapter 5), how the United States is being "McDonaldized" (Chapter 7), whether or not money can buy happiness (Chapter 10), lifestyles of the super-rich (Chapter 10), voice and racial discrimination in the rental market (Chapter 12), the globalization of capitalism (Chapter 14), cohabitation (Chapter 16), home schooling (Chapter 17), how to be successful in college (Chapter 17), prayer and pregnancy (Chapter 18), why abused women don't pack up and leave (Chapter 16), the gentrification of Harlem (Chapter 20), mass hysteria (21), and corporate welfare (Chapter 22).

This third theme is actually a hallmark of the text, as my goal is to make sociology "down to earth." To help students grasp the fascination of sociology, I continuously stress sociology's relevance to their lives. To reinforce this theme, I avoid unnecessary jargon and use concise explanations and clear and simple (but not reductive) language. I often use student-relevant examples to illustrate key concepts, and I have based several of the chapters' opening vignettes on my own experiences in exploring social life. That this goal of sharing sociology's fascination is being reached is evident from the many comments I receive from instructors and students alike that the text helps make sociology "come alive."

◼ Critical Thinking

The fourth theme, critical thinking, focuses on controversial social issues and engages students in examining the various sides of those issues. In these sections, titled **Thinking Critically,** I present objective, fair portrayals of positions, and do not take a side—although I occasionally play the "devil's advocate" in the questions that close each of the topics. These sections can enliven your classroom with a vibrant exchange of ideas. Among the issues addressed are our tendency to conform to evil authority, as uncovered by the Milgram experiments (Chapter 6), bounties paid to kill homeless children in Brazil (Chapter 9), *maquiladoras* on the U.S.-Mexican border (Chapter 9), reparations for slavery (Chapter 12), a consideration of quality of life and our potential to increase our life span (Chapter 13), social class inequality in the treatment of mental and physical illness (Chapter 19), and abortion as a social movement (Chapter 21).

Because these *Thinking Critically* sections are based on controversial social issues that either affect the student's own life or are something that he or she is vitally interested in, they stimulate critical thinking and lively class discussion. They also lend themselves especially well to debates and small-group discussion.

■ Sociology and the New Technology

The fifth theme, sociology and the new technology, investigates an aspect of social life that has come to be central to our existence. We welcome these new tools, for they help us to be more efficient at doing our tasks, from making a living to communicating with people on the other side of the globe. The significance of the new technology goes far beyond the tools and the ease and efficiency they bring to our tasks, however. The new technology also penetrates our being—it shapes our thinking, leading to changed ways of viewing life. We are in the midst of a social revolution that will leave few aspects of our lives untouched.

This theme is introduced in Chapter 2, where technology is defined and presented as a major aspect of culture. It is then discussed throughout the text. Examples include how technology is being used to control workers in order to produce the "maximum security" workplace (Chapter 7), the implications of technology for maintaining global stratification (Chapter 9), and how the consequences of technology differ by social class (Chapter 10). The final chapter (22), "Social Change and the Environment," concludes the book with a focus on this theme.

To highlight this theme, I have written a series of boxes *(Sociology and the New Technology),* on how technology is changing society and affecting our lives.

Among these are the coming bionic competition in sports (Chapter 3), how virtual friendship is replacing some people's flesh-and-blood friends (Chapter 4), dilemmas of cloning (Chapter 6); electronic communities (Chapter 6), cyberslacking and cybersleuthing (Chapter 7), social inequality and the digital divide (Chapter 10), how technology is restructuring work (Chapter 14), the technology that underlies terrorism (Chapter 15), the genetic revolution and genetic privacy (Chapter 19), and unusual reproduction (Chapter 16).

■ The Mass Media and Social Life

In the sixth theme, we stress how the mass media affect our behavior and permeate our thinking. We consider how they even penetrate our consciousness to such a degree that they influence how we perceive our own bodies. As your students consider this theme, they should begin to see the mass media in a different light, which should further stimulate their sociological imagination.

In addition to making this a recurring theme throughout the text, I have also written a series of boxed features called *Mass Media in Social Life* to make it more prominent for students. Among these are an analysis of why Native Americans like Western novels and movies even though Indians are usually portrayed as victims (Chapter 2), the influence of computer games on images of gender (Chapter 3), the worship of thinness—and how this affects our own body images (Chapter 4), the issue of censoring high-tech pornography (Chapter 8), slavery in today's world (Chapter 9), preaching hatred and online censorship (Chapter 12), stimulating greed to stimulate the economy (Chapter 14), and God on the Net (Chapter 18).

New Topics

Because sociology is about social life, as society changes the topics in an introductory text reflect those changes. Consequently, this edition contains numerous new topics. Among them are apology specialists (Chapter 2); genetic engineering (Chapter 3); the coming bioeconomy (Chapter 6); shaming (Chapter 8); voice recognition and racism in the rental market (Chapter 12); reparations for slavery (Chapter 12); terrorism and technology (Chapter 15); the decline in two-parent families (Chapter 16); how people's meanings of cohabitation affect its outcome (Chapter 16); the dilemma of abused women (Chapter 16); home schooling (Chapter 17); an experiment with prayer (Chapter 18); the practice of medicine in the coming bioeconomy (Chapter 19); the health care of Mexican immigrants (Chapter 19); racism in the development of fetal surgery (Chapter 19); the migration of African Americans to the South (Chapter 20); and mass hysteria (Chapter 21).

New Features

Experiencing Sociology   In this new edition, I have included three special photo essays called *Experiencing Sociology.*

■ **Terrorism:** 9–11, the stunning day that changed the United States. We will only realize its impact on society and our own lives as time goes on. A selection of photos in Chapter 15 picks up some of the highlights of this watershed event.

■ **Colombia:** One of the most significant changes in the world is the global rush of poor, rural people to the cities of the Least Industrialized Nations. Some of these settlements are dangerous. I was fortunate to be escorted by an insider through a section of Medellin, Colombia, which you will see in Chapter 20.

■ **The Execution of Timothy McVeigh:** With such a great focus in the national news—amidst concerns about a riot and perhaps even an insurrection—I couldn't resist going to Bloomington, Indiana, where Timothy McVeigh was to be executed. Chapter 21 features my account of this media event, a study in collective behavior—"the riot that never was."

Using ContentSelect   Each chapter ends with a listing of search terms that facilitate chapter-related online research. Students are able to use ContentSelect™, which gives them access to a huge online collection of professional journals.

Special Pedagogical Features

In addition to chapter summaries and reviews, key terms, and a comprehensive glossary, I have included several special features to aid students in learning sociology. *In Sum* sections help students review important points within the chapter before going on to new materials. I have also developed a series of **Social Maps**, which illustrate how social conditions vary by geography.

Chapter-opening vignettes feature down-to-earth illustrations of a major aspect of each chapter's content. Some of these are based on my own experiences. Several come from my research with the homeless, the time I spent with them on the streets and slept in their shelters (Chapters 1, 10, and 19). Others recount my travels in Africa (Chapters 2 and 11) and Mexico (Chapter 20). I also share my experiences when I spent a night with street people at DuPont Circle in Washington, D.C. (Chapter 4). For other vignettes, I use current and historical events

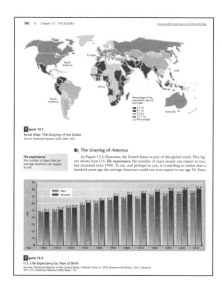

(Chapters 5, 7, 12, 17, 18, 21, and 22), classic studies in the social sciences (Chapters 3, 8, and 13), and even a scene from a novel (Chapter 15). Students have told me that they find the vignettes compelling, that they stimulate interest in the chapter.

On Sources and Terms Sociological data are found in an amazingly wide variety of sources, and this text reflects that variety. Cited throughout this text are standard journals such as the *American Journal of Sociology, Social Problems, American Sociological Review,* and *Journal of Marriage and the Family,* as well as more esoteric journals such as the *Bulletin of the History of Medicine, Chronobiology International,* and *Western Journal of Black Studies.* I have also drawn heavily from standard news sources, especially the *New York Times* and *Wall Street Journal,* as well as more unusual sources such as *El País.* In addition, I cite unpublished papers by sociologists.

Finally, a note on terms. Although still in use, the terms First World, Second World, and Third World are biased. Even though unintentional, to say First World inevitably connotes superiority of some sort—a sort of coming in first place, with other nations following in lesser, inferior positions. To substitute the terms Most Developed Countries, Less Developed Countries, and Least Developed Countries carries the same ethnocentric burden. These terms indicate that our economic state is superior: *We* are "developed," but *they* are not. To overcome this problem, I use neutrally descriptive terms: the Most Industrialized Nations, the Industrializing Nations, and the Least Industrialized Nations. These terms do not carry an ethnocentric value burden, for they indicate only that a nation's amount of industrialization is measurable and relative, without a connotation that industrialization is desirable.

■ Instructor's Supplements

Instructor's Manual

Mark Rubinfeld, Loyola University.

For each chapter in the text, the Instructor's Manual provides an At-a-Glance grid that coordinates use of the other supplements, a chapter summary, learning objectives, a lecture outline, key terms and people (with page references), classroom discussion topics, and a list of key changes in this new edition. The manual also includes a section on how to incorporate the text's website into your course.

Test Bank

Kenneth Mietus, Western Illinois University and Joseph Jacoby, Bowling Green State University.

This heavily revised and expanded test bank contains a multitude of questions in multiple choice, true-false, short answer, and essay formats. A new section contains in-depth questions designed for open-book testing.

Computerized Test Bank The printed Test Bank is also available on Windows or Macintosh CD-ROM through Allyn and Bacon's computerized testing system, TestGen EQ. This fully networkable test generating software is available on a multi-platform CD-ROM. The user-friendly interface allows you to view, edit, and add questions, transfer questions to tests, and print tests in a variety of fonts. Search and sort features allow you to locate questions quickly and to arrange them in whatever order you prefer.

Allyn & Bacon Transparencies for Introductory Sociology Revised for this edition, this package includes more than 125 color acetates featuring illustrations from current Allyn & Bacon Sociology titles, including Henslin.

Companion Website with Online Practice Tests This website is available to all users of the Henslin Sixth Edition text. This site features practice tests, annotated Web resources, interactive maps, detailed interactivities on Census 2000, and a link to ContentSelect™, Allyn and Bacon's online research database. In addition, you will find a Teaching Tool section that will help you to incorporate your Companion Website into your course. There is also a video guide section that contains synopses and sample assignments for hundreds of commercially available videos that contain sociological ideas and themes.

Online Course Management CourseCompass, powered by Blackboard and hosted nationally is Allyn and Bacon's own course management system. CourseCompass helps you manage most aspects of teaching the introductory course. It features pre-loaded content for Henslin Sixth Edition including the Test Bank and an ebook version of the text. A special CourseCompass edition of the text is also available, which includes margin notes and icons that support the accompanying CourseCompass cartridge (Your sales rep can give you additional information.) For colleges and universities with **WebCT**™ and **Blackboard**™ licenses, special course management packages are available in these formats as well.

Sociology Video Program   If you want to use news footage and documentary-style programs to illustrate sociological themes, these videos are from *Nightline, World News Tonight,* and *20/20.* Each video comes with a user's guide. The themes of the first titles are poverty and stratification, race and ethnicity, and marriages, families, and intimate relationships. Other themes will be added.

Sociology Video Library   Videos are available on every major topic in sociology. Some of the videos are from Films for the Humanities and Sciences and Annenberg/CPB.

The Blockbuster Approach: A Guide to Teaching Sociology with Video

By Casey Jordan, Western Connecticut State University

This electronic manual describes hundreds of commercially available videos that represent sociological ideas and themes. Included are samples of in-class discussions; homework assignments, and projects.

■ Presentation Solutions

Text-Specific PowerPoint

Lori Jowell of Tarrant County College

These PowerPoint presentations on CD-ROM, created for the 6th edition, feature lecture outlines for every chapter. PowerPoint software is not required, as a PowerPoint viewer is included on the CD.

The Sociology Digital Media Archive III   Want more electronic presentations in your classroom? This CD-ROM contains hundreds of graphs, charts, and maps to supplement your lectures and illustrate key sociological concepts. It also includes 40 topical lectures with 20–50 PowerPoint slides each. If you have full multimedia capability, you can use the DMA's video segments and links to sociology Web sites.

Sociology PowerPoint Lectures

Prepared by Lori Jowell, Tarrant County Community College

Here is an overview of the topics:

The Sociological Perspective	The Family
Origins of Sociology	Aging and Late Adulthood
Sociological Theory	Abduction
Plastic Surgery	Child Molestation
Scientific Sociology	Handwriting and Dreams
Steps to Doing Research	Social Class and Homelessness
Culture	What is a Social Problem?
Social Experience	Alcohol As a Social Problem
Understanding Socialization	School Violence
Social Interactions	Sexual Deviance
Nonverbal Communication	Tattoos and Body Modification
Gestures	Domestic Violence
Label of Deviance	Teenagers
Crime	Music and Its Influence
Self Defense	AIDS
Violence, Murder, and Aggression	Poverty
Race and Ethnicity	Date Rape
Gender	Eating Disorders
Deluxe Barbie Presentation	The Color Code-Personality Testing
Service Learning	Terrorism

Telecourse Support   Allyn and Bacon provides special assistance for instructors who use the video series from Dallas TeleLearning, *The Sociological Imagination.* They also correlate the questions in their standard test bank with the videos. To help instructors give tests based on the video programs, we also correlate every question in our standard Test Bank with the videos. These telecourse materials are included in the CourseCompass and Blackboard courses for Henslin Sixth Edition.

■ Student Supplements

Study Guide Plus

Gwendolyn E. Nyden, Oakton Community College

This manual provides learning objectives, key terms, self-tests, and glossaries. A separate section on Successful Study Strategies is also included.

Practice Tests with PowerPoint Lecture Outlines

Sharon LeBlond, Cincinnati State Technical and Community College

The practice tests in this manual help students prepare for quizzes and exams. Answers are included at the end of the manual. For this edition we have added lecture outlines that follow the PowerPoint presentation available to instructors. Students may find the outlines useful as they take notes during your lectures.

Study Guide for Speakers of Spanish
This study guide is designed to help native Spanish speakers who are taking a course in English. It includes Spanish translations of chapter summaries and definitions of key terms.

Companion Website with Online Practice Tests
This website features practice texts, annotated Web resources, interactive maps, activities, a detailed section on Census 2000, and a link to the research database ContentSelect. This site features a ContentSelect activity section with key search terms and recommended articles.

ContentSelect Research Database for Sociology (Access Code Required)

(http://www.ablongman.com/contentselect)

Free for your students is this research database. Searchable by keyword, it gives your students access to hundreds of scholarly journals and popular publications. An assigned ISBN is required.

■ Additional Supplements

Sociology iSearch Guide
This free reference guide includes tips, resources, activities, and URLs to help students. The first part introduces students to the basics of the Internet and the World Wide Web. Part two includes over thirty Net activities that tie into the content of the text. Part three lists hundreds of WWW resources for sociologists. The guide also includes information on how to correctly cite research, and a guide to building an online glossary.

Building Bridges: The Allyn & Bacon Guide to Service Learning

Doris Hamner

This manual offers practical advice for students who must complete a service-learning project as part of their required course work.

Careers in Sociology, 2e

W. Richard Stephens, Eastern Nazarene College

This supplement explains how sociology can help students prepare for careers in such fields as law, gerontology, social work, business, and computers. It also examines how sociologists entered the field.

Doing Sociology with Student CHIP: Data Happy!, 3e

By Gregg Lee Carter, Bryant College

This workbook with CHIP software is designed for classes with an empirical orientation. The computer exercises allow students to explore sociological issues using real data.

Acknowledgments

The gratifying response to earlier editions indicates that my efforts at making sociology down to earth have succeeded. The years that have gone into writing this text are a culmination of the many more years that preceded its writing—from graduate school to that equally demanding endeavor known as classroom teaching. No text, of course, comes solely from its author. Although I am responsible for the final words on the printed page, I have received excellent feedback from instructors who used the first five editions. I am especially grateful to

Reviewers of the Fifth Edition
Allison R. Camelot, *California State University at Fullerton*
James M. Cook, *Duke University*
Lorna E. Forster, *Clinton Community College*
Bill Grisby, *University of Northern Colorado*
Tammy Jolley, *University of Arkansas Community College at Batesville*
Ali Kamali, *Missouri Western State College*
Stephen Mabry, *Cedar Valley College*
Mike K. Pate, *Western Oklahoma State College*

Reviewers of the First through Fourth Editions
Francis O. Adeola, *University of New Orleans*
Sandra L. Albrecht, *The University of Kansas*
Richard Alman, *Sierra College*
Gabriel C. Alvarez, *Duquesne University*
Kenneth Ambrose, *Marshall University*
Alberto Arroyo, *Baldwin–Wallace College*
Karren Baird-Olsen, *Kansas State University*
Rafael Balderrama, *University of Texas—Pan American*
Linda Barbera-Stein, *The University of Illinois*

Ronnie J. Booxbaum, *Greenfield Community College*
Cecil D. Bradfield, *James Madison University*
Karen Bradley, *Central Missouri State University*
Francis Broouer, *Worcester State College*
Valerie S. Brown, *Cuyahoga Community College*
Sandi Brunette-Hill, *Carrol College*
Karen Bullock, *Salem State College*
Paul Ciccantell, *Kansas State University*
John K. Cochran, *The University of Oklahoma*
Joan Cook-Zimmern, *College of Saint Mary*
Russell L. Curtis, *University of Houston*
John Darling, *University of Pittsburgh—Johnstown*
Ray Darville, *Stephen F. Austin State University*
Jim David, *Butler County Community College*
Nanette J. Davis, *Portland State University*
Vincent Davis, *Mt. Hood Community College*
Lynda Dodgen, *North Harris Community College*
Terry Dougherty, *Portland State University*
Marlese Durr, *Wright State University*
Helen R. Ebaugh, *University of Houston*
Obi N. Ebbe, *State University of New York—Brockport*
Cy Edwards, Chair, *Cypress Community College*
Rebecca Susan Fahrlander, *Bellevue University*
Louis J. Finkle, *Horry-Georgetown Technical College*
Nicole T. Flynn, *University of South Alabama*
David O. Friedrichs, *University of Scranton*
Bruce Friesen, *Kent State University—Stark*
Norman Goodman, *State University of New York—Stony Brook*
Rosalind Gottfried, *San Joaquin Delta College*
Ramon Guerra, *University of Texas—Pan American*
Donald W. Hastings, *The University of Tennessee—Knoxville*
Lillian O. Holloman, *Prince George's Community College*
Michael Hoover, *Missouri Western State College*
James H. Huber, *Bloomsburg University*
Erwin Hummel, *Portland State University*
Charles E. Hurst, *The College of Wooster*
Nita Jackson, *Butler County Community College*
Jennifer A. Johnson, *Germanna Community College*
Kathleen R. Johnson, *Keene State College*
David Jones, *Plymouth State College*
Irwin Kantor, *Middlesex County College*
Mark Kassop, *Bergen Community College*
Myles Kelleher, *Bucks County Community College*
Mary E. Kelly, *Central Missouri State University*
Alice Abel Kemp, *University of New Orleans*
Diana Kendall, *Austin Community College*
Gary Kiger, *Utah State University*
Gene W. Kilpatrick, *University of Maine—Presque Isle*
Jerome R. Koch, *Texas Tech University*
Michele Lee Kozimor-King, *Pennsylvania State University*
Abraham Levine, *El Camino Community College*
David Maines, *Oakland University*
Ron Matson, *Wichita State University*
Armaund L. Mauss, *Washington State University*
Evelyn Mercer, *Southwest Baptist University*

Robert Meyer, *Arkansas State University*
Michael V. Miller, *University of Texas—San Antonio*
John Mitrano, *Central Connecticut State University*
W. Lawrence Neuman, *University of Wisconsin—Whitewater*
Charles Norman, *Indiana State University*
Patricia H. O'Brien, *Elgin Community College*
Laura O'Toole, *University of Delaware*
Ruth Pigott, *University of Nebraska—Kearney*
Phil Piket, *Joliet Junior College*
Trevor Pinch, *Cornell University*
Daniel Polak, *Hudson Valley Community College*
James Pond, *Butler Community College*
Deedy Ramo, *Del Mar College*
Adrian Rapp, *North Harris Community College*
Ray Rich, *Community College of Southern Nevada*
Barbara Richardson, *Eastern Michigan University*
Salvador Rivera, *State University of New York—Cobleskill*
Howard Robboy, *Trenton State College*
Michael Samano, *Portland Community College*
Michael L. Sanow, *Community College of Baltimore County*
Mary C. Sengstock, *Wayne State University*
Walt Shirley, *Sinclair Community College*
Marc Silver, *Hofstra University*
Roberto E. Socas, *Essex County College*
Susan Sprecher, *Illinois State University*
Mariella Rose Squire, *University of Maine at Fort Kent*
Randolph G. Ston, *Oakland Community College*
Vickie Holland Taylor, *Danville Community College*
Maria Jose Tenuto, *College of Lake County*
Gary Tiederman, *Oregon State University*
Kathleen Tiemann, *University of North Dakota*
Judy Turchetta, *Johnson & Wales University*
Steven Vassar, *Mankato State University*
William J. Wattendorf, *Adirondack Community College*
Jay Weinstein, *Eastern Michigan University*
Larry Weiss, *University of Alaska*
Douglas White, *Henry Ford Community College*
Stephen R. Wilson, *Temple University*
Anthony T. Woart, *Middlesex Community College*
Stuart Wright, *Lamar University*
Mary Lou Wylie, *James Madison University*
Diane Kholos Wysocki, *University of Nebraska—Kearney*
Stacey G. H. Yap, *Plymouth State College*
Joan Cook Zimmern, *College of Saint Mary*

I am also indebted to the fine staff of Allyn and Bacon. I wish to thank Karen Hanson, who first saw the merits of this project and gave it strong support; Jeff Lasser, who has been especially helpful in consultation and who has continued the development of supplemental online sites; Hannah Rubenstein, who made vital contributions to earlier editions of the text on which this one is based; Judy Fiske for constantly hovering over the many details—and supporting my many suggestions;

Kathy Smith for creative copy editing; Myrna Engler for ingenuity in photo research—and a willingness to "keep on looking"; and Dusty Friedman, who has done an outstanding job of overseeing both the routine and the urgent. It is difficult to heap too much praise on such capable people, whose efforts have coalesced with mine to produce this book. The students are the beneficiaries of our combined efforts, whom we constantly kept in mind as we prepared this edition.

Since this text is based on the contributions of many, I would count it a privilege if you would share your teaching experiences with this book, including any suggestions for improving the text. Both positive and negative comments are welcome. It is in this way that I learn.

I wish you the very best in your teaching. It is my sincere desire that *Sociology: A Down-to-Earth Approach* contributes to that success.

Jim Henslin

James M. Henslin, Professor Emeritus
Department of Sociology
Southern Illinois University, Edwardsville

I welcome your correspondence. E-mail is the best way to reach me: henslin@aol.com

About the Author

James M. Henslin, who was born in Minnesota, graduated from high school and junior college in California and from college in Indiana. Awarded scholarships, he earned his Master's and doctorate degrees in sociology at Washington University in St. Louis, Missouri. After this, he was awarded a postdoctoral fellowship from the National Institute of Mental Health, and spent a year studying how people adjust to the suicide of a family member. His primary interests in sociology are the sociology of everyday life, deviance, and international relations. Among his more than a dozen books is *Down to Earth Sociology: Introductory Readings* (Free Press), now in its eleventh edition. This book of readings reflects some of these sociological interests. He has also published widely in sociology journals, including *Social Problems* and *American Journal of Sociology.*

While a graduate student, James Henslin taught at the University of Missouri at St. Louis. After completing his doctorate, he joined the faculty at Southern Illinois University, Edwardsville, where he is Professor Emeritus of Sociology. He says, "I've always found the introductory course enjoyable to teach. I love to see students' faces light up when they first glimpse the sociological perspective and begin to see how society has become an essential part of how they view the world."

Henslin enjoys spending time with his wife, reading, and fishing. His two favorite activities are writing and traveling. He especially enjoys living in other cultures, for this brings him face to face with behaviors and ways of thinking that he cannot take for granted, experiences that "make sociological principles come alive."

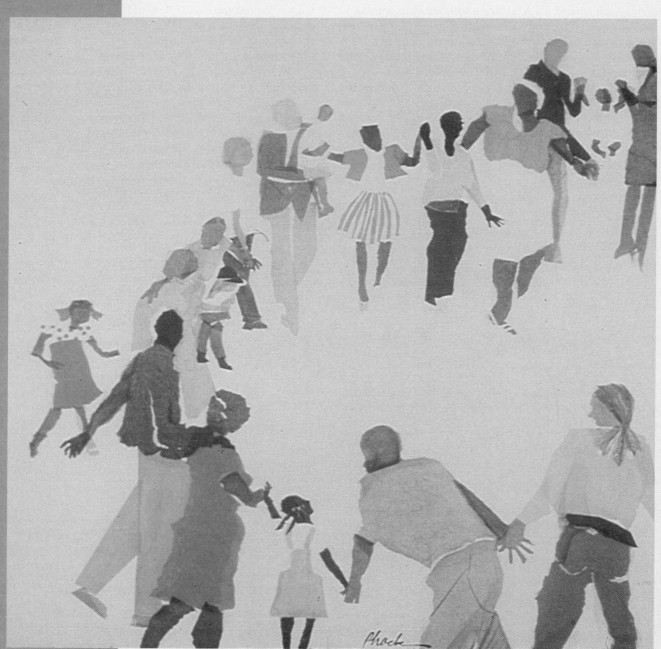

Phoebe Beasley, *Second Circle Dance*, 1987

1

The Sociological Perspective
Seeing the Broader Social Context
The Growing Global Context

Sociology and the Other Sciences
The Natural Sciences
The Social Sciences
The Goals of Science

Origins of Sociology
Tradition Versus Science
Auguste Comte and Positivism
Herbert Spencer and Social Darwinism
Karl Marx and Class Conflict
Emile Durkheim and Social Integration
Max Weber and the Protestant Ethic

The Role of Values in Social Research

Verstehen and Social Facts
Weber and *Verstehen*
Durkheim and Social Facts
How Social Facts and *Verstehen* Fit Together

Sexism in Early Sociology
Attitudes of the Time
Harriet Martineau

Sociology in North America
Early History: The Tension Between Social Reform and Sociological Analysis
Jane Addams and Social Reform
W.E.B. Du Bois and Race Relations
Talcott Parsons and C. Wright Mills: Theory Versus Reform
The Present: The Continuing Tension and the Rise of Applied Sociology

Theoretical Perspectives in Sociology
Symbolic Interactionism
Functional Analysis
Conflict Theory
Levels of Analysis: Macro and Micro
Putting the Theoretical Perspectives Together

Trends Shaping the Future of Sociology

Summary and Review

The Sociological Perspective

E ven from the glow of the faded red-and-white exit sign, its faint light barely illuminating the upper bunk, I could see that the sheet was filthy. Resigned to another night of fitful sleep, I reluctantly crawled into bed, tucking my clothes around my body like a protective cocoon.

The next morning, I joined the long line of disheveled men leaning against the chain-link fence. Their faces were as downcast as their clothes were dirty. Not a glimmer of hope among them.

No one spoke as the line slowly inched forward. When my turn came, I was handed a cup of coffee, some utensils, and a bowl of semiliquid that I couldn't identify. It didn't look like any food I had seen before. Nor did it taste like anything I had ever eaten.

> But I was determined. "I will experience what they experience," I kept telling myself.

My stomach fought the foul taste, every spoonful a battle. But I was determined. "I will experience what they experience," I kept telling myself. My stomach reluctantly gave in and accepted its morning nourishment.

The room was strangely silent. Hundreds of men were eating, each immersed in his own private hell, his head awash with disappointment, remorse, bitterness.

As I stared at the Styrofoam cup that held my coffee, grateful at least for this small pleasure, I noticed what looked like teeth marks. I shrugged off the thought, telling myself that my long weeks as a sociological observer of the homeless were finally getting to me. "That must be some sort of crease from handling," I concluded.

I joined the silent ranks of men turning in their bowls and cups.
When I saw the man behind the counter swishing out Styrofoam
cups in a washtub of water, I began to feel sick to my stomach. I
knew then that the jagged marks on my cup really had come from
a previous mouth.

How much longer did this research have to last? I felt a deep
longing to return to my family—to a welcome world of clean sheets,
healthy food, and "normal" conversations.

The Sociological Perspective

Why were these men so silent? Why did they receive such despicable treatment? What was I doing in that homeless shelter? After all, I hold a respectable, professional position, and I have a home and family.

Sociology offers a perspective, a view of the world. The *sociological perspective* (or imagination) opens a window onto unfamiliar worlds—and offers a fresh look at familiar worlds. In this text you will find yourself in the midst of Nazis in Germany, chimpanzees in Africa, and warriors in South America. But you will also find yourself looking at your own world in a different light. As you view other worlds, or your own, the sociological perspective enables you to gain a new vision of social life. In fact, this is what many find appealing about sociology.

The sociological perspective has been a motivating force in my own life. Ever since I took my first introductory course in sociology, I have been enchanted by the perspective that sociology offers. I have thoroughly enjoyed both observing other groups and questioning my own assumptions about life. I sincerely hope the same happens to you.

Seeing the Broader Social Context

The **sociological perspective** stresses the social contexts in which people live. It examines how these contexts influence people's lives. At the center of the sociological perspective is the question of how groups influence people, especially how people are influenced by their **society**—a group of people who share a culture and a territory.

To find out why people do what they do, sociologists look at **social location,** the corners in life that people occupy because of where they are located in a society. Sociologists look at jobs, income, education, gender, age, and race as significant. Consider, for example, how being identified with a group called *females* or with a group called *males* when we are growing up affects our ideas of who we are and what we should attain in life. Growing up as a male or a female influences not only our aspirations, but also how we feel about ourselves and the way we relate to others in dating and marriage and at work.

Sociologist C. Wright Mills (1959) put it this way: "The sociological perspective enables us to grasp the connection between history and biography." By history, Mills meant that each society is located in a broad stream of events. Because of this, each

sociological perspective
understanding human behavior by placing it within its broader social context

society
a term used by sociologists to refer to a group of people who share a culture and a territory

social location
the group memberships that people have because of their location in history and society

■ *Examining the broad social context in which people live is essential to the sociological perspective, for this context shapes our beliefs and attitudes and sets guidelines for what we do. From this photo, you can see how distinctive those guidelines are for the Yanomamö Indians who live on the border of Brazil and Venezuela. How have these Yanomamö men been influenced by their group? How has your behavior been influenced by your groups?*

society has specific characteristics—such as its ideas about the proper roles of men and women. By biography, Mills referred to the individual's specific experiences. In short, people don't do what they do because of inherited internal mechanisms, such as instincts. Rather, *external* influences—our experiences—become part of our thinking and motivations. The society in which we grow up, and our particular corners in that society, lie at the center of what we do and how we think.

Consider a newborn baby. If we were to take the baby away from its U.S. parents and place it with a Yanomamö Indian tribe in the jungles of South America, you know that when the child begins to speak, his or her words will not be in English. You also know that the child will not think like an American. He or she will not grow up wanting credit cards, for example, or designer jeans, a new car, and the latest video game. Equally, the child will unquestioningly take his or her place in Yanomamö society—perhaps as a food gatherer, a hunter, or a warrior—and he or she will not even know about the world left behind at birth. And, whether male or female, the child will grow up assuming that it is natural to want many children, not debating whether to have one, two, or three children.

People around the globe take their particular world for granted. Something inside us Americans tells us that hamburgers are delicious, small families desirable, and designer clothing attractive. Yet something inside some of the Sinai Desert Arab tribes used to tell them that warm, fresh camel's blood makes a fine drink and that everyone should have a large family and wear flowing robes (Murray 1935; McCabe and Ellis 1990). And that something certainly isn't an instinct. As sociologist Peter Berger (1963) phrased it, that "something" is "society within us."

Although obvious, this point frequently eludes us. We often think and talk about people's behavior as though it were caused by their sex, their race, or some other factor transmitted by their genes. The sociological perspective helps us escape from this cramped personal view by exposing the broader social context that underlies human behavior. It helps us see the links between what people do and the social settings that shape their behavior.

This brings us to *you*—to how *your* social groups have shaped *your* ideas and desires. Over and over in this text you will see that how you look at the world is the result of your exposure to certain groups rather than to others. I think you will enjoy the process of self-discovery that sociology offers.

■ The Growing Global Context

As is evident to all of us—from the labels on our clothing to the components in our cars—our world is becoming a global village. We used to live isolated on farms and in small towns, where beyond the borders of our community lay a world only dimly perceived. Communications used to be so slow that in the War of 1812, the Battle of New Orleans was fought two weeks after the adversaries, the United States and Great Britain, had signed a peace treaty. The armed forces there had not yet heard that the war was over (Volti 1995).

Today, in contrast, instantaneous communications connect us with remote areas of the globe, and a vast economic system connects us not only with Canada and Mexico but also with Belgium, Taiwan, and Indonesia. At the same time that we are immersed in such global interconnections, however, we continue to occupy little corners of life, marked by differences in family background, religion, job, gender, race, and social class. In these corners, we learn distinctive ways of viewing the world.

One of the beautiful—and fascinating—aspects of sociology is that it is able to analyze both parts of our current reality, the changes that incorporate us into a global network and our unique experiences in our smaller corners of life. In this text, we shall examine both of these vital aspects of our lives.

Sociology and the Other Sciences

Just as humans today have an intense desire to unravel the mysteries around them, people in ancient times also attempted to understand their world. Their explanations, however, were not based only on observations, but were also mixed with magic and superstition.

To satisfy their basic curiosities about the world around them, humans gradually developed **science**, systematic methods used to study the social and natural worlds, as well as the knowledge obtained by those methods. **Sociology,** the scientific study of society and human behavior, is one of the sciences that modern civilization has developed.

A useful way of comparing these sciences—and of gaining a better understanding of sociology's place—is to divide them into the natural and the social sciences.

■ The Natural Sciences

The **natural sciences** are the intellectual and academic disciplines designed to comprehend, explain, and predict the events in our natural environment. The natural sciences are divided into specialized fields of research according to subject matter, such as biology, geology, chemistry, and physics. These are further subdivided into even more highly specialized areas. Biology is divided into botany and zoology, geology into mineralogy and geomorphology, chemistry into its inorganic and organic branches, and physics into biophysics and quantum mechanics. Each area of investigation examines a particular "slice" of nature (Henslin 2001a).

■ The Social Sciences

People have not limited themselves to investigating nature. In the pursuit of a more adequate understanding of life, they have also developed fields of science that

science
the application of systematic methods to obtain knowledge and the knowledge obtained by those methods

sociology
the scientific study of society and human behavior

natural sciences
the intellectual and academic disciplines designed to comprehend, explain, and predict events in our natural environment

focus on the social world. These, the **social sciences,** examine human relationships. Just as the natural sciences attempt to objectively understand the world of nature, the social sciences attempt to objectively understand the social world. Just as the world of nature contains ordered (or lawful) relationships that are not obvious but must be discovered through controlled observation, so the ordered relationships of the human or social world are not obvious, and must be revealed by means of repeated observations.

Like the natural sciences, the social sciences are divided into specialized fields based on their subject matter. These divisions are anthropology, economics, political science, psychology, and sociology. And the social sciences, too, are subdivided into further specialized fields. Thus, anthropology is divided into cultural and physical anthropology; economics has macro (large-scale) and micro (small-scale) specialties; political science has theoretical and applied branches; psychology may be clinical or experimental; and sociology has its quantitative and qualitative branches. Since our focus is sociology, let's contrast sociology with each of the other social sciences.

Political Science   *Political science* focuses on politics and government. Political scientists study how people govern themselves. They examine forms of government and how these forms are related to other institutions of society. Political scientists are especially interested in how people attain ruling positions in their society, how they maintain those positions, and the consequences of their actions for those they govern. In studying a constitutional government, such as that of the United States, political scientists also analyze voting behavior.

Economics   *Economics* also concentrates on a single social institution. Economists study the production and distribution of the material goods and services of a society. They want to know what goods are being produced at what rate and at what cost, and how those goods are distributed. They also are interested in the choices that determine production and consumption; for example, why a society produces a certain item instead of another.

Anthropology   *Anthropology* is the sister discipline of sociology. The chief concern of anthropologists is to understand *culture,* a people's total way of life. Culture includes (1) the group's artifacts, such as its tools, art, and weapons; (2) the group's structure, that is, the patterns (such as positions that require respect) that determine how its members interact with one another; (3) a group's ideas and values, especially how its belief system affects people's lives; and (4) the group's forms of communication, especially language. The anthropologists' traditional focus has been on tribal peoples. Anthropologists who are studying for their doctorate usually live with a group. In their reports, they place special emphasis on the group's family (kin) relationships. As there are no "undiscovered" groups left in the world, this focus on tribal groups is giving way to the study of groups in industrialized settings. When anthropologists study the same groups that sociologists do, they place greater emphasis on artifacts, authority (hierarchy), and language, especially kinship terms.

Psychology   The focus of *psychology* is on processes that occur *within* the individual, within what they call the "skin-bound organism." Psychologists focus primarily on mental processes (what occurs in the brain, or the mind). They examine intelligence, emotions, perception, memory, even dreams. Some study how personality is formed. Others focus on mental aberration (psychopathology or mental illness). Many psychologists work as counselors in school and work settings, and in private practice, where they give personality tests, IQ tests, and vocational aptitude tests. As therapists, they focus on resolving personal problems, whether they involve the need to recover from trauma, such as rape, or to free oneself from addiction to drugs, alcohol, or gambling.

social sciences
the intellectual and academic disciplines designed to understand the social world objectively by means of controlled and repeated observations

■ ■ ■ ■ ■

An Updated Version of the Old Elephant Story

It is said that in the recent past five wise men and women, all blindfolded, were led to an elephant and asked to explain what they "saw." The first, a psychologist, feeling the top of the head, said, "This is the only thing that counts. All feeling and thinking take place inside here. To understand this beast, study only this."

The second, an anthropologist, tenderly touched the trunk and the tusks, then smiled and said, "This is really primitive. I feel very comfortable here. Concentrate on these."

The third, a political scientist, feeling the gigantic ears, announced, "This is the power center. What goes in here controls the entire beast. Concentrate your studies here."

The fourth, an economist, feeling the mouth, said, "This is what counts. What goes in here is distributed throughout the body. Concentrate your studies on how it is distributed."

Then came the sociologist (of course!), who, after feeling the entire body, said, "You can't understand the beast by concentrating on only one part. Each is but part of the whole. The head, the trunk and tusks, the ears, the mouth—all are important. But so are the parts of the beast that you haven't mentioned. We must remove our blindfolds so we can see the larger picture. We have to see how everything works together to form the entire animal."

Pausing for emphasis, the sociologist added, "And we also need to understand how this creature interacts with similar creatures. How does its life in groups influence its behaviors?"

I wish I could conclude this tale by saying that the psychologist, the anthropologist, the political scientist, and the economist were dazzled on hearing the wisdom of the sociologist, and amid gasps of wonderment threw away their blindfolds, joined together, and began to examine the entire animal. But, alas and alack! On hearing this sage advice, the specialists stubbornly bound their blindfolds even tighter so they could concentrate all the more on the single part. And if you listened very, very carefully you could even hear them mutter, "The top of the head is mine—stay away from it." "Don't touch the tusks." "Take your hand off the ears." "Stay away from the mouth—that's my area."

■ ■ ■ ■ ■

Sociology   *Sociology* has many similarities to the other social sciences. Like political scientists, sociologists also study how people govern one another, focusing especially on how government affects people's lives. Like economists, sociologists are concerned with what happens to the goods and services of a society—but sociologists place their focus on the social consequences of production and distribution. Like anthropologists, sociologists also study culture; they, too, have an interest in the social consequences of material goods, group structure, and belief systems, as well as in how people communicate with one another. Like psychologists, sociologists are also concerned with how people adjust to the difficulties of life.

Given these overall similarities, then, what distinguishes sociology from the other social sciences? Unlike political scientists and economists, sociologists do not concentrate on a single social institution. Unlike anthropologists, sociologists focus primarily on industrialized societies. And unlike psychologists, sociologists stress factors *external* to the individual to determine what influences people. The Down-to-Earth Sociology box above revisits an old tale about how members of different disciplines perceive the same subject matter.

■ The Goals of Science

The first goal of each scientific discipline is to *explain* why something happens. The second goal is to make **generalizations,** that is, to go beyond the individual case and make statements that apply to a broader group or situation. For example, a sociologist wants to explain not only why Mary went to college or became an armed robber but also why people with her characteristics are more likely than others to go to college or to become armed robbers. To achieve generalizations, sociologists look for **patterns,** recurring characteristics or events. The third scientific goal is to *predict,* to specify what will happen in the future in the light of current knowledge.

generalization
a statement that goes beyond the individual case and is applied to a broader group or situation

patterns
recurring characteristics or events

To attain these goals, scientists do not rely on magic, superstition, or common beliefs but on systematic studies. They examine evidence with an open mind, in such a way that it can be checked by others. Secrecy, prejudice, and other biases go against the grain of science.

Sociologists and other scientists also move beyond **common sense,** those ideas that prevail in a society, and that "everyone knows" are true. Just because "everyone" knows something is true does not make it so. "Everyone" can be mistaken today just as easily as when common sense dictated that the world was flat or that no human could ever walk on the moon. As sociologists examine people's assumptions about the world, their findings may contradict commonsense notions about social life. To test your own "common sense," read the Down-to-Earth Sociology box below.

Sometimes the explorations of sociologists take them into nooks and crannies that people would prefer remain unexplored. For example, a sociologist might study how people make decisions to commit a crime or to cheat on their spouses. Because sociologists want above all to understand social life, they cannot cease their studies because people feel uncomfortable. Because sociologists consider all realms of human life legitimate avenues to explore, their findings sometimes challenge even cherished ideas.

As they examine how groups operate, sociologists often confront attempts to keep things secret. It seems that every organization, every group, nourishes a pet image that it presents to others. Sociologists are interested in knowing what is really going on behind the scenes, however, so they peer beneath the surface to get past that sugar-coated image (Berger 1963). This approach sometimes brings sociologists into conflict with people who feel threatened by that information—which is all part of the adventure, and risk, of being a sociologist.

common sense
those things that "everyone knows" are true

---

down-to-earth
s o c i o l o g y

■ ■ ■ ■ ■
Enjoying A Sociology Quiz—
Sociological Findings Versus Common Sense

Some findings of sociology support commonsense understandings of social life, while others contradict them. Can you tell the difference? To enjoy this quiz, complete *all* the questions before turning the page to check your answers.

1. True/False   More U.S. students are killed in school shootings now than ten or fifteen years ago.

2. True/False   The earnings of U.S. women have just about caught up with those of U.S. men.

3. True/False   When faced with natural disasters such as floods and earthquakes,

people panic and social organization disintegrates.

4. True/False   Most rapists are mentally ill.

5. True/False   Most people on welfare are lazy and looking for a handout. They could work if they wanted to.

6. True/False   Compared with women, men maintain more eye contact in face-to-face conversations.

7. True/False   Couples who live together before marriage are usually more satisfied with their marriages than couples who

do not live together before marriage.

8. True/False   Most husbands of working wives who get laid off from work take up the slack and increase the amount of housework they do.

9. True/False   Men who earn less than their wives do more housework than do men who earn more than their wives.

10. True/False   Students in Japan are under such intense pressure to do well in school that their suicide rate is about double that of U.S. students.

■ ■ ■ ■ ■

Sociological Findings Versus Common Sense— Answers to the Sociology Quiz

1. False. More students were shot to death at U.S. schools in the early 1990s than now (National School Safety Center, 2000). See the box on school shootings on page 525.

2. False. Over the years, the wage gap has narrowed, but only slightly. On average, full-time working women earn only about 65 to 70 percent of what full-time working men earn. This low figure is actually an improvement over earlier years. See Figures 11.5 and 11.6 on pages 328 and 329.

3. False. Following disasters, people develop *greater* cohesion, cooperation, and social organization to deal with the catastrophe.

4. False. Sociologists compared the psychological profiles of prisoners who had been convicted of rape and prisoners who had been convicted of other crimes. Their profiles were similar. Like robbery, rape is a learned behavior. See page 150.

5. False. Most people on welfare are children, the old, the sick, the mentally and physically handicapped, or young mothers with few skills. Less than 2 percent meet the common stereotype of an able-bodied man. See also "Exploring Myths about the Poor" on page 296.

6. False. Women maintain considerably more eye contact (Henley et al. 1985).

7. False. The opposite is true. The reason, researchers suggest, is that many couples who cohabit before marriage are less committed to marriage in the first place—and a key to marital success is firm commitment to one another (Larson 1988).

8. False. Most husbands of working wives who get laid off from work *reduce* the amount of housework they do. See page 476 for an explanation.

9. False. Men who earn less than their wives are *less* likely than other husbands to share housework (Hochschild 1989/2001).

10. False. The suicide rate of U.S. students is about double that of Japanese students (Haynes and Chalker 1997).

Origins of Sociology

Tradition Versus Science

Just how did sociology begin? In some ways it is difficult to answer this question. Even ancient peoples tried to figure out social life. They asked questions about why war exists, why some people become more powerful than others, and why some become rich. However, they often based their answers on superstition, myth, or even the positions of the stars, and did not *test* their assumptions.

Science, in contrast, requires the development of theories that can be tested by systematic research. Measured by this standard, sociology only recently appeared on the human scene. It emerged about the middle of the nineteenth century when social observers began to use scientific methods to test their ideas.

Sociology grew out of social upheaval. The Industrial Revolution had just begun. By the middle of the nineteenth century, Europe was changing from agriculture to factory production. Masses of people were moving to cities in search of work. Their ties to the land—and to a culture that provided them with ready answers—were broken. The city greeted them with horrible working conditions: low pay; long, exhausting hours; dangerous work. To survive, even children had to work in these conditions; some were even chained to factory machines to make certain they could not run away. Life no longer looked the same, and tradition, which had provided the answers to questions about social life, no longer could be counted on.

Tradition was to suffer further blows. The success of the American and French revolutions encouraged people to rethink social life. New ideas arose, including the conviction that individuals possess inalienable rights. As this new idea caught fire, many traditional Western monarchies gave way to more democratic forms. People found the ready answers of tradition, including religion, inadequate.

When tradition reigns, it provides ready answers: "We do this because it has always been done this way." Tradition discourages original thinking. Since the answers are already provided, why search for explanations? Sweeping change, however, does the opposite: By upsetting the existing order, it encourages questioning and demands new answers.

Then there was the imperialism of the time. The Europeans had conquered many parts of the world, and their new colonial empires stretched from Asia and Africa to North America. This exposed them to radically different ways of life, and they began to ask why cultures differ.

Another impetus for the development of sociology was the success of the natural sciences. Just as tradition was breaking down and people were questioning fundamental aspects of life, **the scientific method**—using objective, systematic observations to test theories—was being tried out in chemistry and physics. Many secrets that had been concealed in nature were uncovered. With tradition no longer providing the answers to questions about social life, the logical step was to apply the scientific method to these questions. The result was the birth of sociology.

■ *Auguste Comte (1798–1857), who is credited as the founder of sociology, began to analyze the bases of the social order. Although he stressed that the scientific method should be applied to the study of society, he did not apply it himself.*

■ Auguste Comte and Positivism

This idea of applying the scientific method to the social world, known as **positivism,** apparently was first proposed by Auguste Comte (1798–1857). With the French Revolution still fresh in his mind, Comte left the small, conservative town in which he had grown up and moved to Paris. The changes he experienced in this move, combined with those France underwent in the revolution, led Comte to become interested in what holds society together. What creates social order, he wondered, instead of anarchy or chaos? And then, once society does become set on a particular course, what causes it to change?

As Comte considered these questions, he concluded that the right way to answer them was to apply the scientific method to social life. Just as this method had revealed the law of gravity, so, too, it would uncover the laws that underlie society. Comte called this new science **sociology**—"the study of society" (from the Greek *logos,* "study of," and the Latin *socius,* "companion," or "being with others"). Comte stressed that this new science not only would discover social principles but also would apply them to social reform. Sociologists would reform the entire society, making it a better place to live.

To Comte, however, applying the scientific method to social life meant practicing what we might call "armchair philosophy"—drawing conclusions from informal observations of social life. He did not do what today's sociologists would call research, and his conclusions have been abandoned. Nevertheless, Comte's insistence that we must observe and classify human activities in order to uncover society's fundamental laws is well taken. Because he developed this idea and coined the term *sociology,* Comte often is credited with being the founder of sociology.

the scientific method
the use of objective, systematic observations to test theories

positivism
the application of the scientific approach to the social world

sociology
the scientific study of society and human behavior

■ *Herbert Spencer (1820–1903), who analyzed the evolution of societies, coined the term "survival of the fittest." Spencer thought that helping the poor was wrong, that this merely helped the "less fit" survive.*

■ Herbert Spencer and Social Darwinism

Herbert Spencer (1820–1903), who grew up in England, is sometimes called the second founder of sociology. Spencer disagreed profoundly with Comte that sociology should guide social reform. Spencer thought that societies evolve from lower ("barbarian") to higher ("civilized") forms. As generations pass, the most capable and intelligent ("the fittest") members of a society survive, while the less capable die out. Thus, over time, societies improve. If you help the lower classes, you interfere with this natural process. The fittest members will produce a more advanced society—unless misguided do-gooders get in the way and help the less fit survive.

Spencer called this principle "the survival of the fittest." Although Spencer coined this phrase, it is usually attributed to his contemporary, Charles Darwin, who proposed that organisms evolve over time as they adapt to their environment. Because they are so similar to Darwin's ideas, Spencer's view of the evolution of societies became known as *social Darwinism.*

Spencer's ideas that charity and helping the poor were wrong appalled many. The wealthy industrialists of the time, however, who saw themselves as "the fittest"— and therefore superior—found Spencer's ideas attractive. Not coincidentally, Spencer's views helped them avoid feelings of guilt for living like royalty while people around them went hungry.

Like Comte, Spencer was more of a social philosopher than a sociologist. Also like Comte, Spencer did not conduct scientific studies. He simply developed ideas about society. Spencer gained a wide following in England and the United States, where he was sought after as a speaker, but eventually social Darwinism was discredited.

■ *This eighteenth-century painting (artist unknown) depicts women from Paris joining the French Army on its way to Versailles on October 5, 1789. The French Revolution of 1789 not only overthrew the aristocracy but upset the entire social order. This extensive change removed the past as a sure guide to the present. The events of this period stimulated Auguste Comte to analyze how societies change. His writings are often taken as the origin of sociology.*

■ Karl Marx and Class Conflict

Karl Marx (1818–1883) not only influenced sociology but also left his mark on world history. Marx's influence has been so great that even the *Wall Street Journal*, that staunch advocate of capitalism, has called him one of the three greatest modern thinkers (the other two being Sigmund Freud and Albert Einstein).

Like Comte, Marx thought that people should take active steps to change society. Marx, who came to England after being exiled from his native Germany for proposing revolution, believed that the engine of human history is **class conflict.** He said that the *bourgeoisie* (the controlling class of *capitalists,* those who own the means to produce wealth—capital, land, factories, and machines) are locked in conflict with the *proletariat* (the exploited class, the mass of workers who do not own the means of production). This bitter struggle can end only when members of the working class unite in revolution and throw off their chains of bondage. The result will be a classless society, one free of exploitation, in which all will work according to their abilities and receive according to their needs (Marx and Engels 1848/1967).

Marxism is not the same as communism. Although Marx supported revolution as the only way that the workers could gain control of society, he did not develop the political system called *communism.* This is a later application of his ideas. Indeed, Marx himself felt disgusted when he heard debates about his insights into social life. After listening to some of the positions attributed to him, he shook his head and said, "I am not a Marxist" (Dobriner 1969b:222; Gitlin 1997:89).

Unlike Comte and Spencer, Marx did not think of himself as a sociologist. He spent years studying in the library of the British Museum in London, where he wrote widely on history, philosophy, and, of course, economics and political science. Because of his insights into the relationship between the social classes, especially the class struggle between the "haves" and the "have-nots," many sociologists today claim Marx as a significant early sociologist. He also introduced one of the major perspectives in sociology, conflict theory, which is discussed on pages 30–31.

■ *Karl Marx (1818–1883) analyzed the exploitation of the proletariat (propertyless working classes) by the capitalists (those who own the means of production). He believed that the overthrow of the capitalists by the proletariat was inevitable. Although Marx did not consider himself a sociologist, his ideas have profoundly influenced many sociologists, particularly conflict theorists.*

■ Emile Durkheim and Social Integration

The primary professional goal of Emile Durkheim (1858–1917) was to get sociology recognized as a separate academic discipline. Up to this time, sociology was viewed as part of history and economics. Durkheim, who grew up in eastern France and was educated in both Germany and France, achieved his goal when he received the first academic appointment in sociology at the University of Bordeaux in 1887 (Coser 1977).

Durkheim had another goal: to show how social forces affect people's behavior. To accomplish this, he conducted rigorous research. Comparing the suicide rates of several European countries, Durkheim (1897/1966) found that each country's suicide rate was different, and that each remained remarkably stable year after year. He also found that different groups within a country had different suicide rates, and that these, too, remained stable from year to year. For example, Protestants, males, and the unmarried killed themselves at a higher rate than did Catholics, Jews, females, and the married. From this, Durkheim drew the insightful conclusion that suicide is not simply a matter of individuals here and there deciding to take their lives for personal reasons. Instead, *social factors underlie suicide,* and this is what keeps those rates fairly constant year after year.

Durkheim identified **social integration,** the degree to which people are tied to their social group, as a key social factor in suicide. He concluded that people who have weaker social ties are more likely to commit suicide. This factor, he said, ex-

class conflict
Marx's term for the struggle between capitalists and workers

social integration
the degree to which people feel a part of social groups

■ *The French sociologist Emile Durkheim (1858–1917) contributed many concepts to sociology. When he compared the suicide rates of several countries, he discovered that people are more likely to commit suicide if their ties to others in their communities are weak. Durkheim's identification of the role of social integration in social life remains central to sociology today.*

anomie
Durkheim's term for a condition of society in which people become detached from the norms that usually guide their behavior

plained why Protestants, males, and the unmarried have higher suicide rates. This is how it works, Durkheim said: Protestantism encourages greater freedom of thought and action; males are more independent than females; and the unmarried lack the ties and responsibilities of marriage. In other words, because their social integration is weaker, members of these groups have fewer of the social ties that keep people from committing suicide.

Although strong social bonds help protect people from suicide, Durkheim noted that in some instances strong bonds encourage suicide. An example is people who, torn apart by grief, kill themselves after their spouse dies. Their own feelings are so integrated with those of their spouse that they prefer death rather than life without the one who gave meaning to life.

A hundred years later, Durkheim's study is still quoted. His research was so thorough that the principle he uncovered still applies: People who are less socially integrated have higher rates of suicide. Even today, those same categories that Durkheim identified—Protestants, males, and the unmarried—are more likely to kill themselves.

Durkheim's third concern was that social research be practical. He thought of sociologists as being similar to physicians: Where physicians apply scientific findings to determine the sickness and health of the body, sociologists should do the same for society (Giddens 1978). They should diagnose causes of social ills and develop remedies for them. For example, as is the case today, in Durkheim's time people were concerned that there was too much individualism. Durkheim concluded that the new individualism was not pathological, but a healthy expression of a changing society. Individualism can go too far, however. It then poses the danger of what Durkheim called **anomie**, a breaking down of the controlling influences of society. Under these conditions, people become detached from society and are left with too little moral guidance. This is dangerous, for their desires are no longer regulated by social norms (Coser 1977). Durkheim suggested that sociologists intervene: To prevent anomie, they should create new social groups to stand between the state and the family. These groups, he said, would help meet the need for a sense of belonging that the new, impersonal industrial society was eroding.

In sum, Durkheim's major contribution was his thorough sociological approach to understanding human behavior. Suicide, for example, appears to be such an intensely

■ *Emile Durkheim used the term* anomie *to refer to feeling rootless and normless, lacking a sense of intimate belonging—the opposite of what sociologists mean by* community. *Durkheim believed that modern societies produce a feeling of isolation, much of which comes from the division of labor. In contrast, members of traditional societies, who work alongside family and neighbors and participate in similar activities, experience a high degree of* social integration—*the opposite of anomie. The photo on the right shows workers in Yunnan Province, China picking lichee nuts.*

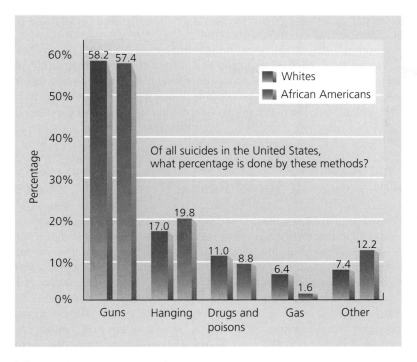

Figure 1.1

How Americans Commit Suicide

Source: Statistical Abstract 2000:Table 138.

Note: Data available only for these groups.

individual act that psychologists should examine it, not sociologists. Yet, as Durkheim illustrated, if we look at human behavior (such as suicide) only in individualistic terms, we miss its *social* basis. For a glimpse of what Durkheim meant, look at Figure 1.1. That African Americans and whites commit suicide in such similar ways indicates something that goes far beyond the individual. Since these patterns are similar year after year, they reflect conditions in society, such as the popularity and accessibility of guns.

■ Max Weber and the Protestant Ethic

Max Weber (Mahx VAY-ber) (1864–1920), a German sociologist and a contemporary of Durkheim, also held professorships in the new academic discipline of sociology. With Durkheim and Marx, Weber is one of the most influential of all sociologists, and you will come across his writings and theories in the coming chapters. Let's look at two issues Weber raised that remain controversial today.

Religion and the Origin of Capitalism   Weber disagreed with Marx's claim that economics is the central force in social change. That role, he said, belongs to religion. Weber (1904/1958) theorized that the Roman Catholic belief system encouraged followers to hold onto traditional ways of life, while the Protestant belief system encouraged its members to embrace change. Protestantism, he said, undermined people's spiritual security. Roman Catholics believed that because they were church members they were on the road to heaven. But Protestants, who did not share in this belief, turned to "signs" that they were in God's will. Financial success became the major sign that God was on their side. Consequently, Protestants began to live frugal lives, saving their money and investing the surplus in order to make even more. This, said Weber, brought about the birth of capitalism.

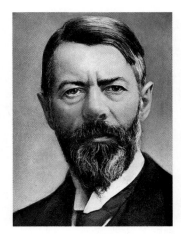

■ *Max Weber (1864–1920) was another early sociologist who left a profound impression on sociology. He used cross-cultural and historical materials to determine how extensively social groups affect people's orientations to life.*

Weber called this self-denying approach to life the *Protestant ethic*. He termed the readiness to invest capital in order to make more money the *spirit of capitalism*. To test his theory, Weber compared the extent of capitalism in Roman Catholic and Protestant countries. In line with his theory, he found that capitalism was more likely to flourish in Protestant countries. Weber's conclusion that religion was the central factor in the rise of capitalism was controversial when he made it, and it continues to be debated today (Hamilton 1996). We'll explore these ideas in more detail in Chapter 7.

The Role of Values in Social Research

Weber raised another issue that remains controversial among sociologists. He said that sociology should be **value free**. By this, he meant that a sociologist's **values**—personal beliefs about what is good or worthwhile in life and the way the world ought to be—should not affect research. Weber wanted **objectivity**, total neutrality, to be the hallmark of social research. If values influence research, he said, sociological findings will be biased.

That bias has no place in research is not a matter of debate. All sociologists agree that no one should distort data to make them fit preconceived ideas or personal values. It is equally clear, however, that because sociologists—like everyone else—are members of a particular society at a given point in history, they, too, are infused with values of all sorts. These values inevitably play a role in our research. For example, values are part of the reason that one sociologist chooses to do research on the Mafia, while another turns a sociological eye on kindergarten students.

Because values can lead to unwitting distortions in how we interpret our findings, sociologists stress **replication**, researchers repeating a study in order to compare their results with the original findings. If values have influenced research findings, replication by other sociologists should uncover this problem and correct it.

Despite this consensus, however, values remain a hotly debated topic in sociology (Haddad and Newby 1999; Orlans 1999; Radelet 2001). The disagreement centers on the proper purposes and uses of sociology. Regarding its *purpose,* some sociologists take the position that their goal should be simply to advance understanding of social life. They should gather data on any topic in which they are interested and then use the best theory available to interpret their findings. Others are convinced that sociologists have the responsibility to focus on the social arrangements that harm people—to investigate what causes poverty, crime, war, and other forms of human exploitation.

Then there is the disagreement over the *uses* of sociology. Those who say that understanding is sociology's proper goal take the position that the knowledge gained by social research belongs to the scientific community and to the world. Accordingly, it can be used by anyone for any purpose. In contrast, those who say that sociologists should focus on harmful social conditions take the position that sociologists should spearhead social reform. They say that sociologists should use their studies to alleviate human suffering and make society a better place to live. These contrasting views are summarized in Figure 1.2.

value free
the view that a sociologist's personal values should not influence social research

values
ideas about what is good or worthwhile in life; attitudes about the way the world ought to be

objectivity
total neutrality

replication
repeating a study in order to check its findings

Figure 1.2
The Debate Over Values

Although this debate is more complicated than the argument summarized here—few sociologists take such one-sided views—this sketch does identify its major issues. Perhaps sociologist John Galliher (1991) best expresses the majority position:

> Some argue that social scientists, unlike politicians and religious leaders, should merely attempt to describe and explain the events of the world but should never make value judgments based on those observations. Yet a value-free and nonjudgmental social science has no place in a world that has experienced the Holocaust, in a world having had slavery, in a world with the ever-present threat of rape and other sexual assault, in a world with frequent, unpunished crimes in high places, including the production of products known by their manufacturers to cause death and injury as has been true of asbestos products and continues to be true of the cigarette industry, and in a world dying from environmental pollution by these same large multinational corporations.

Verstehen and Social Facts

Weber and *Verstehen*

Weber also stressed that to understand human behavior we should use **Verstehen** (a German word meaning "to understand"). Perhaps the best translation of this term is "to grasp by insight." By emphasizing *Verstehen*, Weber meant that the best interpreter of human behavior is someone who "has been there," someone who can understand the feelings and motivations of the people they are studying. In short, we must pay attention to what are called **subjective meanings**, the ways in which people interpret their own behavior. We can't understand what people do, Weber insisted, unless we look at how people view and explain their own behavior.

To better understand this term, let's return to the homeless in our opening vignette. Why were the men so silent? Why were they so unlike the noisy, sometimes boisterous college students who swarm dorms and cafeterias?

Verstehen can help explain this. When I interviewed men in the shelters (and, in other settings, homeless women), they revealed their despair. Because you know—at least on some level—what the human emotion of despair is, you can immediately apply your understanding to their situation. You know that people in despair feel a sense of hopelessness. The future looks bleak, hardly worth plodding toward. Consequently, why is it worth talking about? Who wants to hear another hard-luck story?

By applying *Verstehen*—your understanding of what it means to be human and to face various situations in life—you gain insight into people's behavior. In this case, you can understand their silence, their lack of communication in the shelter.

Durkheim and Social Facts

In contrast to Weber's emphasis on *Verstehen* and subjective meanings, Durkheim stressed what he called **social facts.** By this term, he meant the patterns of behavior that characterize a social group. Examples of social facts in the United States include June being the most popular month for

Verstehen
a German word used by Weber that is perhaps best understood as "to have insight into someone's situation"

subjective meanings
the meanings that people give their own behavior

social facts
Durkheim's term for a group's patterns of behavior

■ *Granted their situation of deprivation, it is not surprising that the homeless are not brimming with optimism. The holiday meal shown here is about as festive as it gets in a homeless shelter.*

weddings, suicide rates being higher among people 65 and older, and more births occurring on Tuesdays than on any other day of the week.

Durkheim said that we must use social facts to interpret social facts. In other words, each pattern reflects some condition of society. People all over the country don't just coincidentally decide to do similar things, whether that be to get married or to commit suicide. If that were the case, in some years middle-aged people would be the most likely to kill themselves, in other years, young people, and so on. *Patterns that hold true year after year indicate that as thousands and even millions of people make their individual decisions, they are responding to conditions in their society.* It is the job of the sociologist, then, to uncover social facts and to explain them through other social facts. In the following section, let's look at how the social facts I mentioned—of weddings, suicide, and births—are explained by other social facts.

■ How Social Facts and *Verstehen* Fit Together

Social facts and *Verstehen* go hand in hand. As a member of U.S. society, you know how June weddings are related to the end of the school year and how this month, now locked in tradition, common sentiment, and advertising, carries its own momentum. As for suicide among the elderly (see Chapter 13), you probably already have a sense of the greater despair that many Americans of this age feel.

But do you know why more Americans are born on Tuesday than on any other day of the week? One would expect Tuesday to be no more common than any other day, and that is how it used to be. But no longer. To understand this change, we need a combination of social facts and *Verstehen*. Four social facts are relevant: First, due to technology, the hospital has become a dominating force in the U.S. medical system. Second, current technology has made delivery by caesarean section safer. Third, as discussed in Chapter 19 (page 571), doctors took over the delivery of babies. Fourth, profit is a top goal of practicing medicine in the United States. As a result of these social facts, an operation that used to be a last resort for emergencies has become so routine that one-fifth (21 percent) of all U.S. babies are now delivered in this

■ *Cesarean deliveries used to be unusual, a last resort to prevent harm to the mother or to save the baby. Today, these deliveries have become routine in the United States. To understand this change, both social facts and* Verstehen *are useful.*

manner (*Statistical Abstract* 2000:Table 90). This is the highest rate of such births in the world (Wolff et al. 1992). To these social facts, we add *Verstehen,* which gives us insight that goes beyond the cold statistics. We can understand that most mothers-to-be prefer to give birth in a hospital and that they do not perceive that they have alternatives. We can also understand that the services of physicians are in high demand and that they schedule deliveries for the time that is most convenient for them. Tuesday is the day that suits them best.

Sexism in Early Sociology

■ Attitudes of the Time

As you may have noticed, all the sociologists we have discussed are men. In the 1800s, sex roles were rigidly defined, with women assigned the roles of wife and mother. In the classic German phrase, women were expected to devote themselves to the four K's: *Kirche, Küchen, Kinder, und Kleider* (church, cooking, children, and clothes). Trying to break out of this mold meant risking severe disapproval.

Few people, male or female, received any education beyond basic reading and writing. Higher education, for the rare few who received it, was reserved for men. A handful of women from wealthy families, however, did pursue higher education. A few even managed to study sociology, although the sexism so deeply entrenched in the universities stopped them from obtaining advanced degrees or becoming professors. In line with the times, their own research was almost entirely ignored.

■ Harriet Martineau

A classic example is Harriet Martineau (1802–1876), who was born into a wealthy family in England. When Martineau first began to analyze social life, she would hide her writing beneath her sewing when visitors arrived, for writing was "masculine" and sewing "feminine" (Gilman 1911:88). Martineau persisted in her interests, however, and she eventually studied social life in both Great Britain and the United States. In 1837, two or three decades before Durkheim and Weber were born, Martineau published *Society in America,* in which she reported on this new nation's customs—family, race, gender, politics, and religion. Despite her insightful examination of U.S. life, which is still worth reading today, Martineau's research met the fate of other early women sociologists and, until recently, has been ignored. Instead, she is known primarily for translating Comte's ideas into English.

Sociology in North America

■ Early History: The Tension Between Social Reform and Sociological Analysis

Transplanted to U.S. soil in the late nineteenth century, sociology first took root at the University of Kansas in 1890; at the University of Chicago in 1892; and at Atlanta University, then an all-black school, in 1897. From there, academic specialties in sociology spread throughout North America. The growth was gradual, however.

■ *Interested in social reform, Harriet Martineau (1802–1876) discovered the writings of Comte. An advocate for the abolition of slavery, she traveled widely and wrote extensively. Her book,* Society in America, *provides a fascinating analysis of U.S. life prior to the Civil War.*

■ *Jane Addams, 1860–1935, a recipient of the Nobel Peace Prize, worked on behalf of poor immigrants. With Ellen G. Starr, she founded Hull-House, a center to help immigrants in Chicago. She was a leader in women's rights (women's suffrage), as well as the peace movement of World War I.*

It was not until 1922 that McGill University gave Canada its first department of sociology. Harvard University did not open its department of sociology until 1930, and the University of California at Berkeley did not follow until the 1950s.

Initially, the department at the University of Chicago, which was founded by Albion Small (1854–1926), dominated sociology. (Small also founded the *American Journal of Sociology* and was its editor from 1895 to 1925.) Members of this first sociology department whose ideas continue to influence today's sociologists include Robert E. Park (1864–1944), Ernest Burgess (1886–1966), and George Herbert Mead (1863–1931), who developed the symbolic interactionist perspective, which we will examine later.

The situation of women in North America was similar to that of European women, and their contributions to sociology met a similar fate. Among the early women sociologists were Jane Addams, Emily Greene Balch, Isabel Eaton, Sophie Germain, Charlotte Perkins Gilman, Alice Hamilton, Florence Kelley, Elsie Clews Parsons, and Alice Paul. Denied faculty appointments in sociology, many turned to social activism (Young 1995).

Because some of these women worked with the poor rather than as professors of sociology, many sociologists classify them as social workers. Today's distinction between sociology and social work is fairly clear cut. There is a profession called social work; people train for it, they are hired to do it, and they have a distinct identity as social workers. They focus on aiding the economically underprivileged and socially maladjusted members of society. They have jobs in hospitals and schools, and many work in the area of public aid. Others set up private practice and counsel patients. Earlier in the development of sociology, however, there often was little distinction between sociology and social work. This fuzziness lasted until recently, and many departments combined sociology and social work. Some still do.

■ Jane Addams and Social Reform

Although many North American sociologists combined the role of sociologist with that of social reformer, none was so successful as Jane Addams (1860–1935). Like Harriet Martineau, Addams came from a background of wealth and privilege. She attended The Women's Medical College of Philadelphia, but dropped out because of illness (Addams 1910/1981). On one of her many trips to Europe, Addams was impressed with work being done to help London's poor. From then on, she tirelessly worked for social justice.

In 1889, Addams co-founded Hull-House, located in Chicago's notorious slums. Hull-House was open to people who needed refuge—to immigrants, the sick, the aged, the poor. With her piercing insights into the social classes, especially how workers were exploited and how peasant immigrants adjusted to industrializing cities, Addams strived to bridge the gap between the powerful and the powerless. Sociologists from nearby University of Chicago were frequent visitors at Hull-House. Her efforts at social reform were so outstanding and so effective that in 1931 she was a co-winner of the Nobel Peace Prize, the only sociologist to win this coveted award.

■ W.E.B. Du Bois and Race Relations

■ *W(illiam) E(dward) B(urghardt) Du Bois (1868–1963) spent his lifetime studying relations between African Americans and whites. Like many early North American sociologists, Du Bois combined the role of academic sociologist with that of social reformer. He was also the editor of Crisis, an influential journal of the time.*

Confronted by the racism of this period, African American professionals also found life difficult. The most notable example is provided by W.E.B. Du Bois (1868–1963), who, after earning a bachelor's degree from Fisk University, became the first African American to earn a doctorate at Harvard (Lemert 1994). After completing his education at the University of Berlin, where he attended lectures by Max Weber, Du Bois taught Greek and Latin at Wilberforce University. He was hired by Atlanta University in 1897, where he remained for most of his career (Du Bois 1935).

It is difficult to imagine the racism that Du Bois encountered. For example, he once saw the fingers of a lynching victim displayed in a Georgia butcher shop (Aptheker 1990). His passionate concern became to eliminate social injustice. Each year between 1896 and 1914, Du Bois published a book on relations between African Americans and whites. Of his almost 2,000 writings, *The Philadelphia Negro* (1899) stands out. In this analysis of how African Americans in Philadelphia coped with racism, Du Bois pointed out that some of the more successful African Americans were breaking their ties with other African Americans in order to win acceptance by whites. This, he said, weakened the African American community by depriving it of their influence. One of Du Bois' most elegantly written books, which preserves a picture of race relations immediately after the Civil War, is *The Souls of Black Folk*. The Down-to-Earth Sociology box below is taken from this book.

---

down-to-earth
s o c i o l o g y

■ ■ ■ ■ ■

Early North American Sociology: Du Bois and Race Relations

The writings of W.E.B. Du Bois, who expressed sociological thought more like an accomplished novelist than like a sociologist, have been neglected in sociology. To help remedy this omission, I reprint the following excerpts from pages 66–68 of *The Souls of Black Folk* (1903). In this book, Du Bois analyzes changes that occurred in the social and economic conditions of African Americans during the thirty years following the Civil War.

For two summers, while he was a student at Fisk, Du Bois taught in a log-hut, segregated school "way back in the hills" of rural Tennessee. The following excerpts help us understand conditions at that time.

It was a hot morning late in July when the school opened. I trembled when I heard the patter of little feet down the dusty road, and saw the growing row of dark solemn faces and bright eager eyes facing me. . . .There they sat, nearly thirty of them, on the rough benches, their faces shading from a pale cream to deep brown, the little feet bare and swinging, the eyes full of expectation, with here and there a twinkle of mischief, and the hands grasping Webster's blue-black spelling-book. I loved my school, and the fine faith the children had in the wisdom of their teacher was truly marvelous. We read and spelled together, wrote a little, picked flowers, sang, and listened to stories of the world beyond the hill. . . .

On Friday nights I often went home with some of the children,—sometimes to Doc Burke's farm. He was a great, loud, thin Black, ever working, and trying to buy these seventy-five acres of hill and dale where he lived; but people said that he would surely fail and the "white folks would get it all." His wife was a magnificent Amazon, with saffron face and shiny hair, uncorseted and barefooted, and the children were strong and barefooted. They lived in a one-and-a-half-room cabin in the hollow of the farm near the spring. . . .

I liked to stay with the Dowells, for they had four rooms and plenty of good country fare. Uncle Bird had a small, rough farm, all woods and hills, miles from the big road; but he was full of tales,—he preached now and then,—and with his children, berries, horses, and wheat he was happy and prosperous. Often, to keep the peace, I must go where life was less lovely; for instance, 'Tildy's mother was incorrigibly dirty, Reuben's larder was limited seriously, and herds of untamed insects wandered over the Eddingses' beds. Best of all I loved to go to Josie's, and sit on the porch, eating peaches, while the mother bustled and talked: how Josie had bought the sewing-machine; how Josie worked at service in winter, but that four dollars a month was "mighty little" wages; how Josie longed to go away to school, but that it "looked liked" they never could get far enough ahead to let her; how the crops failed and the well was yet unfinished; and, finally, how mean some of the white folks were.

For two summers I lived in this little world. . . . I have called my tiny community a world, and so its isolation made it; and yet there was among us but a half-awakened common consciousness, sprung from common joy and grief, at burial, birth, or wedding; from common hardship in poverty, poor land, and low wages, and, above all, from the sight of the Veil* that hung between us and Opportunity. All this caused us to think some thoughts together; but these, when ripe for speech, were spoken in various languages. Those whose eyes twenty-five and more years had seen "the glory of the coming of the Lord," saw in every present hindrance or help a dark fatalism bound to bring all things right in His own good time. The mass of those to whom slavery was a dim recollection of childhood found the world a puzzling thing: it asked little of them, and they answered with little, and yet it ridiculed their offering. Such a paradox they could not understand, and therefore sank into listless indifference, or shiftlessness, or reckless bravado. There were, however, some—such as Josie, Jim, and Ben—to whom War, Hell, and Slavery were but childhood tales, whose young appetites had been whetted to an edge by school and story and half-awakened thought. Ill could they be content, born without and beyond the World. And their weak wings beat against their barriers,—barriers of caste, of youth, of life; at last, in dangerous moments, against everything that opposed even a whim.

*"The Veil" is shorthand for the Veil of Race, referring to how race colors all human relations. Du Bois' hope was that "sometime, somewhere, men will judge men by their souls and not by their skins" (p. 261).

■ ■ ■ ■ ■

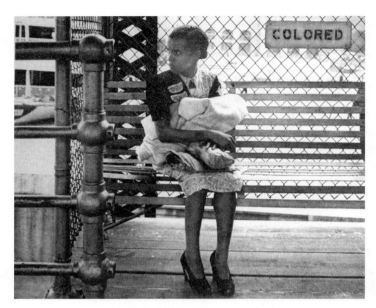

■ In the 1930s, when this photo was taken, racial segregation was a fact of life. Although many changes have occurred since then—and since W.E.B. Du Bois analyzed race relations—race remains a significant factor in the lives of Americans.

Du Bois' insights into race relations were heightened by personal experiences. For example, although he was invited to present a paper at the 1909 meetings of the American Sociological Society, he was too poor to attend, despite his education, faculty position, and accomplishments. When he could afford to attend subsequent meetings, discrimination was so prevalent that he was not permitted to eat or stay at the same hotels as the white sociologists. Later in life, when Du Bois had the money to travel, the U.S. State Department feared that he would criticize the United States and refused to give him a visa (Du Bois 1968).

At first, Du Bois was content to collect and interpret objective data. Later, frustrated at the continued exploitation of blacks, Du Bois turned to social action. Along with Jane Addams and others from Hull-House, he founded the National Association for the Advancement of Colored People, or NAACP (Deegan 1988). Continuing to battle racism both as a sociologist and as a journalist, Du Bois eventually embraced revolutionary Marxism. At age 93, dismayed that so little improvement had been made in race relations, he moved to Ghana, where he is buried (Stark 1989).

Until recently, W.E.B. Du Bois was neglected in sociology, his many contributions unrecognized. As a personal example, during my entire graduate program at Washington University, I was never introduced to Du Bois' books and thought. Today, however, sociologists are rediscovering Du Bois, and he is beginning to receive some long-deserved appreciation.

■ C. Wright Mills was a controversial figure in sociology because of his analysis of the role of the power elite in U.S. society. Today, his analysis is taken for granted by many sociologists.

■ Talcott Persons and C. Wright Mills: Theory Versus Reform

Like Du Bois, and following the advice of Comte, many early North American sociologists combined the role of sociologist with that of social reformer. They saw society, or parts of it, as corrupt and in need of reform. During the 1920s and 1930s, for example, Park and Burgess not only studied prostitution, crime, drug addiction, and juvenile delinquency, but also they offered suggestions for how to alleviate these social problems.

During the 1940s, the emphasis shifted from social reform to social theory. Talcott Parsons (1902–1979), for example, developed abstract models of society that influenced a generation of sociologists. Parsons' detailed models of how the parts of society harmoniously work together did nothing to stimulate social activism.

C. Wright Mills (1916–1962) deplored the theoretical abstractions of this period, and he urged sociologists to get back to social reform. He saw the coalescing of interests on the part of a group he called the *power elite*—the top leaders of business, politics, and the military—as an imminent threat to freedom. Shortly after Mills' death, the United States entered the turbulent era of the 1960s and 1970s. Interest in social activism was sparked, and Mills' ideas became popular among a new generation of sociologists.

■ The Present: The Continuing Tension and the Rise of Applied Sociology

The apparent contradiction of these two aims—analyzing society versus working toward its reform—created a tension in sociology that is still evident today. Some sociologists believe that their proper role is to analyze some aspect of society and to publish their findings in sociology journals. Others say this is not enough—sociologists have an obligation to use their expertise to try to make society a better place in which to live, to help bring justice to the poor.

Somewhere between these extremes has emerged **applied sociology,** the use of sociology to solve problems. (See Figure 1.3, which contrasts basic and applied sociology.) One of the first attempts at applied sociology—and one of the most successful—was the founding of the National Association for the Advancement of Colored People. Today's applied sociologists work in a variety of settings (Guice 1999; Steele et al. 1999). Some work for business firms to solve problems in the workplace. Others do research for the government, where they investigate social problems such as pornography, rape, environmental pollution, or the spread of AIDS. Still others work in high technology. The Down-to-Earth Sociology box on the next page gives an idea of the variety of settings in which applied sociologists work.

applied sociology
the use of sociology to solve problems—from the micro level of family relationships to the macro level of crime and pollution

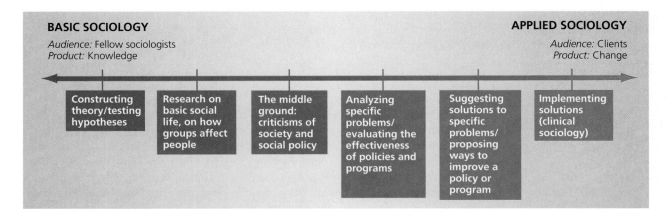

Figure 1.3

Comparing Basic and Applied Sociology
Source: Based on DeMartini 1982.

down-to-earth
s o c i o l o g y

■ ■ ■ ■ ■

Careers in Sociology: What Applied Sociologists Do

Most sociologists teach in colleges and universities. As your instructor is doing in this course, they transmit basic sociological knowledge to the next generation. Applied sociologists, in contrast, work in a wide variety of areas—from counseling children and studying how AIDS is transmitted to making software more "user friendly." (They study how people use new computer products and give feedback to engineers who design those products [Guice 1999].) To give you an idea of this variety, let's look over the shoulders of four applied sociologists.

Leslie Green, who does marketing research at Vanderveer Group in Philadelphia, Pennsylvania, earned her bachelor's degree in sociology at Shippensburg University. To develop strategies to get doctors to prescribe particular drugs, her company invites physicians to discuss prescription drugs. Green sets up the meetings, locates moderators for the discussion groups, and arranges payments to the physicians who participate in the research. "My training in sociology," she says, "helps me in 'people skills.' It helps me to understand the needs of different groups, and to interact with them."

Stanley Capela, whose master's degree is from Fordham University, works as an applied sociologist at HeartShare Human Services in New York. He evalu-

ates how children's programs—such as ones that focus on housing, AIDS, care in group homes, and preschool education for developmentally disabled children—actually work, compared with what they are supposed to do. He spots problems and suggests solutions. One of his assignments was to find out why children waited so long to be adopted, even though there was a long list of eager adoptive parents. He identified the problem as an inefficient information system; that is, the paperwork got bogged down as it was routed through the system. He suggested ways to improve the flow of paperwork.

Laurie Banks, who received her master's degree in sociology from Fordham University, works for the New York City Health Department, where she analyzes statistics. As she examined death certificates, she found that some areas of the city had higher rates of cancer. With its high rates of stomach cancer, one Polish neighborhood stood out. Alerted to this, the Centers for Disease Control conducted interviews in the neighborhood. They traced the cause to eating large amounts of sausage. In another case, Banks compared birth certificates with school records. She found that problems at birth—low birth weight, lack of prenatal care, and birth complications—were linked to low reading skills and behavior problems in school.

Joyce Miller Iutcovich, whose doctorate is from Kent State University, is president of Keystone University Research Corporation in Erie, Pennsylvania. She is also a past president of the Society for Applied Sociology. Iutcovich engages in research and consulting activities primarily for government agencies. Her organization administers the Pennsylvania Substance Abuse and Health Information Clearinghouse, which distributes over 300,000 pieces of literature a month. One of Iutcovich's main projects has been to improve the care given to children in day care. For this, she designed a training program for child care providers and conducts research on caregiver performance for the Pennsylvania Department of Public Welfare. Iutcovich's research has enhanced the training of child care workers, which has improved the quality of care they give children. She has also been able to influence public policy.

From just these few examples, you can catch a glimpse of the variety of work that applied sociologists do. Some work for corporations, some for government and private agencies, and others operate their own firms. You can also see that a doctorate is not necessary to work as an applied sociologist. For another example of applied sociology, see the Down-to-Earth Sociology box on the next page.

■ ■ ■ ■ ■

Applied sociology is not the same as social reform. It is an application of sociology in some specific setting, not an attempt to rebuild society, as early sociologists envisioned. Consequently, a new tension has emerged in sociology. Sociologists who want the emphasis to be on social reform say that applied sociology doesn't even come close to this. It is an application of sociology, but not an attempt to change society. Others, who want the emphasis to remain on discovering knowledge (basic sociology), say that when sociology is applied it is not sociology—even if done by a sociologist. If a sociologist uses sociological principles to help prostitutes escape from pimps, for example, is it still sociology? This issue is discussed in the Down-to-Earth Sociology box on the next page.

At this point, let's consider how theory fits into sociology.

down-to-earth sociology

Sociology or Social Work? Taking Back Children from the Night

What is and is not sociology remains a lively topic among sociologists. Especially when sociologists discuss the application of sociological knowledge, discussions tend to become heated. Where, for example, is the line between sociology and social work? That line can sometimes be very fine. Consider Lois Lee and her work among teen prostitutes. Lois Lee is a sociologist. There is no doubt about this. She earned a Ph.D. in sociology from United States International University in 1981. While she was working on her doctorate, she began to help teenagers who were prostituting themselves. She took them into her home, where she lived with her husband and baby son. In three years, she took in 250 girls.

As Lee focused more and more on helping teen prostitutes, she founded Children of the Night, which reaches the kids by means of "a twenty-four-hour hotline, a street outreach program, a walk-in crisis center, crisis intervention for medical or life-threatening situations, family counseling, job placement, and foster home or group placement." By providing alternatives to prostitution and petty crime, Lee estimates that Children of the Night has helped more than 5,000 runaways and prostitutes get off the streets. Lee's work has brought her national recognition and a presidential award.

Lee credits her success to sociology. She says that sociology gave her insights into the relationships between groups. She says that her sociological training helps her "to understand and move safely through intersecting deviant worlds, to relate positively to police and caretaking agencies while retaining a critical perspective, to know which game to play in which situation."

In a CBS interview, Lee said, "I know what the street rules are. I know what the pimp game is, I know what the con games are, and it's up to me to play that game correctly." She added, "It's all sociology. That's why when people call me a social worker I always correct them."

Many sociologists disagree. They say that Lee is a sociologist who is doing social work. Whether a sociologist, a psychologist, or a social worker helps prostitutes does not change what they do. If a sociologist went into computer sales, for example, he or she would be in

■ *The line between sociology and social work is sometimes drawn fine. As explained in the text, the work of Lois Lee, shown here, helps to blur that finely drawn line.*

business, not sociology, no matter how much insight his or her sociological studies may provide into relationships among customers, managers, and suppliers.

■ ■ ■ ■ ■

Theoretical Perspectives in Sociology

Facts never interpret themselves. In everyday life, we interpret what we observe by using common sense. We place our observations or "facts" into a framework of more-or-less related ideas. Sociologists do this, too, but they place their observations into a conceptual framework called a theory. A **theory** is a general statement about how some parts of the world fit together and how they work. It is an explanation of how two or more "facts" are related to one another. By providing a framework in which to place observations, each theory interprets reality in a distinct way.

Sociologists use three major theories: symbolic interactionism, functional analysis, and conflict theory. Let's first examine the main elements of these theories. (See Table 1.1.) Then let's see how each theory helps us to understand why the divorce rate in the United States is so high.

theory
a general statement about how some parts of the world fit together and how they work; an explanation of how two or more facts are related to one another

TABLE 1.1	**Major Theoretical Perspectives in Sociology**			
Perspective	**Usual Level of Analysis**	**Focus of Analysis**	**Key Terms**	**Applying the Perspectives to the U.S. Divorce Rate**
Symbolic Interactionism	Microsociological—examines small-scale patterns of social interaction	Face-to-face interaction; how people use symbols to create social life	Symbols Interaction Meanings Definitions	Industrialization and urbanization changed marital roles and led to a redefinition of love, marriage, children, and divorce.
Functional Analysis (also called functionalism and structural functionalism)	Macrosociological—examines large-scale patterns of society	Relationships among the parts of society; how these parts are *functional* (have beneficial consequences) or *dysfunctional* (have negative consequences)	Structure Functions (manifest and latent) Dysfunctions Equilibrium	As social change erodes the traditional functions of the family, family ties weaken, and the divorce rate increases.
Conflict Theory	Macrosociological—examines large-scale patterns of society	The struggle for scarce resources by groups in a society; how the elites use their power to control the less powerful	Inequality Power Conflict Competition Exploitation	When men control economic life, the divorce rate is low because women find few alternatives to a bad marriage; the rising divorce rate reflects a shift in the balance of power between men and women.

■ *George Herbert Mead (1863–1931) is one of the founders of symbolic interactionism, a major theoretical perspective in sociology. He taught at the University of Chicago, where his lectures were very popular. Although he wrote little, after his death students compiled his lectures into an influential book,* Mind, Self, and Society.

symbolic interactionism
a theoretical perspective in which society is viewed as composed of symbols that people use to establish meaning, develop their views of the world, and communicate with one another

■ Symbolic Interactionism

We can trace the origins of **symbolic interactionism** to the Scottish moral philosophers of the eighteenth century, who noted that people evaluate their own conduct by comparing themselves with others (Stryker 1990). In the United States, a long line of thinkers added to this analysis, including the pioneering psychologist William James (1842–1910) and the educator John Dewey (1859–1952), who analyzed how people use symbols to encapsulate their experiences. This theoretical perspective was brought to sociology by Charles Horton Cooley (1864–1929), William I. Thomas (1863–1947), and George Herbert Mead (1863–1931). Cooley's and Mead's analyses of how symbols lie at the basis of the self-concept are discussed on pages 70–72.

Symbols in Everyday Life　Symbolic interactionists study how people use *symbols*—the things to which we attach meaning—to develop their views of the world and communicate with one another. Without symbols, our social life would be no more sophisticated than that of animals. For example, without symbols we would have no aunts or uncles, employers or teachers, or even brothers or sisters. I know that this sounds strange, but it is symbols that define for us what such relationships are. There would still be reproduction, of course, but no symbols to tell us how we are related to whom. We would not know to whom we owe respect and obligations, or from whom we can expect privileges—the stuff that our relationships are made of.

Think of it like this: If you think of someone as your aunt or uncle, you behave in certain ways, but if you think of that person as a boyfriend or girlfriend, you behave quite differently. It is the symbol that tells you how you are related to others—and how you should act toward them.

Symbols not only allow relationships to exist, but they also allow society to exist. Without symbols, we could not coordinate our actions with those of other people. We could not make plans for a future date, time, and place. Unable to specify times, materials, sizes, or goals, we could not build bridges and highways. Without symbols, there would be no movies or musical instruments. We would have no hospitals, no government, no religion. The class you are taking could not exist—nor could this book.

In short, symbolic interactionists analyze how our behaviors depend on the ways we define ourselves and others. They study face-to-face interaction, looking at how people work out their relationships and how they make sense out of life and their place in it. They point out that even the *self* is a symbol, for it consists of the ideas we have about who we are. And the self is a changing symbol: As we interact with others, we constantly adjust our views of who we are based on how we interpret the reactions of others. We'll get more into this later.

■ **Applying Symbolic Interactionism** To better understand symbolic interactionism, let's see how changing symbols (meanings) help to explain the high U.S. divorce rate. For background, you should understand that marriage used to be seen as a lifelong commitment, and divorce as an immoral act, a flagrant disregard for public opinion and the abandonment of adult responsibilities.

■ *Symbolic interactionists analyze how family relationships have changed over time, and how these changes are related to divorce. From its particular experiences, each family also develops unique perspectives. How do you think this family views its relationships?*

1. *Emotional satisfaction.* In the early part of the last century, symbolic interactionists observed that the basis for family solidarity was changing. As early as 1933, sociologist William Ogburn noted that personality was becoming more important in mate selection. Then in 1945, sociologists Ernest Burgess and Harvey Locke noted that marriage was coming to depend more and more on mutual affection, understanding, and compatibility. What these sociologists had observed was a fundamental shift in U.S. marriage: Husbands and wives were coming to expect—and demand—greater emotional satisfaction from one another.

As this trend intensified, intimacy became the core of marriage. At the same time, as society grew more complex and impersonal, Americans came to view marriage as a solution to the tensions that society produced (Lasch 1977). This new form, "companionate marriage," contributed to divorce, for it encouraged people to expect that their spouse would satisfy "each and every need." Consequently, sociologists say, marriage became an "overloaded institution."

2. *The love symbol.* Our symbol of love also helps to "overload" marriage. An expectation that "true love" will be a constant source of emotional satisfaction sets people up for crushed hopes, for when dissatisfactions enter marriage, as they inevitably do, spouses tend to blame one another for what they see as the other's failure. Their engulfment in the symbol of love at the time of marriage blinds them to the basic unreality of their expectations.

3. *The meaning of children.* Ideas about childhood have undergone a deep historical shift with far-reaching consequences for the U.S. family (Henslin 1992). In medieval Europe children were seen as miniature adults, and there was no sharp separation between the worlds of adults and children (Ariés 1965). Boys were apprenticed at about age 7, while girls at the same age learned the homemaking duties associated with being a wife. In the United States, just three generations ago children "became adults" when they graduated from eighth grade and went to work. Today's contrast is amazing: From miniature adults, children have been culturally fashioned into impressionable, vulnerable, and innocent beings.

4. *The meaning of parenthood.* These changed notions of childhood have had a deep impact on our ideas of good parenting. Today's parents are expected not only to provide unending amounts of affection, love, and tender care but also to take responsibility for ensuring that their children "reach their potential." Today's child rearing lasts longer and is more demanding, pushing the family into even greater "emotional overload" (Lasch 1977).

5. *Marital roles.* In earlier generations, the responsibilities and privileges of husbands and wives were clearly defined. This meant that newlyweds knew what they could legitimately expect from each other. In contrast, today's much vaguer guidelines leave couples to work out more aspects of their respective roles on their own. Many find it difficult to figure out how to divide up responsibilities for work, home, and children.

6. *Perception of alternatives.* While these changes were taking place, society was making another major shift: More and more women began taking jobs outside the home. As they earned paychecks of their own, many wives began to see alternatives to remaining in unhappy marriages. Symbolic interactionists consider the perception of an alternative an essential first step to making divorce possible.

7. *The meaning of divorce.* As these factors coalesced—greater expectations of emotional satisfaction, changed marital and parental roles, and a new perception of alternatives to an unhappy marriage—divorce steadily increased. (Figure 1.4 shows the increase in divorce in the United States, from practically zero in 1890 to our current 1.1 million divorces a year. The plateau for both marriage and divorce since 1980 is probably due to increased cohabitation.)

As divorce became more common, its meaning changed. Once a symbol of almost everything negative—failure, irresponsibility, even immorality—divorce became infused with new meanings—personal change and the opportunity to begin anew. This symbolic change from failure to self-fulfillment reduced the stigma of divorce, setting the stage for divorce on an even larger scale.

Figure 1.4

U.S. Marriage, U.S. Divorce

Sources: Statistical Abstract 1998: Table 92; earlier editions for earlier years; "Population Update" 2000. The broken lines indicate the author's estimates.

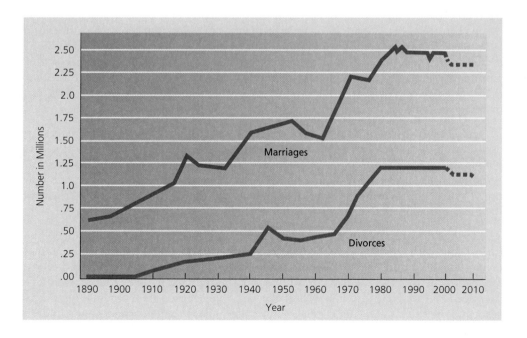

8. *Changes in the law.* The law, itself a powerful symbol, began to reflect these changed ideas about divorce—and to encourage divorce. Where previously divorce was granted only when the most rigorous criteria, such as adultery, were met, legislators now made "incompatibility" grounds for divorce. Eventually, states pioneered "no-fault" divorce, in which couples could dissolve their marriage without accusations of wrongdoing. Some even provide do-it-yourself divorce kits.

IN SUM ■ ■ ■ ■

Symbolic interactionists explain an increasing divorce rate in terms of the changing symbols (or meanings) associated with both marriage and divorce. Changes in people's ideas—about divorce, marital satisfaction, love, the nature of children and parenting, and the roles of husband and wife—have put pressure on today's married couples. No single change is *the* cause, but taken together, these changes provide a strong "push" toward divorce.

Are these changes good or bad? Central to symbolic interactionism is the position that to make a value judgment about change (or anything else) requires a value framework from which to view the change. Symbolic interactionism provides no such value framework. In short, symbolic interactionists, like other sociologists, can analyze social change, but they cannot pass judgment on that change.

■ Functional Analysis

The central idea of **functional analysis** is that society is a whole unit, made up of interrelated parts that work together. Functional analysis, also known as *functionalism* and *structural functionalism,* is rooted in the origins of sociology (Turner 1978). Auguste Comte and Herbert Spencer viewed society as a kind of living organism. Just as a person or animal has organs that function together, they wrote, so does society. Like an organism, if society is to function smoothly, its various parts must work together in harmony.

Emile Durkheim also saw society as being composed of many parts, each with its own function. When all the parts of society fulfill their functions, society is in a "normal" state. If they do not fulfill their functions, society is in an "abnormal" or "pathological" state. To understand society, then, functionalists say that we need to look at both *structure* (how the parts of a society fit together to make the whole) and *function* (what each part does, how it contributes to society).

functional analysis
a theoretical framework in which society is viewed as composed of various parts, each with a function that, when fulfilled, contributes to society's equilibrium; also known as functionalism and structural functionalism

■ *Sociologists who use the functionalist perspectve stress how industrialization and urbanization undermined the traditional functions of the family. Before industrialization, members of the family worked together as an economic unit. As production moved away from the home, it took with it first the father and, more recently, the mother. One consequence is a major dysfunction, the weakening of family ties. This 19th century engraving depicts a carpenter at work while his mother tells stories to the children (and to the adults) and his wife cooks the evening meal.*

Robert Merton and Functionalism

Robert Merton dismissed the organic analogy, but he did maintain the essence of functionalism—the image of society as a whole composed of parts that work together. Merton used the term *functions* to refer to the beneficial consequences of people's actions: Functions help keep a group (society, social system) in equilibrium. In contrast, *dysfunctions* are consequences that harm a society: They undermine a system's equilibrium.

Functions can be either manifest or latent. If an action is *intended* to help some part of a system, it is a *manifest function*. For example, suppose that government officials become concerned about our slowing rate of childbirth. Congress offers a $10,000 bonus for every child born to a married couple. The intention, or manifest function, of the bonus is to increase childbearing. Merton pointed out that people's actions can also have *latent functions;* they can have *unintended* consequences that help a system adjust. Let's suppose that the bonus works, that the birth rate jumps. As a result, the sale of diapers and baby furniture booms. Because the benefits to these businesses were not the intended consequences, they are latent functions of the bonus.

Of course, human actions can also hurt a system. Because such consequences usually are unintended, Merton called them *latent dysfunctions*. Let's assume that the government has failed to specify a "stopping point" with regard to its bonus system. To collect the bonus, some people keep on having children. The more children they have, however, the more they need the next bonus to survive. Large families become common, and poverty increases. Welfare is reinstated, taxes jump, and the nation erupts in protest. Because these results were not intended, and because they harmed the social system, they represent latent dysfunctions of the bonus program.

IN SUM ■ ■ ■ ■

From the perspective of functional analysis, then, the group is a functioning unit, with each part related to the whole. Whenever we examine a smaller part, we need to look for its functions and dysfunctions to see how it is related to the larger unit. This basic approach can be applied to any social group, whether an entire society, a college, or even a group as small as a family.

Applying Functional Analysis Now let's apply functional analysis to the U.S. divorce rate. Functionalists stress that industrialization and urbanization undermined the traditional functions of the family. Let's see how each of the basic functions of the family has changed.

1. *Economic production.* Prior to industrialization, the family was an economic team. At that time, it was difficult to obtain the basic necessities of life, and family members had to cooperate in producing what they needed to survive. When industrialization moved production from home to factory, it disrupted this family team and weakened the bonds that tied family members together. Especially significant was the transfer of the husband/father to the factory, for this isolated him from the family's daily routine. In addition, the wife/mother and children now contributed less to the family's economic survival.

2. *Socialization of children.* As these sweeping changes took place, the government was growing larger and more powerful. It then took over many family functions. To give just one example, schools took away from the family the education of children. In so doing, they assumed much of the responsibility for socializing children. To make certain that families went along with this change, states passed laws requiring school attendance and threatened parents with jail if they did not send their children to school.

3. *Care of the sick and elderly.* As medical training and technology improved, institutionalized medicine grew more powerful. Care of the sick gradually shifted from the family to outside medical specialists. As the central government expanded, its agencies multiplied, and care of the aged changed from a family concern to a government obligation.

■ *In the 1800s, poverty was widespread in the United States. Most people were so poor that they expended their life energies on just getting enough food, fuel, and clothing to survive. Formal education beyond the first several grades was a luxury. This photo depicts the conditions of the people Du Bois worked with. (See the Down-to-Earth Sociology box on page 19.)*

4. *Recreation.* More disposable income became available to Americans, and businesses sprang up to compete for that income. This cost the family a good part of its recreational function, for much entertainment and "fun" changed from home-based, family-centered activities to attendance at paid events.

5. *Sexual control of members.* The vast changes that swept the country also affected the family's role in controlling human sexuality. Traditionally, only sexual relations within marriage were considered legitimate. Although this value was more ideal than real—even the Puritans had a lot of sex outside marriage (Smith and Hindus 1975)—the "sexual revolution" opened many alternatives to marital sex.

6. *Reproduction.* The only family function that seems to have been left untouched is reproduction. Yet even this seemingly inviolable function has not gone unchallenged. A prime example is the greater number of single women who bear children. One third of all U.S. babies are born to an unmarried mother (*Statistical Abstract* 2000:Table 78). Even schools and private agencies have taken over some of the family's control over reproduction. A married woman, for example, can get an abortion without informing her husband, and some U.S. high schools distribute condoms.

A Glimpse of the Past   To see how sharply family functions have changed, it may be useful to take a glimpse of family life in the 1800s.

> When Phil became sick, he was nursed by Ann, his wife. She cooked for him, fed him, changed the bed linen, bathed him, read to him from the Bible, and gave him his medicine. (She did this in addition to doing the housework and taking care of their six children.) Phil was also surrounded by the children, who shouldered some of his chores while he was sick.
>
> When Phil died, the male neighbors and relatives made the casket while Ann, her mother, and female friends washed and dressed the body. Phil was then "laid out" in the front parlor (the formal living room), where friends, neighbors, and relatives viewed him, paying their last respects. From there, friends moved his body to the church for the final message, and then to the grave they themselves had dug.

As you can see, the family used to have more functions. The family handled many aspects of life and death that we now assign to outside agencies. Not only did the care of the sick take place almost exclusively within the family, but death was also a family affair—from preparing the body to burying it. Today we assume that such functions *properly* belong to specialized agencies, and few of us can imagine ourselves preparing the body of a close relative for burial. Such an act may even seem grotesque, almost barbarous, for our current customs also guide our feelings, another fascinating aspect of social life, but one, regrettably, that we do not have time to pursue. (On pages 75–78, we return to the topic of emotions.)

IN SUM ■ ▪ ▪ ▪ ▪

The family has lost many of its traditional functions, while others are presently under assault. Especially significant is that economic production is no longer a cooperative, home-based effort, with husbands and wives depending on one another for their interlocking contributions to a mutual endeavor. Husbands and wives today earn individual paychecks, and increasingly function as separate components of an impersonal, multinational, and even global system. When outside agencies take over family functions, this makes the family more fragile, and an increase in divorce inevitable. The fewer functions that family members have in common, the fewer are their "ties that bind," and these ties are what help husbands and wives get through the inevitable problems they experience.

■ Conflict Theory

Conflict theory provides a third perspective on social life. Unlike the functionalists who view society as a harmonious whole, with its parts working together, conflict theorists stress that society is composed of groups that engage in fierce competition for scarce resources. Although alliances or cooperation may prevail on the surface, beneath that surface lies a struggle for power.

Karl Marx and Conflict Theory   Karl Marx, the founder of conflict theory, witnessed the Industrial Revolution that transformed Europe. He saw that peasants who had left the land to seek work in cities had to work at wages that barely provided enough to eat. The average worker died at age 30, the average wealthy person at age 50 (Edgerton 1992:87). Shocked by this suffering and exploitation, Marx began to analyze society and history. As he did so, he developed **conflict theory.** He concluded that the key to human history is class struggle. In every society, some small group controls the means of production and exploits those who are not in control. In industrialized societies the struggle is between the **bourgeoisie,** the small group of capitalists who own the means to produce wealth, and the **proletariat,** the mass of workers who are exploited by the bourgeoisie. The capitalists also control politics, so that if workers rebel, the capitalists are able to call on the power of the state to control them (Angell 1965).

When Marx made his observations, capitalism was in its infancy and workers were at the mercy of their employers. Workers had none of what we take for granted today—the right to strike, minimum wages, eight-hour days, coffee breaks, five-day work weeks, paid vacations and holidays, medical benefits, sick leave, unemployment compensation, Social Security. Marx's analysis reminds us that these benefits came not from generous hearts, but by workers forcing concessions from their employers.

Conflict Theory Today   Some current conflict sociologists use conflict theory in a much broader sense. Ralf Dahrendorf (b. 1929) sees conflict as inherent in all

conflict theory
a theoretical framework in which society is viewed as composed of groups competing for scarce resources

bourgeoisie
Karl Marx's term for capitalists, those who own the means to produce wealth

proletariat
Marx's term for the exploited class, the mass of workers who do not own the means of production

relations that involve authority. He points out that **authority,** or power that people consider legitimate, permeates every layer of society—whether that be a small group, an organization, a community, or the entire society. People in positions of authority try to enforce conformity, which, in turn, creates resentment and resistance. The result is a constant struggle throughout society to determine who has authority over what (Turner 1978).

Another sociologist, Lewis Coser (b. 1913), pointed out that conflict is most likely to develop among people who are in close relationships. They have worked out ways to distribute responsibilities and privileges, power and rewards. Any change in this arrangement can lead to hurt feelings, to bitterness and conflict. Even in intimate relationships, then, people are in a constant balancing act, with conflict lying uneasily just beneath the surface.

Applying Conflict Theory   To explain why the U.S. divorce rate is high, conflict theorists focus on how men's and women's relationships have changed. For millennia, men have dominated women. Women had few alternatives than to accept their exploitation. Today, however, with industrialization, women can meet their basic survival needs outside of marriage. Industrialization has also fostered a culture in which females participate in social worlds beyond the home. Consequently, today's women refuse to bear burdens that earlier generations accepted as inevitable, and they are much more likely to dissolve a marriage that becomes intolerable—or even unsatisfactory.

IN SUM ■ ▪ ■ ▪ ■

Conflict theorists see marriage as reflecting society's basic inequalities between males and females. The traditional imbalance of power between men and women, which had been taken for granted, changed as women gained power, especially through the paycheck. One consequence is a higher divorce rate as wives strive for more equality and husbands resist their efforts. From the conflict perspective, then, the increase in divorce is not a sign that marriage has weakened, but, rather, a sign that women are making headway in their historical struggle with men.

■ Levels of Analysis: Macro and Micro

A major difference between these three theoretical perspectives is their level of analysis. Functionalists and conflict theorists focus on the **macro level;** that is, they examine large-scale patterns of society. In contrast, symbolic interactionists usually focus on the **micro level,** on **social interaction**—what people do when they are in one another's presence. (See Table 1.1, page 24).

To make this distinction between micro and macro levels clearer, let's return to the example of the homeless, with which we opened this chapter. To study homeless people, symbolic interactionists would focus on the micro level. They would analyze what homeless people do when they are in shelters and on the streets. They would also analyze their communications, both their talk and their **nonverbal interaction** (gestures, silence, use of space, and so on). The observations I made at the beginning of this chapter about the silence in the homeless shelter, for example, would be of interest to symbolic interactionists.

This micro level, however, would not interest functionalists and conflict theorists. They would focus instead on the macro level. Functionalists would examine how changes in the parts of society have increased homelessness. They might look at how changes in the family (fewer children, more divorce) and economic conditions (higher

authority
power that people consider legitimate

macro-level analysis
an examination of large-scale patterns of society

micro-level analysis
an examination of small-scale patterns of society

social interaction
what people do when they are in one another's presence

nonverbal interaction
communication without words through gestures, space, silence, and so on

rents, fewer unskilled jobs, loss of jobs overseas) cause homelessness among people who are unable to find jobs and have no family to fall back on. For their part, conflict theorists would stress the struggle between social classes, especially how the policies of the wealthy force certain groups into unemployment and homelessness. That, they would point out, accounts for the disproportionate number of African Americans who are homeless. Chapter 4 focuses on the distinctions between macro and micro levels of analysis.

■ Putting the Theoretical Perspectives Together

Which theoretical perspective should we use to study human behavior? Which level of analysis is the correct one? As you have seen, these theoretical perspectives provide contrasting pictures of human life. In the case of divorce, these interpretations are quite different from the commonsense understanding that two people were simply "incompatible." Because each theory focuses on different features of social life, each provides a distinctive interpretation. Consequently, it is necessary to use all three theoretical lenses to analyze human behavior. By combining their contributions, we gain a more comprehensive picture of social life.

Trends Shaping the Future of Sociology

Two major trends indicate changing directions in sociology. Let's look again at the relationship of sociology to the reform of society, and then at globalization.

Sociology Full Circle: Reform Versus Research   A tension between social reform and social analysis has always run through sociology. To better understand this tension, some sociologists find it useful to divide sociology into three major periods (Lazarsfeld and Reitz 1989). During the first phase, sociologists stressed the need to do research in order to improve society. One of the first presidents of the American Sociological Society, Albion Small, made this goal explicit. In 1912, Small said that the primary reason for sociology was its "practical application to the improvement of social life." He said that sociologists should use science to gain knowledge, and then use that knowledge to "realize visions" (Fritz 1989). This first phase of sociology lasted until the 1920s.

During the second phase, from the 1920s until World War II, the emphasis switched from making the world a better place to making sociology a respected field of knowledge. Sociologists emphasized **basic** or **pure sociology,** that is, research and theory aimed at making discoveries about life in human groups, but not at making changes in those groups. They achieved this goal within a generation, and almost every college and university in the United States added sociology to its course offerings. It is because of these efforts that you are taking this introductory course in sociology.

We are now in a third phase, which began around the end of World War II. In 1954, the U.S. Supreme Court based a major ruling partially on sociological research. The Court was deciding whether racially segregated public schools were constitutional. Up to this time, states followed a so-called "separate but equal" doctrine and had separate public schools for whites and for blacks. (The schools, as many ob-

pure or basic sociology
sociological research whose purpose is to make discoveries about life in human groups, not to make changes in those groups

servers noted, were separate, but certainly not equal.) In this landmark ruling (*Brown v. the Board of Education of Topeka*), which banned segregated public schools, sociologists testified on the harmful effects of segregation.

This fundamental change in law and its direct impact on education in the United States made sociologists more aware of their potential to bring about social change. Just as sociologists switched from their initial concern with improving society to developing abstract knowledge, today they are seeking ways to apply their research findings. With the development of applied sociology, these efforts have gained momentum. Many sociology departments offer courses in applied sociology; some offer specialties and internships in applied sociology at both the graduate and undergraduate levels.

I want to stress that sociology is not a monolith. We are not all in agreement, moving in lock-step toward a single goal. To divide sociology into three separate phases overlooks as much as it reveals. Even during the first phase, Durkheim and Weber did research for the purpose of gaining academic respectability for sociology. Similarly, during the second phase, many sociologists who wanted to reform society chafed at the emphasis on understanding. And today, many sociologists want the emphasis to remain on basic sociology; they do not view applied sociology as "real" sociology. They say that it is actually social work or psychology masquerading as sociology. Each particular period, however, does have basic emphases, and this division of sociology into three phases does pinpoint major trends. The tension that has run through sociology—between gaining knowledge and applying knowledge—will continue. During this current phase, it is likely that the emphasis on applying sociological knowledge will become stronger.

Globalization   A second major trend, globalization, seems destined to leave its mark on sociology. **Globalization** is the breaking down of national boundaries because of advances in communication, trade, and travel. Currently, the United States dominates sociology. As sociologists William Martin and Mark Beittel (1998) put it, U.S. sociology is the "unrivaled center of the discipline on a world scale." One consequence of this dominance is an emphasis on groups in the United States. We U.S. sociologists tend to look inward, concentrating on events and relationships that occur in our own country. We even base most of our findings on U.S. samples. Globalization is likely to broaden our horizons, directing us to a greater consideration of global issues. This, in turn, is likely to motivate us to try more vigorously to identify universal principles.

Application of Globalization to This Text   With each passing year, the world becomes smaller as we all become more and more connected to the global village. What occurs elsewhere has a direct impact on our lives, and, increasingly, our welfare is tied to that of people in other nations. To help broaden our horizons, in this book we will visit many cultures around the world, examining what life is like for the people there. Seeing how *their* society affects their behavior and orientations to life will help us see how *our* society influences what we do and how we feel about life.

Globalization is one of the most significant events in world history, and you and I are living through it. Throughout this text, I will stress the impact of globalization on your life, especially how it is likely to shape your future. We will also examine the **globalization of capitalism**, focusing on implications of the triumph of this economic system. From time to time, as you read the following pages, you will also confront the developing new world order, which appears destined to play a most significant role in your future.

globalization
the extensive interconnections among nations due to the expansion of capitalism.

globalization of capitalism
capitalism (investing to make profits within a rational system) becoming the globe's dominant economic system

■ ■ ■ ■ ■
Summary and Review

The Sociological Perspective

■ **What is the sociological perspective?**

The **sociological perspective** stresses that people's social experiences—the groups to which they belong and their experiences within these groups—underlie their behavior. C. Wright Mills referred to this as the intersection of biography (the individual) and history (social factors that influence the individual). Pp. 2–4.

Sociology and the Other Sciences

■ **What is science, and where does sociology fit in?**

Science is the application of systematic methods to obtain knowledge and the knowledge obtained by those methods. The sciences are divided into the **natural sciences,** which seek to comprehend, explain, and predict events in the natural environment; and the **social sciences,** which seek to understand the social world objectively by means of controlled and repeated observations. **Sociology** is the scientific study of society and human behavior. Pp. 4–7.

Origins of Sociology

■ **When did sociology first appear as a separate discipline?**

Sociology emerged as a separate discipline in the mid-1800s in western Europe, during the onset of the Industrial Revolution. Industrialization affected all aspects of human existence—where people lived, the nature of their work, how they viewed life, and their interpersonal relationships. Early sociologists who focused on these social changes include Auguste Comte, Herbert Spencer, Karl Marx, Harriet Martineau, Emile Durkheim, and Max Weber. Pp. 8–14.

The Role of Values in Social Research

■ **Should the purpose of social research be only to advance human understanding or also to reform society?**

Sociologists agree that research findings should be **value free,** that the researcher's values and beliefs should be set aside in order to permit objective conclusions. But sociologists do not agree on the uses and purposes of social research. Some believe its purpose should be only to advance understanding of human behavior; others, that its goal should be to reform harmful social arrangements. Pp. 14–15.

Verstehen and Social Facts

■ **How do sociologists use *Verstehen* and social facts to study human behavior?**

According to Weber, to understand why people act as they do, sociologists must try to put themselves in their shoes. He used the German term ***Verstehen,*** "to grasp by insight," to describe this essentially subjective approach. Although not denying the importance of *Verstehen,* Emile Durkheim emphasized the importance of uncovering **social facts,** objective social conditions that influence how people behave. Contemporary sociology uses both approaches to understand human behavior. Pp. 15–17.

Sexism in Early Sociology

■ **What was the position of women in early sociology?**

Sociology appeared during a historical period of widespread sexism. Consequently, few women received the advanced education required to become sociologists. Those who did, such as Harriet Martineau, were ignored. P. 17.

Sociology in North America

■ **When were the first academic departments of sociology established in the United States?**

The earliest departments of sociology were established in the late 1800s at the universities of Kansas, Atlanta, and Chicago. During the 1940s, sociology was dominated by the University of Chicago. Today, no single university or theoretical perspective dominates. In sociology's early years, the contributions of women and minorities were largely ignored. Pp. 17–21.

■ **What is the difference between basic (or pure) and applied sociology?**

Basic (or pure) sociology is sociological research whose purpose is to make discoveries. In contrast, **applied sociology** is the use of sociology to solve problems. Pp. 21–22.

Theoretical Perspectives in Sociology

■ **What is a theory?**

A **theory** is a general statement about how facts are related to one another. A theory provides a conceptual framework for interpreting facts. P. 23.

■ **What are the major theoretical perspectives?**

Sociologists use three primary theoretical frameworks to interpret social life. **Symbolic interactionism** examines how people use symbols to develop and share their views of the world. Symbolic interactionists usually focus on the **micro level**—on small-scale, face-to-face interaction. **Functional analysts,** in contrast, focus on the **macro level**—on large-scale patterns of society. Functional theorists stress that a social system is made up of many parts. When working properly, each part contributes to the stability of the whole, fulfilling a function that contributes to the system's equilibrium. **Conflict theorists** also focus on large-scale patterns of society. They stress that society is composed of competing groups that struggle for scarce resources.

With each perspective focusing on certain features of social life and each providing a unique interpretation, no single theory is adequate. The combined insights of all three perspectives yield a more comprehensive picture of social life. Pp. 24–32.

Trends Shaping the Future of Sociology

■ **What trends are likely to have an impact on sociology?**

Sociology has gone through three phases: The first was an emphasis on reforming society; the second, an emphasis on basic sociology. In today's third phase, we are swinging full circle, coming closer to our roots of applying sociology to social change. **Applied sociology** is likely to continue its influence. A second major trend, **globalization,** is likely to broaden sociological horizons, refocusing research and theory from its concentration on U.S. society. Pp. 32–33.

■ *Where can I read more on this topic?*

Suggested Readings for this chapter are at the back of this book.

Additional Online Resources for This Chapter
www.ablongman.com/henslin6e

- *Content Select* Research Database for Sociology, with suggested key terms and annotated references
- Link to 2000 Census, with activities
- Flashcards of key terms and concepts

- Practice Tests
- Weblinks
- Interactive Maps

using . . .
ContentSelect

Research Database for Sociology

sociological imagination	conflict theory	globalization	social research
sociological perspective	applied sociology	social integration	and values
	captialism		

Helen Hardin, *Robed Journey of the Rainbow Clan,* 1976

2

Culture

What Is Culture?
Culture and Taken-for-
Granted Orientations
to Life
Practicing Cultural
Relativism

Components of Symbolic
Culture
Gestures
Language
Values, Norms,
and Sanctions
Folkways and Mores

Many Cultural Worlds:
Subcultures and
Countercultures

Values in U.S. Society
An Overview of U.S. Values
Value Clusters
Value Contradictions and
Social Change
Emerging Values
Culture Wars:
When Values Clash
Values as Blinders
"Ideal" Versus "Real"
Culture

Cultural Universals
Animals and Language

Technology in the
Global Village
The New Technology
Cultural Lag and Cultural
Change
Technology and Cultural
Leveling

Summary and Review

I had never felt heat like this before. This was *northern* Africa, and I wondered what it must be like closer to the equator. Sweat poured off me as the temperature soared past 110 degrees Fahrenheit.

As we were herded into the building—which had no air conditioning—hundreds of people lunged toward the counter at the rear of the building. With body crushed against body, we waited as the uniformed officials behind the windows leisurely examined each passport. At times like this I wondered what I was doing in Africa.

When I first arrived in Morocco, I found the sights that greeted me exotic—not far removed from my memories of *Casablanca, Raiders of the Lost Ark,* and other movies that over the years had become part of my collective memory. The men, women, and even the children did wear those white robes that reached down to their feet. What was especially striking was that the women were almost totally covered. Despite the heat, they wore not only full-length gowns, but also head coverings that reached down over their foreheads, and veils that covered their faces from the nose down. All you could make out were their eyes—and every eye the same shade of brown.

And how short everyone was! The Arab women looked to be, on average, 5 feet, and the men only about three or four inches taller.

And lines? The concept apparently didn't even exist. Buying a ticket for a bus or train meant pushing and shoving toward the ticket man (always a man—no women were visible in any public position)

As the only blue-eyed, blonde, 6-foot-plus person around, and the only one who was wearing jeans and a pullover shirt, in a world of white-robed short people I stood out like a sore thumb. Everyone stared. No matter where I went, they stared. Wherever I looked, I found brown eyes watching me intently. Even staring back at those many dark brown eyes had no effect. It was so different from home, where, if you caught someone staring at you, the person would immediately look embarrassed and glance away.

And lines? The concept apparently didn't even exist. Buying a ticket for a bus or train meant pushing and shoving toward the ticket man (always a man—no women were visible in any public position), who took the money from whichever outstretched hand he decided on.

And germs? That notion didn't seem to exist here either. Flies swarmed over the food in the restaurants and the unwrapped loaves of bread in the stores. Shopkeepers would considerately shoo off the flies before handing me a loaf. They also offered home delivery. I still remember watching a bread vendor deliver an unwrapped loaf to a woman who stood on a second-floor balcony. She first threw her money to the bread vendor, and he then threw the unwrapped bread up to her. Only, his throw was off. The bread bounced off the wrought-iron balcony railing and landed in the street, which was filled with people, wandering dogs, and the ever-present, defecating burros. The vendor simply picked up the loaf and threw it again. This certainly wasn't his day, for he missed again. But he made it on his third attempt. The woman smiled as she turned back into her apartment, apparently to prepare the noon meal for her hungry family.

Now, standing in the oppressive heat on the Moroccan-Algerian border, the crowd once again became unruly. Another fight had broken out. And once again, the little man in uniform appeared, shouting and knocking people aside as he forced his way to a little wooden box nailed to the floor. Climbing onto this makeshift platform, he shouted at the crowd, his arms flailing about him. The people became silent. But just as soon as the man left, the shoving and shouting began again as the people clamored to get their passports stamped.

The situation had become unbearable. His body pressed against mine, the man behind me decided that this was a good time to take a nap. Determining that I made a good support, he placed his arm against my back and leaned his head against his arm. Sweat streamed down my back at the point where his arm and head touched me.

Finally, I realized that I had to abandon U.S. customs. I pushed my way forward, forcing my frame into every square inch of vacant space that I could create. At the counter, I shouted in English. The official looked up at the sound of this strange tongue, and I thrust my long arms over the heads of three people, shoving my passport into his hand.

What Is Culture?

What is culture? The concept is sometimes easier to grasp by description than by definition. For example, suppose you meet a young woman who has just arrived in the United States from India. That her culture is different from yours is immediately evident. You first see it in her clothing, jewelry, makeup, and hairstyle. Next you hear it in her speech. It then becomes apparent by her gestures. Later, you may hear her express unfamiliar beliefs about the world or about what is valuable in life. All these characteristics are indicative of **culture**—the language, beliefs, values, norms, behaviors, and even material objects that are passed from one generation to the next.

In northern Africa, I was surrounded by a culture quite alien to my own. It was evident in everything I saw and heard. The **material culture**—such things as jewelry, art, buildings, weapons, machines, and even eating utensils, hairstyles, and clothing—provided a sharp contrast to what I was used to seeing. There is nothing inherently "natural" about material culture. That is, it is no more natural (or unnatural) to wear gowns on the street than it is to wear jeans.

I also found myself immersed in a contrasting **nonmaterial culture,** that is, a group's ways of thinking (its beliefs, values, and other assumptions about the world) and doing (its common patterns of behavior, including language, gestures, and other forms of interaction). North African assumptions about crowding to buy a ticket and staring in public are examples of nonmaterial culture. So are U.S. assumptions about not doing either of these things. Like material culture, neither custom is "right." People simply become comfortable with the customs they learn during childhood, and—as in the case of my visit to northern Africa—uncomfortable when their basic assumptions about life are challenged.

■ Culture and Taken-for-Granted Orientations to Life

To develop a sociological imagination, it is essential to understand how culture affects people's lives. Meeting someone from a different culture may make us aware of culture's pervasive influence, but attaining the same level of awareness regarding our own culture is quite another matter. *Our* speech, *our* gestures, *our* beliefs, and *our* customs are usually taken for granted. We assume they are "normal" or "natural," and we almost always follow them without question. As anthropologist Ralph Linton (1936) said, "The last thing a fish would ever notice would be water." So also with people: Except in unusual circumstances, the effects of our own culture generally remain imperceptible to us.

Yet culture's significance is profound; it touches almost every aspect of who and what we are. We came into this life without a language, without values and morality, with no ideas about religion, war, money, love, use of space, and so on. We possessed none of these fundamental orientations that we take for granted and that are so essential in determining the type of people we are. Yet at this point in our lives we all have acquired them. Sociologists call this *culture within us.* These learned and shared ways of believing and of doing (another definition of culture) penetrate our beings at an early age and quickly become part of our taken-for-granted assumptions concerning normal behavior. *Culture becomes the lens through which we perceive and evaluate what is going on around us.* Seldom do we question these assumptions, for, like water to a fish, the framework from which we view life remains largely beyond our ordinary perception.

The rare instances in which these assumptions are challenged, however, can be upsetting. Although as a sociologist I should be able to look at my own culture "from

culture
the language, beliefs, values, norms, behaviors, and even material objects that are passed from one generation to the next

material culture
the material objects that distinguish a group of people, such as their art, buildings, weapons, utensils, machines, hairstyles, clothing, and jewelry

nonmaterial culture
a group's ways of thinking (including its beliefs, values, and other assumptions about the world) and doing (its common patterns of behavior, including language and other forms of interaction)

the outside," my trip to Africa quickly revealed how fully I had internalized my own culture. My upbringing in Western industrialized society had given me strong assumptions about aspects of social life that had become deeply rooted in my being—staring, hygiene, and the use of space. But in this part of Africa these assumptions were useless in helping me get through daily life. No longer could I count on people to stare only surreptitiously, to take precautions against invisible microbes, or to stand in line in an orderly fashion, one behind the other.

As you can tell from the opening vignette, I found these assumptions upsetting, for they violated my basic expectations of "the way people *ought* to be"—although I did not know how firmly I held these expectations until they were so abruptly challenged. When my nonmaterial culture failed me—when it no longer enabled me to make sense out of the world—I experienced a disorientation known as **culture shock.** In the case of buying tickets, the fact that I was several inches taller than most Moroccans and thus able to outreach others helped me to adjust partially to their different ways of doing things. But I never did get used to the idea that pushing ahead of others was "right," and I always felt guilty when I used my size to receive preferential treatment.

An important consequence of culture within us is **ethnocentrism,** a tendency to use our own group's ways of doing things as the yardstick for judging others. All of us learn that the ways of our own group are good, right, proper, and even superior to other ways of life. As sociologist William Sumner (1906), who developed this concept, said, "One's own group is the center of everything, and all others are scaled and rated with reference to it." Ethnocentrism has both positive and negative consequences. On the positive side, it creates in-group loyalties. On the negative side, ethnocentrism can lead to discrimination against people whose ways differ from ours.

The many ways culture affects our lives fascinates sociologists. In this chapter, we'll examine how profoundly culture affects everything we are. This will serve as a basis from which you can start to analyze your previously unquestioned assumptions of reality and thus help you gain a different perspective on social life and your role in it.

IN SUM ■ ■ ■ ■

To avoid losing track of the ideas under discussion, let's pause for a moment to summarize, and in some instances clarify, the principles we have covered.

1. There is nothing "natural" about material culture. Arabs wear gowns on the street and feel that it is natural to do so. Americans do the same with jeans.

2. There is nothing "natural" about nonmaterial culture. It is just as arbitrary to stand in line as it is to push and shove.

3. Culture penetrates deep into our thinking, becoming a taken-for-granted lens through which we see the world and obtain our perception of reality.

4. Culture provides implicit instructions that tell us what we ought to do in various situations. It provides a fundamental basis for our decision making.

5. Culture also provides a "moral imperative"; that is, the culture that we internalize becomes the "right" way of doing things. (I, for example, deeply believed that it was wrong to push and shove to get ahead of others.)

6. Coming into contact with a radically different culture challenges our basic assumptions of life. (I experienced culture shock when I discovered that my deeply ingrained cultural ideas about hygiene and the use of space no longer applied.)

7. Although the particulars of culture differ from one group of people to another, culture itself is universal. That is, all people have culture. There are no exceptions. A society cannot exist without developing shared, learned ways of dealing with the demands of life.

8. All people are ethnocentric, which has both positive and negative consequences.

culture shock
the disorientation that people experience when they come in contact with a fundamentally different culture and can no longer depend on their taken-for-granted assumptions about life

ethnocentrism
the use of one's own culture as a yardstick for judging the ways of other individuals or societies, generally leading to a negative evaluation of their values, norms, and behaviors

■ Practicing Cultural Relativism

To counter our tendency to use our own culture as the standard by which we judge other cultures, we can practice **cultural relativism;** that is, we can try to understand a culture on its own terms. This means to look at how the elements of a culture fit together, without judging those elements as superior or inferior to our own way of life.

Because we tend to use our own culture to judge others, cultural relativism presents a challenge to ordinary thinking. For example, most U.S. citizens appear to have strong feelings against raising bulls for the purpose of stabbing them to death in front of crowds that shout "Olé!" According to cultural relativism, however, bullfighting

cultural relativism
not judging a culture, but trying to understand it on its own terms

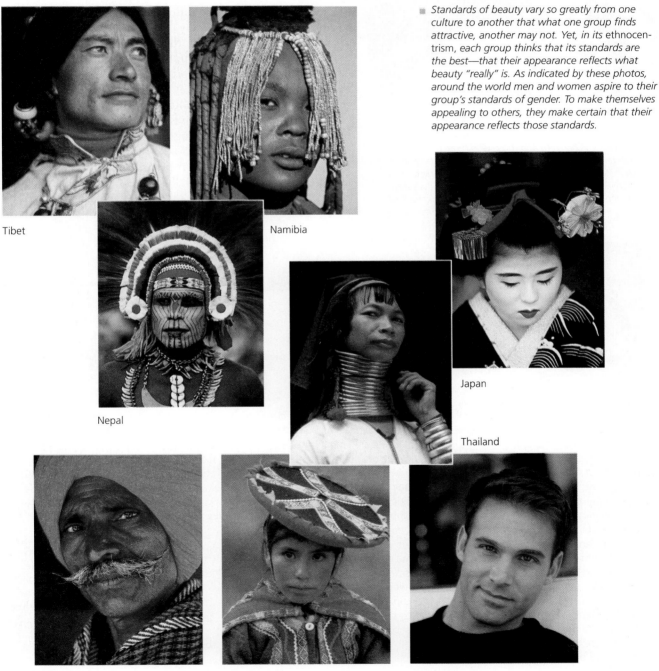

■ Standards of beauty vary so greatly from one culture to another that what one group finds attractive, another may not. Yet, in its ethnocentrism, each group thinks that its standards are the best—that their appearance reflects what beauty "really" is. As indicated by these photos, around the world men and women aspire to their group's standards of gender. To make themselves appealing to others, they make certain that their appearance reflects those standards.

Tibet

Namibia

Nepal

Thailand

Japan

Bangladesh

Peru

United States

must be viewed from the framework of the culture in which it takes place—*its* history, *its* folklore, *its* ideas of bravery, and *its* ideas of sex roles.

You may still regard bullfighting as wrong, of course, if your culture, which is deeply ingrained in you, has no history of bullfighting. We all possess culturally specific ideas about cruelty to animals, ideas that have evolved slowly and match other elements of our culture. In the United States, for example, practices that once were common in some areas—cock fighting, dog fighting, bear-dog fighting, and so on—have been gradually weeded out (Bryant 1993).

None of us can be entirely successful at practicing cultural relativism; we simply cannot help viewing a contrasting way of life through the lens that our own culture provides. Cultural relativism, however, is an attempt to refocus that lens and thereby appreciate other ways of life rather than simply asserting, "Our way is right." For an interesting distinction in cultures, see the Cultural Diversity box on this page.

Although cultural relativism is a worthwhile goal and helps us to avoid cultural smugness, this view has come under attack. In a provocative book, *Sick Societies* (1992), anthropologist Robert Edgerton points out that some cultures endanger their people's health, happiness, or survival. He suggests that we should develop a scale for evaluating cultures on their "quality of life," much as we do for U.S. cities. He also

■ Many Americans perceive bullfighting, which is illegal in the United States, as a cruel activity that should be abolished everywhere. To Spaniards and those who have inherited Spanish culture, however, bullfighting is a beautiful, artistic sport in which matador and bull blend into a unifying image of power, courage, and glory. Cultural relativism requires that we suspend our own perspectives in order to grasp the perspectives of others, something that is much easier described than attained.

cultural diversity

Around the World

Do You Feel Sorry? Hire an Apology Specialist

Americans are often casual about apologies. "Sorry about that" and "Excuse me" slip easily from our lips.

It is not this way for the Chinese and Japanese. For them, to make an apology means to lose face. This is a serious matter, hitting at their sense of identity and understandings about relationships. Apologies are not taken lightly.

In China and Japan, apologies require just the right words, spoken in a precise tone of voice. They even require the right clothing. When the United States mistakenly took the Chinese embassy in Belgrade for a terrorist center? and bombed it, President Clinton apologized on television. Chinese officials were outraged at Clinton, and the Chinese media refused

to broadcast the tape. Why? It was too casual to be a "real" apology. When Clinton made his statement, he was outdoors and wearing a polo shirt.

So who ya gonna call? How about The Apology and Gift Center, a new business in China? The company's 20 employees are somber, middle-aged men and women who have college degrees. They are lawyers, teachers, and social workers who have received additional training in counseling. They know how to say the right words in the right way.

People who feel too embarrassed or inadequate to make an apology themselves come to The Apology and Gift Center, where apology specialists study the details and decide on the best course

of action. They write letters, deliver gifts, and make explanations in person.

Hiring someone to apologize for you may sound strange, but employing someone to plead your case in other matters was a novel idea at one time, too. Today we have lawyers on every street corner—or so it seems.

for your consideration

What is it about U.S. culture that makes it most unlikely that apology specialists will ever become common?

Source: Based on Rosenthal 2001.

asks why we should consider cultures that practice female genital mutilation, gang rape, wife beating, or that sell preteen daughters into prostitution as morally equivalent to those that do not. Cultural values that result in exploitation, he says, are inferior to those that enhance people's lives.

Edgerton's sharp questions and incisive examples bring us to a topic that comes up repeatedly in this text—the disagreements that arise among scholars as they confront changing views of reality. It is such questioning of assumptions that keeps sociology interesting.

■ ■ ■ ■ ■

Components of Symbolic Culture

Sociologists sometimes refer to nonmaterial culture as **symbolic culture,** because its central component is the symbols that people use. A **symbol** is something to which people attach meaning and that they then use to communicate. Symbols are the basis of nonmaterial culture. They include gestures, language, values, norms, sanctions, folkways, and mores. Let's look at each of these components of symbolic culture.

■ Gestures

Gestures, which involve using one's body to communicate with others, are useful shorthand ways to give messages without using words. Although people in every culture of the world use gestures, what a gesture means may change completely from one culture to another. North Americans, for example, communicate a succinct message by raising the middle finger in a short, upward stabbing motion. I wish to stress "North Americans," for that gesture does not convey the same message in South America or most other parts of the world.

I was once surprised to find that this particular gesture was not universal, having internalized it to such an extent that I thought everyone knew what it meant. When I was comparing gestures in Mexico, however, this gesture drew a blank look from friends. After I explained its intended meaning, they laughed and showed me their rudest gesture—placing the hand under the armpit and moving the upper arm up and down. To me, they simply looked as if they were imitating a monkey, but to them the gesture meant "Your mother is a whore"—absolutely the worst possible insult in that culture.

Gestures thus not only facilitate communication but also, because they differ around the world, can lead to misunderstanding, embarrassment, or worse. Once in Mexico, for example, I raised my hand to a certain height to indicate how tall a child was. My hosts began to laugh. It turned out that Mexicans use three hand gestures to indicate height: separate ones for people, animals, and plants. What had amused them was that I had ignorantly used the plant gesture to indicate the child's height. (See Figure 2.1.)

To get along in another culture, then, it is important to learn the gestures of that culture. If you don't, you will not only fail to achieve the simplicity of communication that gestures allow, but you will also miss much of what is happening, run the risk of appearing foolish, and possibly offend people. In some cultures, for example, you would provoke deep offense if you were to offer food or a gift with your left hand, because the left hand is reserved for dirty tasks, such as wiping after going to the bathroom. Left-handed Americans visiting Arabs, please note!

Now suppose for a moment that you are visiting southern Italy. After eating one of the best meals in your life, you are so pleased that when you catch the waiter's eye, you smile broadly and use the standard U.S. "A-OK" gesture of putting your thumb

symbolic culture
another term for nonmaterial culture

symbol
something to which people attach meanings and then use to communicate with others

gestures
the ways in which people use their bodies to communicate with one another

Figure 2.1

Gestures to Indicate Height, Southern Mexico

and forefinger together and making a large "O." The waiter looks horrified, and you are struck speechless when the manager asks you to leave. What have you done? Nothing on purpose, of course, but in that culture that gesture refers to a part of the human body that is not mentioned in polite company (Ekman et al. 1984).

Is it really true that there are no universal gestures? There is some disagreement on this point. Some anthropologists claim that no gesture is universal. They point out that even nodding the head up and down to indicate "yes" is not universal, because in some parts of the world, such as areas of Turkey, nodding the head up and down means "no" (Ekman et al. 1984). However, ethologists, researchers who study biological bases of behavior, claim that expressions of anger, pouting, fear, and sadness are built into our biology and are universal (Eibl-Eibesfeldt 1970:404). They point out that even infants who are born blind and deaf, who have had no chance to *learn* these gestures, express themselves in the same way.

Although this matter is not yet settled, we can note that gestures tend to vary remarkably around the world. It is also significant that certain gestures can elicit emotions; some gestures are so associated with emotional messages that the gestures themselves summon up emotions. For example, my introduction to Mexican gestures took place at a dinner table. It was evident that my husband-and-wife hosts were trying to hide their embarrassment at using their culture's obscene gesture at their dinner table. And I felt the same way—not about *their* gesture, of course, which meant absolutely nothing to me—but about the one I was teaching them.

language
a system of symbols that can be combined in an infinite number of ways and can represent not only objects but also abstract thought

■ *Although most gestures are learned, and therefore vary from culture to culture, some gestures that represent fundamental emotions such as sadness, anger, and fear appear to be inborn. This crying child differs little from a crying child in China—or the United States or anywhere else on the globe. In a few years, however, this child will demonstrate a variety of gestures highly specific to his culture.*

■ Language

The primary way in which people communicate with one another is through **language**—a system of symbols that can be strung together in an infinite number of ways for the purpose of communicating abstract thought. Each word is actually a symbol, a sound to which we have attached a particular meaning so that we can then use it to communicate with one another. Language itself is universal in the sense that all human groups have language, but there is nothing universal about the meanings given to particular sounds. Thus, like gestures, in different cultures the same sound may mean something entirely different—or may have no meaning at all.

The significance of language for human life is difficult to overstate. As will become apparent from the following discussion, *language* allows culture to exist.

Language Allows Human Experience to Be Cumulative   By means of language, one generation can pass significant experiences on to the next, allowing the next generation to build on experiences that it may never undergo. This building process enables humans to modify their behavior in light of what previous generations have learned. Hence the central sociological significance of language: *Language allows culture to develop by freeing people to move beyond their immediate experiences.*

Without language, human culture would be little more advanced than that of the lower primates. To communicate, we would be limited to grunts and gestures, which would minimize the temporal dimension of human life. Our communications would be limited to a small time span: events that are now taking place, those that have just taken place, or those that will take place immediately—a sort of "slightly extended present." You can grunt and gesture, for example, that you want a drink of water, but in the absence of language how could you share ideas concerning past or future events? There would be little or no way to communicate to others what event you had in mind, much less the greater complexities that humans communicate—ideas and feelings about events.

Language Provides a Social or Shared Past   Even without language, an individual would have memories of experiences. Those memories, however, would be extremely limited, for people associate experiences with words and then use words to recall the experience. Such memories as would exist in the absence of language would also be highly individualized, for they could be only rarely and incompletely communicated to others, much less discussed and agreed on. With language, however, events can be codified, that is, attached to words and then recalled so they can be discussed in the present.

Language Provides a Social or Shared Future
Language also extends our time horizons forward. When people talk about past events, they share meanings that allow them to decide how they will or should act in similar circumstances in the future. Because language enables people to agree with one another concerning times, dates, and places, it also allows them to plan activities with one another.

Think about it for a moment. Without language, how could people ever plan future events? How could they possibly communicate goals, purposes, times, and plans? Whatever planning could exist would have to be limited to extremely rudimentary communications, perhaps to an agreement to meet at a certain place when the sun is in a certain position. But think of the difficulty, perhaps impossibility, of conveying just a slight change in this simple arrangement, such as "I can't make it tomorrow, but my neighbor can, if that's all right with you."

Language Allows Shared Perspectives or Understandings   Our ability to speak, then, provides us a social past and future. These two vital aspects of our humanity represent a watershed that distinguishes us from animals. But speech does much more than this.

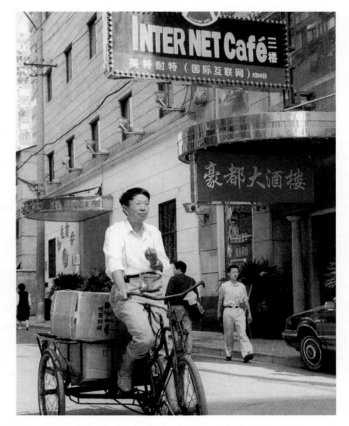

■ *Language is the basis of human culture around the world. The past few years have seen a major development in communication—the ease and speed with which we can "speak" to people across the globe. This development is destined to have vital effects on culture.*

down-to-earth sociology

Emoticons: "Written Gestures" for Expressing Yourself Online

Talking online has become a favorite activity of millions of people. Teenagers rehash the day's events with friends; grandparents keep in touch with grandchildren in different states; hobbyists talk about their special interests; businesspeople seal their deals with the click of a "send" button. All of them love the speed of online communications. They send an e-mail or post a note in a chat room, and in an instant people across the country or in distant lands can read or respond to it.

There is something nagging about online talk, though. It leaves a dissatisfying taste because it is so one-dimensional. People miss the nuances of emotion and overlays of meaning transmitted in face-to-face conversations. Lacking are the gestures and tones of voice that give color and life to our communications, the subtleties by which we monitor and communicate sub-messages. To help fill this gap, computer users have developed a set of symbols to convey their humor, disappointment, sarcasm, and other moods and attitudes. Although these symbols are not as varied or spontaneous as the nonverbal cues of face-to-face interaction, they are useful. Here are some of them. If you tilt your head to the left as you view them, the symbols will be clearer.

:-)	Smile
:-))	Laugh
:-D	Laugh or big grin
:.)	Laughing tears
:-(	Frowning, or Sad
:-((	Very Sad
>:-(	Angry, annoyed
>:-)	Feeling in a devilish mood
:-X	My lips are sealed
;-)	Wink, wink—know what I mean?
:-')	Tongue in cheek
:-P	Sticking out your tongue
:-0	WOW! (What a surprise!)
0:-)	Angel

Some correspondents also use abbreviations to add a touch of whimsy:

GMTA	Great Minds Think Alike
IAB	I Am Bored
ILY	I Love You
IMHO	In My Humble Opinion
J/K	Just Kidding
OIC	Oh, I see
LOL	Laughing Out Loud
OTF	On The Floor (laughing)
ROTF	Rolling On The Floor
ROFLWTIME	Rolling On Floor Laughing With Tears In My Eyes
UGG	You Go, Girl!
WTG	Way To Go!

With e-mail innovations, such shorthand may become unnecessary. Now that we can include video in our e-mail, recipients can see our image and hear our voice. As the cost of video transmitters drops, messages that include verbal and facial cues may replace much written e-mail. As long as written e-mail exists, however, some system of symbols to substitute for gestures will remain.

■ ■ ■ ■ ■

When humans talk with one another, they are exchanging ideas about events; that is, they are exchanging perspectives. Their words are the embodiment of their experiences, distilled and codified into a readily exchangeable form, mutually understandable to people who have learned that language. Talking about events allows people to arrive at the shared understandings that form the basis of social life. As discussed in the Down-to-Earth Sociology box above, to arrive at shared understandings requires shared symbols.

Language Allows Complex, Shared, Goal-Directed Behavior Common understandings also enable people to establish a *purpose* for getting together. Let's suppose you want to go on a picnic. You use speech not only to plan the picnic but also to decide on reasons for the picnic—which may be anything from "because it's a nice day and it shouldn't be wasted studying" to "because it's my birthday." Language permits you to blend individual activities into an integrated sequence. In other words, through discussion you decide where you will go; who will drive; who will bring the hamburgers, the potato chips, the soda; where you will meet; and so on. Only because of language can you participate in such a common yet complex event as a picnic—or build roads and bridges, or attend college classes.

Language and Perception: The Sapir-Whorf Hypothesis   In the 1930s, two anthropologists, Edward Sapir and Benjamin Whorf, became intrigued when they noted that the Hopi Indians of the southwestern United States had no words to distinguish among the past, the present, and the future. English, in contrast, as well as German, French, Spanish, and other languages, distinguishes carefully among these three time frames. From this observation, Sapir and Whorf concluded that the common-sense idea that words are merely labels that people attach to things was wrong. *Language, they concluded, has embedded within it ways of looking at the world.* Thus thinking and perception are not only expressed through language, but are also shaped by language. When we learn a language, we learn not only words, but also a particular way of thinking and perceiving (Sapir 1949; Whorf 1956).

The implications of the **Sapir-Whorf hypothesis,** which alerts us to how extensively language affects us, are far-reaching. *The Sapir-Whorf hypothesis reverses common sense:* It indicates that rather than objects and events forcing themselves onto our consciousness, it is our language that determines our consciousness, and hence our perception, of objects and events. Sociologist Eviatar Zerubavel (1991) gives a good example. Hebrew, his native language, does not differentiate between jam and jelly. Only when Zerubavel learned English could he "see" this difference, which is "obvious" to native English speakers. Similarly, if you learn to classify students as Jocks, Goths, Stoners, Skaters, and Preps, you will perceive a student who asks several questions during class in an entirely different way from someone who does not know these classifications.

Although Sapir and Whorf's observation that the Hopi do not have tenses was incorrect (Edgerton 1992:27), they stumbled onto a major truth about social life. The classifications that we humans develop as we try to make sense of life do influence our perception. The racial-ethnic terms that our culture provides, for example, influence how we see others and ourselves, a point that is discussed in the Cultural Diversity box below.

Sapir-Whorf hypothesis
Edward Sapir and Benjamin Whorf's hypothesis that language creates ways of thinking and perceiving

cultural d·i·v·e·r·s·i·t·y

United States

—in the United States

Race and Language: Searching for Self-Labels

The groups that dominate society often determine the names that are used to refer to racial-ethnic groups. If those names become associated with oppression, they take on negative meanings. For example, the terms *Negro* and *Colored People* came to be associated with tyranny, cruelty, submission, and low status. To overcome these meanings, those referred to by these terms began to identify themselves as *black* or *African American.* They infused these new terms with respect—a basic source of self-esteem which they felt the old terms denied them.

In a twist, African Americans—and to a lesser extent Latinos, Asian Americans, and Native Americans—have changed the rejected term *Colored People* to *People of Color.* Those who embrace this modified term are imbuing it with meanings that offer an identity of respect. The term also has political meanings. It indicates bonds that cross racial-ethnic lines, a growing sense of mutual ties and identity rooted in historical oppression.

There is *always* disagreement about racial-ethnic terms, and this one is no exception. Although most rejected the term *Colored People,* some found in it a sense of respect and claimed it for themselves. The NAACP, for example, stands for the National Association for the Advancement of Colored People. The new term, *People of Color,* arouses similar feelings. Some who would be included in this term claim that it is inappropriate. They point out that this new label still makes color the primary identifier of people. They stress that humans transcend race-ethnicity, that what we have in common as human beings goes much deeper than what you see on the surface. They stress that we should avoid terms that focus on differences in the pigmentation of our skin.

The language of self-reference in a society so conscious of skin color is an ongoing issue. As long as our society continues to place high emphasis on such superficial differences, the search for adequate terms is not likely to ever be "finished." In this quest for terms that strike the right chord, the term *People of Color* may become a historical footnote. If it does, it will be replaced by another term that indicates a changing self-identification in a changing historical context.

IN SUM ■ ■ ■ ■ ■

The sociological significance of language is that it takes us beyond the world of apes and allows culture to develop. Language frees us from the present by providing a past and a future. It gives us the capacity to share understandings about the past and develop common perceptions about the future, as well as to establish underlying purposes for our activities. Consequently, as in the case of planning a picnic, each individual is able to perform a small part of a larger activity, aware that others are carrying out related parts. In this way, a series of separate activities becomes united into a larger whole.

Language also allows us to expand our connections far beyond our immediate, face-to-face groups, so that our *individual* biological and social needs are met by extended networks of people. This development, in turn, leads to far-flung connections with our fellow humans—connections that extend outward from our family and local community and eventually embrace worldwide networks of production and distribution. Although language by no means *guarantees* cooperation among people, language is an *essential* precondition of working together. Without language, the extended cooperative human endeavors on which society is based could not exist (Malinowski 1945; Hertzler 1965; Blumer 1966).

Learning a language means not only learning words but also acquiring the perceptions embedded in that language. In other words, language both reflects and shapes cultural experiences. Precisely because language is such a primary shaper of experience and culture, difficulties arise among people who live among each other but do not share a language, as illustrated in the Cultural Diversity box below.

cultural **d·i·v·e·r·s·i·t·y**

in the United States

Miami—Language in a Changing City

In the years since Castro seized power in Cuba, the city of Miami has been transformed from a quiet southern city to a Latin American mecca. Nothing reflects Miami's essential character today as much as its long-simmering feud over language: English versus Spanish. Half of the city's 360,000 residents have trouble speaking English. Only *one-fourth* of Miami residents speak English at home.

As this chapter stresses, language is a primary means by which people learn—and communicate—their social worlds. Consequently, language differences in Miami reflect not only cultural diversity but also people who live in separate social worlds.

Although its ethnic stew makes Miami culturally one of the richest cities in the United States, the language gap sometimes creates anger and misunderstanding. The aggravation felt by Anglos—which

often seems tinged with hostility—is seen in the bumper stickers that read, "Will the Last American Out Please Bring the Flag?"

But Latinos, now a majority in Miami, are similarly frustrated. Many feel that Anglos should be able to speak at least some Spanish. Nicaraguan immigrant Pedro Falcon, for example, is studying English and wonders why more people don't try to learn his language. "Miami is the capital of Latin America," he says. "The population speaks Spanish."

Language and cultural flare-ups sometimes make headlines in the city. Latinos were outraged when an employee at the Coral Gables Board of Realtors lost her job for speaking Spanish at the office. And protesters swarmed a Publix supermarket after a cashier was fired for chatting with a friend in Spanish.

What's happening in Miami, says University of Chicago sociologist Douglas

Massey, is what happened in cities such as Chicago in the early 1900s. Then, as now, the rate of immigration exceeded the speed with which new residents learned English, creating a pile-up effect in the proportion of non-English speakers. "Becoming comfortable with English is a slow process," he points out, "whereas immigration is fast."

Massey expects Miami's percentage of non-English speakers to grow. But he says that this "doesn't mean in the long run that Miami is going to end up being a Spanish-speaking city." Instead, Massey believes that bilingualism will prevail. "Miami is the first truly bilingual city," he says. "The people who get ahead are not monolingual English speakers or monolingual Spanish speakers. They're people who speak both languages."

Source: Based on Sharp 1992; Usdansky 1992.

In short, *language is the basis of culture*. Like most aspects of culture, its linguistic base is usually invisible to us.

■ Values, Norms, and Sanctions

To learn a culture is to learn people's **values**, their ideas of what is desirable in life. When we uncover people's values, we learn a great deal about them, for values are the standards by which people define good and bad, beautiful and ugly. Values underlie our preferences, guide our choices, and indicate what we hold worthwhile in life.

Every group develops expectations concerning the right way to reflect its values. Sociologists use the term **norms** to describe those expectations, or rules of behavior, that develop out of a group's values. The term **sanctions** refers to the reactions people get for following or breaking norms. A **positive sanction** is an expression of approval given for following a norm, while a **negative sanction** reflects disapproval for breaking a norm.

■ *Many societies relax their* norms *during specified occasions. At these times, known as* moral holidays, *behavior that is ordinarily not permitted is allowed. From a functional standpoint, moral holidays, such as the Mardi Gras held at New Orleans, serve as safety valves, allowing a release of deviance. When the* moral holiday *is over, the usual enforcement of rules follows.*

Positive sanctions can be material, such as a monetary reward, a prize, or a trophy, but in everyday life they usually consist of hugs, smiles, a pat on the back, soothing words, or even handshakes. Negative sanctions can also be material—being fined in court is one example—but negative sanctions, too, are more likely to consist of harsh words or gestures, such as frowns, stares, or raised fists. Getting a raise at work is a positive sanction, indicating that you have followed the norms clustering around work values. If you get fired, however, you are getting a negative sanction, indicating that you have violated these norms. The North American finger gesture discussed earlier is, of course, a negative sanction.

Norms vary from one situation to another. People who talk to God out loud on a bus, for example, are breaking norms. Those who talk to God aloud in church, in contrast, are following the norms for that situation. If they jump up in the middle of the sermon and begin to talk to God, however, they have broken the norm of how and when they are supposed to talk to God in church.

Norms can become rigorous, making people feel stifled. One way some cultures relieve the pressure is through *moral holidays*, specified times when people are allowed to break norms. Moral holidays often center around getting drunk and being rowdy. During moral holidays, such as Mardi Gras, many norms are loosened. Activities for which people would otherwise be arrested are permitted—and expected—including public drunkenness and nudity. The norms are never completely dropped, however—just loosened a bit. Go too far, and the police step in.

Some societies have *moral holiday places*, locations where norms are expected to be broken. Red light districts of our cities are examples. Here prostitutes are allowed to work the streets, bothered only when political pressure builds. If these same prostitutes attempt to solicit customers in adjacent areas, however, they are promptly arrested. Lake of the Ozarks in Missouri, a fairly straight-laced area, has "Party Cove." Here, hundreds of boaters—from those operating cabin cruisers to jet skis—moor their vessels together in a highly publicized cove, where many get drunk and nude, and dance on the boats. In one of the more humorous incidents, boaters complained that a nude woman was riding a jet ski outside of the cove. The water patrol investigated but refused to arrest her because the woman was within the law—she had sprayed shaving cream on certain parts of her body. The Missouri Water Patrol has even announced in the local newspaper that it will not enter this particular cove, supposedly

values
the standards by which people define what is desirable or undesirable, good or bad, beautiful or ugly

norms
the expectations, or rules of behavior, that develop out of values

sanctions
expressions of approval or disapproval given to people for upholding or violating norms

positive sanction
a reward given for following norms, ranging from a smile to a prize

negative sanction
an expression of disapproval for breaking a norm, ranging from a mild, informal reaction such as a frown to a formal prison sentence or an execution

■ *The violation of mores is usually a serious matter. In this case, it is serious enough that the police at this international rugby tournament have swung into action to protect the public from seeing a "disgraceful" sight—at least one so designated by this group. Yet, unlike most violations of mores, this scene also elicits barely suppressed laughter from the police.*

because "there is so much traffic that they might not be able to get out in time to handle an emergency elsewhere."

■ Folkways and Mores

Norms that are not strictly enforced are called **folkways.** We expect people to comply with folkways, but we are likely to shrug our shoulders and not make a big deal about it if they don't. If someone insists on passing you on the left side of the sidewalk, for example, you are unlikely to take corrective action although if the sidewalk is crowded and you must move out of the way, you might give the person a dirty look.

Other norms, however, are taken much more seriously. We think of them as essential to our core values, and we insist on conformity. These are called **mores** (MORE-rays). A person who steals, rapes, or kills has violated some of society's most important mores. As sociologist Ian Robertson (1987:62) put it,

> A man who walks down a street wearing nothing on the upper half of his body is violating a folkway; a man who walks down the street wearing nothing on the lower half of his body is violating one of our most important mores, the requirement that people cover their genitals and buttocks in public.

It should also be noted that one group's folkways may be another group's mores. Although a man walking down the street with the upper half of his body uncovered is deviating from a folkway, a woman doing the same thing is violating a more. In addition, the folkways and mores of a subculture (the topic of the next section) may be the opposite of mainstream culture. For example, to walk down the sidewalk in a nudist camp with the entire body uncovered would conform to that subculture's folkways.

A **taboo** refers to a norm so strongly ingrained that even the thought of its violation is greeted with revulsion. Eating human flesh and having sex with one's parents are examples of such behaviors (Benales 1973; Read 1974; Henslin 2001). When someone breaks a taboo, the individual is usually judged as not fit to live in the same society as others. The sanctions are severe, and may include prison, banishment, or death.

■ ■ ■ ■ ■

Many Cultural Worlds: Subcultures and Countercultures

What common condition do you think this doctor is describing? Here are its possible causes:

[It accompanies] diaphragmatic pleurisy, pneumonia, uremia, or alcoholism . . . Abdominal causes include disorders of the stomach, and esophagus, bowel diseases, pancreatitis, pregnancy, bladder irritation, hepatic metastases, or hepatitis. Thoracic and mediastinal lesions or surgery may be responsible. Posterior fossa tumors or infarcts may stimulate centers in the medulla oblongata. (Chambliss 2001:427)

My best guess is that you don't have the slightest idea what this doctor was talking about. For most of us, he might as well be talking in Greek. Physicians who are lec-

folkways
norms that are not strictly enforced

mores (more-rays)
norms that are strictly enforced because they are thought essential to core values

taboo
a norm so strong that it brings revulsion if violated

turing students in medical school, however, talk like this. In this case, the doctor is describing hiccups!

Physicians form a **subculture**, *a world within the larger world of the dominant culture*. Each subculture has some distinctive way of looking at life. Even if we cannot understand the preceding quote, it makes us aware that the physician's view of life is not quite the same as ours.

U.S. society contains tens of thousands of subcultures. Some are as broad as the way of life we associate with teenagers, others as narrow as those we associate with body builders—or with doctors. Some U.S. ethnic groups also form subcultures: Their values, norms, and foods set them apart. So might their religion, language, and clothing. Occupational groups also form subcultures, as anyone who has hung out with cab drivers (Davis 1959; Henslin 1993), artists (McCall 1980), or construction workers (Haas 1972) can attest. Even sociologists form a subculture. As you are learning, they use a unique language for carving up the world.

Consider this quote from another subculture:

> If everyone applying for welfare had to supply a doctor's certificate of sterilization, if everyone who had committed a felony were sterilized, if anyone who had mental illness to any degree were sterilized—then our economy could easily take care of these people for the rest of their lives, giving them a decent living standard—but getting them out of the way. That way there would be no children abused, no surplus population, and, after a while, no pollution. . . .

> Now let's talk about stupidity. The level of intellect in this country is going down, generation after generation. The average IQ is always 100 because that is the accepted average. However, the kid with a 100 IQ today would have tested out at 70 when I was a lad. You get the concept . . . the marching morons. . . .

> When the . . . present world system collapses, it'll be good people like you who will be shooting people in the streets to feed their families. (Zellner 1995:58, 65)

Welcome to the world of the Survivalists, where the message is much clearer than that of physicians—and much more disturbing.

The values and norms of most subcultures are compatible with the larger society to which they belong. In some cases, however, such as these survivalists, the group's values and norms place it in opposition to the dominant culture. Sociologists use the term **counterculture** to refer to such groups. Heavy metal adherents who glorify Satanism, sexism, hatred, cruelty, violence, and death are an example of a counterculture. Note that motorcycle enthusiasts—who emphasize personal freedom and speed *and* affirm cultural values of success—are members of a subculture. In contrast, the members of an outlaw motorcycle gang—who also stress freedom and speed, but add the values of dirtiness and contempt toward women and work—form part of a counterculture (Watson 1988). Countercultures do not have to be negative, however. Back in the 1800s, the Mormons were a counterculture who challenged the dominant culture's core value of monogamy.

An assault on core values is always met with resistance. To affirm their own values, members of the mainstream culture may ridicule, isolate, or even attack members of the counterculture. The Mormons, for example, were driven out of several states before they finally settled in Utah, which was then a wilderness. Even there the federal government would not let them practice polygyny (one man having more than one wife), and Utah's statehood was made conditional on its acceptance of monogamy (Anderson 1942/1966). Today, the federal and state governments have taken steps against some survivalist groups.

■ *Each* subculture *provides its members with values and distinctive ways of viewing the world.* Subcultures *can form around almost any topic, including, as shown here, the human body itself.*

subculture
the values and related behaviors of a group that distinguish its members from the larger culture; a world within a world

counterculture
a group whose values, beliefs, and related behaviors place its members in opposition to the broader culture

Values In U.S. Society

An Overview of U.S. Values

As you know, the United States is a **pluralistic society,** made up of many different groups. The United States has numerous religious, racial, and ethnic groups, as well as countless interest groups that center around such divergent activities as collecting Barbie dolls and hunting deer. This state of affairs makes the job of specifying U.S. values difficult. Nonetheless, sociologists have tried to identify the underlying core values that are shared by the many groups that make up U.S. society. Sociologist Robin Williams (1965) identified the following:

1. *Achievement and success.* Americans place a high value on personal achievement, especially outdoing others. This value includes getting ahead at work and school, and attaining wealth, power, and prestige.

2. *Individualism.* Americans have traditionally prized success that comes from individual efforts and initiative. They cherish the ideal that an individual can rise from the bottom of society to its very top. If someone fails to "get ahead," Americans generally find fault with that individual, rather than with the social system for placing roadblocks in his or her path.

3. *Activity and work.* Americans expect people to work hard and to be busily engaged in some activity even when not at work. This value is becoming less important.

4. *Efficiency and practicality.* Americans award high marks for getting things done efficiently. Even in everyday life, Americans consider it important to do things fast, and they constantly seek changes to increase efficiency.

5. *Science and technology.* Americans have a passion for applied science, for using science to control nature—to tame rivers and harness winds—and to develop new technology, from motorized scooters to talking computers.

6. *Progress.* Americans expect rapid technological change. They believe that they should constantly build "more and better" gadgets that will help them move toward that vague goal called "progress."

7. *Material comfort.* Americans expect a high level of material comfort. This comfort includes not only nutrition, medical care, and housing, but also late-model cars and recreational playthings—from boats to computer games.

8. *Humanitarianism.* Americans emphasize helpfulness, personal kindness, aid in mass disasters, and organized philanthropy.

9. *Freedom.* This core value pervades U.S. life. It underscored the American Revolution, and Americans today bristle at the suggestion of any limitation on personal freedom. The Mass Media box on the next page highlights an interesting study on how this core value applies to Native Americans.

pluralistic society
a society made up of many different groups

Why Do Native Americans Like Westerns?

U.S. audiences (and even German, French, and Japanese ones) devour westerns. In the United States, it is easy to see why Anglos might like westerns, for it is they who seemingly defy the odds and emerge victorious. It is they who are portrayed as heroes who tame the savage wilderness and defend themselves from cruel, barbaric Indians who are intent on their destruction. But why would Indians like westerns?

Sociologist JoEllen Shively, a Chippewa who grew up on Indian reservations in Montana and North Dakota, observed that westerns are so popular that Native Americans bring bags of paperbacks into taverns to trade with one another. They even call one another "cowboy."

Intrigued, Shively decided to investigate the matter by showing a western movie to adult Native Americans and Anglos in a reservation town. The groups were matched in terms of education, age, income, and percentage of unemployment. To select the movie, Shively (1991, 1992) previewed more than seventy westerns. She chose a John Wayne movie, *The Searchers,* because it not only focuses on conflict between Indians and cowboys but also shows the cowboys defeating the Indians. After the movie, the viewers filled out questionnaires, and she interviewed them.

Shively found something surprising: *All* Native Americans and Anglos identified with the cowboys; *none* identified with the Indians. Anglos and Native Americans, however, identified with the cowboys in quite different ways. Each projected a different fantasy onto the story. While Anglos saw the movie as an accurate portrayal of the Old West and a justification of their own status in society, Native Americans saw it as embodying a free, natural way of life. In fact, Native Americans said that they were the "real cowboys." They said,

■ *Although John Wayne often portrayed an Anglo who kills Indians, Wayne is popular among Indian men. The men tend to identify with cowboys, who reflect their values of bravery, autonomy, and toughness.*

"Westerns relate to the way I wish I could live"; "He's not tied down to an eight-to-five job, day after day"; "He's his own man."

Shively adds,

> What appears to make Westerns meaningful to Indians is the fantasy of being free and independent like the cowboy. . . . Indians . . . find a fantasy in the cowboy story in which the important parts of their ways of life triumph and are morally good, validating their own cultural group in the context of a dramatically satisfying story. (1992)

> To express their real identity—a combination of marginality on the one hand, with a set of values which are about the land, autonomy, and being free—they (use) a cultural vehicle (that

is) written for Anglos about Anglos, but it is one in which Indians invest a distinctive set of meanings that speak to their own experience, which they can read in a manner that affirms a way of life they value, or a fantasy they hold to. (1991)

In other words, values, not ethnicity, are the central issue. If a Native American film industry were to portray Native Americans with the same values that the Anglo movie industry projects onto cowboys, then Native Americans would identify with their own group. Thus, says Shively, Native American viewers make cowboys "honorary Indians," for the cowboys express their values of bravery, autonomy, and toughness.

10. *Democracy*. By this term, Americans refer to majority rule, to the right of everyone to express an opinion, and to representative government.

11. *Equality*. It is impossible to understand Americans without being aware of the central role that the value of equality plays in their lives. Equality of opportunity (part of the ideal culture discussed later), has significantly influenced U.S. history and continues to mark relations between the groups that make up U.S. society.

12. *Racism and group superiority*. Although it contradicts freedom, democracy, and equality, Americans value some groups more than others and have done so throughout their history. The institution of slavery in earlier U.S. society is the most notorious example.

In an earlier publication (Henslin 1975), I updated Williams' analysis by adding these three values.

13. *Education*. Americans are expected to go as far in school as their abilities and finances allow. Over the years, the definition of an "adequate" education has changed, and today a college education is considered an appropriate goal for most Americans. Those who have an opportunity for higher education and do not take it are sometimes viewed as doing something "wrong"—not merely as making a bad choice, but as somehow being involved in an immoral act.

14. *Religiosity*. There is a feeling that "every true American ought to be religious." This does not mean that everyone is expected to join a church, synagogue, or mosque, but that everyone ought to acknowledge a belief in a Supreme Being and follow some set of matching precepts. This value is so pervasive that Americans stamp "In God We Trust" on their money and declare in their national pledge of allegiance that they are "one nation under God."

15. *Romantic love*. Americans feel that the only proper basis for marriage is romantic love. Songs, literature, mass media, and "folk beliefs" all stress this value. They especially love the theme that "love conquers all."

■ *The many groups that compose the United States contribute to its culture. The increasing numbers of Latinos in the United States, for example, are making an impact on music, art, and literature. This is also true of other areas of everyday life, such as this car-hopping contest in California. Cars are outfitted with bionic hydraulic systems, and contestants compete to see whose car can hop the highest or shimmy the most erratically from tire to tire.*

◼️ Value Clusters

As you can see, values are not independent units; some cluster together to form a larger whole. In the **value cluster** surrounding success, for example, we find hard work, education, efficiency, material comfort, and individualism bound up together. Americans are expected to go far in school, to work hard afterward, to be efficient, and then to attain a high level of material comfort, which, in turn, demonstrates success. Success is attributed to the individual's efforts; lack of success is blamed on his or her faults.

◼️ Value Contradictions and Social Change

Not all values fall into neat, integrated packages. Some even contradict one another. The value of group superiority contradicts freedom, democracy, and equality, producing a **value contradiction**. There simply cannot be full expression of freedom, democracy, and equality, along with racism and sexism. Something has to give. One way in which Americans sidestepped this contradiction in the past was to say that freedom, democracy, and equality applied only to some groups. The contradiction was bound to surface over time, however, and so it did with the Civil War and the women's liberation movement. *It is precisely at the point of value contradictions, then, that one can see a major force for social change in a society.*

■ *A value cluster that centers around youthfulness, physical fitness, self-fulfillment, and leisure is becoming central to life in industrial and postindustrial societies. A major reason for the emergence of this value cluster is the greater abundance of material goods, which has freed people from the need to concentrate on survival.*

◼️ Emerging Values

A value cluster of four interrelated core values—leisure, self-fulfillment, physical fitness, and youthfulness—appears to be emerging in the United States. A fifth emerging core value—concern for the environment—can also be identified.

1. *Leisure.* The emergence of leisure as a value is reflected in a huge recreation industry—from computer games, boats, and motor homes to sports arenas, vacation homes, and travel and vacation services.

2. *Self-fulfillment.* This value is reflected in the "human potential" movement, which involves becoming "all one can be," and in books and talk shows that focus on "self-help," "relating," and "personal development."

3. *Physical fitness.* Physical fitness is not a new U.S. value, but increased emphasis is moving it into this emerging cluster. This trend is evident in the "natural" foods craze; people's obsessive concerns about weight and diet; brew bars; the joggers, cyclists, and backpackers who take to the trails; and the mushrooming numbers of health clubs and physical fitness centers.

4. *Youthfulness.* While valuing youth and disparaging old age is not new, some note a new sense of urgency. They attribute this to aging baby boomers, who, aghast at their physical changes, attempt to deny their biological fate. An extreme view is represented by a physician who claims that "aging is not a normal life event, but a disease" (Cowley 1996). It is not surprising, then, that techniques for enhancing a youthful appearance—from cosmetics to surgery—have become popular.

value cluster
a series of interrelated values that together form a larger whole

value contradiction
values that contradict one another; to follow the one means to come into conflict with the other

■ Values, *both those held by individuals and those representing a nation or people, can undergo deep shifts. It is difficult for many of us to grasp the pride with which earlier Americans destroyed trees that took thousands of years to grow, are located only in one tiny speck of the globe, and that we today consider part of the nation's and world's heritage. But this is a value statement, representing current views. The pride expressed on these woodcutters' faces represents another set of values entirely.*

This emerging value cluster is a response to fundamental changes in U.S. society. Americans used to be preoccupied with forging a nation and fighting for economic survival. They now have come to a point in their economic development where millions of people are freed from long hours of work, and millions more are able to retire from work when they still expect decades of life ahead of them. This value cluster centers around helping people to maintain their health and vigor during their younger years and enabling them to enjoy their years of retirement.

5. *Concern for the environment.* During most of U.S. history, the environment was seen as a challenge—a wilderness to be settled, forests to be chopped down, rivers and lakes to be fished, and animals to be hunted. The lack of concern for the environment that characterized earlier Americans is illustrated by the near extinction of the bison and the extinction in 1915 of the passenger pigeon, a bird previously so numerous that its annual migration would darken the skies for days. Today, Americans have developed a genuine and (we can hope) long-term concern for the environment.

This emerging value of environmental concern is also related to the current stage of U.S. economic development, a point that becomes clearer when we note that people act on environmental concerns only after basic needs are met. At this point in their development, for example, the world's poor nations have a difficult time "affording" this value.

■ Culture Wars: When Values Clash

Changes in core values are met with strong resistance by people who hold them dear. They see the change as a threat to their way of life, an undermining of both their present and their future. Efforts to change gender roles, for example, arouse intense controversy, as does support of alternative family forms and changes in sexual behavior. Alarmed at such onslaughts to their values, traditionalists fiercely defend historical family relationships and the gender roles they grew up with. The issue of socialist economic principles versus profit and private property is also at the center of controversy. Today's clash in values is so severe that the term *culture wars* has been coined to refer to it. Compared with the violence directed against the Mormons, however, today's reactions to such controversies are mild.

Values as Blinders

Just as values and their supporting beliefs paint a unique picture of reality, so they also form a view of what life *ought* to be like. Americans value individualism so highly, for example, that they tend to see everyone as free to pursue the goal of success. This value blinds them to the many circumstances that impede people's efforts. The dire consequences of family poverty, parents' low education, and dead-end jobs tend to drop from sight. Instead, Americans cling to the notion that everyone can make it—if they put out enough effort. And they know they are right, for every day, dangling before their eyes are enticing success stories—individuals who have succeeded despite huge handicaps.

"Ideal" Versus "Real" Culture

Many of the norms that surround cultural values are only partially followed. Differences always exist between a group's ideals and what its members actually do. Consequently, sociologists use the term **ideal culture** to refer to the values, norms, and goals that a group considers ideal, worth aspiring to. Success, for example, is part of ideal culture. Americans glorify academic progress, hard work, and the display of material goods as signs of individual achievement. What people actually do, however, usually falls short of the cultural ideal. Compared with their abilities, for example, most people don't work as hard as they could or go as far as they could in school. Sociologists call the norms and values that people actually follow **real culture.**

Cultural Universals

With the amazing variety of human cultures around the world, are there any **cultural universals**—values, norms, or other cultural traits that are found everywhere?

To answer this question, anthropologist George Murdock (1945) combed through data that anthropologists had gathered on hundreds of groups around the world. He drew up a list of customs concerning courtship, cooking, marriage, funerals, games, laws, music, myths, incest taboos, and even toilet training. He found that although such activities are present in all cultures, *the specific customs differ from one group to another.* There is no universal form of the family, no universal way of disposing of the dead. Similarly, the games, rules, songs, stories, and methods of toilet training differ from one culture to another.

Even incest is defined differently from group to group. For example, the Mundugumors of New Guinea extend the incest taboo so far that for each man, seven of every eight women are ineligible marriage partners (Mead 1935/1950). Other groups go in the opposite direction and allow some men to marry their own daughters (La Barre 1954). In certain circumstances, some groups require that brothers and sisters marry one another (Beals and Hoijer 1965). The Burundi of Africa even insist that, in order to remove a certain curse, a son must have sexual relations with his mother (Albert 1963). Such sexual relations are usually allowed only for special people (royalty) or in extraordinary situations (such as when a lion hunter faces a dangerous hunt), and no society permits generalized incest for its members.

In short, although there are universal human activities (speech, music, storytelling, marrying, disposing of the dead, preparing food, and so on), there is no universally accepted way of doing any of them. Humans have no biological imperative that results in one particular form of behavior throughout the world. As indicated in the following Thinking Critically section, a few sociologists do take the position that genes significantly influence human behavior, although almost all sociologists reject this view.

ideal culture
the ideal values and norms of a people, the goals held out for them

real culture
the norms and values that people actually follow

cultural universal
a value, norm, or other cultural trait that is found in every group

thinking
CRITICALLY

Are We Prisoners of Our Genes?
Sociobiology and Human Behavior

A controversial view of human behavior, called **sociobiology** (also known as neo-Darwinism), provides a sharp contrast to the perspective of this chapter, that human behavior is primarily due to culture. Sociobiologists believe that because of natural selection, the basic cause of human behavior is biology.

Charles Darwin (1859), who developed the idea of natural selection, pointed out that the genes of a species—the units that contain the individual's traits—are not distributed evenly among the offspring. The characteristics passed on to some members make it easier for them to survive their environment, increasing the likelihood that they will pass their genetic traits to the next generation. Over thousands of generations, the genetic traits that aid survival tend to become common in a species, while those that do not tend to disappear.

Natural selection explains not only the physical characteristics of animals, but also their behavior, for over countless generations, instincts emerged. Edward Wilson (1975), an insect specialist, claims that human behavior is also the result of natural selection. Human behavior, he said, is no different from the behavior of cats, dogs, rats, bees, or mosquitoes—it has been bred into *Homo sapiens* through evolutionary principles.

Wilson deliberately set out to create a storm of protest, and he succeeded. He went on to claim that religion, competition and cooperation, slavery and genocide, war and peace, envy and altruism—all can be explained by sociobiology. He provocatively added that because human behavior can be explained in terms of genetic programming, sociobiology will eventually absorb sociology—as well as anthropology and psychology.

Obviously, most sociologists find Wilson's position unacceptable. Not only is it a direct attack on their discipline, but also it bypasses the essence of what sociologists focus on: humans developing their own cultures, their own unique ways of life. Sociologists do not deny that biology underlies human behavior—at least not in the sense that it takes a highly developed brain to develop human culture and abstract thought, and that there would be no speech if humans had no tongue or larynx.

But most sociologists find ludicrous the claim that genetic programming causes human behavior (Howe et al. 1992). Pigs act like pigs because they don't have a cerebral cortex, and instincts control their behavior. So it is for spiders, elephants, and so on. But humans possess a self and have abstract thought. They discuss the reasons that underlie what they do. They develop purposes and goals. They consider, reflect, and make choices.

This controversy has turned into much more than simply an academic debate among scientists. Homosexuals, for example, have a personal interest in its outcome. If homosexuality is a lifestyle *choice*, then those who consider that lifestyle to be immoral will use this as a basis for excluding homosexuals from full social participation. If, however, homosexuality has a genetic basis, then choice as a reason for social exclusion is eliminated. Sociologist Peter Conrad (1997) expresses the dominant sociological position when he points out that not all homosexuals have Xq28, the so-called "gay gene," and some people who have this gene are not homosexual. This gene, then, does not determine behavior. Instead, we must look for *social* causes.

In short, sociobiologists and sociologists stand on opposite sides, the one looking at human behavior as determined by genetics, the other looking at

sociobiology
a framework of thought that views human behavior as the result of natural selection and considers biological characteristics to be the fundamental cause of human behavior

human behavior as determined by social learning, by experiences in the human group. Sociologists point out that if humans were prisoners of their genes, we would not have developed such a variety of fascinating ways of life around the world—we would live in a monoculture of some sort.

■ Animals and Language

Let's digress for a moment to follow a fascinating and related issue: Do animals have language? This question has intrigued scientists and nonscientists alike. Do those barks and meows your pets make constitute language?

Social scientists think of language as more complex than mere sounds. They view language as symbols that can be endlessly strung together to communicate abstract thought. Animal sounds, however, appear to be closer to a baby's cries. Although a baby will cry when in pain, this cry of distress, even though it brings a parent running, is not language. The cry is merely a biological response to pain, similar to a reflex.

Social scientists also point out that animals do not have the vocal apparatus necessary to utter the complex sounds that make up language. Do animals lack speech, then, because they lack intelligence (the inability to learn speech), or because they lack the equipment to make the sounds of speech? When Allen and Beatrice Gardner (1969), psychologists at the University of Nevada, learned from Jane Goodall's research that chimps in the wild use many more hand signals than vocal signals, they decided to teach chimps gestures instead of words (Fleming 1974). Their first pupil was Washoe, a female chimpanzee who was born in the wild. In 1966, when Washoe was 1 year old, her language training began. Washoe was like a human baby. She slept a lot, had begun to crawl, and had a daily routine that centered on diapers and bottles.

The Gardners tried to teach Washoe American Sign Language, in which hand signs correspond to individual words. They were encouraged when Washoe began to learn some of the signs, and they were elated when she began to *generalize*, to apply a sign learned in one situation to other situations. For example, they taught her the sign for "open," using three doors in the house trailer she lived in. After learning that sign, Washoe transferred it to all the trailer's doors and drawers, to containers, the refrigerator, and even to the water faucet.

Within a year, Washoe had become inventive and was putting signs together in the equivalent of simple sentences. She even made up combinations, such as joining the sign for "give me" with "tickle" to indicate that she wanted to be tickled. At the end of four years, Washoe could use 160 signs.

At Northwestern University, Irene Pepperberg taught Alex, an African Gray parrot, to name eighty objects, such as wool, walnut, and shower. She also taught the parrot to identify colors, and to tell how many objects are in a group (up to six). Skeptics replied that the only thing that distinguishes Alex from pigeons that learn to peck buttons for food is that his responses sound like English (Stipp 1990).

■ *Do some animals think like humans? This chimp seems to be thinking—but she could simply be scratching her lip. Distinguishing between appearance and reality is often difficult, as is determining whether or not animals have language. Debated for centuries, this question is still not decided. The answer often depends on one's starting point—one's definition of language.*

Do animals have the capacity for language? Such experiments have persuaded some scientists that they do. Others, however, remain unconvinced. For the answer to this question, we must await further evidence.

■ ■ ■ ■ ■

Technology in the Global Village

■ The New Technology

technology
in its narrow sense, tools; its broader sense includes the skills or procedures necessary to make and use those tools

new technology
the emerging technologies of an era that have a significant impact on social life

cultural lag
William Ogburn's term for a situation in which nonmaterial culture lags behind changes in the material culture

The gestures, language, values, folkways, and mores that we have discussed—all are part of symbolic or nonmaterial culture. Culture, as you recall, also has a material aspect, a group's *things,* from its houses to its toys. Central to a group's material culture is its technology. In its simplest sense, **technology** can be equated with tools. In its broader sense, technology also includes the skills or procedures necessary to make and use those tools.

We can use the term **new technology** to refer to the emerging technologies that have a significant impact on social life. People develop minor technologies all the time. Most are slight modifications of existing technologies. Occasionally, however, they develop technologies that make a major impact on human life. It is primarily to these that the term *new technology* refers. For people 500 years ago, the new technology was the printing press. For us, the new technology consists of computers, satellites, and the electronic media.

The sociological significance of technology goes far beyond the tool itself. *Technology sets the framework for a group's nonmaterial culture.* If a group's technology changes, so do people's ways of thinking and how they relate to one another. An example is gender relations. Through the centuries and throughout the world, it has been the custom (the nonmaterial culture of a group) for men to dominate women. Today, with instantaneous communications (the material culture), this custom has become much more difficult to maintain. For example, when women from many nations gathered in Beijing for a U.N. conference in 1995, satellites instantly transmitted their grievances around the globe. Such communications both convey and create discontent, as well as a feeling of sisterhood, motivating women to agitate for social change.

In today's world, the long-accepted idea that it is proper to withhold rights on the basis of someone's sex can no longer hold. What is usually invisible in this revolutionary change is the role of the new technology, which joins the world's nations into a global communication network.

■ *The adoption of new forms of communication by people who not long ago were cut off from events in the rest of the world is bound to change their nonmaterial culture. How do you think this man's thinking and view of the world is changing?*

■ Cultural Lag and Cultural Change

About three generations ago, sociologist William Ogburn (1922/1938), a functional analyst, coined the term **cultural lag.** By this, Ogburn meant that not all parts of a culture change at the same pace. When some part of a culture changes, other parts lag behind.

Ogburn pointed out that *a group's material culture usually changes first, with the nonmaterial culture lagging behind*, playing a game of catch up. For example, when we get sick, we could type our symptoms into a computer and get an immediate printout of our diagnosis and the best course of treatment. In fact, in some tests computers outperform physicians (Waldholz 1991). Yet our customs have not caught up with our technology, and we continue to visit the doctors' office.

Sometimes nonmaterial culture never does catch up. Instead, we rigorously hold onto some outmoded form, one that once was needed, but was long ago bypassed by new technology. A striking example is our nine-month school year. Have you ever wondered why it is nine months long, and why we take summers off? For most of us, this is "just the way it's always been," and we've never questioned it. But there is more to this custom than meets the eye, for it is an example of cultural lag.

In the nineteenth century, when universal schooling came about, the school year matched the technology of the time, which was labor-intensive. For survival, parents needed their children's help at the crucial times of planting and harvesting. Although the invention of highly productive farm machinery eliminated the need for the school year to be so short, generations later we still live with this cultural lag.

■ Technology and Cultural Leveling

For most of human history, communication was limited and travel slow. Consequently, in their relative isolation, human groups developed highly distinctive ways of life as they responded to the particular situations they faced. The unique characteristics they developed that distinguished one culture from another tended to change little over time. The Tasmanians, who lived on a remote island off the coast of Australia, provide an extreme example. For thousands of years, they had no contact with other people. They were so isolated that they did not even know how to make clothing or fire (Edgerton 1992).

Except in such rare instances, humans always had *some* contact with other groups. During these contacts, people learned from one another, adopting some part of the other's way of life. In this process, called **cultural diffusion,** groups are most open to changes in their technology or material culture. They usually are eager, for example, to adopt superior weapons and tools. In remote jungles in South America one can find metal cooking pots, steel axes, and even bits of clothing spun in mills in South Carolina. Although the direction of cultural diffusion today is primarily from the West to other parts of the world, cultural diffusion is not a one-way street—as bagels, woks, hammocks, and sushi bars in the United States attest.

With today's sophisticated technology in travel and communications, cultural diffusion is occurring rapidly. Air travel has made it possible to journey around the globe in a matter of hours. In the not-so-distant past, a trip from the United States to Africa was so unusual that only a few hardy people made it, and newspapers would herald their feat. Today, hundreds of thousands make the trip each year.

The changes in communication are no less vast. Communication used to be limited to face-to-face speech, to written messages that were passed from hand to hand, and to visual signals such as smoke, or light that was reflected from mirrors. Despite newspapers, people in some parts of the United States did not hear that the Civil War had ended until weeks and even months after it was over. Today's electronic communications transmit messages across the globe in a matter of seconds, and we learn almost instantaneously what is happening on the other side of the world.

In fact, travel and communication unite us to such an extent that there is almost no "other side of the world" anymore. One result is **cultural leveling,** a process in which cultures become similar to one another. The globalization of

cultural diffusion
the spread of cultural characteristics from one group to another

cultural leveling
the process by which cultures become similar to one another, and especially by which Western industrial culture is imported and diffused into industrializing nations

"COOL! A KEYBOARD THAT WRITES WITHOUT A PRINTER."

■ *Technological advances are now so rapid that the technology of one generation is practically unrecognizable by the next generation.*

■ *Shown here is a Masai Barbie Doll. Mattel Toys, the U.S. manufacturer, has modified Barbie to match Masai (Kenya) culture by dressing her in a traditional "shuka" dress, beads, shawl, headdress, and anklets. As objects diffuse from one culture to another, they are modified to meet the tastes of the adoptive culture. In this instance, the modification has been done intentionally as part of the globalization of capitalism. Now that Barbie is a Masai, can a Masai Ken be far behind?*

capitalism is bringing not only technology but also Western culture to the rest of the world. Japan, for example, has adopted not only Western economic production but also Western forms of dress and music. These changes, which have been "superimposed" on Japanese culture, have turned Japan into a blend of Western and Eastern cultures.

Cultural leveling is occurring rapidly around the world, as is apparent to any traveler. The Golden Arches of McDonald's welcome today's visitors to Tokyo, Paris, London, Madrid, Moscow, Hong Kong, and Beijing. In Mexico, the most popular piñatas are no longer donkeys but, rather, Mickey Mouse and Fred Flintstone (Beckett 1996). In Beijing, a grade school teacher asked his class if they knew who Mickey Mouse was. One of the students held up a lunchbox with Mickey Mouse on it. As the teacher and the kids scanned the room, they found almost a dozen images of Mickey Mouse. But they didn't find a single image of any character from classical Chinese literature—not one (Hofstadter 2000).

Although the bridging of geography and culture by electronic signals and the exportation of Western icons do not in and of themselves mark the end of traditional cultures, the inevitable result is some degree of *cultural leveling*, some blander, less distinctive way of life—U.S. culture with French, Japanese, and Brazilian accents, so to speak. Although the "cultural accent" remains, something vital is lost forever.

Summary and Review

What Is Culture?

All human groups possess **culture**—language, beliefs, values, norms, and material objects that are passed from one generation to the next. **Material culture** consists of objects (art, buildings, clothing, tools). **Nonmaterial** (or **symbolic**) **culture** is a group's ways of thinking and patterns of behavior. **Ideal culture** is a group's ideal values, norms, and goals. **Real culture** is their actual behavior, which often falls short of their cultural ideals. Pp. 39–40.

■ **What are cultural relativism and ethnocentrism?**

People are naturally **ethnocentric**; that is, they use their own culture as a yardstick for judging the ways of others. In contrast, those who embrace **cultural relativism** try to understand other cultures on those cultures' own terms. Pp. 40–43.

Components of Symbolic Culture

■ **What are the components of nonmaterial culture?**

The central component is **symbols**, anything to which people attach meaning and that they use to communicate with others. Universally, the symbols of nonmaterial culture are **gestures, language, values, norms, sanctions, folkways,** and **mores.** Pp. 43–44.

■ **Why is language so significant to culture?**

Language allows human experience to be goal-directed, cooperative, and cumulative. It also lets humans move beyond the present and share a past, future, and other common perspectives. According to the **Sapir-Whorf hypothesis**, language even shapes our thoughts and perceptions. Pp. 44–49.

■ **How do values, norms, sanctions, folkways, and mores reflect culture?**

All groups have **values,** standards by which they define what is desirable or undesirable, and **norms,** rules or expectations about behavior. Groups use **positive sanctions** to show approval of those who follow their norms, and **negative sanctions** to show disapproval of those who do not. Norms that are not strictly enforced are called **folkways,** while **mores** are norms to which groups demand conformity because they reflect core values. Pp. 49–50.

Many Cultural Worlds: Subcultures and Countercultures

■ **How do subcultures and countercultures differ?**

A **subculture** is a group whose values and related behaviors distinguish its members from the general culture. A **counterculture** holds values that stand in opposition to those of the dominant culture. Pp. 50–51.

Values in U.S. Society

■ **What are the core U.S. values?**

Although the United States is a **pluralistic society,** made up of many groups, each with its own set of values, certain values dominate: achievement and success, individualism, activity and work, efficiency and practicality, science and technology, progress, material comfort, equality, freedom, democracy, humanitarianism, racism and group superiority, education, religiosity, and romantic love. Some values cluster together (**value clusters**) to form a larger whole. **Value contradictions** (such as equality and racism) indicate areas of social tension, which are likely points of social change. Leisure,

physical fitness, self-fulfillment, youthfulness, and concern for the environment are emerging core values. Core values do not change without opposition. Pp. 52–57.

Cultural Universals

■ **Do cultural universals exist?**

Cultural universals are values, norms, or other cultural traits that are found in all cultures. Although all human groups have customs concerning cooking, funerals, weddings, and so on, because the forms these customs take vary from one culture to another, there are no cultural universals. Pp. 57–59.

■ **Do animals have language?**

No animals have language in the sociological sense of the term, although experiments indicate that some animals may have a limited capacity to learn language. Pp. 59–60.

Technology in the Global Village

■ **How is technology changing culture?**

William Ogburn coined the term **cultural lag** to describe how a group's nonmaterial culture lags behind its changing technology. With today's technological advances in travel and communications, **cultural diffusion** is occurring rapidly. This leads to **cultural leveling,** whereby many groups are adopting Western culture in place of their own customs. Much of the richness of the world's diverse cultures is being lost in the process. Pp. 60–62.

■ *Where can I read more on this topic?*

Suggested Readings for this chapter are at the back of this book.

Additional Online Resources for This Chapter
www.ablongman.com/henslin6e

- *Content Select* Research Database for Sociology, with suggested key terms and annotated references
- Link to 2000 Census, with activities
- Flashcards of key terms and concepts

- Practice Tests
- Weblinks
- Interactive Maps

using . . .
ContentSelect

Research Database for Sociology

cultural change	subculture	culture and technology	language and culture
cultural relativism	folkways	ethnocentrism	values and culture

Velino Shije Herrera, *Story Teller*, ca. 1925–1935

3

Socialization

What Is Human Nature?
Feral Children
Isolated Children
Institutionalized Children
Deprived Animals

Socialization into the Self, Mind, and Emotions
Cooley and the Looking-Glass Self
Mead and Role Taking
Piaget and the Development of Reasoning Skills
Kohlberg and the Development of Morality
Gilligan and Gender Differences in Morality
Global Aspects of the Self, Reasoning, and Morality
Freud and the Development of Personality
Socialization into Emotions
The Self and Emotions as Social Control: Society Within Us

Socialization into Gender
Gender Messages in the Family
Gender Messages in the Mass Media

Agents of Socialization
The Family
The Neighborhood
Religion
Day Care
The School
Peer Groups
Sports
The Workplace

Resocialization
Total Institutions

Socialization Through the Life Course
Childhood
Adolescence
Young Adulthood
The Middle Years
The Older Years
The Sociological Significance of the Life Course

Are We Prisoners of Socialization?

Summary and Review

T he old man was horrified when he found out. Life never had been good since his daughter lost her hearing when she was just 2 years old. She couldn't even talk— just fluttered her hands around trying to tell him things. Over the years, he had gotten used to that. But now . . . he shuddered at the thought of her being pregnant. No one would be willing to marry her; he knew that. And the neighbors, their tongues would never stop wagging. Everywhere he went, he could hear people talking behind his back.

> Her behavior toward strangers, especially men, was almost that of a wild animal, manifesting much fear and hostility.

If only his wife were still alive, maybe she could come up with something. What should he do? He couldn't just kick his daughter out into the street.

After the baby was born, the old man tried to shake his feelings, but they wouldn't let loose. Isabelle was a pretty name, but every time he looked at the baby he felt sick to his stomach.

He hated doing it, but there was no way out. His daughter and her baby would have to live in the attic.

. . .

Unfortunately, this is a true story. Isabelle was discovered in Ohio in 1938 when she was about 6½ years old, living in a dark room with her deaf-mute mother. Isabelle couldn't talk, but she did use gestures to communicate with her mother. An inadequate diet and lack of sunshine had given Isabelle a disease called rickets. Her legs

> were so bowed that as she stood erect the soles of her shoes came nearly flat together, and she got about with a skittering gait. Her behavior toward strangers, especially men, was almost that of a wild animal, manifesting much fear and hostility. In lieu of speech she made only a strange croaking sound. (Davis 1940/2001:134)

When the newspapers reported this case, sociologist Kingsley Davis decided to find out what happened to Isabelle after her discovery. We'll come back to that later, but first let's use the case of Isabelle to gain some insight into human nature.

What Is Human Nature?

For centuries, people have been intrigued with the question of what is human about human nature. How much of people's characteristics comes from "nature" (heredity) and how much from "nurture" (the **social environment,** contact with others)? One way to answer this question is to study identical twins who have been reared apart, such as those discussed in the Down-to-Earth Sociology box on the next page. Another way is to examine people who have been reared without human contact. Let's consider such children.

■ Feral Children

Over the centuries, the discovery of **feral** (wild) **children** has been reported from time to time. Supposedly, these children were abandoned or lost by their parents at a very early age and then raised by animals. In the 1700s, a feral child known as "the wild boy of Aveyron" was studied by the scientists of his day (Itard 1962). This boy, who was found in the forests of France in 1798, walked on all fours and pounced on small animals, devouring them uncooked. He could not speak, and he gave no indication of feeling the cold. Other reports of feral children have claimed that on discovery, these children acted like wild animals: They could not speak; they bit, scratched, growled, and walked on all fours; they drank by lapping water, ate grass, tore ravenously at meat, and showed an insensitivity to pain and cold (Malson 1972).

Most social scientists today dismiss the significance of feral children, taking the position that children cannot be raised by animals and that children found in the woods were reared by their parents as infants but then abandoned, probably because they were retarded. But what if this were not the case? Could it be that, if we were untouched by society, we would all by nature be like feral children?

■ Isolated Children

Cases like Isabelle, in our opening vignette, surface from time to time. What can they tell us about human nature? We can first conclude that humans have no natural language, for isolated children like Isabelle are unable to speak.

But maybe Isabelle was mentally impaired, as most scientists claim feral children are, and could not progress through the usual stages of development. When given an

social environment
the entire human environment, including direct contact with others

feral children
children assumed to have been raised by animals, in the wilderness, isolated from other humans

down-to-earth

s o c i o l o g y

■ ■ ■ ■ ■

Heredity or Environment? The Case of Oskar and Jack, Identical Twins

Identical twins share exact genetic heredity. One fertilized egg divides to produce two embryos. If heredity determines personality—or attitudes, temperament, skills, and intelligence—then identical twins should be identical not only in their looks but also in these characteristics.

The fascinating case of Jack and Oskar helps us unravel this mystery. From their experience, we can see the far-reaching effects of the environment—how social experiences override biology.

Jack Yufe and Oskar Stohr are identical twins born in 1932 to a Jewish father and a Catholic mother. They were separated as babies after their parents divorced. Oskar was reared in Czechoslovakia by his mother's mother, who was a strict Catholic. When Oskar was a toddler, Hitler annexed this area of Czechoslovakia, and Oskar learned to love Hitler and to hate Jews. He became involved with the Hitler Youth (a sort of Boy Scout organization, except that this one was designed to instill the "virtues" of patriotism, loyalty, obedience—and hatred).

Jack's upbringing was in almost total contrast to Oskar's. Reared in Trinidad by his father, he learned loyalty to Jews and hatred of Hitler and the Nazis. After the war, Jack emigrated to Israel, where, at the age of 17, he joined a kibbutz. Later, Jack served in the Israeli army.

In 1954, the two brothers met. It was a short meeting, and Jack had been warned not to tell Oskar that they were Jews. Twenty-five years later, in 1979, when they were 47 years old, social scientists at the University of Minnesota brought them together again. These researchers figured that because Jack and

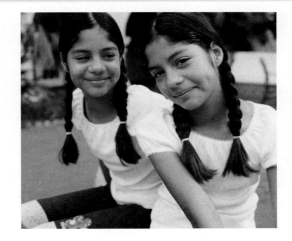

■ *The question of the relative influence of heredity and the environment on human behavior has fascinated and plagued researchers. Identical twins reared apart provide an opportunity to examine this relationship. However, almost all identical twins, including these girls, are reared together, frustrating efforts to separate heredity and environment.*

Oskar had the same genes, whatever differences they showed would have to be due to the environment—to their different social experiences.

Not only did Oskar and Jack have different attitudes toward the war, Hitler, and Jews, but also their basic orientations to life were different. In their politics, Oskar was conservative, while Jack was more liberal. Oskar enjoyed leisure, while Jack was a workaholic. And, as you can predict, Jack was very proud of being a Jew. Oskar, who by this time knew that he was a Jew, wouldn't even mention it.

That would seem to settle the matter. But there was another side to the findings. The researchers also found that Oskar and Jack both liked sweet liqueur and spicy foods, excelled at sports as children but had difficulty with math, and had the same rate of speech. Both flushed the toilet both before and after using it and enjoyed startling people by sneezing in crowded elevators.

for your consideration

Heredity or environment? How much influence does each one have? The question is not yet settled, but at this point it seems fair to conclude that the *limits* of certain physical and mental abilities are established by heredity (such as ability at sports and mathematics), while such basic orientations to life as attitudes are the result of the environment. We can put it this way: For some parts of life, the blueprint is drawn by heredity; but even here the environment can redraw those lines. For other parts, the individual is a blank slate, and it is entirely up to the environment to determine what is written on that slate.

Sources: Based on Begley 1979, Chen 1979, Wright 1995, Reed 2001.

■ ■ ■ ■ ■

intelligence test, she scored practically zero. But after a few months of intensive language training, Isabelle was able to speak in short sentences. In about a year, she could write a few words, do simple addition, and retell stories after hearing them. Seven months later, she had a vocabulary of almost 2,000 words. It took only two years for Isabelle to reach the intellectual level that is normal for her age. She then went on to school, where she was "bright, cheerful, energetic . . . and participated in all school activities as normally as other children" (Davis 1940/2001:135).

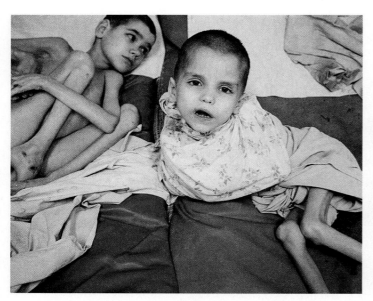

■ *The treatment given these orphaned children in Romania will make it difficult for them to develop into fully functioning adults. If they survive, they will carry scars into adulthood. As explained in the text, it is also likely that their abuse has affected their ability to reason.*

As discussed in the last chapter, language is the key to human development. Without language, people have no mechanism for developing thought. Unlike animals, humans have no instincts that take the place of language. If an individual lacks language, he or she lives in an isolated world, a world of internal silence, without shared ideas, without connections to others.

Without language, there can be no culture—no shared way of life—and culture is the key to what people become. Each of us possesses a biological heritage, but this heritage does not determine specific behaviors, attitudes, or values. It is our culture that superimposes the specifics of what we become onto our biological heritage.

■ Institutionalized Children

But what besides language is required if a child is to develop into what we consider a healthy, balanced, intelligent human being? We find part of the answer in an interesting experiment from the 1930s. Back then, orphanages dotted the United States. Children reared in orphanages often had difficulty establishing close bonds with others—and they tended to have lower IQs. "Common sense" (which we noted in Chapter 1 is unreliable) told everyone that the cause of mental retardation is biological ("They're just born that way"). Two psychologists, H. M. Skeels and H. B. Dye (1939), however, began to suspect another cause. For background on their experiment, Skeels (1966) provides this account of a "good" orphanage in Iowa during the 1930s, where he and Dye were consultants:

> Until about six months, they were cared for in the infant nursery. The babies were kept in standard hospital cribs that often had protective sheeting on the sides, thus effectively limiting visual stimulation; no toys or other objects were hung in the infants' line of vision. Human interactions were limited to busy nurses who, with the speed born of practice and necessity, changed diapers or bedding, bathed and medicated the infants, and fed them efficiently with propped bottles.

Perhaps, thought Skeels and Dye, the absence of stimulating social interaction was the basic problem, not some biological incapacity on the part of the children. To test their controversial idea, they placed in an institution for the mentally retarded thirteen infants whose mental retardation was so obvious that no one wanted to adopt them. Each infant, then about 19 months old, was assigned to a separate ward of women ranging in mental age from 5 to 12 and in chronological age from 18 to 50. The women were pleased with this arrangement. They not only did a good job taking care of the infants' basic physical needs—diapering, feeding, and so on—but also they loved to play with the children, to cuddle them, and to shower them with attention. They even competed to see which ward would have "its baby" walking or talking first. Each child had one woman who became

> particularly attached to him [or her] and figuratively "adopted" him [or her]. As a consequence, an intense one-to-one adult-child relationship developed, which was supplemented by the less intense but frequent interactions with the other adults in the environment. Each child had some one person with whom he [or she] was identified and who was particularly interested in him [or her] and his [or her] achievements. (Skeels 1966)

The researchers left a control group of twelve infants at the orphanage. These infants were also retarded but were higher in intelligence than the other thirteen. They received the usual care. Two and a half years later, Skeels and Dye tested all the children's intelligence. Their findings were startling: Those assigned to the retarded women had gained an average of 28 IQ points while those who remained in the orphanage had lost 30 points.

What happened after these children were grown? Did these initial differences matter? Twenty-one years later, Skeels and Dye did a follow-up study. Those in the control group who had remained in the orphanage had, on average, less than a third-grade education. Four still lived in state institutions, while the others held low-level jobs. Only two had married. In contrast, the average level of education for the thirteen individuals in the experimental group was twelve grades (about normal for that period). Five had completed one or more years of college. One had not only earned a B.A. but also had gone on to graduate school. Eleven had married. All thirteen were self-supporting and had higher-status jobs or were homemakers (Skeels 1966). Apparently, then, one characteristic we take for granted as being a basic "human" trait, high intelligence, depends on early, close relations with other humans.

Let's consider one other case, the story of Genie:

> In 1970, California authorities found Genie, a 13-year-old girl who had been locked in a small room and tied to a chair since she was 20 months old. Apparently her father (70 years old when Genie was discovered) hated children, and probably had caused the death of two of Genie's siblings. Her 50-year-old mother was partially blind and frightened of her husband. Genie could not speak, did not know how to chew, was unable to stand upright, and could not straighten her hands and legs. On intelligence tests, she scored at the level of a 1-year-old. After intensive training, Genie learned to walk and use simple sentences (although they were garbled). As she grew up, her language remained primitive, she took anyone's property if it appealed to her, and she went to the bathroom wherever she wanted. At the age of 21, Genie went to live in a home for adults who cannot live alone. (Pines 1981)

From this pathetic story, we can conclude that not only intelligence but also the ability to establish close bonds with others depends on early interaction. In addition, apparently there is a period prior to age 13 in which language and human bonding must occur for humans to develop high intelligence and the ability to be sociable and follow social norms.

■ Deprived Animals

A final lesson can be gained by looking at animals that have been deprived of normal interaction. In a series of experiments with rhesus monkeys, psychologists Harry and Margaret Harlow demonstrated the importance of early learning. The Harlows (1962) raised baby monkeys in isolation. They gave each monkey two artificial mothers, shown in the photo on this page. One "mother" was only a wire frame with a wooden head, but it did have a nipple from which the baby could nurse. The frame of the other "mother," which had no bottle, was covered with soft terrycloth. To obtain food, the baby monkeys nursed at the wire frame.

When the Harlows (1965) frightened the babies with a large mechanical bear or dog, the babies did not run to the

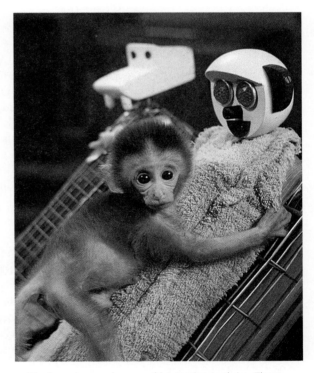

■ *Like humans, monkeys need interaction to thrive. Those raised in isolation are unable to interact satisfactorily with others. In this photograph, we see one of the monkeys described in the text. Purposefully frightened by the experimenter, the monkey has taken refuge in the soft terrycloth draped over an artificial "mother."*

wire frame "mother." Instead, they would cling pathetically to their terrycloth "mother." The Harlows concluded that infant-mother bonding is due not to feeding but, rather, to what they termed "intimate physical contact." To most of us, this phrase means cuddling.

It is also significant that the monkeys raised in isolation were never able to adjust to monkey life. Placed with other monkeys when they were grown, they didn't know how to enter into "monkey interaction"—to play and to engage in pretend fights—and the other monkeys rejected them. Neither did they know how to engage in sexual intercourse, despite futile attempts to do so. The experimenters designed a special device, which allowed some females to become pregnant. After giving birth, however, these monkeys were "ineffective, inadequate, and brutal mothers . . . [who] . . . struck their babies, kicked them, or crushed the babies against the cage floor."

In one of their many experiments, the Harlows isolated baby monkeys for different lengths of time. They found that when monkeys were isolated for short periods (about three months), they were able to overcome the effects of their isolation. Those isolated for six months or more, however, were unable to adjust to normal monkey life. As mentioned, they could not play or engage in pretend fights, and the other monkeys rejected them. In other words, the longer the isolation, the more difficult it is to overcome. In addition, a critical learning stage may exist; if that stage is missed, it may be impossible to compensate for what has been lost. That may have been the case with Genie.

Because humans are not monkeys, we must be careful about extrapolating from animal studies to human behavior. The Harlow experiments, however, support what we know about children who are reared in isolation.

IN SUM ■ ■ ■ ■

Society Makes Us Human Apparently, babies do not develop "naturally" into human adults. Although their bodies grow, if reared in isolation they become little more than big animals. Without the concepts that language provides, they can't experience or even grasp relations between people (the "connections" we call brother, sister, parent, friend, teacher, and so on). And without warm, friendly interaction, they aren't "friendly" in the accepted sense of the term; nor do they cooperate with others. In short, it is through human contact that people learn to be members of the human community. This process by which we learn the ways of society (or of particular groups), called **socialization**, is what sociologists have in mind when they say "Society makes us human."

socialization
the process by which people learn the characteristics of their group—the attitudes, values, and actions thought appropriate for them

self
the unique human capacity of being able to see ourselves "from the outside"; the picture we gain of how others see us

looking-glass self
a term coined by Charles Horton Cooley to refer to the process by which our self develops through internalizing others' reactions to us

■ ■ ■ ■ ■

Socialization into the Self, Mind, and Emotions

At birth, we have no idea that we are separate beings. We don't even know that we are a he or she. How do we develop reasoning skills? Our morality? Our personality? Our emotions? How do we develop a **self**, the picture we have of how others see us, our view of who we are? Let's see how this occurs.

■ Cooley and the Looking-Glass Self

Back in the 1800s, Charles Horton Cooley (1864–1929), a symbolic interactionist who taught at the University of Michigan, concluded that this unique aspect of "humanness" called the self is socially created. He said that *our sense of self develops from interaction with others*. Cooley (1902) coined the term **looking-glass self** to describe the process by which a sense of self develops. He summarized this idea in the following couplet:

Each to each a looking-glass
Reflects the other that doth pass.

The looking-glass self contains three elements:

1. *We imagine how we appear to those around us.* For example, we may think that others perceive us as witty or dull.

2. *We interpret others' reactions.* We come to conclusions about how others evaluate us. Do they like us for being witty? Do they dislike us for being dull?

3. *We develop a self-concept.* Based on our interpretations of how others react to us, we develop feelings and ideas about ourselves. A favorable reflection in this "social mirror" leads to a positive self-concept, a negative reflection to a negative self-concept.

Note that the development of the self does *not* depend on accurate evaluations. Even if we grossly misinterpret how others think about us, those misjudgments become part of our self-concept. Note also that although the self-concept begins in childhood, *its development is an ongoing, lifelong process.* The three steps of the looking-glass self are a part of our everyday lives: As we monitor how others react to us, we continually modify the self. The self, then, is never a finished product—it is always in process, even into old age.

■ Mead and Role Taking

Another symbolic interactionist, George Herbert Mead (1863–1931), who taught at the University of Chicago, added that play is crucial to the development of a self. In play, children learn to **take the role of the other,** that is, to put themselves in someone else's shoes—to understand how someone else feels and thinks and to anticipate how that person will act.

Only gradually do children attain this ability (Mead 1934; Coser 1977). In a simple experiment, psychologist J. Flavel (1968) asked 8- and 14-year-olds to explain a board game to some children who were blindfolded and to others who were not. The 8-year-olds gave the same instructions to everyone, while the 14-year-olds gave more detailed instructions to those who were blindfolded. The younger children could not yet take the role of the other, while the older children could.

As they develop this ability, at first children are able to take only the role of **significant others,** individuals who significantly influence their lives, such as parents or siblings. By assuming their roles during play, such as dressing up in their parents' clothing, children cultivate the ability to put themselves in the place of significant others.

As the self gradually develops, children internalize the expectations of more and more people. The ability to take on roles eventually extends to being able to take the role of "the group as a whole." Mead used the term **generalized other** to

■ *Mead analyzed* taking the role of the other *as an essential part of learning to be a full-fledged member of society. At first, we are able to take the role only of* significant others, *as this child is doing. Later we develop the capacity to take the role of* the generalized other, *which is essential not only for extended cooperation but also for the control of antisocial desires.*

taking the role of the other
putting oneself in someone else's shoes; understanding how someone else feels and thinks and thus anticipating how that person will act

significant other
an individual who significantly influences someone else's life

generalized other
the norms, values, attitudes, and expectations of people "in general"; the child's ability to take the role of the generalized other is a significant step in the development of a self

refer to our perception of how people in general think of us.

Taking the role of others is essential if we are to become cooperative members of human groups—whether they be our family, friends, or co-workers. This ability allows us to modify our behavior by anticipating how others will react—something Genie never learned.

Learning to take the role of the other entails three stages:

1. *Imitation.* Children under 3 can only mimic others. They do not yet have a sense of self separate from others, and they can only imitate people's gestures and words. (This stage is actually not role taking, but it prepares the child for it.)

2. *Play.* During the second stage, from the age of about 3 to 6, children pretend to take the roles of specific people. They might pretend that they are a firefighter, a wrestler, the Lone Ranger, Supergirl, Xena, Batman, and so on. They also like costumes at this stage and enjoy dressing up in their parents' clothing, or tying a towel around their neck to "become" Superman or Wonder Woman.

3. *Games.* This third stage, organized play, or team games, coincides roughly with the early school years. The significance for the self is that to play these games the individual must be able to take multiple roles. One of Mead's favorite examples was that of a baseball game, in which each player must be able to take the role of all the other players. To play baseball, the child not only must know his or her own role but also must be able to anticipate who will do what when the ball is hit or thrown.

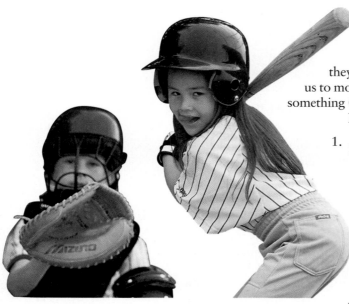

■ To help his students understand the term generalized other, Mead used baseball as an illustration. Why are team sports and organized games such excellent examples to use in explaining this concept?

Mead also said there were two parts of the self, the "*I*" and the "*me.*" The "*I*" is *the self as subject,* the active, spontaneous, creative part of the self. In contrast, the "*me*" is *the self as object.* It is made up of attitudes we internalize from our interactions with others. Mead chose these pronouns because in English "I" is the active agent, as in "I shoved him," while "me" is the object of action, as in "He shoved me." Mead stressed that we are not passive in the socialization process. We are not like computerized robots, passively absorbing the responses of others. Rather, our "I" evaluates the reactions of others and organizes them into a unified whole. Mead added that the "I" even monitors the "me," fine-tuning our actions to help us better match what others expect of us.

Mead also drew a conclusion that some find startling—that *not only the self but also the human mind is a social product.* Mead stressed that we cannot think without symbols. But where do these symbols come from? Only from society, which gives us our symbols by giving us language. If society did not provide the symbols, we would not be able to think, and thus would not possess what we call the mind. Mind, then, like language, is a product of society.

■ Piaget and the Development of Reasoning Skills

An essential part of being human is the ability to reason. How do we learn this skill?

This question intrigued Jean Piaget (1896–1980), a Swiss psychologist who noticed that young children give similar wrong answers when they take intelligence tests. This might mean, he thought, that young children follow some sort of incorrect rule in figuring out answers. This could mean that children go through a common process as they learn how to reason.

To find out, Piaget set up a laboratory where he could give children of different ages problems to solve (Piaget 1950, 1954; Thelen 2000). After years of research, Piaget concluded that children go through four stages as they develop their ability to reason. (If you substitute "reasoning skills" for the term *operational* in the following explanations, Piaget's findings will be easier to understand.)

1. **The sensorimotor stage** (from birth to about age 2) During this stage, the infant's understanding is limited to direct contact with the environment—sucking, touching, listening, seeing. Infants do not think in any sense that we understand. During the first part of this stage, they do not even know that their bodies are separate from the environment. Indeed, they have yet to discover that they have toes. Neither can infants recognize cause and effect. That is, they do not know that their actions cause something to happen.

2. **The preoperational stage** (from about age 2 to age 7) During this stage, children *develop the ability to use symbols*. However, they do not yet understand common concepts such as size, speed, or causation. Although they can count, they do not really understand what numbers mean. Nor do they yet have the ability to take the role of the other. Piaget asked preoperational children to describe a clay model of a mountain range. They did just fine. But when he asked them to describe how the mountain range looked from the perspective of a child who was sitting across from them, they couldn't do so. They could only repeat what they saw from their view.

3. **The concrete operational stage** (from the age of about 7 to 12) Although reasoning abilities are more developed, they remain *concrete*. Children can now understand numbers, causation, and speed, and they are able to take the role of the other and to participate in team games. Without concrete examples, however, they are unable to talk about concepts such as truth, honesty, or justice. They can explain why Jane's answer was a lie, but they cannot describe what truth itself is.

4. **The formal operational stage** (after the age of about 12) Children are now capable of abstract thinking. They can talk about concepts, come to conclusions based on general principles, and use rules to solve abstract problems. During this stage, children are likely to become young philosophers (Kagan 1984). If shown a photo of a slave, for example, a child at the concrete operational stage might have said, "That's wrong!" Now, however, he or she is more likely to ask, "If our county was founded on equality, how could people have owned slaves?"

▩ Kohlberg and the Development of Morality

The development of morality is significant in what humans become. If you have observed young children, you know that they focus on immediate gratification and show little or no concern for others. ("Mine!" a 2-year-old will shout, as she takes a toy from another child.) Yet, at a later age this same child will become considerate of others and concerned with moral issues.

How does this happen? Psychologist Lawrence Kohlberg (1975, 1984, 1986; Walsh 2000) concluded that we go through a sequence of stages as we develop morality. Building on Piaget's work, he found that children begin in the *amoral stage* I just described. For them, there is no right or wrong, just personal needs to be satisfied. From about ages 7 to 10, children are in what Kohlberg called a *preconventional stage*. They have learned rules, and they follow them to stay out of trouble. They view right and wrong as what pleases or displeases their parents, friends, and teachers. Their concern is to avoid punishment. At about age 10, they enter the *conventional stage*. At this stage, morality means to follow the norms and values they have learned. In the *postconventional stage*, which Kohlberg says most people don't reach, people reflect on abstract principles of right and wrong and judge a behavior according to these principles.

■ Gilligan and Gender Differences in Morality

Psychologist Carol Gilligan grew uncomfortable with Kohlberg's conclusions. They didn't seem to match her own experience, and she noted that he had used only boys in his studies. More women had become social scientists by this point, and they were questioning an assumption of male researchers—that female subjects were not necessary, for results of research with boys would be true of girls as well.

Gilligan (1982, 1990) decided to find out if there were differences in how men and women looked at morality. After interviewing about 200 men and women, she found fundamental distinctions. Women, she concluded, are more likely to evaluate morality in terms of *personal relationships*. They want to know how an action affects others. They are more concerned with personal loyalties and with the harm that might come to loved ones. Men, in contrast, tend to think more along the lines of *abstract principles* that define what is right or wrong. An act either matches or violates a code of ethics, and personal relationships have little to do with the matter.

Researchers tested Gilligan's conclusions. When they gave standard tests of moral reasoning to both males and females, they found no gender differences (Wark and Krebs 1996). Instead, they found that both men and women use personal relationships and abstract principles when they make moral judgments. Because of these findings, Gilligan no longer supports her original position (Brannon 1999). The matter is not yet settled, however, for some research does point to differences in moral judgment between men and women (White 1999).

■ Global Aspects of the Self, Reasoning, and Morality

Cooley's conclusions about the looking-glass self and Mead's conclusions about role taking and the mind as a social product appear to be universal. There is less agreement, however, that Piaget's four stages are globally true. Some researchers say that the stages are not as rigid as Piaget concluded, and that children develop reasoning skills much more gradually than this (Berk 1994; Diver-Stamnes and Thomas 1995).

In addition, some adults apparently get stuck in the concreteness of the third stage and never reach the fourth stage, abstract thinking (Kohlberg and Gilligan 1971). College, for example, is a social experience that nurtures the fourth stage, and most people without this experience apparently have less ability for abstract thought. Social experiences, however, can modify these stages, and the stages may differ from one culture to another.

Certainly the *content* of what we learn varies from one culture to another. This, in turn, influences our thinking. For example, Brazilian street children have little or no schooling. Yet through selling candy they develop sophisticated mathematical and bargaining abilities (Saxe 1995). Because children in other cultures have experiences and abilities unlike those of our children, and because their thinking processes revolve around those activities, we cannot assume that the developmental sequences observed in our children are true of children around the globe (Berk 1994).

■ Freud and the Development of Personality

Along with the development of the mind and the self comes the development of personality. Let's look at a theory that has influenced the Western world.

In Vienna during the early 1900s, Sigmund Freud (1856–1939), a physician, founded *psychoanalysis,* a technique for treating emotional problems through long-term, intensive exploration of the subconscious mind. Let's look at that part of his thought that applies to the development of personality.

Freud believed that personality consists of three elements. Each child is born with the first, an **id,** Freud's term for inborn drives for self-gratification. The id of the newborn is evident in cries of hunger or pain. The pleasure-seeking id operates throughout life. It demands the immediate fulfillment of basic needs: attention, safety, food, sex, and so on.

id
Freud's term for our inborn basic drives

But the id's drive for immediate and complete satisfaction runs directly against the needs of other people. As the child comes up against norms and other constraints that block his or her desire, he or she must adapt to survive. To help adapt to these constraints (usually represented by parents), a second component of the personality emerges, which Freud called the **ego.** The ego is the balancing force between the id and the demands of society that suppress it. The ego also serves to balance the id and the **superego,** the third component of the personality, more commonly called the *conscience.*

The superego represents *culture within us,* the norms and values we have internalized from our social groups. As the *moral* component of the personality, the superego provokes feelings of guilt or shame when we break social rules, or pride and self-satisfaction when we follow them.

According to Freud, when the id gets out of hand, we follow our desires for pleasure and break society's norms. When the superego gets out of hand, we become overly rigid in following those norms, finding ourselves bound in a straitjacket of rules that inhibit our lives. The ego, the balancing force, tries to prevent either the superego or the id from dominating. In the emotionally healthy individual, the ego succeeds in balancing these conflicting demands of the id and the superego. In the maladjusted individual, however, the ego cannot control the inherent conflict between the id and the superego, and the result is internal confusion and problem behaviors.

Sociological Evaluation   Sociologists appreciate Freud's emphasis on socialization—that the social group into which we are born transmits norms and values that restrain our biological drives. Sociologists, however, object to the view that inborn and unconscious motivations are the primary reasons that we do what we do. This denies *the central principle of sociology:* that factors such as social class (income, education, and occupation) and our roles in groups underlie human behavior (Epstein 1988; Bush and Simmons 1990).

Feminist sociologists have been especially critical of Freud (Gerhard 2000). Although what we just summarized applies to both females and males, Freud assumed that what is "male" is "normal." He even said that females are inferior, castrated males (Chodorow 1990).

■ Socialization into Emotions

As we have seen, the mind is a social product, and through socialization we acquire the particulars that go into human reasoning. Emotions, too, are not simply the results of biology. They also depend on socialization (Hochschild 1975; 1983; Johnson 1992; Reiser 1999; Turner 2000). This may sound strange. Don't all people get angry? Doesn't everyone cry? Don't we all feel guilt, shame, sadness, remorse, happiness, fear? What has socialization to do with emotions?

Anthropologist Paul Ekman (1980) looked into this question. After studying emotions in several countries, he concluded that everyone experiences six basic emotions: anger, disgust, fear, happiness, sadness, and surprise—and we all show the same facial expressions when we have these emotions. A person from Zimbabwe, for example, could tell from just the look on an American's face that she is angry, disgusted, or fearful, and we could tell from the Zimbabwean's face that he is happy, sad, or surprised. Because we all show the same facial expressions when we experience these six emotions, Ekman concluded that they are built into us biologically, "a product of our genes."

The existence of universal facial expressions for these basic emotions does not mean that socialization has no effect on how we express them. Facial expressions are only one way that we show emotions. Other ways vary with gender. For example, U.S. women are allowed more freedom in how they express happiness, while U.S. men are expected to be more reserved. To express sudden happiness, or a delightful surprise, for example, women are allowed to make "squeals of glee" in public places. Men are not. Such an expression would be a fundamental violation of their gender role.

ego
Freud's term for a balancing force between the id and the demands of society

superego
Freud's term for the conscience, the internalized norms and values of our social groups

Then there are culture, social class, and relationships. Consider culture. Two close Japanese friends who meet after a long separation don't shake hands or hug—they bow. Two Arab men will kiss. Social class is also significant, for it cuts across many other lines, even gender. Upon seeing a friend after a long absence, upper-class women and men are likely to be more reserved in expressing their delight than are lower-class women and men. Relationships also make a big difference. We express our emotions more openly if we are with close friends, more guardedly if we are at a staff meeting with the corporate CEO. A good part of childhood socialization centers on learning these "norms of emotion," how to express our emotions in a variety of settings.

The matter goes deeper than this. Socialization not only leads to different ways of expressing emotions, but even affects what we feel (Clark 1991; 1997). People in one culture may even learn to experience feelings that are unknown in another culture. For example, the Ifaluk, who live on the Western Caroline Islands of Micronesia, use the word *fago* to refer to the feelings they have when they see someone suffer. This comes close to what we call sympathy or compassion. But the Ifaluk also use this term to refer to what they feel when they are around people who are highly admired or respected (Kagan 1984). To us, these are two distinct emotions, and they require separate terms. For a glimpse of a culture in which emotions, values, and behaviors are shockingly different from those we expect, see the Down-to-Earth Sociology box on the next page.

Although Ekman identified only six basic emotions that are universal in feeling and expression, I suspect that other emotions are common to people around the world—and that everyone shows similar facial expressions when they experience them. I suggest that feelings of helplessness, despair, confusion, and shock are among these universal emotions. We need research to find out if I am right.

▪ *Males are socialized to express less emotion than are females, but in certain situations, especially sports, they are allowed to be openly emotional, even demonstrative, with one another. Shown here is Barry Bonds of the San Francisco Giants as he hugs his son, Nikolai, and is congratulated by teammates and staff after his record-breaking 70th home run of the year (against the Houston Astros, October 4, 2001, at Enron Field in Houston, Texas).*

down-to-earth
s o c i o l o g y

◼◼◼◼◼◼

Signs of the Times: Are We Becoming Ik?

Anthropologist Colin Turnbull (1972/ 1995) studied the Ik, a once-proud nomadic people in northern Uganda whose traditional hunting lands were taken from them by the government. Devastated by drought, hunger, and starvation, the Ik turned to a form of extreme individualism in which selfishness, emotional numbness, and lack of concern for others reign supreme. The pursuit of food has become the only good; their society has been replaced by a passionless, numbed association of individuals.

Imagine, for a moment, that you are born into the Ik tribe. After your first three or four years of life, you are pushed out of the hut. From then on, you are on your own. You can sleep in the village courtyard or take shelter, such as you can, against the stockade. With permission, you can sit in the doorway of your parents' house, but you may not lie down or sleep there.

There is no school. No church. Nothing from this point in your life that even comes close to what we call family. You join a group of children aged 3 to 7. The weakest soon die, for only the strongest survive. Later, you join a band of 8- to 12-year olds. At 12 or 13, you split off by yourself.

Socialization usually involves learning some aspect of life from what you see going on around you. Here you see coldness at the center of life. The men hunt, but game is scarce. If they get anything,

they refuse to bring it back to their families, saying, "Each one of them is out seeing what he can get for himself. Do you think they will bring any back for me?"

You also see cruelty at the center of life. When blind Lo'ono trips and rolls to the bottom of the ravine, the adults laugh as she lies on her back, her arms and legs thrashing feebly. When Lolim begs his son to let him in, pleading that he is going to die in a few hours, Longoli drives him away. Lolim dies alone.

The Ik children learn their lesson well: Selfishness is good, the survival of the individual paramount. But the children add a childish glee to the adults' dispassionate coldness. When blind Lolim took ill, the children teased him, kneeling in front of him and laughing as he fell. His grandson crept up and drummed on the old man's bald head with a pair of sticks.

Then there was little Adupa, who managed, for a while, to maintain a sense of awe at what life had to offer. When Adupa found food, she would hold it in her hand, looking at it with wonder and delight. As she raised her hand to her mouth, the other children would jump on her, laughing as they beat her.

for your consideration

From the Ik, we learn that the values we take to be uniquely human are not inherent in humanity. Rather, they arise from

society, and, as such, can be lost when the sense of mutuality that lies at the basis of society breaks down.

It is easy to criticize a society if you don't have to walk in their shoes, so let's turn the critical lens on our own society. Consider how people are treated like things—discarded when they are no longer needed. Corporations fire older workers because they can pay younger ones less—or they relocate an entire factory to a land of cheaper labor. As they leave hundreds and even thousands of workers stranded, managers and owners shrug their shoulders and say, "That's business." For the sake of higher salaries, people sever themselves from kin and community. Successful executives discard same-age spouses, the co-parent of their own children, in exchange for younger, more photogenic "trophy" mates.

Finally, consider how the values we would wish for in friends and family—kindness, generosity, patience, tolerance, cooperation, compassion—are undervalued. If a job requires such talents, it is low in pay and prestige (Maybury-Lewis 1995).

◼ ◼ ◼ ◼ ◼

◼ The Self and Emotions as Social Control: Society Within Us

Much of our socialization is intended to turn us into conforming members of society. Socialization into the self and emotions is an essential part of this process, for both the self and our emotions mold our behavior. Although we like to think we are "free," consider for a moment just some of the factors that influence how we act: the expectations of friends and parents, of neighbors and teachers; classroom norms and college rules; city, state, and federal laws. For example, if in a moment of intense frustration, or out of a devilish desire to shock people, you wanted to tear off your clothes and run naked down the street, what would stop you?

The answer is your socialization—*society within you*. Your experiences in society have resulted in a self that thinks along certain lines and feels particular emotions.

This helps keep you in line. Thoughts such as "Would I get kicked out of school?" and "What would my friends (parents) think if they found out?" represent an awareness of the self in relationship to others. So does the desire to avoid feelings of shame and embarrassment. Our *social mirror,* then—the result of being socialized into a self and emotions—sets up effective controls over our behavior. In fact, socialization into self and emotions is so effective that some people feel embarrassed just thinking about running nude in public!

IN SUM ■ ■ ■ ■

Socialization is essential for our development as human beings. From interaction with others, we receive a self, a mind, and the ability to reason. The net result is that our behavior—and even our thinking and emotions—are shaped according to cultural standards. This is what sociologists mean when they refer to "*society within us.*"

Socialization into Gender

Society also uses **gender socialization** to channel our behavior. By expecting different attitudes and behaviors from us *because* we are male or female, the human group nudges boys and girls in separate directions in life. This foundation of contrasting attitudes and behaviors is so thorough that, as adults, most of us act, think, and even feel according to our culture's guidelines of what is appropriate for our sex.

How do we learn gender messages? The significance of gender is emphasized throughout this book, with a special focus in Chapter 11. For now, though, let's briefly consider the influence of the family and the mass media.

■ Gender Messages in the Family

Our parents are the first significant others who teach us our part in this symbolic division of the world. Sometimes they do so self-consciously, perhaps by bringing into play pink and blue, colors that have no meaning in themselves but that are now associated with gender. But our parents' own gender orientations are so firmly embedded in them that they also teach us **gender roles,** the behaviors and attitudes considered appropriate for our sex, without being aware of what they are doing.

This is illustrated by a classic study done by psychologists Susan Goldberg and Michael Lewis (1969). They asked mothers to bring their 6-month-old infants into their laboratory, supposedly to observe the infants' development. Covertly, however, the researchers also observed the mothers. They found that the mothers kept their daughters closer to them. They also touched their daughters more and spoke more to them.

By the time the children were 13 months old, the girls stayed closer to their mothers during play, and they returned to them sooner and more often than the boys did. When Goldberg and Lewis set up a barrier to separate the children from their mothers, who were holding toys, the girls were more likely to cry and motion for help; the boys, to try to climb over the barrier. Goldberg and Lewis concluded that in our society mothers unconsciously reward daughters for being passive and dependent, but their sons for being active and independent.

These lessons continue throughout childhood. On the basis of their sex, children are given different kinds of toys. Boys are more likely to get guns and "action figures" that destroy enemies. Girls are more likely to get dolls and jewelry. Some parents try to choose "gender neutral" toys, but kids know what is popular, and they feel left

gender socialization
the ways in which society sets children onto different courses in life *because* they are male or female

gender role
the behaviors and attitudes considered appropriate because one is a female or a male

out if they don't have what the other kids have. The significance of toys in gender socialization can be summarized this way: Almost all parents would be upset if someone gave their boy Barbie dolls.

Parents also let their preschool sons roam farther from home than their preschool daughters, and they subtly encourage them to participate in more rough-and-tumble play. They expect their sons to get dirtier and to be more defiant, their daughters to be daintier and more compliant (Gilman 1911/1971; Henslin 2001c). In large part, they get what they expect.

Such experiences in socialization lie at the heart of the sociological explanation of male-female differences. We should note, however, that some sociologists consider biology to be a cause. For example, were the infants in the Goldberg-Lewis study showing built-in biological predispositions, with the mothers merely reinforcing—not causing—those differences? We shall return to this controversial issue in Chapter 11.

■ Gender Messages in the Mass Media

Sociologists stress how this sorting process that begins in the family is reinforced as the child is exposed to other aspects of society. Especially important are the **mass media,** forms of communication that are directed to large audiences. Let's look at how images in advertising, television, movies, and video games, as well as interaction with our peers, reinforce society's expectations of gender.

Advertising   Advertising directed at children depicts boys as more dominant, active, and aggressive than girls. Girls are more likely to be portrayed as giggly and less capable at tasks than boys (Browne 1998). Although changes are taking place (Thomas and Treiber 2000), advertising directed at adults still perpetuates similar stereotypes by portraying men as dominant and rugged and women as sexy and submissive. The result is a spectrum of stereotypical, culturally molded images. Cowboys who roam the wide open spaces are at one end of this spectrum, while at the other end are scantily clad women, whose assets are intended to sell a variety of products, from automobiles to hamburgers. The portrayal of women with unrealistic physical assets makes women feel inadequate (Kilbourne 2001). This, of course, creates demand for an array of products that promise physical enhancement and romantic success.

Television and Movies   Television and movies reinforce stereotypes of the sexes. In movies and on prime-time television, male characters still outnumber female characters. Female characters on television are also more likely to be portrayed in higher-status positions (Vande Berg and Streckfuss 1992). Viewers get the message, for the more television people watch, the more they tend to have restrictive ideas about women's role in society (Signorielli 1989, 1990).

Stereotype-breaking characters are a sign of changing times. Buffy the Vampire Slayer saves her classmates from Evil, while, with tongue in cheek, the Powerpuff Girls are touted as "the most elite kindergarten crime-fighting force ever assembled." Perhaps the most stereotype-breaking of all is *Xena, Warrior Princess,* a television series imported from New Zealand. Portrayed as super dominant, Xena overcomes all obstacles and defeats all foes—whether men or women.

Video Games   Some youths spend countless hours playing video games in arcades and at home. Even college students, especially males, relieve stress by escaping into video games. Sociologists have begun to study how the sexes are portrayed in these games, but how the games affect their players' ideas of gender is unknown at present (Dietz 2000; Sellers 2000). Because these games are on the cutting edge of society, they sometimes also reflect cutting-edge changes in sex roles, as examined in the Mass Media in Social Life box on the next page.

mass media
forms of communication, such as radio, newspapers, and television, that are directed to mass audiences

mass media
in social life

From Xena, Warrior Princess, to Lara Croft, Tomb Raider: Changing Images of Women in the Mass Media

The mass media reflect women's changing role in society. Although media images that portray women as passive, as subordinate, or as mere background objects remain, a new image has broken through. This new image exaggerates changes, but it nonetheless reflects women's active lives outside the home. It also illustrates a fundamental change from submissive to dominant in social relations. As mentioned in the text, Xena, the Warrior Princess, is an outstanding example of this change.

Although it is unusual to call video games a form of the mass media, I think it is appropriate to do so. Like books and magazines, video games are made available to a mass audience. And with digital advances, they have crossed the line from what is traditionally thought of as games to something that more closely resembles interactive movies.

Sociologically, what is significant is that the *content* of video games socializes their users. Gamers are exposed not only to action, but also to ideas as they play. The gender images of video games communicate powerful messages, just as they do in other forms of the mass media.

Lara Croft, an adventure-seeking archeologist and star of *Tomb Raider* and its many sequels, is the essence of the new gender image. Lara is smart, strong, and able to utterly vanquish foes. With both guns blazing, she is the cowboy of the twenty-first century, the term *cowboy* being purposefully chosen, as Lara breaks stereotypical gender roles and assumes what previously was the domain of men. She is the first female protagonist in a field of muscle-rippling, gun-toting macho caricatures (Taylor 1999).

Yet, the old remains powerfully encapsulated in the new. As the photo on this page makes evident, Lara is a fantasy girl for young men of the digital

■ *The mass media not only reflect gender stereotypes but also they play a role in changing them. Sometimes they do both simultaneously. The images of Lara Croft and of Xena, Warrior Princess, not only reflect women's changing role in society, but also, by exaggerating the change, they mold new stereotypes.*

generation. No matter her foe, no matter her predicament, Lara oozes sex. Her form-fitting outfits, which flatter her voluptuous physique, reflect the mental images of the men who fashioned this digital character. So successful has this effort been that boys and young men have bombarded corporate headquarters with questions about Lara's personal life. Lara has caught young men's fancy to such an extent that more than 100 Web sites are devoted to her. Lara is also the star of a movie (with a sequel inevitable) and a comic book. There is even a Lara Croft candy bar.

for your consideration

One reviewer of this text said, "It seems that for women to be defined as equal, we have to become symbolic males—

warriors with breasts." Why is gender change mostly one-way—females adopting traditional male characteristics? Why aren't the media proclaiming a "new man," one with stereotypical female characteristics? To see why men get to keep their gender roles, these two questions should help: Who is moving into the traditional territory of the other? Do people prefer to imitate power or powerlessness?

Finally, consider just how far stereotypes have actually been left behind. The ultimate goal of the video game, after foes are vanquished, is to see Lara in a nightie.

Absorbing Gender Messages: The Peer Group   When sociologist Melissa Milkie (1994) studied a group of junior high school boys, she found that much of their talk centered on the latest movies and TV programs. Of the many images presented in these media, the boys would single out sex and violence. They would joke and laugh about what they had seen, repeat lines, and act out parts for the amusement of one another.

If you know boys in their early teens, you've probably seen behavior like this. You may have been amused, or even have shaken your head in disapproval. As a sociologist, however, Milkie peered beneath the surface. She concluded that the boys were using media images to discover who they are as males. In the experience of these boys, and so many like them throughout our society, to be male is to be obsessed with sex and violence. Not to joke and laugh about murder and promiscuous sex would have marked a boy as a "weenie," a label to be avoided at all costs. These boys were in the process of learning what it is to be a male in our society.

IN SUM   ▪ ▪ ▪ ▪

All of us are born into a society in which "male" and "female" are significant symbols. Sorted into separate groups from childhood, girls and boys come to have sharply different ideas of what to expect of themselves and of one another. We end up with a picture of what males and females are "really" like, and we use that picture to evaluate not just the people around us but also ourselves— our own masculinity or femininity. We are not simply passive consumers of these images. Rather, we select those images that are significant to our situation in life and use them to help construct our pictures of the world.

Because gender serves as a primary basis for **social inequality**—giving privileges and obligations to one group of people while denying them to another—the role of the media and peers is significant and needs to be explored further. We have no studies of how girls use media images to construct their ideas of femininity, and precious few of how boys do so. Perhaps you will become the sociologist to do such research.

▪ ▪ ▪ ▪ ▪

Agents of Socialization

People and groups that influence our self-concept, emotions, attitudes, and behavior are called **agents of socialization.** We have already considered how two of these agents, the family and the mass media, influence our ideas of gender. Now we'll look more closely at how agents of socialization prepare us to take our place in society. We shall first consider the family, then the neighborhood, religion, day care, school and peers, sports, and the workplace.

▪ The Family

Around the world, the first group to have a major impact on humans is the family. Our experiences in the family are so intense that they have a lifelong impact on us. They lay down our basic sense of self, establishing our initial motivations, values, and beliefs. The family gives us ideas about who we are and what we deserve out of life. It is in the family that we begin to think of ourselves as strong or weak, smart or dumb, good-looking or ugly—or somewhere in between. And as already noted, here we begin the lifelong process of defining ourselves as female or male.

social inequality
a social condition in which privileges and obligations are given to some but denied to others

agents of socialization
people or groups that affect our self-concept, attitudes, behaviors, or other orientations toward life

THE FAR SIDE® By GARY LARSON

© 1994 FarWorks, Inc. All Rights Reserved/Dist. by Creators Syndicate

The Far Side® by Gary Larson © 1994 FarWorks, Inc. All Rights Reserved. Used with permission.

"So let's go over it again: You're about a mile up, you see something dying below you, you circle until it's dead, and down you go. Lenny, you stick close to your brothers and do what they do."

To study this process, sociologists have observed parents and young children in public settings, where the act of observing does not interfere with the interaction. Researchers using this unobtrusive technique have noted what they call the "stroller effect" (Mitchell et al. 1992). When parents have their child in a stroller, the father is more likely to be the one who pushes the stroller. If they take the child out of the stroller, the mother is more likely to push the empty stroller, and the father is more likely to carry the child. In this and countless ways, parents send their children subtle gender messages. Most of the ways that parents teach their children about expected differences between men and women involve nonverbal cues, not specific instruction.

The Family and Social Class   One of the main findings of sociologists is how socialization depends on a family's social class. Let's compare how working-class and middle-class parents rear their children. Sociologist Melvin Kohn (1959, 1963, 1976, 1977, 1983; Kohn et al. 1986) found that working-class parents are mainly concerned about their children's outward conformity. They want their children to be obedient, neat, and clean, to follow the rules, and to stay out of trouble. To make their children obey, they tend to use physical punishment. In contrast, middle-class parents focus more on developing their children's curiosity, self-expression, and self-control. They are more concerned about the motivations for their children's behavior, and they are more likely to reason with their children than to use physical punishment.

These findings were a sociological puzzle. Just *why* should working-class and middle-class parents rear their children so differently? Kohn knew that life experiences of some sort held the key, and he found that key in the world of work. Blue-collar workers are usually closely supervised, with their bosses expecting them to do exactly as they are told. Blue-collar parents expect their children's lives to be like theirs, so they stress obedience and conformity. In contrast, middle-class parents, especially those in management and the professions, have more independence at work and are encouraged to take the initiative. Expecting their children to work at similar jobs, they, in turn, socialize them into the qualities they have found valuable.

Kohn still felt puzzled, however, for some working-class parents act more like middle-class parents, and vice versa. As Kohn probed this puzzle, the pieces fell into place. The key was the parents' type of job. Middle-class office workers, for example, have little freedom and are closely supervised. Kohn found that they follow the working-class pattern of child rearing, putting a stress on outward conformity. And some blue-collar workers, such as those who do home repairs, have a good deal of freedom. These workers follow the middle-class model in rearing their children (Pearlin and Kohn 1966; Kohn and Schooler 1969).

■ The Neighborhood

As all parents know, some neighborhoods are better for their children than others. Parents try to move to those neighborhoods—if they can afford them. Their commonsense evaluations are borne out by sociological research. Children from poor neighborhoods are more likely to get in trouble with the law, to become pregnant, to drop out of school, and to end up facing a disadvantaged life (Wilson 1987; Brooks-Gunn et al. 1997).

Sociologists have also documented that the residents of more affluent neighborhoods watch out for the children more than do the residents of poor neighborhoods (Sampson et al. 1999). The adults are more likely to know the local children and their parents, and to help keep the children safe and out of trouble. It is one of the ironies of life that in those neighborhoods that are the riskiest for children (where there is more homicide and child abuse) adults watch out the least for the children, and in neighborhoods where the children least need protecting the adults are more careful.

■ Religion

By influencing values, religion becomes a key component in people's ideas of right and wrong. Religion is so important to Americans that 70 percent belong to a local congregation, and during a typical week two of every five Americans attend a religious service (*Statistical Abstract* 2000:Table 75). Religion is significant even for people reared in nonreligious homes, for religious ideas pervade U.S. society; they provide basic ideas of morality that become significant for us all.

The influence of religion extends to many areas of our lives. For example, participation in religious services teaches us not only beliefs about the hereafter but also ideas about what kinds of dress, speech, and manners are appropriate for formal occasions. Religion is so significant that we shall examine its influence in a separate chapter (Chapter 18).

■ Day Care

It is rare for social science studies to make national news, but occasionally they do. One study that has ignited a debate followed 1,300 children in 10 cities from infancy into kindergarten. Researchers observed the children at home and at day care. (Day care was defined as any care other than by the mother—including care by other relatives and the father.) They also videotaped and made detailed notes on the children's interaction with their mothers (National Institute of Child Health and Human Development 1999; Guensburg 2001). This is what caught the media's attention: The more hours per week that children spend in day care, the weaker the bonds between mothers and children, and the greater the child's behavioral problems—fighting, cruelty, and meanness. Children who spend less time in day care are more affectionate to their mothers and more cooperative. This holds true regardless of the quality of the day care, the family's social class, or whether the child is a girl or a boy.

This study is designed well, and its findings are without dispute. But how do we explain these findings? The cause could be day care. It could be that children who are away from their mothers more are less likely to have their emotional needs met. The researchers suggest that mothers who spend more time with their children are more responsive to their needs because they become more familiar with their "signaling systems." But the cause could be the parents. Perhaps mothers who put their children in day care for more hours are less sensitive to their children in the first place. Or perhaps it is because employed mothers are more tired and stressed than those who stay at home. From this study, we can't determine the cause of the weaker bonding and the behavioral problems.

Then there is the other side of day care. These same researchers also found that the more hours that children spend in day care, the higher they score on language tests (Guensburg 2001). Other researchers have found similar improvement in language skills, especially for children from low-income homes, as well as those from dysfunctional families, those with alcoholic, inept, or abusive parents (Scarr and Eisenberg 1993). As is obvious, we need more studies to be able to tease out the consequences of day care. While this longitudinal study is far from encouraging, it gives us no reason to conclude that day care is producing a generation of "mean but smart" children.

◼ The School

Part of the **manifest function,** or intended purpose, of formal education, is to transmit knowledge and skills, such as reading, writing, and arithmetic. The transmission of such skills is certainly part of socialization, but so are the schools' **latent functions,** its unintended consequences that help the social system. Let's look at this less visible aspect of education.

At home, children learn attitudes and values that match their family's situation in life. At school, they learn a broader perspective that helps prepare them to take a role in the world beyond the family. At home, for example, a child may have been the almost exclusive focus of doting parents, but in school the child learns *universality*—that the same rules apply to everyone, regardless of who their parents are or how special they may be at home. The Cultural Diversity box below explores

manifest functions
the intended consequences of people's actions designed to help some part of a social system

latent functions
the unintended consequences of people's actions that help to keep a social system in equilibrium

cultural **diversity**

in the United States
Caught Between Two Worlds

It is a struggle to learn a new culture, for the behaviors and ways of thinking contrast with the one already learned. This can lead to inner turmoil. One way to handle the conflict is to cut ties with your first culture. This, however, can create a sense of loss that is recognized only later in life.

Richard Rodriguez, a literature professor and essayist, was born in the 1950s to working-class Mexican immigrants. Wanting their son to be successful in their adopted land, his parents named him Richard instead of Ricardo. While his English-Spanish hybrid name indicates the parents' aspirations for their son, it was also an omen of the conflict Richard would experience.

Like other children of Mexican immigrants, Richard's first language was Spanish—a rich mother tongue that gave him his orientation to the world. Until the age of 5, when he began school, Richard knew only fifty words in English. He describes what happened when he began school:

The change came gradually but early. When I was beginning grade school, I noted to myself the fact that the classroom environment was so different in its styles and assumptions from my own family environment that survival would

essentially entail a choice between both worlds. When I became a student, I was literally "remade"; neither I nor my teachers considered anything I had known before as relevant. I had to forget most of what my culture had provided, because to remember it was a disadvantage. The past and its cultural values became detachable, like a piece of clothing grown heavy on a warm day and finally put away.

As happened to millions of immigrants before him, whose parents spoke German, Polish, Italian, and so on, learning English eroded family and class ties and ate away at his ethnic roots. For him, language and education were not simply devices that eased the transition to the dominant culture. Instead, they transformed Richard into a *pocho,* "a Mexican with gringo aspirations." They slashed at the roots that had given him life.

To face such inner turmoil is to confront a fork in the road. Some turn one way and withdraw from the new culture—a clue that helps explain the high dropout rate of Latinos from U.S. schools. Others go in the opposite direction and, cutting ties with their family and cultural roots, wholeheartedly adopt the new culture.

Rodriguez took the second road. He excelled in his new language—so well, in fact, that he graduated from Stanford University and then became a graduate student in English at the University of California at Berkeley. He was even awarded a prestigious Fulbright fellowship to study English Renaissance literature at the British Museum.

But the past wouldn't let Rodriguez alone. Prospective employers were impressed with his knowledge of Renaissance literature, but at job interviews they would ask if he would teach the Mexican novel in translation and be an adviser to Latino students. Rodriguez was haunted by the image of his grandmother, the warmth of the culture he had left behind, the language and thought to which he had become a stranger.

Richard Rodriguez represents millions of immigrants—not just those of Latino origin but those from other cultures, too—who want to be a part of the United States without betraying their past. They fear that to integrate into U.S. culture is to lose their roots. They are caught between two cultures, each beckoning, each offering rich rewards.

Sources: Based on Richard Rodriguez 1975, 1982, 1990, 1991, 1995.

how these new values and ways of looking at the world sometimes even replace those the child learns at home.

Sociologists have also identified a *hidden curriculum* in our schools. This term refers to values that, although not explicitly taught, are part of a school's "message." For example, the stories and examples that are used to teach math and English may bring with them lessons in patriotism, democracy, justice, and honesty. Schools also teach "correct" attitudes toward the economic system (Marger 1987). To learn that the economic system is basically just, for example, is to simultaneously learn that social problems such as poverty and homelessness have nothing to do with economic power, oppression, and exploitation.

Conflict theorists point out that schools teach children to take their place in the work force. This occurs even in kindergarten (Gracey 2001). Children born to wealthy parents go to private schools, where they learn skills and values appropriate to their higher position. Children from poorer homes go to public schools, where they learn that not many of "their kind" will become professionals or leaders. Even in public schools, social class is significant in tracking. Children from blue-collar families are less likely to be placed in the college prep courses. In short, schools around the world reflect and reinforce their nation's social class, economic, and political systems. We will return to this topic in the chapter on education (Chapter 17).

■ Peer Groups

As a child's experiences with agents of socialization broaden, the influence of the family lessens. Entry into school marks only one of many steps in this transfer of allegiance. One of the most significant aspects of education is that it exposes children to **peer groups**, individuals of roughly the same age who are linked by common interests. Examples of peer groups are friends, clubs, gangs, and "the kids in the neighborhood."

Sociologists Patricia and Peter Adler (1998), a husband and wife team, document how the peer group provides an enclave in which boys and girls resist the efforts of parents and schools to socialize them. Observing children at two elementary schools in Colorado, they saw children separate themselves by sex and develop their own worlds with unique norms (Adler et al. 1992). The norms that made boys popular were athletic ability, coolness, and toughness. For girls, popularity was based on family background, physical appearance (clothing and use of makeup), and the ability to attract popular boys. In this children's subculture, academic achievement pulled in opposite directions: For a boy, doing well academically decreased his popularity, while for a girl, getting good grades increased her standing among her peers.

You know from your own experience how compelling peer groups are. It is almost impossible to go against a peer group, whose cardinal rule seems to be "conformity or rejection." Anyone who doesn't do what the others want becomes an "outsider," a "nonmember," an "outcast." For preteens and teens just learning their way around in the world, it is not surprising that the peer group rules.

As a result, the standards of our peer groups tend to dominate our lives. If your peers, for example, listen to rap, heavy metal, rock and roll, country, or gospel, it is

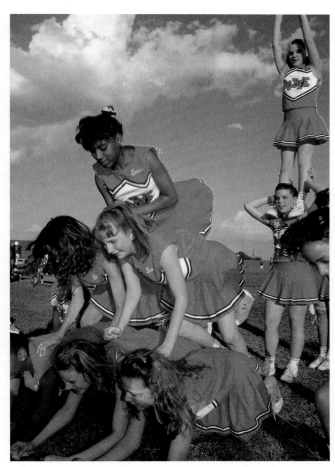

■ Schools are one of the primary agents of socialization. *One of their chief functions is to sort young people into the adult roles thought appropriate for them, and to teach them the attitudes and skills that match those roles. What sorts of attitudes and adult roles do you think these junior high school girls are being socialized into? Is it a function or dysfunction—or both?*

peer group
a group of individuals of roughly the same age who are linked by common interests

■ *Many adults who wish to reduce gender distinctions prefer that grade schoolers of both sexes participate in the same playground activities. Despite the sometimes not-so-subtle suggestions of teachers, however, grade school children insist on separating by sex, where they pursue different interests and activities and develop contrasting norms.*

almost inevitable that you also prefer that kind of music. It is the same for other kinds of music, clothing styles, and dating standards. Peer influences also extend to behaviors that violate social norms. If your peers are college-bound and upwardly striving, that is most likely what you will be; but if they use drugs, cheat, and steal, you are likely to do so, too.

■ Sports

Sports are another powerful socializing agent. Everyone recognizes that sports teach not only physical skills but also values. In fact, "teaching youngsters to be team players" is often given as the justification for financing organized sports. The effects of sports on the self-image are not well understood. Boys often learn that masculinity is related to achievement in sports. The more successful a boy is in sports, the more masculine he is considered to be and the more he is accepted by his peers. Sociologist Michael Messner (1990) points out that this encourages boys to develop *instrumental* relationships—those which are based on what you can get out of them, how useful they are in helping you achieve your goals. This encourages boys to relate instrumentally to girls—who are more likely to have been socialized to construct their identities on meaningful relationships, not on competitive success. As sports become more important in the formation of female identities, we will have to see what the effects are on women.

Our new technology has led to a new problem in sports, which is discussed in the Sociology and the New Technology box on the next page.

sociology & the new technology

Would Bionic Men and Women Be Fair in Sports? The Question of Genetic Engineering

Almost everyone agrees that the use of drugs to enhance sports performance is unfair. Safeguards have been put in place, and the detection of drugs in a winner's body disqualifies that person from competition.

Now comes genetic engineering. With the human genome mapped and technology following rapidly, it is likely that inserting genetic materials in athletes can increase their bulked-up muscle mass or their oxygen-carrying capacity. They will be able to run faster, to jump higher, and to throw further. Where the record for the 26.2 mile marathon is about 2 hours, someone may be able to run it in an hour and a half. The record for the 100 meter sprint, currently at 9.79 seconds, could drop to 6 seconds.

The risks to health would be high. As the president of a biomedical ethics research institute said, inserting genetic materials "is like firing at the bull's-eye of a target with shotgun pellets." When you inject the material, you don't know its exact effects. You might want to strengthen the shoulder muscles of a javelin thrower, for example, but you might enlarge that person's heart, too. Suppose that you add the gene for

human growth hormone, but it turns out that you can't regulate it. The individual could end up with a gigantic head, jaw, hands, and feet.

With health risks high, would athletes take the risk? There is no doubt about the answer. Nearly 200 U.S. athletes who were aspiring for the Olympics were asked if they would take a banned substance that would guarantee them victory in every competition for the next five years—but at the end of the five years it would cause their death. More than half said they would take it.

As genetic manipulation becomes more like a rifle shot than a shotgun blast—and we are closing in on that day—some athletes will seize the opportunity to increase their advantage. Others, seeing this, will do the same. The rush for genetic manipulation will be on.

for your consideration

When Mark McGwire broke the major league home run record in 1998, few were bothered that he used androstenedione, a steroid precursor that is banned in the Olympics and many professional sports. If

genetic engineering can be refined so it poses little risk to athletes, then why not do it? Shouldn't individuals be able to change themselves as much as they like?

Or consider this: What if you were born with special genes that your parents had paid to have inserted while you were an embryo? Why shouldn't you be allowed to participate in sports? You had nothing to do with it. Yet if this were allowed, an army of genetically engineered babies would follow.

Ultimately, genetic engineering will lead to the question of what a human athlete is. If an individual is so finely tuned, so genetically engineered, that he or she can do what the body is not designed to do—is this still human? Or will we end up with someone who, though having the form of a human—should be disqualified from competition with regular humans?

Source: Based on Longman 2001.

■ The Workplace

Another agent of socialization that comes into play somewhat later in life is the workplace. Those initial jobs that we take in high school and college are much more than just a way to earn a few dollars. From the people we rub shoulders with at work, we learn not only a set of skills but also a perspective on the world.

Most of us eventually become committed to some particular line of work, often after trying out many jobs. This may involve **anticipatory socialization**, learning to play a role before entering it. Anticipatory socialization is a sort of mental rehearsal for some future activity. We may talk to people who work in a particular career, read novels about that type of work, or take a summer internship. This allows us to gradually identify with the role, to become aware of what would be expected of us. Sometimes this helps people avoid committing themselves to an unrewarding career, as with some of my students, who tried student teaching, found they couldn't stand it, and moved on to other fields more to their liking.

anticipatory socialization because one anticipates a future role, one learns parts of it now

An intriguing aspect of work as a socializing agent is that the more you participate in a line of work, the more the work becomes a part of your self-concept. Eventually you come to think of yourself so much in terms of the job that if someone asks you to describe yourself, you are likely to include the job in your self-description. You might say, "I am a teacher, accountant, nurse" or whatever.

Resocialization

What does a woman who has just become a nun have in common with a man who has just divorced? The answer is that they both are undergoing **resocialization;** that is, they are learning new norms, values, attitudes, and behaviors to match their new situation in life. In its most common form, resocialization occurs each time we learn something contrary to our previous experiences. A new boss who insists on a different way of doing things is resocializing you. Most resocialization is mild, only a slight modification of things we have already learned.

Resocialization can be intense, however. People who join Alcoholics Anonymous (AA), for example, are surrounded by reformed drinkers who affirm the destructive effects of excessive drinking. Some students experience an intense period of resocialization when they leave high school and start college—especially during those initially scary days before they start to fit in and feel comfortable. To join a cult or to begin psychotherapy is even more profound, for these events expose people to ideas that conflict with their previous ways of looking at the world. If these ideas "take," not only does the individual's behavior change, but he or she also learns a fundamentally different way of looking at life.

Total Institutions

Relatively few of us experience the powerful agent of socialization that Erving Goffman (1961) called the **total institution.** He coined this term to refer to a place in which people are cut off from the rest of society and where they come under almost total control of the officials who run the place. Boot camp, prisons, concentration camps, convents, some religious cults, and some boarding schools, such as West Point, are total institutions.

A person entering a total institution is greeted with a **degradation ceremony** (Garfinkel 1956), an attempt to remake the self by stripping away the individual's current identity and stamping a new one in its place. This unwelcome greeting may involve fingerprinting, photographing, shaving the head, and banning the individual's *personal identity kit* (items such as jewelry, hairstyles, clothing, and other body decorations used to express individuality). Newcomers may be ordered to strip, undergo an examination (often in a humiliating, semi-public setting), and then to put on a uniform that designates their new status. (For prisoners, the public reading of the verdict and being led away in handcuffs by armed police also form part of the degradation ceremony.)

Total institutions are isolated from the public. The walls, bars, or other barriers not only keep the inmates in but also keep outsiders out. Total institutions suppress preexisting statuses: Inmates learn that their previous roles such as spouse, parent, worker, or student mean nothing. The only thing that counts is their current role. Staff members control information and replace the norms of "the outside world" with their own rules, values, and interpretation of life. This helps the institution shape the inmates' ideas and "picture" of the world. Staff members, who control the rewards and punishments, closely supervise the day-to-day lives of the residents. Eating, sleeping, showering, recreation—all are standardized. Under conditions of deprivation, simple rewards for compliance such as sleep, a television program, a

resocialization
the process of learning new norms, values, attitudes, and behaviors

total institution
a place in which people are cut off from the rest of society and are almost totally controlled by the officials who run the place

degradation ceremony
a term coined by Harold Garfinkel to describe an attempt to remake the self by stripping away an individual's self-identity and stamping a new identity in its place

letter from home, extra food, or even a cigarette, are powerful incentives in controlling behavior.

No one leaves a total institution unscathed, for the experience brands an indelible mark on the individual's self and colors the way he or she sees the world. Boot camp, as described in the Down-to-Earth Sociology box below, is brutal but swift. Prison, in contrast, is brutal and prolonged. Neither recruit nor prisoner, however, has difficulty in pinpointing how the institution affected the self.

■ ■ ■ ■ ■

Boot Camp as a Total Institution

The bus arrives at Parris Island, South Carolina, at 3 A.M. The early hour is no accident. The recruits are groggy, confused. Up to a few hours ago, the young men were ordinary civilians. Now, as a sergeant sneeringly calls them "maggots," their heads are buzzed (25 seconds per recruit), and they are quickly thrust into the harsh world of Marine boot camp.

Buzzing their hair is just the first step in stripping away their identity so the Marines can stamp a new one in its place. The uniform serves the same purpose. There is a ban on using the first person "I." Even simple requests must be made in precise Marine style or they will not be acknowledged. ("Sir, Recruit Jones requests permission to make a head call, sir.")

Every intense moment of the next eleven weeks reminds the recruits that they are joining a subculture of self-discipline. Here pleasure is suspect and sacrifice is good. As they learn the Marine way of talking, walking, and thinking, they are denied the diversions they once took for granted: television, cigarettes, cars, candy, soft drinks, video games, music, alcohol, drugs, and sex.

Lessons are bestowed with fierce intensity. When Sgt. Carey checks brass belt buckles, Recruit Robert Shelton nervously blurts, "I don't have one." Sgt. Carey's face grows red as his neck cords bulge. "I?" he says, his face just inches from the recruit. With spittle flying from his mouth, he screams, "'I' is gone!"

"Nobody's an individual" is the lesson that is driven home again and again. "You are a team, a Marine. Not a civilian. Not black or white—not Hispanic or a hyphenated American—but a Marine.

■ Resocialization *is often a gentle process. Usually we are gradually exposed to different ways of thinking and doing. Sometimes, however,* resocialization *can be swift and brutal, as it is during boot camp in the Marines. This private at Parris Island is learning a world vastly unlike the civilian world he left behind.*

You will live like a Marine, fight like a Marine, and, if necessary, die like a Marine."

Each day begins before dawn with close order formations. The rest of the day is filled with training in hand-to-hand combat, marching, running, calisthenics, Marine history, and—always—following orders.

"An M-16 can blow someone's head off at 500 meters," Sgt. Norman says. "That's beautiful, isn't it?"

"Yes, sir!" shout the platoon's fifty-nine voices.

"Pick your nose!" Simultaneously 59 index fingers shoot into nostrils.

The pressure to conform is intense. Those sent packing for insubordination or suicidal tendencies are mocked in cadence during drills. ("Hope you like the sights you see / Parris Island casualty.") As lights go out at 9 P.M. the exhausted recruits perform the day's last task: The entire platoon, in unison, shouts the virtues of the Marines.

Recruits are constantly scrutinized. Subperformance is not accepted, whether it be a dirty rifle or a loose thread on a uniform. The subperformer is shouted at, derided, humiliated. The group suffers for the individual. If a recruit is slow, the entire platoon is punished.

The system works.

After eleven weeks of this treatment, the Beavises and Butt-heads emerge self-disciplined, and physically fit. They are even courteous to their elders. Each time they see a superior, they automatically respond with "Good day, sir." Even skinheads and black separatists have been known to lay aside antagonistic identities and to live and work together as a team.

One of the new Marines (until graduation, they are recruits, not Marines) says, "I feel like I've joined a new society or religion."

He has.

for your consideration

Of what significance is the recruits' degradation ceremony? Why are recruits not allowed video games, cigarettes, or calls home? Why are the Marines so unfair as to punish an entire platoon for the failure of an individual? Use concepts in this chapter to explain why the system works.

Source: Based on Garfinkel 1956; Goffman 1961; "Anybody's Son Will Do," 1983; Ricks 1995.

■ ■ ■ ■ ■

Socialization Through the Life Course

Y
ou are at a particular stage in your life now, and college is a good part of it. You know that you have more stages ahead of you as you go through life. These stages, from birth to death, are called the **life course** (Elder 1975; 1999). The sociological significance of the life course is twofold. First, as you pass through a stage, it affects your behavior and orientations. You simply don't think about life in the same way when you are 30, married, and have a baby and a mortgage, as you do when you are 18 or 20, single, and in college. (Actually, you don't see life the same as a freshman and as a senior.) Second, your life course differs by the historical period of your society and your social location in it. Your social class, race-ethnicity, and gender map out a distinctive world of experience. Consequently, the typical life course differs for males and females, the rich and the poor, and so on. To emphasize this major sociological point, in the sketch that follows I will stress the *historical* setting of people's lives. Because of your particular social location, your own life course may differ from this sketch, which is a composite of stages others have suggested (Levinson 1978; Carr et al. 1995).

life course
the stages of our life as we go from birth to death

▪ In comtemporary Western societies such as the United States, children are viewed as innocent and in need of protection from adult demands such as work and self-support. Ideas of childhood vary historically and cross–culturally. As illustrated by this 1605 painting of Lady Tasburgh and her children, in Europe children were once viewed as miniature adults who assumed adult roles at the earliest opportunity.

▪ Childhood (from birth to about age 12)

To begin, consider how different your childhood would have been if you had grown up during the Middle Ages. When historian Philippe Ariès (1965) examined European paintings from this period, he noticed that children were always dressed in adult clothing. If they were not depicted stiffly posed, as in a family portrait, they were shown engaging in adult activities.

Ariès concluded that at that time and in that place, childhood was not regarded as a special time of life. Rather, children were seen as miniature adults. Ariès pointed out that boys were apprenticed at very early ages. At the age of 7, for example, a boy might leave home for good to learn to be a jeweler or a stonecutter. A girl, in contrast, stayed home until she married, but by the age of 7 she was expected to assume her daily share of the household tasks.

Such practices have not disappeared from the world. I have a vivid memory of a Moroccan blacksmith standing next to an open furnace, nude from the waist up. Sweating profusely in the insufferable tropical heat, his hammer beat rhythmically on glowing, red-hot metal. The blacksmith was about 12 years old.

Parents and teachers in earlier centuries also felt it was their moral duty to use psychological terror to keep children in line. They would lock children in dark closets, frighten them with tales of death and hellfire, and force them to witness gruesome events.

A common moral lesson involved taking children to visit the gibbet [an upraised post on which executed bodies were left hanging from chains], where they were forced to inspect rotting corpses hanging there as an example of what happens to bad children when they grow up. Whole classes were taken out of school to witness hangings, and parents would often whip their children afterwards to make them remember what they had seen. (DeMause 1975)

Industrialization transformed the way we perceive children. When children have the leisure to go to school, they come to be thought of as tender and innocent, as needing more adult care, comfort, and protection. Over time, such attitudes of dependency grow, and today we view children as needing gentle guidance if they are to develop emotionally, intellectually, morally, even physically. We take our view for granted—after all it is only "common sense." Yet, as you can see, our view is not "natural," but is rooted in geography and history.

Childhood, then, is more than biology. Everyone's childhood occurs at some point in history, and is embedded in particular social locations, especially social class and gender. These social factors are as vital as our biology, for they determine what childhood will be like for us. Although a child's *biological* characteristics (such as being small and dependent) are universal, the child's *social* experiences (what happens to that child because of what others expect of him or her) are not. Thus sociologists say that childhood varies from culture to culture.

■ Adolescence (ages 13–17)

Adolescence is not a "natural" age division. It is a social invention. In earlier centuries, people simply moved from childhood into young adulthood, with no stopover in between. The Industrial Revolution brought such an abundance of material surpluses, however, that for the first time in history millions of teenagers were able to remain outside the labor force. At the same time, education became more important for success. The convergence of these two forces in industrialized societies created a gap between childhood and adulthood. In the early 1900s, the term *adolescence* was coined to indicate this new stage in life (Hall 1904), one that has become renowned for inner turmoil.

To ground the self-identity and mark the passage of children into adulthood, tribal societies hold initiation rites. In the industrialized world, however, adolescents must "find" themselves on their own. As they attempt to carve out an identity that is distinct from both the "younger" world being left behind and the "older" world still out of range, adolescents develop their own subcultures, with distinctive clothing, hairstyles, language, gestures, and music. Although these outward patterns are readily visible, we usually fail to realize that adolescence is a social creation: It is contemporary society, not biological age, that makes these years a period of turmoil.

■ Young Adulthood (ages 18–29)

If society invented adolescence, can it also invent other periods of life? Historian Kenneth Keniston suggests that this is happening now. He notes that industrialized societies are adding a period of prolonged youth to the life course, in which people postpone adult responsibilities past adolescence. For millions, the end of high school marks a period of extended education characterized by continued freedom from the need to support oneself. During this time, people are "neither psychological adolescents nor sociological adults" (Keniston 1971).

Somewhere during this period of extended youth, young adults gradually ease into adult responsibilities. They finish school, take a full-time job, engage in courtship

■ *In many societies, manhood is not bestowed upon males simply because they reach a certain age. Manhood, rather, signifies a standing in the community that must be achieved. Shown here is an initiation ceremony in Indonesia, where boys, to lay claim to the status of manhood, must jump over this barrier.*

rituals, get married—and go into debt. The self is considerably more stable during the latter part of this period than it was during adolescence.

■ The Middle Years (ages 30–65)

The Early Middle Years (ages 30–49)   During the early middle years, most people are much surer of themselves and of their goals in life. As with any point in the life course, however, the self can receive severe jolts—in this case from such circumstances as divorce or being fired. It may take years for the self to stabilize after such ruptures.

The early middle years pose a special challenge for many U.S. women, who have been given the message, especially by the media, that they can "have it all." They can be superworkers, superwives, and supermoms—all rolled into one. The reality, however, often consists of conflicting pressures, of too little time and too many demands. Something has to give. Attempts to resolve this dilemma are often compounded by another hard reality—that during gender socialization their husbands learned that child care and housework are not "masculine." In short, adjustments continue in this and all phases of life.

The Later Middle Years (ages 50–65)   During the later middle years, health and mortality begin to loom large as people feel their bodies change, especially if they watch their parents become frail, fall ill, and die. The consequence is a fundamental reorientation in thinking—from *time since birth* to *time left to live* (Neugarten 1976). With this changed orientation, people attempt to evaluate the past and come to terms with what lies ahead. They compare what they have accomplished with how far they had hoped to go. Many people also find themselves caring not only for their own children but also their aging parents. Because of this often crushing set of burdens, people in the later middle years sometimes are called the "sandwich generation."

Life during this stage isn't always stressful. Many people find late middle age to be the most comfortable period of their lives. They enjoy job security and a standard of living higher than ever before; they have a bigger house (one that may even be paid for), newer cars, and more exotic vacations. The children are grown, the self is firmly planted, and fewer upheavals are likely to occur.

As they anticipate the next stage of life, however, most people do not like what they see.

■ The Older Years (about age 65 on)

The Early Older Years   In industrialized societies, the older years begin around the mid-60s. This, too, is recent, for in preindustrial societies, when most people died early, old age was thought to begin around age 40. The improved nutrition, public health, and medical care that industrialization brought delayed the onset of old age. For those in good health, being over 65 is often experienced not as old age, but as an extension of the middle years. People who continue to work or to be active in other rewarding social activities are unlikely to see themselves as old (Neugarten 1977). Although frequency of sex declines, most men and women in their 60s and 70s are sexually active (Denney and Quadagno 1992).

Because we have a self and can reason abstractly, we can contemplate death. Initially death is a vague notion, a remote possibility. But as people see their friends die and their own bodies no longer functioning as before, death becomes less abstract. Increasingly, people feel that "time is closing in" on them.

The Later Older Years   As with the preceding periods of life except the first one, there is no precise beginning point to this last stage. For some, the 75th birthday may mark entry into this period of life. For others, that marker may be the 80th or even the 85th birthday. For most, this stage is marked by growing frailty and illness; for all who reach this stage, by death. For some, the physical decline is slow, and a rare few manage to see their 100th birthday mentally alert and in good physical health.

■ The Sociological Significance of the Life Course

The sociological significance of the life course is that it does not merely represent biology, things that naturally occur to all of us as we add years to our lives. Rather, *social* factors influence our life course. As you just saw, *when* you live makes a huge difference in the course that your life takes. And the difference in time does not have to be vast. Being born just ten years earlier or later may mean that you experience war or peace, an expanding economy or a depression—and those factors vitally affect what happens to you not just during childhood but throughout your life.

Your *social location,* such as social class, gender, and race, is also highly significant. Because of it, your experience of society's events will be similar to people who share your location, but different from people who do not. If you are poor, for example, you likely will feel older faster than most wealthy people for whom life is much less demanding. The life course is also influenced by individual factors—such as your health, or marrying early or entering college late—that may make your life course "out of sequence" or atypical.

For all these reasons, this sketch of the life course may not adequately reflect your own past, present, and future. As sociologist C. Wright Mills (1959) would say, because college recruiters are beating down the door of your school, or failing to do so, you are more inclined to marry, to buy a house, and to start a family—or to postpone these life course events, perhaps indefinitely. In short, changing times change lives, steering the life course into different directions.

■ *This January 1937 photo from Sneedville, Tennessee, shows Eunice Johns, age 9, and her husband, Charlie Johns, age 22. The groom gave his wife a doll as a wedding gift. The new husband and wife planned to build a cabin, and, as Charlie Johns phrased it, "go to housekeepin'." This photo illustrates the cultural relativity of life stages, which we sometimes mistake as fixed. It also is interesting from a symbolic interactionist perspective—that of changing definitions— for while our sensibilities are shocked by such marriages, even though they were not common, they once were taken for granted.*

■■■■■ Are We Prisoners of Socialization?

From our discussion of socialization, you might conclude that sociologists think of people as robots: The socialization goes in, and the behavior comes out. People cannot help what they do, think, or feel, for everything is simply a result of their exposure to socializing agents.

Sociologists do *not* think of people in this way. Although socialization is powerful, and profoundly affects us all, we each have a self. Established in childhood and continually modified by later experience, the self is dynamic. It is not a sponge that passively absorbs influences from the environment, but a vigorous, essential part of our being that allows us to act on our environment (Wrong 1961; Meltzer et al. 1975; Couch 1989).

Indeed, it is precisely because individuals are not robots that their behavior is so hard to predict. The countless reactions of other people merge in each of us. As discussed earlier, even identical twins do not receive identical reactions from others. As the self develops, we internalize or "put together" these innumerable reactions, producing a unique whole that we call the *individual*. Each unique individual uses his or her own mind to reason and to make choices in life.

In this way, *each of us is actively involved in the social construction of the self*. For example, although our experiences in the family lay down the basic elements of our personality, including fundamental orientations to life, we are not doomed to keep those orientations if we do not like them. We can purposely expose ourselves to groups and ideas that we prefer. Those experiences, in turn, will have their own effects on our self. In short, although socialization is powerful, within the limitations of the framework laid down by our social location we can change even the self. And that self—along with the options available within society—is the key to our behavior.

Summary and Review

What Is Human Nature?

■ **How much of our human characteristics come from "nature" (heredity) and how much from "nurture" (the social environment)?**
Observations of isolated, institutionalized, and **feral children** help answer this question, as do experiments with monkeys that have been raised in isolation. Language and intimate social interaction—aspects of "nurture"—are essential to the development of what we consider to be human characteristics. Pp. 66–70.

Socialization into the Self, Mind, and Emotions

■ **How do we acquire a self?**
Humans are born with the *capacity* to develop a **self,** but the self must be socially constructed; that is, its contents depend on social interaction. According to Charles Horton Cooley's concept of the **looking-glass self,** our self develops as we internalize others' reactions to us. George Herbert Mead identified the ability to **take the role of the other** as essential to the development of the self. Mead concluded that even the mind is a social product. Pp. 70–72.

■ **How do children develop reasoning skills?**
Jean Piaget identified four stages that children go through as they develop the ability to reason: (1) *sensorimotor,* in which understanding is limited

to sensory stimuli such as touch and sight; (2) *preoperational,* the ability to use symbols; (3) *concrete operational,* in which reasoning ability is more complex but not yet capable of complex abstractions; and (4) *formal operational,* or abstract thinking. Pp. 72–73.

■ **How do people develop morality?**
Children, who are born without morality, appear to go through a series of stages in learning morality. Kohlberg identified these stages as amoral, preconventional, conventional, and postconventional. As they make moral decisions, both men and women use personal relationships and abstract principles. Pp. 73–74.

■ **How do sociologists evaluate Freud's psychoanalytic theory of personality development?**
Freud viewed personality development as the result of our **id** (inborn, self-centered desires) clashing with the demands of society. The **ego** develops to balance the id and the **superego,** the conscience. Sociologists, in contrast, do not examine inborn or subconscious motivations, but, instead, how social factors—social class, gender, religion, education, and so forth—underlie personality development. Pp. 74–75.

■ **How does socialization influence emotions?**
Socialization influences not only *how* we express our emotions, but also *what* emotions we feel. Socialization into emotions is a major means by which society produces conformity. Pp. 75–78.

Socialization into Gender

■ **How does gender socialization affect our sense of self?**

Gender socialization—sorting males and females into different roles—is a primary means of controlling human behavior. Children receive messages about gender even in infancy. A society's ideals of sex-linked behaviors are reinforced by its social institutions. Pp. 78–81.

Agents of Socialization

■ **What are the main agents of socialization?**

The **agents of socialization** include family, the neighborhood, religion, day care, school, **peer groups,** sports, the **mass media,** and the workplace. Each has its particular influences in socializing us into becoming full-fledged members of society. Pp. 81–88.

Resocialization

■ **What is resocialization?**

Resocialization is the process of learning new norms, values, attitudes, and behavior. Most resocialization is voluntary, but some, as with prisoners in **total institutions,** is involuntary. Pp. 88–89.

Socialization Through the Life Course

■ **Does socialization end when we enter adulthood?**

Socialization occurs throughout the life course. In industrialized societies, the **life course** can be divided into childhood, adolescence, young adulthood, the early middle years, the later middle years, the early older years, and the older older years. Typical Western patterns include obtaining education, becoming independent from parents, building a career, finding a mate, rearing children, and confronting aging. Life course patterns vary by social location such as history, gender, race-ethnicity, and social class, as well as by individual experiences such as health and age at marriage. Pp. 90–93.

■ **Are We Prisoners of Socialization?**

Although socialization is powerful, we are not merely the sum of our socialization experiences. Just as socialization influences human behavior, so humans act on their environment and influence it. Pp. 93–94.

■ *Where can I read more on this topic?*

Suggested readings for this chapter are at the back of this book.

Additional Online Resources for This Chapter
www.ablongman.com/henslin6e

- *Content Select* Research Database for Sociology, with suggested key terms and annotated references
- Link to 2000 Census, with activities
- Flashcards of key terms and concepts

- Practice Tests
- Weblinks
- Interactive Maps

using . . .
ContentSelect

Research Database for Sociology

the life course	gender and	peer groups	resocialization
gender and mass	advertising	personality	socialization
media	human nature	development	

Jacob Lawrence, *Eight Builders*, 1982

4

Social Structure and
Social Interaction

Levels of Sociological Analysis

Macrosociology and Microsociology

The Macrosociological Perspective: Social Structure

The Sociological Significance of Social Structure

Culture

Social Class

Social Status

Roles

Groups

Social Institutions

The Sociological Significance of Social Institutions

An Example: The Mass Media as an Emerging Social Institution

Comparing Functionalist and Conflict Perspectives

Changes in Social Structure

What Holds Society Together?

The Microsociological Perspective: Social Interaction in Everyday Life

Symbolic Interaction

Dramaturgy: The Presentation of Self in Everyday Life

Ethnomethodology: Uncovering Background Assumptions

The Social Construction of Reality

The Need for Both Macrosociology and Microsociology

Summary and Review

My curiosity had gotten the better of me. When the sociology convention finished, I climbed aboard the first city bus that came along. I didn't know where the bus was going, and I didn't know where I was going to spend the night.

"Maybe I overdid it this time," I thought as the bus began winding down streets I had never seen before. Actually, this was my first visit to Washington, D.C., so I hadn't seen any of the streets before. I had no direction, no plans, not even a map. I carried no billfold, just a driver's license shoved into my jeans for emergency identification, some pocket change, and a $10 bill tucked into my socks. My goal was simple: If I saw something interesting, I'd get off and check it out.

"Nothing but the usual things," I mused, as we passed row after row of apartment buildings and stores. I could see myself riding buses the entire night. Then something caught my eye. Nothing spectacular—just groups of people clustered around a large circular area where several streets intersected.

Suddenly one of the men jumped up, smashed the emptied bottle against the sidewalk, and thrust the jagged neck outward in a menacing gesture.

I climbed off the bus and made my way to what turned out to be Dupont Circle. I took a seat on a sidewalk bench and began to observe. As the scene came into focus, I noted several street-corner men drinking and joking with one another. One of the men broke from his companions and sat down next to me. As we talked, I mostly listened.

As night fell, the men said that they wanted to get another bottle of wine. I contributed. They counted their money and asked if I wanted to go with them.

Although I felt my stomach churning—a combination of hesitation and fear—I heard a confident "Sure!" come out of my mouth. As we left the circle, the three men began to cut through an alley. "Oh, no," I thought. "This isn't what I had in mind."

I had but a split second to make a decision. I found myself continuing to walk with the men, but holding back half a step so that none of the three was behind me. As we walked, they passed around the remnants of their bottle. When my turn came, I didn't know what to do. I shuddered to think about the diseases lurking within that bottle. I made another quick decision. In the semidarkness I faked it, letting only my thumb and forefinger touch my lips and nothing enter my mouth.

When we returned to Dupont Circle, the men finished their new bottle of Thunderbird. I couldn't fake it in the light, so I passed, pointing at my stomach to indicate that I was having digestive problems.

Suddenly one of the men jumped up, smashed the emptied bottle against the sidewalk, and thrust the jagged neck outward in a menacing gesture. He glared straight ahead at another bench, where he had spotted someone with whom he had some sort of unfinished business. As the other men told him to cool it, I moved slightly to one side of the group—ready to flee, just in case.

Levels of Sociological Analysis

On this sociological adventure, I almost got myself in over my head. Fortunately, it turned out all right. The man's "enemy" didn't look our way, the broken bottle was set down next to the bench "just in case he needed it," and my introduction to a life that up until then I had only read about continued until dawn.

Sociologists Elliot Liebow (1967/1999), Mitchell Duneier (1999), and Elijah Anderson (1978, 1990, 1999, 2001) have written fascinating accounts about men like these. Although street-corner men may appear to be disorganized—simply coming and going as they please and doing whatever feels good at the moment—Liebow and Anderson analyzed how, like us, these men also are influenced by the norms and beliefs of our society. This will become more apparent as we examine the two levels of analysis that sociologists use.

■ Macrosociology and Microsociology

The first level, **macrosociology,** places the focus on broad features of society. Sociologists who use this approach analyze such things as social class and how groups are related to one another. If macrosociologists were to analyze street-corner men, for example, they would stress that these men are located at the bottom of the U.S. social class system. Their low status means that many opportunities are closed to

macrosociology
analysis of social life focusing on broad features of society, such as social class and the relationships of groups to one another; an approach usually used by functionalists and conflict theorists

them: The men have few job skills, little education, hardly anything to offer an employer. As "able-bodied" men, however, they are not eligible for welfare, even for a two-year limit, so they hustle to survive. As a consequence, they spend their lives on the streets.

Conflict theory and functionalism, both of which focus on the broader picture, are examples of this macrosociological approach. In these theories, the goal is to examine the large-scale social forces that influence people.

In the second level, **microsociology,** sociologists examine **social interaction,** what people do when they come together. Sociologists who use this approach to study street-corner men are likely to focus on the men's rules or "codes" for getting along; their survival strategies ("hustles"); how they divide up money, wine, or whatever other resources they have; their relationships with girlfriends, family, and friends; where they spend their time and what they do there; their language; their pecking order; and so on. With its focus on face-to-face interaction, symbolic interactionism is an example of microsociology.

Because each has a different focus, macrosociology and microsociology yield distinctive perspectives, and both are needed to gain a fuller understanding of social life. We cannot adequately understand street-corner men, for example, without using *macrosociology.* It is essential that we place the men within the broad context of how groups in U.S. society are related to one another—for, just as with ourselves, the social class of these men helps to shape their attitudes and behavior. Nor can we adequately understand these men without *microsociology,* for their everyday situations also form a significant part of their lives.

To see how these two approaches help us to understand social life, let's examine each one. As we do so, you may find yourself feeling more comfortable with one approach than the other. That is what happens with sociologists. For reasons of personal background and professional training, sociologists find themselves more comfortable with one approach and tend to use it in their research. Both approaches, however, are necessary for a full understanding of life in society.

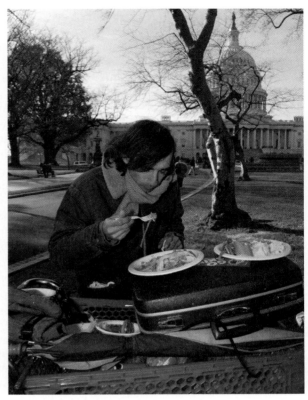

■ *Sociologists use both macro and micro levels of analysis to study social life. Those who use* macrosociology *to analyze the homeless—or any human behavior—focus on broad aspects of society, such as the economy and social classes. Sociologists who use the* microsociological approach *analyze how people interact with one another. Note how this scene invites both levels of analyses: Here you have both social classes (power and powerlessness) and social interaction (the food was delivered by volunteers).*

The Macrosociological Perspective: Social Structure

W hy did the street people in the opening vignette act as they did, staying up all night drinking wine and ready to use a lethal weapon? Why don't *we* act like this? Social structure helps us answer such questions.

■ The Sociological Significance of Social Structure

To better understand human behavior, we need to understand *social structure,* the framework of society that was already laid out before you were born. **Social structure** refers to the typical patterns of a group, such as its usual relationships

microsociology
analysis of social life focusing on social interaction; an approach usually used by symbolic interactionists

social interaction
what people do when they are in the presence of one another

social structure
the framework that surrounds us, consisting of the relationships of people and groups to one another, which give direction to and set limits on behavior

between men and women or students and teachers. *The sociological significance of social structure is that it guides our behavior.*

Because this term may seem vague, let's consider how you experience social structure in your own life. As I write this, I do not know your race-ethnicity. I do not know your religion. I do not know if you are young or old, tall or short, male or female. I do not know if you were reared on a farm, in the suburbs, or in the inner city. I do not know if you went to a public high school or an exclusive prep school. But I do know that you are in college. And that, alone, tells me a great deal about you.

From this one piece of information, I can assume that the social structure of your college is now shaping what you do. For example, let's suppose that today you felt euphoric over some great news. I can be fairly certain (not absolutely, mind you, but relatively certain) that when you entered the classroom, social structure overrode your mood. That is, instead of shouting at the top of your lungs and joyously throwing this book into the air, you entered the classroom in a fairly subdued manner and took your seat.

The same social structure influences your instructor, even if, on the one hand, he or she is facing a divorce or has a child dying of cancer, or, on the other, has just been awarded a promotion or a million-dollar grant. The instructor may feel like either retreating into seclusion or celebrating wildly, but most likely he or she will conduct class in the usual manner. In short, social structure tends to override personal feelings and desires.

Just as social structure influences you and your instructor, so it also establishes limits for street people. They, too, find themselves in a specific social location in the U.S. social structure—although it is quite different from yours or your instructor's. Consequently, they are affected differently. Nothing about their social location leads them to take notes or to lecture. Their behaviors, however, are as logical an outcome of where they find themselves in the social structure as are your own. In their position in the social structure, it is just as "natural" to drink wine all night as it is for you to stay up studying all night for a crucial examination. It is just as "natural" for you to nod and say, "Excuse me," when you enter a crowded classroom late and have to claim a desk on which someone has already placed books as it is for them to break off the head of a wine bottle and glare at an enemy.

In short, people learn their behaviors and attitudes because of their location in the social structure (whether they be privileged, deprived, or in between), and they act accordingly. This is equally true of street people and of ourselves. *The differences in behavior and attitudes are not due to biology (race, sex, or any other supposed genetic factors), but to people's location in the social structure.* Switch places with street people and watch your behaviors and attitudes change!

To better understand social structure, read the Down-to-Earth Sociology box on football on the next page. Because social structure so crucially affects who we are and what we are like, let's look more closely at its major components: culture, social class, social status, roles, groups, and social institutions.

■ Culture

In Chapter 2, we considered culture's far-reaching effects on our lives. At this point, let's simply summarize its main impact. Sociologists use the term *culture* to refer to a group's language, beliefs, values, behaviors, and even gestures. Culture also includes the material objects that are used by a group. Culture is the broadest framework that determines what kind of people we become. If we are reared in Eskimo, Japanese, Russian, or U.S. culture, we will grow up to be like most Eskimos, Japanese, Russians, or Americans. On the outside, we will look and act like them; and on the inside, we will think and feel like them. The specifics will vary by social location— by subculture, age group, race-ethnicity, and gender.

College Football as Social Structure

To gain a better idea of what *social structure* is, think of college football (see Dobriner 1969a). You probably know the various positions on the team: center, guards, tackles, ends, quarterback, running backs, and the like. Each is a *status;* that is, each is a social position. For each of these statuses, there is a *role;* that is, each of these positions has certain expectations attached to it. The center is expected to snap the ball, the quarterback to pass it, the guards to block, the tackles to tackle or block, the ends to receive passes, and so on. Those *role expectations* guide each player's actions; that is, the players try to do what their particular role requires.

Let's suppose that football is your favorite sport and you never miss a home game at your college. Let's also suppose that you graduate, get a great job, and move across the country. Five years later, you return to your campus for a nostalgic visit. The climax of your visit is the biggest football game of the season. When you get to the game, you might

be surprised to see a different coach, but you are not surprised that each playing position is occupied by people you don't know, for all the players you knew have graduated, and their places have been filled by others.

This scenario mirrors *social structure,* the framework around which a group exists. In this football example, that framework consists of the coaching staff and the eleven playing positions. The game

does not depend on any particular individual, but, rather, on *statuses,* the positions that the individuals occupy. When someone leaves a position, the game can go on because someone else takes over that position or status and plays the role. The game will continue even though not a single individual remains from one period of time to the next. Notre Dame's football team endures today even though Knute Rockne, the Gipper, and his teammates are long dead.

Even though you may not play football, you nevertheless live your life within a clearly established social structure. The statuses you occupy and the roles you play were already in place before you were born. You take your particular positions in life, others do the same, and society goes about its business. Although the specifics change with time, the game—whether of life or of football—goes on.

■ ■ ■ ■ ■

Social Class

To understand people, we must examine the particular social locations that they hold in life. Especially significant is *social class*, which is based on income, education, and occupational prestige. Large numbers of people who have similar amounts of income and education and who work at jobs that are roughly comparable in prestige make up a **social class.** It is hard to overemphasize this aspect of social structure, for our social class influences not only our behaviors, but even our ideas and attitudes. We have this in common, then, with the street people described in the opening vignette—both they and we are influenced by our location in the social class structure. Theirs may be a considerably less privileged position, but it has no less influence on their lives. Social class is so significant that we shall spend an entire chapter (Chapter 10) on this topic.

Social Status

When you hear the word *status*, you are likely to think of prestige. These two words are welded together in people's minds. Sociologists, however, use **status** in a different way—to refer to the *position* that an individual occupies. That position may carry a great deal of prestige, as in the case of a judge or an astronaut, or it may bring

social class
a large number of people with similar amounts of income and education who work at jobs that are roughly comparable in prestige

status
the position that someone occupies in society or a social group

little prestige, as in the case of a convenience store clerk or a hamburger flipper at a fast-food restaurant. The status may also be looked down on, as in the case of a street-corner man, an ex-convict, or a bag lady.

All of us occupy several positions at the same time. Simultaneously you may be a son or daughter, a worker, a date, and a student. Sociologists use the term **status set** to refer to all the statuses or positions that you occupy. Obviously your status set changes as your particular statuses change. For example, if you graduate from college and take a full-time job, get married, buy a home, have children, and so on, your status set changes to include the positions of worker, spouse, homeowner, and parent.

Like other aspects of social structure, statuses are part of our basic framework of living in society. The example given earlier of students and teachers who come to class and do what others expect of them despite their particular moods illustrates how statuses affect our actions—and those of the people around us. Our statuses—whether daughter or son, worker or date—serve as guides for our behavior.

Ascribed and Achieved Statuses   An **ascribed status** is involuntary. You do not ask for it, nor can you choose it. Some you inherit at birth such as your race-ethnicity, sex, and the social class of your parents, as well as your statuses as female or male, daughter or son, niece or nephew, and granddaughter or grandson. Others, such as teenager and senior citizen, are related to the life course discussed in Chapter 3, and are given to you later in life.

Achieved statuses, in contrast, are voluntary. These you earn or accomplish. As a result of your efforts you become a student, a friend, a spouse, a rabbi, minister, priest, or nun. Or, for lack of effort (or efforts that others fail to appreciate), you become a school dropout, a former friend, an ex-spouse, or a defrocked rabbi, priest, or nun. In other words, achieved statuses can be either positive or negative; both college president and bank robber are achieved statuses.

Each status provides guidelines for how we are to act and feel. Like other aspects of social structure, they set limits on what we can and cannot do. Because social statuses are an essential part of the social structure, they are found in all human groups.

Status Symbols   People who are pleased with their particular social status may want others to recognize that they occupy that status. To elicit this recognition, they use **status symbols,** signs that identify a status. For example, people wear wedding rings to announce their marital status; uniforms, guns, and badges to proclaim that they are police officers (and to not so subtly let you know that their status gives them authority over you); and "backward" collars to declare that they are Lutheran ministers or Roman Catholic or Episcopal priests.

Some social statuses are negative, and so, therefore, are their status symbols. The scarlet letter in Nathaniel Hawthorne's book by the same title is one example. Another is the CONVICTED DUI (Driving Under the Influence) bumper sticker that some U.S. courts require convicted drunk drivers to display if they wish to avoid a jail sentence.

All of us use status symbols to announce our statuses to others and to help smooth our interactions in everyday life. You might consider your own status symbols. For example, how does your clothing announce your statuses of sex, age, and college student?

Master Statuses   A **master status** is one that cuts across the other statuses that you hold. Some master statuses are ascribed. An example is your sex. Whatever you do, people perceive you as a male or as a female. If you are working your way through college by flipping burgers, people see you not only as a burger flipper and a student, but as a *male* or *female* burger flipper and a *male* or *female* college student. Other master statuses are race and age.

Some master statuses are achieved. If you become very, very wealthy (and it doesn't matter if your wealth comes from an invention or from the lottery—it is still *achieved* as far as sociologists are concerned), your wealth is likely to become a master status. For example, people are likely to say, "She is a very rich burger flipper"—or more likely, "She's very rich, and she used to flip burgers!"

status set
all the statuses or positions that an individual occupies

ascribed statuses
positions an individual either inherits at birth or receives involuntarily later in life

achieved statuses
positions that are earned, accomplished, or involve at least some effort or activity on the individual's part

status symbols
items used to identify a status

master status
a status that cuts across the other statuses that an individual occupies

Similarly, people who become physically disabled or disfigured find, to their dismay, that their condition becomes a master status. For example, a person whose face is scarred from severe burns will be viewed through this unwelcome master status no matter what his or her occupation or accomplishments. People confined to wheelchairs can attest to how their handicap overrides all their other statuses and determines others' perceptions of everything they do.

Although our statuses usually fit together fairly well, some people have a contradiction or mismatch between their statuses. This is known as **status inconsistency** (or discrepancy). A 14-year-old college student is an example. So is a 40-year-old married woman who is dating a 19-year-old college sophomore.

These examples reveal an essential aspect of social statuses: Like other components of social structure, they come with built-in *norms* (that is, expectations) that guide our behavior. When statuses mesh well, as they usually do, we know what to expect of people. This helps social interaction to unfold smoothly. Status inconsistency, however, upsets our expectations. If you met someone mentioned in the preceding examples, how should you act? Are you supposed to treat the 14-year-old as you would a young teenager, or as you would your college classmate? Do you react to the married woman as you would to the mother of your friend, or as you would to a classmate's date?

■ Master statuses *are those that overshadow our other statuses. Shown here is Christopher Reeve, who was paralyzed when he was thrown from a horse. Before his accident, Reeve was a top Hollywood actor, celebrating worldwide success with his role as Superman. Today, his* master status *is that of a person with a disability. He has accepted this status and is a spokesperson for people suffering from spinal cord injuries.*

■ Roles

> All the world's a stage
> And all the men and women merely players.
> They have their exits and their entrances;
> And one man in his time plays many parts . . .
> (William Shakespeare, *As You Like It*, Act II, Scene 7)

Like Shakespeare, sociologists, too, see roles as essential to social life. When you were born, **roles**—the behaviors, obligations, and privileges attached to a status— were already set up for you. Society was waiting with outstretched arms to teach you how it expected you to act as a boy or a girl. And whether you were born poor, rich, or somewhere in between, that, too, attached certain behaviors, obligations, and privileges to your statuses.

The difference between role and status is that you *occupy* a status, but you *play* a role (Linton 1936). For example, being a son or daughter is your status, but your expectations of receiving food and shelter from your parents—as well as their expectation that you show respect to them—is your role.

Roles are like a fence. They allow us a certain amount of freedom, but for most of us that freedom doesn't go very far. Suppose a woman decides that she is not going to wear dresses—or a man that he will not wear suits and ties—regardless of what anyone says. In most situations, they'll stick to their decision. When a formal occasion comes along, however, such as a family wedding or a funeral, they are likely to cave in to norms that they find overwhelming. Almost all of us stay within the fences that mark out what is "appropriate" for our roles. Most of us are little troubled by such constraints, for our socialization is so thorough that we usually *want* to do what our roles indicate is appropriate.

The sociological significance of roles is that they lay out what is expected of people. As individuals throughout society perform their roles, those roles mesh together

status inconsistency
(or discrepancy)
a contradiction or mismatch
between statuses

roles
the behaviors, obligations, and
privileges attached to a status

to form this thing called society. As Shakespeare put it, people's roles provide "their exits and their entrances" on the stage of life. In short, roles are remarkably effective at keeping people in line—telling them when they should "enter" and when they should "exit," as well as what to do in between.

■ Groups

A **group** consists of people who regularly and consciously interact with one another. Ordinarily, the members of a group share similar values, norms, and expectations. Just as social class, statuses, and roles influence our actions, so, too, the groups to which we belong are powerful forces in our lives. In fact, *to belong to a group is to yield to others the right to make certain decisions about our behavior.* If we belong to a group, we assume an obligation to act according to the expectations of other members of that group.

Although this principle holds true for all groups, some groups wield influence over only small segments of our behavior. If you belong to a stamp club, for example, the group's influence may center around your display of knowledge about stamps, and perhaps your attendance at meetings. Other groups, however, such as the family, control many aspects of our behavior. When parents say to their 15-year-old daughter, "As long as you are living under my roof, you had better be home by midnight," they show their expectation that their children, as members of the family, will conform to their ideas about many aspects of life, including their views on curfew. They are saying that so long as the daughter wants to remain a member of the household, her behavior must conform to their expectations.

To belong to any group is to relinquish to others at least some control over our lives. Those social groups that provide little option to belong are called **involuntary memberships** (or involuntary associations). These include our family and the gender, ethnic, and racial groups into which we are born. Groups to which we choose to belong are called **voluntary memberships** (or voluntary associations). These include the scouts, professional associations, church groups, clubs, work groups, and this sociology class. If we want to remain members in good standing, we must conform to what people in these groups expect of us. Both voluntary and involuntary memberships are vital in affecting who we are, for our participation in them shapes our ideas and orientations to life.

■ ■ ■ ■

Social Institutions

At first glance, the term *social institution* may seem to have little relevance to your personal life. The term seems so cold and abstract. In fact, however, **social institutions**—the organized means that each society develops to meet its basic needs—vitally affect your life. By weaving the fabric of society, social institutions shape your behavior. They even color your thoughts. How can this be? Look at what social institutions are: the family, religion, law, politics, economics, education, medicine, science, and the military.

In industrialized societies, social institutions tend to be more formal, in tribal societies more informal. Education in industrialized societies, for example, is highly structured, while in tribal societies it usually consists of informally learning what adults do. Figure 4.1 on the next page summarizes the basic social institutions. Note that each institution has its own roles, values, and norms. Social institutions are so significant that Part IV of this book focuses on them.

group
people who regularly and consciously interact with one another

involuntary memberships
(or involuntary associations) groups in which people are assigned membership rather than choosing to join

voluntary memberships
(or voluntary associations) groups that people choose to join

social institutions
the organized, usual, or standard ways by which society meets its basic needs

Social Institution	Basic Needs	Some Groups or Organizations	Some Values	Some Roles	Some Norms
Family	Regulate reproduction, socialize and protect children	Relatives, kinship groups	Sexual fidelity, providing for your family, keeping a clean house, respect for parents	Daughter, son, father, mother, brother, sister, aunt, uncle, grandparent	Have only as many children as you can afford, be faithful to your spouse
Religion	Concerns about life after death, the meaning of suffering and loss; desire to connect with the Creator	Congregation, synagogue, mosque, denomination, charitable association	Reading and adhering to holy texts such as the Bible, the Koran, and the Torah; honoring God	Priest, minister, rabbi, worshipper, teacher, disciple, missionary, prophet, convert	Attend worship services, contribute money, follow the teachings
Law	Maintain social order	Police, Courts, Prisons	Trial by one's peers, innocence until proven guilty	Judge, police officer, lawyer, defendant, prison guard	Give true testimony, follow the rules of evidence
Politics	Establish a hierarchy of power and authority	Political parties, congresses, parliaments, monarchies	Majority rule, the right to vote as a sacred trust	President, senator, lobbyist, voter, candidate, spin doctor	One vote per person, voting as a privilege and a right
Economics	Produce and distribute goods and services	Credit unions, banks, credit card companies, buying clubs	Making money, paying bills on time, producing efficiently	Worker, boss, buyer, seller, creditor, debtor, advertiser	Maximize profits, "the customer is always right," work hard
Education	Transmit knowledge and skills across the generations	School, college, student senate, sports team, PTA, teachers' union	Academic honesty, good grades, being "cool"	Teacher, student, dean, principal, football player, cheerleader	Do homework, prepare lectures, don't snitch on classmates
Science	Master the environment	Local, state, regional, national, and international associations	Unbiased research, open dissemination of research findings	Scientist, researcher, technician, administrator	Follow scientific method, fully disclose research findings
Medicine	Heal the sick and injured, care for the dying	AMA, hospitals, pharmacies, insurance companies, HMOs	Hippocratic oath, staying in good health, following doctor's orders	Doctor, nurse, patient, pharmacist, medical insurer	Don't exploit patients, give best medical care available
Military	Protection from enemies, support of national interests	Army, navy, air force, marines, coast guard, national guard	To die for one's country is an honor, obedience unto death	Soldier, recruit, enlisted person, officer, prisoner, spy	Be ready to go to war, obey superior officers, don't question orders
Mass Media (an emerging institution)	Disseminate information, mold public opinion, report events	Television networks, radio stations, publishers	Timeliness, accuracy, large audiences, freedom of the press	Journalist, newscaster, author, editor, publisher	Be accurate, fair, timely, and profitable

F igure 4.1

Social Institutions in Industrial and Postindustrial Societies

■ The Sociological Significance of Social Institutions

To understand social institutions is to realize how profoundly social structure affects our lives. Much of their influence lies beyond our ordinary awareness. For example, because of our economic institution, it is common to work eight hours a day for five days every week. There is nothing normal or natural about this pattern, however. Its regularity is only an arbitrary arrangement for dividing work and leisure. Yet this one aspect of a single social institution has far-reaching effects not only in terms of how people structure their time and activities but also in terms of how they deal with family and friends, and how they meet their personal needs and nonwork obligations.

Each of the other social institutions also has far-reaching effects on our lives. By weaving the fabric of society, our social institutions establish the context in which we live, shaping our behavior and coloring our thoughts. Social institutions are so significant that if they were different, we would be different people. We certainly could not remain the same, for social institutions influence our orientations to the social world, and even to life itself.

■ An Example: The Mass Media as an Emerging Social Institution

Far beyond serving simply as sources of information, the mass media influence our attitudes toward social issues, other people, and even our self-concept. Because the media significantly shape public opinion, all totalitarian governments attempt to maintain tight control over them.

The mass media are relatively new in human history, owing their origins to the invention of the printing press in the 1400s. This invention had immediate and profound consequences on virtually all other social institutions. The printing of the Bible altered religion, for instance, while the publication of political broadsides and newspapers altered politics. From these beginnings, a series of inventions—from radio and movies to television and, more recently, the microchip—have made the media an increasingly powerful force.

Indeed, one of the most significant questions we can ask about this new social institution is: Who controls it? That control, which in totalitarian countries is obvious, is much less visible in democratic nations. Functionalists might conclude that the media in a democratic nation represent the varied interests of the many groups that make up that nation. Conflict theorists, in contrast, see the matter quite differently: The mass media—at least a country's most influential newspapers and television stations—represent the interests of the political elite. The wealthy and powerful use the media to mold public opinion and to help preserve their places of privilege.

Since the mass media are so influential in our lives today, the answer to this question of who controls the media is of more than passing interest. This matter is vital for understanding contemporary society.

■ Comparing Functionalist and Conflict Perspectives

Just as the functionalist and conflict perspectives of the mass media differ, so do their views of the nature of social institutions. Let's compare these views.

The Functionalist Perspective   Functionalists stress that no society is without social institutions. This is because social institutions perform vital functions for society. A group may be too small to have

■ The mass media are a major influence in contemporary life. Until 1436, when Johann Gutenberg invented movable type, printing was a slow process, and printed materials were expensive. Today printed materials are common and often cheap. "Cheap" has a double meaning, with its second meaning illustrated in this photo.

people who specialize in education, but it will have its own established ways of teaching skills and ideas to the young. It may be too small to have a military, but it will have some mechanism of self-defense. To survive, every society must meet its basic needs (or **functional requisites**). According to functionalists, that is the purpose of social institutions.

What are those basic needs? Functionalists identify five functional requisites that each society must fulfill if it is to survive (Aberle et al. 1950; Mack and Bradford 1979).

1. *Replacing members.* If a society does not replace its members, it cannot continue to exist. Because reproduction is so fundamental to a society's existence, and because every society has a vital need to protect infants and children, all groups have developed some version of the family. The family gives the newcomer to society a sense of belonging by providing a "lineage," an account of how he or she is related to others. The family also functions to control people's sex drive and to maintain orderly reproduction.

2. *Socializing new members.* Each baby must be taught what it means to be a member of the group into which it is born. To accomplish this, each human group develops devices to ensure that its newcomers learn the group's basic expectations. As the primary "bearer of culture," the family is essential to this process, but other social institutions, such as religion and education, also help meet this basic need.

3. *Producing and distributing goods and services.* Every society must produce and distribute basic resources, from food and clothing to shelter and education. Consequently, every society establishes an *economic* institution, a means of producing goods and services along with routine ways to distribute them.

4. *Preserving order.* Societies face two threats of disorder: one internal, the potential for chaos, and the other external, the possibility of attack. To defend themselves against external conquest, they develop some means of defense, some form of the military. To protect themselves from internal threat, they develop some system of policing themselves, ranging from formal organizations of armed groups to informal systems of gossip.

5. *Providing a sense of purpose.* For people to cooperate with one another and willingly give up personal gains in favor of working with and for others, they need a sense of purpose. They need to be convinced that it is worth sacrificing for the common good. Human groups develop various ways of instilling such beliefs, but a primary one is religion, which attempts to answer questions about ultimate meaning. Actually, all of a society's institutions are involved in meeting this functional requisite; the family provides one set of answers about the sense of purpose, the school another, and so on. All of the answers are interrelated.

The Conflict Perspective Although conflict theorists agree that social institutions were originally designed to meet basic survival needs, they do not see social institutions as working harmoniously for the common good. On the contrary, conflict theorists stress that a society's institutions are controlled by an elite that manipulates them in order to maintain its own privileged position of wealth and power (Useem 1984; Domhoff 1967, 1998, 1999).

As evidence of their position, conflict theorists point out that a fairly small group of people have garnered the lion's share of the nation's wealth. Members of this elite sit on the boards of major corporations and the country's most prestigious universities. They make strategic campaign contributions to influence (or control) the nation's lawmakers, and it is they who make the major decisions in this society: to go to war or to refrain from war, to raise or to lower taxes, to raise or to lower interest rates, to pass laws that favor or impede moving capital, technology, and jobs out of the country.

Feminist sociologists (both women and men) have used conflict theory to gain a better understanding of how social institutions affect gender relations. Their basic

■ *Functionalist theorists have identified five* functional requisites *for the survival of a society. One, providing a sense of purpose, is often met through religious groups. To most people, snake handling, as in this church service in Jolo, West Virginia, is nonsensical. From a functional perspective, however, it makes a great deal of sense. Can you identify its sociological meanings?*

functional requisites
the major tasks that a society must fulfill if it is to survive

insight is that gender, too, is an element of social structure, not simply a characteristic of individuals. In other words, throughout the world, social institutions divide males and females into separate groups, each with unequal access to society's resources.

IN SUM ■ ■ ■ ■ ■

Conflict theorists regard our social institutions as having a single primary purpose—to preserve the social order. They interpret this as preserving the wealthy and powerful in their privileged positions. Functionalists, in contrast, view social institutions as working together to meet universal human needs.

■ Changes in Social Structure

As you can see, this enveloping system that we call social structure powerfully affects our lives. This means that as social structure changes, so, too, do our orientations to life. Consider how culture changes as it responds to evolving values and to new technology, to innovative ideas from home and abroad. Our new era of "globalization" puts us in contact with the customs of many other people. As globalization causes our economy to grow or to stagnate, it opens or closes opportunities and changes our lives, sometimes brutally so. Groups that did not exist, such as the IRS, come into being, and afterward wield extraordinary power over us. The corner in life that we occupy is not independent of these forces, but is pushed and pulled in different directions as social structure changes.

■ What Holds Society Together?

With its many, often conflicting, groups and its extensive social change, how does society manage to hold together? Let's examine two answers sociologists have proposed to this question.

Mechanical and Organic Solidarity   Sociologist Emile Durkheim (1893/1933) found the key to **social cohesion**—the degree to which members of a society feel united by shared values and other social bonds—in what he called **mechanical solidarity.** By this term, Durkheim meant that people who perform similar tasks develop a shared consciousness, a sense of similarity that unites them into a common whole. Think of an agricultural society in which everyone is involved in planting, cultivating, and harvesting. Members of this group have so much in common that they know what most others feel about life. Societies with organic solidarity tolerate little diversity in thinking and attitudes, for their unity depends on similar thinking.

As societies get larger, their **division of labor** (how they divide up work) becomes more specialized. Instead of almost everyone doing the same jobs, some become jewelers, while others become artists, authors, shopkeepers, soldiers, and so on. Rather than splitting society apart, however, the division of labor makes people depend on one another—for the work of each contributes to the welfare of the whole. Because this form of solidarity is based on interdependence, Durkheim called it **organic solidarity.** To see why he used this term, think about how you depend on your teacher to guide you through this introductory course in sociology. At the same time, your teacher needs you and other students in order to have a job. The two of you are *like organs in the same body.* (The "body" in this case is the college or university.) Although each of you performs different tasks, you depend on one another. This creates a form of unity.

The change to organic solidarity meant a new basis for solidarity—not similar views, but separate activities that contribute to the overall welfare of the group. As a result, modern societies can tolerate many differences among people and still manage to work as a whole. Both past and present societies are based on social solidarity, but the types of solidarity differ remarkably.

Gemeinschaft and Gesellschaft   Ferdinand Tönnies (1887/1988) also analyzed this major change. Tönnies used the term *Gemeinschaft* (Guh-MINE-shoft), or "inti-

social cohesion
the degree to which members of a group or a society feel united by shared values and other social bonds

mechanical solidarity
a shared consciousness that people experience as a result of performing the same or similar tasks

division of labor
the splitting of a group's or a society's tasks into specialties

organic solidarity
solidarity based on the interdependence brought about by the division of labor

■ *Warm, ongoing relationships of Gemeinschaft society are apparent in this restaurant in Greece, while the more impersonal relationships of Gesellschaft society are evident in the Cybernet cafe in San Francisco where people ignore one another in favor of electronic interaction via the Internet. Internet interactions do not easily fit standard sociological models—another instance of cultural lag.*

mate community," to describe village life, the type of society in which everyone knows everyone else. He noted that in the society that was emerging, the village's personal ties, family connections, and lifelong friendships were being crowded out by short-term relationships, individual accomplishments, and self-interest. Tönnies called this new type of society *Gesellschaft* (Guh-ZELL-shoft), or "impersonal association." He did not mean that we no longer have intimate ties to family and friends, but, rather, that these ties have shrunk in importance. Contracts, for example, replace handshakes, and work doesn't center around friends and family, but strangers and short-term acquaintances.

How Relevant Are These Concepts Today? I know that *Gemeinschaft, Gesellschaft,* and *mechanical* and *organic solidarity* are strange terms and that Durkheim's and Tönnies' observations must seem like a dead issue. The concern these sociologists expressed, however—that their world was changing from a community in which people are united by shared ideas and feelings to an anonymous association built around impersonal, short-term contacts—are still very real. In large part, this same concern explains the rise of Islamic fundamentalism (Volti 1995). Islamic leaders fear that Western values will uproot their traditional culture, that cold rationality will replace personal relationships among families and clans. They fear, rightly so, that even their views on life and morality will change. Although the terms may sound strange, even obscure, you can see that the ideas remain a vital part of today's world.

IN SUM ■ ■ ■ ■ ■

Whether the terms are *Gemeinschaft* and *Gesellschaft* or *mechanical solidarity* and *organic solidarity,* they indicate that as societies change so do people's orientations to life. *The sociological point is that social structure sets the context for what we do, feel, and think, and ultimately, then, for the kind of people we become.* As you read the Cultural Diversity box on the next page, which describes one of the few remaining *Gemeinschaft* societies in the United States, think of how fundamentally different you would be had you been reared in an Amish family.

Gemeinschaft
a type of society in which life is intimate; a community in which everyone knows everyone else and people share a sense of togetherness

Gesellschaft
a type of society dominated by impersonal relationships, individual accomplishments, and self-interest

cultural diversity

—————in the United States

The Amish–*Gemeinschaft* Community in a *Gesellschaft* Society

In Ferdinand Tönnies' term, the United States is a *Gesellschaft* society. Impersonal associations pervade our everyday life. Local, state, and federal governments regulate many activities. Impersonal corporations hire and fire people not on the basis of personal relationships, but on the basis of the bottom line. And, perhaps even more significantly, millions of Americans do not even know their neighbors.

Within the United States, a handful of small communities exhibits characteristics that depart from those of the mainstream society. One such community is the Old Order Amish, followers of a sect that broke away from the Swiss-German Mennonite church in the 1600s, and settled in Pennsylvania around 1727. Today, about 150,000 Old Order Amish live in the United States. About 75 percent live in just three states: Pennsylvania, Ohio, and Indiana. The largest concentration, about 22,000, reside in Lancaster County, Pennsylvania. The Amish, who believe that birth control is wrong, have doubled in population in just the past two decades.

Because they use horses instead of tractors, most Amish farms are one hundred acres or less. To the five million tourists who pass through Lancaster County each year, the rolling green pastures, white farmhouses, simple barns, horse-drawn buggies, and clotheslines hung with somber-colored garments convey a sense of peace and innocence reminiscent of another era. Although just sixty-five miles from Philadelphia, "Amish country" is a world away.

Amish life is based on separation from the world—an idea taken from Christ's Sermon on the Mount—and obedience to the church's teachings and leaders. This rejection of worldly concerns, writes

sociologist Donald Kraybill in *The Riddle of Amish Culture* (1989), "provides the foundation of such Amish values as humility, faithfulness, thrift, tradition, communal goals, joy of work, a slow-paced life, and trust in divine providence."

The *Gemeinschaft* of village life that Tönnies regretted as being lost to industrialization is very much alive among the Amish. The Amish make their decisions in weekly meetings, where, by consensus, they follow a set of rules, or *Ordnung,* to guide their behavior. Religion and discipline are the glue that holds the Amish together. Brotherly love and the welfare of the community are paramount values. In times of birth, sickness, and death, neighbors pitch in with the chores. In these ways, they maintain the bonds of intimate community.

The Amish are bound by many other ties, including language (a dialect of German known as Pennsylvania Dutch), plain black clothing that has remained unchanged for almost 300 years, and church-sponsored schools. Nearly all Amish marry, and divorce is forbidden. The family is a vital ingredient in Amish life; all major events take place in the home, including weddings, births, funerals, and church services. Amish children attend church schools, but only until the

age of 13. (In 1972, the Supreme Court ruled that Amish parents had the right to take their children out of school after the eighth grade.) To go to school beyond the eighth grade would expose them to values and "worldly concerns" that would drive a wedge between them and their community. The Amish believe that violence is bad, even personal self-defense, and they register as conscientious objectors during times of war. They pay no social security, and they collect none.

The Amish cannot resist all change, of course. Instead, they try to adapt to change in ways that will least disrupt their core values. Because urban sprawl has driven up the price of farmland, almost half of Amish men work at jobs other than farming, most in farm-related businesses or in wood crafts. They go to great lengths to avoid leaving the home. The Amish believe that when a husband works away from home, all aspects of life change—from the marital relationship to the care of the children—certainly an astute sociological insight. They also believe that if a man receives a paycheck he will think that his work is of more value than his wife's.

The Amish's economic success poses a challenge to their traditional values. They frown on showy possessions, viewing them as worldly, so they invest their profits. This, in turn, brings further economic success, resulting in even greater pressures to spend the growing profits. (This process, called "The Protestant Ethic and the Spirit of Capitalism," is discussed later; see pages 188–189.)

Sources: Hostetler 1980; Bender 1990; Kephart and Zellner 1994; Aeppel 1996; Kraybill and Bowman 2001; Savells 2001.

The Microsociological Perspective: Social Interaction in Everyday Life

Whereas the macrosociological approach stresses the broad features of society, the microsociological approach has a narrower focus. Microsociologists examine *face-to-face interaction,* what people do when they are in one another's presence. Let's examine some of the areas of social life that microsociologists study.

Symbolic Interaction

For symbolic interactionists, the most significant part of life in society is social interaction. Symbolic interactionists are especially interested in the symbols that people use. They want to know how people look at things and how this, in turn, affects their behavior and orientations to life. Of the many areas of social life that microsociologists study, let's look at stereotyping, personal space, touching, and eye contact.

Stereotypes in Everyday Life   You are familiar with the way first impressions "set the tone" for interaction. When you first meet someone, you cannot help but notice certain highly visible and distinctive features, especially the person's sex, race, age, and physical appearance. Despite your best intentions, your assumptions about these characteristics shape your first impressions. You probably also know that your assumptions affect how you will act toward that person.

Mark Snyder, a psychologist, wondered if **stereotypes**—our assumptions of what people are like—might be self-fulfilling. That is, since our assumptions shape our reactions, could our reactions produce behaviors that match our stereotype? Snyder (1993) came up with an ingenious way to test this idea. He gave college men a Polaroid snapshot of a woman (supposedly taken just moments before) and told them that they would be introduced to her after they talked with her on the telephone. Actually, photographs showing either a pretty or a homely woman had been prepared before the experiment began. The photo had been chosen at random; it was not of the woman the men would talk to.

stereotypes
assumptions of what people are like, based on previous associations with them or with people who have similar characteristics, or based on information, whether true or false

■ *Physical attractiveness underlies much of our social interaction in everyday life. The experiment reviewed here illustrates how college men modified their interactions on the basis of attractiveness. How do you think women would modify their interactions if they were to meet the two men in these photographs? How about men? Would they change their interactions in the same way?*

We see features of the person, or hear about the person.

We fit what we see or hear into stereotypes, and then expect the person to act in certain ways.

We act toward the person according to our expectations.

From how we act, the person gets ideas of how we perceive him or her.

The behaviors of the person change to match our expectations, thus confirming the stereotype.

Figure 4.2

Self-Fulfilling Stereotypes

The men's stereotypes came into play immediately. As Snyder gave each man the photograph, he asked him what he thought the woman would be like. The men who saw the photograph of the attractive woman said they expected to meet a poised, humorous, outgoing woman. The men who had been given a photo of the unattractive woman described her as awkward, serious, and unsociable. These stereotypes influenced the way the men spoke to the women on the telephone, which, in turn, affected the women's responses. The men who had seen the photograph of a pretty woman were warm, friendly, and humorous. The women they spoke to responded in a warm, friendly, outgoing manner. The men who had seen the photograph of a homely woman were cold, reserved, and humorless on the phone, and the women they spoke to became cool, reserved, and humorless. Keep in mind that the women did not know that their looks had been evaluated and that the photographs were not of them. In short, stereotypes tend to produce behaviors that match the stereotype.

While beauty might be only skin deep, its consequences permeate our lives (Katz 2001). As you have seen, ideas of physical attractiveness affect the ways people react to one another. To be beautiful is to have a decided advantage in social life. For one thing, if you are physically attractive, you are likely to make more money. Studies in both Holland and the United States indicate that advertising firms with better-looking executives have higher revenues (Bosman et al. 1997; Pfann et al. 2000). The researchers suggest that this is because we are more likely to cooperate with people we perceive as good-looking.

Stereotypes also have an impact on what we accomplish. In one experiment, the welding instructor in a vocational training center was told that five men in his training program had an unusually high aptitude for welding (Snyder 1993). Although the five had been chosen at random and knew nothing about the experiment, the effects were dramatic. These men were absent less often than other trainees, learned the basics of welding in about half the usual time, and scored ten points higher than the other men on their final welding test. The difference was noted even by the other trainees, who singled these five out as their preferred co-workers. The men were no different in their initial abilities, but the instructor's stereotype of their abilities influenced how he behaved toward them. This, in turn, changed the men's performance. This principle is illustrated in Figure 4.2.

Stereotypes have no single, inevitable effect. They are not magical. People can resist stereotypes and change outcomes. However, these experiments do illustrate that stereotypes have profound influences—on how we react to one another and even on our abilities. We know that stereotypes of gender, race-ethnicity, and attractiveness are significant in social life. How do they affect those who do the stereotyping and those who are stereotyped? The results we have so far are certainly intriguing, but we need more research on this vital question.

Personal Space   We all surround ourselves with a "personal bubble" that we go to great lengths to protect. We open the bubble to intimates—to our friends, children, parents, and so on—but we're careful to keep most people out of this space. In the hall, we might walk with our books clasped in front of us (a strategy often chosen by females). We carefully line up at the drinking fountain, making certain there is space between us so we don't touch the person in front of us and we aren't touched by the person behind us.

At times we extend our personal space. In the library, for example, you may place your coat on the chair next to you—claiming that space for yourself even though you aren't using it. If you want to really extend your space, you might even spread books in front of the other chairs, keeping the whole table to yourself by giving the impression that others have just stepped away.

The amount of space people prefer varies from one culture to another. South Americans, for example, like to be closer when they speak to others than do people

■ *Social space is one of the many aspects of social life studied by sociologists who have a microsociological focus. What do you see in common in these two photos?*

reared in the United States. Anthropologist Edward Hall (1959) recounts a conversation with a man from South America who had attended one of his lectures.

> He came to the front of the class at the end of the lecture. . . .We started out facing each other, and as he talked I became dimly aware that he was standing a little too close and that I was beginning to back up. Fortunately I was able to suppress my first impulse and remain stationary because there was nothing to communicate aggression in his behavior except the conversational distance. . . .
>
> By experimenting I was able to observe that as I moved away slightly, there was an associated shift in the pattern of interaction. He had more trouble expressing himself. If I shifted to where I felt comfortable (about twenty-one inches), he looked somewhat puzzled and hurt, almost as though he were saying, "Why is he acting that way? Here I am doing everything I can to talk to him in a friendly manner and he suddenly withdraws. Have I done anything wrong? Said something I shouldn't?" Having ascertained that distance had a direct effect on his conversation, I stood my ground, letting him set the distance.

As you can see, despite Hall's extensive knowledge of other cultures, he still felt uncomfortable in this conversation. He first interpreted the invasion of his personal space as possible aggression, for people get close (and jut out their chins and chests) when they are hostile. But when he realized that was not the case, Hall resisted his impulse to move.

After Hall (1969; Hall and Hall 2001) analyzed situations like this, he observed that North Americans use four different "distance zones."

1. *Intimate distance.* This is the zone that the South American unwittingly invaded. It extends to about 18 inches from our bodies. We reserve this space for lovemaking, comforting, protecting, wrestling, hugging, and intimate touching.

2. *Personal distance.* This zone extends from 18 inches to 4 feet. We reserve it for friends and acquaintances and ordinary conversations. This is the zone in which Hall would have preferred speaking with the South American.

3. *Social distance.* This zone, extending out from us about 4 to 12 feet, marks impersonal or formal relationships. We use this zone for such things as job interviews.

4. *Public distance.* This zone, extending beyond 12 feet, marks even more formal relationships. It is used to separate dignitaries and public speakers from the general public.

■ *Norms of touching, including kissing, vary widely around the world. Shown here are two Arab men greeting each other with a kiss in front of the market in Damascus. In contrast, men in North America shake hands. Even after a long absence, and even though they are good friends, at most they will hug briefly or clap one another on the back.*

Touching Not only does frequency of touching differ across cultures, but so does the meaning of touching within a culture. In general, higher-status individuals do more touching. Thus you are much more likely to see teachers touch students and bosses touch secretaries than the other way around. Apparently it is considered unseemly for lower-status individuals to put their hands on superiors. An interesting experiment with surgery patients illustrates how touching can have different meanings. When the nurse came in to tell patients about their coming surgery and after-care, she touched the patients twice, once briefly on the arm when she introduced herself, and then for a full minute on the arm during the instruction period. When she left, she also shook the patient's hand (Thayer 1988).

Men and women reacted differently. Touching had a soothing effect on the women. It lowered their blood pressure and anxiety both before the surgery and for more than an hour afterward. The touching upset the men, however. Their blood pressure and anxiety rose. No one knows the reason for this difference. The experimenters suggest that the men found it harder to acknowledge dependency and fear. Instead of a comfort, the touch was a threatening reminder of their vulnerability. Perhaps. We don't know that answer. For this, too, we need more research.

Eye Contact One way we protect our personal bubble is by controlling eye contact. Letting someone gaze into our eyes—unless the person is our eye doctor—can easily be taken as a sign that we are attracted to that person, and even as an invitation to intimacy. A chain of supermarkets in Illinois, wanting to become "the friendliest store in town," ordered their checkout clerks to make direct eye contact with each customer. Women clerks complained that men customers were taking their eye contact the wrong way, as a sort of invitation to intimacy. Management said they were exaggerating. Their reply was, "We know the kind of looks we're getting back from men," and they refused to make direct eye contact with them.

Let's now turn to dramaturgy, a special area of symbolic interactionism.

■ *"Eye encounters" are a fascinating aspect of everyday life. We use fleeting eye contact for most of our interactions, such as those with clerks or people we pass in the hall between classes. Just as we reserve our close personal space for intimates, so, too, we reserve lingering eye contact for them.*

■ Dramaturgy: The Presentation of Self in Everyday Life

It was their big day, two years in the making. Jennifer Mackey wore a white wedding gown adorned with an 11-foot train and 24,000 seed pearls that she and her mother had sewn onto the dress. Next to her at the altar in Lexington, Kentucky, stood her intended, Jeffrey Degler, in black tie. They said their vows, then turned to gaze for a moment at the four hundred guests. That's when groomsman Daniel Mackey collapsed. As the shocked organist struggled to play Mendelssohn's "Wedding March," Mr. Mackey's unconscious body was dragged away, his feet striking—loudly—every step of the altar stairs.

"I couldn't believe he would die at my wedding," the bride said. (Hughes 1990)

■ *In* dramaturgy, *a specialty within sociology, social life is viewed as similar to the theater. In our everyday lives, we all are actors like those in this cast of* Friends. We, *too, perform roles, use props, and deliver lines to fellow actors—who, in turn, do the same.*

Sociologist Erving Goffman (1922–1982) added a new twist to microsociology when he developed **dramaturgy** (or dramaturgical analysis). By this term he meant that social life is like a drama or a stage play: Birth ushers us onto the stage of everyday life, and our socialization consists of learning to perform on that stage.

Everyday life, Goffman (1997) said, involves playing our assigned roles. We have **front stages** on which to perform them, as did Jennifer and Jeffrey. (By the way, Daniel Mackey didn't really die—he had just fainted.) But we don't have to look at weddings to find front stages. Everyday life is filled with them. Where your teacher lectures is a front stage. And if you make an announcement at the dinner table, you are using a front stage. In fact, you spend most of your time on front stages, for a front stage is wherever you deliver your lines. We also have **back stages,** places where we can retreat and let our hair down. When you close the bathroom or bedroom door for privacy, for example, you are entering a back stage.

The same setting can serve as both a back and a front stage. For example, when you get into your car and look over your hair in the mirror or check your makeup, you are using the car as a back stage. But when you wave at friends or if you give that familiar gesture to someone who has just cut in front of you in traffic, you are using your car as a front stage.

Everyday life brings with it many roles. The same person may be a student, a teenager, a shopper, a worker, a date, as well as a daughter or a son. Although a role lays down the basic outline for a performance, it also allows a great deal of freedom. The particular emphasis or interpretation that we give a role, our "style," is known as **role performance.** Consider your role as son or daughter. You may play the role of ideal daughter or son, being very respectful, coming home

■ Role performance *refers to how we play our roles. One of the major roles we are assigned in life is gender. We learn our "gender lessons" early, and we carefully project images that match cultural stereotypes. The source of humor of Pat on* Saturday Night Live *is* role confusion, *the uncertainty and tentativeness of interaction that results when people don't know whether to react to Pat as a male or as a female.*

dramaturgy
an approach, pioneered by Erving Goffman, analyzing social life in terms of drama or the stage; also called *dramaturgical analysis*

front stage
where performances are given

back stage
where people rest from their performances, discuss their presentations, and plan future performances

role performance
the ways in which someone performs a role within the limits that the role provides; showing a particular "style" or "personality"

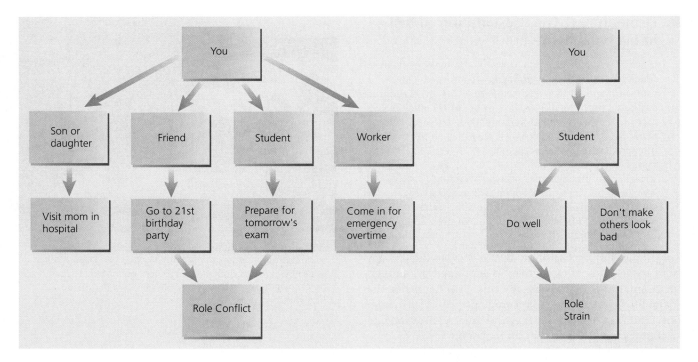

Figure 4.3
Role Strain and Role Conflict

at the hours your parents set, and so forth. Or this description may not even come close to your particular role performance.

Ordinarily our roles are sufficiently separated that conflict between them is minimized. Occasionally, however, what is expected of us in one role is incompatible with the expectations of another role. This problem, known as **role conflict,** makes us uncomfortable, as illustrated in Figure 4.3, in which family, friendship, student, and work roles come clashing together. Usually, however, we manage to avoid role conflict by segregating our roles, which in some instances may require an intense juggling act.

Sometimes the *same* role presents inherent conflict, a problem known as **role strain.** Suppose that you are exceptionally prepared for a particular class assignment. Although the instructor asks an unusually difficult question, you find yourself knowing the answer when no one else does. If you want to raise your hand, yet don't want to make your fellow students look bad, you will experience role strain. As illustrated in Figure 4.3, the difference between role conflict and role strain is that role conflict is conflict *between roles,* while role strain is conflict *within* a role.

A fascinating characteristic of roles is that *we tend to become the roles we play.* That is, roles become incorporated into the self-concept, especially those for which we prepare long and hard and that become part of our everyday lives. When sociologist Helen Ebaugh (1988) interviewed people who had left marriages, police work, the military, medicine, and religious vocations, she found that these roles had become so intertwined with the subjects' self-concepts that leaving them threatened their very identity. The question they struggled with was "Who am I, now that I am not a nun (or physician, wife, colonel, and so on)?" Even years after leaving these roles, many continued to perform them in their dreams.

Having become such a part of the person, these roles linger after the individual has left them. This is illustrated by one of my own respondents, who said:

role conflict
conflicts that someone feels *between* roles because the expectations attached to one role are incompatible with the expectations of another role

role strain
conflicts that someone feels *within* a role

After I left the (Protestant) ministry, I felt like a fish out of water. *Wearing that turned-back collar had become a part of me.* It was especially strange on Sunday mornings when I'd listen to someone else give the sermon. I knew that I should be up there preaching. I felt as though I had left God.

As we go about our everyday lives, we try to control or manage the impressions that we make on others. We all want others to think of us in certain ways, and we use our roles to influence their ideas of us. Goffman called this **impression management.**

To communicate information about the self, we use three types of **sign-vehicles:** the social setting, our appearance, and our manner. The *social setting* is the place where the action unfolds. This is where the curtain goes up on your performance, where you find yourself on stage playing parts and delivering lines. A social setting might be an office, dorm, living room, church, gym, or bar. It is wherever you interact with others. Your social setting includes *scenery,* the furnishings you use to communicate messages, such as desks, blackboards, scoreboards, couches, and so on.

The second sign-vehicle is *appearance,* or how we look when we play our roles. Appearance includes *props,* which are like scenery except that they decorate the person rather than the setting. The teacher has books, lecture notes, and chalk, while the football player wears a special costume called a uniform. Although few of us carry around a football, we all use makeup, hairstyles, and clothing to communicate messages about ourselves. Props and other aspects of appearance give us cues that help us get through everyday life: By letting us know what to expect from others, props tell us how we should react. Think of the messages that props communicate. Some people use clothing to say they are college students, others to say they are older adults. Some use clothing to say they are clergy, others to say they are prostitutes. Similarly, people choose brands of cigarettes, liquor, and automobiles to convey messages about the self.

Even our body is a prop. Its shape proclaims messages about the self. The messages that are attached to various shapes change over time, but, as explored in the Mass Media box on the next page, currently thinness screams desirability.

The third sign-vehicle is *manner,* the attitudes we show as we play our roles. We use manner to communicate information about our feelings and moods. If we show anger or indifference, sincerity or good humor, for example, we indicate to others what they can expect of us as we play our roles.

We become so used to the roles we play in everyday life that we tend to think we are "just doing" things, not that we are like actors on a stage who manage impressions. Yet every time we dress for school, or for any other activity, we are preparing for impression management. Have you ever noticed how your very casually dressed classmates tend to change their appearance on the day they are scheduled to make a report to the class? No one asks them to do so, but their role has changed, and they dress for their slightly modified part. Similarly, you may have noticed that when teenagers begin to date they take several showers a day, stand before a mirror for hours as they comb and recomb their hair, and then change and rechange their clothing until they "get it just right."

Despite our best efforts to manage impressions, however, we sometimes fail. One of my favorite television scenes took place on an old TV show, *The Days and Nights of Molly Dodd.* On this particular episode, Molly Dodd tried to impress a date. She went to the "powder room," a backstage fix-up place reserved for women, where she did the usual things. Satisfied that she looked good, she tried to make a grand entrance, walking confidently, an expectant smile on her face—all the while trailing a long piece of toilet paper from her shoe. The scene is humorous because it highlights an incongruity of elements, which creates *embarrassment.* In dramaturgical terms, embarrassment is a feeling we get when our performance fails.

If we show ourselves to be good role players, we get positive recognition from others. To accomplish this, said Goffman, we often use **teamwork**—two or more

impression management
the term used by Erving Goffman to describe people's efforts to control the impressions that others receive of them

sign-vehicles
the term used by Goffman to refer to how people use social setting, appearance, and manner to communicate information about the self

teamwork
the collaboration of two or more people to manage impressions jointly

mass media
in social life

You Can't Be Thin Enough: Body Images and the Mass Media

An ad for Kellogg's Special K cereal depicts an 18-month-old girl wearing nothing but a diaper, sitting with a worried look on her face (Krane et al. 2001). A bubble caption over her head has her asking the question, "Do I look fat?"

When you stand before a mirror, do you like what you see? To make your body more attractive, do you watch your weight or work out? You have ideas about what you should look like. Where did you get them?

TV ads keep telling us that something is wrong with our bodies. They aren't good enough, and we've got to improve them. The way to improve our bodies, of course, is to buy the advertised products. Wigs, hair pieces, hair transplants, padded brassieres, diet pills, and exercise equipment. Chuck Norris looks so strong and manly as he touts his full body exerciser. Men get the feeling that their body will look like his if they just buy that machine. Female movie stars effortlessly go through tough workouts without even breaking into a sweat. Women get the feeling that men will fight to be near them if they purchase that wonder-working workout machine.

Although we try to shrug off such messages, knowing they are designed to sell products, they still get our attention.

They penetrate our thinking, helping to shape our image of how we "ought" to look. Those models so attractively clothed and coiffed as they walk down the runway, could they be any thinner? For women, the message is clear: You can't be thin enough. The men's message is clear, too: You can't be strong enough.

Man or woman, your body isn't good enough. It needs to be shaped into something it isn't. It sags where it should be firm. It bulges where it should be smooth. It sticks out where it shouldn't,

■ *All of us contrast the reality we see when we look in the mirror with our culture's ideal body types. Calista Flockhart, a top U.S. actress, represents an ideal body type that has developed in some parts of Western culture. These cultural images often make it difficult for large people to maintain positive images of their bodies. These twins in Los Angeles, California have struggled against dominant cultural images.*

people working together to make certain that a performance goes off as planned. When a performance doesn't come off quite right, we use **face-saving behavior.** We may ignore flaws in someone's performance, which Goffman defines as *tact.* Suppose your teacher is about to make an important point. Suppose also that her lecturing has been outstanding and the class is hanging on every word. Just as she pauses for emphasis, her stomach lets out a loud growl. She might then use a face-saving technique by remarking, "I was so busy preparing for class that I didn't get breakfast this morning." It is more likely, however, that both class and teacher will simply ignore the sound, both giving the impression that no one heard a thing—a face-saving technique called *studied nonobservance.* This allows the teacher to make the point, or as Goffman would say, it allows the performance to go on.

face-saving behavior
techniques used to salvage a performance that is going sour

and it doesn't stick out enough where it should.

And—no matter what your weight— it's too much. You've got to be thinner.

Exercise takes time, and it's painful getting in shape. Once you do get in shape, if you slack off it seems to take only a few days for your body to return to its previous slothful, drab appearance. You can't let up, you can't exercise enough, and you can't diet enough.

But who can continue at such a pace, striving for what are unrealistic cultural ideals? A few people, of course, but not many. So liposuction is appealing. Just lie there, put up with a little discomfort, and the doctor will suck the fat right out of you. Surgeons can transform flat breasts into super breasts overnight. They can lower receding hairlines and smooth furrowed brows. They remove lumps with their magical tummy tucks, and take off a decade with their rejuvenating skin peels and face lifts.

With the bosomy girls on *Baywatch* the envy of all, and the impossibly shaped models at *Victoria's Secret* the standard to which they hold themselves, even teens call the plastic surgeon. Parents, anxious lest their child violate peer ideals and trail behind in her race for popularity, foot the bill. In New York City, some parents pay $25,000 to give their daughters a flatter tummy (Gross 1998).

Although peer pressure to alter the body is intense, surgeons keep stoking the fire. A sample ad: "No Ifs, Ands or Butts. You Can Change Your Bottom Line in Hours!"

The thinness craze has moved to the East. Glossy magazines in Japan and China are filled with skinny models and crammed with ads touting diet pills and diet teas. In China, where famine used to abound, a little extra padding was valued as a sign of good health. Today, the obsession is thinness (Rosenthal 1999). Not-so-subtle ads scream that fat is bad. Some teas come with a package of diet pills. Weight-loss machines, with electrodes attached to acupuncture pressure points, not only reduce fat, but they also build breasts. Or so the advertisers claim.

Not limited by some of our rules, advertisers in Japan and China push a soap that supposedly "sucks up fat through the skin's pores" (Marshall 1995). What a dream product! After all, even though those TV models smile as they go through their paces, those exercise machines do look like a lot of hard work.

In the United States, there is another bottom line. Beauty and attractiveness do pay off. Economists studied physical attractiveness and earnings. The result? "Average-looking" men and women earn more than "plain" people. "Good-looking" men and women earn even more. The "ugly" are paid a "pittance" (Hamermesh and Biddle 1994). The net worth of obese women is less than half of their slimmer sisters ("Fat is a Financial Issue" 2000). "Attractive" women have an added cash advantage—they attract and marry higher earning men.

More popularity *and* more money? Maybe you can't be thin enough after all. Maybe those exercise machines are a good investment. If only we could catch up with the Japanese and develop a soap that would suck the fat right out of our pores. You can practically hear the jingle now.

for your consideration

What image do you have of your body? How do cultural expectations of "ideal" bodies underlie your image? Can you recall any advertisement or television program that has affected your body image?

Most advertising and television programs that focus on weight are directed at women. Women are more concerned than men about weight, more likely to have eating disorders, and more likely to express dissatisfaction with their bodies (Honeycutt 1995). Do you think that the targeting of women in advertising creates these attitudes and behaviors? Or do you think that these attitudes and behaviors would exist even if there were no such ads? Why?

Before closing this section, we should note that impression management is not limited to individuals. Families, corporations, colleges, sports teams, in fact probably all groups, try to manage impressions. So do governments. When on September 11, 2001, Arab terrorists hijacked four commercial airliners and flew three of them into the World Trade Center in New York City and the Pentagon in Washington, D.C., the president was in Florida, speaking at a grade school. For his safety, the Secret Service rushed him into hiding, first to a military base in Louisiana, then to another base in Nebraska. Bush first addressed the nation from these secluded locations. To assure the people that the government was still in control, it wouldn't do for the president to speak while in hiding. He had to get back to Washington. The perceived danger to the president was ruled less important than his presence in the White

■ *After the destruction of the World Trade Center on September 11, 2001, the U.S. public, filled with fear, needed reassurance that its government was functioning. The text explains how symbols were used to accomplish this.*

House. To reassure the public, Bush was flown to Washington, escorted by U.S. Air Force F-16 fighter jets, where that same evening he addressed the American people from within the symbol of power, the Oval office.

■ Ethnomethodology: Uncovering Background Assumptions

As discussed in Chapter 1, symbolic interactionists stress that the events of life do not come with built-in meanings. Rather, we give meaning to things by classifying them. When we place objects and events into the classifications provided by our culture, we are doing more than naming things—we are interpreting our world.

Ethnomethodologists study how people make sense of life. They try to uncover people's basic assumptions as they interpret their everyday worlds. To better understand **ethnomethodology**, consider the word's three basic components. "*Ethno*" means folk or people; "*method*" means how people do something; "*ology*" means "the study of." Putting them together, then, *ethno/method/ology* means "the study of how people do things." Specifically, ethnomethodologists study how people use commonsense understandings to get through everyday life.

Let's suppose that during a routine office visit, your doctor remarks that your hair is rather long, then takes out a pair of scissors and offers to give you a haircut. You would feel strange about this situation—for your doctor has violated **background assumptions,** your ideas about the way life is and the way things ought to work. These assumptions, which lie at the root of daily life, are so deeply embedded in our consciousness that we are seldom aware of them, and most of us fulfill them unquestioningly. Thus, your doctor does not offer you a haircut, even if he or she is good at cutting hair and you need one!

The founder of ethnomethodology, sociologist Harold Garfinkel, conducted some interesting exercises designed to uncover our background assumptions. Garfinkel

ethnomethodology
the study of how people use background assumptions to make sense out of life

background assumptions
deeply embedded common understandings, or basic rules, concerning our view of the world and of how people ought to act

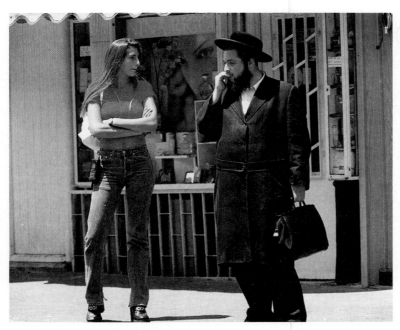

All of us have background assumptions, *deeply ingrained expectations of how the world operates. They lay the groundwork for what we expect will happen in our interactions. How do you think the background assumptions of these two people differ?*

(1967) asked his students to act as though they did not understand the basic rules of social life. Some tried to bargain with supermarket clerks; others would inch close to people and stare directly at them. They were met with surprise, bewilderment, even anger. In one exercise Garfinkel asked students to act as though they were boarders in their own homes. They addressed their parents as "Mr." and "Mrs.," asked permission to use the bathroom, sat stiffly, were extremely courteous, and spoke only when spoken to. As you can imagine, the other family members didn't know what to make of this (Garfinkel 1967):

> They vigorously sought to make the strange actions intelligible and to restore the situation to normal appearances. Reports (by the students) were filled with accounts of astonishment, bewilderment, shock, anxiety, embarrassment, and anger, and with charges by various family members that the student was mean, inconsiderate, selfish, nasty, or impolite. Family members demanded explanations: What's the matter? What's gotten into you? . . . Are you sick? . . . Are you out of your mind or are you just stupid?

In another exercise, Garfinkel asked students to take words and phrases literally. When a student asked his girlfriend what she meant when she said that she had a flat tire, she said:

> What do you mean, "What do you mean?"? A flat tire is a flat tire. That is what I meant. Nothing special. What a crazy question!

Another conversation went like this:

ACQUAINTANCE: How are you?

STUDENT: How am I in regard to what? My health, my finances, my schoolwork, my peace of mind, my . . . ?

ACQUAINTANCE (red in the face): Look! I was just trying to be polite. Frankly, I don't give a damn how you are.

Students who are asked to break background assumptions can be highly creative. The young children of one of my students were surprised one morning when they came down for breakfast to find a sheet spread across the living room floor. On it were dishes, silverware, burning candles—and bowls of ice cream. They, too, wondered what was going on—but they dug eagerly into the ice cream before their mother could change her mind.

IN SUM ■ ■ ■ ■ ■

Ethnomethodologists explore background assumptions, our taken-for-granted ideas about the world, which underlie our behavior. These basic rules of social life are an essential part of the social structure and are violated only with risk. Deeply embedded in our minds, they give us basic directions for living everyday life.

■ The Social Construction of Reality

Symbolic interactionists stress how our ideas help determine our reality. In what has become known as *the definition of the situation,* or the **Thomas theorem,** sociologists W. I. and Dorothy S. Thomas said "If people define situations as real, they are real in their consequences." Consider the following incident:

> On a visit to Morocco, in northern Africa, I decided to buy a watermelon. When I indicated to the street vendor that the knife he was going to use to cut the watermelon was dirty (encrusted with filth would be more apt), he was very obliging. He immediately bent down and began to swish the knife in a puddle on the street. I shuddered as I looked at the passing burros that were freely defecating and urinating as they went by. Quickly, I indicated by gesture that I preferred my melon uncut after all.

For that vendor, germs did not exist. For me, they did. And each of us acted according to our definition of the situation. My perception and behavior did not come from the fact that germs are real but *because I grew up in a society that teaches they are real.* Microbes, of course, *objectively* exist, and whether or not germs are part of our thought world makes no difference to whether we are infected by them. Our behavior, however, does not depend on the *objective* existence of something but, rather, on our *subjective interpretation,* on what sociologists call our *definition of reality.* In other words, it is not the reality of microbes that impresses itself on us, but society that impresses the reality of microbes on us.

Let's consider another example. Do you remember the identical twins, Oskar and Jack, who grew up so differently? As discussed on page 67, Jack was reared in Trinidad and learned to hate Hitler, while Oskar was reared in Germany and learned to love Hitler. Thus what Hitler meant to Oskar and Jack (and what he means to us) depends not on Hitler's acts, but, rather, on how we view his acts, that is, on our definition of the situation.

This is **the social construction of reality.** Our society, or the social groups to which we belong, have their particular views of life. From our groups (the *social* part of this process), we learn specific ways of looking at life—whether that be our view of Hitler (he's good, he's evil), germs (they exist, they don't exist), or *anything else in life.* In short, through our interaction with others, we *construct reality;* that is, we learn ways of interpreting our experiences in life.

Gynecological Examinations To better understand the social construction of reality, let's consider an extended example.

Thomas theorem
William I. and Dorothy S. Thomas' classic formulation of the definition of the situation: "If people define situations as real, they are real in their consequences."

the social construction of reality
the process by which people use their background assumptions and life experiences to define what is real for them

A gynecological nurse, Mae Biggs, and I did research on vaginal examinations. Reviewing about 14,000 cases, we looked at how the medical profession constructs social reality in order to define this examination as nonsexual (Henslin and Biggs 1971/2001). We found that the pelvic examination unfolds much as a stage play does. I will use "he" to refer to the physician because only male physicians participated in this study. Perhaps the results would be different with women gynecologists.

Scene 1 (the patient as person) In this scene, the doctor maintains eye contact with his patient, calls her by name, and discusses her problems in a professional manner. If he decides that a vaginal examination is necessary, he tells a nurse, "Pelvic in room 1." By this statement, he is announcing that a major change will occur in the next scene.

Scene 2 (from person to pelvic) This scene is the depersonalizing stage. In line with the doctor's announcement, the patient begins the transition from a "person" to a "pelvic." The doctor leaves the room, and a female nurse enters to help the patient make the transition. The nurse prepares the "props" for the coming examination and answers any questions the woman might have.

What occurs at this point is essential for the social construction of reality, for *the doctor's absence removes even the suggestion of sexuality.* To undress in front of him could suggest either a striptease or intimacy, thus undermining the reality so carefully being defined, that of nonsexuality.

The patient also wants to remove any hint of sexuality in the coming interaction, and during this scene she may express concern about what to do with her panties. Some mutter to the nurse, "I don't want him to see these." Most women solve the problem by either slipping their panties under their clothes or placing them in their purse.

Scene 3 (the person as pelvic) This scene opens when the doctor enters the room. Before him is a woman lying on a table, her feet in stirrups, her knees tightly together, and her body covered by a drape sheet. The doctor seats himself on a low stool before the woman, tells her, "Let your knees fall apart" (rather than the sexually loaded "Spread your legs"), and begins the examination.

The drape sheet is crucial in this process of desexualization, for it *dissociates the pelvic area from the person:* Bending forward and with the drape sheet above his head, the physician can see only the vagina, not the patient's face. Thus dissociated from the individual, the vagina is dramaturgically transformed into an object of analysis. If the doctor examines the patient's breasts, he also dissociates them from her person by examining them one at a time, with a towel covering the unexamined breast. Like the vagina, each breast becomes an isolated unit dissociated from the person.

In this scene, the patient cooperates in being an object, becoming for all practical purposes a pelvis to be examined. She withdraws eye contact from the doctor, usually from the nurse as well, is likely to stare at the wall or at the ceiling, and avoids initiating conversation.

Scene 4 (from pelvic to person) In this scene, the patient becomes "repersonalized." The doctor has left the examining room; the patient dresses and fixes her hair and makeup. Her reemergence as a person is indicated by such statements to the nurse as, "My dress isn't too wrinkled, is it?" indicating a need for reassurance that the metamorphosis from "pelvic" back to "person" has been completed satisfactorily.

Scene 5 (the patient as person) In this scene, the patient is once again treated as a person rather than as an object. The doctor makes eye contact with her and addresses her by name. She, too, makes eye contact with the doctor, and the usual middle-class interaction patterns are followed. She has been fully restored.

IN SUM ■ ■ ■ ■

To an outsider to our culture, the custom of women going to a male stranger for vaginal examinations might seem bizarre. But not to us. We assume that such behavior is normal, and females in our society are encouraged to participate in this process because they have learned that pelvic examinations are nonsexual. To sustain this definition requires teamwork—patients, doctors, and nurses working together to *socially construct reality.*

Although vaginal examinations are socially constructed as nonsexual, many women cannot rid themselves of uncomfortable feelings during this procedure, especially if their physician is a man. As a consequence, many women prefer to go to women gynecologists. A generation ago, they had little choice, for less than 10 percent of obstetricians and gynecologists were women. Today, about 40 percent are women, and about 72 percent of first-year ob/gyn residents are women (Council on Resident Education in Obstetrics and Gynecology, 2000). We don't yet know how this changed sex ratio will affect pelvic examinations—and perhaps medicine itself. Whatever the particulars may be, the same principles will apply: Team players will work together to maintain agreed-on definitions of the situation.

The social construction of reality is not limited to small segments of social life, such as to medical procedures or watermelons in Africa. Rather, it is an essential part of our everyday lives, for our behavior depends on how we define reality. To understand human behavior—whether that be how people react to microbes, to a photo of Hitler or the swastika, to pelvic examinations, or to anything else in life—we need to know how people define reality.

■ ■ ■ ■ ■

The Need for Both Macrosociology and Microsociology

As noted earlier, both microsociology and macrosociology make vital contributions to our understanding of human behavior. Our understanding of social life would be vastly incomplete without one or the other.

To illustrate this point, let's consider two groups of high school boys studied by sociologist William Chambliss (1973/2001). Both groups attended Hanibal High School. In one group were eight middle-class boys who came from "good" families and were perceived by the community as "going somewhere." Chambliss calls this group the "Saints." The other group consisted of six lower-class boys who were seen as headed down a dead-end road. Chambliss calls this group the "Roughnecks."

Both groups skipped school, got drunk, and did a lot of fighting and vandalism. The Saints were actually somewhat more delinquent, for they were truant more often and engaged in more vandalism. Yet the Saints had a good reputation, while the Roughnecks were seen by teachers, the police, and the general community as no good and headed for trouble.

These reputations followed the boys throughout life. Seven of the eight Saints went on to graduate from college. Three studied for advanced degrees: One finished law school and became active in state politics, one finished medical school, and one went on to earn a Ph.D. The four other college graduates entered managerial or executive training programs with large firms. After his parents divorced, one Saint failed to graduate from high school on time and had to repeat his senior year. Although this boy tried to go to college by attending night school, he never finished. He was unemployed the last time Chambliss saw him.

In contrast, only four of the Roughnecks finished even high school. Two of these boys did exceptionally well in sports and received athletic scholarships to college. They both graduated from college and became high school coaches. Of the two others who graduated from high school, one became a small-time gambler and the other disappeared "up north," where he was last reported to be driving a truck. Both of the two who did not complete high school were sent to state penitentiaries for separate murders.

To understand what happened to the Saints and the Roughnecks, we need to grasp *both* social structure and social interaction. Using *macrosociology,* we can place these boys within the larger framework of the U.S. social class system. This reveals how opportunities open or close to people depending on their social class and how people learn different goals as they grow up in vastly different groups. We can then use *microsociology* to follow their everyday lives. We can see how the Saints manipulated their "good" reputations to skip classes repeatedly and how their access to automobiles allowed them to protect those reputations by transferring their troublemaking to different communities. In contrast, the Roughnecks, who did not have cars, were highly visible. Their lawbreaking, which was limited to a small area, readily came to the attention of the community. Microsociology also reveals how their respective reputations opened doors of opportunity to the first group of boys while closing them to the other.

Thus we need both kinds of sociology, and both are stressed in the following chapters.

Summary and Review

Levels of Sociological Analysis

■ **What two levels of analysis do sociologists use?**
Sociologists use macrosociological and microsociological levels of analysis. In **macrosociology,** the focus is placed on large-scale features of social life, while in **microsociology,** the focus is on **social interaction.** Functionalists and conflict theorists tend to use a macrosociological approach, while symbolic interactionists are more likely to use a microsociological approach. Pp. 98–99.

The Macrosociological Perspective: Social Structure

■ **How does social structure influence our behavior?**
The term **social structure** refers to a society's framework, which forms an envelope around us and establishes limits on our behavior. Social structure consists of culture, social class, social statuses, roles, groups, and social institutions. Together, these serve as foundations for how we view the world.

Our location in the social structure underlies our perceptions, attitudes, and behaviors. Culture lays the broadest framework, while **social class** divides people according to income, education, and occupational prestige. Each of us receives **ascribed statuses** at birth; later we add **achieved statuses.** Our behaviors and orientations are further influenced by the **roles** we play, the **groups** to which we belong, and our experiences with the institutions of our society. These components of society work together to help maintain social order. Pp. 99–104.

Social Institutions

■ **What are social institutions?**
Social institutions are the standard means that a society develops to meet its basic needs. As summarized in Figure 4.1 (page 105), industrialized societies have nine social institutions—the family, religion, law, politics, economics, education, medicine, science, and the military. A tenth, the mass media, is emerging. From the functionalist perspective, social institutions meet

universal group needs, or **functional requisites.** Conflict theorists stress how society's elite uses social institutions to maintain its privileged position. Pp. 104–108.

■ **What holds society together?**

According to Emile Durkheim, in agricultural societies people are united by **mechanical solidarity** (similar views and feelings). With industrialization comes **organic solidarity** (people depend on one another to do their jobs). Ferdinand Tönnies pointed out that the informal means of control of *Gemeinschaft* (small, intimate) societies are replaced by formal mechanisms in *Gesellschaft* (larger, more impersonal) societies. Pp. 108–110.

The Microsociological Perspective: Social Interaction in Everyday Life

■ **What is the focus of symbolic interactionism?**

In contrast to functionalists and conflict theorists, who as macrosociologists focus on the "big picture," symbolic interactionists tend to be microsociologists who focus on face-to-face social interaction. Symbolic interactionists analyze how people define their worlds, and how their definitions, in turn, influence their behavior. P. 111.

■ **How do stereotypes affect social interaction?**

Stereotypes are assumptions of what people are like. When we first meet people, we classify them according to our perceptions of their visible characteristics. Our ideas about those characteristics guide our behavior toward them, which, in turn, may influence them to behave in ways that reinforce our stereotypes. Pp. 111–112.

■ **Do all human groups share a similar sense of personal space?**

In examining how people use physical space, symbolic interactionists stress that we surround ourselves with a "personal bubble," one that we carefully protect. People from different cultures use "personal bubbles" of varying sizes, so the answer to the question is no. Americans typically use four different "distance zones"—intimate, personal, social, and public. Pp. 112–114.

■ **What is dramaturgy?**

Erving Goffman developed **dramaturgy** (or dramaturgical analysis), which analyzes everyday life in terms of the stage. At the core of this analysis is **impression management,** our attempts to control the impressions we make on others. For this, we use the **sign-vehicles** of setting, appearance, and manner. Our performances often call for **teamwork** and **face-saving behavior.** Pp. 115–120.

■ **What is the social construction of reality?**

The phrase **the social construction of reality** refers to how we construct our views of the world, which, in turn, underlie our actions. **Ethnomethodology** is the study of how people make sense of everyday life. Ethnomethodologists try to uncover **background assumptions,** our basic ideas about the way life is. Pp. 120–124.

The Need for Both Macrosociology and Microsociology

■ **Why are both levels of analysis important?**

Because each focuses on different aspects of the human experience, both microsociology and macrosociology are necessary for us to understand social life. Pp. 124–125.

■ *Where can I read more on this topic?*

Suggested Readings for this chapter are at the back of this book.

Additional Online Resources for This Chapter
www.ablongman.com/henslin6e

- *Content Select* Research Database for Sociology, with suggested key terms and annotated references
- Link to 2000 Census, with activities
- Flashcards of key terms and concepts
- Practice Tests
- Weblinks
- Interactive Maps

using . . .

ContentSelect

Research Database for Sociology

role playing	social institution	social structure	stereotypes
social class	social status	division of labor	social groups

Diana Ong, *People*, 1995

5

How Sociologists Do Research

What Is a Valid Sociological Topic?

Common Sense and the Need for Sociological Research

A Research Model
1. Selecting a Topic
2. Defining the Problem
3. Reviewing the Literature
4. Formulating a Hypothesis
5. Choosing a Research Method
6. Collecting the Data
7. Analyzing the Results
8. Sharing the Results

Research Methods
Surveys
Participant Observation (Fieldwork)
Secondary Analysis
Documents
Unobtrusive Measures
Experiments
Deciding Which Method to Use

Gender in Sociological Research

Ethics in Sociological Research
Protecting the Subjects: The Brajuha Research
Misleading the Subjects: The Humphreys Research

How Research and Theory Work Together
The Real World: When the Ideal Meets the Real

Summary and Review

Cindy Hudo, a 21-year-old mother of two in Charleston, South Carolina, who was charged with the murder of her husband, Buba, said:

I start in the car, and I get down the road, and I see Buba walking, and he's real mad. . . . I pull over, you know, and [I said] "I didn't know to pick you up. You know, I'm sorry." And he didn't even say nothing to me. He just started hitting on me. And that's all I wanted to do, was just get home, because I was just self-conscious. I don't want nobody to see him hitting me, because I didn't want him to look bad.

I had to go to work in a half-hour, because I was working a double-shift. And he told me I had forty minutes to get all my furniture out of the house and get my clothes and be out or he was going to throw them out. And I was sitting there, because I could talk him down. You know, because I didn't want to leave him. I just talked to him. I said, "Buba, I don't want to leave." I said, "This is my house." And then he told me . . . (unclear) . . . "my kids." And I said, "No, you're not taking my kids from me. That's too much." And so I said, "Just let me leave. Just let me take the kids. And, you know I'll go, and you know, I won't keep the kids from you or nothing like that." And he said, "I'm going to take them, and you're getting out."

> *I don't want nobody to see him hitting me, because I didn't want him to look bad.*

[After they went inside their trailer, Buba threatened to shoot Cindy. He loaded a shotgun, pointed it at her, and said]: "The only way you're going to get out of this is if you kill me, and I'll—I'll kill you." [Buba gave me the shotgun and] turned around and walked right down the hall, because he knew I wouldn't do nothing. And I just sat there a minute. And I don't know what happened. I just, you know, I went to the bedroom, and I seen him laying there, and I just shot him. He moved. I shot him again because I thought he was going to get up again. . . .

I loved him too much. And I just wanted to help him.

Source: ABC Television, *20/20,* October 18, 1979

What Is a Valid Sociological Topic?

Sociologists do research on just about every area of human behavior. On the macro level, they study such broad matters as race relations (Wilson 2000), the military (Moscos and Butler 1997), and multinational corporations (Kanter et al. 1997a). On the micro level, they study such individualistic matters as pelvic examinations (Henslin and Biggs 1971/2001), how people interact on street corners (Whyte 1989, 2001), and even how people decorate their homes at Christmas (Caplow 1991). In fact, no human behavior is ineligible for sociological scrutiny—whether that behavior is routine or unusual, respectable or reprehensible.

What happened to Cindy and Buba, then, is also a valid topic of sociological research. But exactly *how* would you research spouse abuse? As we look at how sociologists conduct their research, we shall try to answer this question.

Common Sense and the Need for Sociological Research

First, why do we need sociological research? Why can't we simply depend on common sense, on "what everyone knows"? As noted in Chapter 1 (pages 7–8), commonsense ideas may or may not be true. Common sense, for example, tells us that spouse abuse has a significant impact on the lives of the people who are abused.

Although this particular idea is accurate, we need research to test commonsense ideas, because not all such ideas are true. After all, common sense also tells us that if a woman is abused she will pack up and leave her husband. Research, however, shows that the reality of abuse is much more complicated than this. Some women do leave right away, some even after the first incident of abuse. For a variety of reasons, however—the main one being that they feel trapped and don't see viable alternatives—some women suffer abuse for years.

This brings us to the need for sociological research, for we may want to know why some women put up with abuse, while others don't. Or we may want to know something entirely different, such as why men are more likely to be the abusers. Or why some people abuse the people they say they love.

In order to answer a question, we need to move beyond guesswork and common sense. We want to *know* what is really going on. To find out, sociologists do research on about every aspect of social life. Let's look at how they do their research.

■ Because sociologists find all human behavior to be valid research topics, their research runs from the unusual to the routines of everyday life. Their studies range from broad scale social change, such as the globalization of capitalism, to such events as exhibitions of tattooing, piercing, and body painting. Shown here at the Australian Museum in Sydney is Lucky Rich, displaying his stainless steel teeth.

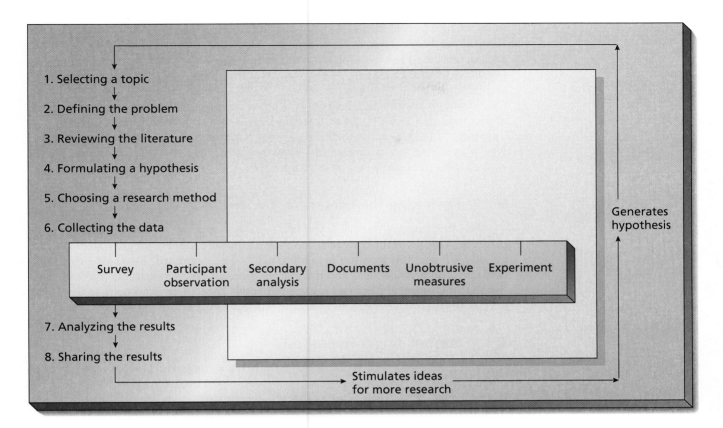

Figure 5.1

The Research Model

Source: Modification of Fig. 2.2 of Schaefer 1989.

A Research Model

As shown in Figure 5.1, scientific research follows eight basic steps. This is an ideal model, however, and in the real world of research some of these steps may run together. Some may even be omitted.

1. Selecting a Topic

The first step is to select a topic. What do you want to know more about? Many sociologists simply follow their curiosity, their drive to know. They become interested in a particular topic, and they pursue it, as I did in studying the homeless. Some sociologists choose a topic because funding is available for that topic, others because a social problem such as domestic violence is in the news, and the sociologist wants to help people better understand it—and perhaps to help solve it. Let's use spouse abuse as our example.

2. Defining the Problem

The second step is to define the problem, to specify what you want to learn about the topic. My interest in the homeless grew until I wanted to learn about homelessness across the nation. Ordinarily, sociologists' interests are much more focused than this. They develop a researchable question that focuses on a specific area or problem. For example, they may want to compare the work experiences of homeless women and men. Or they may want to know what can be done to reduce spouse abuse.

Although sociologists study social problems such as homelessness and spouse abuse, they also conduct research on any aspect of social life that interests them. The "problem" can be as earth shattering as why nations would ever contemplate nuclear war or as simple as wanting to find out why Native Americans like Westerns (see the Mass Media in Social Life box on page 53).

■ 3. Reviewing the Literature

The third step is to review the literature to see what is already written on the problem. This helps the researcher narrow down the problem, identify areas that are already known, and pinpoint areas that need to be examined. Reviewing the literature may also provide ideas about what questions to ask. A researcher may even find out that the problem has been resolved already. Then there is no need to do the research, for no one wants to reinvent the wheel.

■ 4. Formulating a Hypothesis

The fourth step is to formulate a **hypothesis,** a statement of what you expect to find according to predictions from a theory. A hypothesis predicts a relationship between or among **variables,** factors that change, or vary, from one person or situation to another. For example, the statement, "Men who are more socially isolated are more likely to abuse their wives than are men who are more socially integrated" is a hypothesis. Hypotheses need **operational definitions**—that is, precise ways to measure their variables. In this example, we would need operational definitions for three variables: social isolation, social integration, and spouse abuse.

■ 5. Choosing a Research Method

The means by which sociologists collect data are called **research methods** (or research designs). Sociologists use six research methods, selecting the one that will best answer their particular questions. We'll examine these methods in the next section.

■ 6. Collecting the Data

The next step is to gather the data. You have to take care to assure the validity of your data. **Validity** refers to whether the operational definitions really measure what they are intended to measure. For example, how would you measure social isolation and social integration? Perhaps you could find out how often someone interacts with other people. But don't you also have to measure how much the individual identifies with others, or feels a part of a group? This would be a much more difficult matter, but isn't this part of social integration? Even finding the right operational definition for spouse abuse isn't easy. For example, some acts that are accepted as an ordinary part of everyday life in some cultures and subcultures are viewed as abuse by people from other groups. Whose definition of abuse should you use? After grappling with such problems, your operational definitions must make sense *and* be so precise that no one has any question about what you are measuring.

You must also be sure your data are reliable. **Reliability** means that if other researchers use your operational definitions, their findings will be consistent with yours. If your operational definitions are sloppy, husbands who have committed the

hypothesis
a statement of the expected relationship between variables according to predictions from a theory

variable
a factor thought to be significant for human behavior, which varies from one case to another

operational definitions
the way in which a variable in a hypothesis is measured

research method
(or research design)
one of six procedures sociologists use to collect data: surveys, participant observation, secondary analysis, documents, unobtrusive measures, and experiments

validity
the extent to which an operational definition measures what it was intended to measure

reliability
the extent to which research produces consistent results

same act of violence might be included in some research but excluded in other studies. You would end up with erratic results. You might show a 10 percent rate of spousal violence, but another researcher finds it to be 30 percent. This would make your research unreliable.

7. Analyzing the Results

After you gather the data, it is time to analyze them. You can choose from qualitative and quantitative techniques. *Qualitative analysis* would include classifying books, movies, television programs, and people's conversations in order to identify the main themes. The goal is to faithfully reproduce the world of the people you are studying. In my research on cabdrivers (1993), for example, I tried to picture the world as cabbies see it so anyone reading the report would understand not just what cabbies do but also why they do it. Software, such as Nvivo, provides tools to help researchers organize their data.

Quantitative analysis involves crunching numbers. This is especially useful for testing hypotheses, which is done at this stage. The computer has taken much of the drudgery out of analyzing data. What used to take tedious hours, and even days or weeks of mathematical analysis, can now be performed in an instant. The new software can analyze huge amounts of information and help you identify basic patterns. The computer also allows you to try different statistical tests to see which prove the most valuable for analyzing your data. Freed from the time-consuming tasks of number crunching, you are able to spend more time thinking about what those numbers mean. Two basic programs that sociologists learn are Microcase and the Statistical Package for the Social Sciences (SPSS). Some software, such as the Methodologist's Toolchest, provides advice about collecting data and even about ethical issues.

THE FAR SIDE® By GARY LARSON

© 1984 FarWorks, Inc. All Rights Reserved/Dist. by Creators Syndicate

The Far Side® by Gary Larson © 1984 FarWorks, Inc. All Rights Reserved. Used with permission.

"Anthropologists! Anthropologists!"

■ *A major concern of sociologists and other social scientists is that their research methods do not influence their findings. Respondents often change their behavior when they know they are being studied.*

8. Sharing the Results

After analyzing the data, it is time to wrap up the research (or, if it is a broad project, at least some part of it). In this step, you write a report to share your findings with the scientific community. To help others evaluate the research, the report includes a review of these first steps. It also shows how your findings are related to the literature, reviews what has already been published on the topic, and demonstrates how your findings support or refute the theories that apply to the topic.

When research is published, usually in a scientific journal or a book, it "belongs" to the scientific community. Table 5.1 on the next page is an example of published research. These findings are available for **replication**; that is, others can repeat the study to see if they come up with similar results. As finding is added to finding, scientific knowledge builds.

Let's look at the fifth step to see what research methods sociologists use.

replication
repeating a study in order to test its findings

TABLE 5.1 How to Read a Table

Tables summarize information. Because sociological findings are often presented in tables, it is important to understand how to read them. Tables contain six elements: title, headnote, headings, columns, rows, and source. When you understand how these elements work together, you know how to read a table.

1 The **title** states the topic. It is located at the top of the table. What is the title of this table? Please determine your answer before looking at the correct answer at the bottom of the page.

2 The **headnote** is not always included in a table. When it is, it is located just below the title. Its purpose is to give more detailed information about how the data were collected or how data are presented in the table. What are the first seven words of the headnote of this table?

3 The **headings** tell what kind of information is contained in the table. There are three headings in this table. What are they? In the second heading, what does $n = 25$ mean?

4 The **columns** present information arranged vertically. What is the fourth number in the second column and the second number in the third column?

5 The **rows** present information arranged horizontally. In the fourth row, which husbands are more likely to have less education than their wives?

6 The **source** of a table, usually listed at the bottom, provides information on where the data shown in the table originated. Often, as in this instance, the information is specific enough for you to consult the original source. What is the source for this table?

Comparing Violent and Nonviolent Husbands

Based on interviews with 150 husbands and wives in a Midwestern city who were getting a divorce.

Husband's Achievement and Job Satisfaction	Violent Husbands $n = 25$	Nonviolent Husbands $n = 125$
He started but failed to complete high school or college.	44%	27%
He is very dissatisfied with his job.	44%	18%
His income is a source of constant conflict.	84%	24%
He has less education than his wife.	56%	14%
His job has less prestige than his father-in-law's.	37%	28%

Source: Modification of Table 1 in O'Brien 1975.

Some tables are much more complicated than this one, but all follow the same basic pattern. To apply these concepts to a table with more information, see page 364.

ANSWERS

1. Comparing Violent and Nonviolent Husbands
2. Based on interviews with 150 husbands and
3. Husband's Achievement and Job Satisfaction, Violent Husbands, Nonviolent Husbands. The *n* is an abbreviation for number, and $n = 25$ means that 25 violent husbands were in the sample.
4. 56%, 18%
5. Violent Husbands
6. A 1975 article by O'Brien (listed in the References section of this text).

Research Methods

As we review the six research methods (or research designs) that sociologists use, we will continue our example of spouse abuse. As you will see, the method you choose will depend on the questions you want to answer. Because you will want to know what is "average" in your study—so you can have a yardstick for comparison—the ways to measure average are discussed in Table 5.2 below.

Surveys

Let's suppose that you want to know how many wives are abused each year. Some husbands are abused, of course, but let's assume that you are going to focus on wives. An appropriate method for this purpose would be the **survey,** in which you would ask individuals a series of questions. Before you begin your research, however, you must deal with practical matters that face all researchers. Let's look at these issues.

Selecting a Sample   Ideally, you might want to learn about all wives in the world. Obviously, your resources will not permit such a study, and you must narrow your **population,** the target group that you are going to study.

survey
the collection of data by having people answer a series of questions
population
the target group to be studied

TABLE 5.2   Three Ways to Measure "Average"

The Mean
The term *average* seems clear enough. As you learned in grade school, to find the average you add a group of numbers and then divide the total by the number of cases that were added. For example, assume that the following numbers represent men convicted of battering their wives:

321
229
57
289
136
57
1,795

The total is 2,884. Divided by 7 (the number of cases), the average is 412. Sociologists call this form of average the *mean.*

The mean can be deceptive because it is strongly influenced by extreme scores, either low or high. Note that six of the seven cases are less than the mean.

Two other ways to compute averages are the median and the mode.

The Median
To compute the second average, the *median,* first arrange the cases in order—either from the highest to the lowest or the lowest to the highest. In this example, that arrangement will produce the following distribution:

57
57
136
229
289
321
1,795

Then look for the middle case, the one that falls halfway between the top and the bottom. That number is 229, for three numbers are lower and three numbers are higher. When there is an even number of cases, the median is the halfway mark between the two middle cases.

The Mode
The third measure of average, the *mode,* is simply the cases that occur the most often. In this instance the mode is 57, which is way off the mark. Because the mode is often deceptive, and only by chance comes close to either of the other two averages, sociologists seldom use it. In addition, it is obvious that not every distribution of cases has a mode. And if two or more numbers appear with the same frequency, you can have more than one mode.

Let's assume that your resources (money, helpers, time) allow you to investigate spouse abuse only on your campus. Let's also assume that your college enrollment is large, so you won't be able to survey all the married women who are enrolled. Now you must select a **sample,** individuals from among your target population. How you choose a sample is crucial, for your choice will affect the results of your study. For example, to survey only women enrolled in introductory sociology courses, or only those in advanced physics classes, would produce skewed results.

Because you want to generalize your findings to your entire campus, you need a sample that is representative of the campus. How do you get a representative sample?

The best is a **random sample.** This does *not* mean that you stand on some campus corner and ask questions of any woman who happens to walk by. *In a random sample, everyone in your population has the same chance of being included in the study.* In this case, because your population is every married woman enrolled in your college, all married women—whether first-year or graduate students, full- or part-time—must have the same chance of being included in your sample.

How can you get a random sample? First, you need a list of all the married women enrolled in your college. Then you assign a number to each name on the list. Using a table of random numbers, you then determine which of these women become part of your sample. (Random numbers are available on tables in statistics books, or they can be generated by a computer.)

Because a random sample represents the population—in this case married women enrolled at your college—you can generalize your findings to all the married women students on your campus, regardless of whether they were included in the sample.

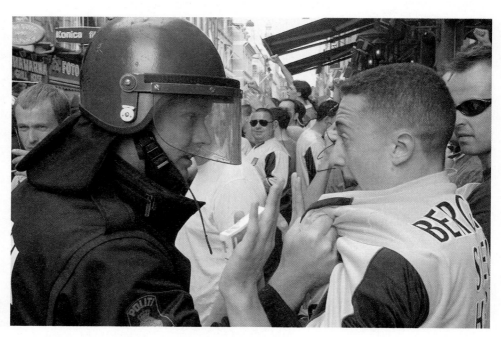

sample
the individuals intended to represent the population to be studied

random sample
a sample in which everyone in the target population has the same chance of being included in the study

▧ *Because sociologists usually cannot interview or observe every member of a group they wish to study, such as the spectators and riot police at this soccer match in Copenhagen, Denmark, they must select a sample that will let them generalize to the entire group. The text explains how samples are selected.*

Doonesbury © G. B. Trudeau. Reprinted with permission of Universal Press Syndicate. All rights reserved.

■ *Improperly worded questions can steer respondents toward answers that are not their own, thus producing invalid results.*

What if you wanted to know only about certain subgroups, such as freshmen and seniors? You could use a **stratified random sample.** You would need a list of the freshmen and senior married women. Then, using random numbers, you would select subsamples of each group. This would allow you to generalize to all the freshmen and senior married women at your college, but you would not be able to draw any conclusions about the sophomores or juniors.

Asking Neutral Questions   After you have decided on your population and sample, your next task is to make certain that your questions are neutral. Your questions must allow **respondents,** the people who answer your questions, to express their own opinions. Otherwise, you will end up with biased answers—which are worthless. For example, if you were to ask, "Don't you think that men who beat their wives should go to prison?" you would be tilting the answer toward agreement with a prison sentence. As you can see, the *Doonesbury* cartoon above illustrates biased questions. For examples of flawed research, see the Down-to-Earth Sociology box on the next page.

Questionnaires and Interviews   Even if you have a representative sample and ask neutral questions, you can still end up with biased findings. **Questionnaires,** the list of questions to be asked, can be administered in ways that are flawed. There are two basic techniques for administering questionnaires. The first is for the respondents to fill them out. These **self-administered questionnaires** allow a larger number of people to be sampled at a lower cost, but the researchers lose control. They don't know the conditions under which people answered the questions. For example, others could have influenced their answers.

The second technique is the **interview.** Researchers ask people questions, either face to face or by telephone. The advantage of this method is that they can ask each question in precisely the same way. The disadvantage is that this is more expensive and time-consuming, and they can complete fewer questionnaires. This can also create **interviewer bias;** that is, the presence of interviewers can affect what people say. For example, some people won't tell an interviewer what they really feel. Instead, they give "socially acceptable" answers. They may be willing to write their true opinions in an anonymous situation, but not to tell them to another person directly. Some even shade their answers to match what they think an interviewer wants to hear.

In some cases, **structured interviews** work best. This type of interview uses **closed-ended questions**—each question is followed by a list of possible answers. Structured interviews are faster to administer, and they make it easier to *code* (categorize) answers so they can be fed into a computer for analysis. Because the answers listed on the questionnaire may not include the respondent's opinions, however, some researchers prefer **unstructured interviews.** Here the interviewer asks **open-ended questions,**

stratified random sample
a sample of specific subgroups of the target population in which everyone in the subgroups has an equal chance of being included in the study

questionnaires
a list of questions to be asked

self-administered questionnaires
questionnaires filled out by respondents

interview
direct questioning of respondents

interviewer bias
effects that interviewers have on respondents that lead to biased answers

structured interviews
interviews that use closed-ended questions

closed-ended questions
questions that are followed by a list of possible answers to be selected by the respondent

unstructured interviews
interviews that use open-ended questions

open-ended questions
questions that respondents are able to answer in their own words

Loading the Dice: How *Not* to Do Research

The methods of science lend themselves to distortion, misrepresentation, and downright fraud. Consider the following information. Surveys show that

- Americans overwhelmingly prefer Toyotas to Chryslers.
- Americans overwhelmingly prefer Chryslers to Toyotas.

- Americans think that cloth diapers are better for the environment than disposable diapers.
- Americans think that disposable diapers are better for the environment than cloth diapers.

Obviously these opposite conclusions cannot both be true. In fact, *both* sets of findings are misrepresentations, although each comes from surveys conducted by so-called independent researchers. These researchers, however, are biased, not independent and objective.

It turns out that some consumer researchers load the dice. Hired by firms that have a vested interest in the outcome of the research, they deliver the results their clients are looking for. There are six basic ways of loading the dice.

1. Choose a biased sample. If you want to "prove" that Americans prefer Chryslers over Toyotas, interview unemployed union workers who trace their job loss to Japanese imports. The answer is predictable. You'll get what you're looking for.

2. Ask biased questions. Even if you choose an unbiased sample, you can phrase questions in such a way that most people see only one logical choice. The diaper study just cited is a case in point. When the disposable diaper companies paid for the survey, the researchers used an excellent sample, but they worded the question this way: "It is estimated that disposable diapers account for less than 2 percent of the trash in today's landfills. In contrast, beverage containers, third-class mail and yard waste are estimated to account for about 21 percent. Given

this, in your opinion, would it be fair to ban disposable diapers?"

Is it surprising, then, that 84 percent of the respondents said that disposable diapers are better for the environment than cloth diapers? Similarly, when the cloth diaper companies funded their survey, they worded the questions to load the dice in their favor.

Consider the following finding, which is every bit as factual as those just cited:

- 80 percent of Americans support foreign aid.

It is difficult to get 80 percent of Americans to agree on anything, but as loaded as this question was it is surprising that there was *only* 80 percent agreement. Incredibly, the question was phrased this way: *"Should the U.S. share at least a small portion of its wealth with those in the world who are in great need?"*

This question is obviously designed to channel people's thinking toward a predetermined answer—quite contrary to the standards of scientific research.

3. List biased choices. Another way to load the dice is to use closed-ended questions that push people into the answers you want. Consider this finding:

- U.S. college students overwhelmingly prefer Levis 501 to the jeans of any competitor.

Sound good? Before you rush out to buy Levis, note what these researchers did: In asking students which jeans would be the most popular in the coming year, their list of choices included *no other jeans* but Levis 501!

4. Discard undesirable results. Researchers can keep silent about results they find embarrassing, or they can continue to survey samples until they find one that matches what they are looking for.

As stressed in this chapter, research must be objective if it is to be scientific. Obviously, none of the preceding results qualifies. The underlying problem with

the research cited here—and with so many surveys bandied about in the media as fact—is that survey research has become big business. Simply put, the vast sums of money offered by corporations have corrupted some researchers.

The beginning of the corruption is subtle. Paul Light, dean at the University of Minnesota, put it this way: "A funder will never come to an academic and say, 'I want you to produce finding X, and here's a million dollars to do it.' Rather, the subtext is that if the researchers produce the right finding, more work—and funding—will come their way." He adds, "Once you're on that treadmill, it's hard to get off."

The first four sources of bias are inexcusable, intentional fraud. The next two sources of bias reflect sloppiness—which is also inexcusable in science.

5. Misunderstand the subjects' world. This route can lead to errors every bit as great as those just cited. Even researchers who use an adequate sample, word their questions properly, and offer adequate choices can end up with skewed results. They may, for example, fail to anticipate that people may be embarrassed to express an opinion that isn't "politically correct." For example, surveys show that 80 percent of Americans are environmentalists. Most Americans, however, are probably embarrassed to tell a stranger otherwise. Today, that would be like going against the flag, motherhood, and apple pie.

6. Analyze the data incorrectly. Even when researchers strive for objectivity, the sample is good, the wording is neutral, and the respondents answer the questions honestly, the results can still be skewed. The researchers may make a mistake in their calculations, such as entering incorrect data into computers. This, too, of course, is inexcusable in science.

Sources: Based on Crossen 1991; Goleman 1993; Barnes 1995; Resnik 2000.

which allow people to answer in their own words. Although open-ended questions allow you to tap the full range of people's opinions, they make it difficult to compare answers. For example, how would you compare these answers to the question "What do you think causes men to abuse their wives?"

"They're sick."

"They haven't been raised right."

"I think they must have had problems with their mother."

"We ought to string them up!"

Establishing Rapport Research on spouse abuse also brings up another significant issue. You may have been wondering if your survey would be worth anything even if you rigorously followed scientific procedures. Will women who have been abused really give honest answers? Will they even admit their victimization to a stranger?

If you were to walk up to a woman on the street and ask if her husband had ever beaten her, there would be little basis for taking your findings seriously. Researchers have to establish **rapport** ("ruh-pour"), a feeling of trust, with their respondents, especially when it comes to sensitive topics, areas of their lives about which people feel embarrassment, shame, or other deep emotions.

We know that once rapport is gained (for example, by first asking nonsensitive questions), victims will talk to researchers about very personal, sensitive issues. A good example is rape. To go beyond police statistics, each year researchers conduct a national crime survey. They interview a random sample of 100,000 Americans, asking them if they have been victims of burglary, robbery, and so on. After establishing rapport, the researchers ask about rape. They find that rape victims will talk about their experiences. The national crime victimization survey shows that rape is *three* times as high as the official statistics indicate (*Statistical Abstract* 2000: page 200).

rapport
a feeling of trust between researchers and subjects

participant observation
(or fieldwork)
research in which the researcher participates in a research setting while observing what is happening in that setting

Participant Observation (Fieldwork)

In the second method, **participant observation,** the researcher *participates* in a research setting while *observing* what is happening in that setting. But how is it possible to study spouse abuse by participant observation? Obviously, this method does not mean that you would be present during the abuse and take notes while it occurs. Spouse abuse, however, is a broad topic, and many questions about abuse cannot be answered adequately by any method other than participant observation.

Let's suppose that you are interested in learning how spouse abuse affects wives. You may want to know how the abuse has changed their relationship with their husbands. How has it changed their hopes and dreams? Or their ideas about men? Certainly it has affected their self-concept as well. But how? Participant observation may be able to provide insight into such questions.

For example, if your campus has a crisis intervention center, you may be able to observe victims of spouse abuse from the time they first report the attack through their participation in counseling. With good rapport, you may even be able to spend time with victims in other settings, observing other aspects of their lives. The victims' statements and interaction with others may be the keys that help you unlock answers about how the abuse has affected

■ *Sociologists who enter a research setting to discover information are following a research method known as* participant observation. *As discussed in the text, sociologists also conduct research in controversial settings. Can you identify the sociologist in this photo at a cockfight in Tarsus, Turkey?*

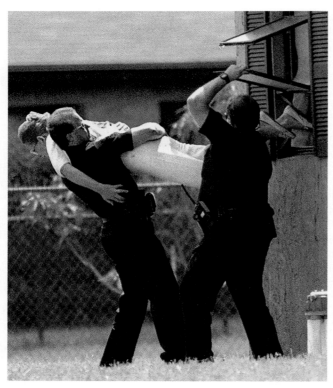

■ *Domestic abuse is one of the most common forms of violence. Until recently, it was treated by the police as a private family matter. Shown here are police pulling a woman from her bathroom window, where she had fled from her armed husband, who was threatening to shoot her.*

their lives. This, in turn, may allow you to make suggestions about how to improve college counseling services.

Participant observers face a problem with **generalizability,** being able to apply their findings to larger populations. Most of their studies are exploratory, documenting in detail the experiences of people in a particular setting. Although such research suggests that other people who face similar situations react in similar ways, it is difficult to know just how far the findings apply beyond their original setting. The results of participant observation, however, can stimulate hypotheses and theories that can be tested in other settings, using other research techniques.

■ Secondary Analysis

In **secondary analysis,** a third research method, researchers analyze data that have already been collected by others. For example, if you were to examine the original data from a study of women who had been abused by their husbands, you would be doing secondary analysis. Ordinarily, researchers prefer to gather their own data, but lack of resources, especially money, may make this impossible. In addition, existing data may contain a wealth of information that wasn't pertinent to the goals of the original researchers, which you can analyze for your own purposes.

Like the other methods, secondary analysis also poses its own problems. How can a researcher who did not carry out the research be sure that the data were systematically gathered and accurately recorded, and that biases were avoided? This problem plagues researchers who do secondary analysis, especially if the original data have been gathered by a team of researchers, not all of whom were equally qualified.

■ Documents

The fourth method sociologists use is the study of **documents,** written sources. To investigate social life, they examine such diverse documents as books, newspapers, diaries, bank records, police reports, immigration files, and records kept by various organizations.

To study spouse abuse, you might examine police reports and court records. These could reveal what proportion of complaints result in arrest and what proportion of the men arrested are charged, convicted, or put on probation. If these were your questions, police statistics would be valuable.

But for other questions, those records would be useless. If you want to know about the victims' social and emotional adjustment, for example, those records would tell you little. Other documents, however, might provide answers. For example, diaries kept by victims could yield insight into their reactions to abuse, showing how their attitudes and relationships change. If you couldn't locate such diaries, you might ask victims to keep diaries. Perhaps the director of a crisis intervention center might ask clients to keep diaries for you—or get the victims' permission for you to examine records of their counseling sessions. To my knowledge, no sociologist has yet studied spouse abuse in this way.

generalizability
the extent to which the findings from one group (or sample) can be generalized or applied to other groups (or populations)

secondary analysis
the analysis of data already collected by other researchers

documents
in its narrow sense, written sources that provide data; in its extended sense, archival material of any sort, including photographs, movies, and so on

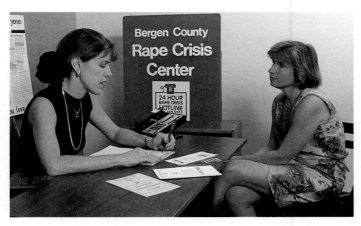

■ *Sociologists use different methods of research to answer different questions. One method that can be used to study spouse abuse is to examine the documents kept by shelters for battered women, which log the number of calls and visits made by victims.*

Of course, I am presenting an ideal situation, a crisis intervention center that opens its arms to you. In actual fact, the center might not cooperate at all. It might refuse to ask victims to keep diaries, and it might not even let you near its records. *Access,* then, is another problem researchers face. Simply put, you can't study a topic unless you can gain access to it.

■ Unobtrusive Measures

The fifth method is **unobtrusive measures,** observing the behavior of people who do not know they are being studied. For example, social researchers studied the level of whisky consumption in a town that was officially "dry" by counting empty bottles in trash cans. To study the degree of fear induced by ghost stories, they measured the shrinking diameter of a circle of seated children (Webb 1966). Some sociologists even examined garbage. They found that more beef is wasted during a beef shortage—presumably because people rush out and buy more than they can store properly (Rathje and Murphy 1992). To study gender differences, one of my graduate students recorded all the graffiti in every public rest room in two towns (Darnell 1971). Researchers have also gone high-tech in their unobtrusive measures. They have outfitted shopping carts with infrared surveillance equipment to trace customers' paths through stores. Retailers use these findings to move items in their stores to more strategic locations (McCarthy 1993).

If you wanted to use unobtrusive measures to study spouse abuse, you could do research at a women's shelter. You could secretly tape conversations among the women, as well as their telephone calls. Or you could use a one-way mirror to observe their interactions, and videotape them. As may be obvious, although such unobtrusive measures might yield rich data, professional ethics would prohibit such a study (Lee 2000).

■ Experiments

A lot of people say that abusers need therapy. But no one knows if therapy really works. Let's suppose that you want to find out. Frankly, no one knows how to change a wife abuser into a loving husband, and knowing if therapy works would certainly be a step in the right direction. To find out, you may want to conduct an **experiment,** for experiments are useful for determining cause and effect. Causation has three necessary conditions, which are discussed in Table 5.3 on the next page.

unobtrusive measures
various ways of observing people who do not know they are being studied

experiment
the use of control groups and experimental groups and dependent and independent variables to test causation

TABLE 5.3 Cause, Effect, and Spurious Correlations

Causation means that a change in one variable is caused by another variable. Three conditions are necessary for causation: correlation, temporal priority, and no spurious correlation. Let's apply each of these conditions to spouse abuse and alcohol abuse.

1. The first necessary condition is **correlation.**

   If two variables exist together, they are said to be correlated. If batterers have drunk alcohol, battering and alcohol abuse are correlated.

   Spouse Abuse   **+**   Alcohol Abuse

   People sometimes assume that correlation is causation. In this instance, they conclude that alcohol abuse causes spouse abuse.

   Alcohol Abuse ——————▶ Spouse Abuse

   But *correlation never proves causation. Either* variable could be the cause of the other. Perhaps battering pushes men into getting drunk.

   Spouse Abuse ——————▶ Alcohol Abuse

2. The second necessary condition is *temporal priority* (one variable must occur before the other).

   Temporal priority means that one thing happens before something else does. For a variable to be a cause (the *independent* variable), it must *precede* that which is changed (the *dependent* variable). If the men had not drunk alcohol until after they beat their wives, obviously alcohol abuse could not be the cause of the spouse abuse. Although the necessity of temporal priority is obvious, in many studies this is not easy to determine.

3. The third necessary condition is *no spurious correlation.* This is the necessary condition that really makes things difficult. Even if we identify correlation and can determine temporal priority, we still don't know that alcohol abuse is the cause. It is possible that we have a *spurious correlation;* that is, the cause may be some underlying third variable that is not easily visible. Some sociologists identify male culture as that underlying third variable.

   Male Culture ——————▶ Spouse Abuse

   Socialized into dominance, some males learn to view women as objects on which to take out their frustration. In fact, this underlying third variable could be a cause of both spouse abuse and alcohol abuse.

But since only some men beat their wives, while all males are exposed to male culture, other variables must also be involved. Perhaps specific subcultures that promote violence and denigrate women lead to both spouse abuse and alcohol abuse.

If so, this does *not* mean that it is the only causal variable, for spouse abuse probably has many causes. Unlike the movement of amoebas or the action of heat on some object, human behavior is infinitely complicated. What is especially important is people's *definitions of the situation,* including their views of right and wrong. To explain spouse abuse, then, we need to add such variables as men's views of violence and their definitions of the relative rights of women and men. It is precisely to help unravel such complicating factors in human behavior that we need the experimental method.

More on Correlations

Correlation simply means that two or more variables are present together. The more often they are found together, the stronger their relationship. To indicate their strength, sociologists use a number called a *correlation coefficient.* If two variables are always related, that is, they are always present together, they have what is called a *perfect positive correlation.* The number 1.0 represents this correlation coefficient. Nature has some 1.0's, such as the lack of water and the death of trees. 1.0's also apply to the human physical state, such as the absence of nutrients and the absence of life. But social life is much more complicated than physical conditions, and there are no 1.0's in human behavior.

Two variables can also have a *perfect negative correlation.* This means that when one variable is present, the other is always absent. The number –1.0 represents this correlation coefficient.

Positive correlations of 0.1, 0.2, and 0.3 mean that one variable is associated with another only 1 time out of 10, 2 times out of 10, and 3 times out of 10. In other words, in most instances the first variable is *not* associated with the second, indicating a weak relationship. The greater the correlation coefficient, the stronger the relationship. A strong relationship *may* indicate causation, but not necessarily. Testing the relationship between variables is the goal of some sociological research.

Let's suppose that a judge likes your idea, and she gives you access to men who have been arrested for spouse abuse. You would randomly divide the men into two groups. (See Figure 5.2 on the next page.) This would help to assure that their individual characteristics (attitudes, number of arrests, severity of crimes, jail time, education, race-ethnicity, age, and so on) are distributed evenly between the groups. You

The Experiment

then would arrange for the men in the **experimental group** to receive some form of therapy. The men in the **control group** would not get therapy.

Your **independent variable,** something that causes a change in another variable, would be therapy. Your **dependent variable,** the variable that may change, would be the men's behavior: whether or not they abuse women after they get out of jail. To make that determination, you would need to rely on a sloppy operational definition: either reports from the wives, or records indicating the men were rearrested for abuse. This is sloppy because some of the women will not report the abuse, and some of the men who abuse their wives will not be rearrested. Yet it may be the best you can do.

Let's assume that you choose rearrest as your operational definition. If you find that the men who received therapy are less likely to be rearrested for abuse, you can attribute the difference to the therapy. If you find no difference in rearrest rates, you can conclude that the therapy was ineffectual. If you find that the men who received the therapy have a *higher* rearrest rate, you can conclude that the therapy backfired.

Ideally, you would test different types of therapy. Perhaps only some work. You might even want to test self-therapy by assigning articles, books, and videos.

As described in the Down-to-Earth Sociology box on the next page, some experiments are not conducted this rigorously. This increases the likelihood that cause and effect will be confused.

■ Deciding Which Method to Use

How do sociologists choose from among these methods? Four primary factors affect their choice. First, *resources* are crucial. Sociologists must match methods with available resources. For example, although they may want to conduct a survey, they may find that finances won't permit it, and instead they turn to the study of documents. The second significant factor is *access to subjects*. If the people who comprise a sample live in remote parts of the country, researchers may have to mail them questionnaires or conduct a telephone survey even if they would prefer face-to-face

experimental group
the group of subjects exposed to the independent variable

control group
the group of subjects not exposed to the independent variable

independent variable
a factor that causes a change in another variable, called the dependent variable

dependent variable
a factor that is changed by an independent variable

down-to-earth
s o c i o l o g y

■ ■ ■ ■ ■

The Hawthorne Experiments

Research from the 1920s, known as the Hawthorne experiments, has become a classic in sociology. This research drives home how necessary it is to accurately identify independent and dependent variables.

The managers of the Hawthorne plant of the Western Electric Company near Chicago wanted to know if different levels of lighting would affect productivity. Several groups of women participated in what are known as the Relay Room Experiments. In the control room, the level of lighting was held constant, while in the experimental room the lighting was varied. To everyone's surprise, output increased in *both* locations. In the experimental room, productivity remained high even when the lights were dimmed to about the level of moonlight—so low that workers could barely see what they were doing!

To solve this mystery, management called in a team of researchers headed by Elton Mayo of the University of Chicago. This team tested thirteen dif-

ferent work conditions. When they changed the workers' pay from hourly wages to piecework (paying them at a set rate for each unit they produce), productivity increased. When they served refreshments, output again went up. When they added two 5-minute rest periods, productivity jumped. When they changed the rest periods to two 10-minute periods, again output increased. When they let the workers go home early, they found the same result. Confused, the researchers restored the original conditions, offering none of these added benefits. The result? Even higher productivity.

The situation grew even more confusing when they observed men workers in what is known as the Bank Wiring Room Study. Here, the researchers didn't change the work conditions at all. They simply observed the men while they worked and interviewed them after work. They expected no change in productivity. What happened was that productivity *dropped*.

None of this made sense. Finally, Mayo concluded that the changes in productivity were due to the research itself. The women, pleased at the attention being paid to them, responded by increasing their efforts. The men, in contrast, were suspicious about why the researchers were observing them. They feared that if they had higher productivity, they would be expected to produce more each day, or that higher productivity might even cost some of them their jobs. Consequently, they decreased their output.

The Hawthorne research is important—not for its findings on worker productivity, but for what it revealed about the research process itself. Today, researchers carefully monitor the *Hawthorne effect,* the change in behavior that occurs when people know they are being studied.

Sources: Based on Roethlisberger and Dickson 1939; Mayo 1966; Baron and Greenberg 1990.

■ ■ ■ ■ ■

---

interviews. The third factor concerns the *purpose of the research,* the questions that the sociologist wishes to investigate and answer. Each method is better for answering some questions than for others. Participant observation, for example, is good for uncovering people's attitudes, while experiments work better for resolving questions of cause and effect. Fourth, *the researcher's background or training* comes into play. In graduate school, sociologists study many methods, but they are able to practice only some of them. Consequently, after graduate school they generally use the methods in which they have had the most training.

Thus, sociologists who have been trained in **quantitative research methods,** which emphasize measurement, numbers, and statistics, are likely to use surveys. Sociologists who have been trained in **qualitative research methods,** which emphasize describing, observing, and interpreting people's behavior, lean toward participant observation. In the Down-to-Earth Sociology box on the next page, you can see how applied sociologists use a combination of quantitative and qualitative methods.

Sociologists sometimes find themselves in the hot seat because of their research. Some poke into private areas of life, which upsets people. Others investigate public matters, but their findings threaten those who have a personal stake in the situation. From the homeless research discussed in the following Thinking Critically section, you can see how significant the choice of research method is, and how using rigorous research methods can land sociologists in the midst of controversy.

quantitative research methods
research in which the emphasis is placed on precise measurement, the use of statistics and numbers

qualitative research methods
research in which the emphasis is placed on observing, describing, and interpreting people's behavior

■ ■ ■ ■ ■

Applied Sociology: Marketing Research as a Blend of Quantitative and Qualitative Methods

If a company is going to survive in the highly competitive business world, it must figure out what consumers need and want, and then supply it—or else convince people that what they need or want is what the company is already producing.

What Marketing Research Is

To increase sales, manufacturers try to improve the "position" of their products. "Position" is marketing jargon for how customers think about a product.

This is where marketing researchers come into play. They find out what customers want, how they select products, how they use them, and what images they hold of a product or service. They also assess how the public will react to a new product or to a change in an established product.

Marketing researchers use both qualitative and quantitative methods. An example of a qualitative method is focus groups. Groups of about ten people are invited to discuss a product. A moderator leads a discussion while other team members observe or videotape the session from behind a one-way mirror. To control for regional variations, the re-searchers may hold other focus groups at the same time in other cities. Sociologist Roger Straus points out that his training in symbolic interactionism has been especially useful for interpreting these results.

Marketing researchers also use quantitative techniques. For example, they may conduct surveys to determine what the public thinks of a new product. They also gather sales data from the "bar codes" found on products. They use statistics to analyze the data, and they prepare tables and graphics to summarize the findings for clients.

A Sociological Controversy

Marketing research occupies a controversial position in sociology. Most of the results of marketing research are proprietary (owned by the client) and are therefore confidential. This means that the findings do not appear in sociology journals and are not used to create social theory. In addition, clients are usually interested only in specific marketing problems, and they seldom commission research on important social issues. For such reasons, many sociologists do not consider marketing research a "legiti-mate" sociological activity. Some even scorn marketing researchers as wasting their sociological talents. They chide them for having "sold out," for using sociological methods to help corporations exploit the public by convincing them to purchase unneeded goods and services.

Marketing researchers, of course, do not see things this way. They argue that marketing research is a neutral activity, that there is no reason to be against it on principle. They add that they do more than just help sell beer and soft drinks. They point out that they have helped colleges attract students and communities assess public needs. They argue that the decision to do research on any topic involves the researcher's own values. This applies to studying how to reduce juvenile delinquency as well as investigating how to sell a particular product. It is unreasonable, they say, for anyone to pass judgment on marketing research—as though other research were morally superior.

Sources: Based on Straus 1991 and communication with Straus 1993.

■ ■ ■ ■ ■

t h i n k i n g
C R I T I C A L L Y

Doing Controversial Research— Counting the Homeless

What could be less offensive than counting the homeless? As sometimes occurs, however, even basic research lands sociologists in the midst of controversy. This is what happened to sociologist Peter Rossi and his associates.

There was a dispute between advocates for the homeless and the federal government. The advocates claimed that 3 to 7 million Americans were homeless; the government claimed that only a quarter of a million people were homeless, just one-twelfth to one-twenty-eighth the number claimed by the advocates. Each side accused the other of gross distortion—the one to place undue pressure on Congress, the other to keep the public from knowing how bad the situation really was.

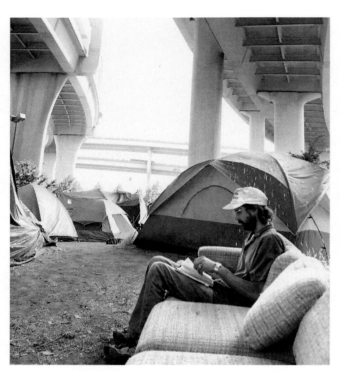

■ As discussed on this page, research sometimes lands sociologists in the midst of controversy. An example is a study conducted to determine how many homeless people there are in the United States. Homeless advocates were not pleased with the results. Shown here is a homeless man in "Dignity Village," an area under a freeway that Portland, Oregon, authorities designated for the homeless.

Only an accurate count could clear up the picture, for both sides were only guessing at the numbers. Peter Rossi and the National Opinion Research Center decided to make an accurate count. They had no vested interest in supporting one side or the other, only in answering this question honestly.

The challenge was immense. The *population* was evident—the U.S. homeless. A *survey* would be appropriate, but how do you survey a *sample* of the homeless? No federal, state, county, or city has a list of the homeless, and only some of the homeless stay at shelters. As for *validity,* to make certain that they were counting only people who were really homeless the researchers needed a good *operational definition* of homelessness. To include people who weren't really homeless would destroy the study's *reliability.* The researchers wanted results that would be consistent if others were to *replicate,* or repeat, the study.

As an operational definition, the researchers used "literally homeless," people "who do not have access to a conventional dwelling and who would be homeless by any conceivable definition of the term." Because a national count would cost about $6 million, far beyond their resources, the researchers decided to count just the homeless in Chicago. By using a *stratified random sample,* they were able to *generalize* to the entire city. The cost was still high, however—about $600,000.

To be able to generalize about the homeless who sleep in shelters, the researchers used a stratified random sample of the city's shelters. For the homeless who sleep in the streets, vacant buildings, and so forth, they used a stratified random sample of the city's blocks. To make doubly certain that their count was accurate, the researchers conducted two surveys. At night, trained teams visited the shelters and searched the alleys, bridges, and vacant houses.

Many found the results startling. On an average night, Chicago has 2,722 homeless people. Because people move in and out of homelessness, between 5,000 and 7,000 are homeless at some point during the year. On warm nights, only two out of five sleep in the shelters, and even in winter only three out of four do so. The median age is 40; 75 percent are men, and 60 percent are African Americans. One in four is a former mental patient, one in five a former prisoner. A homeless person's income from all sources is less than $6 a day. Projecting these findings to the United States results in a national total of about 350,000 homeless people, a figure that is much closer to the government's estimate of 250,000 than it is to the advocates' estimate of 7 to 8 million.

The reactions were predictable. Government officials rubbed their hands in glee. The stunned homeless advocates denied the findings and began a sniping campaign at the researchers.

Remember that Rossi and his associates had no interest in proving which side in the debate was right, only in getting reliable figures. Using impeccable methods, this they did.

The researchers had no intention of minimizing the problem of homelessness. They stressed that 350,000 Americans are so poor that they sleep in city streets, live in shelters, eat out of garbage cans, and suffer from severe health problems. In short, these people live hopeless, desperate lives.

It is good to *know* how many Americans are homeless. Guesses aren't worth much. Even though the number is far less than what the homeless advocates had estimated, this information can still serve their cause: Because there are fewer homeless people than many had thought, it makes the problem more manageable. It means that if we choose to do so, we can put our resources to work with greater certainty of success.

Those whose positions are not supported by research, however, are never pleased, and they tend to take potshots at the researchers. This is one of the risks of doing sociological research, for sociologists never know whose toes they will step on.

Sources: Based on Anderson 1986; Rossi et al. 1986; Rossi et al. 1987; Coughlin 1988; Rossi 1989; Rossi 1991; De Parle 1994; Rossi 1999.

Gender in Sociological Research

As you know, gender is significant in social life. It affects our orientations, our attitudes, and, especially, what happens to us in life. Gender can also be a significant factor in social research, and researchers take steps to prevent gender from biasing their findings. For example, sociologists Diana Scully and Joseph Marolla (1984, 1985) interviewed convicted rapists in prison. They were concerned that their gender might lead to *interviewer bias*—that the prisoners might shift their answers, sharing certain experiences or expressing certain attitudes to Marolla, but saying something else to Scully. To prevent gender bias, each interviewed half the sample. Later in this chapter, we'll look at what they found out.

Gender certainly can be a major impediment in research. In our imagined research on spouse abuse, for example, could a man even do participant observation of women who have been beaten by their husbands? Technically, the answer is yes. But because the women have been victimized by men, they might be less likely to share their experiences and feelings with men. If so, women would be better suited to conduct this research, more likely to achieve valid results. The supposition that these victims are more likely to share their experiences with women than with men, however, is just that—a supposition. Research alone will verify or refute this assumption.

Gender is significant in other ways, too. As sociologists Chloe Bird and Patricia Rieker (1997) point out, it is a mistake to assume that what applies to one sex applies to the other. Women's and men's lives differ significantly, and if we do research on just half of humanity, our research will be vastly incomplete. With today's huge numbers of women sociologists, there is little risk of ignoring women in contemporary research. In the past, however, when almost all sociologists were men, women's lives were neglected.

Gender pops up in unexpected ways in sociological research. I vividly recall an incident in San Francisco. The streets were getting dark, and I was still looking for homeless people. When I saw someone lying down, huddled in a doorway, I approached the individual. As I got close, I began my opening research line, "Hi, I'm Dr. Henslin from. . . ." The individual began to scream and started to thrash wildly. Startled by this sudden, high-pitched scream and by the rapid movements, I quickly backed away. When I later analyzed what had happened, I concluded that I had intruded into a woman's bedroom.

Of course, one can draw another lesson from this incident. Researchers do their best, but they make mistakes. Sometimes these are minor, and even humorous. The woman sleeping in the doorway wasn't frightened. It was only just getting dark, and there were many people on the street. She was just assertively marking her territory and letting me know in no uncertain terms that I was an intruder. If we make a mistake in research, we pick up and go on. As we do so, we take ethical considerations into account, which is the topic of our next section.

Ethics in Sociologal Research

In addition to choosing an appropriate research method, we must also follow the ethics of sociology, which center on assumptions of science and morality (American Sociological Association 1997). Research ethics require openness (sharing findings with the scientific community), honesty, and truth. Ethics clearly forbid the falsification of results. They also condemn plagiarism—that is, stealing someone else's work. Another ethical guideline is that research subjects should not be harmed by the research. Ethics also require that sociologists protect the anonymity of people who provide information. Sometimes they reveal things that are intimate, potentially embarrassing, or otherwise harmful to themselves. Finally, although not all sociologists agree, it generally is considered unethical for researchers to misrepresent themselves.

Sociologists take these ethical standards seriously. To illustrate the extent to which they will go to protect their respondents, consider the research conducted by Mario Brajuha.

■ Protecting the Subjects: The Brajuha Research

Mario Brajuha, a graduate student at the State University of New York at Stony Brook, was doing participant observation of restaurant work. He lost his job as a waiter when the restaurant where he was working burned down—due to a fire of "suspicious origin," as the police said. When detectives learned that Brajuha had

■ Ethics in social research are of vital concern to sociologists. As discussed in the text sociologists may disagree on some of the issue's finer points, but none would approve of slipping LSD to unsuspecting subjects like these marines at Camp Pendleton, South Carolina. This was done to U.S. servicemen in the 1960s under the guise of legitimate testing—just "to see what would happen."

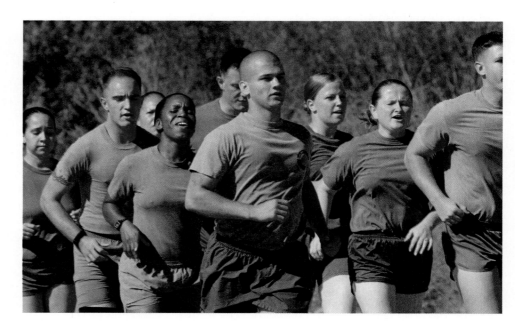

taken field notes (Brajuha and Hallowell 1986), they asked to see them. Because he had promised to keep the information confidential, Brajuha refused. The district attorney then subpoenaed the notes. Brajuha still refused to hand them over. The district attorney threatened to put Brajuha in jail. By this time, Brajuha's notes had become rather famous, and unsavory characters—perhaps those who had set the fire—also wanted to know what was in them. They accompanied their demands with threats of a different nature. Brajuha found himself between a rock and a hard place.

For two years Brajuha refused to hand over his notes, even though he grew anxious and had to appear at several court hearings. Finally, the district attorney dropped the subpoena. When the two men under investigation for setting the fire died, so did the threats to Brajuha, his wife, and their children.

■ Misleading the Subjects: The Humphreys Research

Sociologists agree on the necessity to protect respondents, and they applaud the professional manner in which Brajuha handled himself. Although there is less agreement that researchers should not misrepresent themselves, sociologists who violate this norm can become embroiled in ethical controversy. Let's look at the case of Laud Humphreys, whose research forced sociologists to rethink and refine their ethical stance.

Laud Humphreys, a classmate of mine at Washington University in St. Louis, was an Episcopal priest who decided to become a sociologist. For his Ph.D. dissertation, Humphreys (1970, 1971, 1975) studied social interaction in "tearooms," public restrooms where some men go for quick, anonymous oral sex with other men.

Humphreys found that some restrooms in Forest Park, just across from our campus, were tearooms. He began a participant observation study by hanging around these restrooms. He found that in addition to the two men having sex, a third man—called a "watchqueen"—served as a lookout for police and other unwelcome strangers. Humphreys took on the role of watchqueen, not only watching for strangers but also observing and systematically recording what the men did.

Humphreys decided he wanted to know more about the regular lives of these men. For example, what was the significance of the wedding rings that many of the men wore? He hit on an ingenious technique. Many of the men parked their cars near the tearooms, and Humphreys recorded their license numbers. A friend in the St. Louis police department gave Humphreys each man's address. About a year later, Humphreys arranged for these men to be included in a medical survey conducted by some of the sociologists on our faculty.

Disguising himself with a different hairstyle and clothing, and driving a different car, Humphreys visited their homes. He interviewed the men, supposedly for the medical study. He found that they led conventional lives. They voted, mowed their lawns, and took their kids to Little League games. Many reported that their wives were not aroused sexually or were afraid of getting pregnant because their religion did not allow them to use birth control. Humphreys concluded that heterosexual men were also using the tearooms for a form of quick sex.

This study stirred controversy among sociologists and nonsociologists alike. Humphreys was criticized by many sociologists, and a national columnist even wrote a scathing denunciation of "sociological snoopers" (Von Hoffman 1970). As the controversy grew more heated and a court case loomed, Humphreys feared that his list of respondents might be subpoenaed. He gave me the list to take from Missouri to Illinois, where I had begun teaching. When he called and asked me to destroy it, I burned it in my backyard.

Was this research ethical? This question is not decided easily. Although many sociologists sided with Humphreys—and his book reporting the research won a highly acclaimed award—the criticisms mounted. At first, Humphreys vigorously defended his position, but five years later, in a second edition of his book (1975), he stated that he should have identified himself as a researcher.

How Research and Theory Work Together

Research cannot stand alone. Nor can theory. As sociologist C. Wright Mills (1959) so forcefully argued, research without theory is simply a collection of unrelated "facts." Mills added that theory without research is abstract and empty—it can't represent the way life really is.

Research and theory, then, are both essential for sociology. Every theory must be tested, which requires research. And as sociologists do research, they often come up with surprising findings. Those findings must be explained, and for that we need theory. As sociologists study social life, then, they combine research and theory.

■ The Real World:
When the Ideal Meets the Real

Although we can list the ideals of research, real-life situations often force sociologists to settle for something that falls short of the ideal. Let's look at how two sociologists confronted the ideal and the real in the following Thinking Critically section.

thinking
CRITICALLY

Are Rapists Sick? A Close-Up View of Research

Two sociologists, Diana Scully and Joseph Marolla, were not satisfied with the typical explanation that rapists are "sick," psychologically disturbed, or different from other men. They developed the hypothesis that rape is like most human behavior—it is learned through interaction with others. That is, some men learn to think of rape as appropriate behavior.

To test this hypothesis, it would be best to interview a random sample of rapists. But this is impossible. There is no list of all rapists, so there is no way to give them all the same chance of being included in a sample. You can't even use prison populations to select a random sample, for many rapists have never been caught, some who were caught were found not guilty, and some who were found guilty were given probation. Some, too, who were convicted of rape are innocent. Consequently, Scully and Marolla confronted the classic dilemma of sociologists—either to not do the study or to do it under less than ideal conditions.

They chose to do the study. When they had the opportunity to interview convicted rapists in prison, they jumped at it. They knew that whatever they learned would be more than we already knew. They sent out 3,500 letters to men serving time in seven prisons in Virginia, the state where they were teaching. About 25 percent of the prisoners agreed to be interviewed. They matched these men on the basis of age, education, race, severity of offense, and previous criminal record. This resulted in a sample of 98 prisoners who were convicted of rape and a control sample of 75 men convicted of other offenses.

As noted earlier, the sex of the interviewer can bias research results. To avoid gender bias, Scully and Marolla each interviewed half the sample. It took them 600 hours to gather information on the prisoners, including their psychological, criminal, and sexual history. To guard against lies, they checked what the individuals said against their institutional records. They used twelve scales to measure the men's attitudes about women, rape, and themselves. They also presented nine vignettes of forced sexual encounters to measure the circumstances under which the men defined a situation as rape or viewed the victim as responsible for the rape.

Scully and Marolla discovered something that goes against common sense— that most rapists are not sick, that they are not overwhelmed by uncontrollable urges. The psychological histories of the rapists and the nonrapists were similar. Rapists, they concluded, are emotionally average men who have learned to view rape as appropriate in certain situations. Some rape spontaneously, while others plan their rapes. For some, rape is a form of recreation, and they rape with friends on a regular basis, such as on weekends. Others use rape as a form of revenge, to get even with someone, not necessarily the woman.

Scully and Marolla also found support for what feminists had been pointing out for years, that power was a major element in rape. Here is what one man said:

> Rape gave me the power to do what I wanted to do without feeling I had to please a partner or respond to a partner. I felt in control, dominant. Rape was the ability to have sex without caring about the woman's response. I was totally dominant.

To discover that most rape is calculated behavior—that rapists are not "sick"; that the motivating force is power, not passion; that the behavior stems from the criminal pursuit of pleasure, not from mental illness—is significant. It makes the sociological quest worthwhile.

In comparing their sample of rapists with their control group of nonrapists, Scully and Marolla also found something else significant. The rapists are more likely to believe "rape myths." They are more likely to believe that women cause their own rape by the way they act and the clothes they wear, that a woman who charges rape has simply changed her mind after participating in consensual sex, and that most men accused of rape are innocent.

Connecting Research and Theory

Such findings go far beyond simply adding to our storehouse of "facts." As indicated in Figure 5.1 on page 131, research stimulates both the development of theory and the need for more research. Scully and Marolla suggest that rape myths act as neutralizers, that they allow "potential rapists to turn off social prohibitions against injuring others."

This hypothesis, in turn, pinpoints the need to determine how such myths are transmitted. Which male subcultures perpetuate them? Do the mass media contribute to these myths? Do family, religion, and education create respect for females and help keep males from learning such myths? Or do they somehow contribute to these myths? If so, how?

At some point sociologists will build on this path-breaking research, which was done, as usual, under less than ideal conditions. The resulting theorizing and research may provide the basis for making changes that reduce rape in U.S. society.

Sources: Scully and Marolla 1984, 1985; Marolla and Scully 1986; Scully 1990; Foley et al. 1995.

This is exactly what sociology needs more of—imaginative and sometimes daring research conducted in an imperfect world under less than ideal conditions. This is really what sociology is all about. Sociologists study what people do—whether their behaviors are conforming or deviant, whether they please others or disgust them and arouse intense anger. No matter the behavior that is studied, systematic research methods and the application of social theory take us beyond common sense. They allow us to penetrate surface realities so we can better understand human behavior—and, in the ideal case, make changes to help improve social life.

■ □ ■ ▪
Summary and Review

What Is a Valid Sociological Topic?

Any human behavior is a valid sociological topic, even disreputable behavior. Spouse abuse is an example. Sociological research is based on the sociologist's interests, access to subjects, appropriate methods, and ethical considerations. P. 130.

Common Sense and the Need for Sociological Research

■ **Why isn't common sense adequate?**
Common sense doesn't provide reliable knowledge. When subjected to scientific research, commonsense ideas often are found to be very limited or false. P. 130.

A Research Model

■ **What are the eight basic steps of scientific research?**
1. Selecting a topic, 2. Defining the problem, 3. Reviewing the literature, 4. Formulating a hypothesis, 5. Choosing a research method, 6. Collecting the data, 7. Analyzing the results, 8. Sharing the results. These steps are explained in detail on pp. 131–134.

Research Methods

■ **How do sociologists gather data?**
To gather data, sociologists use six research methods (or research designs): surveys, participant observation, secondary analysis, documents, unobtrusive measures, and experiments. Pp. 135–143.

■ **How do sociologists choose a research method?**
Sociologists choose their research method based on questions to be answered, their access to potential subjects, the resources available, their training, and ethical considerations. Pp. 143–147.

Gender in Sociological Research

■ **What is the relationship between gender and research?**
There are two aspects. First, sociologists used to study men and assume that their findings applied equally to women. As more women became sociologists, this changed. Second, in some kinds of research, such as studying rapists in prison, the gender of the researcher could affect findings. Pp. 147–148.

Ethics in Sociological Research

■ **How important are ethics in sociological research?**
Ethics are of fundamental concern to sociologists, who are committed to openness, honesty, truth, and protecting their subjects from harm. The Brajuha research on restaurants and the Humphreys research on "tearooms" were cited to illustrate ethical issues of concern to sociologists. Pp. 148–149.

How Research and Theory Work Together

■ **What is the relationship between theory and research?**
Theory and research depend on one another. Sociologists use theory to interpret the data they gather. Theory also generates questions that need to be answered by research. Research, in turn, helps to generate theory: When findings don't match what is expected, this indicates the need for new thinking. Pp. 150–151.

■ *Where can I read more on this topic?*
Suggested readings for this chapter are listed at the back of this book.

Additional Online Resources for This Chapter
www.ablongman.com/henslin6e

- *Content Select* Research Database for Sociology, with suggested key terms and annotated references
- Link to 2000 Census, with activities
- Flashcards of key terms and concepts

- Practice Tests
- Weblinks
- Interactive Maps

using . . .

ContentSelect

Research Database for Sociology

sociology and research	controversial research	research bias	research methods
sociology and experiments	ethics and research	gender and research	data analysis

Bernard Bonhomme, *Group of People*, 1999

6

Societies to Social Networks

Social Groups and Societies

The Transformation of Societies

Hunting and Gathering Societies

Pastoral and Horticultural Societies

Agricultural Societies

Industrial Societies

Postindustrial (Information) Societies

Bioeconomic Societies: An Emerging New Type of Society?

Groups Within Society

Primary Groups

Secondary Groups

In-Groups and Out-Groups

Reference Groups

Social Networks

A New Group: Electronic Communities

Group Dynamics

Effects of Group Size on Stability and Intimacy

Effects of Group Size on Attitudes and Behavior

Leadership

The Power of Peer Pressure: The Asch Experiment

Global Consequences of Group Dynamics

Summary and Review

The initiation of Cody Scott into the L. A. Crips had two parts. Here's the first:

> "How old is you now anyway?"
> "Eleven, but I'll be twelve in November."
> I never saw the blow to my head come from Huck. Bam! And I was on all fours . . . Kicked in the stomach, I was on my back counting stars in the blackness. Grabbed by the collar, I was made to stand again. A solid blow to my chest exploded pain on the blank screen that had now become my mind. Bam! Another, then another. Blows rained on me from every direction . . .
> Up until this point not a word had been spoken. . . . Then I just started swinging, with no style or finesse, just anger and the instinct to survive. . . . (This) reflected my ability to represent the set [gang] in hand-to-hand combat. The blows stopped abruptly . . . My ear was bleeding, and my neck and face were deep red . . .

> *It's bein' down when ain't nobody else down with you. It's gettin' caught and not tellin'. Killin' and not caring, and dyin' without fear.*

Scott's beating was followed immediately by the second part of his initiation:

> "Give Cody the pump" [12-gauge pump action shotgun] . . . Tray Ball spoke with the calm of a football coach. "Tonight we gonna rock they world." . . . Hand slaps were passed around the room . . . "Cody, you got eight shots, you don't come back to the car unless they all are gone."
> "Righteous," I said, eager to show my worth. . . .

Hanging close to buildings, houses, and bushes, we made our way, one after the other, to within spitting distance of the Bloods. . . . Huck and Fly stepped from the shadows simultaneously and were never noticed until it was too late. Boom! Boom! Heavy bodies hitting the ground, confusion, yells of dismay, running, . . . By my sixth shot I had advanced past the first fallen bodies and into the street in pursuit of those who had sought refuge behind cars and trees. . . .

A Blood . . . tried to make one last dash . . . to, I think, a porch. I remember raising my weapon and . . . I pulled the trigger and laid him down. . . .

Back in the shack we smoked more pot and drank more beer. I was the center of attention for my acts of aggression. . . .

Tray Ball said. "You got potential, 'cause you eager to learn. Bangin' [being a gang member] ain't no part-time thang, it's full-time, it's a career. It's bein' down when ain't nobody else down with you. It's gettin' caught and not tellin'. Killin' and not caring, and dyin' without fear. It's love for your set and hate for the enemy. You hear what I'm sayin?"

. . . [F]rom that point on Tray Ball became my mentor, friend, confidant, and closest comrade. He allowed me acts of aggression that made my name [Monster] soar with alarming effects. . . . As Monster, however, I had to consistently be more vicious and live up to the name.

Cody adds this insightful remark:

Though never verbally stated, death was looked upon as a sort of reward, a badge of honor, especially if one died in some heroic capacity for the hood . . . The supreme sacrifice was to "take a bullet for a homie [fellow gang member]." The set functioned as a religion. Nothing held a light to the power of the set. If you died on the trigger you surely were smiled upon by the Crip God.

Excerpts from Scott 1993:8–13, 103.

Social Groups and Societies

Groups are the essence of life in society. We become who we are because of our membership in human groups. As we saw in Chapter 3, even our minds are a product of society, or, more accurately phrased, of the groups to which we belong.

In this chapter, we'll consider how groups influence our lives—and even the power that groups wield over us. Although none of us wants to think that we could participate in killings such as those recounted in our opening vignette, don't bet on it. You are going to read some surprising things about groups in this chapter.

Sociologists define *group* in many ways (Carron and Brawley 2000). Albion Small (1905), who was mentioned in Chapter 1 as an early North American sociologist, used this term in a broad sense to mean people who are thought of as belonging together. Sociologists Michael Olmsted and Paul Hare (1978) said that the

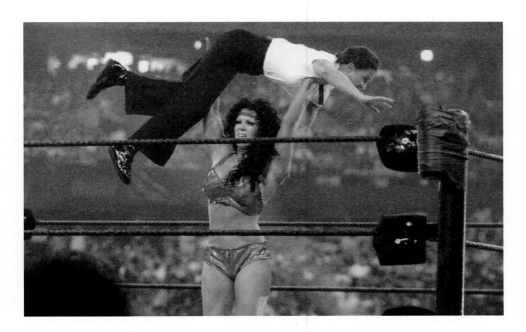

■ As society—the largest and most complex type of group—changes, so, too, do the groups, activities, and, ultimately, the type of people who form that society. This photo taken at Wrestling Mania in Houston, Texas, captures some of the changes that U.S. society has been undergoing in recent years. What social changes can you identify from this photo?

"essential feature of a **group** is that its members have something in common and that they believe what they have in common makes a difference." This will be our definition of *group*.

The largest and most complex group that sociologists study is **society,** which consists of people who share a culture and a territory. The characteristics of a society profoundly affect the groups within it. For example, the former Soviet Union used to have underground artists. They found the Soviet state stifling, and they painted pictures that showed the difficulties of Soviet life. Because the Communist government had set up an extensive spy network, these artists never could be sure that their friends weren't government spies. As a consequence, underground artists were suspicious of one another.

The collapse of the Communist government put out the spark that had given life to these groups, and most members went on to other types of art. Artists who focus on problematic features of Soviet life today—especially the insecurities brought about by the new capitalism—no longer meet furtively in groups or are suspicious of one another. Thousands of other groups in the former Soviet Union have also had to adapt to the new conditions of their society. The sociological principle is this: *As a society changes, so do the nature and types of its groups.*

■ ▪ ▪ ▪ ▪

The Transformation of Societies

To better understand groups, let's first look at the big picture. How did our society—this largest of groups that surrounds us and sets the stage for our life experiences—develop? It certainly did not spring full-blown onto the human scene. As we review its evolution, portrayed in Figure 6.1 on the next page, note how the key is technology. As we summarize these sweeping changes, picture yourself as a member of each society. Consider how your life would be different in each society—how even your thoughts and values would be different.

group
people who have something in common and who believe that what they have in common is significant; also called a social group

society
people who share a culture and a territory

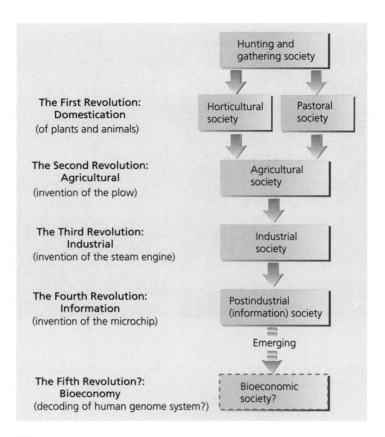

Figure 6.1

The Social Transformations of Society

■ Hunting and Gathering Societies

Societies with the fewest social divisions are called **hunting and gathering societies.** As the name implies, these groups depend on hunting and gathering for their survival. In some, the men do the hunting (of animals), and the women the gathering (of plants). In others, both men and women (and children) gather plants, the men hunt the large animals, and both men and women hunt small animals. Beyond this basic division of labor by sex, there are few social divisions. The groups usually have a **shaman,** an individual thought to be able to influence spiritual forces, but shamans, too, must help obtain food. Although these groups give greater prestige to the men hunters, the women gatherers contribute more food to the group, perhaps even four-fifths of their total food supply (Bernard 1992).

In addition to gender, the major unit of organization is the family. Most group members are related by ancestry or marriage. Because the family is the only distinct social institution in these societies, it fulfills functions that are divided among modern society's many specialized institutions. The family distributes food to its members, educates its children (especially in food skills), nurses its sick, and so on.

Because an area cannot support a large number of people who hunt animals and gather plants (they do not plant—they only gather what is already there), hunting and gathering societies are small. They usually consist of only twenty-five to forty people. These groups are nomadic, moving from one place to another as the food supply of an area gives out. They place a high value on sharing food, which is essential to their survival. Because of disease, drought, and pestilence, children have only

hunting and gathering society
a human group dependent on hunting and gathering for its survival

shaman
a priest (or intermediary with the spirit world) in a tribal society

about a fifty-fifty chance of surviving childhood (Lenski and Lenski 1987).

Of all societies, hunters and gatherers are the most egalitarian. Because what they hunt and gather is perishable and they have no money, the people accumulate few personal possessions. Consequently, no one becomes wealthier than anyone else. There are no rulers, and most decisions are arrived at through discussion. Because their needs are basic and they do not work to store up material possessions, hunters and gatherers have the most leisure of all human groups (Sahlins 1972; Lorber 1994; Volti 1995).

All human groups were once hunters and gatherers, and until several hundred years ago such societies were common. Their demise came when other groups took over the areas on which they depended for their food. Today, only a few remain, such as the pygmies of central Africa, the San of the Namibian desert, and the aborigines of Australia. These groups seem doomed to a similar fate, and it is likely that their way of life will soon disappear from the human scene (Lenski and Lenski 1987).

■ *The simplest forms of societies are called* hunting and gathering societies. *Members of these societies have adapted well to their environments. They are the most egalitarian and have the most leisure of any type of society. The man shown here is a member of a hunting and gathering society in the Brazilian Amazon.*

■ Pastoral and Horticultural Societies

About ten thousand years ago, some groups found that they could tame and breed some of the animals they hunted—primarily goats, sheep, cattle, and camels. Others discovered that they could cultivate plants. As a result, hunting and gathering societies branched into two directions.

The key to understanding the first branching is the word *pasture;* **pastoral societies** are based on the *pasturing of animals.* Pastoral societies developed in arid regions, where lack of rainfall made it impractical to build life around crops. Groups that took this turn remained nomadic, for they followed their animals to fresh pasture. The key to understanding the second branching is the word *horticulture,* or plant cultivation. **Horticultural societies** are based on the *cultivation of plants by the use of hand tools.* Because they no longer had to abandon an area as the food supply gave out, these groups developed permanent settlements.

We can call the domestication of animals and plants the *first social revolution.* As shown in Figure 6.1, it transformed human society. Although the **domestication revolution** was gradual, occurring over thousands of years, it represented a fundamental break with the past and changed human history.

Horticulture may have begun independently in several areas of the globe, including the fertile areas of the Middle East and in Central and South America. Primitive agricultural technology—which consisted of hoes and digging sticks (used to punch holes in the ground for seeds)—may also have spread through *cultural diffusion* (the dispersion of items from one culture to another).

The sociological significance of animal husbandry and plant cultivation is that they *transformed human society.* By creating a more dependable food supply, they ushered in changes that touched almost every aspect of human life. Groups became larger because the more dependable food supply supported more people. With more food than was necessary for survival, no longer did everyone have to produce food. This allowed groups to develop a division of labor, and some people began to work "full time" at making jewelry, tools, weapons, and so on. This led to a surplus of objects, which, in turn, stimulated trade. With trading, groups began to accumulate objects they prized, such as gold, jewelry, and utensils.

pastoral society
a society based on the pasturing of animals

horticultural society
a society based on cultivating plants by the use of hand tools

domestication revolution
the first social revolution, based on the domestication of plants and animals, which led to pastoral and horticultural societies

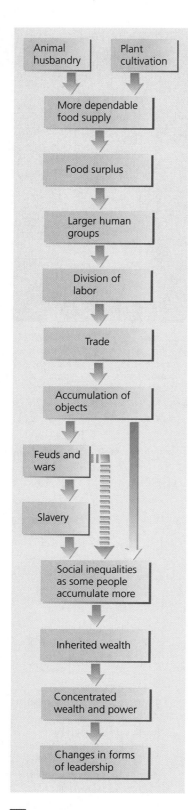

Figure 6.2

Fundamental Consequences
of Animal Husbandry and
Plant Cultivation

As Figure 6.2 illustrates, these changes set the stage for *social inequality.* Some families (or clans) acquired more goods than others. This led to feuds and war, for groups now possessed animals, pastures, croplands, jewelry, and other material goods to fight about. War, in turn, opened the door to slavery, for people found it convenient to let their captives do their drudge work. Social stratification remained limited, however, for the surplus itself was limited. As individuals passed on their possessions to their descendants, wealth grew more concentrated. So did power. At some point during this period, some individuals became chiefs, leaders of groups.

Note the primary pattern that runs through this transformation of group life: the change *from fewer to more possessions and from greater to lesser equality.* Where people were located *within* a society became vital for determining what happened to them in life. Again, Figure 6.2 summarizes how these changes led to social inequality.

■ Agricultural Societies

When the plow was invented about five or six thousand years ago, social life was once again changed forever. Compared with hoes and digging sticks, the use of animals to pull plows was immensely efficient. As the earth was plowed, more nutrients were returned to the soil, making the land more productive. The food surplus of the **agricultural revolution** was unlike anything ever seen in human history. It allowed even more people to engage in activities other than farming. In this new **agricultural society**, people developed cities and the things popularly known as "culture," such as philosophy, art, literature, and architecture. Accompanied by the inventions of the wheel, writing, and numbers, the changes were so profound that this period is sometimes referred to as "the dawn of civilization."

The tendency toward social inequality of previous societies was only a forerunner of what was to come. Inequality became a fundamental feature of life in society. Some people managed to gain control of the growing surplus resources. To protect their expanding privileges and power, this elite surrounded itself with armed men. They even levied taxes on others, who now had become their "subjects." As conflict theorists point out, this concentration of resources and power—along with the oppression of people not in power—was the forerunner of the state.

No one knows exactly how it happened, but during this period females also became subject to males. Sociologist Elise Boulding (1976) theorizes that this change occurred because men were in charge of plowing and the cows. She suggests that when metals were developed, men took on the new job of attaching the metal as tips to the wooden plows and doing the plowing. As a result,

> the shift of the status of the woman farmer may have happened quite rapidly, once there were two male specializations relating to agriculture: plowing and the care of cattle. This situation left women with all the subsidiary tasks, including weeding and carrying water to the fields. The new fields were larger, so women had to work just as many hours as they did before, but now they worked at more secondary tasks. . . . This would contribute further to the erosion of the status of women.

This explanation, however, creates more questions than it answers. Why, for example, did men take over metal work and plowing? Why didn't women? It also does not account for why men control societies in which women are in charge of the cattle. In short, we are left in the dark as to why and how men became dominant, a reason likely to remain lost in human history.

■ Industrial Societies

In the 1700s, another invention turned society upside down. The **Industrial Revolution** began in 1765 when the steam engine was first used to run machinery in Great Britain. Before this, people used a few machines (such as wind and water mills) to harness nature, but most machines depended on human and animal power. The resulting **industrial society** is defined by sociologist Herbert Blumer (1990) as a society in which goods are produced by machines powered by fuels, instead of by the brute force of humans or animals.

With the steam engine, social inequality took another leap. This new technology was far more efficient than anything before it. Just as its surplus was greater, so were its effects on social life. Those who first used the steam engine accumulated such wealth that in many instances their riches outran the imagination of royalty. Gaining an early position in the markets, they were able not only to control the means of production (factories, machinery, tools), but also to dictate people's working conditions. The breakdown of feudal society helped them to control the workers. Masses of people were thrown off the lands that they and their ancestors had farmed as tenants for centuries. Having become homeless, these landless peasants moved to the cities. There they faced the choice of stealing, starving, or working for starvation wages (Chambliss 1964; Michalowski 1985).

Workers had no legal right to safe working conditions, nor the right to unionize. Employment was a private contract between the employer and the individual worker. If workers banded together to protest or to ask for higher wages, they were fired. If they returned to the factory, they were arrested for trespassing on private property. Strikes were illegal, and strikers were savagely beaten by the employer's private security force. On some occasions during the early 1900s, U.S. strikers were shot by private police, and even by the National Guard.

Against these odds, workers gradually won their fight for better working conditions. Wealth then spread to larger segments of society. Eventually, home ownership became common, as did the ownership of automobiles and an incredible variety of consumer goods. Today's typical worker in advanced industrial societies enjoys a high standard of living in terms of material conditions, health care, longevity, and access to libraries and education. Such gains go far beyond what early social reformers could have imagined.

As industrialization progressed, it reversed the pattern set earlier, and equality increased. Indicators of greater equality include better housing and a vast increase in consumer goods, the abolition of slavery, the shift from monarchies to more representative political systems, the right to be tried by a jury of one's peers and to cross-examine witnesses, the right to vote, the right to travel, and greater rights for women and minorities.

It is difficult to overstate the sociological principle that the type of society we live in is the fundamental reason for why we become who we are. To see how industrial society affects your life, note that you would not be taking this course if it were not for industrialization. Clearly you would not have a computer, car, telephone, DVD player, television, or your type of clothing or home. You wouldn't even have electric lights. And on a much deeper level, you would not feel the same about life, or have your particular aspirations for the future. Actually, no aspect of your life would be the same; you would be locked into the attitudes and views that come with an agricultural or horticultural way of life.

■ *The sociological significance of the social revolutions discussed in the text is that the type of society in which we live determines the kind of people we become. It is obvious, for example, that the orientations to life of this worker would differ markedly from those of the man shown on page 159.*

The machinery that ushered in industrial society *was met with ambivalence. While it brought a multitude of welcomed goods, it also brought factory time clocks and the incessant production line. The idea that people had become slaves to the machines they built is illustrated by this classic scene of Charlie Chaplin's in* Modern Times.

agricultural revolution
the second social revolution, based on the invention of the plow, which led to agricultural society

agricultural society
a society based on large-scale agriculture, dependent on plows drawn by animals

Industrial Revolution
the third social revolution, occurring when machines powered by fuels replaced most animal and human power

industrial society
a society based on the harnessing of machines powered by fuels

■ Postindustrial (Information) Societies

If you were to choose one word that characterizes our society, what would it be? Of the many candidates, the word *change* would have to rank high among them. The primary source of the sweeping changes that are transforming our lives is the new technology centering around the microchip. The change is so vast that sociologists say that a new type of society has emerged. They call it the **postindustrial (or information) society.**

What are the main characteristics of this new society? Unlike the industrial society, its hallmark is not raw materials and manufacturing. Rather, its basic component is *information*. Teachers pass on knowledge to students, while lawyers, physicians, bankers, pilots, and interior decorators sell their specialized knowledge of law, the body, money, aerodynamics, and color schemes to clients. Unlike the factory workers of an industrial society, these individuals don't *produce* anything. Rather, they transmit or use information to provide services that others are willing to pay for.

The United States was the first country to have more than 50 percent of its work force in service industries such as education, health, research, the government, counseling, banking, investments, insurance, sales, law, and the mass media. Australia, New Zealand, western Europe, and Japan soon followed. This basic trend away from manufacturing to selling information and services shows no sign of letting up.

The changes have been so profound that they have led to a *fourth social revolution*. The microchip is transforming established ways of life, uprooting old perspectives and replacing them with new ones. This new technology allows us to work at home, and while we ride in cars, trucks, and airplanes to talk to others in distant cities and even to people on the other side of the globe. This tiny device lets us peer farther into the remote recesses of space than ever before. It is changing our shopping patterns as we spend billions of dollars on Internet purchases. And because of it, millions of children spend countless hours struggling against video enemies, at home and in the arcades. For a review of other changes, see the section on the computer in Chapter 22 (pages 676–679).

■ Bioeconomic Societies: An Emerging New Type of Society?

Is another new type of society emerging already? Some social analysts think so (Davis and Meyer 2000; Davis 2001). If so, the society's chief distinguishing characteristic will be an economy that centers around the application of genetic structures—human genetics for medicine, and plant and animal genetics for the production of food. The natural sciences will be reconstituted. Already we see biotechnology replacing botany and biochemistry replacing chemistry (Manavalan 2001). No longer will the transmission of information be limited to numbers, words, sounds, and images, but it will also include smell, taste, and touch (Davis 2001).

If we are witnessing the birth of a new type of society, just when did it begin? There are no firm edges on such momentous changes, and each type of new society overlaps the one it is replacing. We could trace the starting point of the bioeconomic society to 1953, however, when Francis Crick and James Watson identified the double-helix structure of DNA. Certainly the decoding of the human genome in 2001 will turn out to be a significant part of this new society—and perhaps even mark its beginning.

Projecting a new type of society so soon after the arrival of the postindustrial or information society is risky and abounds in controversy. The wedding of genetics and economics may turn out to be simply another part of our information society. But we may be witnessing the birth of a new type of society, one destined to replace the information society. In either case, we can anticipate revolutionary changes in health care (prevention, instead of treating disease), and, with cloning and bioengineering, perhaps even changes in the human species. The Sociology and the New Technology box on the next page examines implications of cloning.

postindustrial (information) society
a society based on information, services, and high technology, rather than on raw materials and manufacturing

Sociology & the new technology

"So, You Want to Be Yourself?" Cloning in the Coming Bioeconomy

No type of society ends abruptly. Instead, there is always overlapping of societies. The information society will mature in the years ahead, and will gradually be overtaken by the bioeconomy. At this point in time, we can only peer over the edge of our current society to glimpse the one that is coming. What will life be like? There are too many issues to deal with in this limited space, so let's consider just one: cloning.

Consider this scenario:

Your four-year-old daughter has drowned, and you can't get over your sorrow. You go to a cloning clinic, where you have stored DNA for all members of your family. You pay the fee, and the technicians, using a salaried, volunteer surrogate mother, bring your daughter back as a newborn.

Will cloned humans become a reality? Without doubt they will. The research is proceeding now, but underground. In fact, the birth may have occurred already in Korea, with the scientists not yet willing to reveal it. The remarkable success of scientists in bioengineering cows that produce medicine in their milk is just the beginning of our new bioeconomic society. Consider the questions these scenarios raise:

Suppose that a couple can't have children. They go through a battery of medical tests. The husband is sterile. The couple talk about the problem for a while, and the wife agrees to have her husband's genetic material implanted. Would this woman, in effect, be rearing her husband as a little boy?

Or suppose that you love your mother dearly, and she is dying. With her permission, you decide to clone her. Who is the clone? Would you be rearing your own mother?

What if a woman gives birth to her own clone? Is the clone her daughter or her sister?

When genetic duplicates appear, the questions of what humans are, what their relationship is to their "parents," and indeed what parents and children are, will be brought up at every kitchen table. In the meantime, since you can't buy a replaceable child just yet, what do you do? You might store your children's DNA for future cloning. Or you may want to store your own DNA. After your death, you can come back to life—and if you've written your will correctly, you will be able to inherit your own estate (Bjerklie et al. 2001).

If such feats become possible, will this give you immortality? Actually, no, for this will not be a resurrection. The cloned individual will be a different person. As ethicist Arthur Caplan says, "If I take twins and shoot one of them, it will be faint consolation to the dead one that the other one is still running around—even though they are genetically identical" (Bjerklie et al. 2001).

for your consideration

As these scenarios show, cloning leads to profound issues. For example, will it be right for people to re-create their dead children? Some would say, "So what? That's their business. People always have complicated reasons for having children, and this will be just another one." Others would give similar answers to the question of whether it would be right to re-create one's parents. Do you agree?

Cloning also leads to issues that deal with the future of society itself. Currently, scientists are plagued by the problem that clones are often deformed. Let's suppose that this problem has been solved, and the cloning of humans becomes routine. Even mass cloning becomes possible. Many object that cloning is immoral, but some will argue the opposite. They will ask why we should leave human reproduction to people who have inferior traits—genetic diseases, low IQs, even the propensity for crime and violence. They will suggest that we select people with the finer characteristics—high creative ability, high intelligence, compassion, a gentle disposition, and a propensity for peace.

Let's assume that scientists have traced these characteristics—as well as the ability and appreciation for poetry, music, mathematics, architecture, and love—to genetics. Do you think that it should be our moral obligation to populate society with people like this—and thus build a society that is better for all—one without terrorism, war, violence, and greed? Could this perhaps be our evolutionary destiny?

Source: Based on Davis and Meyer 2000; Kaebnick 2000; McGee 2000; Bjerklie et al. 2001; Davis 2001.

Although the full implications of the changes swirling around us are unknown—and whether they are part of a new type of society is not the main point. *The sociological significance of these changes is that just as the larger group called society always profoundly affects people's thinking and behavior, so, too, these recent developments will do the same for us.* As society is transformed, we will be swept along with it. The changes will be so extensive that they will transform even how we think about the self and life.

The transformations of society shown in Figure 6.1 (page 158) are not inevitable. Not all the world's societies will go through these stages. Whether any hunting and gathering societies survive, however, remains to be seen. Many countries today are "mixed" types. China is an interesting case. It is mostly agricultural, yet it has a large and growing industrial base. China is also importing vast amounts of the technology that it will take to become an informational society. Some agricultural societies also have a strong anti-modernization movement spearheaded by those who fear the loss of their traditional way of life. This at least partially underlies the terrorist attacks by the Osama bin Laden organizations.

Now that we have reviewed the major historical shifts in societies, let's turn to groups within society. Just how do they affect our lives?

Groups Within Society

Sociologist Emile Durkheim (1933) wondered what could be done to prevent *anomie* (AN-uh-mee), that bewildering sense of not belonging. Durkheim found the answer in small groups. He said that small groups stand as a buffer between the individual and the larger society. If it weren't for these groups, we would feel oppressed by that huge, amorphous entity known as society. By providing intimate relationships, small groups give us a sense of meaning and purpose, helping to prevent anomie.

Before we examine groups in more detail, we should distinguish some terms. Two terms sometimes confused with "group" are *aggregate* and *category*. An **aggregate** consists of individuals who temporarily share the same physical space but who do not see themselves as belonging together. People waiting in a checkout line or drivers parked at a red light are an aggregate. A **category** is a statistic. It consists of people who share similar characteristics, such as all college women who wear glasses or all men over 6 feet tall. Unlike groups, the individuals who make up a category neither interact with one another nor take one another into account. The members of a *group,* in contrast, think of themselves as belonging together, and they interact with one another.

Groups affect your life so extensively that they determine just who you are. If you think this an exaggeration, read on. Let's begin by looking at the types of groups that make up our society.

Primary Groups

Our first group, the family, gives us our basic orientation to life. Later, among friends, we find more intimacy and an additional sense of belonging. These groups are what sociologist Charles Cooley called **primary groups.** By providing intimate, face-to-face interaction, they give us an identity, a feeling of who we are. As Cooley (1909) put it,

> By primary groups I mean those characterized by intimate face-to-face association and cooperation. They are primary in several senses, but chiefly in that they are fundamental in forming the social nature and ideals of the individual.

Producing a Mirror Within It is significant that Cooley calls primary groups the "springs of life." By this, he means that primary groups are essential to our emo-

aggregate
individuals who temporarily share the same physical space but do not see themselves as belonging together

category
people who have similar characteristics

primary group
a group characterized by intimate, long-term, face-to-face association and cooperation

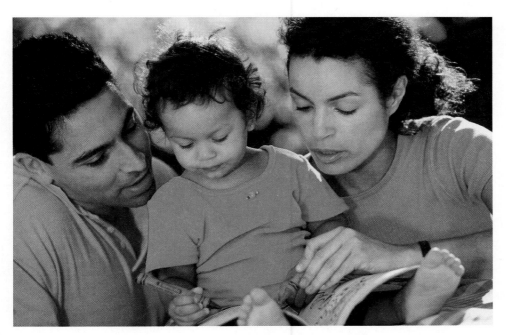

■ **Primary groups** *such as the family play a key role in the development of the self. As a small group, the family also serves as a buffer from the often-threatening larger group known as society. The family has been of primary significance in forming the basic orientations of this Latino couple, as it will be for their daughter.*

tional well-being—whether those groups be the family, friends, or even gangs. As humans, we have an intense need for face-to-face interaction that generates feelings of self-esteem. By offering a sense of belonging, a feeling of being appreciated, and sometimes even loved, primary groups are uniquely equipped to meet this basic human need.

Primary groups are also so significant because their values and attitudes become fused into our identity. We internalize their views, which become the lenses through which we view life. Even as adults—no matter how far we may have come from our childhood roots—early primary groups remain "inside" us, where they continue to form part of the perspective from which we look out onto the world. Ultimately, then, it is difficult, if not impossible, for us to separate the self from our primary groups, for the self and our groups merge into a "we."

■ Secondary Groups

Compared with primary groups, **secondary groups** are larger, more anonymous, formal, and impersonal. Secondary groups are based on some interest or activity, and their members are likely to interact on the basis of specific roles, such as president, manager, worker, or student. Examples are a college class, the American Sociological Association, and the Democratic party.

In hunting and gathering and horticultural societies, the entire society forms a primary group. In industrial and postindustrial societies, secondary groups have become essential to our welfare. They are part of the way we get our education, make our living, and spend our money and leisure time.

As necessary as secondary groups are for contemporary life, they often fail to satisfy our deep needs for intimate association. Consequently, *secondary groups tend to break down into primary groups.* At school and work, we form friendship cliques.

secondary group
compared with a primary group, a larger, relatively temporary, more anonymous, formal, and impersonal group based on some interest or activity, whose members are likely to interact on the basis of specific roles

Our interaction with them is so important that we sometimes feel that if it weren't for our friends, school or work "would drive us crazy." The primary groups we form within secondary groups, then, serve as a buffer between us and the demands that secondary groups place on us.

■ In-Groups and Out-Groups

Groups toward which we feel loyalty are called **in-groups;** those toward which we feel antagonisms, **out-groups.** For Monster Cody in our opening vignette, the gang was an in-group, while the Bloods and all other "enemies" were out-groups. That they—and we—make such a fundamental division of the world has far-reaching consequences for our lives.

Producing Loyalty, a Sense of Superiority, and Rivalries   Identification with a group can generate not only a sense of belonging, but also loyalty and feelings of superiority. These, in turn, often produce rivalries. Usually the rivalries are mild, such as sports rivalries between neighboring towns, where the most extreme act is likely to be the furtive invasion of the out-group's territory in order to steal a mascot, paint a rock, or uproot a goal post. The consequences of in-group membership can also be discrimination, hatred, and, as we saw in our opening vignette, even participation in murder.

Implications for a Socially Diverse Society   It is not surprising that in-group membership leads to discrimination, for, with our strong identifications and loyalties,

"So long, Bill. This is my club. You can't come in."

■ *How our participation in social groups shapes our self-concept is a focus of symbolic interactionists. In this process, knowing who we are* not *is as significant as knowing who we are.*

in-groups
groups toward which one feels loyalty

out-groups
groups toward which one feels antagonisms

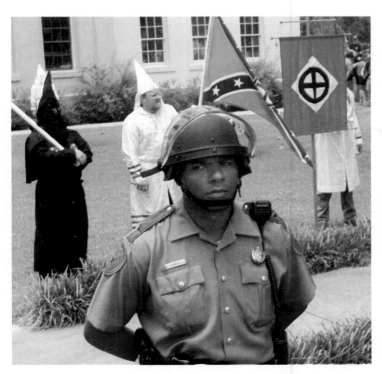

■ *All of us have reference groups—the groups we use as standards to evaluate ourselves. How do you think the reference groups of these members of the KKK who are demonstrating in Jaspar, Texas, differ from those of the police officer who is protecting their right of free speech? Although the KKK and this police officer use different groups to evaluate their attitudes and behaviors, the process is the same.*

we all favor members of our in-groups. This aspect of in- and out-groups is, of course, the basis of many problems in society. It underlies many gender and racial-ethnic divisions. As sociologist Robert Merton (1968) observed, this leads to a fascinating double standard. We view the traits of our in-group as virtues, while we see those *same* traits in out-groups as vices. Men may perceive an aggressive man as assertive, but an aggressive woman as pushy. They may think of a male employee who doesn't speak up as "knowing when to keep his mouth shut," but perceive a quiet woman as too timid to make it in the business world.

To divide the world into "we" and "them" poses a danger for a pluralistic society. As the Jews did for the Nazis, an out-group can come to symbolize evil, arousing fear, contempt, and hatred. After the terrorist bombings of New York and Washington, for some, Arabs became this type of extreme out-group. They saw Arabs as a sinister "them," as untrustworthy, bloodthirsty villains—certainly the opposite of how we evaluate "our" group (no matter what group that may be). Such extreme views often seem to justify attacking the out-group. Many Germans defended the Holocaust as necessary "dirty work." Some Americans defended the sporadic attacks on Arab Americans—and even people who looked like them—following the terrorist bombings. The refusal of some airline pilots to leave the ground until "Arab looking" passengers had been forced to leave the plane also fits this pattern. Economic downturns also help to produce out-groups. Immigrants, for example, may be seen as people who "steal" jobs from friends and family.

There may be attacks on immigrants, a national anti-immigration policy, or a resurgence of neo-Nazis or the Ku Klux Klan.

In short, to divide the world into in-groups and out-groups is a natural part of social life. But in addition to bringing functional consequences, it can also bring highly dysfunctional ones.

■ Reference Groups

Suppose you have just been offered a good job. It pays double what you hope to make even after you graduate from college. You have just two days to make up your mind. If you accept it, you will have to drop out of college. As you consider the matter, thoughts like this may go through your mind: "My friends will say I'm a fool if I don't take the job . . . but Dad and Mom will practically go crazy. They've made sacrifices for me, and they'd be crushed if I didn't finish college. They've always said I've got to get my education first, that good jobs will always be there. . . . But, then, I'd like to see the look on the faces of those neighbors who said I'd never amount to much!"

This is an example of how people use **reference groups,** the groups we use as standards to evaluate ourselves. Your reference groups may include your family, neighbors, teachers, classmates, co-workers, and the Scouts or the members of a church, synagogue, or mosque. If you are like Monster Cody in our opening vignette, the "set" would be the main reference group. You don't even have to belong to a reference group; it can be a group to which you aspire. For example, if you are thinking about going to graduate school, graduate students or members of the profession you want to join may form a reference group whose standards you consider as you evaluate your grades or writing skills.

reference groups
Herbert Hyman's term for the groups we use as standards to evaluate ourselves

Providing a Yardstick   Reference groups exert tremendous influence over our lives. For example, if you want to become a corporate executive, you might start to dress more formally, try to improve your vocabulary, read the *Wall Street Journal,*

■ *We all use* reference groups *to evaluate our accomplishments, failures, values, and attitudes. We compare what we see in ourselves with what we perceive as normative in these groups. As is evident in these two photos, the reference groups these youths are using are not likely to lead them to the same social destination.*

and change your major to business or law. In contrast, if you want to become a rock musician, you might wear several earrings in one ear, dress in ways your parents and many of your peers consider extreme, read *Rolling Stone,* drop out of college, and hang around clubs and rock groups.

Exposure to Contradictory Standards in a Socially Diverse Society   From these examples, you can see that the yardsticks provided by reference groups operate as a form of social control. When we see ourselves as measuring up to the yardstick, we feel no conflict. If our behavior, or even aspirations, do not match the standards held by a reference group, however, the mismatch can lead to inner turmoil. For example, to want to become a corporate executive would create no inner turmoil for most of us, but it would if we had grown up in an Amish home, for the Amish strongly disapprove of such aspirations for their children. They ban high school and college education, three-piece suits, and corporate employment. Similarly, if you wanted to become a soldier and your parents were dedicated pacifists, you likely would feel deep conflict, as your parents would hold quite different aspirations for you.

Given the social diversity of our society as well as our social mobility, many of us are exposed to contradictory ideas and standards from the many groups that become significant to us. The "internal recordings" that play contradictory messages from these reference groups, then, are one cost of social mobility.

Social Networks

If you are a member of a large group, you probably regularly associate with a few people within that group. In a sociology class I was teaching at a commuter campus, six women who didn't know one another chose to work together on a project. They got along well, and they began to sit together. Eventually they planned a Christmas party at one of their homes. These clusters, or internal factions, are called **cliques.** The links between people—their cliques, as well as their family, friends, acquaintances, and even "friends of friends"—are called **social networks.** Think of a social network as ties that extend outward from yourself, gradually encompassing more and more people.

The Small World Phenomenon   Although we live in a huge society, we don't experience social life as an ocean of nameless, strange faces. Instead, we interact within social networks that connect us to the larger society. Social scientists have wondered just how extensive the connections are between social networks (Watts 1999). If you list everyone you know, and each of those individuals lists everyone he or she knows, and you keep doing this, would almost everyone in the United States eventually be included on those lists?

It would be too cumbersome to test this hypothesis by drawing up such lists, but psychologist Stanley Milgram (1967) hit on an ingenious way to find out just how interconnected our social networks are. In what has become a classic experiment known as "the small world phenomenon," he selected names at random from across the United States. Some he designated as "senders," others as "receivers." Milgram addressed letters to the receivers and asked the senders to mail the letters to someone they knew on a first-name basis who they thought might know the receiver. These people, in turn, were asked to mail the letter to someone they knew who might know the receiver, and so on. The question was, Would the letters ever get to the receivers? If so, how long would the chain be?

clique
a cluster of people within a larger group who choose to interact with one another; an internal faction

social network
the social ties radiating outward from the self that link people together

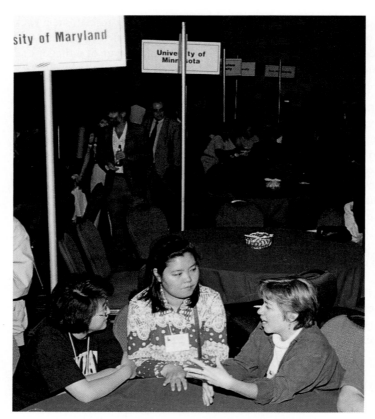

■ *Why do people get ahead in life? Is it because of their abilities? Although personal abilities and efforts are important for success, so are* social networks, *which open and close doors of opportunity. Despite the official program of sociology conventions, for example, much of the "real" business centers around renewing and extending social networks.*

Think of yourself as part of this experiment. What would you do if you were a sender, but the receiver lived in a state in which you know no one? You would send the letter to someone you knew who might know someone in that state. And this is just what happened. None of the senders knew the receivers, and in the resulting chains some links broke; that is, after receiving a letter, some people didn't send it on. Surprisingly, however, most letters did reach their intended receivers. Even more surprising, the average chain was made up of only *five* links.

Global Considerations   Milgram's experiment shows just how small our world really is, and it gives us insight into why strangers from different parts of the country sometimes find they have a mutual acquaintance. If our social networks are so interrelated that almost everyone in the United States is connected by just five links, how many links connect us to everyone on earth? This experiment is yet to be done.

Implications for a Socially Diverse Society   One reason that overcoming social inequality (the topic of Chapters 9–13) is so difficult is that our own social networks contribute to inequality. This topic is explored in the Cultural Diversity box on the next page.

cultural d-i-v-e-r-s-i-t-y

in the United States

How Our Social Networks Perpetuate Social Inequality

Consider some of the principles we have reviewed. People tend to form in-groups with which they identify; they use reference groups to evaluate their attitudes and behavior; and they interact in social networks. Our in-groups, reference groups, and social networks are likely to consist of people whose backgrounds are similar to our own. This means that, for most of us, just as social inequality is built into society, so it is built into our own relationships. One consequence is that *we tend to perpetuate social inequality.*

To see why, suppose that an outstanding job—great pay, interesting work, with opportunity for advancement—has just opened up where you work. Who are you going to tell? Most likely it will be someone you know, someone you like, or someone to whom you owe a favor. And most likely your social network is made up of people who look much like yourself—especially their race, age, and social class. This tends to keep good jobs moving in the direction of people whose characteristics are similar to those of the people already in an organization. You can see how our social networks both reflect the inequality that characterizes our society and help to perpetuate it.

Consider a network of white men who are established in an organization. As they learn of opportunities (jobs, investments, real estate, and so on), they share this information with their networks. Opportunities and good jobs flow to people who have characteristics similar to their own. Those who benefit from this information, in turn, reciprocate with similar information when they learn of it. This locks out from these opportunities people who have different characteristics, such as women and minorities, while it perpetuates the "good old boys'" network. No intentional discrimination need be involved.

To overcome this barrier, women and minorities do **networking.** They develop their own social networks to help advance their careers. To make acquaintances who will prove valuable to them, like the "good old boys," they, too, go to parties, join clubs, churches, synagogues, mosques, and political parties. Women cultivate a network of women, and African American leaders cultivate a network of African American leaders. As a result, the network of African American leaders is so tight that one-fifth of the entire national African American leader-

ship are personal acquaintances. Add some "friends of a friend," and *three-fourths* of the entire leadership belong to the same network (Taylor 1992). Women who reach top positions end up in a circle so tight that the term "new girl" network is being used, especially in the field of law. Remembering those who helped them and sympathetic to those who are trying to get ahead, these women tend to steer their business to other women. Like the "good old boys" who preceded them, the new insiders also justify their exclusionary practice (Jacobs 1997).

for your consideration

The perpetuation of social inequality does not require purposeful discrimination. Just as it is built into society, so social inequality is built into our personal relationships. How do you think your own social network helps to perpetuate social inequality? How do you think we can break this cycle? The key must center on creating diversity in social networks.

■ A New Group: Electronic Communities

In the 1990s, due to our new technology, a new type of human group, the **electronic community,** made its appearance. On the Internet hundreds of thousands of people meet in "news groups" to communicate electronically about almost any conceivable topic, from donkey racing and bird-watching to sociology and quantum physics. Most news groups are simply an interesting, new way of communicating. Some, however, meet our definition of *group:* people who interact with one another and who think of themselves as belonging together.

Some of these groups pride themselves on the distinctive nature of their interest and knowledge—factors that give them a common identity and bind them together. This new form of group is explored in the Sociology and the New Technology box on the next page.

networking
using one's social networks for some gain

electronic community
individuals who regularly interact with one another on the Internet and who think of themselves as belonging together

sociology &

the new
technology

Electronic Communities:
Cybercommunications and Our Changing Culture

A new technology can transform society. As you have seen in this chapter, the domestication of animals and the invention of the plow and the steam engine brought wholesale changes to people's lives. The microchip is in the process of transforming our society. Let's consider just "talk" and intimacy.

Throughout most of human history, "talk" meant face-to-face communication. The invention of writing allowed people who were far apart to "talk" to one another—and leave a record of what they "said." The invention of the printing press in 1436 multiplied the power of "long-distance talk." As it did so, it transformed religion and politics. With Bibles available to the masses, no longer did the Roman Catholic Church remain the exclusive interpreter of God's Word. Political tracts, pouring off the press, encouraged independent political thought. The new religious and political thought, in turn, undermined the church and monarchy, ushering in Protestant religions and constitutional forms of government.

If we think of the media as passive channels of information, as mere "holders" and "senders" of messages, we miss the sociological point. The media shape our lives. Just as the printing press encouraged new ways of thinking, which

THE FAR SIDE® BY GARY LARSON

© 1982 FarWorks, Inc. All Rights Reserved/Dist. by Creators Syndicate

The Far Side® by Gary Larson © 1982 FarWorks, Inc. All Rights Reserved. Used with permission.

In the days before television

■ ■ ■ ■ ■

Group Dynamics

group dynamics
the ways in which individuals affect groups and the ways in which groups influence individuals

small group
a group small enough for everyone to interact directly with all the other members

As you know from personal experience, the lively interaction *within* groups—who does what with whom—has profound consequences for how you adjust to life. Sociologists use the term **group dynamics** to refer to how groups influence us and how we affect groups. Let's consider how the size of a group makes a difference, and then examine leadership, conformity, and decision making.

Before doing this, we should see how sociologists define the term *small group.* In a **small group,** there are few enough members that each one can interact directly with all the other members. Small groups can be either primary or secondary. A wife, undermined the power of church and government, so, too, our new technology is doing much more than just bringing us new forms of "talk."

Consider how the Internet is extending the boundaries of our homes, schools, and businesses. While remaining within our four walls, we "travel" electronically around the world. We share information with people we have never met, and develop friendships with people across the globe.

The result is the electronic community, a type of group that until now was unknown in human history. Electronic communities can center on any shared interest, whether it be antique cars, radical politics, or deviant sex. Some communities are based on giving support. When people who suffer from cancer share their experiences with fear, pain, surgery, radiation, and chemotherapy, they break the depressing isolation that hems them in. Those who suffer from other debilitating diseases do the same.

Some even form an *electronic primary group.* As they communicate online, they come to identify with one another, develop a sense of intimacy, and share personal information. Online friends become so significant that they build their lives around each other. They rush to their computer the first thing in the morning. There they eagerly read e-mail from their Internet friends, and visit "chat rooms," where they discuss the latest development in their "real" (not online) relationships. Only then do they dress and go to work. After work, they rush back to their virtual world. For them, the people they "meet" electronically are as real as their family—and sometimes have a greater impact on their lives.

A historical shift in the nature of human relationships may be in sight. Already a new form of social intimacy is emerging. With the Net, people need never meet in order to identify on a personal, even intimate, basis. They experience closeness without permanence, and depth without commitment (Cerulo et al. 1992). It is likely that electronic primary groups will affect not only our social interactions, but also our culture, and even our sense of self.

for your consideration

Has Internet intimacy affected your life at all? Do you distance yourself from others nearby, while you foster intimacy with people in faraway places? Do you only wave to your next door neighbors, and know little about them, while you contact your Net friends often and know intimate details about their lives? Are you experiencing a changing sense of community?

Social researchers first reported that the longer people were online, the more their relationships with family and friends declined. More recent studies indicate that we aren't seeing these negative effects. Gregarious people remain outgoing in both their virtual and real worlds. Eighty-five percent of Net users report no change in the time they spend with family and friends (Guernsey 2001). And in what seems to be a positive note, teenagers are using the Net to explore their identity in new ways (Turkle 1995; Goldsborough 2001). Where do you fit in this scenario?

husband, and children, as well as workers who take their breaks together, are primary small groups, while bidders at an auction and passengers on a flight from Saint Louis to Minneapolis are secondary small groups.

■ Effects of Group Size on Stability and Intimacy

Writing in the early 1900s, sociologist Georg Simmel (1858–1918) noted the significance of group size. He used the term **dyad** for the smallest possible group, which consists of two people. Dyads, which include marriages, love affairs, and close

dyad
the smallest possible group, consisting of two people

■ *Japanese who work for the same firm think of themselves more as a group or team, Americans more as individuals. Japanese corporations use many techniques to encourage group identity, such as making group exercise a part of the work day. Similarity of appearance and activity helps to fuse group identity and company loyalty.*

friendships, show two distinct qualities. First, they are the most intense or intimate of human groups. Because only two people are involved, the interaction is focused on them. Second, because dyads require that both members participate and be committed, they are the most unstable of social groups. If one member loses interest, the dyad collapses. In larger groups, in contrast, even if one member withdraws, the group can continue, for its existence does not depend on any single member (Simmel 1950).

A **triad** is a group of three people. As Simmel noted, the addition of a third person fundamentally changes the group. With three people, interaction between the first two decreases. This can create strain. For example, with the birth of a child, hardly any aspect of a couple's relationship goes untouched. Attention focuses on the baby, and interaction between the husband and wife diminishes. Despite the difficulty that this presents—including in many instances the husband's jealousy that he is getting less attention from his wife—the marriage usually becomes stronger. Although the intensity of interaction is less in triads, they are inherently stronger and give greater stability to a relationship.

Yet, as Simmel noted, triads, too, are inherently unstable. It is not uncommon for two members to feel stronger bonds with one another, and then a **coalition** tends to form. A coalition occurs when some group members align themselves against others. In the case of the triad, two members act as a dyad, leaving the third member feeling hurt and excluded. Another characteristic of triads is that they often produce an arbitrator or mediator, someone who tries to settle disagreements between the other two. In one-child families, you can often observe both of these characteristics of triads—coalitions and arbitration.

The general principle is this: *As a small group grows larger, it becomes more stable, but its intensity, or intimacy, decreases.* To see why, look at Figure 6.3. As each new person comes into a group, the connections among people multiply. In a dyad, there is only 1 relationship; in a triad, 3; in a group of four, 6; in a group of five, 10. If we expand the group to six, we have 15 relationships, while a group of seven yields 21 relationships. If we continue adding members, we soon are unable to follow the connections: A group of eight has 28 possible relationships; a group of nine, 36 relationships; a group of ten, 45; and so on.

triad
a group of three people

coalition
the alignment of some members of a group against others

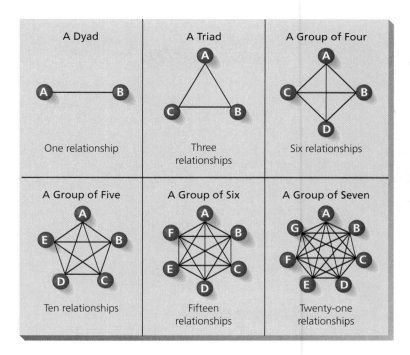

Figure 6.3

The Effects of Group Size on Relationships

It is not only the number of relationships that makes larger groups more stable. As groups grow, they also tend to develop a more formal structure to accomplish their goals. For example, leaders emerge and more specialized roles come into play. This often results in such familiar offices as president, secretary, and treasurer. This structure provides a framework that helps the group survive over time.

■ Effects of Group Size on Attitudes and Behavior

Imagine that your social psychology professors have asked you to join a few students to discuss your adjustment to college life. When you arrive, they tell you that to make the discussion anonymous they want you to sit unseen in a booth. You will participate in the discussion over an intercom, talking when your microphone comes on. The professors say they will not listen to the conversation, and they leave.

You find the format somewhat strange, to say the least, but you go along with it. You have not seen the other students in their booths, but when they talk about their experiences, you find yourself becoming wrapped up in the problems they begin to share. One student even mentions how frightening he has found college because of his history of epileptic seizures. Later, you hear this individual breathe heavily into the microphone. Then he stammers and cries for help. A crashing noise follows, and you imagine him lying helpless on the floor.

Nothing but an eerie silence follows. What do you do?

Your professors, John Darley and Bibb Latané (1968), staged the whole thing, but you don't know this. No one had a seizure. In fact, no one was even in the other booths. Everything, except your comments, was on tape.

Some participants were told they would be discussing the topic with just one other student, others with two, others with three, and so on. Darley and Latané found that all students who thought they were part of a dyad rushed out to help. If they

■ *Group size has a significant influence on how people interact. When a group changes from a dyad (two people) to a triad (three people), the relationships among the participants undergo a shift. How do you think the birth of this girl affected the relationship between her mother and father?*

Groups also mold our orientation to life. What assumptions of the world do you think this girl is growing up with?

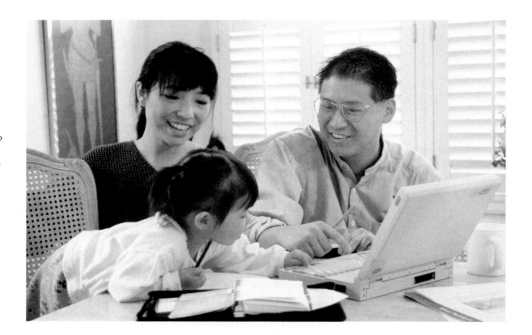

thought they were part of a triad, only 80 percent went to help—and they were slower in leaving the booth. In six-person groups, only 60 percent went to see what was wrong—and they were even slower.

This experiment demonstrates how deeply group size influences our attitudes and behavior—it even affects our willingness to help one another. Students in the dyad clearly knew it was up to them to help the other student. The professor was gone, and if they didn't help there would be no help. In the larger groups, including the triad, students felt *a diffusion of responsibility:* Giving help was no more their responsibility than anyone else's.

You probably have observed the second consequence of group size firsthand. When a group is small, its members are informal, but as the group grows, they lose their sense of intimacy and become more formal. No longer can the members assume that the others are "insiders" in sympathy with what they say. Now they must take a "larger audience" into consideration, and instead of merely "talking," they begin to "address" the group. Their speech becomes more formal, and their body language stiffens.

You probably have observed a third aspect of group dynamics, too. In the early stages of a party, when only a few people are present, almost everyone talks with everyone else. But as others arrive, the guests break into several smaller groups. Some hosts, who want their guests to mix together, make a nuisance of themselves trying to achieve *their* idea of what a group should be like. The division into small groups is inevitable, however, for it follows the basic sociological principles we have just reviewed. Because the addition of each person rapidly increases connections (in this case, "talk lines"), conversation becomes more difficult. The guests break into smaller groups where they can see each other and comfortably interact directly with one another.

■ Leadership

All groups, no matter what their size, have leaders, although they may not hold formal positions in the group. A **leader** is someone who influences the behaviors, opinions, or attitudes of others. Some people are leaders because of their personalities, but leadership involves much more than this, as we shall see.

leader
someone who influences other people

Types of Leaders   Groups have two types of leaders (Bales 1950, 1953; Cartwright and Zander 1968). The first is easy to recognize. This person, called an **instrumental leader** (or *task-oriented leader*), tries to keep the group moving toward its goals. These leaders try to keep group members from getting sidetracked, reminding them of what they are trying to accomplish. The **expressive leader** (or *socioemotional leader*), in contrast, usually is not recognized as a leader, but he or she certainly is. This person is likely to crack jokes, to offer sympathy, or to do other things that help lift the group's morale. Both types of leadership are essential: the one to keep the group on track, the other to increase harmony and minimize conflicts.

It is difficult for the same person to be both an instrumental and an expressive leader, for these roles contradict one another. Because instrumental leaders are task oriented, they sometimes create friction as they prod the group to get on with the job. Their actions often cost them popularity. Expressive leaders, in contrast, who stimulate personal bonds and reduce friction, are usually more popular (Olmsted and Hare 1978).

Leadership Styles   Let's suppose that the president of your college has asked you to head a task force to determine how the college can improve race relations on campus. Although this position requires you to be an instrumental leader, you can adopt a number of **leadership styles,** or ways of expressing yourself as a leader. The three basic styles are those of **authoritarian leader,** one who gives orders; **democratic leader,** one who tries to gain a consensus; and **laissez-faire leader,** one who is highly permissive. Which should you choose?

Social psychologists Ronald Lippitt and Ralph White (1958) carried out a classic study of these leadership styles. Boys matched for IQ, popularity, physical energy, and leadership were assigned to "craft clubs" made up of five boys each. The experimenters trained adult men in the three leadership styles. As the researchers peered through peepholes, taking notes and making movies, each adult rotated among the clubs, playing all three styles to control possible effects of their individual personalities.

The *authoritarian* leaders assigned tasks to the boys and told them exactly what to do. They also praised or condemned their work arbitrarily, giving no explanation for why it was good or bad. The *democratic* leaders held discussions with the boys, outlining the steps that would help them reach their goals. They also suggested alternative approaches and let the boys work at their own pace. When they evaluated the projects, they gave "facts" as the bases for their decisions. The *laissez-faire* leaders were passive. They gave the boys almost total freedom to do as they wished. They offered help when asked, but made few suggestions. They did not evaluate the boys' projects, either positively or negatively.

The results? The boys who had authoritarian leaders grew dependent on their leader and showed a high degree of internal solidarity. They also became either aggressive or apathetic, with the aggressive boys growing hostile toward their leader. In contrast, the boys who had democratic leaders were friendlier, more "group minded," and looked to one another for mutual approval. They did less scapegoating, and when the leader left the room they continued to work at a steadier pace. The boys with laissez-faire leaders asked more questions, but they made fewer decisions. They were notable for their lack of achievement. The researchers concluded that the democratic style of leadership works best. Their conclusion, however, may have been biased, as the researchers favored a democratic style of leadership in the first place, and they did the research during a highly charged political period (Olmsted and Hare 1978). Apparently, this same bias in studies of leadership continues (Cassel 1999).

You may have noted that only boys and men were involved in this experiment. It is interesting to speculate how the results might differ if we were to repeat the experiment with all-girl groups and with mixed groups of girls and boys—and if we used both men and women as leaders. Perhaps you will become the sociologist to study such variations of this classic experiment.

instrumental leader
an individual who tries to keep the group moving toward its goals; also known as a task-oriented leader

expressive leader
an individual who increases harmony and minimizes conflict in a group; also known as a socioemotional leader

leadership styles
ways in which people express their leadership

authoritarian leader
a leader who leads by giving orders

democratic leader
a leader who leads by trying to reach a consensus

laissez-faire leader
an individual who leads by being highly permissive

■ *Adolf Hitler was voted the most influential person of the twentieth century. He also was among the most evil. Why did so many people follow Hitler? That question stimulated the research discussed on these pages. Shown here is Hitler on his birthday, April 20, 1943, with Hermann Goering, the commander of the Luftwaffe (air force).*

Leadership Styles in Changing Situations   Different situations require different styles of leadership. Suppose, for example, that you are leading a dozen backpackers in California's Sierra Madre mountains, and it is time to make dinner. A laissez-faire style would be appropriate if the backpackers had brought their own food—or perhaps a democratic style if the meal were to be communally prepared. Authoritarian leadership—you telling all the hikers how to prepare their meals—would create resentment. This, in turn, would likely interfere with meeting the primary goal of the group, which in this case is to have a good time while enjoying nature.

Now assume the same group but a different situation: One of your party is lost, and a blizzard is on its way. This situation calls for you to take charge and be authoritarian. To simply shrug your shoulders and say, "You figure it out," would invite disaster—and probably a lawsuit.

Who Becomes a Leader?   Are leaders born with characteristics that propel them to the forefront of a group? No sociologist would agree with such a premise. In general, people who become leaders are seen by group members as strongly representing their values, or as able to lead a group out of a crisis (Trice and Beyer 1991). Leaders also tend to be more talkative and to express determination and self-confidence.

These findings may not be surprising, as such traits appear related to leadership. Researchers, however, have also discovered traits that seem to have no bearing on the ability to lead. For example, taller people and those judged better looking are more likely to become leaders (Stodgill 1974; Crosbie 1975). The taller and more attractive are also likely to earn more, but that is another story (Deck 1968; Feldman 1972; Katz 2001).

Many other factors underlie people's choice of leaders, most of which are quite subtle. A simple experiment performed by social psychologists Lloyd Howells and Selwyn Becker (1962) uncovered one of these factors. Forming groups of five people who did not know one another, they seated them at a rectangular table, three on one side and two on the other. After discussing a topic for a set period of time, each group chose a leader. The findings are startling: Although only 40 percent of the people sat on the two-person side, 70 percent of the leaders emerged from that side. The explanation is that we tend to direct more interactions to people facing us than to people to the side of us.

■ The Power of Peer Pressure: The Asch Experiment

How influential are groups in our lives? To answer this, let's look first at *conformity* in the sense of going along with our peers. Our peers have no authority over us, only the influence that we allow.

Imagine that you are taking a course in social psychology with Dr. Solomon Asch and you have agreed to participate in an experiment. As you enter his laboratory, you see seven chairs, five of them already filled by other students. You are given the sixth. Soon the seventh person arrives. Dr. Asch stands at the front of the room next to a covered easel. He explains that he will first show a large card with a vertical line on it, then another card with three vertical lines. Each of you is to tell him which of the three lines matches the line on the first card (see Figure 6.4).

Dr. Asch then uncovers the first card with the single line and the comparison card with the three lines. The correct answer is easy, for two of the lines are obviously wrong, and one exactly right. Each person, in order, states his or her answer aloud. You all answer correctly. The second trial is just as easy, and you begin to wonder why you are there.

Then on the third trial something unexpected happens. Just as before, it is easy to tell which lines match. The first student, however, gives a wrong answer. The second gives the same incorrect answer. So do the third and the fourth. By now you are wondering what is wrong. How will the person next to you answer? You can hardly believe it when he, too, gives the same wrong answer. Then it is your turn, and you give what you know is the right answer. The seventh person also gives the same wrong answer.

On the next trial, the same thing happens. You know the choice of the other six is wrong. They are giving what to you are obviously wrong answers. You don't know what to think. Why aren't they seeing things the same way you are? Sometimes they do, but in twelve trials they don't. Something is seriously wrong, and you are no longer sure what to do.

When the eighteenth card is finished, you heave a sigh of relief. The experiment is finally over, and you are ready to bolt for the door. Dr. Asch walks over to you with a big smile on his face, and thanks you for participating in the experiment. He explains that you were the only real subject in the experiment! "The other six were stooges. I paid them to give those answers," he says. Now you feel real relief. Your eyes weren't playing tricks on you after all.

What were the results? Asch (1952) tested fifty people. One-third (33 percent) gave in to the group half the time, giving what they knew to be wrong answers. Another two of five (40 percent) gave wrong answers, but not as often. One of four (25 percent) stuck to their guns and always gave the right answer. I don't know how I would do on this test (if I knew nothing about it in advance), but I like to think that I would be part of the 25 percent. You probably feel the same way about yourself. But why should we feel that we wouldn't be like *most* people?

The results are disturbing, and more researchers have replicated Asch's experiment than any other study (Levine 1999). In our "land of individualism," the group is so powerful that most people are willing to say things that they know are not true. And this was a group of strangers! How much more conformity can we expect when our group consists of friends, people we value highly and depend on for getting along in life? Again, perhaps you will become the sociologist to run that variation of Asch's experiment, perhaps using female subjects.

Even more disturbing are the results of the experiment described in the following Thinking Critically section.

Card 1

Card 2

The cards used by Solomon Asch in his classic experiment on group conformity

Figure 6.4

Asch's Cards
Source: Asch 1952:452–453

t h i n k i n g
CRITICALLY

If Hitler Asked You to Execute a Stranger, Would You? The Milgram Experiment

Imagine that you are taking a course with Dr. Stanley Milgram (1963, 1965), a former student of Dr. Asch. Assume that you do not know about the Asch experiment and have no reason to be wary. You arrive at the laboratory to participate in a study on punishment and learning. You and a second student draw lots for the roles of "teacher" and "learner." You are to be the teacher. When you see that the learner's chair has protruding electrodes, you are glad that you are the teacher. Dr. Milgram shows you the machine you will run. You see that one side of the control panel is marked "Mild Shock, 15 volts," while the center says "Intense Shock, 350 Volts" and the far right side reads "DANGER: SEVERE SHOCK."

"As the teacher, you will read aloud a pair of words," explains Dr. Milgram. "Then you will repeat the first word, and the learner will reply with the second word. If the learner can't remember the word, you press this lever on the shock generator. The shock will serve as punishment, and we can then determine if punishment improves memory." You nod, now very relieved that you haven't been designated the learner.

"Every time the learner makes an error, increase the punishment by 15 volts," instructs Dr. Milgram. Then, seeing the look on your face, he adds, "The shocks can be extremely painful, but they won't cause any permanent tissue damage." He pauses, and then says, "I want you to see." You then follow him to the "electric chair," and Dr. Milgram gives you a shock of 45 volts. "There. That wasn't too bad, was it?" "No," you mumble.

The experiment begins. You hope for the learner's sake that he is bright, but unfortunately he turns out to be rather dull. He gets some answers right, but you have to keep turning up the dial. Each turn makes you more and more uncomfortable. You find yourself hoping that the learner won't miss another answer. But he does. When he received the first shocks, he let out some moans and groans, but now he is screaming in agony. He even protests that he suffers from a heart condition.

How far do you turn that dial?

By now, you probably have guessed that there was no electricity attached to the electrodes and the "learner" was a stooge who only pretended to feel pain. The purpose of the experiment was to find out at what point people refuse to participate. Does anyone actually turn the lever all the way to "DANGER: SEVERE SHOCK"?

Milgram wanted the answer because of the Nazi slaughter of Jews, gypsies, homosexuals, people with disabilities, and others whom they designated as "inferior." That millions of ordinary people did nothing to stop the deaths seemed bizarre, and Milgram wanted to see how ordinary, intelligent Americans might react in an analogous situation.

Milgram was upset by what he found. Many "teachers" broke into a sweat and protested to the experimenter that this was inhuman and should be stopped. But when the experimenter calmly replied that the experiment must go on, this assurance from an "authority" ("scientist, white coat, university laboratory") was enough for most "teachers" to continue, even though the "learner" screamed in agony. Even "teachers" who were "reduced to twitching, stuttering wrecks" continued to follow orders.

Milgram varied the experiments (Miller 1986). He used both men and women and put some "teachers" and "learners" in the same room, where the "teacher" could clearly see the suffering. He had some "learners" pound and kick the wall during the first shocks and then go silent. The results varied. When there was no verbal feedback from the "learner," 65 percent of the "teachers" pushed the lever all the way to 450 volts. Of those who could see the "learner," 40 percent turned the lever all the way. When

▪ In the 1960s, U.S. social psychologists ran a series of creative but controversial experiments. Among these were Stanley Milgram's experiments, described in the text. From this photo of the "learner" being prepared for the experiment, you can get an idea of how convincing the situation would be for the "teacher."

Milgram added a second "teacher," a stooge who refused to go along with the experiment, only 5 percent of the "teachers" turned the lever all the way, a result that bears out some of Asch's findings.

A stormy discussion about research ethics erupted. Not only were researchers surprised and disturbed by what Milgram found, but also they were alarmed at his methods. Universities began to require that subjects be informed of the nature and purpose of social research. Researchers agreed that to reduce subjects to "twitching, stuttering wrecks" was unethical, and almost all deception was banned.

■ ■ ■ ■ ■

for your consideration . . .

What is the connection between Milgram's experiment and the actions of Monster Cody in our opening vignette? Considering how significant these findings are, do you think that the scientific community overreacted to Milgram's experiments? Should we allow such research? Consider both the Asch and Milgram experiments, and use symbolic interactionism, functionalism, and conflict theory to explain why groups have such influence over us.

■ Global Consequences of Group Dynamics

In our era of nuclear and biological weapons, one of the disturbing implications of the Asch and Milgram experiments is **groupthink.** Sociologist Irving Janis (1972, 1982) coined this term to refer to the collective tunnel vision that groups sometimes develop: Members think alike and any suggestion of alternatives is taken as a sign of disloyalty. Even moral judgments must be put aside, for the "team" is convinced that its welfare depends on a single course of action. Groupthink may lead to overconfidence and a disregard for the risks that the group is taking (Hart 1991; Flippen 1999). The Asch and Milgram experiments help us see how groupthink can develop.

Suppose you are a member of the president's inner circle. It is midnight, and the president has just called an emergency meeting to deal with a terrorist attack. At first, various options are presented. Eventually, these are narrowed to only a few choices, and at some point everyone seems to agree on what now seems "the only possible course of action." At that juncture, expressing doubts will bring you into conflict with *all* the other important people in the room. To criticize will mark you as not being a "team player." So you keep your mouth shut, with the result that each step commits you—and them—more and more to the "only" course of action.

We can choose from numerous examples from around the globe, but, as Janis points out, U.S. history provides a fertile field for illustrating groupthink: the refusal of President Franklin D. Roosevelt and his chiefs of staff to believe that the Japanese might attack Pearl Harbor, and the subsequent decision to continue naval operations as usual; President Kennedy's invasion of Cuba; and U.S. policies in Vietnam. Watergate is especially noteworthy, for it plunged the United States into political crisis, and for the first time in history a U.S. president was forced to resign.

In each of these cases, options closed as officials committed themselves to a single course of action. To question the decision would have marked one as disloyal, as not a "team player." Those in power plunged ahead, no longer able to see different perspectives, no longer trying to objectively weigh evidence as it came in, but interpreting everything as supporting their one "correct" decision. Like Milgram's subjects, they became mired in actions that as individuals they would have considered unacceptable. In some cases, they found themselves pursuing policies that they otherwise might have considered morally repugnant.

groupthink
Irving Janis' term for a narrowing of thought by a group of people, leading to the perception that there is only one correct answer, in which to even suggest alternatives becomes a sign of disloyalty

This type of moral reevaluation—and the threat to a free society that it brings—is not limited to the events of another era. It continues, as witnessed by the approval of targeted assasinations by the CIA. Perhaps one of the most startling examples occurred in 2001, when respectable journalists and politicians openly discussed the option of torturing Arab suspects who wouldn't talk. They even defended torture as moral—"the lesser of two evils."

Preventing Groupthink　　Groupthink is a danger that faces government leaders, who tend to surround themselves with an inner circle that closely reflects their own views. Isolated at the top, they can become cut off from information that does not support their own opinions. It is obvious that the extreme emotions that follow a terrorist attack can provide fertile ground for groupthink. Perhaps the key to preventing the mental captivity and intellectual paralysis known as groupthink is the widest possible circulation—especially among a nation's top government officials—of research that has been freely conducted by social scientists and information that has been freely gathered by media reporters.

If this conclusion comes across as an unabashed plug for sociological research and the free exchange of ideas, it is. Giving free rein to diverse opinions can effectively curb groupthink, which—if not prevented—can lead to the destruction of a society and, in today's world of sophisticated nuclear, biological, and chemical weapons, the obliteration of the earth's inhabitants.

Summary and Review

Social Groups and Societies

■ **What is a group?**

Sociologists use many definitions of groups, but, in general, **groups** are people who have something in common and who believe that what they have in common is significant. **Societies** are the largest and most complex groups that sociologists study. Pp. 156–157.

The Transformation of Societies

■ **What inventions are linked to the change from one type of society to another?**

On their way to postindustrial society, humans passed through four types of societies. Each emerged from a social revolution that was linked to new technology. The **domestication revolution,** which brought the pasturing of animals and the cultivation of plants, transformed **hunting and gathering societies** into **pastoral** and **horticultural societies.** Then the invention of the plow ushered in the **agricultural society,** while the **Industrial Revolution,** brought about by machines that were powered by fuels, led to the **industrial society.** The computer chip ushered in a new type of society called **postindustrial** (or **information**) **society.** Another new type of society, the **bioeconomic society,** may be emerging. Pp. 157–164.

■ **How is social inequality linked to the transformation of societies?**

Social equality was greatest in hunting and gathering societies, but over time social inequality grew. The root of the transition to social inequality was the accumulation of a food surplus, made possible through the domestication revolution. This surplus stimulated the division of labor, trade, accumulation of material goods, the subordination of females by males, the emergence of leaders, and the development of the state. Pp. 157–164.

Groups Within Society

■ **How do sociologists classify groups?**

Sociologists divide groups into primary groups, secondary groups, in-groups, out-groups, reference groups, and networks. The cooperative, intimate, long-term, face-to-face relationships provided by **primary groups** are fundamental to our sense of self. **Secondary groups** are larger, relatively temporary, more anonymous, more formal, and more impersonal than primary groups. **In-groups** provide members with a strong sense of identity and belonging. **Out-groups** also foster identity by showing in-group members what they are *not*. **Reference groups** are groups whose standards we mentally refer to as we evaluate ourselves. **Social networks** consist of social ties that link people together. The new technology has given birth to a new type of group, the **electronic community.** Pp. 164–172.

Group Dynamics

■ **How does a group's size affect its dynamics?**

The term **group dynamics** refers to how individuals affect groups and how groups influence individuals. In a **small group,** everyone can interact directly with everyone else. As a group grows larger, its intensity decreases but its stability increases. A **dyad,** consisting of two people, is the most unstable of human groups, but it provides the most intense or intimate relationships. The addition of a third person, forming a **triad,** fundamentally alters relationships. Triads are unstable, as **coalitions** (the alignment of some members of a group against others) tend to form. Pp. 172–176.

■ **What characterizes a leader?**

A **leader** is someone who influences others. **Instrumental leaders** try to keep a group moving toward its goals, even though this causes friction and they lose popularity. **Expressive leaders** focus on creating harmony and raising group morale. Both types are essential to the functioning of groups. Pp. 176–177.

■ **What are the three main leadership styles?**

Authoritarian leaders give orders, **democratic leaders** try to lead by consensus, and **laissez-faire leaders** are highly permissive. An authoritarian style appears to be more effective in emergency situations, a democratic style works best for most situations, and a laissez-faire style is usually ineffective. Pp. 177–178.

■ **How do groups encourage conformity?**

The Asch experiment was cited to illustrate the power of peer pressure, the Milgram experiment to illustrate the influence of authority. Both experiments demonstrate how easily we can succumb to **groupthink,** a kind of collective tunnel vision. Preventing groupthink requires the free circulation of contrasting ideas. Pp. 178–182.

■ *Where can I read more on this topic?*

Suggested readings for this chapter are at the back of this book.

Additional Online Resources for This Chapter
www.ablongman.com/henslin6e

- *Content Select* Research Database for Sociology, with suggested key terms and annotated references
- Link to 2000 Census, with activities
- Flashcards of key terms and concepts
- Practice Tests
- Weblinks
- Interactive Maps

using . . .
ContentSelect

Research Database for Sociology

postindustrial societies	cliques	leadership styles	agricultural societies
social diversity	social inequality	peer pressure	industrial societies
social networks	electronic communities	group dynamics	
		clubs	

Jean–Pierre Stora, *Business City*, 1995

7

The Rationalization of Society
Why Did Society Change?
Marx: Capitalism Broke Tradition
Weber: Religion Broke Tradition

Formal Organizations and Bureaucracy
Formal Organizations
The Characteristics of Bureaucracies
"Ideal" Versus "Real" Bureaucracy
Dysfunctions of Bureaucracies
The Perpetuation of Bureaucracies
The Sociological Significance of Bureaucracies

Voluntary Associations
Functions of Voluntary Associations
Shared Interests
The Problem of Oligarchy

Working for the Corporation
The "Hidden" Corporate Culture

Humanizing the Corporate Culture
Attempts to Humanize the Work Setting
The Conflict Perspective
Technology and the Control of Workers

U.S. and Japanese Corporations
How the Corporations Differ
The Myth Versus Reality

Summary and Review

Bureaucracy and Formal Organizations

This was the most exciting day Jennifer could remember. Her first day at college. So much had happened so quickly. Her senior year had ended with such pleasant memories: the prom, graduation—how proud she had felt at that moment. But best of all had been her SAT scores. Everyone, especially Jennifer, had been surprised at the results—she had outscored everyone in her class.

"Yes, they're valid," her advisor had assured her. "You can be anything you want to be."

Those words still echoed in Jennifer's mind. "Anything I want to be," she thought.

Then came the presidential scholarship! Full tuition for four years. It went beyond anything Jennifer had ever dreamed possible. She could hardly believe it, but it was really true.

"Your Social Security number, please!"

These abrupt words snapped Jennifer out of her reverie. After waiting in line for an hour, she had finally reached the registration desk. She quickly mumbled the nine digits that would identify her as an incoming student.

"What?" asked the clerk. Jennifer repeated the numbers more clearly.

"I can't give you a class card. You haven't paid your fees."

"What do you mean? I'm on scholarship."

> "I can't help what it says there. The only thing that counts is what it says here,"

"Evidently not, or else you'd be in the computer," replied the clerk, rolling her eyes.

"But I am."

"If you were, it would say so here."

"But I really am. Look," Jennifer said as she took the prized letter out of her purse.

"I can't help what it says there. The only thing that counts is what it says here," the clerk said, gesturing toward the computer. "You'll have to go over to Forsyth Hall to clear it up." Then looking past Jennifer, she called to the next student: "Next!"

Jennifer felt thoroughly confused. Dejected, she crossed the quadrangle to Forsyth and joined a double line of students that stretched from the building to the courtyard.

No one told Jennifer that this was the line for deferring tuition. The "problems" line was the shorter one in the basement.

You can understand Jennifer's dismay. Things could have been clearer—a lot clearer. The problem is that many colleges must register thousands of students, most of whom are going to start classes on the same day. To make the job manageable, colleges have broken down the registration process into separate steps. Each step is an integrated part of the entire process. Computerized advance registration has facilitated this process, but as Jennifer found out, things don't always go as planned.

This chapter looks at how society is organized to "get its job done." As you read it, you may be able to trace the source of some of your frustrations to this social organization—as well as see how your welfare depends on it.

The Rationalization of Society

In the previous chapter, we discussed how societies have undergone transformations so extensive that whole new types of societies have emerged. We also saw that we are now in the midst of one of those earth-shattering transformations. Underlying our information society (which may be merging into a bioeconomic society) is a high emphasis on **rationality,** the idea that efficiency and practical results should dominate human affairs. Let's examine how this approach to life—which today we take for granted—came about.

■ Why Did Society Change?

Until recently, people were immersed in a **traditional orientation** to life—the idea that the past is the best guide for the present. In this view, what exists is good because it has passed the test of time. Customs—and relationships based on them—have served people well, and they should not be abandoned lightly. A central orientation of a traditional society is to protect the status quo. Change is viewed with suspicion and comes about slowly, if at all.

rationality
the acceptance of rules, efficiency, and practical results as the right way to approach human affairs

traditional orientation
the idea, characteristic of tribal, peasant, and feudal societies, that the past is the best guide for the present

TABLE 7.1	A Model of Production in Traditional and Nontraditional Societies

Traditional Societies (Horticultural, Agricultural)	Nontraditional Societies (Industrial, Postindustrial)
1. Production is done by family members and same-sex groups (men's and women's groups).	1. Production is done by workers hired for the job.
2. Production takes place in the home, or in fields and other areas adjacent to the home.	2. Production takes place in a centralized location set up for this purpose. (Some decentralization is occurring in the information society.)
3. Tasks are assigned according to personal relationships (men, women, and children do specific tasks based on custom).	3. Tasks are assigned according to agreements and training.
4. Relationships are based on history ("the way it's always been").	4. Relationships are based on contracts, which change as the situation changes.
5. Relationships are diffuse (vague, covering many areas of life).	5. Relationships are specific; contracts (even if not written) specify conditions.
6. Relationships are long-term, often lifelong.	6. Relationships are short-term, for the length of the contract.
7. The "how" of production is not evaluated; the issue is, "We want to keep doing it the way we've always done it."	7. The "how" of production is evaluated; the issue is, "How can we make this more efficient?"
8. It is assumed that arrangements will continue indefinitely.	8. Arrangements are evaluated periodically, to decide whether to continue or to change them.
9. People are evaluated according to how they fulfill their traditional roles.	9. People are evaluated according to the "bottom line" (the organization's goals).

Note: This model is an ideal type. Rationality is never totally absent from any society, and no society (or organization) is based entirely on rationality. Even the most rational organizations (those that most carefully and even ruthlessly compute the "bottom line") have traditional components. To properly understand this table, consider these nine characteristics as being "more" or "less" present.

The traditional orientation to life stands in the way of industrialization. As Table 7.1 shows, the traditional orientation is based on personal relationships. Deep obligation and responsibility, which are often lifelong, permeate society. What counts in production is not who is best at doing something, but the relationships that people have to one another. Based on origins that are lost in history, everyone—even children—has an established role to play. The past is prized, and it rules the present.

Capitalism requires an entirely different way of looking at life. If a society is to industrialize, a deep shift must occur in people's thinking. Tradition ("This is the way we've always done it") must be replaced with *rationality* ("Let's find the most efficient way to do it"). As Table 7.1 shows, personal relationships are replaced by impersonal, short-term contracts. The "bottom line" (results) becomes the primary concern, and rule-of-thumb methods give way to explicit ways of measuring results.

It is difficult to overstate the significance of the change from tradition to rationality, for it flies in the face of human history. Judging things from the bottom line instead of by personal relationships goes against the basic orientation of all human societies until recent times. It is like a wife saying to her husband, "I'm going to evaluate how much you've contributed to the family budget and how much time you've put in on household tasks—and I'll keep or replace you on that basis." Since

■ *As college registration illustrates,* bureaucracies *break tasks down into their component parts and have specialists handle each part. The efficiency of this procedure is sometimes lost on the clientele being served. Shown here is freshmen orientation at Duke University.*

this was such a fundamental switch, then, how did the **rationalization of society**—the widespread acceptance of rationality and the construction of a social organization largely built around this idea—come about?

◼ Marx: Capitalism Broke Tradition

An early sociologist, Karl Marx (1818–1883), was one of the first to note how tradition had given way to rationality. As he thought about why this change had taken place, he concluded that capitalism had broken the bonds of tradition. As people who had money experimented with capitalism, they saw that it was more efficient. They were impressed that it produced things they wanted in much greater abundance and yielded high profits. This encouraged them to invest capital in manufacturing. As capitalism spread, traditional thinking receded. Gradually, the rationality of capitalism replaced the traditional approach to life. Marx's conclusion: The change to capitalism changed the way people thought about life.

◼ Weber: Religion Broke Tradition

To sociologist Max Weber (1864–1920), this problem was as intriguing as an unsolved murder is to a detective. Weber wasn't satisfied with Marx's answer, and he kept searching for the solution. He found the clue when he noted that capitalism thrived only in certain parts of Europe. "There has be a reason for this," he mused. As Weber pursued the matter, he began to think that religion held the key. He noted that capitalism flourished in Protestant countries, while Roman Catholic countries held on to tradition and were relatively untouched by capitalism.

But why did Roman Catholics cling to the past, while Protestants embraced change? Weber's answer to this puzzle has been the source of controversy ever since he first proposed it in his influential book, *The Protestant Ethic and the Spirit of Capitalism* (1904–1905). Weber concluded that Roman Catholic doctrine emphasized the acceptance of present arrangements, not change: "God wants you where you are. You owe allegiance to the Church, to your family, to your community and country. Accept your lot in life and remain rooted." Weber argued that Protestant theology, in contrast, opened its followers to change. Weber was intimately familiar with Calvinism, his mother's religion. Calvinists (followers of the teachings of John Calvin, 1509–1564) believed that people are destined before birth for either heaven or hell—and they do not know their destiny until after they die. Weber said that this teaching filled Calvinists with an anxiety that pervaded their lives. Salvation became their chief concern—they wanted to know *now* where they were going after death.

To resolve their spiritual dilemma, Calvinists hit upon an ingenious solution: God surely did not want those chosen for heaven to be ignorant of their destiny. Therefore, those who were in God's favor would know it—they would receive a sign from God. But what sign? The answer, claimed Calvinists, was found not in mystical, spiritual experiences, but in things that people could see and measure. The sign of God's approval was success: Those whom God had predestined for heaven would be blessed with visible success in this life.

This idea transformed the lives of Calvinists. It motivated them to work hard, and because Calvinists also believed that thrift is a virtue, their dedication to work led to an accumulation of money. They could not spend this money on themselves, however, for to purchase items beyond the basic necessities was considered sinful. **Capitalism,** the investment of capital in the hope of producing profits, became an outlet for their excess money. The success of those investments, in turn, became a fur-

rationalization of society
a widespread acceptance of rationality and a social organization largely built around this idea

capitalism
the investment of capital with the goal of producing profits

ther sign of God's approval. In this way, Calvinists transformed worldly success into a spiritual virtue. Other branches of Protestantism, although not in agreement with the notion of predestination, also adopted the creed of thrift and hard work. Consequently, said Weber, Protestant countries embraced capitalism.

But what has this to do with rationalization? Simply put, capitalism demands rationalization, the careful calculation of practical results. If profits are your goal, you must compute income and expenses. You must calculate inventories and wages, the cost of producing goods and how much they bring in. You must determine "the bottom line." Efficiency, then, not tradition, becomes the drumbeat to which you march. If they are inefficient, traditional ways of doing things are replaced, for what counts are the results. Weber's equation: A changed way of thinking (God will give a sign to the elect) produced capitalism.

Who is correct? Weber, who concluded that Protestantism produced rationality, which then paved the way for capitalism? Or Marx, who concluded that capitalism produced rationality? No analyst has yet reconciled these two opposing answers to the satisfaction of sociologists: The two views still remain side by side.

■ *In traditional societies, religion was a dominant force. In this photo of Antequera, Spain, the cathedral makes it evident how tradition dominated village life. Max Weber and Karl Marx disagreed about why societies changed from a traditional orientation to a rational one.*

Formal Organizations and Bureaucracy

Regardless of whether Marx or Weber was right about its cause, rationality was a totally different way of approaching life. As this new orientation came to permeate society, it led to new types of organizations. One result was **formal organizations,** secondary groups designed to achieve explicit objectives. Formal organizations have become a central feature of our lives. Most of us are born within them, we are educated in them, we spend our working lives in them, and we are buried by them.

■ Formal Organizations

Prior to industrialization, there were few formal organizations. The guilds of western Europe during the twelfth century are an example. People who performed the same type of work organized to control their craft in a local area. They set prices and standards of workmanship (Bridgwater 1953; Volti 1995). Much like modern unions, guilds also prevented outsiders (nonmembers of the guild) from working at the particular craft. Another example of an early formal organization is the army, with its hierarchical structure of senior officers, junior officers, and ranks. Formal armies, of course, go back to early history.

formal organization
a secondary group designed to achieve explicit objectives

■ *The division of labor, a central characteristic of formal organizations, is not new. In this painting of Italian farm life by Francesco Bassano (1549–1592), you can see the intricate division of labor that farm production required in the 1500s. Note the many specialized tasks these people are doing. Can you identify what is different about today's division of labor?*

With industrialization, secondary groups became common. Today we take their existence for granted and, beginning with grade school, all of us spend a good deal of time in them. Formal organizations tend to develop into bureaucracies, and in general, the larger the formal organization, the more likely it is to be bureaucratic.

■ The Characteristics of Bureaucracies

What do the Soviet army, the U.S. postal service, the Mormon Church, and your college have in common? The sociological answer is that they all are **bureaucracies.** As Weber (1913/1947) pointed out, bureaucracies have

1. *Clear-cut levels, with assignments flowing downward and accountability flowing upward.* Each level assigns responsibilities to the level beneath it, while each lower level is accountable to the level above it for fulfilling those assignments. The bureaucratic structure of a typical university is shown in Figure 7.1 on the following page.

2. *A division of labor.* Each worker has a specific task to fulfill, and all the tasks are coordinated to accomplish the purpose of the organization. In a college, for example, a teacher does not run the heating system, the president does not teach, and a secretary does not evaluate textbooks. These tasks are distributed among people who have been trained to do them.

3. *Written rules.* In their attempt to become efficient, bureaucracies stress written procedures. In general, the longer a bureaucracy exists, the larger it grows, and

bureaucracy
a formal organization with a hierarchy of authority; a clear division of labor; emphasis on written rules, communications, and records; and impersonality of positions

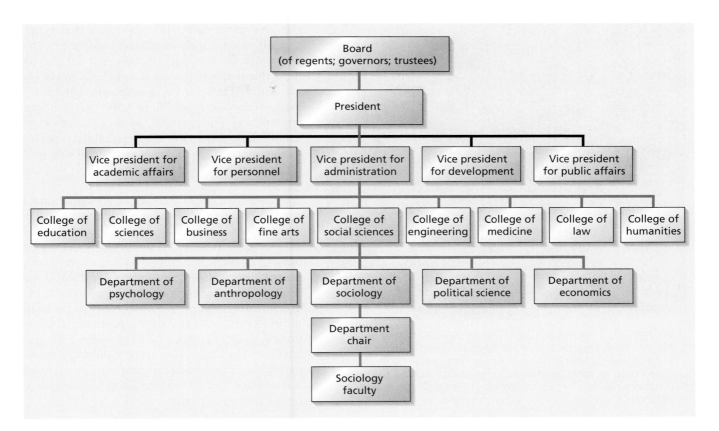

F igure 7.1

The Typical Bureaucratic Structure of a Medium-Sized University
This is a scaled-down version of a university's bureaucratic structure. The actual lines of a university are likely to be much more complicated than those depicted here. A large university may have a chancellor and several presidents under the chancellor, with each president responsible for a particular campus. Although in this figure extensions of authority are shown only for the vice president for administration and the College of Social Sciences, each of the other vice presidents and colleges has similar positions. If the figure were to be extended, departmental secretaries would be shown, and eventually, somewhere, even students.

the more written rules it has. The rules of some bureaucracies cover just about every imaginable situation. In my university, for example, the rules are published in handbooks: separate ones for faculty, students, administrators, civil service workers, and perhaps others that I don't even know exist.

4. *Written communications and records.* Records are kept of much of what occurs in a bureaucracy ("Fill that out in triplicate"). In some, workers spend a fair amount of time sending memos and e-mail back and forth. Sometimes, workers must detail their activities in written reports. My university, for example, requires that each quarter faculty members summarize the number of hours they spent on specified activities. They must also submit an annual report listing what they accomplished in teaching, research, and service—all accompanied by copies of publications, testimonies to service, and written teaching evaluations from each course. These materials go to committees that evaluate the performance of each faculty member.

■ *This 1907 photo indicates one way that technology has changed our lives. The little drawers that the women are searching contain customer records of the Metropolitan Life Insurance Company. Today, this entire bank of records could be stored on a personal computer. We also could use the computer to search or modify the records, infinitesimally faster—and certainly much easier on the legs—than standing on the ladder.*

5. *Impersonality*. It is the office that is important, not the individual who holds the office. You work for the organization, not for the replaceable person who heads some post in the organization. Each worker is a replaceable unit, for many others are available to fulfill each particular function. For example, when a professor retires or dies, someone else is appointed to take his or her place. This makes you a small cog in a large machine.

These five characteristics help bureaucracies reach their goals. They also allow them to grow and endure. One bureaucracy in the United States, the postal service, has become so large that one out of every 150 employed Americans works for it (*Statistical Abstract* 2000:645, 936). If the head of a bureaucracy dies, retires, or resigns, the organization continues without skipping a beat, for unlike a "mom and pop" operation, its functioning does not depend on the individual who heads it. The expansion (some would say domination) of bureaucracies in contemporary society is illustrated by the Down-to-Earth Sociology box on the following page.

■ *Today's armies, no matter what country they are from, are bureaucracies. They have a strict hierarchy of rank, division of labor, impersonality (an emphasis on the office, not the person holding it), and they stress written records, rules, and communications—essential characteristics identified by Max Weber. Though its outward appearance may differ from Western standards, this army in India is no exception to this principle.*

The McDonaldization of Society

The thousands of McDonald's restaurants that dot the U.S. landscape—and increasingly, the world—have a significance that goes far beyond the convenience of ready-made hamburgers and milk shakes. As sociologist George Ritzer (1993, 2001) says, our everyday lives are being "McDonaldized." Let's see what he means by this.

The McDonaldization of society—the standardization of everyday life—does not refer just to the robotlike assembly of food. As Ritzer points out, this process is occurring throughout society—and it is transforming our lives. Want to do some shopping? Shopping malls offer one-stop shopping in controlled environments. Planning a trip? Travel agencies offer "package" tours. They will transport middle-class Americans to ten European capitals in fourteen days. All visitors experience the same hotels, restaurants, and other scheduled sites—and no one need fear meeting a "real" native. Want to keep up with the world? *USA Today* spews out McNews—short, bland, unanalytic pieces that can be digested between gulps of the McShake or the McBurger.

■ *McDonald's in Tokyo, Japan*

Efficiency brings dependability. You can expect your burger and fries to taste the same whether you buy them in Los Angeles or Beijing. Efficiency also lowers prices. But efficiency does come at a cost. Predictability washes away spontaneity, changing the quality of our lives. It produces a sameness, a bland version of what used to be unique experiences. In my own travels, for example, had I taken packaged tours I never would have had the enjoyable, eye-opening experiences that have added so much to my appreciation of human diversity.

For good or bad, our lives are being McDonaldized, and the predictability of packaged settings seems to be our social destiny. When education is rationalized, no longer will our children have to put up with real professors, who insist on discussing ideas endlessly, who never come to decisive answers, and who come saddled with quirks and idiosyncrasies. Our programmed education will eliminate the need for discussion of social issues—we will have packaged solutions to them, definitive answers like those we find in mathematics and engineering—and on television. Computerized courses will teach the same answers to everyone—the approved, "politically correct" ways to think about social issues. Mass testing will assure that students regurgitate the programmed responses.

Our coming prepackaged society will be efficient, of course. But it also means that we will be trapped in the "iron cage" of bureaucracy—just as Weber warned would happen.

■ ■ ■ ■ ■

■ "Ideal" Versus "Real" Bureaucracy

Just as people often act differently from the way the norms say they should, so it is with bureaucracies. The characteristics of bureaucracies identified by Weber are **ideal types;** that is, they are a composite of characteristics based on many specific examples. Think of the judges at a dog show. They have a mental image of how each particular breed of dog should look and behave, and they judge each individual dog according to that mental image. Each dog will rank high on some of these characteristics, and lower on others. In the same way, a particular organization will rank higher or lower on the traits of a bureaucracy, yet still qualify as a bureaucracy. Instead of labeling a particular organization as a "bureaucracy" or "not a bureaucracy," it probably makes more sense to think in terms of the *extent* to which it is bureaucratized (Udy 1959; Hall 1963).

As with culture, then, a bureaucracy often differs from its ideal image. The actual lines of authority ("going through channels"), for example, may be different from those portrayed on organizational charts such as the one shown in Figure 7.1. For example, suppose that before being promoted, the university president taught in

the McDonaldization of society
the process by which ordinary aspects of life are rationalized and efficiency comes to rule such things as food preparation

ideal type
a composite of characteristics based on many specific examples ("ideal" in this case means a description of the abstracted characteristics, not what one desires to exist)

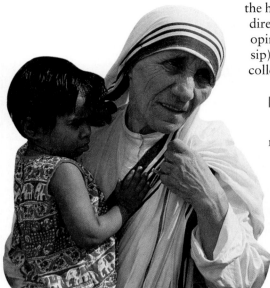

■ *In this chapter, we discuss how bureaucracies have become a powerful and overwhelming force in social life. Even Mother Teresa, one of the most famous religious figures of the late twentieth century, was unable to overcome bureaucratic red tape in her attempt to help New York City's homeless.*

the history department. As a result, friends from that department may have direct access to him or her. If they wish to provide "input" (ranging from opinions about how to solve problems to personal grievances or even gossip), these individuals may skip their chairperson or even the dean of their college, and go directly to the president.

■ Dysfunctions of Bureaucracies

Although in the long run no other form of social organization is more efficient, as Weber recognized, bureaucracies also have a dark side. Let's look at some of their dysfunctions.

Red Tape: A Rule Is a Rule   Bureaucracies can be so bound by red tape that their rules impede the purpose of the organization (Pandey and Kingsley 2000). Some rules (or "correct procedures" in bureaucratic jargon) are enough to try the patience of a saint.

> In the Bronx, Mother Teresa spotted a structurally sound abandoned building and wanted to turn it into a homeless shelter. But she ran head on into a rule: The building must have an elevator for people with disabilities. Not having the funds for the elevator, Mother Teresa struggled to get permission to bypass this rule. Two frustrating years later, she gave up. The abandoned building is still rotting way. (Tobias 1995)

Obviously this rule about elevators was not intended to stop Mother Teresa from ministering to the down and out. But, hey, rules is rules!

Lack of Communication Between Units   Each unit within a bureaucracy performs specialized tasks, which are designed to contribute to the organization's goals. At times, units fail to communicate with one another and end up working at cross purposes. In Granada, Spain, for example, the local government was concerned about the run-down appearance of buildings along one of its main streets. Consequently, one unit of the government fixed the fronts of these buildings, repairing concrete, iron, and stonework. The results were impressive, and the unit was proud of what it had accomplished. The only problem was that another unit of the government had slated these same buildings for demolition (Arías 1993). Because neither unit of this bureaucracy knew what the other was doing, one beautified the buildings while the other made sure they ended up as a heap of rubble.

Bureaucratic Alienation   Treated in terms of roles, rules, and functions rather than as individuals, many workers begin to feel more like objects than people. Marx termed these reactions **alienation,** which he said comes from being cut off from the finished product of one's labor. He pointed out that before industrialization, workers used their own tools to produce an entire product, such as a chair or table. Now the capitalists own the tools (machinery), and assign each worker only a single step or two in the entire production process. Relegated to repetitive tasks that seem remote from the final product, workers lose a sense of identity with what they produce. They come to feel estranged not only from their products but also from their work environment.

alienation
Marx's term for the experience of being cut off from the product of one's labor that results in a sense of powerlessness and normlessness

Resisting Alienation   Because workers want to feel valued and want to have a sense of control over their work, they resist alienation. Forming primary groups at work is a major form of that resistance. Workers band together in informal settings— at lunch, around desks, or for a drink after work. There they give one another approval for jobs well done and express sympathy for the shared need to put up with cantankerous bosses, meaningless routines, and endless rules. They relate to one another not just as workers, but as people who value one another. They flirt, laugh and tell jokes, and talk about their families and goals. Adding this multidimensionality to their work relationships maintains their sense of being individuals rather than mere cogs in a machine.

Consider a common sight. While visiting an office, you see work areas that are decorated with family and vacation photos. The sociological implication is that of workers striving to resist alienation. By staking a claim to individuality, the workers are rejecting an identity as machines that exist to perform functions.

The Alienated Bureaucrat   Not all workers succeed in resisting alienation. Some who become alienated remain in the organization because they see no viable alternative or because they have "only so many years until retirement." They hate every minute of work, and it shows—in their attitudes toward clients, toward fellow workers, and toward authority in the organization. The alienated bureaucrat does not take initiative, will not do anything for the organization beyond what is absolutely required, and uses rules to justify doing as little as possible. If Jennifer in this chapter's opening vignette had come across a more alienated bureaucrat behind the registration window, she might have been asked, "What's the matter with you—can't you read? Everyone else manages to pay their fees on time. Why can't you? I don't know what kind of students they're sending us nowadays." If the clerk had been even more alienated, he or she might have denied knowledge of where Jennifer should go to get the problem resolved.

Despite poor attitude and performance, alienated workers often retain their jobs. Some keep their jobs because of seniority, while others threaten expensive, time-consuming, and embarrassing legal action if anyone tries to fire them. Some alienated workers are shunted off into small bureaucratic corners, where they spend the day doing trivial tasks and have little chance of coming in contact with the public. This treatment, of course, only alienates them further.

Bureaucratic Incompetence   In a tongue-in-cheek analysis of bureaucracies, Laurence Peter proposed what has become known as the **Peter principle:** Each employee of a bureaucracy is promoted to his or her *level of incompetence* (Peter and Hull 1969). People who perform well in a bureaucracy come to the attention of those higher up the chain of command and are promoted. If they continue to perform well, they are again promoted. This process continues until they are promoted to a level at which they can no longer handle the responsibilities well—their level of incompetence. There they hide behind the work of others, taking credit for the accomplishments of employees under their direction.

Although the Peter principle contains a grain of truth, if it were generally true, bureaucracies would be staffed by incompetents, and these organizations would not succeed. In reality, bureaucracies are remarkably successful. Sociologists Peter Evans and James Rauch (1999) examined the government bureaucracies of 35 developing countries. They found that prosperity comes to the countries that have central bureaucracies that hire workers on the basis of merit and offer them rewarding careers.

■ The Perpetuation of Bureaucracies

Bureaucracies have become a standard feature of modern life because they are a powerful form of social organization. They harness people's energies in order to reach specific goals. Once in existence, however, bureaucracies tend to take on a life of their own. In a process called **goal displacement,** even after the organization achieves its goal and no longer has a reason to continue, continue it does.

A classic example is the National Foundation for the March of Dimes, organized in the 1930s to fight polio (Sills 1957). At that time, the origin of polio was a mystery. The public was alarmed and fearful, for overnight a healthy child could be stricken

Peter principle
a bureaucratic "law" according to which the members of an organization are promoted for good work until they reach their level of incompetence, the level at which they can no longer do good work

goal displacement
a goal displaced by another goal; in this context, the adoption of new goals by an organization; also known as *goal replacement*

■ *The March of Dimes was founded by President Franklin Roosevelt in the 1930s to fight polio. When a vaccine for polio was discovered in the 1950s, the organization did not declare victory and disband. Instead, it kept the organization intact by creating new goals—fighting birth defects. Sociologists use the term* goal displacement *to refer to this process of adopting new goals. "Fighting birth defects" is now being replaced by an even vaguer goal, "Breakthroughs for Babies." This new goal displacement may guarantee the organization's existence forever, for it is a goal so elusive it can never be reached. (Can we ever run out of the need for "breakthroughs"?)*

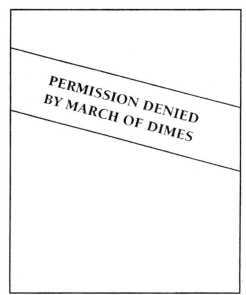

with this crippling disease. Parents lived in fear, because no one knew whose child would be next. To raise money to discover the cause and find a cure, the March of Dimes was founded. This organization placed posters of children on crutches near cash registers in almost every store in the United States. (See the photo above.) The U.S. public took the campaign to heart and contributed heavily. The March of Dimes raised money beyond its wildest dreams. During the 1950s, Dr. Jonas Salk developed a vaccine for polio, and this threat was wiped out almost overnight. The public breathed a collective sigh of relief.

What then? Did the organization fold? After all, its purpose had been fulfilled. But, as you know, the March of Dimes is still around. Faced with the loss of their jobs, the professional staff that ran the organization quickly found a way to keep its bureaucracy intact by pursuing a new enemy—birth defects. Their choice of enemy is particularly striking, for it is doubtful that we will ever run out of birth defects—and thus unlikely that these people will ever run out of jobs. But then came a new threat to the organization's existence—the mapping of the human genome system. This could one day eliminate birth defects. To ward off this threat, the March of Dimes has adopted a new slogan, "Breakthroughs for Babies." This latest goal should ensure the organization's existence forever—for it is so vague that we are not likely to ever run out of the need for "breakthroughs."

Organizations are sensitive about sociologists analyzing their activities, and the March of Dimes is no exception. When I tried to get permission to reprint a copy of their current poster, I was denied that permission—*unless I changed my analysis to make it more favorable to the organization.* As you can see from the missing photo above, I refused to do so. Sociologists regularly confront such obstacles in their work.

■ The Sociological Significance of Bureaucracies

Perhaps the main sociological significance of bureaucracies is that they represent a fundamental change in how people relate to one another (see Table 7.1 on page 187). When work is rooted in personal relationships, much more is at stake than performing tasks efficiently and keeping an eye on the bottom line. Seeing that all relatives and friends have jobs, for example, was once the determining factor in making decisions. Bureaucracies, or the rationalization of society, changed all this (Volti 1995).

Voluntary Associations

Although bureaucracies have become the dominant form of organization for large, task-oriented groups, even more common are voluntary associations. Let's examine their characteristics.

Back in the 1830s, Alexis de Tocqueville, a Frenchman, traveled across the United States, observing the customs of this new nation. His report, *Democracy in America* (1835), became widely read in Europe and in the United States. It is still quoted for its insights into the American character. One of de Tocqueville's observations was that Americans joined a lot of **voluntary associations,** groups made up of volunteers who organize on the basis of some mutual interest.

Over the years, Americans have maintained this pattern and are very proud of it. A visitor entering one of the thousands of small towns that dot the U.S. landscape is often greeted with a highway sign proclaiming some of the town's volunteer associations: Girl Scouts, Boy Scouts, Kiwanis, Lions, Elks, Eagles, Knights of Columbus, Chamber of Commerce, American Legion, Veterans of Foreign Wars, and perhaps a host of others. One type of voluntary association is so prevalent that a separate sign sometimes indicates which varieties are present in the town: Roman Catholic, Baptist, Lutheran, Methodist, Episcopalian, and so on. Not listed on these signs are many other voluntary associations, such as political parties, unions, health clubs, the National Right to Life, the National Organization for Women, Alcoholics Anonymous, Gamblers Anonymous, Association of Pinto Racers, and Citizens United For or Against This and That.

Americans love voluntary associations, and use them to express a wide variety of interests. Some groups are local, consisting of only a few volunteers; others are national, with a paid professional staff. Some are temporary, organized to accomplish some specific task, such as arranging for Fourth of July fireworks. Others, such as the Scouts and political parties, are permanent—large, secondary organizations with clear lines of command—and they are also bureaucracies.

■ Functions of Voluntary Associations

Whatever their form, voluntary associations are numerous because they meet people's basic needs. People do not *have* to belong to these organizations. They join because they obtain benefits from their participation. Functionalists have identified seven functions of voluntary associations.

1. Voluntary organizations advance particular interests. For example, adults who are concerned about children's welfare volunteer for the Scouts because they think kids are better off joining this group than hanging out on the street. In short, voluntary associations get things done, whether that means arranging for the fireworks to go off on time or making people familiar with the latest legislation on abortion.

2. Voluntary groups offer people an identity. Some even provide a sense of purpose in life. As in-groups, they give their members a feeling of togetherness, of belonging. In many cases, they give them a sense of doing something worthwhile. This function is so important for some individuals that their participation in voluntary associations becomes the center of their lives.

3. Voluntary associations help govern the nation and maintain social order. Groups that help "get out the vote" or assist the Red Cross in coping with disasters are obvious examples.

voluntary association
a group made up of volunteers who have organized on the basis of some mutual interest

The first two functions apply to all voluntary associations. In a general sense, so does the third. Although few organizations focus on politics, voluntary associations help to incorporate individuals into society, which helps to maintain social order.

Sociologist David Sills (1968) identified four other functions, which apply only to some voluntary associations.

4. Some voluntary groups mediate between the government and the individual. For example, some provide a way for people to put pressure on lawmakers.

5. By providing training in organizational skills, some groups help individuals climb the occupational ladder.

6. Other groups help bring people into the political mainstream. The National Association for the Advancement of Colored People (NAACP) is an example of such a group.

7. Finally, some voluntary associations pave the way to social change. Groups such as Greenpeace oppose the taken-for-granted definitions of "normal" when it comes to the environment. Their challenges to established boundaries often indicate the direction of social change.

Shared Interests

Voluntary associations, then, represent no single interest or purpose. They can be reactionary, resisting new ways of doing things, or they can be visionary, standing at the vanguard of social change. Despite their diversity, however, a common thread runs through voluntary associations. That thread is mutual interest. Although the particular interest varies from group to group, shared interest in some view or activity is the tie that binds their members together.

Motivations for joining these groups differ. Some people join because they hold strong convictions concerning the stated purpose of the organization, others simply because membership helps them politically or professionally. Some may even join because they have romantic interests in a group member.

With so many motivations for joining, and because the commitment of some members is fleeting, voluntary associations often have high turnover. Some people move in and out of groups almost as fast as they change clothes. Within each organization, however, is an inner circle—individuals who actively promote the group, who stand firmly behind the group's goals, and who are firmly committed to maintaining the organization itself. If this inner circle loses its commitment, the group is likely to fold.

The Problem of Oligarchy

An interesting, and disturbing, aspect of voluntary associations is that the leaders often grow distant from their members and become convinced that they can trust only the inner circle to make the group's important decisions. To see this principle at work, let's look at the Veterans of Foreign Wars (VFW).

Sociologists Elaine Fox and George Arquitt (1985) studied three local posts of the VFW, a national organization of former U.S. soldiers who have served in foreign wars. They found that although the leaders conceal their attitudes from the other members, they view the rank and file as a bunch of ignorant boozers. Because the leaders can't stand the thought that such people might represent them to the community and at national meetings, a curious situation arises. Although the VFW constitution makes rank-and-file members eligible for top leadership positions, they never become leaders. In fact, the leaders are so effective in controlling these top positions that even be-

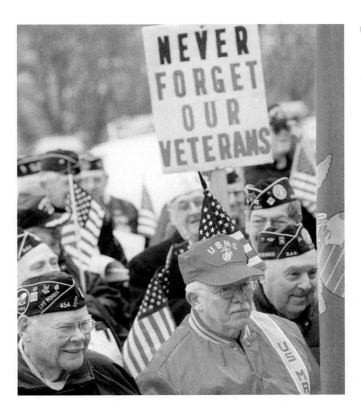

■ In a process called the iron law of oligarchy, a small, self-perpetuating elite tends to take control of formal organizations. Veterans' organizations are no exception to this principle, as sociological studies have shown.

fore an election they can tell you who is going to win. "You need to meet Jim," the sociologists were told. "He's the next post commander after Sam does his time."

At first, the researchers found this puzzling. The election hadn't been held yet. As they investigated further, they found that leadership is actually decided behind the scenes. The elected leaders appoint their favored people to chair the key committees. This makes the members aware of their accomplishments, and they elect them as leaders. The inner circle, then, maintains control over the entire organization simply by appointing members of their inner circle to highly visible positions.

Like the VFW, most organizations are run by only a few of their members (Cnaan 1991). Building on the term *oligarchy*, a system in which many are ruled by a few, sociologist Robert Michels (1876–1936) coined the term **the iron law of oligarchy** to refer to how organizations come to be dominated by a small, self-perpetuating elite. The majority of members are passive, and an elite inner circle keeps itself in power by passing the leadership positions from one clique member to another.

What many find disturbing about the iron law of oligarchy is that people are excluded from leadership because they don't represent the inner circle's values, background, or even their images of themselves. This is true even of organizations that are strongly committed to democratic principles. For example, U.S. political parties—supposedly the backbone of the nation's representative government—have fallen prey to it. Run by an inner circle, they pass their leadership positions from one elite member to another. This principle is also demonstrated by the U.S. Senate. With their control of statewide political machinery, access to free mailing, and even the free use of tax dollars to produce videos that can be sent by e-mail, about 90 percent of U.S. senators who choose to run are reelected (*Statistical Abstract* 2000:Table 462).

The iron law of oligarchy is not without its limitations, of course. Members of the inner group must remain attuned to the opinions of the other members, regardless of

the iron law of oligarchy Robert Michels' phrase for the tendency of formal organizations to be dominated by a small, self-perpetuating elite their personal feelings. If the oligarchy gets too far out of line, it runs the risk of a grassroots rebellion that would throw the elite out of office. This threat often softens the iron law of oligarchy by making the leadership responsive to the membership. In addition, because not all organizations become captive to an elite, this is a tendency, not an inevitability (Fisher 1994; Jarley et al. 2000).

Working for the Corporation

Since you are likely to end up working in a bureaucracy, let's look at how its characteristics may affect your career.

The "Hidden" Corporate Culture

Who gets ahead in large corporations? Although we might like to think that success comes from intelligence and hard work, many factors other than merit underlie salary increases and promotions. As sociologist Rosabeth Moss Kanter (1977, 1983) stresses, the *corporate culture* contains "hidden values." These values create a self-fulfilling prophecy that affects people's corporate careers.

It works like this: Corporate and department heads have ideas about who the best workers and colleagues are, and who is most likely to succeed. People who match their ideas have backgrounds similar to them—and they even look like them. These people are given better access to information, networking, and "fast track" positions. They then perform better and become more committed to the organization—thus confirming the initial expectation. In contrast, those judged to be outsiders are thought to have lesser abilities. Because of this, they are given fewer opportunities and challenges. Working at a level beneath their capacity, they come to think poorly of themselves, become less committed to the organization, and don't perform as well—thus confirming the initial expectation.

The hidden values that created this self-fulfilling prophecy remain invisible. What is visible are the promotions of people with superior performances and greater commitment to the company, not the low expectations and closed opportunities that produced these attitudes and accomplishments.

You can see how these hidden values contribute to the iron law of oligarchy we just reviewed. Because of this self-fulfilling prophecy, the inner circle reproduces itself by favoring people who "look" like its own members, generally white and male. Women and minorities, who don't match the stereotype, are often "showcased"—placed in highly visible positions with little power in order to demonstrate how progressive the company is. There, however, they often hold "slow-track" positions, where accomplishments seldom come to the attention of top management.

Kanter found that the level people reach in an organization shapes their behavior, and even their attitudes. In general, the higher people go, the higher their morale. "This is a good company," they say to themselves. "They recognize my abilities." With their greater satisfaction, people in higher office also tend to be more helpful to subordinates and more flexible in their style of leadership. In contrast, people who don't get very far in the organization are frustrated and tend to have lower morale. They are also likely to be rigid supervisors and strong defenders of whatever privileges they have.

A significant part of bureaucracies lies below the surface. Because workers tend to see only the level that is readily visible, they usually ascribe differences in people's behaviors and attitudes to their personalities. Sociologists probe beneath the surface, however, to examine how corporate culture shapes people's attitudes, and, by extension, the quality of their work.

As corporations grapple with growing diversity, the hidden corporate culture is likely to give way, but only slowly and grudgingly. In the following Thinking Critically section, we'll consider other aspects of diversity in the workplace.

thinking
CRITICALLY

Managing Diversity in the Workplace

Times have changed. In San Jose, California, the *Nguyens* outnumber the *Joneses* by nearly 50 percent. More than half of U.S. workers are minorities, immigrants, and women. Diversity in the workplace is much more than skin color. Diversity includes ethnicity, gender, age, religion, social class, and sexual orientation.

In the past, the idea was for people to join the "melting pot," to give up their distinctive traits and become like the dominant group. Today, with the huge successes of the civil rights and women's movements, people are more likely to prize their distinctive traits. Realizing that assimilation (being absorbed into the dominant culture) is probably not the wave of the future, three of four Fortune 500 companies have "diversity training." They hold lectures and workshops so employees can learn to work with colleagues of diverse cultures and racial-ethnic backgrounds.

Coors Brewery is a prime example of this change. Coors went into a financial tailspin after one of the Coors brothers gave a racially charged speech in the 1980s. Today, Coors offers diversity workshops, has sponsored a gay dance, and has paid for a corporate-wide mammography program. The company even had rabbis certify its suds as kosher. Its proud new slogan: "Coors cares" (Cloud 1998). Now, that's quite a change.

What Coors cares about, of course, is the bottom line. It's the same with the other corporations. Blatant racism and sexism once made no difference to profitability. Today, they do. To promote profitability, companies must promote diversity—or at least pretend to. The sincerity of corporate heads is not what's important; diversity in the workplace is.

Diversity training has the potential to build bridges, but it can backfire. Directors of these programs can be so incompetent that they create antagonisms and reinforce stereotypes. At a diversity training session at the U.S. Department of Transportation, for example, women groped men as the men ran by. Blacks and whites were encouraged to insult one another and to call one another names (Reibstein 1996). The intention may have been good (understanding the other through role reversal and getting hostilities "out in the open"), but the approach was moronic. Instead of healing, these behaviors wound and leave scars.

■ ■ ■ ■ ■
for your consideration . . .

Do you think that the growing diversity in today's workplace provides a glimpse into our future? If so, how? How can we develop diversity training that fosters mutual respect? Can you suggest practical ways to develop workplaces that are not divided by gender and race-ethnicity?

Humanizing the Corporate Culture

Bureaucracies have transformed society by harnessing people's energies to specific goals and monitoring progress to those goals. Weber (1946) predicted that because bureaucracies were so efficient and had the capacity to replace themselves, they would come to dominate social life. More than any prediction in sociology, this one has withstood the test of time (Rothschild and Whitt 1986; Perrow 1991).

Attempts to Humanize the Work Setting

Bureaucracies appear likely to remain our dominant form of social organization, and most of us, like it or not, are destined to spend our working lives in bureaucracies. Many people have become concerned about the negative side of bureaucracies, and would like to make them more humane. **Humanizing a work setting** means to organize work in such a way that it develops rather than impedes human potential. Humanized work settings offer access to opportunities on the basis of ability and contributions rather than personal characteristics. They distribute power more equally and have fewer rigid rules and more open decision making.

Can bureaucracies adapt to such a model? Contrary to some images, not all bureaucracies are unyielding, unwieldy monoliths. There is nothing in the nature of bureaucracies that makes them *inherently* insensitive to people's needs or that prevents them from humanizing corporate culture.

But what about the cost of such changes? The United States is in a global economic competition. Japan and western Europe—and now China—are formidable rivals. To humanize corporate culture, however, does not require huge expense. Sociologist Rosabeth Moss Kanter (1983) compared forty-seven companies that were rigidly bureaucratic with competitors of the same size that were more flexible. She found that the more flexible companies were more profitable—probably because their greater flexibility encouraged greater creativity, productivity, and company loyalty.

Quality Circles   In light of such findings, many corporations have experimented with humanizing their work settings. They are not motivated by some altruistic urge to make life better for their workers, but by the same motivation as always, the bottom line. It is in their self-interest to make their company more competitive. Thousands of U.S. firms use *quality circles*. A group of workers and a manager or two meet regularly to try to improve the quality of both working conditions and the company's products.

Most of these companies report that quality circles yield few benefits. Perhaps this is because many companies are set in their ways, and they don't take the suggestions of their workers seriously. Whatever the reason for the disappointing results, companies such as Whirlpool and GE have abandoned quality circles. Each company continues to solicit ideas from its employees, however. GE, which has switched to town hall type meetings, rewards workers with cash and stock options (Naj 1993).

A surprising twist is that manufacturing companies that use quality circles report more repeated motion injuries, such as carpal tunnel syndrome (Fairris and Brenner 2001). Apparently this unexpected consequence of quality circles is due to higher pressure on employees to increase their pace of work.

Employee Stock Ownership Plans   If workers are shareholders, it is thought that their company loyalty and productivity will increase. Consequently, many companies let their employees buy the firm's stock either at a discount or as part of their salary. About ten million U.S. workers own part of 11,000 companies. What are the results? Some studies show that these companies are more profitable than other firms

humanizing a work setting organizing a workplace in such a way that it develops rather than impedes human potential

(White 1991; Logue and Yates 2000). Other studies, however, report that their profits are about the same, although their productivity may be higher (Blassi and Conte 1996). We need more definitive research on this matter.

If the employees own all the company stock, it should eliminate problems between workers and management. This should be obvious—after all, the workers and owners are the same people. But this is not the case. United Airline pilots, for example, who own the largest stake in their airline, staged a work slowdown during their 2001 contract negotiations, forcing the cancellation of thousands of flights. The machinists, who are also owners, followed suit. The machinists' union even threatened to strike. As passengers fled the airline, United racked up huge losses, and its stock plummeted (Zuckerman 2001). The irony is that the company's losses were the worker-owners' losses.

Profitability, not ownership, appears to be the key to reducing worker-management conflict. Unprofitable firms put more pressure on their employee-owners, while profitable companies are quicker to resolve problems.

Work Teams Work teams are used by one of five U.S. companies. It is a wonder that they are not more common. These self-managed teams, which stimulate creative ideas and solutions to problems, instill a greater sense of loyalty to the company. Employees work harder, have less absenteeism, and are more productive. Workers in these groups also react more quickly to threats posed by technological change and competitors' advances. No less a behemoth than IBM has found that people work more effectively in small groups than in a centralized command structure (Drucker 1992).

The concepts we discussed in the last chapter help to explain these results. In small work groups, people form primary relationships, and their identities become intertwined with their group. This reduces alienation, for rather than being lost in a bureaucratic maze, their individuality is appreciated, their contributions more readily recognized. The group's successes become the individual's successes—as do its failures—and these reflect positively or negatively on the individual. As a consequence of their expanded personal ties, workers make more of an effort. The results have been so good that, in what is known as "worker empowerment," some self-managed teams even replace bosses as the ones who control everything from schedules to hiring and firing (Lublin 1991).

Corporate Day Care Another way to humanize the work setting is to set up day care facilities at work. This eases the strain on parents, allowing them to work and still keep an eye on a baby or young child. Parents are able to spend time with their children during breaks and lunch hours. Mothers can even nurse their children at the child care center. The parents are also able to observe how their child is taken care of.

Most U.S. companies offer no child care at all. In the face of global competition, especially cheap labor in the Least Industrialized Nations, can U.S. firms afford child care? Surprisingly, child care can reduce labor costs. When the Union Bank of Monterey, California, decided to measure the cost of its day care, they found that the annual turnover of employees who used its day care was just one-fourth that

■ Humanizing the work setting *means to make the work site a pleasant place that meets the needs of workers. You can see how on-site day care simplifies life for this father—both he and his daughter go to the same place at the same time. You can also see how this keeps the day care workers on their toes, for the parents are popping in and out throughout the day. Such services cost companies less than they appear to, for they reduce worker turnover.*

of those who did not use it. Users of the center were also absent from work less, and they had shorter maternity leaves. The net cost? After subtracting the center's costs from these savings, the bank saved more than $200,000 (Solomon 1988).

Providing back-up child care falls somewhere in between offering on-site child care and no child care at all. With this approach, parents use their own babysitter, but if the sitter can't make it, parents can use the center's back-up services, allowing them to get to work—and to work without worry (Narayan 1994).

As the number of women in management increases, it is likely that more U.S. firms will offer child care services as part of a benefits package designed to attract and hold capable workers.

The Cooperative An alternative organizational form is the cooperative, introduced to the United States during the 1840s (Rothschild and Whitt 1986). Cooperatives are owned by members who collectively make decisions, determine goals, evaluate resources, set salaries, and assign work tasks. There is no overarching hierarchy, and all members can participate in the decisions of the organization. There are about five thousand cooperatives in the United States. These organizations attempt to achieve some specific social good, such as distributing higher quality food at lower prices. They also attempt to provide a high level of personal satisfaction for their members as they work toward their goals. Because all members can participate in decision making, cooperatives spend huge amounts of time in deciding even routine matters. The economic results of cooperatives are mixed. Many are less profitable than private organizations, others more so. A few have been so successful that they have been bought out by Wall Street firms.

■ The Conflict Perspective

Conflict theorists point out that it does not matter how work is structured. The basic relationship between workers and owners is always confrontational (Edwards 1979; Derber and Schwartz 1988). Workers and owners walk different paths in life, with owners exploiting workers to extract greater profits and workers trying to resist that exploitation. Because their basic interests are fundamentally opposed, these critics argue, attempts by employers to humanize the work setting (or to manage diversity) are mere window dressing, efforts to conceal their fundamental goal of exploiting workers. It is just another attempt to manipulate workers into actively cooperating in their own exploitation. This analysis does not apply to cooperatives because they are owned by the workers.

■ Technology and the Control of Workers

The microchip has brought a higher quality of manufactured goods and reduced drudgery in our lives. Records are much easier to keep, and we can type just one letter and let the computer print it out and address it to ten individuals—or to ten thousand. Working on my computer, I can modify this sentence, this paragraph, or any section of this book with ease. The other side of the computer is its potential for abuse. Computers make it easier for governments to operate a police state by monitoring our every move. The Big Brother in Orwell's classic novel, *1984,* may turn out to be a computer.

Perhaps, as Orwell suggests, our destiny is to be oppressed by technology, to become servants to a master computer, but if so, we won't be able to tell for a while. In the meantime, we can see that the computer has allowed managers to increase surveillance without face-to-face supervision. For example, sitting in their office, managers know the exact number of keystrokes workers make each minute. They know precisely how long each worker takes for each telephone call. Workers who fall below the average are singled out for discipline. It does not matter that the slower workers may be more polite or more helpful, only that the computer reports slower performance.

As sociologist Gary Marx (1985, 1986, 1995) says, we may be moving to a "maximum-security" workplace. Computers are able to measure motion, air currents, vibrations, odors, pressure changes, and voice stress. Video cameras need only a pinhole through which to spy. To prevent employees from punching in someone else's time card, a leading hotel uses a device to scan their workers' eyes. It compares these images with computerized data on file. A truck driver at Safeway, who used to enjoy his job, says, "No one was looking over your shoulder, and you felt like a human being." But now he says he feels "pushed around." A computer in the dashboard of his truck, called, appropriately, a Tripmaster, not only keeps track of his speed, but also his shifting, "excessive" idling, and even when and how long he stops for a coffee break. The driver says he will retire early.

The maximum-security workplace seems an apt term, but with the computer's awesome capacities, the surveillance of the workplace may be just one aspect of a coming "maximum-security society" (Marx 1995). The Sociology and the New Technology box below discusses how computers are being used to monitor workers who think that their actions have gone unnoticed.

sociology & the new technology

Cyberslackers and Cybersleuths: Surfing at Work

Few people work constantly at their jobs. Most of us take breaks and, at least once in a while, goof off. We meet fellow workers at the water cooler, and we talk in the hallway. Much of this interaction is good for the company, for it bonds us to fellow workers and ties us to our jobs.

Our personal lives may may even cross over into our workday. Some of us make personal calls from the office. Bosses know that we need to check in with our child's preschool or make arrangements for a babysitter. They expect such calls. Some even wink as we make a date or nod as we arrange to have our car worked on. And most bosses make personal calls of their own from time to time. It's the abuse that bothers bosses, and it's not surprising that they fire anyone who talks on the phone all day for personal reasons.

The latest wrinkle at work is *cyberslacking*, using computers at work for personal purposes. Most workers fritter away some of their workday online (Greengard 2000). They trade stocks, download music, gamble, and play games. They read books, shop, exchange jokes, send personal e-mail, and visit online red-light districts. Some cyberslackers even operate their own businesses online. Others spend most of their "working" hours battling virtual enemies. One computer programmer became a national champion playing *Starcraft* at work.

Some workers defend their cyberloafing. They argue that since their work invades their homes—forcing them to work in the evening and on weekends—employers should accommodate their personal lives. Some Web sites protect cyberslackers: They feature a panic button in case the boss pokes her head in your office. Click the button and a phony spreadsheet pops onto your screen while typing sounds emerge from your speakers.

Companies have struck back. Xerox fired 40 employees for downloading pornography at work (Naughton 1999). Dow Chemical fired 200 "workers" for cyberloafing (Greengard 2000). And then there is the cybersleuth. With specialized software, cybersleuths can examine everything employees read online, everything they write, and every Web site they visit. They can even bring up every word they've erased. What some workers don't know (and what some of us forget) is that "delete" does not mean *delete*. Our computer keeps a hidden diary, even of what we've erased. With a few clicks, the cybersleuth, like magic ink, makes our "deleted" information visible, exposing our hidden diary for anyone to read.

for your consideration

Do you think that cybersleuthing is an abuse of power? An invasion of privacy? Or do employers have a right to check on what their employees are doing with company computers on company time? Can you think of a less invasive solution to cyberslacking?

U.S. and Japanese Corporations

How were the Japanese able to arise from the defeat of World War II—including the nuclear devastation of two of their main cities—to become a giant in today's global economy? Some analysts trace part of the answer to the way their corporations are organized.

How the Corporations Differ

One analyst, William Ouchi (1981), pinpointed five ways in which Japanese corporations differ from those of the United States. You will be surprised at how different they are. But are these differences in handling executives myth or reality?

Hiring and Promoting Teams   In *Japan,* teamwork is central. College graduates who join a corporation are all paid about the same starting salary. They also get raises as a team. To learn about the company, they are rotated as a team through the various levels of the organization. They develop intense loyalty to one another and to their company, for the welfare of one represents the welfare of all. Only in later years are individuals singled out for recognition. When there is an opening in the firm, outsiders are not even considered.

In the *United States,* personal achievement is central. An employee is hired on the basis of what the firm thinks that individual can contribute. Employees try to outperform others, and they strive for raises and promotions as signs of personal success. The individual's loyalty is to himself or herself, not to the company. Outsiders are considered for openings in the firm.

Lifetime Security   In *Japan,* lifetime security is taken for granted. Employees can expect to work for the same firm for the rest of their lives. In return for not being laid off or fired, the firm expects them to be loyal to the company, to stick with it

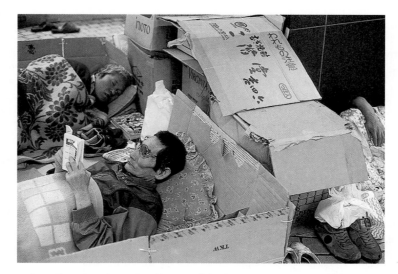

■ *For a time, Americans stood in awe of the Japanese corporate model. Research, however, has uncovered serious flaws. Lifetime job security, for example, is a myth. These homeless men are living in the Shinjuko train station in Tokyo. Note how they have followed the Japanese custom of placing their shoes outside before entering their "home."*

through good and bad times. Workers do not go job shopping, for their careers—and many aspects of their lives—are wrapped up in this one firm.

In the *United States,* lifetime security is unusual. It is limited primarily to teachers, who receive what is called *tenure.* Companies lay off workers in slow times. To remain competitive they even reorganize and fire entire divisions. Workers, too, "look out for number one." They seek better pay and opportunities elsewhere. Job shopping and job hopping are common.

Almost Total Involvement   In *Japan,* work is like a marriage: The worker and the company are committed to each other. The employee supports the company with loyalty and long hours at work, while the company supports its workers with lifetime security, health services, recreation, sports and social events, even a home mortgage. Involvement with the company does not stop when the workers leave the building. They join company study and exercise groups, and are likely to spend evenings with co-workers in bars and restaurants.

In the *United States,* work is a specific, often temporary contract. Workers are hired to do a certain job. When they have done that job, they have fulfilled their obligation to the company. Their after-work hours are their own. They go home to their private lives, which usually are separate from the firm.

Broad Training   In *Japan,* workers move from one job to another within the company. Not only are they not stuck doing the same thing for years on end, but also they gain a broader picture of the corporation and how the specific jobs they are assigned fit into the bigger picture.

In the *United States,* workers are expected to perform one job, to do it well, and then to be promoted upward to a job with more responsibility. Their understanding of the company is largely tied to the particular corner they occupy, often making it difficult for them to see how their job fits into the overall picture.

Decision Making by Consensus   In *Japan,* decision making is a lengthy process. Each person who will be affected by a decision is consulted. After lengthy deliberations, a consensus emerges, and everyone agrees on which suggestion is superior. This makes workers feel that they are an essential part of the organization, not simply cogs in a giant machine.

In the *United States,* the person in charge of the unit to be affected does as much consulting with others as he or she thinks necessary and then makes the decision.

■ The Myth Versus Reality

Peering beneath the surface reveals a reality that differs from the myth that has grown up around the Japanese corporation. Lifetime job security, for example, is elusive, and only about a third of Japanese workers find it. Most workers are also required by law to retire at age 60, whether they have the savings to support themselves or not (Clark and Ogawa 1997). Japanese corporations have begun to tie pay to productivity. They have found that paying the same wages to almost everyone in the same age group makes the company less competitive in the global market. Management by consensus is also a myth. This was not how decisions were made at Sony, one of Japan's most successful companies (Nathan 1999). Akio Morita, Sony's founder, was an entrepreneur from the same mold as Bill Gates. Morita didn't send memos up and down the line, as the myth would have you believe. Instead, he relied on his gut feeling about products. When he thought up the Walkman, Morita didn't discuss it until consensus emerged. Instead, he simply ordered it to be manufactured. And he made quick decisions. Over lunch, he decided to buy CBS Records. The cost was $2 billion. The Cultural Diversity box on the following page, with which we close this chapter, explores other aspects of the Japanese myth.

Around the World
Japanese and U.S. Corporations in an Age of Greed

Do you know which of these statements is false?

- The Japanese are more productive than Americans.
- The living standard of Americans has fallen behind that of the Japanese.
- Japanese workers enjoy lifetime job security.
- The Japanese are paid less than Americans.

From what you just read, you know that the third one is false. So are the other three.

A while back, Japanese corporations seemed invincible. There was even talk that the United States had won World War II, but had lost the economic war. Impressed with Japan's success, many nations, including the United States, sent executives to Japan to study their companies. U.S. corporations then copied parts of that model.

Cracks in the facade soon appeared. Small at first, they grew, destroying some of Japan's major corporations. These com-panies had been built on personal relationships, on mutual obligations that transcend contracts. This had been a key to creating fierce loyalty, a corporate strength that turned out to be an Achilles heel. When Japan's economy went into a nose-dive, companies refused to lay off workers. Layoffs were not part of their corporate culture. Costs mounted while profits disappeared, sinking them in a sea of red ink.

In a surprise move, Japan studied U.S. corporations to see why they were more efficient. Flying in the face of their tradition, Japanese corporations began to lay off workers and to offer merit pay. Toyota and Honda began to give bonuses to managers who met their goals, a standard U.S. practice, but one that had been unthinkable in Japan (Schlesinger and Sapsford 1993; Reitman and Suris 1994; Shirouzu and Williams 1995; Kanabayashi 1996).

One of the biggest surprises was Ford's takeover of Mazda. With Mazda teetering on the edge of bankruptcy, its creditors decided that Ford knew more about building and marketing cars than Mazda and invited Ford to manage the company. In true U.S. fashion, Ford laid off workers and renegotiated contracts with suppliers. With its work force slashed from 46,000 to 36,000, Mazda again became profitable. The process isn't over: After Ford turned Mazda around, Renault took over Nissan Motor (Shirouzu 2000). A much leaner, meaner Japanese production machine is emerging.

The real bottom line is that we live in a global marketplace—of ideas as well as products. The likely result will be that both the West and Japan will feed off each other. Japanese corporations will learn how to compete more effectively in global capitalism's cutthroat production and marketing. It is not as apparent, however, that U.S. corporations will learn the cooperation that underlies the Japanese corporation—for it may not increase the bottom line.

Summary and Review

The Rationalization of Society

■ **How did the rationalization of society come about?**

The term **rationalization of society** refers to a transformation in people's thinking and behaviors—one that shifts the focus from following time-honored ways to being efficient in producing results. Max Weber, who developed this term, traced this change to Protestant theology, which he said brought about capitalism. Karl Marx attributed rationalization to capitalism itself. Pp. 186–189.

Formal Organizations and Bureaucracy

■ **What are formal organizations?**

Formal organizations are secondary groups designed to achieve specific objectives. Their dominant form is the **bureaucracy**, which Weber said consists of a hierarchy, a division of labor, written rules and communications, and impersonality of positions—characteristics that make bureaucracies efficient and enduring. Pp. 189–194.

■ **What dysfunctions are associated with bureaucracies?**

The dysfunctions of bureaucracies include alienation, red tape, lack of communication between units, **goal displacement,** and incompetence (as seen in the **Peter principle**). In Weber's view, the impersonality of bureaucracies tends to produce **alienation** among workers—the feeling that no one cares about them and that they do not really fit in. Marx's view of alienation is somewhat different—workers do not identify with the product of their labor because they participate in only a small part of the production process. Pp. 194–196.

Voluntary Associations

■ **What are the functions of voluntary associations?**

Voluntary associations are groups made up of volunteers who organize on the basis of common interests. These associations further mutual interests, provide a sense of identity and purpose, help to govern and maintain order, mediate between the government and the individual, give training in organizational skills, help provide access to political power, and pave the way for social change. Pp. 197–198.

■ **What is "the iron law of oligarchy"?**

Sociologist Robert Michels noted that formal organizations have a tendency to become controlled by an inner circle that limits leadership to its own members. The dominance of a formal organization by an elite that keeps itself in power is called **the iron law of oligarchy.** Pp. 198–200.

Working for the Corporation

■ **How does the corporate culture affect workers?**

The term **corporate culture** refers to an organization's traditions, values, and unwritten norms. Much of corporate culture, such as its hidden values, is not readily visible. Often, a self-fulfilling prophecy is at work: People who match a corporation's hidden values tend to be put on tracks that enhance their chance of success, while those who do not match those values are set on a course that minimizes their performance. Pp. 200–201.

Humanizing the Corporate Culture

■ **What does it mean to humanize the work setting?**

Humanizing a work setting means to organize it in a way that develops rather than impedes human potential. Among the attempts to make bureaucracies more humane are quality circles, work teams, and corporate day care. Employee stock ownership plans give workers a greater stake in the outcomes of their work organizations, but they do not prevent worker-management conflict. Cooperatives are an alternative to bureaucracies. Conflict theorists see attempts to humanize work as a way of manipulating workers. Pp. 202–205.

U.S. and Japanese Corporations

■ **How do Japanese and U.S. corporations differ?**

The Japanese corporate model contrasts sharply with the U.S. model in terms of hiring and promotion, lifetime security, interaction of workers outside the work setting, broad training of workers, and collective decision making. Much of this model is a myth, an idealization of reality, and does not reflect Japanese corporate life today. Pp. 206–208.

■ *Where can I read more on this topic?*

Suggested readings for this chapter are at the back of this book.

Additional Online Resources for This Chapter
www.ablongman.com/henslin6e

- *Content Select* Research Database for Sociology, with suggested key terms and annotated references
- Link to 2000 Census, with activities
- Flashcards of key terms and concepts

- Practice Tests
- Weblinks
- Interactive Maps

using . . .
ContentSelect

Research Database for Sociology

Karl Marx	bureaucracy	alienation	Japanese corporate
Max Weber	oligarchy	corporate culture	model
capitalism	McDonaldization	corporation	

What Is Deviance?

How Norms Make Social Life Possible

Sanctions

Shaming and Degradation Ceremonies

Competing Explanations of Deviance: Sociology, Biology, and Psychology

The Symbolic Interactionist Perspective

Differential Association Theory

Control Theory

Labeling Theory

The Functionalist Perspective

Can Deviance Really Be Functional for Society?

Strain Theory: How Social Values Produce Deviance

Illegitimate Opportunity Structures: Social Class and Crime

The Conflict Perspective

Class, Crime, and the Criminal Justice System

Power and Inequality

The Law as an Instrument of Oppression

Reactions to Deviance

Street Crime and Prisons

The Death Penalty

Legal Change

The Trouble with Official Statistics

The Medicalization of Deviance: Mental Illness

The Need for a More Humane Approach

Summary and Review

8

Deviance and Social Control

I n just a few moments I was to meet my first Yanomamo, my first primitive man. What would it be like? . . . I looked up (from my canoe) and gasped when I saw a dozen burly, naked, filthy, hideous men staring at us down the shafts of their drawn arrows. Immense wads of green tobacco were stuck between their lower teeth and lips, making them look even more hideous, and strands of dark-green slime dripped or hung from their noses. We arrived at the village while the men were blowing a hallucinogenic drug up their noses. One of the side

> they would "clean" their hands by spitting a quantity of slimy tobacco juice into them, rub them together, and then proceed with the examination.

effects of the drug is a runny nose. The mucus is always saturated with the green powder, and the Indians usually let it run freely from their nostrils. . . . I just sat there holding my notebook, helpless and pathetic. . . .

The whole situation was depressing, and I wondered why I ever decided to switch from civil engineering to anthropology in the first place. . . . (Soon) I was covered with red pigment, the result of a dozen or so complete examinations. . . . These examinations capped an otherwise grim day. The Indians would blow their noses into their hands, flick as much of the mucus off that would separate in a snap of the wrist, wipe the residue into their hair, and then carefully examine my face, arms, legs, hair, and the contents of my pockets. I said (in their language), "Your hands are dirty"; my comments were met by the Indians in the following way: they would "clean" their hands by spitting a quantity of slimy tobacco juice into them, rub them together, and then proceed with the examination.

This is how Napoleon Chagnon describes his eye-opening introduction to the Yanomamo tribe of the rain forests of Brazil. His ensu-
ing months of fieldwork continued to bring surprise after surprise, and
often Chagnon (1977) could hardly believe his eyes—or his nose.

*W*here would we start if we were to list the deviant behaviors of these people?
With the way they appear naked in public? Use hallucinogenic drugs? Let
mucus hang from their noses? Or with the way they rub hands that are filled with
mucus, spittle, and tobacco juice over a frightened stranger who doesn't dare to
protest? Perhaps. But it isn't this simple, for as we shall see, deviance is relative.

What Is Deviance?

deviance
the violation of rules or norms

crime
the violation of norms that are
written into law

*S*ociologists use the term **deviance** to refer to any violation of norms, whether
the infraction is as minor as jaywalking, as serious as murder, or as humorous as Chagnon's encounter with the Yanomamo. This deceptively simple definition
takes us to the heart of the sociological perspective on deviance, which sociologist
Howard S. Becker (1966) identified this way: *It is not the act itself, but the reactions to the act, that make something deviant.* In
other words, people's behaviors must be viewed from the framework of the culture in which they take place. To Chagnon, the behaviors were frighteningly deviant, but to the Yanomamo they
represented normal, everyday life. What was deviant to Chagnon
was *conformist* to the Yanomamo. From their viewpoint, you
should check out strangers as they did, and nakedness is good, as
are hallucinogenic drugs and letting mucus be "natural."

Chagnon's abrupt introduction to the Yanomamo allows us to
see the *relativity of deviance,* a major point made by symbolic interactionists.. Because different groups have different norms, *what
is deviant to some is not deviant to others.* This principle holds
within a society as well as across cultures. Thus acts that are acceptable in one culture—or in one group within a society—may be
considered deviant in another culture, or by another group within
the same society. This idea is explored in the Cultural Diversity
box on the next page.

This principle also applies to a specific form of deviance
known as **crime,** the violation of rules that have been written into
law. In the extreme, an act that is applauded by one group may be
so despised by another group that they punish it by death. Making a huge profit on a business deal is one example. Americans
who do this are admired. They may even write a book about it or
seek public office. In China, however, until recently this same act
was a crime called *profiteering.* Anyone found guilty was hanged
in a public square as a lesson to all.

Unlike the general public, sociologists use the term *deviance*
nonjudgmentally, to refer to any act to which people respond negatively. When sociologists use this term, it does not mean they
agree that an act is bad, just that people judge it negatively. To so-

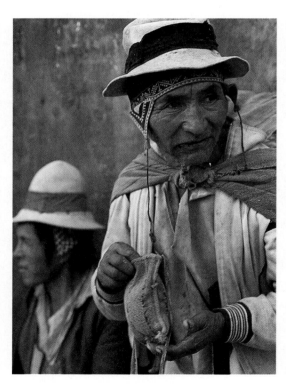

■ *This Aymara Indian in Bolivia has just taken a pinch
of coca leaves from the sack made for this purpose by
his wife or mother. For centuries, the Indians of Bolivia
and nearby countries have chewed coca leaves as a
stimulant. It would be the deviant who would not
participate in this custom, affirming the sociological
point that deviance is relative.*

cultural d·i·v·e·r·s·i·t·y

—Around the World

Human Sexuality in
Cross-Cultural Perspective

Anthropologist Robert Edgerton (1976) reported how differently human groups react to similar behaviors. Of the many examples he cites, let's look at sexuality to illustrate how a group's *definition* of an act, not the act itself, determines whether or not it will be considered deviant.

Norms of sexual behavior vary so widely around the world that what is considered normal in one society may be considered deviant in another. The Pokot people of northwestern Kenya, for example, place high emphasis on sexual pleasure and expect that both a husband and his wife will reach orgasm. If a husband does not satisfy his wife, he is in trouble. Pokot men often engage in adulterous affairs, and should a husband's failure to satisfy his wife be attributed to his adultery, his wife

and her female friends will tie him up when he is asleep. The women will shout obscenities at him, beat him, and, as a final gesture of their utter contempt, slaughter and eat his favorite ox before releasing him. His hours of painful humiliation are intended to make him henceforth more dutiful concerning his wife's conjugal rights.

People can also become deviants for failing to understand that the group's ideal norms may not be its real norms. As with many groups, the Zapotec Indians of Mexico profess that sexual relations should take place exclusively between husband and wife. Yet the *only* person in one Zapotec community who had had no extramarital affairs was considered deviant. Evidently these people have an un-

spoken understanding that married couples will engage in affairs, but be discreet about them. When a wife learns that her husband is having an affair, she usually has one, too.

One Zapotec wife did not follow this covert norm. Instead, she would praise her own virtue to her husband—and then voice the familiar "headache" excuse. She also informed the other husbands and wives in the village whom their spouses were sleeping with. As a result, this virtuous woman was condemned by everyone in the village. Clearly, covert norms can conflict with formal norms—another illustration of the gap between ideal and real culture.

---

ciologists, then, all of us are deviants of one sort or another, for we all violate norms from time to time.

To be considered deviant, a person does not even have to *do* anything. Sociologist Erving Goffman (1963) used the term **stigma** to refer to characteristics that discredit people. These include violations of norms of ability (blindness, deafness, mental handicaps) and norms of appearance (a facial birthmark, obesity). They also include involuntary memberships, such as being a victim of AIDS or the brother of a rapist. The stigma becomes a person's master status, defining him or her as deviant. Recall from Chapter 4 that a master status cuts across all other statuses that a person occupies.

■ How Norms Make Social Life Possible

No human group can exist without norms, for *norms make social life possible by making behavior predictable.* What would life be like if you could not predict what others would do? Imagine for a moment that you have gone to a store to purchase milk:

> Suppose the clerk says, "I won't sell you any milk. We're overstocked with soda, and I'm not going to sell anyone milk until our soda inventory is reduced."
>
> You don't like it, but you decide to buy a case of soda. At the checkout, the clerk says, "I hope you don't mind, but there's a $5 service charge on every fifteenth customer." You, of course, are the fifteenth.
>
> Just as you start to leave, another clerk stops you and says, "We're not working any more. We decided to have a party." Suddenly a stereo begins to blast, and everyone in the store begins to dance. "Oh, good, you've brought the soda," says a different clerk, who takes your package and passes sodas all around.

stigma
"blemishes" that discredit a person's claim to a "normal" identity

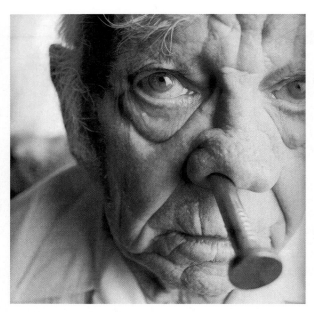

■ *Much of our interaction is based on* background assumptions, *the unwritten, taken-for-granted "rules" that underlie our everyday lives. We don't have a "rule" that specifies, "Adults, don't shove a spike up your nose," yet we all know this rule exists. Shown here is Melvin Burkhart from Gibsonton, Florida, whose claim to fame is breaking this particular unspecified rule.*

Life is not like this, of course. You can depend on grocery clerks to sell you milk. You can also depend on paying the same price as everyone else, and not being forced to attend a party in the store. Why can you depend on this? Because we are socialized to follow norms, to play the basic roles society assigns to us.

Without norms, we would have social chaos. Norms lay out the basic guidelines for how we should play our roles and interact with others. In short, norms bring about **social order,** a group's customary social arrangements. Our lives are based on these arrangements, which is why deviance often is perceived as so threatening: Deviance undermines predictability, the foundation of social life. Consequently, human groups develop a system of **social control,** formal and informal means of enforcing norms.

■ Sanctions

As discussed in Chapter 2, people do not strictly enforce folkways, but they become very upset when someone breaks a more. Expressions of disapproval of deviance, called **negative sanctions,** range from frowns and gossip for breaking folkways to imprisonment and capital punishment for breaking mores. In general, the more seriously the group takes a norm, the harsher the penalty for violating it. We will discuss prison and the death penalty later. **Positive sanctions,** in contrast— from smiles to formal awards—are used to reward people for conforming to norms. Getting a raise is a positive sanction, being fired a negative sanction. Getting an *A* in basic sociology is a positive sanction, getting an *F* a negative one.

Most negative sanctions are informal. You probably will merely stare when someone dresses in what you consider to be inappropriate clothing, or just gossip if a married person you know spends the night with someone other than his or her spouse. Whether you consider the breaking of a norm simply an amusing matter that warrants no severe sanctions or a serious infraction that does, however, depends on your perspective. If a woman appears at your college graduation ceremonies in a swimsuit, you may stare and laugh, but if this is *your* mother, you are likely to feel that different sanctions are appropriate. Similarly, if it is *your* father who spends the night with an 18-year-old college freshman, you are likely to do more than gossip.

■ Shaming and Degradation Ceremonies

Shaming is another sanction. Shaming is especially effective when it is used by members of a primary group. For this reason, it is often used to keep children in line. It is also effective in small communities, where the individual's reputation is at stake. As our society grew large and urban, it lost its sense of community, and shaming lost its effectiveness. Some are trying to bring shaming back. One Arizona sheriff, for example, makes the men in his jail wear pink underwear (Boxer 2001).

Shaming can be the centerpiece of public ritual, intended to mark the violator as a deviant and hold him or her up for all the world to see. In Nathaniel Hawthorne's *The Scarlet Letter,* town officials forced Hester Prynne to wear a scarlet A sewn on her dress. The A stood for adulteress. Wherever she went, Pryne had to wear this badge of shame, and the community expected her to wear it every day for the rest of her life.

Sociologist Harold Garfinkel (1956) gave the name **degradation ceremony** to formal attempts to brand someone as an outsider. The individual is called to account before the group, witnesses denounce him or her, the offender is pronounced guilty,

social order
a group's usual and customary social arrangements, on which its members depend and on which they base their lives

social control
a group's formal and informal means of enforcing its norms

negative sanction
a punishment or negative reaction for disapproved behavior, for deviance

positive sanction
a reward or positive reaction for approved behavior, for conformity

degradation ceremonies
rituals designed to strip an individual of his or her identity as a group member; for example, a court martial or the defrocking of a priest

and steps are taken to strip the individual of his or her identity as a group member. In some court martials, officers who are found guilty stand at attention before their peers while the insignia of rank are ripped from their uniforms. This procedure dramatizes that the individual is no longer a member of the group. Although Hester Prynne was not banished from the group physically, she was banished morally; her degradation ceremony proclaimed her a *moral* outcast from the community. The scarlet A marked her as "not one" of them.

Although we don't use scarlet As today, informal degradation ceremonies still occur. Consider what happened to Joseph Gray (Chivers 2001):

■ Degradation ceremonies *are intended to humiliate norm violators and mark them as "not members" of the group. This photo was taken by the U.S. army in 1945 after U.S. troops liberated Cherbourg, France. Members of the French resistance shaved the heads of these women, who had "collaborated" (had sexual contact with) the occupying Nazis. They then marched the shamed women down the streets of the city, while the public shouted insults and spat on them.*

> Joseph Gray, a fifteen-year veteran of the New York City police force, was involved in a fatal accident. The *New York Times* and New York television stations reported that Gray had spent the afternoon drinking in a topless bar before plowing his car into a vehicle carrying a pregnant woman, her son, and her sister. All three died. Gray was accused of manslaughter and drunk driving.

The news media hammered this story to the public. Three weeks later, as Gray left police headquarters after resigning from his job, an angry crowd gathered around him. Gray hung his head in public disgrace as Victor Manuel Herrera, whose wife and son were killed in the crash, followed him, shouting, "You're a murderer!"

IN SUM ■ ■ ■ ■ ■

In sociology, the term *deviance* refers to all violations of social rules, regardless of their seriousness. The term is not a judgment about the behavior. Deviance is relative, for what is deviant in one group may be conformist in another. Consequently, we must consider deviance from *within* a group's own framework, for it is *their* meanings that underlie their behavior. The following Thinking Critically section focuses on this issue.

thinking CRITICALLY

Is It Rape, Or Is It Marriage? A Study in Culture Clash

Surrounded by cornfields, Lincoln, Nebraska, is about as provincial as a state capital gets. Most of its residents have little experience with people from different ways of life. Their baptism into cultural diversity came as a shock.

The wedding was traditional and followed millennia-old Islamic practices (Annin and Hamilton 1996). A 39-year-old Iraqi refugee had arranged for his two eldest daughters, ages 13 and 14, to marry two fellow Iraqi refugees, ages 28 and 34. A Muslim cleric flew in from Ohio to perform the ceremony.

Nebraska went into shock. So did the refugees. What is marriage in Iraq is rape in Nebraska. The husbands were charged with rape, the girls' father with child abuse, and their mother with contributing to the delinquency of minors.

The event made front page news in Saudi Arabia, where people shook their heads in amazement at Americans. Nebraskans shook their heads in amazement, too.

In Fresno, California, a young Hmong refugee took a group of friends to a local college campus. There they picked up the girl he had selected to be his wife (Sherman 1988; Lacayo 1993). The young men brought her to his house, where he had sex with her. The young woman, however, was not in agreement with this plan.

The Hmong call this *zij poj niam*, marriage by capture. For them, this is an acceptable form of mate selection, one that mirrors Hmong courtship ideals of strong men and virtuous, resistant women. The Fresno District Attorney, however, called it kidnapping and rape.

■ ■ ■ ■ ■

for your consideration . . .

To apply *symbolic interactionism* to these real-life dramas, ask how the perspectives of the people involved explain why they did what they did. To apply *functionalism*, ask how the U.S. laws that were violated are "functional" (that is, what are their benefits, and to whom?). To apply *conflict theory*, ask what groups are in conflict in these examples. (Do not focus on the individuals involved, but on the groups to which they belong.)

Understanding events in terms of different theoretical perspectives does not tell us what reaction is "right" when cultures clash. Remember that science can analyze causes and consequences, but it cannot determine what actions are right or wrong. Any sense of moral violation that you may feel about these cases comes from your system of values—which brings us, once again, to the initial issue—the relativity of deviance.

■ Competing Explanations of Deviance: Sociology, Biology, and Psychology

Since norms are essential for society, why do people violate them? To better understand the reasons, it is useful to know how sociological explanations differ from biological and psychological ones.

Psychologists and *sociobiologists* explain deviance by looking for answers *within* individuals. They assume that something in the makeup of people leads them to become deviant. By contrast, sociologists look for answers in factors *outside* the individual. They assume that something in the environment influences people to become deviant.

Biological explanations focus on **genetic predispositions** to such deviances as juvenile delinquency and crime (Lombroso 1911; Wilson and Herrnstein 1985; Hauser et al. 1995; Lalumiere and Quinsey 2000). Biological explanations include (but are not restricted to) the following three theories: (1) intelligence—low intelligence leads to crime; (2) the "XYY" theory—an extra Y chromosome in males leads to crime; and (3) body type—people with "squarish, muscular" bodies are more likely to commit **street crime,** acts such as mugging, rape, and burglary.

How have these theories held up? Not very well. Most people with these supposedly "causal" characteristics do not become criminals. Some criminals are very

genetic predispositions inborn tendencies, in this context, to commit deviant acts

street crime crimes such as mugging, rape, and burglary

intelligent, and most people of low intelligence do not commit crimes. Most men who commit crimes have the normal "XY" chromosome combination, and most men with the "XYY" combination do not become criminals. In addition, no women have this combination of genes, so this explanation can't be applied to female criminals. Criminals also exhibit the full range of body types, and most people with "squarish, muscular" bodies do not become street criminals.

Psychologists focus on abnormalities *within* the individual, on what are called **personality disorders.** Their supposition is that deviating individuals have deviating personalities (Heilbrun 1990; Krueger and Caspi 2000; Barnes 2001), that subconscious motivations drive them to deviance. No specific childhood experience, however, is invariably linked with deviance. For example, children who had "bad toilet training," "suffocating mothers," or "emotionally aloof fathers" may become embezzling bookkeepers—or good accountants. Just as students, teachers, and police officers represent a variety of bad—and good—childhood experiences, so do deviants. Similarly, people with "suppressed anger" can become freeway snipers or military heroes—or anything else. In short, there is no inevitable outcome of any childhood experience, and deviance is not associated with any particular personality.

Sociologists, in contrast, search for factors *outside* the individual. They look for social influences that "recruit" some people rather than others to break norms. To account for why people commit crimes, for example, sociologists examine such external influences as socialization, subcultural membership, and social class. *Social class,* a concept discussed in depth in Chapter 10, refers to people's relative standing in terms of education, occupation, and especially income and wealth.

Knowing how relative deviance is, sociologists ask a crucial question: "Why should we expect to find something constant within people to account for a behavior that is conforming in one society and deviant in another?"

To see how sociologists explain deviance, let's contrast the three sociological perspectives—symbolic interactionism, functionalism, and conflict theory.

Unlike biology and psychology, which look within *individuals* for explanations of human behavior, sociological explanations focus on external *experiences,* such as people's associations or group memberships. Sociological explanations of human behavior have become widely accepted and now permeate society, as illustrated by this teenager, whom I photographed as we were exiting the Staten Island Ferry in New York City.

The Symbolic Interactionist Perspective

As we examine symbolic interactionism, it will become more evident why sociologists are not satisfied with explanations that are rooted in biology or personality. A basic principle of symbolic interactionism is that each of us uses symbols to interpret the situations we face—and we act according to our interpretations, not according to some blind predisposition. Let's consider how our membership in groups influences our behaviors and our views of life.

◼ Differential Association Theory

The Theory   Contrary to theories built around biology and personality, sociologists stress that people *learn* deviance. Edwin Sutherland coined the term **differential association** to indicate that we learn to deviate or to conform to society's norms

personality disorders
the view that a personality disturbance of some sort causes an individual to violate social norms

differential association
Edwin Sutherland's term to indicate that associating with some groups results in learning an "excess of definitions" of deviance, and, by extension, in a greater likelihood that one will become deviant

mostly by the *different* groups we *associate* with (Sutherland 1924, 1947; Sutherland et al. 1992). On the most obvious level, some boys and girls join Satan's Servants, while others join the Scouts. As sociologists have repeatedly demonstrated, what they learn influences them toward or away from deviance (Alarid et al. 2000; Erickson et al. 2000).

Sutherland's theory is actually more complicated than this, but he basically said that deviance is learned. This goes directly against the view that deviance is biological or is due to personality. Sutherland stressed that the different groups to which we belong (our "*different*ial association") give us messages about conformity and deviance. We may receive mixed messages, but we end up with more of one than the other (an "excess of definitions," as Sutherland put it). The end result is an imbalance—attitudes that tilt us more in one direction than the other. Consequently, we conform or deviate.

Families   Since our family is so important for teaching us attitudes, it probably is obvious to you that the family makes a big difference in whether we learn deviance or conformity. Researchers have confirmed this informal observation. They have found that delinquents are more likely to come from families that get in trouble with the law. They studied 25,000 delinquents who were locked up in high-security state institutions (Beck et al. 1988). They found that 25 percent had a father who had been in prison, 25 percent a brother or sister, 9 percent a mother, and 13 percent some other relative. Of all jail inmates across the United States, about half have a father, mother, brother, or sister who has served time (*Sourcebook of Criminal Justice Statistics* 1997:483). In short, families that are involved in crime tend to set their children on a lawbreaking path.

Friends, Neighborhoods, and Subcultures   Just as you may also have observed, if someone's friends are delinquent, that person is likely to be delinquent (Haynie 2001). In fact, the longer someone has delinquent friends, the more likely he or she is to be delinquent (Warr 1993). Much delinquency is clustered in certain neighborhoods, and children from those neighborhoods are likely to become delinquent (Miller 1958; Wolfgang and Ferracuti 1967; Baskin and Sommers 1998). This, of course, comes as no surprise to parents, who generally are eager to get their kids out of "bad" neighborhoods and away from "bad" friends. Although they may not know the term *differential association*, they know how it works.

Sociologist Ruth Horowitz (1983, 1987), who did participant observation in a lower-class Chicano neighborhood in Chicago, discovered how associating with people who have a certain concept of "honor" can propel young men to deviance. The formula is simple. "A real man has honor. An insult is a threat to one's honor. Therefore, not to stand up to someone is to be less than a real man."

Now suppose you are a young man growing up in this neighborhood. You likely would do a fair amount of fighting, for you would interpret many things as attacks on your honor. You might even carry a knife or a gun, for words and fists wouldn't always be sufficient. Along with members of your group, you would define fighting, knifing, and shooting quite differently from the way most people do.

Members of the Mafia also intertwine ideas of manliness with violence. For them, *to kill is a measure of their manhood*. Not all killings are accorded the same respect, however, for "the more awesome and potent the victim, the more worthy and meritorious the killer" (Arlacchi 1980). Some killings are done to enforce norms. A member of the Mafia who gives information to the police, for

■ *To experience a sense of belonging is a basic human need. Membership in groups, especially peer groups, is a primary way that people meet this need. Regardless of the orientation of the group—whether to conformity or to deviance—the process is the same. Shown here is a gang from Brooklyn, New York, flashing their gang signs at Coney Island. Gang membership helps provide a vital sense of belonging.*

example, has violated *omertá* (the Mafia's vow of secrecy). Such an offense can never be tolerated, for it threatens the very existence of the group. This example further illustrates just how relative deviance is. Although killing is deviant to mainstream society, for members of the Mafia, *not* to kill after certain rules are broken—such as when someone "squeals" to the cops—is the deviant act.

Prison or Freedom?   An issue that comes up over and over again in sociology is whether we are prisoners of socialization. Symbolic interactionists stress that we are not mere pawns in the hands of others. We are not destined by our group memberships to think and act as our groups dictate. Rather, we *help produce our own orientations to life*. Our choice of membership (differential association), for example, helps to shape the self. For instance, one college student may join a feminist group that is trying to change the treatment of women in college; another may associate with a group of women who shoplift on weekends. Their choice of groups points them in two different directions. The one who associates with shoplifters may become even more oriented toward criminal activities, while the one who joins the feminist group may develop an even greater interest in producing social change.

◼ Control Theory

Inside most of us, it seems, are strong desires to do things that would get us in trouble—inner drives, temptations, urges, hostilities, and so on. Yet most of us stifle these desires most of the time. Why?

The Theory   Sociologist Walter Reckless (1973), who developed **control theory**, stresses that two control systems work against our motivations to deviate. Our *inner controls* include our internalized morality—conscience, religious principles, ideas of right and wrong. Inner controls also include fears of punishment, feelings of integrity, and the desire to be a "good" person (Hirschi 1969; Rogers 1977; Baron 2001). Our *outer controls* consist of people—such as family, friends, and the police—who influence us not to deviate (Costello and Vowell 1999). Control theory is sometimes classified as a functional theory, because when our outer controls operate well, we conform to social norms and thereby do not threaten the status quo. However, symbols and meanings are central to this theory, so, it can also be classified as a symbolic interactionist theory.

As sociologist Travis Hirschi (1969) noted, the stronger our bonds are with society, the more effective our inner controls are. Bonds are based on *attachments* (feeling affection and respect for people who conform to society's norms), *commitments* (having a stake in society that you don't want to risk, such as a respected place in your family, a good standing at college, a good job), *involvements* (putting time and energy into approved activities), and *beliefs* (believing that certain actions are morally wrong). This theory can be summarized as *self*-control, says Hirschi. The key to learning high self-control is socialization, especially in childhood. Parents help their children develop self-control by supervising them and punishing their deviant acts (Gottfredson and Hirschi 1990).

Applying the Theory   Consider drug use. Suppose that some friends have invited you to a night club. When you get there, you notice that everyone seems unusually happy, almost giddy would be the word. They seem to be ecstatic in their animated conversations and dancing. Your friends tell you that almost everyone here has taken the drug ecstasy, and they invite you to take some with them.

What do you do? Let's not explore the question of whether taking ecstasy in this setting is a deviant or a conforming act. That is a separate issue. Instead, concentrate on the pushes and pulls you would feel. The pushes toward taking the drug: your friends, the setting, and your curiosity. Then there are the inner controls: the inner voices of your conscience and your parents, perhaps of your teachers, as well as your

control theory
the idea that two control systems—inner controls and outer controls—work against our tendencies to deviate

■ *Drugs and drug use are one of the most interesting areas of deviance. Drugs have social reputations. They are thought of as good or bad. "Good" drugs are not necessarily harmless, nor are "bad" drugs necessarily harmful. Alcohol is an example of a "good" drug that kills thousands of Americans a year. Marijuana is an example of a "bad" drug that kills no one. Drug use also goes through fads. Shown here is one of those fads, a rave party in a New York City night club, where activities are based around the use of ecstasy.*

fears of arrest and of the dangers of illegal drugs. There are also the outer controls—perhaps the uniformed security guard looking in your direction.

So, what *did* you do? Which was stronger, your inner and outer controls or the pushes and pulls toward taking the drug? It is you who can best weigh these influences, for they differ with each of us.

■ Labeling Theory

Symbolic interactionists have developed **labeling theory,** which focuses on the significance of the labels (names, reputations) that we are given. Labels tend to become a part of our self-concept, which helps to set us on paths that propel us into or divert us from deviance. Let's look at how people react to society's labels—from "whore" and "pervert" to "cheat" and "slob."

Rejecting Labels: How People Neutralize Deviance Most people resist the negative labels that others try to pin on them. Some are so successful that even though they persist in deviance, they still consider themselves conformists. For example, even though they beat up people and vandalize property, some delinquents consider themselves to be conforming members of society. How do they do it?

Sociologists Gresham Sykes and David Matza (1988) studied boys who were in this situation. They found that they used five **techniques of neutralization** to deflect society's norms.

Denial of Responsibility Some boys said, "I'm not responsible for what happened because . . . " and then were quite creative about the "becauses." They said that what happened was an "accident." Other boys saw themselves as "victims" of society. What else could you expect? They were like billiard balls shot around the pool table of life.

Denial of Injury Another favorite explanation of the boys was "What I did wasn't wrong because no one got hurt." They would define vandalism as "mischief," gang fights as a "private quarrel," and stealing cars as

labeling theory
the view, developed by symbolic interactionists, that the labels people are given affect their own and others' perceptions of them, thus channeling their behavior either into deviance or into conformity

techniques of neutralization
ways of thinking or rationalizing that help people deflect society's norms

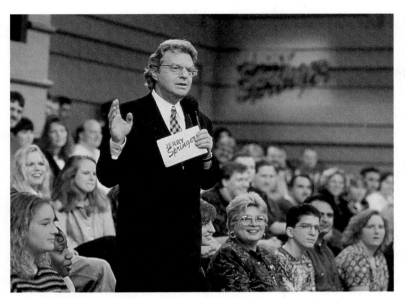

■ *The exhibit of deviants on* The Jerry Springer Show *offers viewers a sense of being participants in forbidden events. As Springer and others like him continue to parade deviants before the public, the shock and surprise wear off, making the deviance seem "more" normal. What is occurring is the* mainstreaming *of deviance—the disapproved moving into the mainstream, or becoming more socially acceptable.*

"borrowing." They might acknowledge that what they did was illegal, but claim that they were "just having a little fun."

Denial of a Victim Some boys thought of themselves as avengers. Vandalizing a teacher's car was done to get revenge for an unfair grade, while shoplifting was a way to even the score with "crooked" store owners. In short, even if the boys did accept responsibility and admit that someone had gotten hurt, they protected their self-concept by claiming that the people "deserved what they got."

Condemnation of the Condemners Another technique the boys used was to deny that others had the right to judge them. They might accuse people who pointed their fingers at them of being "a bunch of hypocrites": The police were "on the take," teachers had "pets," and parents cheated on their taxes. In short, they said, "Who are *they* to accuse *me* of something?"

Appeal to Higher Loyalties A final technique the boys used to justify antisocial activities was to consider loyalty to the gang more important than following the norms of society. They might say, "I had to help my friends. That's why I got in the fight." Not incidentally, the boy may have shot two members of a rival group, as well as a bystander!

IN SUM ■ ■ ■ ■

These five techniques of neutralization have implications far beyond these boys, for it is not only delinquents who try to neutralize the norms of mainstream society. Look again at these five techniques: (1) "I couldn't help myself"; (2) "Who really got hurt?"; (3) "Don't you think she deserved that, after what *she* did?"; (4) "Who are *you* to talk?"; and (5) "I had to help my friends—wouldn't you have done the same thing?" Don't such statements have a familiar ring? All of us attempt to neutralize the moral demands of society, for such neutralizations help us sleep at night.

Embracing Labels: The Example of Outlaw Bikers   Although most of us re- sist attempts to label us as deviant, there are those who revel in a deviant identity. Some teenagers, for example, make certain by their clothing, choice of music, and hairstyles that no one misses their rejection of adult norms. Their status among fel- low members of a subculture, within which they are almost obsessive conformists, is vastly more important than any status outside it.

One of the best examples of a group that embraces deviance is motorcycle gangs. Sociologist Mark Watson (1988) did participant observation with outlaw bikers. He rebuilt Harleys with them, hung around their bars and homes, and went on "runs" (trips) with them. He concluded that outlaw bikers see the world as "hostile, weak, and effeminate." They pride themselves on looking "dirty, mean, and generally unde- sirable" and take pleasure in provoking shocked reactions to their appearance. Hold- ing the conventional world in contempt, they also pride themselves on getting into trouble, laughing at death, and treating women as lesser beings whose primary value is to provide them with services—especially sex. Outlaw bikers also look at them- selves as losers, a factor that becomes woven into their unusual embrace of deviance.

The Power of Labels: The Saints and the Roughnecks   We can see how pow- erful labeling is by referring back to the study of the "Saints" and the "Roughnecks" that was cited in Chapter 4 (pages 124–125). As you recall, both groups of high school boys were "constantly occupied with truancy, drinking, wild parties, petty theft, and vandalism." Yet their teachers looked on the Saints as "headed for success" and the Roughnecks as "headed for trouble." By the time they finished high school, not one Saint had been arrested, while the Roughnecks had been in constant trouble with the police.

Why did the community see these boys so differently? Chambliss (1973/2001) concluded that this split vision was due to *social class*. As symbolic interactionists em- phasize, social class vitally affects our perceptions and behavior. The Saints came from respectable, middle-class families, the Roughnecks from less respectable, work- ing-class families. These backgrounds led teachers and the authorities to expect good behavior from the Saints but trouble from the Roughnecks. And, like the rest of us, teachers and police saw what they expected to see.

The boys' social class also affected their visibility. The Saints had automobiles, and they did their drinking and vandalism out of town. Without a car, the Rough- necks hung around their own street corners, where their boisterous behavior drew the attention of police and confirmed the ideas that the community already had of them.

The boys' social class also equipped them with distinct *styles of interaction*. When police or teachers questioned them, the Saints were apologetic. Their show of respect for authority elicited a positive reaction from teachers and police, allowing them to escape school and legal problems. The Roughnecks, said Chambliss, were "almost the polar opposite." When questioned, they were hostile. Even when they tried to assume a respectful attitude, everyone could see through it. Consequently, while teachers and police let the Saints off with warnings, they came down hard on the Roughnecks.

Although what happens in life is not determined by labels alone, the Saints and the Roughnecks did live up to the labels that the community gave them. As you re- call, all but one of the Saints went on to college. One earned a doctorate, one became a lawyer, one a doctor, and the others business managers. In contrast, only two of the Roughnecks went to college. They earned athletic scholarships and became coaches. The other Roughnecks did not fare so well. Two of them dropped out of high school, later became involved in separate killings, and received long prison sentences. One became a local bookie, and no one knows the whereabouts of the other.

How do labels work? Although the matter is complex, because it involves the self-concept and reactions that vary from one individual to another, we can note that labels open and close doors of opportunity. Unlike in sociology, in everyday usage, the label "deviant" is a way of judging people. This label can lock people out of con- forming groups and push them into almost exclusive contact with people who have similar labels.

IN SUM ■ ■ ■ ■

Symbolic interactionists examine how people's definitions of the situation underlie their deviation from or conformance to social norms. They focus on group membership (differential association), how people balance pressures to conform and to deviate (control theory), and the significance of the labels that are given to people (labeling theory).

The label *deviant* involves competing definitions and reactions to the same behavior. This central point of symbolic interactionism is explored in the Mass Media box below.

mass media
in social life

Pornography on the Internet: Freedom Versus Censorship

Pornography vividly illustrates one of the sociological principles discussed in this chapter—the relativity of deviance. It is not the act, but reactions to the act, that make something deviant. Consider one of today's major issues, pornography on the Internet.

Web surfers have a wide choice of pornography. Some sites are even indexed: heterosexual or gay, single or group, teenagers, cheerleaders, and older women who "still think they have it." Some offer only photographs, others video. Live sites are available, such as one that bills itself as "direct from Amsterdam." Sign on, and you can command your "model" to do anything your heart desires. Both male and female "models" are available, and the per minute charges are hefty.

What is the problem? Why can't people exchange nude photos electronically if they want to? Or watch others having sex online, if someone offers that service? Although some object to any kind of sex site, what disturbs many are the sites that feature bondage, torture, rape, bestiality (humans having sex with animals), and sex with children.

The Internet abounds with chat rooms, where people "meet" online to discuss some topic. No one is bothered by the chat rooms where the topic is Roman architecture or rap music or turtle racing. But those whose focus is how to torture women are another matter. So are those that offer lessons on how to

seduce grade school children—or that extol the delights of having sex with three-year-olds.

The state and federal governments have passed laws against child pornography, and the FBI seizes computers and searches them for illegal pictures. The courts levy fines and send some violators to prison. To exchange pictures of tortured and sexually abused women, however, remains legal.

for your consideration

Some feel that no matter how much they may disagree with a point of view or find it repugnant, communication about it (including photos) must be allowed. If we let the government censor these activities, it will censor other activities.

Do you think it should be legal to exchange photos of women being sexually abused or tortured? Should it be legal to discuss ways to seduce children? If not, on what basis should they be banned? If we should make these activities illegal, then what other communications should we prohibit? On what basis?

Assume that such photos and chat rooms remain legal. If so, should schools and public libraries be allowed to install filters to screen out designated Internet sites? One side insists that such filters violate the First Amendment's guarantee of free speech, the other that it is only a reasonable precaution to protect children (Schwartz 2001). What do you think?

Finally, can you disprove the central point of the symbolic interactionists—that an activity is deviant only because people decide that it is deviant? You may use examples cited in this box, or any others that you wish. You cannot invoke God or moral absolutes in your argument, however, as they are outside the field of sociology. As you will recall from the first chapter of this book, sociology cannot decide moral issues. This applies even to extreme cases.

The Functionalist Perspective

When we think of deviance, its dysfunctions are likely to come to mind. Functionalists, in contrast, are as likely to stress the functions of deviance as they are to stress its dysfunctions.

Can Deviance Really Be Functional for Society?

Most of us are upset by deviance, especially crime, and assume that society would be better off without it. The classic functionalist theorist Emile Durkheim (1893/1933, 1893/1964), however, came to a surprising conclusion. Deviance, he said, including crime, is functional for society, for it contributes to the social order. Its three main functions are:

1. *Deviance clarifies moral boundaries and affirms norms.* A group's ideas about how people should act and think mark its *moral boundaries.* Deviant acts challenge those boundaries. To call a deviant member into account is to say, in effect, "You broke an important rule, and we cannot tolerate that." To punish deviants affirms the group's norms and clarifies what it means to be a member of the group.

2. *Deviance promotes social unity.* To affirm the group's moral boundaries by punishing deviants fosters a "we" feeling among the group's members. In saying, "You can't get by with that," the group collectively affirms the rightness of its own ways.

3. *Deviance promotes social change.* Groups do not always agree on what to do with people who push beyond their accepted ways of doing things. Some group members may even approve the rule-breaking behavior. Boundary violations that gain enough support become new, acceptable behaviors. Thus, deviance may force a group to rethink and redefine its moral boundaries, helping groups, and whole societies, to change their customary ways.

Strain Theory: How Social Values Produce Deviance

Functionalists argue that crime is a *natural* part of society, not an aberration or some alien element in our midst. Indeed, they say, some mainstream values actually generate crime. To understand what they mean, consider what sociologists Richard Cloward and Lloyd Ohlin (1960) identified as the crucial problem of the industrialized world: the need to locate and train the most talented people of every generation—whether they were born into wealth or into poverty—so they can take over the key technical jobs of modern society. When children are born, no one knows which ones will have the ability to become dentists, nuclear physicists, or engineers. To get the most talented people to compete with one another, society tries to motivate *everyone* to strive for success. It does this by arousing discontent—making people feel dissatisfied with what they have so they will try to "better" themselves.

Most people, then, end up with strong desires to reach **cultural goals** such as wealth or high status, or to achieve whatever other objectives society holds out for them. However, not everyone has equal access to society's **institutionalized means,** the legitimate ways of achieving success. Some people find their path to education and good jobs blocked. These people experience *strain* or frustration, which may motivate them to take a deviant path.

cultural goals
the legitimate objectives held out to the members of a society

institutionalized means
approved ways of reaching cultural goals

TABLE 8.1	How People Match Their Goals to Their Means			
Do They Feel the Strain That Leads to Anomie?	Mode of Adaptation	Cultural Goals	Institutionalized Means
No	Conformists	Accept	Accept
Yes	Innovators	Accept	Reject
	Ritualists	Reject	Accept
	Retreatists	Reject	Reject
	Rebels	Reject/Replace	Reject/Replace

This perspective, known as **strain theory,** was developed by sociologist Robert Merton (1956, 1968). People who experience strain, he said, are likely to feel *anomie,* a sense of normlessness. Because mainstream norms (such as work or education) don't seem to be getting them anywhere, they find it difficult to identify with these norms. They may even feel wronged by the system, and its rules may seem illegitimate (Anderson 1978).

Table 8.1 compares people's reactions to cultural goals and institutionalized means. The first reaction, which Merton said is the most common, is *conformity,* using socially acceptable means to try to reach cultural goals. In industrialized societies most people try to get good jobs, a good education, and so on. If well-paid jobs are unavailable, they take less desirable jobs. If they are denied access to Harvard or Stanford, they go to a state university. Others take night classes and go to vocational schools. In short, most people take the socially acceptable road.

Four Deviant Paths　The remaining four responses, which are deviant, represent reactions to anomie. Let's look at each. *Innovators* are people who accept the goals of society but use illegitimate means to try to reach them. Drug dealers, for instance, accept the goal of achieving wealth. But they reject the legitimate avenues for doing so. Other examples are embezzlers, robbers, and con artists.

The second deviant path is taken by people who become discouraged and give up on achieving cultural goals. Yet they still cling to conventional rules of conduct. Merton called this response *ritualism.* Although ritualists have given up on excelling and advancing in position, they survive by following the rules of their job. Teachers whose idealism is shattered (who are said to suffer from "burnout"), for example, remain in the classroom, where they teach without enthusiasm. Their response is considered deviant because they cling to the job although they have abandoned the goal, which may have been stimulating young minds or making the world a better place.

People who choose the third deviant path, *retreatism,* reject both cultural goals and the institutionalized means of achieving them. Those who drop out of the pursuit of success by way of alcohol or drugs are retreatists. Such people even stop trying to appear as though they share the goals of their society.

The final type of deviant response is *rebellion.* Convinced that their society is corrupt, rebels, like retreatists, reject both society's goals and its institutionalized means. Unlike retreatists, however, they seek to replace existing goals with new ones. Revolutionaries are the most committed type of rebels.

strain theory
Robert Merton's term for the strain engendered when a society socializes large numbers of people to desire a cultural goal (such as success) but withholds from many the approved means to reach that goal; one adaptation to the strain is crime, the choice of an innovative means (one outside the approved system) to attain the cultural goal

IN SUM ■ ■ ■ ■ ■

Strain theory underscores the main sociological point about deviance, namely, that deviants are the product of society. Due to their social location, some people experience greater pressures to deviate from society's norms, others much less. Simply put, if a society emphasizes the goal of material success, groups deprived of access to this goal will be more involved in property crime.

■ Illegitimate Opportunity Structures: Social Class and Crime

One of the more interesting sociological findings in the study of deviance is that the social classes have distinct styles of crime. Let's see how unequal access to the institutionalized means to success helps explain this.

Street Crime Functionalists point out that industrialized societies have no trouble socializing the poor into wanting to own things. Like others, the poor are bombarded with messages urging them to buy everything from designer jeans and DVD players to new cars. Television and movies show vivid images of the middle class enjoying luxurious lives. These images reinforce the myth that all full-fledged Americans can afford society's many goods and services.

In contrast, the school system, the most common route to success, fails the poor. It is run by the middle class, and there the children of the poor confront a bewildering world, one at odds with their background. Their grammar and nonstandard language may be liberally sprinkled with what the middle class considers obscenities. Their ideas of punctuality and neatness, as well as their poor preparation in paper-and-pencil skills, are a mismatch with their new environment. Facing such barriers, the poor are more likely than their more privileged counterparts to drop out of school. Educational failure, in turn, closes the door on many legitimate avenues to financial success.

Not infrequently, however, a different door opens to the poor, one that sociologists Richard Cloward and Lloyd Ohlin (1960) called **illegitimate opportunity structures.** Woven into the texture of life in urban slums, for example, are robbery, burglary, drug dealing, prostitution, pimping, gambling, and other remunerative

illegitimate opportunity structures
opportunities for crimes that are woven into the texture of life

■ *This 1871 wood engraving depicts children as they are being paid for their day's work in a London brickyard. In early capitalism, most street criminals came from the marginal working class, as did these children. It is the same today.*

■ ■ ■ ■ ■

Islands in the Street: Urban Gangs in the United States

For more than ten years, sociologist Martín Sánchez Jankowski (1991) did participant observation of thirty-seven Irish, African American, Puerto Rican, Chicano, Dominican, Jamaican, and Central American gangs in Boston, Los Angeles, and New York City. The gangs earned money through gambling, arson, mugging, armed robbery, wholesaling drugs to pushers, and selling moonshine, guns, stolen car parts, and protection. Jankowski ate, slept, and sometimes fought with the gangs, but by mutual agreement he did not participate in drugs or other illegal activities. He was seriously injured twice during the study.

Contrary to stereotypes, Jankowski did not find that the motive for joining was to escape a broken home (there were as many members from intact as from broken homes) or to seek a substitute family (as many boys said they were close to their families as said they were not). Rather, the boys joined to gain access to money, to have recreation (including girls and drugs), to maintain anonymity in committing crimes, to get protection, and to help the community. This last reason may seem surprising, but in some neighborhoods gangs protect residents from outsiders. The boys also saw the gang as an alternative to the dead-end—and deadening—jobs held by their parents.

Neighborhood residents are ambivalent about gangs. On the one hand, they fear the violence. On the other hand, many adults once belonged to gangs, the gangs often provide better protection than the police, and gang members are the children of people who live in the neighborhood.

Particular gangs will come and go, but gangs will likely always remain part of the city. As functionalists point out, gangs fulfill needs of poor youth who live on the margins of society.

for your consideration

What are the functions that gangs fulfill (the needs they meet)? Suppose that you have been hired as an urban planner by the City of Los Angeles. How could you arrange to meet the needs that gangs fulfill in ways that minimize violence and encourage youth to follow mainstream norms?

■ ■ ■ ■ ■

crimes, commonly called "hustles" (Liebow 1967/1997; Bourgois 1994; Anderson 1978, 1990, 2001). For many of the poor, the "hustler" is a role model—glamorous, in control, the image of "easy money," one of the few people in the area who comes close to attaining the cultural goal of success. For such reasons, then, these activities attract disproportionate numbers of the poor. As discussed in the Down-to-Earth Sociology box above, gangs are one way that the illegitimate opportunity structure beckons disadvantaged youth.

White-Collar Crime The more privileged social classes are not crime-free, of course, but for them different illegitimate opportunities beckon. They find *other forms* of crime to be functional. Rather than mugging, pimping, and burglary, the more privileged encounter "opportunities" for evading income tax, bribing public officials, embezzling from employers, participating in fraud, and so on. Physicians, for example, never hold up cabbies, but many do cheat Medicare. Sociologist Edwin Sutherland (1949) coined the term **white-collar crime** to refer to crimes that people of respectable and high social status commit in the course of their occupations.

Although the general public seems to think that the lower classes are more prone to crime, numerous studies show that white-collar workers also commit many crimes (Weisburd et al. 1991; Croall 2001). This difference in perception is largely due to visibility. While crimes that the poor commit are given much publicity, the crimes of the more privileged classes seldom make the evening news and go largely unnoticed. Yet "crime in the suites," which runs about $400 billion a year (Zeune 2001), costs more than "crime in the streets." This refers only to dollar costs. No one has yet figured out a way to compare, for example, the suffering experienced by a rape victim with the pain felt by an elderly couple who lost their life savings to white-collar fraud.

You probably have shopped at some of these criminal enterprises. Sears, for example, defrauded the poor of over $100 million. These were people so poor they

white-collar crime Edwin Sutherland's term for crimes committed by people of respectable and high social status in the course of their occupations; for example, bribery of public officials, securities violations, embezzlement, false advertising, and price fixing could no longer afford to pay for what they had purchased at Sears, and they had filed for bankruptcy. To avoid a criminal trial, Sears pleaded guilty. When the Sears case made national headlines, it frightened the parent companies of Macy's and Bloomingdale's, which settled with debtors out of court (McCormick 1999).

Although white-collar crime is not as dramatic as street killings, abduction, or rape—and thus generally considered less newsworthy—it, too, can cause physical injury and death. When Odwalla, Inc. sold apple juice contaminated with dangerous bacteria, 14 children came down with a disease that ravaged their kidneys. One of them died (Belluck 1998). No totals are available on the number of Americans killed by unsafe products, but the government does tally the number of fatal work injuries. This comes to 6,000 a year (*Statistical Abstract* 2000: Table 709). Some deaths, but we don't know how many, are the result of executive decisions to put profits ahead of workers' safety. If court hearings bear out the allegations made at the time I am writing this book, one of the most notorious of white-collar crimes was the decision by Firestone executives to let faulty tires remain on U.S. vehicles—even though they were recalling them in Saudi

■ More than 100 people have died from accidents involving Firestone tires. Shown here is Victor Rodriguez, whose 10-year-old son was killed when a Firestone tire on their Ford Explorer blew out in San Antonio, Texas. The fault may be Firestone's, for manufacturing defective tires; or it may lie with Ford, for equipping the vehicles with tires that were too small; or it may be a combination of both. If so, this would be a case of white collar crime *that kills. White-collar murderers are unlikely to ever spend a single day in jail for their crimes.*

Arabia and Venezuela. As illustrated by the photo on this page, the consequences were devastating. These tires cost the lives of 200 Americans (White et al. 2001).

The greatest concern of Americans, however, is street crime. They fear the violent stranger who will change their life forever. As the Social Map below shows, the chances of such an encounter depend on where you live. From this map, you can also see that some regions are safer than others. In general, the northern states are the safest, the southern states the most dangerous.

Gender and Crime A major change in the nature of crime is the growing number of female offenders. As Table 8.2 shows, women are committing a larger pro-

Figure 8.1

Social Map: Some States Are Safer: Violent Crime in the United States

Violent crimes are murder, rape, robbery, and aggravated assault. Rates vary widely among the states. One's chances of becoming a victim to these crimes are ten times higher in some states. With a rate of 89 per 100,000 people, North Dakota has the lowest rate of violence, while New Mexico, at 961, has the highest rate. The U.S. average rate is 466 (the total of the states' average divided by 50). This total does not include Washington, D.C., whose rate of 1,719, is three and a half times the national average.

Source: Statistical Abstract 2000: Table 331.

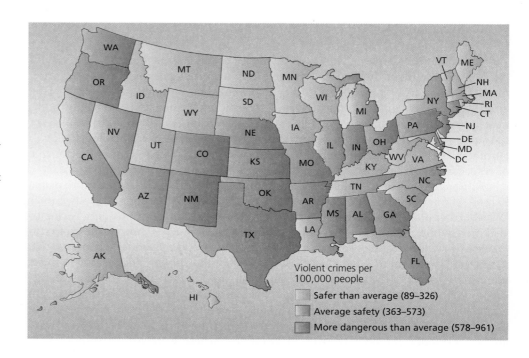

| TABLE 8.2 | What a Difference 10 Years Makes: Women and Crime | | | | | | | |

Of all those arrested, what percentage are women?

Crime	1988	1998[1]	Change	Crime	1988	1998[1]	Change
Car Theft	10.1	15.7	+55%	Robbery	8.5	10.0	+18%
Burglary	8.4	12.5	+49%	Forgery and Counterfeiting	33.9	38.9	+15%
Aggravated Assault	13.4	19.6	+46%	Larceny/Theft	30.5	34.7	+14%
Vandalism	10.9	15.2	+39%	Drugs	15.5	17.5	+13%
Drunk in Public	9.3	12.8	+38%	Arson	13.1	14.7	+12%
Stolen Property (Buying, Possessing)	11.8	15.5	+31%	Weapons (Carrying, Possessing)	7.7	7.9	+3%
Drunken Driving	11.9	15.6	+31%	Murder	12.2	11.2	−8%
Embezzlement	37.9	48.8	+29%	Gambling	15.4	10.4	−32%

[1]Latest year available
Source: Statistical Abstract 1990:Table 298; 2000:Table 345.

portion of almost all crimes—from drugs to burglary. The exceptions are murder and illegal gambling. As more women have joined the professions and corporate world, they, too, have been enticed by its illegitimate opportunities, and their involvement in embezzlement, fraud, and forgery has increased.

IN SUM ■ ■ ■ ■

Functionalists conclude that much street crime is the consequence of socializing everyone into equating success with material possessions, while denying many in the lower social classes the means to attain that success. People from higher social classes encounter different opportunity structures to commit crimes.

The Conflict Perspective

Class, Crime, and the Criminal Justice System

The federal government accused two multinational corporations, Grumann and SmithKline, of fraud, of claiming fake charges that cost the taxpayers millions of dollars. No executives went to jail. The corporations paid fines—and then the government awarded them more contracts. (Pasztor 1993; Tanouye 1997)

Contrast this event with stories you often read in newspapers about young men who are sentenced to several years in prison for stealing cars. How can a legal system that is supposed to provide "justice for all" be so inconsistent? According to conflict theorists, this question is central to the analysis of crime and the **criminal justice system**—the police,

criminal justice system
the system of police, courts, and prisons set up to deal with people who are accused of having committed a crime

courts, and prisons that deal with people who are accused of having committed crimes. Let's see if conflict theorists have an answer.

Power and Inequality

Conflict theorists look at power and social inequality as the main characteristics of society. They stress that a group at the top, a power elite, controls the criminal justice system. This group makes certain that laws are passed that will protect its power. Other norms, such as those that govern informal behavior (chewing with a closed mouth, appearing in public with combed hair, and so on), may come from other sources, but they simply are not as important. Such norms influence our everyday behavior, but they do not determine who gets sent to prison and who does not.

Conflict theorists see the most fundamental division in industrial society as that between the few who own the means of production and the many who do not, those who sell their labor and the privileged few who buy it. Those who buy labor, and thereby control workers, make up the **capitalist class;** those who sell their labor form the **working class.** Toward the most depressed end of the working class is the **marginal working class:** people with few skills who are subject to layoffs and whose jobs are low paying, part time, or seasonal. This class is marked by unemployment and poverty. From its ranks come most of the prison inmates in the United States. Desperate, these people commit street crimes, and because their crimes threaten the social order that keeps the elite in power, they are severely punished.

The Law as an Instrument of Oppression

According to conflict theorists, the idea that the law operates impartially and administers a code that is shared by all is a cultural myth promoted by the capitalist class.

These theorists see the law as an instrument of oppression, a tool designed to maintain the powerful in their privileged position (Spitzer 1975; MacDonald 1995; Chambliss 2000). Because the working class has the potential to rebel and overthrow the current social order, when its members get out of line, they are arrested, tried, and imprisoned.

For this reason, the criminal justice system does not focus on the owners of corporations and the harm they do to the masses through unsafe products, wanton pollution, and price manipulations. Instead, it directs its energies against violations by the working class (Platt 1978; Coleman 1989; Chambliss 2000). The violations of the capitalist class cannot be totally ignored, however, for if they became too outrageous or oppressive, the working class might rise up in revolution. To prevent this, occasionally a flagrant violation by a member of the capitalist class is prosecuted. The publicity given to the case helps to stabilize the social system by providing visible evidence of the "fairness" of the criminal justice system.

Usually, however, the powerful are able to bypass the courts altogether, appearing instead before an agency that has no power to imprison (such as the Federal Trade Commission). These agencies are directed by people from wealthy backgrounds who sympathize with the intricacies of the corporate world. This means that most cases of illegal sales of stocks and bonds, price fixing, trade restraint, collusion, and so on are handled by "gentlemen overseeing gentlemen." Is it surprising, then, that the typical sanction is a token fine? In contrast, the property crimes of the masses are handled by courts that do have the power to imprison. Burglary, armed robbery, and theft committed by the poor threaten not only the sanctity of private property but, ultimately, the positions of the powerful.

When groups that have been denied access to power gain that access, we can expect to see changes in the legal system. This is precisely what is occurring now. Racial-ethnic minorities and homosexuals, for example, have more political power today than ever before. In line with conflict theory, a

capitalist class
the wealthy who own the means of production and buy the labor of the working class

working class
those who sell their labor to the capitalist class

marginal working class
the most desperate members of the working class, who have few skills, little job security, and are often unemployed

■ Social class divides people into distinct ways of life, so much so that even crimes differ by class. Shown here is Marc Rich (I would love to have made up such a name for purposes of illustration, but in an ironical twist, this is the man's real name), who, among other crimes, was accused of failing to pay $48 million in taxes. Obviously Rich's opportunity structure differs from that of someone in the middle or lower class. In a controversial act, on his last day in office President Bill Clinton pardoned Rich—another illustration of Rich's unique opportunity structure.

new category of crime has been formulated. We analyze this change in the Thinking Critically section on pages 235–236.

From the perspective of conflict theory, the small penalties imposed for crimes committed by the powerful are typical of a legal system that has been designed by the elite (capitalists) to control workers, to keep themselves in power, and, ultimately, to stabilize the social order. From this perspective, law enforcement is a cultural device through which the capitalist class carries out self-protective and repressive policies.

Reactions to Deviance

Whether it involves cheating on a sociology quiz or holding up a liquor store, any violation of norms invites reaction. Let's look at some of these reactions.

Street Crime and Prisons

Today, we don't make people wear scarlet letters, but we do remove them from society and make them wear prison uniforms. And we still use degradation ceremonies—in this case, a public trial and the public pronouncement that someone is "unfit" to live among "decent, law-abiding people" for some specified period of time. Figure 8.2 illustrates the remarkable growth in the U.S. prison population. This huge number does *not* include jail inmates. If we add these, the total comes to over two million. The United States not only has more prisoners than any other nation, but a larger percentage of its population in prison as well ("Coming to . . ." 2001). As Table 8.3 shows, about 94 percent of prisoners are men, and almost half are African Americans. That prisoners come from a subpopulation that is not as rooted in society as most people is evident when you look at the education totals on this table. Notice how marriage—one of the major techniques society has of "anchoring" us—provides protection from prison.

As noted, because social class funnels some people into the criminal justice system and others away from it, official statistics on crime have an inherent social class bias. This becomes especially apparent if you look at the education totals on this table. You can see how people's chances of ending up in prison increase if they do not complete

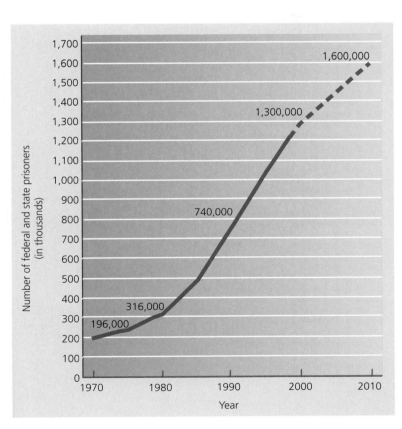

Figure 8.2

How Much Is Enough? The Explosion in the Number of U.S. Prisoners
To better understand the significance of this growth, compare it with the growth of the U.S. population. Between 1970 and 1998, the U.S. population grew 32 percent, while the U.S. prison population grew *17 times as fast* (563 percent). If the U.S. prison population had grown at the same rate as the U.S. population, there would be about 259,000 prisoners, one-fifth of the actual number.
Source: Statistical Abstract 1995:Table 349; 2000:Table 371.

T A B L E 8.3 Inmates in U.S. State Prisons		
Characteristics	Percentage of Prisoners with These Characteristics	Percentage of U.S. Population with These Characteristics
Age		
17 and younger	0.6%	25.9%
18–24	21.3%	10.2%
25–34	45.7%	16.6%
35–44	22.7%	15.7%
45–54	6.5%	10.7%
55–64	2.4%	8.2%
65 and older	0.7%	12.7%
Race		
African American	46.5%	12.1%
White	33.3%	72.7%
Latino	17.0%	12.5%
Others	3.2%	2.7%
Sex		
Male	93.7%	49.0%
Female	6.3%	51.0%
Marital Status		
Never Married	57.1%	23.5%
Divorced	18.6%	9.9%
Married	16.6%	59.7%
Education		
Less than high school	43.0%	17.9%
High school graduate	43.6%	33.8%
Some college	10.7%	17.2%
College graduate	2.7%	31.1%

Source: Sourcebook of Criminal Justice Statistics 1999:Table 6.37; Statistical Abstract 1998:Tables 16, 61, 262; 2000:Table 16; Figure 12.6 of this text.

high school—and how unlikely it is for a college graduate to have this unwelcome destination in life.

For the past 15 years or so, the United States has followed a "get tough" policy. "Three strikes and you're out" laws (a mandatory sentence, sometimes life imprisonment, upon conviction for a third felony) have become common. While few of us would feel sympathy if a man convicted of a third rape (or a third murder) were sent to prison for life, as discussed in the following Thinking Critically section, these laws have had unanticipated consequences.

t h i n k i n g
CRITICALLY

"Three Strikes and You're Out!" Unintended Consequences of Well-Intended Laws

In the 1980s, violent crime soared. Americans were fearful, and they demanded that their lawmakers do something. Politicians heard the message, and they responded by passing the "three strikes" law. Anyone convicted of a third felony receives an automatic mandatory sentence. Judges are not allowed to consider the circumstances. Some mandatory sentences carry life imprisonment.

In their haste to appease the public, the politicians did not limit these laws to *violent* crimes. And they did not consider that some minor crimes are considered felonies. As the functionalists would say, this has led to unanticipated consequences.

Here are some actual cases (Cloud 1999).

■ In Iowa, a man was sentenced to 10 years for stealing $30 worth of steaks from a grocery store.

■ In California, a 21-year-old anthropology major was sentenced to 10 years for mailing sheets of LSD to her boyfriend.

■ In Los Angeles, a 27-year-old man was sentenced to 25 years for stealing a pizza.

■ In Alabama, a husband, father, Vietnam veteran, and owner of a roofing business bought a pound of marijuana. Thirteen years earlier, he had been arrested for several petty crimes—crimes that didn't even carry a prison sentence. He was sentenced to life in prison without parole.

■ In New York City, a man who was about to be sentenced for selling crack said to the judge, "I'm only 19. This is terrible." He then hurled himself out of a courtroom window, plunging to his death sixteen stories below.

■ In Sacramento, a man who passed himself off as Tiger Woods to go on a $17,000 shopping spree was sentenced to 200 years in prison (Reuters 2001).

■ ■ ■ ■ ■

for your consideration . . .

Apply the symbolic interactionist, functionalist, and conflict perspectives to mandatory sentencing. For *symbolic interactionism,* what do these laws represent to the public? How does your answer differ depending on what part of "the public" you are referring to? For *functionalism,* who benefits from these laws? What are some of their dysfunctions? For the *conflict perspective,* what groups are in conflict? Who has the power to enforce their will on others?

A major problem with prisons is that they fail to teach their clients to stay away from crime. Our **recidivism rate**—the percentage of former prisoners who are

recidivism rate
the proportion of people who are rearrested

■ *Charles Manson, shown here, has been confined in a California maximum security prison since ordering several murders, including one in which the fetus was ripped out of a pregnant woman, Sharon Tate. Manson is an example of why many people, despairing of rehabilitation, call for retribution, deterrence, and incapacitation. Manson is up for parole.*

rearrested—is extremely high. If you were to survey the average prison, you would find that three out of every four prisoners has been in prison before. You would also find that half of these recidivists have been convicted of violent crimes (*Sourcebook of Criminal Justice Statistics* 1999:Table 6.39). Finally, you would find that when they are released, roughly two-thirds of them will be rearrested within just three years ("Coming to . . . " 2001). It is safe to conclude that if—and this is a big if—the purpose of prisons is to teach people that crime doesn't pay, they are a colossal failure.

■ The Death Penalty

Capital punishment, the death penalty, is the most extreme and controversial measure the state takes. Apart from the moral and philosophical controversy surrounding the death penalty, people object to its biases. The death penalty is not administered evenly. Consider geography: Where people commit murder greatly affects their chances of being put to death by the state. The Social Map below shows this unevenness.

The death penalty also shows gender, social class, and racial-ethnic bias. It is almost unheard of for a woman or a rich person to be put to death by the state. It happens, but rarely. About 1.4 percent of prisoners on death row are women (*Sourcebook of Criminal Justice Statistics* 2000:Table 6.84). Instead of bias in favor of women, however, these totals may reflect the relative frequency and severity of their crimes.

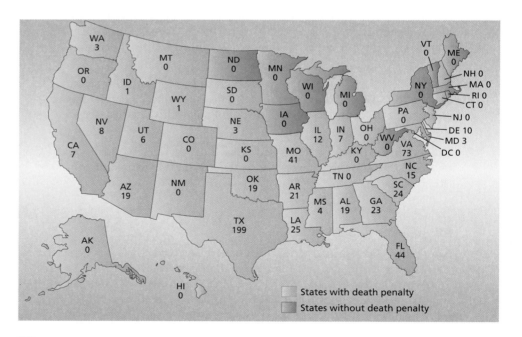

States with death penalty
States without death penalty

▪️igure 8.3

Social Map: Executions in the United States
Executions since 1977, when the death penalty was reinstated.
Source: Statistical Abstract 2000:Table 376.

capital punishment
the death penalty

The bias that once put an end to the death penalty, though, was flagrant. Donald Partington (1965), a lawyer, examined all executions for rape and attempted rape in Virginia between 1908 and 1963. For these crimes, 2,798 men were convicted. Fifty-six percent were whites, 44 percent blacks. Of these, 41 men were executed for rape and 13 for attempted rape. *All* were black. *Not one* of the whites was executed.

After listening to evidence like this, in 1972 the Supreme Court ruled in *Furman* v. *Georgia* that the death penalty was unconstitutionally applied. The execution of prisoners stopped—but not for long. The states wrote new laws, and in 1977 they again began to execute prisoners. Since then, 63 percent of those put to death have been white and 37 percent African American (*Statistical Abstract* 2000:Table 375). Table 8.4 shows the race-ethnicity of the 3,771 prisoners now on death row.

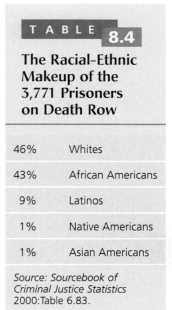

TABLE 8.4	
The Racial–Ethnic Makeup of the 3,771 Prisoners on Death Row	
46%	Whites
43%	African Americans
9%	Latinos
1%	Native Americans
1%	Asian Americans

Source: Sourcebook of Criminal Justice Statistics 2000:Table 6.83.

■ Legal Change

Did you know that it is a crime in Iran and Afghanistan for women to wear makeup? A crime in Illinois for merchants to sell meat before noon on Sundays? You probably know that it is a crime to drink alcohol while driving your car, but did you know that this is legal in Texas? As stressed in this chapter, deviance, including the form called *crime,* is relative. It varies from one society to another, and from group to group within a society. It also varies from one time period to another, as opinions change or as different groups gain access to power.

Let's consider legal change.

thinking
CRITICALLY

Changing Views: Making Hate a Crime

B ecause crime consists of whatever acts authorities decide to assign that label, new crimes emerge from time to time. A prime example is juvenile delinquency, which Illinois lawmakers designated a separate type of crime in 1899. Juveniles committed crimes prior to this time, of course, but these youths were not considered to be a separate type of lawbreaker. They were just young people who committed crimes, and they were treated the same as adults who committed the same crime. New technology also leads to new crimes. Motor vehicle theft, a separate crime in the United States, obviously did not exist before the automobile was invented

In the 1980s, another new crime was born when state governments developed the classification **hate crime.** This is a crime that is motivated by *bias* (dislike, hatred) against someone's race-ethnicity, religion, sexual orientation, disability, or national origin. Prior to this, of course, people attacked others or destroyed their property out of these same motivations, but in those cases the motivation was not the issue. If someone injured or killed another person because of that person's race-ethnicity, religion, sexual orientation, national origin, or disability, he or she was charged with assault or murder. Today, motivation has become a central issue, and hate crimes carry more severe sentences than do crimes that involve the same act but without hatred as the motive. Table 8.5 summarizes the victims of hate crimes.

hate crime
crimes to which more severe penalties are attached because they are motivated by hatred (dislike, animosity) of someone's race-ethnicity, religion, sexual orientation, disability, or national origin

TABLE 8.5	Hate Crimes
Directed Against	**Number of Victims**
Race-Ethnicity	
African Americans	3,663
Whites	1,003
Latinos	620
Asian Americans	372
Native Americans	66
Religion	
Jews	1,235
Catholics	65
Protestants	62
Islamics	23
Sexual Orientation	
Male Homosexual	1,005
Female Homosexual	270
Homosexuals (general)	177
Heterosexuals	17
Disabilities	
Physical	14
Mental	13

Source: Statistical Abstract 2000:Table 338.

We can be certain that the "evolution" of crime is not yet complete. As society changes and as different groups gain access to the seat of power, we can expect the definitions of crime to change accordingly.

■ ■ ■ ■ ■

for your consideration . . .

Why do we need a separate classification called hate crime? Why aren't the crimes of assault, robbery, murder, and so on adequate? How do you think your social location (race-ethnicity, gender, social class, sexual orientation, or physical ability) affects your opinion?

■ The Trouble with Official Statistics

Both the findings of symbolic interactionists (that stereotypes operate when authorities deal with groups such as the Saints and the Roughnecks) and the conclusion of conflict theorists (that the criminal justice system exists to serve the ruling elite) demonstrate the need for caution in interpreting official statistics. Crime statistics do not have an objective, independent existence. They are not like oranges that you pick out in a grocery store. Rather, crime statistics are a human creation. They are produced within a specific social and political context for some particular purpose. Change that context, and the statistics would change.

Consider this: According to official statistics, working-class boys are clearly more delinquent than middle-class boys. Yet, as we have seen, *who actually gets arrested for what* is affected by social class, a point that has far-reaching implications. As symbolic interactionists point out, the police follow a symbolic system as they enforce the law. Their ideas of "typical criminals" and "typical good citizens," for example, permeate their work. The more a suspect matches their "criminal profile," the more likely that person is to be arrested. **Police discretion,** the decision of whether or not to arrest someone or even to ignore a matter, is a routine part of police work. Consequently, official crime statistics always reflect these and many other biases.

IN SUM ■ ■ ▪ ■

Reactions to deviants vary from such mild sanctions as frowns and stares to such severe responses as imprisonment and death. Some sanctions are formal—court hearings, for example—although most are informal, as when friends refuse to talk to each other. One sanction is to label someone a deviant, which can have powerful consequences for the person's life, especially if the label closes off conforming activities and opens deviant ones. The degradation ceremony, in which someone is publicly labeled "not one of us," is a powerful sanction. So is imprisonment. Official statistics must be viewed with caution, for they reflect biases.

■ The Medicalization of Deviance: Mental Illness

Another way in which society deals with deviance is to "medicalize" it. Let's look at what this entails.

Neither Mental nor Illness? To *medicalize* something is to make it a medical matter, to classify it as a form of illness that properly belongs in the care of physicians. For the past hundred years or so, especially since the time of Sigmund Freud (1856–1939), the Viennese physician who founded psychoanalysis, there has been a growing tendency toward the **medicalization of deviance.** In this view, deviance, including crime, is a sign of mental sickness. Rape, murder, stealing, cheating, and so on are external symptoms of internal disorders, consequences of a confused or tortured mind.

Thomas Szasz (1986, 1996, 1998), a renegade in his profession of psychiatry, argues that *mental illnesses are neither mental nor illness. They are simply problem behaviors.* Some forms of so-called mental illnesses have organic causes; that is, they are *physical* illnesses that result in unusual perceptions or behavior. Some depression, for example, is caused by a chemical imbalance in the brain, which can be treated by drugs. The depression, however, may show itself as crying, long-term sadness, and lack of interest in family, work, school, or one's appearance. When a person becomes deviant in ways that disturb others, and when these others cannot find a satisfying explanation for why the person is "like that," they conclude that a "sickness in the head" causes the inappropriate, unacceptable behavior.

All of us have troubles. Some of us face a constant barrage of problems as we go through life. Most of us continue the struggle, encouraged by relatives and friends, motivated by job, family responsibilities, and life goals. Even when the odds seem hopeless, we carry on, not perfectly, but as best we can.

police discretion
the practice of the police, in the normal course of their duties, to arrest someone for an offense or to overlook the matter

medicalization of deviance
to make deviance a medical matter, a symptom of some underlying illness that needs to be treated by physicians

■ People whose behaviors violate norms often are called mentally ill. "Why else would they do such things?" is a common response to deviant behaviors that we don't understand. Mental illness is a label that contains the assumption that there is something wrong "within" people that "causes" their disapproved behavior. The surprise with this man, who changed his legal name to "Scary Guy," is that he speaks at schools across the country, where he promotes acceptance, awareness, love, and understanding.

Some people, however, fail to cope well with the challenges of daily life. Overwhelmed, they become depressed, uncooperative, or hostile. Some strike out at others, while some, in Merton's terms, become retreatists and withdraw into their apartments or homes, not wanting to come out. These are *behaviors, not mental illnesses,* stresses Szasz. They may be inappropriate coping devices, but they are coping devices, nevertheless, not mental illnesses. Thus, Szasz concludes that "mental illness" is a myth foisted on a naive public by a medical profession that uses pseudoscientific jargon in order to expand its area of control and force nonconforming people to accept society's definitions of "normal."

Szasz's extreme claim forces us to look anew at the forms of deviance that we usually refer to as mental illness. To explain behavior that people find bizarre, he directs our attention not to causes hidden deep within the "subconscious," but, instead, to how people learn such behaviors. Asking, "What is the origin of inappropriate or bizarre behavior?" then becomes similar to asking, "Why do some women steal?" "Why do some men rape?" "Why do some teenagers cuss their parents and stalk out of the room, slamming the door?" *The answers depend on those people's particular experiences in life, not on an illness in their mind.* In short, some sociologists find Szasz's renegade analysis refreshing because it indicates that *social experiences,* not some illness of the mind, underlie bizarre behaviors—as well as deviance in general.

The Homeless Mentally Ill

Jamie was sitting on a low wall surrounding the landscaped courtyard of an exclusive restaurant. She appeared unaware of the stares that were elicited by her layers of mismatched clothing, her dirty face, and the shopping cart that overflowed with her meager possessions.

Every once in a while Jamie would pause, concentrate, and point to the street, slowly moving her finger horizontally. I asked her what she was doing.

"I'm directing traffic," she replied. "I control where the cars go. Look, that one turned right there," she said, now withdrawing her finger.

"Really?" I said.

After a while she confided that her cart talked to her.

"Really?" I said again.

"Yes," she replied. "You can hear it, too." At that, she pushed the shopping cart a bit.

"Did you hear that?" she asked.

When I shook my head, she demonstrated again. Then it hit me. She was referring to the squeaking wheels!

I nodded.

When I left, Jamie was pointing to the sky, for, as she told me, she also controlled the flight of airplanes.

To most of us, Jamie's behavior and thinking are bizarre. They simply do not match any reality we know. Could you or I become like Jamie?

Suppose for a bitter moment that you are homeless and have to live on the streets. You have no money, no place to sleep, no bathroom. You do not know *if* you are going to eat, much less where. You have no friends or anyone you can trust, and you live in constant fear of rape and violence. Do you think this might be enough to drive you over the edge?

Consider just the problems involved in not having a place to bathe. (Shelters are often so dangerous that the homeless prefer to take their chances and sleep in public settings.) At first, you try to wash in the toilets of gas stations, bars, the bus station, or a shopping center. But you are dirty, and people stare when you enter and call the management when they see you wash your feet in the sink. You are thrown out and told in no uncertain terms never to come back. So you get dirtier and dirtier. Eventually you come to think of being dirty as a fact of life. Soon, maybe, you don't even care. The stares no longer bother you, at least not as much.

No one will talk to you, and you withdraw more and more into yourself. You begin to build a fantasy life. You talk openly to yourself. People stare, but so what?

They stare anyway. Besides, they are no longer important to you.

Jamie might be mentally ill. Some organic problem, such as a chemical imbalance in her brain, might underlie her behavior. But perhaps not. How long would it take us to exhibit bizarre behaviors if we were homeless—and hopeless? The point is that *just being on the streets can cause mental illness*—or whatever we want to label socially inappropriate behaviors that we find difficult to classify. *Homelessness and mental illness are reciprocal:* Just as "mental illness" can cause homelessness, so the trials of being homeless, of living on cold, hostile streets, can lead to unusual and unacceptable thinking and behaviors.

■ The Need for a More Humane Approach

As Durkheim (1895/1964:68) pointed out, deviance is inevitable—even in a group of saints.

> Imagine a society of saints, a perfect cloister of exemplary individuals. Crimes, properly so called, will there be unknown; but faults which appear [invisible] to the layman will create there the same scandal that the ordinary offense does in ordinary [society].

With deviance inevitable, one measure of a society is how it treats its deviants. Our prisons certainly don't say much good about U.S. society. Filled with the poor, they are warehouses of the unwanted. They reflect patterns of broad discrimination in our larger society. White-collar criminals continue to get by with a slap on the wrist while street criminals are punished severely. Some deviants, who fail to meet current standards of admission to either prison or mental hospital, take refuge in shelters and cardboard boxes in city streets. Although no one has *the* answer, it does not take much reflection to see that there are more humane approaches than these.

Because deviance is inevitable, the larger issues are to find ways to protect people from deviant behaviors that are harmful to themselves or others, to tolerate those that are not harmful, and to develop systems of fairer treatment for deviants. In the absence of fundamental changes that would bring about a truly equitable social system, most efforts are, unfortunately, Band-Aid solutions. What we need is a more humane social system, one that would prevent the social inequalities that are the focus of the next four chapters.

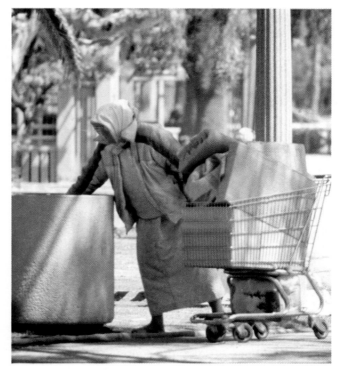

■ The homeless are located at the bottom of the U.S. social class ladder. One might even say that their status is so low that they occupy the space beneath its lowest rung. Why do you think a society as wealthy as the United States has homeless people?

Summary and Review

What Is Deviance?

From a sociological perspective, **deviance** (the violation of norms) is relative. What people consider deviant varies from one culture to another and from group to group within the same society. As symbolic interactionists stress, it is not the act itself, but the reactions to the act, that make something deviant. All groups develop systems of **social control** to punish **deviants,** those who violate its norms. Pp. 212–216.

■ How do sociological and individualistic explanations of deviance differ?

To explain why people deviate, sociobiologists and psychologists look for reasons *within* the individual, such as **genetic predispositions** or **personality**

disorders. Sociologists, in contrast, look for explanations *outside* the individual, in social relations. Pp. 216–217.

The Symbolic Interactionist Perspective

■ **How do symbolic interactionists explain deviance?**

Symbolic interactionists have developed several theories to explain deviance such as **crime** (the violation of norms that are written into law). According to **differential association theory,** people learn to deviate by associating with others. According to **control theory,** each of us is propelled toward deviance, but most of us conform because of an effective system of inner and outer controls. People who have less effective controls deviate. Pp. 217–220.

Labeling theory focuses on how labels (names, reputations) help to funnel people into or away from deviance. People who commit deviant acts often use **techniques of neutralization** to continue to think of themselves as conformists. Pp. 220–223.

The Functionalist Perspective

■ **How do functionalists explain deviance?**

Functionalists point out that deviance, including criminal acts, is functional for society. Functions include affirming norms and promoting social unity and social change. According to **strain theory,** societies socialize their members into desiring **cultural goals.** Many people are unable to achieve these goals in socially acceptable ways—that is, by **institutionalized means.** *Deviants,* then, are people who either give up on the goals or use deviant means to attain them. Merton identified five types of responses to cultural goals and institutionalized means: conformity, innovation, ritualism, retreatism, and rebellion. **Illegitimate opportunity theory** stresses that some people have easier access to illegal means of achieving goals. Pp. 224–229.

The Conflict Perspective

■ **How do conflict theorists explain deviance?**

Conflict theorists take the position that the group in power (the **capitalist class**) imposes its definitions of deviance on other groups (the **working class** and the marginal working class). From the conflict perspective, the law is an instrument of oppression used to maintain the power and privilege of the few over the many. The marginal working class has little income, is desperate, and commits highly visible property crimes. The ruling class directs the **criminal justice system,** using it to punish the crimes of the poor while diverting its own criminal activities away from this punitive system. Pp. 229–231.

Reactions to Deviance

■ **What are common reactions to deviance in the United States?**

In following a "get-tough" policy, the United States has imprisoned millions of people. African Americans and Latinos comprise a disproportionate percentage of U.S. prisoners. In line with conflict theory, as groups gain political power, their views are reflected in the criminal code. **Hate crime** legislation was considered in this context. Pp. 231–236.

■ **Are official statistics on crime reliable?**

The conclusions of both symbolic interactionists (that the police operate with a large measure of discretion) and conflict theorists (that the legal system is controlled by the capitalist class) indicate that we must be cautious when using crime statistics. Pp. 236–237.

■ **What is the medicalization of deviance?**

The medical profession has attempted to **medicalize** many forms of **deviance,** claiming that they represent mental illnesses. Thomas Szasz disagrees, claiming that they are problem behaviors, not mental illnesses. Research on homeless people illustrates how problems in living can lead to bizarre behavior and thinking. Pp. 237–239.

■ **What is a more humane approach?**

Deviance is inevitable, so the larger issues are to find ways to protect people from deviance that harms themselves and others, to tolerate deviance that is not harmful, and to develop systems of fairer treatment for deviants. P. 239.

■ *Where can I read more on this topic?*

Suggested readings for this chapter are at the back of this book.

Additional Online Resources for This Chapter
www.ablongman.com/henslin6e

- *Content Select* Research Database for Sociology, with suggested key terms and annotated references
- Link to 2000 Census, with activities
- Flashcards of key terms and concepts

- Practice Tests
- Weblinks
- Interactive Maps

using . . .
ContentSelect

Research Database for Sociology

deviance	control theory	capital punishment	criminal justice
stigma	labeling theory	hate crime	system
social control	strain theory	urban gangs	mental illness
social order	white collar	gender and crime	homelessness
street crime	crime		

Franklin McMahon, *Crossroads Housing Section, Capetown*, 1985

9

Global Stratification

Systems of Social Stratification

Slavery

Caste

Estate

Class

Global Stratification and the Status of Females

What Determines Social Class?

Karl Marx: The Means of Production

Max Weber: Property, Prestige, and Power

Why Is Social Stratification Universal?

The Functionalist Perspective: Motivating Qualified People

The Conflict Perspective: Class Conflict and Scarce Resources

Lenski's Synthesis

How Do Elites Maintain Stratification?

Ideology Versus Force

Comparative Social Stratification

Social Stratification in Great Britain

Social Stratification in the Former Soviet Union

Global Stratification: Three Worlds

The Most Industrialized Nations

The Industrializing Nations

The Least Industrialized Nations

Modifying the Model

How the World's Nations Became Stratified

Colonialism

World System Theory

Dependency Theory

Culture of Poverty

Evaluating the Theories

Maintaining Global Stratification

Neocolonialism

Multinational Corporations

Technology and Global Domination

A Concluding Note

Summary and Review

*L*et's contrast three "average" families from around the world:

For Getu Mulleta, 33, and his wife, Zenebu, 28, of rural Ethiopia, life is a constant struggle to keep themselves and their seven children from starving. They live in a 320-square-foot manure-plastered hut with no electricity, gas, or running water. They have a radio, but the battery is dead. Surviving on $130 a year, the family farms teff, a cereal grain.

The Mulletas' poverty is not due to a lack of hard work. Getu works about 80 hours a week, while Zenebu puts in even more hours. "Housework" for Zenebu includes fetching water, making fuel pellets out of cow dung for the open fire over which she cooks the family's food, and cleaning animal stables. Like other Ethiopian women, she eats after the men.

In Ethiopia, the average male can expect to live to 48, the average female to 50.

The Mulletas' most valuable possession is their oxen. Their wishes for the future: more animals, better seed, and a second set of clothing.

In Guadalajara, Mexico, Ambrosio and Carmen Castillo Balderas and their five children, ages 2 to 10, live in a four-room house. They also have a walled courtyard, where the family spends a good deal of time. They even have a washing machine, which is hooked up to a garden hose that runs to a public water main several hundred yards away. Like most Mexicans, they do not have a telephone, nor do they own a car.

> *Unlike many, however, they own a refrigerator, a stereo, and a recent proud purchase that makes them the envy of their neighbors, a television.*

Unlike many, however, they own a refrigerator, a stereo, and a recent proud purchase that makes them the envy of their neighbors, a television.

Ambrosio, 29, works full time as a wholesale distributor of produce. He also does welding on the side. The family's total annual income is $3,600. They spend 57 percent of their income on food. Carmen works about 60 hours a week taking care of their children and keeping their home spotless. The neatness of their home stands in stark contrast to the neighborhood, which is lined with littered dirt roads. As in many other Mexican neighborhoods, public utilities and road work do not keep pace with people's needs.

The average life expectancy for males in Mexico is 70. For females, it is 76.

The Castillo Balderas' most valued possessions are their refrigerator and television. Their wish for the future: a truck.

Springfield, Illinois, is home to the Kellys—Rick, 36, Patti, 34, Julie, 10, and Michael, 7. The Kellys live in a four-bedroom, 2,100-square-foot, carpeted ranch-style house, with central heating and air conditioning, a basement, and a two-car garage. Their home is equipped with a refrigerator, washing machine, clothes dryer, dishwasher, garbage disposal, vacuum cleaner, food processor, microwave, and toaster. They also own three radios, a CD player, four telephones (one cellular), two televisions, a camcorder, VCR, DVD player, tape recorder, Gameboy, Nintendo, and a computer, printer, and scanner, not to mention two blow dryers, an answering machine, a blender, an electric can opener, and an electric toothbrush. This doesn't count the stereo-radio-CD players in their pickup and car.

Rick works 40 hours a week as a cable splicer for a telephone company. Patti teaches school part time. Together they make $46,737, plus benefits. The Kellys can choose from among dozens of superstocked supermarkets. They spend $3,935 for food they eat at home, and another $2,691 eating out, a total of 14 percent of their annual income.

In the United States, the average life expectancy is 74 for males, 80 for females.

On the Kellys' wish list are a new SUV, a 40-gigabyte computer, a flat screen TV, a digital camera, a fax machine, a Palm Pilot, a boat, a camping trailer, an ATV, and, oh yes, further down the road, a vacation cabin.

Sources: Menzel 1994; Population Reference Bureau 1995; *Statistical Abstract* 2000:Tables 116, 733, 743.

■ *"Worlds Apart" could be the title for these photos, which illustrate how life chances depend on global stratification. On the left is the Mulleta family of Ethiopia, featured in the opening vignette, standing in front of their home with all their material possessions. On the right is the Skeen family of Texas, surrounded by their possessions.*

Systems of Social Stratification

Some of the world's nations are wealthy, others poor, and some in between. This layering of nations, and of groups of people within a nation, is called *social stratification*. Social stratification is one of the most significant topics we shall discuss in this book, for it affects our life chances—from, as you saw in the opening vignette, our access to material possessions to the age at which we die.

Social stratification also affects the way we think about life. If you had been born into the Ethiopian family, for example, you would be illiterate and would expect your children to be the same. You also would expect hunger to be a part of life and would not be too surprised when people die young. To be born into either of the other two families, however, would give you quite a different picture of the world.

Social stratification is a system in which groups of people are divided into layers according to their relative power, property, and prestige. It is important to realize that social stratification does not refer to individuals. It is a *way of ranking large groups of people in a hierarchy that shows their relative privileges.*

It is also important to note that *every society stratifies its members.* Some, like agricultural societies, draw firm lines that separate group from group, while others, like hunting and gathering societies, show greater equality. Regardless of its forms, however, the existence of social stratification is universal. Let's look at four major systems of social stratification: slavery, caste, estate, and class.

▪ Slavery

Slavery, whose essential characteristic is *ownership of some people by others*, has been common in world history. The Old Testament even lays out rules for how the Israelites should treat their slaves. So does the Koran. The Romans had slaves, as did

social stratification
the division of large numbers of people into layers according to their relative power, property, and prestige: applies to both nations and to people within a nation, society, or other group

slavery
a form of social stratification in which some people own other people

■ Slavery *is an age-old system of social stratification. This 1769 broadside from Charleston, South Carolina, reminds us that this form of stratification was once the custom in the United States.*

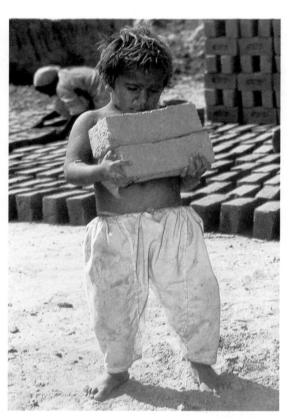

■ *This little Pakastani boy does backbreaking work each day in the brick kilns in the village of Batapur. He is a bonded laborer, a status that is close to that of slave. He cannot quit work, for, like his family, he must work to pay off debt that passes from generation to generation.*

the Africans and Greeks. In classical Greece and Rome, slaves did the work, freeing citizens to engage in politics and the arts. Slavery was least common among nomads, especially hunters and gatherers, and most common in agricultural societies (Landtman 1938/1968). As we examine the major causes and conditions of slavery, you will see how remarkably it has varied around the world.

Causes of Slavery   Contrary to popular assumption, slavery was not usually based on racism, but on one of three other factors. The first was debt. In some cultures, an individual who could not pay a debt could be enslaved by the creditor. The second was crime. Instead of being killed, a murderer or thief might be enslaved by the family of the victim as compensation for their loss. The third was war and conquest. When one group of people conquered another, they often enslaved some of the vanquished (Starna and Watkins 1991). Historian Gerda Lerner (1986) notes that the first people enslaved through warfare were women. When premodern men raided a village or camp, they killed the men, raped the women, and then brought the women back as slaves. The women were valued for sexual purposes, for reproduction, and for their labor.

Roughly twenty-five hundred years ago, when Greece was but a collection of city-states, slavery was common. A city that became powerful and conquered another city would enslave some of the vanquished. Both slaves and slaveholders were Greek. Similarly, when Rome became the supreme power about two thousand years ago, following the custom of the time the Romans enslaved some of the Greeks they had conquered. More educated than their conquerors, some of these slaves served as tutors in Roman homes. Slavery, then, was a sign of debt, of crime, or of defeat in battle. It was not a sign that the slave was inherently inferior.

Conditions of Slavery   The conditions of slavery have varied widely around the world. *In some cases, slavery was temporary.* Slaves of the Israelites were set free in the year of jubilee, which occurred every fifty years. Roman slaves ordinarily had the right to buy themselves out of slavery. They knew what their purchase price was, and some were able to meet this price by striking a bargain with their owner and selling their services to others. Such was the case with some of the educated Greek slaves. In most instances, however, slavery was a lifelong condition. Some criminals, for example, became slaves when they were given life sentences as oarsmen on Roman war ships. There they served until death, which often came quickly to those in this exhausting service.

Slavery was not necessarily inheritable. In most places, the children of slaves were automatically slaves themselves. But in some instances, the child of a slave who served a rich family might even be adopted by that family, becoming an heir who bore the family name along with the other sons or daughters of the household. In ancient Mexico, the children of slaves were always free (Landtman 1938/1968:271).

Slaves were not necessarily powerless and poor. In almost all instances, slaves owned no property and had no power. Among some groups, however, slaves could accumulate property and even rise to high positions in the community. Occasionally, a slave might even become wealthy, loan money to the master, and, while still a slave, own slaves himself or herself (Landtman 1938/1968). This, however, was rare.

Slavery in the New World   A gray area between a contract and slavery is **indentured service** (Main 1965; Elkins 1968). Many people who wanted to start a new life in the American colonies were unable to pay their passage. Ship captains would transport them on credit, and colonists would "buy their paper" when they arrived. This arrangement provided passage for the penniless, payment for the ship's captain, and servants for wealthier colonists for a set number of years. During that specified period, the servants were required by law to serve their master. If they ran away, they became outlaws and were captured and forcibly returned. At the end of the period of indenture, they became full citizens, able to live where they chose and free to sell their labor.

When there were not enough indentured servants to meet their growing need for labor, the colonists tried to enslave Indians. This attempt, however, failed miserably. One reason was that when Indians escaped they knew how to survive in the wilderness and were able to make their way back to their tribe. The colonists then turned to Africans, who were being brought to North and South America by the Dutch, English, Portuguese, and Spanish.

Because slavery has a broad range of causes, some analysts conclude that racism didn't lead to slavery, but, rather, slavery led to racism. Finding it profitable to make people slaves for life, U.S. slave owners developed an **ideology,** beliefs that justify social arrangements. They developed the view that the slaves were inferior. Some even said that they were not fully human. In short, the colonists developed elaborate justifications for slavery, built on the presumed superiority of their own group.

To make slavery even more profitable, slave states passed laws that made slavery *inheritable;* that is, the babies born to slaves became the property of the slave owners (Stampp 1956). These children could be sold, bartered, or traded. To strengthen their control, slave states passed laws making it illegal for slaves to hold meetings or to be away from the master's premises without carrying a pass (Lerner 1972). As sociologist W. E. B. Du Bois (1935/1966:12) noted, "gradually the entire white South became an armed camp to keep Negroes in slavery and to kill the black rebel."

Patterns of legal discrimination did not end after the Civil War. For example, until 1954 the states operated two separate school systems. Even until the 1950s, in order to keep the races from "mixing," it was illegal in Mississippi for a white and an African American to sit together on the same seat of a car! The reason there was no outright ban on blacks and whites being in the same car was to allow for African American chauffeurs.

indentured service
a contractual system in which someone sells his or her body (services) for a specified period of time in an arrangement very close to slavery, except that it is voluntarily entered into

ideology
beliefs about the way things ought to be that justify social arrangements

■ *As discussed in the text, slavery still exists. In this photo, a representative of the Liason Agency Network (on the left) is buying the freedom of the Sudanese slaves (in the background).*

Slavery Today Slavery has again reared its ugly head, this time in Sudan, Mauritania, and Benin (Hentoff 1998; Jacobs 1999; Marshall 2001). This region has a long history of slavery, and it was not until 1980 that slavery was officially abolished in Mauritania, and not until 1987 in Sudan (Ayittey 1998). Although officially abolished, slavery continues. Enslavement of members of the Dinka tribe in Sudan is the topic of the Mass Media box below.

mass media
in social life

What Price Freedom? Slavery Today

Children of the Dinka tribe in rural Sudan don't go to school. They work. Their families depend on them to tend the cattle that are so important to their way of life.

On the morning of the raid, ten-year-old Adhieu had been watching the cattle. "We were very happy because we would soon leave the cattle camps and return home to our parents. But in the morning, there was shooting. There was yelling and crying everywhere. My uncle grabbed me by the hand, and we ran. We swam across the river. I saw some children drowning. We hid behind a rock."

By morning's end, 500 children were either dead or enslaved. Their attackers were their fellow countrymen—Arabs from northern Sudan. The children who were captured were forced to march hundreds of miles north. Some escaped on the way. Others tried to—and were shot (Akol 1998).

Tens of thousands of Dinkas have been killed or enslaved since civil war broke out in Sudan in the 1980s. Yet the Arab-led government—the National Islamic Front—insists that slavery does not exist. It claims it is an invention of foreign politicians, Christian humanitarians, and hostile foreign media (Akol 1998). But there are too many witnesses, too much documentation by human rights groups. There also are devastating accounts by journalists: Public television (PBS) has even run film footage of captive children in chains. And then there are the slaves who managed to escape, who recount their ordeal in horrifying detail. The reasonable question is not whether slavery exists in Sudan, but to

what extent the Sudanese government encourages and supports this trafficking in human bodies (Dottridge 2001).

The United States bombed Kosovo into submission for its crimes against humanity, yet it has remained silent in the face of this outrage. A cynic might say that Kosovo was located at a politically strategic spot in Europe, whereas Sudan occupies an area of Africa in which the U.S. and European powers have little interest. A cynic might add that these powers fear Arab retaliation, which might take the form of oil embargoes and terrorism. A cynic might also suggest that outrages against black Africans are not as significant to these powers as those against white Europeans.

Appalled by the lack of response on the part of the world's most powerful governments, private groups have been spurred into action. Foremost among them is Christian Solidarity International (CSI), based in Zurich, Switzerland. The technique this human rights group uses is controversial. Arab "retrievers" go to northern Sudan, where they either buy or abduct slaves. Walking by night and hiding by day, they elude security forces and bring the slaves south. There, CSI pays the retrievers $50 per slave (Mabry 1999).

As CBS news cameras rolled, the rescuer paid the slave trader $50,000 in Sudanese pounds. At $50 per person, the bundle of bills was enough to free 1,000 slaves. The liberated slaves, mostly women and children, were then free to return to their villages (Jacobs 1999).

CSI has been severely criticized. Critics claim that buying slaves, even to free them, encourages slavery. The money

provides motivation to enslave people in order to turn around and sell them. Fifty dollars is a lot of money in Sudan, where the average income for an entire year is $1,550 (Haub and Cornelius 2001). It is also the value of two or three goats (Gaviak 2000).

That is a bogus argument, replies CSI. What is intolerable is to leave women and children in slavery where they are deprived of their freedom and families, and beaten and raped by brutal masters.

CSI claims to have purchased the freedom of about 40,000 slaves (Dottridge 2001). No one knows how many people remain in slavery.

for your consideration

What do you think about buying the freedom of slaves? Can you suggest a workable alternative? Why do you think the U.S. government has remained inactive about this issue for so long, when it invades other countries for human rights abuses? Do you think that, perhaps, its excursions into such places as Haiti and Kosovo were pretexts for political motives, that they had little to do with human rights? If not, why the silence in the face of slavery?

The media coverage of this issue has motivated many Americans to become active in freeing slaves. High schools nationwide—and even grade schools—are raising money to participate in slave buy-back programs (Schaefer 1999). If you were a school principal, would you encourage this practice? Why or why not?

■ In a caste system, *status is determined by birth and is lifelong.* At birth, these women in Bagepalli, India, received not only membership in a lower caste but also, because of their gender, a predetermined position in that caste and in the division of labor. They are carrying firewood that took the entire day to gather.

▪ Caste

The second system of social stratification is caste. In a **caste system,** status is determined by birth and is lifelong. Someone born into a low-status group will always have low status, no matter how much that person may accomplish in life. In sociological terms, the basis of a caste system is ascribed status (discussed on page 102). Achieved status cannot change an individual's place in this system.

Societies with this form of stratification try to make certain that the boundaries between castes remain firm. They practice **endogamy,** marriage within their own group, and prohibit intermarriage. To reduce contact between castes, they even develop elaborate rules about *ritual pollution,* teaching that contact with inferior castes contaminates the superior caste.

caste system
a form of social stratification in which one's status is determined by birth and is lifelong

endogamy
marriage within one's own group

India's Religious Castes India provides the best example of a caste system. Based not on race but on religion, India's caste system has existed for almost three thousand years (Chandra 1993a, 1993b). India's four main castes, or *varnas,* are depicted in Table 9.1. These four castes are subdivided into thousands of subcastes, or *jati,* with each *jati* having an occupational specialty. For example, knife sharpening is done by members of a particular subcaste.

The lowest group listed on Table 9.1, the Harijan, make up India's "untouchables." If a Harijan touches someone of a higher caste, that person becomes unclean. Even the shadow of an untouchable can contaminate. Early morning and late afternoons are especially risky, for the long shadows of these periods pose a danger to everyone higher up the caste system. Consequently, Harijans are not even allowed in some villages during these times. Anyone who becomes contaminated must follow *ablution,* or washing rituals, to restore purity (Lannoy 1975).

Although the Indian government formally abolished the caste system in 1949, centuries-old practices cannot be so easily eliminated, and the caste system remains part

TABLE 9.1	India's Caste System
Caste	**Occupation**
Brahman	Priests or scholars
Kshatriya	Nobles and warriors
Vaishya	Merchants and skilled artisans
Shudra	Common laborers
Harijan (Dalit)	The outcastes; degrading labor

of everyday life in India. The ceremonies people follow at births, marriages, and deaths, for example, are dictated by caste (Chandra 1993a). The upper castes dread the upward mobility of the untouchables, whom they detest. On occasion, they even resist it with violence and ritual suicide (Crossette 1996; Filkins 1997; Deliege 2001).

South Africa   Until recently, South Africa provided another example of social stratification based on caste. Europeans of Dutch descent, a numerical minority called Afrikaaners, controlled the government, the police, and the military. They used these sources of power to enforce a system called **apartheid** (ah-PAR-tate), the separation of the races. Everyone was classified by law into one of four racial groups: Europeans (whites), Africans (blacks), Coloureds (mixed races), and Asians. These classifications determined where people could live, work, and go to school. It also established where they could swim or see movies—for by law whites were not allowed to mix socially with the others.

After decades of trade sanctions, sports boycotts, and other pressure, Afrikaaners reluctantly dismantled their caste system. Black Africans no longer carry special passes, public facilities are integrated, and all racial-ethnic groups have the right to vote and to hold office. Although apartheid has been dismantled, its legacy haunts South Africa (Krog 1999). Whites still dominate the country's social institutions, and most blacks remain uneducated and poor. Many new rights—such as the right to higher education, to eat in restaurants, even to see a doctor—are of little use to people who can't afford them. Political violence has been replaced by old-fashioned crime. South Africa's murder rate, the highest in the world, runs *nine times* higher than the extraordinary U.S. rate ("South African . . . " 2001). Apartheid's legacy of prejudice, bitterness, and hatred is destined to fuel race relations for generations.

A U.S. Racial Caste System   Before leaving the subject of caste, we should note that when slavery ended in the United States, it was replaced by a *racial caste system,* in which everyone was marked for life at birth (Berger 1963/2001). In this system, *all* whites, no matter if they were poor and uneducated, considered themselves to have a higher status than *all* African Americans. As in India and South Africa, the upper caste, fearing pollution from the lower caste, prohibited intermarriage and insisted on separate schools, hotels, restaurants, and even toilets and drinking fountains in public facilities. When any white met any African American on a southern sidewalk, the African American had to move aside—which the untouchables of India still must do when they meet someone of a higher caste (Deliege 2001).

■ Estate

During the middle ages, Europe developed a unique system of stratification. The **estate system,** as it was known, consisted of three groups, or estates. The *first* estate was made up of the nobility, the wealthy and powerful families that ruled the country. They owned the land, which was the source of wealth at that time. The nobility did no farming themselves, or any "work," for that matter. Work was considered beneath their dignity, something to be done by servants. The nobility's responsibility was to administer their lands and fortunes, and to live "genteel" lives worthy of their high position.

The *second* estate consisted of the clergy. The Roman Catholic Church was a political power at this time. It owned vast amounts of land and collected taxes from commoners; everyone who lived within the boundaries of a parish had to pay a set amount. The church's power was so great that to be crowned, a king had to obtain the pope's permission.

Inheritance customs gave the nobility and the church another intricate connection. To prevent its vast lands from being carved into smaller chunks, the nobility practiced *primogeniture,* allowing only firstborn sons to inherit land. The other sons

apartheid
the separation of races as was practiced in South Africa

estate stratification system
the stratification system of medieval Europe, consisting of three groups or estates: the nobility, clergy, and commoners

CAPITAL AND LABOUR.

■ *This cartoon of political protest appeared in London newspapers in 1843. It illustrates the severe exploitation of labor that occurred after the estate system of social stratification broke down and peasants were forced to leave the land and find work elsewhere. Depicted here are the extremes of early capitalism. Scenes such as these stimulated Marx's analysis of social class.*

had to look around for some way to support themselves, and joining the clergy was a favored way. (Other methods were becoming an officer in the military or practicing law.) The church was attractive because priests had a lifetime position and were guaranteed a comfortable living. At that time, the church sold offices, and the wealthy could buy the position of bishop, for example, which guaranteed a high income.

The *third* estate consisted of the commoners. These were the farmers (known as serfs), the carpenters, the harness makers, the servants, and all the other people who made up society. Born into the third estate, and with practically no way to move out of it, they died there, too. The rare person who made it out of the third estate was a man who was knighted for performing an extraordinary feat for the king. Exceptional bravery in battle could lead to knighthood. But this was rare, and membership in this estate, as in the others, was lifelong.

Women in the Estate System Women belonged to the estate of their husbands. Women in the first estate had no occupation, for, like their husbands, work was considered beneath their dignity. Their responsibility was to administer the household, overseeing the servants. Women were not members of the second estate, as the Roman Catholic clergy did not marry. Women of the third estate shared the hard life of their husbands, including physical labor and food shortages. In addition, they faced the real peril of rape by men of the first estate. A few commoners who caught the eye of men of the first estate did marry and join them in the first estate. This, however, was rare.

■ Class

As we have seen, stratification systems based on slavery, caste, and estate are rigid. The lines drawn between people are so firm that there is little or no movement from one group to another. A **class system,** in contrast, is much more open, for it is based primarily on money or material possessions. It, too, begins at birth, when individuals are ascribed the status of their parents, but, unlike these other systems, people can change their social class by what they achieve (or fail to achieve) in life. In

class system
a form of social stratification based primarily on the possession of money or material possessions

addition, no laws specify people's occupations on the basis of birth or prohibit marriage between the classes.

A major characteristic of the class system, then, is its relatively fluid boundaries. A class system allows **social mobility,** that is, movement up or down the class ladder. The potential for improving one's life—or for falling down the class ladder—is a major force that drives people to go far in school and to work hard. In the extreme, the family background that a child inherits at birth may present such obstacles that he or she has little chance of climbing very far—or it may provide such privileges that it makes it almost impossible to fall down the class ladder.

■ Global Stratification and the Status of Females

In every society of the world, gender is a basis for social stratification. In no society is gender the sole basis for stratifying people, but gender cuts across *all* systems of social stratification—whether slavery, caste, estate, or class (Huber 1990). As we explored briefly in the estate system, on the basis of their gender, people are sorted into categories and given different access to the good things available in their society.

Apparently these distinctions always favor males. It is remarkable, for example, that in *every* society of the world men's earnings are higher than women's. Men's dominance is even more evident when we consider female circumcision (see the box on page 317). That most of the world's illiterate are females drives home women's relative position. Of the several hundred million adults who cannot read, about 60 percent are women ("Fighting Illiteracy . . . " 2000). Because gender is so significant for what happens to us in life, we shall devote a separate chapter to this topic (Chapter 11).

What Determines Social Class?

I n the early days of sociology, a disagreement arose about the meaning of social class. Let's compare how Marx and Weber analyzed the issue.

■ Karl Marx: The Means of Production

As discussed in Chapter 1, Karl Marx (1818–1883) witnessed the effects of societies in upheaval. When the feudal system broke up, masses of peasants were displaced from their traditional lands and occupations. Fleeing to cities, they competed for the few available jobs. Offered only a pittance for their labor, they dressed in rags, went hungry, and slept under bridges and in shacks. In contrast, the factory owners built mansions, hired servants, and lived in the lap of luxury. Seeing this great disparity between owners and workers, Marx concluded that social class depends on a single factor—the **means of production**—the tools, factories, land, and investment capital used to produce wealth (Marx 1844/1964; Marx and Engels 1848/1967).

Marx argued that the distinctions people often make among themselves—such as clothing, speech, education, paycheck, or, today, even the type of car they drive— are superficial matters. These things camouflage the only dividing line that counts. There are just two classes of people, said Marx: the **bourgeoisie,** those who own the means of production, and the **proletariat,** those who work for the owners. In short, people's relationship to the means of production determines their social class.

Marx did recognize other groups: farmers and peasants; a *lumpenproletariat* (marginal people such as beggars, vagrants, and criminals); and a middle group of self-employed professionals. Marx did not consider these groups social classes, however, for they lacked **class consciousness**—a shared identity based on their position in the

social mobility
movement up or down the social class ladder

means of production
the tools, factories, land, and investment capital used to produce wealth

bourgeoisie (capitalists)
Karl Marx's term for the people who own the means of production

proletariat (workers)
Karl Marx's term for the people who work for those who own the means of production

class consciousness
Karl Marx's term for awareness of a common identity based on one's position in the means of production

Taken at the end of the 1800s, these photos illustrate the contrasting worlds of social classes produced by capitalism. The sleeping boys shown in this classic 1890 photo by Jacob Riis sold newspapers in London. They did not go to school, and they had no home. The children on the right, Cornelius and Gladys Vanderbilt, are shown in front of their parents' estate. They went to school and did not work. You can see how the life situations illustrated in these photos would have produced different orientations to life—and, therefore, politics, ideas about marriage, values, and so on—the stuff of which life is made.

means of production. They did not perceive themselves as exploited workers whose plight could be solved by collective action. Consequently, Marx thought of these groups as insignificant in the coming workers' revolution destined to overthrow capitalism.

The capitalists will grow even wealthier, Marx said, and the hostilities will increase. When workers come to realize that capitalists are the source of their oppression, they will unite and throw off the chains of their oppressors. In a bloody revolution, they will seize the means of production and usher in a classless society, where no longer will the few grow rich at the expense of the many. What holds back the workers' unity and their revolution is **false consciousness**, workers mistakenly thinking of themselves as capitalists. For example, workers with a few dollars in the bank may forget that they are workers and instead see themselves as investors, or as capitalists who are about to launch a successful business.

The only distinction worth mentioning, then, is whether a person is an owner or a worker. This decides everything else, Marx stressed, for property determines people's lifestyles, shapes their ideas, and establishes their relationships with one another.

false consciousness
Karl Marx's term to refer to workers identifying with the interests of capitalists

■ Max Weber: Property, Prestige, and Power

Max Weber (1864–1920) became an outspoken critic of Marx. Weber argued that property is only part of the picture. Social class, he said, is made up of three components—property, prestige, and power (Gerth and Mills 1958; Weber 1922/1968). Some call these the three P's of social class. (Although Weber used the terms *class*, *status*, and *power*, some sociologists find *property*, *prestige*, and *power* to be clearer terms. To make them even clearer, you may wish to substitute *wealth* for *property*.)

Property (or wealth), said Weber, is certainly significant in determining a person's standing in society. On that he agreed with Marx. But, added Weber, ownership is not the only significant aspect of property. For example, some powerful people, such as managers of corporations, *control* the means of production although they do not *own* them. If managers can control property for their own benefit—awarding themselves huge bonuses and magnificent perks—it makes no practical difference that they do not own the property that they so generously use for their own benefit.

The text describes the many relationships among Weber's three components of social class: property, prestige, and power. Colin Powell is an example of power that was converted into prestige—which was then converted back into power.

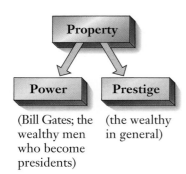

(Bill Gates; the wealthy men who become presidents)

(the wealthy in general)

(Ronald Reagan)

(Olympic gold medalists who endorse products)

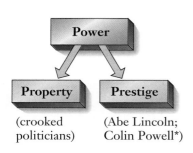

(crooked politicians)

(Abe Lincoln; Colin Powell*)

Figure 9.1

Weber's Three Components of Social Class: Interrelationships Among Them

*Colin Powell illustrates the circularity of these components. Powell's power as Chairman of the Joint Chiefs of Staff led to prestige. Powell's prestige, in turn, led to power when he was called from retirement to serve as Secretary of State in the George W. Bush administration.

Prestige, the second element in Weber's analysis, is often derived from property, for people tend to look up to the wealthy. Prestige, however, can also be based on other factors. Olympic gold medalists, for example, may not own property, yet they have high prestige. Some are even able to exchange their prestige for property—such as those who are paid a small fortune for claiming that they start their day with "the breakfast of champions." In other words, property and prestige are not one-way streets: Although property can bring prestige, prestige can also bring property.

Power, the third element of social class, is the ability to control others, even over their objections. Weber agreed with Marx that property is a major source of power, but he added that it is not the only source. For example, prestige can be turned into power. Perhaps the best example is Ronald Reagan, an actor who became president of the most powerful country in the world. Figure 9.1 shows how property, prestige, and power are interrelated.

IN SUM ■ ■ ▪ ▪ ▫

For Marx, social class was based solely on a person's relationship to the means of production. One is either a member of the bourgeoisie or the proletariat. Weber argued that social class is a combination of property, prestige, and power.

■ ▪ ▪ ▪ ▫

Why Is Social Stratification Universal?

What is it about social life that makes all societies stratified? We shall first consider the explanation proposed by functionalists, which has aroused much controversy in sociology, then explanations proposed by conflict theorists.

■ The Functionalist View: Motivating Qualified People

Functionalists take the position that the patterns of behavior that characterize a society exist because they are functional for that society. Because social inequality is universal, inequality must help societies survive. But how?

Davis and Moore's Explanation Two functionalists, Kingsley Davis and Wilbert Moore (1945, 1953), wrestled with this question. They concluded that stratification of society is inevitable because:

1. Society must make certain that its positions are filled.

2. Some positions are more important than others.

3. The more important positions must be filled by the more qualified people.

4. To motivate the more qualified people to fill these positions, society must offer them greater rewards.

Let's look at two examples to flesh out this functionalist argument. The position of college president is more important than that of a student because the president's decisions affect many more people. Any mistakes he or she makes carry implications for a large number of people, including many students. The same is true for a general compared with a private. The decisions of a general affect careers and paychecks, and may even determine life and death.

Positions with greater responsibility also require greater accountability. College presidents and army generals are accountable—to boards of trustees and to the leader of a country, respectively—for how they perform. How can society motivate highly qualified people to enter its higher-pressure positions? What keeps people from avoiding them and seeking only less demanding jobs?

The answer, said Davis and Moore, is that society offers greater rewards for its more responsible, demanding, and accountable positions. If these jobs didn't offer greater prestige, salaries, and benefits, why would anyone strive for them? Thus, a salary of $2 million, a country club membership, a private jet, and a chauffeured limousine may be necessary in order to get the most highly qualified people to compete with one another for some positions, while a $30,000 salary without fringe benefits is enough to get hundreds of less qualified people to compete for less demanding positions. It is the same with positions that require rigorous training. If you can get the same pay with a high school diploma, why suffer through the many tests and term papers that college requires?

The functionalist argument is simple and clear. Society works better if its most qualified people hold its most important positions. For example, to get highly talented people to become surgeons—to undergo many years of rigorous training and then cope with life-and-death situations on a daily basis, as well as withstand the Sword of Damocles known as malpractice suits—society must provide a high payoff.

Tumin's Critique of Davis and Moore   Note that Davis and Moore tried to explain *why* social stratification is universal, not to *justify* social inequality. Nevertheless, their view makes many sociologists uncomfortable, for they see it as coming close to justifying the inequalities in society.

Melvin Tumin (1953) was the first sociologist to point out what he saw as major flaws in the functionalist position. Here are three of his arguments.

First, the functionalists say that the most important positions bring the higher rewards, but how do we know if this is true? How do you determine which are the most important positions? You can't measure importance by a position's rewards, for that argument is circular. You must have an independent way to measure importance. For example, is a surgeon really more important to society than a garbage collector, since the garbage collector helps to prevent contagious diseases?

Second, if stratification worked as Davis and Moore described it, society would be a **meritocracy;** that is, all positions would be awarded on the basis of merit. If so, ability should predict who goes to college. Instead, family income is the best predictor—the more a family earns, the more likely their children are to go to college. Similarly, while some people do get ahead through ability and hard work, others simply inherit wealth and the opportunities that go with it. Moreover, a stratification system that places most men above most women does not live up to the argument that talent and ability are the bases for holding important positions. In short, factors far beyond merit give people their positions in society.

Third, if social stratification is so functional, it ought to benefit almost everyone. Social stratification, however, is *dysfunctional* for many. Think of the people who could have made invaluable contributions to society had they not been born in slums and had to drop out of school and take menial jobs to help support the family—or the many who, born female, are assigned "women's work," thus ensuring that they do not maximize their mental abilities.

■ The Conflict Perspective: Class Conflict and Scarce Resources

Conflict theorists don't just criticize details of the functionalist perspective. Rather, they attack its basic premise. Conflict, not function, they stress, is the basis of social stratification. In every society, groups struggle with one another to gain a larger share of the society's resources. Whenever a group gains power, it uses that

meritocracy
a form of social stratification in which all positions are awarded on the basis of merit

power to extract what it can from the groups beneath it. This elite group also uses the social institutions to keep other groups weak and itself in power.

Mosca's Argument   Italian sociologist Gaetano Mosca argued that every society will be stratified by power. This is inevitable, he said in an 1896 book entitled *The Ruling Class,* because:

1. No society can exist unless it is organized. This requires leadership of some sort in order to coordinate people's actions and get society's work done.

2. Leadership (or political organization) means inequalities of power. Some people take leadership positions, while others follow.

3. Human nature is self-centered. Therefore, people in power will use their positions to seize greater rewards for themselves.

There is no way around these facts of life, added Mosca. They make social stratification inevitable, and every society will stratify itself along lines of power.

Marx's Argument   If he were alive to hear the functionalist argument, Karl Marx would be enraged. From his point of view, the people in power are not there because of superior traits, as the functionalists would have us believe. That view is simply an ideology the elite use to justify their being at the top—and to seduce the oppressed into believing that their welfare depends on keeping society stable. Human history is the history of class struggle, of those in power using society's resources to benefit themselves and to oppress those beneath them—and of oppressed groups trying to overcome their domination.

Marx predicted that the workers would revolt. The day will come, he said, when class consciousness will overcome the ideology that now blinds them. When the workers realize their common oppression, they will rebel against the capitalists. The struggle to control the means of production may be covert at first, taking the form of work slowdowns or industrial sabotage. Ultimately, however, resistance will break out into the open. The revolution will not be easy, for the bourgeoisie control the police, the military, and even education, where they implant false class consciousness in the workers' children.

Current Modifications of Conflict Theory   Some sociologists have refocused conflict theory. C. Wright Mills (1956), Ralf Dahrendorf (1959), Randall Collins (1988; 1999), and James Schellenberg (1996), for example, stress how groups *within the same class* compete for scarce resources. They struggle for power, money, education, housing, and even prestige—whatever benefits society has to offer. The result is conflict not only between labor unions and corporations, but also between the young and the old, women and men, and racial and ethnic groups. Unlike functionalists, then, conflict theorists hold that just beneath the surface of what may appear to be a tranquil society lies conflict that is barely held in check.

▪ Lenski's Synthesis

Despite vast differences between the functionalist and conflict views, some analysts have tried to synthesize them. Sociologist Gerhard Lenski (1966) suggested we can reconcile these views by looking at whether or not a group has surpluses. The functionalists are right, he said, when it comes to groups that do not accumulate a surplus. These groups, such as hunting and gathering societies, give a greater share of their resources to those who take on important tasks, such as risking their lives in battle. For societies that have surpluses, however, Lenski says that the conflict theorists are right. In these societies, a struggle breaks out to control the surpluses. Some group wins, becoming an elite that sets up ways to protect its privileges. This builds social inequality into the society, resulting in a full-blown system of social stratification.

How Do Elites Maintain Stratification?

Suppose that you are part of the ruling elite of your society. What can you do to make sure you don't lose your privileged position? The key lies in controlling ideas and information, and, in the least effective means of all, the use of force.

■ Ideology Versus Force

Medieval Europe provides a good example of the power of ideology. At that time, land was the primary source of wealth. The land was owned by only the nobility and the church. Almost everyone was a peasant (or commoner) who worked for these powerful landowners. The peasants farmed the land, took care of the livestock, and built the roads and bridges. Each year, they had to turn over a designated portion of their crops to their feudal lord. Year after year, for centuries, they did so. Why?

Controlling Ideas Why didn't the peasants rebel and take over the land themselves? There were many reasons, not the least of which was that the nobility and church controlled the army. Coercion, however, only goes so far, for it breeds hostility and nourishes rebellion. How much more effective it is to get the masses to *want* to do what the ruling elite desires. This is where *ideology* (beliefs that justify the way things are) comes into play, and the nobility and clergy used it to great effect. They developed an ideology known as the **divine right of kings**—the idea that the king's authority comes directly from God. The king delegates authority to nobles, who as God's representatives must be obeyed. To disobey is a sin against God; to rebel means physical punishment on earth and eternal suffering in hell.

Controlling people's ideas can be remarkably more effective than using brute force. Although this particular ideology no longer governs peoples' minds today, the elite in every society develops ideologies to justify its position at the top. For example, around the world schools teach that their country's form of government—*whatever form of government that may be*—is the best. Religious leaders teach that we owe obedience to authority, that laws are to be obeyed. To the degree that their ideologies are accepted by the masses, the elite remains securely in power.

Controlling Information and Using Technology
To maintain their positions of power, elites also try to control information. In dictatorships this is accomplished through the threat of force, for dictators can—and do—imprison editors and reporters for publishing critical reports. Some do so just for writing unflattering articles (Timerman 1981). Lacking such power, the ruling elites of democracies manipulate the media by selectively releasing information—and by withholding information "in the interest of national security."

The new technology is another tool for the elite. Telephones can be turned into microphones even when they are off the hook. Machines can read the entire contents

> **divine right of kings**
> the idea that the king's authority comes directly from God

■ The divine right of kings *was an ideology that made the king God's direct representative on earth—to administer justice and punish evildoers. This theological-political concept was supported by the Roman Catholic Church, whose representatives crowned the king. Depicted here is Charlemagne, who, crowned by Pope Leo III in 800, established what is known as the Holy Roman Empire. This painting is by Jean Victor Schnetz.*

of a computer in a second, without leaving a trace. Face-recognition systems—introduced at Super Bowl XXXV in Tampa, Florida—can scan a crowd of thousands, instantly matching the scans with digitized files of individuals. With these devices, the elite can monitor citizens' activities without their being aware that they are being observed. Dictatorships have few checks on how they employ such technology, but in democracies, checks and balances, such as constitutional rights and requiring court orders for search and seizure, at least partially curb their abuse.

The new technology is a two-edged sword. Just as it gives the elite powerful tools for monitoring citizens, it also makes it more difficult for them to control information. The new technology of satellite communications, e-mail, and the Internet pays no respect to international borders. Whether government officials like it or not, on the Internet information flies around the globe in seconds. Internet users also have free access to PGP (Pretty Good Privacy), a code that no government has been able to break.

IN SUM ■ ■ ■ ■ ■

To maintain stratification within a society, the elite tries to dominate their society's institutions. In a dictatorship, the elite makes the laws. In a democracy, the elite influences the laws. In both, the legal establishment enforces the laws. The elite also controls the police and military and can give orders to crush a rebellion—or even to run the post office or air traffic control if workers strike. As noted, force has its limits, and a nation's elite generally finds it preferable to maintain its stratification system by peaceful means, especially by influencing the thinking of its people.

■ ■ ■ ■ ■

Comparative Social Stratification

Now that we have examined systems of social stratification, considered why stratification is universal, and looked at how elites keep themselves in power, let's compare social stratification in Great Britain and in the former Soviet Union.

■ Social Stratification in Great Britain

Great Britain is often called England by Americans, but England is only one of the countries that make up the island of Great Britain. The others are Scotland and Wales. In addition, Northern Ireland is part of the United Kingdom of Great Britain and Northern Ireland.

Like other industrialized countries, Great Britain has a class system that can be divided into a lower, middle, and upper class. Great Britain's population is about evenly divided between the middle class and the lower (or working) class. A tiny upper class, perhaps 1 percent of the population, is wealthy, powerful, and highly educated.

Compared with Americans, the British are very class conscious. Like Americans, they recognize class distinctions on the basis of the type of car a person drives, or the stores someone patronizes. But the most striking characteristics of the British class system are language and education. This often shows up in differences in speech, which have a powerful impact on British life. Accent almost always betrays class. As soon as someone speaks, the listener is aware of that person's class—and treats him or her accordingly (Sullivan 1998).

Education is the primary way by which the British perpetuate their class system from one generation to the next. Almost all children go to neighborhood schools, but the children of Great Britain's privileged 5 percent—who own *half* the nation's wealth—attend exclusive private boarding schools (known as "public" schools). There they are trained in subjects considered "proper" for members of the ruling class. An astounding 50 percent of the students at Oxford and Cambridge, the country's most prestigious universities, come from this 5 percent of the population. To illustrate how powerfully this system of stratified education affects the national life of Great Britain, sociologist Ian Robertson (1987) said,

> [E]ighteen former pupils of the most exclusive of them, Eton, have become prime minister. Imagine the chances of a single American high school producing eighteen presidents!

■ Social Stratification in the Former Soviet Union

Heeding Karl Marx's call for a classless society, Vladimir Ilyich Lenin (1870–1924) and Leon Trotsky (1879–1940), led a revolution in Russia. They, and the nations that followed their banner, never claimed to have achieved the ideal of communism, in which all contribute their labor to the common good and receive according to their needs. Instead, they used the term *socialism* to describe the intermediate step between capitalism and communism, in which social classes are abolished but some inequality remains.

To tweak the nose of Uncle Sam, the socialist countries would trumpet their equality and point a finger at glaring inequalities in the United States. They, too, however, were marked by huge disparities in privilege. Their major basis of stratification was membership in the Communist Party. This often decided who would gain admission to the better schools or obtain the more desirable jobs. The equally qualified son or daughter of a nonmember would be turned down, for such privileges came with demonstrated loyalty to the Party.

Even the Communist Party was highly stratified. Most members occupied a low level, where they fulfilled such tasks as spying on other workers. For this, they might get easier jobs in the factory or occasional access to special stores to purchase hard-to-find goods. The middle level consisted of bureaucrats who were given better than average access to resources and privileges. At the top level was a small elite: party members who enjoyed not only power but also limousines, imported delicacies, vacation homes, and even servants and hunting lodges. As with other stratification systems around the world, women held lower positions in the Party. This was evident at each year's May Day celebration when the top members of the Party reviewed the latest weapons paraded in Moscow's Red Square. Photos of these events showed only men.

The leaders of the USSR became frustrated as they saw the West thrive. They struggled with a bloated bureaucracy, the inefficiencies of central planning, workers who did the minimum because they could not be fired, and a military so costly that it spent one of every eight of the nation's rubles (*Statistical Abstract* 1993:1432; table dropped in later editions). Their ideology did not call for their citizens to be deprived, and in an attempt to turn things around, the Soviet leadership initiated reforms. They allowed elections to be held in which more than one candidate ran for an office. (Prior to this, voters had a choice of only one candidate per office.) They also sold

■ *Russia's reluctant embrace of capitalism has brought many changes. One is a new affluence—which is matched by a new poverty. Both are evident in this photo from Moscow.*

huge chunks of state-owned businesses to the public. Overnight, making investments to try to turn a profit changed from being a crime into a respectable goal.

Russia's transition to capitalism took a bizarre twist. As authority broke down, a powerful Mafia emerged. These criminal groups are headed by gangsters, corrupt government officials, and crooked businessmen. Some have the help of agents of the KGB (Russian secret police). In a ruthless drive for wealth, these groups assassinate bank presidents and other business leaders who refuse to cooperate with them (Goble 1996; Zarakhovich 2001). They control half of Russia's economy (Foster 1998), and are stashing capital in offshore retreats, especially in such watering and wintering spots as Marbella on Spain's Costa del Sol.

Russia's "wild west" days are bound to disappear as the central government reestablishes its authority. At that time, this group of organized criminals will take its place as part of Russia's new capitalist class.

Global Stratification: Three Worlds

As noted at the beginning of this chapter, just as the people within a nation are stratified by power, prestige, and property, so are the world's nations. Until recently, a simple model consisting of First, Second, and Third Worlds was used to depict global stratification. *First World* referred to the industrialized capitalist nations, *Second World* to the communist nations, and *Third World* to any nation that did not fit into the first two categories. The breakup of the Soviet Union in 1989 made these terms outdated. In addition, although *first, second,* and *third* did not mean "best," "better," and "worst," they sounded like it. An alternative classification some now use—developed, developing, and undeveloped nations—has the same drawback. By calling ourselves "developed," it sounds as though we are mature and the "undeveloped" nations somehow retarded.

Consequently, I have chosen more neutral, descriptive terms: *Most Industrialized, Industrializing,* and *Least Industrialized* nations. We can measure industrialization with no judgment implied as to whether a nation's industrialization represents "development," ranks it "first," or is even desirable at all.

The intention is to depict on a global level the three primary dimensions of social stratification: property, power, and prestige. The Most Industrialized Nations have much greater property (wealth), power (they do get their way in international relations), and prestige (they are looked up to as world leaders). The three families sketched in the opening vignette illustrate the far-reaching effects of global stratification.

■ The Most Industrialized Nations

The Most Industrialized Nations are the United States and Canada in North America; Great Britain, France, Germany, Switzerland, and the other industrialized nations of western Europe; Japan in Asia; and Australia and New Zealand in the area of the world known as Oceania. Although there are variations in their economic systems, these nations are capitalistic. As Table 9.2 shows, although these nations have only 16 percent of the world's people, they have 31 percent of the earth's land. Their wealth is so enormous that even their poor live better and longer lives than do the average citizens of the Least Industrialized Nations. The Social Map on the next two pages shows the tremendous disparities in income among the world's nations.

■ The Industrializing Nations

The Industrializing Nations include most of the nations of the former Soviet Union and its former satellites in eastern Europe. As Table 9.2 shows, these nations account for 20 percent of the earth's land and 16 percent of its people.

The dividing points between the three "worlds" are soft, making it difficult to know how to classify some nations. This is especially the case with the Industrializing Nations. Exactly how much industrialization must a nation have to be in this category? Although soft, these categories do pinpoint essential differences among nations. Most people who live in the Industrializing Nations have much lower incomes and standards of living than those who live in the Most Industrialized Nations. Most, however, are better off than those who live in the Least Industrialized Nations. For example, on such measures as access to electricity, indoor plumbing, automobiles, telephones, and even food, citizens of the Industrializing Nations rank lower than those in the Most Industrialized Nations, but higher than those in the Least Industrialized Nations. As you saw in the opening vignette, this principle applies even to life expectancy.

TABLE 9.2	Distribution of the World's Land and Population	
	Land	Population
Most Industrialized Nations	31%	16%
Industrializing Nations	20%	16%
Least Industrialized Nations	49%	68%

Sources: Computed from Kurian 1990, 1991, 1992.

The Most Industrialized Nations

	Nation	Income per Person
1	Luxembourg	$41,200
2	Switzerland	$39,980
3	Norway	$34,310
4	Denmark	$33,040
5	Japan	$32,350
6	Singapore	$30,170
7	United States	$29,240
8	Austria	$26,830
9	Germany	$26,570
10	Sweden	$25,580
11	Belgium	$25,380
12	Iceland	$25,000
13	Netherlands	$24,780
14	Finland	$24,280
15	France	$24,210
16	Hong Kong	$23,660
17	United Kingdom	$21,410
18	Australia	$20,640
19	Italy	$20,090
20	Canada	$19,170
21	Ireland	$18,710
22	Israel	$16,180
23	New Zealand	$14,600
24	Taiwan	$13,410

The Industrializing Nations

	Nation	Income per Person
25	Spain	$14,100
26	Greece	$11,740
27	Portugal	$10,670
28	Slovenia	$9,840
29	Malta	$9,330
30	South Korea	$8,600
31	Argentina	$8,030
32	Seychelles	$6,910
33	Uruguay	$6,070
34	Czech Republic	$5,150
35	Chile	$4,990
36	Brazil	$4,630
37	Hungary	$4,510
38	Poland	$3,910
39	Mexico	$3,840
40	Slovakia	$3,680
41	Malaysia	$3,670
42	Venezuela	$3,530
43	South Africa	$3,310
44	Turkey	$3,160
45	Colombia	$2,470
46	Russia	$2,260
47	Thailand	$2,150

The Oil-Rich Nations

	Nation	Income per Person
164	United Arab Emirates	$23,800
165	Qatar	$21,300
166	Kuwait	$17,000
167	Bahrain	$13,000
168	Oman	$9,500
169	Saudi Arabia	$6,910
170	Libya	$6,570

The Least Industrialized Nations

	Nation	Income per Person		Nation	Income per Person
48	Croatia	$4,620	69	Fed States of Micronesia	$1,920
49	Gabon	$4,120	70	El Salvador	$1,810
50	Mauritius	$3,870	71	Dominican Republic	$1,750
51	Lebanon	$3,560	72	Ecuador	$1,700
52	Saint Lucia	$3,510	73	Iran	$1,650
53	Estonia	$3,360	74	Guatemala	$1,640
54	Botswana	$3,310	75	Marshall Islands	$1,610
55	Grenada	$3,140	76	Algeria	$1,550
56	Panama	$3,080	77	Jamaica	$1,550
57	Dominica	$3,040	78	Swaziland	$1,520
58	Costa Rica	$2,770	79	Jordan	$1,510
59	Belize	$2,670	80	Romania	$1,360
60	Iraq	$2,560	81	Kazakhstan	$1,340
61	Fiji	$2,460	82	Vanuatu	$1,340
62	Peru	$2,440	83	Suriname	$1,320
63	Latvia	$2,430	84	Egypt	$1,290
64	Lithuania	$2,260	85	Morocco	$1,240
65	Belarus	$2,180	86	Uzbekistan	$1,220
66	Namibia	$2,110			
67	Tunisia	$2,110			
68	Paraguay	$2,000			

Figure 9.2

Social Map: Global Stratification: Income* of the World's Nations

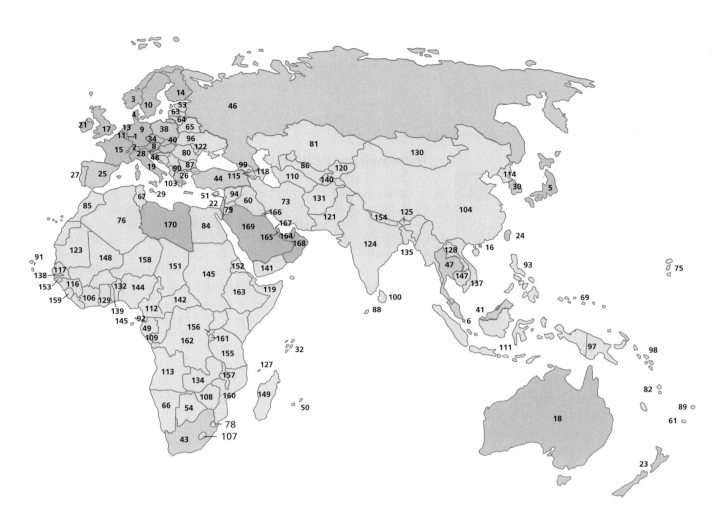

The Least Industrialized Nations

Nation	Income per Person	Nation	Income per Person	Nation	Income per Person	Nation	Income per Person
87 Bulgaria	$1,200	106 Cote d'Ivoire	$710	127 Comoros	$400	146 Sudan	$290
88 Maldives	$1,180	107 Lesotho	$680	128 Laos	$400	147 Cambodia	$280
89 Western Samoa	$1,140	108 Zimbabwe	$675	129 Ghana	$390	148 Mali	$250
90 Macedonia	$1,100	109 Congo	$670	130 Mongolia	$390	149 Madagascar	$250
91 Cape Verde	$1,090	110 Turkmenistan	$640	131 Afghanistan	$380	150 Burkina Faso	$245
92 Equatorial Guinea	$1,060	111 Indonesia	$640	132 Benin	$380	151 Chad	$230
		112 Cameroon	$630	133 Haiti	$380	152 Eritrea	$230
93 Philippines	$1,050	113 Angola	$620	134 Zambia	$370	153 Guinea-Bissau	$230
94 Syria	$1,020	114 North Korea	$580	135 Bangladesh	$350	154 Nepal	$220
95 Bolivia	$1,010	115 Armenia	$560	136 Kenya	$350	155 Tanzania	$220
96 Ukraine	$980	116 Guinea	$550	137 Vietnam	$350	156 Rwanda	$210
97 Papua-New Guinea	$930	117 Senegal	$520	138 Gambia	$340	157 Malawi	$200
		118 Azerbaijan	$510	139 Togo	$340	158 Niger	$200
98 Solomon Islands	$870	119 Somalia	$500	140 Tajikistan	$330	159 Sierra Leone	$170
99 Georgia	$860	120 Kyrgystan	$480	141 Yemen	$330	160 Mozambique	$170
100 Sri Lanka	$810	121 Pakistan	$470	142 Central African Republic	$320	161 Burundi	$140
101 Guyana	$800	122 Moldova	$460	143 Uganda	$310	162 Congo, Democratic Republic of	$110
102 Cuba	$790	123 Mauritania	$440	144 Nigeria	$300		
103 Albania	$760	124 India	$440	145 Sao Tome and Principe	$290	163 Ethiopia	$100
104 China	$750	125 Bhutan	$430				
105 Honduras	$740	126 Nicaragua	$410				

*Income is the country's per capita gross national product measured in U.S. dollars. Since some totals vary widely from year to year, they must be taken as approximate.

Sources: Famighetti 1999, *Statistical Abstract* 2000:Table 1364, Haub and Cornelius 2001.

The benefits of industrialization are uneven. Large numbers of people in the Industrializing Nations remain illiterate and desperately poor. Conditions can be gruesome, as discussed in the following Thinking Critically section.

Open Season: Children As Prey

What is childhood like in the Industrializing Nations? The answer depends on who your parents are. If you are the son or daughter of rich parents, childhood can be pleasant—a world filled with luxuries, and even servants. If you are born into poverty, but living in a rural area where there is plenty to eat, life can still be good—although there may be no books, television, and little education. If you live in a slum, however, life can be horrible—worse even than in the slums of the Most Industrialized Nations. Let's take a glance at what is happening to children in the slums of Brazil.

There is not enough food—this would be no surprise—as well as broken homes, alcoholism, drug abuse, and a high crime rate. From your knowledge of slums in the Most Industrialized Nations, you would expect these things. What you may not expect, however, are the brutal conditions in which Brazilian slum *(favela)* children live.

Sociologist Martha Huggins (1993; 2000) reports that poverty is so deep that children and adults swarm over garbage dumps to try to find enough decaying food to keep them alive. And you might be surprised to discover that in Brazil the owners of these dumps hire armed guards to keep the poor out—so they can sell the garbage for pig food. And you might be shocked to learn that the Brazilian police and death squads murder about 2,000 children a year. Some

■ *Poverty in the Least Industrialized Nations is so severe that some families survive by picking through garbage. This photo from Rio de Janeiro, Brazil, shows some of the 600 people whose survival depends on plucking from the city's dump any bit or piece that seems even remotely reusable.*

associations of shop owners even hire hit men and auction designated victims off to the lowest bidder! The going rate is half a month's salary—figured at the low Brazilian minimum wage.

Life is cheap in the poor nations—but death squads for children? To understand this, we must first note that Brazil has a long history of violence. Brazil also has a high rate of poverty, only a tiny middle class, and is controlled by a small group of families who, under a veneer of democracy, make the country's major decisions. Hordes of homeless children, with no schools or jobs, roam the streets. To survive, these street children wash windshields, shine shoes, beg, and steal. These children, part of the "dangerous classes," as they are known, threaten the status quo.

The "respectable" classes see these children as nothing but trouble. They hurt business, for customers feel intimidated when they see a group of begging children clustered in front of stores. Some shoplift; others dare to sell items that place them in competition with the stores. With no effective social institutions to care for these children, one solution is to kill them. As Huggins notes, murder sends a clear message—especially if it is accompanied by ritual torture—gouging out the eyes, ripping open the chest, cutting off the genitals, raping the girls, and burning the victim's body.

Not all life is bad in the Industrializing Nations, but this is about as bad as it gets.

■ ■ ■ ■ ■

for your consideration . . .

Do you think there is anything the Most Industrialized Nations can do about this situation? Or is it any of their business? Is it, though unfortunate, just an "internal" affair that is up to the Brazilians to handle as they wish?

The Least Industrialized Nations

In the Least Industrialized Nations, most people are peasant farmers living on farms or in villages. These nations account for 49 percent of the earth's land and 68 percent of the world's people.

It is difficult to imagine the poverty that plagues the Least Industrialized Nations. In Luanda, the capital of Angola, for example, skinny street children live in sewers (McNeil 1999). I have seen this same thing in Medellín, Colombia. Although wealthy nations have their pockets of poverty, *most* people in these nations live on less than $1,000 a year, in many cases considerably less. Most of them have no running water, indoor plumbing, central water supply, or access to trained physicians. Because modern medicine has cut infant mortality but not births, the population of most of these nations is growing quickly. This places even greater burdens on their limited facilities, causing them to fall farther behind each year. The twin specters of poverty and death at an early age stalk these countries.

Modifying the Model

This classification of countries into Most Industrialized, Industrializing, and Least Industrialized is helpful in that it pinpoints gross differences among them. But it also presents problems. As mentioned, just how much industrialization does a nation need in order to be classified as Most Industrialized or Industrializing? Also, in Chapter 6 we noted that several nations have become "postindustrial." Does this new stage require a separate classification? Finally, the oil-rich nations of the Middle East

An Alternative Model of Global Stratification

Four Worlds of Development

1. Most Industrialized Nations

2. Industrializing Nations

3. Least Industrialized Nations

4. Oil-rich, nonindustrialized nations

are not industrialized, but by providing the oil and gasoline that fuel the machinery of the Most Industrialized Nations, they have become immensely wealthy. Consequently, to classify them simply as Least Industrialized glosses over significant distinctions, such as their modern hospitals, extensive prenatal care, pure water systems, abundant food and shelter, high literacy, and even computerized banking (see the Social Map on pages 262–263).

Kuwait, on whose formal behalf the United States and other Most Industrialized Nations fought Iraq in the Gulf War, is an excellent example of the problem. Kuwait is so wealthy that almost none of its citizens works for a living. The government simply pays them a generous annual salary just for being citizens. Migrant workers from the poor nations do most of the onerous chores that daily life requires, while highly skilled workers from the Most Industrialized Nations run the specialized systems that keep Kuwait's economy going—and, as with the Gulf War, apparently fight its wars for it as well. Table 9.3 reflects this significant distinction.

How The World's Nations Became Stratified

How did the globe become stratified into such distinct worlds? The obvious answer is that the poorer nations have fewer resources than the richer nations. As with so many "obvious" answers, however, this one, too, falls short. Many of the Industrializing and Least Industrialized Nations are rich in natural resources, while one Most Industrialized Nation, Japan, has few. Four theories explain how global stratification came about.

◼ Colonialism

The first theory, **colonialism,** focuses on how the countries that industrialized first got the jump on the rest of the world. Beginning in Great Britain about 1750, industrialization spread throughout western Europe. Plowing some of their immense profits into powerful armaments and fast ships, these countries invaded weaker nations, making colonies out of them (Harrison 1993). After subduing them, the more powerful countries left behind a controlling force in order to exploit their labor and natural resources. At one point, there was even a free-for-all among the industrialized European countries as they rushed to divide up an entire continent. As Africa was sliced into pieces, even tiny Belgium got into the act and acquired the Congo, which was *seventy-five* times larger than itself.

Whereas the more powerful European countries would plant their national flags in a colony and send their representatives to run the government, the United States, after it industrialized, usually chose to plant corporate flags in a colony and let these corporations dominate the territory's government. Central and South America are prime examples of such U.S. *economic colonies.* No matter what the form, and whether it was benevolent or harsh, the purpose was the same—to exploit the nation's people and resources for the benefit of the "mother" country.

Colonialism, then, shaped many of the Least Industrialized Nations. In some instances, the Most Industrialized Nations were so powerful that to divide their spoils, they drew lines across a map, creating new states without regard for tribal or cultural considerations (Kifner 1999). Britain and France did just this in North Africa and

colonialism
the process by which one nation takes over another nation, usually for the purpose of exploiting its labor and natural resources

parts of the Middle East, which is why the national boundaries of Libya, Saudi Arabia, Kuwait, and other countries are so straight. This legacy of European conquests still erupts into tribal violence, because tribes with no history of national identity were arbitrarily incorporated into the same political boundaries.

■ World System Theory

To explain how global stratification came about, Immanuel Wallerstein (1974, 1979, 1984, 1990) developed **world system theory.** He analyzed how industrialization led to four groups of nations. Those that industrialized first (Britain, France, Holland, and later Germany) grew rich and powerful. He calls these the *core nations*. The nations around the Mediterranean grew dependent on trade with these core nations, and their economies stagnated. Wallerstein calls this group the *semiperiphery*. The economies of the eastern European countries, which sold cash crops to the core nations, developed even less. This third group is the *periphery*, or fringe nations. A fourth group of nations was left out of the development of capitalism altogether. This *external area* includes most of Africa and Asia. As capitalism expanded, the relationships among these groups of nations changed. Most notably, Asia is no longer left out of capitalism.

The **globalization of capitalism**—the adoption of capitalism around the world— has created extensive ties among the world's countries. Production and trade now so interconnect the world's countries that events around the globe affect us all. Sometimes this is immediate, as happens when a revolution interrupts the flow of raw materials, or if terrorists managed to get their hands on nuclear weapons. At other times the effects are like a slow ripple, as when a government's policies impede its ability to compete in world markets. All of today's societies, then, no matter where they are located, are part of a *world system*.

This interconnection is more evident in some instances, especially in the case of Mexico and the United States. The following Thinking Critically section explores implications of Mexico's *maquiladoras*.

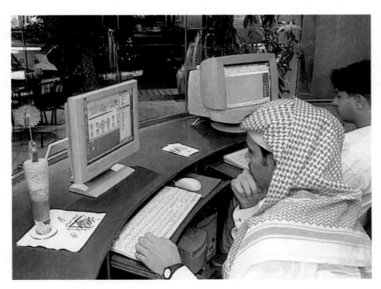

■ *The world's people always have been part of an interconnected system of water and air, and, ultimately, part of a food chain. Now they also are interconnected by a global system of telecommunications. This photo was taken in Riyadh, the capital of Saudi Arabia, at an Internet cafe called The Rendezvous.*

world system theory
economic and political connections that tie the world's countries together

globalization
the extensive movement of capital and ideas among nations due to the expansion of capitalism

thinking
CRITICALLY

When Globalization Comes Home:
Maquiladoras South of the Border

When Humberto drives his truck among Ciudad Juarez's shanties—patched together from packing crates, discarded tires, and cardboard—women and children flock around him. Humberto is the water man, and his truckload of water means life.

Two hundred thousand Mexicans are rushing to Juarez each year, fleeing the hopelessness of the rural areas in pursuit of a better life. They didn't have running water or plumbing in the country anyway, and here they have the possibility of a job, a weekly check that will buy food for the kids.

The pay is $10 a day.

This may not sound like much, but it is more than twice the minimum daily wage in Mexico.

In the 1960s, Mexico and the United States began an industrialization program along the border to help reduce Mexico's unemployment. Then in the 1990s came NAFTA, the North American Free Trade Agreement that allows companies to import materials to Mexico without paying tax, and to then export the finished products into the United States, again without tax. Assembly-for-export plants, known as *maquiladoras,* sprang up along the Mexican border. You can see why. Few taxes and $10 a day for workers starved for jobs—less than U.S. workers make in an hour.

It was a win-win deal for the multinational corporations, and GE, GM, IBM, Sony, Samsung, and thousands of other companies rushed in.

Some get an even sweeter deal. They pay their workers the minimum wage of $4—for 10-hour days with a 30 minute break (Darweesh 2000).

That these workers have to live in shacks, with no running water or sewage, is not their concern.

Then there is the pollution. Juarez pumps 75 million gallons of untreated sewage into the Rio Grande—every day. Other *maquiladora* towns along the border do the same.

There is also the loss of jobs for U.S. workers. Along the sewage-infested Rio Grande sit 6 of the 15 poorest cities in the United States. NAFTA didn't bring poverty to these cities. They were poor before, but residents resent the jobs they've seen move across the border (Thompson 2001).

■ *A photo taken inside a maquiladora in Tijuana, Mexico. Car parts shipped from the United States are assembled here, and then shipped back to the United States.*

■ *This is where the workers live.*

The work conditions are also hazardous to health. To keep up with fast-paced machines, some workers stand in awkward positions for hours. The safety guards on the machines that assemble auto parts are removed to speed up production (Brown 2000). Some workers are exposed to hazardous chemicals—and the safety instructions are written in English (Abeil 1999).

What if workers organize and demand better pay and conditions? The main obstacle is that cheaper labor beckons, and the multinationals can move their *maquiladoras*. Guatemala and Honduras will gladly take them. So will China, where workers make $1 a day (Skiba 2001). Many *maquiladoras* are already moving farther south in Mexico, where the workers are even more desperate and will work for less (Chen 2001).

Workers do have unions. It's just that the companies ignore them. And the Mexican government supports the companies. At a conference between U.S. and Mexican representatives on the topic of freedom of association, workers unfurled a banner calling for recognition of their union. The goon squads beat the demonstrators and drove them from the meeting hall (Brown 2000).

This is what "freedom of association" means in Mexico.

Many Mexicans would say that this presentation is one-sided. "Sure there are problems," they say, "but that is always how it is when a country industrializes. Don't you realize that the *maquiladoras* bring jobs to people who have no work? They also bring roads, telephone lines, and electricity to undeveloped areas." "In fact," says Vicente Fox, the president of Mexico, "workers at the *maquiladoras* make more than the average salary in Mexico—and that's what we call fair wages" (Fraser 2001).

■ ■ ■ ■ ■

for your consideration . . .

Let's apply our three theoretical perspectives to see where reality lies. Conflict theorists say that capitalists weaken the bargaining power of workers by exploiting divisions among them. In what is known as the *split labor market,* to lower the cost of labor, capitalists pit one group of workers against another. What examples of this do you see here?

When functionalists analyze a situation, they identity its functions and dysfunctions. What functions and dysfunctions of *maquiladoras* do you see?

Do *maquiladoras* represent exploitation or opportunity? As symbolic interactionists point out, reality is a perspective based on one's experience. What multiple realities do you see here?

■ Culture of Poverty

An entirely different explanation of global stratification was proposed by economist John Kenneth Galbraith (1979). Galbraith claimed that the cultures of the Least Industrialized Nations held them back. Building on the ideas of anthropologist Oscar Lewis (1966a, 1966b), Galbraith argued that some nations are crippled by a **culture of poverty,** a way of life that perpetuates poverty from one generation to the next. He explained it this way: Most of the world's poor live in rural areas, where they barely eke out a living from the land. Their marginal life offers little room for error or risk, so they tend to stick closely to tried-and-true, traditional ways. To experiment with new farming techniques could be a disaster, for if these techniques fail, this leads to hunger and death. Their religion also encourages them to accept their situation, for it teaches fatalism, that their lot in life is God's will.

■ Evaluating the Theories

Most sociologists prefer colonialism and world system theory. To them, an explanation based on a culture of poverty places blame on the victim—the poor nations themselves. It points to characteristics of the poor nations, rather than to international arrangements that benefit the Most Industrialized Nations at the expense of the poor nations. But even taken together, these theories yield only part of the picture. None of these theories, for example, would have led anyone to expect that after World War II, Japan—which had a religion that stressed fatalism, which had two major cities destroyed by atomic bombs, and which had been stripped of its colonies—would become an economic powerhouse able to turn the Western world on its head.

Each theory, then, yields but a partial explanation, and the grand theorist who will put the many pieces of this puzzle together has yet to appear.

Maintaining Global Stratification

Regardless of how the world's nations became stratified, why do the same countries remain rich year after year, while the rest stay poor? Let's look at two explanations of how global stratification is maintained.

■ Neocolonialism

Sociologist Michael Harrington (1977) argued that colonialism fell out of style and was replaced by **neocolonialism.** When World War II changed public sentiment about sending soldiers and colonists to weaker countries, the Most Industrialized Nations turned to the international markets as a way to control the Least Industrialized Nations. These powerful nations determine how much they will pay for tin from Bolivia, copper from Peru, coffee from Brazil, and so forth. They also move hazardous industries into the Least Industrialized Nations.

As many of us to our sorrow learn, owing a large debt and falling behind on payments puts us at the mercy of our creditors. So it is with neocolonialism. The *policy* of selling weapons and other manufactured goods to the Least Industrialized Nations on credit turns those countries into eternal debtors. The capital they need to develop their own industries goes instead to the debt, which becomes bloated with mounting interest. Keeping these nations in debt makes them submit to trading terms dictated by the neocolonialists (Carrington 1993; S. Smith 2001).

Thus, although the Least Industrialized Nations have their own governments—whether elected or dictatorships—they remain almost as dependent on the Most Industrialized Nations as they were when those nations occupied them.

culture of poverty
a culture that perpetuates poverty from one generation to the next

neocolonialism
the economic and political dominance of the Least Industrialized Nations by the Most Industrialized Nations

Multinational Corporations

Multinational corporations, companies that operate across many national boundaries, also help to maintain the global dominance of the Most Industrialized Nations. In some cases, multinational corporations exploit the Least Industrialized Nations directly. A prime example is the United Fruit Company. For decades, the company controlled national and local politics in Central America. It ran these nations as fiefdoms for the company's own profit while the U.S. Marines waited in the wings in case the company's interests needed to be backed up.

Most commonly, however, multinational corporations help to maintain international stratification simply by doing business. A single multinational may do mining in several countries, do manufacturing in many others, and run transportation and marketing networks around the globe. No matter where the profits are made, or where they are reinvested, the primary beneficiaries are the Most Industrialized Nations, especially the one in which the multinational corporation has its world headquarters. As Michael Harrington (1977) stressed, the real profits are made in processing the products and in controlling their distribution—and these profits are withheld from the Least Industrialized Nations. For more on multinational corporations, see pages 423–428.

Multinational corporations try to work closely with the elite of the Least Industrialized Nations (Waldman 1995; Squeo and Pearl 2000). This elite, which lives a sophisticated upper-class life in the major cities of its home country, sends its children to prestigious universities, such as Oxford, the Sorbonne, and Harvard. The multinational corporations funnel investments to this small circle of power, whose members favor projects such as building laboratories and computer centers in the capital city, projects that do not help the vast majority of their people, who live in poor, remote villages where they eke out meager livings on small plots of land.

The end result is an informal partnership between multinational corporations and the elite of the Least Industrialized Nations. To gain access to the country's raw materials, labor, and market, the corporations pay off the elite. (These are politely called "subsidies," not bribes.) The elite use their payoffs not only to buy their genteel lifestyle, but also to purchase advanced weapons from multinational corporations, which they use to oppress their people and maintain their dominance. Both elites and corporations benefit from political stability, which is necessary for keeping their diabolical partnership alive.

This, however, is not the full story. Multinational corporations also play a role in changing international stratification. This is an unintentional by-product of their worldwide search for cheap resources and labor. By moving manufacturing from the Most Industrialized Nations to the Least Industrialized Nations, they not only exploit cheap labor but also bring jobs and money to these nations. Although workers in the Least Industrialized Nations are paid a pittance, it is more than they can earn elsewhere. With new factories come opportunities to develop skills and a capital base. This does not occur in all nations, but the Pacific Rim nations, nicknamed the "Asian tigers," are a remarkable case in point. They have developed such a strong capital base that they have begun to rival the older capitalist nations. As has become painfully apparent, these countries also are subject to capitalism's infamous "boom and bust" cycles. Many workers in the *maquiladoras* that you just read about will have their dreams smashed as capitalism moves into its next downturn.

Technology and Global Domination

The race between the Most and Least Industrialized Nations to develop and apply the new technologies is like a race between a marathon runner and a one-legged man. Can the outcome be in doubt? The vast profits piled up by the multinational corporations allow the Most Industrialized Nations to invest huge sums in the latest technology. Gillette, for example, spent $100 million simply so

multinational corporations companies that operate across many national boundaries; also called transnational corporations it could adjust its production "on an hourly basis" (Zachary 1995). These millions came from just one U.S. company. Many Least Industrialized Nations would love to have $100 million to invest in their entire economy, much less to use for fine-tuning the production of razor blades. In short, in the quest to maintain global domination, the new technologies pile up even more advantages for the Most Industrialized Nations.

■ ■ ■ ■ ■

A Concluding Note

Let's return to the three families in our opening vignette. Remember that these families represent distinct worlds of money and power, that is, global stratification. Their life chances—from access to material possessions to the opportunity for education and even the likely age at which they will die—are profoundly affected by the global stratification we've looked at. This division of the globe into interconnected units of nations with more or less wealth and more or less power and prestige, then, is much more than a matter of theoretical interest. In fact, it is *your* life we are talking about.

■ ■ ■ ■ ■

Summary and Review

Systems of Social Stratification

▪ What is social stratification?

Social stratification refers to a hierarchy of relative privilege based on power, property, and prestige. Every society stratifies its members, and in every society men as a group are placed above women as a group. P. 245.

▪ What are four major systems of social stratification?

Four major stratification systems are slavery, caste, estate, and class. The essential characteristic of **slavery** is that some people own other people. Initially, slavery was based not on race but on debt, punishment, or defeat in battle. Slavery could be temporary or permanent, and was not necessarily passed on to one's children. North American slaves had no legal rights, and the system was gradually buttressed by a racist **ideology.** In a **caste system,** status is determined by birth and is lifelong. The **estate system** of feudal Europe consisted of the nobility, clergy, and commoners. A **class system** is much more open than these other systems, for it is based primarily on money or material possessions. Industrialization encourages the formation of class systems. Gender cuts across all forms of social stratification. Pp. 245–252.

What Determines Social Class?

Karl Marx argued that a single factor determines social class: If you own the means of production, you belong to the **bourgeoisie;** if you do not, you are one of the **proletariat.** Max Weber argued that three elements determine social class: *property, prestige,* and *power.* Pp. 251–254.

Why Is Social Stratification Universal?

To explain why stratification is universal, functionalists Kingsley Davis and Wilbert Moore argued that in order to attract the most capable people to fill its important positions, society must offer them greater rewards. Melvin Tumin said that if this view were correct, society would be a **meritocracy,** with all positions awarded on the basis of merit. Gaetano Mosca argued that stratification is inevitable because every society must have leadership, which by definition means inequality. Conflict theorists argue that stratification comes about because resources are limited, and an elite emerges as groups struggle against one another for them. Gerhard Lenski suggested a synthesis between the functionalist and conflict perspectives. Pp. 254–256.

How Do Elites Maintain Stratification?

To maintain social stratification within a nation, the ruling class uses an ideology that justifies current arrangements. It also controls information and uses technology, and, when all else fails, depends on brute force. Pp. 257–258.

Comparative Social Stratification

■ **What are key characteristics of stratification systems in other nations?**
The most striking features of the British class system are speech and education. In Britain, accent reveals social class, and almost all of the elite attend "public" schools (the equivalent of our private schools). In what is now the former Soviet Union, communism was supposed to abolish class distinctions. Instead, it merely ushered in a different set of classes. Pp. 258–260.

Global Stratification: Three Worlds

■ **How are the world's nations stratified?**
The model presented here divides the world's nations into three groups: the Most Industrialized, the Industrializing, and the Least Industrialized. This layering represents relative property, power, and prestige. The oil-rich nations are an exception. Pp. 260–266.

How the World's Nations Became Stratified

■ **Why are some nations rich and others poor?**
The main theories that seek to account for global stratification are **colonialism, world system theory,** and the **culture of poverty.** Pp. 266–270.

Maintaining Global Stratification

■ **How do elites maintain global stratification?**
There are two basic explanations for why the world's countries remain stratified. **Neocolonialism** is the ongoing dominance of the Least Industrialized Nations by the Most Industrialized Nations. The second explanation points to the influence of **multinational corporations.** The new technology gives further advantage to the Most Industrialized Nations. Pp. 270–272.

■ *Where can I read more on this topic?*
Suggested readings for this chapter are at the end of this book.

Additional Online Resources for This Chapter
www.ablongman.com/henslin6e

- *Content Select* Research Database for Sociology, with suggested key terms and annotated references
- Link to 2000 Census, with activities
- Flashcards of key terms and concepts

- Practice Tests
- Weblinks
- Interactive Maps

using . . .
ContentSelect

Research Database for Sociology

apartheid	Marxism	slavery	stratification
colonialism	meritocracy	social stratification	the ruling class
globalization	multinational corporations		

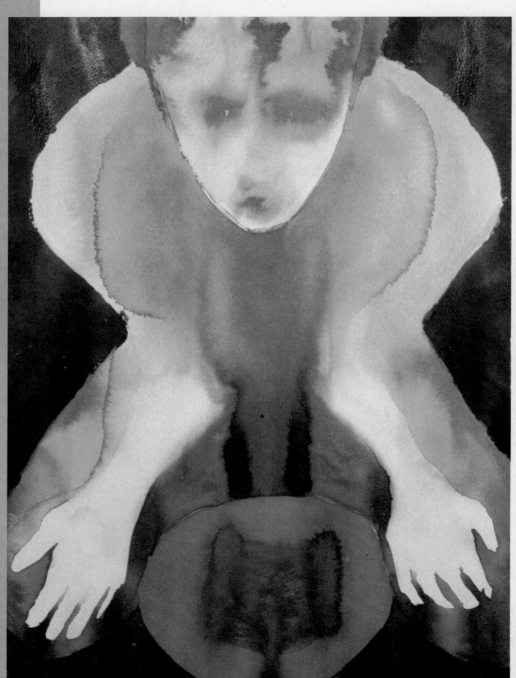

Graham Dean, *Beg*, 1991

Social Class in the United States

What Is Social Class?

Wealth

Power

Prestige

Status Inconsistency

Sociological Models of Social Class

Updating Marx

Updating Weber

Social Class in the Automobile Industry

Consequences of Social Class

Physical Health

Mental Health

Family Life

Education

Religion

Politics

Crime and the Criminal Justice System

Social Class and the New Technology

Social Mobility

Three Types of Social Mobility

Women in Studies on Social Mobility

The Pain of Social Mobility

Poverty

Drawing the Poverty Line

Who Are the Poor?

Children of Poverty

The Dynamics of Poverty

Why Are People Poor?

Welfare Reform

Deferred Gratification

Where Is Horatio Alger? The Social Functions of a Myth

Summary and Review

h, New Orleans, that fabled city on the Gulf. Images from its rich past floated through my head—pirates, wealth, intrigue. Memories from a pleasant vacation stirred my thoughts—the exotic French Quarter with its enticing aroma of Creole food and sounds of earthy jazz drifting through the air.

The shelter for the homeless, however, forced me back to an unwelcome reality. The shelter was the same as those I had visited in the North, West, and East—only dirtier. The dirt, in fact, was the worst that I had encountered during my research, and this shelter was the only one to insist on payment in exchange for sleeping in one of its filthy beds.

> *I was startled by a sight so out of step with the misery and despair I had just experienced that I stopped in midtrack.*

The men looked the same—disheveled and haggard, wearing that unmistakable expression of despair—just like the homeless anywhere in the country. Except for the accent, you wouldn't know what region of the country you were in. Poverty wears the same tired face, I realized. The accent may differ, but the look remains the same.

The next morning, I felt indignation swell within me. I had grown used to the sights and smells of abject poverty. Those no longer surprised me. But now, just a block or so from the shelter, I was startled by a sight so out of step with the misery and despair I had just experienced that I stopped in midtrack.

I was confronted by life-size, full-color photos that were mounted on the transparent plastic shelter covering a bus stop. Staring back at me were finely dressed men and women proudly strutting about as they modeled elegant suits, dresses, diamonds, and furs.

A wave of disgust swept over me. "Something is cockeyed in this society," I thought, my mind refusing to stop juxtaposing these images with the suffering I had just witnessed.

*O*ccasionally the reality of social class hits home with brute force. This was one of those moments. The disjunction that I felt in New Orleans was triggered by the ads, but it was not the first time that I had experienced this sensation. Whenever my research abruptly transported me from the world of the homeless to one of another social class, I felt unfamiliar feelings of disjointed unreality. Each social class has its own way of being, and because these fundamental orientations to the world contrast so sharply, the classes do not mix well.

What Is Social Class?

"There are the poor and the rich—and then there are you and I, neither poor nor rich." This is just about as far as most Americans' consciousness of social class goes. Let's try to flesh out this idea.

Our task is made somewhat difficult because sociologists have no clear-cut, agreed-on definition of social class. As noted in the last chapter, conflict sociologists (of the Marxist orientation) see only two social classes: those who own the means of production and those who do not. The problem with this view, say most sociologists, is that it lumps too many people together. Physicians and corporate executives with incomes of $400,000 a year are lumped together with hamburger flippers who work at McDonald's for $13,000 a year.

Most sociologists agree with Weber that there is more to social class than just a person's relationship to the means of production. Consequently, most sociologists use the components Weber identified and define **social class** as a large group of people who rank close to one another in wealth, power, and prestige. These three elements separate people into different lifestyles, give them different chances in life, and provide them with distinct ways of looking at the self and the world.

Let's look at how sociologists measure these three components of social class.

Wealth

The primary dimension of social class is wealth. **Wealth** consists of property and income. *Property* comes in many forms, such as buildings, land, animals, machinery, cars, stocks, bonds, businesses, and bank accounts. *Income* is money received as wages, rents, interest, royalties, or the proceeds from a business.

social class
according to Weber, a large group of people who rank close to one another in wealth, power, and prestige; according to Marx, one of two groups: capitalists who own the means of production or workers who sell their labor

wealth
property and income

■ *In the United States, a mere 0.5 percent of the population owns over a quarter of the nation's wealth. Very few minorities are numbered among this 0.5 percent. An outstanding exception is Oprah Winfrey, whose ultra-successful career in entertainment, bringing her over $250 million a year, has made her one of the 400 richest Americans. Winfrey is shown here as she launched the premiere issue of* O, The Oprah Magazine, *at a press breakfast in New York City. Oprah has given millions of dollars to benefit minority children.*

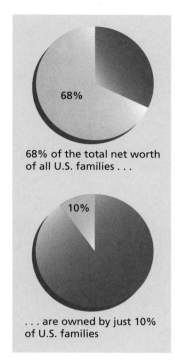

68% of the total net worth of all U.S. families . . .

. . . are owned by just 10% of U.S. families

Source: Beeghley 2000.

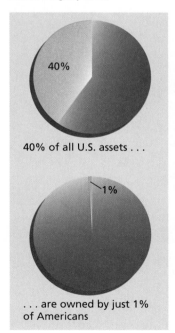

40% of all U.S. assets . . .

. . . are owned by just 1% of Americans

Source: Western 2000.

Figure 10.1

Distribution of Wealth of Americans

Distinction Between Wealth and Income   Wealth and income are sometimes confused, but they are not the same. Some people have much wealth and little income. For example, a farmer may own much land (a form of wealth), but a little bad weather, combined with the high cost of fertilizers and machinery, can cause the income to disappear. Others have much income and little wealth. For example, an executive with a $200,000 annual income may be debt ridden. Below the surface prosperity—exotic vacations, country club membership, private schools for the children, fancy sports cars, and an elegant home in an exclusive suburb—he or she may be overextended, the fancy cars in danger of being repossessed, and the mortgage payments "past due." Typically, however, wealth and income go together.

Who owns the wealth in the United States? One answer, of course, is "everyone." Although this statement has some merit, it overlooks how the nation's wealth is divided among "everyone." Let's look at how the two forms of wealth—property and income—are distributed among Americans.

Distribution of Wealth   Overall, Americans are worth a hefty sum, about $26 trillion (*Statistical Abstract* 2000:Table 766). This counts all real estate, stocks, bonds, and business assets in the entire country. Figure 10.1 shows how highly concentrated this wealth is. Most, 68 percent, is owned by only *10 percent* of the nation's

Some U.S. incomes are higher than Mt. Everest

29,028 feet

If a 1½-inch child's block equals $500 of income, the average American is only 7 feet off the ground, the average family just 12 feet, while the income of some families propels them past the top of Mount Everest.

7 feet

12 feet

Average American

Average U.S. Family

Figure 10.2

Inequality of U.S. Income

families. And the higher up the income ladder we go, the more concentrated this wealth becomes. As sociologist Leonard Beeghley (2000) observes, *the super-rich, the richest 1 percent of U.S. families, are worth more than the entire bottom 90 percent of Americans.* As you can see from Figure 10.1, this 1 percent owns 40 percent of all the wealth in the United States.

Distribution of Income How is income distributed in the United States? Economist Paul Samuelson (Samuelson and Nordhaus 2000) put it this way: "If we made an income pyramid out of a child's blocks, with each layer portraying $500 of income, the peak would be far higher than Mount Everest, but most people would be within a few feet of the ground."

Actually, if each block were 1½ inches tall, the typical American would be just 7 *feet off the ground,* for the average per capita income in the United States is about $29,000 per year. (This average income includes every American, even children.) The typical family climbs a little higher, for most families have more than one worker, and together they average about $47,000 a year. Yet compared with the few families who are on the mountain's peak, the average U.S. family would find itself only 12 feet off the ground (*Statistical Abstract* 2000:Tables 727, 746). Figure 10.2 portrays these differences.

The fact that some Americans enjoy the peaks of Mount Everest while most—despite their efforts—make it only 7 to 12 feet up the slope presents a striking image of income inequality in the United States. Another picture emerges if we divide the U.S. population into five equal groups and rank them from highest to lowest income. As Figure 10.3 shows, the top 20 percent of the population receives *almost half* (47.2 percent) of all income in the United States. In contrast, the bottom 20 percent of Americans receives only 4.3 percent of the nation's income.

Two features of Figure 10.3 are outstanding. First, notice how consistent income inequality remains through the years. Second, the changes that do occur indicate *growing inequality. The richest 20 percent of U.S. families have grown richer, while the poorest 20 percent have grown poorer.* Despite numerous antipoverty programs, the poorest 20 percent of Americans receive *less* of the nation's income today than they did in the

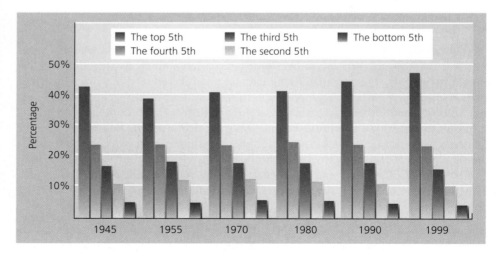

Figure 10.3

Growing Inequality: The Percentage of the Nation's Income Received by Each Fifth of U.S. Families Since World War II
Note: The distribution of U.S. income—salaries, wages, and all other money received, except capital gains and government subsidies in the form of food stamps, health benefits, or subsidized housing.
Source: Statistical Abstract 1947; 2001:Table 670.

T A B L E 10.1	Highest-Paid CEOs	
Executive	**Company**	**Annual Compensation**
Sanford I. Weill	Citigroup	$224 million
John T. Chambers	Cisco Systems	$157 million
Kenneth L. Lay	Enron	$140 million
L. Dennis Kozlowski	Tyco	$125 million
John F. Welch, Jr.	GE	$123 million
Joseph P. Nacchio	Qwest	$97 million
W. J. Sanders	Advanced Micro Devices	$92 million

Source: "Executive Pay," 2001.

1940s (a drop from 5.4 percent to 4.3 percent). The richest 20 percent, in contrast, receive *more* than ever (an increase from about 41 percent to just over 47 percent).

The most affluent group in the United States is the chief executive officers (CEOs) of the nation's largest corporations. The *Wall Street Journal* surveyed the 350 largest U.S. companies to find out what they paid their CEOs ("The Boss's Pay," 2001). Their median compensation (including salaries, bonuses, and stock options) came to $2,902,000 a year. (Median means that half received more than this amount, and half less.) The CEOs' income—which does *not* include their interest, dividends, rents, and capital gains—is *90 times* higher than the average pay of U.S. workers (*Statistical Abstract* 2000:Table 694). Table 10.1 above lists the seven highest paid executives. (The bankruptcy of Enron in 2002, with the spectacle of Kenneth Lay pleading the fifth before Congress, demonstrates that the economic foundation of this income is not always secure.)

Imagine how you could live with an income like this. And this is precisely the point. Beyond cold numbers lies a dynamic reality that profoundly affects people's lives. The difference in wealth between those at the top and those at the bottom of the U.S. class structure means vastly different lifestyles. For example, a colleague of mine who was teaching at an exclusive eastern university piqued his students' curiosity when he lectured on poverty in Latin America. That weekend, one of his students borrowed his parents' corporate jet and pilot, and in class the next Monday he and his friends related their personal observations on poverty in Latin America. Americans who are at the low end of the income ladder, in contrast, lack the funds to travel even to a neighboring town for the weekend: Their choices revolve around whether to spend the little they have at the laundromat or on milk for the baby. In short, divisions of wealth represent not "mere" numbers, but choices that make vital differences in people's lives, a topic explored in the Down-to-Earth Sociology box on the next page.

■ *Bill Gates, a cofounder of Microsoft Corporation, is the wealthiest person in the world. His fortune of $90 billion continues to increase as his company develops new products. His 40,000-square-foot home (sometimes called a "technopalace") in Seattle, Washington, is appraised at $110 million. In addition to being the wealthiest person in history, Gates has also given more money to the poor and minorities than any individual in history.*

How the Super-Rich Live

It's good to see how other people live. It helps give us a different perspective for viewing life. Let's take a glimpse at the life of John Castle (his real name). After earning a degree in physics at MIT and an MBA at Harvard, John went into banking and securities, where he made more than $100 million (Lublin 1999).

Wanting to be close to someone famous, John bought President John F. Kennedy's "Winter White House," an oceanfront estate in Palm Beach, Florida. John spent $11 million to remodel the 13,000-square-foot house so it would be more to his liking. Among those changes: adding bathrooms numbers 14 and 15. He likes to show off John F. Kennedy's bed and also the dresser that has the drawer labeled "black underwear," carefully hand-lettered by Rose Kennedy.

If John gets bored at his beachfront estate—or tired of swimming in the Olympic-size pool where JFK swam the weekend before his assassination—he entertains himself by riding one of his thoroughbred horses at his nearby 10-acre ranch. If this fails to ease his boredom, he can relax aboard his custom-built 45-foot Hinckley yacht.

The yacht is a real source of diversion. He once boarded it for an around-

■ *How do the super-rich live? It is difficult to even imagine their lifestyles, but this entrance to a home on Palm Island, off Miami, Florida, can give you some idea of what they are like.*

the-world trip. He didn't stay on board, though—just joined the cruise from time to time. A captain and crew kept the vessel sailing in the right direction, and whenever John felt like it he would fly in and stay a few days. Then he would fly back to the States to direct his business. He did this about a dozen times, flying perhaps 150,000 miles. An interesting way to go around the world.

How much does a custom-built Hinckley yacht cost? John can't tell you. As he says, "I don't want to know what anything costs. When you've got enough money, price doesn't make a difference. That's part of the freedom of being rich."

Right. And for John, being rich also means paying $1,000,000 to charter a private jet to fly Spot, his Appaloosa horse, back and forth to the vet. John didn't want Spot to have to endure a long trailer ride. Oh, and of course, there was the cost of Spot's medical treatment, another $500,000.

Other wealthy people put John to shame. Wayne Huizenga, the CEO of AutoNation, bought a 2,000-acre country club, complete with an 18-hole golf course, a 55,000-square foot clubhouse, and 68 slips for visiting vessels. The club is so exclusive that its only members are Wayne and his wife.

■ ■ ■ ■ ■

Power

Like many people, you may have said to yourself, "Sure, I can vote, but somehow the big decisions are always made despite what I might think. Certainly *I* don't make the decision to send soldiers to Kuwait or Afghanistan. *I* don't launch missiles against Kosovo or Baghdad. *I* don't decide to raise taxes or lower interest rates. It isn't *I* who decides to change welfare benefits."

And then another part of you may say, "But I do participate in these decisions through my representatives in Congress, and by voting for president." True enough—as far as it goes. The trouble is, it just doesn't go far enough. Such views of being a participant in the nation's "big" decisions are a playback of the ideology we learn at an early age—an ideology that Marx said is put forward by the elites to both legitimate and perpetuate their power. Sociologists Daniel Hellinger and Dennis Judd (1991) call this the "democratic facade" that conceals the real source of power in the United States.

Back in the 1950s, sociologist C. Wright Mills (1956) was criticized for insisting that **power**—the ability to carry out your will despite resistance—was concentrated in the hands of a few, for his analysis contradicted the dominant ideology of equality. As discussed in earlier chapters, Mills coined the term **power elite** to refer to those who make the big decisions in U.S. society.

Mills and others have stressed how wealth and power coalesce in a group of like-minded individuals who share ideologies and values. They belong to the same private clubs, vacation at the same exclusive resorts, and even hire the same bands for their daughters' debutante balls. These shared backgrounds and vested interests reinforce their view of the world and of their special place in it (Domhoff 1998, 1999). This elite wields extraordinary power in U.S. society. Although there are exceptions, *most* U.S. presidents have come from this group—millionaire white men from families with "old money" (Baltzell and Schneiderman 1988).

Continuing in the tradition of Mills, sociologist William Domhoff (1990, 1998) argues that this group is so powerful that no major decision of the U.S. government is made without its approval. He analyzed how this group works behind the scenes with elected officials to determine both the nation's foreign and domestic policy—from setting Social Security taxes to imposing trade tariffs. Although Domhoff's conclusions are controversial—and alarming—they certainly follow logically from the principle that wealth brings power, and extreme wealth brings extreme power.

■ Prestige

Occupations and Prestige   What are you thinking about doing after college? Chances are you don't have the option of lolling under palm trees at the beach. Almost all of us have to choose an occupation and go to work. Look at Table 10.2 on the next page to see how the one you are considering stacks up in terms of **prestige** (respect or regard). Because we are moving toward a global society, this table also shows how the rankings given by Americans compare with those of the residents of sixty other countries.

Why do people give more prestige to some jobs than to others? If you look at Table 10.2, you will notice that the jobs at the top share four features:

1. They pay more.

2. They require more education.

3. They entail more abstract thought.

4. They offer greater autonomy (freedom, or self-direction).

If we turn this around, we can see that people give less prestige to jobs that are low-paying, require less preparation or education, involve more physical labor, and are closely supervised. In short, the professions and white-collar jobs are ranked at the top of the list, blue-collar jobs at the bottom.

One of the more interesting aspects of these rankings is how consistent they are across countries and over time. For example, people in every country rank college professors higher than nurses, nurses higher than social workers, and social workers higher than janitors. Similarly, the occupations that were ranked high back in the 1970s still rank high today—and likely will rank high in the years to come.

power
the ability to get your way despite the desires of other people

power elite
C. Wright Mills' term for the top people in U.S. corporations, military, and politics who make the nation's major decisions

prestige
respect or regard

TABLE 10.2 Occupational Prestige: How the United States Compares with 60 Countries

Occupation	United States	Average of 60 Countries	Occupation	United States	Average of 60 Countries
Supreme court judge	85	82	Professional athlete	51	48
College president	82	86	Undertaker	51	34
Physician	82	78	Social worker	50	56
Astronaut	80	80	Electrician	49	44
College professor	78	78	Secretary	46	53
Lawyer	75	73	Real estate agent	44	49
Dentist	74	70	Farmer	44	47
Architect	71	72	Carpenter	43	37
Psychologist	71	66	Plumber	41	34
Airline pilot	70	66	Mail carrier	40	33
Electrical engineer	69	65	Jazz musician	37	38
Civil engineer	68	70	Bricklayer	36	34
Biologist	68	69	Barber	36	30
Clergy	67	60	Truck driver	31	33
Sociologist	65	67	Factory worker	29	29
Accountant	65	55	Store sales clerk	27	34
Banker	63	67	Bartender	25	23
High school teacher	63	64	Lives on public aid	25	16
Author	63	62	Bill collector	24	27
Registered nurse	62	54	Cab driver	22	28
Pharmacist	61	64	Gas station attendant	22	25
Chiropractor	60	62	Janitor	22	21
Veterinarian	60	61	Waiter or waitress	20	23
Classical musician	59	56	Bellhop	15	14
Police officer	59	40	Garbage collector	13	13
Actor or actress	55	52	Street sweeper	11	13
Athletic coach	53	50	Shoe shiner	9	12
Journalist	52	55			

Sources: Treiman 1977, Appendices A and D; Nakao and Treas 1991.

Displaying Prestige To get a sense of payoff, people want others to acknowledge their prestige. In times past, in some countries only the emperor and his family could wear purple—for it was the royal color. In France, only the nobility could wear lace. In England, no one could sit while the king was on his throne. Some kings and queens required that subjects walk backward as they left the room—so no one would "turn their back" on the "royal presence."

Concern with displaying prestige has not let up. For some, it is almost an obsession. Military manuals specify precisely who must salute whom. The U.S. president enters a room only after others are present (to show that *he* isn't the one waiting for *them*). They must also be standing when he enters. In the courtroom, bailiffs, sometimes armed, make certain that everyone stands when the judge enters.

The display of prestige permeates society. In Los Angeles, some people list their address as Beverly Hills and then add their correct ZIP code. When East Detroit changed its name to East Pointe to play off its proximity to swank Grosse Pointe, property values shot up (Fletcher 1997). Many pay more for clothing that bears a "designer" label. Prestige is often a primary factor in deciding which college to attend. Everyone knows how the prestige of a generic sheepskin from Regional State College compares with a degree from Harvard, Princeton, Yale, or Stanford.

Interestingly, status symbols vary with social class. Clearly, only the wealthy can afford certain items, such as yachts. But beyond affordability lies a class-based preference in status symbols. For example, Yuppies (young upwardly mobile professionals) are quick to flaunt labels, BMW's ("beemers"), and other material symbols to show that they have "arrived," while the rich, more secure in their status, often downplay such images. The wealthy see designer labels of the "common" classes as cheap and showy. They, of course, flaunt their own status symbols, such as $30,000 Rolex watches.

■ *Acceptable display of prestige and high social position varies over time and from one culture to another. Shown here is Elisabeth d'Autriche, queen of France from 1554 to 1592. It certainly would be difficult to outdress her at a party.*

■ Status Inconsistency

Ordinarily a person has a similar rank on all three dimensions of social class—wealth, power, and prestige. The homeless men in the opening vignette are an example. Such people are **status consistent.** Sometimes that match is not there, however, and someone has a mixture of high and low ranks, a condition called **status inconsistency.** This leads to some interesting situations.

Sociologist Gerhard Lenski (1954, 1966) pointed out that each of us tries to maximize our **status,** our social ranking. Thus individuals who rank high on one dimension of social class but lower on others expect people to judge them on the basis of their highest status. Others, however, trying to maximize their own position, may respond to them according to their lowest status.

A classic study of status inconsistency was done by sociologist Ray Gold (1952). He found that after apartment-house janitors unionized, they made more money than some of the tenants whose garbage they carried out. Tenants became upset when they saw their janitors driving more expensive cars than they did. Some attempted to "put the janitor in his place" by making "snotty" remarks to him. For their part, the janitors took secret pride in knowing "dirty" secrets about the tenants, gleaned from their garbage.

Individuals with status inconsistency, then, are likely to confront one frustrating situation after another. They claim the higher status, but are handed the lower. The sociological significance of this condition is that such people tend to be more politically radical (Lenski 1954, Mateju and Kreidl 2001). An example is college professors. Their prestige is very high, as we saw in Table 10.2, but their incomes are relatively low. Hardly anyone in U.S. society is more educated, and yet college

status consistency
ranking high or low on all three dimensions of social class

status inconsistency
(or **status discrepancy**)
ranking high on some dimensions of social class and low on others

status
social ranking

■ *Status discrepancy is common for lottery winners, whose new wealth is vastly greater than their education and occupational status. Shown here are John and Sandy Jarrell of Chicago, after they learned that they were one of 13 families to share a $295 million jackpot. How do you think their $22 million will affect their lives?*

professors don't even come close to the top of the income pyramid. In line with Lenski's prediction, the politics of most college professors are left of center. This hypothesis may also hold true among academic departments; that is, the higher a department's pay, the less radical are its politics. Teachers in departments of business and medicine, for example, are among the most highly paid in the university—and they also are the most politically conservative.

Sociological Models of Social Class

The question of how many social classes there are is a matter of debate. Sociologists have proposed several models, but no model has gained universal support. There are two main models: one that builds on Marx, the other on Weber.

■ Updating Marx

Marx argued that there are just two classes—capitalists and workers—with membership based solely on a person's relationship to the means of production (see Figure 10.4). Sociologists have criticized this view because these categories are too broad. For example, because executives, managers, and supervisors don't own the means of production, they would be classified as workers. But what do these people have in common with assembly-line workers? Similarly, the category of "capitalist" takes in too many types. Some people employ a thousand workers, and their decisions directly affect a thousand families. Compare these people with a man I know in Godfrey, Illinois, who used to fix cars in his back yard. As Frank gained a following, he quit his regular job, and in a few years he put up a building with five bays and an office. Frank is now a capitalist, for he employs five or six mechanics and owns the tools and

Capitalists
(Bourgeoisie, those who own the means of production)

Workers
(Proletariat, those who work for the capitalists)

Inconsequential Others
(beggars, etc.)

Figure 10.4

Marx's Model of Social Class

the building (the "means of production"). But what does he have in common with a factory owner who controls the lives of one thousand workers? Not only is Frank's work different, but so are his lifestyle and the way he looks at the world.

Sociologist Erik Wright (1985) resolved this problem by regarding some people as members of more than one class at the same time. They occupy what he called **contradictory class locations.** By this, Wright means that people's position in the class structure can generate contradictory interests. For example, the automobile-mechanic-turned-business-owner may want his mechanics to have higher wages since he, too, has experienced their working conditions. At the same time, his current interests—making profits and remaining competitive with other repair shops—lead him to resist pressures to raise wages.

Because of such contradictory class locations, Wright modified Marx's model. As summarized in Table 10.3, Wright identified four classes: (1) *capitalists,* business owners who employ many workers; (2) *petty bourgeoisie,* small business owners, (3) *managers,* who sell their own labor but also exercise authority over other employees; and (4) *workers,* who simply sell their labor to others. As you can see, this model allows finer divisions than the one Marx proposed, yet it maintains the primary distinction between employer and employee. Problems persist, however. For example, where do the professions fit? In which category would we place college professors? And as you know, there are huge differences between managers. An executive at GM, for example, may manage a thousand workers, while a shift manager at MacDonald's may be responsible for only a handful. They, too, have little in common.

TABLE 10.3
Wright's Modification of Marx's Social Class Model
1. Capitalists
2. Petty bourgeoisie
3. Managers
4. Workers

contradictory class location
Erik Wright's term for a position in the class structure that generates contradictory interests

■ Updating Weber

Sociologists Joseph Kahl and Dennis Gilbert (Gilbert and Kahl 1993; Gilbert 1997) developed a six-class model to portray the class structure of the United States and other capitalist countries. Think of their model—Figure 10.5 on the next page—as a ladder. Our discussion starts with the highest rung and moves downward. In line with Weber, on each lower rung you find less wealth, less power, and less prestige. Note that in this model education is also a primary measure of class.

The Capitalist Class   Only about 1 percent of the population occupies the top rung of the class ladder. As we saw in Figure 10.1, this 1 percent is so wealthy that its members are worth more than the entire bottom 90 percent of the nation. They own 40 percent of the nation's entire wealth. Their power is so great that their decisions open or close jobs for millions of people. They also have direct access to top politicians. This small elite even helps to shape the consciousness of the nation: They own our newspapers, magazines, radio and television stations, and control the boards of directors of our colleges and universities. The super-rich perpetuate themselves in privilege by passing to their children their assets and influential social networks.

The capitalist class can be divided into "old" and "new" money. The longer that wealth has been in a family, the more it adds to the family's prestige. Their children seldom mingle with "common" folk—instead, they attend exclusive private schools where they learn views of life that support their privileged position. They don't work for wages; instead, many study business or enter the field of law so they can manage the family fortune. These old-money capitalists (also called "blue-bloods") wield vast power as they use their extensive political connections to protect their huge economic empires (Persell et al. 1992; Domhoff 1990, 1999).

■ *Sociologists use income, education, and occupational prestige to measure social class. For most people, this classification works well. But not for everyone. Entertainers sometimes are difficult to fit in. To what social class does Christine Aguilera belong?*

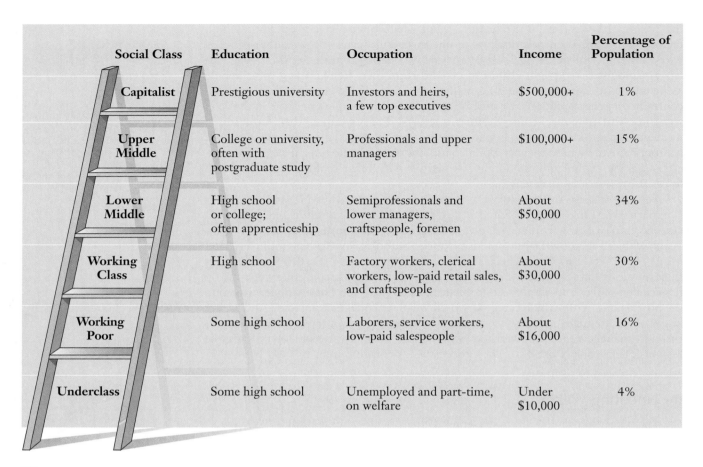

Social Class	Education	Occupation	Income	Percentage of Population
Capitalist	Prestigious university	Investors and heirs, a few top executives	$500,000+	1%
Upper Middle	College or university, often with postgraduate study	Professionals and upper managers	$100,000+	15%
Lower Middle	High school or college; often apprenticeship	Semiprofessionals and lower managers, craftspeople, foremen	About $50,000	34%
Working Class	High school	Factory workers, clerical workers, low-paid retail sales, and craftspeople	About $30,000	30%
Working Poor	Some high school	Laborers, service workers, low-paid salespeople	About $16,000	16%
Underclass	Some high school	Unemployed and part-time, on welfare	Under $10,000	4%

Figure 10.5

The U.S. Social Class Ladder

Source: Based on Gilbert and Kahl 1993 and Gilbert 1997; income estimates are modified from Duff 1995.

At the lower end of the capitalist class are the *nouveau riche,* those who have "new money." They are outsiders to this upper class. Although they have made fortunes in business, the stock market, inventions, entertainment, or sports, they have not attended the "right" schools, and they lack the influential social networks that come with old money. Not blue-bloods, they aren't trusted to have the right orientations to life. Donald Trump, for example, is not listed in the *Social Register,* the "White Pages" of the blue-bloods that lists the most prestigious and wealthy one-tenth of 1 percent of the U.S. population. Trump says he "doesn't care," but he reveals his true feelings by adding that his heirs will be in it (Kaufman 1996). He probably is right, for the children of the new-moneyed can ascend into the top part of the capitalist class—if they go to the right schools *and* marry old money.

Many in the capitalist class are philanthropic. They establish foundations and give huge sums to "causes." Their motivations vary. Some feel guilty because they have so much while others have so little. Others feel a responsibility—even a sense of fate or purpose—to use their money for doing good. Still others seek prestige, acclaim, or fame.

The Upper Middle Class   Of all the classes, the upper middle class is the one most shaped by education. Almost all members of this class have at least a bachelor's degree, and many have postgraduate degrees in business, management, law, or medicine. These people manage the corporations owned by the capitalist class or else operate their own business or profession. As Gilbert and Kahl (1982) say, these positions may not grant prestige equivalent to a title of nobility in the Germany of Max Weber, but they certainly represent the sign of having "made it" in contemporary America. . . .Their income is sufficient to purchase houses and cars and travel that become public symbols for all to see and for advertisers to portray with words and pictures that connote success, glamour, and high style.

Consequently, parents and teachers push children to prepare for upper-middle-class jobs. About 15 percent of the population belong to this class.

The Lower Middle Class   About 34 percent of the population belong to the lower middle class. Members of this class have jobs that call for them to follow orders given by those who have upper-middle-class credentials. Their technical and lower-level management positions bring them a good living, although they feel threatened by taxes and inflation. They enjoy a comfortable, mainstream lifestyle, and many anticipate being able to move up the social class ladder.

The distinctions between the lower middle class and the working class on the next lower rung are more blurred than those between other classes. In general, however, members of the lower middle class work at jobs that have slightly more prestige, and their incomes are generally higher.

The Working Class   About 30 percent of the U.S. population belong to this class of relatively unskilled blue-collar and white-collar workers. Compared with the lower middle class, they have less education and lower incomes. Their jobs are also less secure, more routine, and more closely supervised. One of their greatest fears is being laid off during a recession. With only a high school diploma, the average member of the working class has little hope of climbing up the class ladder. Job changes usually bring "more of the same," so most concentrate on getting ahead by achieving seniority on the job rather than by changing their type of work.

The Working Poor   Members of this class, about 16 percent of the population, work at unskilled, low-paying, temporary and seasonal jobs, such as sharecropping, migrant farm work, housecleaning, and day labor. Most are high school dropouts. Many are functionally illiterate, finding it difficult to read even the want ads. They are not likely to vote (Gilbert and Kahl 1993; Beeghley 2000), for they feel that no matter what party is elected to office, their situation won't change.

Although they work full time, millions of the working poor depend on help such as food stamps to supplement their meager incomes (O'Hare 1996b). It is easy to see how you can work full time and still be poor. Suppose that you are married and have a baby 3 months old and another child 3 years old. Your spouse stays home to care for them, so earning the income is up to you. But as a high-school dropout, all you can get is a minimum wage job. At $5.25 an hour, you earn $210 for 40 hours. In a year, this comes to $10,920—before deductions. Your nagging fear—and daily nightmare—is of ending up "on the streets."

The Underclass   On the lowest rung, and with next to no chance of climbing anywhere, is the **underclass**. Concentrated in the inner city, this group has little or no connection with the job market. Those who are employed, and some are, do menial, low-paying, temporary work. Welfare, if it is available, along with food stamps and food pantries, are their main support. Most members of other classes consider these people the ne'er-do-wells of society. Life is the toughest in this class, and it is filled with despair. About 4 percent of the population fall into this class.

The homeless men described in the opening vignette of this chapter, and the women and children like them, are part of the underclass. These are the people whom most Americans wish would just go away. Their presence on our city streets bothers passersby from the more privileged social classes—which includes just about everyone. "What are those obnoxious, dirty, foul-smelling people doing here, cluttering up my city?" appears to be a common response. Some people respond with sympathy and a

underclass
a group of people for whom poverty persists year after year and across generations

desire to do something. But what? Almost all of us just shrug our shoulders and look the other way, despairing of a solution and somewhat intimidated by their presence.

The homeless are the "fallout" of our developing postindustrial economy. In another era, they would have had plenty of work. They would have tended horses, worked on farms, dug ditches, shoveled coal, and run the factory looms. Some would have explored and settled the West. Others would have been lured to California, Alaska, and Australia by the prospect of gold. Today, however, with no frontiers to settle, factory jobs scarce, and farms that are becoming technological marvels, we have little need for unskilled labor.

■ Social Class in the Automobile Industry

The automobile industry illustrates the social class ladder. The Fords, for example, own and control a manufacturing and financial empire whose net worth is truly staggering. Their power matches their wealth, for through their multinational corporation their decisions affect production and employment in many countries. The family's vast fortune, and its accrued power, are now several generations old. Consequently, Ford children go to the "right" schools, know how to spend money in the "right" way, and can be trusted to make family and class interests paramount in life. They are without question at the top level of the *capitalist* class.

Next in line come top Ford executives. Although they may have an income of several hundred thousand dollars a year (and some, with stock options and bonuses, earn several million dollars annually), most are new to wealth and power. Consequently, they would be classified at the lower end of the capitalist class.

A husband and wife who own a Ford agency are members of the *upper middle class*. Their income clearly sets them apart from the majority of Americans, and their reputation in the community is enviable. More than likely they also exert greater-than-average influence in their community, but their capacity to wield power is limited.

A Ford salesperson, as well as people who work in the dealership office, belongs to the *lower middle class*. Although there are some exceptional salespeople, even a few who make a lot of money selling prestigious, expensive cars to the capitalist class, salespeople at a run-of-the-mill Ford agency are lower middle class. Compared with the owners of the agency, their income is less, their education is likely to be less, and their work is less prestigious.

Mechanics who repair customers' cars are members of the *working class*. A mechanic who is promoted to supervise the repair shop joins the lower middle class.

Those who "detail" used cars (making them appear newer by washing and polishing the car, painting the tires, spraying "new car scent" into the interior, and so on) belong to the *working poor*. Their income and education are low, the prestige accorded their work minimal. They are laid off when selling slows down.

Ordinarily, the *underclass* is not represented in the automobile industry. It is conceivable, however, that the agency might hire a member of the underclass to do a specific job such as mowing the grass or cleaning up the used car lot. In general, however, personnel at the agency do not trust members of the underclass and do not want to associate with them—even for a few hours. They prefer to hire someone from the working poor for such jobs.

■ ■ ■ ■ ■

Consequences of Social Class

Each social class can be thought of as a broad subculture with distinct approaches to life. This means that social class affects people's health, family life, and education. It also influences their religion and politics, even their experiences with crime and the criminal justice system. Let's look at these consequences of social class, as well as how the new technology is related to social class.

■ Physical Health

Social class is so significant that it even affects our chances of living and dying. The principle is simple: The lower a person's class, the more likely that individual is to die before the expected age. This principle holds true at all ages. Infants born to the poor are more likely than other infants to die before their first birthday. In old age—whether 75 or 95—a larger proportion of the poor die each year than do the wealthy. The two primary reasons for this are lifestyle and medical care.

Social class shapes people's lifestyles, which, in turn, affect their health. Those in the lower social classes are more likely to smoke, eat more fats, abuse drugs and alcohol, exercise less, and practice unsafe sexual behavior (Chin et al. 2000). This, to understate the matter, does not increase people's health.

The second reason for the unequal death rates is unequal access to medical care. Consider this example:

> Terry Takewell (his real name) was a 21-year-old diabetic who lived in a trailer park in Somerville, Tennessee. When Zettie Mae Hill, Takewell's neighbor, found the unemployed carpenter drenched with sweat from a fever, she called an ambulance. Takewell was rushed to nearby Methodist Hospital. There he had an outstanding bill of $9,400. A notice had been posted in the emergency room telling staff members to alert supervisors if Takewell ever returned.
>
> By the time the hospital administrator was informed of the admission, Takewell was already in a hospital bed. The administrator went to Takewell's room, helped him to his feet, and escorted him to the parking lot. There, neighbors found him under a tree and took him home.
>
> Takewell died about twelve hours later.
>
> Zettie Mae Hill is still torn up about it. She wonders if Takewell would be alive today if she had directed his ambulance to a different hospital. She said, "I didn't think a hospital would just let a person die like that for lack of money." (Based on Ansberry 1988)

Why was Terry Takewell denied medical treatment and his life cut short? The fundamental reason is that in the United States health care is not a citizen's right, but a commodity for sale. The result is a two-tier system of medical care—superior care for those who can afford the cost, and inferior care for those who cannot. Unlike the middle and upper classes, few poor people have a personal physician, and they often spend hours waiting in crowded public health clinics. After waiting most of a day, some don't even get to see a doctor; instead, they are told to come back the next day (Fialka 1993). And when the poor are hospitalized, they are likely to find themselves

■ *The photos of these two women were taken "at home." The woman in her chateau in Geneva, Switzerland (above) and the woman at Simferopol, Crimea (right) are both shown in their living rooms. From the contrast evident in these photos, can you see how social class makes such a vital difference in people's life chances? Can you see why these women are likely to see the world in highly distinctive ways, and why their politics and even their religions are likely to differ?*

in understaffed and underfunded public hospitals, where they are treated by rotating interns who do not know them and cannot follow up on their progress.

■ Mental Health

Social class also affects our mental health. From the 1930s until now, sociologists have found that the mental health of the lower classes is worse than that of the higher classes (Faris and Dunham 1939; Srole et al. 1978; Lundberg 1991; Miller 1994). Greater mental problems are part of the stress that accompanies poverty. Compared with middle- and upper-class Americans, the poor have less job security, lower wages, more unpaid bills, more divorce, more alcoholism, greater vulnerability to crime, and more physical illnesses—often accompanied by the threat of eviction hanging over their heads. Such conditions deal severe blows to people's emotional well-being.

People higher up the social class ladder experience stress, of course, but their stress is generally less and their coping resources greater. Not only can they afford vacations, psychiatrists, and counselors, but *their class position gives them greater control over their lives, a key to good mental health*. Happiness, a component of mental health, is explored in the Down-to-Earth Sociology box on the next page.

■ Family Life

Social class plays an especially significant role in family life. Of its many consequences in this vital area, let's look at choice of spouse, divorce, and child rearing.

Choice of Husband or Wife Members of the capitalist class place strong emphasis on family tradition. They stress the family's ancestors, history, and even a sense of purpose or destiny in life (Baltzell 1979; Aldrich 1989). Children of this class learn that their choice of husband or wife affects not just themselves but the entire family, that their spouse will have an impact on the "family line." Because of these background expectations, the field of "eligible" marriage partners is much narrower than it is for the children of any other social class. In effect, parents in this class play a strong role in their children's mate selection.

Divorce The more difficult life of the lower social classes, especially the many tensions that come from insecure jobs and inadequate incomes, leads to higher marital friction and a greater likelihood of divorce. Consequently, children of the poor are more likely to grow up in broken homes.

Child Rearing As discussed on page 82, sociologist Melvin Kohn (1977) found significant class differences in child rearing. Lower-class parents are more concerned that their children conform to conventional norms and obey authority figures. Middle-class parents, in contrast, encourage their children to be more creative and independent. They also tolerate a wider range of behaviors, except in speech, where they are less tolerant of bad grammar and curse words.

Kohn concluded that lower- and middle-class parents rear their children differently because their occupations give them different visions of their children's futures. Lower-class parents are closely supervised in their jobs, and they anticipate that their children will work at similar jobs. Consequently, they try to teach their children to defer to authority. In contrast, parents from the more privileged classes enjoy greater creativity and self-expression at work. Anticipating similar work for their children, they encourage them to express greater freedom. Out of these contrasting orientations also arise different ways of enforcing discipline; lower-class parents are more likely to use the stick, while the middle classes rely more on verbal persuasion.

■ Education

As we saw in Figure 10.5, education increases as one goes up the social class ladder. It is not just the amount of education that changes, but also the type of education. Children of the capitalist class bypass public schools. They attend exclusive

down-to-earth
s o c i o l o g y

Can Money Buy Happiness?

Do you think you would be happier if you didn't have to worry about paying bills? Or if you could pay cash for a new car and afford exotic vacations?

If you answered yes, you are correct. The middle class are happier than the poor, and the rich are happier than the middle class.

Research also shows that:

■ Women are generally happier than men.

■ Whites are generally happier than African Americans.

■ Married people are generally happier than unmarried people.

■ Americans aren't as happy today as they were a generation ago.

■ Women are especially less happy now than they were a generation ago.

Some of these findings have puzzled researchers. The finding that whites are generally happier than African Americans isn't a puzzle because it follows the principle that happiness generally increases with income. But since Americans are richer today than they were a generation ago, they should also be happier. Yet the national average of hap-

piness has declined. Researchers have suggested several solutions to this paradox. First, to get their higher incomes, Americans work more hours than they used to—and their jobs are less secure. Second, Americans divorce more and get married less than they did in the past—and the divorced and single generally aren't as happy as the married. A third explanation focuses on the finding that the decline in happiness has occurred almost entirely among women. Although women are still generally happier than men, their average level of happiness has dropped while that of men has hardly budged. The reason, suggest researchers, is the many more millions of women who have entered the work force. They face not only the

pressures of work, but also at home they shoulder about the same responsibilities that their non-employed mothers did.

Then there is this explanation: We really are happier, but we don't know it! Over the years, our expectations have increased, and we now demand more out of life than we used to. We aren't as satisfied with eating at home, for example, or having just three channels on TV to watch. We demand restaurant meals, larger houses, newer cars, gourmet food, and exotic vacations. Since happiness revolves around having our expectations met, as our expectations go up, our ability to meet those expectations has to keep pace or our happiness declines.

Oh, well, an extra ten or twenty grand a year will help.

for your consideration

Of the four explanations for the general decline in the happiness of Americans in the face of a rising standard of living, which one do you think is the best? Why?

Based on Leonhardt 2001.

private schools where they are trained to take a commanding role in society. Prep schools such as Phillips Exeter Academy, Groton School, and Woodberry Forest School teach upper-class values and prepare their students for prestigious universities (Beeghley 2000; Higley 2001). Keenly sensitive to the significance of private schools, aspiring members of the upper middle class do their best to get their children in prestigious preschools; they even elicit letters of recommendation for their 2- and 3-year-olds. Such differences in parental expectations and resources are a major reason why children from the more privileged classes do better in school and are more likely to enter and to graduate from college.

■ Religion

One area of social life that we might think would be unaffected by social class is religion. ("People are just religious, or they are not. What does social class have to do with it?") As we shall see in Chapter 18, however, the classes tend to cluster in different denominations. Episcopalians, for example, are more likely to recruit from the middle and upper classes. Baptists draw heavily from the lower classes, and Methodists are more middle class. Patterns of worship also follow class lines: The lower classes are attracted to spontaneous worship services and louder music, while the middle and upper classes prefer more "subdued" worship.

■ Politics

As has been stressed throughout this text, symbolic interactionists emphasize that people see events from their own corner in life. Political views are no exception to this principle, and the rich and the poor walk different political paths. The higher people are on the social class ladder, the more likely they are to vote for Republicans. In contrast, most members of the working class believe that the government should intervene in the economy to make citizens financially secure, and most are Democrats. Although the working class is more liberal on *economic* issues (policies that increase government spending), it is more conservative on *social* issues (such as opposing abortion and the Equal Rights Amendment) (Lipset 1959; Houtman 1995). People toward the bottom of the class structure are also less likely to be politically active—to campaign for candidates, or even to vote (Gilbert and Kahl 1997; Soss 1999; Beeghley 2000).

■ Crime and the Criminal Justice System

If justice is supposed to be blind, it certainly is not when it comes to one's chances of being arrested (Henslin 2000). In Chapter 8 (pages 226–228) we discussed how the upper and lower social classes have different styles of crime. The white-collar crimes of the more privileged classes are more likely to be dealt with outside the criminal justice system, while the street crimes of the lower classes are dealt with by the police and courts. One consequence of this class standard is that members of the lower classes are more likely to be in prison, on probation, or on parole. In addition, since people tend to commit crimes in or near their own neighborhoods, the lower classes are more likely to be robbed, burglarized, or murdered.

■ Social Class and the New Technology

If the United States does not keep pace with global change and remain competitive by producing low-cost, quality goods, its economic position will decline. Opportunities will dwindle; there will be fewer jobs and shrinking paychecks. To compete in this global economic race, the United States is incorporating advanced technology in all spheres of life.

For the capitalist class, the new technology is a dream come true: By minimizing the obstacles of national borders, capitalists can move factories to countries with cheap labor and maximize profits through global integration. Components can be produced in one country, assembled in another, and the product marketed throughout the world. The upper middle class are well prepared for the change. Their education enables them to take a leading role in managing this global system for the capitalist class, or for using the new technology to advance in their chosen professions.

Below these two most privileged classes, however, the new technology adds to the insecurity to life. As job markets shift, the skills of many in the lower middle class become outdated. This strikes fear in those who work at specialized crafts, for new technology can reduce or even eliminate the need for their narrow, specialized skills.

People in lower management are more secure, for they can transfer their skills from one job to another.

From this middle point on the ladder down, technology hits people the hardest. The working class is ill prepared to cope with the changes, and the threat of plant closings haunts them. The working poor are even more vulnerable, for they have even less to offer in the new job market. As unskilled jobs dry up, many workers are consigned to the industrial garbage bin.

The underclass, technologically illiterate, is left behind. This point was driven home to me when I saw the homeless sitting dejected in the shelters. Of what value were these high school dropouts, our technological know-nothings, to this new society that is undergoing its piercing birth pains? With no productive place, their base of social belonging and self-esteem has been pulled out from under them.

In short, the new technology opens and closes opportunities for people largely by virtue of where they are located on the social class ladder, a topic discussed in the New Technology box below.

sociology & the new technology

Closing the Digital Divide: The Technology Gap Facing the Poor and Minorities

Consider this:

- Ninety-one percent of children whose family has an annual income of $75,000 or more have computers at home, compared with 22 percent of children in families with annual incomes less than $20,000 a year (Lewin 2001a).

- A high-income urban family is 20 times more likely to have Internet access than a low-income rural family.

- A white child in a poor family is three or four times more likely to have Internet access than an African American or Latino child in a poor family.

- A child in a wealthy Asian American family is 34 times more likely to have Internet access than a child in a poor African American or Latino family ("Haves and Have-Nots" 2000).

- Of all racial-ethnic groups, Native Americans have the least access to computers. Only half have telephones at home (Romero 2000).

The term *digital divide* refers to this unequal access to computers and the

Internet. As you can see, this technology gap marks the social classes, geographical areas, and racial-ethnic groups.

Sociologists focus on the *structural* basis of wealth and poverty. That is, they examine how advantage and disadvantage are *built into society*—how birth forces some people to face many obstacles, while others face few. To level the playing field, the question is not how we can destroy the advantages that some have, but, rather, how we can reduce obstacles and increase opportunities for others.

If computers were only for playing cyber games, the digital divide would not be an issue. But in today's technological world, children who have less access to computers and the Internet face a major hurdle in life. To have weak computer skills means to be cut off from information and work opportunities.

for your consideration

What do you think can be done to overcome the digital divide? For example, should the government pay to connect every U.S. home to the Internet and buy a computer for every child, beginning in kindergarten? Why or why not?

Let's look at the problem this way: The Internet has become a gigantic library that spans the globe. Would we ever allow our city or school libraries to let some ethnic groups in more often than others? Would we allow them to let in the wealthy, but close the door on the poor? Finally, do you think that this analogy is fair, since libraries are funded by tax dollars but home computers and Internet access are paid for by individuals?

Social Mobility

No aspect of life, then—from marriage to education—goes untouched by social class. Because life is so much more satisfying in the more privileged classes, people strive to climb the social class ladder. What affects their chances?

■ Three Types of Social Mobility

There are three basic types of social mobility: intergenerational, structural, and exchange. **Intergenerational mobility** refers to a change that occurs between generations—when grown-up children end up on a different rung of the social class ladder from the one their parents occupy. If the child of someone who sells used cars graduates from college and buys a Saturn dealership, that person experiences **upward social mobility.** Conversely, if a child of the dealership's owner parties too much, drops out of college, and ends up selling cars, he or she experiences **downward social mobility.**

We like to think that individual efforts are the reason people move up the class ladder, and their faults the reason they move down. In these examples, we can identify hard work, sacrifice, and ambition on the one hand, versus indolence and alcohol abuse on the other. Although individual factors such as these do underlie social mobility, sociologists consider **structural mobility** to be the crucial factor. This second basic type of mobility refers to changes in society that cause large numbers of people to move up or down the class ladder.

To better understand structural mobility, think of how opportunities opened when computers were invented. New types of jobs appeared overnight. Huge numbers of people took workshops and crash courses, switching from blue-collar to white-collar work. Although individual effort certainly was involved—for some seized the opportunity while others did not—the underlying cause was a change in the *structure* of work. Consider the opposite—how opportunities close during a depression, and millions of people are forced downward on the class ladder. In this instance, too, their changed status is due less to individual behavior than to *structural* changes in society.

The third type of social mobility, **exchange mobility**, occurs when large numbers of people move up and down the social class ladder, but, on balance, the proportions of the social classes remain about the same. Suppose that a million or so working-class people are trained in computers, and they move the class ladder. Suppose also that due to a surge in imports about a million skilled workers have to take lower-status jobs. Although millions of people change their social class, there is, in effect, an *exchange* among them. The net result more or less balances out, and the class system remains basically untouched.

■ Women in Studies on Social Mobility

The United States is famous worldwide for its intergenerational mobility. That children can pass up their parents on the social class ladder is one of the attrac-

intergenerational mobility the change that family members make in social class from one generation to the next

upward social mobility movement up the social class ladder

downward social mobility movement down the social class ladder

structural mobility movement up or down the social class ladder that is attributable to changes in the structure of society, not to individual efforts

exchange mobility about the same numbers of people moving up and down the social class ladder, such that, on balance, the social class system shows little change

■ *The term* structural mobility *refers to changes in society that push large numbers of people either up or down the social class ladder. A remarkable example was the stock market crash of 1929, when thousands of people suddenly lost immense amounts of wealth. People who once "had it made" found themselves standing on street corners selling apples or, as depicted here, selling their possessions at fire-sale prices.*

tions of this country. To find out how extensive this mobility is, sociologists used to study only men. In classic studies, they concluded that about half of sons passed their fathers; about one-third stayed at the same level, and only about one-sixth fell down the class ladder (Blau and Duncan 1967; Featherman and Hauser 1978; Featherman 1979).

Fathers and sons? How about the other half of the population? Feminists pointed out this obvious omission (Davis and Robinson 1988). They also objected to the assumption that women had no class position of their own—sociologists had simply assigned them the class of their husbands. The defense was that too few women were in the labor force to make a difference.

With huge numbers of women now working for pay, more recent studies include women (Breen and Whelan 1995; Beeghley 2000). Sociologists Elizabeth Higginbotham and Lynn Weber (1992), for example, studied 200 women from working-class backgrounds who became professionals, managers, and administrators in Memphis. They found that almost without exception, the women's parents had encouraged them while they were still little girls to postpone marriage and get an education. This study confirms findings that the family is of utmost importance in the socialization process and that the primary entry to the upper middle class is a college education. At the same time, note that if there had not been a *structural* change in society, the millions of new positions that women occupy would not exist.

▪ The Pain of Social Mobility

You know that to be knocked down the social class ladder is painful, but were you aware that climbing it also brings pain? Sociologist Steph Lawler (1999) interviewed British women who had moved to the middle class through education or marriage. The women were caught between two worlds—their working-class background and their current middle-class life. The gap in their relationship with their mothers was especially bothersome. The tension centered around their new tastes in furniture, food, and speech. Even the way they reared their children became a matter of dispute. Sociologists Richard Sennett and Jonathan Cobb (1972/1988), who studied social mobility in Boston, also found a gap between parents and children. The working-class parents had made deep sacrifices so their children could go to college, they expected their children to appreciate their sacrifices. Because the children's educated world was so distant from that of their parents, however, the children had grown aloof, and the two had difficulty even talking to one another. The parents felt betrayed and were bitter.

In short, social class separates people into worlds so distinct that communication and mutual understanding become difficult. To change one's social class is to tear oneself from one's roots. As you may recall, Richard Rodriguez, featured in the Perspectives box on page 84, found that his climb up the social class ladder had wrenching costs.

■ ▫ ■ ▪ ■

Poverty

Many Americans find the "limitless possibilities" on which the American dream is based to be elusive. As illustrated in Figure 10.5 on page 286, the working poor and underclass together form about one-fifth of the U.S. population. This translates into a huge number, about 60 million people. Who are these people?

poverty
lacking resources to meet your basic needs

■. Drawing the Poverty Line

To determine who is poor, the U.S. government uses a **poverty line.** This measure was set in the 1960s, when poor people were thought to spend about one-third of their incomes on food. Based on this assumption, each year the government computes a low-cost food budget and multiplies it by 3. Families whose incomes are less than this amount are classified as poor; those whose incomes are higher—even by a dollar—are determined to be "not poor."

This official measure of poverty is grossly inadequate. Poor people actually spend only about 20 percent of their incomes on food, so to determine a poverty line we really ought to multiply their food budget by five instead of three (Uchitelle 2001). No political party in power wants to do this, as redrawing the line would make it appear that poverty increased under their watch. Another problem with the poverty line is that some mothers work and have to pay for child care, but they are treated the same as mothers who don't have this expense. The poverty line is also the same for everyone across the nation, even though the cost of living is higher in some states. Nor, for some reason, does the government count food stamps as income.

That a change in the poverty line would instantly make millions of people poor—or take away their poverty—would be a laughable matter, if it weren't so serious. The government uses the poverty line to decide who will receive help and who will not. Although this line is arbitrary, it is the official measure of poverty. Using it, let's see who in the United States is poor. Before we do this, though, compare your ideas of the poor with the myths explored in the Down-to-Earth Sociology box below.

poverty line
the official measure of poverty; calculated to include those whose incomes are less than three times a low-cost food budget

---

down-to-earth
s o c i o l o g y

Exploring Myths About the Poor

Myth 1 Most poor people are lazy. They are poor because they do not want to work.
Half of the poor are either too old or too young to work. About 40 percent are under age 18, and another 10 percent are age 65 or older. About 30 percent of the working-age poor work at least half the year.

Myth 2 Poor people are trapped in a cycle of poverty that few escape.
The poverty population is *dynamic.* Most poverty lasts less than a year (Gottschalk et al. 1994). Only 12 percent remain in poverty for five or more consecutive years (O'Hare 1996a). Most children who are born in poverty are *not* poor as adults (Ruggles 1989).

Myth 3 Most of the poor are African Americans and Latinos.
As shown in Figure 10.7, the poverty rates of African Americans and Latinos are much higher than that of whites. Because there are so many more whites in the U.S. population, however, *most poor Americans are white.* Fifty-five percent of the poor are white, 21 percent African American, 19 percent Latino, 3 percent Asian American, and 1 percent Native American (*Statistical Abstract* 2000:Tables 44, 754; total is 99 percent due to rounding).

Myth 4 Most of the poor are single mothers and their children.
Although about 38 percent of the poor do match this stereotype, 34 percent of the poor live in married-couple families, 22 percent

live alone or with nonrelatives, and 6 percent live in other settings.

Myth 5 Most of the poor live in the inner city.
This one is close to fact, as about 42 percent do live in the inner city. But 36 percent live in the suburbs, and 22 percent live in small towns and rural areas.

Myth 6 The poor live on welfare.
About half of the income of poor adults comes from wages and pensions, about 25 percent from welfare, and about 22 percent from Social Security.

Sources: Primarily O'Hare 1996a and O'Hare 1996b, with other sources as indicated

■ ■ ■ ■ ■

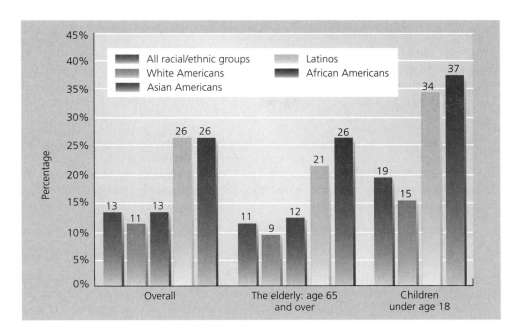

Figure 10.6

Poverty in the United States, by Age and Race-Ethnicity

Note: The poverty line on which this figure is based is $16,400 for a family of four. The source includes only these groups, and does not include Asian American children. .

Source: Statistical Abstract 2000: Tables 754, 757, 758.

■ Who Are the Poor?

Geography   As you can see from the Social Map below, the poor are not evenly distributed among the states. The clustering of poverty in the South is a pattern that has prevailed for more than 100 years.

A second aspect of geography is also significant. About 56 million Americans live in rural areas. Of these, 9 million are poor. At 16 percent, their rate of poverty is

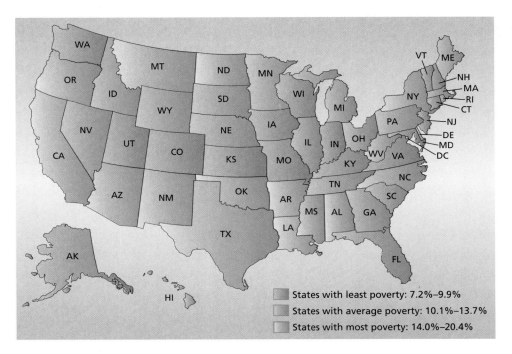

Figure 10.7

Patterns of Poverty

Note: Poverty varies tremendously by state. In the extreme, poverty is about three times as common in New Mexico (20.4%) than it is in Maryland (7.2%).

Source: Statistical Abstract 2000:Table 759.

higher than the national average of 13 percent. The rural poor are less likely to be single parents, and more likely to be married and to have jobs. Compared with urban Americans, the rural poor are less skilled and less educated, and the jobs available to them pay less than similar jobs in urban areas (Dudenhefer 1993).

The greatest predictor of whether Americans are poor is not geography, however, but race-ethnicity, education, and the sex of the person who heads the family. Let's look at these three factors.

Race-Ethnicity   One of the strongest factors in poverty is race-ethnicity. As Figure 10.6 on page 297 shows, only 11 percent of white Americans are poor, but 26 percent of African Americans and Latinos live in poverty. At 13 percent, the poverty rate of Asian Americans is close to that of white Americans. Although their poverty rate is the lowest, because there are so many more white Americans, most poor people are white.

Education   As you know, education is a vital factor in poverty, but you may not have known just how powerful it is. From Figure 10.8 you can see that only 2 of 100 people who finish college end up in poverty, but one of every four or five people who drop out of high school is poor. As you can see, the chances of someone being poor decrease with each higher level of education. Although this principle applies regardless of race-ethnicity, you can see how race-ethnicity makes an impact at every level of education.

The Feminization of Poverty   The other major predictor of poverty is the sex of the person who heads the family. Compared with men, women are more likely to be poor (*Statistical Abstract* 2000:Tables 750, 751). Women who head families average less than two-thirds the income of men who head families (*Statistical Abstract* 2000:Table 748). Consequently, most poor families are headed by women. The three major causes of this phenomenon, called the **feminization of poverty**, are divorce, births to single women, and the lower wages paid to women.

Old Age   As Figure 10.6 on page 297 shows, the elderly are less likely than the general population to be poor. It used to be that growing old increased people's chances of being poor, but government policies to redistribute income—Social Security and subsidized housing, food, and medical care—slashed the rate of poverty among the elderly. This figure also shows how the prevailing racial-ethnic patterns carry over into old age. You can see how much more likely an elderly African American or Latino is to be poor than is an elderly white person.

feminization of poverty
a trend in U.S. poverty whereby most poor families are headed by women

Figure 10.8

Who Ends Up Poor? Poverty by Education and Race-Ethnicity

Source: Statistical Abstract 2000:Table 761.

■ *Beyond the awareness of most Americans are the rural poor, such as this family in Louisiana. This family is typical of the rural poor: white and headed by a woman. What do you think the future holds for these children?*

◆ Children of Poverty

Children are more likely to live in poverty than are adults or the elderly. This holds true regardless of race-ethnicity, but from Figure 10.6 you can see how much greater poverty is among Latino and African American children. That about 14 million U.S. children are reared in poverty is shocking when one considers the wealth of this country and the supposed concern for the well-being of children. This tragic aspect of poverty is the topic of the following Thinking Critically section.

thinking

CRITICALLY

The Nation's Shame: Children in Poverty

One of the most startling statistics in sociology is shown in Figure 10.6: One of every five U.S. children lives in poverty. About one of seven white children and one of three Latino and African American children are poor. These figures translate into incredible numbers—approximately *14 million* children live in poverty: 6 million white children, 4 million Latino children, and 4 million African American children.

The main cause for this high rate of child poverty, says sociologist and former U.S. Senator Daniel Moynihan, is an increase in births outside marriage. In 1960, one of twenty U.S. children was born to a single woman. Today that total is *more than six times higher,* and single women now account for one of three (33 percent) of all U.S. births. Figure 10.9 shows the striking relationship between births to single women and social class. For women above the poverty line, only 6 percent of births are to single women; for women below the poverty line this rate is more than *seven* times higher.

Regardless of the causes of childhood poverty—and there are many—what is most significant is that these millions of children face all of the suffering and obstacles to a satisfying life that poverty entails. They are more likely to die in infancy, to go hungry, to be malnourished, to develop more slowly, and to have more health problems. They also are more likely to drop out of school, to become involved in criminal activities, and to have children while still in their teens—thus perpetuating the cycle of poverty.

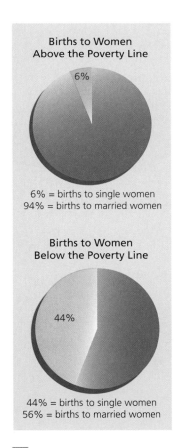

Births to Women Above the Poverty Line

6%

6% = births to single women
94% = births to married women

Births to Women Below the Poverty Line

44%

44% = births to single women
56% = births to married women

Figure 10.9

How Many Births to Single Mothers?

Note: Totals were available only for white women.
Source: Murray 1993.

■ ■ ■ ■ ■

for your consideration . . .

Many social analysts—liberals and conservatives alike—are alarmed at this increase in child poverty. They emphasize that it is time to stop blaming the victim, and, instead, to focus on the *structural* factors that underlie child poverty. To relieve this problem, they say, we must take immediate steps to establish national programs of child nutrition and health care. Solutions will require at least three fundamental changes: (1) removing obstacles to employment; (2) improving education; and (3) strengthening the family. To achieve these changes, what specific programs would *you* recommend?

Sources: Moynihan 1991; Sandefur 1995; *Statistical Abstract* 1997:Table 1338; 2000: Tables 22, 78, 754, 757.

■ The Dynamics of Poverty

Some have suggested that the poor tend to get trapped in a **culture of poverty** (Harrington 1962; Lewis 1966a). They assume that the values and behaviors of the poor "make them fundamentally different from other Americans, and that these factors are largely responsible for their continued long-term poverty" (Ruggles 1989:7).

Lurking behind this concept is the idea that the poor are lazy people who bring poverty on themselves. Certainly some individuals and families match this stereotype—many of us have known them. But is a self-perpetuating culture—one that is transmitted across generations and that locks people in poverty—the basic reason for U.S. poverty?

Researchers who followed 5,000 U.S. families since 1968 uncovered some rather surprising findings. Contrary to common stereotypes, most poverty is short, lasting only a year or less. Most poverty comes about because of a dramatic life change such as divorce, the loss of a job, or even the birth of a child (O'Hare 1996a). As Figure 10.10 shows, only 12 percent of poverty lasts five years or longer. Contrary to the stereotype of lazy people content to live off the government, few poor people enjoy poverty—and they do what they can to *not* be poor.

Yet from one year to the next, the number of poor people remains about the same. This means that the people who move out of poverty are replaced by people who move *into* poverty. Most of these newly poor will also move out of poverty within a year. Some people even bounce back and forth, never quite making it securely out of poverty. Poverty, then, is dynamic, touching a lot more people than the official totals indicate. Although 13 percent of Americans may be poor at any one time, twice that number, about one-fourth of the U.S. population, is or has been poor for at least a year.

■ Why Are People Poor?

Two explanations for poverty compete for our attention. The first, which sociologists prefer, focuses on *social structure*. Sociologists stress that *features of society* deny some people access to education or learning job skills. They emphasize racial, ethnic, age, and gender discrimination, as well as changes in the job market—the closing of plants, drying up of unskilled jobs, and an increase in marginal jobs that pay poverty wages.

A competing explanation focuses on the *characteristics of individuals* that are assumed to contribute to poverty. Individualistic explanations that sociologists reject outright as worthless stereotypes are laziness and lack of intelligence. Individualistic explanations that sociologists reluctantly acknowledge include dropping out of school, bearing children in the teen years, and averaging more children than women in the other social classes. Most sociologists are reluctant to speak of such factors in this context, for they appear to blame the victim, something that sociologists bend over backward not to do.

The tension between these competing explanations is of more than just theoretical interest. Each explanation affects our perception and has practical consequences, as is illustrated in the following Thinking Critically section.

culture of poverty
the assumption that the values and behaviors of the poor make them fundamentally different from other people, that these factors are largely responsible for their poverty, and that parents perpetuate poverty across generations by passing these characteristics to their children

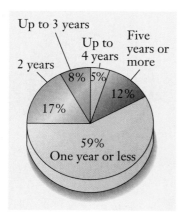

Figure **10.10**

How Long Does Poverty Last?
Source: Gottschalk et al. 1994:89.

thinking

CRITICALLY

The Welfare Debate: The Deserving and the Undeserving Poor

T hroughout U.S. history, Americans have divided the poor into two types: the deserving and the undeserving. The deserving poor are people who, in the public mind, are poor through no fault of their own. Most of the working poor, such as the Lewises, are considered deserving:

> Nancy and Ted Lewis are in their early 30s and have two children. Ted works three part-time jobs, earning $12,000 a year; Nancy takes care of the children and house and is not employed. To make ends meet, the Lewises rely on food stamps, Medicaid, and housing subsidies.

The undeserving poor, in contrast, are viewed as having brought on their own poverty. They are freeloaders who waste their lives in sloth, alcohol and drug abuse, and promiscuous sex. They don't deserve help, and, if given anything, will waste it on their dissolute lifestyles. Some would see Joan as an example:

> Joan, her mother, and her three brothers and two sisters lived on welfare. Joan started having sex at 13, bore her first child at 15, and, now, at 23, is expecting her fourth child. Her first two children have the same father, the third a different father, and Joan isn't sure who fathered her coming child. Joan parties most nights, using both alcohol and whatever drugs are available. Her house is filthy, the refrigerator usually empty, and social workers have threatened to take away her children.

This division of the poor into deserving and undeserving underlies the heated debate about welfare. "Why should we use *our* hard-earned money to help *them*? They are just going to waste it. Of course, there are those who want to get on their feet, and helping them is okay."

▪ ▪ ▪ ▪ ▪

for your consideration . . .

Why do people make a division between deserving and undeserving poor? Should we let some people starve because they "brought poverty upon themselves"? Should we let children go hungry because their parents are unmarried and uneducated? Or because they are drug abusers? Does "unworthy" mean that we should not offer assistance to people who "squander" the help they are given?

In contrast to thinking of poor people as deserving or undeserving, use the sociological perspective to explain poverty without blaming the victim. What *social* conditions (conditions of society) create poverty? What *social* conditions produce the lifestyles that the middle class so despises?

▪ Welfare Reform

After decades of criticism, U.S. welfare was restructured in 1996. A federal law—the Personal Responsibility and Work Opportunity Reconciliation Act—required states to place a lifetime cap on welfare assistance and to require welfare recipients to look for work and to take available jobs. The maximum length of time someone can collect welfare is five years. Many states have a shorter time frame. Unmarried teen parents must attend school and live at home or in some other adult-supervised setting.

This law set off a storm of criticism. Some called it an attack on the poor. Defenders replied that the new rules would rescue people from poverty. They would transform welfare recipients into self-supporting and hard-working citizens—and reduce welfare costs. Some states put up new signs, changing "Welfare Center" to "Job Placement Center." National welfare rolls plummeted, dropping by half (Bernstein 2000). This is only the rosy part of the picture, however. Some former welfare recipients have no job, but they are not on welfare because they have used up their time limit. Many are barely getting by, living with the fear of losing their jobs in an economic downturn. Some skip meals because there isn't enough money for food (Sengupta 2001).

Consider one of the "success stories":

> JoAnne Sims, 37, lives in Erie, New York, with her 7-year-old daughter Jamine. JoAnne left welfare, and now earns $6.75 an hour as a cook for Head Start. Her 37-hour week brings $239.75 before deductions. With the help of medical benefits and a mother who provides child care, JoAnne "gets by." She says, "From what I hear, a lot of us who went off welfare are still poor . . . let me tell you, it's not easy." (Peterson 2000)

Conflict theorists have an interesting interpretation of welfare. They say that its purpose is not to help people, but, rather to maintain an army of reserve workers. It is designed to keep the unemployed alive during economic downturns until they are needed during the next economic boom. Reducing the welfare rolls through the 1996 law fits this model, as it occurred during the longest economic boom in U.S. history. Recessions are inevitable, however, and just as inevitable, surging unemployment. In line with conflict theory, we can predict that with each recession welfare rules will be softened—in order to keep the reserve army of the unemployed ready for the next time they are needed.

■ Deferred Gratification

deferred gratification
forgoing something in the present in the hope of achieving greater gains in the future

One consequence of a life of deprivation punctuated by emergencies—*and of seeing the future as more of the same*—is a lack of **deferred gratification,** giving up things in the present for the sake of greater gains in the future. It is difficult to practice this middle-class virtue if one does not have a middle-class surplus—or middle-class hope.

Back in 1967, sociologist Elliot Liebow noted this precise problem among black street-corner men. Their jobs were low-paying and insecure, their lives pitted with emergencies. With the future looking exactly like the present, and any savings they did manage gobbled up by emergencies—either theirs or their friends' and relatives'—saving for the future was pointless. The only thing that made sense from their perspective was to enjoy what they could at the moment. Immediate gratification, then, was not the cause of their poverty, but its consequence. Cause and consequence loop together, however, for their immediate gratification helped perpetuate their poverty. For another look at this "looping," see the Down-to-Earth Sociology box on the next page, in which I share my personal experiences with poverty.

If both causes are at work, why do sociologists emphasize the structural explanation? Reverse the situation for a moment. Suppose that members of the middle class drove old cars that ran only half the time, faced threats from the utility company to shut off the electricity and heat, and had to make a choice between buying medicine and food and diapers or paying the rent. How long would they practice deferred gratification? Their orientations to life would likely make a sharp U-turn.

Sociologists, then, do not view the behaviors of the poor as the cause of their poverty, but, rather, as the result of their poverty. Poor people would welcome the middle-class opportunities that would allow them the chance to practice the middle-class virtue of deferred gratification. Without those opportunities, though, they just can't afford it.

■ A culture's dominant ideology is reinforced in many ways, including in its literature. As discussed in the text, Horatio Alger provided inspirational heroes for thousands of boys. The central theme of these many novels, immensely popular in their time, was rags to riches. Through rugged determination and self-sacrifice, a boy could overcome seemingly insurmountable obstacles to reach the pinnacle of success.

■ Where Is Horatio Alger?
The Social Functions of a Myth

In the late 1800s, Horatio Alger was one of the country's most talked-about authors. The rags-to-riches exploits of his fictional boy heroes and their startling successes in overcoming severe odds motivated thousands of boys of that period. Although Alger's characters have disappeared from U.S. literature, they remain alive and well in the psyche of Americans. From real-life examples of people from humble

■ ■ ■ ■ ■
Poverty: A Personal Journey

I was born in poverty. My parents, who could not afford to rent a house or apartment, rented the tiny office in their minister's house. That is where I was born.

My father began to slowly climb the social class ladder. His fitful odyssey took him from laborer to truck driver to the owner of a series of small businesses (tire repair shop, bar, hotel), then to vacuum cleaner salesman, and back to bar owner. He converted a garage into a house. Although it had no indoor plumbing or insulation (in northern Minnesota!), it was a start. Later, he bought a house, and then he built a new home. After that we moved into a trailer, and then back to a house. My father's seventh grade education was always an obstacle. Although he never became wealthy, poverty did become a distant memory for him.

My social class took a leap—from working to upper middle—when, after attending college and graduate school, I became a university professor. I entered a world that was unknown to my parents, a world much more pampered and privileged. I had opportunities to do research, to publish, and to travel to exotic places. My reading centered on sociological research, and I read books in Spanish as well as in English. My father, in contrast, never read a book in his life, and my mother read only detective stories and romance paperbacks. One set of experiences isn't "better" than the other, just significantly different in determining what windows of perception it opens onto the world.

My interest in poverty, which was rooted in my own childhood experiences, stayed with me. I traveled to a dozen or so skid rows across the United States and Canada, talking to homeless people and staying in their shelters. In my own town, I spent considerable time with people on welfare, observing how they lived. I constantly marveled at the connections between *structural* causes of poverty (low education and skills, undependable transportation, the lack of unskilled jobs) and its *personal* causes (the *culture of poverty*—alcohol and drug abuse, multiple out-of-wedlock births, frivolous spending, all-night partying, and a seeming incapacity to keep appointments—except to pick up the welfare check).

Sociologists haven't unraveled this connection, and as much as we might *like* for only the structural causes to apply, clearly *both* are at work (Duneier 1999:122). The situation can be illustrated by looking at the perennial health problems I observed among the poor—the constant colds, runny noses, back aches, and injuries. The health problems stemmed from the *social structure* (less access to medical care, lesser trained or less capable physicians, drafty houses, lack of education regarding nutrition, and more dangerous jobs). At the same time, *personal* characteristics—hygiene, eating habits, and overdrinking—caused health problems. Which was the cause and which the effect? Both, of course, for one fed into the other. The medical problems (which were based on both personal and structural causes) fed into the poverty these people experienced, making them less able to perform their jobs successfully—or even to show up at work regularly. What an intricate puzzle for sociologists!

■ ■ ■ ■ ■

origins who climbed far up the social class ladder, Americans know that anyone can get ahead if they really try. In fact, they believe that most Americans, including minorities and the working poor, have an average or better-than-average chance of getting ahead—obviously a statistical impossibility (Kluegel and Smith 1986).

The accuracy of the **Horatio Alger myth** is less important than the belief that limitless possibilities exist for everyone. Functionalists would stress that this belief is functional for society. On the one hand, it encourages people to compete for higher positions, or, as the song says, "to reach for the highest star." On the other hand, it places blame for failure squarely on the individual. If you don't make it—in the face of ample opportunities to get ahead—the fault must be your own. The Horatio Alger myth helps to stabilize society, then, for since the fault is viewed as the individual's, not society's, current social arrangements can be regarded as satisfactory. This reduces pressures to change the system.

As Marx and Weber pointed out, social class penetrates our consciousness, shaping our ideas of life and our "proper" place in society. When the rich look at the world around them, they sense superiority and anticipate control over their own destiny. When the poor look around them, they are more likely to sense defeat, and to anticipate that their lives will be buffeted by unpredictable forces. Both rich and poor know the dominant ideology, that their particular niche in life is due to their own efforts, that the reasons for success—or failure—lie solely with the self. Like the fish that don't notice the water, people tend not to perceive the effects of social class on their own lives.

Horatio Alger myth
the belief that due to limitless possibilities anyone can get ahead if he or she tries hard enough

Summary and Review

What Is Social Class?

■ What is meant by the term social class?

Most sociologists have adopted Weber's definition of **social class** as a large group of people who rank close to one another in terms of wealth, power, and prestige. **Wealth,** consisting of property and income, is concentrated in the upper classes. The distribution of wealth in the United States has changed little since World War II, but the changes that have occurred have been toward greater inequality. **Power** is the ability to get one's way even though others resist. C. Wright Mills coined the term **power elite** to refer to the small group that holds the reins of power in business, government, and the military. **Prestige** is often linked to occupational status. Pp. 276–281.

People's rankings of occupational prestige have changed little over the decades and are similar from country to country. Globally, the occupations that bring greater prestige pay more, require more education and abstract thought, and offer greater autonomy. Pp. 281–283.

■ What is meant by the term status inconsistency?

Status is social ranking. Most people are **status consistent;** that is, they rank high or low on all three dimensions of social class. People who rank higher on some dimensions than on others are status inconsistent. The frustrations of **status inconsistency** tend to produce political radicalism. Pp. 283–284.

Sociological Models of Social Class

■ What models are used to portray the social classes?

Erik Wright developed a four-class model based on Marx: (1) capitalists (owners); (2) petty bourgeoisie (small business owners); (3) managers; and (4) workers. Kahl and Gilbert developed a six-class model based on Weber. At the top is the capitalist class. In descending order are the upper middle class, the lower middle class, the working class, the working poor, and the **underclass.** Pp. 284–288.

Consequences of Social Class

■ How does social class affect people's lives?

Social class leaves no aspect of life untouched. It affects our chances of benefiting from the new technology, dying early, becoming ill, receiving good health care, and getting divorced. Social class membership also affects child rearing, educational attainment, religious affiliation, political participation, and contact with the criminal justice system. Pp. 288–293.

Social Mobility

■ What are the three types of social mobility?

The term **intergenerational mobility** refers to changes in social class from one generation to the next. **Exchange mobility** is the movement of large numbers of people from one class to another, with the net result that the relative proportions of the population in the classes remain about the same. The term **structural mobility** refers to changes in society that lead large numbers of people to change their social class. Pp. 294–295.

Poverty

■ Who are the poor?

Poverty is unequally distributed in the United States. Minorities, children, women-headed households, and rural Americans are more likely than others to be poor. The poverty rate of the elderly is less than that of the general population. Pp. 295–300.

■ Why are people poor?

Some social analysts believe that characteristics of *individuals,* such as the desire for immediate gratification, cause poverty. Sociologists, in contrast, examine *structural* features of society, such as employment opportunities, to find the causes of poverty. Sociologists generally conclude that life orientations are a consequence, not the cause, of people's position in the social class structure. Pp. 300–302.

■ How is the Horatio Alger myth functional for society?

The **Horatio Alger myth**—the belief that anyone can get ahead if only he or she tries hard enough—encourages people to strive to get ahead. It also deflects blame for failure from society to the individual. Pp. 302–303.

■ *Where can I read more on this topic?*

Suggested readings for this chapter are at the end of this book.

All URLs listed are current as of the printing of this book. URLs often change. Please check our Web site, **http://www.abacon.com/henslin,** for updates.

Additional Online Resources for This Chapter
www.ablongman.com/henslin6e

■ *Content Select* Research Database for Sociology, with suggested key terms and annotated references
■ Link to 2000 Census, with activities
■ Flashcards of key terms and concepts

■ Practice Tests
■ Weblinks
■ Interactive Maps

using . . .
ContentSelect

Research Database for Sociology

culture of poverty	poverty line	the capitalist class	welfare reform
feminization	social class	underclass	working poor
of poverty	social mobility	wealth and income	

11

Sex and Gender

Issues of Sex and Gender

Gender Differences
in Behavior: Biology
or Culture?

The Dominant Position
in Sociology

Opening the Door
to Biology

**Gender Inequality in
Global Perspective**

Sex Typing of Work

Prestige of Work

Other Areas of Global
Discrimination

**How Females Became
a Minority Group**

The Origins of Patriarchy

**Gender Inequality in the
United States**

Fighting Back: The Rise
of Feminism

Gender Inequality
in Education

Gender Inequality
in Everyday Life

**Gender Inequality
in the Workplace**

The Pay Gap

The Glass Ceiling and the
Glass Escalator

The "Mommy Track"

Sexual Harassment

Gender and Violence

Feminism and Gendered
Violence

Solutions

**The Changing Face
of Politics**

**Glimpsing the Future—
With Hope**

Summary and Review

I n Tunis, the capital of Tunisia, on Africa's northern coast, I met some U.S. college students, with whom I spent a couple of days. When they said that they wanted to see Tunis' red light district, I wondered if it would be worth the trip. I already had seen other red light districts, including the unusual one in Amsterdam where the state licenses the women, requires medical checkups (certificates must be posted so customers can check them), sets the prices, and pays the prostitutes social security benefits upon retirement. The women sit behind lighted picture windows while customers stroll along the canal side streets and browse from the outside.

> The wharf was crowded with men who were eyeing the women.

This time, the sight turned my stomach.

We ended up on a wharf that extended into the Mediterranean. Each side was lined with a row of one-room wooden shacks, each one crowded up against the next. In front of each open door stood a young woman. Peering from outside into the dark interiors, I could see that each door led to a tiny room with a well-worn bed.

The wharf was crowded with men who were eyeing the women. Many of them wore sailor uniforms from countries that I couldn't identify.

As I looked more closely, I could see that some of the women had runny sores on their legs. Incredibly, with such visible evidence of their disease, customers still entered. Evidently the low price (at that time $2) was too much to resist.

With a sickening feeling in my stomach and the desire to vomit,
I kept a good distance between myself and the beckoning women.
One tour of the two-block area was more than sufficient.

Out of sight, I knew, was a group of men whose wealth derived
from exploiting these women who were condemned to live short lives
punctuated by fear and misery.

I n this chapter, we examine **gender stratification**—males' and females' unequal access to power, prestige, and property. Gender is especially significant because it is a *master status;* that is, it cuts across *all* aspects of social life. No matter what we attain in life, we carry the label *male* or *female*. These labels carry images and expectations about how we should act. They not only guide our behavior, but also serve as a basis of power and privilege.

In this chapter's fascinating journey, we shall look at inequality between the sexes around the world and in the United States. We shall explore whether it is biology or culture that makes us the way we are, and review sexual harassment, unequal pay, and violence against women. This excursion will provide a good context for understanding the power differences between men and women that lead to situations such as the one just described in our opening vignette. It should also give you insight into your own experiences with gender.

Issues of Sex and Gender

W hen we consider how females and males differ, the first thing that usually comes to mind is **sex**, the *biological characteristics* that distinguish males and females. *Primary sex characteristics* consist of a vagina or a penis and other organs related to reproduction. *Secondary sex characteristics* are the physical distinctions between males and females that are not directly connected with reproduction. Secondary sex characteristics become clearly evident at puberty when males develop more muscles and a lower voice, and gain more body hair and height, while females form more fatty tissue and broader hips, and develop breasts.

Gender, in contrast, is a *social*, not a biological characteristic. **Gender** consists of whatever a group considers proper for its males and females. Consequently, gender varies from one society to another. Whereas *sex* refers to male or female, *gender* refers to masculinity or femininity. In short, you inherit your sex, but you learn your gender as you are socialized into the behaviors and attitudes your culture asserts are appropriate for your sex.

The expectations associated with gender vary around the world, as illustrated in the photo montage on the next page. They vary so greatly that some sociologists suggest we replace masculinity and femininity with masculinities and femininities (Beynon 2002).

The sociological significance of gender is that it is a device by which society controls its members. Gender sorts us, on the basis of sex, into different life experiences. It opens and closes doors to power, property, and even prestige. Like social class, gender is a structural feature of society.

Before examining inequalities of gender, let's consider why the behaviors of men and women differ.

gender stratification
males' and females' unequal access to power, prestige, and property on the basis of their sex

sex
biological characteristics that distinguish females and males, consisting of primary and secondary sex characteristics

gender
the social characteristics that a society considers proper for its males and females; masculinity or femininity

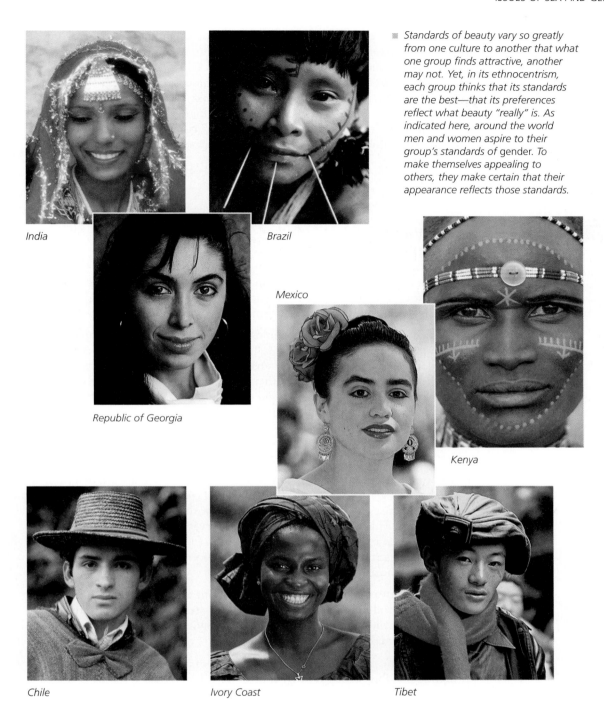

India

Brazil

Mexico

Republic of Georgia

Kenya

Chile

Ivory Coast

Tibet

■ Standards of beauty vary so greatly from one culture to another that what one group finds attractive, another may not. Yet, in its ethnocentrism, each group thinks that its standards are the best—that its preferences reflect what beauty "really" is. As indicated here, around the world men and women aspire to their group's standards of gender. To make themselves appealing to others, they make certain that their appearance reflects those standards.

■ Gender Differences in Behavior: Biology or Culture?

Why are most males more aggressive than most females? Why do women enter "nurturing" occupations such as nursing in far greater numbers than men? To answer such questions, many people respond with some variation of "They're just born that way."

Is this the correct answer? Certainly biology plays a significant role in our lives. Each of us begins as a fertilized egg. The egg, or ovum, is contributed by our mother, the sperm that fertilizes the egg by our father. At the very moment the egg is fertilized our sex is determined. Each of us receives twenty-three pairs of chromosomes

■ *Cynthia Fuchs Epstein, whose position in the ongoing "nature versus nurture" debate is summarized here.*

from the ovum and twenty-three from the sperm. The egg has an X chromosome. If the sperm that fertilizes the egg also has an X chromosome, we become a girl (XX). If the sperm has a Y chromosome, we become a boy (XY).

That's the biology. Now, the sociological question is, Does this biological difference control our behavior? Does it, for example, make females more nurturing and submissive and males more aggressive and domineering? Almost all sociologists take the side of "nurture" in this "nature versus nurture" controversy, but some do not, as you can see from the following Thinking Critically section.

thinking
CRITICALLY

Biology Versus Culture— Culture Is the Answer

F or sociologist Cynthia Fuchs Epstein (1986, 1988, 1989), differences between the behavior of males and females are solely the result of social factors— specifically, socialization and social control. Her argument is as follows:

1. A reexamination of the anthropological record shows greater equality between the sexes in the past than we had thought. In earlier societies, women, as well as men, hunted small game, made tools, and gathered food. In today's hunting and gathering societies, the roles of both women and men are broader and less rigid than those created by stereotypes. For example, the Agta and Mbuti are egalitarian. This proves that hunting and gathering societies exist in which women are not subordinate to men. Anthropologists claim that in these societies there is a separate but equal status of women at this level of development.

2. The types of work that men and women do in each society are determined not by biology but by social arrangements. Few people can escape these arrangements, and almost everyone works within his or her allotted narrow range. This gender division of work serves the interests of men, and it is enforced by both informal customs and formal laws. When these socially constructed barriers are removed, women's work habits are similar to those of men.

3. Biology "causes" some human behaviors, but these are limited to those involving reproduction or differences in body structure. These differences are relevant for only a few activities, such as playing basketball or "crawling through a small space."

4. Female crime rates are rising in many parts of the world. This indicates that aggression, which is often considered a biologically dictated male behavior, is related instead to social factors. When social conditions permit, such as when women become lawyers, they, too, become "adversarial, assertive, and dominant." Not incidentally, another form of this "dominant behavior" is the challenge women have made in scholarly journals to the biased views about human nature proposed by men.

In short, rather than "women's incompetence or inability to read a legal brief, perform brain surgery, [or] to predict a bull market," social factors—socialization, gender discrimination, and other forms of social control—create gender differences in behavior. Arguments that assign "an evolutionary and genetic basis" to explain differences between the behaviors of women and men are simplistic. They "rest on a dubious structure of inappropriate, highly selective, and poor data, oversimplification in logic and in inappropriate inferences by use of analogy."

thinking
CRITICALLY

Biology Versus Culture— Biology Is the Answer

S ociologist Steven Goldberg (1974, 1986, 1993) finds it astonishing that anyone should doubt "the presence of core-deep differences in males and females, differences of temperament and emotion we call masculinity and femininity." Goldberg's argument—that it is not environment but inborn differences that "give masculine and feminine direction to the emotions and behaviors of men and women"—is as follows:

1. The anthropological record shows that all societies for which evidence exists are (or were) **patriarchies** (societies in which men dominate women). Stories about long-lost **matriarchies** (societies in which women dominate men) are myths.

2. In all societies, past and present, the highest statuses are associated with men. In every society, politics is ruled by "hierarchies overwhelmingly dominated by men."

3. The reason why men dominate societies is that they "have a lower threshold for the elicitation of dominance behavior . . . a greater tendency to exhibit whatever behavior is necessary in any environment to attain dominance in hierarchies and male-female encounters and relationships." Men are more willing "to sacrifice the rewards of other motivations—the desire for affection, health, family life, safety, relaxation, vacation and the like— in order to attain dominance and status."

4. Just as a 6-foot woman does not prove the social basis of height, so exceptional individuals, such as highly achieving and dominant women, do not refute "the physiological roots of behavior."

In short, only one interpretation of why every society from that of the Pygmy to that of the Swede associates dominance and attainment with men is valid. Male dominance of society is "an inevitable resolution of the psychophysiological reality." Socialization and social institutions merely *reflect*—and sometimes exaggerate—inborn tendencies. Any interpretation other than inborn differences is "wrongheaded, ignorant, tendentious, internally illogical, discordant with the evidence, and implausible in the extreme." The argument that males are more aggressive because they have been socialized that way is the equivalent of a claim that men can grow moustaches because boys have been socialized that way.

To acknowledge this reality is *not* to defend discrimination against women. Whether or not one approves what societies have done with these basic biological differences is not the issue. The point is that biology leads males and females to different behaviors and attitudes—regardless of how we feel about this or wish it were different.

■ *Steven Goldberg, whose position in the ongoing "nature versus nurture" debate is summarized here.*

■ The Dominant Position in Sociology

The dominant sociological position is that social factors, not biology, are the reasons we behave the way we do. Our visible differences of sex do not come with meanings built into them. Rather, each human group makes its own interpretation of these physical differences and on that basis assigns males and females to separate groups. There, people learn what is expected of them and are given different access to their society's privileges.

patriarchy
a society in which men dominate women

matriarchy
a society in which women dominate men

Most sociologists find compelling the argument that if biology were the principal factor in human behavior, all around the world we would find women to be one sort of person and men another. In fact, however, ideas of gender vary greatly from one culture to another—and, as a result, so do male-female behaviors. The Tahitians in the South Pacific stand in remarkable contrast to our usual expectations of gender. They don't give their children names that are identifiable as male or female, and they don't divide their labor on the basis of gender. They expect *both* men and women to be passive, yielding, and to ignore slights. Neither males nor females are competitive in trying to attain material possessions (Gilmore 1990).

■ Opening the Door to Biology

The matter of "nature" versus "nurture" is not so easily settled, however, and some sociologists acknowledge that biological factors are involved in some human behavior other than reproduction and childbearing (Udry 2000). For example, Alice Rossi, a feminist sociologist and former president of the American Sociological Association, has suggested that women are better prepared biologically for "mothering" than are men. She (1977, 1984) says that women are more sensitive to the infant's soft skin and to their nonverbal communications. Rossi stresses that the issue is not either biology or society. It is that nature provides biological predispositions, which are then overlaid with culture.

To see why the door to biology is opening, just slightly, in sociology, let's consider a medical accident and a study of Vietnam veterans.

A Medical Accident The drama began in 1963, when 7-month-old identical twins were taken to a doctor to be circumcised (Money and Ehrhardt 1972). The inept physician, who was using electrocautery (a heated needle), turned the electric current too high and accidentally burned off the penis of one of the boys. You can imagine the parents' reaction of disbelief, followed by horror, as the truth sank in.

What can be done in a situation like this? The damage was irreversible. The parents were told that their boy could never have sexual relations. After months of soul-searching and tearful consultations with experts, the parents decided that their son should have a sex change operation. When he was 17 months old, surgeons castrated the boy, using the skin to construct a vagina. The parents then gave the child a new name, Brenda, dressed him in frilly clothing, let his hair grow long, and began to treat him as a girl. Later, physicians gave Brenda female steroids to promote female pubertal growth.

At first, the results were promising. When the twins were 4 years old, the mother said (remember that the children are biologically identical):

> One thing that really amazes me is that she is so feminine. I've never seen a little girl so neat and tidy. . . . She likes for me to wipe her face. She doesn't like to be dirty, and yet my son is quite different. I can't wash his face for anything. . . . She is very proud of herself, when she puts on a new dress, or I set her hair. . . . She seems to be daintier. (Money and Ehrhardt 1972)

About a year later, the mother described how their daughter imitated her while their son copied his father:

> I found that my son, he chose very masculine things like a fireman or a policeman. . . . He wanted to do what daddy does, work where daddy does, and carry a lunch kit. . . . [My daughter] didn't want any of those things. She wants to be a doctor or a teacher. . . . But none of the things that she ever wanted to be were like a policeman or a fireman, and that sort of thing never appealed to her. (Money and Ehrhardt 1972)

If the matter were this clear-cut, we could use this case to conclude that gender is entirely up to nurture. Seldom are things in life so simple, however, and a twist occurs in this story. Despite this promising start and her parents' coaching, Brenda did not adapt well to femininity. She preferred to mimic her father shaving, rather than her mother putting on makeup. She rejected dolls, favoring guns and her brother's toys. She liked rough and tumble games and insisted on urinating standing up. Classmates teased her and called her a "caveman" because she walked like a boy. At age 14, she was expelled from school for beating up a girl who teased her. Despite estrogen treatment, she was not attracted to boys, and at age 14, in despair over her inner turmoil, she was thinking of suicide. In a tearful confrontation, her father told her about the accident and her sex change.

"All of a sudden everything clicked. For the first time, things made sense, and I understood who and what I was," the twin says of this revelation. Bruce (his new name) then requested male hormone shots, and later had surgery to partially reconstruct a penis. At age 25, he married a woman and adopted her children (Diamond and Sigmundson 1997).

The Vietnam Veterans Study   In many studies, researchers have found that boys and men who have higher levels of testosterone tend to be more aggressive. Some of the findings are intriguing. In one study, researchers compared the testosterone levels of college men in a "rowdy" fraternity with those of men in a fraternity that had a reputation for academic success and social responsibility. Men in the "rowdy" fraternity had higher levels of testosterone (Dabbs et al. 1996). In another study, researchers compared the levels of testosterone in prisoners who had committed property crimes with those of prisoners who had committed sex crimes and acts of violence against people. Those who had committed the crimes of sex and violence had higher levels of testosterone (Dabbs et al. 1995). The samples were small, and you never knew if the findings of a particular study were due to chance.

Then in 1985, the U.S. government began a health study of Vietnam veterans. To be certain the study was representative, the researchers chose a random sample of 4,462 men. Among the data they collected was a measurement of testosterone for each veteran. Now, unexpectedly, sociologists had a large random sample available, and it is providing surprising clues about human behavior.

This sample supports earlier studies showing that men who have higher levels of testosterone tend to be more aggressive and to have more problems as a consequence. When the veterans with higher testosterone were boys, they were more likely to get in trouble with parents and teachers and to become delinquents. As adults, they are more likely to use hard drugs, to get into fights, to end up in lower-status jobs, and to have more sexual partners. Knowing this, you probably won't find it surprising to learn that they are also less likely to marry—certainly their low-paying jobs and trouble with authorities make them less appealing candidates for marriage. Those who do marry are less likely to share problems with their wives. They also are more likely to have affairs, to hit their wives, and, it follows, to get divorced (Dabbs and Morris 1990; Booth and Dabbs 1993).

Fortunately for us sociologists, the Vietnam veterans study does not leave us with biology as the sole basis for behavior. Not all men with high testosterone get in trouble with the law, do poorly in school, or mistreat their wives. A chief difference, in fact, is social class. High-testosterone men from higher social classes are less likely to be involved in antisocial behaviors than are high-testosterone men from lower social classes (Dabbs and Morris 1990). *Social* factors (socialization, life goals,

■ *Sociologists stress the social factors that underlie human behavior, the experiences that mold us, funneling us into different directions in life. The study of Vietnam veterans discussed in the text is one indication of how the sociological door is slowly opening to also consider biological factors in human behavior. Shown here are men of the 173rd Airborne Brigade in a "search and destroy" patrol in Tuy Province, Vietnam, in June 1966.*

self-definitions), then, also play a part. Uncovering the social factors and discovering how they work in combination with testosterone will be of high sociological interest.

IN SUM ■ ■ ■ ■ ■

We shall have to await further studies, but the initial findings are intriguing. They indicate that some behavior that we sociologists usually assume to be due entirely to socialization is also influenced by biology. The findings are preliminary, but significant and provocative. In the years to come, this should prove to be an exciting—and controversial—area of sociological research. One level of research will be to determine if any behaviors are due only to biology. The second level will be to discover how social factors modify biology. The third level will be, in sociologist Janet Chafetz's (1990:30) phrase, to determine how "different" becomes translated into "unequal."

Gender Inequality in Global Perspective

Some analysts speculate that in hunting and gathering societies women and men were social equals (Leacock 1981; Hendrix 1994). Apparently horticultural societies also had less gender discrimination than does our contemporary world (Collins et al. 1993). In these societies, women may have contributed about 60 percent of the group's total food. Yet, after reviewing the historical record, historian and feminist Gerda Lerner (1986) concluded that "there is not a single society known where women-as-a-group have decision-making power over men (as a group)."

Let's take a brief overview of some of this global inequality.

Sex Typing of Work

Anthropologist George Murdock (1937) surveyed 324 premodern societies around the world. He found that in all of them activities are **sex typed.** In other words, every society associates activities with one sex or the other. He also found that activities that are considered "female" in one society may be considered "male" in another. In some groups, for example, taking care of cattle is women's work, while other groups assign this task to men.

Metalworking was the exception; it was considered men's work in all the societies Murdock examined. Three other pursuits—making weapons, pursuing sea mammals, and hunting—were almost universally the domain of men. In a few societies, however, women participated in these activities. Although Murdock found no specific work that was universally assigned to women only, he did find that making clothing, cooking, carrying water, and grinding grain were almost always female tasks. In a few societies, however, such activities were regarded as men's work.

From Murdock's cross-cultural survey, we can conclude that nothing about biology requires men and women to be assigned different work. Anatomy does not have to equal destiny when it comes to occupations, for as we have seen, pursuits that are considered feminine in one society may be deemed masculine in another, and vice versa.

sex typing
the association of behaviors with one sex or the other

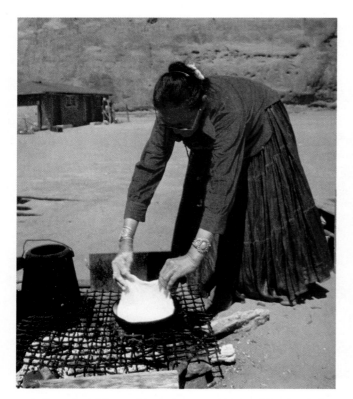

■ *Anthropologist George Murdock surveyed 324 traditional societies worldwide. In all of them, some work was considered "men's work", while other tasks were considered "women's work". He found that almost universally cooking is considered women's work. This Navaho woman is making fry bread over an open fire in Monument Valley, Arizona.*

Prestige of Work

You might ask whether this division of labor really illustrates social inequality. Does it perhaps simply represent arbitrary forms of dividing up labor, not gender discrimination?

That could be the case, except for this finding: *Universally, greater prestige is given to male activities—regardless of what those activities are* (Linton 1936; Rosaldo 1974). If taking care of goats is men's work, then the care of goats is considered important and carries high prestige, but if it is women's work, it is considered less important and given less prestige. Or, to take an example closer to home, when delivering babies was "women's work" and was done by midwives, it was given low prestige. But when men took over this task, its prestige increased sharply (Ehrenreich and English 1973). In short, it is not the work that provides the prestige, but the sex with which the work is associated.

Other Areas of Global Discrimination

Let's briefly consider four additional aspects of global gender discrimination. Later, when we focus on the United States, we shall examine these topics in greater detail.

Education   Two figures illustrate how extensively females are discriminated against in education: Almost 1 billion adults around the world cannot read; two-thirds are women ("State of . . . " 2001). Approximately 130 million children are not enrolled in grade school; about two-thirds are girls (Ashford 1995). Table 11.1 illustrates this point further. From this table, you can see that females usually are less literate than males—but not

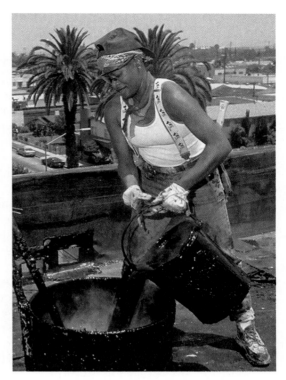

■ *Throughout history, women have been denied the right to pursue various occupations on the basis of presumed biological characteristics. As society—and sex roles—have changed, women have increasingly entered occupations traditionally reserved for men.*

| TABLE 11.1 | Literacy and Gender: Literacy Rates in Least Industrialized and Industrializing Nations |

Country	Women	Men	Country	Women	Men	Country	Women	Men
Nepal	14%	41%	Laos	44%	69%	Zimbabwe	80%	90%
Sierra Leone	18%	45%	Iraq	45%	71%	Dominican Republic	82%	82%
Mali	23%	39%	Nigeria	47%	67%	South Africa	82%	82%
Mozambique	23%	58%	Guatemala	49%	62%	Venezuela	90%	92%
Ethiopia	25%	46%	Gabon	53%	74%	Lebanon	90%	95%
Bangladesh	26%	49%	Ghana	54%	76%	Colombia	91%	91%
Morocco	31%	57%	Papua New Guinea	63%	81%	Thailand	92%	96%
Sudan	35%	58%	Kenya	70%	86%	Costa Rica	95%	95%
India	36%	66%	Turkey	72%	92%	Cuba	95%	96%
Egypt	39%	64%	Indonesia	78%	90%	Uruguay	98%	97%

Source: UNESCO: Institute for Statistics, 2000.

always. In four of the countries listed, females and males have identical literacy rates, and in one their rate is slightly higher.

Politics   That women lack equal access to national decision making can be illustrated by this global fact: No national legislature in the entire world has as many women as men. Women come closest to having equal representation in Norway, where 40 percent of the legislators are women, but in some countries, such as South Korea and Egypt, the total is only 1 or 2 percent (Riley 1997; Ashford 2001). In Kuwait and United Arab Emirates, women can't even vote (Crossette 1995a, b). In most nations, women hold only about 11 percent of the seats in parliaments and congresses (Ashford 2001).

The Pay Gap   In every nation, women average less pay than men. In the United States, full-time working women average about 70 percent of what men are paid (see Figure 11.6 on page 329), while in South Korea women make only half of what men earn (Monk-Turner and Turner 2000).

Violence Against Women   A global human rights issue is violence against women. Infamous historical examples are foot binding in China, witch burning in Europe, and *suttee* (burning the living widow with her dead husband's body) in India. Today we have rape, wife beating, female infanticide, and forced prostitution, which was likely the case in our opening vignette. Perhaps today's most notorious current example is female circumcision, the topic of the Perspectives box on the next page.

■ *Foot binding, a form of violence against women, was practiced in China. This photo of a woman in Canton, China, is from the early 1900s. The woman's tiny feet, which made it difficult for her to walk, were a "marker" of status, indicating that her husband was wealthy and did not need her labor. It also made her dependent on him.*

cultural d-i-v-e-r-s-i-t-y

Africa

Around the World

Female Circumcision

Female circumcision is common in parts of Muslim Africa and in some parts of Malaysia and Indonesia. Often called female genital mutilation (FGM) by Westerners, this practice is also known as clitoral excision, clitoridectomy, infibulation, and labiadectomy, depending on how much of the tissue is removed. Worldwide, between 100 million and 200 million females have been circumcised.

In some cultures, only the girl's clitoris is cut off; in others, much more is removed. In Sudan, the Nubia cut away most of the girl's genitalia, then sew together the remaining outer edges. They bind the girl's legs from ankles to waist for several weeks while scar tissue closes up the vagina. They leave a small opening the size of a pencil for the passage of urine and menstrual fluids.

Among most groups, the surgery takes place between the ages of 4 and 8. In some cultures, it occurs seven to ten days after birth. In others, it is not performed until girls reach adolescence. Because the surgery is usually done without anesthesia, the pain is so excruciating that adults must hold the girl down. In urban areas, physcians sometimes perform the operation; in rural areas, it is usually performed by a neighborhood woman.

Shock, bleeding, infection, infertility, and death are among the risks. Vaginal spasms, painful intercourse, and lack of orgasms are common consequences. Because the tiny opening makes urination and menstruation difficult, urinary tract infections are common as urine and menstrual flow build up behind the opening.

When a woman marries, the opening is cut wider to permit sexual intercourse. In some groups, this is the husband's responsibility. Before a woman gives birth, the opening is enlarged further. After

birth, the vagina is again sutured shut, a cycle of surgically closing and opening that begins anew with each birth.

A woman who was circumcised at 12, described her ordeal this way:

"Lie down there," the excisor suddenly said to me, pointing to a mat on the ground. No sooner had I laid down than I felt my frail, thin legs grasped by heavy hands and pulled wide apart. I lifted my head. Two women on each side of me pinned me to the ground. I would have given anything at that moment to be a thousand miles away. Then a shooting pain brought me back to reality. I underwent the ablation of the labia minor and then of the clitoris. The operation seemed to go on forever. I was in the throes of agony, torn apart both physically and psychologically. It was the rule that girls of my age did not weep in this situation. I broke the rule. I cried and screamed with pain. Never have I felt such excruciating pain!

Afterwards they forced me, not only to walk back to join the other girls who had already been excised, but to dance with them. I was doing my best, but then I fainted. . . . It was a month before I was completely healed. When I was better, everyone mocked me, as I hadn't been brave, they said. (Walker and Parmar 1993: 107–108)

What are the reasons for this custom? Some groups believe that it reduces female sexual desire, thus making it more likely that a woman will be a virgin at marriage, and, afterward, will remain faithful to her husband. Others think that it enhances fertility and vaginal cleanliness.

Feminists call female circumcision a form of ritual torture to control female sexuality. They point out that men dominate the societies that practice it. Mothers

cooperate with the surgery because in these societies an uncircumcised woman is considered impure and is not allowed to marry. Grandmothers insist that the custom continue out of concern that their granddaughters marry well.

Some immigrants to the United States take their daughters back to their homeland for the operation. Others pool their money and fly in an excisor who performs the surgery on several girls. In 1997, the United States passed a law that makes arranging or performing female circumcision punishable by up to five years in prison.

Change is coming in the nations that practice female circumcision. In a landmark case in Kenya, two young girls obtained a court order restraining their father from having them circumcised. Their community was shocked, but an attorney reminded the court that Kenya had signed human rights agreements.

for your consideration

Do you think that Western nations should try to make African nations stop this custom? Or would this be ethnocentric, the imposition of Western values on other cultures? As one Somali woman said, "The Somali woman doesn't need an alien woman telling her how to treat her private parts." What legitimate basis do you think there is for members of one culture to interfere with another?

Sources: Based on Mahran 1978, 1981; Ebomoyi 1987; Lightfoot-Klein 1989; Merwine 1993; Walker and Parmar 1993; Chalkley 1997; Collymore 2000; "Kenya" . . . 2001.

How Females Became a Minority Group

A round the world, gender is *the* primary division between people. Every society sets up barriers to provide unequal access to power, property, and prestige on the basis of sex. Consequently, sociologists classify females as a **minority group.** Because in most countries females outnumber males, you may think this strange. This term, however, refers to people who are discriminated against on the basis of physical or cultural characteristics, and it applies to females (Hacker 1951). For an overview of gender discrimination in a changing society, see the Cultural Diversity box below.

Have females always been a minority group? As we just saw, some analysts speculate that in horticultural and hunting and gathering societies women and men may have been social equals—or that at least there was much less gender discrimination than we have today. How did it happen, then, that around the world women came to be systematically discriminated against? Let's consider the primary theory that has been proposed.

The Origins of Patriarchy

minority group
a group that is discriminated against on the basis of its members' physical or cultural characteristics

The major theory of the origin of patriarchy—men dominating society—points to the social consequences of human reproduction (Lerner 1986; Friedl 1990). In early human history, life was short, and in order to reproduce the human group, many children had to be born. Because only females get pregnant, carry a child for nine months, give birth, and nurse, women were limited in their activities for a con-

cultural d·i·v·e·r·s·i·t·y

Around the World

"Pssst. You Wanna Buy a Bride?" China in Transition

N guyen Thi Hoan, age 22, thanked her lucky stars. A Vietnamese country girl, she had just arrived in Hanoi to look for work, and while she was still at the bus station a woman offered her a job in a candy factory.

It was a trap. After Nguyen had loaded a few sacks of sugar, the woman took her into the country to "get supplies." There some men took her to China, which was only 100 miles away. Nguyen was put up for auction, along with a 16-year-old Vietnamese girl. Each brought $350, a small fortune in China. Nguyen was traded from one bride dealer to another until she was taken to a Chinese village. There she was introduced to her new husband, who had paid $700 for her (Marshall 1999).

Why are tens of thousands of women kidnapped and sold as brides in China each year (Rosenthal 2001a)? First, parts of China have a centuries-long tradition of bride selling. Second, China has a shortage of women. The government enforces a "one couple-one child" policy. Since sons are preferred, female infanticide has become common (a topic explored on page 609). One result is a shortage of women of marriageable age. In some provinces, for every 100 women there are over 120 men. Yet 100 percent of the men are expected to marry and produce heirs (Rosenthal 2001a).

Actually, Nguyen was lucky. Some kidnapped women are sold as prostitutes.

Bride selling and forced prostitution are millennia old practices. But China is

also entering a new era, which is bringing with it new pressures for Chinese women. Ideas of beauty are changing, and blonde, blue-eyed women are becoming a fetish. As a consequence, Chinese women feel a pressure to "Westernize" their bodies. Surgeons promise to give them bigger breasts and Western-looking eyes. A Western style of advertising is gaining ground, too: Scantily clad women now perch on top of sports cars (Chen 1995; Johansson 1999; Yat-ming Sin and Hon-ming Yau 2001).

China in transition . . . It is bringing back the old, bride selling, while moving toward the new, Western ideas of beauty and advertising. In both the old and new, women are commodities for the consumption of men.

siderable part of their lives. To survive, an infant needed a nursing mother. With a child at her breast or in her uterus, or one carried on her hip or on her back, women were physically encumbered. Consequently, around the world women assumed tasks that were associated with the home and child care, while men took over the hunting of large animals and other tasks that required greater speed and absence from the base camp for longer periods of time (Huber 1990).

As a consequence, men became dominant. It was they who left camp to hunt animals, who made contact with other tribes, who traded with these other groups, and who quarreled and waged war with them. It was also the men who made and controlled the instruments of death, the weapons used for hunting and warfare. It was they who accumulated possessions in trade, and gained prestige by triumphantly returning with prisoners of war or with large animals to feed the tribe. In contrast, little prestige was given to the ordinary, routine, taken-for-granted activities of women—who were not seen as risking their lives for the group. Eventually, men took over society. Their weapons, items of trade, and knowledge gained from contact with other groups became sources of power. Women became second-class citizens, subject to men's decisions.

Is this theory correct? Remember that the answer lies buried in human history, and there is no way of testing it. Male dominance may be due to some entirely different cause. For example, anthropologist Marvin Harris (1977) proposed that because most men are stronger than most women and hand-to-hand combat was necessary in tribal groups, men became the warriors and women the reward to entice them to do battle. Frederick Engels proposed that patriarchy developed with the origin of private property (Lerner 1986; Mezentseva 2001). He could not explain why private property should have produced male dominance, however. Gerda Lerner (1986) suggests that patriarchy may even have had different origins in different places.

Whatever its origins, a circular system of thought evolved. Men came to think of themselves as inherently superior—based on the evidence that they dominated society.

■ *A theory of how patriarchy originated centers on childbirth. Because only women give birth, they assumed tasks associated with home and child care, while men hunted and performed other survival tasks that required greater strength, speed, and absence from home. As this woman from the Kpelle tribe in Liberia pounds palm fruit, she also takes care of her children. As you can see, her daughter is already practicing her adult role.*

■ *The burqua worn by Arab women is viewed by many as a form of male domination, a way to suppress women's individuality, freedom, and sexuality. After the Taliban were deposed by U.S. troops, one of the first things some women did was to throw off their burquas and veils.*

They surrounded many of their activities with secrecy, and constructed elaborate rules and rituals to avoid "contamination" by females, whom they openly deemed inferior by that time. Even today, patriarchy is always accompanied by cultural supports designed to justify male dominance—such as certain activities not being "appropriate" for women.

As tribal societies developed into larger groups, men, who enjoyed their power and privileges, maintained their dominance. Long after hunting and hand-to-hand combat ceased to be routine, and even after large numbers of children were no longer needed in order to reproduce the human group, men held on to their power. Male dominance in contemporary societies, then, is a continuation of a millennia-old pattern whose origin is lost in history.

Gender Inequality in the United States

Gender inequality is not some accidental, hit-or-miss affair. Rather, the institutions of each society work together to maintain the group's particular forms of inequality. Customs, often venerated throughout history, both justify and maintain these arrangements. Although men have resisted sharing their privileged positions with women, change has come.

Fighting Back: The Rise of Feminism

To see how far we have come, it is useful to see where we used to be. In early U.S. society, the second-class status of women was taken for granted. A husband and wife were legally one person—him (Chafetz and Dworkin 1986). Women could not serve on juries, nor could they vote, make legal contracts, or hold property in their own name. How could times have changed so much that these examples sound like fiction?

A central lesson of conflict theory is that power yields privilege; like a magnet, it draws society's best resources to the elite. Because men tenaciously held on to their privileges and used social institutions to maintain their position, basic rights for women came only through prolonged and bitter struggle.

Feminism, the view that biology is not destiny and that stratification by gender is wrong and should be resisted, met with strong opposition—both by men who had privilege to lose and by women who accepted their status as morally correct. In 1916, feminists, then known as suffragists, founded the National Women's Party. In January 1917, they formed a picket line around the White House. After picketing continuously for six months, the picketers were arrested. Hundreds were sent to prison, including Lucy Burns and Alice Paul, two leaders of the National Women's Party. The extent to which these women had threatened male prerogatives is demonstrated by their treatment in prison.

> Two men brought in Dorothy Day [the editor of a periodical that espoused women's rights], twisting her arms above her head. Suddenly they lifted her and brought her body down twice over the back of an iron bench. . . . They had been there a few minutes when Mrs. Lewis, all doubled over like a sack of flour, was thrown in. Her head struck the iron bed and she fell to the floor senseless. As for Lucy Burns, they handcuffed her wrists and fastened the handcuffs over [her] head to the cell door. (Cowley 1969)

feminism
the philosophy that men and women should be politically, economically, and socially equal; an organized activity on behalf of this principle

This "first wave" of the women's movement had a radical branch that wanted to reform all the institutions of society, and a conservative branch that concentrated on winning the vote for women (Chafetz and Dworkin 1986; Freedman 2001). The

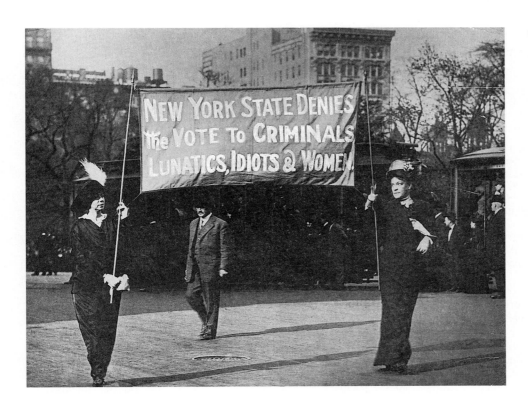

The women's struggle for equal rights has been long and hard. Shown here is a 1919 photo from the "first wave" of the U.S. women's movement. Only against enormous opposition from men did U.S. women win the right to vote. They first voted in national elections in 1920.

conservative branch dominated, and after the vote was won in 1920 the movement basically dissolved.

The "second wave" began in the 1960s. Sociologist Janet Chafetz (1990) points out that up to this time most women thought of work as a temporary activity intended to fill the time between completing school and getting married. As more women took jobs, however, and many began to think of paid work as a career, they started to compare their working conditions with those of men. This shift in their reference group radically changed the way they viewed their working conditions. The result was a "second wave" of protest and struggle against gender inequalities. The goals of this second wave (which continues today) are broad—they range from changing women's work roles to changing policies on violence against women.

This second wave of the women's movement also has its liberal and conservative branches. Although each holds a different view of what gender equality should look like, the two share several goals, including equality in job opportunities and pay. Both liberals and conservatives have a radical wing. The radicals on the liberal side call for hostility toward men; radicals on the conservative side favor a return to traditional family roles. All factions—whether radical or conservative—claim to represent the "real" needs of today's women. It is from these claims and counterclaims that the women's movement will continue to take shape and affect public policy.

Apparently, a "third wave" of feminism is emerging. In this third wave, the focus is switching from equal opportunity for women (although this goal remains) to the values that underlie work and the social institutions. Feminists point out that these values—power, competition, emotional invulnerability, toughness, autonomy, and independence—represent "male" qualities. These values need to be supplemented, if not replaced, with "female" values—cooperation, openness about vulnerability, gentleness, connection, and interdependence (England 2000). If this is really the beginning of a third wave, not just a switch in focus, we can assume that it, too, will have its liberal, conservative, and radical branches.

down-to-earth sociology

Making the Invisible Visible—The Deadly Effects of Sexism

Medical researchers were perplexed. Reports were coming in from all over the country: Women were twice as likely as men to die after coronary bypass surgery. Researchers at Cedars-Sinai Medical Center in Los Angeles checked their own records. They found that of 2,300 coronary bypass patients, 4.6 percent of the women died as a result of the surgery, compared with 2.6 percent of the men.

These findings presented a sociological puzzle. To solve it, researchers first turned to biology (Bishop 1990). In coronary bypass surgery, a blood vessel is taken from one part of the body and stitched to a coronary artery on the surface of the heart. Perhaps this operation was more difficult to perform on women because they have smaller coronary arteries. To find out, researchers measured the amount of time that surgeons kept patients on the heart-lung machine while they operated. They were surprised to

learn that women spent *less* time on the machine than men. This indicated that the operation was not more difficult to perform on women.

As the researchers probed, a surprising answer unfolded—unintended sexual discrimination. Physicians had not taken the chest pains of their women patients as seriously as they took the complaints of their men patients. They were *ten* times more likely to give men exercise stress tests and radioactive heart scans. They also sent men to surgery on the basis of abnormal stress tests, but waited until women showed clear-cut symptoms of coronary heart disease before sending them to surgery. Having surgery after the disease is further along reduces the chances of survival.

So does this: When women and men who have heart pain go to hospital emergency rooms, doctors are more likely to admit the men and to send the women home (Seiker and Pope 2000).

Does the sex of the physician matter? These studies don't tell us, but it does when it comes to ordering Pap smears and mammography (Lurie et al. 1993). Researchers examined the records of 98,000 patients and found that women physicians are more likely to order these screening tests. As more women become doctors, this bias in death may decline.

for your consideration

In short, gender bias is so pervasive that it operates beneath our level of awareness and is so severe that it can be a matter of life or death. It is important to note that the doctors in these studies were unaware that they were discriminating. They had no intention of doing so. In what ways does gender bias affect your own perceptions and behavior?

Although women enjoy fundamental rights today, gender inequality continues to play a central role in social life. In some instances, this can even be a life-and-death matter, as with the medical situations discussed in the Down-to-Earth Sociology box above. Let's look at gender relations in education and everyday life, and then, in greater detail, at discrimination in the world of work.

■ Gender Inequality in Education

In education, too, a glimpse of the past sheds light on the present. About a century ago, leading educators claimed that women's wombs dominated their minds, and higher education put a burden on women's frail capacities. Dr. Edward Clarke, of Harvard University's medical faculty, expressed the dominant sentiment this way:

> A girl upon whom Nature, for a limited period and for a definite purpose, imposes so great a physiological task, will not have as much power left for the tasks of school, as the boy of whom Nature requires less at the corresponding epoch. (Andersen 1988)

Because women were so much weaker, Clarke urged them to study only one-third as much as young men—and not to study at all during menstruation.

Over the years, such ideas were discarded. Until recently, however, college was seen as more valuable for men, and fewer women went to college. This created an educational gap between men and women that remains: Overall in the United States,

28 percent of men have completed college compared to 24 percent of women (*Statistical Abstract* 2001:Table 216.) This gap is closing fast. More women than men now go to college, and they earn 56 percent of all bachelor's degrees and 57 percent of all master's degrees (*Statistical Abstract* 2001:Tables 272, 287, 288). As Figure 11.1 shows, women also complete their bachelor's degrees faster than men. If this continues, it won't be long until the gap is reversed.

Another gap that is closing is illustrated on Figure 11.2. As this figure illustrates, the proportion of professional degrees earned by women has increased sharply. The greatest change is in dentistry: In 1970 across the entire United States, only 34 women earned this degree. Today, about 1,500 women become dentists each year (*Statistical Abstract* 2001: Table 289).

Women earning more degrees than men, graduating from college faster, and entering the professions in larger numbers is certainly a major break with the past. If we probe beneath the surface, however, we find old practices. Women's sports, for example, are often underfunded because they are not considered as important as men's sports (Rishe 1999). And whenever I attend a high school football or basketball game, I still see a group of girls in short, brightly colored skirts wildly cheering the boys from the sidelines—but no such group of boys leading organized cheers for the girls when they play *their* sports.

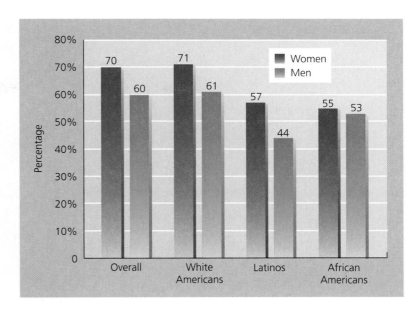

Figure 11.1

Of Those Who Go to College, How Many Receive a Bachelor's Degree Within 5 Years?
Source: Statistical Abstract 1999:Table 328.

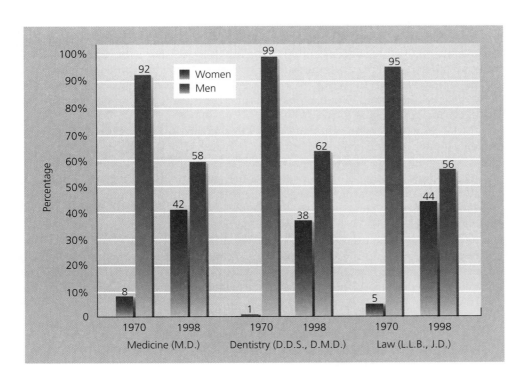

Figure 11.2

Gender Changes in Professional Degrees
Source: Statistical Abstract 2001: Table 289.

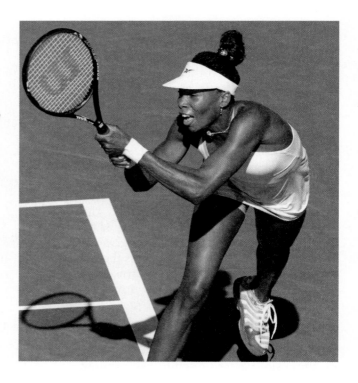

■ *From grade school through college, male sports are emphasized. Despite vast changes, including federal laws, women's sports often remain underfunded and girls' and womens' sports talents undeveloped. Shown here is a remarkable exception, Venus Williams, who has taken the tennis world by storm. Venus, who was coached by her father since she was 4 years old, turned professional at age 14.*

Then there is the matter of *gender tracking;* that is, degrees tend to follow gender, which reinforces male-female distinctions. Here are two extremes: Men earn 83 percent of bachelor's degrees in the "masculine" field of engineering, while women are awarded 88 percent of bachelor's degrees in the "feminine" field of library "science" (*Statistical Abstract* 2000:Table 320). Because gender socialization gives men and women different orientations to life, they enter college with gender-linked aspirations. It is their socialization—not some presumed innate characteristics—that channels men and women into different educational paths.

If we follow students into graduate school, we see that with each passing year the proportion of women drops. Table 11.2 gives us a snapshot of doctoral programs in the sciences. Note how aspirations (enrollment) and accomplishments (doctorates earned) are sex linked. In five of these doctoral programs, men outnumber women, in two they are even, and in one, women outnumber men. In *all* of them, women are less likely to complete the doctorate.

If we follow those who earn doctoral degrees to their teaching careers at colleges and universities, we find gender stratification in rank and pay. Throughout the United States, women are less likely to be awarded the rank of full professor, the highest-paying and most prestigious rank. Professors are paid more than the lower ranks (instructor, assistant professor, and associate professor). In both private and public colleges, professors average more than twice the salary of instructors (*Statistical Abstract* 2000:Table 313). Even when women do become full professors, they average less pay than men who are full professors (Wood 2001).

Beyond the pay gap is a less visible issue, that of subtle discrimination. Women professors get smaller labs, their work is not taken as seriously as men's, and *they* are not taken as seriously. As Barbara Grosz, a professor at Harvard, put it (Zernike 2001)

> The first time you're mistaken for a secretary is funny. The 99th time is not. The first time the guys (men professors) don't include you in the conversation at a meeting, you think, "I'm not interested anyway." But a whole year of these conversations—there's this kind of constant erosion.

TABLE 11.2	Doctorates in Science, By Sex					
Field	Students Enrolled		Doctorates Conferred		Completion Ratio* (Higher or Lower Than Expected)	
	Women	Men	Women	Men	Women	Men
Computer sciences	27%	73%	17%	83%	−37	+13
Engineering	19%	81%	13%	87%	−32	+7
Agriculture	40%	60%	28%	72%	−30	+20
Mathematics	35%	65%	25%	75%	−29	+15
Physical sciences	28%	72%	23%	77%	−18	+7
Social sciences	50%	50%	41%	59%	−18	+18
Biological sciences	50%	50%	44%	56%	−12	+12
Psychology	70%	30%	67%	33%	−4	+3

*The formula for the completion ratio is X minus Y divided by X, where X is the proportion enrolled in a program and Y is the proportion granted doctorates.
Source: Statistical Abstract 2000:Tables 995, 997.

■ Gender Inequality in Everyday Life

Of the many aspects of gender discrimination in everyday life that we could examine, we have space to look only at two: the general devaluation of femininity in U.S. society, and male dominance of conversation.

General Devaluation of Things Feminine

Leaning against the water cooler, two men—both minor executives—are nursing their cups of coffee, discussing last Sunday's Giants game, postponing for as long as possible the moment when work must finally be faced.

A [man] vice president walks by and hears them talking about sports. Does he stop and send them back to their desks? Does he frown? Probably not. Being a man, he is far more likely to pause and join in the conversation, anxious to prove that he, too, is "one of the boys," feigning an interest in football that he may very well not share at all. These men—all the men in the office—are his troops, his comrades-in-arms.

Now, let's assume that two women are standing by the water cooler discussing whatever you please: women's liberation, clothes, work, any subject—except football, of course. The vice president walks by, sees them, and moves down the hall in a fury, cursing and wondering whether it is worth the trouble to complain—but to whom?—about all those bitches standing around gabbing when they should be working. "Don't they know," he will ask, in the words of a million men, "that this is an office?" (Korda 1973:20–21)

As indicated in this scenario—and in the professor's quote that closed the last section—women's interests, attitudes, and contributions are not taken as seriously as those of men. Masculinity is valued more highly, for it represents strength and success; femininity is devalued, for it is perceived as weakness and lack of accomplishment.

Sociologist Samuel Stouffer produced a classic study of World War II combat soldiers. In *The American Soldier* (1949), he reported that officers used feminine terms as insults to motivate soldiers. To show less-than-expected courage or endurance was to risk the charge of not being a man. An officer might say, "Whatsa matter, Bud—got lace on your drawers?" A generation later, accusations of femininity were still used as motivating insults to prepare soldiers to fight in Vietnam. Drill sergeants would mock their troops by saying, "Can't hack it, little girls?" (Eisenhart 1975). The practice continues. Male soldiers who show hesitation during maneuvers are mocked by others, who call them girls (Miller 2001).

In sports, we see the same thing. Sociologist Douglas Foley (2001) notes that football coaches insult boys who don't play well by saying that they are "wearing skirts," and sociologist Donna Eder (1995) notes that junior high boys call one another "girl" if they don't hit hard enough in football. Sociologists Jean Stockard and Miriam Johnson (1980), who observed boys playing basketball, heard boys who missed a basket being called a "woman." In professional hockey, players who are not rough enough on the ice are called "girls" (Gallmeier 1988:227).

This name-calling is sociologically significant. As Stockard and Johnson (1980:12) point out, these insults are a devaluation of females. As they noted, "There is no comparable phenomenon among women, for young girls do not insult each other by calling each other 'man.' "

Gender Inequality in Conversation   If you have noticed that men are more likely to interrupt a conversation, your observation is correct. Sociologists not only confirm this, but they also report that men are more likely to control changes in topics. They note that talk between a man and a woman is often more like talk between an employer and an employee than between social equals (Hall 1984; West and Garcia 1988; Smith-Lovin and Brody 1989; Tannen 1990, 2001). Even in college classes, men interrupt their instructors more often than do women. This is especially true if the instructor is a woman (Brooks 1982). In short, conversations between men and women mirror their relative positions of power in society.

Derogatory terms and conversation represent only the tip of the iceberg, for underlying these aspects of everyday life is a structural inequality based on gender that runs throughout society. Let's examine that structural feature in the workplace.

Gender Inequality in the Workplace

To examine the work setting is to make visible basic relations between men and women. Let's begin with one of the most remarkable areas of gender inequality at work, the pay gap.

◼ The Pay Gap

One of the chief characteristics of the U.S. work force is a steady growth in the numbers of women who work outside the home for wages. Figure 11.3 shows that in 1890 about one of every five workers was a woman. By 1940, this ratio had grown to one of four, by 1960 to one of three, and today it is almost one of two.

Women who work for wages are not evenly distributed throughout the United States, and where a woman lives makes a difference in how likely she is to work out-

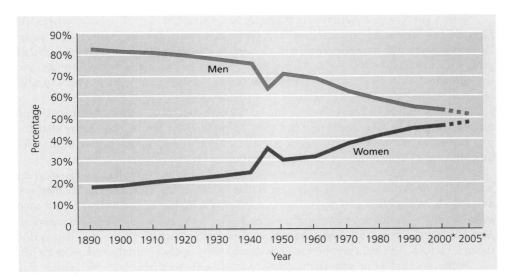

Figure 11.3

Women's and Men's Proportion of the U.S. Labor Force

Note: Pre 1940 totals include women 14 and over; totals for 1940 and after are for women 16 and over. Broken lines are the author's projections.

Sources: 1969 *Handbook on Women Workers,* 1969:10; *Manpower Report to the President,* 1971:203, 205; Mills and Palumbo, 1980:6, 45; *Statistical Abstract* 2000:Table 647.

side the home. From the Social Map below, you can see the geographical patterns. These apparently reflect regional-subcultural differences of which we currently have little understanding.

Chances are, you are going to go to work after you complete college. (You might like to sit under a palm tree and drink piña coladas instead, but chances are you won't be able to retire right after college.) How would you like to earn an extra million dollars on your job? If this sounds appealing, read on. I'm going to reveal how you can make an extra $2,000 or so a month between the ages of 25 and 65.

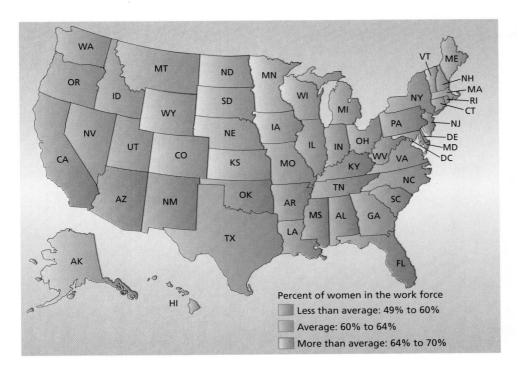

Figure 11.4

Percent of Women in the Work Force

Source: Statistical Abstract 2000: Table 648.

Is this hard to do? Actually, it is simple for some, but impossible for others. As Figure 11.5 shows, all you have to do is be born a male and graduate from college. If we compare full-time workers, this is how much more the *average male* college graduate earns over the course of his career. Hardly any single factor pinpoints gender discrimination better than this million dollars. From Figure 11.5, you can also see that the pay gap shows up at all levels of education.

The pay gap is so great that, as Figure 11.6 shows, U.S. women who work full time average only 70 percent of what men are paid. This figure also shows that the pay gap used to be even worse. And it does not occur only in the United States. All industrialized nations have a gender pay gap.

What logic can underlie the gender pay gap? Earlier we saw that college degrees are gender linked, so perhaps this gap is due to career choices. Maybe women are more likely to choose lower-paying jobs, such as teaching grade school, whereas men are more likely to go into better-paying fields, such as business, law, and engineering. Actually, this is true, and researchers have found that about *half* the pay gap is due to such factors. The balance, however, is due to gender discrimination (Kemp 1990).

Depending on your sex, then, you are likely either to benefit from gender discrimination—or to be its victim. Because the pay gap will be so important in your own work life, let's follow some college graduates to see how it actually comes about. Economists Rex Fuller and Richard Schoenberger (1991) examined the starting salaries of the business majors at the University of Wisconsin, of whom 47 percent were women. They found that the women's starting salaries averaged 11 percent ($1,737) less than the men's.

You might be able to think of valid reasons for this initial pay gap. For example, the women might have been less qualified. Perhaps they had lower grades. Or maybe they completed fewer internships. If so, they would deserve lower salaries.

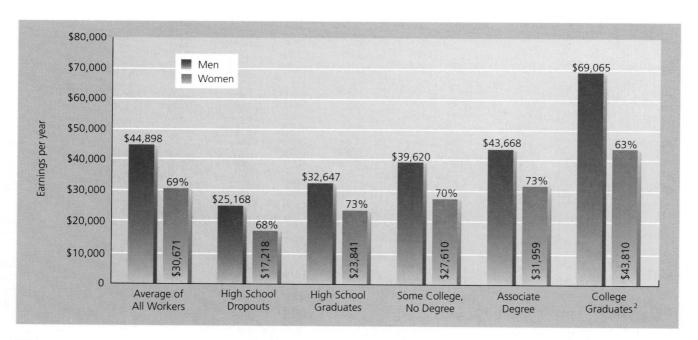

F igure 11.5

The Gender Pay Gap, by Education[1]

[1]Full-time workers in all fields.

[2]Bachelor's and all higher degrees, including professional degrees.

Source: Statistical Abstract 2000:Table 752.

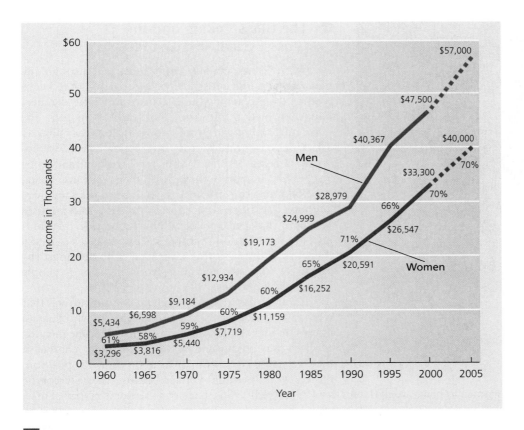

Figure 11.6

What Percentage of Men's Income Do Women Earn?
The Gender Gap Over Time

Note: The income jump from 1990 to 1995 could be due to a statistical procedure. The 1995 source (for 1990 income) uses "median income," while the 1997 source (for 1995 income) merely says "average earnings." How the "average" is computed is not stated. For a review of this distinction, see Table 5.2. Broken lines indicate the author's estimates.

Source: Beeghley 1989:239; *Statistical Abstract* 1995:Table 739; 2000:Table 752.

To find out, Fuller and Schoenberger reviewed the students' college records. To their surprise, they found that the women had *higher* grades and *more* internships. In other words, if women were equally qualified, they were offered lower salaries—and if they were more qualified, they were offered lower salaries—a classic lose-lose situation.

What happened after these graduates had been on the job a while? Did things even out, so that after a few years the women and men earned about the same? Fuller and Schoenberger checked their salaries five years later. Instead of narrowing, the pay gap had grown even wider. By this time, the women earned 14 percent ($3,615) less than the men.

As a final indication of the extent of the U.S. gender pay gap, consider this. Of the nation's top 500 corporations (the so-called "Fortune 500"), only 5 are headed by women (Hehir 2001). And 5 is a record-breaking number! I examined the names of the CEOs of the 350 largest U.S. corporations, and I found that your best chance to reach the top is to be named (in this order) John, Robert, James, William, or Charles. Edward, Lawrence, and Richard are also advantageous. Amber, Katherine, Leticia, and Maria, however, apparently draw a severe penalty. Naming your baby girl John or Robert might seem a little severe, but it could help her get to the top. (I say this only slightly tongue-in-cheek.)

■ *Shown here is Anne Mulcahy, president and CEO of Xerox Corporation. What sets Mulcahy apart is that she broke through the glass ceiling to head one of the most well-known companies in the United States.*

The Glass Ceiling and the Glass Escalator

What keeps women from breaking through the *glass ceiling*, the mostly invisible barrier that keeps women from reaching the executive suite? Researchers have identified a "pipeline" that leads to the top—the marketing, sales, and production positions that directly affect the corporate bottom line (Reich 1995). Stereotyped as being better at "support," women tend to be steered into human resources or public relations. There, successful projects are not appreciated in the same way as those that bring in corporate profits—and bonuses for their managers. Felice Schwartz, founder of Catalyst, an organization that focuses on women's issues in the workplace, put it this way: Men, who dominate the executive suite, stereotype potential leaders as people who look like themselves (Lopez 1992).

Another reason the glass ceiling is so powerful is that women lack mentors, successful executives who take an interest in them and teach them the ropes. Some men executives fear gossip and sexual harassment charges if they get close to a woman in a subordinate position. Others don't mentor women because they stereotype women as being weak (Lancaster 1995; Reich 1995). Lack of a mentor is no trivial matter, for supposedly all top executives have had a coach or mentor (Lancaster 1995).

The glass ceiling is cracking, however, and more women are reaching the executive suite. A look at women who've broken through the glass ceiling reveals highly motivated women with a fierce competitive spirit who are willing to give up sleep and recreation for the sake of career advancement. They also learn to play by "men's rules," developing a style that makes men comfortable. In the background of about three-fourths of these women is a supportive husband who shares household duties and adapts his career to the needs of his executive wife (Lublin 1996).

Sociologist Christine Williams (1995) interviewed men and women who worked as nurses, elementary school teachers, librarians, and social workers. She found that instead of bumping into a glass ceiling, the men in these traditionally female occupations had climbed aboard a *glass escalator*. That is, compared with women, the men were accelerated into higher-level positions, given more desirable work assignments, and paid higher salaries. The motor that drives the glass escalator is gender— the stereotype that because someone is male he is more capable.

■ *One of the frustrations felt by many women in the labor force is that no matter what they do, they hit a glass ceiling. Another is that to succeed they feel forced to abandon characteristics they feel are essential to their self.*

The "Mommy Track"

Most employed wives face greater role conflict than do their husbands. They are more likely to be the caretakers of the marriage, to nurture it through the hard times. They also tend to spend more time in maintaining family ties (such as sending greeting and thank you cards). Most wives, even though employed full time, also spend more time taking care of the children and doing housework.

To help resolve this conflict, Felice Schwartz (1989) suggested that corporations offer women a choice of two parallel career paths. The "fast track" consists of the high-powered, demanding positions that may require sixty or seventy hours of work per week—regular responsibilities, emergencies, out-of-town meetings, and a briefcase jammed with work that has to be done at night and on weekends. With such limited time outside of work, family life often suffers. Women can choose this "fast track" if they wish. Or, instead, they may choose a "mommy track," which would emphasize both career and family. Less would be expected of a woman on the "mommy track," for her commitment to the firm would be lower and her commitment to her family higher.

That, of course, say critics, is exactly what is wrong with this proposal. A "mommy track" will encourage women to be satisfied with lower aspirations, lower pay, and fewer promotions. It will confirm men's stereotypes of women executives. And unless we have a "daddy track," it also assumes that child rearing is women's work (Starrels 1992). The "mommy track," critics conclude, would encourage women to slow up in the race to climb the corporate ladder, keep men in executive power, and relegate women to an inferior position in corporate life.

Schwartz replied that she was really proposing a "zigzag track" (Shellenbarger 1995b). "In my ideal world," she said, "parents, including men, would slow down when their kids were small. Later they would go back to the mainstream. If you choose this intermittent route upward, you would make it to the top slower than someone equally able who took the straight vertical route. The goal," she added, "is to balance family and career."

Critics suggest that a better way to resolve the conflict between work and family is for husbands to take on greater responsibilities at home and for firms to provide on-site day care, flexible work schedules, and parental leave without loss of benefits. Some maintain that the choice between family and career is artificial, that there are ample role models of family-oriented, highly successful women, from Sandra Day O'Connor and Ruth Bader Ginsberg, Justices of the U.S. Supreme Court, to Ann Fisher, astronaut and physician.

Sexual Harassment

Sexual harassment—unwelcome sexual attention at work or at school, which may affect a person's job performance or create a hostile work environment—was not recognized as a problem until the 1970s. Before this, women considered unwanted sexual comments, touches, looks, and pressure to have sex to be a personal matter.

With the prodding of feminists, women began to perceive unwanted sexual advances at work and school as part of a *structural* problem. That is, they began to see them not simply as a man here and there doing obnoxious things because he was attracted to a woman, but, rather, as men abusing their positions of authority in order to force unwanted sexual activities on women. Since women have moved into positions of authority, they, too, have become sexual harassers (Wayne et al. 2001). With most authority vested in men, however, most sexual harassers are men.

As symbolic interactionists stress, terms affect our perception. Because we have the term *sexual harassment,* we perceive actions in a different light than did our predecessors. The meaning of sexual harassment is vague and shifting, however, and court cases constantly change what this term does and does not include. Originally sexual desire was an element of sexual harassment, but no longer. In a case that went to the U.S. Supreme Court, a homosexual who had been tormented by his supervisors

sexual harassment
the abuse of one's position of authority to force unwanted sexual demands on someone

and fellow workers when he was working on an oil rig sued his employer. The Court ruled that sexual desire is not necessary, that sexual harassment laws also apply to homosexuals who are harassed by heterosexuals on the job (Felsenthal 1998).

Central to sexual harassment is the abuse of power, a topic that is explored in the following Thinking Critically section.

thinking
CRITICALLY

Sexual Harassment of Women in the Military

The news spread like wildfire across the United States. Several male Army sergeants at Aberdeen Proving Ground in Maryland were accused of sexually abusing their female trainees (McIntyre 1997). The female recruits, many in their late teens, had been entrusted to the care of severe, demanding drill sergeants. There's nothing new about this; the Army uses rugged training to socialize *all* its recruits. What was new, however, were widespread accusations of sexual harassment, of using power—including intimidation and threats—to force sex on unwilling recruits. The accused drill sergeants, who said the sex was consensual, were tried and found guilty of rape. One married sergeant, who had pleaded guilty to having consensual sex with 11 trainees (adultery is a crime in the Army), was convicted of raping another 6 trainees a total of 18 times and was sentenced to 25 years in prison.

Some took an "I told you so" attitude. Their view was, you can't have coed dormitories unless you're looking for trouble. These are red-blooded men in the prime of their life, and the recruits are young, desirable, and, in some cases, naive. It is absolutely stupid to have them sleep under the same roof. If we are going to prepare women for combat, they need to be trained in separate military camps under the supervision of women. If men are brought in to assist, they should leave at the end of the day or sleep in separate barracks.

Others, who were also shocked by the rapes, took the attitude that the system was fine, but a few sergeants had gone bad. Training men and women together is the only way to assure equality, they insisted. Training must involve all phases of military life. To prevent such problems, however, we must impose greater controls over those in charge. From those to whom we entrust responsibility, we can demand accountability. Recruits need to be told to report immediately all violations of touching or even of seductive language.

Then another bombshell hit. After the recruits made their accusations, the Army appointed a blue-ribbon panel to investigate sexual harassment in its ranks. When Sgt. Major Gene McKinney, the highest-ranking of the Army's 410,000 noncommissioned officers, was appointed to this committee, former subordinates accused him of sexual harassment (Shenon 1997). McKinney was relieved of duties and court-martialed. He was found not guilty of sexual harassment, but guilty of obstruction of justice. McKinney was reprimanded and demoted. His embittered accusers claimed the Army had sacrificed them for McKinney.

A civilian panel investigated. It recommended that the services remain integrated, but that platoons (the smallest units, with fifty soldiers) be segregated by sex (Mersereau 1998). The Navy didn't like this recommendation and said it wanted men and women to work together and to sleep in the

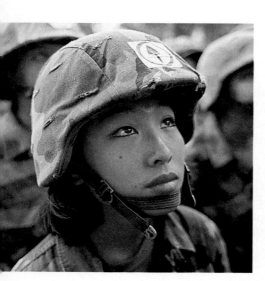

■ *Marine recruits at basic training in Parris Island, South Carolina.*

same building, as they would on a ship. The Army and Navy continued as they were. The Marines did, too, but their practice has always been to keep men and women almost completely separate (Ricks 1998). A survey of 29,000 military personnel shows that sexual harassment and rapes in the military continue (Antecol and Cobb-Clark 2001).

■ ■ ■ ■ ■

for your consideration . . .

How can we set up a structure to minimize sexual harassment in the military? Can we do this and still train men and women together? Can we do this and still have them sleep in the same barracks? Be specific about the structure you would establish.

■ □ ■ ■ ■

Gender and Violence

The high rate of violence in the United States shocks foreigners and frightens many Americans. Only a couple of generations ago, many Americans left their homes and cars unlocked. Today, fearful of carjackings, they lock their cars even while driving, and, fearful of rape and kidnappings, they escort their children to school. Lurking behind these fears is the gender inequality of violence—the fact that females are much more likely to be victims of males, not the other way around. Let's briefly review this almost one-way street in gender violence.

On pages 317 and 318, we examined violence against women in other cultures, and in Chapter 16 we shall review violence in the home. Here, due to space limitations, we can review only briefly some primary features of violence.

Forcible Rape   Being raped is a common fear of U.S. women. And this fear is far from groundless. Rape is so common that each year between 2 and 3 of every 1,000 females age 12 and over in the entire United States are raped. The official rate is 8.1 per 10,000. Surveys of crime victims, however, show that only one-third (32 percent) of rapes are reported, giving us a real rate of 24 per 10,000. Females of all ages are victims, but the typical rape victim is 16 to 24 years old. Contrary to stereotypes, most rape victims know their assailant; only one-fourth of rapes are committed by strangers (*Statistical Abstract* 2000:Tables 336, 341, 342, and page 200).

An aspect of rape that is usually overlooked is the rape of men in prison. With prison officials reluctant to let the public know about the horrible conditions behind bars, our studies are far from perfect. Those we have, however, indicate that about 15 to 20 percent of men in prison are raped. From court cases, we know that some guards even punish prisoners who displease them by placing them in cells with known sexual predators (Donaldson 1993; Lewin 2001b).

Date Rape   What has shocked so many about date rape (also known as *acquaintance rape*) is studies showing that it does not consist of a few isolated events (Collymore 2000; Goode 2001). In an often-cited study, about 21 percent of the women in the introductory psychology courses at Texas A&M University reported that they had been forced to have sexual intercourse (Muehlenhard and Linton

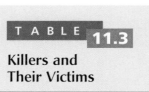

TABLE 11.3

Killers and Their Victims

The Victims	
Male	*Female*
75%	25%

The Killers	
Male	*Female*
89%	11%

Note: Some victims are so badly decomposed that their sex is unknown. If this small percentage is removed from the data, the total for female victims drops to 24.4%.

Source: Statistical Abstract 2000:Tables 334, 345.

1987). In a more recent study, researchers surveyed the students in a representative sample of courses at Marietta College, a private school in Ohio (Felton et al. 2001). They found what is probably a more reasonable total, that 2.5 percent of the women had been physically forced to have sex. They also found that about as many men (23 percent) as women (24 percent) had given in to pressure to have sex when they didn't want to, but—and this is no surprise—none of the men had been physically forced to have sex.

Most date rapes go unreported. A primary reason is that the victim feels partially responsible because she knows the person and was with him voluntarily. However, as a physician who has treated victims of date rape has said, "Would you feel responsible if someone hit you over the head with a shovel—just because you knew the person?" (Carpenito 1999).

Murder   Table 11.3 summarizes how gender fits into U.S. patterns of murder. Note that although females make up a little over 51 percent of the U.S. population, they don't even come close to making up 51 percent of the nation's killers. Note also that one-fourth of all murder victims are female—and nine times out of ten the killer is a male.

Violence in the Home   Women are also the typical victims of family violence. Spouse battering, marital rape, and incest are discussed in Chapter 16, pages 496–498. A particular form of violence against women, genital circumcision, is the focus of the Perspectives box on page 317.

Women in the Criminal Justice System   There is another side to gender and violence. Although women are much less likely to kill, when they do kill, judges are more likely to be more lenient with them. As Table 11.4 shows, women are more likely than men to be given probation for murder (as well as for robbery, burglary, and all crimes listed on this table). It is possible that sexual stereotypes underlie these decisions—such as the idea that women are less of a menace than men and

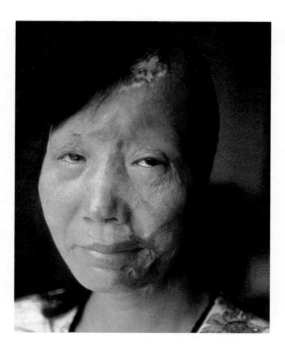

■ *Violence against females is a global problem, but it is worse in some places than others. When Wu Fang from Fenghuo village in Shaanxi province, China, was beaten by her husband, she asked for a divorce. Her husband said he would rather see her in a coffin than divorce. When Wu Fang ran away, the town lord had her brought back—so she would not "tarnish" the name of the village. For throwing acid on her, her husband was executed.*

TABLE 11.4 Going Easier on Women

When Men and Women Are Convicted of the Same Crime, Who Gets Off Easier?*

Crime	Prison		Probation	
	Men	Women	Men	Women
Murder	97%	89%	1%	5%
Robbery	78%	67%	9%	13%
Burglary	55%	43%	19%	23%
Aggravated Assault	54%	30%	18%	26%
Larceny	42%	28%	24%	34%
Fraud	39%	31%	28%	41%
Drug Dealing	50%	37%	20%	26%
Weapons	49%	28%	22%	30%

*This table examines the extremes of sentencing; totals do not add to 100 percent because of jail sentences and unspecified "other" dispositions.
Source: Sourcebook of Criminal Justice Statistics 1997:Table 5.50.

should be given another chance. It is also possible that women defendants have less of a criminal history ("rap sheet") when they are charged with crimes. We need research on this topic.

Feminism and Gendered Violence

Feminist sociologists have been especially effective in bringing violence against women to the public's attention. Some use symbolic interactionism, pointing out that to associate strength and virility with violence—as is done in so many areas of U.S. culture—is to promote violence. Others use conflict theory. They argue that as gender relations change, men lose power, and that some men become violent against women as a way to reassert their declining power and status (Reiser 1999). Perhaps this is the underlying reason for the violence featured in the Mass Media box on the next page.

Solutions

There is no magic bullet for this problem of gendered violence, but to be effective any solution must break the connection between violence and masculinity. This would require an educational program that incorporates schools, churches, homes, and the media. Given the gun-slinging heroes of the Wild West and other American icons, as well as the violent messages so prevalent in today's mass media, it is difficult to be optimistic that a change will come any time soon.

Our next topic, women in politics, however, gives us much more reason for optimism.

mass media
in social life

Beauty and Pain
How Much Is an Ad Worth?

The studio audience at *Super Jockey*, a popular television program in Japan, waits expectantly. They've seen it before, and they can't get enough. A young woman, clad in a revealing bikini, walks onto the stage. Cringing with fear, she is lowered into a glass tank of scalding hot water.

The studio audience eagerly watches the woman through the glass. The national audience watches at home. Both break into laughter as the girl writhes in pain.

To make sure the young woman gets the full treatment, a man standing behind the tank ladles hot water over the woman's breasts—just as though he were basting a chicken. As her flesh quickly reddens, the television camera zooms in for a close-up shot of her breasts.

Most women last only three or four seconds.

The camera follows as the young woman scrambles out of the tub, where she jumps up and down in pain and rubs ice all over her body.

The audience howls with glee.

Why do the women do it? For every second they stay in the hot water, they get one second on the program to advertise any product they wish. Most advertise their place of employment, their pain a favor to their boss (Strauss 1998).

It is often difficult to understand other cultures. *Super Jockey* wouldn't be tolerated in the United States. If some television company tried to air a U.S. version, protests would erupt. The studio would be picketed, its sponsors boycotted.

Instead of trying to explain the intricacies of a culture that finds such behavior amusing (*Super Jockey* is a comedy show), we might wish to turn the focus onto our own culture. Why do we find the rape of women a source of entertainment? How can I say that we do? It is apparent from *our* television. I'm not talking about some dry, historical documentary on Public Television. I'm referring to TV "dramas," police shows, detective shows, and other programs in which the story line centers on women who are raped. Of course, in order to make sure this kind of entertainment

gets a seal of approval, producers see to it that the rapist is apprehended and punished. As further evidence that this entertainment is meritorious, the rapist may commit suicide, get shot by the police, or get run down by a car as he tries to escape into his netherworld.

If you think that I've stretched things a bit, consider how entertaining our society finds the murder of women. The Halloween shocker-thriller-slasher films are outstanding examples. Audiences that are simultaneously titillated and terror-stricken watch, riveted, as crazed, masked killers hunt down college coeds with knives, axes, even chain saws. Audiences seem to find the screams of the victims especially entertaining. And the prettier, shapelier, and more skimpily clad the victim, the higher the entertainment value.

It is difficult to understand cultures, especially to explain why people find certain things amusing or entertaining. Why would Japanese and Americans find the victimization of women to be such a scintillating source of entertainment?

The Changing Face of Politics

What do these nations have in common?

Canada in North America
Argentina, Bolivia, and Nicaragua in Latin America
Britain, France, Ireland, and Portugal in western Europe
The Philippines in Asia
Israel in the Mideast
Poland in eastern Europe
India, Pakistan, and Sri Lanka on the subcontinent

The answer is that all have had a woman president or prime minister. To this list, we can add even such bastions of male chauvinism as Haiti, Turkey, and Bangladesh (Harwood and Brooks 1993).

Then why not the United States? Why don't women, who outnumber men, take political control of the nation? Eight million more women than men are of voting age, and more women than men vote in U.S. national elections. As Table 11.5 shows, however, men greatly outnumber women in political office. Despite the gains women have made in recent elections, since 1789 about 1,800 men have served in the U.S. Senate, but only 24 women have served, including the 9 current senators. Not until 1992 was the first African American woman (Carol Moseley-Braun) elected to the U.S. Senate (National Women's Political Caucus 1998; *Statistical Abstract* 2001:Table 390).

Why are women underrepresented in U.S. politics? First, women are still underrepresented in law and business, the careers from which most politicians come. Further, most women do not perceive themselves as belonging to a class of people who need to organize politically in order to overcome domination. Most women also find that the irregular hours kept by those who run for office are incompatible with their role as mother. Fathers, in contrast, whose ordinary roles are more likely to take them away from home, do not feel this same conflict. Women are also less likely to have a supportive spouse who is willing to play an unassuming background role while providing solace, encouragement, child care, and voter appeal. Finally, preferring to hold on tightly to their positions of power, men have been reluctant to incorporate women into centers of decision making or to present them as viable candidates.

These factors are changing, however, and we can expect more women to seek and gain political office. As we saw in Figure 11.2 (on page 323), more women are going into law. The same is true for business. There they are doing more traveling and making statewide and national contacts. Increasingly, child care is seen as a mutual responsibility of both mother and father. This generation, then, is likely to mark a fundamental change in women's political participation, and it appears to be only a matter of time until a woman occupies the Oval Office.

TABLE 11.5	U.S. Women in Political Office*	
	Percentage of Offices Held by Women	Number of Offices Held by Women
National Office		
U.S. Senate	9%	9
U.S. House of Representatives	13%	56
State Office		
Governors	6%	3
Lt. Governors	38%	19
Attorneys general	22%	11
Secretaries of state	28%	14
Treasurers	32%	16
State auditors	8%	4
State legislators	23%	1,672
Local Office		
Mayors[a]	18%	177
County	22%	12,525
School district	27%	27,702

*These totals, from 1999 and 2000, do not include women elected to the judiciary, women appointed to state cabinet-level positions, women elected to executive posts by the legislature, or members of a university board of trustees.

[a]Of cities with a population over 30,000.

Source: National Women's Political Caucus 1998; *Statistical Abstract* 2000:Tables 463, 471, 472; 2001:Tables 390, 397.

Glimpsing the Future—With Hope

By playing a fuller role in the decision-making processes of our social institutions, women are going against the stereotypes and role models that lock males into exclusively male activities and push females into roles that are considered feminine. As structural barriers fall and more activities are degendered, both males and females will be free to pursue activities that are more compatible with their abilities and desires as individuals.

As sociologists Janet Chafetz (1974), Janet Giele (1978), and Judith Lorber (1994) have pointed out, the ultimate possibility is a new conception of the human personality. At present, structural obstacles, accompanied by supporting socialization and stereotypes, cast most males and females into fairly rigid roles. Overcoming these obstacles and abandoning traditional stereotypes will give males and females new perceptions of themselves and one another. Both females and males will then be free to feel and to express needs and emotions that present social arrangements deny them. Females will likely perceive themselves as more in control of their environment and to explore this aspect of the human personality. Males will likely feel and express more emotional sensitivity—to be warmer, more affectionate and tender, and to give greater expression to anxieties and stresses that their gender now forces them to suppress. In the future, we may discover that such "greater wholeness" of males and females entails many other dimensions of the human personality.

As females and males develop a new consciousness of themselves and their own potential, relationships between them will change. Certainly distinctions between the sexes will not disappear. There is no reason, however, for biological differences to be translated into social inequalities. The reasonable goal is to have an appreciation of sexual differences coupled with equality of opportunity—which may well lead to a transformed society (Gilman 1911/1971; Offen 1990). If this happens, as sociologist Alison Jaggar (1990) observed, gender equality can become less a goal than a background condition for living in society.

Summary and Review

Issues of Sex and Gender

■ What is gender stratification?

The term **gender stratification** refers to unequal access to power, prestige, and property on the basis of sex. Each society establishes a structure that, on the basis of sex and gender, opens and closes doors to its privileges. P. 308.

■ How do sex and gender differ?

Sex refers to biological distinctions between males and females. It consists of both primary and secondary sex characteristics. **Gender,** in contrast, is what a society considers proper behaviors and attitudes for its male and female members. Sex physically distinguishes males from females; gender defines what is "masculine" and "feminine." P. 308.

■ Why do the behaviors of males and females differ?

The "nature versus nurture" debate refers to whether differences in the behaviors of males and females are caused by inherited (biological) or learned (cultural) characteristics. Almost all sociologists take the side of nurture. In recent years, however, sociologists have begun to cautiously open the door to biology. Pp. 309–314.

Gender Inequality in Global Perspective

■ Is gender stratification universal?

George Murdock surveyed information on tribal societies and found not only that all of them have sex-linked activities, but also that all of them give greater prestige to male activities. **Patriarchy,** or male dominance, does appear to be universal. Besides work, other areas of discrimination include education, politics, and violence. Pp. 314–317.

How Females Became a Minority Group

■ How did females become a minority group?

The main theory that attempts to explain how females became a **minority group** in their own societies focuses on the physical limitations imposed by childbirth. The origins of this discrimination, however, are lost in history, and no one knows for sure how it began. Pp. 318–320.

Gender Inequality in the United States

■ Is the feminist movement new?

In what is called the "first wave," feminists made political demands for change in the early 1900s—and were met with hostility, and even violence. The "second wave" began in the 1960s and continues today. A "third wave" may be emerging. Pp. 320–322.

■ What forms does gender stratification in education take?

Although more women than men attend college, each tends to select "feminine" or "masculine" fields. Women are underrepresented in most doctoral programs in science, and they are less likely to complete these programs. Fundamental change is indicated by the growing numbers of women in law and medicine. Pp. 322–325.

■ **Is there gender inequality in everyday life?**
Two indications of gender inequality in everyday life are the general devaluation of femininity and the male dominance of conversation. Pp. 325–326.

Gender Inequality in the Workplace

■ **How does gender inequality show up in the workplace?**
Even though women are a high proportion of the work force, all occupations show a gender gap in pay. For college graduates, the lifetime pay gap runs a million dollars in favor of men. **Sexual harassment** also continues to be a reality of the workplace. Pp. 326–333.

Gender and Violence

■ **What forms does violence against women take?**
The victims of battering, rape, incest, and murder overwhelmingly are females. Female circumcision is a special case of violence against females. Conflict theorists point out that men use violence to maintain their power and privilege. Pp. 333–336.

The Changing Face of Politics

■ **What is the trend in gender inequality in politics?**
A traditional division of gender roles—women as child care providers and homemakers, men as workers outside the home—used to keep women out of politics. Women continue to be underrepresented in politics, but the trend toward greater political equality is firmly in place. Pp. 336–337.

Glimpsing the Future—With Hope

■ **How might changes in gender roles and stereotypes affect our lives?**
In the United States, women are playing a fuller role in the decision-making processes of our social institutions. Men, too, are reexamining their traditional roles. A new conception of the human personality may develop, one that allows both males and females to pursue their individual interests unfettered by gender. Pp. 337–338.

■ *Where can I read more on this topic?*
Suggested Readings for this chapter are found at the back of this book.

Additional Online Resources for This Chapter
www.ablongman.com/henslin6e

- *Content Select* Research Database for Sociology, with suggested key terms and annotated references
- Link to 2000 Census, with activities
- Flashcards of key terms and concepts
- Practice Tests
- Weblinks
- Interactive Maps

using . . .
ContentSelect

Research Database for Sociology

date rape	feminism	gender violence	sexism
female circumcision	gender inequality	patriarchy	sexual harassment
	gender stratification	rape	the glass ceiling

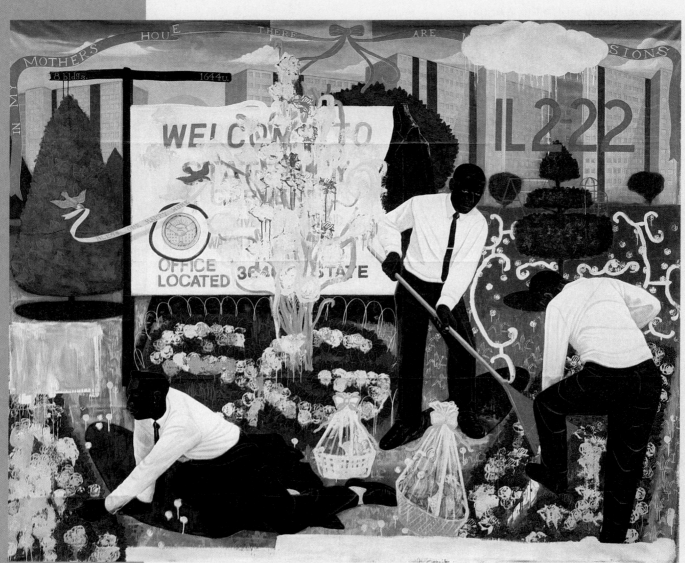

Kerry James Marshall, *Merry Mansions*, 1994

Race and Ethnicity

Laying the Sociological Foundation
Race: Myth and Reality
Ethnic Groups
Minority Groups and Dominant Groups
How People Construct Their Racial-Ethnic Identity
Prejudice and Discrimination
Individual and Institutional Discrimination

Theories of Prejudice
Psychological Perspectives
Sociological Perspectives

Global Patterns of Intergroup Relations
Genocide
Population Transfer
Internal Colonialism
Segregation
Assimilation
Multiculturalism (Pluralism)

Race and Ethnic Relations in the United States
White Europeans
Latinos
African Americans
Asian Americans
Native Americans

Looking Toward the Future
The Immigration Debate
Affirmative Action
Toward a True Multicultural Society

Summary and Review

T he date: July 10, 1941

The place: Jedwabne, Poland

The Germans had just invaded this area of Poland, "liberating" it from the Soviet Union. When the German soldiers arrived, one of the first questions the Polish villagers asked was, "Is it OK to kill Jews?"

The question itself is strange, the event that followed—one of the most ghastly of the war—even stranger. When the Germans said this was permitted, the villagers launched a massive killing spree. Half of this little Polish town killed the other half, murdering about 1,600 of their neighbors.

> Some Jews hid in a barn. The villagers found them, set the barn on fire, and burned their neighbors alive.

The men killed some of their neighbors with bricks and clubs. They knifed one and then cut out his eyes and tongue. They hacked the head off one man and kicked it around like a soccer ball.

When word got to the next village, the townspeople rushed over—not to help, but to watch.

The savagery was too much even for the Germans. They suggested that the villagers let at least one family from each profession live. The villagers replied that they already had enough workers.

Filled with bloodlust, the villagers continued their killing spree. To escape the torture, mothers fled in panic with their children to a pond. They drowned their children and then themselves, a cruel, unwelcome, but less painful death.

Some Jews hid in a barn. The villagers found them, set the barn on fire, and burned their neighbors alive. Then they searched the town to see if they had missed any Jews. They found a few sick at home and some children cowering under beds. They roped the children together by their legs and dragged them away. Then they stuck them with pitchforks and pitched them onto the smoldering coals of the barn.

The Germans didn't participate. They just offered advice from time to time—and photographed the events for their scrapbooks.

—Based on Fisher 2001; Gross 2001; Will 2001.

Laying the Sociological Foundation

Seldom do race and ethnic relations degenerate to the brutal extent that they did in this little town in Poland, but in our own society troubled race relations constantly confront us in newspaper headlines and TV news. Sociology can contribute greatly to our understanding of this aspect of social life. To begin, let's consider to what extent race itself is a myth.

Race: Myth and Reality

With its 6 billion people, the world offers a fascinating variety of human shapes and colors. People see one another as black, white, red, yellow, and brown. Eyes come in various shades of blue, brown, and green. Lips are thick and thin. Hair is straight, curly, kinky, black, white, and red—and, of course, all shades of brown.

As humans spread throughout the world, their adaptations to diverse climates and other living conditions resulted in this profusion of complexions, colors, and shapes. Genetic mutations added distinct characteristics to the peoples of the globe. In this sense, the concept of **race**—a group with inherited physical characteristics that distinguish it from another group—is a reality. Humans do, indeed, come in a variety of colors and shapes.

In two senses, however, race is a myth, a fabrication of the human mind. The *first* fabrication is the idea that any race is superior to others. All races have their geniuses—and their idiots. As with language, one is not better than the others.

Ideas of racial superiority abound, however. They are not only false, but also dangerous. Adolf Hitler, for example, believed that the Aryans were a superior race, responsible for the cultural achievements of Europe. The Aryans, he said, were destined to establish a higher culture and usher in a new world order. This destiny required them to avoid the "racial contamination" that would come from breeding with inferior races, and to isolate or destroy races that might endanger Aryan culture.

When Hitler's views were put into practice, the world was left an appalling legacy—the Nazi slaughter of those they deemed inferior: Jews, Slavs, gypsies, homosexuals, and people with mental and physical disabilities. Dark images of gas ovens and emaciated bodies stacked like cordwood haunted the world's nations. At Nuremberg, the Allies, flush with victory, put the top Nazi officials on trial, exposing their heinous deeds to a shocked world. Their public executions, everyone assumed, marked the end of such grisly acts.

Obviously, they didn't. In the summer of 1994 in Rwanda, Hutus slaughtered between 800,000 and one million Tutsis—mostly with machetes (Gourevitch 1995). A few years later, the Serbs in Bosnia killed Muslims, giving us the new term "ethnic cleansing." As these events sadly attest, **genocide,** the attempt to destroy a people because of their presumed race or ethnicity, remains alive and well. Although the killings may not be accompanied by swastikas and gas ovens, the goal is the same.

The *second* myth is that "pure" races exist. Humans show such a mixture of physical characteristics—in skin color, hair texture, nose shape, head shape, eye color,

race
inherited physical characteristics that distinguish one group from another

genocide
the systematic annihilation or attempted annihilation of a people based on their presumed race or ethnicity

and so on—that there are no "pure" races. Instead of falling into distinct types that are clearly separate from one another, human characteristics flow endlessly together. The mapping of the human genome system shows that humans are strikingly homogenous, that so-called racial groups differ from one another only once in a thousand subunits of the genome (Angler 2000). As with Tiger Woods (discussed in the Cultural Diversity box below), these minute gradations make any attempt to draw lines purely arbitrary.

cultural **d·i·v·e·r·s·i·t·y**

in the United States

Tiger Woods and the Emerging Multiracial Identity: Mapping New Ethnic Terrain

Tiger Woods, perhaps the top golfer of all time, calls himself Cablinasian (Leland and Beals 1997). Woods invented this term as a boy to try to explain to himself just who he was—a combination of Caucasian, Black, Indian, and Asian. Woods wants to embrace both sides of his family. To be known by a racial identity that applies to just one of his parents is to deny the other parent.

Like many of us, Tiger Woods' racial-ethnic heritage is difficult to specify. Some, who like to count things, put Woods at one-quarter Thai, one-quarter Chinese, one-quarter white, an eighth Native American, and an eighth African American. From this chapter, you know how ridiculous such computations are, but the sociological question is why many consider Tiger Woods an African American. The U.S. racial scene is indeed complex, but a good part of the reason is simply that this is the label the media chose. "Everyone has to fit somewhere" seems to be our attitude. If they don't, we grow uncomfortable. And for Tiger Woods, the media chose African American.

The United States once had a firm "color line"—barriers between racial-ethnic groups that you didn't dare cross, especially in dating or marriage. This invisible barrier has broken down, and today such marriages are common (Kent et al. 2001). Several campuses have interracial student organizations. Harvard has two, one just for students who have one African American parent (Leland and Beals 1997).

As we march into unfamiliar ethnic terrain, our classifications are bursting at the seams. Kwame Anthony Appiah, of Har-

■ *Tiger Woods, after winning the British Open Golf Championship at St. Andrews, Scotland.*

vard's Philosophy and Afro-American Studies Departments, says, "My mother is English; my father is Ghanaian. My sisters are married to a Nigerian and a Norwegian. I have nephews who range from blond-haired kids to very black kids. They are all first cousins. Now according to the American scheme of things, they're all black—even the guy with blond hair who skis in Oslo" (Wright 1994).

Until recently, the U.S. census, which is taken every ten years, made everyone choose from Caucasian, Negro, Indian, and Oriental. Everyone was sliced and diced and packed into one of these restrictive classifications. After years of complaints, the list was expanded. In the year 2000 census, everyone had to declare that they were or were not "Spanish/

Hispanic/Latino." Then they had to mark "one or more races" that they "consider themselves to be." They could choose from White; Black, African American, or Negro; American Indian or Alaska Native; Asian Indian, Chinese, Filipino, Japanese, Korean, Vietnamese, Native Hawaiian, Guamanian or Chamorro, Samoan, and other Pacific Islander. Finally, if these didn't do it, you could check a box called "Some Other Race" and then write whatever you wanted. Seven million Americans classified themselves as multiracial (Kent et al. 2001).

Perhaps the census should list Cablinasian. Of course there should be GASH for the German-African-Swedish-Hispanic Americans, BITE for those of Botswanian-Indonesian-Turkish-English descent, and STUDY for the Swedish-Turkish-Uruguan-Danish-Yugoslavian Americans. As you read farther in this chapter, you will see why these terms make as much sense as the categories we currently use.

for your consideration

Just why do we count people by "race" anyway? Why not eliminate race from the U.S. census? (Race became a factor in the census during slavery when five blacks were counted the same as three whites to determine how many representatives a state could send to Congress!) Why is race so important to some people? Perhaps you can use the materials in this chapter to answer these questions.

Although large groupings of people can be classified by blood type and gene frequencies, even these classifications do not uncover "race." Rather, they are so arbitrary that biologists and anthropologists cannot even agree on how many races there are. They have drawn up many lists, each containing a different number of "races." Ashley Montagu (1964; 1999), a physical anthropologist, pointed out that some scientists have classified humans into only two "races," while others have found as many as two thousand. Montagu (1960) himself classified humans into forty "racial" groups. As the Down-to-Earth Sociology box below illustrates, even a plane ride can change our race!

The *idea* of race, of course, is far from a myth. Firmly embedded in our culture, it is a powerful force in our everyday lives. That no race is superior and that even experts cannot decide how people should be biologically classified into races is not what counts. "I know what I see, and you can't tell me any different" seems to be the common attitude. As noted in Chapter 4, sociologists W. I. and Dorothy Thomas observed that "If people define situations as real, they are real in their consequences." In other words, people act on beliefs, not facts. As a result, we always have people like Hitler, the Polish villagers in our opening vignette, the Hutus in Rwanda, and the Serbian killers in Bosnia. While few people hold such extreme views, most people appear to be ethnocentric enough to believe, at least just a little, that their own race is superior to others.

down-to-earth sociology

Common Sense and Sociology: What Is Race?

At the beginning of this text (pages 7–8), I mentioned that common sense and sociology often conflict. This is especially so when it comes to race. According to common sense, our racial classifications represent biological differences between people. Sociologists, in contrast, stress that what we call races are *social* classifications, not biological categories.

Sociologists point out that *our "race" depends more on the society in which we live than on our biological characteristics.* For example, the racial categories common in the United States are merely one of *numerous* ways that people around the world classify physical appearances. Although groups around the world use different categories, each group assumes that its categories are natural, merely a response to visible biology.

To better understand this essential sociological point—that race is more social than it is biological—consider this: In the United States, children born to the same parents are all of the same race. "What could be more natural?" Americans assume. But in Brazil, children born to the same parents may be of different races—if their appearances differ. "What could be more natural?" assume Brazilians.

Consider how Americans usually classify a child born to a "black" mother and a "white" father. Why do they usually say that the child is "black"? Wouldn't it be equally as logical to classify the child as "white"? Similarly, if a child's grandmother is "black," but all her other ancestors are "white," the child is often considered "black." Yet she has much more "white blood" than "black blood." Why, then, is she considered "black"? Certainly not because of biology. Rather, such thinking is a legacy of slavery. Whites—in an attempt to preserve the "purity" of their "race" in the face of numerous children whose fathers were white slave masters and mothers were black slaves—classified anyone with even a "drop of black blood" as "not white."

This sounds ridiculous, but *even a plane trip can change a person's race.* In the city of Salvador in Brazil, people classify one another by color of skin and eyes, breadth of nose and lips, and color and curliness of hair. They use at least seven terms for what we call white and black. Consider again a U.S. child who has "white" and "black" parents. If she flies to Brazil, she is no longer "black"; she now belongs to one of their several "whiter" categories (Fish 1995).

On the flight just mentioned, did the girl's "race" actually change? Our common sense revolts at this, I know, but it actually did. We want to argue that because her biological characteristics remain unchanged, her race remains unchanged. This is because we think of race as biological, when *it really is a label we use to describe perceived biological characteristics.* Simply put, the race we "are" depends on *where* we are—on who is doing the classifying.

And our classifications are fluid, not fixed. You can see change occurring even now in those used in the United States. The category "multiracial," for example, indicates changing thought.

for your consideration

How would you ever explain this primary sociological point that race is more a social classification than a biological one to "Joe Six-Pack"? Can you come up with any arguments to refute it? How do you think our racial-ethnic categories will change in the future?

IN SUM ■ ■ ■ ■

Race, then, lies in the eye of the beholder. Humans show such a mixture of physical characteristics—in skin color, hair texture, nose shape, head shape, eye color, and so on—that there is no inevitable, much less universal, way to classify our many biological differences. Instead of falling into distinct types clearly separate from one another, human characteristics flow endlessly together. Because racial classifications are arbitrary, the categories people use differ from one society to another, and they change over time. In this sense, then, race and its accompanying idea of racial superiority are myths.

■ Ethnic Groups

Whereas people use the term *race* to refer to supposed biological characteristics that distinguish one people from another, **ethnicity** and **ethnic** apply to cultural characteristics. Derived from the word *ethnos* (a Greek word meaning "people" or "nation"), ethnicity and ethnic refer to people who identify with one another on the basis of common ancestry and cultural heritage. Their sense of belonging may center on their nation of origin, distinctive foods, dress, language, music, religion, or family names and relationships.

People often confuse the terms *race* and *ethnic group*. For example, many people, including many Jews, consider the Jews a race. Jews, however, are more properly considered an ethnic group, for it is their cultural characteristics, especially their

■ Although this strange-looking person could be a cartoon character, this is a serious photo of Adolf Hitler taken in 1924. Hitler is wearing lederhosen, *traditional clothing of Bavaria, Germany.*

The reason I selected this photo is to illustrate how seriously we must take all preaching of hatred and of racial supremacy, even though it seems to come from harmless or even humorous sources. This comical-appearing man caused the horrific scene on the right, which greeted the British army when it liberated the concentration camp in Buchenwald, Germany. They found thousands of people dying of starvation and diseases amidst piles of rotting corpses awaiting mass burial.

ethnic (and **ethnicity**) having distinctive cultural characteristics

■ Because ideas of race and ethnicity are such a significant part of society, all of us are classified according to those ideas. This photo illustrates the difficulty such assumptions posed for Israel. The Ethiopians, shown here as they arrived in Israel, although claiming to be Jews, looked so different from other Jews that it took several years for Israeli authorities to acknowledge this group's "true Jewishness."

religion, that bind them together. Wherever Jews have lived in the world, they have intermarried. Consequently, Jews in China may look mongoloid, while some Swedish Jews are blue-eyed blonds. This matter is strikingly illustrated in the photo on the previous page. Ethiopian Jews look so different from European Jews that when they immigrated to Israel many European Jews felt that they could not be *real* Jews.

■ Minority Groups and Dominant Groups

Sociologist Louis Wirth (1945) defined a **minority group** as people who are singled out for unequal treatment *and* who regard themselves as objects of collective discrimination. Either physical (racial) or cultural (ethnic) differences can serve as the basis of the unequal treatment. Wirth added that the discrimination excludes minorities from full participation in the life of their society.

Surprisingly, a minority group is not necessarily a *numerical* minority. For example, before India's independence in 1947, a handful of British colonial rulers discriminated against tens of millions of Indians. Similarly, when South Africa practiced apartheid, a smaller group of Dutch discriminated against a much larger number of blacks. And all over the world, females are a minority group. Accordingly, sociologists refer to those who do the discriminating not as the *majority*, but, rather, as the **dominant group**, for they have greater power, privileges, and social status.

Possessing political power and unified by shared physical and cultural traits, the dominant group uses its position to discriminate against those with different—and supposedly inferior—traits. The dominant group considers its privileged position to be the result of its own innate superiority.

Emergence of Minority Groups A group becomes a minority in one of two ways. The *first* is through the expansion of political boundaries. With the exception of females, tribal societies contain no minority groups. Everyone shares the same culture, including the same language, and belongs to the same group. When a group expands its political boundaries, however, it produces minority groups if it incorporates people with different customs, languages, values, and physical characteristics into the same political entity and discriminates against them. For example, after defeating Mexico in war, the United States took over the Southwest. The Mexicans living there, who had been the dominant group, were transformed into a minority group, a master status that has influenced their lives ever since. Referring to his ancestors, one Latino said, "We didn't move across the border—the border moved across us."

A *second* way in which a group becomes a minority is through migration. This can be voluntary, as with the millions of people who have chosen to move from Mexico to the United States, or involuntary, as with the millions of Africans who were brought in chains to the United States. (The way females became a minority group represents a third way, but, as reviewed in the previous chapter, no one knows just how this occurred.)

Shared Characteristics Anthropologists Charles Wagley and Marvin Harris (1958) noted that no matter where they live in the world, minorities share these five characteristics:

1. Membership in a minority group is an ascribed status; that is, it is not voluntary, but comes through birth.

2. The physical or cultural traits that distinguish minorities are held in low esteem by the dominant group.

3. Minorities are unequally treated by the dominant group.

4. Minorities tend to marry within their own group.

5. Minorities tend to feel strong group solidarity (a sense of "we-ness").

minority group
people who are singled out for unequal treatment, and who regard themselves as objects of collective discrimination

dominant group
the group with the most power, greatest privileges, and highest social status

These conditions—especially when combined with collective discrimination—tend to create a shared sense of identity among minorities, and, in many instances, even a sense of common destiny.

How People Construct Their Racial–Ethnic Identity

Some of us have a greater sense of ethnicity than others. We feel firm boundaries between "us" and "them." Others have assimilated so extensively into the mainstream culture that they are only vaguely aware of their ethnic origins. With interethnic marrying common, some do not even know the countries from which their families originated—nor do they care. If asked to identify themselves ethnically, they respond with something like "I'm Heinz 57—German and Irish, with a little Italian and French thrown in—and I think someone said something about being one-sixteenth Indian, too."

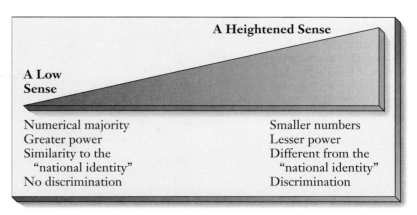

Figure 12.1

A Sense of Ethnicity
Source: Based on Doane 1997.

Why do some people feel an intense sense of ethnic identity, while others feel hardly any? Figure 12.1 portrays four factors, identified by sociologist Ashley Doane, that heighten or reduce our sense of ethnic identity. From this figure, you can see that the keys are relative size, power, appearance, and discrimination. If your group is relatively small, has little power, looks different from most people in society, and is an object of discrimination, you will have a heightened sense of ethnic identity. In contrast, if you belong to the dominant group that holds most of the power, look like most people in the society, and feel no discrimination, you are likely to experience a sense of "belonging"—and wonder why ethnic identity is such a big deal.

We can use the term **ethnic work** to refer to how people construct their ethnicity. For people who have a strong ethnic identity, this term refers to how they enhance and maintain their group's distinctions—from clothing, food, and language to religion and holidays. For people whose ethnic identity is not as firm, it refers to attempts to recover their ethnic heritage, such as trying to trace family lines. Millions of Americans are engaged in ethnic work, which has confounded the experts who thought that the United States would be a **melting pot,** with most of its groups quietly blending into a sort of ethnic stew. In recent years, however, Americans have become fascinated with their "roots," increasingly proud of their ethnic backgrounds, and, some, very assertive of their ethnicity. Consequently, some analysts think that "tossed salad" is more appropriate than "melting pot."

Whites make up 69 percent of the U.S. population, minorities (African Americans, Asian Americans, Latinos, and Native Americans) 29 percent. Another 1 or 2 percent claim membership in more than one group. As the Social Map on the next page shows, the distribution of dominant and minority groups among the states seldom comes close to the national average. This is because minority groups tend to be clustered in regions. The extreme distributions are represented by Maine, which has only 2 percent minority, and by Hawaii, where the national average is reversed and minorities outnumber Anglos 71 percent to 29 percent.

Prejudice and Discrimination

Prejudice and discrimination are common throughout the world. In Mexico, Hispanic Mexicans discriminate against Native American Mexicans; in Israel, Ashkenazi Jews, primarily of European descent, discriminate against Sephardi Jews from the Muslim world; and in Japan, the Japanese discriminate against just about anyone who isn't Japanese, especially immigrant Koreans and the descendants of the Eta

ethnic work
activities designed to discover, enhance, or maintain ethnic and racial identification

melting pot
the view that Americans of various backgrounds would blend into a sort of ethnic stew

Figure 12.2

Social Map: The Distribution of Dominant and Minority Groups in the United States

These totals, for 1999, indicate how unevenly distributed U.S. minority groups are. The extremes are Hawaii with 71% minority and Maine with 2 percent minority.

Source: Statistical Abstract 2000: Table 25.

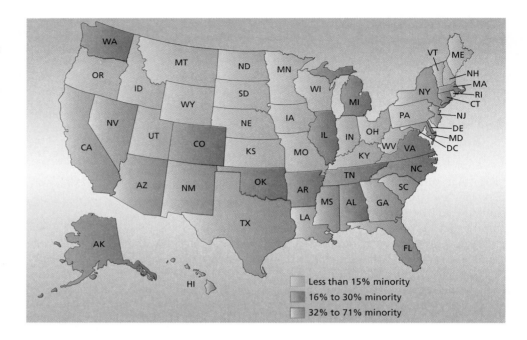

Less than 15% minority

16% to 30% minority

32% to 71% minority

caste. The Eta, now renamed the Burakumin, still bear a stigma because they used to do the society's dirty work—handling dead animals (stripping the hides and tanning the leather) and serving as Japan's executioners and prison guards (Mander 1992; Deliege 2001). In some places the elderly discriminate against the young, in others the young against the elderly. And all around the world men discriminate against women.

As you can see from this list, **discrimination** is an *action*—unfair treatment directed against someone. When the basis of discrimination is race, it is known as **racism,** but discrimination can be based on many characteristics other than race—including age, sex, height, weight, income, education, marital status, sexual orientation, disease, disability, religion, and politics. Discrimination is often the result of an *attitude* called **prejudice**—a prejudging of some sort, usually in a negative way. There is also positive prejudice, which exaggerates the virtues of a group, as when people think that some group (usually their own) is more capable than others. Most prejudice, however, is negative and involves prejudging a group as inferior.

The Extent of Prejudice   Sociologists have found that ethnocentrism is so common that each racial or ethnic group views other groups as inferior in at least some ways. In a random sample of adults in the Detroit area, sociologists Maria Krysan and Reynolds Farley (1993) found that whites and African Americans tend to judge Latinos as less intelligent than themselves. Using a probability sample (from which we can generalize), sociologists Lawrence Bobo and James Kluegel (1991) found that older and less educated whites are more prejudiced than are younger and more educated whites. Details of their findings are shown in Figure 12.3. Other studies show that Latinos and Asian Americans have their own prejudices (Brockerhoff 2000; Charles 2000).

If you grow up in a society that features racial-ethnic stereotypes in everyday life, is it possible not to be prejudiced? Yes, but only with difficulty. Psychologist Anthony Greenwald, who created the "Implicit Association Test," found that 90 to 95 percent of us are prejudiced, even though we don't know it. In one version of this test, good and bad words with photos of African Americans and whites are flashed on the screen. Subjects are quicker to associate positive words (such as love, peace, and baby) with whites and negative words (such as cancer, bomb, and devil) with blacks. Here's the clincher: This is true for *both* white and black subjects (Chamberlain 1998; Berreby 2000; Dasgupta et al. 2000). Greenwald concludes that almost all of us carry "mental imprints" of our culture that lead to biased perception.

discrimination

an *act* of unfair treatment directed against an individual or a group

racism

prejudice and discrimination on the basis of race

prejudice

an *attitude* or prejudging, usually in a negative way

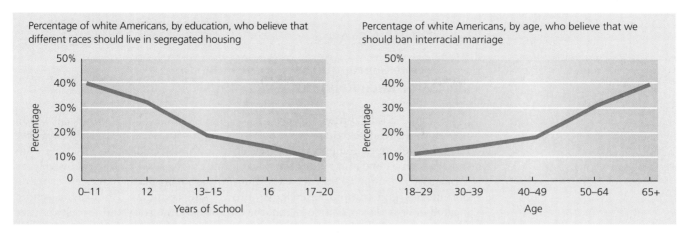

Percentage of white Americans, by education, who believe that different races should live in segregated housing

Percentage of white Americans, by age, who believe that we should ban interracial marriage

Figure 12.3

A Measure of Preferred Social Distance
Source: Bobo and Kluegel 1991.

Members of some groups are more prejudiced than others. At the University of Alabama, sociologist Donald Muir (1991) measured the attitudes of white students who belonged to fraternities and sororities and compared them to those of nonmembers. He asked a variety of questions—from their ideas about dating African Americans to their view on attending classes together. On all measures, fraternity members were more prejudiced than the nonfrats. Research on other campuses supports this finding (Morris 1991). Let's take a closer look at race relations on U.S. campuses.

■ *In the 1920s and 1930s, the Ku Klux Klan was a powerful political force in the United States. To get a sense of the prevailing mood at the time, consider the caption that accompanied this photo of the Ku Klux Klan women from Freeport, New York, when it appeared in the papers: "Here's the Ladies in Their Natty Uniforms Marching in the Parade." Which theories would be most useful to explain this upsurge in racism among mainstream whites of the time?*

thinking
CRITICALLY

Self-Segregation: Help or Hindrance for Race Relations on Campus?

Only after a long, bitter, and violent struggle was federal civil rights legislation prohibiting racial segregation on college campuses passed in the 1960s. These laws did not mark the end of self-segregation, however; certain practices continued, such as one area of a cafeteria or lounge being used almost exclusively by a particular group. In recent years, minority students have requested separate dormitories and campus centers. At Brown University, an Ivy League school located in Providence, Rhode Island, the old rows of fraternity and sorority houses have been replaced by Harambee House (for African Americans), Hispanic House, Slavic House, East Asian House, and German House. Cornell University offers "theme dorms" for African Americans, Hispanics, and Native Americans.

Controversy surrounds this self-segregation of racial-ethnic groups. On one side is William H. Gray III, the head of the United Negro College Fund. Both African American and Latino students drop out of college at a much higher rate, Gray says, so colleges should do everything they can to make minority students feel welcome and accepted.

Critics call the trend toward separate housing a "separatist movement" that divides students into "small enclaves." Administrators at the University of Pennsylvania appointed a commission to study campus life. The committee concluded that when students self-segregate, they lose opportunities for wider interaction with diverse groups of students. Since students tend to socialize with the people they live with, separate housing inhibits the mixing of different groups, depriving students of the rich experiences that come through intercultural contacts.

Joshua Lehrer, a Brown University student who is white, says that some racial and ethnic groups "are separating themselves from everybody else, yet complain when society separates them. Can you really have it both ways?" he asks.

■ ■ ■ ■ ■

for your consideration . . .

Compare separate racial-ethnic housing on college campuses with three patterns discussed in this chapter: segregation, assimilation, and multiculturalism. Is self-segregation permissible if minority students desire it, but not if white students want it? Explain your position.

Sources: Bernstein 1993; Jordon 1996; Terry 2000.

■ Individual and Institutional Discrimination

Sociologists stress that we need to move beyond thinking in terms of **individual discrimination,** the negative treatment of one person by another. Although such behavior creates problems, it is primarily a matter of one individual treating another badly. With their focus on the broader picture, sociologists encourage us to examine **institutional discrimination,** that is, to see how discrimination is woven into the fabric of society. Let's look at two examples.

Home Mortgages and Car Loans   Mortgage lending provides an excellent illustration. As shown in Figure 12.4, race-ethnicity is a significant factor in getting a mortgage. When bankers looked at the statistics shown in this figure, they cried foul. It might *look* like discrimination, they said, but the truth is that whites have better

individual discrimination
the negative treatment of one person by another on the basis of that person's perceived characteristics

institutional discrimination
negative treatment of a minority group that is built into a society's institutions; also called *systemic discrimination*

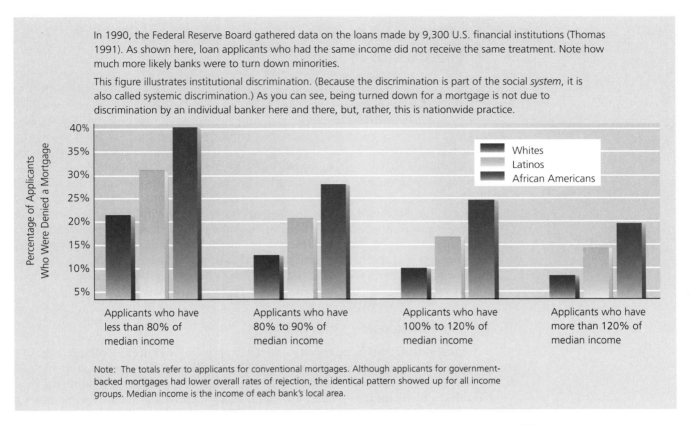

In 1990, the Federal Reserve Board gathered data on the loans made by 9,300 U.S. financial institutions (Thomas 1991). As shown here, loan applicants who had the same income did not receive the same treatment. Note how much more likely banks were to turn down minorities.

This figure illustrates institutional discrimination. (Because the discrimination is part of the social *system*, it is also called systemic discrimination.) As you can see, being turned down for a mortgage is not due to discrimination by an individual banker here and there, but, rather, this is nationwide practice.

Note: The totals refer to applicants for conventional mortgages. Although applicants for government-backed mortgages had lower overall rates of rejection, the identical pattern showed up for all income groups. Median income is the income of each bank's local area.

Figure 12.4

Race-Ethnicity and Mortgages: An Example of Institutional Discrimination

credit histories. To see if this were true, researchers went over the data again, comparing the credit histories of applicants. Not only did they check for late payments, but they also compared the applicants' debts, loan size relative to income, and even characteristics of the property they wanted to buy. The lending gap did narrow a bit, but the bottom line was that even when applicants were identical in all these areas, African Americans and Latinos were *60 percent* more likely to be rejected than whites (Thomas 1992; Passell 1996).Other studies show that African Americans are charged more than whites for their car loans (Henriques 2001). In short, it is not a matter of a banker here or there discriminating according to personal prejudices; rather, discrimination is built into the country's financial institutions.

Health Care Discrimination does not have to be deliberate. It can occur without the awareness of either those doing the discriminating or those being discriminated against. An example is medical care for heart problems. Regardless of their age, sex, or income, white patients are two to three times more likely than black patients to receive coronary bypass surgery (Wenneker and Epstein 1989; Winslow 1992). Treatment after a heart attack follows a similar pattern. A study of 40,000 Medicare patients shows that whites are more likely than blacks to be given cardiac catheterization, a test to detect blockage of blood vessels. This study holds a surprise: Black *and* white doctors are equally as likely to give this preventive care more often to whites (Stolberg 2001).

Why is race a factor in medical decisions? Researchers simply do not know at present. With both white and black doctors involved, we can be certain that physicians *do not intend* to discriminate. In ways we do not yet understand, discrimination is built into medicine. Race apparently works like gender. Just as women's higher death rates in coronary bypass surgery can be traced to attitudes about gender (see page 322), so race serves as a subconscious reason for giving or denying access to advanced medical procedures.

■ ■ ■ ■ ■

Theories of Prejudice

Why are people prejudiced? A commonsense explanation is that they or someone they know has been hurt by a member of a racial or ethnic group, and they transfer their feelings to other members of that group. In some cases, this may be true, but a classic piece of research shows that much more is usually involved. Psychologist Eugene Hartley (1946) asked people how they felt about several groups. Besides blacks, Jews, and so on, he included the Wallonians, Pireneans, and Danireans—names he had made up. Most people who expressed dislike for Jews and blacks also expressed dislike for these three fictitious groups. Hartley's study shows that prejudice does not depend on negative experiences with others. It also reveals that people who are prejudiced against one racial or ethnic group tend to be prejudiced against other groups. People can be, and are, prejudiced against people they have never met—and even against groups that do not exist!

Social scientists have developed several theories to explain prejudice. Let's look first at psychological explanations, then at sociological ones.

■ Psychological Perspectives

Frustration and Scapegoats In 1939, psychologist John Dollard suggested that prejudice is the result of frustration. People who cannot strike out at the real source of their frustration (such as low wages) look for someone to blame for their troubles. This **scapegoat**—often a racial, ethnic, or religious minority—becomes a target on which they vent their frustrations. Gender and age also provide common bases for scapegoating.

Even mild frustration can increase prejudice. A team of psychologists led by Emory Cowen (1959) first measured the prejudice of a sample of students. Then they gave the students two puzzles to solve, making sure they did not have enough time to solve them. After the students had worked furiously on the puzzles, the experimenters shook their heads in disgust and said they couldn't believe they hadn't finished such a simple task. They then retested the students; their scores on prejudice had increased. The students had directed their frustrations outward, onto people who had nothing to do with their problem.

The Authoritarian Personality Have you ever wondered if personality is a cause of prejudice? Maybe some people are more inclined to be prejudiced, and others more fair-minded. For psychologist Theodor Adorno, who had fled from the Nazis, this was no idle speculation. With the horrors he had observed still fresh in his mind, Adorno wondered if there might be a certain type of person who is more likely to fall for the racist spewings of people like Hitler, Mussolini, and the Ku Klux Klan.

To find out, Adorno (1950) tested about two thousand people, ranging from college professors to prison inmates. He gave them three tests. They measured ethnocentrism, anti-Semitism, and support for strong, authoritarian leaders. Adorno found that people who scored high on one test also scored high on the other two. For example, people who agreed with anti-Semitic statements also said that governments should be authoritarian and that foreign ways of life pose a threat to the "American" way.

Adorno concluded that highly prejudiced people are insecure conformists. They have deep respect for authority and are submissive to superiors. He termed this the **authoritarian personality**. These people see things as either right or wrong. Ambiguity disturbs them, especially in matters of religion or sex. They become anxious when they confront norms and values that differ from their own. To define people who differ from themselves as inferior assures them that their own positions are right.

scapegoat
an individual or group unfairly blamed for someone else's troubles

authoritarian personality
Theodor Adorno's term for people who are prejudiced and rank high on scales of conformity, intolerance, insecurity, respect for authority, and submissiveness to superiors

Adorno's research stirred the scientific community, stimulating more than a thousand research studies. In general, the researchers found that people who are older, less educated, less intelligent, and from a lower social class are more likely to be authoritarian. Critics say that this doesn't indicate a particular personality, just that the less educated are more prejudiced—which we already knew (Yinger 1965; Ray 1991).

■ Sociological Perspectives

Sociologists find psychological explanations inadequate. They stress that the key to understanding prejudice is not an individual's *internal* state, but, rather, factors *outside* the individual. Thus, sociologists focus on how some environments foster prejudice, while others discourage it. This topic is explored in the Mass Media box below. With this background, let's compare functionalist, conflict, and symbolic interactionist perspectives on prejudice.

---

mass media in social life

Preaching Hatred: Crime or Inalienable Right?

The Internet is a marvelous source of information—and misinformation. Anyone can put up a Web site and fill it with distortions of truth or even with outright lies. People of all ages, from all walks of life, can nurse grudges, seek revenge for perceived wrongs, and fan hatred.

Such negative communications can be upsetting, especially those that champion hatred. Consider these statements:

Civil Rights come out of the barrel of a gun, and we mean to give the niggers and Jews all the civil rights they can handle. . . . Our security team will see that no live targets escape from the range. Any who refuse to run or can't for any reason will be fed to the dogs. The dogs appreciate a good feed as much as we do.
  —Invitation to a summer conference held by the Aryan Nations at Hayden Lake, Idaho. The group's founder, Richard Butler, is a former Lockheed executive. (Quoted in Murphy 1999)

Who's pimping the world? The hairy hands of the Zionist. . . . The so-called Jew claims that there were six million in Nazi Germany. I am here today to tell you that there is absolutely no . . . evidence to substantiate, to prove that six million so-called Jews

lost their lives in Nazi Germany. . . . Don't let no hooked-nose, bagel-eating, lox-eating, perpetrating-a-fraud so-called Jew who just crawled out of the ghettoes of Europe just a few days ago . . .
  —Khalid Abdul Muhammad (Quoted in Herbert 1998)

Hatred knows no racial-ethnic boundaries; the first statement was made by a white, the second by an African American.

The issue of what to do about hate speech is perplexing. Some want to ban it, while others say that censorship of any speech threatens the free speech of us all. Canada has taken action. Ingrid Rimland of San Diego runs a Web site on which she sells anti-Semitic literature and publicizes the views of Ernst Zundel. Zundel, an immigrant from Germany who has lived in Canada for forty years, denies the Holocaust took place and preaches anti-Semitism. Canadian authorities accused Zundel of controlling the San Diego Web site and charged him under laws that prohibit the use of telephone lines to spread hate messages based on race, religion, or ethnic origin (Stone 1999).

There is a technological solution. The Anti-Defamation League, a human rights group, developed a "hate filter." When

this software is installed on a computer, it blocks access to Web sites that promote intolerance: the Ku Klux Klan, skinheads, and neo-Nazis, as well as those that spew hatred for homosexuals or other groups.

for your consideration

Should we ban statements of hatred from the mass media? Should we perhaps make it illegal to utter such statements, and punish their authors for breaking the law? Or should we allow the promotion of hatred in the mass media, regardless of its inflammatory nature, regardless of how it twists the facts and incites prejudice and hatred? Is there a middle ground, perhaps installing hate filters in grade and middle schools?

Do you think that censoring this one type of speech could be one step toward banning other kinds of speech? For example, once we prohibit a specific kind of speech, what is to stop the government from censoring criticism of its leadership, claiming it is a threat to "national security"?

Functionalism   In a telling scene from a television documentary, journalist Bill Moyers interviewed Fritz Hippler, a Nazi intellectual who at age 29 was put in charge of the entire German film industry. Hippler said that when Hitler came to power the Germans were no more anti-Semitic than the French, probably less so. He was told to create anti-Semitism. Obediently, Hippler produced movies that contained vivid scenes comparing Jews to rats—their breeding threatening to infest the population.

Why was Hippler told to create hatred? Prejudice and discrimination were functional for the Nazis. The Jews provided a convenient scapegoat, a common enemy against which the Nazis could unite a Germany that had been brought to its knees by defeat in World War I and bled by war reparations and rampant inflation. In addition, the Jews owned businesses, bank accounts, art work, and other property that the Nazis could confiscate. They also held key positions (university professors, reporters, judges, and so on), which the Nazis could replace with their own flunkies. In the end, hatred also showed its dysfunctional side, as the Nazi officials who were hanged at Nuremberg discovered.

When state machinery is harnessed to hatred as it was by the Nazis—who exploited the schools, police, courts, mass media, and almost all aspects of the government—prejudice becomes practically irresistible. Recall the identical twins featured in the Down-to-Earth Sociology box on page 67. Oskar and Jack had been separated as babies. Jack was brought up as a Jew in Trinidad, while Oskar was reared as a Catholic in Czechoslovakia. Under the Nazi regime, Oskar learned to hate Jews; he was unaware that he was a Jew himself.

That prejudice is functional and is shaped by the social environment was demonstrated by psychologists Muzafer and Carolyn Sherif (1953). In a boys' summer camp, they assigned friends to different cabins and then had the cabins compete in sports. In just a few days, strong in-groups had formed, and even former lifelong friends were calling one another "crybaby" and "sissy" and showing intense dislike for one another.

Sherif's study teaches us several important lessons about social life. Note how it is possible to arrange the social environment so we generate either positive or negative feelings about people, and how prejudice arises when groups are pitted against one another in an "I win, you lose" situation. You can also see that prejudice is functional, how it creates in-group solidarity. And, of course, it is obvious how dysfunctional prejudice is, how it destroys human relationships.

Conflict Theory   Conflict theorists also analyze how groups are pitted against one another, but they focus on how this arrangement benefits those with power. They begin by noting that workers want better food, health care, housing, and education. Good jobs are necessary to attain these common interests. If workers are united, they can demand higher wages and better working conditions. If capitalists can keep workers divided, they can hold wages down. To do so, capitalists use two main weapons.

The first weapon is to keep workers insecure. The fear of unemployment works especially well. The unemployed serve as a **reserve labor force** for capitalists. They draw on this group to expand production during economic booms, and when the economy contracts, they release these workers to rejoin the ranks of the unemployed. The lesson is not lost on workers who still have jobs. They fear eviction and having their cars and furniture repossessed. Many know they are just one paycheck from ending up "on the streets." This helps keep workers docile.

The second weapon is to exploit racial and ethnic strife. To pit worker against worker weakens their bargaining power. Sowing fear and suspicion among racial-ethnic groups—such as by letting whites know that blacks are waiting to take their

reserve labor force
the unemployed; unemployed workers are thought of as being "in reserve"—capitalists take them "out of reserve" (put them back to work) during times of high production and then lay them off (put them back in reserve) when they are no longer needed

jobs, or by getting blacks to view Latinos as a threat to theirs—also produces docile workers. The result is a **split labor market,** workers divided along racial-ethnic and gender lines (Du Bois 1935/1992; Minchin 1999; Brueggemann 2000).

The consequences are devastating, say conflict theorists. It is just like the boys in the Sherif experiment. African Americans, Latinos, whites, and so on see themselves as able to make gains only at one another's expense. This rivalry shows up along even finer racial-ethnic lines, such as that in Miami between Haitians and African Americans, who distrust each other as competitors. Divisions among workers deflect anger and hostility away from the capitalists and direct these powerful emotions toward other racial and ethnic groups. Instead of recognizing their common class interests and working for their mutual welfare, workers learn to fear and distrust one another.

Symbolic Interactionism   While conflict theorists focus on the role of the capitalist class in exploiting racial and ethnic divisions, symbolic interactionists examine how labels affect perception and create prejudice.

How Labels Create Prejudice   Symbolic interactionists stress that *the labels we learn affect the way we see people.* Labels cause **selective perception;** that is, they lead us to see certain things and blind us to others. If we apply a label to a group, we tend to see its members as all alike. We shake off evidence that doesn't fit (Simpson and Yinger 1972). Racial and ethnic labels are especially powerful. They are shorthand for emotionally laden stereotypes. The term *nigger,* for example, is not neutral. Nor are *honky, spic, mick, kike, limey, kraut, dago,* or any of the other scornful words people use to belittle ethnic groups. Such words overpower us with emotions, blocking out rational thought about the people to whom they refer (Allport 1954).

Stereotypes and Discrimination: The Self-Fulfilling Prophecy   Some stereotypes not only justify prejudice and discrimination—they even produce the behavior depicted in the stereotype. Let's consider Group X. Negative stereotypes characterize Group X as lazy. If they are lazy, they don't deserve good jobs. ("They are lazy and undependable and wouldn't do well.") This attitude creates a *self-fulfilling prophecy.* Because they are denied jobs that require high dedication and energy, most members of Group X are limited to doing "dirty work," the kind of work thought appropriate for "that kind" of people. Since much dirty work is sporadic, members of Group X are often seen standing around street corners. The sight of their idleness reinforces the original stereotype of laziness. The discrimination that created the "laziness" in the first place passes unnoticed.

Symbolic interactionists stress that we are not born with prejudice. Instead, we learn prejudice through interaction with others. At birth each of us joins some particular family and racial or ethnic group, where we learn beliefs and values. There, as part of our basic orientations to the world, we learn to like—or dislike—members of other groups and to perceive them positively or negatively. If discrimination is common, we learn to practice it routinely. Just as we learn any other attitudes and customs, then, in the same way we learn prejudice and discrimination.

Two groups that have gained national attention and concern from citizens and government alike are the neo-Nazis and the Ku Klux Klan. What would happen if a Jew attended the meetings of these groups that make hatred of Jews part of their identity? Would he or she survive? In the Down-to-Earth Sociology box on the next page, sociologist Raphael Ezekiel, a Jew, reveals some of the insights he gained during his remarkable study of these groups.

split-labor market
workers split along racial, ethnic, gender, age, or any other lines; this split is exploited by owners to weaken the bargaining power of workers

selective perception
seeing certain features of an object or situation, but remaining blind to others

down-to-earth sociology

The Racist Mind

Sociologist Raphael Ezekiel wanted to get a close look at the racist mind. As a Jew, he faced a unique problem. The best way to study racism from the inside is to do participant observation (see pp. 139–140). Would this be possible for him? Openly identifying himself as a Jew, Ezekiel asked Ku Klux Klan and neo-Nazi leaders if he could interview them and attend their meetings. Surprisingly, they agreed. Ezekiel published his path-breaking research in a book, *The Racist Mind* (1995). Here are some of the insights he gained during his fascinating sociological adventure:

> [The leader] builds on mass anxiety about economic insecurity and on popular tendencies to see an Establishment as the cause of economic threat; he hopes to teach people to identify that Establishment as the puppets of a conspiracy of Jews. [He has a] belief in exclusive categories. For the white racist leader, it is profoundly true . . . that the socially defined collections we call races represent fundamental categories. A man is black or a man is white; there are no in-betweens. Every human belongs to a racial category, and all the members of one category are radically different from all the members of other categories. Moreover, race represents the essence *of* the person. A truck is a truck, a car is a car, a cat is a cat, a dog is a dog, a black is a black,

a white is a white. . . . These axioms have a rock-hard quality in the leaders' minds; *the world is made up of racial groups.* That is what exists for them.

> Two further beliefs play a major role in the minds of leaders. First, life is war. The world is made of distinct racial groups; life is about the war between these groups. Second, events have secret causes, are never what they seem superficially. . . . Any myth is plausible, as long as it involves intricate plotting. . . . It does not matter to him what others say. . . . He lives in his ideas and in the little world he has created where they are taken seriously. . . . Gold can be made from the tongues of frogs; Yahweh's call can be heard in the flapping swastika banner. (pp. 66–67)

Who is attracted to the neo-Nazis and Ku Klux Klan? Here is what Ezekiel discovered:

> [There is a] ready pool of whites who will respond to the racist signal. . . . This population [is] always hungry for activity—or for the talk of activity—that promises dignity and meaning to lives that are working poorly in a highly competitive world. . . . Much as I don't want to believe it, [this] movement brings a sense of meaning—at least for a while—to some of the discontented. To struggle in a cause that transcends the individual lends mean-

ing to life, no matter how ill-founded or narrowing the cause. For the young men in the neo-Nazi group . . . membership was an alternative to atomization and drift; within the group they worked for a cause and took direct risks in the company of comrades. . . .

> When interviewing the young neo-Nazis in Detroit, I often found myself driving with them past the closed factories, the idled plants of our shrinking manufacturing base. The fewer and fewer plants that remain can demand better educated and more highly skilled workers. These fatherless Nazi youths, these high-school dropouts, will find little place in the emerging economy . . . a permanently underemployed white underclass is taking its place alongside the permanent black underclass. The struggle over race merely diverts youth from confronting the real issues of their lives. Not many seats are left on the train, and the train is leaving the station. (pp. 32–33)

for your consideration

Use functionalism, conflict theory, and symbolic interaction to explain (1) how the leaders and followers of these hate groups view the world, and (2) why some people are attracted to the message of hate.

Global Patterns of Intergroup Relations

Sociologists have studied racial-ethnic relations around the world. They have found six basic patterns that characterize the dominant group and the minorities. These patterns are shown in Figure 12.5. Let's look at each.

■ Genocide

Stereotypes (or labels) are a powerful force in our lives. Symbolic interactionists point out that they can even persuade people who believe that hurting others, much less killing them, is wrong, to participate in mass murder.

Inhumanity ←——————————————————————————→ Humanity

Rejection   Acceptance

Genocide	Population Transfer	Internal Colonialism	Segregation	Assimilation	Multiculturalism (Pluralism)
The dominant group tries to destroy the minority group (e.g., Germany and Rwanda)	The dominant group expels the minority group (e.g., reservations for Native Americans)	The dominant group exploits the minority group (e.g., low-paid, menial work)	The dominant group structures the social institutions to maintain minimal contact with the minority group (e.g., the U.S. South before the 1960s)	The dominant group absorbs the minority group (e.g., American Czechoslovakians)	The dominant group encourages racial and ethnic variation; when fully successful, there is no longer a dominant group (e.g., Switzerland)

Figure 12.5

Global Patterns of Intergroup Relations: A Continuum

Last century's most notorious examples of genocide were Hitler's attempt to destroy all Jews and the Hutus' attempt to destroy all Tutsis. One of the horrifying aspects of these slaughters was that those who participated did not crawl out from under a rock someplace. As you saw in our opening vignette, sometimes it was the neighbors who were the killers. The murderers were ordinary citizens whose participation was facilitated by labels that singled out the victims as enemies worthy of death (Huttenbach 1991; Browning 1993; Simmons 1998; Gross 2001).

To better understand how ordinary people can participate in genocide, let's look at an example from the 1800s. The U.S. government and white settlers labeled Native Americans as "savages." To define the Native Americans as less than human made it easier to justify killing them in order to take over their resources. It made the conscience rest easier as they slaughtered those who resisted their advance toward the West. Most Native Americans, however, died not from bullets but from diseases that the whites brought with them. The Native Americans had no immunity against these diseases, such as measles and the flu (Dobyns 1983; Schaefer 2000). The settlers also ruthlessly destroyed the Native Americans' food supply (buffalos, crops). As a result, about *95 percent* of Native Americans died (Garbarino 1976; Thornton 1987; Churchill 1997).

The same thing was happening in other places. In South Africa, the Boers, or Dutch settlers, viewed the native Hottentots as jungle animals, and they totally wiped them out. In Tasmania, the British settlers stalked the local aboriginal population, hunting them for sport and sometimes even for dog food.

Labels are powerful forces in human life. Labels that dehumanize others help people to **compartmentalize**—to separate their acts from their sense of being good and moral people. To regard members of a group as less than human means that it is okay to treat them inhumanely. Thus people can kill—and still retain a good self-concept (Bernard et al. 1971; Markhusen 1995). In short, *labeling the targeted group as less than fully human facilitates genocide.*

■ Population Transfer

There are two types of **population transfer:** indirect and direct. *Indirect* population transfer is achieved by making life so unbearable for members of a group that they leave "voluntarily." Under the bitter conditions of czarist Russia, for example, millions of Jews made this "choice." *Direct transfer* occurs when a dominant group expels a minority. Examples include the relocation of Native Americans to reservations and the transfer of Americans of Japanese descent to internment camps during World War II.

In the 1990s, a combination of genocide and population transfer occurred in Bosnia and Kosovo, parts of the former Yugoslavia. A hatred nurtured for centuries

compartmentalize
to separate acts from feelings or attitudes

population transfer
forcing a minority group to move

had been kept under wraps during Tito's iron-fisted rule from 1944 to his death in 1980. After Tito's death, these suppressed, smoldering hatreds came to the surface and Yugoslavia split into warring factions. When the Serbs gained power, Muslims rebelled and began guerilla warfare. The Serbs vented their hatred by what they termed **ethnic cleansing:** They terrorized villages with killing and rape, forcing survivors to flee in fear.

■ Internal Colonialism

In Chapter 9, the term *colonialism* was used to refer to one way that the Most Industrialized Nations exploit the Least Industrialized Nations (pp. 266 and 267). Conflict theorists use the term **internal colonialism** to refer to how a country's dominant group exploits minority groups for its economic advantage. The dominant group manipulates the social institutions to suppress minorities and deny them access to the society's benefits. Slavery, reviewed in Chapter 9, is an extreme example of internal colonialism, as was the South African system of *apartheid*. Although the dominant Afrikaaners despised the minority, they found its presence necessary. As Simpson and Yinger (1972) put it, who else would do the hard work?

■ Segregation

Internal colonialism is often accompanied by **segregation**—the separation of racial or ethnic groups. Segregation allows the dominant group to maintain social distance from the minority and yet to exploit their labor as cooks, cleaners, chauffeurs, housekeepers, nannies, factory workers, and so on. In the U.S. South until the 1960s, by law African Americans and whites had to use separate public facilities such as hotels, schools, swimming pools, bathrooms, and even drinking fountains. In thirty-eight states, laws prohibited marriage between blacks and whites. Violators could be sent to prison (Mahoney and Kooistra 1995). It took until 1967 to repeal the last law of this type (Spickard 1989). In Israel, Palestinians who work for the dominant Israelis have to carry passes and go through armed checkpoints in the morning and return to their own areas at the end of the day.

Racial-ethnic segregation in housing is still a fact of life for most Americans. In the Cultural Diversity box on the next page, you can see how residential segregation is related to internal colonialism.

■ Assimilation

Assimilation is the process by which a minority is absorbed into the mainstream culture. There are two types. In *forced assimilation* the dominant group refuses to allow the minority to practice its religion, speak its language, or follow its customs. Prior to the fall of the Soviet Union, for example, the dominant group, the Russians, required that Armenian children attend schools where they were taught in Russian. Armenians could honor only Russian, not Armenian, holidays. *Permissible assimilation*, in contrast, allows the minority to adopt the dominant group's patterns in its own way and at its own speed. In Brazil, for example, where an ideology favors the blending of the country's diverse racial types into a "Brazilian stock," racial and ethnic groups are encouraged to intermarry.

■ Multiculturalism (Pluralism)

A policy of **multiculturalism,** also called **pluralism,** permits or even encourages racial and ethnic variation. Minority groups are able to maintain their separate identities, yet freely participate in their country's social institutions, from education to

ethnic cleansing
a policy to eliminate an ethnic group; includes forcible expulsion and genocide. The term emerged in 1992 among the Serbians during their policy of expelling Croats and Muslims from territories claimed by them during the Yugoslav wars

internal colonialism
the policy of economically exploiting minority groups

segregation
the policy of keeping racial or ethnic groups apart

assimilation
the process of being absorbed into the mainstream culture

multiculturalism (also called **pluralism)**
a philosophy or political policy that permits or encourages ethnic differences

cultural diversity

in the United States and Around the World
"You Can Work for Us, But You Can't Live Near Us"

Never before had so many people crowded in the city hall on Glen Cove, Long Island. What drew them was nothing less than the future of their community, which had become an ethnic and social class crucible. At the front sat the well-groomed Long Islanders in their designer suits and docksiders. Behind them, seated and standing, were men in soiled jeans and work boots whose calloused hands bespoke their occupations as landscape laborers and construction workers. Most of them had fled the civil war in their home country of El Salvador, seeking peace and jobs in the United States.

The meeting was called to order by the town mayor, the son of Italian immigrants, who had launched a campaign to rid the town of a day labor shape-up point, an area where men gathered on the sidewalks in the early mornings to look for day jobs. Some days before, the mayor had ordered the Immigration and Naturalization Service to raid the area. This evening he proposed an ordinance making it illegal for groups of five or more to assemble on city streets for the purpose of seeking work. The mayor and other city residents testified that the men made cat calls at women and urinated in public. Concerned citizens called the shape-up an eyesore. Representatives of the immigrants countered by affirming the immigrants' constitutional right to freedom of assembly and argued that they were not loitering in the streets but waiting peacefully on the sidewalks.

The larger issue that haunted the Long Islanders, one they were reluctant to ac-

knowledge publicly but a few admitted to me privately, was the fear that the immigrants gave the impression that the town was in decline. Such a perception in suburbia jeopardizes real estate values—the bedrock of U.S. middle-class security. On Long Island, as in many similar areas, even the hint of racial or ethnic turnover frightens homeowners and potential buyers. In Glen Cove, this fear led to the campaign to get rid of the shape-up, the single most vivid image of the ethnically distinct people residing in the community.

What never was discussed in the town meeting nor came up in casual conversation was that the immigrants had been attracted to the area precisely because the suburbanites desired their inexpensive labor. Almost all the landscapers on Long Island are now Salvadoran, while many families depend on immigrant women to come into their homes to clean their houses and to take care of their children and elderly. Immigrants, especially from El Salvador and other Latin American countries, toil in the island's restaurant kitchens, factories, industrial laundries, and in gleaming office buildings at night. They do the jobs that U.S. workers do not want to do or cannot afford to do because they pay too little to support their families.

When the Salvadorans and other immigrants arrived on Long Island, seeking their futures, they first lived primarily in communities

with high minority populations. But as the immigrants moved closer to their jobs, their numbers swelled in more traditional bedroom communities like Glen Cove. These other towns also began to adopt "not in my backyard" policies by passing new ordinances or enforcing old ones, even by refusing to let undocumented immigrant children attend their public schools. Old timers felt that such measures could stem the decline in their way of life. What they overlooked was how immigrant labor is preserving their standard of living.

Sarah Maher
University of Vermont
Salvadorans in Suburbia

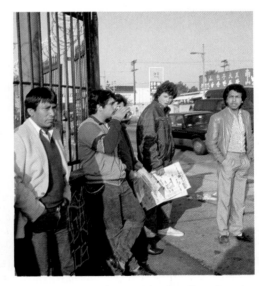

▪ *Day laborers lined up, waiting for offers of work*

politics. Switzerland provides an outstanding example of multiculturalism. The Swiss are made up of four ethnic groups—French, Italians, Germans, and Romansh. The groups have kept their own languages, and they live peacefully in political and economic unity. Multiculturalism has been so successful that none of these groups can properly be called a minority.

■ ■ ■ ■ ■

Race and Ethnic Relations in the United States

As I have stressed, racial classifications are arbitrary and ever-changing. Nevertheless, as part of everyday life, we classify one another as belonging to distinct racial-ethnic groups (see Figure 12.6). Most of us also have strong racial-ethnic self-identities. Let's explore some of the consequences of that membership and identity.

A Note on Terms   To write on race-ethnicity is like stepping into a minefield: One never knows where to expect the next explosion. Even basic terms are controversial. The term African American, for example, is rejected by some who say that this

Figure 12.6

U.S. Racial and Ethnic Groups

aThe totals for the groups of Americans of European descent should be taken as broadly accurate only. The data in *Statistical Abstract* have been adjusted downward by 5.23 percent to match the 2000 census data reported in the 2001 source. This decline would not apply across the board, but it is the best that can be done to resolve the conflicting totals we have at the moment.

bIncludes "British."

cIncludes "Scottish-Irish."

dMost Latinos trace at least part of their ancestry to Europe.

eIn descending order, the largest six groups of Asian Americans are Chinese, Filipinos, Japanese, Asian Indians, Koreans, and Vietnamese.

fIncludes Native American, Eskimo, and Aleut.

Source: Statistical Abstract 2000: Tables 16, 26, 50; Kent et al. 2001.

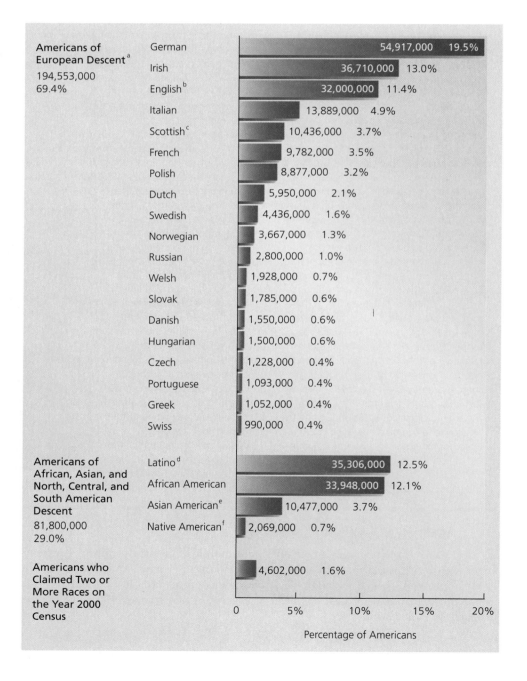

Americans of European Descent[a]
194,553,000
69.4%

Group	Number	Percentage
German	54,917,000	19.5%
Irish	36,710,000	13.0%
English[b]	32,000,000	11.4%
Italian	13,889,000	4.9%
Scottish[c]	10,436,000	3.7%
French	9,782,000	3.5%
Polish	8,877,000	3.2%
Dutch	5,950,000	2.1%
Swedish	4,436,000	1.6%
Norwegian	3,667,000	1.3%
Russian	2,800,000	1.0%
Welsh	1,928,000	0.7%
Slovak	1,785,000	0.6%
Danish	1,550,000	0.6%
Hungarian	1,500,000	0.6%
Czech	1,228,000	0.4%
Portuguese	1,093,000	0.4%
Greek	1,052,000	0.4%
Swiss	990,000	0.4%

Americans of African, Asian, and North, Central, and South American Descent
81,800,000
29.0%

Group	Number	Percentage
Latino[d]	35,306,000	12.5%
African American	33,948,000	12.1%
Asian American[e]	10,477,000	3.7%
Native American[f]	2,069,000	0.7%

Americans who Claimed Two or More Races on the Year 2000 Census
4,602,000   1.6%

Percentage of Americans
0   5%   10%   15%   20%

term properly includes white immigrants from South Africa. They also say that it does not include Oscar Peterson, the jazz musician—because he is Canadian (author's file). Many of these people identify themselves as blacks, rather than as African Americans. Similarly, some Latinos prefer the term *Hispanic American,* while others reject it, saying that it ignores the Indian side of their heritage. Some would limit the term *Chicanos*—commonly used to refer to Americans from Mexico—to those who have a sense of oppression and ethnic unity; they say it does not apply to those who have assimilated.

No term that I use here, then, will satisfy everyone. Terms for racial-ethnic identity are constantly changing, and they take on newly charged political meaning from time to time. With this as background, let's review the major groups in the United States, going from the largest to the smallest.

JUST SO.

Hoodlum. "Tain't their color I mind s'much—(hic) it's their (hic) habits I 'bject to."

■ *Almost all racial-ethnic groups, including white ethnics, have experienced prejudice and discrimination. The objects of scorn in this cartoon, which appeared in U.S. newspapers in 1879, are Irish immigrants. The Irish were despised at the time, and were often depicted drunk. In a surprising twist, the Chinese immigrants in this cartoon are portrayed positively as hard workers.*

■ White Europeans

Perhaps the single event that best crystallizes the racial view of the nation's founders occurred at the first Continental Congress of the United States. There they passed the Naturalization Act of 1790, declaring that only white immigrants could apply for citizenship. Their sense of superiority and privilege was not limited to their views of race. These **WASPs** (white Anglo-Saxon Protestants) also viewed white Europeans from countries other than England as inferior. They greeted **white ethnics**—immigrants from Europe whose language and other customs differed from theirs—with negative stereotypes. They especially despised the Irish, viewing them as dirty, lazy drunkards, but they also painted Germans, Poles, Jews, Italians, and so on with similarly broad brush strokes.

The cultural and political dominance of the WASPs placed pressure on immigrants to blend into the mainstream culture. The children of most immigrants embraced the new way of life and quickly came to think of themselves as Americans rather than as Germans, French, Hungarians, and so on. They dropped their distinctive customs, especially their language, often viewing them as symbols of shame. This second generation of immigrants was sandwiched between two worlds, that of their parents from "the old country" and their new home. Their children, the third generation, had an easier adjustment, for they had fewer customs to discard. As immigrants from other parts of Europe assimilated into this Anglo culture, the meaning of WASP expanded to include people of this descent.

Because the English settled the colonies, they established the culture to which later immigrants had to conform—from the dominant language to the dominant religion. Highly ethnocentric, they considered the customs of any group that differed from theirs as inferior. In short, it was the European colonists who, taking power and determining the national agenda, controlled the destiny of the nation and dominated and exploited other ethnic groups. Throughout the years, other ethnic groups have had to react to this institutional and cultural dominance of western Europeans, which still sets the stage for current ethnic relations.

■ Latinos (Hispanics)

Before reviewing major characteristics of Latinos, it is important to stress that *Latino* and *Hispanic* do not refer to a race, but to ethnic groups. Latinos may identify themselves racially as black, white, or Native American.

Numbers, Origins, and Location   When birds still nestled in the trees that were used to build the *Mayflower,* Latinos had already established settlements in Florida and New Mexico (Bretos 1994). Today, Latinos are the largest minority group

WASP
a White Anglo-Saxon Protestant; narrowly, an American of English descent; broadly, an American of western European ancestry

white ethnics
white immigrants to the United States whose culture differs from that of WASPs

■ *When the U.S. government took control of what is now the southwestern United States, Mexicans living there were transformed from the dominant group into a minority group. To try to maintain their culture, Chicanos,* Americans of Mexican origin, *do ethnic work, such as this dance by the Ballet Folklorico de Yale College, at a Cinco de Mayo celebration. As assimilation progresses, customs from the homeland become similar to museum pieces—bits of history to be examined, perhaps admired, but remote from everyday life.*

in the United States. As shown in Figure 12.7, about 21 million people trace their origin to Mexico, 3 million to Puerto Rico, 1 million to Cuba, and almost 5 million to Central or South America, primarily Venezuela and Colombia. Officially tallied at 35 million in the year 2000 census, the actual number of Latinos is higher, because, not surprisingly, many who are in the country illegally avoid contact with both public officials and census forms. Each year, more than 1 million people are apprehended at the border or at points inland and are deported to Mexico (*Statistical Abstract* 2000:Table 349). Perhaps another million or so manage to enter the United States. Many migrate for temporary work and then return to their homes and families.

To gain an understanding of how vast these numbers are, we can note that there are millions more Latinos in the United States than there are Canadians in Canada (31 million). To Midwesterners, such a comparison often comes as a surprise, for Latinos are absent from vast stretches of mid-America. As shown in Figure 12.8, 69 percent are concentrated in just four states: California, Texas, New York, and Florida. Latinos are the largest minority group in several major cities, including Los Angeles, San Antonio, Miami, and Houston.

Spanish Language   The Spanish language distinguishes most Latinos from other U.S. ethnic groups. With 20 million people speaking Spanish at home, the United States has become one of the largest Spanish-speaking nations in the world (*Statistical Abstract* 2000:Table 51, adjusted). Because about half of Latinos are unable to speak English, or can do so only with difficulty, many millions face a major obstacle to getting good jobs.

The growing use of Spanish has become a matter of controversy. Perceiving the prevalence of Spanish as a threat, Senator S. I. Hayakawa of California initiated an "English only" movement in 1981. The constitutional amendment he sponsored never got off the ground, but 23 states have passed a law declaring English their official language (Schaefer 2000).

Diversity   For Latinos, country of origin is highly significant. Those from Puerto Rico, for example, feel little in common with people from Mexico, Venezuela, or El Salvador—just as earlier immigrants from Germany, Sweden, and England felt they had little in common with one another. A sign of these divisions is the preference many have

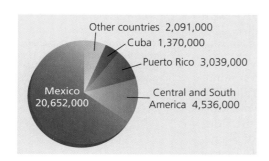

Figure 12.7

Country of Origin of U.S. Latinos

Source: Statistical Abstract 2000:Table 45.

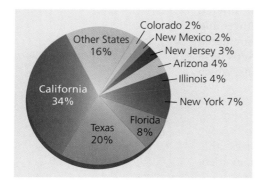

Figure 12.8

Where U.S. Latinos Live

Source: Statistical Abstract 2000:Table 25.

■ In reaction to the millions of recent Latino immigrants who speak Spanish, an "English-only" movement has developed in the United States. Twenty-three states have passed laws declaring that English is their official language. One wonders which version of English the legislators had in mind.

to refer to themselves in terms of their country of origin, such as Puerto Rican or Cuban American, rather than as Latino or Hispanic.

As with other ethnic groups, Latinos, too, are separated by social class. The half-million Cubans who fled Castro's rise to power in 1959, for example, were mostly well-educated, well-to-do professionals or businesspeople. In contrast, the 100,000 "boat people" from Cuba who fled in 1980 were mostly lower-class refugees, people with whom the earlier arrivals would not have even associated in Cuba—and do not associate with here. The earlier arrivals, firmly established in Florida and in control of many businesses and financial institutions, distance themselves from the more recent immigrants.

These divisions of national origin and social class are a major obstacle to political unity. One consequence is a severe underrepresentation in politics. Although Latinos make up 12.5 percent of the U.S. population, and we could expect 12 or 13 U.S. Senators to be Latino, none are. Latinos hold only 4 percent of the seats in the U.S. Congress and just 1 percent of elected local offices (*Statistical Abstract* 2000:Table 471; 2001:Table 390.).

Fragmented among themselves, Latinos also find that a huge gulf separates them from African Americans (Flippen 2001). With highly distinct histories and cultures, the relationship of these two groups is often tinged with hostility. As Latinos have become more visible in U.S. society and more vocal in their demands for equality, they have come face to face with African Americans who fear that Latino gains in jobs and at the ballot box will come at their expense. Together, Latinos and African Americans make up one-fourth of the U.S. population. It is likely that these two groups will increasingly come to recognize that their unity will produce an unstoppable political force.

Comparative Conditions Table 12.1 on the next page shows how Latinos compare with other groups. You can see that compared with European Americans and with Asian Americans, Latinos are worse off on all the indicators of well-being shown in this table. You can also see how similar their rankings on these indicators are to those of African Americans. This table also illustrates the significance of country of origin. You can see that Cuban Americans score higher on these indicators of well-being, while Puerto Rican Americans score far worse. Table 12.2 on page 365 shows that almost half of Latinos do not complete high school, and only 11 percent graduate from college. In a postindustrial society that increasingly requires advanced skills, these totals indicate that a large number of people will be left behind.

T A B L E 12.1 Race-Ethnicity and Comparative Well-Being

	Median Family Income	Percentage of White Income	Percentage Unemployed	Percentage of White Unemployment	Percentage Below Poverty Line	Percentage of White Poverty	Percentage Owning Their Homes	Percentage of White Home Ownership
White Americans	$49,023	—	2.5%	—	10.5%	—	70%	—
African Americans	$29,404	60%	8.0%	320%	26.1%	249%	46%	66%
Latinos	$29,608	60%	4.4%	176%	25.6%	244%	45%	64%
Country of origin								
Mexico	$27,883	57%	4.5%	180%	27.1%	258%	49%	70%
Puerto Rico	$28,953	59%	5.1%	204%	30.9%	294%	33%	47%
Cuba	$39,530	81%	2.9%	116%	13.6%	130%	58%	83%
Central and South America	$32,676	67%	4.1%	164%	19.9%	190%	35%	50%
Asian Americans[a]	$52,826	108%	2.8%	112%	12.5%	119%	52%	74%
Native Americans	$21,619	44%	NA[b]	NA	31.2%	297%	NA	NA

[a]Includes Pacific Islanders.
[b]Not available.
Source: *Statistical Abstract 2000*:Tables 41, 42, 44, 45.

	Less than High School Education	High School Education	1–3 Years of College	College Graduate	Number of Doctorates Awarded	Percentage of all Doctorates Awarded
White Americans	16%	34%	25%	26%	24,143	78%
African Americans	23%	36%	26%	15%	1,577	5%
Latinos	44%[a]	45%	NA	11%	1,298	4%
Asian Americans	16%	22%	20%	42%	2,720	9%
Native Americans	20%[a,b]	69%	NA	11%	185	0.6%

TABLE 12.2 Education and Race-Ethnicity

Note: NA = Not Available. Totals except for doctorates refer to persons 25 years and over.
[a]Totals for Latinos and Native Americans are not listed in the same way in the source as they are for other groups.
[b]Author's estimate, based on the changes made by the other groups between 1990 and 1998.
Source: Statistical Abstract 2000:Tables 41, 42, 44, 45, 997.

■ African Americans

After slavery was abolished, in a practice known as *Jim Crow,* the South passed laws to segregate blacks and whites. In 1896, the Supreme Court ruled in *Plessy v. Ferguson* that state laws requiring "separate but equal" accommodations for blacks were a reasonable use of state power. Whites used this ruling to strip blacks of the political power they had gained after the Civil War. They prohibited blacks from voting in "white" primaries. It was not until 1944 that the Supreme Court ruled that African Americans could vote in southern primaries, and not until 1954 that they had the legal right to attend the same public schools as whites (Schaefer 2000). Well into the 1960s, the South was still openly—and legally—practicing segregation.

The Struggle for Civil Rights

It was 1955, in Montgomery, Alabama. As specified by law, whites took the front seats of the bus, while blacks went to the back. As the bus filled up, blacks had to give up their seats to whites.

When Rosa Parks, a 42-year-old African American woman and secretary of the Montgomery NAACP, was told she would have to stand so white folks could sit, she refused (Bray 1995). She stubbornly sat there while the bus driver raged and whites felt insulted. Her arrest touched off mass demonstrations, led fifty thousand blacks to boycott the city's buses for a year, and thrust an otherwise unknown preacher into a historic role.

Rev. Martin Luther King Jr., who had majored in sociology at Morehouse College in Atlanta, Georgia, took control. He organized car pools and preached non-violence. Incensed at this radical organizer and at the stirrings in the normally compliant black community, segregationists also put their beliefs into practice—by bombing homes and dynamiting churches.

Rising Expectations and Civil Strife
The barriers came down, but they came down slowly. Not until 1964 did Congress pass the Civil Rights Act, making it illegal to discriminate in restaurants, hotels, theaters, and other public places. Then in 1965, Congress passed the Voting Rights Act, banning the fraudulent literacy tests that the South had used to keep African Americans from voting.

■ *Until the 1960s, the South's public facilities were racially segregated. Some were reserved for whites only, others for blacks only. This apartheid was broken by blacks and whites who worked together and risked their lives to bring about a fairer society. Shown here is a 1963 sit-in at a Woolworth's lunch counter in Jackson, Mississippi. Sugar, ketchup, and mustard are being poured over the heads of the demonstrators.*

Encouraged by these gains, African Americans experienced what sociologists call **rising expectations;** that is, they believed better conditions would soon follow. The lives of the poor among them, however, changed little, if at all. Frustrations built, finally exploding in Watts in 1965, when African Americans in that Los Angeles ghetto took to the streets in the first of what have been termed "the urban revolts." When King was assassinated by a white supremacist on April 4, 1968, inner cities across the nation again erupted in fiery violence. Under threat of the destruction of U.S. cities, Congress passed the sweeping Civil Rights Act of 1968.

Continued Gains   Since then, African Americans have made remarkable political, educational, and economic gains. At 9 percent, African Americans have *quadrupled* their membership in the U.S. House of Representatives in the past 30 years (Rich 1986; *Statistical Abstract* 2001:Table 390). As college enrollments increased, the middle class expanded. Today, half of all African American families make more than $25,000 a year. One in three makes more than $35,000 a year, one of four more than $50,000, and one of eight more than $75,000 (*Statistical Abstract* 2000:Table 743). Although the poverty rate of African Americans is among the highest (see Table 12.1), contrary to stereotypes the average African American family is not poor.

The extent of African American political prominence was highlighted when Jesse Jackson (another sociology major) competed for the Democratic presidential nomination in 1984 and 1988. Political progress was further confirmed in 1989 when L. Douglas Wilder of Virginia became the nation's first elected African American governor. The political prominence of African Americans came to the nation's attention again in 2000 when Alan Keyes competed for the Republican presidential nomination.

Current Losses   Despite these gains, African Americans continue to lag behind in politics, economics, and education. No U.S. Senator is African American, when based on the percentage of the population we would expect 12. As Table 12.1 shows, African Americans average only 60 percent of white income, have more unemployment and poverty, and are less likely to own their home. As Table 12.2 shows, only 15 percent have graduated from college. That one in three African American families has an

rising expectations
the sense that better conditions are soon to follow, which, if unfulfilled, increase frustration

income over $35,000 is only part of the story. The other part is that about one of every six families makes less than $10,000 a year (*Statistical Abstract* 2000:Table 743).

Two worlds of African American experience have developed—one educated and affluent, the other uneducated and poor. Concentrated among the poor are those with the least hope, the highest despair, and the violence that so often dominates the evening news. African American males are *seven* times as likely to be homicide victims as are white males. Compared with white females, African American females are more than *four* times as likely to be murdered (*Statistical Abstract* 2000:Table 335). Homicide is now the leading cause of death for African American males ages 15 to 24. Each year, more African American males are killed by other African Americans than died in the entire nine years of the war in Vietnam.

■ As discussed in the text, sociologists disagree about the relative significance of race and social class in determining social and economic conditions of African Americans. William Julius Wilson, shown here, is an avid proponent of the social class side of this debate.

Race or Social Class? A Sociological Debate   This division of African Americans into "haves" and "have-nots" has fueled a sociological controversy. Sociologist William Julius Wilson (1978, 1987, 2000) argues that social class has become more important than race in determining the life chances of African Americans. Prior to civil rights legislation, he says, the African American experience was dominated by race. Throughout the United States, African Americans were excluded from avenues of economic advancement—from good schools and good jobs. When civil rights legislation opened new opportunities, African Americans seized them. Following the path taken by other ethnic groups, as African Americans advanced economically, they, too, moved out of the inner city. Just as legislation began to open doors to African Americans, however, manufacturing jobs dried up and many blue-collar jobs were moved to the suburbs. As a result, while better-educated African Americans were able to obtain middle-class, white-collar jobs, a large group of African Americans—those with poor education and lack of skills—was left behind, trapped by poverty in the inner city.

The result, says Wilson, is two worlds of African American experience. One group is stuck in the inner city, lives in poverty, attends poor schools, and faces dead-end jobs or welfare. This group is filled with hopelessness and despair, combined with apathy or hostility. In contrast, those who have moved up the social class ladder live in comfortable homes in secure neighborhoods. They work at well-paid jobs and send their children to good schools. Their middle-class experiences and lifestyle have changed their views on life, and their aspirations and values now have little in common with those of African Americans who remain poor. According to Wilson, then, social class—not race—has become the most significant factor in the lives of African Americans.

Some sociologists reply that this analysis overlooks the discrimination that continues to underlie the African American experience (Feagin 1999). Sociologist Charles Willie (1991), for example, notes that even when they do the same work, whites average higher pay than do African Americans. This, he argues, points to racial discrimination, not to social class. The Down-to-Earth Sociology box on the next page highlights this discrimination.

What is the answer to this debate? Wilson would reply that it is not an either-or question. My book is titled *The **Declining** Significance of Race*, he would say, not *The Absence of Race*. Certainly racism is still alive, he would add, but today social class is more central to the African American experience than is racial discrimination. The answer, then, is to provide jobs—for the availability of work offers hope, and work provides an anchor to a responsible life (Wilson 1996, 2000).

Continued Discrimination and Social Class   African Americans who occupy higher statuses not only enjoy greater opportunities but also face less discrimination. The discrimination they encounter, however, is no less painful (Duneier 1999). Middle-class and wealthy African Americans, for example, report being pulled over by police who assume their expensive cars must be stolen. Christopher Darden

down-to-earth
sociology

What You Reveal by Your Voice: Racism in the Rental Market

Blatant expressions of discrimination have become a thing of the past. There was a time when whites could burn crosses with impunity at the homes of blacks. Some even lynched African Americans and Asian Americans without fear of the law. Today cross burning and lynching will be investigated and prosecuted. If local officials don't make an arrest, the FBI will step in. Similarly, discrimination in public accommodations was once standard. Today, no hotel, restaurant, or gas station would refuse service on the basis of race-ethnicity. This, too, has become a criminal matter.

With times so changed, some may think that racism is a thing of the past. Although overt racism has been relegated to the back shelves of social life, racism is alive and well, as sociologist Douglas Massey of the University of Pennsylvania documents (Massey and Lundy 2001). In his undergraduate course in research methods were whites who spoke what is called White Middle Class English, African Americans who spoke a dialect known as Black English Vernacular, and other African Americans who spoke middle-class English with a black accent.

As you know, Americans often identify one another racially by their speech. Massey used this feature of everyday life to test discrimination in the housing market. He and his students designed standard identities for members of these linguistic groups (assigning them similar income, for example). They also developed a standard script, the one group translating it into Black English Vernacular. The students called on 79 apartments that were advertised for rent in newspa-

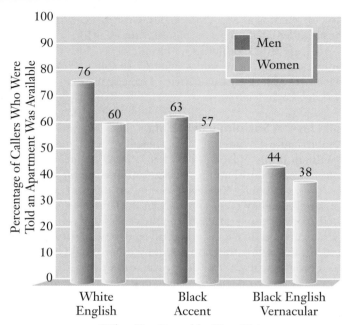

What You Reveal by Your Voice:
Racism in the Rental Market

Figure 12.9

Callers Who Were Told an Apartment Was Available
Source: Massey and Lundy 2001.

pers. The study was done blindly, with the white and black students not knowing how the others were being treated.

Compared with whites, African Americans were less likely to speak to rental agents, who often used answering machines to screen calls. They also were less likely to be told that an apartment was available, more likely to have to pay an application fee, and more likely to have credit mentioned. Figure 12.9 shows the

percentage of callers who were told that an apartment was available. Students who posed as lower-class blacks (speakers of Black English Vernacular) had the least access to apartments.

As you can see from this figure, in line with last chapter's topic, in all instances, for both whites and blacks, discrimination was worse against women.

■ ■ ■ ■ ■

(1997:97), an African American prosecutor in the O. J. Simpson case, says that the police stop him about five times a year:

> I know the rules of the game, and I put them to work instinctively. Don't move. Don't turn around. Don't give some rookie an excuse to shoot you. Don't ask questions, no matter how badly you might want to know the answer to "Why are you stopping us, but no other cars on the street? Why aren't you stopping any of those white people?"
> "You've got a bad tail light," the cop would say. Or, "You were weaving a little." But you know what the real crime was: suspicion of being black.

The following Thinking Critically section highlights a proposal to compensate for injustices to African Americans.

CRITICALLY

Reparations for Slavery: Justice or Foolishness?

The subtitle of this section is intended to frame the stark contrasts that surround the debate about reparations for slavery. The issue itself is simple. The enslavement of millions of Africans was a gross injustice. Since the slaves were never paid for 240 years of work, their descendents should be. This is both a moral and a legal issue.

The argument for reparations, or compensation, contains related matters. The first is that the greater wealth of today's white Americans is built on the centuries of unpaid labor of black slaves. The second is that today's unequal conditions between African Americans and whites (the "racial deficit") in education, housing, and income are a legacy of slavery (Marable 2001).

Simply put, reparations are a form of back wages. These back wages will be paid either directly to the descendents of slaves or into a reparations trust fund targeted not to individuals but to poor black communities with the greatest need.

Opponents of reparations agree that slavery was a horrible crime against humanity. They stress that it occurred a long time ago and that it is not a black and white issue. It was Africans who sold African prisoners to white slavers in the first place. Secondly, most of today's whites are descended from people who immigrated to the United States after slavery ended. It is not only that they had nothing to do with slavery—neither did their ancestors. In addition, if reparations were paid, the money would be coming not only from whites but also from taxes paid by Latinos, Asian Americans, and Native Americans, as well as immigrants from hundreds of countries—none of whom had anything to do with slavery either. Not incidentally, it would also come from taxes that have been paid by African Americans.

Shelby Steele, a psychologist and an African American, argues that it is time to move beyond "thinking of ourselves as victims." He says that "we need to build a positive black identity, an identity built around ingenuity and personal responsibility. We should busy ourselves with the hard work of development, not try to manipulate white guilt" (Steele 2001).

■ ■ ■ ■ ■

for your consideration . . .

There are finer points on both sides of the argument, but these are the basic issues that are argued. What is your opinion of reparations?

Ideas, including our opinions, are not located in a social vacuum. They are rooted both in history and in our particular location in society. Can you identity how your social location underlies your opinions about this controversial topic? To do so, consider your racial-ethnic background, when your ancestors arrived in the United States, your social class, the ideas of your parents, and especially the opinions of your friends. How do these factors influence your views of what is moral and logical in this issue?

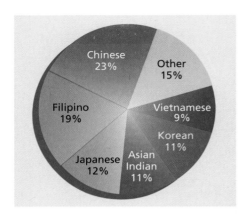

Figure 12.10

The Ethnic Background
of Asian Americans

Source: Statistical Abstract 2000:
Table 26.

Asian Americans

I have stressed in this chapter that our racial-ethnic categories are based more on social considerations than biological ones. This point is again obvious when we examine the category Asian American. As Figure 12.10 shows, those who are called Asian Americans came to the United States from many nations. With no unifying culture or "race," why should they ever be clustered together in a single category? Think about it. What culture or race-ethnicity do Samoans and Vietnamese have in common? Or Laotians and Pakistanis? Or Native Hawaiians and Chinese? Or people from India and those from Guam? Yet all these groups—and more—are lumped together and called Asian Americans. Apparently the U.S. government is not satisfied until it is able to pigeonhole everyone into a racial-ethnic category.

Since Asian American is a standard term, however, let's look at the characteristics of the nearly 11 million people who are lumped together and assigned this label.

A Background of Discrimination   From the time they arrived on these shores, Asian Americans met discrimination. Lured by gold strikes in the West and a vast need for unskilled workers to build the railroads, 200,000 Chinese immigrated between 1850 and 1880. Feeling threatened by competing cheap labor, Anglos formed mobs and vigilante groups to intimidate the Chinese. In 1850, California passed the Foreign Miner's Act, which required Chinese (and Latinos) to pay a fee of $20 a month—when wages were a dollar a day. When the famous golden spike was driven at Promontory, Utah, in 1869 to mark the completion of the railroad to the west coast, white workers prevented Chinese workers from being in the photo—even though Chinese made up 90 percent of Central Pacific Railroad's labor force (Hsu 1971). The California Supreme Court ruled that Chinese testimony against whites was inadmissible in court (Carlson and Colburn 1972). In 1882, Congress passed the Chinese Exclusion Act, suspending all Chinese immigration for 10 years. Four years later, the Statue of Liberty was dedicated. The tired, the poor, and the huddled masses it was intended to welcome were obviously not Chinese.

When immigrants from Japan arrived, they met *spillover bigotry,* a stereotype that lumped Asians together, depicting them as sneaky, lazy, and untrustworthy. After

■ *Amid fears that Japanese Americans were "enemies within" who would sabotage industrial and military installations on the West Coast, in the early days of World War II Japanese Americans were transferred to "relocation camps." Many returned home after the war to find that their property had been vandalized.*

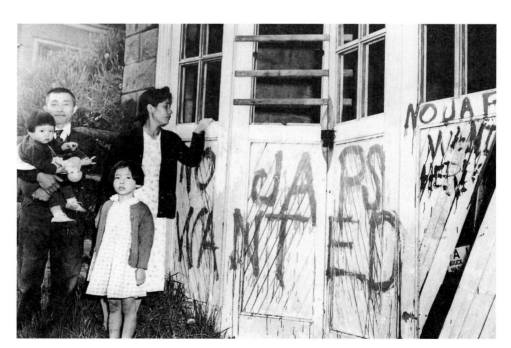

Japan attacked Pearl Harbor in 1941, conditions grew worse for the 110,000 Japanese Americans who called the United States their home. U.S. authorities feared that Japan would invade the United States and that the Japanese Americans would fight on Japan's side. They also feared that Japanese Americans would sabotage military installations on the West Coast. Although no Japanese American had been involved in even a single act of sabotage, on February 19, 1942, President Franklin D. Roosevelt ordered that everyone who was *one-eighth Japanese or more* be placed in special prisons (called "relocation camps"). They were charged with no crime, and they had no trials. Japanese ancestry was sufficient cause for being imprisoned.

A World of Striking Contrasts Most Asian Americans live in the West, as can be seen in Figure 12.11. The three largest groups of Asian Americans—of Chinese, Filipino, and Japanese descent—are concentrated in Los Angeles, San Francisco, Honolulu, and New York City. From Table 12.1 (page 364), you can see that Asian Americans have a higher annual income than any other racial-ethnic group listed on this table. This has led to an assumption that all Asian Americans are successful, a stereotype that masks huge ethnic differences. Look at the poverty rate of Asian Americans shown on this table. Although 12.5 percent is less than any other minority group, it means that about one and a half million Asian Americans live in poverty. Their poverty is not evenly distributed; poverty is unusual among Chinese and Japanese Americans, but it clusters among Americans from Southeast Asia.

Reasons for Success The general success of Asian Americans can be traced to three major factors: family life, educational achievement, and assimilation into mainstream culture.

Of all ethnic groups, including whites, Asian American children are the most likely to grow up with two parents and the least likely to be born to a single mother (Lee 1998; *Statistical Abstract* 2000:Table 85). Most grow up in close-knit families that stress self-discipline, thrift, and hard work (Suzuki 1985; Bell 1991). This early socialization provides strong impetus for the other two factors.

The second factor is their high rate of college graduation. As Table 12.2 on page 365 shows, 42 percent of Asian Americans complete college. To realize how stunning this is, compare this with the other groups shown on this table. Their educational achievement, in turn, opens doors to economic success.

Assimilation, the third factor, is indicated by several measures. With about two of five marrying someone of another racial-ethnic group, Asian Americans have the highest intermarriage rate of any minority. They also are the most likely to live in integrated neighborhoods (Lee 1998). Japanese Americans, the financially most successful of Asian Americans, are the most assimilated (Bell 1991; Schaefer 2000). About 73 percent say that their best friend is not a Japanese American.

Asian Americans are becoming more prominent in politics. With 64 percent of its citizens being Asian American, Hawaii has elected Asian American governors and sent several Asian American senators to Washington (Lee 1998, *Statistical Abstract* 2000:Table 25). The first Asian American governor outside of Hawaii is Gary Locke, who in 1996 was elected governor of Washington, a state in which Asian Americans make up less than 6 percent of the population.

▪ Native Americans

Diversity of Groups Thanks to countless grade B Westerns, many Americans hold stereotypes of Native Americans who lived on the frontier. They see them as wild, uncivilized savages, a single group of people subdivided into separate tribes. The European immigrants to the Colonies, however, encountered diverse groups of people with a variety of cultures—from nomadic hunters and gatherers to people living in wooden houses in settled agricultural communities. Altogether, they spoke over 700 languages (Schaefer 2000). Each group had its own norms and values—and the usual

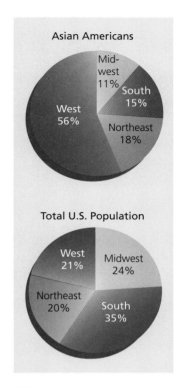

Figure **12.11**
Residence of Asian Americans
Source: Statistical Abstract 2000: Table 26.

ethnocentric pride in its own culture. Consider what happened in 1744. When the colonists of Virginia offered college scholarships for "savage lads," the Iroquois replied:

> "Several of our young people were formerly brought up at the colleges of Northern Provinces. They were instructed in all your sciences. But when they came back to us, they were bad runners, ignorant of every means of living in the woods, unable to bear either cold or hunger, knew neither how to build a cabin, take a deer, or kill an enemy. . . . They were totally good for nothing."
>
> They added, "If the English gentlemen would send a dozen or two of their children to Onondaga, the great Council would take care of their education, bring them up in really what was the best manner and make men of them." (Nash 1974; in McLemore 1994)

Native Americans, who numbered between 5 and 10 million, had no immunity to the diseases the Europeans brought with them. With deaths due to disease—and warfare, a much lesser cause—their number was reduced to about *one-twentieth* its original size. A hundred years ago, the Native American population reached a low point of a half million. Native Americans, who now number about 2 million (see Figure 12.6 on page 360), speak 150 different languages. Like Latinos and Asian Americans, they do not think of themselves as a single people that justifies a single label.

From Treaties to Genocide and Population Transfer At first, relations between the European settlers and the Native Americans were by and large peaceful. The Native Americans accommodated the strangers, as there was plenty of land for both. As wave after wave of settlers continued to arrive, however, Pontiac, an Ottawa chief, saw the future—and didn't like it. He convinced several tribes to unite in an effort to push the Europeans into the sea. He almost succeeded, but failed when the English were reinforced by fresh troops (McLemore 1994).

A pattern of deception evolved. The U.S. government would make treaties to buy some of a tribe's land, with the promise to honor forever the tribe's right to what it had not sold. European immigrants, who continued to pour into the United States, would disregard these boundaries. The tribes would resist, with death tolls on both sides. Washington would then intervene—not to enforce the treaty, but to force the tribe off its lands. In its relentless drive westward, the U.S. government embarked on a policy of genocide. It assigned the U.S. cavalry the task of "pacification," which translates as slaughtering Native Americans who "stood in the way" of this territorial expansion.

The acts of cruelty perpetrated by the Europeans against Native Americans appear endless, but two were especially grisly. The first was the distribution of blankets contaminated with smallpox—under the guise of a peace offering. The second was the Trail of Tears, a forced march of a thousand miles from the Carolinas and Georgia to Oklahoma. Fifteen thousand Cherokees were forced to make this midwinter march in light clothing. Conditions were so bad that 4,000 died. The symbolic end to Native American resistance came in 1890 with a massacre at Wounded Knee, South Dakota. Of 350 men, women, and children, the U.S. cavalry gunned down 300 and buried them in a mass grave (Thornton 1987; Lind 1995; Johnson 1998). These acts took place after the U.S. government changed its policy from genocide to population transfer and began to confine Native Americans to specified areas called *reservations*.

The Invisible Minority and Self-Determination Native Americans can truly be called the invisible minority. Because about 50 percent live in rural areas and one-third in just three states—Oklahoma, California, and Arizona—most other Americans are hardly conscious of a Native American presence in the United States. The isolation of 54 percent of Native Americans on reservations further reduces their visibility (*Statistical Abstract* 2000:Table 43).

The systematic attempts of European Americans to destroy the Native Americans' way of life and their resettlement onto reservations continue to have deleterious effects. Of all U.S. minorities, Native Americans are the worst off. Table 12.1 on page 364 shows their high rate of poverty. Their rates of suicide and alcoholism are also higher, while their life expectancy is lower than that of the nation as a whole

■ *Of all the oppressive acts perpetrated against the Native Americans by the dominant Anglos, the Trail of Tears was certainly one of the most brutal. This painting presents a sanitized version of events; most victims walked (some were barefoot, although it was winter), and dead bodies were left strewn along the trail. Also, it is unlikely that any Native American was allowed to possess a rifle.*

(U.S. Department of Health and Human Services 1990; Lester 1997). Table 12.2 on page 365 also shows that their education lags behind the rest of the nation; only 11 percent graduate from college.

These negative conditions are the consequence of Anglo domination. In the 1800s, U.S. courts determined that Native Americans did not own the land on which they had been settled and had no right to develop their resources. Native Americans were made wards of the state and treated like children by the Bureau of Indian Affairs (Mohawk 1991). Then, in the 1960s, Native Americans won a series of legal victories that restored both their control over the land and their right to determine economic policy. As a result, many Native American tribes have opened businesses on their lands—ranging from industrial parks serving metropolitan areas to fish canneries.

It is the casinos, though, that have attracted the most attention. In 1988, the federal government passed a law that allowed Native Americans to operate gambling establishments on reservations. Over 160 tribes opened casinos, which generate about $6 billion a year (McLemore et al. 2001). Some tribes have struck it rich. The Mdewakanton Dakota Sioux in Minnesota has only 270 members. Its casino nets $900,000 a year for each man, woman, and child (Farney 1998; "Reservations . . . " 2000). The most successful tribe, however, is the Pequot of Connecticut. With only 310 members, they bring in more than $2 million a day (Zielbauer 2000).

A highly controversial issue is *separatism*. Because Native Americans were independent peoples when the Europeans arrived and they never willingly joined the United States, many tribes maintain the right to remain separate from the U.S. government and U.S. society. The chief of the Onondaga tribe in New York, a member of the Iroquois Federation, summarizes the issue this way:

> For the whole history of the Iroquois, we have maintained that we are a separate nation. We have never lost a war. Our government still operates. We have refused the U.S. government's reorganization plans for us. We have kept our language and our traditions, and when we fly to Geneva to UN meetings, we carry Hau de no sau nee passports. We made some treaties that lost some land, but that also confirmed our separate-nation status. That the U.S. denies all this doesn't make it any less the case. (Mander 1992)

One of the most significant changes is **pan-Indianism.** This emphasis on common elements that run through Native American cultures is an attempt to develop an identity that goes beyond the tribe. Whether Native Americans wish to work together as in pan-Indianism or to stress separatism and to identify solely with their own tribe, to assimilate into the dominant culture or to remain apart from it, to move to cities

pan-Indianism
a movement that focuses on common elements in Native-American culture in order to develop a mutual self-identity and to work toward the welfare of all Native Americans

or to remain on reservations, to operate casinos or to engage only in traditional activities—"Such decisions must be ours," say the Native Americans. "We are sovereign, and we will not take orders from the victors of past wars."

■ ■ ■ ■ ■

Looking Toward the Future

Back in 1903, sociologist W. E. B. Du Bois said, "The problem of the twentieth century is the problem of the color line—the relation of the darker to the lighter races of men." Incredibly, a hundred years later, the color line remains one of the most volatile topics facing the nation.

In another hundred years, will yet another sociologist lament that the color of people's skin still affects human relationships? Granted our past, it seems that although racial-ethnic walls will diminish, even crumble at some points, the color line is not likely to disappear. Two issues we are currently grappling with are immigration and affirmative action.

◗ The Immigration Debate

Throughout its history, the United States has both welcomed immigration and feared its consequences. The gates opened wide (numerically, if not in attitude) for a massive wave of immigrants in the late nineteenth and early twentieth centuries. During the past 20 years, a second great wave of immigration has brought close to a million new residents to the United States each year (*Statistical Abstract* 2000:Table 4). Unlike the first wave, which was almost exclusively from western Europe, this second wave is more diverse. In fact, it is changing the U.S. racial-ethnic mix. If current trends in immigration (and birth) persist, in a little over 50 years the "average" American will trace his or her ancestry to Africa, Asia, South America, the Pacific Islands, the Middle East—to almost anywhere but white Europe. This change is discussed in the Cultural Diversity box on the next page.

In some states, the future is arriving much sooner than this. In California, ethnic and racial minorities already constitute the majority. California has 17 million minorities and 16 million whites (*Statistical Abstract* 2001:Table 23). Californians who request new telephone service from Pacific Bell can speak to customer service representatives in Spanish, Korean, Vietnamese, Mandarin, Cantonese—or in English.

As in the past, there is concern that "too many" immigrants will alter the character of the United States. "Throughout the history of American immigration," write sociologists Alejandro Portés and Ruben Rumbaut (1990), "a consistent thread has been the fear that the 'alien element' would somehow undermine the institutions of the country and would lead it down the path of disintegration and decay." A widespread fear in the early 1900s was that the immigrants from southern Europe, then arriving in huge numbers, would bring communism with them. The fears and controversy have not let up. Today, some fear that Spanish-speaking immigrants threaten the primacy of the English language. In addition, the age-old fear that immigrants will take jobs away from native-born Americans remains strong. Finally, minority groups that struggled for political representation fear that newer groups will gain political power at their expense.

◗ Affirmative Action

The role of affirmative action in our multicultural society lies at the center of a national debate about race and ethnic relations. In this policy, initiated by President Kennedy in 1961, goals based on race (and sex) are used in hiring, promotion, and college admission. Sociologist Barbara Reskin (1998) examined the results of affirmative action. In agreement with earlier studies (Badgett and Hartmann 1995), she concluded that although it is difficult to separate the results of affirmative action

cultural diversity

in the United States

Glimpsing the Future: The Shifting U.S. Racial-Ethnic Mix

During the next twenty-five years, the population of the United States is expected to grow by about 22 percent. To see what the U.S. population will look like in twenty-five years, can we simply multiply the current racial-ethnic mix by 22 percent? The answer is a resounding no. As you can see from the figure below, some groups will grow much more than others, giving us a different-looking United States. Some of the changes in the U.S. racial-ethnic mix will be dramatic. In twenty-five years, one of every nineteen Americans is expected to have an Asian background, and one of every six a Latino background.

Two basic causes underlie this fundamental shift: immigration and birth rates. By far, immigration is the most important. That the racial-ethnic groups have different rates of immigration and birth rates will change their proportions of the U.S. population. You can see how the proportion of non-Hispanic whites is expected to shrink, that of Native Americans to remain the same, and that of African Americans to increase slightly. With both vast immigration and higher-than-average birth rates, in fifty years about one of four Americans is expected to be of Latino ancestry.

for your consideration

This shifting racial-ethnic mix is one of the most significant events occurring in the United States. To better understand its implications, apply the three theoretical perspectives.

Use the conflict perspective to identify the groups likely to be threatened by this change. Over what resources are struggles likely to develop? What impact do you think this changing mix might have on European Americans? On African Americans? On Latinos? On Asian Americans? On Native Americans? What changes in immigration laws (or their enforcement) can you anticipate?

To apply the symbolic interactionist perspective, consider how groups might perceive one another differently as their proportion of the population changes.

To apply the functionalist perspective, try to determine how each racial-ethnic group will benefit from this changing mix. How will other parts of society (such as businesses) benefit? What dysfunctions can you anticipate?

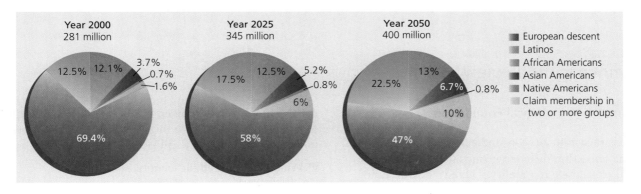

Figure 12.12

Projections of the Racial-Ethnic Makeup of the U.S. Population

I modified the projections for 50 years from now based on the new census category of membership in two or more groups and trends in interethnic marriage.

Sources: Statistical Abstract 2000:Table 16; Kent et al. 2001.

from economic booms and busts and the greater numbers of women in the work force, affirmative action has had a modest impact.

The results may have been modest, but the reaction to this program has been anything but modest. Affirmative action has been at the center of controversy for more than a generation. Liberals, both white and minority, say that this program is the most direct way to level the playing field of economic opportunity. If whites are passed over, this is an unfortunate cost we must pay if we are to make up for past discrimination. Conservatives, in contrast, both white and minority, agree that opportunity should be open to all, but claim that putting race (or sex) ahead of people's training and ability to perform a job is reverse discrimination. Because of their race (or sex), qualified people who had nothing to do with past inequity are discriminated against. They add that affirmative action stigmatizes the people who benefit from it, because it suggests that they hold their jobs because of race (or sex), rather than merit.

This national debate crystallized with a series of controversial rulings. Perhaps the most significant was *Proposition 209*, a 1996 amendment to the California state constitution that banned preferences to minorities and women in hiring, promotion, and college admission. Despite appeals by a coalition of civil rights groups, the U.S. Supreme Court upheld this California law. Since then, the state of Washington adopted a similar law, and the courts have stopped several other states from considering race in university admissions and state hiring (Wilgoren 2001). The issue of the proper role of affirmative action in a multicultural society is likely to remain center stage for quite some time.

■ *The United States is the most racially-ethnically diverse society in the world. This can be our central strength, with our many groups working together to build a harmonious society, a stellar example for the world. Or it can be our Achilles heel, with us breaking into feuding groups, a Balkanized society that marks an ill-fitting end to a grand social experiment. Our reality will probably fall somewhere between these extremes.*

■ Toward a True Multicultural Society

The potential is for the United States to become a society in which its racial-ethnic groups not only coexist, but also respect one another and work for mutually beneficial goals. In a true multicultural society, the minority groups that make up the United States will participate fully in the nation's social institutions while maintaining their cultural integrity. To reach this goal will require that we understand that "the biological differences that divide one race from another add up to a drop in the genetic ocean." For a long time, we have given racial categories an importance they never merited. Now we need to figure out how to reduce them to the irrelevance they deserve. In short, we need to make real the abstraction called equality that we profess to believe (Cose 2000).

Summary and Review

Laying the Sociological Foundation

■ How is race both a reality and a myth?
In the sense that different groups inherit distinctive physical traits, race is a reality. There is, however, no agreement regarding what constitutes a particular race, or of how many races there are. In the sense of one race being superior to another and of there being pure races, race is a myth. The *idea* of race is powerful, shaping basic relationships among people. Pp. 342–345.

■ How do race and ethnicity differ?
Race refers to inherited biological characteristics; **ethnicity,** to cultural ones. Members of ethnic groups identify with one another on the basis of common ancestry and cultural heritage. Pp. 345–346.

■ What are minority and dominant groups?
Minority groups are people who are singled out for unequal treatment by members of the **dominant group,** the group with more power, privilege, and social status. Minorities originate with migration or the expansion of political boundaries. Pp. 346–347.

■ What heightens ethnic identity, and what is "ethnic work"?
A group's size, power, physical characteristics, and amount of discrimination heighten or reduce ethnic identity. **Ethnic work** is the process of constructing an ethnic identity. For people with strong ties to their culture of origin, ethnic work involves enhancing and maintaining group distinctions. For those without a firm ethnic identity, ethnic work is an attempt to recover one's ethnic heritage. P. 347.

■ Are prejudice and discrimination the same thing?
Prejudice is an attitude, **discrimination** an act. Some people who are prejudiced do not discriminate, while others who are not prejudiced do. Pp. 347–350.

■ **How do individual and institutional discrimination differ?**

Individual discrimination is the negative treatment of one person by another, while **institutional discrimination** is discrimination built into social institutions. Institutional discrimination often occurs without the awareness of either the perpetrator or the object of discrimination. Health care after heart attacks is one example. Pp. 350–351.

Theories of Prejudice

■ **How do psychologists explain prejudice?**

Psychological theories of prejudice stress **authoritarian personalities** and frustration displaced toward scapegoats. Pp. 352–353.

■ **How do sociologists explain prejudice?**

Sociological theories focus on how different social environments increase or decrease prejudice. Functionalists stress the benefits and costs that come from discrimination. Conflict theorists look at how the groups in power exploit racial and ethnic divisions in order to hold down wages and otherwise maintain power. Symbolic interactionists stress how labels create **selective perception** and self-fulfilling prophecies. Pp. 353–356.

Global Patterns of Intergroup Relations

■ **What are the major patterns of minority and dominant group relations?**

Beginning with the least humane, they are **genocide, population transfer, internal colonialism, segregation,** assimilation, and **multiculturalism (pluralism).** Pp. 356–359.

Race and Ethnic Relations in the United States

■ **What are the major ethnic groups in the United States?**

From largest to smallest, the major ethnic groups are European Americans, Latinos, African Americans, Asian Americans, and Native Americans. P. 360.

■ **What are some issues in race-ethnic relations and characteristics of minority groups today?**

Latinos are divided by social class and country of origin. African Americans are increasingly divided into middle and lower classes, with two sharply contrasting worlds of experience. On many measures, Asian Americans are better off than white Americans, but their well-being varies with country of origin. For Native Americans, the primary issues are poverty, nationhood, and settling treaty obligations. The overarching issue for minorities is overcoming discrimination. Pp. 360–374.

Looking Toward the Future

■ **What main issues dominate race-ethnic relations?**

The main issues are immigration, affirmative action, and how to develop a true multicultural society. The answers affect our future. Pp. 374–376.

■ *Where can I read more on this topic?*

Suggested Readings for this chapter are at the back of this book.

Additional Online Resources for This Chapter
www.ablongman.com/henslin6e

- *Content Select* Research Database for Sociology, with suggested key terms and annotated references
- Link to 2000 Census, with activities
- Flashcards of key terms and concepts

- Practice Tests
- Weblinks
- Interactive Maps

using . . .
ContentSelect

Research Database for Sociology

affirmative action	ethnic cleansing	immigration	racism
cultural diversity	ethnicity	melting pot	segregation
dominant group	genocide	prejudice	

Frida Kahlo, *Dona Rosita Morillo*, 1941

13

The Elderly

Aging in Global Perspective
The Social Construction of Aging
Effects of Industrialization
The Graying of America

The Symbolic Interactionist Perspective
Deciding When You Are Old
What Does Old Age Mean?
Changing Perceptions of the Elderly
The Influence of the Mass Media

The Functionalist Perspective
Disengagement Theory
Activity Theory
Continuity Theory

The Conflict Perspective
Social Security Legislation
Intergenerational Conflict
Fighting Back

Problems of Dependency
Isolation and Gender
Nursing Homes
Elder Abuse
The Elderly Poor

The Sociology of Death and Dying
Industrialization and the New Technology
Death as a Process
Hospices
Suicide and Age

Looking Toward the Future

Summary and Review

I n 1928, Charles Hart, who was working on his Ph.D. in anthropology, did fieldwork with the Tiwi, who lived on an island off the northern coast of Australia. Because every Tiwi belonged to a clan, they assigned Hart to the bird (Jabijabui) clan and told him that a particular woman was his mother. Hart described the woman as "toothless, almost blind, withered." He added that she was "physically quite revolting and mentally rather senile." He then recounted this remarkable event:

> The Tiwi, like many other hunting and gathering peoples, sometimes got rid of their ancient and decrepit females.

[T]oward the end of my time on the islands an incident occurred that surprised me because it suggested that some of them had been taking my presence in the kinship system much more seriously than I had thought. I was approached by a group of about eight or nine senior men, all of whom I knew. They were all senior members of the Jabijabui clan and they had decided among themselves that the time had come to get rid of the decrepit old woman who had first called me son and whom I now called mother. As I knew, they said, it was Tiwi custom, when an old woman became too feeble to look after herself, to "cover her up." This could only be done by her sons and brothers and all of them had to agree beforehand, since once it was done, they did not want any dissension among the brothers or clansmen, as that might lead to a feud. My "mother" was now completely blind, she was constantly falling over logs or into fires, and they, her senior clansmen, were in agreement that she would be better out of the way. Did I agree?

I already knew about "covering up." The Tiwi, like many other hunting and gathering peoples, sometimes got rid of their ancient and decrepit females. The method was to dig a hole in the ground in some lonely place, put the old woman in the hole and fill it in with earth until only her head was showing. Everybody went away for a day or two and then went back to the hole to discover to their surprise, that the old woman was dead, having been too feeble to raise her arms from the earth. Nobody had "killed" her; her death in Tiwi eyes was a natural one. She had been alive when her relatives last saw her. I had never seen it done, though I knew it was the custom, so I asked my brothers if it was necessary for me to attend the "covering up."

They said no and that they would do it, but only after they had my agreement. Of course I agreed, and a week or two later we heard in our camp that my "mother" was dead, and we wailed and put on the trimmings of mourning. (Hart and Pilling 1970:154)

Aging in Global Perspective

We won't deal with the question of whether it was moral or ethical for Hart to agree that the old woman should be "covered up." What is of interest for our purposes is how the Tiwi treated their frail elderly—or, more specifically, their frail *female* elderly. You probably noticed that the Tiwi "covered up" only old women. As noted in Chapter 11, females are discriminated against throughout the world. As this case makes evident, in some places that discrimination extends even to death.

Every society must deal with the problem of people growing old, and of some becoming very frail. Although few societies choose to bury old people alive, all societies must decide how to allocate limited resources among their citizens. As the proportion of the population that is old increases, which is happening in many nations, those decisions generate tensions between the generations.

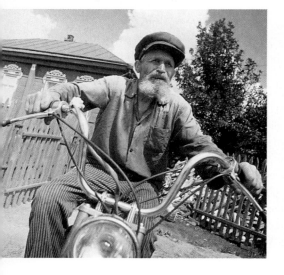

■ This Abkhasian man says he is 115 years old. Reasons for the Abkhasians' apparent longevity are explained in the text. Because birth records in this society do not reach back to the 1800s, however, we cannot be certain of the claims made by the Abkhasians.

■ The Social Construction of Aging

The way the Tiwi treated frail elderly women reflects one extreme of how societies cope with aging. Another extreme, one that reflects an entirely different attitude, is illustrated by the Abkhasians, an agricultural people who live in a mountainous region of Georgia, a republic of the former Soviet Union. Rather than "covering up" their elderly, the Abkhasians pay them high respect and look to them for guidance. They would no more dispense with one of their elderly in this manner than we would "cover up" a sick child.

The Abkhasians may be the longest-lived people on earth. Many claim to live past 100—some beyond 120 and even 130 (Benet 1971). Although it is difficult to document the accuracy of these claims (Haslick 1974; Harris 1990), government records indicate that an extraordinary number of Abkhasians do live to a very old age.

Three main factors appear to account for their long lives. The first is their diet, which consists of little meat, much fresh fruit, vegetables, garlic, goat cheese, cornmeal, buttermilk, and wine. The second is their lifelong physical activity. They do slow down after age 80, but even after the age of 100 they still work about four hours a day. The third factor—a highly developed sense of community— goes to the very heart of the Abkhasian culture. From childhood, each individual is integrated into a primary group, and remains so throughout life. There is no such thing as a nursing home, nor do the elderly live alone. Because they continue to work and contribute to the group's welfare, the elderly aren't a burden to anyone. They don't vegetate, nor do they feel the need to "fill time" with bingo and shuffleboard. In short, the elderly feel no sudden rupture between what they "were" and what they "are."

The examples of the Tiwi and the Abkhasians reveal an important sociological principle—that, like gender, aging is *socially constructed*. That is, nothing in the nature of aging summons forth any particular set of attitudes. Rather, attitudes toward the aged are rooted in society and, therefore, differ from one social group to another. As we shall also see, even the age at which people are considered old depends not on biology, but on culture.

■ Effects of Industrialization

As noted in previous chapters, industrialization is a worldwide trend. The higher standard of living that it brings includes more food, better public health practices (especially a purer water supply), and more effective ways of fighting the diseases that kill children. Consequently, when a country industrializes, more of its people reach older ages. The Social Map on the next page illustrates this principle. You can see that the industrialized countries have the highest percentage of elderly. The range among nations is broad, from just 1 of 45 citizens in nonindustrialized Cote d'Ivoire to *eight* times higher than this, to almost 1 of 5 in post-industrial Italy (*Statistical Abstract* 2000:Table 1353).

As a nation's elderly population increases, so, too, does the bill its younger citizens pay to provide for their needs. This bill has become a major social issue. Although Americans complain that Social Security taxes are too high, the U.S. rate of 14 percent is comparatively low. Hungarian workers are hit the hardest; they pay 40 percent of their wages into social security. At about 37 percent, Austria, France, and Holland follow closely behind (*Statistical Abstract* 2000:Table 1386). People in the Least Industrialized Nations pay no social security taxes. There, families are expected to take care of their own elderly, with no help from the government.

With industrialization continuing without letup and with the proportion of the elderly population continuing to increase, future liabilities for care of the elderly have alarmed analysts. An outstanding case is Germany. By the year 2020, about 30 percent of Germans will be over the age of 60. In order to continue to furnish them the high level of care that they now receive, Germany will have to tax nearly *all* the income of its future workers (Wessel 1995). Obviously, this is impossible, but no one has yet come up with a workable solution to the problem.

■ Central to a group's culture are ways of viewing reality. Living for centuries in isolation on Bathurst and Melville Islands off the northern coast of Australia, the Tiwi, featured in the vignette on "covering up," developed a unique culture. Shown here is Wurabuti, who has prepared himself to lead his uncle's funeral dance. To be certain that his uncle's ghost will not recognize him, Wurabuti is wearing a "shirt" painted with ocher and clay, a topknot of cockatoo feathers, and a beard of goose feathers.

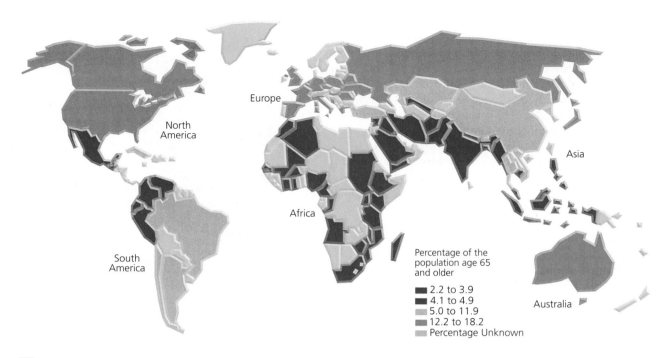

Figure 13.1

Social Map: The Graying of the Globe
Source: Statistical Abstract 2000:Table 1353.

■ The Graying of America

life expectancy
the number of years that an average newborn can expect to live

As Figure 13.2 illustrates, the United States is part of this global trend. This figure shows how U.S. **life expectancy,** the number of years people can expect to live, has increased since 1900. To me, and perhaps to you, it is startling to realize that a hundred years ago the average American could not even expect to see age 50. Since

Figure 13.2

U.S. Life Expectancy by Year of Birth
Sources: Historical Statistics of the United States, Colonial Times to 1970, Bicentennial Edition, Part I, Series B, 107–115; *Statistical Abstract* 2000:Table 116.

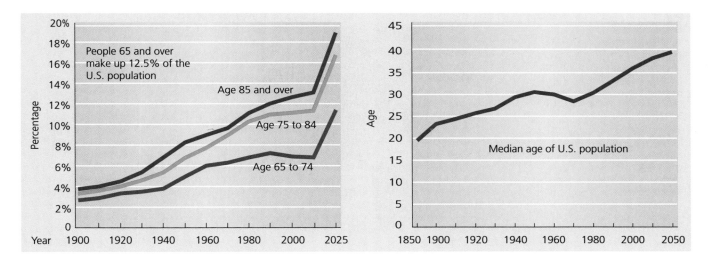

Figure 13.3

The Graying of America

Source: Statistical Abstract 2000:Table 14.

then, we've added about *30* years to our life expectancy, and Americans born today can expect to live into their 70s or 80s.

The term **graying of America** refers to this increasing percentage of older people in the U.S. population. As Figure 13.3 shows, in 1900 only 4 percent of Americans were age 65 and older. Today almost 13 percent are. The average 65-year-old can expect to live another eighteen years (*Statistical Abstract* 2000:Table 118). U.S. society has become so "gray" that the median age has *doubled* since 1850, and today there are seven million *more* elderly Americans than there are teenagers (*Statistical Abstract* 2000:Table 19). Despite this change, as Table 13.1 shows, on a global scale Americans rank fifteenth in life expectancy.

TABLE 13.1			U.S. Life Expectancy in Global Perspective			
World Rank	Country	Life Expectancy at Birth	World Rank	Country	Life Expectancy at Birth
1	Hong Kong	82.4	9	Holland	78.3
2	Japan	80.7	10	Sweden	78.2
3	Australia	79.8	11	Belgium	77.8
4	Canada	79.4	12	Switzerland	77.8
5	Italy	79.0	13	Great Britain	77.7
6	France	78.8	14	Germany	77.4
7	Spain	78.8	15	United States	77.1
8	Greece	78.4			

Source: Statistical Abstract 1997:Table 1336; 2000:Table 1355.

graying of America
a term that refers to the rising proportion of older people as a percentage of the U.S. population

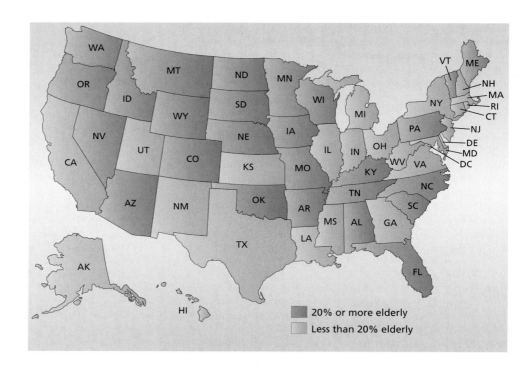

Figure 13.4

As Florida Goes, So Goes the Nation: The Year 2025

Note: The growing proportion of the elderly in the U.S. population is destined to have profound effects on U.S. society. By the year 2025, one-fifth of the population of 27 states is expected to be 65 or older. Today, at 19 percent, only Florida comes close to this.

Source: U.S. Bureau of the Census, 1996, U.S. Department of Commerce, PPL-47; *Statistical Abstract* 2000: Table 24.

20% or more elderly

Less than 20% elderly

life span
The maximum length of life of a species

As anyone who has ever visited Florida has noticed, the elderly population is not evenly distributed around the country. (As Jerry Seinfeld sardonically noted, "There's a law that when you get old you've got to move to Florida.") The Social Map above shows how uneven this distribution is expected to be in a couple of decades.

Race-Ethnicity and Aging   Just as the percentages of elderly differ among the states, so the percentage varies among the racial-ethnic groups that make up the United States. As you can see from Table 13.2, compared with other groups, a larger proportion of white Americans is age 65 and older. Latinos have the smallest proportion of elderly. The difference is so great that the proportion of elderly whites (14.8 percent) is more than twice that of Latinos (5.9 percent). As we saw in Chapter 12, minorities are growing faster than whites. As a consequence, their representation among the U.S. elderly is also increasing. Differences in cultural attitudes about aging, family relationships, work histories, and health practices will be important areas of sociological investigation in coming years.

Although more people are living to old age, the maximum length of life possible, the **life span,** has not increased. Experts disagree, however, on what that maximum is. It is at least 122, for this was the well-documented age of Jeanne Louise Calment of France at her death in 1998. If the reports on the Abkhasians are correct (and this is a matter of controversy), the human life span may

T A B L E   13.2   **Race-Ethnicity and Aging**

What Percentage of These Groups Are Elderly?

	Age			
	65–74	75–84	85+	Total 65 and Over
Whites	7.5%	5.4%	1.9%	14.8%
African Americans	4.9%	2.6%	1.0%	8.5%
Asian Americans	4.7%	2.6%	0.7%	8.0%
Native Americans	4.0%	2.4%	1.0%	7.4%
Latinos	3.5%	1.8%	0.6%	5.9%
U.S. Average	6.6%	4.5%	1.6%	12.7%

Source: Statistical Abstract 2000: Tables 14, 18.

exceed even this number by a comfortable margin. It is also likely that due to advances in genetics the human life span will increase shortly. Some geneticists even think it is possible that we may be able to double our life span (Recer 2000).

The Symbolic Interactionist Perspective

To better understand how aging is socially constructed, let's look beyond biology to some of the symbols associated with age. How does culture signal to us that we are "old"? How do stereotypes and the mass media affect our perceptions of aging?

Deciding When You Are Old

You probably can remember when you thought that a 12-year-old was "old"—and anyone older than that, beyond reckoning. You probably were 5 or 6 at the time. Similarly, to a 12-year-old, someone of 21 seems "old." To someone who is 21, 30 may mark the point at which one is no longer "young," and 40 may seem very old. And so it keeps on going. "Old" gradually recedes further and further from the self. To people who turn 40, 50 seems old; at 50, the late 60s look old—not the early 60s, for the passing of years seems to accelerate as we age, and at 50 the 60s don't seem so far away.

In Western culture, most people have difficulty in applying the label "old" to themselves. In the typical case, they have become used to what they see in the mirror. The changes have taken place gradually, and each change, if it has not exactly been taken in stride, has been accommodated. Consequently, it comes as a shock, when they meet a friend they have not seen in years, to see how much that person has changed. At class reunions, *each* person can hardly believe how much older *the others* appear!

If there is no single point at which people automatically cross a magical line and become "old," what, then, makes someone "old"? We can point to several factors that spur people to apply the label of old to themselves.

The first factor is *biology.* One person may experience "signs" of aging earlier than others: wrinkles, balding, aches, difficulty in doing some things that he or she used to take for granted. Consequently, one person will *feel* "old" at an earlier or later age than others.

A second factor is *personal history* or biography. A woman who gave birth at 16 may have a daughter who in turn has a child at 18, making the woman a biological grandmother at age 34. It is most unlikely that she will begin to play any stereotypical role—spending the day in a rocking chair, for example—but *knowing* that she is a grandmother has an impact on her self-concept. At a minimum, she must *deny* that she is old. An accident that limits someone's mobility may also make that person feel old sooner than others.

Then there is **gender age,** the relative value that a culture places on men's and women's ages. For example, graying hair on men, even some wrinkles, may be seen as signs of "maturity"; on women, those same features may be interpreted as signs of being "old." "Mature" and "old," of course, carry quite different meanings in Western cultures; the first is desired, the second shunned. Similarly, around the world, most men are able to marry much younger spouses than women can. Maria might be an exception and marry Bill, who is fourteen years younger than she. But in most marriages in which there is a fourteen-year age gap between husband and wife, the odds greatly favor

■ *Maud Farris-Luse in Coldwater, Michigan, is the world's oldest living person whose age can be authenticated. She was born January 21, 1887. The world's record for age that has been documented by a birth certificate was held by Jeanne Calment of France, who died in 1998 at the age of 122.*

gender age
the relative values of men's and women's ages in a particular culture

■ *When does old age begin? Because biology doesn't determine the onset of old age, each culture develops and follows its own norms for when old age begins and for age-appropriate behavior. Due to longer lives and medical enhancements, those norms in U.S. culture are much less firm than they used to be. Shown here is Barbara Streisand, at age 59, with her husband, James Brolin, 61.*

the wife being the younger of the pair. Biology, of course, has nothing to do with this socially constructed reality of appearance and marriage ages.

The fourth factor in deciding when people label themselves as "old" is *timetables,* the signals societies use to inform their members that old age has begun. Since there is no automatic age at which people become "old," these timetables vary around the world. One group may choose a particular birthday, such as the 60th or 65th, to signal the onset of old age. Other groups may not even have birthdays, making such numbers meaningless. In the West, retirement is sometimes a cultural signal of the beginning of old age.

■ What Does Old Age Mean?

To help pinpoint how people's experiences of old age involve factors other than biology, let's look at three cross-cultural examples.

The first example is from the United States. The statement I just made about some groups not celebrating birthdays may have sounded like an exaggeration. Only after they moved to reservations, however, did Native Americans adopt the Anglo custom of counting birthdays. For traditional Native Americans today, the signal for old age remains more the inability to perform productive social roles than any particular birthday. Consequently, those unable to continue in these roles tend to think of themselves as old—regardless of their age. In one survey, for instance, a Native American woman who had many disabilities described herself as elderly. She was 37 (Kramer 1992).

Consider this fictionalized conversation between two Tiwi men:

> Bashti looked in envy at Masta. Masta strutted just a bit as he noticed Bashti glance his way. He knew what Bashti was thinking. Had he not thought the same just twenty years earlier? Then he had no wife; now he had three. Then he had no grand hut. Now he did, plus one for each wife. Then he had no respect, no power, no wealth. Now he was looked up to by everyone. "Ah, the marvels and beauty of gray hair," Masta thought. Bashti hung his head as he slouched toward the fringe of the group. "But my turn will come. I, too, will grow old," he thought, finding some comfort in his low status.

Why would a Tiwi man look forward to growing old, something that few people in the United States do? Traditional Tiwi society was a **gerontocracy,** a society run by the elderly. The old men held the power and controlled everything. Their power was so inclusive that the old men married *all* the women—both young and old—leaving none for the young men. Only at the age of 40 or so was a man able to marry (Hart and Pilling 1970). (In Tiwi society, females were the pawns, and aging was of no advantage to a woman. Indeed, in the opening vignette, we saw one of the disadvantages that old age brought to Tiwi women.)

A third example is traditional Eskimo society, which also provides a rich contrast to the postindustrialized world.

> Shantu and Wishta fondly kissed their children and grandchildren farewell. Then, sadly, but with resignation at the sacrifice they knew they had to make for their family, they slowly climbed onto the ice floe. The painful goodbyes were made as the large slab of ice inched into the ocean currents. Shantu and Wishta would now starve. But they were old, and their death was necessary, for it reduced the demand on the small group's scarce food supply.
>
> As the younger relatives watched Shantu and Wishta recede into the distance, each knew that their turn to make this sacrifice would come. Each hoped that they would face it as courageously.

Growing old in traditional Eskimo society meant a "voluntary" death. Survival in their harsh environment was so precarious that all, except very young children, had to pull their own weight. The food supply was so limited that nothing was left over to give to anyone who could not participate in the closely integrated tasks required for survival.

gerontocracy
a society (or some other group) run by the elderly

IN SUM ■ ■ ■ ■

Symbolic interactionists stress that, by itself, old age has no particular meaning. There is nothing about old age that automatically summons forth responses of honor and respect (as with the Abkhasians), envy (as with the Tiwi), or resignation (as with the traditional Eskimo). This perspective helps us see the role of culture in how we view the process of growing old—how the social modifies the biological.

Changing Perceptions of the Elderly

At first, the audience sat quietly as the developers explained their plans to build a high-rise apartment building. After a while, people began to shift uncomfortably in their seats. Then they began to show open hostility.

"That's too much money to spend on those people," said one.

"You even want them to have a swimming pool?" asked another incredulously.

Finally, one young woman put their attitudes in a nutshell when she asked, "Who wants all those old people around?"

When physician Robert Butler (1975, 1980) heard these responses to plans to build apartments for senior citizens, he began to realize how deep antagonistic feelings against the elderly can run. He coined the term **ageism** to refer to prejudice, discrimination, and hostility directed against people because of their age. Let's see how ageism developed in U.S. society.

Shifting Meanings As we have seen, there is nothing inherent in old age to summon forth any particular attitude, negative or not. Old age may even have had positive meanings in early U.S. society (Cottin 1979; Kart 1990; Clair et al. 1993). In Colonial times, because few people made it to old age, growing old was seen as an accomplishment. With no pensions, the elderly continued to work at jobs that changed little over time. They were viewed as storehouses of knowledge about work skills and about how to live a long life.

The coming of industrialization, however, eroded these bases of respect. With improved sanitation and medical care, more people reached old age. No longer was being elderly an honorable distinction. The new forms of mass production made

ageism
prejudice, discrimination, and hostility directed against people because of their age; can be directed against any age group, including youth

■ Stereotypes, which play such a profound role in social life, are a basic area of sociological investigation. In contemporary society, the mass media are a major source of stereotypes.

PEANUTS® by Charles M. Schulz

As she contemplates her future, Zhao Chunlan, a 71-year-old widow, smiles shyly, but with evident satisfaction. She has heard about sons abandoning their aged parents. She has even heard whispering about abuse.

But Zhao has no such fears.

It is not that her son is so devoted that he would never swerve from his traditional duty to his mother. Rather, it is a piece of paper that has eased Zhao's mind. Her 51-year-old son has signed a support agreement: He will cook her special meals, take her to regular medical checkups, even give her the largest room in his house and put the family's color television in it (Sun 1990).

The high status of the elderly in China is famed around the world: They are considered a source of wisdom, given honored seating at both family and public gatherings—even venerated after death in ancestor worship.

Although this outline may represent more ideal than real culture, it appears to generally hold true. Industrialization, however, which is bringing a longer life expectancy, is tearing at the bonds between generations. So is a national policy that allows each married couple only one child. With fewer young people, the percentage of the population that is over 65 is mushrooming. Already numbering 88 million, 7 percent of the population, China's elderly

may soar to 40 percent in just fifty years (Kinsella and Taeuber 1993; *Statistical Abstract* 2000:Tables 1352, 1353).

Because China has no national social security system, children must provide for their elders (Chang 2000). Many local officials have become alarmed by signs that parent-child bonds are weakening, and they require adult children to sign support agreements for their aged parents. One province has hit on an ingenious device: In order to get a marriage license, a couple must sign a contract pledging to support their parents after they reach age 60 (Sun 1990). "I'm sure he would do right by me, anyway," says Zhao, "but this way I know he will."

young workers as productive as the elderly. Coupled with mass education, this stripped away the elderly's superior knowledge (Cowgill 1974). In the Cultural Diversity box above, you can see how a similar process is occurring in China now as it, too, industrializes.

We have seen a basic principle of symbolic interactionism—that people perceive both themselves and others according to the symbols of their culture. Thus, as the meaning of old age was transformed—when it changed from an asset to a liability—not only did younger people come to view the elderly differently, but also the elderly began to perceive themselves in a new light. A sign of how they, too, internalized this shift in meanings is the way people lie about their age: They used to claim they were older than they were, but now they say they are younger than they are (Clair et al. 1993).

Because most U.S. elderly can take care of themselves financially—in fact, many are well-off—the meaning of old age is changing once again. In addition, members of the baby boom generation have now entered their 50s. With their vast numbers and better health and financial strength, they are destined to positively affect our images of the elderly. The next step in this symbolic shift, now in process, is to celebrate old age as a time of renewal—not simply as a period that precedes death, but, rather, as another stage of growth.

■ The Influence of the Mass Media

In Chapter 3 (pages 79–81), we noted that the mass media help to shape our ideas about both gender and relationships between men and women. As a powerful source of symbols, the media also influence our ideas of the elderly, a topic that is discussed in the following Mass Media box.

mass media
in social life

Shaping Our Perceptions of the Elderly

The mass media profoundly influence our lives. What we hear and see on television and in the movies, the songs we listen to, the books and magazines we read—all become part of our world view. Without our knowing it, the media shape our images of people. They influence how we view minorities, the dominant group, men, women, and children, people with disabilities, people from other cultures—and the elderly.

The shaping is subtle, so much so that it is usually beneath our awareness. The elderly, for example, are underrepresented on television and in most popular magazines. The covert message is that the elderly are of little consequence and can be safely ignored. Or consider how the media reflect and reinforce stereotypes of *gender age*. Older male news anchors are likely to be retained, while female anchors who turn the same age are more likely to be transferred to less visible positions. Similarly, in movies older men are more likely to play romantic leads—and opposite much younger rising stars.

Then there is advertising. The American Association of Retired Persons (AARP) points out that television ads often depict the elderly as being feeble or foolish, or as passing their time in rocking chairs (Goldman 1993). The reason for this, claims the AARP, is that younger people dominate advertising firms, and their ads reflect their negative images of older people. They pick out the "worst traits of the group, making everyone believe that old is something you don't want to be."

The message is not lost. As we add years, we go to great lengths to deny that we are growing old. This plays into advertisers' hands, who exploit our fears of losing our youth so they can sell us their hair dyes, skin creams, and other products that supposedly conceal even the appearance of old age (Vernon et al. 1990; Vasil and Wass 1993; Ryan and Wentworth 1999).

As discussed in the text, the elderly's affluence is growing. This translates into economic power, something that advertisers and producers must take into consideration. It is inevitable, then, that the media's images of the elderly will change. An indication of that change is shown in the photo to the right. We might also note the sexism that still clings to these changing images—the primary depiction is that of older men and younger women.

■ *Age is much more than biology. The point at which old age begins, for example, differs from one culture to another. In some cultures, Michael Douglas, 57, would be considered an old man, but he is still portrayed as the romantic lead opposite much younger actresses. Douglas is shown here with his wife, Catherine Zeta-Jones, age 32.*

The Functionalist Perspective

Functionalists analyze how the parts of society work together. Among the components of society are **age cohorts,** people who were born at roughly the same time and who pass through the life course together. Age cohorts significantly affect our lives. For example, if the age cohort nearing retirement is large (a "baby boom" generation), many jobs open at roughly the same time. If it is small (a "baby bust" generation), however, fewer jobs open. Let's look at disengagement theory and activity theory, which focus on the adjustments to retirement.

■ Disengagement Theory

Elaine Cumming and William Henry (1961) analyzed how society prevents disruption when the elderly leave their positions of responsibility. In what is called **disengagement theory,** they explained how it would be disruptive if the elderly left their positions only when they died or became incompetent. To prevent this, pensions

age cohort
people born at roughly the same time who pass through the life course together

disengagement theory
the view that society prevents disruption by having the elderly vacate (or disengage from) their positions of responsibility so the younger generation can step into their shoes

are offered to entice the elderly to hand over their positions to younger people. Retirement (or disengagement), then, is a mutually beneficial agreement between two parts of society. It helps smooth the transition between the generations.

Cumming (1976) also examined disengagement from the individual's perspective. She pointed out that disengagement begins during middle age, long before retirement, when someone senses that the end of life is closer than its start. The individual does not immediately disengage, however, but, realizing that time is limited, begins to assign priority to goals and tasks. Disengagement begins in earnest when children leave home, then increases with retirement and eventually widowhood.

Evaluation of the Theory   Almost from the time it was formulated, disengagement theory came under attack (Hatch 2000). Anthropologist Dorothy Jerrome (1992) points out that it contains an implicit bias against older people—assumptions that the elderly disengage from productive social roles, and then sort of sink into oblivion. Her own research shows that instead of disengaging, the elderly *exchange* one set of roles for another. The new roles, which often center around friendship, are no less satisfying than the earlier roles. They are less visible to researchers, however, who tend to have a youthful orientation—and who show their bias by assuming that productivity is the measure of self-worth.

Retirement, too, is changing. Computers, modems, and the new types of work have blurred the dividing line between work and retirement. Less and less does retirement mean to hit a wall and to abruptly stop working. Many workers just slow down. Some continue at their jobs, but put in fewer hours. Others switch careers, even though they are in their 60s. Some may move to a warmer climate, but take their work with them. Many never "retire"—at least not in the sense of sinking into a recliner or being forever on the golf course. If disengagement theory is ever resurrected, it must come to grips with this fundamental change.

■ Activity Theory

Are retired people more satisfied with life? Are intimate activities more satisfying than formal ones? Such questions are the focus of **activity theory,** which assumes that the more activities elderly people engage in, the more they find life satisfying. Although we could consider this theory from other perspectives, because its focus is how disengagement is functional or dysfunctional, it can be considered from the functionalist perspective.

Evaluation of the Theory   The results are mixed. In general, researchers have found that more active people are more satisfied. But not always. A study of retired people in France found that some people are happier when they are more active, others when they are less involved (Keith 1982). Similarly, most people find informal, intimate activities, such as spending time with friends, to be more satisfying than formal activities. But not everyone does. In one study, 2,000 retired U.S. men reported formal activities to be as important as informal ones. Even solitary activities, such as doing home repairs, had about the same impact as intimate activities on these men's life satisfaction (Beck and Page 1988). It is similarly the case with seeing adult children. The amount of interaction with adult children that increases satisfaction differs for each person—when, in their words, they see their children "frequently enough" (Hatch 2000).

activity theory
the view that satisfaction during old age is related to a person's amount and quality of activity

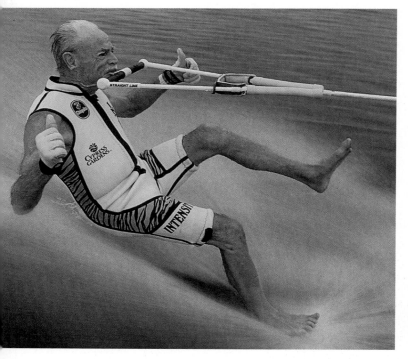

■ As the numbers of U.S. elderly grow, a new emphasis is being placed on their well-being. Researchers are exploring the elderly's mental and social development, as well as the causes of physical well-being. As research progresses, do you think we will reach the point where the average old person will be in this man's physical condition?

In short, just counting the amount of interaction or activities of elderly people is simplistic, and this theory, too, has been rejected. If it is ever resurrected, researchers must take into account what activities *mean* to people.

■ Continuity Theory

Another theory of how people adjust to growing old is continuity theory. As its name implies, the focus of this theory is how people adjust to change by continuing some aspect of their lives, such as the roles they are used to or their coping techniques. Researchers have found that people who have multiple roles (wife, author, mother, intimate friend, church member, etc.) are better equipped to handle the changes that growing old entails. They have also found that people from higher social classes have greater resources to meet the challenges of old age, and they adjust better to aging.

Evaluation of the Theory   The basic criticism of continuity theory is that it is too broad (Hatch 2000). We all have anchor points based on our experiences, and we all rely on them to make adjustments to the changes we encounter in life. This applies to people of all ages beyond infancy. This theory is really a collection of loosely connected ideas, with no specific application to the elderly.

IN SUM ■ ■ ■ ■

The *broader* perspective of the functionalists is how society's parts work together to keep society running smoothly. Although it is inevitable that younger workers replace the elderly, this transition could lead to disruptions. To entice the elderly out of their positions so younger people can take over, the elderly are offered pensions. Functionalists also use a *narrower* perspective to focus on how the elderly adjust to their retirement. The findings of this narrower perspective are too mixed to be of much value—except that those with better resources (including multiple roles) adjust better to old age.

■ ■ ■ ■ ■

The Conflict Perspective

From the conflict perspective, the guiding principles of social life are competition, disequilibrium, and change. So it is with society's age groups. Regardless of whether the young and old recognize it, they are part of a basic struggle that threatens to throw society into turmoil. The passage of Social Security legislation is an example of this struggle.

■ Social Security Legislation

In the 1920s, before Social Security provided an income for the aged, two-thirds of all citizens over 65 had no savings and could not support themselves (Holtzman 1963; Hudson 1978). Only one-fifth of workers were able to retire before they died (O'Rand and Henretta 1999). The fate of workers sank even deeper during the Great Depression, and in 1930, Francis Townsend, a physician, started a movement to rally older citizens. He soon had one-third of all Americans over 65 enrolled in his Townsend clubs. They demanded that the federal government impose a national sales tax of 2 percent to provide $200 a month for every person over 65 (about $2,400 a month in today's money). In 1934, the Townsend Plan went before Congress. Because it called for such high payments and many were afraid that it would destroy people's incentive to save for the future, Congress looked for a way to reject the plan without appearing to oppose the elderly. When President Roosevelt announced his own, more modest Social Security plan in 1934, Congress embraced it (Schottland 1963; Amenta et al. 1999).

This legislation required that workers retire at 65. It did not matter how well people did their work, nor how much they needed the pay. For decades, the elderly protested. Finally, in 1986 Congress eliminated mandatory retirement. Today, almost 90 percent of Americans retire by age 65, but most do so voluntarily. No longer can they be forced out of their jobs simply because of their age.

Conflict theorists point out that Social Security did not come about because members of Congress had generous hearts. Rather, Social Security emerged from a struggle between competing interest groups. As conflict theorists stress, equilibrium is only a temporary balancing of social forces, one that can be upset at any time. Perhaps more direct conflict may emerge in the future. Let's consider that possibility.

■ Intergenerational Conflict

Will the future bring conflict between the elderly and the young? Although violence is not likely, if you listen closely, you can hear the grumbling—complaints that the elderly are getting more than their share of society's resources. The huge costs of Social Security and Medicare have become a national concern. These two programs alone account for *one of every three* tax dollars (*Statistical Abstract* 2001:Table 463). As Figure 13.5 shows, Social Security taxes were $781 million in 1950; now they run about *500 times* higher. The Down-to-Earth Sociology box on the next page examines stirrings of resentment that threaten to become widespread.

Some form of conflict seems inevitable. The graying of the United States leaves fewer working people to pay for the benefits received by the increasing millions who collect Social Security. This and other problems are discussed in the following Thinking Critically section.

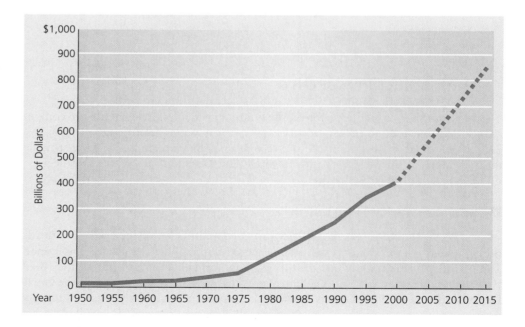

Figure 13.5

Costs of Social Security

Source: Statistical Abstract 1997:Table 518; 2000:Table 533. Broken line indicates the author's projections.

thinking
CRITICALLY

Exploding the Myth of U.S. Budget Surpluses: Can We Pay the Elderly's Social Security Out of Thin Air?

E ach month the Social Security Administration mails checks to 45 million people. Across the country, 181 million U.S. workers pay into the Social Security system, looking to it to provide for their basic necessities—and even a little more than that—in their old age (*Statistical Abstract* 2000:Tables 606, 608).

How dependable is Social Security? The short answer is "Don't bet your old age on it."

The first problem is well known. Social Security is not a bank account. The money taken from our checks is not deposited into our individual accounts. No

---

down-to-earth
s o c i o l o g y

■ ■ ■ ■ ■

Changing Sentiment About the U.S. Elderly

M ost U.S. elderly used to be poor. With Social Security, the elderly's rate of poverty dropped dramatically. As we saw in Figure 10.6 on page 297, today's elderly have a low rate of poverty. As you know, many elderly travel about the country in motor homes and spend a lot of money on recreation. Is their changed situation leading to a new sentiment about the elderly?

There are indications that it is. Sena- tor Alan Simpson called the elderly "greedy geezers," and "oldsters in Bermuda shorts teeing off near their second homes in Florida" who demand government handouts (Duff 1995). Teresa Anderson (1985) felt resentful when she had to pay more than her par- ents for an identical room in the same motel. She said, "My parents work and own several pieces of property. Some- thing is wrong when people are auto- matically entitled to a 'senior citizen discount' regardless of need."

Some even argue that we should ra- tion medical care for the elderly (Perrin 1994). Considering costs, asks Daniel Callahan (1987), why should we perform open-heart surgery on people in their 80s? This only prolongs their life by two or three years. Doesn't it make more sense to use those same resources to give a kidney transplant to a child, whose life might be prolonged by fifty years?

Robert Samuelson (1988) proposes that we eliminate tax breaks for the elderly, such as their extra standard deduction on federal income tax forms. He also suggests that we reduce the cost-of-living adjustments in Social Se- curity. He accuses the elderly's powerful lobby, the American Association of Retired Persons (AARP), of using mis- leading stereotypes. He says, "In the real world, the stereotypes of the elderly

■ *Attitudes toward the elderly have undergone major shifts during the short history of the United States. As the economic circumstances of the elderly improve, attitudes are changing once again.*

as sedentary, decrepit, and poor have long vanished, but in politics the cliché is promoted and perpetuated." He accuses the AARP of outright hypocrisy: "They in- sist (rightfully) that age alone doesn't rob people of vitality and independence, while also arguing (wrongfully) that age alone entitles them to special treatment." They can't have it both ways, he says.

for your consideration

Use information in this chapter to analyze why perceptions of the elderly are changing. Note two sides of the coin. On one side are the higher living stan- dards—higher than any 65-plus generation in U.S. history. One in three golfers is over 65, as are 60 percent of cruise vaca- tioners. On the other side are those who live in poverty— 20 percent of the unmarried, 26 percent of African Americans, 21 percent of Latinos, 12 per- cent of Asian Americans, and 9 percent of whites (*Statistical Abstract* 2000:Table 758). Note also the contrasting images— on one hand, "blood-sucking vultures"; on the other hand, "pathetic creatures saving pen- nies to buy the best meal they can afford—dog food."

■ ■ ■ ■ ■

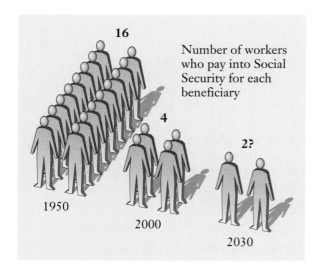

Number of workers who pay into Social Security for each beneficiary

16

4

2?

1950

2000

2030

Figure 13.6

Fewer Workers Supporting a Larger Number of Retirees

Source: Social Security Administration; *Statistical Abstract* 2000:Tables 606, 608.

money in the Social Security system is attached to anyone's name. At retirement, we don't withdraw the money we paid into Social Security. Instead, the government writes checks on money that it collects from current workers. When these workers retire, they, too, will be paid, not from their own savings, but from money collected from others who are still working.

The Social Security system is like a giant chain letter—it works as long as enough new people join the chain. If you join early enough, you'll collect much more than you paid in—but if you join toward the end, you're simply out of luck. And, say some conflict theorists, we are nearing the end of the chain. The shift in the **dependency ratio,** the number of people who collect Social Security compared with the number of workers who contribute to it, is especially troubling. As Figure 13.6 shows, sixteen workers used to support each person who was collecting Social Security. Now the dependency ratio has dropped to four to one. In another generation, it should hit two to one.

When this happens, Social Security taxes could become so high that they stifle the country's economy. To prevent this, Congress raised Social Security taxes and established a Social Security trust fund. Supposedly, this fund has trillions of dollars.

The second problem with Social Security takes us to the root of the crisis, or, some say, fraud. In 1965, President Lyndon Johnson was bogged down in a war in Vietnam. To conceal the war's costs from the public, he hit on an ingenious solution—to prohibit the Social Security Administration from investing in anything but U.S. Treasury bonds—a form of government IOUs. This put the money collected for Social Security into the general fund, where Johnson could siphon it off to finance the war. Today's politicians still do this. They use the term "off budget" to refer to the Social Security money they spend. And each year, they spend it all.

Suppose that you buy a $10,000 U.S. Treasury bond. The government takes your $10,000 and hands you a document that says it owes you $10,000 plus interest. This is how Social Security works. The Social Security Administration (SSA) collects the money from workers, pays the retired, disabled, and survivors of deceased workers, and then hands the excess over to the U.S. government. The government, in turn, gives SSA gigantic IOUs in the form of U.S. Treasury bonds. The government spends the money on whatever it wants—whether that means building roads and schools or subsidizing tobacco crops.

The government's boasts of huge budget surpluses are lies. *There are no surpluses,* and there never have been. These so-called budget surpluses are a sleight-of-hand manipulation of the people's money. The government spends billions more than it takes in. By putting the Social Security money in the general account, it looks like there is more income than expenditures. But there isn't. Many people don't believe that politicians would try to pull the wool over our eyes in such a gigantic way, but so it is. A glance at *Statistical Abstract of the United States,* available in your library, will clarify the government's magical bookkeeping. Table 532 in the 2000 edition reports a federal government surplus of $167 billion for 2000. Yet the *same* table shows that between 1999 and 2000 the federal government's debt increased by $80 billion.

Think of it this way: Suppose you were spending more money than you make—but to hide it you dip into Aunt Mary's bank account and put some of her money in your own account. If you don't count what you owe Aunt Mary, you have a surplus. The government simply does not count those huge IOUs it owes the elderly—and it reports a fraudulent surplus to the public.

This arrangement is a politician's dream. Each month the government wipes the Social Security trust fund clean. Politicians grab the money and hand out the IOUs.

dependency ratio
the number of workers required to support dependent persons—those 65 and older and those 15 and under

The Gramm-Rudman law, which was designed to limit the amount of federal debt, does *not* count funds "borrowed" from Social Security. (In their terms, it is "off budget.") It is as though this government spending does not exist—and to politicians it doesn't. To them, Social Security is a gigantic machine that produces billions from thin air. Those are just numbers on paper, not money that has been confiscated from workers.

As one analyst said, the Social Security trust fund isn't a fund and you shouldn't trust it (Sloan 2001).

■ ■ ■ ■ ■

for your consideration . . .

Here are three proposals to solve this problem.

1. Raise the retirement age to 70.

2. Use the excess Social Security taxes to pay off the national debt. The debt could be paid off before the dependency ratio drops much further, making the money spent on interest (now $220 billion a year) available for Social Security payments. For this to work, the government could not increase its spending, almost an impossibility for politicians.

3. Change the entire system. Put what workers pay as Social Security taxes into their own individual retirement accounts. A board, independent of the government, would select money managers to invest these accounts in real estate, stocks, and bonds. Annually, the board would review the performance of the money managers, retaining those who do the best job and replacing the others. All investment results would be published and would be available for public inspection.

Think in terms of your own Social Security. Do you prefer to retain the current Social Security system? Do you prefer one of these three proposals? None is perfect. What problems might each have? Can you think of a better alternative?

Sources: Smith 1986; Smith 1987; Hardy 1991; Genetski 1993; Stevenson 1998, *Statistical Abstract* 2000. Government publications that list Social Security receipts as deficits can be found in *Monthly Treasury Statement of Receipts and Outlays,* the *Winter Treasury Bulletin,* and the *Statement of Liabilities and Other Financial Commitments of the United States Government.*

Figure 13.7 on the next page shows how medical costs for the elderly have soared. Because of this, some fear that children's health care is being shortchanged and that Congress will be forced to "choose between old people and kids." What especially alarms some are the data shown in Figure 13.8. As the condition of the elderly has improved, that of children has worsened. Although critics are pleased that the elderly are better off than they were, they are bothered that this improvement has come at the cost of the nation's children.

But has it really? Conflict sociologists Meredith Minkler and Ann Robertson (1991) point out that while the figures themselves are true, the comparison is misleading. The money that went to the elderly did *not* come from the children. Would anyone say that the money the government gives to flood victims comes from the children? Of course not. Politicians make choices about where to spend taxes, and they could very well have decided to increase spending on *both* the elderly and children. They simply have not done so. As conflict theorists point out, framing the issue as a case of money going to one group at the expense of another group is an attempt to divide the working class. If the working class can be made to think that it must choose between pathetic children and suffering old folks, it will be divided and unable to work together to improve U.S. society.

Figure 13.7

Health Care Costs for the Elderly and Disabled

Medicare is intended for the elderly and disabled, Medicaid for the poor. About 29 percent of Medicaid payments ($41 billion) goes to the elderly. Medicaid payments include payments on the AFDC program (*Statistical Abstract* 2000:Table 172). Broken lines indicate the author's projections.

Source: Statistical Abstract, various years, and 2000:Tables 169, 173.

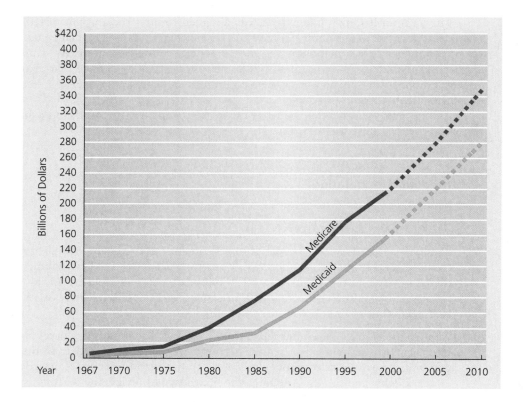

Figure 13.8

Trends in Poverty

Note: For some years the government totals for youth refer to people under 18, for other years to people under 16 or 15. Broken lines indicate the author's projections.

Source: Congressional Research Service, *Statistical Abstract* 2000: Table 757.

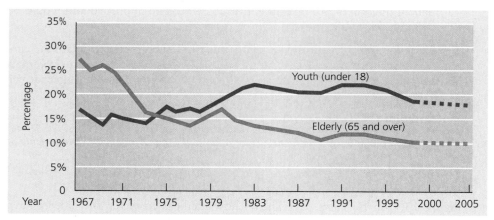

■ Fighting Back

Some organizations work to protect the hard-won gains of the elderly. Let's consider two.

The Gray Panthers   The Gray Panthers, who claim 50,000 members, are aware of the danger of dividing the working class along age lines (Collins 2001). This organization, founded in the 1960s by Margaret Kuhn (1905–1995), encourages people of all ages to work for the welfare of both the old and the young. On the micro level, the goal is to develop positive self-concepts (Kuhn 1990). On the macro level, the goal is to build a base so broad that it can challenge institutions that oppress the poor, whatever their age—and to fight attempts to pit people against one another along age lines. One indication of their effectiveness is that Gray Panthers frequently testify before congressional committees concerning pending legislation (Fitzpatrick 2001).

The American Association of Retired Persons   The AARP also combats negative images of the elderly. This 35-million member organization is politically powerful (Garcia 2001). It monitors proposed federal and state legislation and mobilizes its members to act on issues affecting their welfare. The AARP can trigger tens of thousands of telephone calls, telegrams, and letters from irate elderly citizens. To protect their chances of reelection, politicians know better than to cross swords with the AARP. As you can expect, critics claim that the organization is too powerful, that it is able to muster forces to claim more than its share of the nation's resources.

All this helps prove our point, say conflict theorists. Age groups are just one of society's many groups that are struggling for scarce resources, with conflict the inevitable result.

Before we close this chapter, let's look at problems of dependency and the sociology of death and dying.

Problems of Dependency

"When I get old, will I be able to take care of myself? Will I become frail and not be able to get around? Will I end up poor and in some nursing home, in the hands of strangers who don't care about me?" These are common concerns. Let's examine the dependency of the elderly: isolation, nursing homes, abuse, and poverty.

Isolation and Gender

Contrary to some stereotypes, most U.S. elderly are *not* isolated. Because most women live longer than most men, however, women are more likely than men to lose their spouse and to experience isolation (Brewer 2001). As you can see from Figure 13.9, 74 percent of elderly men live with their wives, but only 42 percent of elderly women live with their husbands. The intense feelings of loss and isolation that widowhood brings, then, are more likely to be experienced by women. This difference in mortality also means that women are much more likely to take care of frail husbands than husbands are to care for frail wives. It also means that most patients of nursing homes are women.

Nursing Homes

In one nursing home, the nurses wrote in the patient's chart that she had a foot lesion. She actually had gangrene and maggots in her wounds (Rhone 2001). In another nursing home—supposedly a premier retirement home in Southern California—a woman suffered a stroke in her room. Her "caretakers" didn't discover her condition for 15 hours. She didn't survive (Morin 2001).

Although most elderly are cared for by their families, a million and a half Americans age 65 and over are in nursing homes. This comes to about 4 percent of the nation's elderly (*Statistical Abstract* 2001:Tables 11, 176). Some return home after only a few weeks or a few months. Others die after a short stay. Overall, about one half of elderly women and one-third of elderly men spend at least some time in nursing homes.

Nursing home residents are *not typical* of the elderly. Most (50.4 percent) are age 85 or older (*Statistical Abstract* 2001:Table 176). Those in nursing homes are likely to be widowed, or to never have married and thus are without family to take care of them. More than half are incontinent (unable to control their bladder), and two-thirds are disorientated or have memory loss (Treas 1995).

It is difficult to say good things about nursing homes. The literature on nursing homes, both popular and scientific, is filled with horror stories—reports of patients who have been neglected, beaten, raped, and robbed. Events like those in the quotation that opens this section are all too common. Not all nursing homes are like this, of course. Perhaps most are even halfway decent. Some even provide a pleasant decor and aides that care about their patients. Even these, however, have a tendency to

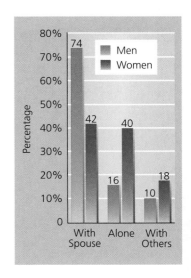

Figure 13.9

Where Do the U.S. Elderly Live?

Source: Statistical Abstract 2000: Table 40.

■ *The residents of nursing homes are not typical of the elderly. They are in worse helath and generally more isolated. In addition, as you may infer from this photo, they often are given drugs to keep them docile.*

strip away human dignity. Consider what sociologist Sharon Curtin (1976) found in one of these superior nursing homes:

> Miss Larson entered Montcliffe the last week of October. . . . Shortly after her admission, I arrived at 7 a.m. to find the night nurse indignant and angry. Miss Larson had climbed over the side rails during the night, and had been found in the bathroom. "She didn't ring or call out," said the nurse. . . . "Why, she might have been hurt, and she is so confused. I want the doctor to order me more sedation. We can't have her carrying on, and disturbing all the other patients."
>
> I walked in the room and Miss Larson was in restraints. . . . "Get me out of these!" she ordered. "How dare they try to stop me from getting out of bed. I always have to relieve myself at night; and they never answer my bell."
>
> Miss Larson was not confused; but in a place where all the patients are so sedated that they scarcely move a muscle during the night, she was counted a nuisance. I did not want them to increase her sedation; barbiturates frequently make old people confused and disoriented. Even if she was a pain in the neck, I like her better awake and making some sense. The problem was she had no rights. She was old, sick, feeble. Therefore she must shut up, lie still, take what little was offered and be grateful. And if she did that, she would be a "good girl."

The elderly resent being treated like children—in an institution or anywhere else. They resist, as did Miss Larson, but resistance is usually fruitless. We can add that such callous treatment doesn't come cheap. Nursing care is so expensive that 70 percent of residents without family go broke within just three months (Ruffenbach 1988; Treas 1995).

But all these criticisms of nursing homes pale in comparison with this finding, which is probably the single greatest indictment of all: Compared with the elderly who have similar conditions and remain in the community, those who are placed in nursing homes tend to get sicker and to die sooner (Wolinsky et al. 1997). Because of this, we can note—with only a trace of irony—that one of the major functions of nursing homes is to help dispose of the frail and unwanted elderly. In other words, they are the equivalent of the Tiwi's practice of "covering up," which we reviewed in the chapter's opening vignette.

Nursing homes do serve vital functions. They provide care for the elderly who have no families, or who are so sick that their families can no longer care for them. Sometimes nursing homes even help family relationships. A study of a well-run, middle-class nursing home showed that 70 percent of residents who were parents either grew closer to their family or maintained an already close relationship. Thirty percent continued to be alienated from their children. Often, affection between the aged parent and adult children had been strained by the parent's physical or mental condition. With professional care, the condition of patients improved, and many adult children felt free to again provide emotional support to the parent (Smith and Bengston 1979).

After numerous complaints about nursing home abuses as well as much prodding by the AARP to change nursing homes from warehouses of bodies to places of treatment and human care, in 1987 Congress passed the Nursing Home Reform Amendments. This law provides a bill of rights for nursing home residents. It gives them the right to privacy, to be informed about their treatment and to refuse it, to keep personal belongings, to review medical records, to complain without reprisal, and to be unfettered—not tied to a chair or a bed as Miss Larson was. As with any other law, of course, this one, too, is only as good as its enforcement. For an example of an excellent system of institutionalized care, see the Cultural Diversity box below.

Technology and Nursing Homes   You probably are aware of how important social interaction is for your well being. It is the same for the elderly. Isolation can even lead to mental and physical deterioration. Researchers have found that an active social life helps to prevent the deterioration of the brain that can lead to Alzheimer's and Parkinson's diseases. Social isolation is not the cause of these brain

cultural diversity

Around the World

Alzheimer's Disease: Lessons from Sweden

"I'm ready," shouted Clay from the bedroom.

"That was fast," thought Virginia, his wife of forty-eight years. "He never gets ready for church that fast."

Virginia walked into the bedroom, and there, smiling and ready to leave for church, stood Clay—absolutely naked except for three watches strapped to his left wrist. Virginia told me this story later that morning when I asked her how things were going.

As people grow old, among their fears is that of "losing their mind." By this they mean senility, or, more technically, Alzheimer's disease.

How do we care for people when they get like Clay?

Clay is in good hands. His wife is still healthy, and she lovingly makes certain that he eats nourishing meals, is included in social events—and wears clothes when he goes out.

But what about the many who don't have close, caring relatives? For them, senility means institutionalization—which, even if it does not mirror the horror stories we all have heard, is certainly a far cry

■ *Former president Ronald Reagan suffers from Alzheimer's disease. This disease devastates the thinking process, making its victims unable to carry out the ordinary routines on which everyday life depends. As the percentage of the aged in our society increases, so will the number of people who suffer from this disease—and the caregiving that will become necessary.*

from the loving care that someone like Virginia gives.

Institutionalization, however, does not have to be a bad experience. To see the potential for positive care, we can turn to Sweden, which since the 1980s has been

pioneering group homes for victims of Alzheimer's disease (Malmberg and Sundström 1996). The group homes consist of six to eight small apartments fanning outward from a shared kitchen and living room. Residents have their own accommodations, but a trained and well-paid staff is available around the clock. The goal is to mirror a home environment in which residents are lovingly cared for, where they are treated as individuals, and where they participate in everyday activities. The benefits go far beyond personalized care; secondary problems associated with Alzheimer's—depression, restlessness, and anxiety—apparently decrease.

for your consideration

The group home model pioneered by Sweden is exemplary, but expensive. In the United States, what chance do you think we have for providing group homes like this for victims of Alzheimer's? Suppose that we did provide such homes, but could not afford them for all Alzheimer's victims—how should they be rationed?

conditions—which can strike anyone—but people who are socially isolated are more likely to come down with them (Ross 2000).

Social activity comes in many forms. Some residents of nursing homes find that the computer and Internet help them overcome isolation and depression. Sending and receiving e-mail is turning out to be especially valuable. It can help the elderly to keep in contact with relatives and friends, who may be dispersed throughout the country, and, in our emerging global society, throughout the world. To see why learning how to send e-mail would reduce depression, loneliness, and boredom, imagine yourself in advanced age, in declining health, and confined to a nursing home. Your spouse and friends are deceased, and your children live several states away. Now think how encouraged you would feel if you received this message from your granddaughter (an actual message sent to a woman in her 90s, who took a course in e-mail offered in her nursing home): "Dear Grandma, I can't believe you just sent me e-mail. You're the coolest grandma in California" (Crary 1999).

Elder Abuse

Stories of elder abuse abound—and so does the abuse itself. In interviews with a random sample of nursing home staff, 40 percent admitted that during the preceding year they had abused patients psychologically. Ten percent admitted to abusing patients physically (Pillemer and Hudson 1993). Most abuse of the elderly, however, takes place not in nursing homes but at home. Most abusers are not paid staff, but family members, who hit, verbally and emotionally abuse, or financially exploit their aged relatives (Pillemer and Wolf 1987). The most likely abuser is the spouse (Nachman 1991; Pillemer and Suitor 1993).

Why do spouses, children, and other relatives abuse their own elderly? Sociologists Karl Pillemer and Jill Suitor (1993) interviewed more than 200 people who were caring for family members who suffered from Alzheimer's disease. One husband told them,

> Frustration reaches a point where patience gives out. I've never struck her, but sometimes I wonder if I can control myself. . . . This is . . . the part of her care that causes me the frustration and the loss of patience. What I tell her, she doesn't register. Like when I tell her, "You're my wife." "You're crazy," she says.

From this husband's statement, we can glean some insight into the stress that comes with caring for a person who is dependent, demanding, and in some cases violent (Pillemer and Suitor 1993; Korbin et al. 1994). Since most people who care for the elderly undergo stress but are not violent toward those they care for, however, we do not have the answer to why some caregivers become violent. For this, we must await future research.

More important than understanding the causes of abuse, however, is preventing nursing home residents from being abused in the first place. An important step in this direction is laws that require background checks of nursing home workers. At a minimum, we can screen out people who have been convicted of such crimes as rape. This is similar to requiring background checks of nursery school workers in order to screen out people who have been convicted of molesting children. Most states have passed such laws. These laws are only a first step to solving this problem. They will not prevent abuse, only avoid the obvious.

The Elderly Poor

Many elderly live in nagging fear of poverty. Since they do not know how long they will live, nor what the rate of inflation will be, they fear that they will outlive their savings. How realistic is this fear? Although we cannot speak to any individual case, we can look at the elderly as a group.

Gender and Poverty As reviewed in Chapter 11, during their working years most women have lower incomes than men. As Figure 13.10 shows, this pattern follows

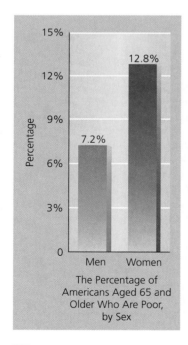

Figure 13.10

Gender and Poverty in Old Age

Source: Statistical Abstract 2000: Table 40.

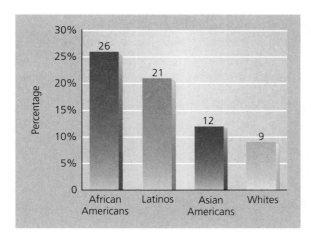

Figure 13.11
Poverty and Race-Ethnicity
Source: Statistical Abstract 2000:
Table 758.

women and men into their old age. As you can see, elderly women are about 80 percent more likely than elderly men to be poor.

Race–Ethnicity and Poverty   The elderly also reflect the racial and ethnic patterns of the general society. As Figure 13.11 shows, elderly whites are the least likely to be poor. As you can see, compared with whites, poverty is twice as common among elderly Latinos and three times as common among elderly African Americans. For elderly Asian Americans, the gap is much smaller, yet their poverty runs a third higher than that of whites.

A Decline in Poverty   Poverty among the elderly was once (in the 1960s) so severe that one of every three elderly Americans lived below the poverty line. In response to public demand, the federal government established anti-poverty programs and fattened Social Security checks. Legislation also gave workers vested rights in their pension plans. (Employers had to set aside the retirement money in secure accounts.) This led to one of the few success stories in the government's campaign

■ *In old age, as in other stages in the life course, having enough money for one's needs and desires makes life more pleasant and satisfying. This elderly woman, who must live out of her car, is not likely to find this time of her life satisfying. Income, however, is hardly the sole determiner of satisfaction during old age. As indicated in the text, integration in a community in which one is respected is a crucial factor. Thus, these elderly women who get together for a weekly game of poker are likely to find this time of life more satisfying than the isolated homeless woman.*

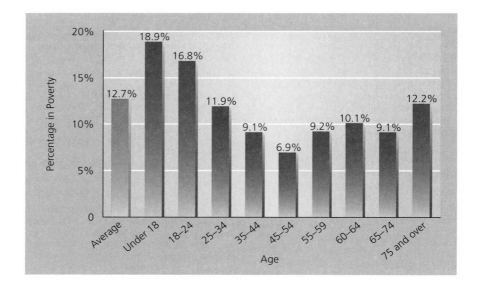

Figure 13.12

Poverty and Age

Source: Statistical Abstract 2000: Table 757.

against poverty. As Figure 13.12 shows, this campaign has been so successful that today's elderly are less likely than the average American to be poor.

The Sociology of Death and Dying

In a fascinating subfield of sociology, death and dying, sociologists stress how death, like old age, is much more than a biological event. They examine how culture shapes the ways that people experience death. Let's look at some of their findings.

Industrialization and the New Technology

Before industrialization, the sick were taken care of at home, and they died at home. Because life was short, *most* children saw a sibling or parent die (Blauner 1966). As noted in Chapter 1 (page 29), the family even prepared corpses for burial.

Industrialization radically altered the circumstances of dying—which has been transformed into an event that is managed by professionals in hospitals. Consequently, most Americans have never seen anyone die. Fictional deaths on television are the closest most come to witnessing death. In effect, dying has become an event that takes place behind closed doors—isolated, disconnected, remote.

This change has made the process of dying strange and alien to us. We try to put on a mask of immortality and hide from the fact of death. We have developed elaborate ways to refer to death without using the word itself, which uncomfortably reminds us of our human destiny. We carefully construct a language of avoidance, using terms such as "gone," "passed on," "no longer with us," "passed through the pearly gates," and "at peace now."

New technologies not only removed the dying from our presence, but also are bringing us a new experience of death. They have produced what sociologists Karen Cerulo and Janet Ruane (1996) call *technological lifespace.* This term refers to a form of existence that is neither life nor death as we usually define it. The self of a "brain dead" person, for example, is gone—dead—yet technology can keep the body alive. What used to be firm—the boundary between life and death—in some instances has now become murky, for technological lifespace is a kind of bridge between life and death.

As people grow older, the reality of death becomes more real. With each passing year, the elderly see more of their friends and relatives die. Much of their talk may center on those people—how they miss them, and how she "went" so suddenly, or how he lingered on. Fears about dying often focus more on the "how" of death than on death itself. The elderly are especially fearful of dying alone or in pain. One of their biggest fears is cancer, which seems to strike out of the blue.

■ Death as a Process

Psychologist Elisabeth Kübler-Ross (1969/1981) became curious about how people cope when they find out that they are going to die soon. After interviewing people who had been informed that they had an incurable disease, she concluded that people who come face to face with their own death go through five stages:

1. *Denial.* At first, people cannot believe that they are going to die. ("The doctor must have made a mistake. Those test results can't be right.") They avoid the topic of death and situations that might remind them of it.

2. *Anger.* After a while, they acknowledge that they are going to die, but they see their death as unjust. ("I didn't do anything to deserve this. So-and-so is much worse than I am, and he's in good health. It isn't right that I should die.")

3. *Negotiation.* Next, the individual tries to get around death by making a bargain with God, with fate, or even with the disease itself. ("I need one more Christmas with my family. I never appreciated them as much as I should have. Don't take me until after Christmas, and then I'll be ready.")

4. *Depression.* In this stage, people are resigned to their death, but they grieve because their life is about to end, and they have no power to change the course of events.

5. *Acceptance.* In this final stage, people come to terms with their impending death. They put their affairs in order—make wills, pay bills, instruct their children to take care of the surviving parent. They also express regret at not having done certain things when they had the chance. Devout Christians are likely to talk about the hope of salvation and their desire to be in heaven with Jesus.

Dying is more individualized than Kübler-Ross's model indicates. Not everyone, for example, tries to make bargains. What is important sociologically is that death is a process, not just an event. People who know they are going to die face a sharply different reality from the one experienced by those of us who think we will be alive years from now. That reality of impending death powerfully affects their thinking and behavior. Let me share an intimate event from my own life.

> When my mother was informed that she had inoperable cancer, she immediately went into a vivid stage of denial. If she later went through anger or negotiation, she kept it to herself. After a short depression, she experienced a longer period of questioning why this was happening to her. She then moved quickly into stage 5, which occurred very much as Kübler-Ross described it. After her funeral, my two brothers and I went to her apartment, as she had instructed us. There, to our surprise, attached to each item in every room—from the bed and the television to the boxes of dishes and knick-knacks—was a piece of masking tape with one of our names on it. At first we found this strange. We knew she was an orderly person, but to this extent? As we sorted through her things, reflecting on why she had given certain items to whom, we began to appreciate the "closure" she had given to this aspect of her material life.

■ Hospices

In earlier generations, when few people made it to age 65 or beyond, death at an early age was taken for granted—much as people take it for granted today that most people *will* see 65. In fact, due to advances in medical technology, *most* deaths in the

■ *In this hospice in St. Paul, Minnesota, a grandson uses a "pocket talker" (a portable microphone with attached earpiece) to talk to his ninety-nine-year-old grandmother.*

United States (about 75 percent) occur after age 65. Now that we live longer because of medical technology and better public health practices, we have a greater concern about the *how* of dying. Few elderly want to burden their children with their own death. They also want to die with dignity, surrounded with the comforting presence of friends and relatives. Hospitals, to put the matter bluntly, are awkward places in which to die. There people experience what sociologists call *institutional death*—they die surrounded by strangers in formal garb, in an organization that puts its routines ahead of patients' needs.

Hospices emerged as a solution to these problems, including the great expense of hospitalization. Hospices attempt to lower costs and to reduce the emotional and physical burden on dying people and their friends and relatives. A central idea of hospices is that the control of dying belongs to the people who are dying and their families. The term **hospice** originally referred to a place, but now it generally refers to home care (Cloud 2000). Services are brought into a dying person's home—from counseling to such down-to-earth help as providing babysitters or driving the person to a doctor or lawyer. At any one time, about 80,000 people are in hospice care in the United States (*Sociological Abstract* 2000:Table 206).

Whereas hospitals are dedicated to prolonging life, hospices are dedicated to providing dignity in death and to make people comfortable in what Kübler-Ross (1989) called the *living-dying interval*, that period between discovering that death is imminent and death itself. In the hospital, the focus is on the patient; in the hospice, the focus switches to both the dying person and his or her friends and family. In the hospital, the goal is to make the patient well; in the hospice, it is to relieve pain and suffering. In the hospital, the primary concern is the individual's physical welfare; in the hospice, although medical needs are met, the primary concern is the individual's social—and in some instances, spiritual—well-being.

■ Suicide and Age

We noted in Chapter 1 how Durkheim stressed that suicide has a *social* base. Suicide, he said, is much more than an individual act. Each country, for example, has its own suicide rate, which remains quite stable year after year. In the United States, we can predict with almost certainty that 31,000 people will commit suicide this year. If we are off by more than 1,000, it would be a surprise. As we saw in Figure 1.1. (page 13), we can also predict with certainty that Americans will choose firearms as the most common way to kill themselves, and that hanging will come in second. We can also be certain that this year males will be more likely than females to take their lives. It is this way year after year.

Statistics often fly in the face of the impressions we get from the mass media, and here we have such an example. Although the suicides of young people are given high publicity, such deaths are relatively rare. The suicide rate of adolescents is *lower* than that of almost all other ages. Because adolescents have such a low death rate, however, suicide does rank as their third leading cause of death—after accidents and homicide (*Statistical Abstract* 2000:Table 128).

These findings on suicide are an example of the primary sociological point stressed throughout this text: Recurring patterns of human behavior—whether education, marriage, work, crime, use of the Internet, or even suicide—represent underlying social forces. Consequently, if no basic changes take place in the social conditions under which the groups that make up U.S. society live, you can expect these same patterns of suicide five to ten years from now.

hospice
a place, or services brought into someone's home, for the purpose of bringing comfort and dignity to a dying person

Looking Toward the Future

We have reviewed several key issues in aging—from the social construction of "old" to problems with nursing homes and the mythical Social Security surplus. We also caught a glimpse of aging in other societies. To close the chapter, I would like you to reflect on some exciting and, perhaps, disturbing scientific breakthroughs that may have a direct impact on your own life.

thinking
CRITICALLY

How Long Do You Want to Live?
Pushing Past the Limits of Biology

How would you like to live to 150? To 200?

Such a question may strike you as absurd. But with our new and still developing technology, science may stretch the life span to limits unheard of since biblical days.

We are just at the beginning stages of genetic engineering, and ahead of us may lie a brave new world. Predictions are that technicians will be able to snip out our bad DNA and replace it with more compliant bits. The caps at the end of our chromosomes, the telomeres, shrink as we age, causing the cells to die. An enzyme called telomerase may be able to modify this process, allowing cells to reproduce many more times than they do now (Nuland 1999).

Already—just by manipulating a gene or two—scientists have been able to double the life span of worms, flies, and mice. Humans have these same genes (Recer 2000). A doubled human life span would take the longest living people past 200.

We are only peering over the edge of the future, glimpsing what might be possible. Some optimistic molecular biologists predict that we will find ways to grow spare body parts. From the same stem cells we will grow livers, hearts, kidneys, fingers—whatever you need.

Spare body parts? Apparently they're on the way. If the growing of body parts becomes routine, I can envision the day when the organ and limb salespeople take over. Can't you just hear it now? "Such a deal! I got a new kidney coming in Tuesday. Everybody's gonna want it, but for some reason I like you, and I'm gonna give you a special price."

Back in grade school, my teachers told me stories about Ponce de León, an explorer from Spain who searched for the fountain of youth. He eventually "discovered" Florida, but the fountain of youth eluded him. In our perpetual search for immortality, could we, finally, have found what eluded Ponce de León?

■ ■ ■ ■ ■
for your consideration . . .

Let's assume that biomedical science does stretch the human life span, that living to be 200 or so becomes common. If people retire at age 65, how could society afford to support them for 135 years? People can't work much past this, for—and this may be the basic flaw in this brave new world scenario—even with new body parts, the world would not be filled with 200-year-olds who functioned as though they were 25. They would be old people, subject to the diseases and debilities that come with advancing age. If Medicare costs are bulging at the seams now, what would they be like in such a world?

Finally, how would you answer this question: Is the real issue how we can live longer, or how we can live better?

Summary and Review

Aging in Global Perspective

■ **How are the elderly treated around the world?**

No single set of attitudes, beliefs, or policies regarding the aged characterizes the world's nations. Rather, they vary from exclusion and killing, to integration and honor. The global trend is for more people to live longer. P. 380.

■ **What does the social construction of aging mean?**

Nothing in the nature of aging summons forth any particular set of attitudes. Rather, attitudes toward the elderly are rooted in society and differ from one social group to another. Pp. 380–381.

■ **What does the term "graying of America" mean?**

The phrase **graying of America** refers to the growing proportion of Americans who reach old age. Since the costs of Social Security and health care for the elderly have become a social issue, sentiment about the elderly seems to be shifting. Pp. 382–385.

The Symbolic Interactionist Perspective

■ **What factors influence perceptions of aging?**

Symbolic interactionists stress that, by itself, reaching any particular age has no meaning. They identify four factors that influence when people label themselves as "old": biological changes, biographical events, **gender age,** and cultural timetables. Cross-cultural comparisons—for example, the traditional Native Americans, Tiwi, and Eskimos—demonstrate the role of culture in determining how individuals experience aging. **Ageism,** negative reactions to the elderly, is based on stereotypes, which, in turn, are influenced by the mass media. Pp. 385–389.

The Functionalist Perspective

■ **How is retirement functional for society?**

Functionalists focus on how the withdrawal of the elderly from positions of responsibility benefits society. **Disengagement theory** examines retirement as a device for ensuring that a society's positions of responsibility will be passed smoothly from one generation to the next. **Activity theory** examines how people adjust when they disengage from productive roles. **Continuity theory** focuses on how people adjust to growing old by continuing their roles and coping techniques. Pp. 389–391.

The Conflict Perspective

■ **Is there conflict among different age groups?**

Social Security legislation is an example of one generation making demands on another generation for limited resources. As the **dependency ratio,** the number of workers who support one retired person, drops, workers may become resentful. The Social Security Trust Fund may be a gigantic fraud perpetrated by the power elite on the nation's elderly. The argument that benefits to the elderly come at the cost of benefits to children is fallacious. Organizations such as the Gray Panthers and the AARP recognize the potential for conflict between age groups. Pp. 391–397.

Problems of Dependency

■ **What are some of the problems that today's elderly face?**

Women are more likely to live alone and to be poor. At any one time, about 4 percent of the elderly live in nursing homes. Because of widespread abuse, the U.S. Congress passed a bill of rights to protect nursing home residents. The most common abusers of the elderly, however, are members of their own family. Poverty in old age, greatly reduced through government programs, reflects the gender and racial-ethnic patterns of poverty in the general society. Pp. 397–402.

The Sociology of Death and Dying

■ **How does culture affect the meaning—and experience— of death and dying?**

Like old age, death is much more than a biological event. Industrialization, for example, brought modern medicine, hospitals, and the custom of dying in a formal setting surrounded by strangers. Kübler-Ross identified five stages in the dying process, which, though insightful, do not characterize all people. **Hospices** are a cultural device designed to overcome the negative aspects of dying in hospitals. Suicide shows distinct patterns by age, sex, and method. It is possible that science will increase the human **life span.** Pp. 402–405.

■ *Where can I read more on this topic?*

Suggested Readings for this chapter are at the back of this book.

All URLs listed are current as of the printing of this book. URLs often change. Please check our Web site, **http://www.abacon.com/henslin,** for updates.

Additional Online Resources for This Chapter
www.ablongman.com/henslin6e

- *Content Select* Research Database for Sociology, with suggested key terms and annotated references
- Link to 2000 Census, with activities
- Flashcards of key terms and concepts

- Practice Tests
- Weblinks
- Interactive Maps

using . . .

ContentSelect

Research Database for Sociology

Alzheimer's disease	elder abuse	gender age	nursing home
American Association of Retired Persons	elderly	hospice	old age
	ethnicity and death	life expectancy	

Franklin McMahon, *Making Butter Cookies*, 1970

14

The Economy

The Transformation of
Economic Systems

Preindustrial Societies:
The Birth of Inequality

Industrial Societies:
The Birth of the Machine

Postindustrial Societies: The
Birth of the Information Age

Bioeconomic Societies:
The Merger of Biology
and Economics

The Transformation of
the Medium of Exchange

Earliest Mediums of Exchange

Medium of Exchange in
Agricultural Societies

Medium of Exchange in
Industrial Societies

Medium of Exchange in
Postindustrial Societies

World Economic Systems

Capitalism

Socialism

Ideologies of Capitalism
and Socialism

Criticisms of Capitalism
and Socialism

The Convergence of
Capitalism and Socialism

The Functionalist View
of the Globalization
of Capitalism

The New Global Division
of Labor

Ownership and Management
of Corporations

Functions on a Global Scale

The Conflict View
of the Globalization
of Capitalism

The Inner Circle of Corporate
Capitalism

Interlocking Directorates

Global Investing

Work in U.S. Society

The Decline of Agriculture
and the Transition to
Postindustrial Society

Women and Work

The Underground Economy

Shrinking Paychecks

Patterns of Work and Leisure

Facing the Future:
Implications of
Global Capitalism

Global Trade: Inequalities
and Conflict

New Technologies
and Downsizing:
Utopia or Nightmare?

Summary and Review

The Nike story is a fascinating example of entrepreneurial opportunity in the United States and of the globalization of capitalism.

Phil Knight was a distance runner on the track team at the University of Oregon. After he completed Stanford Business School in the late 1960s, Knight began to import running shoes from Japan and sell them out of the back of his car. As you can imagine, sales were

> They found that workers in Indonesia, Vietnam, and Thailand were willing to work for even less.

slow, and a day of rain would wipe out sales altogether. But Knight was able to see potential far beyond the trunk of his car, and he and his former track coach decided to create their own brand of running shoes.

The two needed some sort of symbol for their new brand, but they couldn't come up with anything. They hired a design student at Portland State University. They paid him $35 to think up the "Swoosh."

What is the Nike "Swoosh" worth today? Maybe $6 billion.

In the early years, Nike ran small factories in New Hampshire and Maine. Nike closed those factories in the 1980s. They were paying their workers between $8 and $11 an hour at the time. Workers in Korea and Taiwan were willing to make the same shoes for $1 an hour—and they were happy to get it.

In the 1990s, Nike relocated its manufacturing plants again. They found that workers in Indonesia, Vietnam, and Thailand were willing to work for even less.

A pair of Nike shoes that sells for $80 or $100 in the United States costs the company about $2.60 for labor.

Based on Patillo-McCoy 1999.

▪ Although the term market *is used to refer to the mechanisms by which people establish value so they can exchange goods and services, its original meaning referred to a direct exchange of goods, as shown in this photo of a market in Copacabana, Bolivia. In peasant societies, where such markets are still a regular part of everyday life, people find the social interaction every bit as rewarding as the goods and money that they exchange.*

*W*e live in a global economy, and this chapter focuses on the consequences of this fact for the future of the United States—and for our own lives.

■ ▪ ▪ ▪ ▪

The Transformation of Economic Systems

*I*n Mexico, the market is a bustling scene. Farmers sell fruits and vegetables, as well as poultry, goats, and caged songbirds. Others sell homemade blankets, serapes, huaraches, pottery, belts. Women bend over open fires cooking tacos, which their customers wolf down with soft drinks. The market is a combined business and social occasion: As people make their purchases, they catch each other up on the latest gossip. Such scenes used to characterize the world, but now they are limited primarily to the Least Industrialized Nations. The closest people come in the United States is a flea market, a farmer's market, or a street fair.

Today, the term *market* means much more than such settings and activities. Market has kept its original meaning of buying and selling, but it now refers to things much more impersonal. The **market**, a system of producing and distributing goods and services, today means the Dow Jones Industrial Average in New York City, and the Nikkei Index in Tokyo. Market also means the movement of vast amounts of goods across international borders, even across oceans and continents. Market means brokers taking orders for Boeing, speculators trading international currencies, and futures traders making huge bets on whether oil, wheat, and pork bellies will go up or down—and, of course, it also refers to buying a hamburger and fries at a local fast food chain.

The market, or as sociologists prefer to call it, the **economy,** is essential to our welfare. It means inflation or deflation, high or low interest rates, high or low unemployment, economic recession or economic boom. The economy affects our chances of going to college, of buying a home, of having to work at a boring, dead-end job or of being on a fast track in an up-and-coming company.

Today, the economy, which many sociologists consider the most important of our social institutions, differs radically from all but our most recent past. To better understand how global forces affect the U.S. economy—and your life, let's begin with a review of sweeping historical changes.

▪ Preindustrial Societies: The Birth of Inequality

The earliest human groups, *hunting and gathering societies,* had a **subsistence economy.** Groups of perhaps twenty-five to forty people lived off the land. They gathered what they could and moved from place to place as their food supply ran low. Because there was little or no excess food or other items, they did little trading with other groups. With no excess to accumulate, everybody possessed about the same as everyone else.

Then people discovered how to breed animals and cultivate plants. This produced a surplus and ushered in social inequality. The more dependable food supply in *pastoral and horticultural societies* allowed humans to settle down in a single place. Human groups grew larger, and some individuals began to devote their ener-

market
any process of buying and selling; on a more formal level, the mechanism that establishes values for the exchange of goods and services

economy
a system of distribution of goods and services

subsistence economy
a type of economy in which human groups live off the land with little or no surplus

gies to tasks other than producing food. Some people became leather workers, others weapon makers, and so on. This new division of labor produced a surplus, and groups traded items with one another. The primary sociological significance of surplus and trade is this: They set the stage for *social inequality*, for some people accumulated more possessions than others. The effects of that change remain with us today.

The invention of the plow ushered in the next major change. The plow multiplied food production, allowing *agricultural societies* to develop. As more people were freed from food production, more specialized divisions of labor followed. The result was an even greater surplus. As trade expanded, trading centers developed. Trading centers turned into cities, and power passed from the heads of families and clans to a ruling elite. The result was even greater social, political, and economic inequality.

■ Industrial Societies: The Birth of the Machine

In 1765, another invention changed the world. Machines powered by fuels, instead of humans and animals, brought a surplus unlike anything in history. In the new *industrial society*, inequality increased even more. A handful of individuals opened factories, exploiting the labor of many. The owners became wealthy and were able to manipulate the political machinery for their own purposes. This set the stage for the bloody battles that followed, when workers unionized to improve their working conditions.

Then came more efficient machines. As the surpluses grew even greater, the emphasis slowly changed from producing goods to consuming them. In 1912, sociologist Thorstein Veblen coined the term **conspicuous consumption** to describe this change in people's orientations. Veblen noted that the Protestant ethic identified by Weber—an emphasis on hard work, savings, and a concern for salvation (discussed on pages 188–189)—was being replaced by an eagerness to show off wealth by the "elaborate consumption of goods."

conspicuous consumption
Thorstein Veblen's term for a change from the Protestant ethic to an eagerness to show off wealth by the elaborate consumption of goods

 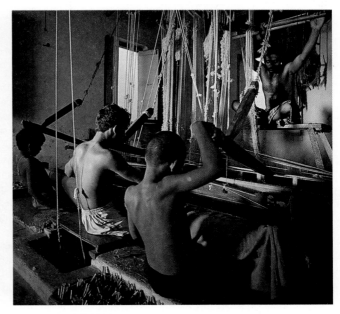

■ *One of the negative consequences of early industrialization in the West was the use of child labor. In the photo on the left, of the U.S. textile industry in the 1800s, you can see spindle boys at work in a Georgia cotton mill. Today's Least Industrialized Nations are experiencing the same negative consequence as they industrialize. The photo on the right shows boys at work in a contemporary textile factory in Varanas, India. About the only improvement is that the child workers in India are able to sit down as they exhaust their childhood.*

■ Postindustrial Societies: The Birth of the Information Age

In 1973, sociologist Daniel Bell noted that a new type of society was emerging. This new society, which he called the *postindustrial society,* has six characteristics: (1) a service sector so large that *most* people work in it; (2) a vast surplus of goods; (3) even more extensive trade among nations; (4) a wider variety and quantity of goods available to the average person; (5) an information explosion; and (6) a *global village*—that is, the world's nations are linked by fast communications, transportation, and trade. The Down-to-Earth Sociology box below discusses how interconnected the global village has become.

■ Bioeconomic Societies: The Merger of Biology and Economics

It is usually easier to analyze an event after you've passed through it than one you are experiencing. Nevertheless, we may be on the verge of yet another new type of society, one being ushered in by advances in biology, especially the deciphering of the human genome system in 2001. While the specifics of this new society are yet to unfold, the marriage of biology and economics will yield even greater surpluses and greater possibilities for trade. The global village will continue to expand. This new society may also lead to longer and healthier lives. As history is our guide, it also may create even greater inequality between the rich and poor nations.

The broad changes in societies may seem to be abstract matters, but they are far from irrelevant to your life. Whenever society changes, so do our lives. Consider the

---

down-to-earth
s o c i o l o g y

■ ■ ■ ■ ■

"Your Name is What? You Live Where? But You Sound Like You're Right Next Door."

"Hi. I'm Nancy Morrison from Chicago. May I help you?"

You are likely to be greeted with something like this when you call about your credit card or to inquire why something you ordered hasn't arrived yet. Or maybe you will talk to Susan Sanders from Newark, New Jersey.

Nothing surprising in this. It happens all the time. The accent is so perfect that even someone from Chicago or Newark wouldn't know the difference.

It just happens that the individual who is greeting you is Nishara Hydedrabad—or Narayana Ramdas. She doesn't live in Chicago or Newark, or even in the United States, for that matter. She lives in Bangalore, India.

Your call has been routed to a highly trained worker 8,000 miles away. In training sessions, she and her fellow workers watch *Friends* and *Ally McBeal.* They must

be able to reconstruct the dialogue, so they can master the nuances of English. They have to know, for example, that when a customer says, "No way, Jose" that there is no Jose.

In role playing sessions, their trainer poses as a caller and interrogates them on U.S. movies, TV programs, and sports. If a customer moves into unfamiliar territory, they are taught to say, "Can we get back to business?"

The value of these call centers to U.S. and other companies is so great that India is becoming "the back office for the world." Among many other companies, General Electric and British Airways have set up huge phone banks in Bangalore to handle a daily barrage of customer inquiries.

And what a competitive advantage the corporations find in India. "Susan" is a college graduate, and for her this isn't

a stopgap job, but a career. She gets paid a huge salary compared to most Indians. She earns somewhere between $1,600 and $2,100—a year.

for your consideration

How is technology shrinking the global village? Explain how the activities in this Indian call center are an example of the impression management discussed in Chapter 4 (pages 115–120). Do you think that it is a fair business practice to have Indian telephone workers take on pseudo American identities? Are "Susan" and "Nancy" exploited by the multinational corporations? Or do they benefit from them?

Based on Landler 2001.

■ ■ ■ ■ ■

information explosion. When you graduate from college, you will do some form of "knowledge work." Instead of working in a factory, you will manage information, or design, sell, or service products. The type of work you do has profound implications for your life. It produces social networks, creates attitudes, and even affects how you view yourself and the world.

It is the same with the global village. Think of the globe as divided into three neighborhoods—the three worlds of industrialization and postindustrialization we reviewed in Chapter 9 (pages 260–265). Some nations are located in the poor part of the village. Their citizens barely eke out a living from menial work. Some of them even starve to death—while their fellow villagers in the rich neighborhood feast on the best that the globe has to offer. It's the same village, but what a difference the neighborhood makes.

Now visualize any one of the three neighborhoods. Again you will see gross inequalities. Not everyone who lives in the poor neighborhood is poor, and some areas of the rich neighborhood are packed with poor people. Because the United States is the global economic leader, occupying the most luxurious mansion in the best neighborhood and is spearheading the new bioeconomy, let's look at U.S. trends.

The Transformation of the Medium of Exchange

As each type of economy evolved, so, too, did the **medium of exchange,** the means by which people value and exchange goods and services. As we review this transformation, you'll see how the medium of exchange not only reflects the state of a country's development but also contributes to it.

Earliest Mediums of Exchange

As noted, the lack of surplus in hunting and gathering and pastoral and horticultural societies meant that there was little to trade. Whatever trading did occur was by **barter,** directly exchanging one item for another. The surplus that stimulated trade in later societies led to new ways of valuing goods and services so people could exchange them. Let's look at how the medium of exchange was transformed.

Medium of Exchange in Agricultural Societies

Although bartering continued in agricultural societies, people increasingly came to use **money,** a medium of exchange that places a value on items. In most places, money consisted of gold and silver coins. A coin's weight and purity determined the amount of goods or services it could purchase. In some places people made purchases with **deposit receipts.** These receipts transferred ownership to a specified number of ounces of gold or bushels of grain, or to a specified amount of other goods that were on deposit in a warehouse or bank. Toward the end of the agricultural period, deposit receipts became formalized into **currency** (paper money). Each piece of paper represented a specific amount of gold or silver on deposit in a warehouse. Currency and deposit receipts represented **stored value.** No more currency or deposit receipts could be issued than the amount of gold or silver in the warehouse. Gold and silver coins continued to circulate alongside the deposit receipts and currency.

Medium of Exchange in Industrial Societies

With few exceptions, in industrial societies bartering became a thing of the past. Gold was replaced by paper currency, which, in the United States, could be exchanged for gold stored at Fort Knox. This policy was called the **gold standard.** As long as each dollar represented a specified amount of gold, the number of dollars that

medium of exchange
the means by which people value goods and services in order to make an exchange, for example, currency, gold, and silver

barter
the direct exchange of one item for another

money
any item (from seashells to gold) that serves as a medium of exchange; today, currency is the most common form

deposit receipts
a receipt stating that a certain amount of goods is on deposit in a warehouse or bank; the receipt is used as a form of money

currency
paper money

stored value
the backing of a currency by goods that are stored and held in reserve

gold standard
paper money backed by gold

Figure 14.1

Declining Value of the
U.S. Dollar

Source: Modified from "Alternative
Investment Market Letter," November 1991.

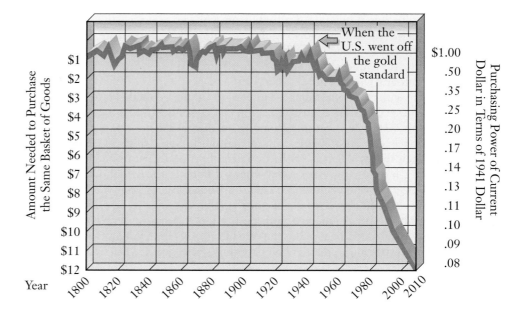

could be issued was limited. Toward the end of this period, U.S. paper money could
no longer be exchanged for gold or silver. Instead, there was **fiat money,** currency issued by a government that is not backed by stored value.

When fiat money replaced stored value, coins made of precious metals disappeared from circulation. People considered these coins more valuable, and they were
unwilling to part with them. Gold coins disappeared first, followed by the largest silver coin, the dollar. Then, as inferior metals (copper, zinc, and nickel) replaced the
smaller silver coins, people began to hoard these silver coins, and they, too, disappeared from circulation.

Even without a gold standard that restrains the issuing of currency to stored
value, governments have a practical limit on the amount of paper money they can
issue. In general, prices increase if a government issues currency at a rate higher than
the growth of its **gross domestic product (GDP),** the total goods and services that a
country produces. This condition, **inflation,** means that each unit of currency will
purchase fewer goods and services. Governments try to control inflation, for it is a
destabilizing influence.

As you can see from Figure 14.1, as long as the gold standard limited the amount
of currency, the purchasing power of the dollar remained relatively stable. When the
United States left the gold standard in 1937, the dollar no longer represented stored
value, and it plunged in value. Today, the dollar is but a shadow of its former self,
retaining only about 9 percent of its original purchasing power.

In industrialized societies, checking accounts became common. A *check* is actually a type of deposit receipt, for it is a promise that the writer of the check has deposited enough currency in the warehouse (the bank or credit union) to cover the
check. The latter part of the industrial period saw the invention of the **credit card.**
This device allows its owner, who has been approved for a specified amount, to purchase goods without an immediate exchange of money—either metal, currency, or
check. The credit card owner is billed for the purchase.

■ **Medium of Exchange in Postindustrial Societies**

During the first part of the postindustrial (or information) society, paper money circulated freely. Paper money became less common, being gradually replaced by checks
and credit cards. The next development was the **debit card.** This device electronically
withdraws the cost of an item from the card holder's bank account. Like the check, the
debit card is a type of deposit receipt, for it transfers ownership of currency on deposit.

fiat money
currency issued by a government that is not backed by
stored value

**gross domestic product
(GDP)**
the amount of goods and
services produced by a nation

inflation
an increase in prices

credit card
a device that allows its owner
to purchase goods but to be
billed later

debit card
a device that allows its owner
to charge purchases against his
or her bank account

The latest evolution of money is e-cash. **E-cash** consists of digital money that is stored on the user's computer. E-cash can be encoded in e-mail and sent over the Internet. In effect, the new medium of exchange is itself a part of the information explosion.

TABLE 14.1	**Comparing Socialism and Capitalism**

Socialism	Capitalism
1. The public owns the means of production.	1. Individuals own the means of production.
2. Central committees plan production no competition.	2. The owners determine production based on competition.
3. There is no profit motive in the distribution of goods and services.	3. The pursuit of profit is the reason for distributing goods and services.

■ ▢ ▪ ▢

World Economic Systems

Now that we have sketched the main economic changes in history, let's compare capitalism and socialism, the two main economic systems in force today. Table 14.1 presents a summary of this discussion.

◗ Capitalism

People who live in a capitalist society may not understand its basic tenets, even though they see them reflected in their local shopping malls and fast-food chains. If we distill the many businesses of the United States to their basic components, we see that **capitalism** has three essential features: (1) *private ownership of the means of production* (individuals own the land, machines, and factories, and decide what they will produce); (2) *market competition* (an exchange of items between willing buyers and sellers); and (3) *the pursuit of profit* (selling something for more than it costs).

Some people believe that the United States is an example of pure capitalism. Pure capitalism, however, known as **laissez-faire capitalism** (literally meaning "hands off"), means that the government doesn't interfere in the market. Such is not the case in the United States. The current form of U.S. capitalism is **welfare** or **state capitalism.** Private citizens own the means of production and pursue profits, but they do so within a vast system of laws designed to protect the welfare of the population.

Suppose that you discover what you think is a miracle tonic: It will grow hair, erase wrinkles, and dissolve excess fat. If your product works, you will become an overnight sensation—not only a multimillionaire, but also the toast of television talk shows.

■ *This advertisement from 1885 represents an early stage of capitalism, when individuals were free to manufacture and market products with little or no interference from the government. Today, the production and marketing of goods take place under detailed, complicated government regulations.*

e–cash
digital money that is stored on computers

capitalism
an economic system characterized by the private ownership of the means of production, the pursuit of profit, and market competition

private ownership of the means of production
the ownership of machines and factories by individuals, who decide what shall be produced

market competition
the exchange of items between willing buyers and sellers

laissez-faire capitalism
unrestrained manufacture and trade (literally, "hands off" capitalism)

welfare (state) capitalism
an economic system in which individuals own the means of production, but the state regulates many economic activities for the welfare of the population

Before you count your money—and your fame—however, you must reckon with **market restraints,** the laws and regulations of welfare capitalism that limit your capacity to produce and sell. First, you must comply with local and state rules. You must obtain a business license and a state tax number that allows you to buy your ingredients without paying sales taxes. Then come the federal regulations. You cannot simply take your product to local stores and ask them to sell it; you first must seek approval from federal agencies that monitor compliance with the Pure Food and Drug Act. This means you must prove that your product will not cause harm to the public. In addition, you must be able to substantiate your claims—or else face being shut down by state and federal agencies that monitor the market for fraud. Your manufacturing process is also subject to federal, state, and local laws concerning hygiene and the disposal of hazardous wastes.

Suppose that you overcome these obstacles, and your business prospers. Other federal agencies will monitor your compliance with laws concerning discrimination by race, sex, and disability, minimum wages, and Social Security taxes. State agencies will examine your records to see if you have paid unemployment taxes and sales taxes. Finally, the Internal Revenue Service will look over your shoulder and demand a share of your profits (up to 39.1 percent). In short, the U.S. economic system is highly regulated and is far from an example of laissez-faire capitalism.

To see how welfare or state capitalism developed in the United States, let's go back to an earlier era. When capitalism was in its infancy in the 1800s, you could have made your "magic" potion at home and sold it at any outlet willing to handle it. You could have advertised that it cured baldness, erased wrinkles, and dissolved fat, for no agency existed to monitor your product or your claims. (See the 1885 poster on page 415.) In fact, this is precisely what thousands of individuals did at that time. They made "elixirs" in their basements and gave them whimsical names such as "Grandma's Miracle Medicine" and "Elixir of Health and Happiness." A single product could claim that it restored sexual potency, purged the intestines, and made people more intelligent. These tonics often made people feel better, for many elixirs were braced with alcohol—and even cocaine (Ashley 1975). (Coca-Cola was a "pick me up" during this period, for until 1903 it contained cocaine. This is what the *Coca* of Coca Cola refers to.) To protect the public's health, in 1906 the federal government passed the Pure Food and Drug Act and began to regulate products.

John D. Rockefeller's remarkable success in unregulated markets helps explain why the government began to regulate capitalism. After a ruthless drive to eliminate competition, Rockefeller managed to corner the U.S. oil and gasoline market. He would slash prices and then double them after driving out the competition. He would even sabotage competitors' pipelines and refineries (Josephson 1949). With his competitors crippled or eliminated, his company, Standard Oil, was able to dictate prices to the entire nation. Rockefeller had achieved the capitalist's dream, a **monopoly,** the control of an entire industry by a single company.

Rockefeller had played the capitalist game too well, however, for he had wiped out one of its essential components, competition. Consequently, to protect this cornerstone of capitalism, the federal government passed antimonopoly legislation and broke up Standard Oil. Today, the top firms in each industry—such as Ford Motors in automobiles and General Electric in household appliances—must obtain federal approval before acquiring another company in the same industry. If the government determines that one firm dominates a market, it can force that company to **divest** (sell off) some of its businesses.

Another characteristic of welfare capitalism is that although the government supports competition, it establishes its own monopoly over what it calls "common good" items. These are items presumed essential for the common

market restraints
laws and regulations that limit the capacity to manufacture and sell products

monopoly
the control of an entire industry by a single company

divest
to sell off

■ Shown here is John D. Rockefeller, perhaps the richest man in the world when this photo was taken in 1937. In his older years, Rockefeller developed the unusual habit of giving both poor and rich people "shiny, new dimes." He is photographed here as he gave dimes to wealthy friends who had just played a round of golf with him. Since Rockefeller made a percentage from almost every gallon of gasoline sold in the United States, if he had dug a little deeper, he may have been able to give away shiny new quarters.

good of the citizens, such as soldiers, war supplies, highways, and sewers.

Socialism

Socialism also has three essential components: (1) the public ownership of the means of production; (2) central planning; and (3) the distribution of goods without a profit motive.

In socialist economies, the government owns the means of production. It owns not only the factories, but also the land, railroads, oil wells, and gold mines. Unlike capitalism, in which **market forces**— supply and demand—determine what will be produced and the prices that will be charged, a central committee decides products and prices. The committee decides how many toothbrushes, toilets, and shoes the country needs. It also decides which factories will produce them, what price will be charged for the items, and where they will be distributed.

Socialism is designed to eliminate competition, for goods are sold at predetermined prices regardless of the demand for an item or the cost to produce it. Profit is not the goal, nor is encouraging consumption of goods in low demand (by lowering the price), nor limiting the consumption of hard-to-get goods (by raising the price). Rather, the goal is to produce goods for the general welfare and to distribute them according to people's needs, not their ability to pay.

In a socialist economy *everyone* works for the government. The members of the central committee who set production goals are government employees, as are the supervisors who implement those goals, the factory workers who produce the merchandise, the truck drivers who move it, and the clerks who sell it. Those who buy the items may work at different jobs—in offices, on farms, in day care centers—but they, too, are government employees.

■ *Successful capitalists can buy most things in life. Donald Trump could be flashing a victory sign to signify that he can afford to sit in the front row at a title fight at Madison Square Garden in New York City. Or his victory sign could indicate that he is able to afford a trophy girlfriend. Sitting next to Trump, age 54, is his girlfriend, Melania Knauss, age 27.*

■ *Throughout most of the twentieth century, capitalism and communism were pitted against one another in a deadly struggle. Each thought of itself as the correct economic form, and each viewed the other as an evil obstacle to be eradicated. In support of this view of essential goodness and evil, proponents of each system launched global propaganda campaigns. Shown here is a painting of Vladimir Lenin, leader of the worldwide workers' revolution. This 1930 painting by Alexander Gerassimow (1881–1963) hangs in the Tretyakov Gallery in Moscow.*

socialism
an economic system characterized by the public ownership of the means of production, central planning, and the distribution of goods without a profit motive

market forces
the law of supply and demand

Just as capitalism does not exist in a pure form, neither does socialism. Although the ideology of socialism calls for resources to be distributed according to need, not the ability to pay, in line with the functionalist argument of social stratification presented in Chapter 9 (pages 254–255), socialist countries found it necessary to offer higher salaries for some jobs. Only then could they entice capable people to take greater responsibilities. As a result, in socialist countries factory managers always earned more than factory workers. By narrowing the huge pay gaps that characterize capitalist nations, however, socialist nations established considerably greater equality of income.

Dissatisfied with the greed and exploitation of capitalism and the lack of freedom and individuality of socialism, Sweden and Denmark developed **democratic socialism** (also called *welfare socialism*). In this form of socialism, both the state and individuals produce and distribute goods and services. The government owns and runs the steel, mining, forestry, and energy concerns, as well as the country's telephones, television stations, and airlines. Remaining in private hands are the retail stores, farms, factories, and most service industries.

■ Ideologies of Capitalism and Socialism

> **democratic socialism**
> a hybrid economic system in which capitalism is mixed with state ownership

Not only do capitalism and socialism have different approaches to producing and distributing goods, but also they represent distinct ideologies. *Capitalists* believe that market forces should determine both products and prices. They also believe that greed is good. It is healthy for people to strive after profits, for this stimulates them to develop new products. The Mass Media box below examines how capitalists create demand for their products.

---

mass media
in social life

Greed Is Good—Selling the American Dream

Advertising is such an integral part of our lives that being deluged with ads almost appears to be our human destiny. When we open a newspaper or magazine, we expect to find pages that proclaim the virtues of products and firms. We turn on the television and are assailed with commercials for ten minutes of every half hour. Some social analysts even claim that the purpose of television is to round up an audience to watch the commercials, that the programs are mere diversions from the medium's real objective of selling products!

Advertising is so powerful that it can produce the desire to consume products for which we previously felt no need whatsoever. U.S. kitchens, filled with gadgets that slice and dice, attest to this power.

Advertising's power to make people gluttons goes beyond kitchen gadgets that are soon consigned to back drawers

and garage sales. Many Americans would not think of going out in public without first shampooing, rinsing, conditioning, and blow-drying their hair. Many feel the need to apply an underarm deodorant so powerful that it overcomes the body's natural need to sweat. For many women, public appearance also demands the application of foundation, lipstick, eye shadow, mascara, rouge, powder, and perfume. For many men, after-shave lotion is essential. And only after covering the body with clothing that displays designer labels do Americans feel that they are presentable to the public.

Advertising influences not only what we put on our bodies, what we eat, and what we do for recreation, but also how we feel about ourselves. Our ideas of whether we are too fat, too skinny, too hippy, too buxom, whether our hair is too oily or too dry, our body too hairy, or our skin too rough are largely a conse-

quence of advertising. As we weigh our self-image against the idealized images that bombard us in our daily fare of commercials, we conclude that we are lacking something. Advertising assures us that there is salvation—some new product that promises to deliver exactly what we lack.

The approach is ingenious in its simplicity: Create discontent by presenting ideal images that are impossible to attain. And it works. We grow dissatisfied with ourselves. And we snatch the advertisers' solution: We strive to consume more of the never-ending products that the corporations offer us—those they have decided we need.

The American Dream . . . built on greed, discontent, enticing images, and the promise of redemption. Of course, dreams often strangely juxtapose realities.

Socialists, in contrast, believe that profit is immoral. Karl Marx said that an item's value is based on the work that goes into it. The only way there can be profit, he stressed, is by paying workers less than the value of their labor. Profit, then, is the *excess value* withheld from workers. Socialists believe that the government should protect workers from this exploitation. To do so, it should own the means of production, using them not to produce profit, but to produce items that match people's needs, not their ability to pay.

Adherents to these ideologies paint each other in such stark colors that *each perceives the other as a system of exploitation.* Capitalists view socialists as violating basic human rights of freedom of decision and opportunity. Socialists see capitalists as violating the basic human right of freedom from poverty. With each side claiming moral superiority while viewing the other as a threat to its very existence, the last century witnessed the world split into two main blocs. In what was known as the *Cold War,* the West armed itself to defend capitalism, the East to defend socialism.

Criticisms of Capitalism and Socialism

The primary criticism leveled against capitalism is that it leads to social inequality. Capitalism, say its critics, produces a tiny top layer of wealthy, powerful people, who exploit a vast bottom layer of poorly paid workers. Many of these workers are unemployed and underemployed (**underemployment** is having to work at a job beneath your training and abilities or being able to find only part-time work). Another major criticism is that the tiny top layer wields vast political power. Those few who own the means of production reap huge profits, accrue power, and are able to get legislation passed that goes against the public good.

The primary criticism leveled against socialism is that it does not respect individual rights (Berger 1991). Others (in the form of some government body) control people's lives. They decide where people will live, where they will go to school, where they will work, and how much they will be paid. In China, they even decide how many children women may bear (Mosher 1983). Critics also argue that central planning is grossly inefficient and that socialism is not capable of producing much wealth. They say that its greater equality really amounts to giving almost everyone an equal chance to be poor.

The Convergence of Capitalism and Socialism

Regardless of the validity of these mutual criticisms, as nations industrialize they grow alike. They urbanize, produce similar divisions of labor (such as professionals and skilled technicians), and encourage higher education. Even similar values emerge (Kerr 1960, 1983). By itself, this tendency would make capitalist and socialist nations grow more alike, but another factor also brings them closer to one another (Form 1979): Despite their incompatible ideologies, both capitalist and socialist systems have adopted features of the other.

That capitalism and socialism are growing similar is known as **convergence theory.** This view points to a possible hybrid or mixed economy for the future. A fundamental change in socialist countries gives evidence for convergence theory. Russia and China suffered from shoddy goods, they were plagued by shortages, and their standard of living severely lagged behind the West. To try to catch up, in the 1980s and 1990s Russia and China reinstated market forces. Private ownership of property

underemployment
the condition of having to work at a job beneath one's level of training and abilities, or of being able to find only part-time work

convergence theory
the view that as capitalist and socialist economic systems each adopt features of the other, a hybrid (or mixed) economic system will emerge

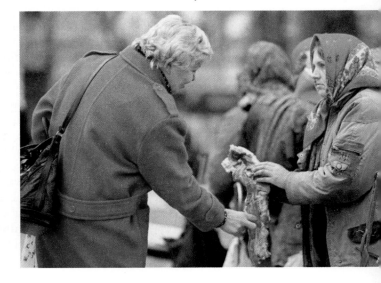

■ *Although most people under communist rule lived in poverty, they were assured jobs that provided basic food and shelter. With today's erratic transition to capitalism, citizens of the former Soviet Union no longer have that assurance. Shown here is a scene in Kiev, the capital of Ukraine, where people are learning capitalism, that is, to buy and sell for profit. How many customers will finger this piece of meat before someone buys it?*

cultural d·i·v·e·r·s·i·t·y

Around the World

No Cash? No Problem! Barter in the Former Soviet Union

About 50 miles from the town of Bila Tserkva, you'll see a few tires piled alongside the highway. By the time you get to Bila Tserkva, the stacks of black tires have grown thicker and higher until they seem to line both sides of the road like thick rubber walls (Brzezinski 1997).

Welcome to Russia's transition to capitalism. This is payday at the tire plant in Bila Tserkva. With cash in short supply, workers are paid in tires. In other towns, workers get paid in airplanes, televisions, clothing, even tombstones, sex toys, and toilet bowls. Some laid-off workers get their unemployment benefits in manure

(Paddock 1998; Schmemann 1998; Powell 1999). In Volgograd, workers are paid in brassieres. So many brassieres will get you into the latest Sylvester Stallone movie—or buy you a hat, a pair of shoes, an ice cream cone. . . .

In the cash-strapped former Soviet Union, it's not just individuals who use goods instead of cash. In Smolensk, the cannery pays its taxes in canned beef. It uses canned meat to pay for the cows and pigs it slaughters; aluminum to make the cans; equipment to can the meat; electricity to run the equipment; and cardboard boxes to ship the cans (Paddock 1998).

Barter chains have developed. Ukraine's electric utility company receives payment in goods ranging from military uniforms to steel tubing. The company passes the steel tubing on to the Russian company that supplies it with electricity, which, in turn, uses the tubing in its pipelines. The uniforms? It gives these to Russia's Ministry of Defense in lieu of taxes.

When city workers in Tatarstan arrived at city hall, they found 600 new trucks parked on the front lawn. The trucks were payment on the local truck maker's tax bill. The workers were lucky—they might have been greeted with piles of tires or brassieres.

became legal, and the state auctioned off many of its industries. Even making a profit—which had been a crime previously—was encouraged. They even invited their former arch-enemies, Western corporations, to open up shop. In China, capitalists have been invited to join the Communist Party (Eckholm 2001). For a glimpse of Russia's transition to capitalism, see the Cultural Diversity box above.

Changes in capitalism also support this theory. The United States has adopted many socialist practices. One of the most obvious is extracting money from some individuals to pay for benefits it gives to others. Examples include unemployment compensation (taxes paid by workers are distributed to those who no longer produce a profit); subsidized housing (shelter, paid for by the many, is given to the poor and elderly, with no motive of profit); welfare (taxes from the many are distributed to the needy); a minimum wage (the government, not the employer, determines the minimum that workers receive); and Social Security (the retired do not receive what they paid into the system, but, rather, money that the government collects from current workers). Such embracing of socialist principles means that the United States has produced its own version of a mixed type of economy.

Perhaps, then, convergence is unfolding before our very eyes. On the one hand, capitalists now assume that their system should provide workers at least minimal support during unemployment, extended illness, and old age. On the other hand, socialist leaders have reluctantly admitted that profit and private ownership do motivate people to work harder.

The matter, however, is not this simple. That each has adopted features of the other is only part of the picture. The systems remain far from "converged." Although it is considerably muted compared to what it was in the heady days of the cold war, the struggle between the systems continues. Russian and Polish citizens, for example, longing for greater stability, have voted Communists back into top government positions. In the United States, Republicans try to roll back socialistic measures and return to a purer capitalism, while Democrats resist. Meanwhile the Chinese, longing to transform themselves into the world's number one capitalist nation, await the death of the elderly rulers who are barricaded in their "Kremlin" fortress.

The Functionalist View of the Globalization of Capitalism

Sun Microsystems uses a single phone number to offer round-the-globe, round-the-clock technical service. The number is staffed by teams in California, England, and Australia. They electronically hand work off as a team when another country comes on line.

When the Turkish economy plunged, Goodyear didn't let its tire plant in Turkey sit idle. Instead, using flexible tire-making technology, Goodyear swiftly regeared its tire models and redirected output to the rest of Europe. (Zachary 1995)

The globalization of capitalism may be the most significant economic change in the past 100 years. Its impact on our lives may rival that of the Industrial Revolution itself. As Louis Gallambos, a historian of business, says, "This new global business system will change the way everyone lives and works." (Zachary 1995)

The New Global Division of Labor

To apply functionalism to the globalization of capitalism, we must first step back a moment and look at work itself. Work is functional for society. Only because people work do we have electricity, hospitals, schools, automobiles, and homes. Beyond this obvious point, however, lies a basic sociological principle: *Work binds us together.* As you may recall from Chapter 4, Emile Durkheim noted that in preindustrial societies people do similar work and directly share most aspects of life. Because of this, they look at the world in similar ways. Durkheim used the term **mechanical solidarity** to refer to the sense of unity that comes from doing similar activities.

The industrialization of society, in contrast, brings a division of labor. Because people no longer share the same activity, they feel less solidarity with one another. Grape pickers in California, for example, may feel they have little in common with workers who make aircraft in Missouri. Yet, each worker performs a specific function and contributes to the welfare of the others. They are *like the separate organs that make up the same body.* Durkheim called this type of unity **organic solidarity.**

Durkheim observed the beginning of what has turned out to be a global process. Today, organic solidarity engulfs the world. We now have a *global division of labor,* and each of us depend on workers around the globe. People who live in California or New York—or even Michigan—depend on workers in Tokyo to produce cars. Tokyo workers, in turn, depend on Saudi Arabian workers for oil, South American workers to operate ships, and miners in South Africa for palladium for their catalytic converters. Although we do not feel a sense of unity with one another—in fact, we may feel threatened and hostile—interdependence links us all in the same global economic web. This process does not occur without cultural hurdles, of course, a topic of the Cultural Diversity box on the next page.

mechanical solidarity
Durkheim's term for the unity that comes from being involved in similar occupations or activities
organic solidarity
Durkheim's term for the interdependence that results from people needing others to fulfill their jobs

■ *As recounted in the opening vignette about Nike, in their march toward globalization multinational companies locate their corporate headquarters in one country, manufacture their basic components in another country, assemble them in still another, and sell the finished product throughout the world. Shown here is a Nike assembly plant in Indonesia.*

cultural d·i·v·e·r·s·i·t·y

Around the World
Doing Business in the Global Village

The World

The globalization of capitalism means that businesspeople face cultural hurdles as they sell products in other cultures. At times, even experienced firms don't manage to break through cultural barriers. General Motors, for example, was successful in marketing its automobile, the Nova, in the United States. When GM tried to export that success south of the border, Mexicans snickered, and few would buy the car. Finally, someone let the company in on the secret: In Spanish, *"No va"* is an entire sentence that means "It doesn't go" or "It doesn't work."

Ford did no better when it tried to sell its Pinto in Brazil. People there snickered, too. It turns out that pinto is Portuguese slang for "little penis." Ford changed the car's name to Corcel, "the horse" (Archbold and Harmon 2001).

Many U.S. companies are trying to market to Mexico's growing middle class and to Spanish-speaking Americans. Some of them have stumbled over their Spanish. When Parker Pen tried to translate "It won't leak in your pocket and embarrass you," it came out, "It won't leak in your pocket and make you pregnant." Frank Perdue's cute chicken slogan, "It takes a strong man to make a tender

chicken" didn't fare any better. It came out: "It takes an aroused man to make a chicken affectionate."

Even Coca-Cola, with its many years of cross-cultural experience, stumbled when it tried to market Coke in China. The name came out as "Bite the wax tadpole." And when American Airlines launched a "Fly in Leather" campaign to promote its leather seats in first class, the Mexican campaign stumbled just a bit. "Fly in Leather" (vuela en cuero), while literally correct, came out as Fly Naked. I suppose that slogan did appeal to some.

Some businesspeople have managed to avoid such problems. They have seized profit opportunities in cultural differences. For example, Japanese women are embarrassed by the sounds they make in public toilets. To drown out the offensive sounds, they flush the toilet an average of 2.7 times a visit (Iori 1988). This wastes a lot of water, of course. Seeing this cultural trait as an opportunity, a U.S. entrepreneur developed a battery-powered device that is mounted in the toilet stall. When a woman activates the device, it emits a 25-second flushing sound. A toilet-sound duplicator may be useless in our

culture, but the Japanese have bought thousands of them.

Let's suppose that you decide to publish a magazine in Japan. Your market research shows that a magazine about sports heroes would be popular. It wouldn't surprise you to know that your readers expect you to chronicle their idol's career, height, and hobbies. But you would miss something essential if you didn't learn that the Japanese also expect to read about their hero's blood type. They view it as a sort of zodiac birth sign (Ono 1993). And you might learn that Japanese mothers save their baby's umbilical cord in a wooden box. If you could get hold of a sports hero's umbilical cord, you could make a small fortune (Shirouzu 1995).

If you opened a golf course in Japan, you would need to understand why golfers there fear shooting a hole-in-one. This obligates them to buy expensive gifts for their fellow players, to throw a drinking party, and to plant a commemorative tree to mark their "joy." Entrepreneurs have seized this cultural opportunity, too. To ward off such a catastrophe, they sell policies that for $100 provide $5,000 hole-in-one insurance (Hardy 1993a).

■ Ownership and Management of Corporations

Capitalism is driving today's global interdependence. It's triumph as the world's dominant economic force can be traced to a social invention called the corporation. A **corporation** is a business that is treated legally as a person. A corporation can make contracts, incur debts, sue and be sued. Its liabilities and obligations, however, are separate from those of its owners. For example, each shareholder of Ford Motor Company—whether he or she has 1 or 100,000 shares—owns a portion of the company. However, Ford, not its individual owners, is responsible for fulfilling its contracts and paying its debts. To indicate how corporations now dominate the economy, sociologists use the term **corporate capitalism.**

One of the most surprising, but functional, aspects of corporations is their *separation of ownership and management.* Unlike most businesses, the owners, those who own the company's stock, do not run the day-to-day affairs of the company. Instead, managers run the corporation, and they are able to treat it *as though it were their own* (Cohen 1990; Zampa and McCormick 1991). The result is the "ownership of wealth

corporation
the joint ownership of a business enterprise, whose liabilities and obligations are separate from those of its owners

corporate capitalism
the domination of the economic system by giant corporations

without appreciable control, and control of wealth without appreciable ownership" (Berle and Means 1932). Sociologist Michael Useem (1984) put it this way:

> When few owners held all or most of a corporation's stock, they readily dominated its board of directors, which in turn selected top management and ran the corporation. Now that a firm's stock [is] dispersed among many unrelated owners, each holding a tiny fraction of the total equity, the resulting power vacuum allow[s] management to select the board of directors; thus management [becomes] self-perpetuating and thereby acquire[s] de facto control over the corporation.
>
> Management determines its own salaries, sets goals and awards itself bonuses for meeting them, authorizes market surveys, hires advertising agencies, determines marketing strategies, and negotiates with unions. The management's primary responsibility to the owners is to produce profits.

What makes this separation of ownership and management work is profits. When stock options and bonuses are tied to the company's performance, managers are highly motivated to make profits. At the annual stockholders' meeting, the owners consider broad company matters, including the selection of a board of directors and a firm to audit the company's books. As long as the managers report good profits, the stockholders rubber-stamp their recommendations. It is so unusual for this not to happen that when it doesn't take place it is called a **stockholders' revolt.** The irony of this term is generally lost, but remember that in such cases it is not the workers but the owners who are rebelling!

■ *The globalization of capitalism means the dominance of markets by the main capitalist countries. Mattell, a U.S. corporation, ships Barbie and Ken around the world. Along with these dolls goes a reflection of U.S. culture, in this case an image of a way of life, one destined to shape people's thinking and aspirations.*

■ Functions on a Global Scale

The globalization of capitalism is leading to a new world structure. We are now seeing the world's nations separate into three primary trading blocks: North and South America, dominated by the United States; Europe, dominated by Germany; and Asia, dominated by Japan. Functionalists stress not only how this new global division benefits the multinational giants, but also how it benefits the citizens of the world.

Consider free trade. Free trade leads to greater competition, which, in turn, drives the search for greater productivity. This lowers prices and brings a higher standard of living. Free trade also has dysfunctions. As production moves to countries where labor costs are lower, millions of U.S., U. K., French, and German workers lose their jobs. Our opening vignette about Nike touched on this. Functionalists point out that this is merely a temporary dislocation. As the Most Industrialized Nations lose production jobs, their workers shift into service and high-tech jobs. Meanwhile, the unemployed of the poor nations are given work and the chance for a better life.

■■■■■
The Conflict View of the Globalization of Capitalism

Conflict theorists say that to place the focus on global interdependence is to miss the point. What we should look at is how the wealthy benefit at the expense of workers. Let's see what they mean by this.

■ The Inner Circle of Corporate Capitalism

The **multinational corporations**—corporations that operate across national borders—are headed by a group that Michael Useem (1984) calls the *inner circle.* Members of this inner circle, though in competition with one another, are united by a

stockholders' revolt
the refusal of a corporation's stockholders to rubber-stamp decisions made by its managers

multinational corporations
Corporations that have manufacturing, service, distribution systems in several countries.

mutual interest in preserving capitalism (Mizruchi and Koenig 1991). Within their own country, they consult with high-level politicians, promote legislation favorable to big business, and serve as trustees for the most influential foundations and universities. They also promote political candidates who stand firmly for the private ownership of property. On a global level, they promote the ideology of capitalism and move capital from one nation to another in their search for greater and more immediate profits.

Table 14.2 lists the world's largest corporations. You can see how the United States and Japan dominate world trade. Together, they account for 18 of the world's

TABLE 14.2 The World's Largest Corporations

Rank	Name	Country	Revenue	Profit (Loss)	Employees
1	General Motors	U.S.	$177 billion	$6.0 billion	388,000
2	Wal-Mart	U.S.	$167 billion	$5.4 billion	1,140,000
3	Exxon Mobil	U.S.	$164 billion	$7.9 billion	106,000
4	Ford Motors	U.S.	$163 billion	$7.3 billion	365,000
5	Daimler Chrysler	Germany	$160 billion	$6.1 billion	467,000
6	Mitsui	Japan	$119 billion	$0.3 billion	38,000
7	Mitsubishi	Japan	$118 billion	$0.2 billion	42,000
8	Toyota	Japan	$116 billion	$3.0 billion	215,000
9	General Electric	U.S.	$112 billion	$10.7 billion	340,000
10	Itochu	Japan	$109 billion	($0.8 billion)	53,000
11	Royal Dutch/Shell	Netherlands	$105 billion	$8.6 billion	96,000
12	Sumitomo	Japan	$96 billion	$0.3 billion	33,000
13	Nippon Telephone	Japan	$94 billion	($0.6 billion)	224,000
14	Marubeni	Japan	$92 billion	$0 billion	32,000
15	Axa	France	$88 billion	$2.2 billion	92,000
16	IBM	U.S.	$88 billion	$7.7 billion	307,000
17	BP Amoco	Great Britain	$84 billion	$5.0 billion	80,000
18	Citigroup	U.S.	$82 billion	$9.8 billion	177,000
19	Volkswagen	Germany	$80 billion	$0.9 billion	306,000
20	Nippon Life Insurance	Japan	$79 billion	$3.4 billion	71,000
21	Siemens	Germany	$75 billion	$1.8 billion	443,000
22	Allianz	Germany	$74 billion	$2.4 billion	114,000
23	Hitachi	Japan	$72 billion	$0.2 billion	398,000
24	Matsushita Electric	Japan	$66 billion	$0.9 billion	290,000
25	Nisshoiwa	Japan	$65 billion	$0.1 billion	18,000

Source: Kahn 2001.

largest 25 companies. Based on revenues, Japan, with 11 of the world's top 25 corporations, is the world leader. But as its losses and meager profits show, Japan has been fighting an economic depression for over ten years. Based on profits, the United States dominates world trade. The profits of its 7 corporations shown in this table are much greater than those of all the other 18 combined.

If the giant corporations cannot attain a monopoly, they strive for an **oligopoly**—several large companies that dominate a single industry, such as gasoline, breakfast cereal, or light bulbs. If they achieve this, then they can divide the market among themselves. They are also able to dictate the quality and prices of their products. To get legislation that gives them special tax breaks, oligopolies also cultivate political connections. (Some simply say that they "buy" politicians.)

One of the more significant, and to some, sinister, developments in capitalism is today's merger of giant corporations from different nations. Merging, or one buying another, reduces competition. This, too, makes it easier to set prices and quality and to trounce smaller competitors. In short, mergers consolidate the power of the multinational corporations and make it easier for them to dominate global markets.

Consolidation of power is one of the primary goals of these corporations. The inner circle looks for cooperative politicians and develops a cozy relationship with them. If they find hostility, some are not above plotting murder and overthrowing governments. In 1973, a U.S. multinational, the International Telephone & Telegraph Company (ITT), joined the CIA in a plot to unseat Chile's elected government. They first attempted to bring about the economic collapse of Chile. When this failed, they plotted a coup d'état, which led to the assassination of the Chilean president, Salvador Allende (Coleman 1995).

U.S. economic power is so integrated with politics that the inner circle can even get the U.S. president to pitch their products. If this sounds like an exaggeration, consider this report from the Associated Press (October 29, 1995):

> The White House celebrated Saudi Arabia's $6 billion purchase of U.S.-made airplanes Thursday, calling it a victory for both American manufacturers and the Clinton administration. . . . President Clinton helped broker the sale. . . . Prince Bandar bin Sultan, [Saudi Arabia's] minister of defense and aviation, credited Clinton for closing the purchase. *Clinton personally pitched the quality of the U.S. planes to Saudi King Fahd.* (Italics added)
> . . . (T)he Clinton Administration worked this sale awfully damn hard because of the president's commitment to promoting U.S. business abroad. . . . He has done that routinely, instructed his ambassadors and his diplomats to put the economic interests of Americans forward as they conduct their diplomacy.

Although the president wasn't selling toothpaste, it was the same principle.

In short, the interests of the heads of the multinational corporations and the top political leaders converge. Together, they form a *power elite,* with top government leaders dedicated to promoting the interests of the country's economic leaders. We shall return to this topic in the next chapter.

■ Interlocking Directorates

Conflict theorists stress how the powerful use **interlocking directorates** (Mizruchi and Koenig 1991). The elite serve as directors of several companies. Their fellow members on those boards also sit on the boards of other companies, and so on. Like a spider's web that starts at the center and then fans out in all directions, the top companies are interlocked into a network (Mintz and Schwartz 1985). The chief executive officer of a firm in England, who sits on the board of directors of half a dozen other companies, said:

> If you serve on, say, six outside boards, each of which has, say, ten directors, and let's say out of the ten directors, five are experts in one or another subject, you have a built-in panel of thirty friends who are experts who you meet regularly, automatically each month, and you really have great access to ideas and information. You're joining a club, a very good club. (Useem 1984)

This concentration of power minimizes competition, for a director is not going to approve a plan that will be harmful to another company in which he or she (mostly

oligopoly
the control of an entire industry by several large companies

interlocking directorates
the same people serving on the board of directors of several companies

Figure 14.2
Social Map:
The Globalization
of Capitalism:
U.S. Ownership
in Other Countries
Source: Statistical Abstract
2000:Table 1317.

he) has a stake. The top executives of the top U.S. companies are part of the powerful capitalist class described on pages 285–286. They even get together in recreational settings, where they renew their sense of solidarity, purpose, and destiny (Domhoff 1997).

Global Investing

The two figures on these pages illustrate how corporations have outgrown their national boundaries. The world map shows the investments that U.S. corporations have made in other countries. Cross-border investments are not a one-way street, however, as the U.S. map shows. If you buy a book from New York's Random House, you are making a purchase from Bertelsmann, a German company. Macy's (of the famous Macy's Thanksgiving Day parade) is owned by Campeau, a Canadian company. And if you buy a package of Tums, you are buying a product from an old-line U.S. company that is now owned by Beecham Group, a British corporation.

Although we have started to take the presence of multinational corporations for granted—as well as their cornucopia of products—their power and presence are new to the world scene. As they do business around the globe, they become more and more detached from the interests and values of their country of origin. A U.S. executive made this revealing statement, "The United States does not have an automatic call on our resources. There is no mind-set that puts the country first" (Kennedy 1993). These corporate giants move investments and production from one part of the globe to another—with no concern for consequences other than profits. How their adding—or withdrawing—of investments affects workers is of no concern to them. With profit as their moral guide, the conscience of multinational corporations is dominated by dollar signs.

Figure 14.2 *(Continued)*

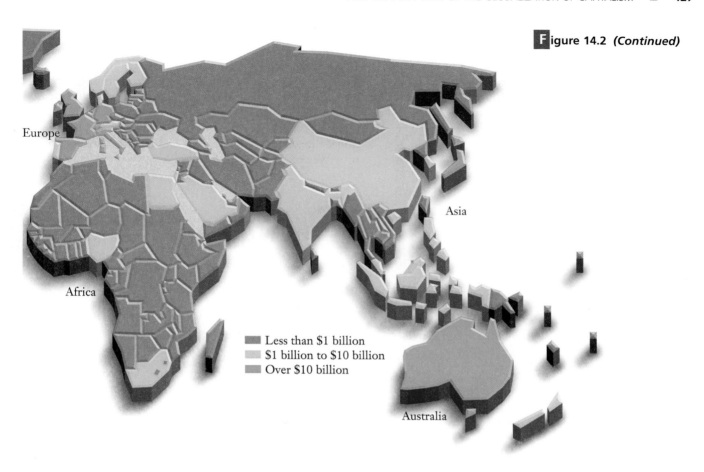

Less than $1 billion
$1 billion to $10 billion
Over $10 billion

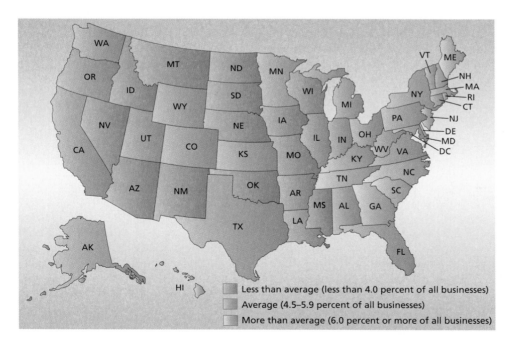

Figure 14.3

Social Map:
The Globalization
of Capitalism: Foreign
Ownership of U.S. Business

Businesses in which at least 10 percent of the voting interest is controlled by a non-U.S. owner. Does not include banks.

Source: Statistical Abstract 2000: Table 1314.

Less than average (less than 4.0 percent of all businesses)
Average (4.5–5.9 percent of all businesses)
More than average (6.0 percent or more of all businesses)

This primary allegiance to profits and market share, rather than to any nation, is of sociological significance. The shift in orientation is so new, however, that we don't yet know its implications. But we can consider two stark contrasts. The first: Removed from tribal loyalties and national boundaries, the global interconnections of the multinational corporations may be a force for global peace. The second: They could create a New World Order dominated by a handful of corporate leaders. If so, we all may find ourselves at the mercy of a global elite directed by the heads of the world's corporate giants. We will discuss this possibility in the next chapter.

■ ■ ■ ■ ■

Work in U.S. Society

With this broad, even global, background, let's turn our focus on work in U.S. society.

■ The Decline of Agriculture and the Transition to Postindustrial Society

At various times in this text, I have used the term *postindustrial society* to describe the United States. Figure 14.4 illustrates why this term is appropriate. This figure shows a change that is without parallel in human history. In the 1800s, most U.S. workers were farmers. Today, farmers make up about 2 percent of the work force. With the technology of the 1800s, a typical farmer produced enough food for only five people. With today's powerful machinery and hybrid seeds, he or she now feeds about eighty. In 1940, about half of U.S. workers wore a blue collar; then changing technology shrank the market for blue-collar jobs. White-collar work continued its ascent, reaching the dominant position it holds today. Figure 14.4 illustrates nothing less than the transition to a new society. Because of this change, your life is different—not just your work—but also your attitudes and even the way you view the world.

■ Women and Work

One of the chief characteristics of the U.S. work force has been a steady increase in the numbers of women who work for wages outside the home. Over the past century, the number steadily increased, and today almost one of two U.S. workers is a woman. As you can see from Figure 14.5, this ratio is one of the highest in the industrialized world.

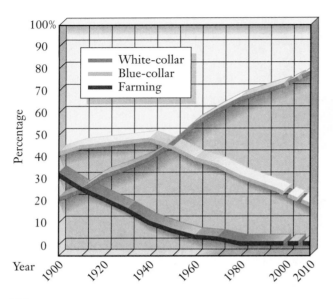

Figure **14.4**

The Revolutionary Change in the U.S. Work Force

Note: From 1900 to 1940, "workers" refers to people age 14 and over, from 1970 to people age 16 and over. Broken lines are the author's projections.

Source: Statistical Abstract, various years, and 2000:Table 671.

Figure **14.5**

Women Make Up What Percentage of the Labor Force in the Most Industrialized Nations?

Source: Statistical Abstract 1999: Table 1376; 2000:Table 671.

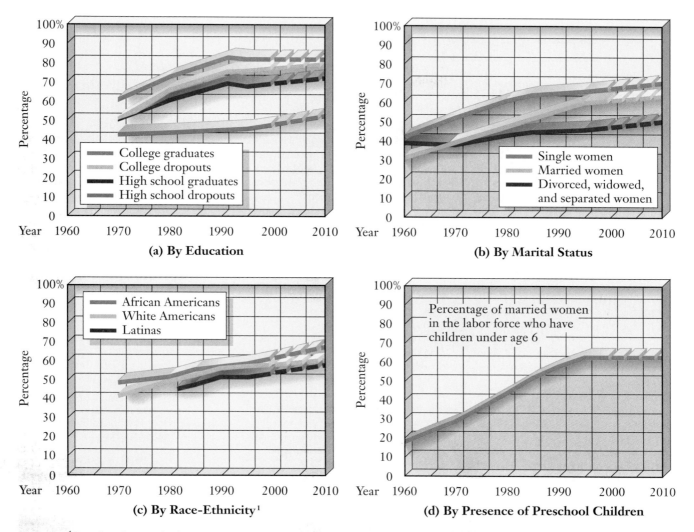

¹Data for other racial-ethnic groups unavailable in the source; no data for Latinas for 1970–1980.

Figure 14.6

Percentage of Women in the U.S. Labor Force

Source: Statistical Abstract 1995: Tables 627, 629, 637, 639; 2000: Tables 644, 647, 651, 653.

How likely it is for a woman to be in the labor force depends on several factors. Figure 14.6a shows how working for wages increases with each level of education. This is probably because women who have more education also find more satisfying work—and get higher pay. Figure 14.6b shows the influence of marital status. You can see that single women are the most likely to work for wages, married women follow closely behind, and divorced, widowed, and separated women are the least likely to be in the work force. From Figure 14.6c, you can see that race-ethnicity makes little difference.

Researchers have found distinctions between women and men in the world of work. First, women tend to be more concerned than men with maintaining a balance between their work and family lives (Statham et al. 1988). Second, men and women tend to follow different models for success: Men tend to emphasize individualism, power, and competition, while women are more likely to stress collaboration, persuasion, and helping (Miller-Loessi 1992). Finally, a primary concern of many women is the extent to which they must adopt the male model in order to be successful in their careers. You should note that these findings represent tendencies. Although they characterize the average woman or man, many people diverge from them.

As discussed in Chapter 11, women face discrimination at work. The Down-to-Earth Sociology box on the next page explores how some women cope with this discrimination.

down-to-earth

s o c i o l o g y

■ ■ ■ ■ ■

Women in Business: Maneuvering the Male Culture

I work for a large insurance company. Of its twenty-five hundred employees, about 75 percent are women. Only 5 percent of the upper management positions, however, are held by women.

I am one of the more fortunate women, for I hold a position in middle management. I am also a member of the twelve-member junior board of directors, of whom nine are men and three are women.

Recently one of the female members of the board suggested that the company become involved in Horizons for Tomorrow, a program designed to provide internships for disadvantaged youth. Two other women and I spent many days developing a proposal for our participation.

The problem was how to sell the proposal to the company president. From past experiences, we knew that if he saw it as a "woman's project" it would be shelved into the second tier of "maybes." He hates what he calls "aggressive bitches."

We three decided, reluctantly, that the proposal had a chance only if it were presented by a man. We decided that Bill was the logical choice. We also knew that we had to "stroke" Bill if we were going to get his cooperation.

We first asked Bill if he would "show us how to present our proposal." (It is ridiculous to have to play the role of the "less capable female," but, unfortunately, the corporate culture sometimes dictates this strategy.) To clinch matters, we puffed up Bill even more by saying, "You're the logical choice for the next chairmanship of the board."

Bill, of course, came to our next planning session, where we "prepped" *him* on what to say.

At our meeting with the president, we had Bill give the basic presentation. We then backed *him* up, providing the background and rationale for why the president should endorse the project. As we answered the president's questions, we carefully deferred to Bill.

The president's response? "An excellent proposal," he concluded, "an appropriate project for our company."

To be successful, we had to maneuver through the treacherous waters of the "hidden culture" (actually not so "hidden" to women who have been in the company for a while). The proposal was not sufficient on its merits, for the "who" behind a proposal is at least as significant as the proposal itself.

"We shouldn't have to play these games," Laura said, summarizing our feelings.

But we all know that we have no choice. To become labeled "pushy" is to commit "corporate suicide"—and we're no fools.

Source: Written by an insurance executive in the author's introductory sociology class who, out of fear of retaliation at work, has chosen to remain anonymous.

■ ■ ■ ■ ■

The Quiet Revolution   Because the change has been so gradual and its implications so profound, sociologists use the term **quiet revolution** to refer to the consequences that have occurred because so many women have joined the paid labor force. This has meant a transformation of consumer patterns, interactions at work, orientations, self-concepts, and relationships with boyfriends, husbands, and children. One of the most significant aspects of the quiet revolution is indicated by Figure 14.6d on page 429. Note how few mothers of preschool children used to work for wages. Their percentage now equals the average of all U.S. women. We discuss implications of these changes in Chapter 16.

■ The Underground Economy

The underground economy. It has a sinister ring—suggestive of dope deals struck in alleys and wads of bills hastily exchanged. The underground economy is this, but it is a lot more—and it is usually a lot more innocent. If you pay the plumber with a check made out to "cash," if you purchase a pair of sunglasses from a street vendor or a kitchen gadget at a yard sale, if you so much as hand a neighbor's kid a $20 bill to mow the lawn or to baby sit, you are participating in the underground economy. (Pennar and Farrell 1993)

the quiet revolution
the fundamental changes in society that occur as a result of vast numbers of women entering the work force

underground economy
exchanges of goods and services that are not reported to the government and thereby escape taxation

Also known as the informal economy and the off-the-books economy, the **underground economy** consists of economic activities—whether legal or illegal—that people don't report to the government. What interests most of us is not unreported baby-sitting money, but the illegal activities that people cannot report even if they want to. As a 20-year-old child care worker who also works as a prostitute two or three nights a week told me, "Why do I do this? For the money! Where else can I make this kind of money in a few hours? And it's all tax free." Drug dealing is perhaps the largest single source of illegal income, for billions of dollars flow from users to sellers and their networks of growers, importers, processors, transporters, dealers, and enforcers. These particular networks are so huge that each year the police arrest more than a million Americans for illegal drug activities (*Statistical Abstract* 2000:Table 345).

The million or so illegal immigrants who enter the United States each year are also part of the underground economy. Often called *undocumented workers* (referred to as *los sin documentos* in Spanish), they work for employers who don't pay attention to their fake Social Security cards, or for those who pay them in cash. Of the 43 restaurant workers who were killed when terrorists struck the World Trade Center, 12 were working with fake Social Security cards (Cleeland 2001). Some enter on their own, but smugglers bring in many (Henslin 2000:275). The undocumented workers from China work primarily in Chinese restaurants and in New York's garment industry. Many from India and Pakistan work in fast food restaurants (Rosenbaum 1998). Those from Mexico and Central and South America are concentrated in California and Texas, but they disperse throughout the country. They pick lettuce on farms, sew garments in clandestine sweat shops, clean rooms in hotels, and serve food at restaurants. For the most part, they do the low-paying and dirty jobs that U.S. citizens try to avoid. The rest of us benefit from their labor, for they bring us cheaper goods and services.

Because of its subterranean nature, no one knows the size of the underground economy, but it probably runs 10 to 15 percent of the regular economy (Pennar and Farrell 1993). Since the official gross domestic product of the United States is about $9 trillion (*Statistical Abstract* 2000:Table 715), the underground economy probably runs about $1 trillion a year. It is so huge that it distorts the official statistics of the country's gross domestic product, and costs the IRS more than $100 billion a year in lost taxes.

■ The term underground economy *has a sinister ring to it. Part of the underground economy does consist of drug deals furtively transacted in back alleys, but the term refers to any unreported, untaxed commercial transaction. Most are as innocuous, and common, as that depicted in this photo of The Annex, a weekend flea market in New York City.*

■ Shrinking Paychecks

U.S. workers are some of the most productive in the world (*Statistical Abstract* 2000:Table 1384). One might think, therefore, that their pay would be increasing. This brings us to a disturbing trend.

Until about 1970, gains in productivity did translate into paychecks that allowed workers to buy more goods. But how things have changed. Look at Figure 14.7 on the next page. The gold bars show current dollars, the dollars the average worker finds in his or her paycheck. From this, it appears that U.S. workers are making a lot more than they used to. They bring home more than *four* times as many dollars as workers did in 1970. Back in 1970, workers averaged only a little over $3 an hour; now it is almost $14. The green bars, which show the *buying power* of these paychecks, strip away the illusion. They show that inflation has whittled away the value of those dollars. Today's workers can't buy as much with their $14 as workers in 1970 could with their "measly" $3 an hour. The question is not "How could you live on just $3 back then?" but, rather, "How can you live on just $14 an hour today?"

■ Patterns of Work and Leisure

Suppose that it is 1860 and you work for a textile company in Lowell, Massachusetts. When you arrive at work one day, you find that the boss has posted a new work rule: All workers will have to come in at the same time and remain until quitting time. Like the other workers, you feel outrage. You join them as they shout, "This is slavery!" and march out of the plant, indignant at such a preposterous rule. (Zuboff 1991)

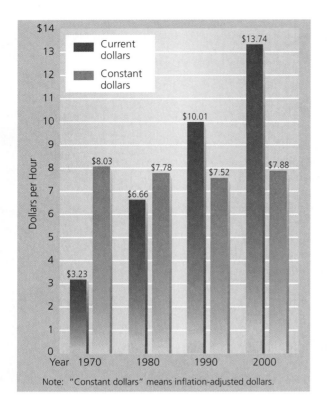

Figure 14.7

Average Hourly Earnings of U.S. Workers in Current and Constant (1982) Dollars
Source: Statistical Abstract 1999:Table 698; 2001:Table 616.

leisure
time not taken up by work or
required activities

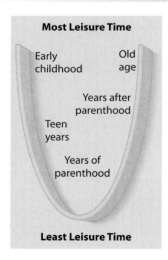

Figure 14.8

Leisure and the Life Course:
The "U" Curve of Leisure

This is a true story. The workers were angry because up until then they had been able to come and go when they wanted. Let's consider how patterns of work and leisure are related to the transformation of economies.

Effects of Industrialization   Hunting and gathering societies provided enormous amounts of **leisure,** time not taken up by work or required activities such as eating and sleeping. Assuming they didn't live in a barren place or have to deal with some unusual event, such as drought or pestilence, it did not take long for them to hunt and gather what they needed for the day. In fact, *most of their time was leisure,* and the rhythms of nature were an essential part of their lives. Agricultural economies also allowed much leisure, for, at least in the western hemisphere, work peaked with the spring planting, let up in the summer, and then peaked again with the fall harvest. During the winter work again receded, for by this time the harvest was in, animals had been slaughtered, food had been canned and stored, and a wood supply had been laid up.

Industrialization, however, broke this harness to seasonal rhythms. Going against all of human history, rhythms now were dictated by bosses and machines. Workers resisted this change. They insisted on moving to their traditional rhythms. After working for several weeks—or even just days—a worker would disappear, only to reappear when money ran out. For most, enjoying leisure was considerably more important than amassing money (Weber 1958/1904–1905). Bosses, in contrast, wanted to profit from regular, efficient production, and they began to insist that all workers start work at the same time. To workers, that seemed like slavery. Today, work patterns that are artificially imposed on us have become part of the taken-for-granted cultural rhythms that coordinate our lives.

Trends in Leisure   It is not the activity itself that makes something leisure, but the purpose for which it is done. Consider driving a car. If you do it for pleasure, it is leisure, but if you are an on-duty police officer or if you must commute to the office, it is work. If done for enjoyment, horseback riding and reading a book are leisure—but these activities are work for jockeys and students.

Patterns of leisure change with the life course, following the U-curve shown on Figure 14.8. Young children enjoy the most leisure, but teenagers still have considerably more leisure than their parents. Parents with small children have the least leisure, but after the children leave home, leisure picks up again. After the age of 60 or so, the amount of leisure for adults peaks.

Compared with early industrialization, workers today have far more leisure. A hundred years ago the work week was half again as long as today's, for then workers had to be at their machines 60 hours a week. When workers unionized, they demanded a shorter work week. Over the years, the work week has gradually shrunk. In Germany the work week is 35 hours, with Friday afternoons usually off. Volkswagen was the world's first global corporation to adopt a 30-hour work week (Rifkin 1995). In addition, German workers get six weeks of paid vacation a year. A strange thing has happened recently in the United States: This trend toward more leisure has reversed course. U.S. workers now average 1,978 hours of work a year, the highest of any industrialized nation ("Americans Work More" 2001).

Telecommuting (Teleworking)   Just as the Industrial Revolution took workers from home to factory, so our current technological revolution has allowed several million workers to return home (Wells 2001). There they do their work, while they "commute" electronically with their company. Corporations save office space, and workers avoid traffic jams. Productivity usually increases, but managers fret about a loss of control over workers. Many feel that if workers are out of sight, they aren't really working. For their part, workers often fear that their career will be sabotaged because they are out of touch with office politics.

Work is always more than work. The paycheck is the typical motivation for taking a job, but friendships with fellow workers are also valued. This is a problem for teleworkers, who miss the camaraderie of their office mates. E-mail helps, but it isn't the same as face-to-face interaction, of seeing the look on Bob's and Mary's faces when they tell a joke or repeat the latest office gossip. Many teleworkers find work at home, though inviting, to be a soulless experience. Here is what a student who read this text reported:

> My husband is still working as a software engineer. His company "wired" most of their employees for home offices. So he now works from home and has a boss in another state whom he rarely sees in person. He misses his "community" at the office and often, out of the blue, will just go in for a few hours for no good reason. He's usually disappointed, though, because most everyone else works at home, and he finds few people to chat with. His company recognizes this as a big problem. It's hard to keep the team spirit, so they have tried to gently "mandate" once a week togetherness lunches. But it's not the same as everyday contact.

■ *As capitalism globalizes, it is not just the products but also the cultures of the dominant capitalist nations that are exported around the world. As the premier producer and exporter of images, Hollywood makes a global impact. Shown here in Xian, China, is what has become a global icon.*

Facing the Future: Implications of Global Capitalism

We can catch a glimpse of the future by looking at two trends that are firmly in place: global trade and the new technology.

■ Global Trade: Inequalities and Conflict

The giant multinational corporations are carving up the world into major trading blocs and pushing for the reduction or elimination of tariffs. As a result, we can expect trade among nations to increase beyond anything the world has ever seen. U.S. corporations will continue to support an expansion in global trade, for world markets have become crucial for their success. For example, with the huge costs of making movies (the average movie now runs $50 million), the U.S. movie industry would go broke if it weren't for global distribution.

Not all nations will benefit equally, of course, and some nations will not benefit at all. The Most Industrialized Nations (even as they move through their postindustrial phase) will continue to garner the lion's share of the world's wealth. A major concern is that economic inequality will increase between the richer and the poorer nations. The growing wealth of the nations that control global trade does not sit easily with the Least Industrialized Nations. Their continued poverty, combined with pressures from their mushrooming populations, provides fertile ground for the recruitment of terrorists. If they are able, they will vent their frustrations against those nations they perceive are exploiting them.

■ New Technologies and Downsizing: Utopia or Nightmare?

Computer-driven production will continue to reduce the number of workers who are needed to make the goods we use. As I wrote back in 1975,

> Although it may sound as though it is taken from some utopian scheme, it has been estimated that the day will come when only 2 percent of the population will be needed to produce all the manufactured goods our total population needs. That day may not be far off as Ford Motor Company now takes only six workers to produce a single car while it took 104 workers for the same task in 1910 . . . it is possible that a single plant with but a single worker can produce all the bread needed in southern California. . . . Whether such changes represent a utopian dream come true or not, for displaced workers it can well be a nightmare. (p. 341)

Utopia or nightmare? From a symbolic interactionist standpoint, it all depends on your point of view. As conflict theorists stress, that point of view depends on where you stand in the production process. The jobs that the new technology destroys are not located at the top levels of the multinationals, nor are they held by the capitalists who own the company stock. For the most part, these people are immune from such disruptions. Although they must modify their investment strategies to match changing markets, the new technology allows them to lower production costs, increase profits, and fatten their dividend checks. The people who bear the brunt of the change are low-level workers who live from paycheck to paycheck. It is they who suffer the ravages of uncertainty, the devastation of job loss, and, often, the wrenching adjustments that come from being forced from their jobs.

Let's close this chapter, then, with a Thinking Critically section that focuses on the far-reaching implications of this global transformation of our economy.

thinking
CRITICALLY

What Type of New Society? New Technology and the Restructuring of Work

The fear of being automated out of a job plagues many workers. They have seen machines displace people who worked at their side, the lucky ones getting "early retirement," the others nothing.

But does technology actually take away jobs? On the one hand, there is no doubt that technology causes job after job to become obsolete. On this score, the workers' fears are not irrational. The automobile industry makes about as many cars as it did 30 years ago, but it employs less than half as many production workers. The number of workers at U.S. Steel has dropped from 120,000 to just 20,000—yet production remains the same (Volti 1995). Computerized automation will continue to erase millions of U.S. manufacturing jobs.

But there is another side to the story, for technology also creates jobs. The automobile industry wiped out the livelihood of stable hands, but it put tens of thousands more to work in the new steel and gasoline industries. These jobs are in addition to mechanics, salespeople, and advertisers, as well as the work done in the body shops that dot our landscape.

Each new technology, then, both destroys old jobs and creates new ones. Some of these jobs—as with those in the gasoline stations that automobiles require—are readily visible. Others are less evident. The technology that went into airplanes, for example, not only spawned pilots, mechanics, and reservation clerks, but also stimulated global tourism. To put this in a nutshell: *Most* of us work at jobs that did not even exist a hundred years ago.

And the future? New technologies are inevitable. The basic question is whether the new technologies will destroy jobs faster than they create them. For the millions of workers who find their jobs pulled out from under them, this question is of more than theoretical interest.

Consider two futures (Rifkin 1995). The one is a technoparadise of abundance and leisure. With few workers needed, work is spread around, and the work week is only 10 or 15 hours. Yet everyone is able to possess goods in abundance. Having restored the leisure that humans used to enjoy in their early days as hunters and gatherers, creative leisure becomes a chief characteristic of the new society. Some spend time in intellectual pursuits, studying the sciences, philosophy, languages. Some follow the arts—painting, poetry, the theater. Many travel. Parents spend much more time with their children. Others, of course, just watch more soap operas, play more video games, or sit transfixed, with beer in one hand and remote in the other, through endless hours of televised sports.

The second future is a divided society. One group, smaller and affluent, lives among a larger group of impoverished workers and those dispossessed from the work force. The contrasts are so great that it is almost like a country inside a country. Millions, surviving in hopelessness, accept meager handouts that are grudgingly given. Displaced from job opportunities, the nation's youth produce a violent criminal subculture. Frightened and confused at the increasing violence, the affluent lock themselves behind gated communities.

We can't turn back the clock. New technology is here to stay, and, as always, it will continue to change the shape of work. The basic issue, then, is how we, as a society, react. The transformation of work is inevitable, but the consequences of that restructuring are not.

■ As conflict theorists stress, in order to keep labor costs low and profits high, capitalist economies use a reserve labor force that pits one worker against another. This poorly paid gold miner in South Africa, working under the debilitating conditions you see in this photo, is an expendable part of the profit system that drives the economic machinery called capitalism. If this worker protests his working conditions, he will be fired immediately, for waiting in the wings are thousands of unemployed workers eager to take his place.

■ ■ ■ ■ ■

for your consideration . . .

Which of these futures appears to be more likely? In answering this question, refer to the discussion in this chapter about the effects of the new technologies on work, the globalization of capitalism, and the growing power of multinational corporations.

The growing gap between the "haves" and the "have-nots" of our society is an ominous trend. Look at the inverted pyramid shown in Figure 14.9 on the next page. This figure provides a snapshot of how the nation's income is divided. Each rectangle on the left represents a fifth of the U.S. population. The rectangles on the right represent the proportion of the nation's income that goes to each of these fifths. The result is an inverted pyramid. Note that *47 percent* of the entire country's

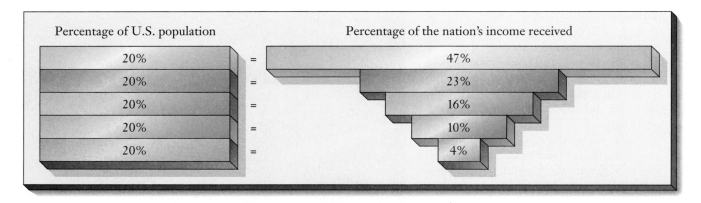

Percentage of U.S. population		Percentage of the nation's income received
20%	=	47%
20%	=	23%
20%	=	16%
20%	=	10%
20%	=	4%

Figure 14.9
The Inverted Income Pyramid:
The Proportion of Income Received by Each Fifth of the U.S. Population
Source: Statistical Abstract 2000:Table 745.

income goes to just one-fifth of Americans, while only *4 percent* goes to the poorest fifth. This gap is now greater than it has been in generations. Rather than bringing equality, then, the postindustrial economy has perpetuated and enlarged the income inequalities of the industrial economy. What implications of this division of the nation's wealth do you see for our future?

Summary and Review

The Transformation of Economic Systems

■ **How are economic systems linked to types of societies?**

The earliest societies, hunting and gathering, were **subsistence economies:** Small groups lived off the land and produced little or no surplus. Economic systems grew more complex as people discovered how to domesticate and cultivate (pastoral and horticultural societies), farm (agricultural societies), and manufacture (industrial societies). Each of these methods allowed people to produce a *surplus,* which fostered trade. Trade, in turn, brought social inequality as some people accumulated more than others. Service industries dominate the postindustrial socieites. Pp. 410–413.

The Transformation of the Medium of Exchange

■ **How has the medium of exchange evolved?**

A **medium of exchange** is any means by which people exchange goods and services. In hunting and gathering and pastoral and horticultural societies, people **bartered** goods and services. In agricultural societies, **money** came into use, which evolved into **currency,** or paper money, representing a specific

amount of gold or silver on deposit. Postindustrial societies rely increasingly on electronic transfer of funds in the form of **credit cards, debit cards,** and **e-cash.** Pp. 413–415.

World Economic Systems

■ **How do the major economic systems differ?**

The world's two major economic systems are capitalism and socialism. In **capitalism,** private citizens own the means of production and pursue profits. In **socialism,** the state owns the means of production and determines production with no goal of profit. Adherents of each have developed ideologies that defend their own systems and paint the other as harmful. Following **convergence theory,** each system has adopted features of the other. Pp. 415–421.

The Functionalist View of the Globalization of Capitalism

From the functionalist perspective, work is a basis of social solidarity. Traditional societies have **mechanical** solidarity; people perform similar tasks and identify with one another. Industrialization brings **organic solidarity,** interdependence based on the division of labor. This process has continued, and we now are developing a global division of labor. Corporations, with their separation of ownership and management, underlie the success of capitalism. Pp. 421–423.

The Conflict View of the Globalization of Capitalism

Conflict theorists, who focus on power, note that global capitalism is a means by which capitalists exploit workers. At the top of the major corporations is an inner circle. While workers lose jobs to automation, the inner circle maintains its political power and profits from the new technology. The term **corporate capitalism** indicates that giant corporations dominate capitalism today. Pp. 423–428.

Work in U.S. Society

■ **How has the workforce changed?**

In the transition to a postindustrial society, the number of farm workers has plummeted, blue-collar work has decreased, and almost everyone works at service jobs. The proportion of women in the labor force is

almost one in two, one of the highest ratios in the industrialized world. Pp. 428–430.

■ **What is the underground economy?**

The **underground economy** consists of any economic activity not reported to the government, from babysitting to prostitution. The size of the underground economy runs perhaps 10 to 15 percent of the regular economy. Pp. 430–431.

■ **How have patterns of work and leisure changed?**

In hunting and gathering societies, most time was leisure. In agricultural societies, work was dictated by the seasons. Industrialization reduced workers' leisure, but workers have now gained some leisure back. Americans work more hours per week than do the workers of any industrialized nation. Pp. 431–433.

Facing the Future: Implications of Global Capitalism

Due to expanding global trade, new technologies, and downsizing, the nature of work will continue to be transformed. Choices made now can lead either to a better society or to a nightmare. Pp. 433–436.

■ *Where can I read more on this topic?*

Suggested Readings for this chapter are at the back of this book.

Additional Online Resources for This Chapter
www.ablongman.com/henslin6e

- *Content Select* Research Database for Sociology, with suggested key terms and annotated references
- Link to 2000 Census, with activities
- Flashcards of key terms and concepts
- Practice Tests
- Weblinks
- Interactive Maps

using . . .
ContentSelect
Research Database for Sociology

capitalism	postindustrial	subsistence economy	underemployment
global village	society	telecommuting	work and leisure
monopoly	socialism		

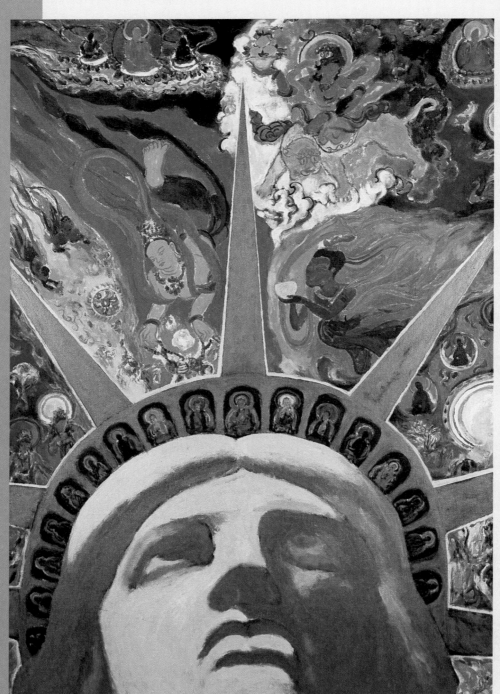

Tsing-Feng Chen, *Greetings from the East*, 1985

15

Politics

Micropolitics and Macropolitics

Power, Authority, and Violence
Authority and Legitimate Violence
Traditional Authority
Rational-Legal Authority
Charismatic Authority
Authority as Ideal Type
The Transfer of Authority

Types of Government
Monarchies: The Rise of the State
Democracies: Citizenship as a Revolutionary Idea
Dictatorships and Oligarchies: The Seizure of Power

The U.S. Political System
Political Parties and Elections
Democratic Systems in Europe
Voting Patterns
Lobbyists and Special-Interest Groups
PACs in U.S. Elections

Who Rules the United States?
The Functionalist Perspective: Pluralism
The Conflict Perspective: The Power Elite, or Ruling Class
Which View Is Right?

War and Terrorism: A Means to Implement Political Objectives
Is War Universal?
How Common Is War?
Why Nations Go to War
Costs of War
Sowing the Seeds of Future Wars
Nuclear, Biological, and Chemical Terrorism
War and Dehumanization

A New World Order?

Summary and Review

In 1949, George Orwell wrote *1984*, a book about a future in which the government, known as "Big Brother," dominates society, dictating almost every aspect of each individual's life. Even to love someone is considered a sinister activity, a betrayal of the supreme love and total allegiance that all citizens owe Big Brother.

Despite the danger, Winston and Julia fall in love. They meet furtively, always with the threat of discovery hanging over their heads. When informers turn them in, expert interrogators separate Julia and Winston, and proceed swiftly to quash their affection in order to restore their loyalty to Big Brother.

> *...they realize that each has betrayed the other. Their love is gone. Big Brother has won.*

Then follows a remarkable account of Winston and his tormentor, O'Brien. Winston is strapped into a chair so tightly that he can't even move his head. O'Brien explains that although inflicting pain is not always enough to break a person's will, everyone has a breaking point. There is some worst fear that will push anyone over the edge.

O'Brien tells Winston that he has discovered his worst fear. He then sets a cage with two giant, starving sewer rats on the table next to Winston. O'Brien picks up a hood connected to the door of the cage and places it over Winston's head. He then explains that when he presses the lever, the door of the cage will slide up, and the rats will shoot out like bullets and bore straight into Winston's face. Winston's eyes, the only part of his body that he can move, dart back and forth, revealing his terror. Speaking so quietly that Winston has to strain to hear him, O'Brien adds that the rats sometimes attack the eyes first, but sometimes they burrow through the cheeks and devour the tongue. When O'Brien places his hand on the lever, Winston realizes that the only way out is for someone else to take his place. But who? Then he hears his own voice screaming, "Do it to Julia! . . . Tear her face off! Strip her to the bones. Not me! Julia! Not me!"

Orwell does not describe Julia's interrogation, but when Julia and Winston see each other later they realize that each has betrayed the other. Their love is gone. Big Brother has won.

Winston's misplaced loyalty had made him a political heretic, for every citizen had the duty to place the state above all else in life. To preserve the state's dominance over the individual, Winston's allegiance had to be stripped from Julia. As you see, it was.

lthough seldom this dramatic, politics is always about power and authority, the focus of this chapter.

Micropolitics and Macropolitics

The images that come to mind when we think of *politics* are those of government: kings, queens, coups, dictatorships, running for office, voting. These are examples of politics, but this term is much broader. It refers to power relations wherever they exist, including those in your own life. As Weber (1922/1968) said, **power** is the ability to get your way even over the resistance of others. If two or three employees try to impress their new boss—who is going to decide which one of them will be promoted to manager—this is an example of jockeying for power, and of politics. So are parents' efforts to enforce a curfew despite protests from a reluctant daughter or son. Ever struggle over the TV remote control? This, too, is an attempt to gain power—and, thus, of politics. *Every group, then, is political, for in every group there is a power struggle of some sort.* Symbolic interactionists use the term **micropolitics** to refer to the exercise of power in everyday life (Schwartz 1990).

In contrast, **macropolitics**—the focus of this chapter—refers to the exercise of large-scale power over a large group. Governments, whether the dictatorship faced by Winston or the elected forms in the United States and Canada, are examples of macropolitics. Let's turn, then, to macropolitics, considering first the matter of authority.

Power, Authority, and Violence

To exist, every society must have a system of leadership. Some people must have power over others. As Max Weber (1913/1947) pointed out, we perceive power as either legitimate or illegitimate. Legitimate power is called **authority**. This is power that people accept as right. In contrast, illegitimate power—called **coercion**—is power that people do not accept as just.

power
the ability to carry out your will, even over the resistance of others

micropolitics
the exercise of power in everyday life, such as deciding who is going to do the housework

macropolitics
the exercise of large-scale power, the government being the most common example

authority
power that people accept as rightly exercised over them; also called *legitimate power*

coercion
power that people do not accept as rightly exercised over them; also called *illegitimate power*

Imagine that you are on your way to buy a great DVD player on sale for $250. As you are on your way to the store, a man jumps out of an alley and shoves a gun in your face. He demands your money. Frightened for your life, you hand over the $250. After filing a police report, you head back to college to take a sociology exam. You are running late, so you step on the gas. As the needle hits 85, you see flashing blue and red lights in your rear-view mirror. Your explanation about the robbery doesn't faze the officer—nor the judge who hears your case a few weeks later. She first lectures you on safety and then orders you to pay $50 in court costs plus $10 for every mile an hour over 65. You pay the $250.

The mugger, the police officer, and the judge—each has power, and in each case you part with $250. What, then, is the difference? The difference is that the mugger has no authority. His power is illegitimate—he has no *right* to do what he did. In contrast, you acknowledge that the officer has the right to stop you and that the judge has the right to fine you. They have authority, or legitimate power.

▪ Authority and Legitimate Violence

As sociologist Peter Berger observed, it makes little difference whether you willingly pay the fine that the judge levies against you, or refuse to pay it. The court will get its money one way or another.

> There may be innumerable steps before its application [violence], in the way of warnings and reprimands. But if all the warnings are disregarded, even in so slight a matter as paying a traffic ticket, the last thing that will happen is that a couple of cops show up at the door with handcuffs and a Black Maria (billy club). Even the moderately courteous cop who hands out the initial traffic ticket is likely to wear a gun—just in case. (Berger 1963)

The *government*, then, also called the **state**, claims a monopoly on legitimate force or violence. This point, made by Max Weber (1946, 1922/1968)—that the state claims the exclusive right to use violence and the right to punish everyone else who does—is crucial to our understanding of politics. If someone owes you a debt, you cannot imprison that person or even forcibly take the money. The state, however, can. The ultimate proof of the state's authority is that you cannot kill someone because he or she has done something that you consider absolutely horrible—but the state can. As Berger (1963) summarized this matter, *"Violence is the ultimate foundation of any political order."*

Before we explore the origins of the modern state, let's first look at a situation in which the state loses legitimacy.

The Collapse of Authority   Sometimes the state oppresses its people, and they resist their government just as they do a mugger. The people cooperate reluctantly—with a smile if that is what is required—while they eye the gun in the hand of the government's representatives. But, as they do with a mugger, when they get the chance, they take up arms to free themselves. **Revolution**, armed resistance with the intent to overthrow a government, is not only a people's rejection of a government's claim to rule over them but also a rejection of its monopoly on violence. In a revolution, people claim that right for themselves. If successful, they establish a new state in which they claim the right to monopolize violence.

What some see as coercion, however, others see as authority. Consequently, while some people are ready to take up arms against a government, others remain loyal to it, willingly defend it, and perhaps even die for it. *The more that its power is seen as legitimate, then, the more stable a government is.*

But just why do people accept power as legitimate? Max Weber (1922/1968) identified three sources of authority: traditional, rational-legal, and charismatic. Let's examine each.

▪ The ultimate foundation of any political order is violence. At no time is this more starkly demonstrated than when a government takes human life. Shown in this 1910 photo from Sing Sing Prison is a man about to be executed.

state
a political entity that claims monopoly on the use of violence in some particular territory; commonly known as a country

revolution
armed resistance designed to overthrow a government

■ For centuries, widows in Mediterranean countries, such as this widow in Lebanon, were expected to wear black and mourn for their husbands the rest of their lives. Widows conformed to this expression of lifetime sorrow for their deceased husband not because of law, but because of custom. As industrialization erodes traditional authority, fewer widows follow this practice.

traditional authority
authority based on custom

rational-legal authority
authority based on law or written rules and regulations; also called *bureaucratic authority*

Traditional Authority

Throughout history, the most common basis for authority has been tradition. **Traditional authority,** which is based on custom, is the hallmark of tribal groups. In these societies, custom dictates basic relationships. For example, birth makes a particular individual the chief, king, or queen. As far as members of that society are concerned, this is the right way to determine who shall rule because "We've always done it this way."

Gender relations often give us a window on traditional authority. For example, in the villages of Spain widows are expected to wear only black until they remarry. See the photo on this page. This generally means that they wear black for the rest of their lives. By law, a widow is free to wear any color she wishes, but not by custom. Tradition, decreeing black, is so strong that if a widow were to violate this dress code, she would be perceived as having profaned the memory of her deceased husband and would be ostracized by the community.

When a traditional society industrializes, this transformation undermines traditional authority. Social change brings new experiences. This opens up new perspectives on life, and no longer does traditional authority go unchallenged. Thus, in Spain you can still see old women dressed in black from head to toe—and you immediately know their marital status. Younger widows, however, are likely to be indistinguishable from other women.

Although traditional authority declines with industrialization, it never dies out. In postindustrial societies, for example, parents exercise authority over their children *because* parents always have had such authority. From generations past, we inherit the idea that parents should discipline their children, choose their doctors and schools, and teach them religion and morality.

Rational-Legal Authority

The second type of authority, **rational-legal authority,** is not based on custom but on written rules. *Rational* means reasonable, and *legal* means part of law. Thus *rational-legal* refers to matters agreed to by reasonable people and written into law (or regulations of some sort). The matters agreed to may be as broad as a constitution that specifies the rights of all members of a society or as narrow as a contract between two individuals. Because bureaucracies are based on written rules, rational-legal authority is sometimes called *bureaucratic authority.*

Rational-legal authority comes from the position that someone holds, not from the person who holds that position. In a democracy, for example, the president's authority comes from the office, as specified in a written constitution, not from custom or the individual's personal characteristics. In rational-legal authority, everyone—no matter how high the office—is subject to the organization's written rules. In governments based on traditional authority, the ruler's word may be law, but in those based on rational-legal authority, the ruler's word is subject to the law.

Charismatic Authority

A few centuries back, in 1429, the English controlled large parts of France. When they wouldn't allow the coronation of a new French king, a farmer's daughter heard a voice telling her that God had a special assignment for her—that she should put on men's clothing, recruit an army, and go to war against the English. Inspired, Joan of Arc raised an army, conquered cities, and defeated the English. Later that year, her visions were fulfilled as she stood next to Charles VII while he was crowned king of France. (Bridgwater 1953)

Joan of Arc is an example of **charismatic authority,** the third type of authority Weber identified. (*Charisma* is a Greek word that means a gift freely and graciously given [Arndt and Gingrich 1957].) A charismatic individual is someone people are drawn to because they believe that person has been touched by God or has been endowed by nature with exceptional qualities (Lipset 1993). The armies did not follow Joan of Arc because it was the custom to do so, as in traditional authority. Nor did they risk their lives alongside her because she held a position defined by written rules, as in rational-legal authority. Instead, people followed her because they were drawn to her outstanding traits. They saw her as a messenger of God, fighting on the side of justice, and they accepted her leadership because of these appealing qualities.

The Threat Posed by Charismatic Leaders A king owes allegiance to tradition, and a president to written laws. To what, however, does a charismatic leader owe allegiance? Because their authority is based on their personal ability to attract followers, charismatic leaders pose a threat to the established political system. They lead followers according to personal inclination, not according to the paths of tradition or the regulations of law. Accordingly, they can inspire followers to disregard—or even to overthrow—traditional and rational-legal authorities.

This means that charismatic leaders pose a threat to the established order. Consequently, traditional and rational-legal authorities are often quick to oppose charismatic leaders. If they are not careful, however, their opposition may arouse even more positive sentiment in favor of the charismatic leader, causing him or her to be viewed as a martyr. Occasionally the Roman Catholic church faces such a threat, as when a priest claims miraculous powers that appear to be accompanied by amazing healings. As people flock to this individual, they bypass parish priests and the formal

■ *One of the best examples of charismatic authority is Joan of Arc, shown here at the coronation of Charles VII, whom she was instrumental in making king. Uncomfortable at portraying Joan of Arc wearing only a man's coat of armor, the artist has made certain she is wearing plenty of makeup, and also has added a ludicrous skirt.*

■ *Charismatic authorities can be of any morality, from the saintly to the most bitterly evil. Like Joan of Arc, Adolf Hitler attracted throngs of people, providing the stuff of dreams and arousing them from disillusionment to hope. This poster from the 1930s, titled* Es Lebe Deutschland *("Long Live Germany"), illustrates the qualities of leadership that Germans of that period saw in Hitler.*

charismatic authority
authority based on an individual's outstanding traits, which attract followers

ecclesiastical structure. This transfer of allegiance from the organization to an individual threatens the church hierarchy. Consequently, church officials may encourage the priest to withdraw from the public eye, perhaps to a monastery, to rethink matters. Thus the threat is defused, rational-legal authority reasserted, and the stability of the organization maintained.

■ Authority as Ideal Type

Weber's classifications—traditional, rational-legal, and charismatic—represent ideal types of authority. As noted on page 193, ideal type does not refer to what is ideal or desirable, but to a composite of characteristics found in many real-life examples. A particular leader, then, may show a combination of characteristics.

An example is John F. Kennedy, who combined rational-legal and charismatic authority. As the elected head of the U.S. government, Kennedy represented rational-legal authority. Yet his mass appeal was so great that his public speeches aroused large numbers of people to action. When in his inaugural address Kennedy said, "Ask not what your country can do for you; ask what you can do for your country," millions of Americans were touched. When Kennedy proposed a Peace Corps to help poorer countries, thousands of idealistic young people volunteered for challenging foreign service.

Charismatic and traditional authority can also overlap. The Ayatollah Khomeini of Iran, for example, was a religious leader, holding the traditional position of ayatollah. His embodiment of the Iranian people's dreams, however, as well as his austere life and devotion to principles of the Koran, gave him such mass appeal that he was also a charismatic leader. Khomeini's followers were convinced that he had been chosen by God, and his speeches could arouse tens of thousands of followers to action.

In rare instances, then, traditional and rational-legal leaders possess charismatic traits. This is unusual, however, and most authority is clearly one type or another.

■ The Transfer of Authority

The orderly transfer of authority from one leader to another is crucial for social stability. Under traditional authority, people know who is next in line. Under rational-legal authority, people may not know who the next leader will be, but they do know how that person will be selected. South Africa provides a remarkable example of the orderly transfer of authority under a rational-legal organization. This country had been ripped apart by decades of racial strife, including horrible killings committed by each side. Yet, by maintaining its rational-legal authority, the country was able to peacefully transfer power from the dominant group led by President de Klerk to the minority group led by Nelson Mandela.

Charismatic authority, however, has no such rules of succession. This makes it less stable than either traditional or rational-legal authority. Because charismatic authority is built around a single individual, the death or incapacitation of a charismatic leader can mean a bitter struggle for succession. Consequently, some charismatic leaders make arrangements for an orderly transition of power by appointing a successor. This does not guarantee orderly succession, of course, for the followers may not perceive the designated heir in the same way as they did the charismatic leader. A second strategy is for the charismatic leader to build an organization. As the organization develops a system of rules or regulations, it transforms itself into a rational-legal organization. Weber used the term the **routinization of charisma** to refer to the transition of authority from a charismatic leader to either traditional or rational-legal authority.

routinization of charisma
the transfer of authority from a charismatic figure to either a traditional or a rational-legal form of authority

■ *Crucial for society is the orderly transfer of power. One of the most remarkable transfers occurred in South Africa. Under this country's constitutional system, power was transferred from the white dominated government headed by Fredrik Willem De Klerk (on the left) to Nelson Mandela (on the right).*

Types of Government

How do the various types of government—monarchies, democracies, dictatorships, and oligarchies—differ? As we compare them, let's also look at how the institution of the state arose, and why the concept of citizenship was revolutionary.

▪ Monarchies: The Rise of the State

Early societies were small and needed no extensive political system. They operated more like an extended family. As surpluses developed and societies grew larger, cities evolved—perhaps about 3500 B.C. (Fischer 1976). **City-states** then came into being, with power radiating outward from a city like a spider's web. Although the city controlled the immediate area around it, the areas between cities remained in dispute. Each city-state had its own **monarchy,** a king or queen whose right to rule was passed on to their children. If you drive through Spain, France, or Germany, you can still see evidence of former city-states. In the countryside, you will see only scattered villages. Farther on, your eye will be drawn to the outline of a castle on a faraway hill. As you get closer, you will see that the castle is surrounded by a city. Several miles farther, you will see another city, also dominated by a castle. Each city, with its castle, was once a center of power.

City-states often quarreled, and wars were common. The victors extended their rule, and eventually a single city-state was able to wield power over an entire region. As the size of these regions grew, the people slowly began to identify with the larger region. That is, they began to see distant inhabitants as "we" instead of "they." What we call the *state*—the political entity that claims a monopoly on the use of violence within a territory—came into being.

▪ Democracies: Citizenship as a Revolutionary Idea

The United States had no city-states. Each colony, however, was small and independent like a city-state. After the American Revolution, the colonies united. With the greater strength and resources that came from political unity, they conquered almost all of North America, bringing it under the power of a central government.

The government formed in this new country was called a **democracy.** (Derived from two Greek words—*demos* [common people] and *kratos* [power]—*democracy* literally means "power to the people.") Because of the bitter antagonisms associated with the revolution against the British king, the founders of the new country were distrustful of monarchies. They wanted to put political decisions into the hands of the people. This was not the first democracy the world had seen, but such a system had been tried before only with smaller groups. Athens, a city-state of Greece, practiced democracy two thousand years ago, with each free male above a certain age having the right to be heard and to vote. Members of some Native American tribes, such as the Iroquois, also elected their chiefs, and in some, women were able to vote and to hold the office of chief. (The Incas and Aztecs of Mexico and Central America had monarchies.)

Because of their small size, tribes and cities were able to practice **direct democracy.** That is, they were small enough for the eligible voters to meet together, express their opinions, and then vote publicly—much like a town hall meeting today. As populous and spread out as the United States was, however, direct democracy was impossible, and **representative democracy** was invented. Certain citizens (at first

city-state
an independent city whose power radiates outward, bringing the adjacent area under its rule

monarchy
a form of government headed by a king or queen

democracy
a system of government in which authority derives from the people; the term comes from two Greek words that translate literally as "power to the people"

direct democracy
a form of democracy in which the eligible voters meet together to discuss issues and make their decisions

representative democracy
a form of democracy in which voters elect representatives to govern and make decisions on their behalf

▪ Democracy *was a heritage left by the British rule of India. The people take elections seriously, and the government transfers power peacefully from one party and candidate to another. Shown here are ballot boxes being delivered to remote areas of the northern Indian state of Assam.*

mass media
in social life

Politics and Democracy in a Technological Society
"Politics is just like show business."—RONALD REAGAN

Is the new technology a threat to democracy? Politicians use computers, telephone link-ups, faxes, e-mail, and Web sites to take the pulse of the public—and to convey their platforms and their biases. Instead of tuning in and passively listening to a politician's speech, we now can talk back to candidates and leaders via chat rooms, "electronic town meetings," and call-in radio and TV talk shows.

This shift to interactive communication lies at the heart of a debate over the health and future of our democracy. Critics charge that when those who are elected to govern use the new technology to constantly "take the public's temperature," they give more attention to minute shifts in public opinion than they do to the business of governing. When politicians use polls to "fine tune" their public posturing, the positions they take on issues are not based on personal conviction. In other words, politicians now campaign nonstop.

The Internet has become a major issue. "Televoting" could replace our representational democracy with a form of direct democracy. Voters could sign petitions with digital signatures, and then online decide issues that politicians now resolve for them. They could even make laws online.

Some fear that the Internet isn't safe for voting. With no poll watchers, undue influence (threats, promises, or gifts in return for votes) would go undetected. Others raise a more fundamental issue: Direct democracy might detour the U.S. Constitution's system of checks and balances, which was designed to safeguard us from the "tyranny of the majority." To determine from a poll that 51 percent of adults hold a certain opinion on an issue is one thing—that information can guide our leaders. But to have 51 percent of televoters determine a law is not the same as having elected representatives publicly argue the merits of a proposal and then try to balance the interests of the many groups that make up their constituency.

Some point with alarm to the election of Jesse Ventura as governor of Minnesota. He ran as an independent, and for much of his campaign Ventura had no physical headquarters. Ventura fans sent e-mail to their friends and contacts, encouraging them to pass on the message. Even two-thirds of Ventura's fund-raising pledges arrived by e-mail.

■ Crucial for society is the orderly transfer of power. Under its constitutional system, the United States is remarkably stable: Power is transferred peacefully—even when someone of an unusual background wins an election. Jesse Ventura, shown here, is governor of Minnesota.

for your consideration
Do you think direct democracy would be superior to representative democracy? What is wrong with emphasizing image over substance? So what if we are replacing reasoned leadership with nonstop campaigning? How does an e-mail campaign compare with 30-second "sound bites"? Do you think Ventura's election breathed fresh air into the stale world of politics—or does it indicate that the Internet poses a danger to U.S. politics? Or is it something else entirely? How can we use the mass media to improve government?

Sources: "Democracy and Technology" 1995; Diamond and Silverman 1995; Grossman 1995; Fineman 1999; Raney 1999; Seib 2000.

only male white landowners) voted for men to represent them in Washington. Later the vote was extended to nonowners of property, to African American men, then to women, and to others. Our new communications technologies, which make "electronic town meetings" possible, may also allow a new form of direct democracy. This issue is explored in the Mass Media box above.

Today we take the concept of citizenship for granted. What is not evident to us is that the idea had to be conceived in the first place. There is nothing natural about citizenship—it is simply one way in which people choose to define themselves. Throughout most of human history, people were thought to *belong* to a clan, to a tribe, or even to a ruler. The idea of **citizenship**—that by virtue of birth and residence people have basic rights—is quite new to the human scene (Turner 1990; Eisenstadt 1999).

The concept of representative democracy based on citizenship, perhaps the greatest gift the United States has given to the world, was revolutionary. Power was to be vested in the people themselves, and government was to flow from the people. That this concept was revolutionary is generally forgotten, but its implementation meant

citizenship
the concept that birth (and residence) in a country impart basic rights

the reversal of traditional ideas. It made the government responsive to the people's will, not the people to the government's will. To keep the government responsive to the needs of its citizens, people had not only the right, but the obligation, to express dissent. In a widely quoted statement, Thomas Jefferson observed that

> a little rebellion now and then is a good thing. . . . It is a medicine necessary for the sound health of government. . . . God forbid that we should ever be twenty years without such a rebellion. . . . The tree of liberty must be refreshed from time to time with the blood of patriots and tyrants. It is its natural manure. (In Hellinger and Judd 1991)

The idea of **universal citizenship**—of *everyone* having the same basic rights by virtue of being born in a country (or by immigrating and becoming a naturalized citizen)—flowered very slowly, and came into practice only through fierce struggle. When the United States was founded, for example, this idea was still in its infancy. Today it seems inconceivable to Americans that anyone should be denied the right to vote, hold office, make a contract, testify in court, or own property on the basis of gender or race-ethnicity. For earlier generations of white Americans, however, it seemed just as inconceivable that women, African Americans, Native Americans, Asian Americans, and the poor should be allowed such rights.

Over the years, then, rights have been extended, and in the United States citizenship and its privileges now apply to all. No longer does property, sex, or race-ethnicity determine the right to vote, to testify in court, and so on. These characteristics, however, do influence whether one votes, as we shall see in a later section on voting patterns.

■ Dictatorships and Oligarchies: The Seizure of Power

If an individual seizes power and then dictates his will onto the people, the government is known as a **dictatorship.** If a small group seizes power, the government is called an **oligarchy.** The occasional coups in Central and South America, in which military leaders seize control of a country, are examples of oligarchies. Although one individual may be named president, it often is a group of high-ranking military officers, working behind the scenes, that makes the decisions. If their designated president becomes uncooperative, they remove him from office and appoint another.

Monarchies, dictatorships, and oligarchies vary in the amount of control they exert over their citizens. **Totalitarianism** is almost *total* control of a people by the government. As our opening vignette demonstrated, totalitarian regimes tolerate no opposing opinion. In Nazi Germany, for example, Hitler organized a ruthless secret police force, the Gestapo, which searched for any sign of dissent. Spies even watched how moviegoers reacted to newsreels, reporting those who did not respond "appropriately" (Hippler 1987). Today, Saddam Hussein acts as ruthlessly toward Iraqis.

In totalitarian regimes, the names of those who rule may change, but the techniques of control remain similar. Threats and terror force citizens to comply and allow the dictator to remain in power. Privacy is viewed as a threat to the regime, and the police may keep a dossier on each citizen. A description of Nazi Germany could just as well be applied to the Soviet Union under Stalin or to Iraq under Saddam Hussein. New technology allows greater control. The East German secret police under the Soviets sprayed radioactive substances onto the floors of rooms where dissidents met. The substances got onto their shoes. To follow those who had been present, the police wore vibrating Geiger counters. Usually they used a safe radioactive level, but they made errors. To see who was getting West Germany's deutschmarks, the Stasi sprayed some bills with scandium. It turned out that if more than one note was in a man's pocket, the effect on his fertility came close to castration ("East Germany . . . " 2001).

People around the world find great appeal in the freedom inherent in citizenship and representative democracy. Those who have no say in their government's decisions, or who face prison or even death for expressing dissent, find in these ideas the hope for a brighter future. With today's electronic communications, people no longer remain ignorant of whether they are more or less privileged politically than others.

universal citizenship
the idea that everyone has the same basic rights by virtue of being born in a country (or by immigrating and becoming a naturalized citizen)

dictatorship
a form of government in which power is seized by an individual

oligarchy
a form of government in which power is held by a small group of individuals; the rule of the many by the few

totalitarianism
a form of government that exerts almost total control over the people

This knowledge produces pressure for greater citizen participation in government. As electronic communications develop further, this pressure will increase.

The U.S. Political System

With this global background, let's examine the U.S. political system. We shall consider the two major political parties and elections, compare the U.S. political system with other democratic systems, and examine voting patterns and the role of lobbyists and PACs.

Political Parties and Elections

After the founding of the United States, numerous political parties emerged, but by the time of the Civil War, two parties dominated U.S. politics (Burnham 1983): the Democrats, who in the public mind are associated with the working class, and the Republicans, who are associated with wealthier people. Each party nominates candidates, and in pre-elections, called *primaries,* the voters decide which candidates will represent their party. Each candidate then campaigns, trying to appeal to the most voters. The Social Map below shows how Americans align themselves with political parties.

Although the Democrats and Republicans represent different philosophical principles, each party appeals to a broad membership, and it is difficult to distinguish a conservative Democrat from a liberal Republican. The extremes are easy to discern, however. Deeply committed Democrats support legislation that transfers income from the richer to the poorer, or that controls wages, working conditions, and competition. Dyed-in-the-wool Republicans oppose such legislation.

Those elected to Congress may cross party lines. That is, some Democrats vote for legislation proposed by Republicans, and *vice versa.* This happens because office-holders support their party's philosophy but not necessarily its specific proposals. Thus, when it comes to a particular bill, such as raising the minimum wage, some conservative Democrats may view the measure as unfair to small employers, or too costly, and vote with the Republicans against the bill. At the same time, liberal Republicans—feeling that the proposal is just, or sensing a dominant sentiment in voters back home—may side with its Democratic backers.

Figure 15.1

Social Map:
U.S. Political Parties

Which party dominates, Democrat or Republican?

Note: Based on the composition of the states' upper and lower houses. Votes for president may differ. For states whose upper and lower houses are dominated by different parties, the total number of legislators was used. In case of ties, or as with Nebraska, no party designation, percentage vote for president was used.

Source: Statistical Abstract 2001: Table 395.

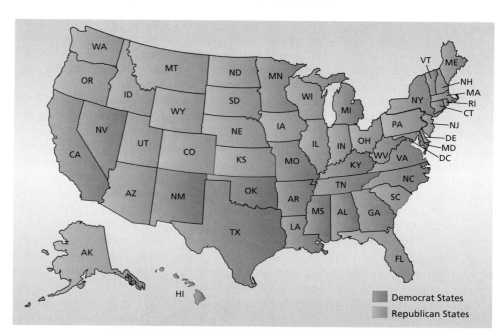

| | Democrat States |
| | Republican States |

Regardless of their differences and their public quarrels, the Democrats and Republicans represent *different slices of the center.* Although each may ridicule its opposition and promote different legislation, each party firmly supports such fundamentals of U.S. political philosophy as free public education; a strong military; freedom of religion, speech, and assembly; and, of course, capitalism—especially the private ownership of property.

Third parties also play a role in U.S. politics, but to have any influence they, too, must support these centrist themes. Any party that advocates radical change is doomed to a short life of little political consequence. Because most Americans consider a vote for a third party a waste, third parties do notoriously poorly at the polls. Two exceptions are the Bull Moose party, whose candidate, Theodore Roosevelt, won more votes in 1912 than Taft, the Republican presidential candidate, and the United We Stand (now Reform) party, founded by billionaire Ross Perot, which won 19 percent of the vote in 1992, but only 8 percent in 1996, and less than 1 percent in 2000 (Bridgwater 1953; *Statistical Abstract* 1995:Table 437; 2000:Table 456; election 2000 reports).

■ As Latinos have grown in numbers, so has their political prominence. Shown here at a news conference in San Jose, California, is Arturo Vargas, executive director of the National Association of Latino Elected Officials. People have many reasons for voting the way they do. For some, the ethnicity of the candidate is important.

■ Democratic Systems in Europe

We tend to take our political system for granted and assume that any other democracy looks like ours—even down to having two major parties. Such is not the case. To gain a comparative understanding, let's look at the European system.

Although both their system and ours are democracies, there are fundamental distinctions between the two (Domhoff 1979, 1983; Lind 1995). First, elections in most of Europe are not winner-take-all. In the United States, elections are determined by a simple majority. For example, if a Democrat wins 51 percent of the votes cast in an electoral district, he or she takes office. The Republican candidate, who may have won 49 percent, loses everything. In contrast, most European countries base their elections on a system of **proportional representation;** that is, the seats in the national legislature are divided according to the proportion of votes each political party receives. If one party wins 51 percent of the vote, for example, that party is awarded 51 percent of the seats; while a party with 49 percent of the votes receives 49 percent of the seats.

Second, proportional representation encourages minority parties, while the winner-take-all system discourages them. The proportional representation system of most European countries means that if a party gets 10 percent of the voters to support its candidate, it will get 10 percent of the seats. This system encourages the formation of **noncentrist parties,** those that propose less popular or even offbeat ideas. For example, a party may make its central platform a return to the gold standard, or the shutting down of nuclear power reactors. In the United States, in contrast, 10 percent of the votes means 0 seats. So does 49 percent of the votes. This pushes parties to the center, for to have any chance of "taking all," a party must strive to obtain broad support. For this reason, the United States has **centrist parties.**

In the proportional representation system, to win even just a few seats in the national legislature is important. It allows even a tiny party to gain access to the media throughout the year. This publicity helps keep its issues alive. Small parties also gain power beyond their numbers. Because votes are fragmented among the many parties that compete in national elections, seldom does a single party gain a majority of the seats in the legislature. To muster the required votes, the party with the most seats must align itself with one or more of the smaller parties and form a **coalition government.** A party with only 10 or 15 percent of the seats, then, may be able to trade its vote on some issues for the larger party's support on others. Because coalitions often fall apart, these governments tend to be less stable than that of the United States. Italy, for example, has had fifty-eight different governments since World War II, compared with the United States, which has had eleven presidents since then. To add greater stability, the Italians have voted that three-fourths of their Senate seats will be decided on the winner-take-all system (Melloan 1993b; D'Emilio 2000).

proportional representation
an electoral system in which seats in a legislature are divided according to the proportion of votes each political party receives

noncentrist party
a political party that represents marginal ideas

centrist party
a political party that represents the center of political opinion

coalition government
a government in which a country's largest party aligns itself with one or more smaller parties

■ Voting Patterns

Year after year, Americans show consistent voting patterns. From Table 15.1, you can see that the percentage of people who vote increases with age. The exception is those ages 21 to 24. This table also shows how significant race-ethnicity is. Non-Hispanic whites are more likely to vote than are African Americans, while Latinos are the least

TABLE 15.1 Who Votes in U.S. Elections?	1980	1984	1988	1992	1996	2000
Overall						
Americans Who Vote	59%	60%	57%	61%	54%	55%
Age						
18–20	36	37	33	39	31	28
21–24	38	44	46	33	24	24
25–34	55	58	48	53	43	44
35–44	64	64	61	64	55	55
45–64	69	70	68	70	64	64
65 and up	65	68	69	70	67	68
Sex						
Male	59	59	56	60	53	53
Female	59	61	58	62	56	56
Race/Ethnicity[a]						
Whites	61	61	59	64	56	56
African Americans	51	56	52	54	51	54
Latinos	30	33	29	29	27	28
Education						
Grade school only	43	43	37	35	28	27
High school dropout	46	44	41	41	34	34
High school graduate	59	59	55	58	49	49
College dropout	67	68	65	69	61	60
College graduate	80	79	78	81	73	72
Marital Status						
Married	NA	NA	NA	NA	NA	50
Divorced	NA	NA	NA	NA	NA	38
Labor Force						
Employed	62	62	58	64	55	56
Unemployed	41	44	39	46	37	35
Income[c]						
Under $5,000	38	39	35	NA	NA	21[b]
$5,000 to $9,999	46	49	41	NA	NA	24
$10,000 to $19,999	54	55	48	NA	NA	30
$15,000 to $24,999	59	63	56	NA	NA	35
$25,000 to $34,999	67	74	64	NA	NA	40
$35,000 to 49,999	74	74	70	NA	NA	44
$50,000 to $74,999	NA	NA	NA	NA	NA	50
$75,000 and over	NA	NA	NA	NA	NA	57

[a]Only these racial-ethnic groups are listed in all sources.

[b]Because the breakdown of voting by income for the year 2000 is not contained in the 2001 source, data for 1998 from U.S. Census Bureau, *Current Population Report,* P20–523, 2000: Tables 1, 5, 7, 8, 9 is used.

[c]For years preceding 1998, the category $35,000 to $49,999 is actually $35,000 and over, except for 1998, which is an average of $35,000 to $49,900 and over $50,000.

Sources: Statistical Abstract 1991:Table 450; 1997:Table 462; *Statistical Abstract* 2001:Table 401.

—in the United States

The Politics of Immigrants: Power, Ethnicity, and Social Class

That the United States is the land of immigrants is a truism. Every schoolchild knows that since the English Pilgrims landed on Plymouth Rock, successive groups have crossed the Atlantic Ocean to reach U.S. shores. Some, such as the Irish immigrants in the late 1800s and early 1900s, left to escape brutal poverty and famine. Others, such as the Jews of czarist Russia, fled persecution. Some sought refuge from lands ravaged by war. Others, called *entrepreneurial immigrants,* came for better economic opportunities. Still others were *sojourners* who planned to return home after a temporary stay. Some, not usually called immigrants, came in chains, held in bondage by early immigrants.

Today, the United States is in the midst of its second largest wave of immigration. In the first, in the early 1900s, immigrants came to account for 13 percent of the U.S. population. Almost all of those immigrants came from Europe. Today, immigrants make up about 8 percent of the population, and the mix is far more diverse. Only 14 percent of immigrants come from Europe. Most are from Asia, Mexico, the Caribbean, and South and Central America. Since 1980, more than 15 million legal

immigrants have settled in the United States. Another 5 million are here illegally.

In the last century, U.S.-born Americans feared that immigrants would bring socialism or communism with them. Today some fear that the millions of immigrants from Spanish-speaking countries threaten the primacy of the English language. As in the last century, the fear that immigrants will take jobs away from U.S.-born Americans remains strong. In addition, African Americans fear a loss of political power as immigrants from Mexico and Central and South America swell the Latino population.

After they are in the country, what path to political activity do immigrants take? In general, they first organize as a group on the basis of *ethnicity* rather than *class.* They respond to common problems, especially discrimination and those associated with adapting to a new way of life. This first step in political activity is a reaffirmation of their cultural identity. As sociologists Alejandro Portés and Ruben Rumbaut note, "By mobilizing the collective vote and by electing their own to office, immigrant minorities have learned the rules of the democratic game and absorbed its values in the process."

Irish immigrants to Boston illustrate this pattern of banding together on the basis of ethnicity. They built a power base that put the Irish in political control of the city and, ultimately, saw John F. Kennedy, one of their own, sworn in as president of the United States.

As Portés and Rumbaut observe, immigrants don't become "American" overnight. Instead, they begin by fighting for their own interests as a group—as Irish, Italians, and so on. Only after they attain enough political power to overcome discrimination do immigrant groups become "like everyone else"—that is, like those who have power. At this point of political power—when a group has representation somewhat proportionate to its numbers—a major change occurs. Social class then becomes more significant than race-ethnicity. This, then, is the typical path that immigrants follow in their socialization into the U.S. political system.

Sources: Portés and Rumbaut 1990; Salholz 1990; Prud'Homme 1991; James 1993; *Statistical Abstract* 1999:Table 10; 2000:Tables 7, 46.

likely to vote. The significance of race-ethnicity is so great that Latinos are less than half as likely to vote as are non-Hispanic whites. A crucial aspect of the socialization of newcomers to the United States is to learn the U.S. political system, the topic of the Cultural Diversity box on this page.

Table 15.1 also shows that voting increases with education. College graduates are more than twice as likely to vote as those who don't complete high school. Employment and income are also significant. People who make more than $35,000 a year are twice as likely to vote as those who make less than $5,000. Finally, note that women are slightly more likely than men to vote.

Social Integration How can we explain the voting patterns shown in Table 15.1? Look at the extremes. Whites who are older, more educated, affluent, and employed are the most likely to vote. Those least likely to vote are Latinos who are poor, younger, less educated, and unemployed. From these extremes, we can draw this principle: *The more that people feel they have a stake in the political system, the* *more likely they are to vote.* They have more to protect, and they feel that voting can make a difference. In effect, people who have been more rewarded by the political and economic system feel more socially integrated. They vote because they perceive that elections directly affect their own lives and the type of society in which they and their children live.

Alienation and Apathy   In contrast, those who gain less from the system—in terms of education, income, and jobs—are more likely to feel alienated from politics. Looking at themselves as outsiders, many feel hostile to the government. Some feel betrayed, believing that politicians have sold out to special-interest groups. They are convinced that all politicians are liars. Minorities who feel the U.S. political system is a "white" system are less likely to vote.

From Table 15.1, we see that many highly educated people with good incomes also stay away from the polls. Many people do not vote because of **voter apathy,** or indifference. Their view is that "next year will just bring more of the same, regardless of who is president." A common attitude of those who are apathetic is "What difference will my one vote make when there are millions of voters?" Many see little difference between the two major political parties.

Alienation and apathy are so common that *half* of the eligible voters do not vote for president, and *two-thirds* of the nation's eligible voters don't bother to vote for candidates for Congress (*Statistical Abstract* 2000:Table 480).

voter apathy
indifference and inaction on the part of individuals or groups with respect to the political process

The Gender Gap in Voting   Historically, men and women have voted the same way. Now, as Table 15.2 illustrates, when they go to the ballot box, they are somewhat more likely to vote for different presidential candidates. Where men are split between Democrats and Republicans, women are more likely to vote for Democratic candidates. In addition to this gender gap, this table also illustrates the much larger racial-ethnic gap in politics. Note how few African Americans vote for a Republican presidential candidate.

As we saw in Table 15.1, voting patterns reflect life experiences, especially economic circumstances. On average, women earn less than men and African Americans earn less than whites. As a result, at this point in history women and African Americans tend to look more favorably on government programs that redistribute income.

■ Lobbyists and Special-Interest Groups

Suppose that you are president of the United States, and you want to make milk and bread more affordable for the poor. As you check into the matter, you find that prices are high because the government is paying farmers billions of dollars a year in price supports (*Statistical Abstract* 1996:Table 1091; 2000:Table 1107). You propose to eliminate these subsidies.

Immediately, large numbers of people leap into action. They contact their senators and representa-

TABLE 15.2 How the Two-Party Presidential Vote Is Split	1988	1992	1996	2000
Women				
Democrat	50%	61%	65%	56%
Republican	50%	39%	35%	44%
Men				
Democrat	44%	55%	50%	44%
Republican	56%	45%	50%	56%
African Americans				
Democrat	92%	94%	99%	97%
Republican	8%	6%	1%	3%
Whites				
Democrat	41%	53%	54%	45%
Republican	59%	47%	46%	55%
Latinos				
Democrat	NA	NA	NA	61%
Republican	NA	NA	NA	39%
Asian Americans				
Democrat	NA	NA	NA	62%
Republican	NA	NA	NA	38%

Source: Statistical Abstract 1999:Table 464; Gallup Poll 2000, *Los Angeles Times Exit Poll*, November 7, 2001.

tives and hold news conferences. Your office is flooded with calls, faxes, and e-mail. Reuters and the Associated Press distribute pictures of farm families—their Holsteins grazing contentedly in the background—and inform readers how your harsh proposal will destroy these hard-working, healthy, happy good Americans who are struggling to make a living. President or not, you have little chance of getting your legislation passed.

What happened? The dairy industry went to work to protect its special interests. A **special-interest group** consists of people who think alike on a particular issue and who can be mobilized for political action. The dairy industry is just one of thousands of such groups that employ **lobbyists,** people who are paid to influence legislation on behalf of their clients. Special-interest groups and lobbyists have become a major force in U.S. politics. Members of Congress who want to be re-elected must pay attention to them, for they represent blocs of voters who share a vital interest in the outcome of specific bills. Well financed and able to contribute huge sums, lobbyists can deliver votes to you—or to your opponent.

Some members of Congress who lose an election or retire become lobbyists. They know their way around Washington, and, unlike other lobbyists, they have access to the floor of the House and Senate. Those who headed powerful committees can demand over a million dollars a year. Those lower in the pecking order get $200,000 or so. What about the laws that prohibit departing members from lobbying during the first year after they leave Congress? They skirt these laws by calling themselves "strategic advisors," not lobbyists. They direct other lobbyists, and—drawing one of Washington's fine moral lines—supposedly do not make direct contacts for a year (Wayne 2000).

Another law is also easily skirted. To prevent special-interest groups from unduly influencing legislation, the law limits the amount that any individual, corporation, or special-interest group can give a candidate, and requires all contributions over $1,000 to be reported. To get around this law, special-interest groups form **political action committees (PACs).** These organizations solicit contributions from many donors—each contribution being within the legal limit—and then use the large total to influence legislation.

PACs are powerful, for they bankroll lobbyists and legislators. To influence politics, about 4,000 PACs shell out $220 million a year directly to their candidates (*Statistical Abstract* 2000:Tables 484, 485). PACs also contribute millions in indirect ways. Some give "honorariums" to senators who agree to say a few words at a breakfast. A few PACs represent broad social interests such as protecting the environment. Most, however, stand for the financial interests of specific groups, such as the dairy, oil, banking, and construction industries. Those PACs with the most clout in terms of money and votes gain the ear of Congress. To politicians, the sound of money talking apparently sounds like the voice of the people.

■ PACs in U.S. Elections

Suppose that you want to run for the Senate. To have a chance of winning, not only do you have to shake hands around the state, be photographed hugging babies, and eat a lot of chicken dinners at local civic organizations, but also you must send out hundreds of thousands of pieces of mail to solicit votes and financial support. During the home stretch, television ads may run $700,000 a week (Harwood 1994). If you are an *average* candidate for the Senate, you will spend over $5 million on your campaign. To run for the House will cost a paltry $600,000 (*Statistical Abstract* 2000:Tables 462, 488).

Now suppose that it is only a few weeks from the election, the polls show you and your opponent neck and neck, and your war chest is empty. The representatives of a couple of PACs pay you a visit. One says that his organization will pay for a mailing, while the other offers to buy television and radio ads. You feel somewhat favorable toward their positions anyway, and you accept. Once elected, you owe them.

special-interest group
a group of people who have a particular issue in common who can be mobilized for political action

lobbyists
people who influence legislation on behalf of their clients

political action committee (PAC)
an organization formed by one or more special-interest groups to solicit and spend funds for the purpose of influencing legislation

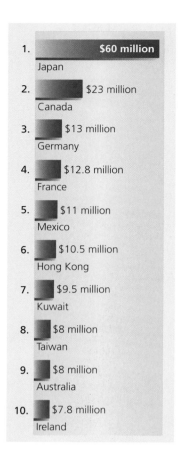

1.	**$60 million**
	Japan
2.	$23 million
	Canada
3.	$13 million
	Germany
4.	$12.8 million
	France
5.	$11 million
	Mexico
6.	$10.5 million
	Hong Kong
7.	$9.5 million
	Kuwait
8.	$8 million
	Taiwan
9.	$8 million
	Australia
10.	$7.8 million
	Ireland

Figure 15.2

Foreign Lobbyists:
The Top 10 Spenders
Source: Engelberg and Tolchin 1993.

anarchy
a condition of lawlessness or
political disorder caused by the
absence or collapse of governmental authority

pluralism
the diffusion of power
among many interest groups,
preventing any single group
from gaining control of the
government

checks and balances
the separation of powers
among the three branches
of U.S. government—legislative, executive, and judicial—
so that each is able to nullify
the actions of the other two,
thus preventing the domination of any single branch

When legislation that affects their interests comes up for vote, their representatives call you—at your unlisted number at home—and tell you how they want you to vote. It would be political folly to double-cross them.

It is said that the first duty of a politician is to get elected—and the second duty is to get reelected. If you are an average senator, to finance your reelection campaign you must raise $2,400 *every single day* of your six-year term. It is no wonder that money has been dubbed the "mother's milk of politics."

Criticism of Lobbyists and PACs   The major criticism leveled against lobbyists and PACs is that their money, in effect, buys votes. Rather than representing the people who elected them, legislators support the special interests of groups that have the ability to help them stay in power. The influence of foreign lobbyists has been a target of especially harsh criticism. As shown in Figure 15.2, the top ten foreign lobbyists spend $163 million annually to influence votes. Japan has hired more than 100 former U.S. government officials to pressure members of Congress to reduce quotas and duties on imports of its products. During election years, Japan contributes to *both* presidential candidates. Critics argue that the playing field is not level, for Japan has made it a crime for foreigners to influence its legislation (Judis 1990; Duffy 1992).

Even if the United States were to outlaw PACs, special-interest groups would not disappear from U.S. politics. Lobbyists walked the corridors of the Senate long before PACs, and since the time of Alexander Graham Bell they have carried the unlisted numbers of members of Congress. For good or ill, lobbyists play an essential role in the U.S. political system.

Who Rules the United States?

With lobbyists and PACs holding such influence, just whom do U.S. senators and representatives really represent? This question has led to a lively debate among sociologists.

◼ The Functionalist Perspective: Pluralism

Functionalists view the state as having arisen out of the basic needs of the social group. To protect themselves from oppressors, people formed a government and gave it the monopoly on violence. The risk is that the state can turn that force against its own citizens. To return to the example used earlier, states have a tendency to become muggers. Thus, people must find a balance between having no government—which would lead to **anarchy**, a condition of disorder and violence—and having a government that protects them from violence, but that also may itself turn against them. When functioning well, then, the state is a balanced system that protects its citizens—from one another *and* from government.

What keeps the U.S. government from turning against its citizens? Functionalists say that **pluralism**, a diffusion of power among many interest groups, prevents any one group from gaining control of the government and using it to oppress the people (Polsby 1959; Dahl 1961, 1982; Engeman 2001). To keep the government from coming under the control of any one group, the founders of the United States set up three branches of government: the executive branch (the president), the judiciary branch (the courts), and the legislative branch (the Senate and House of Representatives). Each is sworn to uphold the Constitution, which guarantees rights to citizens, and each can nullify the actions of the other two. This system, known as **checks and balances,** was designed to ensure that power remains distributed and that no one branch of government dominates.

Our pluralist society has many parts—women, men, racial-ethnic groups, farmers, factory and office workers, religious organizations, bankers, bosses, the unemployed, the retired—as well as such broad categories as the rich, middle class, and poor. No group dominates. Rather, as each group pursues its own interests, it is balanced by other groups that are pursuing theirs. To attain their goals, groups must negotiate and compromise with one another. This minimizes conflict. Because these groups have political muscle to flex at the polls, and politicians need votes, politicians try to design policies that please as many groups as they can. This, say functionalists, makes the political system responsive to the people, and no one group rules.

■ The Conflict Perspective: The Power Elite, or Ruling Class

Conflict theorists disagree. If you focus on the lobbyists scurrying around Washington, they say, you get a blurred image of superficial activities. What really counts is the big picture, not its fragments. The important question is who holds the power that determines the country's overarching policies. For example, who determines how many Americans will be out of work by raising or lowering interest rates? Who sets policies that transfer jobs from the United States to countries where labor costs less? And the ultimate question of power: Who is behind the decision to go to war?

Sociologist C. Wright Mills (1956) took the position that the country's most important matters are not decided by lobbyists or even by Congress. Rather, the decisions that have the greatest impact on the lives of Americans—and people across the globe—are made by a **power elite.** As depicted in Figure 15.3, the power elite consists of the top leaders of the largest corporations, the most powerful generals and admirals of the armed forces, and certain elite politicians—the president, his cabinet, and select senior members of Congress who chair the major committees. It is they who wield power, who make the decisions that direct the country and shake the world.

Are the three groups that make up the power elite—the top business, political, and military leaders—equal in power? Mills said they were not, but he didn't point to the president and his staff or even to the generals and admirals as the most powerful. The most powerful, he said, are the corporate heads. Because all three segments of the power elite view capitalism as essential to the welfare of the country, business interests, Mills said, come foremost in setting national policy. (Remember the incident mentioned in the previous chapter (page 425) of the U.S. president selling airplanes.)

Sociologist William Domhoff (1990, 1999) uses the term **ruling class** to refer to the power elite. He focuses on the 1 percent of Americans who belong to the super

■ The Great Depression transformed Americans' attitudes about government intervention in economic matters. Shown here is a 1947 poster that was displayed in post offices and other public buildings throughout the country.

power elite
C. Wright Mills's term for those who rule the United States: the top people in the leading corporations, the most powerful generals and admirals of the armed forces, and certain elite politicians

ruling class
another term for the power elite

The top corporate, military , and political leaders

Congress
Other legislators
Interest-group leaders
Local opinion leaders

The masses of people— unorganized, exploited, and mostly disinterested

Most Power

Least Power

Figure 15.3

Power in the United States: The Model Proposed by C. Wright Mills
Source: Based on Mills 1956.

rich, the powerful capitalist class analyzed in Chapter 10 (pages 285–286). Members of this class control our top corporations and foundations, even the boards that oversee our major universities. It is no accident, says Domhoff, that from this group the president chooses most members of his cabinet and appoints ambassadors to the most powerful countries of the world.

Conflict theorists point out that we should not think of the power elite (or ruling class) as some secret group that meets together in order to agree on specific matters. Rather, because their backgrounds and orientations to life are so similar, those who make up the power elite share the same values and goals. All have attended prestigious private schools, they belong to exclusive clubs, and they are millionaires many times over. There is no grand conspiracy to control the country, but, instead, decisions flow from their mutual interest in solving the problems that face big business. Because their political connections extend to the top centers of power, this elite determines the economic and political conditions under which the rest of the country operates (Domhoff 1990, 1998). We shall return to this line of inquiry later.

Which View Is Right?

The functionalist and conflict views of power in U.S. society cannot be reconciled. Either competing interests block any single group from being dominant, as functionalists assert, or a power elite oversees the major decisions of the United States, as conflict theorists maintain. The answer may have to do with the level you look at. Perhaps at the middle level of power (depicted in Figure 15.3), the competing groups do keep each other at bay, and none is able to dominate. If so, the functionalist view would apply to this level. But which level holds the key to U.S. power? Perhaps the functionalists have not looked high enough, and activities at the peak remain invisible to them. On that level, does an elite dominate? In order to protect its mutual interests, does a small group make the major decisions of the United States?

The answer is not yet conclusive. For this, we must await more research.

War and Terrorism: A Means to Implement Political Objectives

As we have noted, an essential characteristic of the state is that it claims a monopoly on violence. At times, a state may direct that violence against other nations. **War**, armed conflict between nations (or politically distinct groups), is often part of national policy. Let's look at this aspect of politics.

Is War Universal?

Although human aggression and individual killing characterize all human groups, war does not. War is simply *one option* that groups may choose for dealing with disagreements, but not all societies choose this option. The Mission Indians of North America, the Arunta of Australia, the Andaman Islanders of the South Pacific, and the Eskimos of the Arctic, for example, had procedures to handle aggression and quarrels, but they did not have organized battles that pitted one tribe or group against another. These groups do not even have a word for war (Lesser 1968).

How Common Is War?

One of the contradictions of humanity is that people long for peace while at the same time they glorify war. The glorification of war can be seen by noting how major battles hog the center of a country's retelling of its history and how monuments to generals, patriots, and battles are scattered throughout the land. From May Day pa-

war
armed conflict between nations or politically distinct groups

rades in Moscow's Red Square to the Fourth of July celebrations in the United States and the Cinco de Mayo victory marches in Mexico, war and revolution are interwoven into the fabric of daily life.

War is so common that a cynic might say it is the normal state of society. Sociologist Pitirim Sorokin (1937) counted the wars in Europe from 500 B.C. to A.D. 1925. He documented 967 wars, an average of one war every two to three years. Counting years or parts of a year in which a country was at war, at 28 percent Germany had the lowest record of warfare. Spain's 67 percent gave it the dubious distinction of being the most war-prone. Sorokin found that Russia, the land of his birth, had experienced only one peaceful quarter-century during the entire previous thousand years. Since the time of William the Conqueror, who took power in 1066, England was at war an average of 56 out of each 100 years. Spain fought even more often. It is worth noting the history of the United States in this regard: Since 1850, it has intervened militarily around the world about 160 times, an average of *once a year* (Kohn 1988; current events).

Why Nations Go to War

Why do nations choose war to handle their disputes? Sociologists answer this question by focusing not on factors *within* humans, such as aggressive impulses, but by looking for *social* causes—conditions in society that encourage or discourage combat between nations.

Sociologist Nicholas Timasheff (1965) identified three essential conditions of war. The first is a cultural tradition of war. Because their nation has fought wars in the past, the leaders of a group see war as an option for dealing with serious disputes with other nations. The second is an antagonistic situation in which two or more states confront incompatible objectives. For example, each may want the same land or resources. The third is a "fuel" that heats the antagonistic situation to a boiling point, so that people cross the line from thinking about war to actually engaging in it. Timasheff identified seven such "fuels." He found that war is likely if a country's leaders see the antagonistic situation as an opportunity to achieve one or more of these objectives:

1. Revenge: settling "old scores" from previous conflicts

2. Power: dictating their will to a weaker nation

3. Prestige: saving the nation's "honor"

4. Unity: uniting rival groups within their country

5. Position: protecting or exalting their own position

6. Ethnicity: bringing under their rule "our people" who are living in another country

7. Beliefs: forcibly converting others to religious or political beliefs

Costs of War

One side effect of the new technologies stressed in this text is a higher capacity to inflict death. During World War I, bombs claimed fewer than 3 of every 100,000 people in England and Germany. With World War II's more powerful airplanes and bombs, these deaths increased a hundredfold, to 300 of every 100,000 civilians (Hart 1957). With today's higher killing capacity, if a war were fought with nuclear bombs, the death rate could run 100 percent. War is also costly in terms of money. As shown in Table 15.3, the United States has spent $4 trillion on nine major wars.

Despite its massive costs in lives and property, warfare remains a common way to pursue political objectives. For about seven years, the

TABLE 15.3
What U.S. Wars Cost

War of 1812	$615,000,000
Mexican War	$1,076,000,000
American Revolution	$1,918,000,000
Spanish-American War	$5,961,000,000
Civil War	$45,990,000,000
Korean War	$262,062,000,000
World War I	$369,580,000,000
Vietnam War	$553,088,000,000
World War II	$2,953,716,000,000
Total	$4,194,006,000,000

Note: The source lists the costs in 1967 dollars. To account for inflation, I increased these amounts by 350 percent, and added the costs of service-connected benefits. Where a range was listed, I used the mean.

The military costs for the U.S. involvement in Grenada, Panama, Kuwait, Somalia, Haiti, Kosovo, and Afghanistan are not listed in the source. Also not included are interest payments on war loans. Nor are these costs reduced by the financial benefits to the United States, such as the acquisition of California and Texas in the Mexican War. Also not included are ongoing expenditures by the military, currently about $290 billion a year.

Source: Statistical Abstract 1993:Table 553; 2000: Table 566.

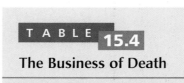

The Business of Death

The 5 Largest Arms Sellers	
1. United States	$31.8 billion
2. Great Britain	$6.6 billion
3. France	$5.9 billion
4. Russia	$2.3 billion
5. China	$1.1 billion

The 10 Largest Arms Consumers	
1. Saudi Arabia	$11.6 billion
2. Taiwan	$9.2 billion
3. Japan	$2.6 billion
4. Great Britain	$2.1 billion
5. Kuwait	$2.0 billion
6. Egypt	$1.6 billion
7. Turkey	$1.6 billion
8. United States	$1.6 billion
9. United Arab Emirates	$1.4 billion
10. South Korea	$1.1 billion
11. Israel	$1.1 billion

Source: Statistical Abstract 2000: Table 571.

United States fought in Vietnam—at a cost of 59,000 American and about 2 million Vietnamese lives (Herring 1989; Hellinger and Judd 1991). For nine years, the Soviet Union waged war in Afghanistan—with a death toll of about 1 million Afghans and perhaps 50,000 Soviet soldiers (Armitage 1989; Binyon 2001). An eight-year war between Iran and Iraq cost about 400,000 lives. Cuban mercenaries in Africa and South America brought an unknown number of deaths. Civil wars in Africa, Asia, and South America claimed hundreds of thousands of lives, mostly of civilians. Also unknown is how many lives were lost in the brief wars against Iraq (Desert Storm) and the terrorists in Afghanistan.

■ Sowing the Seeds of Future Wars

Selling advanced war technology to the Least Industrialized Nations sows the seeds of future wars. When a Least Industrialized Nation buys high-tech weapons, its neighbors get nervous, sparking an arms race among them (Cole and Lubman 1994; Ricks 1994). Table 15.4 shows that the United States is the chief merchant of death. Great Britain and France place a distant second and third. This table also shows the major customers in the business of death. Two matters are of interest. First, Egypt, a country so poor that it can hardly keep its people from starving, is one of the biggest spenders. Either its power elite is drastically insecure (and seeks to bolster its power through these tremendous expenditures), or else it is incredibly secure because of the weapons it has purchased. Second, the purchases of arms by Saudi Arabia, Kuwait, and United Arab Emirates indicate that U.S. dollars spent on oil tend to return to the United States. There is, in reality, an exchange of arms and oil.

The seeds of future wars are also sown by nuclear proliferation. Some Least Industrialized Nations, such as India, Pakistan, and China, have nuclear weapons. Iran, Iraq, Libya, and North Korea are furiously trying to develop their own nuclear arsenals. In the hands of a terrorist or a dictator who uses them to settle personal or nationalistic grudges, these weapons can mean nuclear blackmail or nuclear attack.

After the cold war ended, the United States and Russia announced that they no longer were aiming their nuclear missiles at the other's cities. But this was misinformation, for they still do (Barry and Thomas 2001). Although Russia offered the United States troops and bases for its war on terrorism in Afghanistan, these countries continue to eye each other suspiciously. Neither Russia nor the United States is wholly convinced that the other has truly peaceful intentions. G-7 is especially concerned that Russia's democratic reform may be undermined by inflation, currency collapse, and organized crime. They also fear that reactionary politicians will attempt to restore Russia's faded glory through military might. Russia's nuclear arsenal sits uneasily, an ominous threat to the global coalitions G-7 has worked out. As a consequence, despite Russia's weakened state, G-7 invites Russia to its annual summits.

■ Nuclear, Biological, and Chemical Terrorism

Hatred between ethnic groups spans generations, sometimes continuing for centuries. Groups nurture their bitterness by endlessly chronicling the atrocities committed by their archenemy. One consequence is armed conflict, which continuously erupts somewhere in the world as one group seizes an opportunity to attack its enemy—or to try to remove its yoke of oppression.

Nourished hatreds also make terrorism a danger. If a weaker group seeks to attack a more powerful group, one of its few—and very inviting—options is suicide terrorism. This tactic shocks the world and captures headlines, as it has done time after time when Palestinians use it against Israelis. The most dramatic example of suicide terrorism, of course, was the attack on the World Trade Center and the Pentagon under the direction of Osama bin Laden. Despite the several thousand deaths from this attack

September 11, 2001

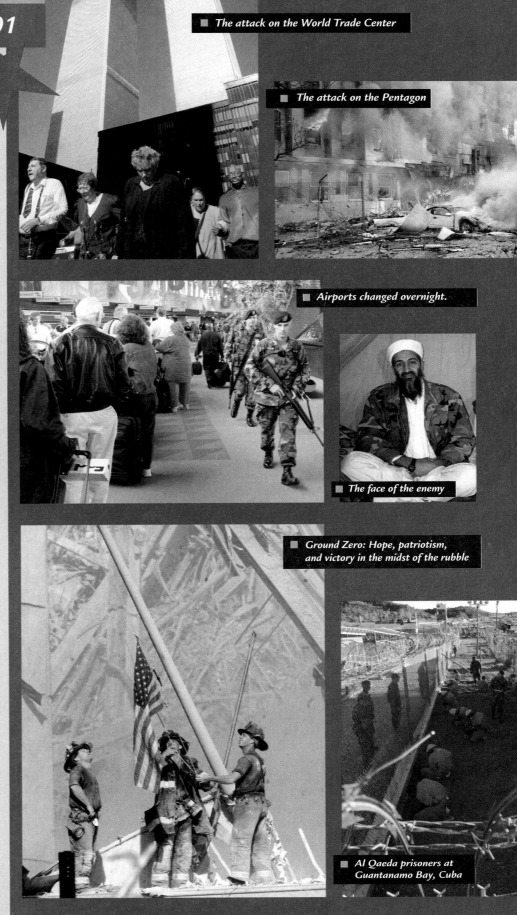

The attack on the World Trade Center

The attack on the Pentagon

Airports changed overnight.

The face of the enemy

Ground Zero: Hope, patriotism, and victory in the midst of the rubble

Al Qaeda prisoners at Guantanamo Bay, Cuba

September 11, 2001, goes down in U.S. history as the equivalent of December 7, 1941, when Japan attacked Pearl Harbor. The destruction of the World Trade Center and a large portion of the Pentagon was similar to the destruction of the U.S. Naval fleet moored at Pearl Harbor. Each attack came unexpectedly. Each was brutal in its destruction. And each changed the United States.

Each attack was followed by a surge of patriotism. Groups that disagreed vehemently with one another paused to put their differences aside for the common good. For a moment, Democrats and Republicans quit quarreling, suddenly seeing eye to eye on issues that had to do with survival. Even comedians revised their jokes and skits, replacing material that could be perceived as critical of the president or unpatriotic.

Almost overnight, Americans looked at the world in a different light. What had been taken for granted became uncertain. Americans became cautious and suspicious. Troops appeared in civilian areas. People who looked like the attackers became suspect, and in some instances were the target of attacks. In each event, Americans felt that their freedom was at stake, that what they call the "American way of life" was being challenged, even that Western civilization itself was threatened. In each instance, the nation mobilized to fight an enemy in far-off lands.

Sociologically, one can expect these reactions. During times of crisis, people's interests and concerns narrow. Survival comes first, and things that previously had been important recede. Only after survival is assured do other items regain their significance.

The photos in this collage illustrate some of these events and principles.

Sociology

& the new technology

Technology and Terrorism

To make their point, terrorists strive for drama, creating events that capture people's attention. It isn't so much the damage that is the goal of terrorists, but the publicity that comes from the act, as well as the fear it engenders. A well-placed bomb in a holiday crowd will not bring a government to its knees. It may, in fact, strengthen the nation's resolve. But the ability to penetrate security and to inflict even a minor wound on a much more powerful foe makes it known that the terrorists are a force to be reckoned with. For those who share their sentiments, the terrorist act is a unifying device, a means of arousing support for their cause.

Nowhere in the history of the world, at least up to this point, has a terrorist act been more dramatic than the destruction on September 11, 2001, of New York's World Trade Center. The simultaneous attack on the Pentagon, shocking in its own right, also represented an alarming penetration of the command center of the armed forces of the United States.

These attacks were not the long-anticipated assault through high technology—the use of nuclear, biological, or chemical weapons. They were low-tech. The main weapon was box cutters, a common tool of businesses, readily available at the local hardware store for a dollar or two. The jet planes and the jet fuel were advanced technology, of course, but they were old technology. They had been around for 40 years or so. Terrorists hit upon the idea of using this old technology to create powerful weapons. They turned commercial airliners into missiles laden with jet fuel, transforming them into flying bombs to deliver their message.

Often overlooked is the technology that made the message so effective—the communications system that undergirds our news media. The satellites and transmission systems allowed the attacks to be transmitted instantaneously around the world. Targeting Manhattan meant that scores of television cameras would be trained on the target. With our technologically connected world, the horror would be immediately transmitted around the globe—to be replayed over and over again to horror-stricken audiences transfixed before their electronic screens. To choose a target in a place that did not have this technology would not have had the same effect (Hafner 2001).

for your consideration

What "message" did the terrorists intend to deliver? Were they successful? Did their "message" backfire on them? How has life in the United States changed because of this attack? Where else, and in what ways, has it changed people's lives?

and its enormous impact on the United States, as discussed in the Sociology and the New Technology box above, the hijacked planes were relatively weak tools.

The real danger lies in nuclear, chemical, and biological weapons. Unleashed against a civilian population, such weapons could cause millions of deaths. With the anthrax that was mailed to a few select victims in 2001, Americans caught a glimpse of how easily such weapons can be unleashed. The availability of nuclear, chemical, and biological weapons because of the breakup of the Soviet empire makes further terrorism on U.S. soil a chilling possibility. This topic is discussed in the Down-to-Earth Sociology box on the next page.

■ War and Dehumanization

Proud of his techniques, the U.S. trainer was demonstrating to the South American soldiers how to torture a prisoner. As the victim screamed in anguish, the trainer was interrupted by a phone call from his wife. His students could hear him say, "A dinner and a movie sound nice. I'll see you right after work." Hanging up the phone, he then continued the lesson. (Stockwell 1989)

War exacts many costs in addition to killing people and destroying property. One is its effect on morality. Exposure to brutality and killing often causes **dehumanization,** the process of reducing people to objects that do not deserve to be treated as humans.

As we review findings on dehumanization and see how it breeds callousness and cruelty, perhaps we can better understand how O'Brien in the opening vignette could have unleashed rats into someone's face. Consider the four characteristics of dehumanization (Bernard et al. 1971):

dehumanization
the act or process of reducing people to objects that do not deserve the treatment accorded humans

down-to-earth
s o c i o l o g y

■ ■ ■ ■ ■
Biological Terrorism

Consider this scenario:

Over a period of years, agents of a nation whose leaders hate the United States and want to settle a grudge quietly infiltrate the country. Most are admitted as students at universities. All have been highly trained by their country's secret police. On a predetermined day, at a specified hour, they release anthrax and smallpox into the air of 20 major cities. Within days, a third of Americans are dead.

This scenario haunts U.S. officials. There will be no warning, no attempt to hold the United States hostage in order to extort billions of dollars. Money is not the goal. The motive is revenge for humiliation suffered at U.S. hands. The goal will be no less than to wipe out the United States itself.

The White House conducted an exercise to play out what might happen if terrorists, armed with genetically modified germs, decided to strike. Officials were alarmed at how easily such an attack could be carried out and at the millions who would die (Broad and Miller 1998). Alarmed, government officials have stockpiled vaccines around the country and have trained emergency medical teams in major cities (Broad and Petersen 2001). All military personnel, including National Guard and reserve units, are being vaccinated against anthrax.

Then there is President Clinton's "secret" directive that in case of such an attack the inhabitants of a city are *not* to be evacuated. Instead, the military will block roads and at gunpoint will stop people from fleeing cities and spreading the disease. Highly likely is a military takeover of state and local governments in order to fight the chaos (Miller and Broad 1999). This may well explain why the U.S. military is openly discussing the legality of martial law (Davies 2000). It may also explain the strange event that occurred after the attack on the World Trade Center—the roads and bridges leading to and from Manhattan were blocked. For several hours, the people who were already in Manhattan, including those who had escaped the World Trade Center, were not allowed to leave the island. In the meantime, specialists were dispatched to the rubble to determine if biological agents had been released in the attack.

An ancient Chinese proverb says: "May you live in exciting times." This seemingly innocuous saying is actually a curse; it expresses the hope that an enemy's life will be upset. We do live in exciting times. Let's hope that the curse that envelops us—proliferating nuclear, chemical, and biological weapons, interstate and interethnic rivalries and domination, aspiring nationalism, and the growing threat of terrorism—does not mean our destruction.

■ ■ ■ ■ ■

1. *Increased emotional distance from others.* People stop identifying with others, no longer seeing them as having qualities similar to themselves. They come to be seen as subhumans, not as people, but as "the enemy," or objects of some sort.

2. *An emphasis on following procedures.* Regulations are not questioned, for they are seen as a means to an end. People are likely to say, "I don't like doing this, but I have to follow rules," or "We all have to die some day. What difference does it make if these people die now?"

3. *Inability to resist pressures.* One's own ideas of morality take a back seat to fears of losing one's job, losing the respect of one's peers, or having one's integrity and loyalty questioned.

4. *A diminished sense of personal responsibility.* People come to see themselves as only small cogs in a large machine. They are not responsible for what they do, for they are simply following orders. The higher-ups who give the orders are thought to have more complete or even secret information that justifies what is being done. They think, "The higher-ups are in a position to judge what is right and wrong, but in my humble place, who am I to question these acts?"

A Vietnam vet who read this section remarked, "You missed the major one we used. We killed kids. Our dehumanizing technique was a saying, 'The little ones are the soldiers of tomorrow.'"

Dehumanization numbs the conscience. As in the vignette that opened this section, even acts of torture become dissociated from one's "normal self." Brutality and killing, though regrettable, are seen as tools that help to get a job done. Torturing and killing somehow fit into the larger scheme of things—and someone has to do the "dirty work." The individual clothes such acts in patriotic language: They are "the soldier's duty." Those who make the decisions are the ones who are responsible—soldiers simply follow orders.

As sociologist Tamotsu Shibutani (1970) stressed, dehumanization is aided by the tendency for prolonged conflicts to be transformed into a struggle between good and evil. The enemy, of course, represents evil in the equation. To fight against absolute evil sometimes requires the suspension of moral standards—for one is dealing with an abnormal situation, opposing an enemy that is less than human, and fighting for the precarious survival of good (Markhusen 1995). War, then, exalts treachery, cruelty, and killing—and medals are given to glorify actions that would be condemned in every other context of social life.

As soldiers participate in acts that they, too, would normally condemn, they neutralize their morality. This insulates them from acknowledging their behaviors as evil, which would threaten their self-concept and mental adjustment. Surgeons, highly sensitive to patients' needs in ordinary medical situations, become capable of mentally removing an individual's humanity. By thinking of Jews as "people who are going to die anyway," German surgeons during World War II were able to mutilate them just to study the results.

Dehumanization does not always insulate the self from guilt, however, and its failure to do so can bring severe personal consequences. During the war, while soldiers are surrounded by army buddies who agree that the enemy is less than human and deserves inhuman treatment, such definitions ordinarily remain intact. After returning home, however, the dehumanizing definitions more easily break down. Many soldiers then find themselves seriously disturbed by what they did during the war. Although most eventually adjust, some cannot, such as this soldier from California who wrote this note before putting a bullet through his brain (Smith 1980):

> I can't sleep anymore. When I was in Vietnam, we came across a North Vietnamese soldier with a man, a woman, and a three-or four-year-old girl. We had to shoot them all. I can't get the little girl's face out of my mind. I hope that God will forgive me . . . I can't.

A New World Order?

The globalization of capitalism, accompanied by the worldwide flow of information, capital, and goods discussed in the previous chapter, is little affected by national boundaries. The United States, Canada, and Mexico have formed a North American Free-Trade Association (NAFTA), to which all of South America may eventually belong. Some South American countries have even adopted the dollar as an official currency, even as their national currency coexists alongside it. Transcending their national boundaries, most European countries have formed an economic and political unit (the European Union, or EU). They, too, have adopted a cross-national currency, the Euro. The EU has also established a "rapid reaction force" of 60,000 troops under a unified command (Cohen 2001). Transcending national borders, the United Nations has sent out "peace keeping" troops to nations from Korea to Kosovo.

Will this process continue until there is but one state or empire that envelops the earth itself? This is a distinct possibility, deriving perhaps not only from these historical trends but also from a push by a powerful group of capitalists who profit from global free trade (Domhoff 1990). Although the trend is in full tilt, we are unlikely to see its conclusion during our lifetimes, for national boundaries and national patriotism die only a hard death. As borders shift, as occurred with the breakup of the Soviet Union, previously unincorporated nations such as Lithuania and Azerbaijan demand their independence and the right to full statehood. The Cultural Diversity box on the next page explores this tension between nations and states.

nationalism
a strong identity with a nation, accompanied by the desire for that nation to be dominant

cultural d·i·v·e·r·s·i·t·y

Around the World

Roadblocks in the Path to the New World Order: The Globalization of Capitalism Versus the Resurgence of Nationalism

The world has about five thousand nations. What makes each a *nation* is that its people share a language, culture, territory, and political organization. A *state,* in contrast, claims a monopoly on violence over a territory. A state may contain many nations. The Kayapo Indians are but one nation within the state called Brazil. The Chippewa and Sioux are two nations within the state called the United States. The world's five thousand nations have existed for hundreds, some even for thousands, of years. In contrast, most of the world's 194 states have been around only since World War II.

Most modern states are empires; that is, they have incorporated nations into their boundaries—usually by conquest. Some states have far better records than others, but overall, no ideology, left or right, religious or sectarian, has protected nations or promoted pluralism much better or worse than any other. The last century probably saw more genocides and *ethnocides* (the destruction of an ethnic group) than any other.

For nation peoples, group identity transcends political affiliation. Clearly, the Palestinians who live within Israel's borders do not identify themselves as Israelis. But did you know that the Oromos in Ethiopia have more members than do three-quarters of the states in the United Nations, and that they do not think of themselves as Ethiopians? The 22 million Kurds don't consider themselves first and foremost to be Iranians, Iraqis, Syrians, or Turks. There are about 450 nations in Nigeria, 350 in India, 180 in Brazil, 130 in the former USSR, and 90 in Ethiopia. That nations are squeezed into states with

■ *Shown here are Russian troops in what remains of downtown Grozny, the capital of Chechnya. Russia bombed the city in order to stop the former colony from gaining independence.*

which they don't identify is the nub of the problem.

In most states, power resides in the hands of an elite that operates by a simple credo: Winner takes all. The elite control foreign investment and aid, and use both to enforce their power. They control exports, levy taxes—and buy the weapons. They confiscate the resources of the nations, whether those take the form of Native American land in North and South America or oil from the Kurds in Iraq. When nations resist, the result is open conflict—and sometimes genocide.

About half of the debt of the least industrialized states and nearly all debt in Africa comes from the purchase of weapons, which the states use to suppress their own citizens. Most of the world's 22 million refugees are victims of such conflicts, as are most of the 100 million internally displaced people who have been uprooted from their homelands.

A vicious cycle forms. The appropriation of a nation's resources leads to conflict, conflict leads to insecurity and the

purchase of weapons, weapons purchases lead to debt, and debt leads to the appropriation of more resources. This self-feeding cycle helps to ensure that elites of the least industrialized states will cooperate with G-7, which supplies the arms, as it divides the globe's resources among its members.

G-7's march to a New World Order has met a serious obstacle, the resurgence of **nationalism**—identity with and loyalty to a nation. Because it promotes loyalty to smaller groups instead of to the regional divisions into which G-7 wants to carve the globe, nationalism threatens the evolving New World Order. The shooting wars increase—fought over issues and animosities that are rooted in history. Not only are such events only faintly understood by those who are not a party to them, but also they have been kept vividly alive in the folklore and collective memory of these nations. These wars threaten the fragile coalitions that G-7 is building as it divides up the world's resources.

G-7 will continue to divide the globe into regional trading blocs, and we will continue to witness this oppositional struggle. We will see seemingly contradictory outcomes: the formation of global coalitions matched by the simultaneous outbreak of small-scale shooting wars as nations struggle for independence.

The end result? It is sufficient to note how greatly the scales are tipped in favor of the most industrialized states and the multinational corporations. David is not likely to defeat Goliath this time.

Sources: Clay 1990; Ohmae 1995; Jáuregui 1996; Marcus 1996; Alter 2000, Hechter 2000; Fletcher 2001.

If global political and economic unity does come about, it is fascinating to speculate on what type of government may emerge. Certainly a world order holds potential benefits for human welfare. We could have global peace. And if we have a benevolent government, our lives and participation in politics could be quite satisfying. But we must be mindful of Hitler. If his conquests had resulted in world domination, not only would we all be speaking German, but also we would be living under a single dictator in a world totalitarian regime based on racial identification. If the world's resources and people come under the control of a dictatorship or an oligarchy, then, the future for humanity could be bleak, perhaps similar to that of Winston and Julia in our opening vignette.

Summary and Review

Micropolitics and Macropolitics

■ **What is the difference between micropolitics and macropolitics?**

The essential nature of politics is **power,** and every group is political. The term **micropolitics** refers to the exercise of power in everyday life. **Macropolitics** refers to large-scale power, such as governing a nation. P. 440.

Power, Authority, and Violence

■ **How are authority and coercion related to power?**

Authority is power that people view as legitimately exercised over them, while **coercion** is power they consider unjust. The **state** is a political entity that claims a monopoly on violence over some territory. If enough people consider a state's power illegitimate, **revolution** is possible. Pp. 440–441.

■ **What kinds of authority are there?**

Max Weber identified three types of authority. Power in **traditional authority** derives from custom—patterns set down in the past serve as rules for the present. Power in **rational legal authority** (also called *bureaucratic authority*) is based on law and written procedures. In **charismatic authority,** power is based on loyalty to an individual to whom people are attracted. Charismatic authority, which undermines traditional and rational-legal authority, has built-in problems in transferring authority to a new leader. Pp. 442–444.

Types of Government

■ **How are the types of government related to power?**

In a **monarchy,** power is based on hereditary rule; in a **democracy,** power is given to the ruler by citizens; and in a **dictatorship,** power is seized by an individual or small group. Pp. 445–447.

The U.S. Political System

■ **What are the main characteristics of the U.S. political system?**

The United States has a "winner take all" system, in which elections are determined by a simple majority. Most European democracies, in contrast, have **proportional representation;** legislative seats are allotted according to the percentage of votes each political party receives. Pp. 448–449.

Voter turnout is higher among people who are more socially integrated—those who sense a greater stake in the outcome of elections, such as the more educated and well-to-do. **Lobbyists** and **special-interest groups,** such as **political action committees** (PACs), play a significant role in U.S. politics. Pp. 450–454.

Who Rules the United States?

■ **Is the United States controlled by a ruling class?**

In a view known as **pluralism,** functionalists say that no one group holds power, that the country's many competing interest groups balance one another. Conflict theorists, who focus on the top level of power, say that the United States is governed by a **power elite,** a ruling class made up of the top corporate, political, and military leaders. At this point, the matter is not settled. Pp. 454–456.

War and Terrorism: A Means to Implement Political Objectives

■ **How is war related to politics—and what are its costs?**

War is a means of attempting to reach political objectives. Because of technological advances in killing, the costs of war in terms of human lives have escalated. The Least Industrialized Nations, which can least afford it, spend huge amounts on technologically advanced weapons. Another cost is dehumanization, whereby people no longer see others as worthy of human treatment. This paves the way for torture and killing. Pp. 456–462.

A New World Order?

■ **Is humanity headed toward a one-world political order?**

The global expansion of communications, transportation, and trade, the widespread adoption of capitalism, the retreat of socialism, and the trend toward regional economic and political unions may indicate that a world political system is developing. The oppositional trend is a fierce **nationalism.** If a New World Order develops, the possible consequences for human welfare range from excellent to calamitous. Pp. 462–464.

■ *Where can I read more on this topic?*

Suggested Readings for this chapter are at the back of this book.

Additional Online Resources for This Chapter
www.ablongman.com/henslin6e

- *Content Select* Research Database for Sociology, with suggested key terms and annotated references
- Link to 2000 Census, with activities
- Flashcards of key terms and concepts

- Practice Tests
- Weblinks
- Interactive Maps

using . . .
ContentSelect

Research Database for Sociology

dictatorship	oligarchy	special interest groups	totalitarianism
lobbyists	ruling class	terrorism	war
new world order			

Noma, *Family Embrace*, 2000

16

The Family

Marriage and Family in Global Perspective
What Is a Family?
Common Cultural Themes

Marriage and Family in Theoretical Perspective
The Functionalist Perspective: Functions and Dysfunctions
The Conflict Perspective: Gender and Power
The Symbolic Interactionist Perspective: Gender and the Meanings of Marriage

The Family Life Cycle
Love and Courtship in Global Perspective
Marriage
Childbirth
Child Rearing
The Family in Later Life

Diversity in U.S. Families
African American Families
Latino Families
Asian American Families
Native American Families
One-Parent Families
Families Without Children
Blended Families
Gay and Lesbian Families

Trends in U.S. Families
Postponing Marriage
Cohabitation
Unmarried Mothers
The Sandwich Generation and Elder Care

Divorce and Remarriage
Problems in Measuring Divorce
Children of Divorce
The Absent Father and Serial Fatherhood
The Ex-Spouses
Remarriage

Two Sides of Family Life
The Dark Side of Family Life: Battering, Child Abuse, Marital Rape, and Incest
The Bright Side of Family Life: Successful Marriages

The Future of Marriage and Family

Summary and Review

H old still. We're going to be late," said Sharon as she tried to put shoes on 2-year-old Michael, who kept squirming away.

Finally succeeding with the shoes, Sharon turned to 4-year-old Brittany, who was trying to pull a brush through her hair. "It's stuck, Mom," Brittany said.

"Well, no wonder. Just how did you get gum in your hair? I don't have time for this, Brittany. We've got to leave."

Getting to the van fifteen minutes behind schedule, Sharon strapped the kids in, and then herself. Just as she was about to pull away, she remembered that she had not checked the fridge for messages.

"Just a minute, kids. I'll be right back."

Running into the house, she frantically searched for a note from Tom. She vaguely remembered him mumbling something about being held over at work. She grabbed the Post-It and ran back to the van.

"He's picking on me," complained Brittany when her mother climbed back in.

"Oh, shut up, Brittany," Sharon said. "He's only 2. He can't pick on you."

"Yes, he did," Brittany said, crossing her arms defiantly as she stretched out her foot to kick her brother's seat.

"Oh, no! How did Mikey get that smudge on his face? Did you do that, Brit?"

> *"Yes, he did," Brittany said, crossing her arms defiantly as she stretched out her foot to kick her brother's seat.*

Brittany crossed her arms again, pushing out her lips in her classic pouting pose.

As Sharon drove to the day care center, she tried to calm herself. "Only two more days of work this week, and then the weekend. Then I can catch up on housework and have a little relaxed time with the kids. And Tom can finally cut the grass and buy the groceries," she thought. "And maybe we'll even have time to make love. Boy, that's been a long time."

At a traffic light, Sharon found time to read Tom's note. "Oh, no. That's what he meant. He has to work Saturday. Well, there go those plans."

What Sharon didn't know was that her boss also had made plans for Sharon's Saturday. And that their emergency Saturday babysitter wouldn't be available. And that the van would break down on the way home from work. That Michael was coming down with chicken pox. That Brittany would follow next. That . . .

T hat there isn't enough time to get everything done is a common complaint of most of us. But it is especially true for working parents of young children, who find themselves without the support systems taken for granted just a generation ago: stay-at-home moms who were the center of the neighborhood, a husband whose sole income was enough to support a wife and several children, a safe neighborhood where even small children could play outside, and a grandma who could pitch in during emergencies.

Those days are gone forever. Today, more and more families are like Sharon and Tom's. They are harried, pressured, working more and seemingly making less, and, certainly, having less time for one another—and for their children. In this chapter, we shall try to understand what is happening to the U.S. family, and to families worldwide.

Marriage and Family in Global Perspective

T o better understand U.S. patterns of marriage and family, let's first sketch a cross-cultural portrait. The perspective it yields will give us a context for interpreting our own experience in this vital social institution.

What Is a Family?

"What is a family, anyway?" asked William Sayres (1992) at the beginning of an article on this topic. By this question, he meant that although the family is so significant to humanity that it is universal—every human group in the world organizes its members in families—the world's cultures display so much variety that the term

■ Often one of the strongest family bonds is that of mother and daughter. The young artist of this painting, an eleventh grader, wrote: "This painting expresses the way I feel about my future with my child. I want my child to be happy and I want her to love me the same way I love her. In that way we will have a good relationship so that nobody will be able to take us apart. I wanted this picture to be alive, that is why I used a lot of bright colors."

family is difficult to define. For example, although the Western world regards a family as a husband, wife, and children, other groups have family forms in which men have more than one wife (**polygyny**) or women more than one husband (**polyandry**). (See the photo on the next page.) How about the obvious? Can we define the family as the approved group into which children are born? This would overlook the Banaro of New Guinea. In this group, a young woman must give birth before she can marry—and she *cannot* marry the father of her child (Murdock 1949).

And so it goes. For just about every element you might regard as essential to marriage or family, some group has a different custom. Consider the sex of the bride and groom. Although in almost every instance the bride and groom are female and male, there are exceptions. In some Native American tribes, a man or woman who wanted to be a member of the opposite sex went through a ceremony (*berdache*) and was *declared* a member of the opposite sex. From then on, not only did the "new" man or woman do the tasks associated with his or her new sex, but also the individual was allowed to marry. In this instance, the husband and wife were of the same biological sex. In the contemporary world, Denmark (in 1989), Norway (in 1993), Sweden (in 1995), and Holland (in 1998) have legalized same-sex marriages.

Even to say that the family is the unit in which children are disciplined and that parents are responsible for their material needs is not universally true. Among the Trobriand Islanders, the wife's eldest brother is responsible for making certain that his sister's children have food and for disciplining them when they get out of line (Malinowski 1927). Finally, even sexual relationships don't universally characterize a husband and wife. The Nayar of Malabar never allow a bride and groom to have sex. After a three-day celebration of the marriage, they send the groom packing—and never allow him to see his bride again (La Barre 1954). (In case you're wondering, the groom comes from another tribe. Nayar women are allowed to have sex, but only with approved lovers—who can never be the husband. This system keeps family property intact—along matrilineal lines.)

Such remarkable variety means that we have to settle for a broad definition. A **family** consists of people who consider themselves related by blood, marriage, or adoption. A **household,** in contrast, consists of people who occupy the same housing unit—a house, apartment, or other living quarters.

polygyny
a form of marriage in which men have more than one wife

polyandry
a form of marriage in which women have more than one husband

family
two or more people who consider themselves related by blood, marriage, or adoption

household
people who occupy the same housing unit

■ *Polygyny is outlawed in the United States. It also violates contemporary Mormon teaching. About 30,000 men who claim to be Mormons, but who are rejected by the Mormon church, still practice polygyny. Shown here is Tom Green from Snake Valley, Utah, with his five wives and some of their 29 children. A couple of his wives were pregnant when this photo was taken. Green was put in prison for violating Utah's polygamy laws and for marrying one of his wives when she was just 13 years old.*

nuclear family
a family consisting of a husband, wife, and child(ren)

extended family
a nuclear family plus other relatives, such as grandparents, uncles and aunts, who live together

family of orientation
the family in which a person grows up

family of procreation
the family formed when a couple's first child is born

marriage
a group's approved mating arrangements, usually marked by a ritual of some sort

endogamy
the practice of marrying within one's own group

exogamy
the practice of marrying outside one's group

incest taboo
the rule that prohibits sex and marriage among designated relatives

We can classify families as **nuclear** (husband, wife, and children) and **extended** (including people such as grandparents, aunts, uncles, and cousins in addition to the nuclear unit). Sociologists also refer to the **family of orientation** (the family in which an individual grows up) and the **family of procreation** (the family formed when a couple have their first child). Finally, regardless of its form, **marriage** can be viewed as a group's approved mating arrangements—usually marked by a ritual of some sort (the wedding) to indicate the couple's new public status.

■ Common Cultural Themes

Despite this diversity, several common themes do run through marriage and family. As Table 16.1 illustrates, all societies use marriage and family to establish patterns of mate selection, descent, inheritance, and authority. Let's look at these patterns.

Mate Selection   Each human group establishes norms to govern who marries whom. Norms of **endogamy** specify that people should marry *within* their own group. Groups may prohibit interracial marriage, for example. In contrast, norms of **exogamy** specify that people must marry *outside* their group. The best example is the **incest taboo,** which prohibits sex and marriage among designated relatives. In some societies, these norms are written into law, but in most cases they are informal. In the United States most whites marry whites and most African Americans marry African Americans—not because of any laws but because of informal norms.

Descent   How are you related to your father's father or to your mother's mother? The explanation is found in your society's **system of descent,** the way people trace

TABLE 16.1

Common Cultural Themes: Marriage in Traditional and Industrialized Societies

Characteristic	Traditional Societies	Industrialized (and Postindustrialized) Societies
What is the structure of marriage?	*Extended* (marriage embeds spouses in a large kinship network of explicit obligations)	*Nuclear* (marriage brings fewer obligations toward the spouse's relatives)
What are the functions of marriage?	Encompassing (see the six functions listed on p. 473)	More limited (many functions are fulfilled by other social institutions)
Who holds authority?	Highly *patriarchal* (authority is held by males)	Although some patriarchal features remain, authority is more evenly divided
How many spouses at one time?	Most have one spouse (*monogamy*), while some have several (*polygamy*)	One spouse
Who selects the spouse?	The spouse is selected by the parents, usually the father	Individuals choose their own spouse
Where does the couple live?	Couples most commonly reside with the groom's family (*patrilocal residence*), less commonly with the bride's family (*matrilocal residence*)	Couples establish a new home (*neolocal residence*)
How is descent figured?	Most commonly figured from male ancestors (*patrilineal* kinship), less commonly from female ancestors (*matrilineal* kinship)	Figured from male and female ancestors equally (*bilateral kinship*)
How is inheritance figured?	Rigid system of rules; usually patrilineal, but may be matrilineal	Highly individualistic; usually bilateral

kinship over generations. To us, a **bilateral system** seems natural—for we think of ourselves as related to *both* our mother's and our father's side of the family. "Doesn't everyone?" you might ask. Interestingly, this is only one logical way to reckon descent. In a **patrilineal system,** descent is traced only on the father's side, and children are not considered related to their mother's relatives. In a **matrilineal system,** descent is figured only on the mother's side, and children are not considered related to their father's relatives. The Naxi of China, for example, don't even have a word for father (Hong 1999).

Inheritance Marriage and family—in whatever form is customary in a society—are also used to compute rights of inheritance. In the bilateral system, property is passed to both males and females, in the patrilineal system only to males, and in the matrilineal system (the rarest form) only to females. Each system matches a people's ideas of justice and logic.

Authority Historically, some form of **patriarchy,** a social system in which men dominate women, has formed a thread that runs through all societies. Contrary to what many think, there are no historical records of a true **matriarchy,** a social system in which women as a group dominate men as a group. Our marriage and family customs, then, developed within a framework of patriarchy. Although U.S. family patterns are becoming more **egalitarian,** or equal, many of today's customs still point to their patriarchal origin. Naming patterns, for example, reflect patriarchy. Despite some changes, the typical bride still takes the groom's last name, and children usually receive the father's last name. For information on a society that systematically promotes equality in marriage, see the Cultural Diversity box on the next page.

system of descent
how kinship is traced over the generations

bilateral (system of descent) a system of reckoning descent that counts both the mother's and the father's side

patrilineal (system of descent) a system of reckoning descent that counts only the father's side

matrilineal (system of descent) a system of reckoning descent that counts only the mother's side

patriarchy
authority vested in males; male control of a society or group

matriarchy
authority vested in females; female control of a society or group

egalitarian
authority more or less equally divided between people or groups, in this instance between husband and wife

Around the World

Promoting Gender Equality: Family Life in Sweden

Swedish lawmakers hold a strong image of what good family life is. That image centers on equality in marriage and on the welfare of children. Lawmakers bolster this image with laws designed to put women and men on equal footing in marriage, to give mothers and fathers equal responsibility for the home and children, and to protect the financially weaker party in the event of divorce.

At the center of family laws is the welfare of children. Health care for mothers and children, for example, is free. This includes obstetric care and all health care during pregnancy. Maternity centers offer free health checks and courses in preparation for childbirth. Fathers are encouraged to attend the childbirth classes.

When a child is born, the parents are eligible for fifteen months' leave of absence with pay. Both cannot receive compensation at the same time; the parents decide how they will split the fifteen months between them. For the first twelve months the state pays 90 percent of gross income, and then a generous fixed rate for the remaining three months. The paid leave does not have to be taken all at once, but can be spread over eight years. The parents can stay at home full time, or they can work part time for a longer period. Because most mothers take all the leave, the law now includes a "father's month," one month that cannot be transferred to the mother.

The government also guarantees other benefits. When a child is born, the father is entitled to ten days leave of absence with full pay. When a child is sick, either parent can care for the child and receive full pay for missed work—up to sixty days a year per child. Moreover, by law local governments must offer child care. And if a husband becomes violent or threatens his wife, the woman can have a security alarm installed in their home free of charge.

Swedish divorce laws have been drawn up with an eye to what is considered best for the child. Local governments are required to provide free counseling to any parent who requests it. If both parties agree and if they have no children under the age of 16, a couple is automatically entitled to a divorce. Otherwise the law requires a six-month cooling-off period so parents can more calmly consider what is best for their children. Joint custody of children is automatic, unless one of the parents opposes it. The children must live with only one of the parents. The parent who does not live with the children is required to pay child support in proportion to his or her finances. If the parent fails to do so, the social security system makes the payments.

for your consideration

How does the Swedish system compare with that of the United States? What "system" for watching out for the welfare of children does the United States have, anyway?

Sources: Based on The Swedish Institute 1992; Froman 1994; Bernhardt and Goldscheider 2001.

Marriage and Family in Theoretical Perspective

A global perspective reveals that human groups have chosen many forms of mate selection, numerous ways to trace descent, and so on. Although these patterns are arbitrary, each group sees its own forms of marriage and family as natural. Now let's see what picture emerges when we apply the three sociological perspectives.

■ The Functionalist Perspective: Functions and Dysfunctions

Functionalists stress that to survive, a society must meet certain basic needs, or functions. When functionalists look at family, they examine how it is related to other parts of society, especially how the family contributes to the well-being of society.

Why the Family Is Universal Functionalists note that although the form of marriage and family varies from one group to another, the family is universal because it fulfills six needs that are basic to the survival of every society. As described on pages 28–29, these needs, or functions, are (1) economic production, (2) socialization of children, (3) care of the sick and aged, (4) recreation, (5) sexual control, and (6) reproduction. To make certain that these functions are performed, every human group adopted some form of the family.

Functions of the Incest Taboo Functionalists note that the incest taboo helps families avoid *role confusion*. This, in turn, facilitates the socialization of children. For example, if father-daughter incest were allowed, how should a wife treat her daughter—as a daughter, as a subservient second wife, or even as a rival? Should the daughter consider her mother as a mother, as the first wife, or as a rival? Would her father be a father or a lover? And would the wife be the husband's main wife, a secondary wife—or even the "mother of the other wife" (whatever role that might be)? Maternal incest would also lead to complications every bit as confusing as these.

The incest taboo also forces people to look outside the family for marriage partners. Anthropologists theorize that *exogamy* was especially functional in tribal societies, for it forged alliances between tribes that otherwise might have killed each other off. Today, exogamy extends a bride's and groom's social networks beyond their nuclear family by building relationships with their spouse's family.

Isolation and Emotional Overload Functionalists also analyze dysfunctions that arise from the relative isolation of the nuclear family. Unlike extended families, which are enmeshed in kinship networks, members of nuclear families can count on fewer people for material and emotional support. This makes nuclear families vulnerable to "emotional overload." That is, the stress that comes with crises such as the loss of a job—or even the routine pressures of a harried life, as depicted in our opening vignette—is spread among fewer people. This places greater strain on each family member. In addition, the relative isolation of the nuclear family makes it vulnerable to a "dark side"—incest and various other forms of abuse, matters we examine later in this chapter.

■ The Conflict Perspective: Gender and Power

As you recall, central to conflict theory is the struggle over scarce resources. The recurring struggle over who does housework is actually a struggle over limited resources—time, energy, and the leisure to pursue interesting activities.

The Power Struggle Over Housework Most men resist doing housework. As Figure 16.1 shows, even wives who work outside the home full time end up doing much more housework than their husbands. The lesser effort that husbands make seems such a strain to them, however, that even when his wife does almost all the

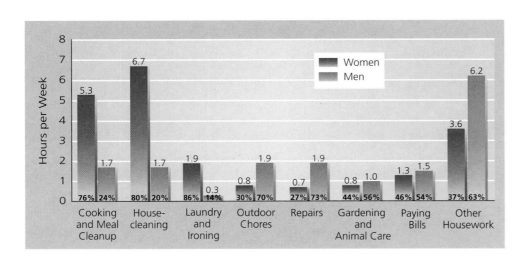

Figure 16.1

In Two-Paycheck Marriages, Who Does the Housework?

Note: Based on a national sample. Cooking and meal cleanup are combined from the original data.

Source: Bianchi et al. 2000.

cooking and cleaning, the husband is likely to see himself as splitting the work fifty-fifty (Galinsky et al. 1993). Things are so one-sided that wives are *eight* times more likely than husbands to feel that the division of housework is unfair (Sanchez 1994).

And no wonder. Wives who put in an eight-hour day of working for wages average eleven hours more child care and housework each week than their husbands do (Bianchi and Spain 1996). *Incredibly, this is the equivalent of twenty-four 24-hour days a year.* Sociologist Arlie Hochschild (1989) calls this the working wife's "second shift." To stress the one-sided nature of the second shift, she quotes this satire by Garry Trudeau in the *Doonesbury* comic strip:

> A "liberated" father is sitting at his word processor writing a book about raising his child. He types: "Today I wake up with a heavy day of work ahead of me. As Joannie gets Jeffry ready for day care, I ask her if I can be relieved of my usual household responsibilities for the day. Joannie says, 'Sure, I'll make up the five minutes somewhere.' "

Not surprisingly, the burden of the second shift creates deep discontent among wives (Risman 1998). These problems, as well as how wives and husbands cope with them, are discussed in the following Thinking Critically section.

thinking
CRITICALLY

The Second Shift—Strains and Strategies

To find out what life is like in two-paycheck marriages, for nine years sociologist Arlie Hochschild (1989) and her research associates interviewed and reinterviewed over fifty families. Hochschild also did participant observation with a dozen of them. She "shopped with them, visited friends, watched television, ate with them, and came along when they took their children to day care."

Although men are doing more housework today than they did just a few years ago (Bianchi et al. 2000), most feel that the *second shift*—the household duties that follow the day's work for pay—is the wife's responsibility. But as the wives cook, clean, and take care of the children after their job at the office or factory, many feel tired and emotionally drained. Some pride themselves on being the "supermom" who can do it all, but most just grit their teeth and bear it, doing the extra work, but resenting it. Not uncommonly, these feelings show up in the bedroom, where the wives show a lack of interest in sex.

The strains from working the second shift affect not only the marital relationship, but also the wife's self-concept. Here is how one woman tried to lift her flagging self-esteem:

> After taking time off for her first baby, Carol Alston felt depressed, "fat," and that she was "just a housewife." For a while she became the supermarket shopper who wanted to call down the aisles, "I'm an MBA! I'm an MBA!"

To pick up more of the burden, some husbands cut down on their commitment to a career. Others cut back on movies, seeing friends, doing hobbies. Most men, however, engage in "strategies of resistance." Hochschild identified the following:

■ *Waiting it out.* Many men never volunteer to do housework. Since many wives dislike asking, because it feels like "begging," this strategy often works. Some men make this strategy even more effective by showing irritation or becoming glum when they are asked, which discourages the wife from asking again.

■ *Playing dumb.* When they do housework, some men become incompetent. They can't cook rice without burning it; when they go to the store, they forget grocery lists; they never can remember where the broiler pan is. Hochschild did not claim that husbands do these things on purpose, but, rather, by withdrawing their mental attention from the task, they "get credit for trying and being a good sport"—but in such a way that they are not chosen next time.

■ *Needs reduction.* An example of this strategy is the father of two who explained that he never shopped because he didn't "need anything." He didn't need to iron his clothes because he "[didn't] mind wearing a wrinkled shirt." He didn't need to cook because "cereal is fine." As Hochschild observed, "Through his reduction of needs, this man created a great void into which his wife stepped with her 'greater need' to see him wear an ironed shirt . . . and cook his dinner."

■ *Substitute offerings.* Expressing appreciation to the wife for being so organized that she can handle both work for wages and the second shift at home can be a substitute for helping—and a subtle encouragement for her to keep on working the second shift.

■ ■ ■ ■ ■

for your consideration . . .

Hochschild (1991) is confident that the problem of the second shift can be resolved. Based on the materials just presented

1. Identify the underlying *structural* causes of the problem of the second shift.

2. Based on your answer to number 1, identify *structural* solutions to this problem.

3. Determine how a working wife and husband might best reconcile the issues of the second shift.

■ The Symbolic Interactionist Perspective: Gender and the Meanings of Marriage

As noted in Chapter 1, symbolic interactionists focus on the meanings that people give to their lives. Let's apply this perspective to some surprising findings about husbands and housework.

ARLO & JANIS ® by Jimmy Johnson

■ *The cartoonist has beautifully captured the reduction of needs strategy discussed by Hochschild.*

The first finding is probably what you expect—the closer a husband's and wife's earnings, the more likely they are to share housework. Although husbands in such marriages don't share housework equally, they share more than other husbands. This finding, however, may be surprising: When husbands get laid off, most *decrease* their housework. *And husbands who earn less than their wives do the least housework.*

How can we explain this? It would seem that husbands who get laid off or who earn less than their wives would want to balance things out by doing more around the house, not less. Researchers suggest that the key is *gender role*. If a wife earns more than her husband, it threatens his masculinity—he takes this as a sign that he has failed in his traditional role of provider. To do housework—"women's work" in his eyes—threatens his masculinity even further. By avoiding housework, he "reclaims" his masculinity (Hochschild 1989; Brines 1994).

The Family Life Cycle

We have seen how the forms of marriage and family vary widely, and we have examined marriage and family from the three sociological perspectives. Now let's discuss love, courtship, and the family life cycle.

Love and Courtship in Global Perspective

Until recently, social scientists thought that romantic love originated in western Europe during the medieval period (Mount 1992). When anthropologists William Jankowiak and Edward Fischer (1992) surveyed the data available on 166 societies around the world, however, they found that this was not so. **Romantic love**—people being sexually attracted to one another and idealizing the other—showed up in 88 percent of these groups. The role of love, however, differs sharply from one society to another. As the Cultural Diversity box on the next page details, for example, Indians don't expect love to occur until *after* marriage—if then.

Because love plays such a significant role in Western life—and often is thought to be the *only* proper basis for marriage—social scientists have probed this concept with the tools of the trade: experiments, questionnaires, interviews, and observations. In a fascinating experiment, psychologists Donald Dutton and Arthur Aron discovered that fear breeds love (Rubin 1985). Here's what they did. About 230 feet above the Capilano River in North Vancouver, British Columbia, a rickety footbridge sways in the wind. It makes you feel like you won't make it across, that you might fall into the rocky gorge below. A more solid footbridge crosses only ten feet above a shallow stream. The experimenters had an attractive woman approach men who were crossing these bridges. She told them she was studying "the effects of exposure to scenic attractions on creative expression." She

romantic love
feelings of erotic attraction accompanied by an idealization of the other

■ Romantic love *reaches far back into history, as illustrated by this Etruscan sarcophagus. The Etruscans, reaching their peak of civilization in 500 B.C. in what is now Italy, were vanquished by Rome about one hundred years later. The artist has portrayed the couple's mutual affection and satisfaction.*

Around the World

East Is East and West Is West...
Love and Arranged Marriage in India

After Arun Bharat Ram returned to India with a degree from the University of Michigan, his mother announced that she wanted to find him a wife. Arun would be a good "catch" anywhere: 27 years old, educated, well mannered, intelligent, handsome—and, not incidentally, heir to a huge fortune.

Arun's mother already had someone in mind. Manju came from a solid, middle-class family and was also a college graduate. Arun and Manju met in a coffee shop at a luxury hotel—along with both sets of parents. He found her pretty and quiet. He liked that. She was impressed that he didn't boast about his background.

After four more meetings, one where the two young people met by themselves, the parents asked their children if they were willing to marry. Neither had any major objections.

The Prime Minister of India and fifteen hundred other guests came to the wedding.

"I didn't love him," Manju says. "But when we talked, we had a lot in common." She then adds, "But now I couldn't live without him. I've never thought of another man since I met him."

Although India has undergone extensive social change, Indian sociologists estimate that parents still arrange about 95 percent of marriages. Today, however, as with Arun and Manju, couples have veto power over their parents' selection. Another innovation is that the couple are allowed to talk to each other before the wedding—unheard of just a generation ago.

Why do Indians have arranged marriages? And why does this practice persist today, even among the educated and upper classes? We can also ask why the United States has such an individualistic approach to marriage.

To answer these questions takes us to a basic sociological principle: *A group's marriage practices match its values and its patterns of social stratification.* Individual mate selection matches U.S. values of individuality and independence, while arranged marriages match Indian values of children deferring to parental authority. Arranged marriages also reaffirm caste lines by channeling marriage within the same caste.

To Indians, allowing unrestricted dating would be to entrust important matters to inexperienced young people. It also would encourage premarital sex, which, in turn, would break down family lines. (Virginity at marriage assures the upper castes that they know the fatherhood of the children.) Consequently, Indians socialize their children to think that parents have superior wisdom in these matters. In the United States, family lines are less important, and caste is an alien concept.

Even ideas of love differ. For Indians, love is a peaceful emotion, based on long-term commitment and devotion to family. Indians also think of love as something that can be "created" between two people. To do so, one needs to arrange the right conditions. Marriage is one of those right conditions.

These different backgrounds have produced contrasting approaches to love and marriage. *For Indians, marriage produces love—while for Americans, love produces marriage.* Americans see love as having a mysterious element, a passion that suddenly seizes an individual. Indians see love as a peaceful feeling that develops when a man and a woman are united in intimacy and share common interests and goals in life.

for your consideration

What advantages do you see to the Indian approach to love and marriage? Could you see the Indian system working in the United States? Why or why not? Do you think that love can be created? Or does love suddenly "seize" people? What do you think love is?

Sources: Based on Gupta 1979; Bumiller 1992; Sprecher and Chandak 1992; Whyte 1992; Dugger 1998; Sampat 1999.

showed them a picture, and they wrote down their associations. The sexual imagery in their stories showed that the men on the unsteady, frightening bridge were more sexually aroused than the men on the solid bridge. More of these men also called the young woman afterward—supposedly to get information about the study.

You may have noticed that this research was really about sexual attraction, not love. The point, however, is that romantic love usually begins with sexual attraction. Finding ourselves sexually attracted to someone, we spend time with that person. If we discover mutual interests, we may label our feelings "love." Apparently, then, romantic love has two components. The first is emotional, a feeling of sexual attraction. The second is cognitive, a label that we attach to our feelings. If we attach this label, we describe ourselves as being "in love."

Marriage

In the typical case, marriage in the United States is preceded by "love," but, contrary to folklore, whatever love is, it certainly is not blind. That is, love does not hit people willy-nilly, as if Cupid had shot darts blindly into a crowd. If it did, marital patterns would be unpredictable. An examination of who marries whom, however, reveals that love is socially channeled.

The Social Channels of Love and Marriage   When we marry, we generally think that we have freely chosen our spouse. With few exceptions, however, our choices follow highly predictable social channels, especially age, education, social class, race, and religion. For example, a Latina with a college degree whose parents are both physicians is likely to fall in love with and marry a Latino slightly older than herself who has graduated from college. Similarly, a girl who drops out of high school and whose parents are on welfare is likely to fall in love with and marry a man who comes from a background similar to hers.

Sociologists use the term **homogamy** to refer to the tendency of people who have similar characteristics to marry one another. Homogamy occurs largely as a result of *propinquity,* or spatial nearness. That is, we tend to "fall in love" and marry people who live near us or whom we meet at school, church, or work. The people with whom we associate are far from a random sample of the population, for social filters produce neighborhoods, schools, and churches that follow racial-ethnic and social class lines.

As with all social patterns, there are exceptions. Although 94 percent of Americans who marry choose someone of their same racial background, 6 percent do not. Because there are 59 million married couples in the United States, those 6 percent add up, totaling three and a half million couples.

One of the more dramatic changes in U.S. marriage is a sharp increase in interracial marriages. We can trace this change back to the norm-shattering 1960s. Among the many changes ushered in during this period was a breaking of the "color line" in courtship. As you can see from Figure 16.2, interracial marriages also show distinct patterns.

Childbirth

The popular image is that the arrival of a baby makes a couple deliriously happy. The facts are somewhat different.

Marital Satisfaction   Sociologist Martin Whyte (1992), who interviewed wives in the Detroit area, found that marital satisfaction usually *decreases* with the birth of a child (Whyte 1992; Bird 1997). To understand why, recall from Chapter 6 that a dyad (just two persons) provides greater intimacy than a triad (after adding a third person, interaction must be shared). To move from the theoretical to the practical, think about the implications for marriage of coping with a fragile newborn's 24-hour-a-day needs of being fed, soothed, and diapered—while having less sleep and heavier expenses.

Social Class   Sociologist Lillian Rubin (1976, 1992b) compared fifty working-class couples with twenty-five middle-class couples. She found that social class made a significant difference in how couples adjust to the arrival of children. For the average working-class couple, the first baby arrived just nine months after marriage. They hardly had time to adjust to being husband and wife before they were thrust into the demanding roles of mother and father. The result was financial problems, bickering, and interference from in-laws. The young husbands weren't ready to "settle down," and they resented getting less attention from their wives. A working-class husband who became a father just five months after getting married made a telling remark to Rubin when he said, "There I was, just a kid myself, and I finally had someone to

Figure **16.2**

The Racial Background of Husbands and Wives in Marriages Between Whites and African Americans

Source: Statistical Abstract 2000: Table 54.

homogamy
the tendency of people with similar characteristics to marry one another

take care of me. Then suddenly, I had to take care of a kid, and she was too busy with him *to take care of me*" (italics added).

In contrast, the middle-class couples postponed the birth of their first child, which gave them more time to adjust to each other. On average, their first baby arrived three years after marriage. Their greater financial resources also worked in their favor, making life a lot easier and marriage more pleasant.

■ Child Rearing

Who's minding the kids while the parents are at work? A while back such a question would have been ridiculous, for the mother was at home taking care of the children. As with Sharon in our opening vignette, however, that assumption no longer holds. With three of five U.S. mothers working for wages, who is taking care of the children?

Married Couples and Single Mothers   Figure 16.3 compares the child care arrangements of married couples and single mothers. As you can see, their overall

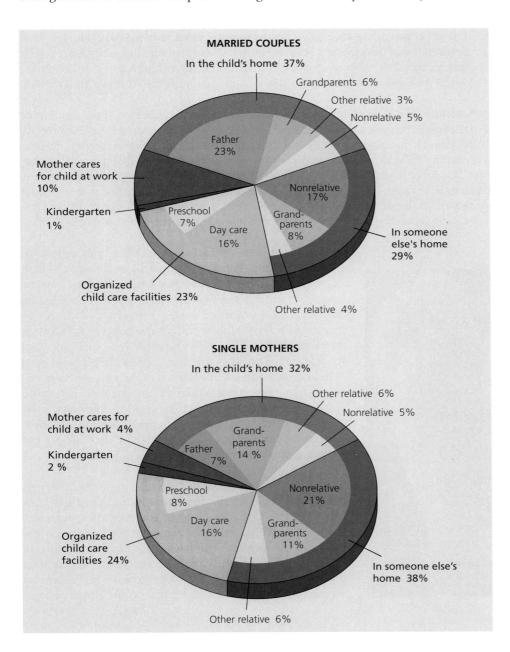

Figure 16.3
Who Takes Care of Preschoolers While Their Mothers Are at Work?
Source: O'Connell 1993.

child care arrangements are similar. For each group, about one of three preschoolers is cared for in the child's home. The main difference is the role of the child's father while the mother is at work. For married couples, almost one of four children is cared for by the father, while for single mothers this plummets to only one of fourteen. As you can see, grandparents step in to help fill the gap left by the absent father.

Day Care   As Figure 16.3 shows, about one of six children is in day care. The broad conclusions of research on day care were reported in Chapter 3 (page 83). Apparently only a minority of U.S. day care centers offer high-quality care as measured by stimulating learning activities, safety, and emotional warmth (Bergmann 1995; Blau 2000). A primary reason for this dismal situation is the abysmal salaries paid to day care workers, which average $10,000 a year (Casper and O'Connell 1997; *Statistical Abstract* 2000:Table 1300).

It is difficult for parents to judge the quality of day care, since they don't know what takes place when they are not there. Two factors, however, best predict that children will receive quality care: staff who have had training in early childhood development and a small number of children assigned to each day care worker (Blau 2000). The Internet is providing an innovative solution to some parents' nagging fears that their children might be neglected or even abused. Closed circuit television cameras pipe images onto the Web. Parents at work can visit each room of the day care center via cyberspace, and thus monitor their toddler's activities and care (Rabinovitz 1998).

Nannies   For upper-middle-class parents, nannies have become popular. Part of their attraction is one-on-one care. Another reason is that they provide in-home care, which reduces the chances of a child catching illnesses and eliminates the need to transport the child to an unfamiliar environment. A recurring problem is tensions between the parents and the nanny: jealousy that the nanny may be the one to see the first step, hear the first word, or be called mommy; different discipline styles; disdain on the part of the nanny that the mother isn't staying home with her child; and the child crying when the nanny leaves, but not when the mother goes to work.

■ No adequate substitute has been found for the family. Although its form and functions vary around the world, the family remains the primary socializer of children.

Social Class   Social class makes a huge difference in child rearing. As noted on page 82, sociologist Melvin Kohn found that parents socialize their children into the norms of their work worlds. Because members of the working class are more closely supervised and are expected to follow explicit rules, their concern is less with their children's motivation and more with their outward conformity. Thus they are more apt to use physical punishment. In contrast, middle-class parents, who are expected to take more initiative on the job, are more concerned that their children develop curiosity, self-expression, and self-control. They are also more likely to withdraw privileges or affection than they are to use physical punishment.

Birth Order   Birth order is also important. Parents tend to discipline their firstborns more than their later children, and to give them more attention. When the second child arrives, the firstborn competes to remain the focus of attention. Researchers suggest that this instills in firstborns a greater drive for success, which is why they are more likely than their siblings to earn higher grades in school, to go to college, and to go further in college.

Firstborns are even more likely to become astronauts, to appear on the cover of *Time* magazine, and to become president of the United States. Although subsequent children may not go as far, most are less anxious about being successful, and more relaxed in their relationships (Snow et al. 1981; Goleman 1985; Storfer 2000). Firstborns are also more likely to defend the status quo and to support conservative causes, later-borns to upset the apple cart and to support liberal causes (Sulloway 1997).

Although such tendencies are strong, they are only that—tendencies. Firstborns can be liberal, for example, or even conservative on some issues and liberal on others (Freese et al. 1999). *There are no inevitable outcomes of birth order, social class, or any other social characteristic.*

■ The Family in Later Life

The later stages of family life bring their own pleasures to be savored and problems to be solved. Let's look at the empty nest, retirement, and widowhood.

The Empty Nest   When the last child leaves home, the husband and wife are left, as at the beginning of their marriage, "alone together." This situation, sometimes called the **empty nest,** is thought to signal a difficult time of adjustment for women, because they have devoted so much energy to a child-rearing role that is now gone. Sociologist Lillian Rubin (1992a), who interviewed both career women and home-makers, found that this picture is largely a myth. Contrary to the stereotype, she found that women's satisfaction generally *increases* when the last child leaves home. A typical statement was made by a 45-year-old woman, who leaned forward in her chair as though to tell Rubin a secret:

> To tell you the truth, most of the time it's a big relief to be free of them, finally. I suppose that's awful to say. But you know what, most of the women I know feel the same way. It's just that they're uncomfortable saying it because there's all this talk about how sad mothers are supposed to be when the kids leave home.

Similar findings have come from other researchers, who report that most mothers feel relieved at being able to spend more time on themselves. Many couples also report a renewed sense of intimacy at this time (Mackey and O'Brien 1995). This closeness appears to stem from four causes: The couple is free of the many responsibilities of child rearing, they have more leisure, their income is at its highest, and they have fewer financial obligations.

The Not-So-Empty Nest   An interesting twist on leaving home has taken place in recent years. With prolonged education and the high cost of establishing a household, U.S. children are leaving home later. In addition, many who strike out on their own find the cost or responsibility too great and return to the home nest. As a result, 42 percent of all U.S. 24- to 29-year-olds are still living with their parents (*Statistical Abstract* 2000:Tables 12, 70).

Widowhood   Women are more likely than men to become widowed and to have to face the wrenching problems this entails. Not only does the average wife live longer than her husband, but also she has married a man older than herself. The death of a spouse tears at the self, clawing at identities that had merged through the years. Now that the one who had become an essential part of the self is gone, the survivor, as in adolescence, is forced once again to wrestle with the perplexing question "Who am I?"

When death is unexpected, the adjustment is more difficult (Hiltz 1989). Survivors who know that death is impending make preparations that smooth the transition—from arranging finances to psychologically preparing themselves for being alone. Saying goodbye and cultivating treasured last memories help them to adjust to the death of an intimate companion.

empty nest
a married couple's domestic situation after the last child has left home

Diversity in U.S. Families

It is important to note that there is no such thing as *the* American family. Rather, family life varies widely throughout the United States. The significance of social class, noted earlier, will continue to be evident as we examine diversity in U.S. families.

■ African American Families

Note that the heading reads African American *families*, not *the* African American family. There is no such thing as *the* African American family any more than there is *the* white family or *the* Latino family. The primary distinction is not between African Americans and other groups, but between social classes. Because African Americans who are members of the upper class follow the class interests reviewed in Chapter 10—preservation of privilege and family fortune—they are especially concerned about the family background of those whom their children marry (Gatewood 1990). To them, marriage is viewed as a merger of family lines. Children of this class marry later than children of other classes.

Middle-class African American families focus on achievement and respectability. Both husband and wife are likely to work outside the home. A central concern is that their children go to college, get good jobs, and marry well—that is, marry people like themselves, respectable and hardworking, who want to get ahead in school and pursue a successful career.

African American families in poverty face all the problems that cluster around poverty (Wilson 1987, 1996; Anderson 2001). Because the men are likely to have few skills and to be unemployed, it is difficult for them to fulfill the cultural roles of husband and father. Consequently, these families are likely to be headed by a woman and to have a high rate of births to single women. Divorce and desertion are also more common than among other classes. Sharing scarce resources and "stretching kinship" are primary survival mechanisms. That is, people who have helped out in hard times are considered brothers, sisters, or cousins to whom one owes obligations as though they were blood relatives (Stack 1974). Sociologists use the term *fictive kin* to refer to this stretching of kinship.

From Figure 16.4, you can see that, compared with other groups, African American families are the least likely to be headed by married couples and the most likely

■ There is no such thing as the African American family, any more than there is the Native American, Asian American, Latino, or Irish American family. Rather, each racial-ethnic group has different types of families, with the primary determinant being social class.

This African American family is observing Kwanzaa, a relatively new festival, that celebrates African heritage. Can you explain how Kwanzaa is an example of *ethnic work*, a concept introduced in Chapter 9?

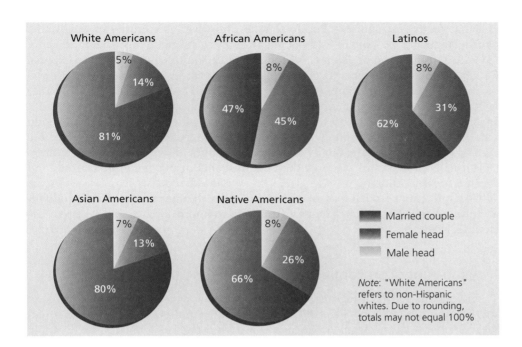

Figure 16.4

Family Structure:
The Percentage of
U.S. Households Headed
by Men, Women, and
Married Couples
Source: Statistical Abstract 2000:
Tables 41, 42, 44, 45.

to be headed by women. Because of a *marriage squeeze*—an imbalance in the sex ratio, in this instance fewer unmarried men per 1,000 unmarried women—African American women are more likely than other racial-ethnic groups to marry men who are less educated than themselves (South 1991).

■ Latino Families

As Figure 16.4 shows, the proportion of Latino families headed by married couples and women falls in between that of whites and that of African Americans. The effects of social class on families, which I just sketched, also apply to Latinos. In addition, families differ by country of origin. Families from Cuba, for example, are more likely to be headed by a married couple than are families from Puerto Rico (*Statistical Abstract* 2000:Table 45).

■ *Although there is no such thing as the Latino family, in general, Latinos place high emphasis on extended family relationships.*

What really distinguishes Latino families, however, is culture—especially the Spanish language, the Roman Catholic religion, and a strong family orientation coupled with a disapproval of divorce. Although there is some debate among the experts, another characteristic seems to be **machismo**—an emphasis on male strength and dominance. In Chicano families (those originating from Mexico), the husband-father plays a stronger role than in either white or African American families (Vega 1990). Machismo apparently decreases with each generation in the United States (Hurtado et al. 1992; Wood 2001). The wife-mother, however, generally makes most of the day-to-day decisions for the family and does the routine disciplining of the children. She is usually more family centered than her husband, displaying more warmth and affection for her children.

Generalizations have limits, of course, and as with other ethnic groups, individual Latino families vary considerably from one to another (Baca Zinn 1994; Carrasquillo 1994).

■ Asian American Families

As you can see from Figure 16.4 on the previous page, the structure of Asian American families is almost identical to that of white families. Apart from this broad characteristic, because Asian Americans come from twenty countries, their family life varies considerably, reflecting their many cultures. In addition, as with Latino families, the more recent their immigration, the more closely their family life reflects the family life of their country of origin (Kibria 1993; Glenn 1994).

Despite such differences, sociologist Bob Suzuki (1985), who studied Chinese American and Japanese American families, identified several distinctive characteristics. Although Asian Americans have adopted the nuclear family, they have retained Confucian values that provide a distinct framework for family life: humanism, collectivity, self-discipline, hierarchy, respect for the elderly, moderation, and obligation. Obligation means that each individual owes respect to other family members and is responsible for never bringing shame on the family. Asian Americans tend to be more permissive than Anglos in child rearing and more likely to use shame and guilt rather than physical punishment to control their children's behavior.

■ Native American Families

Perhaps the single most significant issue that Native American families face is whether to follow traditional values or to assimilate into the dominant culture (Yellowbird and Snipp 1994; Garrett 1999). This primary distinction creates vast differences among families. The traditionals speak native languages and emphasize distinctive Native American values and beliefs. Those that have assimilated into the broader culture do not.

Figure 16.4 depicts the structure of Native American families. You can see how close it is to that of Latinos. In general, Native American parents are permissive with their children and avoid physical punishment. Elders play a much more active role in their children's families than they do in most U.S. families: They not only provide child care, but also they teach and discipline children. Like others, Native American families differ by social class.

■ *To search for the Native American family would be fruitless. There are rural, urban, single-parent, extended, nuclear, rich, poor, traditional, and assimilated Native American families, to name just a few. Shown here is an Apache family in Whiteriver, Arizona. You may want to consider the man's clothing in light of the Mass Media box on page 53.*

From this brief review, you can see that race-ethnicity signifies little for understanding family life. Rather, social class and culture hold the keys. The more resources a family has, the more it assumes the characteristics of a middle-class nuclear family. Compared with the poor, middle-class families have fewer children and fewer unmarried mothers, and place greater emphasis on educational achievement and deferred gratification.

■ One-Parent Families

One-parent families have become a matter of general concern. They are discussed by TV talk show hosts and politicians alike. Figure 16.5 shows how the percentage of U.S. children who live with both parents has dropped, going from 85 percent in 1970 to 68 percent today. Two primary reasons underlie this change. The first is the high divorce rate, which each year forces a million children from two-parent homes to one-parent homes (*Statistical Abstract* 1999:Table 159). The second is the increase in births to women who are not married. Overall, 33 percent of U.S. children are born to unmarried women (*Statistical Abstract* 2000:Table 85). With the divorce rate stabilizing, we can expect the number of children who live with only one parent to stop increasing (O'Hare 2001).

The primary reason for the concern, however, may have less to do with children being reared by one parent and more to do with most one-parent families being poor. The poverty is not a coincidence. Most one-parent families are headed by women. Although 90 percent of children of divorce live with their mothers, most divorced women earn less than their former husbands. And most mothers who have never married have little education and few marketable skills. They are condemned to bouncing from one minimum-wage job to another, with welfare sandwiched in between.

To understand the typical one-parent family, then, we need to view it through the lens of poverty, for that is its primary source of strain. The results are serious, not just for these parents and their children, but for society as a whole. Children from single-parent families are more likely to drop out of school, to get arrested, to have emotional problems, and to get divorced (McLanahan and Sandefur 1994; Menaghan et al. 1997). If female, they are more likely to bear children while still unmarried teenagers. The cycle of poverty is so powerful that *nearly half* of all welfare recipients are current or former teenage parents (Corbett 1995).

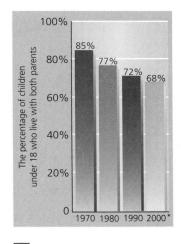

Figure 16.5

The Decline in Two-Parent Families

*The author's estimate. Year 1998 is 68%.

Source: Statistical Abstract 1995: Table 79; 2000:Table 69.

■ Families Without Children

Overall, about 14 percent of U.S. married couples never have children (*Statistical Abstract* 2000:Table 95). The percentage differs by education. As Figure 16.6 on the next page shows, the more education a woman has, the more likely she is to expect to bear no children. This figure shows that race-ethnicity is also significant. As you can see, Latinas are much less likely to expect to remain childless than are white and African American women.

Why do some couples choose not to have children? The main reason is a sense of freedom—to be able to change jobs or to have more spontaneity in their lives (Lunneborg 1999). Some avoid children so they will have more money, others to bypass stress. Some simply do not like children. Many seek a spouse who shares their view about remaining childless, or as they prefer to call it, childfree. Some women see their marriage as too fragile to withstand the strains a child would bring. Others

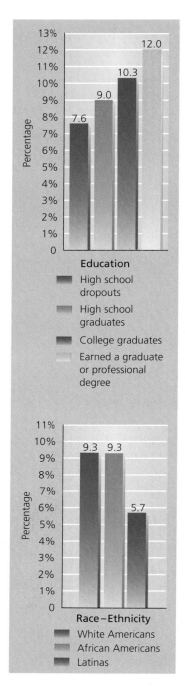

blended family
a family whose members were once part of other families

believe they would be stuck at home—bored, lonely, and with diminishing career opportunities (Gerson 1985). The most common reason, though, is summarized by this statement in a newsletter:

> We are DINKS (dual incomes, no kids). We are happily married. I am 43, my wife is 42. We have been married for almost twenty years. . . . Our investment strategy has a lot to do with our personal philosophy: "You can have kids—or you can have everything else!"

With trends firmly in place—more education and careers for women; legal abortion; technological advances in contraception; the high cost of rearing children; and an emphasis on possessing more and more materials things—the proportion of women who never bear children is likely to increase.

Many childless couples, however, are not childless by choice. Some adopt, while a few turn to the solutions featured in the Sociology and New Technology box on the next page.

■ Blended Families

An increasingly significant type of family in the United States is the **blended family,** one whose members were once part of other families. Two divorced people who marry and each bring their children into a new family unit become a blended family. With divorce common, millions of children spend some of their childhood in blended families. One result is more complicated family relationships. Consider this description written by one of my students:

> I live with my dad. I should say that I live with my dad, my brother (whose mother and father are also my mother and father), my half sister (whose father is my dad, but whose mother is my father's last wife), and two stepbrothers and stepsisters (children of my father's current wife). My father's wife (my current stepmother, not to be confused with his second wife who, I guess, is no longer my stepmother) is pregnant, and soon we all will have a new brother or sister. Or will it be a half brother or half sister?
>
> If you can't figure this out, I don't blame you. I have trouble myself. It gets very complicated around Christmas. Should we all stay together? Split up and go to several other homes? Who do we buy gifts for, anyway?

■ Gay and Lesbian Families

In 1989, Denmark became the first country to legalize marriage between people of the same sex. Since then, Holland, Norway, and Sweden have made same-sex marriages legal. In 2000, Vermont became the first state to legalize what they call "gay unions." Except for the name, "gay unions" are marriages. Partners are treated as married couples for purposes of inheritance, property transfers, medical decisions, insurance, and state income taxes. If they want to split up, they must go through "dissolution" proceedings in Family Court. By retaining the term "marriage" for heterosexual couples, Vermont hoped to soften criticism of its pathbreaking law. This didn't work, and across the state Vermonters protested. If other states follow Vermont's lead, it seems inevitable that some will use the term marriage to refer to same-sex unions.

Gay and lesbian families are not evenly distributed throughout the United States. Rather, they are highly urban, with about half concentrated in just 20 cities. The greatest concentrations are in San Francisco, Los Angeles, Atlanta, New York City, and Washington, D.C. About one-fifth of gay and lesbian couples were previously married to heterosexuals. Twenty-two percent of lesbian couples and 5 percent of gay couples have children (Bianchi and Casper 2000).

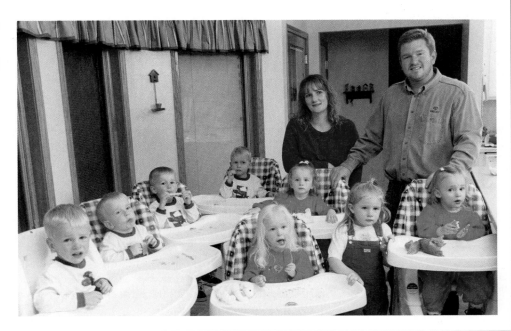

The Brave New World of High-Tech Reproduction: Where Technology Outpaces Law and Sometimes Common Sense

Jaycee has five parents—or none, depending on how you look at it. The story goes like this. Luanne and John Buzzanca were infertile. Although they spent more than $100,000 on treatments, nothing worked. Then a fertility clinic mixed a man's sperm with a woman's egg. Both the man and the woman remained anonymous. A surgeon implanted the fertilized egg in Pamela Snell, who gave birth to Jaycee (Davis 1998a; Foote 1998).

Her job as surrogate mother completed, Pamela handed Jaycee over to Luanne, who was waiting at her beside. Luanne's husband, John, would have been there, but he had filed for divorce just a month before.

Luanne asked John for child support. John refused, and Luanne sued. The judge ruled that John didn't have to pay. He said that because Jaycee had been conceived in a petri dish with an egg and sperm from anonymous donors, John wasn't the baby's father. The judge added that Luanne wasn't the baby's mother either.

Five parents—or none? Welcome to the brave—and very real—new world of high-tech reproduction. Although most children conceived with the aid of high-tech procedures claim only two parents, reproductive technologies have made such scenarios a nightmare for the unsuspecting.

for your consideration

In our new, high-tech world, what is a mother? Is Pamela Snell, who gave birth to Jaycee, a mother? Strangely, she is not. Is the donor of the egg a mother? Biologically, yes, but legally, no. Is Luanne a mother? Fortunately, for Jaycee's sake, a higher court ruled that she is.

What is a father? Consider this case. Elizabeth Higgins of Jacksonville, Indiana, had difficulty conceiving. She gave eggs to Memorial Hospital. Her husband gave sperm. A hospital technician mistakenly mixed someone else's sperm with Mrs. Higgins' eggs. The fertilized eggs were implanted in Mrs. Higgins, who gave birth to twin girls. Mrs. Higgins is white, her husband black. Mr. Higgins was bothered because the girls had only Caucasian features, and he couldn't bond with them. Mr. and Mrs. Higgins separated. They sued the hospital for child support, arguing that the hospital, not Mr. Higgins, is the father (Davis 1998b).

If a hospital can be a father in this brave new world, then what's a grandparent? A man in New Orleans donated sperm to a fertility clinic. He died, and his girlfriend decided to be artificially inseminated with his sperm. The grieved parents of the man were upset that their son, although dead, could still father children. They also feared that those children, who would be their grandchildren, would have a legal claim to their estate (Davis 1998b).

How would you apply common sense to these many cases?

■ The McCaughey septuplets of Carlisle, Iowa, with their parents, Bobby and Kenny, and their 6 year-old sister, Mikayla.

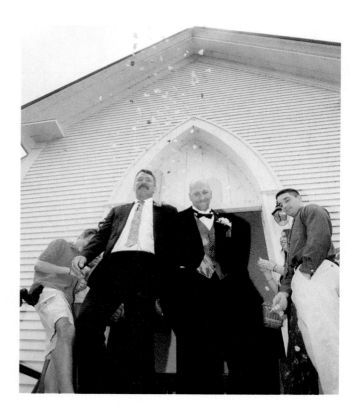

■ *With same-sex marriages now legal in several European countries, how long will it be until they are legal in the United States? Shown here is the first couple to be united under Vermont's pathbreaking "civil union" law.*

What are gay marriages like? Like everything else in life, same-sex couples cannot be painted with a single brush stroke. As with heterosexual couples, social class is significant, and orientations to life differ with education, occupation, and income. Sociologists Blumstein and Schwartz (1985) interviewed same-sex couples and found their main struggles to be housework, money, careers, problems with relatives, and sexual adjustment—the same problems that face heterosexual couples. Same-sex couples are more likely to break up, however, and one argument for legalizing gay marriages is that these relationships will become more stable.

Trends in U.S. Families

As is apparent from this discussion, patterns of marriage and family life in the United States are undergoing a fundamental shift. Other indicators of this change, which we shall now examine, include the postponement of marriage, cohabitation, single motherhood, divorce, and remarriage.

■ Postponing Marriage

Figure 16.7 illustrates one of the most significant trends in U.S. marriage. As you can see, the average age of first-time brides and grooms declined from 1890 to about 1950. In 1890 the typical first-time bride was 22, but by 1950 she had just left her teens. For about twenty years, there was little change. Then in 1970 the average age started to increase sharply. *Today's average first-time bride and groom are older than at any time in U.S. history.*

cohabitation
unmarried couples living together in a sexual relationship

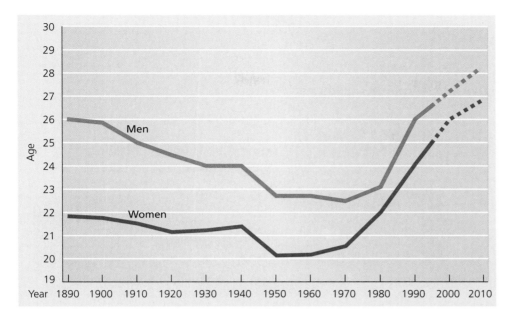

Figure 16.7

The Median Age at Which Americans Marry for the First Time

Note: The broken lines indicate the author's estimate.
Source: Statistical Abstract 1999:Table 158.

Figure 16.8

**Americans Ages 20–24
Who Have Never Married**
*Author's estimate.
Source: Statistical Abstract* 1993:
Table 60; 2000:Table 55.

Since postponing marriage is today's norm, it may come as a surprise to many readers to learn that *most* U.S. women used to marry before they turned 25. Look at Figure 16.8. You can see that the percentage of younger Americans who have not married has soared. The percentage of unmarried women of this age is now *double* what it was in 1970.

Why did this change occur? A sharp increase in cohabitation is a good part of the reason. Although Americans have postponed the age at which they first marry, they have *not* postponed the age at which they first set up housekeeping with someone of the opposite sex. Let's look at this trend in cohabitation.

■ Cohabitation

Figure 16.9 shows the remarkable increase in **cohabitation,** adults living together in a sexual relationship without being married. It is important to grasp what a significant change this figure represents. Cohabitation is *eight times* more common today than it was 30 years ago. Half of the couples who marry today have lived together before marriage. A generation ago, it was 8 percent (Bianchi and Casper 2000). This broad change in behavior has changed attitudes. For example, when hiring executives, some corporations now pay for live-in partners to attend orientation sessions.

Commitment is the essential difference between cohabitation and marriage. In marriage, the assumption is permanence; in cohabitation, couples agree to remain together for "as long as it works out." For marriage, individuals make public vows that legally bind them as a couple; for cohabitation, they simply move in together. Marriage requires a judge to authorize its termination; if a cohabiting relationship sours, the couple separate and tell their friends that it didn't work out. Perhaps the single statement that pinpoints the difference in commitment is this: Cohabiters are less likely than married couples to have a joint bank account (Brines and Joyner 1999). The Down-to-Earth Sociology box on the next page discusses cohabitation and commitment in greater detail.

Broken line indicates author's estimate

Figure 16.9

**Cohabitation in the
United States**
Source: Statistical Abstract 1995:
Table 60; 2000:Table 57.

■ ■ ■ ■ ■

"What Do You Mean You Want Us to Live Together?"

One of the most remarkable statistics in sociology is the rapid increase of cohabitation in the United States. Hardly any statistic shows such a sharp upward curve as that depicted in Figure 16.9. This increase in cohabitation is directly related to two fundamental changes in U.S. culture.

The first is changed ideas of sexual morality. It is difficult for today's college students to grasp the sexual morality of those who came of age before the 1960s sexual revolution. At that time, most people considered sex before marriage to be immoral. It existed, to be sure, but furtively, and often with guilt. To live together before marriage was called "shacking up," and the couple was thought to be "living in sin." A double standard operated. It was the woman's responsibility to say no to sex before marriage. Consequently, she was considered to be the especially sinful one in cohabitation.

The second cultural change is the sharp increase in the U.S. divorce rate. Throughout the twentieth century, the rate of divorce increased in the United States. Although the rate has now leveled off and even dropped somewhat, it remains at almost the highest level in U.S. history. Youth who reach adulthood today are more likely to have seen their parents divorce than any generation that came before them. This makes marriage seem like a fragile thing, something that requires great commitment, although it is not likely to last regardless of what you put into it. This is scary, threatening. Cohabitation reduces the fear and threat by offering a relationship of intimacy without the long-term commitment of marriage.

From the outside, all cohabitation may look the same. And certainly cohabitation has common features, especially that of an unmarried man and woman living together in a sexual relationship. But sociologists have found essential differences in what cohabitation means for the couples. Table 16.2 shows the four types of cohabitation sociologists have identified. For about 10 percent of couples, cohabitation is a substi-

TABLE 16.2		Commitment in Cohabitation: Does It Make a Difference?				
			After 5 to 7 Years			
					Of Those Still Together	
Level of Commitment	*Percent of Couples*		*Split Up*	*Still Together*	*Married*	*Cohabiting*
Substitute for Marriage	10%		35%	65%	25%	40%
Step toward Marriage	46%		31%	69%	52%	17%
Trial Marriage	15%		51%	49%	28%	21%
Coresidential Dating	29%		46%	54%	33%	21%

Source: Bianchi and Casper 2000.

tute for marriage. These couples consider themselves married, but for some reason don't want a marriage certificate. Some object to marriage on philosophical grounds ("What difference does a piece of paper make?"); others do not yet have a legal divorce from a spouse. In the most common type of cohabitation, however—involving almost half of cohabiters—the couples view cohabitation as one of a series of steps on the path to marriage. For them, cohabitation is more than "going steady," but less than engagement. Another 15 percent of couples are simply "giving it a try." They want to see what marriage to one another might be like. For the least committed—about 29 percent, cohabitation is a form of dating. It provides a more dependable source of sex and some emotional support.

Do these distinctions make a difference? Let's look at these couples a half dozen years after they began to live together. As you can see from Table 16.2, couples who viewed cohabitation as a substitute for marriage are the least likely to marry and the most likely to still be cohabiting a few years later. For cou-

ples who saw cohabitation as a step toward marriage, the outcomes are just the opposite. These couples are the most likely to marry and the least likely to still be cohabiting. The outcomes for the couples who were "trying" cohabitation are about the same as for those for whom cohabitation was a form of steady dating. They both are the least likely to remain together.

for your consideration

Can you classify cohabiting couples you know into these four types? Do you think there are other types? If so, what would they be? The distinction between couples who see cohabitation as a step toward marriage and those who see it as a trial marriage is fuzzy. Based on your experiences, can you clarify this distinction? Finally, what functions does cohabitation serve?

■ ■ ■ ■ ■

Unmarried Mothers

Earlier we discussed the steady increase in births to single women in the United States. To better understand this trend, we can place it in global perspective. As Figure 16.10 shows, the United States is not alone in this increase. Of the ten industrialized nations for which we have data, all except Japan have experienced sharp increases in births to single women. The U.S. rate is far from the highest; it falls in the middle third of these nations.

From this figure, it seems fair to conclude that industrialization sets in motion social forces that encourage out-of-wedlock births. There are several problems with this conclusion, however. Why was the rate so low in 1960? Industrialization had been in process for many decades prior to that time. Why are the rates in the bottom four nations only a fraction of those in the top two nations? Why does Japan's rate remain so consistently low? Why are Sweden's and Denmark's so high? With only a couple of minor exceptions, the ranking of these nations today is the same as it was in 1960. By itself, then, industrialization is too simple an answer. A fuller explanation must focus on customs and values embedded within these cultures. For that answer, we will have to await further research.

Figure 16.10

Births to Unmarried Women in Ten Industrialized Nations
Note: The broken lines indicate the author's estimates.
Source: Statistical Abstract 1993: Table 1380; 1998:Table 1347.

The Sandwich Generation and Elder Care

The *sandwich generation* refers to people who find themselves sandwiched between two generations, responsible for both their children and their own aging parents. Typically between the ages of 40 and 55, these people find themselves pulled in two strongly compelling directions. Overwhelmed by two sets of competing responsibilities, they are plagued with guilt and anger because they can be only in one place at a time.

Concerns about elder care have gained the attention of the corporate world, and about 25 percent of large companies offer some kind of elder care assistance to their employees (Gardner 1998). This assistance includes seminars, referral services, and flexible work schedules designed to help employees meet their responsibilities without missing so much work (Shellenbarger 1994b). Some experts believe that companies may respond more positively to the issue of elder care than to child day care. Why? Most CEOs are older men whose wives stayed home to take care of their children, so they don't understand the stresses of balancing work and child care. Nearly all have aging parents, however, and many have faced the turmoil of trying to cope with work, family, and aging parents.

With people living longer, this issue is likely to become increasingly urgent.

Divorce and Remarriage

The topic of family life would not be complete without considering divorce. Let's first try to determine how much divorce there really is.

Problems in Measuring Divorce

You probably have heard that the U.S. divorce rate is 50 percent, a figure that is popular with reporters. The statistic is true in the sense that each year about half as many divorces are granted as there are marriages performed. Each year, there are about 2,360,000 marriages and 1,135,000 divorces in the United States ("Population Today" 2002).

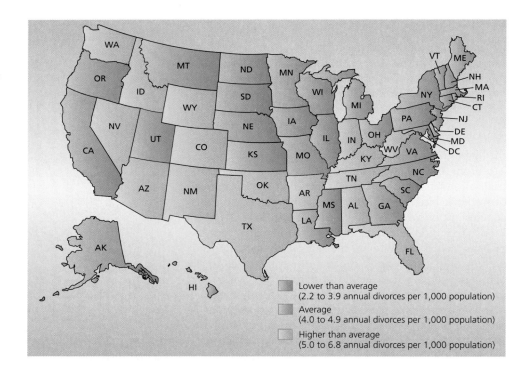

Figure 16.11

Social Map: The "Where" of U.S. Divorce

Note: Data for Indiana and Louisiana are from an earlier edition.

Source: Statistical Abstract 2000: Table 150.

    Lower than average
    (2.2 to 3.9 annual divorces per 1,000 population)

    Average
    (4.0 to 4.9 annual divorces per 1,000 population)

    Higher than average
    (5.0 to 6.8 annual divorces per 1,000 population)

With these statistics, what is wrong with saying that the divorce rate is 50 percent? The real question is why these two numbers should be compared in the first place. The couples who divorced do not—with rare exceptions—come from the group that married that year. The one number has *nothing* to do with the other, so these statistics in no way establish the divorce rate.

What figures should we compare, then? Couples who divorce are drawn from the entire group of married people in the country. Since the United States has 59,000,000 married couples, and only 1,135,000 of them obtained divorces in a year, the divorce rate is 1.9 percent, not 50 percent. A couple's chances of still being married at the end of a year are 98 percent—not bad odds—and certainly much better odds than the mass media would have us believe. As the Social Map above shows, however, the "odds," if we want to call them that, change depending on where you live.

Over time, of course, those annual 1.9 percentages add up. A third way of measuring divorce, then, is to ask, "Of all U.S. adults, what percentage are divorced?" Figure 16.12 answers this question. You can see that the divorce rate has risen among

Figure 16.12

What Percentage of Americans Are Divorced?

Source: Statistical Abstract 1995: Table 58; 2000:Table 53.

Only these racial-ethnic groups are listed. Years 2000 and 2010 are the author's estimate, based on totals for the late 1990s.

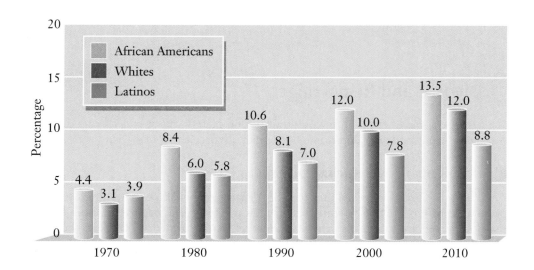

all the groups shown in this figure, but at a slower rate among Latinos. Again, a cross-cultural comparison helps to place U.S. statistics in perspective—but the news is not good. As Table 16.3 shows, the United States has—by far—the highest divorce rate in the industrialized world. If current trends persist, half or even more of all U.S. marriages may end in divorce (Stewart et al. 1997). But contrary forces are also at work, for the U.S. divorce rate peaked around 1980, and has declined since then.

The Down-to-Earth Sociology box below reports some "curious" findings about divorce, while factors that make marriage successful are summarized at the end of this chapter.

■ Children of Divorce

Each year, more than 1 million U.S. children learn that their parents are divorcing (*Statistical Abstract* 1999:Table 159). Most divorcing parents become so wrapped up in their own problems that they are unable to prepare their children for the divorce—even if they knew how to do so. When the break comes, children become confused and insecure. For security, many cling to the unrealistic idea that their parents will be reunited (Wallerstein and Kelly 1992). To help resolve the conflict, they may side with one parent and reject the other.

What are the effects of divorce on children? The children of divorce appear to have more hostility, anxiety, and nightmares, and to not do as well in school (Guidubaldi et al. 1987). The studies, however, generally compare children of divorce with children from average homes. The problem is that children whose parents divorce don't come from average homes. They come from conflict-ridden homes. The real question, then, is how children of divorce compare with children whose parents have high conflict but remain married. When sociologist Susan Jekielek (1998) made this comparison, she found that children whose parents divorce do slightly better emotionally than children who must live with their parents' conflict. Other research supports this finding (Stewart et al. 1997).

TABLE 16.3 Divorce Rates in Ten Industrialized Nations	1960	1970	1980	1990	1995[1]
United States	10	15	23	21	20
Denmark	6	8	11	13	12
Canada	2	6	10	11	11
Great Britain	2	5	12	13	13
Sweden	5	7	11	12	14
Germany	4	5	6	8	9
France	3	3	6	8	9
Netherlands	2	3	8	8	10
Japan	4	4	5	5	6
Italy	NA	1	1	2	2

[1]Latest year available.
Rates are per 1,000 women. Strangely, this is the only way the source presents them.
Source: Statistical Abstract 1992:Table 1364; 1998:Table 1346.

---

down-to-earth
s o c i o l o g y

You Be the Sociologist: Curious Divorce Patterns

Sociologists Alex Heckert, Thomas Nowak, and Kay Snyder (1995) did secondary analysis (see page 140) of data gathered from a nationally representative sample of 5,000 U.S. households. Here are three of their findings:

1. If a wife earns more than her husband, the marriage is more likely to break up; if a husband earns more than his wife, divorce is less likely.

2. If the wife's health is poorer than her husband's, the marriage is more likely to break up; if the husband's health is poorer than his wife's, divorce is less likely.

3. The more housework a wife does, the less likely a couple is to divorce.

Can you explain these findings? You be the sociologist. Please develop your own explanations before looking at the answers on the next page.

(continued)

■ ■ ■ ■ ■

You Be the Sociologist: Curious Divorce Patterns *(continued)*

What do the findings mean? Heckert, Nowak, and Snyder suggest these explanations:

1. A wife who earns more than her husband has more alternatives to an unsatisfying marriage; a wife who earns less is more dependent.

2. Social pressure is greater for a wife to take care of a husband in poor health than it is for a husband to take care of a wife in poor health.

3. Who does the most housework is an indication of a husband's

and wife's relative bargaining power. Wives with the most bargaining power are the least likely to put up with unsatisfying marriages.

■ ■ ■ ■ ■

What helps children adjust to divorce? Again, conflict is a crucial factor. Torn apart by a loyalty conflict, children whose parents continue to fight and want them to take sides do the worst (Stewart et al. 1997). Children who do the best are those who experience little conflict, feel loved, live with a parent who is making a good adjustment, and have consistent routines; in addition, the family has adequate money to meet its needs. Preliminary studies also indicate that adjustment is better if the child lives with the parent of the same sex (Lamb 1977; Clingempeel and Repucci 1982; Peterson and Zill 1986; Wallerstein and Kelly 1992). Children also adjust better if a second adult can be counted on for support (Hayashi and Strickland 1998). Urie Bronfenbrenner (1992) says this person makes the third leg of a stool, giving stability to the smaller family unit. Any adult can be the third leg, he says—a relative, friend, mother-in-law, or even co-worker—but the most powerful stabilizing third leg is the father, the ex-husband.

The effects of divorce follow children into adulthood. For example, compared with adults who grew up in intact families, grown-up children of divorced parents have less contact with either their father or their mother (Webster and Herzog 1995). They are also less likely to marry and more likely to divorce (Diekmann and Engel-

■ *It is difficult to capture the anguish of the children of divorce, but when I read these lines by the fourth-grader who drew these two pictures, my heart was touched:*

Me alone in the park . . .
All alone in the park.
My Dad and Mom are divorced
that's why I'm all alone.

This is me in the picture with my son.
We are taking a walk in the park.
I will never be like my father.
I will never divorce my wife and kid.

hardt 1999; Wallerstein, Lewis, and Kelly 2000; Amato 2001). How much difficulty they experience in relationships, however, depends mainly on how their mother adjusts to the divorce. Those whose mothers did not remarry, who remarried and then divorced again, or who interfered with the children's relationship with their father have the greatest difficulty in romance. In short, mothers who establish more stable intimate relationships after divorce build a more nourishing environment that helps their children learn to develop intimate relationships.

■ The Absent Father and Serial Fatherhood

With divorce common and with mothers usually granted custody of the children, a new fathering pattern has emerged. In this pattern, known as **serial fatherhood,** a divorced father maintains high contact with his children during the first year or two after the divorce. As the man develops a relationship with another woman, he begins to play a fathering role with the woman's children and reduces contact with his own children. With another breakup, this pattern may repeat. Only about one-sixth of children who live apart from their fathers see their dad as often as every week. Actually, *most* divorced fathers stop seeing their children altogether (Ahlburg and De Vita 1992; Furstenberg and Harris 1992; Seltzer 1994). Apparently, for many men, fatherhood has become a short-term commitment.

■ The Ex-Spouses

Anger, depression, and anxiety are common feelings at divorce. But so is relief. Women are more likely than men to feel that the divorce is giving them a "new chance" in life. A few couples manage to remain friends through it all—but they are the exception. The spouse who initiates the divorce usually gets over it sooner (Kelly 1992; Wang and Amato 2000).

Divorce does not necessarily mean the end of a couple's relationship. Some divorced couples maintain contact because of their children. For others, the "continuities," as sociologists call them, represent lingering attachments (Vaughan 1985; Masheter 1991). The former husband may help his former wife hang a picture and move furniture, or she may invite him over for a meal. Some couples even continue to make love after their divorce.

After divorce, a couple's cost of living increases—two homes, two utility bills, and so forth. But the financial impact is different for men and for women. Divorce usually brings greater economic hardship for women (Smock et al. 1999; Wang and Amato 2000). This is especially true for mothers of small children, whose standard of living drops about 37 percent (Seltzer 1994). The higher a woman's education, the better prepared she is to survive financially after the divorce (Dixon and Rettig 1994).

■ Remarriage

Despite the number of people who emerge from the divorce court swearing "Never again!" most do marry again. But they aren't remarrying as quickly as they used to. In the 1960s, the average woman remarried in about two years. Today she waits five years to remarry (*Statistical Abstract* 1999:Table 160). Comparable data are not available for men.

As Figure 16.13 shows, most divorced people marry other divorced people. You may be surprised that the women most likely to remarry are young mothers and those who have not graduated from high school (Glick and Lin 1986). Apparently women who are more educated and more independent (no children) can afford to be more selective. Men are more likely than women to remarry, perhaps because they have a larger pool of potential mates.

serial fatherhood
a pattern of parenting in which a father, after divorce, reduces contact with his own children, serves as a father to the children of the woman he marries or lives with, then ignores them after moving in with or marrying another woman; this pattern repeats

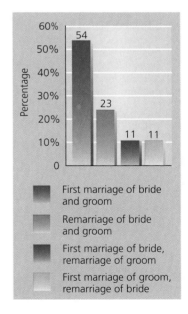

Figure 16.13

The Marital History of U.S. Brides and Grooms

Source: Statistical Abstract 2000: Table 145.

How do remarriages work out? The divorce rate of remarried people *without* children is the same as that of first marriages. Those who bring children into a new marriage, however, are more likely to divorce again (MacDonald and DeMaris 1995). The reason may be a lack of clear norms to follow (Coleman et al. 2000). As sociologist Andrew Cherlin (1989) notes, we lack satisfactory names for stepmothers, stepfathers, stepbrothers, stepsisters, stepaunts, stepuncles, stepcousins, and stepgrandparents. At the very least, these are awkward terms to use, but they also represent ill-defined relationships.

Two Sides of Family Life

Let's first look at situations in which marriage and family have gone seriously wrong and then try to answer the question of what makes marriage work.

The Dark Side of Family Life: Battering, Child Abuse, Marital Rape, and Incest

The dark side of family life involves events that people would rather keep in the dark. We shall look at battering, child abuse, rape, and incest.

Battering   To study spouse abuse, some sociologists have focused on just a few victims (Goetting 2001). Others have interviewed nationally representative samples of U.S. couples (Straus 1980; Straus, Gelles, and Steinmetz 1980; Straus and Gelles 1988; Straus 1992). Although not all sociologists agree (Dobash et al. 1992, 1993; Pagelow 1992), Murray Straus concludes that husbands and wives are about equally likely to attack one another. When it comes to the effects of violence, however, gender equality vanishes (Gelles 1980; Straus 1980, 1992). As Straus points out, even though *she* may throw the coffeepot first, it is generally *he* who lands the last and most damaging blow. Consequently, many more wives than husbands seek medical attention because of marital violence. A good part of the reason, of course, is that most husbands are bigger and stronger than their wives, putting women at a disadvantage in this literal battle of the sexes. The Down-to-Earth Sociology box on the next page discusses why some women remain with their abusive husbands.

Violence against women is related to the sexist structure of society, which we reviewed in Chapter 11, and to the socialization we reviewed in Chapter 3. Because they grew up with norms that encourage aggression and the use of violence, some men feel it is their right to control women. When frustrated in a relationship—or even by causes outside it—some men turn violent toward their wives and lovers. The basic sociological question is how to socialize males to handle frustration and disagreements without resorting to violence (Rieker et al. 1997). We do not yet have this answer.

Child Abuse

My wife and I answered an ad about a lakeside house in a middle-class neighborhood that was for sale by owner. As the woman showed us through the house, which was immaculate, we were surprised to see a plywood box in the youngest child's bedroom. About 3 feet high, 3 feet wide, and 6 feet long, the box was perforated with holes and had a little door with a padlock. Curious, I asked what it was. The woman replied matter-of-factly that her son had a behavior problem, and this was where they locked him for "time out." She added that other times they would tie him to a float, attach a line to the dock, and put him in the lake.

We left as soon as we could. With thoughts of a terrorized child filling my head, I called the state child abuse hotline.

▪ Due to the efforts of feminists, spouse battering has become a focus of national concern, the topic of a publicity-educational campaign, and the object of changed laws. Unlike the situation of just a few years ago, wife beating is no longer considered a private matter to be settled between married couples.

■ ■ ■ ■ ■

"Why Doesn't She Just Leave?" The Dilemma of Abused Women

"**W**hy would she ever put up with violence?" is the question on everyone's mind. From the outside, it looks so easy. Just pack up and leave. "I know I wouldn't put up with anything like that."

And yet this is not what typically happens. Women tend to stay with their men after they are abused. Some stay only a short while, to be sure, but others remain in abusive situations for years. Why?

Sociologist Ann Goetting (1999) asked this question, too. To get the answer, she interviewed women who had made the break. She wanted to find out what it was that set them apart. How were they able to leave, when so many women can't seem to? She found these characteristics in the women who made the break:

1. They had a positive self-concept.

Simply put, they believed that they deserved better.

2. They broke with traditional values.

They did not believe that a wife had to stay with her husband no matter what.

3. They found adequate finances.

For some this was easy, but for others it was not. To accumulate enough to get out, some of the women saved for years, putting back just a little each week.

4. They had supportive family and friends.

A support network served as a source of encouragement to help them rescue themselves.

If you take the opposite of these four characteristics, you have the answer to why some women put up with abuse: They don't think they deserve anything better, they believe it is their duty to stay, they don't think they can make it financially, and they lack a supportive network. These four factors are not of equal importance for all women, of course. For some, the lack of finances is the most significant, while for others it is their low self-concept. For all, the supportive network—or the lack of one—plays a significant role.

for your consideration

Based on these findings, what would you say to a woman whose husband abused her?

How do you think battered women's shelters fit into this explanation?

What other parts of this puzzle can you think of—such as the role of love?

■ ■ ■ ■ ■

As you can tell, what I saw upset me. Most of us are bothered by child abuse—helpless children being victimized by their own parents, the very adults who are supposed to love, protect, and nurture them. The most gruesome of these cases make the evening news: The 4-year-old girl who was beaten and raped by her mother's boyfriend, who passed into a coma and then three days later passed out of this life; the 6- to 10-year-old children whose stepfather videotaped them engaging in sex acts. Unlike these cases, which made headlines in my area, most child abuse is never brought to our attention: the children who live in filth, who are neglected—left alone for hours or even days at a time—or who are beaten with extension cords—cases like the little boy I learned about when I went house hunting.

We do know that child abuse is extensive. Each year, about 3 million U.S. children are reported to the authorities as victims of abuse or neglect. About 1 million of these cases are substantiated (*Statistical Abstract* 2000:Table 366).

Marital Rape   Sociologists have found that marital rape is more common than is usually supposed. For example, between one-third and one-half of women who seek help at shelters for battered women are victims of marital rape (Bergen 1996). But these women make up a special group; they are not representative of U.S. women. To get a better answer, sociologist Diana Russell (1990) used a sampling technique that allows generalization. She found that 14 percent of married women report that their husbands have raped them. Similarly, 10 percent of a representative sample of Boston women interviewed by sociologists David Finkelhor and Kersti Yllo (1985, 1989) reported that their husbands had used physical force to compel them to have sex. Compared with victims of rape by strangers or acquaintances, victims of marital rape are less likely to report the rape (Mahoney 1999).

Finkelhor's and Yllo's in-depth interviews with fifty victims showed that marital rape most commonly occurs during either separation or the breakup of a marriage. They found three types of marital rape.

Nonbattering rape (40 percent). The husband forces his wife to have sex but has no intention of hurting her physically. These instances generally involve conflict over sex, such as when the husband feels insulted because his wife refuses to have sex.

Battering rape (48 percent). In addition to sexually assaulting his wife, the husband intentionally inflicts physical pain to retaliate for some supposed wrongdoing on her part.

Perverted rape (6 percent). These husbands, who apparently are sexually aroused by the violent elements of rape, force their wives to submit to unusual sexual acts. Anger and hostility can also motivate this type of rape. (The remaining 6 percent are mixed, containing elements of more than one type.)

Incest   Sexual relations between certain relatives (for example, between brothers and sisters or between parents and children) constitute **incest.** Incest is most likely to occur in families that are socially isolated (Smith 1992). As with marital rape, sociological research has destroyed assumptions that incest is not common. Sociologist Diana Russell (n.d.) found that incest victims who experience the most difficulty are those who were victimized the most often, whose assaults occurred over longer periods of time, and whose incest was "more intrusive," for example, sexual intercourse as opposed to sexual touching.

Who are the offenders? Russell found that uncles are the most common offenders, followed by first cousins, fathers (stepfathers especially), brothers, and, finally, relatives ranging from brothers-in-law to stepgrandfathers. Other researchers report that brother-sister incest is several times more common than father-daughter incest (Canavan et al. 1992). Incest between mothers and sons is rare.

■ The Bright Side of Family Life: Successful Marriages

Successful Marriages   After examining divorce and family abuse, one could easily conclude that marriages seldom work out. This would be far from the truth, however, for about two of every three married Americans report that they are "very happy" with their marriages (Cherlin and Furstenberg 1988; Whyte 1992). To find out what makes marriage successful, sociologists Jeanette and Robert Lauer (1992) interviewed 351 couples who had been married fifteen years or longer. Fifty-one of these marriages were unhappy, but the couples stayed together for religious reasons, family tradition, or "for the sake of the children." Of the others, the 300 happy couples, all:

1. Think of their spouse as their best friend

2. Like their spouse as a person

3. Think of marriage as a long-term commitment

4. Believe that marriage is sacred

5. Agree with their spouse on aims and goals

6. Believe that their spouse has grown more interesting over the years

7. Strongly want the relationship to succeed

8. Laugh together

incest
sexual relations between specified relatives, such as brothers and sisters or parents and children

Sociologist Nicholas Stinnett (1992) used interviews and questionnaires to study 660 families from all regions of the United States and parts of South America. He found that happy families:

1. Spend a lot of time together

2. Are quick to express appreciation

3. Are committed to promoting one another's welfare

4. Do a lot of talking and listening to one another

5. Are religious

6. Deal with crises in a positive manner

Other sociologists have found that the better a couple gets along with their in-laws, the happier the marriage (Bryant et al. 2001).

Symbolic Interactionism and the Misuse of Statistics Many of my students express concerns about their own marital future, a wariness born out of the divorce of their parents, friends, neighbors, relatives—even their pastors and rabbis. They wonder about their chances of having a successful marriage. Because sociology is not just about abstract ideas, but is really about our lives, it is important to stress that we are individuals, not statistics. That is, if the divorce rate were 33 percent or 50 percent, this would *not* mean that if we marry, our chances of getting divorced are 33 percent or 50 percent. That is a misuse of statistics, and a common one at that. Divorce statistics represent all marriages and have absolutely *nothing* to do with any individual marriage. Our own chances depend on our unique situations—and especially the way we approach marriage.

To make this point clearer, let's apply symbolic interactionism. From a symbolic interactionist perspective, we create our own worlds. That is, our experiences don't come with built-in meanings. Rather, we interpret our experiences, and act accordingly. Simply put, if we think of our marriage as likely to fail, we increase the likelihood that it will fail; if we think that our marriage will work out well, the chances of a good marriage increase. In other words, we tend to act according to our ideas, creating a sort of self-fulfilling prophecy. For example, if we think our marriage may fail, we are more likely to run when things become difficult. The folk saying "There are no guarantees in life" is certainly true, but it does help to have a vision that a good marriage is possible and that it is worth achieving.

The Future of Marriage and Family

What can we expect of marriage and family in the future? Despite its many problems, marriage is in no danger of becoming a relic of the past. Marriage is so functional that it exists in every society. Consequently, the vast majority of Americans will continue to find marriage vital to their welfare.

Certain trends are firmly in place. Cohabitation, births to single women, and age at first marriage will increase. More married women will join the work force, and they will continue to gain marital power. Equality in marriage, however, is not even on the horizon. The number of elderly will continue to increase, and more couples will find themselves sandwiched between caring for their parents and rearing their own children. The reduction in our divorce rate is another matter entirely. We don't know how long our current plateau will last or if it will be followed by a higher or lower rate.

Finally, our culture will continue to be haunted by distorted images of marriage and family: the bleak ones portrayed in the mass media and the rosy ones painted by cultural myths. Sociological research can help correct these distortions and allow us to see how our own family experiences fit into the patterns of our culture. Sociological research can also help to answer the big question of how to formulate social policy that will support and enhance family life.

Summary and Review

Marriage and Family in Global Perspective

▪ What is a family—and what themes are universal?

Family is difficult to define. For just about every element one might consider essential, there are exceptions. Consequently, **family** is defined broadly—as people who consider themselves related by blood, marriage, or adoption. Sociologists and anthropologists have documented extensive variation in family customs—from cultures in which babies are married to those in which husbands and wives refrain from sexual relations for years at a time. Universally, **marriage** and family are mechanisms for governing mate selection, reckoning descent, and establishing inheritance and authority. Pp. 468–472.

Marriage and Family in Theoretical Perspective

▪ What is the functionalist perspective on marriage and family?

Functionalists examine the functions and dysfunctions of family life. Examples include the **incest taboo** and how weakened family functions increase divorce. Pp. 472–473.

▪ What is the conflict perspective on marriage and family?

Conflict theorists examine how marriage and family help perpetuate inequalities, especially the subservience of women. Power struggles in marriage, such as those over housework, are an example. Pp. 473–475.

▪ What is a symbolic interactionist perspective on marriage and family?

Symbolic interactionists examine how the contrasting experiences and perspectives of men and women are played out in marriage. They stress that only by grasping the perspectives of wives and husbands can we understand their behavior. Pp. 475–476.

The Family Life Cycle

▪ What are the major elements of the family life cycle?

The major elements are love and courtship, marriage, childbirth, child rearing, and the family in later life. Most mate selection follows predictable patterns of age, social class, race-ethnicity, and religion. Childbirth and child-rearing patterns also vary by social class. Pp. 476–481.

Diversity in U.S. Families

▪ How significant is race-ethnicity in family life?

The primary distinction is social class, not race or ethnicity. Families of the same social class are likely to be similar, regardless of their racial or ethnic makeup. Pp. 482–485.

▪ What other diversity in U.S. families is there?

Also discussed were one-parent, childless, **blended,** and gay and lesbian families. Each has its unique characteristics, but social class is significant in determining their primary characteristics. Poverty is especially significant for one-parent families, most of which are headed by women. Pp. 485–488.

Trends in U.S. Families

▪ What major changes characterize U.S. families?

Two changes are postponement of first marriage and an increase in **cohabitation.** With more people living longer, many middle-aged couples find themselves sandwiched between rearing their children and caring for their parents. Pp. 488–491.

Divorce and Remarriage

▪ What is the current divorce rate?

Depending on what figures you choose to compare, you can produce almost any rate you wish, from

75 percent to just 1.9 percent. However you figure it, the U.S. divorce rate is higher than any other industrialized nation. Pp. 491–493.

How do children and their parents adjust to divorce?

Divorce is difficult for children, whose adjustment problems often continue into adulthood. Most divorced fathers do not maintain ongoing relationships with their children. Financial problems are usually greater for the former wives. Although most divorced people remarry, their rate of remarriage has slowed considerably. Pp. 493–496.

Two Sides of Family Life

What are the two sides of family life?

The dark side is abuse—spouse battering, child abuse, marital rape, and **incest**, acts that revolve around the misuse of family power. The bright side is families that produce intense satisfaction for spouses and their children. Pp. 496–499.

The Future of Marriage and Family

What is the likely future of marriage and family?

We can expect cohabitation, births to single women, and age at first marriage to increase. The growing numbers of women in the work force are likely to continue to shift the marital balance of power. Pp. 499–500.

Where can I read more on this topic?

Suggested Readings for this chapter are at the back of this book.

Additional Online Resources for This Chapter
www.ablongman.com/henslin6e

- *Content Select* Research Database for Sociology, with suggested key terms and annotated references
- Link to 2000 Census, with activities
- Flashcards of key terms and concepts

- Practice Tests
- Weblinks
- Interactive Maps

using . . .
ContentSelect

Research Database for Sociology

absent fathers	cohabitation	incest	successful
blended family	divorce and	mate selection	marriage
children of divorce	remarriage	single mothers	

17

The Development of Modern Education

Education in Earlier Societies

Industrialization and Universal Education

Education in Global Perspective

Education in the Most Industrialized Nations: Japan

Education in the Industrializing Nations: Russia

Education in the Least Industrialized Nations: Egypt

The Functionalist Perspective: Providing Social Benefits

Teaching Knowledge and Skills

Cultural Transmission of Values

Social Integration

Gatekeeping

Replacing Family Functions

Other Functions

The Conflict Perspective: Reproducing the Social Class Structure

The Hidden Curriculum

Tilting the Tests: Discrimination by IQ

Stacking the Deck: Unequal Funding

The Correspondence Principle

The Bottom Line: Family Background and the Educational System

The Symbolic Interactionist Perspective: Fulfilling Teacher Expectations

The Rist Research

The Rosenthal-Jacobson Experiment

How Do Teacher Expectations Work?

Problems in U.S. Education—and Their Solutions

Problems: Mediocrity and Violence

Solutions: Retention, Safety, Standards, and Other Reforms

Summary and Review

Education

There wasn't much for teenagers to do in Littleton, Colorado. Not much happened in this quiet town of 35,000, a middle-class suburb southwest of Denver. Some of the high school kids liked to draw attention to themselves by wearing black trenchcoats and black shirts with swastikas. They called themselves the Trenchcoat Mafia and tossed around a few phrases in German.

"Just kids. They'll grow out of it," was the typical adult response. "We all went through something ourselves."

The Trenchcoat Mafia had their own table in the cafeteria and their group picture in the yearbook. The caption: "Who says we're different? Insanity's healthy. . . . Stay alive, stay different, stay crazy! Oh, and stay away from CREAM SODA!!"

Just another high school group: jocks, Goths, stoners, geeks, preppies. Every school has some.

The jocks despised the Trenchcoat Mafia. They threw them into lockers and called them scumbags, faggots, and inbreeds. They threw rocks and bottles at them from moving cars.

Two seniors, Eric Harris and Dylan Klebold, honors students and members of the Trenchcoat Mafia, talked about killing their classmates, especially the jocks. Eric even had his own Web page, where he described whom he wanted to kill and how he wanted to do it. As a class project, Eric and Dylan made a video in which they pretended to kill the classmates they didn't like. Just talk. But as the killing on *Doom,* the video game they loved, no longer satisfied,

As bombs went off and shots rang out, students ran in terror, cowering in closets and under tables.

the boys hatched a plan for real killing. It was risky. Maybe they would survive, maybe not. But if not, they would go out in a blaze of glory. Hitler's birthday would be perfect.

As bombs went off and shots rang out, students ran in terror, cowering in closets and under tables. Harris and Klebold went from room to room in search of victims. In the library, they found students hiding under a table. "Do you believe in God?" asked one of the shooters. "Yes," replied Cassie Bernall. "There is no God," the gunman retorted, as he placed a gun against her head and squeezed the trigger.

The boys killed twelve of their fellow students and one teacher before they turned their guns on themselves. They wounded twenty-three students.

—Based on Bai 1999; Gibbs 1999.

acculturation
the transmission of culture from one generation to the next

■ *Violence in U.S. schools has become a major concern of parents, the public, and politicians. Shown here is a scene outside Columbine High School in Littleton, Colorado, an upper-middle-class suburb of Denver, where two students went on a shooting rampage in 1999. They sought athletes, minorities, and Christians for victims. After wounding 23 students and killing 12 students and a teacher, the two killed themselves.*

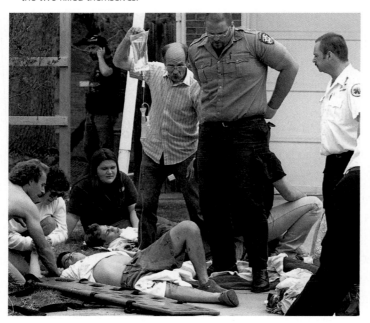

T he events at Columbine High School have been seared into the nation's consciousness. School shootings have confused just about everyone. No one has the full explanation for why they are occurring, or what we can do to prevent them. When we return to this topic, we are going to find a surprise, but, first, let's take a broad look at education.

The Development of Modern Education

W e shall look first at education in earlier societies, then trace the development of universal education.

■ Education in Earlier Societies

Earlier societies had no separate social institution called education. They had no special buildings called schools, and no people who earned their living as teachers. Rather, as an integral part of growing up, children learned what was necessary to get along in life. If hunting or cooking were the essential skills, then people who already possessed those skills taught them. *Education was synonymous with acculturation,* learning a culture. It still is in today's tribal groups.

In some societies, when a sufficient surplus developed—as in Arabia, China, North Africa, and classical Greece—a separate institution developed. Some people then devoted themselves to teaching, while those who had the leisure—the children of the wealthy—became their students. In ancient China, for example, Confucius taught a few select pupils, while in Greece, Aristotle, Plato, and Socrates

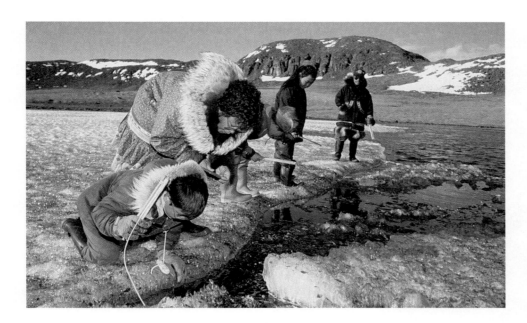

■ *In hunting and gathering societies, there is no separate social institution called* education. *As with this Eskimo child, children learn their adult economic roles from their parents and other kin.*

taught science and philosophy to upper-class boys. Education, then, came to be something quite distinct from informal acculturation. **Education** is a group's *formal* system of teaching knowledge, values, and skills. Such instruction stood in marked contrast to the learning of traditional skills such as farming or hunting, for it was intended to develop the mind.

Education, which flourished during the period roughly marked by the birth of Christ, slowly died out. During the Dark Ages of Europe, monks kept the candle of enlightenment burning. Except for a handful of the wealthy and some members of the nobility, only the monks could read and write. Although the monks delved into philosophy, they focused on learning Greek, Latin, and Hebrew so that they could study the Bible and writings of early church leaders. The Jews also kept formal learning alive as they studied the Torah.

Formal education remained limited to those who had the leisure to pursue it. (The word *school* comes from the Greek word σχωλή *[scholē]* meaning "leisure.") Industrialization transformed education, for the new machinery and new types of jobs meant that workers had to be able to read, to write, and to work accurately with figures—the classic three R's of the nineteenth century (Reading,'Riting, and 'Rithmetic).

■ Industrialization and Universal Education

After the American Revolution, the founders of the new republic were concerned that the country lacked unity, that its many religious and ethnic groups (nationalities) would make the nation unstable. To help create a uniform national culture, Thomas Jefferson and Noah Webster proposed universal schooling. Standardized texts would instill patriotism and teach the principles of representative government (Hellinger and Judd 1991). If this new political experiment were to succeed, they reasoned, it would need educated voters who are capable of making sound decisions. A national culture remained elusive, however, and in the 1800s the country remained politically fragmented. Many states even considered themselves to be near-sovereign nations.

Education reflected this disunity. There was no comprehensive school system, just a hodgepodge of independent schools. Public schools even charged tuition. Some Lutherans, Presbyterians, and Roman Catholics operated their own schools (Hellinger and Judd 1991). Children of the rich attended private schools. Children of the poor received no formal education—nor did slaves. High school was considered higher

education
a formal system of teaching knowledge, values, and skills

■ *This 1893 photo of a school in Hecla, Montana, taught by Miss Blanche Lamont, provides a glimpse into the past, when free public education, pioneered in the United States, was still in its infancy. In these one-room rural schools, a single teacher had charge of grades 1 to 8. Children were assigned a grade not by age but by mastery of subject matter. Occasionally, adults who wished to learn to read, to write, or to add and subtract would join the class. Attendance was sporadic, for the family's economic survival came first.*

mandatory education laws
laws that require all children to attend school until a specified age or until they complete a minimum grade in school

education (hence the name *high* school), and only the wealthy could afford it. College, too, was beyond the reach of almost everyone.

Horace Mann, an educator from Massachusetts, found this situation deplorable. Even the average family could not afford to send its children to grade school. In 1837 he proposed that "common schools," supported through taxes, be established throughout his state. Mann's idea spread, and state after state began to support free public education. It is no coincidence that universal education and industrialization occurred at the same time. Political and civic leaders saw that the economy was changing, and they recognized the need for an educated work force. They also feared the influx of foreign values and, like the founders of the country, looked on public education as a way to "Americanize" immigrants (Hellinger and Judd 1991).

By 1918, all U.S. states had **mandatory education laws** requiring children to attend school, usually until they had completed the eighth grade or turned 16, whichever came first. In the early 1900s, graduation from the eighth grade marked the end of education for most people. "Dropouts" at that time were students who did not complete grade school.

As industrialization progressed and as fewer people made their living from farming, formal education came to be thought of as essential to the well-being of society. As you can see from Figure 17.1, college graduation in the United States is now *twice* as common as high school graduation used to be. Sixty-six percent of all high school graduates enter college, the highest rate of any nation (*Statistical Abstract* 2000:Table 295).

One-fourth of Americans still don't make it through high school, however, which condemns most of them to a difficult economic life. As you can see from the Social Map on the next page, the rate of high school graduation is far from evenly distributed across the states. You may wish to compare the clustering of states on this Social Map with the one on page 297 that shows the distribution of poverty.

Figure 17.1

Educational Achievement in the United States

Note: Americans 25 years and over. Asterisk indicates author's estimate.

Source: National Center for Education Statistics, 1991:Table 8; *Statistical Abstract* 2000:Table 249.

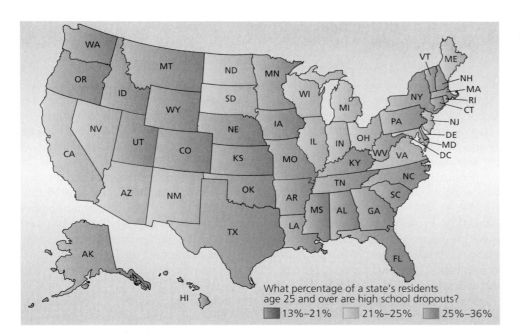

Figure 17.2

Social Map: Not Making It: Dropping Out of High School

Note: The states vary widely. The extremes range from 13.4 percent in Alaska to 35.7 percent in Mississippi.

Source: Statistical Abstract 2000: Table 253.

What percentage of a state's residents age 25 and over are high school dropouts?

■ 13%–21%   □ 21%–25%   ■ 25%–36%

Education in Global Perspective

To glimpse the variety of education around the world and to see how education is directly related to a nation's economy, let's look at education in three countries. Keep in mind that these are examples. No single nation represents the wide variety of education that characterizes these three levels of industrialization.

Education in the Most Industrialized Nations: Japan

A central sociological principle of education is that a nation's education reflects its culture. Because a core Japanese value is solidarity with the group, the Japanese discourage competition among individuals. Even in the work force, people who are hired together work as a team. They are not expected to compete with one another for promotions, but, instead, they are promoted as a group (Ouchi 1993). Japanese education reflects this group-centered ethic. Children in grade school work as a group, all mastering the same skills and materials. Teachers stress cooperation and respect for elders and others in positions of authority. By law, Japanese schools all use the same textbooks (Haynes and Chalker 1997).

In a fascinating cultural contradiction, college admissions procedures in Japan are highly competitive. Like the Scholastic Assessment Test (SAT) required of U.S. college-bound high school seniors, Japanese seniors who want to attend college must take a national test. Only the top scorers in Japan, however—rich and poor alike—are admitted to college. In contrast, even U.S. high school graduates who perform poorly on these tests can find some college to attend—as long as their parents can pay the tuition.

■ *The poverty of some of the Least Industrialized Nations defies the imagination of most people who have been reared in the industrialized world. Their educational systems are similarly marked by poverty. This photo shows an outdoor school in Hunza, Pakistan.*

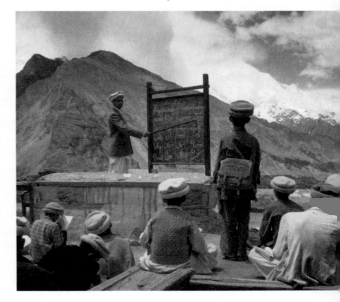

Education in the Industrializing Nations: Russia

After the Revolution of 1917, the Soviet Communist party attempted to upgrade the nation's educational system. At that time, as in most countries, education was limited to children of the elite. Following the sociological principle that education reflects culture, the new government made certain that socialist values dominated its schools, for it saw education as a means to undergird the new political system. As a result, schoolchildren were taught that capitalism was evil and that communism was the salvation of the world.

Education, including college, was free. Schools stressed mathematics and the natural sciences, and few courses in the social sciences were taught (Taylor and Mechitov 1994). Just as the economy was directed from central headquarters, so was education. With orders issued out of Moscow, schools throughout the country followed the same state-prescribed curriculum. All students in the same grade used the same textbooks. To prevent the development of thinking that might be contrary to communism, students memorized the materials and were discouraged from discussing them (Bridgman 1994).

Post-Soviet Russians are in the midst of "reinventing" education. For the first time, private, religious, and even foreign-run schools are allowed, and teachers can encourage students to question and to think for themselves. The problems that these Russians confronted are mind-boggling. Not only did they have to retrain tens of thousands of teachers who were used to teaching pat political answers, but also school budgets shrank, while inflation spiraled upward. Teachers stampeded out of education into fields that, with the new capitalism, paid many times what teachers were earning.

Because it is true of education everywhere, we can safely predict that Russia will develop an educational system that reflects its culture. This system will glorify its historical exploits and reinforce its values and world views. One difficulty for Russians at this point is that their values and world views are changing rapidly. The transition to capitalism is transforming basic ideas about profit and private property—and their educational system is destined to reflect those changed values.

Education in the Least Industrialized Nations: Egypt

Education in the Least Industrialized Nations stands in sharp contrast to that in the industrialized world. Even if the Least Industrialized Nations have mandatory attendance laws, they are not enforced. Because most of their people work the land or take care of families, they find little need for education. In addition, most of these nations simply cannot afford extensive formal education. As we saw from Figure 9.2 (pages 262–263), most people in the Least Industrialized Nations live on less than $1,000 a year. Consequently, in some nations most children do not go to school beyond the first couple of grades. Figure 17.3 contrasts education in China and the United States. As was once common around the globe, it is primarily the wealthy in the Least Industrialized Nations who have the means and the leisure for formal education—especially anything beyond the basics. As an example, let's look at education in Egypt.

Several centuries before the birth of Christ, Egypt's world-renowned centers of learning produced such acclaimed scientists as Archimedes and Eukleides. The primary areas of study during this classic period were physics, astronomy, geometry, geography, mathematics, philosophy, and medicine. The largest library in the world was at Alexandria. Fragments from the papyrus manuscripts of this library, which burned to the ground, have been invaluable in deciphering ancient manuscripts. After Egypt suffered defeat in war, however, education declined, never again to rise to its former prominence.

WHO IN CHINA AND THE UNITED STATES GOES TO:

China / United States

97% / 100%
Grade School

40% / 99%
Junior High School

12% / 90%
High School

4% / 75%
College and Post-High School Specialized Education

Figure 17.3

Education in a Most Industrialized (Postindustrial) Nation and a Least Industrialized Nation

Note: These are initial attendance rates, not completion rates. The U.S. junior high school total is the author's estimate.

Source: Brauchli 1994.

Although the Egyptian constitution guarantees five years of free grade school for all children, many poor children receive no education at all. For those who do, qualified teachers are few and classrooms are crowded. Only 39 percent of women and 64 percent of men can read and write ("Egypt," 1998). Those who go beyond the five years of grade school attend a preparatory school for three years. High school also lasts for three years. During the first two years, all students take the same courses, but during the third year they specialize in arts, science, or mathematics. All high school students take a monthly examination and a national exam at the end of the senior year.

The Functionalist Perspective: Providing Social Benefits

A central position of functionalism is that when the parts of society are working properly, each contributes to the well-being or stability of that society. The positive things that people intend their actions to accomplish are known as **manifest functions.** The positive consequences that they did not intend are called **latent functions.** Let's look at these functions.

Teaching Knowledge and Skills

Education's most obvious manifest function is to teach knowledge and skills—whether the traditional three R's or their more contemporary counterparts, such as computer literacy. Each generation must train the next to fulfill the group's significant positions. Because our postindustrial society needs highly educated people, the schools supply them.

Often what counts is not the learning, but the *certification* of learning. Sociologist Randall Collins (1979) observed that we have become a **credential society.** By this, he means that employers use diplomas and degrees as *sorting* devices. For example, they assume that college graduates are responsible people, for presumably they have shown up on time for numerous classes, have turned in scores of assignments, and have demonstrated basic writing and thinking skills. The job skills a position requires can then be grafted onto this foundation, which has been certified by the college.

In some cases, job skills must be mastered before an individual is allowed to do certain work. On-the-job training was once adequate for physicians, engineers, and airline pilots, but with changes in information and technology this is no longer the case. This is precisely why doctors display their credentials so prominently. They stand before you certified by an institution of higher learning, their framed degrees declaring that they have completed rigorous training programs and are licensed to work on your body.

Cultural Transmission of Values

Another manifest function of education is the **cultural transmission** of values, a process by which schools pass a society's core values from one generation to the next. Some of the transmitted values are not even recognized as such. For example, the fact that instruction takes place almost exclusively in English, the dominant language of the society, reflects an intimate evolution from British institutions. Similarly, the architecture of school buildings reflects Western culture. Unlike the thatched-roof schools of some tropical societies, the distinctive appearance of U.S. schools identifies them as schools on sight.

To better understand the connection between education and values, let's look at how the U.S. educational system transmits individualism, competition, and patriotism.

manifest functions
intended beneficial consequences of people's actions

latent functions
unintended beneficial consequences of people's actions

credential society
the use of diplomas and degrees to determine who is eligible for jobs, even though the diploma or degree may be irrelevant to the actual work

cultural transmission
in reference to education, the ways in which schools transmit a society's culture, especially its core values

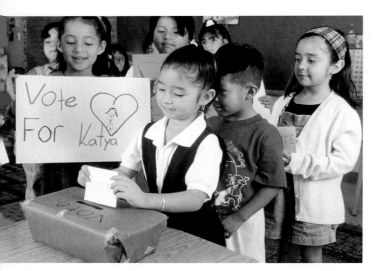

■ *Among the major functions of education is the cultural transmission of values such as patriotism and good citizenship. Another function of education, social integration, also is apparent from this photo, for the students are learning that despite their individual identities, they all are Americans.*

Individualism and Competition   Individualism is a thread that runs throughout the U.S. educational system. Where Japanese schools stress that the individual is only one part of a larger, integrated whole, U.S. students learn that the individual is on his or her own. Pervasive but often subtle, such instruction begins in the early grades when teachers point out the success of a particular student. They might say, for example, "Everyone should be like José," or, "Why can't you be like María, who got all the answers right?" By such seemingly innocuous comments, teachers thrust one child ahead of the rest, holding the individual up for praise.

Competitive games in the classroom and schoolyard provide an apt illustration of how schools transmit this core value. In the classroom, a teacher may divide the class into competitive groups for a spelling bee, while on the playground, children are encouraged to play competitive games and sports. The school's formal sports program—baseball, football, basketball, soccer, hockey, volleyball, and so on—pits team against team in head-to-head confrontations, driving home the lesson that the competitive spirit is highly valued. Although organized sports stress teamwork, the individual is held up for praise. The custom of nominating a "most valuable player" (emphasizing which of these persons is *the* best) reinforces the related lesson of individualism.

Patriotism   Finally, as in schools around the world, U.S. schools teach patriotism. U.S. students learn that the United States is the best country in the world; Russians are taught that no country is better than Russia; and French, German, Japanese, and Afghani students all learn the same about their respective countries. Grade school teachers in every country extol the virtues of the society's founders, their struggle for freedom from oppression, and the goodness of the country's basic social institutions.

In the United States, grade school teachers wax eloquent when it comes to George Washington's exploits—whether real or mythical (and each society tends to develop myths about its own early heroes). Being told that Washington threw a silver dollar across the Potomac and chopped down a cherry tree creates vivid memories that children bring into adulthood. Any suspicions about whether Washington wasted the silver dollar or how such a good person could have chopped down a valued tree are hushed by the teacher, who stresses Washington's virtues: strength and accuracy in throwing the silver dollar, and honesty about what he did to the cherry tree.

■ Social Integration

Schools also bring about *social integration,* that is, they help to mold students into a more cohesive unit. When children enter school, they come from many different backgrounds. Their speech patterns, dress, and attitudes may differ from the mainstream. In the classroom and on the playground, those backgrounds take new shape. The end result is that schools help socialize students into the mainstream culture.

The classroom itself helps to produce social integration. When students salute the flag and sing the national anthem, for example, they become aware of the "greater government," and their sense of national identity grows. One of the best indicators of how education promotes political integration is the millions of immigrants who have attended U.S. schools, learned mainstream ideas and values, and given up their earlier national and cultural identities as they became Americans (Violas 1978; Rodriguez 1995; Carper 2000).

This integrative function of education goes far beyond similarities of appearance or speech. *To forge a national identity is to stabilize the political system.* If people identify with a society's social institutions and *perceive them as the basis of their wel-*

fare, they have no reason to rebel. This function is especially significant when it comes to the lower social classes, from which most social revolutionaries are drawn. The wealthy already have a vested interest in maintaining the status quo, but to get the lower classes to identify with the social system *as it is* goes a long way toward preserving the system in its current state.

People with disabilities often have found themselves left out of the mainstream of society. To overcome this, U.S. schools have added a new manifest function, **mainstreaming,** or inclusion. This means that schools try to incorporate students with disabilities into regular social activities. As a matter of routine policy, students with disabilities used to be placed in special schools. There, however, they learned to adjust to a specialized world; this left them ill prepared to cope with the dominant world. The educational philosophy then changed to one that encourages or even requires students with disabilities to attend regular schools. For people who cannot walk, wheelchair ramps are provided; for those who cannot hear, "signers" (interpreters who use their hands) may attend classes with them. Most students who are blind attend special schools, as do people with severe learning disabilities. Overall, one half of students with disabilities now attend school in regular classrooms ("State of American Education," 2000).

■ *In recent years, social integration, a traditional function of public education, has been extended. In a process called mainstreaming (also known as inclusion by educators), children who used to be sent to special schools now attend regular schools. Shown here is a class in Highland Park, California (near Los Angeles). This child with disabilities is the victim of a drive-by shooting.*

Gatekeeping

Gatekeeping, or determining which people will enter what occupations, is another function of education. One type of gatekeeping is *credentialing*—using diplomas and degrees to determine who is eligible for a job—which opens the doors of opportunity for some and closes it to others. Gatekeeping is often accomplished by **tracking,** sorting students into different educational programs on the basis of their perceived abilities. Some U.S. high schools funnel students into one of three tracks: general, college prep, or honors. Students on the lowest track are likely to go to work after high school, or to take vocational courses at a community college. Those on the highest track usually enter more prestigious colleges. Those in between usually attend a local college or regional state university. The impact is lifelong, affecting opportunities for jobs, income, and lifestyle. Although schools have retreated from formal tracking, an informal system continues, and the results are similar (Lucas 1999).

Gatekeeping sorts people on the basis of merit, said functionalists Talcott Parsons (1940), Kingsley Davis, and Wilbert Moore (1945). They pioneered a view known as **social placement,** arguing that some jobs require few skills and can be performed by people of lesser intelligence. Other jobs, however, such as that of physician, require high intelligence and advanced education. To motivate capable people to postpone gratification and to put up with years of rigorous education, rewards of high income and prestige are held out. Thus, functionalists look on education as a system that, to the benefit of society, sorts people according to their abilities and ambition.

Replacing Family Functions

Over the years, the functions of U.S. schools have expanded, and they now rival some family functions. Child care is an example. Grade schools do double duty as babysitters for parents who both work, or for single mothers in the work force. Child care always has been a latent function of formal education, for it was an unintended consequence of schooling. Now, however, because most families have two wage earners, child care has become a manifest function. Some schools even offer child care both before and after formal classes. Another function schools are performing is giving

mainstreaming
helping people to become part of the mainstream of society

gatekeeping
the process by which education opens and closes doors of opportunity; another term for the social placement function of education

tracking
the sorting of students into different educational programs on the basis of real or perceived abilities

social placement
a function of education that funnels people into a society's various positions

sex education and birth control advice. This has stirred controversy, for some families resent this function being taken from them. Such disagreements over values has fueled a movement for alternative schooling, a topic discussed in the Down-to-Earth Sociology box below.

■ Other Functions

Education also fulfills other functions. For example, because most students are unmarried, high schools and colleges serve as *matchmaking* institutions. It is here that many young people find their future spouses. The sociological significance is that schools funnel people into marriage with mates of similar background, interests, and education. Schools also establish *social networks*. Some adults maintain friendships from high school and college; others develop networks that benefit their careers. Finally, schools also help to *stabilize employment*. To keep millions of young

down-to-earth
s o c i o l o g y

■ ■ ■ ■ ■

Home Schooling: The Search for Quality and Values

"You're doing what? You're going to teach your kids at home?" is the typical, incredulous response to parents who decide to home school their children. "How can you teach? You're not trained."

The unspoken question is, "What's wrong with you? Do you want your kids to be dumb and social misfits?"

The home schooling movement was small at first, just a trickle of parents who were dissatisfied with the rigidity of the school bureaucracy, the lax discipline, incompetent teachers, low standards, unsafe conditions, and, in some instances, of hostility to their religion.

The trickle has grown. While not yet a raging river, the number of children

who are being taught at home is roughly the size of the public school systems of Los Angeles and Chicago combined. The best estimate is that more than 1 million children are being home schooled (Hill 2000; Lines 2000).

Home schooling seems to have burst onto the U.S. scene, but, surprisingly, it is not new. In the colonial era, home

■ These four children in North Carolina are being home schooled by their mother. The text reports the surprising results of home schooling.

people in school is to keep them out of the labor market, protecting the positions of older workers.

Another function is to provide employment. With 53 million students in grade and high schools, and another 15 million enrolled in college, U.S. education is big business. Primary and secondary schools provide jobs for 2.8 million teachers, while another million teach in colleges and universities (*Statistical Abstract* 2000:Tables 239, 270, 315). Millions more work as support personnel—aides, administrators, bus drivers, janitors, and secretaries. Another several million earn their living in industries that service schools—from building schools to manufacturing pencils, paper, and desks. Overall, the United States spends $330 billion a year on its elementary and secondary schools, and another $200 billion on its colleges and universities (*Statistical Abstract* 2000:Tables 275, 308).

To see how you can make college more functional for yourself, consider the findings reviewed in the Down-to-Earth Sociology box on the next page.

---

schooling was the *typical* form of education (Carper 2000). Today's home-schooling movement, which is restoring this earlier pattern, reflects a fascinating shift in U.S. politics. Contemporary home schooling was begun by political and religious liberals in the 1950s and 1960s. Their objection was that the schools were too conservative. Shortly after this, the schools became more liberal, and in the 1970s and 1980s, political and religious conservatives embraced home schooling (Lines 2000; Stevens 2001).

Does home schooling work? Can parents who are not trained as teachers actually teach? The early results of testing home schoolers were promising, but they were limited to small groups or to single states. Then in 1990, a national sample of 2,000 home schoolers showed that these students did better than students who were in public schools. Could this really be true?

To find out, researchers tested 21,000 home schoolers across the nation (Rudner 1999). The results are astounding. The median scores for every test at every grade were in the 70th to 80th percentiles. The home schoolers outscored both public and Catholic school students.

The basic reason for the stunning success of home schooling appears to be the parents' involvement in their children's education. Home schoolers receive an intense, one-on-one education. Their curriculum—although it includes the basics that are required by the state—is designed around the student's interests and needs. Ninety percent of students are taught primarily by their mothers, ten percent by their fathers (Lines 2000). Ninety-eight percent of the fathers are in the labor force, but only 22 percent of the mothers. The parents' income is also above average.

What about the children's socialization? Do home-schooled kids become social misfits? The studies show that they do just fine on this level, too. They actually have fewer behavior problems than children who attend conventional schools (Lines 2000). Home-schooled children are not isolated. As part of their educational experience, their parents take them to libraries, museums, factories, and nursing homes (Medline 2000). For social activities, many of the children meet with other children who are being home schooled. There also are home-schooling associations that

run conferences and even hold sporting events.

What we do not know, of course, is what these home schoolers' test scores would have been if they had been taught in public schools. With their parents' concern and involvement in their education, they likely would have done very well there, too. Finally, although the Rudner study was large, about 21,000 students, it was not a random sample, and we cannot say how the *average* home schooler is doing. But, then, we have no random sample of all public school students, either.

for your consideration

Why do you think home schooling is turning out to be so successful? At current rates of growth, it won't be long before 2 million U.S. children are being taught at home. Do you think this movement may eventually become a threat to U.S. public schools? Would you like to have been home schooled? Would you consider home schooling your children?

■ ■ ■ ■ ■

down-to-earth
s o c i o l o g y

■ ■ ■ ■ ■

How to Get More Out of College—and Still Enjoy It

Why is college a great experience for some students, and a miserable one for others? How can you learn more and also enjoy college more? Derek Bok, the president of Harvard, pondered these questions. Then he asked a statistician, Richard Light, to find the answers. For 10 years, Light and a team of researchers interviewed 1,600 Harvard students. They compared the students who enjoyed college and got a lot out of it with those who did not. We can distill their findings into 8 rules for making college a great experience.

1. *Meet the faculty.* As Light (2001) says, "Each semester, get to know one faculty member reasonably well—and get that teacher to know you reasonably well. At the end of four years—two semesters each—you have eight professors to write recommendations for you. You will also feel more connected to your college."

2. *Take small classes.* Classes with less than 15 students provide enough interaction for you to get to know other students, and to get to know your professor.

3. *Study in groups.* You can learn by yourself, of course, but the students who discussed their assignments in groups of four to six not only understood the material better, but also felt more connected with their subject matter and their college.

4. *Write, Write, Write.* Not many students like to hear this, as it seems to represent work. And it does. But the students who wrote more felt more engaged with their courses. Light says it is better to take a course that requires several short papers rather than one long paper. If you get the long paper wrong, you are sunk. With the shorter papers, you can make a mid-course correction.

5. *Take a foreign language.* Not only do you learn about another culture and way of thought, but also you get to apply these first four principles. Classes in foreign languages usually are small, require that you work in groups, demand short papers, and, with all of their interaction, allow you to get to know your teacher.

6. *Treat college like a buffet.* Parents often advise their college-bound children to "get your required courses out of the way." Students who fill their first year or two with required courses feel less satisfied. It is better to think of college as a buffet. You can fill your plate with whatever you want. The only thing is that you don't yet know what you want. So try different courses. This does not mean that you never serve yourself a main meal, just that when you are ready to major, you will have a better idea of your interests. You won't be wondering if that course in Bulgarian history or the Sociology of Social Movements held the key to your future.

7. *Work in long stretches.* To squeeze in 20 minutes here and there for homework produces less learning and satisfaction than to immerse yourself in the subject. Light recommends keeping a time log for a few weeks so you can evaluate how you use time and determine how to find longer stretches of time.

8. *Hold the drum.* Get involved in outside activities—in music, sports, drama, political discussion groups—whatever your

interest might be. Students who do this are happier and more successful in college

One young woman told her advisor how unhappy she was. Her advisor said that she was too involved in her studies, that she should get involved in outside activities, such as the band. The woman moaned that she had no talent. Her advisor became irritated and said, "Then ask if you can hold the drum." Years later, when this woman was asked why she enjoyed college so much, she said that she had held the drum in the band. The band, it turned out, got her involved in pep rallies and football games and introduced her to a diverse range of students.

Harvard took these findings so seriously that it changed some policies. It encouraged faculty to assign homework to be done in groups and began to offer more classes later in the day so discussions could continue over dinner.

for your consideration
How can you apply these eight findings to your own life?

Based on Light 2001, Zernike 2001a.

■ ■ ■ ■ ■

■ ■ ■ ■ ■

The Conflict Perspective: Reproducing the Social Class Structure

Unlike functionalists, who look at the benefits of education, conflict theorists examine how education helps the elite to maintain their dominance. They stress that *education reproduces the social class structure*. By this, they mean that education perpetuates a society's social divisions. For example, regardless of children's abilities, the more well-to-do are likely to take college preparatory courses and the poor, vocational courses. Both inherit the corresponding life opportunities laid down before they were born.

Let's look, then, at how education reproduces the social class structure.

■ The Hidden Curriculum

The term **hidden curriculum** refers to the unwritten rules of behavior and attitudes that schools teach in addition to the formal curriculum (Gillborn 1992). Examples are obedience to authority and conformity to mainstream norms. Conflict theorists note how the hidden curriculum helps to perpetuate social inequalities.

To understand this central point, consider the way "proper" English is taught. Middle-class schools—whose teachers know where their students are headed—stress "proper" English and "good" manners. In contrast, the teachers in inner-city schools—who also know where *their* students are headed—allow ethnic and street language in the classroom. Each is helping to reproduce the social class structure. That is, each is preparing students to work in positions similar to those of their parents. The social class of some children destines them for higher positions. For these, they need "refined" speech and manners. The social destiny of others is closely supervised, low-status jobs. For these, they need only to obey rules (Bowles and Gintis 1976; Olneck and Bills 1980). Teaching these students "refined" speech and manners would be needless effort.

From the conflict perspective, even kindergarten has a hidden curriculum, as the Down-to-Earth Sociology box on the next page illustrates.

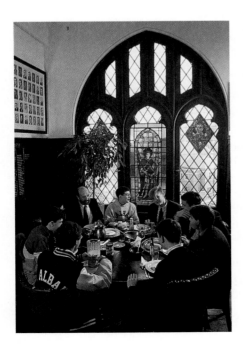

■ Conflict theorists stress that education reproduces a country's social class system. To support this position, they point out that the U.S. social classes attend different schools, where they are taught by teachers of different backgrounds, and where they learn contrasting perspectives of the world and their place in it. Shown here are students lunching with their teacher at St. Alban's School in Washington, D.C.

hidden curriculum
the unwritten goals of schools, such as obedience to authority and conformity to cultural norms

Kindergarten as Boot Camp

After he did participant observation in a kindergarten, sociologist Harry Gracey (1999) concluded that kindergarten is a sort of boot camp for education. Here, tender students from diverse backgrounds are molded into a compliant group that will, on command, unthinkingly follow classroom routines. "Show and tell," for example, does more than allow children to be expressive. It also teaches them to talk only when they are asked to speak. ("It's your turn, Jarmay.") The format also teaches children to request permission to talk ("Who knows what Adela has?") by raising a hand and being acknowledged. This ritual also teaches children to acknowledge the teacher's ideas as superior. She is the one who has the capacity to evaluate students' activities and ideas.

Gracey found a *hidden curriculum* in the other activities he observed. Whether students were drawing pictures, listening to records, eating snacks, or resting,

the teachers would scold talkative students and give approval to those who conformed. In short, the children received the message that the teacher—and, by inference, the entire school system—is the authority.

This, Gracey concluded, is not a side issue—it is *the* purpose of kindergarten. The teacher's job is to teach children to "follow orders with unquestioning obedience." It is to "create and enforce a rigid social structure in the classroom through which they effectively control the behavior of most of the children for

most of the school day." This produces three kinds of students: (1) "good" students, those who submit to school-imposed discipline and come to identify with it; (2) "adequate" students, those who submit to the school's discipline but do not identify with it; and (3) "bad" students, those who refuse to submit to school routines. Children in the third category are called "problem children." To bring them into line, a tougher drill sergeant—the school psychologist—is called in. If that doesn't work, the problem children are drugged into docility with Ritalin.

Gracey notes that these early lessons extend beyond the classroom. As a boot camp, kindergarten prepares students for the routines of the work world, both on the assembly line and at the office. It helps turn the children into docile workers who follow the routines imposed by "the company."

Tilting the Tests: Discrimination by IQ

Even intelligence tests play a part in keeping the social class system intact. For example, how would you answer the following question?

A symphony is to a composer as a book is to a(n) _____.

_____ *paper* _____ *sculptor* _____ *musician* _____ *author* _____ *man*

You probably had no difficulty coming up with "author" as your choice. Wouldn't any intelligent person have done so?

In point of fact, this question raises a central issue in intelligence testing. Not all intelligent people would know the answer. This question contains *cultural biases*. Children from some backgrounds are more familiar with the concepts of symphonies, composers, sculptors, and musicians than are other children. Consequently, the test is tilted in their favor (Turner 1972; Ashe 1992).

Perhaps asking a different question will make the bias clearer. How would you answer this question?

If you throw dice and "7" is showing on the top, what is facing down?

_____ *seven* _____ *snake eyes* _____ *box cars*

_____ *little Joes* _____ *eleven*

This question, suggested by Adrian Dove (n.d.), a social worker in Watts, is slanted toward a lower-class experience. It surely is obvious that this *particular* cultural bias tilts the test so that children from some social backgrounds will perform better than others.

It is no different with IQ (intelligence quotient) tests that use such words as *composer* and *symphony*. A lower-class child may have heard about rap, rock, hip hop, or jazz but not about symphonies. In other words, IQ tests measure not only intelligence but also culturally acquired knowledge. Whatever else we can say, the cultural bias built into the IQ tests used in schools is clearly *not* tilted in favor of the lower classes. One consequence is that minorities and the poor are assigned to less demanding courses (Weiler 1998; Lucas 1999). This destines them for lower-paying jobs in adult life. Thus, conflict theorists view IQ tests as another weapon in an arsenal designed to maintain the social class structure across the generations.

■ Stacking the Deck: Unequal Funding

To see how funding for education differs by geography, look at the Social Map on this page. You can see that where students live is significant for determining how much is spent on their education. Conflict theorists go beyond this observation, however. They stress that in all states the deck is stacked against the poor. Because public schools are largely supported by local property taxes, the richer communities (where property values are higher) have more to spend on their children. The poorer communities end up with much less. Consequently, the richer communities can offer higher salaries and take their pick of the most highly qualified and motivated teachers. They can afford to buy the latest textbooks, computers, and software, as well as to teach courses in foreign language, music, and so on.

Because U.S. schools reflect the U.S. social class system, the children of the privileged emerge from grade school best equipped for success in high school. In turn, they come out of high school best equipped for success in college. They have been given the tools to maintain their dominance. The children of the poor are blown away in this competition, much as a one-legged runner would be in a race against Jackie Joyner-Kersee.

In short, because education's doors of opportunity swing wide open for some but have to be pried open by others, conflict theorists say that the educational system reproduces (or perpetuates) the social class structure. In fact, they add, this is one of its primary purposes.

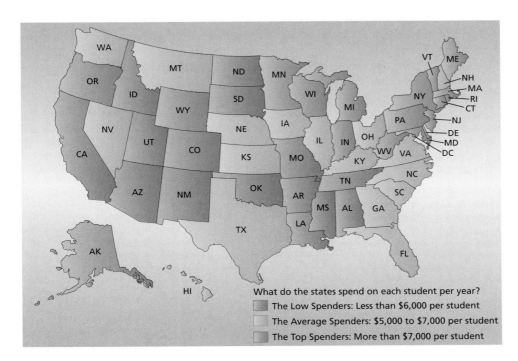

Figure 17.4

Social Map: The Unequal Funding of Education

Note: Some states spend more than twice as much on their students. The range is from $4,059 in Utah to $10,611 in Alaska.

Source: Statistical Abstract 2000: Table 275.

What do the states spend on each student per year?
The Low Spenders: Less than $6,000 per student
The Average Spenders: $5,000 to $7,000 per student
The Top Spenders: More than $7,000 per student

■ The Correspondence Principle

Conflict sociologists Samuel Bowles and Herbert Gintis (1976) used the term **correspondence principle** to refer to how schools reflect society. This term means that what is taught in a nation's schools *corresponds* to the characteristics of that society. The following list provides some examples.

Characteristics of Society	Characteristics of Schools
1. Capitalism	1. Promote competition
2. Social inequality	2. Provide unequal funding of schools
3. Racial-ethnic prejudice	3. Funnel minorities into job training programs that demand little intellect
4. Bureaucratic structure of corporations	4. Provide a model of authority in the classroom
5. Need for submissive workers	5. Make students submissive, as in the kindergarten boot camp
6. Need for dependable workers	6. Promote punctuality in attendance and homework
7. Need to maintain armed forces	7. Promote patriotism (to fight for capitalism)

Thus, conclude conflict theorists, the U.S. educational system is designed to turn most students into dependable workers who will not question their bosses. It also is intended to produce some innovators in thought and action, but who can still be counted on to be loyal to the social system as it exists (Olneck and Bills 1980).

■ The Bottom Line: Family Background and the Educational System

The end result of unequal funding, IQ tests, and so on is this: Family background is more important than test scores in predicting who attends college. Back in 1977, sociologist Samuel Bowles compared the college attendance of the brightest 25 percent of high school students with the intellectually weakest 25 percent. Figure 17.5 shows the results. Of the *brightest* 25 percent of high school students, 90 percent of those from affluent homes went to college, while only half of those from low-income homes did so. Of the *weakest* students, 26 percent from affluent homes went to college, while only 6 percent from poorer homes did so. Other sociologists have confirmed this finding. The principle is this: If you rank families from the poorest to the richest, as the family's income increases so does the likelihood that their children will attend college (Manski 1992–1993).

Conflict theorists point out that the educational system reproduces not only the U.S. social class structure, but also its divisions of race and ethnicity. From Figure 17.6, you can see that, compared with whites, African Americans and Latinos are

Figure 17.5

Who Goes to College? The Role of Social Class and Personal Ability in Determining College Attendance
Source: Bowles 1977.

correspondence principle
the sociological principle that schools correspond to (or reflect) the social structure of society

Students' Test Scores

Students' Background	High	Low
Rich	90%	26%
Poor	50%	6%

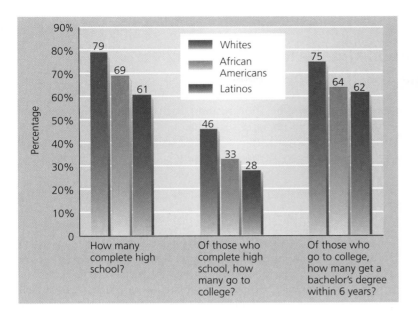

Figure 17.6

The Funneling Effects of Education: Race and Ethnicity
Note: The source gives totals only for these three groups.
Source: Statistical Abstract 1999:Tables 304, 328.

less likely to complete high school, less likely to go to college, and, if they go to college, less likely to graduate. Those without college degrees are more likely to end up with low-paying, dead-end jobs. As you know, the type of college you attend is also important. As Table 17.1 shows, of those who attend college, whites, African Americans, and Asian Americans are almost equally likely to be found at four-year private colleges. This figure does not support the conflict view, but, rather, shows increasing equality. From Table 17.1, however, you can see the continued disadvantage of Latinos and Native Americans in the U.S. educational system today.

IN SUM ■ ■ ■ ■

Conflict theorists stress that a major purpose of the educational system is to *reproduce social inequality,* to help keep the social class structure intact from one generation to the next. A variety of techniques funnel the children of the poor into community college job training programs and the children of the middle classes into state universities and small private colleges. The offspring of the elite, in contrast, are funneled into exclusive boarding high schools, where they are taught in small classes by well-paid teachers (Persell et al. 1992). The social network that these privileged children inherit includes contacts with the admissions officers of the nation's most elite colleges. Some of these networks are so efficient that *half* of the graduating classes of these private schools attend Harvard, Yale, and Princeton (Persell and Cookson 1986).

TABLE 17.1

Of Those Who Go to College, What Percentage Attends Each Type of College?

Racial-Ethnic Group	Public College	Private College	2-Year College	4-Year College
Whites	77%	23%	37%	63%
African Americans	78%	22%	42%	58%
Asian Americans	79%	21%	40%	60%
Latinos	85%	15%	56%	44%
Native Americans	87%	13%	50%	50%

Source: Statistical Abstract 2000:Table 298.

■ ■ ■ ■ ■

The Symbolic Interactionist Perspective: Fulfilling Teacher Expectations

Functionalists look at how education benefits society, and conflict theorists examine how education perpetuates social inequality. Symbolic interactionists, in contrast, study face-to-face interaction in the classroom. They have found that the expectations of teachers have profound consequences for their students.

■ The Rist Research

Why do some people get tracked into college prep courses and others into vocational ones? There is no single answer, but in what has become a classic study, sociologist Ray Rist came up with some intriguing findings. Rist (1970) did participant observation in an African American grade school with an African American faculty. He found that after only eight days in the classroom, the kindergarten teacher felt that she knew the children's abilities well enough to assign them to three separate worktables. To Table 1, Mrs. Caplow assigned those she considered to be "fast learners." They sat at the front of the room, closest to her. Those whom she saw as "slow learners," she assigned to Table 3, located at the back of the classroom. She placed "average" students at Table 2, in between the other tables.

This seemed strange to Rist. He knew that the children had not been tested for ability, yet their teacher was certain that she could identify the bright and slow children. Investigating further, Rist found that social class was the underlying basis for assigning the children to the different tables. Middle-class students were separated out for Table 1, children from poorer homes to Tables 2 and 3. The teacher paid the most attention to the children at Table 1, who were closest to her, less to Table 2, and the least to Table 3. As the year went on, children from Table 1 perceived that they were treated better and came to see themselves as smarter. They became the leaders in class activities and even ridiculed children at the other tables, calling them "dumb." Eventually, the children at Table 3 disengaged themselves from many classroom activities. At the end of the year, only the children at Table 1 had completed the lessons that prepared them for reading.

This early tracking stuck. Their first-grade teacher looked at the work they had accomplished and placed students from Table 1 at her Table 1. She treated her tables much as the kindergarten teacher had, and the children at Table 1 again led the class.

The children's reputations continued to follow them. The second-grade teacher reviewed their scores and also divided her class into three groups. The first she named the "Tigers" and, befitting their name, gave them challenging readers. Not surprisingly, the Tigers came from the original Table 1 in kindergarten. The second group she called the "Cardinals." They came from the original Tables 2 and 3. Her third group consisted of children she had failed the previous year, whom she called the "Clowns." The Cardinals and Clowns were given less advanced readers.

Rist concluded that *each child's journey through school was determined by the eighth day of kindergarten!* This research, as with that done on the Saints and Roughnecks (reported in Chapter 4), demonstrates the power of labels. They can set people on courses of action that affect the rest of their lives

What occurred was a **self-fulfilling prophecy**. This term, coined by sociologist Robert Merton (1949), refers to a false assumption of something that is going to happen but which then comes true simply because it was predicted. For example, if

self-fulfilling prophecy
Robert Merton's term for an originally false assertion that becomes true simply because it was predicted

people believe an unfounded rumor that a bank is going to fail, they all rush to the bank to demand their money. The prediction—although originally false—is now likely to come true.

■ The Rosenthal-Jacobson Experiment

All of us know about teacher expectations—that some teachers have higher standards and expect work of a higher quality. Teacher expectations, however, also work at a subtle level. In what has become a classic experiment, social psychologists Robert Rosenthal and Lenore Jacobson (1968) tried out a new test in a San Francisco grade school. They tested the children's abilities and then told the teachers which students would probably "spurt" ahead during the year. They instructed the teachers to watch these students' progress, but not to let the students or their parents know about the test results. At the end of the year, they tested the students again and found that the IQs of the predicted "spurters" had jumped ten to fifteen points higher than those of the other children.

You might think that Rosenthal and Jacobson became famous for developing such a powerful scholastic aptitude test. Actually, their "test" was another of those covert experiments. Rosenthal and Jacobson had simply given routine IQ tests to the children and had then *randomly* chosen 20 percent of the students as "spurters." These students were *no* different from the others in the classroom. A self-fulfilling prophecy had taken place: The teachers expected more from those particular students, and the students responded. In short, expect dumb and you get dumb. Expect smart, and you get smart.

Although attempts to replicate this experiment have had mixed results (Pilling and Pringle 1978), a good deal of research confirms that students who are expected to do better generally do (Seaver 1973; Snyder 1993).

■ How Do Teacher Expectations Work?

Sociologist George Farkas (1990a, 1990b, 1996) became interested in how teacher expectations affect grades. Using a stratified sample of students in a large school district in Texas, he found that *even though they had the same test scores,* girls averaged higher course grades than did boys. Asian Americans also received higher grades than did African Americans, Latinos, and whites who had the same test scores.

At first, this may sound like more of the same old news—another case of discrimination. But this explanation doesn't fit, which is what makes the finding fascinating. Look who the victims are. It is most unlikely that the teachers would be prejudiced against boys and whites. To interpret these unexpected results, Farkas used symbolic interactionism. He observed that some students "signal" to their teachers that they are "good students." They show an eagerness to cooperate, and they quickly agree with what the teacher says. They also show that they are "trying hard." The teachers pick up these signals and reward these "good students" with better grades. Girls and Asian Americans, the researcher concludes, are better at displaying these characteristics so coveted by teachers.

We do not have enough information on how teachers form their expectations or how they communicate them to students. Nor do we know much about how students "signal" messages to teachers. Perhaps you will become the educational sociologist who will shed more light on this significant area of human behavior.

The Sociology and New Technology box on the next page discusses how technology is producing new forms of student-teacher interaction and "signaling."

the new technology

Internet University: No Walls, No Ivy, No All Night Parties

Distance learning, courses taught to students who are not physically present with their instructor, is not new. For decades, we have had correspondence courses.

Today, however, telecommunications are transforming distance learning. Satellites, computers, television, and CD-ROMs are changing the face of education so radically that cyber colleges soon may be part of mainstream education. Columbia, Stanford, Chicago, and Carnegie Mellon are partners in Cardean University, which offers an MBA program and is expanding into law. Up to $1 million is being spent to develop each online course (McCormick 2000). The founders envision a student body of *millions* of people around the world. They also envision small classes where students work together online to solve course-related problems. Com-

puter-mounted cameras may allow everyone in the class to see everyone else simultaneously. Spider-web diagrams will let the instructor know who is e-mailing others—and who is holding back. Tucked deeper in the software is a program to allow the deans to scrutinize the instructors. The deans will get reports, for example, that let them know

how long it takes instructors to answer e-mail.

Why should formal education be limited to walled classrooms? Think of the possibilities of the Net. We could study human culture and compare notes on eating, dating, or burial customs with fellow students in Thailand, Iceland, South Africa, Germany, Egypt, China, and Australia. We could write a joint paper in which we compare our experiences with one another and with those described in the text, and then submit our paper to our mutual instructor.

Will we eventually go from kindergarten to grad school with classmates from around the world? While this may sound intriguing, no walls also means no joking in the hallway or dorm, no flirting after class, no getting together over a cup of coffee. . . .

Problems in U.S. Education— and Their Solutions

To conclude this chapter, let's examine two problems facing U.S. education— and consider their potential solutions.

■ Problems: Mediocrity and Violence

The Rising Tide of Mediocrity   All Arizona high school sophomores took a math test. It covered the math that sophomores should know. One of eight passed. Meanwhile, in New York, to get its students to graduate, the state had to drop its passing grade to 55 out of 100 (Steinberg 2000). Some New York City schools are so bad that the city and state have given up and turned them over to private, for-profit companies (Wyatt 2000). Perhaps nothing so captures what is wrong with U.S. schools than this event, reported by sociologist Thomas Sowell (1993b):

> [A]n international study of 13-year-olds . . . found that Koreans ranked first in mathematics and Americans last. When asked if they thought they were "good at mathematics," only 23 percent of the Korean youngsters said "yes"—compared to 68 percent of American 13-year-olds. The American educational dogma that students should "feel good about themselves" was a success in its own terms—though not in any other terms.

Scores on the Scholastic Assessment Test (SAT) indicate this same problem. As Figure 17.7 shows, the math scores have recovered, but the verbal scores are still much lower than they were years ago.

The president of the American Federation of Teachers came up with a unique defense of the decline in SAT scores: The low test scores, he said, mean that teachers are doing a *better* job! They are getting more students to stay in high school and to go on to college. Students from poorer academic backgrounds, who used to drop out of high school, now become part of the test results (Sowell 1993b). Perhaps this is the reason. But if it is, it indicates not success, but a severe underlying problem—teachers giving inferior education to disadvantaged students.

Others suggest that SAT scores have declined because children find television and video games more appealing than reading (Rigdon and Swasy 1990). Students who read little acquire a smaller vocabulary and less rigor in thought and verbal expression. Sociologists Donald Hayes and Loreen Wolfer (1993) are convinced that the culprit is the "dummied down" textbooks that pervade U.S. schools. Some point their fingers at less homework, fewer term papers, grade inflation, and burned-out teachers who are more interested in collecting paychecks than in educating their students. Some of the examples they offer are startling, such as the college freshman who couldn't understand why she was doing poorly in college since she had placed third in her Chicago high school graduating class. Testing showed that she ranked in the lowest 2 percent of the nation's high school graduates (Kotlowitz 1992).

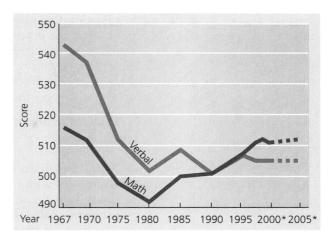

Figure 17.7

National Results of the Scholastic Assessment Test (SAT)

Note: Broken lines indicate the author's estimate.

Source: Statistical Abstract 2000: Table 284.

How to Cheat on the SATs   If you receive poor grades this semester, wouldn't you like to use a magic marker to, presto!, change them into higher grades? I suppose every student would. Now imagine that you had that power. Would you use it?

Some people in authority apparently have found such a magic marker, and they are using it to raise our embarrassingly low national SAT scores. Table 274 of the 1996 edition of the *Statistical Abstract of the United States* says that in 1995 only 8.3 percent of students earned 600 or more on the verbal portion of the SAT test. The very next edition, in 1997, however, holds a pleasant surprise. Table 276 tells us that it was really 21.9 percent of students who scored 600 or higher in 1995. Later editions of this source retain the higher figure. What a magic marker!

In the twinkle of an eye, we get another bonus. Somehow, between 1996 and 1997 the scores of *everyone* who took the test in previous years improved. Now that's the kind of power we all would like to have. Students, grab your report cards. Workers, change those numbers on your paycheck.

It certainly is easier to give simpler tests than to do better teaching. And this is what has happened to the SAT. The test is now shorter and students have more time to answer fewer questions. To make the verbal part easier, the test on antonyms was dropped (Manno 1995; Stecklow 1995). Results of previous years were then "rescored" to match the easier test. This "dummying down" of the SAT is yet another form of grade inflation, the topic to which we shall now turn.

Grade Inflation, Social Promotion, and Functional Illiteracy   High school teachers used to give about twice as many C's as A's, but now there are more A's than C's. Since grades went up while learning went down, some of today's A's are the C's of years past. Another sign of **grade inflation** is that *one-third* of all college freshmen have an overall high school grade point average of A. This is more than *twice* what it was in 1970 (*Statistical Abstract* 2000:Table 302). Grade inflation has also hit the Ivy League. At Harvard University, *half* of the course grades are now A's and A-'s. To match his colleagues' grading, one Harvard professor even gives an official, inflated grade for the student's transcript—and then in private gives a grade that reflects his true evaluation of the student's learning (Mansfield 2001).

grade inflation
higher grades given for the same work; a general rise in student grades without a corresponding increase in learning or test scores

Grade inflation in the face of declining standards has been accompanied by **social promotion,** the practice of passing students from one grade to the next even though they have not mastered basic materials. One result is **functional illiteracy,** people having difficulty with reading and writing even though they have graduated from high school. Some high school graduates cannot fill out job applications; others can't figure out if they get the right change at the grocery store.

The Influence of Peer Groups   Two psychologists and a sociologist, who studied 20,000 high school students in California and Wisconsin, found that the peer group is the most important factor on how teenagers do in school (Steinberg et al. 1996). Simply put: Those who hang out with good students tend to do well; those who hang out with friends who do poorly in school do poorly. Student subcultures include informal norms about how well teenagers should do in school. Some groups have norms of classroom excellence, while others sneer at getting good grades. The applied question that arises from this research, of course, is how to build educational achievement into student culture.

Violence in Schools   Many U.S. schools have deteriorated to the point that safety is an issue. To get into some schools, students must pass through metal detectors, and uniformed guards have become a permanent fixture in them. Some grade schools even supplement their traditional fire drills with "drive-by shooting drills" (Toch 1993; Grossman 1995).

And what about school shootings, such as the event with which we opened this chapter? For a surprising analysis, read the Mass Media box on the next page.

■ Solutions: Retention, Safety, Standards, and Other Reforms

It is one thing to identify problems, and quite another to find solutions for them. Let's consider some solutions to the problems we just reviewed.

A Secure Learning Environment   The first step in offering a good education is to make students safe and free from fear. With the high rate of violence in U.S. society, we can expect some violence to spill over into the schools. To minimize that spillover, school administrators can expel all students who threaten the welfare of others. They also can refuse to tolerate threats, violence, and weapons. A zero tolerance policy for guns on school property is not unreasonable.

Higher Standards   Within a secure learning environment, then, we can take other steps to improve the quality of education. To offer a quality education, we need quality teachers. Our schools compete with private industry for the same pool of college graduates. If the starting salary in other fields is higher than it is in education, those fields will attract the brighter, more energetic graduates. Figure 17.8 on page 526 highlights the abysmal job we are doing in this competition.

What else can we do to improve the quality of education? A study by sociologists James Coleman and Thomas Hoffer (1987) provides helpful guidelines. They wanted to see why the test scores of students in Roman Catholic schools average 15 to 20 percent higher than those of students in public schools. Is it because Catholic schools attract better students, while public schools have to put up with everyone? To find out, Coleman and Hoffer tested 15,000 students in public and Catholic high schools.

Their findings? From the sophomore through the senior years, students at Catholic schools pull ahead of public school students by a full grade in verbal and math skills. The superior test performance of students in Catholic schools, they concluded, is due not to better

social promotion
passing students to the next grade even though they have not mastered basic materials

functional illiterate
a high school graduate who has difficulty with basic reading and math

■ On average, students in Roman Catholic schools score higher on national tests than students in public schools. Is it because Roman Catholic schools have better students, or because they do better teaching? The text reports the sociological findings.

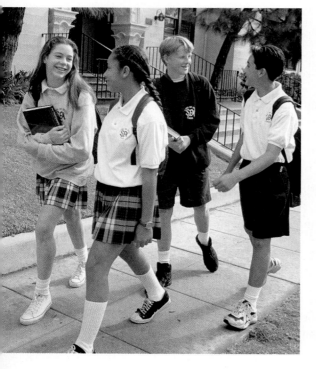

mass media
in social life

School Shootings: When Myth Gives Way to Panic

The media sprinkle their reports of school shootings with such dramatic phrases as "alarming proportions," "outbreak of violence," and "out of control." They give us the impression that schools all over the nation are set to erupt in gunfire. The public views the shootings as convincing evidence that something is seriously wrong with society. Parents used to consider schools safe havens, but no longer. Those naïve thoughts have been shattered by the bullets that have sprayed our schools—or at least by the media's portrayal of growing danger and violence in our schools.

Have our schools really become war zones, as the mass media would have us believe? Certainly events such as those at Columbine High School are disturbing, but we need to probe deeper than newspaper headlines and televised images in order to understand their social significance.

When we do, we find that the media's sensationalist reporting has created a myth. Contrary to "what everyone knows," *there is no trend toward*

■ *This picture was taken when Drew Golden was 6 years old. Five years later, when Drew was 11, he teamed up with 13-year-old Mitch Johnson. Together, they ambushed their middle school teachers and classmates in Jonesboro, Arkansas. They wounded nine students and one teacher and killed four girls and one teacher.*

TABLE 17.2 — Exploding a Myth: Deaths at U.S. Schools[a]

School Year	Shooting Deaths	Other Homicides[b]	Total by Gender Boys	Total by Gender Girls	Total
1992–1993	45	11	49	7	56
1993–1994	41	12	41	12	53
1994–1995	16	5	18	3	21
1995–1996	29	7	26	10	36
1996–1997	15	11	18	8	26
1997–1998	36	8	27	17	44
1998–1999	25	6	24	7	31
1999–2000	16	16	26	6	32
2000–2001	18	5	18	5	23
Mean, 1992–2001	27	9.0	27.4	8.3	35.8

[a]Includes all school-related homicides, even those that occurred on the way to or from school; includes suicides; includes school personnel killed at school by other adults; includes adults who had nothing to do with the school but who were found dead on school property.

[b]Beating, hanging, jumping, stabbing, and strangling.

Source: National School Safety Center, 2002.

greater school violence. Despite the dramatic school shootings that make headlines, as Table 17.2 shows, shooting deaths at schools are *not* increasing. As you can see, even during the 1998–1999 school year, when the Columbine killers went on their lethal rampage, the number of shooting deaths at U.S. schools was *below* average.

This is not to say that school shootings are not a serious problem. Even one student being wounded or killed is too many. But, contrary to the impression fostered by the media, we are *not* seeing an escalation of school shooting deaths.

This is why we need sociology: to quietly, dispassionately search for facts so we can better understand the events that shape our lives. The first requirement for solving any problem is accurate data, for we do not want to create solutions based on hysteria. The information presented in this box may not make for sensational headlines, but it does serve to explode the myths that the media have spread.

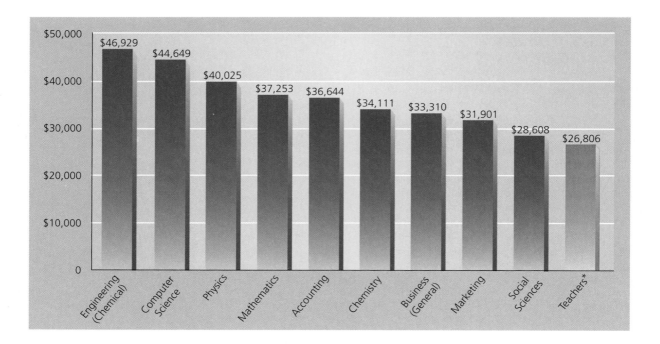

Figure 17.8

Starting Salaries of U.S. College Graduates: Public School Teachers Compared
with Private Industry

Sources: Statistical Abstract 2000:Table 316; Howard and Gould 2001.

students, but to higher standards. Catholic schools have not watered down their curricula as have public schools. The researchers also underscored the importance of parental involvement. Parents and teachers in Catholic schools reinforce each other's commitment to learning.

These findings support the basic principle reviewed earlier about teacher expectations: Students perform better when they are expected to do well. To this, you might want to reply, "Of course. I knew that. Who wouldn't?" Somehow, however, this basic principle is lost on many teachers, who end up teaching at a low level, and lost on most school administrators, who accept low student performance. The reason, actually, is probably not their lack of awareness of such basics, but, rather, the organization that entraps them, a bureaucracy in which ritual replaces performance. To understand this point better, you may wish to review Chapter 7.

Ultimately, then, we must expect more not only of students, but also of teachers and administrators. They, too, must be held accountable to higher standards. One way to do this is to peg their salaries, or at least bonuses, to the performance of their students. Of course, we have to make certain that the test results are legitimate. Unfortunately, some teachers and administrators will cheat for money—giving students the answers and throwing out low tests (Kantrowitz and McGinn 2000).

Other Reforms—From Vouchers to Charter Schools   There is no lack of proposals for improving schools, but perhaps the one that has gained the most media attention—both because it is so controversial and because it holds such potential—is *vouchers*. The state would give the parents of each school-age child a voucher to be spent on the school of the parents' choice. As you can see from Figure 17.4 (page 517), the states have a great deal of money to work with, and the amount available per pupil would be large. Public and private schools—even those operated by individuals and businesses—would compete for the vouchers. With each school's test results published in local newspapers and available online, parents would be able to shop around for the school they like best. One major objection is that vouchers might be used to finance religious schools.

A second step in school reform is the creation of charter schools. **Charter schools** are public schools that, although financed by tax money, are owned and administered by independent groups. They are *chartered* by the state or some state agency to use innovative techniques in order to improve academic standards. There is no single model. Some charter schools are owned and run by parents, others by for-profit corporations. Some charter schools are in the inner city, others in the suburbs. Some are open the entire year. One is operated almost entirely online. One trait they have in common is a freedom from teachers' unions and the public school bureaucracy. As you can imagine, teachers' unions and public school administrators have fought the creation of charter schools. Although these schools have great promise, it is too soon to tell if they will meet their potential (Manno and Finn 1998, Perreault 2000, Lin 2001).

Many applaud charter schools as a way of bringing educational reform and yet avoiding the political controversy of vouchers, that of funding religious schools. Opponents, however, fear that charter schools, like vouchers, will doom public schools by siphoning off their resources. Proponents of these reforms are unfazed by this objection. They say that public schools need to compete in the marketplace. If they don't produce better results, they *should* fold. It is no wonder that public school teachers and administrators fear reform.

Reform in anything needs a guiding principle. I suggest that this serve as the guiding principle in reforming education: The problem is *not* the ability of the students, but, rather, the educational system. This principle is central in the results reported in the following Thinking Critically section, with which we close this chapter.

charter schools
schools that, although financed by taxes, are owned and run by private groups

thinking
CRITICALLY

Breaking Through the Barriers: Restructuring The Classroom

Jaime Escalante taught in an East Los Angeles inner-city school that was plagued with poverty, crime, drugs, and gangs. In this self-defeating environment, he taught calculus. His students scored so highly on national tests that officials suspected cheating. They asked his students to retake the test. They did. This time, they earned even higher scores.

How did Escalante do it?

First, Escalante had to open his students' minds to the possibility of success, that they could learn. Most Latino students were tracked into craft classes where they made jewelry and birdhouses. "Our kids are just as talented as anyone else. They just need the opportunity to show it," Escalante said. "They just don't think about becoming scientists or engineers."

Students also need to see learning as a way out of the barrio, as the path to good jobs. Escalante arranged for foundations to provide money for students to attend the colleges of their choice. Students learned that if they did well, their poverty wouldn't stop them.

Escalante also changed the system of instruction. He had his students think of themselves as a team, of him as the coach, and the national math exams as a

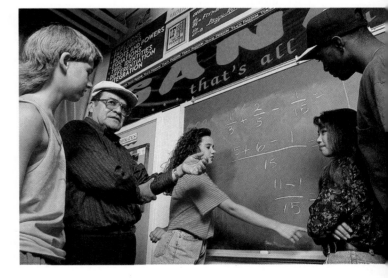

■ *To say that today's schoolchildren can't learn as well as previous schoolchildren is a case of blaming the victim. As discussed in the text, Jaime Escalante (shown here) demonstrated that teachers can motivate even highly deprived students to study hard and to excel in learning. His experience challenges us to rethink our approach to education.*

sort of Olympics for which they were preparing. To foster team identity, students wore team jackets, caps, and T-shirts with logos that identified them as part of the math team. Before class, his students did "warm-ups" (hand clapping and foot stomping to a rock song).

Escalante's team had practice schedules as rigorous as a championship football team. Students had to sign a contract that bound them to participate in a summer math program, to complete the daily homework, and to attend Saturday morning and after-school study sessions. To remind students that self-discipline pays off, Escalante covered his walls with posters of sports figures—Michael Jordan, Babe Ruth, Jackie Joyner-Kersee, and Scottie Pippin.

The sociological point is this: The problem was not the ability of the students. Their failure to do well in school was not due to something within them. The problem was the system, the way classroom instruction was designed. When Escalante changed the system of instruction—and brought in hope—both attitudes and performance changed.

■ ■ ■ ■ ■

for your consideration . . .

What principles discussed in this or earlier chapters did Escalante apply? What changes do you think we can make in education to bring about similar results all over the country?

Sources: Based on Barry 1989; Meek 1989; Escalante and Dirmann 1990; Hilliard 1991.

■ ■ ■ ■ ■

Summary and Review

The Development of Modern Education

◼ **How did modern education develop?**

In most of human history, **education** consisted of informal learning, equivalent to **acculturation**. In some earlier societies, centers of formal education did develop, such as among the Arabs, Chinese, Greeks, and Egyptians. Because modern education came about in response to industrialization, formal education is much less common in the Least Industrialized Nations. Pp. 504–506.

Education in Global Perspective

◼ **How does education compare among the Most Industrialized, Industrializing, and Least Industrialized Nations?**

In general, formal education reflects a nation's economy. Consequently, education is extensive in the Most Industrialized Nations, undergoing vast change in the Industrializing Nations, and spotty in the Least Industrialized Nations. Japan, Russia, and Egypt provide examples of education in countries at three levels of industrialization. Pp. 507–509.

The Functionalist Perspective: Providing Social Benefits

◼ **What is the functionalist perspective on education?**

Among the functions of education are the teaching of knowledge and skills, providing credentials, **cultural transmission** of values, social integration, **gatekeeping**, and **mainstreaming**. Functionalists also note that education has replaced some traditional family functions. Pp. 509–514.

The Conflict Perspective: Reproducing the Social Class Structure

◼ **What is the conflict perspective on education?**

The basic view of conflict theorists is that *education reproduces the social class structure;* that is, through such mechanisms as unequal funding and operating different schools for the elite and for the masses, education perpetuates a society's basic social inequalities from one generation to the next. Pp. 515–519.

The Symbolic Interactionist Perspective: Fulfilling Teacher Expectations

■ **What is the symbolic interactionist perspective on education?**

Symbolic interactionists focus on face-to-face interaction. In examining what occurs in the classroom, they have found that student performance tends to conform to teacher expectations, whether they are high or low. Pp. 520–522.

Problems in U.S. Education—and Their Solutions

■ **What are the chief problems that face U.S. education?**

In addition to violence, the major problems are low achievement as shown by SAT scores, **grade** inflation, social promotion, and **functional illiteracy.** Pp. 522–524.

■ **What are the potential solutions to these problems?**

The primary solution is to restore high educational standards, which can be done only after providing basic security for students. Any solution for improving quality must be based on expecting more of *both* students and teachers. Pp. 524–528.

■ *Where can I read more on this topic?*

Suggested Readings for this chapter are found at the back of this book.

All URLs listed are current as of the printing of this book. URLs often change. Please check our Web site, **http://www.abacon.com/henslin,** for updates.

Additional Online Resources for This Chapter
www.ablongman.com/henslin6e

- *Content Select* Research Database for Sociology, with suggested key terms and annotated references
- Link to 2000 Census, with activities
- Flashcards of key terms and concepts

- Practice Tests
- Weblinks
- Interactive Maps

using . . .
ContentSelect

Research Database for Sociology

acculturation	grades	mainstreaming	school shootings
cultural bias	home schooling	private schools	virtual university
gatekeeping			

Jacob Lawrence, Eight Studies for the Book of Genesis, No. 3. And God said "Let the earth bring forth the grass, trees, fruits and herbs" 1989

18

Religion

What Is Religion?

The Functionalist
Perspective
Functions of Religion
Functional Equivalents
of Religion
Dysfunctions of Religion

The Symbolic
Interactionist
Perspective
Religious Symbols
Rituals
Beliefs
Religious Experience
Community

The Conflict Perspective
Opium of the People
A Reflection of Social
Inequalities
A Legitimation of Social
Inequalities

Religion and the Spirit
of Capitalism

The World's Major
Religions
Judaism
Christianity
Islam
Hinduism
Buddhism
Confucianism

Types of Religious
Groups
Cult
Sect
Church
Ecclesia
Variations in Patterns
When Religion and
Culture Conflict

Religion in the
United States
Characteristics of Members
Characteristics of Religious
Groups
Secularization of Religion
and Culture

The Future of Religion

Summary and Review

The first report was stunning. About a hundred armed agents of the Bureau of Alcohol, Tobacco, and Firearms (ATF) attacked the compound of the Branch Davidians, an obscure religious group in Waco, Texas. Four of the agents were shot to death. So were six men who tried to defend the compound. Then came a fifty-one-day standoff, televised to the U.S. public, in which the ATF and FBI did strange things such as bombarding the compound with loud music day and night. At 6 A.M. on the fifty-first day of the siege, following on-again, off-again negotiations with David Koresh, the 33-year-old leader of the group, a tank rammed the compound's main building. It pumped in gas consisting of chemicals that, by international law, the U.S. military was unable to use against Iraqi soldiers. As a second tank punched holes in the walls, the women

> A tank rammed the compound's main building. It pumped in gas consisting of chemicals that, by international law, the U.S. military was unable to use against Iraqi soldiers.

and children fled to the second floor. The men shot futilely at the tanks. An explosion rocked the compound, and the buildings burst into flames. Eighty men, women, and children were burned to death. Some of the charred bodies of the twenty-five children were found huddled next to their mothers. The government removed the bodies, sealed off the area, and bulldozed the charred remains of the buildings. Survivors claimed that the government had set the fire. The government said the Branch Davidians had set it, that they had committed suicide by fire.

sacred
Durkheim's term for things set apart or forbidden, that inspire fear, awe, reverence, or deep respect

profane
Durkheim's term for common elements of everyday life

religion
according to Durkheim, beliefs and practices that separate the profane from the sacred and unite its adherents into a moral community

church
according to Durkheim, one of the three essential elements of religion—a moral community of believers; a second definition is the type of religious organization described on page 549, a large, highly organized group with formal, sedate worship services and little emphasis on personal conversion

e will return to this event later in the chapter. But first, let's turn to a sociological analysis of religion.

What Is Religion?

All human societies are organized by some form of the family, as well as by some kind of economic system and political order. As we have seen, these key social institutions touch on aspects of life that are essential to human welfare. This chapter examines religion, another universal social institution.

Sociologists who do research on religion analyze the relationship between society and religion and study the role that religion plays in people's lives. They do not seek to prove that one religion is better than another. Nor is their goal to verify or disprove anyone's faith. As mentioned in Chapter 1, sociologists have no tools for deciding that one course of action is more moral than another, much less that one religion is "the" correct one. Religion is a matter of faith; sociologists deal with empirical matters, things they can observe or measure. Thus sociologists study the effects of religious beliefs and practices on people's lives. They also analyze how religion is related to stratification systems. Unlike theologians, however, sociologists cannot evaluate the truth of a religion's teachings.

In 1912 Emile Durkheim published an influential book, *The Elementary Forms of the Religious Life,* in which he tried to identify the elements common to all religions. After surveying religions around the world, Durkheim could find no specific belief or practice that all religions share. He did find, however, that all religions develop a community around whatever their practices and beliefs are. All religions also separate the sacred from the profane. By **sacred,** Durkheim referred to aspects of life having to do with the supernatural that inspire awe, reverence, deep respect, even fear. By **profane,** he meant aspects of life that are not concerned with religion or religious purposes but, instead, are part of the ordinary aspects of everyday life. Durkheim (1912/1965) concluded:

> A religion is a unified system of beliefs and practices relative to sacred things, that is to say, things set apart and forbidden—beliefs and practices which unite into one single moral community called a Church, all those who adhere to them.

Thus, Durkheim said, a **religion** is defined by three elements:

1. *Beliefs* that some things are sacred (forbidden, set apart from the profane)

2. *Practices* (rituals) centering around the things considered sacred

3. *A moral community* (a church) resulting from a group's beliefs and practices

Durkheim used the word **church** in an unusual sense, to refer to any "moral community" centered on beliefs and practices regarding the sacred. In Durkheim's sense, *church* refers to Buddhists bowing before a shrine, Hindus dipping in the Ganges River, and Confucianists offering food to their ancestors. Similarly, the term *moral community* does not imply morality in the sense familiar to most of us. A moral community is simply people who are united by their religious practices—and that would include sixteenth-century Aztec priests who each day gathered around an altar to pluck out the beating heart of a virgin.

To better understand the sociological approach to religion, let's see what pictures emerge when we apply the three theoretical perspectives.

■ *From his review of world religions, Durkheim concluded that all religions have beliefs, practices, and a moral community. Part of Hindu belief is that the Ganges is a holy river and bathing in it imparts spiritual benefits. Each year, millions of Hindus participate in this rite of ablution (purification).*

The Functionalist Perspective

Functionalists stress that religion is universal because it meets basic human needs. What are some of the functions—and dysfunctions—of religion?

■ Functions of Religion

Questions About Ultimate Meaning   Around the world, religions provide answers to perplexing questions about ultimate meaning—such as the purpose of life, why people suffer, and the existence of an afterlife. Those answers give people a sense of purpose. Instead of seeing themselves buffeted by random events in an aimless existence, believers see their lives as fitting into a divine plan.

Emotional Comfort   The answers that religion provides about ultimate meaning also comfort people by assuring them that there is a purpose to life, even to suffering. Similarly, religious rituals that enshroud crucial events such as illness and death provide emotional comfort at times of crisis. The individual knows that others care and can find consolation in following familiar rituals.

Social Solidarity   Religious teachings and practices unite believers into a community that shares values and perspectives ("we Jews," "we Christians," "we Muslims"). The religious rituals that surround marriage, for example, link the bride and groom with a broader community that wishes them well. So do other religious rituals, such as those that celebrate birth and mourn death.

Guidelines for Everyday Life   The teachings of religion are not all abstractions. They also provide practical directions on how to live our everyday lives. For example, four of the Ten Commandments delivered by Moses to the Israelites concern God, but the other six contain instructions on how to live everyday life, from how to get along with parents, employers, and neighbors to warnings about lying, stealing, and having affairs.

The consequences for people who follow these guidelines can be measured. People who attend church are less likely to abuse alcohol and illegal drugs than are people who don't go to church (Ostling 2001). This holds true for both adults and teens. In general, churchgoers follow a healthier lifestyle, and they live longer than those who don't go to church. A related function of religion is discussed in the Down-to-Earth Sociology box on the next page.

Social Control   Religion not only provides guidelines for everyday life, but also controls people's behaviors. Most norms of a religious group apply only to its members, but some set limits on nonmembers also. An example is religious teachings that are incorporated into criminal law. In the United States, for example, blasphemy and adultery were once crimes for which people could be arrested, tried, and sentenced. Laws that prohibit the sale of alcohol before noon on Sunday are another example.

Adaptation   Religion can help people adapt to new environments. For example, it isn't easy for immigrants to adjust to the customs of a new land. By keeping their native language alive and preserving familiar rituals and teachings, religion provides continuity with the immigrants' cultural past.

The handful of German immigrants who settled in Perry County, Missouri, in the 1800s, for example, even brought their Lutheran minister with them. Their sermons and hymns continued to be in German, and their children attended a school in which the minister conducted classes in German. Out of this small group grew the Lutheran Church-Missouri Synod, which, despite its name, is an international

down-to-earth sociology

■ ■ ■ ■ ■ News Flash! Prayer Works!

That prayer works would not be a news item for many believers. They pray, and they see results. They see lives changed, and even physical healings.

For scientists at Columbia University, however, that prayer actually works shocked them and made national news. The researchers, headed by the chairman of the Department of Obstetrics and Gynecology at Columbia University, were so astounded by their findings that at first they didn't know what to do with them. They didn't want to report their findings, for fear that their scientific colleagues would laugh at or ridicule them.

Their research was so scientifically solid, however, and the results so unambiguous that they decided the only thing they could do was to publish their findings.

What so astounded them?

The setting was a fertility program at Cha General Hospital in Seoul, South Korea. Being treated were women who wanted to have children but were having difficulty getting pregnant. One of the physicians suggested that prayer might make a difference in whether or not the women became pregnant. The medical researchers knew that prayer could not possibly make a difference.

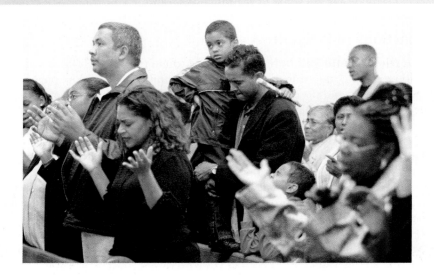

But, after all, what could they lose by trying?

To find out, the researchers set up a research design that would meet the standards of science (see Figure 18.1). Background information was gathered on the next 219 patients. A statistician in Korea collected the data and photographs of the women and sent them to another statistician in the United States.

(Twenty patients were lost to the sample due to fragmentary e-mail transmission.) This second statistician matched the remaining 199 women by age, reason for infertility, and length of infertility. The women were then randomly assigned by a computer to either the experimental group (those who would be prayed for) or the control group (those who would not receive prayer).

---

denomination that numbers about 2.5 million members. Little by little, this group's descendants and converts entered mainstream U.S. culture. Today, except for Luther's basic teachings and a few church practices, little remains of the past, for just as it helped the immigrants adapt to a new environment, so the religion itself changed to reflect that same environment.

Support for the Government   Most religions provide support for the government. An obvious example is the way many churches so prominently display the U.S. flag. For their part, governments reciprocate by supporting God—as witnessed by the way U.S. presidents, whether they are believers or not, invariably ask God to bless the nation in their inaugural speeches.

Some governments sponsor a particular religion, ban all others, provide financial support for building churches and seminaries, and even pay salaries to the clergy. These religions are known as **state religions.** During the sixteenth and seventeenth centuries in Sweden, the government sponsored Lutheranism; in Switzerland, Calvin-

state religion
a government-sponsored religion

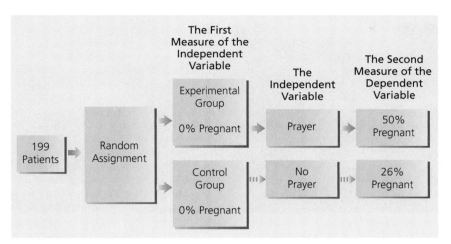

Figure 18.1

The Experimental Outcome
of Prayer for Infertile
Patients Undergoing
In Vitro Fertilization–
Embryo Transfer

[a]Pregnancy was determined by the
presence of a heartbeat detected
by untrasound.

The U.S. statistician sent photographs of the women who were to be prayed for to members of Christian denominations in the United States, Canada, and Australia. One group prayed for the women, a second group prayed that the prayers of the first group would be effective, and a third group prayed for the first two groups.

Those who were praying lived continents away from the women who were being prayed for. They prayed for three weeks.

This was a double blind experimental design. The women did *not* know they were being prayed for. (They still don't.) This eliminated the *placebo effect*—the possibility that suggestion or hope or some other emotion might be at work. Even the medical staff that was treating the women did *not* know about the experiment. This eliminated the possibility that the staff might somehow treat some women differently. All women received identical medical treat-ment, IVT-ET (*in vitro* fertilization-embryo transfer).

The results?

The women who were prayed for became pregnant *twice* as often as the women who did not have people praying for them.

Based on Cha et al. 2001; Nagourney 2001.

ism; and in Italy, Roman Catholicism. In other instances, even though the government sponsors no particular religion, religious beliefs are so established in a nation's life that the country's history and social institutions are sanctified by being associated with God. For example, U.S. officials—even those who do not belong to any particular religion—take office by swearing that they will, in the name of God, fulfill their duty. Similarly, Congress opens each session with a prayer led by its own chaplain, some schoolchildren recite the pledge of allegiance daily (including the phrase "one nation under God"), and coins bear the inscription "In God We Trust." Sociologist Robert Bellah (1970) referred to this phenomenon as **civil religion.**

Social Change   Although religion is often so bound up with the prevailing social order that it resists social change, occasionally religion spearheads change. In the 1960s, for example, the civil rights movement, which fought to desegregate public facilities and abolish racial discrimination at southern polls, was led by religious leaders, especially leaders of African American churches such as Martin Luther King, Jr.

civil religion
Robert Bellah's term for religion that is such an established feature of a country's life that its history and social institutions become sanctified by being associated with God

■ *Religion can promote social change, as was evident in the U.S. civil rights movement. Dr. Martin Luther King, Jr., a Baptist minister, shown here in his famous "I have a dream" speech, was the foremost leader of this movement.*

Churches also served as centers at which demonstrators were trained and rallies were organized.

■ Functional Equivalents of Religion

These functions—except for prayer and pregnancy—can also be fulfilled by other components of society. If some other component answers questions about ultimate meaning, provides emotional comfort and guidelines for daily life, and so on, sociologists call it a **functional equivalent** of religion. Thus, for some people, Alcoholics Anonymous is a functional equivalent of religion (Chalfant 1992). For others, psychotherapy, humanism, transcendental meditation, or even a political party performs similar functions.

Some functional equivalents are difficult to distinguish from a religion (Brinton 1965; Luke 1985). For example, communism had its prophets (Marx and Lenin), sacred writings (everything written by Marx, Engels, and Lenin, but especially the *Communist Manifesto*), high priests (the heads of the Communist party), sacred buildings (the Kremlin), shrines (Lenin's body on display in Red Square), rituals (the annual May Day parade in Red Square), and even martyrs (Cuba's Ché Guevara). Soviet communism was avowedly atheistic and tried to wipe out all traces of Christianity, Judaism, and Islam from its midst. It even tried to replace baptisms and circumcisions with state-sponsored rituals that dedicated the child to the state. The Communist party also composed its own rituals for weddings and funerals.

As sociologist Ian Robertson (1987) pointed out, however, there is a fundamental distinction between a religion and its functional equivalent. Although the substitute may perform similar functions, its activities are not directed toward God, gods, or the supernatural.

■ Dysfunctions of Religion

Functionalists also examine ways in which religion is *dysfunctional,* that is, how it can bring harmful results. Two main dysfunctions are war and religious persecution.

War and Terrorism History is filled with wars based on religion—commingled with politics. Between the eleventh and fourteenth centuries, for example, Christian monarchs conducted nine bloody Crusades in an attempt to wrest control of the Holy Land from the Muslims. Unfortunately, war and terrorism are not just a relic

functional equivalent
in this context, a substitute that serves the same functions (or meets the same needs) as religion, for example, psychotherapy

Ein erschröckliche geschicht/so zu Derneburg in der Graff-
schafft Reinstepn/am Harz gelegen/von dreyen Zauberin/vnnd zwayen
Mañen/In ettlichen tagen des Monats Octobris Im 1 5 5 5. Jare ergangen ist.

■ Woodcuts (prints made from engraved blocks of wood coated with ink to leave an impression on paper) were used to illustrate books shortly after the printing press was invented. This woodcut commemorates a dysfunction of religion, the burning of witches at the stake. This particular event occurred at Derneburg, Germany, in 1555.

of the past. In recent years, we have seen Protestants and Catholics slaughter one another in Northern Ireland, while Jews and Muslims in Israel have done the same thing. The terrorists who crashed the commercial airliners into the New York World Trade Center and the Pentagon believed they were in a *jihad*, a holy war, and that dying in a suicide mission gave them a ticket to paradise.

Religion as Justification for Persecution   Beginning in the 1200s and continuing into the 1800s, in what has become known as the Inquisition, special commissions of the Roman Catholic church tortured women to make them confess that they were witches, and then burned them at the stake. In 1692, Protestant leaders in Salem, Massachusetts, executed 21 men and women who were accused of being witches. (The last execution for witchcraft was in Scotland in 1722 [Bridgwater 1953].) Similarly, it seems fair to say that the Aztec religion had its dysfunctions—at least for the virgins who were offered to appease angry gods. In short, religion has been used to justify oppression and any number of brutal acts.

■ ■ ■ ■ ■

The Symbolic Interactionist Perspective

Symbolic interactionists focus on the meanings that people give their experiences, especially how they use symbols. Let's apply this perspective to religious symbols, rituals, and beliefs to see how they help to forge a community of like-minded people.

■ Religious Symbols

Suppose that it is about two thousand years ago and you have just joined a new religion. You have come to believe that a recently crucified Jew named Jesus is the Messiah, the Lamb of God offered for your sins. The Roman leaders are persecuting the followers of Jesus. They hate your religion because you and your fellow believers will not acknowledge Caesar as God.

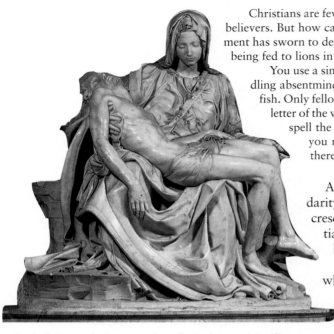

▪ *Symbolic interactionists stress that a basic characteristic of humans is that they attach meaning to objects and events and then use representations of those objects or events to communicate with one another. Some religious symbols are used to communicate feelings of awe and reverence. Michaelangelo's Pietà, depicting Mary tenderly holding her son, Jesus, after his crucifixion, is one of the most acclaimed symbols in the Western world. It is admired for its beauty by believers and nonbelivers alike.*

Christians are few in number, and you are eager to have fellowship with other believers. But how can you tell who is a believer? Spies are all over. The government has sworn to destroy this new religion, and you do not relish the thought of being fed to lions in the Coliseum.

You use a simple technique. While talking with a stranger, as though doodling absentmindedly in the sand or dust, you casually trace the outline of a fish. Only fellow believers know the meaning—that, taken together, the first letter of the words in the Greek sentence "Jesus (is) Christ the Son of God" spell the Greek word for *fish*. If the other person gives no response, you rub out the outline and continue the interaction as usual. If there is a response, you eagerly talk about your new faith.

All religions use symbols to provide identity and social solidarity for their members. For Muslims, the primary symbol is the crescent moon and star; for Jews, the Star of David; for Christians, the cross. For members, these are not ordinary symbols, but sacred emblems that evoke feelings of awe and reverence. In Durkheim's terms, religions use symbols to specify what is sacred and to separate the sacred from the profane.

A symbol is a condensed way of communicating. Worn by a fundamentalist Christian, for example, the cross says, "I am a follower of Jesus Christ. I believe that He is the Messiah, the promised Son of God, that He loves me, that He died to take away my sins, that He rose from the dead and is going to return to earth, and that through Him I will receive eternal life."

That is a lot to pack into one symbol—and it is only part of what the symbol means to a fundamentalist believer. To people in other traditions of Christianity, the cross conveys somewhat different meanings—but to all Christians, the cross is a shorthand way of expressing many meanings. So it is with the Star of David, the crescent moon and star, the cow (expressing to Hindus the unity of all living things), and the various symbols of the world's many other religions.

▪ Rituals

Rituals, ceremonies or repetitive practices, are also symbols that help unite people into a moral community. Some rituals, such as the bar mitzvah of Jewish boys and the Holy Communion of Christians, are designed to create in the devout a feeling of closeness with God and unity with one another. Rituals include kneeling and praying at set times, bowing, crossing oneself, singing, lighting candles and incense, scripture readings, processions, baptisms, weddings, funerals, and so on.

▪ Beliefs

Symbols, including rituals, develop from beliefs. The belief may be vague ("God is") or highly specific ("God wants us to prostrate ourselves and face Mecca five times each day"). Religious beliefs include not only *values* (what is considered good and desirable in life—how we ought to live) but also a **cosmology,** a unified picture of the world. For example, the Jewish, Christian, and Muslim belief that there is only one God, the Creator of the universe, who is concerned about the actions of humans and who will hold us accountable for what we do, is a cosmology. It presents a unifying picture of the universe.

rituals
ceremonies or repetitive practices; in this context, religious observances or rites, often intended to evoke a sense of awe of the sacred

cosmology
teachings or ideas that provide a unified picture of the world

Religious Experience

The term **religious experience** refers to a sudden awareness of the supernatural or a feeling of coming in contact with God. Some people undergo a mild version, such as feeling closer to God when they look at a mountain or listen to a certain piece of music. Others report a life-transforming experience. St. Francis of Assisi, for example, said that he became aware of God's presence in every living thing.

Some Protestants use the term **born again** to describe people who have undergone such a life-transforming religious experience. These people say they came to the realization that they had sinned, that Jesus had died for their sins, and that God wants them to live a new life. Their worlds become transformed. They look forward to the Resurrection and to a new life in heaven, and they see relationships with spouses, parents, children, and even bosses in a new light. They also report a need to make changes in how they interact with others so that their lives reflect their new, personal commitment to Jesus as their "Savior and Lord." They describe a feeling of beginning life anew, hence the term *born again*.

Community

Finally, the shared meanings that come through symbols, rituals, and beliefs (and for some, a religious experience) unite people into a moral community. People in a moral community feel a bond with one another, for their beliefs and rituals bind them together while at the same time separating them from those who do not share their unique symbolic world. Mormons, for example, feel a "kindred spirit" (as it is often known) with other Mormons. Baptists, Jews, Jehovah's Witnesses, and Muslims feel the same toward members of their respective faiths.

As a symbol of their unity, members of some religious groups address one another as "brother" or "sister." "Sister Luby, we are going to meet at Brother and Sister Maher's on Wednesday" is a common way of expressing a message. The terms *brother* and *sister* are intended to symbolize a relationship so close that the individuals consider themselves members of the same family.

Community is powerful, not only because it provides the basis for mutual identity, but also because it establishes norms that govern the behavior of its members. Members either conform, or they lose their membership. In Christian churches, for example, an individual whose adultery becomes known, and who refuses to ask forgiveness, may be banned from the Church. He or she may be formally excommunicated, as in the Catholic tradition, or more informally "stricken from the rolls," as is the usual Protestant practice.

Removal from the community is a serious matter for people whose identity is bound up in the community. Sociologists John Hostetler (1980), William Kephart, and William Zellner (1994) describe the Amish practice of *shunning*—ignoring an offender in all situations. Persons who are shunned are treated as though they do not exist (for if they do not repent by expressing sorrow for their act they have ceased to exist as members of the community). The shunning is so thorough that even family members, who themselves remain in good standing in the congregation, are not allowed to talk to the person being shunned. This obviously makes for some interesting meals.

religious experience
a sudden awareness of the supernatural or a feeling of coming in contact with God

born again
a term describing Christians who have undergone a life-transforming religious experience so radical that they feel they have become new persons

■ One of the functions of religion is to create community. To help accomplish this, religions often use rituals to help unite their members. Shown here is a candlelight vigil held by the Falun Gong, a religious movement outlawed by the Chinese government as a dangerous religious cult.

The Conflict Perspective

The conflict perspective has an entirely different focus. Conflict theorists examine how religion supports the status quo and helps to maintain social inequalities.

■ Opium of the People

In general, conflict theorists are highly critical of religion. Karl Marx, an avowed atheist who believed that the existence of God was impossible, set the tone for conflict theorists with his most famous statement on this subject: "Religion is the sigh of the oppressed creature, the sentiment of a heartless world. . . . It is the opium of the people" (Marx 1844/1964). By this statement, Marx meant that oppressed workers escape into religion. For them, religion is like a drug that helps them forget their misery. By diverting their thoughts to future happiness in a coming world, religion takes their eyes off their suffering in this one, thereby greatly reducing the possibility that they will rebel against their oppressors.

■ A Reflection of Social Inequalities

Conflict theorists stress that religious teachings and practices are a mirror of a society's inequalities. Gender inequality illustrates this point. When men completely dominated U.S. society, U.S. churches and synagogues ordained only men, limiting women to such activities as teaching children in Sunday school or preparing meals for congregational get-togethers—things that were considered appropriate "feminine" activities. As women's roles in the broader society changed, however, religion reflected those changes. First, many religious groups allowed women to vote. Then, as women attained prominent positions in the business world and professions, some Protestant and Jewish groups allowed women to be ordained. Similarly, just as women still face barriers in secular society, so some congregations still refuse to ordain women. In some congregations the barriers remain so high that women are still not allowed to vote.

■ A Legitimation of Social Inequalities

Conflict theorists say that religion not only mirrors the social inequalities of the larger society, but also legitimates them. By this, they mean that religion teaches that the existing social arrangements of a society represent what God desires. For example, during the Middle Ages, Christian theologians decreed the "divine right of kings." This doctrine meant that God determined who would become king, and set him on the throne. The king ruled in God's place, and it was the duty of a king's subjects to be loyal to him (and to pay their taxes). To disobey the king was to disobey God.

In what was perhaps the supreme technique of legitimating the social order (and one that went even a step further than the "divine right of kings"), the religion of ancient Egypt held that the Pharaoh was a god. The Emperor of Japan was similarly declared divine. If this were so, who could ever question his decisions? Today's politicians would give their right arm for such a religious teaching. Deification endorsed by religion!

Conflict theorists point to many other examples of how religion legitimates the social order. In India, Hinduism supports the caste system by teaching that an individual who tries to change caste will come back in the next life as a member of a lower caste—or even as an animal. In the decades before the American Civil War, Southern ministers used scripture to defend slavery, saying that it was God's will—while northern ministers legitimated *their* region's social structure by using scripture to denounce slavery as evil (Ernst 1988; Nauta 1993; White 1995).

Religion and the Spirit of Capitalism

Max Weber disagreed with the conflict perspective that religion merely reflects and legitimates the social order, and that religion impedes social change by encouraging people to focus on the afterlife. In contrast, Weber saw religion's focus on the afterlife as a source of profound social change.

Like Marx, Weber observed the industrialization of European countries. Weber became intrigued with the question of why some societies embraced capitalism while others clung to their traditional ways. Tradition is strong and tends to hold people in check, yet some societies had been transformed by capitalism, while others remained untouched. As he explored this puzzle, Weber concluded that religion held the key to **modernization**—the transformation of traditional societies to industrial societies.

To explain his conclusions, Weber wrote *The Protestant Ethic and the Spirit of Capitalism* (1904–1905/1958). Because Weber's argument was presented in Chapter 7 (pages 188–189), it is only summarized here.

1. Capitalism is not just a superficial change. Rather, capitalism represents a fundamentally different way of thinking about work and money. *Traditionally, people worked just enough to meet their basic needs, not so that they could have a surplus to invest.* To accumulate money (capital) as an end in itself, not just to spend it, was a radical departure from traditional thinking. People even came to consider it a duty to invest money in order to make profits, which, in turn, they reinvested to make more profits. Weber called this new approach to work and money the **spirit of capitalism.**

2. Why did the spirit of capitalism develop in Europe, and not, for example, in China or India, where the people had similar material resources, education, and so on? According to Weber, *religion was the key.* The religions of China and India, and indeed Roman Catholicism in Europe, encouraged a traditional approach to life, not thrift and investment. Capitalism appeared when Protestantism came on the scene.

3. What was different about Protestantism, especially Calvinism? John Calvin taught that God had predestined some people to heaven, others to hell. Neither church membership nor feelings about your relationship with God could assure you that you were saved. You wouldn't know your fate until after you died.

4. This doctrine created intense anxiety among Calvin's followers: "Am I predestined to hell or to heaven?" they wondered. As Calvinists wrestled with this question, they concluded that church members have a duty to prove that they are one of God's elect, and to live as though they are predestined to heaven—for good works are a demonstration of salvation.

5. This conclusion motivated Calvinists to lead moral lives *and* to work hard, to not waste time, and to be frugal—for idleness and needless spending were signs of worldliness. Weber called this self-denying approach to life the **Protestant ethic.**

6. As people worked hard and spent money only on necessities (a pair of earrings or a second pair of dress shoes would have been defined as sinful luxuries), they accumulated money. Because it couldn't be spent, this capital was invested—which led to a surge in production.

7. Thus, a change in religion (from Catholicism to Protestantism, especially Calvinism) led to a fundamental change in thought and behavior (the *Protestant ethic*). The result was the *spirit of capitalism.* Thus capitalism originated in Europe, and not in places where religion did not encourage capitalism's essential elements: the accumulation of capital and its investment and reinvestment.

Although Weber's analysis has been influential, it has not lacked critics (Kaelber 2001). Hundreds of scholars have attacked it, some for overlooking the lack of capitalism in Scotland (a Calvinist country), others for failing to explain why the Industrial Revolution was born in England (not a Calvinist country). Hundreds of other scholars

modernization
the transformation of traditional societies into industrial societies

spirit of capitalism
Weber's term for the desire to accumulate capital as a duty—not to spend it, but as an end in itself—and to constantly reinvest it

Protestant ethic
Weber's term to describe the ideal of a self-denying, highly moral life, accompanied by hard work and frugality

have defended Weber's argument. There is currently no historical evidence that can definitively prove or disprove Weber's thesis.

At this point in history, the Protestant ethic and the spirit of capitalism are not confined to any specific religion or even to any one part of the world. Rather, they have become cultural traits that have spread to societies around the world (Greeley 1964; Yinger 1970). U.S. Catholics have about the same approach to life as do U.S. Protestants. In addition, Hong Kong, Japan, Malaysia, Singapore, South Korea, and Taiwan—not exactly Protestant countries—have embraced capitalism (Levy 1992).

■ ■ ■ ■ ■

The World's Major Religions

The largest of the thousands of religions in the world are listed in Table 18.1. Let's briefly review six of them.

■ Judaism

The origin of Judaism is traced to Abraham, who lived about four thousand years ago in Mesopotamia. Jews believe that God (Jahweh) made a covenant with Abraham, selecting his descendants as a chosen people and promising to make them "as numerous as the sands of the seashore" and to give them a special land that would be theirs forever. The sign of this covenant was the circumcision of males, which was to be performed when a boy was eight days old. Descent is traced through Abraham and his wife, Sarah, their son Isaac, and their grandson Jacob (also called Israel).

Joseph, a son of Jacob, was sold by his brothers into slavery and taken to Egypt. Following a series of hair-raising adventures, Joseph became Pharaoh's right-hand man. When a severe famine hit Canaan, where Jacob's family was living, Jacob and his eleven other sons fled to Egypt. Under Joseph's leadership, they were welcome. A subsequent Pharaoh, however, enslaved the Israelites. After about four hundred years, Moses, an Israelite who had been adopted by Pharaoh's daughter, confronted Pharaoh. He persuaded Pharaoh to release the slaves, which at that time numbered about 2 million. Moses led them out of Egypt, but before they reached their Promised Land, the Israelites spent forty years wandering in the desert. Sometime during those years, Moses delivered the Ten Commandments from Mount Sinai. Abraham, Isaac, Jacob, and Moses hold revered positions in Judaism. The events of their lives and the recounting of the early history of the Israelites are contained in the first five books of the Bible, called the Torah.

The founding of Judaism marked a fundamental change in religion, for it was the first religion based on **monotheism,** the belief that there is only one God. Prior to Judaism, religions were based on **polytheism,** the belief that there are many gods. In Greek religion, for example, Zeus was the god of heaven and earth, Poseidon the god of the sea, and Athena the goddess of wisdom. Other groups followed **animism,** believing that all objects in the world have spirits, some of which are dangerous and must be outwitted.

Contemporary Judaism in the United States comprises three main branches: Orthodox, Reform, and Conservative. Orthodox Jews adhere to the laws espoused by Moses. They

monotheism
the belief that there is only one God

polytheism
the belief that there are many gods

animism
the belief that all objects in the world have spirits, some of which are dangerous and must be outwitted

T A B L E **18.1**	The World's Largest Religions[a]
Religion	**Number of Followers**
Christians	1,900,000,000
Muslims	1,200,000,000
Hindus	762,000,000
Chinese folk religions	379,000,000
Buddhists	354,000,000
Sikhs	22,000,000
Jews	14,000,000
Spiritualists	12,000,000
Baha'is	7,000,000
Confucians	6,000,000
Jains	4,000,000
Shintoists	3,000,000

[a]*Note:* The classification of religions is often confusing. Animists, for example, although numerous, are not listed as a separate group in the source, while an amorphous classification of "new religions" is. It is often difficult to tell what groups are encompassed in what categories.
Source: Statistical Abstract 1999:Table 1348.

eat only foods prepared in a designated manner (kosher), observe the Sabbath in a traditional way, and segregate males and females in their religious services. During the 1800s, a group that wanted to make their practices more compatible with U.S. culture broke from this tradition. This liberal group, known as Reform Judaism, mostly uses English in its religious ceremonies and has reduced much of the ritual. The third branch, Conservative Judaism, falls somewhere between the other two. No branch has continued polygyny (allowing a man to have more than one wife), the original marriage custom of the Jews, which was outlawed by rabbinic decree about a thousand years ago.

■ *Religion, which provides community and identification, is passed from the older to the younger. Shown here are older orthodox Jews in Miami Beach as they bind prayers around the arms of adolescent boys. The boys, in turn, will replace their elders and transmit their religion to the next generation.*

The history of Judaism is marked by conflict and persecution. The Israelites were conquered by Babylon, and were again made slaves. After returning to Israel and rebuilding the temple, they were later conquered by Rome, and after their rebellion at Masada in A.D. 70 failed, they were exiled for almost two thousand years into other nations. During those centuries, they faced prejudice, discrimination, and persecution (called **anti-Semitism**) by many peoples and rulers. The most horrendous example was Hitler's attempt to eliminate the Jews as a people in the Nazi Holocaust of World War II. Under the Nazi occupation of Europe and North Africa, about 6 million Jews were slaughtered. Many died in gas ovens that were constructed for just this purpose.

Central to Jewish teaching is the requirement to love God and do good deeds. Good deeds begin in the family, where each member has an obligation toward the others. Sin is a conscious choice to do evil, and must be atoned for by prayers and good works. Jews consider Jerusalem their holiest city and believe that the Messiah will one day appear there, bringing redemption for them all.

■ Christianity

Christianity, which developed out of Judaism, is also monotheistic. Christians believe that Jesus Christ is the Messiah whom God promised the Jews.

Jesus was born in poverty, and traditional Christians believe he was born to a virgin. Within two years of his birth, Herod, named king of Palestine by Caesar, who had conquered Israel, was informed that people were saying a new king had been born. When Herod sent soldiers to kill Jesus, Jesus' parents fled with him to Egypt. After Herod died, they returned, settling in the small town of Nazareth.

At about the age of 30, Jesus began a preaching and healing ministry. His teachings challenged the contemporary religious establishment, and as his popularity grew the religious leaders plotted to have him killed by the Romans. Christians interpret the death of Jesus as a blood sacrifice made to atone for their sins. They believe that through his death they have peace with God and will inherit eternal life.

The twelve main followers of Jesus, called *apostles,* believed that Jesus rose from the dead. They preached the need to be "born again," that is, to accept Jesus as Savior, give up selfish ways, and live a devout life. The new religion spread rapidly, and after an initial period of hostility on the part of imperial Rome—during which time believers were fed to the lions in the Coliseum—in A.D. 317 Christianity became the empire's official religion.

During the first thousand years of Christianity, there was only one church organization, directed from Rome. During the eleventh century, after disagreement over doctrine and politics, Greek Orthodoxy was established. It was headquartered in Constantinople (now Istanbul, Turkey). During the Middle Ages, the Roman Catholic church, which was aligned with the political establishment, grew corrupt. Some Church offices, such as that of bishop, were sold for a set price, and, in a situation that touched off the Reformation led by Martin Luther in the sixteenth century, the forgiveness of sins (including those not yet committed) could be purchased by buying an "indulgence."

anti-Semitism
prejudice, discrimination, and persecution directed against Jews

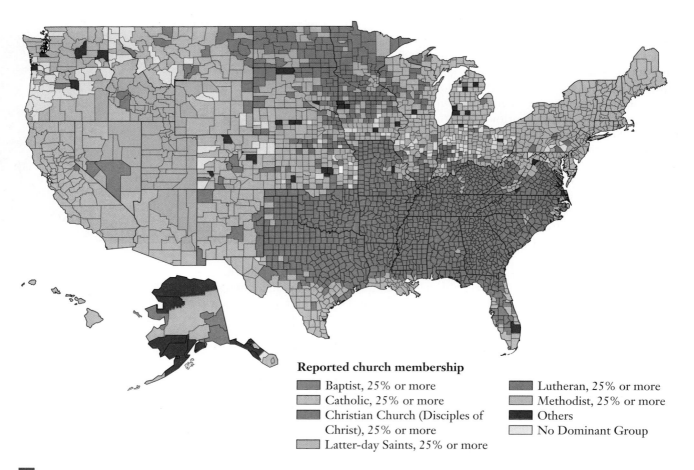

Reported church membership

- Baptist, 25% or more
- Catholic, 25% or more
- Christian Church (Disciples of Christ), 25% or more
- Latter-day Saints, 25% or more
- Lutheran, 25% or more
- Methodist, 25% or more
- Others
- No Dominant Group

Figure 18.2

Social Map: Church Membership: Dominant Religion, by County

Source: Bradley et al. 1992

Although Martin Luther's original goal was to reform the Church, not divide it, the Reformation began a splintering of Christianity. It coincided with the breakup of feudalism, and as the ancient political structure came apart, people clamored for independence not only in political ideology but also in religious thought. Today, Christianity is the most popular religion in the world, with about 2 billion adherents. Christians are divided into hundreds of groups, some with doctrinal differences so slight that only members of the group can appreciate the extremely fine distinctions that, they feel, significantly separate them from others. The Social Map above shows how some of these groups are distributed in the United States.

■ Islam

Islam, whose followers are known as Muslims, began in the same part of the world as Judaism and Christianity. Islam, the world's third monotheistic religion, has over a billion followers. It was founded by Muhammad, who was born in Mecca (now in Saudi Arabia) in about A.D. 570. Muhammad married Khadija, a wealthy widow. About the age of 40, he reported that he had had visions from God. These, and his teachings, were later written down in a book called the Koran. Few paid attention to Muhammad, although Ali, his son-in-law, believed him. When he found out that there was a plot to murder him, Muhammad fled to Medina, where he found a more receptive audience. There he established a *theocracy* (a government based on the principle that God is king, God's laws the statutes of the land, and priests the earthly administrators of God). In A.D. 630 he returned to Mecca, this time as a conqueror (Bridgwater 1953).

After Muhammad's death, a struggle for control over the empire he had founded split Islam into two branches that remain today, the Sunni and the Shi'ite. The Shi'ites believe that the *imam* (the religious leader) is inspired as he interprets the Koran. They are generally more conservative and are inclined to **fundamentalism,** the belief

fundamentalism

the belief that true religion is threatened by modernism and that the faith as it was originally practiced should be restored that modernism threatens religion and that the faith as it was originally practiced should be restored. The Sunni, who do not share this belief, are generally more liberal, more accepting of social change.

Like the Jews, Muslims trace their ancestry to Abraham. Abraham fathered a son, Ishmael, by Hagar, his wife Sarah's Egyptian maid (Genesis 25:12). Ishmael had twelve sons, from whom a good portion of today's Arab world is descended. For them also, Jerusalem is a holy city. The Muslims consider the Bibles of the Jews and the Christians to be sacred but take the Koran as the final word. They believe that the followers of Abraham and Moses (Jews) and Jesus (Christians) changed the original teachings and that Muhammad restored their purity. It is the duty of each Muslim to make a pilgrimage to Mecca during his or her lifetime. Unlike the Jews, the Muslims continue to practice polygyny. They limit a man to four wives, however.

Because of immigration from the Mideast and conversions of African Americans, Islam has grown rapidly in the past few decades in the United States. This topic is explored in the Cultural Diversity box below.

cultural d·i·v·e·r·s·i·t·y

in the United States

The New Neighbor: Islam in the United States

In a scene that is growing increasingly familiar, instead of going into a church or synagogue to pray and worship, many Americans take off their shoes, face Mecca, and kneel with their faces to the floor.

Called by some the fastest growing religion in the United States, Islam is making its presence felt. Islam's growth is fueled by two main sources. The primary source is the millions of immigrants from the Middle East and Asia who have arrived in the United States since the 1980s. Like the immigrants before them, these refugees from Muslim countries brought along their religion as part of their culture. The second source is African Americans. Although believers represent a cross-section of African Americans, the call of Islam is heard most loudly in the inner city (Peart 1993). Overall, U.S. Muslims are about 42 percent African American, 25 percent South Asian, 12 percent Arab, and the remainder from a mix of backgrounds (Power 1998).

The appeal of Islam to African Americans is the message of black pride, self-improvement, and black power. Although U.S. Muslims are divided among about twenty groups, the appeal is similar: morality (no drugs, crime, or extramarital

■ *Universally, children are socialized into the religion of their group. The kindergarten students shown here at the Al-Ghazaly Islamic school in Jersey City, New Jersey, are learning how to pray.*

sex), respect for women, and black empowerment. Among all groups, modest clothing is required. Among some, ultra-conservative codes govern behavior: Men and women sit apart in public, women wear robes that cover them from head to toe, and one-on-one dating is prohibited (Tapia 1994). Many men embrace the authority that Islam ascribes to them. For many, both men and women, Islam is a way to connect with African roots.

For many Americans, Louis Farrakhan is synonymous with U.S. Islam. Although he is the most visible and vocal Muslim leader, the group he heads, the Nation of Islam,

has only about 10,000 members (Brooke 1995). The Chicago-based Muslim American Society, headed by W. Dean Mohammed, has 200,000 members (Miller 1999).

Just as their organizations are diverse, so their opinions are wide-ranging. With regard to race, for example, some believe the races are equal; others believe African Americans are superior and whites are devils. Similarly, some groups stress black separatism, while others emphasize the need to start businesses and run for office (Miller 1999).

Alarmed that Islam has gained so many converts, some African American Christians are counterattacking. They hold Muslim Awareness seminars in order to warn Christians away from Islam (Tapia 1994). A former Black Muslim who is now a Christian evangelist and who sees it as his duty to counter Islam, says the difference is grace. "Islam is a works-oriented religion, but Christianity is built on God's grace in Jesus."

"His is just a slave religion," retort some Muslims.

The many mosques that are taking their place in the midst of churches and synagogues can be taken as a sign of a maturing multicultural society.

◼ Hinduism

Unlike the other religions described, Hinduism has no specific founder. Going back about four thousand years, Hinduism is the chief religion of India. The term *Hinduism,* however, is Western, and in India the closest term is *dharma* (law). Unlike Judaism, Christianity, and Islam, Hinduism has no canonical scripture, that is, no texts thought to be inspired by God. Instead, several books, including the *Brahmanas, Bhagavad-Gita,* and *Upanishads,* expound on moral qualities that people should strive to develop. They also delineate the sacrifices people should make to the gods.

Hindus are *polytheists;* that is, they believe that there are many gods. They believe that one of these gods, Brahma, created the universe. Brahma, along with Shiva (the Destroyer) and Vishnu (the Preserver), form a triad that is at the center of modern Hinduism. A central belief is *karma,* spiritual progress. There is no final judgment, but, instead, **reincarnation,** a cycle of life, death, and rebirth. Death involves only the body, and each person's soul comes back in a form that matches the individual's moral progress in the previous life (which centers on proper conduct in following the rules of one's caste). If an individual reaches spiritual perfection, he or she has attained *nirvana.* This marks the end of the cycle of death and rebirth, when the soul is reunited with the universal soul. When this occurs, *maya,* the illusion of time and space, has been conquered.

Some Hindu practices have been modified as a consequence of social protest—especially child marriage and *suttee,* the practice of cremating a surviving widow along with her deceased husband (Bridgwater 1953). Other ancient rituals remain unchanged, such as *kumbh mela,* a purifying washing in the Ganges River, which takes place every twelve years, and in which many millions participate.

reincarnation
in Hinduism and Buddhism, the return of the self after death in a different form

◼ Buddhism

In about 600 B.C., Siddhartha Gautama founded Buddhism. (Buddha means the "enlightened one," a term Gautama was given by his disciples.) Gautama was the son of an upper-caste Hindu ruler in an area north of Benares, India. At the age of 29, he renounced his life of luxury and became an ascetic. Through meditation, he discovered the "four noble truths," which emphasize self-denial and compassion.

1. Existence is suffering.
2. The origin of suffering is desire.
3. Suffering ceases when desire ceases.
4. The way to end desire is to follow the "noble eightfold path."

The noble eightfold path consists of

1. Right belief
2. Right resolve (to renounce carnal pleasure and to harm no living creature)
3. Right speech
4. Right conduct
5. Right occupation or living
6. Right effort
7. Right-mindedness (or contemplation)
8. Right ecstasy

The central symbol of Buddhism is the eight-spoked wheel. Each spoke represents one aspect of the path. As with Hinduism, the ultimate goal of Buddhism is the cessation of rebirth and thereby of suffer-

■ *Depictions of Buddha are found throughout the world. Many Buddhists have small statues in their homes and businesses, at which they make daily food offerings. This statue is located at Sukhothai, Thailand.*

ing. Buddhists teach that all things are temporary, even the self. Because all things are destined to pass away, there is no soul (Reat 1994).

Buddhism spread rapidly. In the third century B.C., the ruler of India adopted Buddhism and sent missionaries throughout Asia to spread the new teaching (Bridgwater 1953). By the fifth century A.D., Buddhism reached the height of its popularity in India, after which it died out. Buddhism, however, had been adopted in Ceylon, Burma, Tibet, Laos, Cambodia, Thailand, China, Korea, and Japan, where it flourishes today. Vigorous communities of Buddhists have also developed in the United States.

■ Confucianism

About the time that Gautama lived, K'ung Fu-tsu (551–479 B. C.) was born in China. Confucius (his name strung together in English), a public official, was distressed by the corruption that he saw in government. Unlike Gautama, who urged withdrawal from social activities, Confucius urged social reform and developed a system of morality based on peace, justice, and universal order. His teachings were incorporated into writings called the *Analects*.

The basic moral principle of Confucianism is to maintain *jen,* sympathy or concern for other humans. The key to jen is to sustain right relationships—being loyal and placing morality above self-interest. In what is called the "Confucian Golden Rule," Confucius stated a basic principle for jen: to treat those who are subordinate to you as you would like to be treated by people superior to yourself. Confucius taught that right relationships within the family (loyalty, respect) should be the model for society. He also taught the "middle way," an avoidance of extremes.

Confucianism was originally atheistic, simply a set of moral teachings without reference to the supernatural. As the centuries passed, however, local gods were added to the teachings, and Confucius himself was declared a god. Confucius' teachings became the basis for the government of China. About A.D. 1000, the emphasis on meditation gave way to a stress on improvement through acquiring knowledge. This emphasis remained dominant until the twentieth century. By this time, the government had become rigid, and respect for the existing order had replaced respect for relationships (Bridgwater 1953). Following the Communist revolution of 1949, political leaders attempted to weaken the people's ties with Confucianism. They partially succeeded, but Confucianism remains embedded in Chinese culture.

Types of Religious Groups

Sociologists have identified four types of religious groups: cult, sect, church, and ecclesia. The summary presented here is a modification of analyses by sociologists Ernst Troeltsch (1931), Liston Pope (1942), and Benton Johnson (1963). Figure 18.3 illustrates the relationship between each of these four types of groups.

■ Cult

The word *cult* conjures up bizarre images—shaven heads, weird music, brainwashing—even ritual suicide may come to mind. Cults, however, are not necessarily weird, and few practice "brainwashing" or bizarre rituals. In fact, *all religions began as cults* (Stark 1989). A **cult** is simply a new or different religion whose teachings and practices put it at odds with the dominant culture and religion. Because the term cult arouses such negative meanings in the public mind, however, some scholars prefer to use *new religion* instead.

Cults often begin with the appearance of a **charismatic leader,** an individual who inspires people because he or she seems to have extraordinary qualities. **Charisma** refers to an outstanding gift or to some exceptional quality. Finding something highly

cult
a new religion with few followers, whose teachings and practices put it at odds with the dominant culture and religion

charismatic leader
literally, someone to whom God has given a gift; more commonly, someone who exerts extraordinary appeal to a group of followers

charisma
literally, an extraordinary gift from God; more commonly, an outstanding, "magnetic" personality

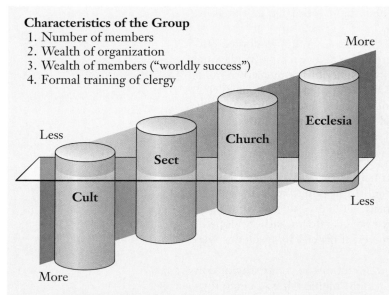

Characteristics of the Group
1. Number of members
2. Wealth of organization
3. Wealth of members ("worldly success")
4. Formal training of clergy

The Group Emphasizes
1. The need to reject society
   (the culture is a threat to true religion)
2. That it is rejected by society (the group feels hostility)
3. Hostility toward other religions
4. Hostility from other religions
5. Personal salvation
6. Emotional expression of religious beliefs
7. Revelation (God speaks directly to people)
8. God's direct intervention in people's lives
   (such as providing guidance or healing)
9. A duty to spread the message (evangelism)
10. A literal interpretation of scripture
11. A literal heaven and hell
12. That a conversion experience is necessary

Note: Any religious organization can be placed somewhere on this continuum, based on its having "more" or "less" of these characteristics.

Figure 18.3

Religious Groups:
From Hostility to Acceptance
Sources: Based on Troeltsch 1931; Pope 1942; and Johnson 1963.

appealing about the individual—in some instances, almost a magnetic charm—people feel drawn to both the person and the message.

The most popular religion in the world began as a cult. Its handful of followers believed that an unschooled carpenter who preached in remote villages in a backwater country was the Son of God, that he was killed and came back to life. Those beliefs made the early Christians a cult, setting them apart from the rest of their society. Persecuted by both religious and political authorities, these early believers clung to one another for support. Many cut off associations with their friends, who didn't accept the new message. To others, the early Christians must have seemed deluded and brainwashed.

So it was with Islam. When Muhammad revealed his visions and said that God's name was really Allah, only a few people believed him. To others, he must have seemed crazy, deranged.

Each cult (or new religion) is met with rejection on the part of society. Its message is considered bizarre, its approach to life strange. Its members antagonize the majority, who are convinced that they have a monopoly on the truth. The new message may claim revelation, visions, visits from God and angels, some form of enlightenment, or seeing the true way to God. The cult demands intense commitment, and its followers, who are confronting a hostile world, pull together in a tight circle, separating themselves from nonbelievers.

Most cults fail. Not many people believe the new message, and the cult fades into obscurity. Some, however, succeed and make history. Over time, large numbers of people may come to accept the message and become followers of the religion. If this happens, the new religion changes from a cult to a sect.

■ Sect

A **sect** is larger than a cult, but its members still feel tension between their views and the prevailing beliefs and values of the broader society. A sect may even be hostile to its society. At the very least, its members remain uncomfortable with many of the emphases of the dominant culture, and nonmembers, in turn, tend to be uncomfortable with members of the sect.

Ordinarily, sects are loosely organized and fairly small. They emphasize personal salvation and an emotional expression of one's relationship with God. Clapping, shouting, dancing, and extemporaneous prayers are hallmarks of sects. Like cults, sects also stress **evangelism,** the active recruitment of new members.

If a sect grows, its members tend to gradually make peace with the rest of society. To appeal to a broader base, the sect shifts some of its doctrines, redefining matters to remove some of the rough edges that created tension between it and the rest of society. As the members become more respectable in the eyes of the society, they

sect
a group larger than a cult that still feels substantial hostility from and toward society

evangelism
an attempt to win converts

feel less hostility and little, if any, isolation. If a sect follows this course, as it grows and becomes more integrated into society, it changes into a church.

Church

At this point, the religious group is highly bureaucratized—probably with national and international headquarters that give direction to the local congregations, enforce rules about who can be ordained, and control finances. The relationship with God has grown less intense. The group is likely to have less emphasis on personal salvation and emotional expression. Worship services are likely to be more sedate, with sermons more formal, and written prayers read before the congregation. Rather than being recruited from the outside by fervent, personal evangelism, most new members now come from within, from children born to existing members. Rather than joining through conversion—seeing the new truth—children may be baptized, circumcised, or dedicated in some other way. At some designated age, children may be asked to affirm the group's beliefs in a confirmation or bar mitzvah ceremony.

Ecclesia

Finally, some groups become so well integrated into a culture, and so strongly allied with their government, that it is difficult to tell where one leaves off and the other takes over. In these *state religions*, also called **ecclesia**, the government and religion work together to try to shape society. There is no recruitment of members, for citizenship makes everyone a member. The majority of the society, however, may belong to the religion in name only. The religion is part of a cultural identification, not an eye-opening experience. How extensively religion and government intertwine in an ecclesia is illustrated by Sweden. In the 1860s, all citizens had to memorize Luther's *Small Catechism* and be tested on it yearly (Anderson 1995). Today, Lutheranism is still the state religion, but most Swedes come to church only for baptisms, marriages, and funerals.

While cults and sects see God as personally involved with and concerned about an individual's life, requiring an intense and direct response, ecclesias envision God as more impersonal and remote. Church services reflect this view of the supernatural, for they tend to be highly formal, directed by ministers or priests who, after undergoing rigorous training in approved schools or seminaries, follow prescribed rituals.

Examples of ecclesia include the Church of England (whose very name expresses alignment between church and state), the Lutheran church in Sweden and Denmark, Islam in Iran and Iraq, and, during the time of the Holy Roman Empire, the Roman Catholic church, which was the official religion for the region that is now Europe.

Variations in Patterns

Obviously, not all religious groups go through all these stages—from cult to sect to church to ecclesia. Some die out because they fail to attract enough members. Others, such as the Amish, remain sects. And, as is evident from the few countries that have state religions, very few religions ever become ecclesias.

In addition, these classifications are not perfectly matched in the real world. For example, although the Amish are a sect, they place little or no emphasis on recruiting others. The early Quakers, another sect, shied away from emotional expressions of their beliefs. They would quietly meditate in church, with no one speaking, until God gave someone a message to share with others. Finally, some groups that become churches may retain a few characteristics of sects, such as an emphasis on evangelism or a personal relationship with God.

ecclesia
a religious group so integrated into the dominant culture that it is difficult to tell where the one begins and the other leaves off; also called a *state religion*

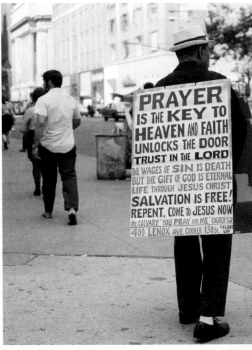

■ Americans are a religious people, and one cannot understand them or their history unless one takes this into account. Most Americans consider religion to be a private matter, but some violate this background assumption and take to the streets with their message.

Although all religions began as cults, not all varieties of a particular religion begin that way. For example, some **denominations**—"brand names" within a major religion, such as Methodism or Reform Judaism—may begin as splinter groups. A group within a church may disagree with *some* aspects of the church's teachings (not its major message) and break away to form its own organization. An example is the Southern Baptist Convention, which was formed in 1845 to defend the right to own slaves (Ernst 1988; Nauta 1993; White 1995).

■ When Religion and Culture Conflict

As we have seen, cults and sects represent a break with the past. Consequently, they challenge the social order. Three major patterns of adaptation occur when religion and the culture in which it is embedded find themselves in conflict.

First, the members of a religion may reject the dominant culture and have as little as possible to do with nonmembers of their religion. Like the Amish, they may withdraw into closed communities. As noted in the Cultural Diversity box on page 110, the Amish broke away from Swiss-German Mennonites in 1693. They try to preserve the culture of their ancestors, who lived in a simpler time when there were no televisions, movies, automobiles, or even electricity. To do so, they emphasize family life and traditional male and female roles. They continue to wear the style of clothing that their ancestors wore three hundred years ago, to light their homes with oil lamps, and to speak German at home and in church. They also continue to reject radio, television, motorized vehicles, and education beyond the eighth grade. They do mingle with non-Amish when they shop in town—where they are readily distinguishable by their form of transportation (horse-drawn carriages), clothing, and speech.

In the *second* pattern, a cult or sect rejects only specific elements of the prevailing culture. For example, religious teachings may dictate that immodest clothing—short skirts, swimsuits, low-cut dresses, and so on—is immoral, or that wearing makeup or going to the movies is wrong. Most elements of the main culture, however, are accepted. Although specific activities are forbidden, members of the religion are able to participate in most aspects of the broader society. They resolve this mild tension either by adhering to the religion or by "sneaking," doing the forbidden acts on the sly.

In the *third* pattern, the society rejects the religious group. In the extreme, as with the early Christians, leaders may even try to destroy it. The Roman emperor declared the followers of Jesus to be enemies of Rome and ordered them to be hunted down and destroyed. The Mormons provide another example. Their rejection of Roman Catholicism and Protestantism as corrupt, along with their belief in polygyny, led to their persecution. In 1831, they left Palmyra, New York, and moved first to Kirtland, Ohio, and subsequently to Independence, Missouri. When the persecution continued, they moved to Nauvoo, Illinois. There a mob murdered the founder of the religion, Joseph Smith, and his brother Hyrum. The Mormons decided to escape the dominant culture altogether by founding a community in the wilderness. In 1847, they settled in the Great Salt Lake Valley of what is today the state of Utah (Bridgwater 1953).

Our opening vignette focused on another example. Let's return to it.

thinking

CRITICALLY

How to Destroy a Cult: The U.S. Government Versus the Branch Davidians

After the killing of Koresh and eighty or so of his followers at Waco, rumors persisted that federal agents had used flammable devices to burn down the compound. For six years, the FBI denied the rumors. Journalists continued to track down leads, and in 1999, the Texas Rangers revealed that federal agents

denomination
a "brand name" within a major religion, for example, Methodist or Baptist

had used incendiary devices. They also revealed that the U.S. Army's supersecret Delta Force had been involved in the attack.

What crimes could have justified this lethal assault against the Branch Davidians? The government first said that it took action because the group had violated firearms laws. Later, agents changed their story to make saving the children their primary goal. Was the death of those children—and their parents—just an ironic twist of events that marked the stunning end to a strange group? Or was it part of a conspiracy by U.S. government agencies to put an end to groups that dare to challenge their authority?

Koresh's teachings certainly were bizarre. He taught that he was Jesus Christ returned to earth. Many have made this same claim, but Koresh's twist was that he had returned in sinful form so he could better understand sinners. As a sinner, Koresh had a voracious sexual appetite. He demanded—and received—sex from the men's wives, while insisting that the men remain celibate. Some reports, perhaps sponsored by the government, indicate that he also had sex with their daughters, some as young as 12 and 13 years old. Koresh also taught that Armageddon was on its way, that one day the government would attack them. About this, he was right.

Since the official version has been published in the mass media, let's consider the case for the other side. This analysis is written from the conflict perspective. It assumes a conspiracy on the part of the elite to destroy a group that posed a threat to its power.

First, Koresh was no recluse. He drove around the area, shopped in stores, and ate in restaurants. The government could have arrested him in public, with no confrontation. Second, after the government's first assault, Koresh let anyone leave who wanted to go. Some parents and twenty-one children did leave. After studying these children, the worst the government could come up with was that some children had been spanked for disobedience. They also reported that the children had been taught Bible stories and songs. Third, the accounts of the survivors don't support government claims. Sheila Martin, whose husband, a Harvard-trained attorney, died in the fire along with four of their children, says that people don't know how nice it was to live there. "Those were the happiest days of my life," she said.

On the other hand, there may have been child abuse. But does child abuse explain an armed attack by government agents? Unlikely. Rather, the ATF's first accounts that the Branch Davidians had stockpiled weapons is the key to explain the government's desire to annihilate the group. In the months before their destruction, the Branch Davidians had purchased thousands of dollars of guns and ammunition. Their purchases were legal, but the government became concerned about reports of a heavily armed strange group, holed up in a compound. Who knows what such a group might do? The solution was to destroy it.

■ On April 19, 1993, the U.S. Bureau of Alcohol, Tobacco, and Firearms attacked the Branch Davidian compound in Waco, Texas. The leader of the cult and over 80 followers, including children, died in this fire.

■ ■ ■ ■ ■

for your consideration . . .

If this analysis is correct, what groups might be targeted next? Perhaps it will be militant Islamic groups. Government agents have already infiltrated them. Other candidates are the survivalist groups. They believe the U.S. government is the Antichrist and reject the government's authority. Like the Branch Davidians, some have armed themselves and retreated into compounds. The Prophet's Church Universal and Triumphant, for example, under the leadership of Elizabeth Clare, has built underground shelters near Yellowstone National Park—and is rumored to have stockpiled arms. Dozens of other groups, which teach that society is about to collapse, have, like Koresh, stockpiled weapons in order to defend themselves.

Can we expect more Wacos? It is difficult to see how the government can sit idly by while groups with paramilitary structures arm themselves, denounce the government as the Antichrist—and perhaps refuse to pay taxes. With the public outcry over the death of the Waco children, however, future attacks may be more restrained—and they probably won't be televised.

Sources: Barkun 1993; Chua-Eoan 1993; Corbin 1993; Dillin 1993; Lacayo 1993b; Pressley 1993; Tye 1993; Gotschall 1994; Paul 1994; "Faddish Justice" 1995; Isikoff 1999; Kuntz 1999.

Religion in the United States

With its hundreds of denominations and sects, how can we generalize about religion in the United States? What do these many religious groups have in common? It certainly isn't doctrine (church teaching), but doctrine is not the focus of sociology. Sociologists, rather, are interested in the relationship between society and religion, and the role that religion plays in people's lives. To better understand religion in U.S. society, then, we shall focus first on characteristics of members of religious groups, and then on the groups themselves.

Characteristics of Members

About 70 percent of Americans belong to a church or synagogue. Let's look at the characteristics of people who hold formal membership in a religion. (The source does not contain information on members of mosques.)

Region Membership is not evenly distributed around the country. As Table 18.2 shows, membership is highest in the South and Midwest. Why is membership in the West so much lower? This may be due to the West being the newest region in the nation and having the highest net migration. If so, when its residents have put down firmer roots, the West's percentage of religious membership will increase.

Social Class Religion in the United States is stratified by social class. As can be seen from Figure 18.4 on the next page, each religious group draws members from all social classes, but some are "top-heavy" and others "bottom-heavy." The most top-heavy are the Episcopalians and Jews; the most bottom-heavy are the Baptists and Evangelicals. This figure is further confirmation that churchlike groups tend to appeal more to the successful, while the more sectlike groups appeal to the less successful.

Americans have a tendency to change their religion. About 40 percent of Americans belong to a denomination that is different from the one in which they were reared (Sherkat and Wilson 1991). People who change their social class are also likely to change their denomination. Upwardly mobile people are likely to seek a religion that draws more people from their new social class. An upwardly mobile Baptist, for example, may become a Methodist or a Presbyterian. For Roman Catholics, the situation is somewhat different. Because each parish is a geographical unit, an upwardly mobile individual who moves into a more affluent neighborhood is likely to automatically transfer into a congregation that has a larger proportion of affluent members.

TABLE 18.2

Church and Synagogue Membership

Percentage of Population, by Region

Region	Membership
South	75%
Midwest	72%
East	67%
West	60%

Note: The source does not have totals for mosque membership.

Source: Statistical Abstract 2000:Table 75.

F igure 18.4

Income and Religious Affiliation

Source: Compiled from data in *Gallup Opinion Index,* 1987:20–27, 29.

Race and Ethnicity   It is common for religions around the world to be associated with race and ethnicity: Islam with Arabs, Judaism with Jews, Hinduism with Indians, and Confucianism with Chinese. Sometimes, as with Hinduism and Confucianism, a religion and a particular country are almost synonymous. Christianity is not associated with any one country, although it is associated primarily with Western culture.

In the United States, all major religious groups draw from the nation's many racial and ethnic groups. Like social class, however, race and ethnicity tend to cluster. People of Latino or Irish descent are likely to be Roman Catholics, those of Greek origin to belong to the Greek Orthodox church. African Americans are likely to be Protestants, more specifically Baptists, or to belong to fundamentalist sects.

Although many churches are integrated, it is with good reason that Sunday morning between 10 and 11 A.M. has been called "the most segregated hour in the United States." African Americans tend to belong to African American churches, while most whites see only whites in theirs. The segregation of churches is based not on law, but on custom.

Age   As shown in Table 18.3, the chances that an American belongs to a church or synagogue generally increase with age. The surveys on which this table is based usually show a smaller percentage of membership among those between the ages of 18 and 29. It could be that this latest survey is tapping a resurgence of religion among younger Americans. A possible—and intriguing—explanation for the large increase at ages 50 to 64 and the still larger increase among people over 65 is that religious people outlive those who do not affiliate with a church or synagogue. Each year, as alcohol abuse and other forms of unhealthy lifestyles take their toll, there remains a larger percentage of church members—whose lifestyles are more sedate, more conforming.

■ Characteristics of Religious Groups

Let's examine the major features of religious groups in the United States.

Diversity   With its 350,000 congregations and hundreds of denominations, no religious group even comes close to being a dominant religion in the

T A B L E 18.3

Church and Synagogue Membership

Percentage of Population, by Age

Age	Membership
18–29	68%
30–49	64%
50–64	72%
65+	82%

Note: The source does not have totals for mosque membership.

Source: Statistical Abstract 2000: Table 759.

United States (*Statistical Abstract* 2000:Table 74). Table 18.4 illustrates some of this remarkable diversity, as did the box on U.S. Islam on page 545.

Pluralism and Freedom It is the U.S. government's policy not to interfere with religions. The government's position is that its obligation is to ensure an environment in which people can worship as they see fit. Religious freedom is so extensive that anyone can start his or her own church and proclaim himself or herself a minister, revelator, or any other desired term. At times, however, the government grossly violates its hands-off policy, as with the Branch Davidians, which we discussed in the Thinking Critically section on pages 550–552.

Competition and Recruitment The many religious groups of the United States compete for clients. They even advertise in the Yellow Pages of the telephone directory and insert appealing advertising—under the guise of news—in the religious section of the Saturday or Sunday edition of the local newspapers. Because of this intense competition, some groups modify their message, making it closer to what their successful competitors are offering (Greeley and Hout 1999).

Commitment Americans are a religious people. Ninety-four percent report that they believe in God, and about 43 percent attend religious services each week

TABLE 18.4 The Largest U.S. Religious Groups[a]

1. Roman Catholic	62,000,000	15. Church of the Nazarene	600,000
2. Baptist	36,400,000	16. Islamic[b]	500,000
3. Pentecostal	11,500,000	17. Reformed Churches	500,000
4. Methodist	8,600,000	18. Salvation Army	500,000
5. Lutheran	8,200,000	19. Unitarian Universalist	500,000
6. Jews	6,000,000	20. Brethren	400,000
7. Mormon	5,100,000	21 Buddhist	400,000
8. Churches of Christ	4,900,000	22. Christian and Missionary Alliance	300,000
9. African (and Christian) Methodist	4,500,000	23. Community Churches	300,000
10. Presbyterian	4,000,000	24. Evangelical Church	300,000
11. Eastern Orthodox	3,300,000	25. Armenian Church	200,000
12. Episcopal Church	2,400,000	26. Congregationalist	200,000
13. Jehovah's Witnesses	1,000,000	27. Hindu	200,000
14. Seventh Day Adventist	800,000	28. Mennonite	200,000

[a]All totals must be taken as approximate. Some groups ignore reporting forms. Totals are rounded to the nearest 100,000.
[b]Some popular sources list U.S. Muslims at 6 million. The actual number may fall between these extremes.
Source: Statistical Abstract: 2000:Table 74.

PEANUTS® by Charles M. Schulz

■ *In its technical sense, to evangelize means to "announce the Good News" (that Jesus is the Savior). In its more common usage, to evangelize means to make converts. As* Peanuts *so humorously picks up, evangelization is sometimes accomplished through means other than preaching.*

(*Statistical Abstract* 2000:Table 75). They back up their commitment with generous support for religion and its charities. Each year Americans donate about $75 billion to religious causes (*Statistical Abstract* 2000:Table 640). To appreciate the significance of this huge figure, keep in mind that, unlike a country in which there is an ecclesia, those billions of dollars are not taxes but voluntary contributions.

Toleration   The general religious toleration of Americans can be illustrated by three prevailing attitudes: (1) "All religions have a right to exist—as long as they don't try to brainwash anyone or bother me." (2) "With all the religions to choose from, how can anyone tell which one—if any—is true?" (3) "Each of us may be convinced about the truth of our religion—and that is good—but to try to convert others is a violation of the individual's dignity."

Fundamentalist Revival   The fundamentalist Christian churches are undergoing a revival. They teach that the Bible is literally true and that salvation comes only through a personal relationship with Jesus Christ. They also denounce what they see as the degeneration of U.S. culture: sex on television, in movies, and in videos; abortion; corruption in public office; premarital sex cohabitation; and drug use. Their answer to these problems is firm, simple, and direct: People whose hearts are changed through religious conversion will change their lives. The mainstream churches, which offer a more remote God and less emotional involvement, fail to meet the basic religious needs of large numbers of Americans. The Down-to-Earth Sociology box on the next page describes a group whose needs are not met by mainstream religious groups.

One result is that mainstream churches are losing members while the fundamentalists are gaining them. Figure 18.5 on page 557 depicts this change. The exception is the Roman Catholic church, whose growth in North America is due primarily to heavy immigration from Mexico and other Roman Catholic countries.

The Electronic Church   What began as a ministry to shut-ins and those who do not belong to a church has blossomed into its own type of church. Its preachers, called "televangelists," reach millions of viewers and raise millions of dollars. Some of its most famous ministries are those of Robert Schuller (the "Crystal Cathedral") and Pat Robertson (the 700 Club).

Many local ministers view the electronic church as a competitor. They complain that it competes for the attention and dollars of their members. The electronic church replies that its money goes to good causes and that through its conversions it feeds members into the local churches, strengthening, not weakening, them.

down-to-earth
s o c i o l o g y

▪ ▪ ▪ ▪ ▪
Bikers and Bibles

The Bible Belt churchgoers in Eureka Springs, Arkansas, stare as Herbie Shreve, unshaven, his hair hanging over the collar of his denim vest, roars into town on his Harley Davidson. With hundreds of other bikers in town, it is going to be a wild weekend of drinking, nudity, and fights.

But not for Herbie. After pitching his tent, he sets up a table at which he offers other bikers free ice water and religious tracts. "No hard sell. They seek us out when it's the right time," says Herbie.

The ministry began when Herbie's father, a pastor, took up motorcycling to draw closer to his rebellious teen-age son. As the pair rode around the heartland of America, they often were snubbed by fellow Christians when they tried to attend church. So Herbie's father hatched plans for a motorcycle ministry. "Jesus said, 'Go out to the highways and hedges,' and that always stuck with me," says the elder Shreve. "I felt churches ought to be wherever the people are."

They founded the Christian Motorcyclists Association (CMA), headquartered in Hatfield, Arkansas. It now has 33,000 members in more than 300 chapters in the United States and Canada. Members of the CMA call themselves "weekend warriors."

"Riding for the Son" is emblazoned on their T-shirts and jackets—something

▪ Some Christian groups make evangelism, the conversion of others, a primary goal. One such group is the Christian Motorcyclists' Association. Its members say that they want to get people "to reverse direction, from the highway to hell to the highway to heaven." Regular churchgoers often find the appearance of CMA members offensive.

that would make them stand out almost anywhere, but especially in the midst of the nudity and drunkenness.

No CMA member has ever been harmed by a biker. But they have come

close. In the early days, bikers at a rally surrounded Herbie's tent and threatened to burn it down. "Some of those same people are friends of mine today," says the elder Shreve.

Stepping over a biker who has passed out in front of his tent, Herbie goes through the campground urging last night's carousers to join them by a lake for a Sunday service. Four years ago no one took him up on it. Today twenty bikers straggle down to the dock.

Herbie's brief sermon is plain-spoken. He touches on the biker's alienation— the unpaid bills, the oppressive bosses, the righteous church ladies "who are always mad and always right." He tells them that Jesus loves them, and that they can call him anytime. "I'll help fix your life," he says.

CMA has several conversions this weekend. "You just stay at it. You don't know when their hearts are touched. Look at these guys," Herbie says, pointing to fellow CMA members. "They were all bikers headed for hell, too. Now they follow the Son."

Herbie gets on his Harley. In town, the traditional churchgoers stare as he roars past, his long hair sweeping behind him.

Sources: Based on Graham 1990; Shreve 1991.

▪ ▪ ▪ ▪ ▪

The Internet and Religion   As with so many aspects of life, the Internet has begun to have an impact on religion. We will focus on this change in the concluding section.

▪ Secularization of Religion and Culture

The term **secularization** refers to the process by which worldly affairs replace spiritual interests. (The term **secular** means "belonging to the world and its affairs.") As we shall see, both religions and cultures can become secularized.

The Secularization of Religion

secularization
the process by which spiritual concerns are replaced by worldly concerns

secular
belonging to the world and its affairs

As the model, fashionably slender, paused before the head table of African American community leaders, her gold necklace glimmering above the low-cut bodice of her emerald-green dress, the hostess, a member of the Church of God in Christ, said, "It's now OK to wear more revealing clothes—as long as it's done in good taste." Then she added, "You couldn't do this when I was a girl, but now it's OK—and you can still worship God." (Author's files)

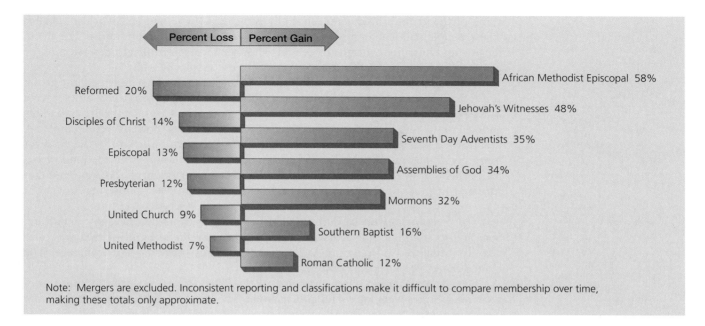

Percent Loss | Percent Gain

Reformed 20%
Disciples of Christ 14%
Episcopal 13%
Presbyterian 12%
United Church 9%
United Methodist 7%

African Methodist Episcopal 58%
Jehovah's Witnesses 48%
Seventh Day Adventists 35%
Assemblies of God 34%
Mormons 32%
Southern Baptist 16%
Roman Catholic 12%

Note: Mergers are excluded. Inconsistent reporting and classifications make it difficult to compare membership over time, making these totals only approximate.

Figure **18.5**

U.S. Churches: Gains and Losses in Ten Years

Sources: Yearbook of American and Canadian Churches 1993: Table 2; *Statistical Abstract* 1985: Table 74; 1995:Table 84, the latest year available.

When I heard these words, I grabbed a napkin and quickly jotted them down, my sociological imagination stirred by their deep implication. As strange as it may seem, this simple event pinpoints the essence of why the Christian churches in the United States have splintered. Let's see how this could possibly be.

The simplest answer to why Christians don't have just one church, or at most several, instead of the hundreds of sects and denominations that dot the U.S. landscape, is disagreements about doctrine (church teaching). As theologian and sociologist Richard Niebuhr pointed out, however, there are many ways of settling doctrinal disputes beside splintering off and forming another religious organization. Niebuhr (1929) suggested that the answer lies more in *social* change than it does in *religious* conflict.

The explanation goes like this. As noted earlier, when a sect becomes more churchlike, tension between it and the mainstream culture lessens. Quite likely, when a sect is first established, its founders and first members are poor, or at least not very successful in worldly pursuits. Feeling like strangers in the dominant culture, they derive a good part of their identity from their religion. In their church services and lifestyle, they stress how different their values are from those of the dominant culture. They are also likely to emphasize the joys of the coming afterlife, when they will be able to escape from their present pain.

As time passes, the group's values—such as frugality and the avoidance of gambling, alcohol, and drugs—help later generations become successful. As they attain more education and become more middle class, the group's members grow more respectable in the eyes of society. They no longer experience the alienation that was felt by the founders of their group. Life's burdens don't seem as heavy, and the need for relief through an afterlife becomes less pressing. Similarly, the pleasures of the world no longer appear as threatening to the "true" belief. As illustrated by the woman at the fashion show, they then attempt to harmonize their religious beliefs with their changing ideas about the culture.

This process is called the **secularization of religion**—shifting the focus from spiritual matters to the affairs of this world. Anyone familiar with today's mainstream Methodists would be surprised to know they once were a sect. Methodists used to ban playing cards, dancing, and theater attendance. They even considered circuses to be sinful. As Methodists grew more middle-class, however, they began to change their views on sin. They then began to dismantle the barriers that they had constructed between themselves and the outside world (Finke and Stark 1992). Secularization leads to a splintering of the group, for accommodation with the secular culture displeases

secularization of religion
the replacement of a religion's spiritual or "otherworldly" concerns with concerns about "this world"

some of the group's members, especially those who have had less worldly success. These people still feel a gulf between themselves and the broader culture. For them, tension and hostility continue to be real. They see secularization as a desertion of the group's fundamental truths, a "selling out" to the secular world.

After futile attempts by die-hards to bring the group back to its senses, the group splinters. Those who protested the secularization of Methodism, for example, were kicked out—even though *they* represented the values around which the group had organized in the first place. The dissatisfied—who by now are viewed as complainers—then form a sect that once again stresses its differences from the world, the need for more personal, emotional religious experiences, and salvation from the pain of living in this world. As time passes, the cycle repeats—adjustment to the dominant culture by some, continued dissatisfaction by others, and further splintering.

The Secularization of Culture   Just as religion can secularize, so can culture. Sociologists use the term **secularization of culture** to refer to a culture that was once heavily influenced by religion, but no longer retains much of that influence. The United States provides an example.

Despite attempts to reinterpret history, the Pilgrims and most of the founders of the United States were highly religious people. The Pilgrims were even convinced that God had guided them to found a new land, while many of the founders felt that God had guided them to develop a new form of government.

The clause in the Constitution that mandates the separation of church and state was *not* an attempt to keep religion out of government, but a (successful) device to avoid the establishment of a state religion like that in England. Here, people were to have the freedom to worship as they wished. The assumption of the founders was even more specific—that Protestantism represented the true religion.

The phrase in the Declaration of Independence, "All men are created equal," refers to a central belief in God as the creator of humanity. A member of the clergy opened Congress with prayer. Many colonial laws were based on principles derived explicitly from the Old and New Testaments. In some colonies, blasphemy was a crime, as was failing to observe the Sabbath. Similarly, adultery was a crime; in some places it even carried the death penalty. Even public kissing between husband and wife was considered an offense, punishable by placement in the public stocks (Frumkin 1967). In other words, religion permeated U.S. culture. It was part and parcel of how the Colonists saw life. Their lives, laws, and other aspects of the culture reflected their religious beliefs.

Today, U.S. culture has been secularized; the influence of religion on public affairs has greatly lessened. No longer are laws based on religious principles. It has even become illegal to post the Ten Commandments in civic buildings. In general, ideas of what is "generally good" have replaced religion as an organizing principle for the culture.

Underlying the secularization of culture is *modernization,* a term that refers to a society industrializing, urbanizing, developing mass education, and adopting science and advanced technology. The significance of modernization goes far beyond these surface changes. Science and advanced technology bring with them a secular view of the world that begins to permeate society. They provide explanations for many aspects of life that people traditionally attributed to God. As a consequence, people come to depend much less on religion to explain life events. Its satisfactions and problems—from births to deaths—are attributed to natural causes. When a society has secularized thoroughly, even religious leaders may turn to answers provided by biology, philosophy, psychology, sociology, and so on.

Although the secularization of its culture means that religion has become less important in U.S. public life, *personal* religious involvement among Americans has not diminished. Instead, it has *increased.* As we saw, ninety-four percent believe there is a God and 77 percent believe there is a heaven. Not only do 70 percent claim membership in a church or synagogue, but on any given weekend 43 percent of all Americans

secularization of culture
the process by which a culture becomes less influenced by religion

report that they attended a worship service (Woodward 1989; Gallup 1990; *Statistical Abstract* 2000:Table 75).

Table 18.5 underscores the paradox of how religious participation has increased while the culture has secularized. The proportion of Americans who belong to a church or synagogue is now *four* times higher than it was when the country was founded. Church membership, of course, is only a rough indicator of how significant religion is in people's lives. Some church members are not particularly religious, while many intensely religious people—Lincoln, for one—never join a church.

The Future of Religion

A group of prominent intellectuals once foresaw an end to religion. As science advanced, they said, it would explain everything. It would transform human thought and replace religion, which was merely mistaken pre-scientific thinking. In 1966 Anthony Wallace, one of the world's best-known anthropologists at the time, made the following observation:

> The evolutionary future of religion is extinction. Belief in supernatural beings . . . will become only an interesting historical memory. . . . doomed to die out, all over the world, as a result of the increasing adequacy and diffusion of scientific knowledge.

Wallace and the many other social analysts who took this position were wrong. Religion thrives in the most advanced scientific nations, in capitalist and in socialist countries. It is evident that these analysts did not understand the fundamental significance of religion in people's lives.

Humans are inquiring creatures. They are aware that they have a past, a present, and a future. They reflect on their experiences to try to make sense out of them. One of the questions people develop as they reflect on life concerns the purpose of it all. Why are we born? Is there an afterlife? If so, where are we going, and what will it be like when we get there? Out of these concerns arises this question: If there is a God, what does God want of us in this life? Does God have a preference about how we should live?

Science, including sociology, cannot answer such questions. By its very nature, science cannot tell us about four main concerns that many people have: (1) the existence of God; (2) the purpose of life; (3) the existence of an afterlife; and (4) morality. About the first, science has nothing to say (no test tube has either isolated God or refuted God's existence). As to the second, although science can provide a definition of life and describe the characteristics of living organisms, it has nothing to say about ultimate purpose. As to the third, science can offer no information, for it has no tests to prove or disprove a "hereafter." As to the fourth, science can demonstrate the consequences of behavior but not the *moral* superiority of one action compared with another. This means that science cannot even prove that loving your family and neighbor is superior to hurting and killing them. Science can describe death and compute consequences, but it cannot dictate the moral superiority of any action, even in such an extreme example.

There is no doubt that religion will last as long as humanity lasts, for what could replace it? And if something did, and answered such questions, would it not be religion under another name?

To glimpse the cutting edge of religious change, we'll close with a look at the online marketing of religion.

TABLE	**18.5**

Growth in Religious Membership: The Percentage of Americans Who Belong to a Church or Synagogue

Year	Percentage Who Claim Membership
1776	17%
1860	37%
1890	45%
1926	58%
1975	71%
1999	70%

Sources: Finke and Stark 1992; *Statistical Abstract* 2000:Table 75.

■ *A basic principle of symbolic interactionism is that meaning is not inherent in an object or event, but is determined by people as they interpret the object or event. Old bones and fossils are an excellent illustration of this principle. Does this skull of homo erectus "prove" evolution? Does it "disprove" creation? Such "proof" and "disproof" lie in the eye of the beholder, as evidenced by the recent rise of "scientific creationism," now gaining adherents in U.S. universities.*

mass media
in social life

God on the Net: The Online Marketing of Religion

Muslims in France download sermons and join an invisible community of worshippers at virtual mosques. Jews in Sweden type messages that fellow believers in Jerusalem download and insert in the Western Wall. Christians in California make digital donations to the Crystal Cathedral. Buddhists in Japan seek enlightenment online. The Internet helps to level the pulpit: On the Net, the leader of a pagan group can compete directly with the Pope.

The Internet is making religious rebellion easier, too. And it has become harder for organizations to punish their rebels. Jacques Gaillot is a French bishop who is critical of the Roman Catholic church. The church hierarchy exiled him to the Saharan desert of North Africa, a strategy that used to work well. Instead of being silenced in his remote outpost, however, Gaillot logged onto the Internet, where he now preaches to a virtual congregation via Real Audio (Huffstutter 1998).

No one knows the outcome, but the times, they are a' changin'. Some say that we are on the edge of a religious reformation as big as the one set off by Gutenberg's invention of the printing press.

Could be. Here are some of the developments in religion made possible by the Internet:

■ New churches that exist only in cyberspace

■ Chat rooms directed by rabbis

■ Video and audio feeds of sermons

■ Online donations by credit card

■ Mailing lists for those devoted to witchcraft

■ Online counseling for spiritual problems

Will virtual religion satisfy? Will it prove to be an adequate replacement for the warm embrace of a fellow believer? Will it bring comfort to someone in mourning the way a sympathetic touch can? For some, not at all. For others, yes. We are gazing into the future. To what extent this new medium will affect our religious lives—and perhaps even alter the face of religion—remains to be seen.

Summary and Review

What Is Religion?

Durkheim identified three essential characteristics of **religion:** beliefs that set the **sacred** apart from the **profane, rituals,** and a moral community (a **church**). P. 532.

The Functionalist Perspective

■ **What are the functions and dysfunctions of religion?**

Among the functions of religion are answering questions about ultimate meaning, providing emotional comfort, social solidarity, guidelines for everyday life, social control, adaptation, support for the government, and fostering social change. Groups or activities that provide these same functions are called **functional equivalents** of religion. Among the dysfunctions of religion are war, terrorism, and religious persecution. Pp. 533–537.

The Symbolic Interactionist Perspective

■ **What aspects of religion do symbolic interactionists study?**

Symbolic interactionists focus on the meanings of religion for its followers. They examine religious symbols, **rituals,** beliefs, **religious experiences,** and the sense of community provided by religion. Pp. 537–539.

The Conflict Perspective

■ **What aspects of religion do conflict theorists study?**

Conflict theorists examine the relationship of religion to social inequalities, especially how religion reinforces a society's stratification system. P. 540.

Religion and the Spirit of Capitalism

■ **What does the spirit of capitalism have to do with religion?**

Max Weber disagreed with Marx's conclusion that religion impedes social change. In contrast, Weber saw religion as a primary source of social change. He analyzed how Protestantism gave rise to **the Protestant ethic,** which stimulated what he called **the spirit of capitalism.** The result was capitalism, which transformed society. Pp. 541–542.

The World's Major Religions

■ **What are the world's major religions?**

Judaism, Christianity, and Islam, all **monotheistic** religions, can be traced to the same Old Testament roots. Hinduism, the chief religion of India, has no specific founder, as do Judaism (Abraham), Christianity (Jesus), Islam (Muhammad), Buddhism (Gautama), and Confucianism (K'ung Fu-tsu). Specific teachings and history of these six religions are given in the text. Pp. 542–547.

Types of Religious Groups

■ **What types of religious groups are there?**

Sociologists divide religious groups into cults, sects, churches, and ecclesias. All religions began as **cults.** Those that survive tend to develop into **sects** and eventually into **churches.** Sects, often led by **charismatic leaders,** are unstable. Some are perceived as threats and are persecuted by the state. **Ecclesias,** or state religions, are rare. Pp. 547–552.

Religion in the United States

■ **What are the main characteristics of religion in the United States?**

Membership varies by region, social class, age, and race-ethnicity. The major characteristics are diversity, pluralism and freedom, competition, commitment, toleration, a fundamentalist revival, and the electronic church. Pp. 552–556.

■ **What is the connection between secularization of religion and the splintering of churches?**

Secularization of religion, a change in a religion's focus from spiritual matters to concerns of "this world," is the key to understanding why churches divide. Basically, as a cult or sect changes to accommodate its members' upward social class mobility, it changes into a church. Left dissatisfied are members who are not upwardly mobile. They tend to splinter off and form a new cult or sect, and the cycle repeats itself. Cultures permeated by religion also secularize. This, too, leaves many members dissatisfied and promotes social change. Pp. 556–559.

The Future of Religion

Although industrialization led to the **secularization of culture,** this did not spell the end of religion, as many social analysts assumed it would. Because science cannot answer questions about ultimate meaning, the existence of God or an afterlife, or provide guidelines for morality, the need for religion will remain. In any foreseeable future, religion—or its **functional equivalents**—will prosper. The Internet is likely to have far-reaching consequences on religion. Pp. 559–560.

■ *Where can I read more on this topic?*

Suggested Readings for this chapter are found at the back of this book.

Additional Online Resources for This Chapter
www.ablongman.com/henslin6e

- *Content Select* Research Database for Sociology, with suggested key terms and annotated references
- Link to 2000 Census, with activities
- Flashcards of key terms and concepts
- Practice Tests
- Weblinks
- Interactive Maps

using . . .
ContentSelect

Research Database for Sociology

religious experience	Judaism	Hinduism	cult
religion and the spirit of capitalism	Christianity	Buddhism	Protestant ethic
	Islam		

Sir Roy Calne, F.R.S., *Papworth 91 Combined Heart/Lung/Liver Transplant Operation, 1991*

19

Medicine

Sociology and the Study of Medicine

The Symbolic Interactionist Perspective

The Role of Culture in Defining Health and Illness
The Components of Health

The Functionalist Perspective

The Sick Role

The Conflict Perspective

Effects of Global Stratification on Health Care
Establishing a Monopoly on U.S. Health Care

Historical Patterns of Health

Physical Health
Mental Health

Issues in Health Care

Medical Care: A Right or a Commodity?
Social Inequality
Malpractice Suits and Defensive Medicine
Medical Incompetence
Depersonalization: The Medical Cash Machine
Conflict of Interest
Medical Fraud
Sexism in Medicine
The Medicalization of Society
Medically Assisted Suicide
Curbing Costs: Issues in Private and National Health Insurance

Threats to Health

AIDS
The Globalization of Disease
Drugs: Alcohol and Nicotine
Disabling Environments
Misguided, Foolish, and Callous Experiments

The Search for Alternatives

Treatment or Prevention?
Health Care in Global Perspective

The Future of Medicine

Summary and Review

I had decided that it was not enough to just study the homeless—I had to help them. I learned that a homeless shelter in St. Louis was planning to help poor people save on utilities by installing free wood stoves in their homes. This would help keep them from being forced onto the streets. It wasn't exactly applied sociology, but I volunteered.

I was a little anxious about the coming training session on how to install stoves, as I had never done anything like this. As I entered the homeless shelter on that Saturday morning, I found the building in semi-darkness. "They must be saving on electricity," I thought to myself. Then I was greeted with an unnerving sight. Two police officers were chasing a nude man, who was running through the halls. They caught him. I watched as the elderly man, looking confused, struggled to put on his clothing. From the police I learned that he had ripped the wires out of the shelter's main electrical box; that was why there were no lights on.

I asked the officers where they were going to take the man, and they replied, "To Malcolm Bliss" (the state hospital). When I said, "I guess he'll be in there for quite a while," they replied, "Probably just a day or two. We picked him up last week—he was crawling under cars at a traffic light—and they let him out in two days."

> We picked him up last week—he was crawling under cars at a traffic light—and they let him out in two days.

The police then explained that one must be a danger to others or to oneself in order to be admitted to the hospital as a long-term patient. Visualizing this old man crawling under stopped cars at an intersection, and considering how he had risked electrocution by ripping out the electrical wires with his bare hands, I marveled at the definition of "danger" that the psychiatrists must be using.

medicine
one of the major social institutions that sociologists study; a society's organized ways of dealing with sickness and injury

■ Shamans *in tribal groups act as both priest and physician. These religious healers follow rituals intended to maintain harmony between humans and spiritual forces—to release good forces to heal people, or to release the individual from evil forces that are harming the person's health. This Dayak shaman in Borneo, Indonesia, wears amulets as he performs a ceremonial dance.*

Sociology and the Study of Medicine

This incident points to a severe problem with U.S. medical care. In this chapter, we will examine why the poor often receive second-rate medical care and, in some instances, abysmal treatment. We'll also look at how skyrocketing costs have created ethical dilemmas such as whether medical care should be rationed.

As we consider these issues, the role of sociology in studying **medicine**—a society's standard ways of dealing with illness and injury—will become apparent. For example, because U.S. medicine is a profession, a bureaucracy, and a big business, sociologists study how it is influenced by self-regulation, the bureaucratic structure, and the profit motive. Sociologists also study how illness and health are much more than biological matters—how, for example, they are related to cultural beliefs, lifestyle, and social class. Because of these emphases, the sociology of medicine is one of the applied fields of sociology, and many medical schools and even hospitals have sociologists on their staffs.

The Symbolic Interactionist Perspective

Let's begin, then, by examining how culture influences health and illness. This takes us to the heart of the symbolic interactionist perspective.

The Role of Culture in Defining Health and Illness

Suppose that one morning you look in the mirror and see strange blotches covering your face and chest. Hoping against hope that it is not serious, you rush to a doctor. If the doctor said that you had "dyschromic spirochetosis," your fears would be confirmed.

Now, wouldn't everyone around the world draw the conclusion that your spots are symptoms of a disease? No, not everybody. In one South American tribe this skin condition is so common that the few individuals who *aren't* spotted are seen as the unhealthy ones. They are even excluded from marriage because they are "sick" (Ackernecht 1947; Zola 1983).

Consider mental "illness" and mental "health." People aren't automatically "crazy" because they do certain things. Rather, they are defined as "crazy" or "normal" according to cultural guidelines. If an American talks aloud to spirits that no one else can see, and takes direction from them, he or she is likely to be defined as insane—and, for everyone's good, locked up. In some tribal societies, in contrast, someone who talks to invisible spirits might be honored for being in close contact with the spiritual world—and, for everyone's good, be declared a **shaman,** or spiritual intermediary, who would then diagnose and treat medical problems.

"Sickness" and "health," then, are not absolutes, as we might suppose. Rather, they are matters of definition. Around the world, each culture provides guidelines that its people use to determine whether they are "healthy" or "sick." As discussed in the Cultural Diversity box, those guidelines also tell you what your illness is. This is another example of how the social construction of reality plays a vital role in our lives.

shaman
the healing specialist of tribal groups who attempts to control the spirits thought to cause a disease or injury; commonly called a witch doctor

cultural d·i·v·e·r·s·i·t·y

Around the World

"You Don't Know What *Empacho* Is? What Kind of a Doctor Are You?"

How do you know what illness you have when you don't feel good? You know what you are suffering from because of your culture. You are given a word, such as flu, fever, or cold. Not surprisingly, the same symptoms will have different names in different cultures. This is to be expected, for languages differ. The significance of different names, however, can extend far beyond the terms that are used. The name can imply different causes of the problem and the need for different cures. The difference can be so great that some illnesses exist in one culture and not another.

Mexicans, for example, suffer from *empacho,* but U.S. physicians haven't even heard of this health problem. *Empacho* is food stuck in the intestines. It leads to severe stomach aches. Massage sometimes relieves *empacho,* helping to get the food unstuck and moving along. So do teas and herbs.

So what happens when immigrants from Mexico go to U.S. doctors who have never heard of *empacho*? The doctor thinks the patient is dumb for thinking that food gets stuck in the intestines, and the

patient thinks the doctor is dumb for not knowing about such a common sickness.

As these immigrants make a gradual transition to U.S. ways, they will adopt a new way of thinking about illness. In the meantime, in order to adequately treat these patients, physicians need to understand their culture. *Empacho* is not just a different name. It is a way of thinking. *Empacho* is real for these immigrants. To dismiss *empacho* as folklore and useless knowledge is to show disdain for the patient. Also, if the doctor doesn't even know about *empacho*—which everyone

knows about—how can he be trusted to treat other ailments?

for your consideration

The culture conflict is clear. Both patient and doctor have learned different ways of viewing reality. The symptoms are evident to both, but the meaning is entirely different to the Mexican immigrant and the U.S. physician. How do you think the physician can use *empacho* to treat the patient?

■ *How do you think this doctor's assumptions of the cause and proper treatment of illness might contrast with those of the immigrant parents of her patient?*

Health
Excellent Functioning

P H Y S I C A L · M E N T A L · S O C I A L · S P I R I T U A L

Poor Functioning
Illness

Figure 19.1

A Continuum of Health
and Illness

health
a human condition measured
by four components: physical,
mental, social, and spiritual

sick role
a social role that excuses
people from normal obli-
gations because they are sick
or injured, while at the same
time expecting them to seek
competent help and cooperate
in getting well

■ The Components of Health

Back in 1941, international "health experts" identified three components of **health:** physical, mental, and social (World Health Organization 1946). They missed the focus of our previous chapter, however, and I have added a spiritual component to Figure 19.1. Even the dimensions of health, then, are subject to debate.

If we were to agree on the components of health, we would still be left with the question of what makes someone physically, mentally, socially, or spiritually "healthy." Again, as symbolic interactionists stress, these are not objective matters but, rather, matters whose definitions vary from culture to culture. In a pluralistic society, they even differ from one group to another.

As with religion in the previous chapter, then, the concern of sociologists is not to define "true" health or "true" illness. Instead, it is to analyze the effects that people's ideas of health and illness have on their lives, and even the ways in which people determine that they are sick.

The Functionalist Perspective

Functionalists begin with an obvious point: If society is to function well, its people need to be healthy enough to perform their normal roles. This means that societies must set up ways to control sickness. One way they do this is to develop a system of medical care. Another way is to make rules to keep too many people from "being sick." Let's look at how this works.

■ The Sick Role

Do you remember when your throat began to hurt and when your mom or dad took your temperature the thermometer registered 102°F? Your parents took you to the doctor, and despite your protests that tomorrow was the first day of summer vacation (or some other important event), you had to spend the next three days in bed taking medicine. You were forced to play what sociologists call the "sick role." What do they mean by this term?

Elements of the Sick Role   Talcott Parsons, the functionalist who first analyzed the **sick role,** pointed out that it has four elements—you are not held responsible for being sick, you are exempt from normal responsibilities, you don't like the role, and you will get competent help so you can return to your routines. If people don't seek competent help, they are considered responsible for being sick. They are denied the right to claim sympathy from others and to be excused from their normal routines. People who seek help are given sympathy and encouragement; the others are given the cold shoulder for wrongfully claiming the sick role.

Ambiguity in the Sick Role   Instead of a fever of 102°F, suppose the thermometer registers 99.5°F. Do you then "become" sick or not? That is, do you decide to claim the sick role? Because most instances of illness are not as clear-cut as, say, a heart attack or a limb fracture, decisions to claim the sick role often are based more on social considerations than physical conditions. Let's also suppose that you are facing a midterm, you are unprepared for it, and you are allowed to make it up if you are ill. The more you think about the test, the worse you are likely to feel—which makes the need to claim the sick role seem more legitimate. Now assume that the thermometer still shows 99.5, but you have no test and your friends are coming over to take you out to celebrate your twenty-first birthday. You are not likely to play the sick role. Note that in both cases your physical condition is the same.

Gatekeepers to the Sick Role   Parents and physicians are the primary gatekeepers to the sick role. That is, they mediate between children's feelings of illness and their claim to being sick. Before parents call the school to excuse a child's absence, they decide whether the child is faking or has genuine symptoms that are serious enough to warrant keeping him or her home from school. For adults, physicians are gatekeepers of the sick role. If employers and teachers receive a "doctor's excuse" (official permission for someone to play the sick role), they have no need to pass judgment on the individual's claim.

Gender Differences in the Sick Role   Try to figure out this riddle. On average, women are healthier than men, and they live longer. Yet they are also sick more often and go to doctors more frequently (*Statistical Abstract* 2000:Tables 191, 192, 211). How can both statements be true? Apparently, the answer is that women are more willing than men to claim the sick role when they don't feel well (Klonoff and Landrine 1992). The sick role does not match the *macho* image that most boys and men try to project. Most men try to follow the cultural ideal that they should be strong, keep their pain to themselves, and "tough it out." Women in contrast, are given a model that they should share their feelings and seek help from others. Gender roles, then, apparently underlie this riddle of why women can be healthier than men and yet be sick and go to doctors more often.

The Conflict Perspective

As stressed in earlier chapters, the primary focus of conflict theorists is how people struggle over scarce resources. Since medical treatment is one of those resources, let's examine this competition in global perspective and then see how one group developed a monopoly on U.S. health care.

Effects of Global Stratification on Health Care

In Chapter 9 (pages 266–267), we saw how the nations that industrialized first obtained the economic and military power that brought them riches and allowed them to dominate the globe. This also led to global stratification of medical care, a matter of life and death for people around the world. For example, open heart surgery has become routine in the Most Industrialized Nations. The Least Industrialized Nations, however, cannot afford the technology that open heart surgery requires. This contrast is starkly illustrated by the photos on the next page. So it is with AIDS. In the United States and other rich nations, those who suffer from AIDS have had their lives extended by expensive medicines. People with AIDS in the Least Industrialized Nations can't afford these medicines. For them, AIDS is a death sentence.

Life expectancy tells the story. Whereas most people in the industrialized world can expect to live to about 75, *most* people in Afghanistan, Cambodia, Congo, Ethiopia, and Kenya die before they reach 50. In Zimbabwe, the average person is

■ *Global stratification in health care is starkly contrasted in these photos. It is difficult to believe, but the photo on the left is a hospital room. It was taken in Nagaland, India. As you would expect, the tuberculosis patients in this hospital have a high rate of mortality. The photo on the right, of open heart surgery in Louisville, Kentucky, illustrates medical treatment in the Most Industrialized Nations. As discussed in the text, due to stratification within nations, not everyone has equal access to such advanced technology.*

dead by age 37. Figure 19.2 lists the countries where fewer than 7 of every 1,000 babies die before they are a year old. You can see that almost all of them are industrialized nations. The contrast is stark—of every 1,000 babies born in Angola, 195 never reach their first birthday (*Statistical Abstract* 2000:Table 1355).

Global stratification even helps to determine what diseases we get. Suppose that you had been born in a Least Industrialized Nation located in the tropics. During your much shorter life, you would face illness and death from four major sources: malaria (from mosquitoes), internal parasites (from contaminated water), diarrhea (from food and soil contaminated with human feces), and malnutrition. You would not face heart disease and cancer, for they are "luxury" diseases; that is, they characterize the industrialized world where people live long enough to get them. As na-

Figure 19.2

How Many Babies Die Before Their First Birthday?

Note: All countries listed in the source with an infant mortality rate below that of the United States. That this is not a complete list is evident from Austria, Switzerland, Hong Kong, and Sweden being dropped from the source, all of which had lower rates in the 1997 edition. Infant mortality is defined as the number of babies that die before their first birthday, per 1,000 live births.

Source: Statistical Abstract 2000: Table 1355.

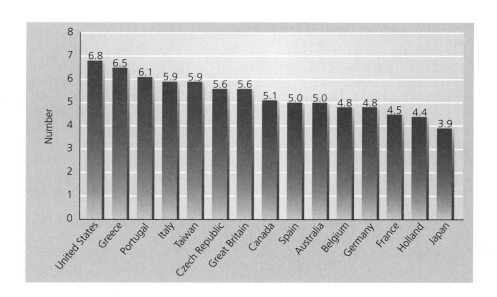

tions industrialize and their people live longer, they trade in the things that used to be their primary killers and begin to worry about cancer and heart attacks instead.

There is also the matter of social stratification *within* the Least Industrialized Nations. Many diseases that ravage the poor people in these countries could be brought under control if more funds were spent on public health. Cheap drugs can prevent malaria, while safer water supplies and higher food production would go a long way toward eliminating the other major killers. The meager funds that these countries have at their disposal, however, are not spent this way. Instead, having garnered the lion's share of the country's resources, the elite lavish it on themselves. They even send a few students to top medical schools in the West. This gives them access to advanced technology—from X–rays to life support systems. In contrast, the poor of these nations go without even basic medical services and continue to die at an early age.

▉ Establishing a Monopoly on U.S. Health Care

Let's turn our focus to medicine in the United States. How did medicine become the largest business in the country? How did it become the only legal monopoly in the United States? To find the answers, we need to understand how medicine became professionalized.

The Professionalization of Medicine   Imagine that you are living in the American colonies in the 1700s and that you want to become a physician. There are no required courses. No entrance exams. In fact, there are no medical schools. You won't need *any* formal education at all. You can simply ask a physician to train you. In return for the opportunity to learn, you'll be his assistant and will help him with menial tasks. When *you* think that you have learned enough, you'll hang out a shingle and proclaim yourself a doctor. The process is much the same as what an automobile mechanic goes through today. In fact, you can even skip the apprenticeship if you wish, and simply hang out your shingle—just like a mechanic. If you can convince people you are good, you'll make a living. If not, you'll turn to something else.

In the 1800s, things began to change. A few medical schools opened, and there was some licensing of physicians. The medical schools of this period were like religions are today: They competed for clients and made different claims to the truth. One medical school would teach a particular idea about what caused illness and how to treat it, while another medical school would teach something else. Training was short, and often not even a high school diploma was required. There was no clinical training, and lectures went unchanged from year to year. The medical school at Harvard University took only two school years to complete—and the school year lasted only four months (Starr 1982; Rosenberg 1987; Riessman 1994).

Then came the 1900s. In 1906, the United States had 160 medical schools. The Carnegie Foundation asked Abraham Flexner, a renowned educator, to evaluate them. Even the most inadequate schools opened their doors to Flexner, for they thought that gifts from the Carnegie Foundation would follow (Rodash 1982). In some schools, the laboratories consisted only of "a few vagrant test tubes squirreled away in a cigar box." Other schools had libraries with no books. Flexner, of course, recommended higher standards. He also suggested that philanthropies fund the most promising schools. With more funds, these schools upgraded their facilities and were able to attract more capable faculty and students. In the face of higher standards and greater competition, most of the other schools had to close their doors.

The Flexner report (1910) led to the **professionalization of medicine.** When sociologists use the term *profession,* they mean something quite specific. What happened was that physicians began to (1) undergo a rigorous education; (2) claim a theoretical understanding of illness; (3) regulate themselves; (4) assert that they were performing a service for society (rather than just following self-interest); and (5) take authority over clients (Goode 1960).

professionalization of medicine
the development of medicine into a field in which education becomes rigorous, and in which physicians claim a theoretical understanding of illness, regulate themselves, claim to be doing a service to society (rather than just following self-interest), and take authority over clients

■ As hard as it is to believe, doctors used to be available at the beck and call of patients. They would come to a patient's home, diagnose the illness, prescribe medication, and even sit up all night with the critically ill—all for a modest fee. This photo is from the 1950s.

The Monopoly of Medicine   When medicine became a profession, it also became a monopoly, and this is the key to understanding our current situation. The group that gained control over U.S. medicine set itself up as *the* medical establishment. This group was able to get laws passed to restrict medical licensing to graduates of schools they controlled. By controlling the education and licensing of physicians, the medical establishment silenced most competing philosophies of medicine. The WASP males who took control also either refused to admit women and minorities to medical schools or severely limited their enrollment.

Eliminating the competition paved the way for medicine to become big business. The monopoly was so thorough that by law only a select group of men—a sort of priesthood of medicine—were allowed to diagnose and treat medical problems. Only they knew what was right for people's health. Only they could scribble the secret language (Latin) on special pieces of parchment (prescription forms) for translators (pharmacists) to decipher (Miner 2001). This select group was able to shape itself into the most lucrative profession in the country—for its members set their own fees and had little competition. This group of men became so powerful that it was even able to take childbirth away from midwives—the focus of the Down-to-Earth sociology box on the next page.

This approach, **fee-for-service** (payment to a physician in exchange for diagnosis and treatment), which made medicine a *business,* usually went unquestioned. Then, as monopolies do, the medical monopoly drove up the price of health care. This led to a public outcry: Because the poor couldn't afford medical treatment, the government should pay for it. The AMA fought every proposal for the government to fund medical care. Physicians were convinced that government funding would "socialize" medicine—that it would eliminate the fee-for-service system and turn doctors into government employees.

In the 1960s, proponents of government funding won. *Medicaid* (government-paid medical care for the poor) and *Medicare* (government-sponsored medical insurance for the elderly) were established. Physicians' fears proved groundless. Instead of leading to the socialization of medicine, these programs gave physicians millions of additional customers. People who previously could not afford medical services now had their medical expenses paid by the government. As Figure 13.5 on page 392 illustrates, these costly programs have put billions of dollars into physicians' pockets.

From its humble origins, medicine has grown into the largest business in the United States. This business consists not only of physicians, but also of nurses, physi-

fee-for-service
payment to a physician to diagnose and treat a patient's medical problems

To Establish a Monopoly, Eliminate Your Competition: How Physicians Defeated Midwives

Midwifery helps us understand the professionalization of medicine and provides insight into the founding of the U.S. medical establishment. In the United States, as in Europe and elsewhere, pregnancy and childbirth were considered natural events, and women were thought best equipped to help other women deal with them. Consequently, midwives delivered babies. Some midwives were trained; others were neighborhood women who had experience in childbirth. In many European countries, midwives were licensed by the state—as they still are.

As medicine became professionalized, physicians wanted to expand their business. Their desire for expansion, however, ran up against two major obstacles. The first was ignorance; they didn't know anything about delivering babies. It was considered indecent for a man to know much about pregnancy, much less to help a woman give birth. The second was the midwives, whom the physicians came to see as business competitors.

The physicians bribed some midwives to sneak them into the bedrooms where women were giving birth. To say "sneaked" is no exaggeration, for some physicians crawled on their hands and knees so that the mother-to-be wouldn't know a man was present. Most physicians weren't fortunate enough to find such cooperative midwives, however, and they had to train with mannequins. Gradually, physicians did gain admission to childbirth, but a veil of indecency persisted; doctors had to fumble blindly under a sheet in a darkened room, their head decorously turned aside.

■ The text discusses how physicians were able to eliminate their competition in delivering babies. In some states, midwives have made a comeback. Shown here is a midwife after she delivered a baby at the parents' home.

As physicians gained political power, they launched a ruthless campaign against their competitors. They attacked midwives as "dirty, ignorant, and incompetent," even calling them a "menace to the health of the community." Using their new political clout in the AMA, physicians succeeded in persuading many states to pass laws that made it illegal for anyone but a physician to deliver babies. Some states, however, continued to allow nurse-midwives to practice. The struggle is not yet over, and nurse-midwives and physicians sometimes still clash over who has the right to deliver babies.

Conflict theorists emphasize that this was a gender struggle—men sought to take control over what had been women's work. They stress that political power was central to the way physicians expanded their domain. Symbolic interactionists, without denying the political aspect, stress the social construction of reality. The key, they say, is the information campaign that physicians launched to eliminate midwives, convincing the public that pregnancy and childbirth were not natural processes, but medical conditions that required the assistance of an able man. This new definition, which flew in the face of the millennia-old tradition of women helping women to have babies, turned childbirth into "men's work." The prestige of the work went up—and so did the price.

Sources: Wertz and Wertz 1981; Rodash 1982; Danzi 1989; Rothman 1994.

cian extenders, hospital personnel, pharmacists, insurance and pharmaceutical companies, corporations that own hospitals and nursing homes, and the huge research, manufacturing, and sales force that sells drugs and medial technology. The medical monopoly is so powerful that it lobbies all the state legislatures and the U.S. Congress. Like sports, some hospitals even pay million-dollar sign-up bonuses to lure big-name surgeons (McCartney 1993).

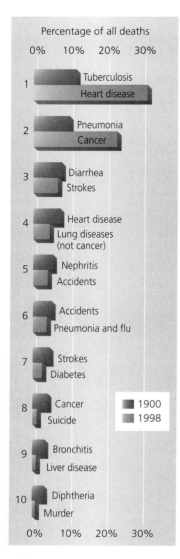

Percentage of all deaths

| | 0% | 10% | 20% | 30% |

1 Tuberculosis
   Heart disease

2 Pneumonia
   Cancer

3 Diarrhea
   Strokes

4 Heart disease
   Lung diseases
   (not cancer)

5 Nephritis
   Accidents

6 Accidents
   Pneumonia and flu

7 Strokes
   Diabetes

8 Cancer   ■ 1900
   Suicide   ■ 1998

9 Bronchitis
   Liver disease

10 Diphtheria
   Murder

| | 0% | 10% | 20% | 30% |

Figure 19.3

The Top Ten Causes of Death in the United States, 1900 and 1998

Sources: National Center for Health Statistics, *Statistical Abstract* 2001:Table 107.

epidemiology
the study of disease and disability patterns in a population

■ ■ ■ ■
Historical Patterns of Health

Let's look at how health and illness in the United States have changed. This will take us into the field of **epidemiology,** the study of how medical disorders are distributed throughout a population.

■ Physical Health

Leading Causes of Death   One way to see how the physical health of Americans has changed is to compare the leading causes of death in two time periods. To get an idea of how dramatic this change is, look at Figure 19.3. Note that half of the leading causes of death in 1900 don't even appear on today's list. Heart disease and cancer, which placed fourth and eighth in 1900, have now jumped to the top of the list, while tuberculosis and diarrhea, which were the number one and number three killers in 1900, don't even show up in today's top ten. Similarly, murder and suicide didn't make the top ten in 1900, but they do now. These shifts indicate that extensive changes have occurred in society. Disease, then, is not only a biological event. It is also *social,* following the contours of social change.

Were Americans Healthier in the Past?   A second way to see how the physical health of Americans has changed is to ask if they are healthier—or sicker—than they used to be. This question brings us face to face with the definitional problem discussed earlier. "Healthy" by whose standards? An additional problem is that many of today's diseases went unrecognized in the past. One way around these problems is to look at mortality rates. If Americans used to live longer, we can assume they were healthier. Because most people today live longer than their ancestors, however, we can conclude that contemporary Americans are healthier.

Some may think this conclusion flies in the face of abundant evidence to the contrary: polluted air and water, and the high rates of heart disease and cancer shown in Figure 19.3. And it does. Sometimes older people say, "When I was a kid, cancer wasn't even around. I never knew anyone who died from cancer, and now it seems everyone does." What they overlook is that most cancers strike older people, and when life expectancy is shorter, there is less chance that people will die from cancer. Also, in the past most cancer went unrecognized. People were simply said to have died of "old age" or "heart failure."

■ Mental Health

When it comes to mental health, we have no way to make good comparisons. We may picture a past in which the elderly had lower suicide rates, less mental illness, and so on, but we need solid measures of mental illness or mental health, not anecdotes. The idyllic past—where everyone grew up in a happy home with two loving parents, married for life, and lived in harmony with the rest of the world—never existed. All groups have their share of mental problems—and commonsense beliefs that mental illness is worse today represent a perception, not measured reality. Such perceptions may be true, of course, but the *opposite* could also be true. Since we don't even know how extensive mental illness is today (Miller 1993; Scheff 1999), we certainly can't judge how much there was in the past.

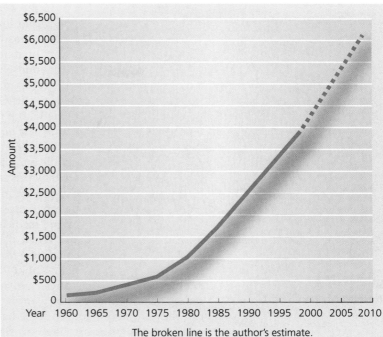

The broken line is the author's estimate.

Issues in Health Care

L et's turn to issues in health care in the United States.

■ Medical Care: A Right or a Commodity?

A primary controversy in the United States is whether medical care is a right or a privilege. If it is a right, then all citizens should have easy access to good medical care. If it is a privilege, then, as with automobiles, clothing, and other commodities, the rich will have access to one type of care, and the poor to another. Currently, medical care is not the right of citizens. It is a commodity to be sold at the highest price. Those with the money can buy better quality, while the poor and uninsured must go without—or wait for handouts. The attempts to address this disparity with some system of national medical care have been futile.

Related to this issue is the skyrocketing cost of medical care. As shown in Figure 19.4, in 1960 the average American spent $150 a year on health care. Today the average American spends about $4,500. To grasp what this means, consider this. In 1960, a 17-inch black-and-white television also cost about $150. If television prices had risen at the same rate as health care, a 17-inch *black-and-white* television would now cost about $4,500. The reasons for this increase in medical costs include the growing numbers of elderly and the new medical technology. The result of health care being an expensive commodity is a *two-tier system of medical care*—superior care for those who can afford the cost, and inferior care for those who cannot. Again, this is like new sports cars for the wealthy, and broken-down used cars for the poor.

Figure 19.4

The Soaring Cost of Medical Care: What the Average American Pays Each Year

Source: Statistical Abstract 2000:Table 153 (and earlier years).

■ Social Inequality

The opening vignette, which described the nude man in the homeless shelter who was being taken to the state mental hospital, lays bare the two-tier system of medical care. A middle-class or rich person who had mental problems would go to a private psychiatrist, not to a state mental hospital. Of course, he or she would not have been in that shelter in the first place.

Since 1939, sociologists have found an inverse correlation between mental problems and social class. In other words, the lower the social class, the higher the proportion of mental problems. This finding has been confirmed in numerous studies (Faris and Dunham 1939; Hudson 1988; Ross and Willigen 1997; Croudace et. al 2000). Sociologists have little difficulty understanding why people in the lower social classes have greater mental problems, for these people bear the stresses that come with poverty. Compared with middle- and upper-class Americans, the poor have less job security, lower wages, and more unpaid bills and insistent bill collectors. They are also more likely to divorce, to be victims of violent crime, and to abuse alcohol. Such conditions deal severe blows to emotional well-being.

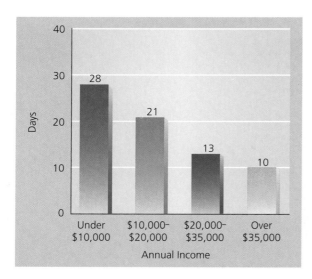

Figure 19.5

Number of Days Sick

Note: Number of days people were so sick or injured that they cut down on their usual activities for more than half a day; includes days off work and school.

Source: Statistical Abstract 2000: Table 211.

In the 1960s, politicians and psychiatrists came up with a policy that brought shame to the mental health establishment. Called **deinstitutionalization,** the plan was to open the locked wards of state mental hospitals, release the patients, and give them counseling and medications on the outside. The patients were released, but the outpatient services were not put in place. As a result, U.S. streets were flooded with former mental patients who had no income and nowhere to go. The streets became their home.

Needless to say, these were poor people. Members of the middle and upper classes who had mental problems were counseled by private psychiatrists and, if hospitalized, went to expensive private mental hospitals. The rich were treated with "talk" therapy (various forms of psychotherapy), while the poor were given "medicinal straitjackets" (medication to sedate them).

When it comes to physical illnesses, we find similar inequalities. As Figure 19.5 shows, the poor are more likely to get sick. Unlike the middle and upper classes, however, few poor people have a personal physician, and some of them spend hours waiting in crowded public health clinics. After waiting most of a day, some don't even get to see a doctor; they are simply told to come back the next day (Fialka 1993). Finally, when hospitalized, the poor are likely to find themselves in understaffed and underfunded public hospitals, where they are treated by rotating interns who do not know them and cannot follow up on their progress.

■ Malpractice Suits and Defensive Medicine

Some analysts have observed that physicians used to kill more patients than they cured. Given that physicians didn't know about germs and didn't wash before surgery or childbirth, this may be true. In the 1800s, doctors thought that sickness was caused by "bad fluids," and they had four techniques for getting rid of these fluids: (1) bleeding (cutting a vein or using leeches to drain out "bad" blood); (2) blistering (applying packs so hot they burned the skin, draining out the bad pus); (3) vomiting (feeding patients liquids that made them vomit up the bad fluids); and (4) purging (feeding patients substances that caused diarrhea).

In light of today's superior treatment, one might think malpractice suits would be a thing of the past. The opposite, however, is true. Back then, the law didn't allow patients to recover damages. The thinking was, "People make mistakes," and that included doctors. Today, physicians are held to much higher standards—and not excused for making mistakes. Damage awards are high, and doctors are anxious. One physician told me, "I'm looking for something else to do, because medicine is no longer fun. Every time I treat a patient, I wonder if this is the one who is going to turn around and sue me."

To protect themselves, physicians practice **defensive medicine.** They consult with colleagues and order lab tests not because the patient needs them but because they want to leave a paper trail in case they are sued. These consultations and tests—done for the doctor's benefit, not the patient's—are one of the major reasons for the increase in the nation's annual medical bill (Volti 1995; Hammerstein 2000). To reduce the costs of defensive medicine, the state of Maine has instituted physician checklists. If doctors follow them, malpractice suits are dismissed (Felsenthal 1993). Although physicians complain about a "paint-by-numbers" approach to medicine, many prefer this to the threat of lawsuits.

■ Medical Incompetence

Did you hear about the woman who had a problem with her lungs—and her doctor did a hysterectomy? No, I'm not making this up. It happened in New York City (Steinhauer and Fessenden 2001). Another doctor operated on the wrong side of a

deinstitutionalization
the release of patients from mental hospitals into the community, supposedly while receiving treatment within a network of outpatient services

defensive medicine
medical practices done not for the patient's benefit but in order to protect a physician from malpractice suits

patient's brain, and yet another removed the wrong kidney—leaving the cancerous one intact. Still other physicians operate on the wrong patient altogether (Steinhauer 2001). Although not an everyday event, these things do happen. In fact, there is a serious proposal that the patient and doctor sign their names in ink at the point where an incision is to be made, so no doctor will remove the wrong body part.

Few would disagree that if a surgeon removes the wrong breast, the patient has the right to sue her doctor. But are some malpractice suits unfair? Certainly. Some patients sue doctors for trivial matters, others for matters over which they have no control. Yet, despite the rigors of medical education, medical incompetence is extensive. The Institute of Medicine, a branch of the National Academy of Sciences, reports that each year between 44,000 and 98,000 Americans die at the hands of doctors. *If the number of Americans killed by medical errors were an official classification of death, it would rank as one of the top ten leading causes of death* (Steinhauer and Fessenden 2001).

Many proposals have been made to reduce these needless deaths (what the medical profession calls "adverse events"). Because many patients die from cross-reactions of prescription drugs, some suggest that doctors enter all prescriptions online. A computer program would check patient records, causing the monitor to flash a warning if a doctor tries to prescribe a drug that can interfere with other medications.

These proposals have merit, but the proposal that gets at the heart of the matter is the one made by the Institute of Medicine. It recommends that we establish a Federal Center for Patient Safety. All medical deaths and injuries would be reported to the Center. Just as the Federal Aviation Agency investigates each plane crash, the Center would investigate each medical injury and death. Based on the cause it pinpointed, it would set up guidelines designed to reduce the number of similar events.

■ Depersonalization: The Medical Cash Machine

Sociologist Sue Fisher (1986), who was examined for an ovarian mass, gives this account:

> On my initial visit a nurse called me into an examination room, asked me to undress, gave me a paper gown to put on and told me the doctor would be with me soon. I was stunned. Was I not even to see the doctor before undressing? . . . How could I present myself as a competent, knowledgeable person sitting undressed on the examining table? But I had a potentially cancerous growth, so I did as I had been told.
>
> In a few minutes the nurse returned and said, "Lie down. The doctor is coming." Again I complied. The doctor entered the examining room, nodded in my direction while reading my chart, and proceeded to examine me without ever having spoken to me.

One of the main criticisms leveled against the medical profession is **depersonalization,** the practice of dealing with people as though they were cases and diseases, not individuals. Many patients have the impression that they are being treated by a cash machine—a physician who, while talking to them, is impatiently counting minutes and tabulating dollars so that he or she can move on to the next customer and make more money. After all, any extra time spent with a patient is money down the drain.

Some students start medical school with lofty motives. They want to "treat the whole person," yet they

depersonalization
dealing with people as though they were objects; in the case of medical care, as though patients were merely cases and diseases, not persons

■ *In one of the most brazen attempts to justify cigarette smoking, Philip Morris reported that the Czech government saved $1,227 every time a smoker dies. The report led to a public outcry, and Philip Morris quickly backpedaled, saying it had been misunderstood. Following the company's reasoning, we ought to encourage smoking in grade school, for the sooner people die the more the government saves.*

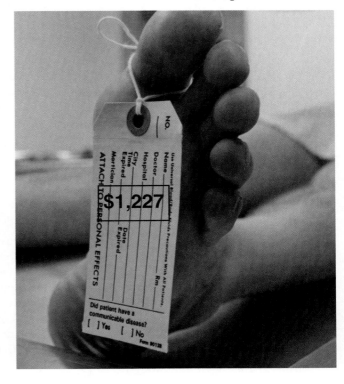

learn to depersonalize patients. Sociologists Jack Haas and William Shaffir (1993), who did participant observation at McMaster University in Canada, discovered how this happens. As vast amounts of material are thrown at medical students, their feelings for patients are overpowered by the need to be efficient. Consider this student's report:

> Somebody will say, "Listen to Mrs. Jones's heart. It's just a little thing flubbing on the table." And *you forget about the rest of her* . . . and it helps in learning in the sense that you can go in to a patient, put your stethoscope on the heart, listen to it, and walk out. . . . The advantage is that *you can go in a short time and see a patient, get the important things out of the patient, and leave* (italics added).

This student's statement to the researchers illustrates the extent to which patients become objects.

> You don't know the people that are under anesthesia—just practice putting the tube in, and the person wakes up with a sore throat, and well, it's just sort of a part of the procedure. . . . Someone comes in who has croaked (and you say), "Well, come on. Here is a chance to practice your intubation" (inserting a tube in the throat).

■ Conflict of Interest

As part of her treatment for cancer, Julia Lippman needed intravenous feeding at home. Her doctor told her to cancel the arrangements she had made with a company that provided such services and to use a company called T^2 instead. If she didn't, he added, he would not be responsible for her treatment. It turned out that he had invested in T^2 (Rodwin 1993).

The medical cash machine generates conflicts of interest. Some doctors make hidden income by referring patients to a hospital, pharmacy, or medical supply company of which they are part owner. Others make money under the table by prescribing one drug instead of another. If a doctor prescribes a lot of its drug, some companies award the doctor an all-expense-paid trip to a medical conference (Zuger 1999; Petersen 2001). Others pay for their golf outings or send them on cruises. Such conflicts of interest make it difficult to know if a doctor is basing a course of treatment on the patient's best interest—or on the best interest of the doctor's bank account.

■ Medical Fraud

With 2 million Medicare claims filed every day, physicians with Medicare patients are not likely to be audited. Many have not been able to resist the temptation to cheat. The following are not isolated incidents—they are just some of the most outrageous.

> Some doctors have charged for services they supposedly performed on patients who were dead. A psychiatrist in California had sex with his patient—and charged Medicaid for the time. Another doctor billed for abortions on women who were not pregnant. One had even had a hysterectomy. This same doctor even claimed that he performed two abortions within a month on the same patient. Another doctor billed Medicare for treating a 22-year-old for diaper rash (Geis et al. 1995).

Medical suppliers have also been guilty of outrageous fraud. A wheelchair van service, for example, billed Medicare $62,000 for just one patient, who supposedly made a $260 trip every two days for sixteen months (Schatz 1995). An ophthalmologist tried to pocket an extra $14,000 by performing unnecessary eye operations. He left fourteen people with impaired vision (Geis et al. 1995). Worse yet is medical fraud that endangers people's lives. One pharmacist sold expired pacemakers (Schatz 1995). Another, a highly respected pharmacist in Kansas City who was worth $10 million, couldn't resist piling up just a few more bucks. He diluted the drugs he provided for patients in chemotherapy (Belluck 2001).

Sexism in Medicine

In Chapter 12 (page 351), we examined racism in medicine. Now let's look at sexism in medicine, which also carries serious consequences. In the Down-to-Earth Sociology box on page 322, we saw that physicians don't take women's health complaints as seriously as they do those of men. As a result, women with heart disease are operated on at a later stage, making it more likely that they will die from their surgery.

The sexism involving heart disease was so subtle that the physicians were not even aware that they were discriminating against women. Some sexism in medicine, in contrast, is blatant. One of the best examples is bias *against* women's reproductive organs. Sue Fisher (1986), whose encounter with depersonalized medicine was cited earlier, did participant observation in a hospital. When she heard doctors recommend total hysterectomy (removal of both the uterus and the ovaries) even when no cancer was present, she asked why. The doctors explained that the uterus and ovaries are "potentially disease-producing" organs. They also said that these organs are unnecessary after the childbearing years, so why not remove them?

Since few women feel the same way, in order to make money, surgeons have to "sell" the operation. Here is how one doctor explained his "hard sell" to sociologist Diana Scully (1994):

> You have to look for your surgical procedures; you have to go after patients. Because no one is crazy enough to come and say, "Hey, here I am. I want you to operate on me." You have to sometimes convince the patient that she is really sick—if she is, of course [laughs], and that she is better off with a surgical procedure.

To "convince" a woman to have this surgery, the doctor tells her that, unfortunately, the examination has turned up fibroids in her uterus—and they *might* turn into cancer. This statement is often sufficient, for it frightens women, who picture themselves dying from cancer. To clinch the sale, the surgeon withholds the rest of the truth—that the fibroids probably will not turn into cancer and that she has several nonsurgical alternatives.

Underlying this sexism is male dominance of medicine in the United States. This is not a worldwide characteristic of medicine. For example, while only one of four U.S. physicians is a woman, in the former Soviet Union the ratio was reversed and three out of four physicians were women (Knaus 1981; *Statistical Abstract* 2000:Table 669). The sex ratio is changing. In 1970, only 8 percent of U.S. medical degrees went to women. Today it is 41 percent (*Statistical Abstract* 2000:Table 322). This change should reduce sexism in medical practice, including that described in the Down-to-Earth Sociology box on the next page.

The Medicalization of Society

As we have seen, childbirth and women's reproductive organs have come to be defined as medical matters. Sociologists use the term **medicalization** to refer to the process of turning something that was not previously considered a medical issue into a medical matter. Examples include acne, anxiety, balding, depression, sagging buttocks and chins, small breasts, "over" and "under" weight, and wrinkles.

As usual, the three theoretical perspectives give us three views of the medicalization of these human conditions. Symbolic interactionists would stress that there is nothing inherently medical about acne, balding, sagging chins, and so on. It is all a matter of definition: People used to consider such matters as normal problems of life; now they are starting to redefine them as medical problems. Functionalists would stress that the medicalization of such conditions helps the medical establishment by broadening its customer base. They would also point out another functional aspect of medicalization—that it provides people with someone who will listen to their problems—and sometimes helps them. Conflict sociologists would argue that this process indicates the growing power of the medical establishment: The more conditions of life that physicians can medicalize, the greater their profits and power.

medicalization
the transformation of something into a matter to be treated by physicians

down-to-earth sociology

The Doctor-Nurse Game

Leonard Stein (1988), a physician who worked with nurses and doctors for many years, said that their interactions are like a game. Because physicians have the higher status, nurses must try to give the impression that the doctor is always in control. Although nurses spend more time with patients and are often more familiar with their needs, never can they be perceived as making recommendations to the doctor. Consequently, nurses disguise their recommendations. Consider this dialog between a nurse and a doctor whom the nurse has called at 1 A.M. The rotating resident does not know the patient.

"This is Dr. Jones." (*an open and direct communication*)

"Dr. Jones, this is Nurse Smith on 2W. Mrs. Brown learned today that her father died, and she is unable to fall asleep." (*On the surface, this is simply a factual statement—the patient has learned of a death in the family and is unable to sleep. But it contains a hid-* den recommendation. The nurse has diagnosed the cause of the sleeplessness and has suggested that a sedative be prescribed.*)

The doctor replies: "What sleeping medication has been helpful to Mrs. Brown in the past?" (*On the surface, this question is a mere request for a fact. It is, however, a request for a recommendation of what to prescribe.*)

"Pentobarbital, 100 milligrams, was quite effective the night before last." (*On the surface, this is just factual information. Actually, however, it is a specific recommendation from the nurse to the physician—one that includes not only the name of the medicine, but also the dosage.*)

"Pentobarbital, 100 milligrams before bedtime, as needed for sleep. Got it?" (*At this point, the doctor speaks with audible authority—a little louder, a little firmer.*)

"Yes, I have, and thank you very much, doctor."

The two have successfully played the doctor-nurse game. The lower-status person has made a recommendation to the higher-status person. The nurse did this in a covert manner that required neither the nurse nor the physician to acknowledge what really occurred. The participants played the game so well that they did not threaten their relative statuses.

When I interviewed Stein, he said that the doctor-nurse game is breaking down because of the larger number of men who have entered nursing, the feminist movement that has challenged male authority, and the growing number of women physicians. As a consequence, nurses have become less subservient, and physicians are less able to exert unquestioned authority.

Some version of the game will continue to be played, however, as long as status differences remain. The rules will simply be modified to meet changing circumstances.

■ ■ ■ ■ ■

■ Medically Assisted Suicide

I started the intravenous dripper, which released a salt solution through a needle into her vein, and I kept her arm tied down so she wouldn't jerk it. This was difficult as her veins were fragile. And then once she decided she was ready to go, she just hit the switch and the device cut off the saline drip and through the needle released a solution of thiopental that put her to sleep in ten to fifteen seconds. A minute later, through the needle flowed a lethal solution of potassium chloride. (Jack Kevorkian, as quoted in Denzin 1992)

The topic of suicide fascinates the U.S. public. A how-to book on suicide, *Final Exit*, sold more than a half million copies. The Hemlock Society, a group that advocates voluntary **euthanasia** (mercy killing) for terminally ill people, has grown to eighty chapters. Oregon passed a law allowing medically assisted suicide. Opponents called it legalized murder, and the U.S. Attorney General ordered the Drug Enforcement Administration to arrest any doctor who prescribed drugs for suicide (Verhovek 2001).

With new technology that can keep the body alive even after the heart, lungs, and other vital organs no longer function on their own, a burning question that has yet to be answered is, "Who has the right to pull the plug?" Should someone's body be kept alive for years even though his or her mind is no longer functioning? To resolve this issue, some people sign a **living will**—a declaration about what they want medical personnel to do in case they become dependent on artificial life support systems.

euthanasia
mercy killing

living will
a statement people in good health sign that clearly expresses their feelings about being kept alive on artificial life support systems

Our technology and the acts of Kevorkian have brought us face to face with matters of death that are both disturbing and difficult to resolve. Should "medically assisted suicide" be legal? The following Thinking Critically section explores these issues.

thinking
CRITICALLY

Should Doctors Be Allowed to Kill Patients?

Except for the name, this is a true story:

> Bill Simpson, who was in his seventies, had battled leukemia for years. After doctors removed his spleen, he developed an abdominal abscess. It took another operation to drain it. A week later, the abscess filled, and Bill required more surgery. Again the abscess returned. Simpson began to drift in and out of consciousness. His brother-in-law suggested euthanasia. The surgeon injected a lethal dose of morphine into Simpson's intravenous feeding tubes.

At a medical conference, a cancer specialist who had treated thousands of patients announced that he had kept count of those who had asked him to help them die. "There were 127 men and women," he said. Then he added, "And I saw to it that 25 of them got their wish." Thousands of other physicians have done the same (Nuland 1995).

The public seems to hold two dominant images of people who undergo euthanasia. One impression is of an individual who is devastated by chronic pain. The doctor mercifully helps to end that pain by performing euthanasia. The second is of a brain-dead individual—a human vegetable—who lies in a hospital bed, kept alive only by machines. How accurate are these images?

We have the example of Holland. There euthanasia remains illegal, but it is practiced openly. The Royal Dutch Medical Association has even set standards for euthanasia, and the government honors its standards. Although physicians must report each death in which they assist, *60 percent* go unreported. In about 1,000 cases a year, physicians kill their patients without the patients' express consent. In one instance, a doctor ended the life of a nun because he thought she would like this but was afraid to ask because it was against her religion. In another case, a physician terminated a patient with breast cancer who said that she did *not* want euthanasia. In the doctor's words, "It could have taken another week before she died. I just needed this bed" (Hendin 1997, 2000).

Some Dutch are concerned that they could be euthanized if they have a medical emergency. They carry "passports" that instruct medical personnel that they wish to live. Most Dutch, however, support euthanasia. Many carry another "passport," one that instructs medical personnel to carry out euthanasia (Shapiro 1997).

Dr. Jack Kevorkian, the author of the quote that opened this section, gave the authorities a rough time. He helped 120 people commit suicide. He even taunted the authorities, sometimes dumping bodies off at motels or leaving them in vans. Kevorkian was careful. He provided the "death machine" and the drugs, but he never touched the lever that released the drugs. Michigan prosecutors tried Kevorkian for murder four times, but juries refused to convict him. Then, Kevorkian went too far. He played a videotape on national television, showing him giving a lethal injection to a man who was dying from Lou Gehrig's disease. Prosecutors put Kevorkian on trial again. He was convicted of second degree murder and was sentenced to 10 to 25 years in prison.

■ ■ ■ ■ ■

for your consideration . . .

Do you think that physicians should have the right to assist in suicides? As is evident from research from Holland, physician-assisted deaths have a way of expanding. In addition to what is reported here, Dutch doctors also kill newborn babies who have serious birth defects (Smith 1999). Their justification is that these children would not have "quality of life." Would you support this?

Sources: Gomez 1991; Markson 1992; Angell 1996; Smith 1999.

■ Curbing Costs: Issues in Private and National Health Insurance

We have seen some of the reasons why the price of medical care in the United States has soared: advanced—and expensive—technology for diagnosis and treatment, a growing elderly population, tests performed as defensive measures rather than for medical reasons, and health care that is regarded as a commodity to be sold to the highest bidder. As long as these conditions are in place, the price of medical care will continue to outpace inflation. Let's look at some attempts to reduce costs.

HMOs   Health Maintenance Organizations, or HMOs are medical companies that negotiate an annual fee in exchange for providing medical care for a corporation's employees. Whatever money is left over at the end of the year is the HMO's profit. If they bid too low, they lose money. While this arrangement eliminates unnecessary medical treatment, it also puts pressure on doctors to reduce *necessary* treatment.

The results are anything but pretty. Over her doctor's strenuous objections, a friend of mine was discharged from the hospital even though she was still bleeding and running a fever. Her HMO representative said he would not authorize another day in the hospital. A lung specialist in Washington Heights, New York, fought with his HMO for three hours to get permission to do a procedure on a woman who was coughing up life-threatening amounts of blood (Steinhauer 1999). After suffering a heart attack, a man in Kansas City, Missouri, needed surgery that could be performed only at Barnes Hospital in St. Louis, Missouri. The HMO said, "Too bad. That hospital is out of our service area." The man died while appealing the HMO decision (Spragins 1996).

The basic question, of course, is: At what human cost do we reduce spending on medical treatment?

health maintenance organization (HMO)
a health care organization that provides medical treatment to its members for a fixed annual cost

Diagnosis-Related Groups   To curb spiraling costs, the federal government has classified all illnesses into diagnosis-related-groups (DRGs) and has set a specified amount that it will pay for the treatment of each illness. Hospitals make a profit if they move patients through the system quickly, if they discharge patients before the allotted amount is spent. As a consequence, some patients are discharged before they

■ *The cartoonist has captured an unfortunate reality of U.S. medicine.*

FRANK & ERNEST by ® Bob Thaves

are fully ready to go home. Others are refused admittance because they appear to have a "worse than average" case of a particular illness. In other words, they might take longer to treat and would cost the hospital money instead of making it a profit (Easterbrook 1987; Feinglass 1987).

National Health Insurance A young woman who was five months pregnant was taken to a hospital complaining of stomach pains. The hospital refused to admit her, because she had no money or credit. As they were about to transfer her to a hospital for the poor, she gave birth. The baby was stillborn. The hospital went ahead and transferred the woman—dead baby, umbilical cord, and all (Ansberry 1988).

Dumping, the practice of refusing to treat unprofitable patients and sending them to public hospitals, is one consequence of a system that puts profit ahead of patient care. Most cases are less dramatic than that of the woman and her stillborn baby, but the same principle applies. With 44 million Americans—primarily the poor—uninsured (*Statistical Abstract* 2000:Table 177), pressure has grown for the government to provide national health insurance. The Social Map below shows how the uninsured are distributed among the states.

Advocates of national health insurance point out that centralized, large-scale purchases of medical and hospital supplies will reduce costs. They also stress how inadequate medical care is for the poor. Such horror stories as the one I just related make their point. Opponents stress the red tape of national health insurance. They ask if federal agencies—such as those that run the postal service—inspire so much confidence that they should be entrusted with administering something so vital as the nation's health care. This debate is not new, and even if some form of national health insurance is adopted, the argument is likely to continue.

Rationing Medical Care The most controversial suggestion for how to reduce medical costs is to ration medical care. We cannot afford to provide all the available technology to everyone, goes the argument, so we have to ration it. No easy answer has been found for this pressing matter, which is becoming the center of a national debate. This dilemma is the focus of the Sociology and the New Technology box on the next page.

dumping
the practice of sending unprofitable patients to public hospitals

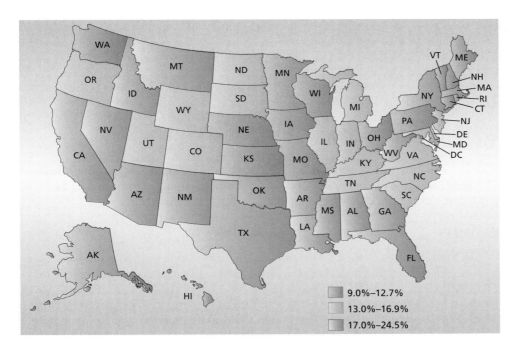

Figure 19.6

Social Map: Who Lacks Medical Insurance?

Note: The range is broad, from a low of 9 percent who lack medical insurance in Nebraska to a high of 24.5 percent in Texas.

Source: Statistical Abstract 2000: Table 178.

9.0%–12.7%
13.0%–16.9%
17.0%–24.5%

sociology & the new technology

Who Should Live, and Who Should Die? The Dilemma of Rationing Medical Care

Visiting a doctor or a hospital is not without risk. We have seen that doctors kill somewhere between 50,000 and 100,000 patients a year. But today's risk is small compared to that of earlier times, when physicians bled and purged their patients in an effort to cure them. Today's physicians are well trained, and medical care is based on scientific studies. Our new technology even allows us to cure medical conditions that just a short time ago doomed people to early deaths. In other instances, the medical condition can't be cured, but, with treatment, the patient is able to live a long and satisfying life.

And therein lies the rub. Even though some particular medical technology is essential for treatment, there isn't enough of it to go around to everyone who needs it. Other technology is so costly that it could bankrupt society if it were made available to everyone who had a particular condition. Who, then, should receive the benefits of our new medical technology?

Consider dialysis, the use of machines to cleanse the blood of people who are suffering from kidney disease. Currently, dialysis is available to anyone who needs it, and the cost runs several billion dollars a year. Four percent of all Medicare goes to pay for the dialysis of just one-fourth of 1 percent of Medicare patients. Great Britain, which faces this same problem, rations dialysis to people under the age of 55 (Volti 1995).

Open heart surgery is a technological wonder, but its costs are astounding. One percent of all the money the nation spends on its medical bills goes to pay for the bypass surgeries of just four-hundredths of 1 percent of the population. Medical treatment at the end of people's lives also helps us understand the issue. Of all Medicare money, about one-fourth is spent to maintain patients during just the last year of their lives. Almost a third of this amount is spent during just the last month of life (Volti 1995).

The situation will worsen. Medical technology—and its spiraling costs—continue to advance. So does the number of elderly people, who need medical treatment the most.

How should we spend our limited resources? At the heart of this issue lie questions not only of cost, but also of fairness, of how to distribute the benefits of advanced medical technology in an equitable manner.

The dilemma is harsh: If we ration medical treatment, many sick people will die. If we don't, we may go bankrupt.

for your consideration

But how should we decide who should receive treatment and who should be denied it? Should wealth or fame be part of the decision? Or should there be a lottery? In more specific terms: Should a baseball icon be given a liver transplant even though there is little chance that it will substantially prolong his life? This is what happened to Mickey Mantle, whose liver had been ravaged by years of hard drinking, by hepatitis C, and by cancer, which had spread to other parts of his body. Mantle waited just 2 days for a new liver. He died less than 3 months after receiving it. If the liver had been put in a healthy individual, it is likely that person would still be alive.

Use ideas, concepts, and principles from this and other chapters to develop a proposal for solving this pressing issue. Also note how this dilemma changes shape if you view it from the contrasting perspectives of conflict theory, functionalism, and symbolic interactionism.

Threats to Health

Let's look at five threats to health both in the United States and worldwide: AIDS; the globalization of disease; drugs; disabling environments; and misguided, foolish, and callous experiments.

■ AIDS

In 1981, the first case of AIDS (acquired immune deficiency syndrome) was documented. Since then, this virus that attacks the human immune system has killed almost 500,000 Americans. As you can see from Figure 19.7, in the United States this disease has been brought under control. New infections peaked in 1993, and deaths peaked in 1995. For Americans, AIDS has turned into a chronic disease that you live with, rather than die of. Today, about 450,000 Americans are living with AIDS (or HIV, the virus that

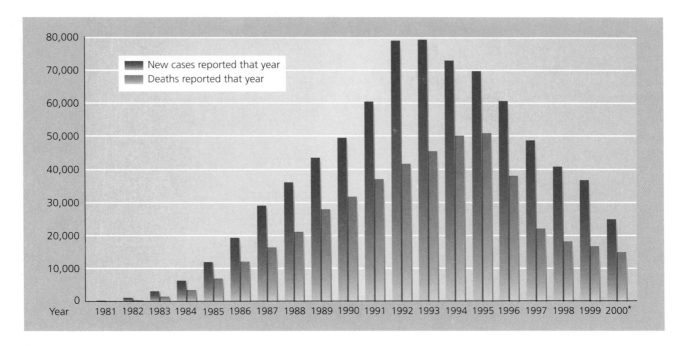

Figure 19.7

The Growth of AIDS in the United States

Source: Centers for Disease Control 2001:Tables 21, 28.

causes AIDS) (Centers for Disease Control 2001). The average cost to treat a U.S. AIDS patient is $20,000 a year, making the nation's AIDS medical bill about $9 billion a year.

Globally, in contrast, AIDS has not been brought under control. About 20 million people have died from this disease, but the worst is yet to come. As Figure 19.8 so graphically illustrates, Africa is the hardest hit region of the world. In sub-Saharan Africa, AIDS is the leading cause of death. In some counties there, AIDS is expected to wipe out half the teenagers (Nullis 2000). Botswana, in southern Africa, has the highest rate of AIDS in the world, with more than one in three adults infected. If the United States had the same rate, about 100 million Americans would have AIDS. Worldwide, each minute, 11 people are infected with HIV—ten of them are in sub-Saharan Africa (Will 2000).

Let's look at some of the major characteristics of this disease.

Origin   The question of how AIDS originated baffled scientists for two decades, but it appears to be solved (Kolata 2001). They have traced genetic sequences back to the Congo. Apparently, the virus was present in chimpanzees and was then transmitted to humans. How this occurred is not known, but the best guess is that hunters were exposed to the animals' blood as they slaughtered them for meat.

The Transmission of AIDS   The only way a person can become infected with AIDS is if bodily fluids pass from one person to another. AIDS is most commonly transmitted through the exchange of blood and semen, but nursing babies can also get AIDS through the milk of their infected mothers. Since the AIDS virus is present in all bodily fluids (including sweat, tears, spittle, and urine), some people think that AIDS can also be transmitted in these forms. The U.S. Centers for Disease Control, however, say that AIDS cannot be transmitted by casual contact in which traces of these fluids would be exchanged.

Patterns of transmission vary from one society to another. In some, for example, most people get AIDS from heterosexual sex, while in others

Figure 19.8

AIDS: A Global Glimpse

Source: Based on Haub and Cornelius 2000.

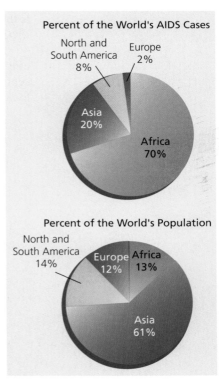

■ *AIDS is devastating huge areas of Africa. In some countries, one-third or more of the population has AIDS. Millions of children have been orphaned. Governments that first ignored the problem are now trying to battle AIDS. This anti-AIDS billboard is posted in Kampala, Uganda.*

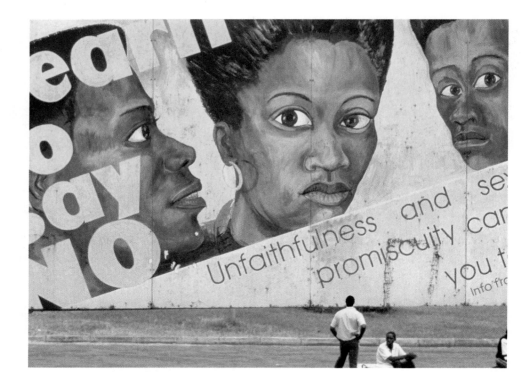

most victims get the disease from homosexual sex. Patterns also differ for men and women within the same society. Figure 19.9 compares the patterns for men and women in the United States.

Gender, Race-Ethnicity, and AIDS Although many people think of AIDS as a man's disease, in parts of Africa, AIDS strikes males and females equally. In the United States, each year women make up a larger proportion of new cases. In 1982, only 6 percent of AIDS cases were women, but today women account for 25 percent of all new cases (Centers for Disease Control 1997:Tables 3, 10; 2001:Table 5). AIDS is the seventh leading cause of death of both U.S. men and women ages 15 to 24 (*Statistical Abstract* 2000:Table 129).

As shown in Table 19.1 on the next page, the risk of AIDS is also related to race-ethnicity. The reason for this is not genetic; that is, no racial-ethnic group is more susceptible to AIDS because of biological factors. Rather, risks differ because of *social* factors, such as rates of intravenous drug use and the use of condoms.

Figure 19.9

How Americans Get AIDS

Source: Centers for Disease Control, 2001:Table 5.

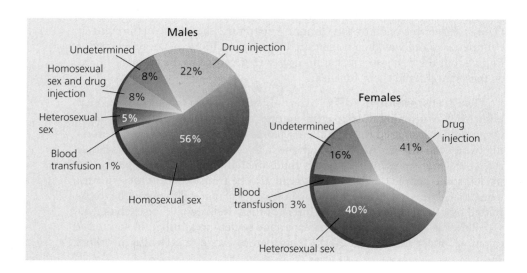

The Stigma of AIDS   One of the most significant sociological aspects of AIDS is the stigma it carries. This provides another example of how social factors are essential to health and illness. Some people refuse even to be tested because they fear the stigma they would bear if they tested HIV-positive. One unfortunate consequence is the continuing spread of AIDS by people who "don't want to know." Even some governments put their heads in the sand. Chinese officials, for example, refuse to admit how extensive the spread of AIDS is becoming in their country (Rosenthal 2001c). If this disease is to be brought under control, its stigma must be overcome: AIDS must be viewed like any other lethal disease—as the work of a destructive biological organism.

Is There a Cure for AIDS?   Figure 19.7 on page 583 shows how AIDS in the United States increased dramatically, peaked, and then declined. With such a remarkable decline, have we found a cure for AIDS?

With thousands of scientists conducting research, the media have heralded each new breakthrough as a possible cure. The most promising treatment to date, the one that lies behind the drop in deaths, was spearheaded by David Ho, a virologist (virus researcher). If patients in the early stages of the disease take a "cocktail" of drugs (a combination of protease inhibitors, AZT, and 3TC), all signs of the virus can be erased from their bodies. Their immune systems then rebound (Gorman 1997). No one is calling this a cure, however, for apparently the virus lingers undetected, ready to flourish if the drugs are withdrawn.

While most praise this new treatment, some researchers have issued a dire warning (Rotello 1996). They suggest that the cocktail may become this decade's penicillin. When penicillin was introduced, everyone was ecstatic about its effectiveness. However, over the years, the microbes that penicillin targets mutated, producing "super germs" against which we have no protection. If this is the case with AIDS, then a new, "super-AIDS" virus could hit the world with more fury than its first devastating wave.

TABLE 19.1	Aids and Race-Ethnicity	
	Percentage of U.S. Population	Percentage of New AIDS Cases
Whites	69.4%	36.5%
Latinos	12.5%	20.0%
African Americans	12.1%	42.1%
Asian Americans	3.7%	1.0%
Native Americans	0.7%	0.4%

Source: Centers for Disease Control 2001:Table 9 and Figure 12.6 on page 360 of this text.

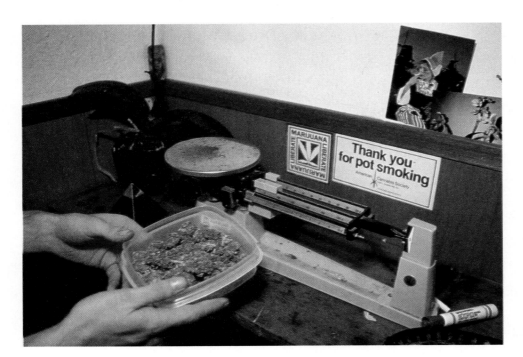

■ *A controversy surrounding AIDS is the "semilegal" marijuana clubs in San Francisco. Here marijuana is sold openly to people seeking to combat the side effects of AIDS treatments.*

■ The Globalization of Disease

> The year was 1918. Men and women, seemingly healthy the day before, collapsed and quickly died. In the morning, men wheeled carts down the streets to pick up corpses that were left on porches like last night's trash. In a matter of months, a half million Americans died. Worldwide, the death toll reached between 20 million and 40 million. (Phillips 1998)

What silent killer had so abruptly hit the United States and most of the world? Incredibly, it was the flu. For some reason, still unknown, a particularly lethal variety of the common flu bug suddenly appeared.

Medical researchers fear that something like this will happen again. If it does, a new social condition may make it even more deadly. Global travel has destroyed the natural frontiers that used to contain diseases. Today, in a matter of just hours, airline passengers can spread a disease around the world. Because older diseases have mutated and have produced "super bugs" that are immune to antibiotics, the resulting number of deaths could make the 1918 death toll seem puny by comparison.

Such are the fears. Twenty-eight new diseases have recently appeared on the world scene. Antibiotics are ineffective against many of them. Because some of these new diseases are lethal, we may have to resort to an old remedy—isolating people in asylums. When the Ebola virus made its surprise appearance in 1976, with its particularly hideous form of death, the only way it could be contained was to isolate an entire region of Zaire (Olshansky 1997).

Tuberculosis holds special fears. It was once thought that the battle against TB had been won, but this disease has had a resurgence. It now is the leading cause of infectious deaths among adults worldwide. Today, more people die globally from TB than perished in its peak of destruction in the 1800s (Garrett 1999). Drug-resistant strains of TB are common in Russian prisons. Prisoners still in need of treatment are released, taking the disease with them into the general population. Some think that Russia is becoming an incubator of drug-resistant tuberculosis that will be thrust upon the world (Zuger 2000). Already, to treat patients who have TB that does not respond to drugs, U.S. surgeons are returning to a technique that they had abandoned decades ago: removing lungs and other infected body parts (Belkin 1999).

■ Drugs: Alcohol and Nicotine

Many drugs, both legal and illegal, harm their users. Let's examine some of the health consequences of alcohol and nicotine, the two most frequently used legal drugs in the United States.

Alcohol Alcohol is *the* standard recreational drug of Americans. The *average* adult American consumes 39 gallons of alcoholic beverages per year—about 34 gallons of beer, 3 gallons of wine, and 2 gallons of whiskey, vodka, or other distilled spirits. Alcohol is so popular that Americans drink more beer than they do milk, coffee, tea, fruit juices, or bottled water (*Statistical Abstract* 2000:Table 238).

As you know, despite laws that ban alcohol consumption before the age of 21, underage drinking is common. Table 19.2 shows that about three out of four high school students drink alcohol during their senior year. This drug is so popular that

TABLE 19.2   **What Drugs Have High School Seniors Used...**

	In the Past Year?	In the Past Month?
Alcohol	73.2%	50.0%
Nicotine (cigarettes)	NA	31.4%
Marijuana	36.5%	21.6%
Amphetamines	10.5%	5.0%
MDMA (Ecstasy)	8.2%	3.6%
Barbiturates	6.2%	3.0%
Hallucinogens	8.1%	2.6%
Cocaine	5.0%	2.1%
LSD	6.6%	1.6%
Heroin	1.5%	0.7%
. . .		
How many have been drunk?	51.8%	32.3%

Source: Johnston et al. 2001:Table 2-2.

two of every three college students have drunk alcohol during this past month. If getting drunk is the abuse of alcohol, then, without doubt, alcohol abuse among young people is also popular. As Table 19.2 shows, about half of all high school seniors have been drunk during the past year, one-third during just the past month.

Table 19.3, which lists the use of several drugs, shows an interesting social change. Women college students now drink more often than men college students. Men, however, are slightly more likely to use most of the drugs shown on this table.

Is alcohol bad for health? This beverage cuts both ways. About two drinks a day for men and one drink a day for women *reduces* the risk of heart attacks and strokes (Greenberg 1999; Kazman 1999). (Women weigh less on average and produce fewer enzymes that metabolize alcohol.) Moderate alcohol consumption also helps people survive heart attacks ("Moderate Drinking . . . " 2001). Beyond these amounts, however, alcohol consumption *increases* the risk of a variety of diseases, from cancer to stroke. It also increases the likelihood of birth defects. Each year, 750,000 Americans seek treatment for alcohol problems; about 20,000 die from alcohol abuse (*Statistical Abstract* 2000:Tables 142, 224).

TABLE 19.3	What Drugs Have Full-Time College Students Used?			
	In the Past Year?		In the Past Month?	
	Men	*Women*	*Men*	*Women*
Alcohol	80.3%	85.3%	67.0%	67.6%
Nicotine (cigarettes)	41.4%	41.2%	29.7%	27.1%
Marijuana	36.1%	32.5%	22.9%	18.0%
MDMA (Ecstasy)	9.3%	8.9%	2.6%	2.3%
Amphetamines	7.1%	6.3%	2.6%	3.2%
LSD	6.4%	2.8%	1.1%	0.7%
Cocaine	5.3%	4.4%	1.3%	1.5%
Barbiturates	4.7%	2.9%	1.7%	0.7%
Heroin	0.4%	0.7%	0.2%	0.3%

Source: Johnston et al. 2001:Tables 8–2, 8–3.

Finally, if you are a college student, is alcohol good for your grades? As Table 19.4 makes evident, the more college students drink, the worse they do in their classes.

Nicotine

Let's suppose that you have a ticket to fly to some exotic destination. There will be 200 passengers plus crew on board your plane. You are excited about your trip, but on the way to the airport, the radio program you are listening to is interrupted by an announcement that five U.S. jets will be hijacked that day. All will crash—and all passengers and crew will die. There is no doubt that five planes will go down, that 1,000 terrified passengers will perish. The airlines, however, are still going to operate.

Do you still fly? After all, the chances are good that *yours* will not be one of the five.

My best guess is that you turn around and go home, that U.S. airports will be eerily silent that day.

Nicotine—with its progressive emphysema and several types of cancer—kills about 390,000 Americans each year. This is the equivalent of five fully loaded, 200-passenger jets with full crews crashing each and every day—leaving no survivors. Who in their right mind would take the risk that *their* plane will not be among them? Yet this is the risk that smokers take.

Nicotine, by far the most lethal of all recreational drugs, is harmful in other ways, too. Sociologist Erich Goode (1989) points out that smokers are three times as likely as nonsmokers to die before they reach the age of 65. Smokers in their thirties are *six* times as likely than nonsmokers of the same age to have a heart attack (Winslow 1995). Smoking even doubles the risk of blindness in old age (Lagnado 1996).

An antitobacco campaign that stresses the health hazards of smoking has been successful. It has ended smoking on U.S. airlines and produced legislation that requires restaurants and offices to establish nonsmoking areas. It is even illegal to light up in a bar in California (Haldane 2001). Figure 19.10 on the next page shows how this antismoking message has hit home. In three decades, cigarette smoking has been cut in *half* among U.S. men, and it has dropped by a third among U.S. women.

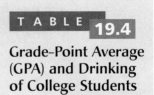

TABLE 19.4

Grade-Point Average (GPA) and Drinking of College Students

GPA	Number of Drinks per Week	
	Men	*Women*
A	5	2
B	7	3
C	9	4

Source: Presley et al. 1993.

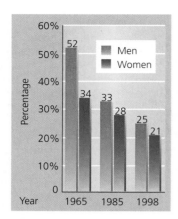

Figure 19.10

Who Is Still Smoking?
The Percentage of Americans
Who Smoke Cigarettes
Source: Statistical Abstract 1993:
Table 210; 2000:Table 227.

disabling environment
an environment that is harmful
to health

■ *Do you think this magazine ad is designed
to make cigarettes appealing to male
youth? Although tobacco industry officials
denied that they were trying to entice
youth to smoke, the evidence such as this
ad is overwhelmingly against them. After
pressure from the U.S. Congress, Camel
stopped its Joe Camel ads.*

*In my opinion, it is not an exaggeration
to call the U.S. tobacco industry criminal. At
its feet must be laid countless painful deaths.
Among those torturous deaths, I count
those of my mother and my only sister.*

Yet millions of Americans—who wouldn't think of flying if they knew that even one jet were going to crash—continue to smoke. Why? The two major reasons are addiction and advertising. Nicotine may be as addictive as heroin (Tolchin 1988). While this may sound far-fetched, consider Buerger's disease:

In this disease, the blood vessels, especially those supplying the legs, become so constricted that circulation is impaired whenever nicotine enters the bloodstream.

If a patient continues to smoke, gangrene may eventually set in. First a toe may have to be amputated, then the foot at the ankle, then the leg at the knee, and ultimately at the hip. . . . Patients are informed that if they will only stop smoking, it is virtually certain that the otherwise inexorable march of gangrene up the legs will be curbed. Yet surgeons report that some patients with Buerger's disease vigorously puff away in their hospital beds following a second or third amputation. (Brecher et al. 1972)

The second reason is advertising. Even though cigarette ads were banned from television in the 1980s, cigarettes continue to be advertised in newspapers and magazines. The tobacco industry has a huge advertising budget, spending $8 billion a year to encourage people to smoke (Holland 2001). The industry targets youth, often by associating cigarette smoking with success, high fashion, and independence. With the tobacco industry's political clout and 40,000 Americans depending on the industry for their livelihood, attempts to stop cigarette advertising have failed (*Statistical Abstract* 2000:Table 673). However, Joe Camel, the industry's most blatant attempt to lure youthful smokers, has been banned. (See the photo below.)

■ Disabling Environments

A **disabling environment** is one that is harmful to people's health. The health risk of some occupations is evident: Lumberjacking, riding rodeo bulls, and taming lions are obvious examples. In many occupations, however, people become aware of the risk only years after they worked at jobs they thought were safe. For example, several million people worked with asbestos during and after World War II. The federal government estimates that one-quarter of them will die of cancer from having breathed asbestos dust. It is likely that many other substances that we have not yet identified also cause slowly developing cancers—including, ironically, some asbestos substitutes (Meier 1987; Hawkes 2001).

Industrialization increased the world's standard of living and brought better health to hundreds of millions of people. Ironically, it also threatens to disable the basic environment of the human race, posing what may be the greatest health hazard of all time. The burning of carbon fuels is leading to the *greenhouse effect,* a warming of the earth that may change the globe's climate, melt the polar ice caps, and flood the earth's coastal shores. Chlorofluorocarbon gases used in refrigerators and air conditioners have punched a hole in the *ozone shield,* the protective layer of the earth's upper stratosphere that screens out most of the sun's ultraviolet rays. High-intensity ultraviolet radiation is harmful to most forms of life. In humans, it causes skin cancer and cataracts. The pollution of land, air, and water, especially through nuclear waste, pesticides, herbicides, and other chemicals, poses additional risks to life on our planet.

Identifying environmental threats to world health is only the first step. The second is to introduce short- and long-term policies to reduce such problems. The sociology of the environment is discussed on pages 680–687.

■ Misguided, Foolish, and Callous Experiments

At times, physicians and government officials behave so arrogantly that they callously disregard the health of the people they are sworn to protect. Let's look at two notorious instances.

The Tuskegee Syphilis Experiment   Imagine that you are living in Macon County, Alabama, during the Depression years. You are dirt poor. You live in a little country shack with a dirt floor and no electricity or running water. You never finished grade school, and you make a living, such as it is, by doing odd jobs. You haven't been feeling quite right lately, but you have no money to see a doctor.

Then you rub your eyes in disbelief. It is just like winning the lottery. You've been offered free medical examinations at Tuskegee University—free rides to and from the clinic, hot meals on examination days, and free treatment for minor ailments. Your survivors are even guaranteed a burial payment. You eagerly accept.

You have just become part of what is surely slated to go down in history as one of the most callous experiments of all time, outside of the infamous Nazi experiments. With heartless disregard for human life, the U.S. Public Health Service told 399 African American men that they had joined a social club and burial society called "Miss Rivers' Lodge." They also told them that they had "bad blood," and if they went to a private doctor, they would lose their benefits.

What the men were *not* told was that they had syphilis. For forty years, the "Public Health Service" let their disease go untreated just "to see what happened." There was even a control group of 201 men free of the disease (Jones 1993).

By the way, there was one further benefit for the men—free autopsies to determine the ravages of syphilis on their bodies.

The Cold War Experiments   Now assume that you are a soldier stationed in Nevada, and the U.S. Army orders your platoon to march through an area in which an atomic bomb has just been detonated. Because you are a soldier, you obey. Nobody knows much about radiation, and you don't know that the army is using you as a guinea pig: It wants to see if you'll be able to withstand the fallout—without any radiation equipment. Or suppose you are a patient at the University of Rochester in 1946, and your doctor, whom you trust implicitly, says he is going to give you something "to help you." You are pleased. But the injection, it turns out, is uranium (Noah 1994). He and a team of other doctors are conducting an experiment to find out how much uranium it will take to damage your kidneys ("U.S. Department of Energy, Advisory Committee").

Like the Tuskegee experiment, radiation experiments like these were conducted on unsuspecting subjects simply because government officials wanted information. There were others, too. Some soldiers were given LSD. And in Palmetto, Florida, officials released whooping cough viruses into the air, killing a dozen innocent children (Conahan 1994).

Playing God   To most of us, it is incredible that government officials and medical personnel would so callously disregard human life, but it obviously happens. Those in official positions sometimes reach a point where they think they can play God and determine who shall live and who shall die. And, obviously, the most expendable citizens are the poor and powerless. It is inconceivable that an experiment such as the syphilis study would have been forced on the wealthy and powerful. The elite are protected from such callous disregard of human rights and life. The only way the poor can be protected against such gross abuse of professional positions is if we publicize each known instance of abuse and insist on vigorous prosecution of those who direct and carry out such experiments.

Do such things still happen? You can decide for yourself. Consider how medical researchers developed fetal surgery. The idea of operating on unborn children was intriguing. It held the possibility of extending medical knowledge and getting the names of the pioneers in prestigious medical journals. But would such surgery even be possible? To find out could cost lives. To reduce the risk, the researchers first experimented with animals. Their next stop in refining their skills and extending their knowledge was surgery on pregnant Puerto Rican women. Now that the procedures are proven, the main patients are the unborn of the white and affluent (Casper 1998). The steps taken in this process expose an underlying assumption about the value of life. It is almost as though the researchers viewed themselves as climbing an evolutionary ladder.

The Search for Alternatives

What alternatives are there to the way U.S. medicine is usually practiced? One suggestion is to shift the emphasis from the treatment of disease to the prevention of disease. After considering this approach to medical care, we will look at the health care systems of other countries. Perhaps these two closing topics will suggest new ideas for you to follow, or to avoid.

■ Treatment or Prevention?

Effects of Values and Lifestyles   The impact of values and lifestyle on health becomes apparent if we contrast Utah (home of the Mormons, who disapprove of alcohol, coffee, soft drinks, and tobacco) with its adjacent state of Nevada (home of a gambling industry that fosters a rather different lifestyle). Although these two states have similar levels of income, education, urbanization, and medical care, Nevadans are more likely to die from cancer, strokes, heart attacks, and lung disease. They also are more likely to be murdered and to commit suicide (*Statistical Abstract* 2000:Table 130). The difference in their rates of disease and death is the result of the way people in each state live their lives. In short, many threats to health are preventable.

Prevention implies both an individual and a group responsibility. On the individual level, exercising regularly, eating nutritious food, maintaining an optimal weight, practicing sexual monogamy, and avoiding smoking and alcohol abuse go a long way toward preventing disease. Following these guidelines can add years to your life—and can make those years healthy and enjoyable ones.

On the group level, one alternative is preventive medicine. Instead of focusing on treating disease, U.S. medicine could make "wellness" its goal. What would implementing a national policy of "prevention, not intervention" require? First, the medical establishment would have to change its basic philosophy, not an easy task to accomplish. Essentially, physicians, nurses, and hospitals would have to be convinced that prevention is profitable. One possibility is that a group of doctors and a hospital could be paid an annual fee for keeping people well (Cooper 1993). Second, the public's attitude would have to be turned around so they, too, could see the benefits of "wellness." This would require educational programs in the schools. In addition, the media would need to show how healthy living habits—good nutrition, exercise, safe sex, and drug avoidance—lead to better health and a longer life. For example, what we eat is a significant factor in many types of cancer. An educational program to replace fatty, low-fiber foods with a diet rich in fruits, green tea, and leafy, green vegetables would go a long way toward saving lives. Unfortunately, rather than making such basic changes, most Americans seem to prefer that their doctors prescribe drugs.

On a broader scale, we could focus on comprehensive prevention—trying to eliminate or at least reduce disabling environments and the use of harmful drugs. Stronger legal action can be taken against businesses that spew industrial waste into the air and use our rivers and oceans as industrial sewers, as well as those that use advertising to seduce youths to use harmful drugs. Finally, since we live in a global village, the creation and maintenance of a health-producing environment requires international controls and cooperation.

■ Health Care in Global Perspective

The search for alternatives also leads us to examine health care in other nations. Consequently, we shall close this chapter with a comparison of health care in the three worlds of industrialization. As with education (see pages 507–509), no one country can adequately

■ Each culture makes basic assumptions about the causes and cures of health problems. The traditional assumptions of Eastern medical practitioners, usually ridiculed by Western physicians, are now being taken seriously by some. Acupuncture, for example, is gradually gaining acceptance in the West, although it does not fit Western assumptions of cause and cure.

illustrate the varieties of medicine that are practiced in nations in a particular stage of industrialization. Nevertheless, the countries highlighted in the Cultural Diversity box below do illustrate major characteristics of health care around the world. Examining their practices helps us place both positive and negative aspects of the U.S. health care system in cultural perspective.

cultural d·i·v·e·r·s·i·t·y

Around the World
Health Care in Sweden, Russia, and China

Health Care in the Most Industrialized Nations: Sweden

Sweden has the most comprehensive health care system in the world. National health insurance is financed by both contributions from the state and employers. It covers all Swedish citizens and alien residents. Most physicians work for the government, and, except for a small consultation fee, medical and dental treatment is free. The government reimburses travel expenses for patients. Only minimal fees are charged for prescriptions and hospitalization (Swedish Institute 1990).

Medical treatment is just one component of Sweden's cradle-to-grave system of social welfare. For example, people who are sick or who must stay home with sick children receive 90 percent of their salaries. Swedes are given parental leave upon the birth of a child, and are guaranteed a pension.

Sweden's system of socialized medicine is inefficient, however. Swedes have not solved the twin problems of eliminating waiting lines and motivating physicians to "get down to work." Because the salaries of medical personnel are guaranteed, regardless of how many patients they see, the system has poor productivity. When reporters visited Sweden's largest hospital on a weekday morning, when 80 of 120 surgeons were on duty, they found 19 of 24 operating rooms idle. Their photos of empty operating rooms— at a time when there was a one- to two-year waiting period for hip replacements and cataract surgery—provoked a public outcry (Bergström 1992).

With public pressure to change the situation, in 1999, Swedish lawmakers made a U-turn. They decided that competition creates efficiency and they should abandon the socialized model. They have begun to do this, and they are gradually turning the health care system over to the private sector. The government has sold some hospitals to private companies and is contracting out services instead of providing them through government employees ("Social Darwinism . . . " 2001). We don't yet know what the Swedish medical system will look like by the time this transition is complete.

Health Care in the Industrializing Nations: Russia

Russia's painful transition to capitalism has brought its economic and political system to the verge of collapse. It can't pay its debts, and it is barely being kept afloat by emergency loans from the World Bank—and this only because the Most Industrialized Nations fear a nuclear holocaust should Russia dissolve into anarchy.

Russia's health care system is similarly in tatters. Under the communists, Russia had established a system that made health care available to most. Like the rest of the nation's systems of production, the health care system was centralized. The state owned the medical schools and determined how many doctors would be trained and in what specialties. The state set the salaries for doctors, paid them, and determined where they would practice.

This medical system has fallen apart, and the health of the population has declined. An example is Moscow's ambulance system. It used to be efficient—dial 03 and an ambulance would arrive within minutes. Now an ambulance can take eight to twelve *hours* to arrive, because drivers are using the ambulances as freelance cabs, and they keep emergency cases waiting (Field 1998).

The only hospitals comparable to those in the United States are reserved for the elite (Light 1992). In the rest, conditions are deplorable. Patients must bring their own linens, medicines, and syringes with them to the hospital. Some hospitals do not even have a doctor on staff. Surgical scalpels are resharpened until they break. Sometimes even razor blades are used for surgery (Donelson 1992). Some doctors face the choice of operating without anesthetic or not operating at all (Paddock 1999). Physicians are paid so little that in order to have food, they have to grow potatoes. They walk to work because they cannot afford the equivalent of a dime to take a bus (Goldberg and Kishkovsky 2000).

The bright spot is that physicians continue to work despite their low status and miserable pay. Many are motivated by idealism and the desire to help, coupled with the hope that things will get better. A second bright spot is that some doctors are making the transition to private practice, which could be the beginning of a new medical system built on the rubble of the old (Goldberg and Kishkovsky 2000).

In the meantime, Russia's medical system remains shattered. Perhaps no event more pinpoints the disarray than this:

Three patients lay unconscious in the intensive care unit, kept alive only by the Siberian hospital's life support system. Two were elderly; one was 39.

On Wednesday, the hospital received a telegram from the local power company: "You haven't paid your bill for five years. You owe us $94,931. Pay up, or we'll shut off your electricity." The next morning, at 6 A.M., the company shut off the power. Forty minutes later, all three patients were dead. (Paddock 1999)

(continued)

cultural d-i-v-e-r-s-i-t-y

Around the World

Health Care in Sweden, Russia, and China (continued)

The years of environmental degradation under the communists have also taken their toll. Serious birth defects have jumped to four times the U.S. rate. A likely culprit is radiation pollution from decades of nuclear irresponsibility (Specter 1995). Table 19.5 shows what is perhaps the single best indicator of the deterioration of Russian health, the drop in life expectancy that began in the 1960s (Cockerham 1997). Life expectancy is not only a medical issue, but also a barometer of a society's health.

Health Care in the Least Industrialized Nations: China
Because this nation of 1.2 billion people has a vast shortage of trained physicians, hospitals, and medicine, most Chinese see "barefoot doctors," people who have only a basic knowledge of medicine, are paid low wages, and travel from village to village. With its emphases on medicinal herbs and acupuncture, Chinese medicine differs from that of the West. Although Westerners have scoffed at the Chinese approach, some have found reason to change their minds. For example, one of the herbs that the Chinese have used for a thousand years or more to treat liver disease has been tested by Western societies; it reduces liver cancer (Tanouye 1995).

As China makes its transition to capitalism, its medical system, too, has disintegrated (Rosenthal 2001d). Changes include payment for medical treatment

T A B L E 19.5 Indicators of Health	Sweden	United States	Russia	China
Life expectancy	79.2 years	77.1 years	67.2 years	70.3 years
Infant mortality[a]	3.9	6.8	20.3	28.9
Birth rate[b]	11.7	14.2	9.0	16.1
Death rate[b]	10.8	8.7	13.8	6.7
Health costs as a percent of Gross Domestic Product	8.6	14.0	2.3	NA

[a]Per 1,000 live births.
[b]Per 1,000 population.
Source: Field 1998; *Statistical Abstract* 1998:Tables 1345, 1348; 2000:Tables 1355, 1358.

that used to be free. Now a hospital stay can cost 600 to 700 yuan; the average monthly wage is 200 yuan. Physician salaries are as low as $7.25 a month (Chu 1998). Some doctors take extra jobs because they cannot survive on their salaries. Some medical personnel demand payment before they will give medical treatment, as with the surgeons who, arms scrubbed and held high in the air, refused to enter the operating room until the patient's relatives had stuffed their pockets with cash (Sampson 1992).

for your consideration
No nation has discovered the perfect medical system, and each

country faces a medical crisis of "too much demand at too great a cost" (Moore and Winslow 1993). How would you say that the U.S. medical system is superior—and inferior—to each of these systems? Is there one that you would pick over the U.S. system? Why? Short of instituting socialized medicine, which goes against the U.S. value system, propose changes that will overcome the deficiencies of the U.S. medical system reviewed in this chapter—and that will maintain its strengths.

■ The Future of Medicine

It is always risky to predict the future, for unexpected events cause twists and turns in the path we are following. Some trends are strong however, and we can expect U.S. medicine to continue its fee-for-service approach, to be marked by social inequalities, that even larger numbers of women will become doctors. The search for alternative treatment will become more popular, and, despite widespread knowledge of their health risks, alcohol and nicotine will continue to be abused. Cigarette smoking, however, will continue to decrease.

These trends, firmly in place, will be overshadowed by rapid advances in our knowledge of human genes and the development of a new technology to apply that knowledge to benefit human health. These changes in knowledge and technology are going to transform the face of medicine, and, with it, our expectations of health and medical treatment. Some of the implications of these changes are discussed in the Sociology and the New Technology box below, with which we close this chapter.

genomics
the study of genes and how they relate to health and illness

Sociology & the new technology

Genetic Profiling: Medicine in the Coming Bioeconomy

You and a friend come down with the same disease. You both go to the same doctor. After examining the two of you, she uploads your genetic charts to a pharmaceutical company that formulates a medicine to match each of your unique genetic structures. When you get to the drug store, waiting for you are separate designer medicines, made to attack the disease at the molecular level.

Your doctor gives you the bad news. You have an incurable heart disease—at least it used to be incurable. Now, however, you pop over to the New Organ Clinic, where you place an order for a new heart. The heart will be a perfect match, since it will be grown from your own cells. You've just extended your life by another 50 years or so.

Are these scenarios far-fetched? Not at all. **Genomics,** the study of genes and how they relate to health and illness, is destined to change the face of medicine. That pivotal event in 2001, the mapping of the human genome system, combined with stem cell research, is expected to make these scenarios a reality during our lifetimes.

And more than this. At birth, the genetic sequence of each child will be recorded on discs. These records will allow physicians to fix health problems *before* they show up. Instead of waiting for symptoms to appear, doctors will examine your genetic record to discover the diseases that are your biological destiny—and then snip out the bad molecules and splice in new ones so you never suffer those problems.

At least this is how it will be if you are wealthy.

■ *The emerging bioeconomy (assuming that one is emerging) can be dated to the mapping of the human genome system in 2001. But it also could be traced to 1953, when the double-helix structure of DNA was identified. Although discoveries and inventions can set societies on new paths, new types of societies have no clear-cut beginnings, nor does the previous one have a clear-cut ending.*

No new technology comes without its downside. Not only will genetic discs feed social inequality, but also they will be a treasure trove of information for insurers and future employers. Being able to predict future medical conditions will bring *medical profiling*. Who wants to insure someone if they know they are going to come down with a debilitating disease? Who wants to hire them? In fact, who wants to marry them?

for your consideration

Assume that you have just graduated from college. With fresh BA in hand, you go for your first job interview. The interviewer says you seem perfect for the job, and then asks for a copy of your genetic disc. Do you think prospective employers should have access to your genetic structure? You can apply symbolic interactionism to this question. How would your answer change if you are the employer? Doesn't it only seem fair that employers should be able to hire healthier workers?

Assume that you have just applied for health insurance. The insurer not only wants your medical history, but also asks for your medical disc. Do you think you should have to comply? Why or why not?

Assume that you have fallen in love and you are thinking about marriage. One evening, as you are discussing plans for the future, your loved one turns to you and says, "I love you dearly, but we can't get married until we have our medical discs examined by bioresearchers. And if we have no unique health risks, then . . . " Do you agree to this?

Based on Cowley and Underwood 2000; Licata 2001; Wilensky 2001.

■ ■ ■ Summary and Review

Sociology and the Study of Medicine

■ **What is the role of sociology in the study of medicine?**

Sociologists study medicine as a social institution. As practiced in the United States, three of its primary characteristics are professionalization, bureaucracy, and the profit motive. P. 564.

The Symbolic Interactionist Perspective

■ **What is the symbolic interactionist perspective on health and illness?**

Health is not only a biological matter; but also it is intimately related to society. Illness is also far from an objective matter, for illness is always viewed from the framework of culture. The definitions applied to physical and mental conditions vary from one group to another. Pp. 564–566.

The Functionalist Perspective

■ **What is the functionalist perspective on health and illness?**

Functionalists stress that in return for being excused from their usual, responsible activities, people have to accept the **sick role.** They must assume responsibility for seeking competent medical help and cooperate in getting well so they can quickly resume normal activities. Pp. 566–567.

The Conflict Perspective

■ **What is the conflict perspective on health and illness?**

Health care is one of the scarce resources over which groups compete. On a global level, health care follows the stratification that we studied in Chapter 9. The best health care is available in the dominant nations, the worst in the dependent nations.

In the American colonies, no training or licensing was necessary if one wanted to call oneself a doctor. Even until the early 1900s, medical training was a hit-or-miss affair. In 1910, the education of physicians came under the control of a group of men who eliminated most of their competition and turned medicine into a monopoly and the largest business in the United States. Pp. 567–571.

Historical Patterns of Health

■ **How have health patterns changed over time?**

Patterns of disease in the United States have changed so extensively that of today's top ten killers, five did not even show up on the 1900 top ten list. Because most Americans live longer than their ancestors did, we can conclude that contemporary Americans are healthier. For mental illness, we have no idea how today compares with the past, for we have no baselines from which to make comparisons. P. 572.

Issues in Health Care

■ **How does treating health care as a commodity lead to social inequalities?**

Because health care is a commodity to be sold to the highest bidder, the United States has a two-tier system of medical care in which the poor receive inferior health care for both their mental and physical illnesses. Pp. 573–574.

■ **What are some other problems in U.S. health care?**

One problem is **defensive medicine,** which refers to medical procedures that are done for the physician's benefit, not for the benefit of the patient. Intended to protect physicians from lawsuits, these tests and consultations add huge amounts to the nation's medical bill. Other problems are incompetence, **depersonalization,** conflict of interest, medical fraud, and sexism. Pp. 574–578.

■ **Why is medically assisted suicide an issue now?**

Due to advanced technology, people can be kept technically alive even when they have no brain waves. Physicians who openly assist in suicides have come under severe criticism. Research findings on **euthanasia** in Holland have fueled this controversy. Pp. 578–580.

■ **What attempts have been made to cut medical costs?**

Health maintenance organizations (HMOs) and diagnosis-related groups (DRGs) are among the measures that have been taken to reduce medical costs. National health insurance, which has run into immense opposition, has been proposed. The most controversial proposal is to ration medical care. Pp. 580–582.

Threats to Health

■ **What are some threats to the health of Americans?**

Discussed here are AIDS, which is declining in the United States but is devastating countries in Africa; the globalization of disease; alcohol and nicotine; **disabling environments;** and unethical experiments, of which the Tuskegee syphilis experiments and the Cold War radiation experiments are two examples. Pp. 582–589.

The Search for Alternatives

■ **Are there alternatives to our current health care system?**

The primary alternative discussed here is a change in focus from treatment to prevention. Other alternatives may be found by examining health care systems in other countries. Health care in Sweden, Russia, and China were reviewed. Pp. 590–592.

The Future of Medicine

■ **How will the practice of medicine change?**

Genomics is going to change the face of medical practice. Knowledge of our genetic structure will allow designer medicines, the treatment of diseases before they appear, and the growth of replacement organs, including hearts. P. 593.

■ *Where can I read more on this topic?*

Suggested Readings for this chapter are found at the back of this book.

Additional Online Resources for This Chapter
www.ablongman.com/henslin6e

- *Content Select* Research Database for Sociology, with suggested key terms and annotated references
- Link to 2000 Census, with activities
- Flashcards of key terms and concepts
- Practice Tests
- Weblinks
- Interactive Maps

using . . .
ContentSelect

Research Database for Sociology

AIDS	genomics	mental health	the medicalization
alcohol	health and illness	nicotine	of society
death	medicine and suicide		

Loren MacIver, *Downstairs*

20

Population and Urbanization

POPULATION IN GLOBAL PERSPECTIVE
A Planet with No Space for Enjoying Life?
The New Malthusians
The Anti-Malthusians
Who Is Correct?
Why Are People Starving?

Population Growth
Why Do the Least Industrialized Nations Have So Many Children?
Implications of Different Rates of Growth
The Three Demographic Variables
Problems in Forecasting Population Growth

URBANIZATION
The Development of Cities
The Process of Urbanization
U.S. Urban Patterns

Models of Urban Growth
The Concentric Zone Model
The Sector Model
The Multiple-Nuclei Model
The Peripheral Model
Critique of the Models

City Life: Alienation and Community
Who Lives in the City?
Urban Sentiment: Finding a Familiar World
The Norm of Noninvolvement and the Diffusion of Responsibility

Urban Problems and Social Policy
Suburbanization
Disinvestment and Deindustrialization
The Rural Rebound
The Potential of Urban Revitalization

Summary and Review

The image still haunts me. There stood Celia, age 30, her distended stomach visible proof that her thirteenth child was on its way. Her oldest was only 14 years old! A mere boy by our standards, he had already gone as far in school as he ever would. Each morning, he joined the men to work in the fields. Each evening around twilight, we saw him return home, exhausted from hard labor in the subtropical sun.

> There stood Celia, age 30, her distended stomach visible proof that her thirteenth child was on its way.

My wife and I, who were living in Colima, Mexico, had eaten dinner in Celia's and Angel's home, which clearly reflected the family's poverty. A thatched hut consisting of only a single room served as home for all fourteen members of the family. At night, the parents and younger children crowded into a double bed, while the eldest boy slept in a hammock. As in many other homes in the village, the others slept on mats spread on the dirt floor.

The home was meagerly furnished. It had only a gas stove, a table, and a cabinet where Celia stored her few cooking utensils and clay dishes. There were no closets; clothes were hung on pegs in the walls. There also were no chairs, not even one. We were used to the poverty in this village, but this really startled us. The family was so poor that they could not afford even a single chair.

Celia beamed as she told us how much she looked forward to the birth of her next child. Could she really mean it? It was hard to imagine that any woman would want to be in her situation.

Yet Celia meant every word. She was as full of delightful anticipation as she had been with her first child—and with all the others in between.

How could Celia have wanted so many children—especially when she lived in such poverty? That question bothered me. I couldn't let it go until I had the solution. This chapter helps provide an answer.

POPULATION IN GLOBAL PERSPECTIVE

Celia's story takes us into the heart of **demography,** the study of the size, composition, growth, and distribution of human populations. It brings us face to face with the question of whether we are doomed to live in a world so filled with people that there will be practically no space for anybody. Will our planet be able to support its growing population? Or are chronic famine and mass starvation the sorry fate of most earthlings? Let's look at how this concern began, and then at what today's demographers say about it.

A Planet with No Space for Enjoying Life?

The story begins with the lowly potato. When the Spanish conquistadors found that people in the Andes ate this vegetable, which was unknown in Europe, they brought it home with them. At first, Europeans viewed it suspiciously, but gradually the potato became the main food of the lower classes. With more abundant food, fertility increased, the death rate dropped, and Europe's population soared, almost doubling during the 1700s (McKeown 1977; McNeill 1999).

Thomas Malthus (1766–1834), an English economist, saw this surging growth as a sign of doom. In 1798, he wrote a book that became world famous, *An Essay on the Principle of Population.* In it, Malthus proposed what became known as the **Malthus theorem.** He argued that while population grows geometrically (from 2 to 4 to 8 to 16 and so forth), the food supply increases only arithmetically (from 1 to 2 to 3 to 4 and so on). This meant, he claimed, that if births go unchecked, the population of a country, or even of the world, will outstrip its food supply.

demography
the study of the size, composition, growth, and distribution of human populations

Malthus theorem
an observation by Thomas Malthus that although the food supply increases only arithmetically (from 1 to 2 to 3 to 4 and so on), population grows geometrically (from 2 to 4 to 8 to 16 and so forth)

■ *In earlier generations, large farm families were common. (My own father came from a Minnesota farm family of ten children.) Having many children was functional—there were many hands to help with crops, food production, and food preparation. As the country industrialized and urbanized, this changed to a dysfunction— children became expensive and nonproducing. Consequently, the size of families shrank as we entered Stage 3 of the* demographic transition, *and today U.S. families of this size are practically nonexistent.*

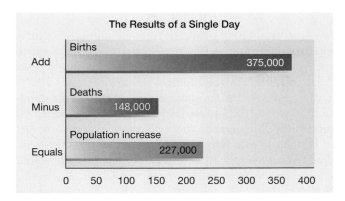

The Results of a Single Day

The Accumulating Increase

The New Malthusians

Was Malthus right? This question became a matter of heated debate among demographers. One group, which can be called the *New Malthusians,* is convinced that today's situation is at least as grim, if not grimmer, than anything Malthus ever imagined. For example, *the world's population is growing so fast that in just the time it takes you to read this chapter, another fifteen thousand to twenty thousand babies will be born!* By this time tomorrow, the earth will have an additional quarter of a million people to feed. This increase goes on hour after hour, day after day, without letup. For an illustration of this growth, see Figure 20.1.

The New Malthusians point out that the world's population is following an **exponential growth curve.** This means that if growth doubles during approximately equal intervals of time, it suddenly accelerates. To illustrate the far-reaching implications of exponential growth, sociologist William Faunce (1981) told a parable about a poor man who saved a rich man's life. The rich man was grateful and said that he wanted to reward the man for his heroic deed.

> The man replied that he would like his reward to be spread out over a four-week period, with each day's amount being twice what he received on the preceding day. He also said he would be happy to receive only one penny on the first day. The rich man immediately handed over the penny and congratulated himself on how cheaply he had gotten by. At the end of the first week, the rich man checked to see how much he owed and was pleased to find that the total was only $1.27. By the end of the second week he owed only $163.83. On the twenty-first day, however, the rich man was surprised to find that the total had grown to $20,971.51. When the twenty-eighth day arrived the rich man was shocked to discover that he owed $1,342,177.28 for that day alone and that the total reward had jumped to $2,684,354.56!

This is precisely what alarms the New Malthusians. They claim that humanity has just entered the "fourth week" of an exponential growth curve. Figure 20.2 shows why they think the day of reckoning is just around the corner. They point out that it took all

Figure 20.1

How Fast Is the World's Population Growing?

Source: "Population Today," 2002.

exponential growth curve
a pattern of growth in which numbers double during approximately equal intervals, thus accelerating in the latter stages

Figure 20.2

World Population Growth Over 2,000 Years

Source: Modified from Piotrow 1973:4.

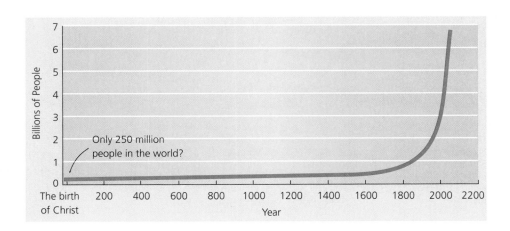

of human history for the world's population to reach its first billion around 1800. It then took about one hundred thirty years (until 1930) to add the second billion. Just thirty years later (1960), the world population hit 3 billion. The time it took to reach the fourth billion was cut in half, to only fifteen years (1975). It then took just twelve more years (1987) for the total to hit 5 billion, and another twelve for it to reach 6 billion (in 1999).

To illustrate this increase, the New Malthusians have come up with some mind-boggling statistics. They note that before the Industrial Revolution, it took 1,600 years for the world's population to double, but the most recent doubling took just forty years—*forty* times as fast (Cohen 1996). They also point out that between 8000 B.C. and A.D. 1750 the world added an average of only 67,000 people a year—but now that many people are being added *every seven hours* (Weeks 1994).

It is obvious, claim the New Malthusians, that there is going to be less and less for more and more.

■ The Anti-Malthusians

All of this seems obvious, and no one wants to live shoulder-to-shoulder and fight for scraps. How, then, can anyone argue with the New Malthusians?

An optimistic group of demographers, whom we can call the *Anti-Malthusians*, see a far different picture. They believe that Europe's **demographic transition** provides a more accurate glimpse into the future. This transition is diagrammed in Figure 20.3. During most of its history, Europe was in Stage 1. Its population was about the same from year to year, for high death rates offset the high birth rates. Then came Stage 2, the "population explosion" that so upset Malthus. Europe's population surged because birth rates remained high, while death rates went down. Finally, Europe made the transition to Stage 3: The population stabilized as people brought their birth rates into line with their lower death rates.

This, say the Anti-Malthusians, is precisely what will happen in the Least Industrialized Nations. Their current surge in growth simply indicates that they have reached Stage 2 of the demographic transition. Hybrid seeds and medicine imported from the Most Industrialized Nations have cut their death rates, but their birth rates remain high. When they move into Stage 3, as surely they will, we will wonder what all the fuss was about.

■ Who Is Correct?

As you can see, both the New Malthusians and the Anti-Malthusians have looked at historical trends and projected them onto the future. The New Malthusians project

demographic transition
a three-stage historical process of population growth: first, high birth rates and high death rates; second, high birth rates and low death rates; and third, low birth rates and low death rates; a fourth stage has begun to appear in the Most Industrialized Nations, as depicted in Figure 20.3.

Figure 20.3

The Demographic Transition

Note: The standard demographic transition is depicted by Stages 1–3. Stage 4 has recently been suggested by some Anti-Malthusians.

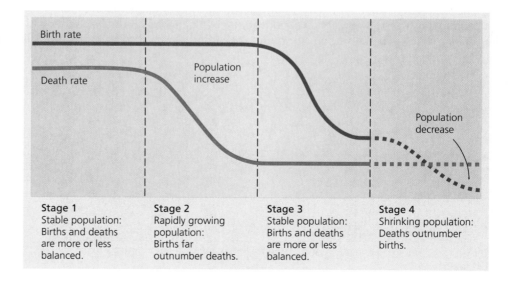

| Stage 1 Stable population: Births and deaths are more or less balanced. | Stage 2 Rapidly growing population: Births far outnumber deaths. | Stage 3 Stable population: Births and deaths are more or less balanced. | Stage 4 Shrinking population: Deaths outnumber births. |

continued world growth and are alarmed. The Anti-Malthusians project Stage 3 of the demographic transition onto the Least Industrialized Nations and are reassured.

There is no question that the Least Industrialized Nations are in Stage 2 of the demographic transition. The question is, will these nations enter Stage 3? After World War II, the West exported its hybrid seeds, herbicides, and techniques of public hygiene around the globe. Death rates plummeted in the Least Industrialized Nations as their food supply increased and health improved. Their birth rates stayed high, however, and their populations mushroomed. Just as Malthus had done 200 years before, demographers predicted worldwide catastrophe if something were not done immediately to halt the population explosion (Ehrlich and Ehrlich 1972, 1978).

We can use the conflict perspective to understand what happened when this message reached the leaders of the industrialized world. They saw the mushrooming populations of the Least Industrialized Nations as a threat to the balance of power they had so carefully worked out. With swollen populations, the poorer countries might demand a larger share of the earth's resources. The leaders found the United Nations to be a willing tool, and they used it to spearhead efforts to reduce world population growth. The results have been remarkable. The birth rates of the Least Industrialized Nations have dropped from an average of 2.1 percent a year in the 1960s to 1.4 percent today (Haub and Yinger 1994; Haub and Cornelius 2001).

The New Malthusians and Anti-Malthusians have greeted this news with significantly different interpretations. The New Malthusians stress that the populations of the Least Industrialized Nations have not stopped growing—their growth has just slowed. A slower growth rate still spells catastrophe—it just takes longer for it to hit (Ehrlich and Ehrlich 1997). For the Anti-Malthusians, however, this slowing of growth is the signal they had been waiting for—Stage 3 of the demographic transition is on its way. First the death rate in the Least Industrialized Nations fell—now, just as the anti-Malthusians predicted, their birth rates are also falling.

The Anti-Malthusians also argue that our future will be the opposite of what the New Malthusians worry about: There will be too few children in the world, not too many. The world's problem will not be a population explosion, but **population shrinkage**—populations getting smaller. They point out that births in 65 countries have already dropped so low that those countries no longer produce enough children to maintain their populations. Of the 42 countries of Europe, 40 are in this situation (McDonald 2001). They all fill more coffins than cradles. Table 20.1 lists the ten nations with the world's lowest birth rates. As you look at this table, keep in mind that it takes an average of 2.1 children per couple to reproduce a population. (The extra .1 child makes up for those who die or fail to reproduce.)

Some Anti-Malthusians even predict a "demographic free fall" (Mosher 1997). As more nations enter Stage 4 of the demographic transition, the world's population will peak at about 7 or 8 billion, then begin to grow smaller. Two hundred years from now, they say, we will have a lot fewer people on earth.

Who is right? It simply is too early to tell. Like the proverbial pessimists who see the glass of water half empty, the New Malthusians interpret changes in world population growth

population shrinkage the process by which a country's population becomes smaller because its birth rate and immigration are too low to replace those who die and emigrate

TABLE 20.1		**Extremes in Childbirth**	
Where Do Women Give Birth to the Fewest Children?		**Where Do Women Give Birth to the Most Children?**	
Country	Number of Children	Country	Number of Children
1. Bulgaria	1.1	1. Niger	7.5
2. Czech Republic	1.1	2. Congo	7.2
3. Estonia	1.2	3. Oman	7.1
4. Italy	1.2	4. Somalia	7.0
5. Latvia	1.2	5. Uganda	6.9
6. Macao	1.2	6. Angola	6.8
7. Russia	1.2	7. Burkina Faso	6.8
8. San Marino	1.2	8. Western Sahara	6.8
9. Slovenia	1.2	9. Ethiopia	6.7
10. Spain	1.2	10. Mali	6.7

Sources: Haub and Cornelius 2001.

◼ *Photos of starving people, such as this mother and her child, haunt Americans and other members of the Most Industrialized Nations. Many of us wonder why, when some are starving, we should live in the midst of such abundance, often overeating and even casually scraping excess food into the garbage. The text discusses reasons for such unconscionable disparities.*

negatively. And like the optimists who see the same glass half full, the Anti-Malthusians view the figures positively. Sometime during our lifetime we should know the answer.

▣ Why Are People Starving?

Pictures of starving children gnaw at our conscience. We live in such abundance, while these children and their parents starve before our very eyes. Why don't they have enough food? Is it because there are too many of them, or simply that the abundant food produced around the world does not reach them?

The Anti-Malthusians make a point that seems irrefutable. As Figure 20.4 shows, *the amount of food produced for each person in the world is now much more than it was in 1950.* Although the world's population has more than doubled during this time, improved seeds and fertilizers have made more food available for *each* person on earth. Even more food may be on the way, for scientists have found how to

Figure 20.4

How Much Food Does the World Produce Per Person?

Note: 1979–1981 = 100
Years 1975 to 1991 are U.N. figures; years prior to 1975 have been recomputed from Simon to 1979–1981 base; years beyond 1998 are the author's projections.

Sources: Simon 1981:58; United Nations Statistical Yearbook: 1985–1986:Table 7; and 1990–1991: Table 4, *Statistical Abstract* 1999: Table 1394, and earlier years.

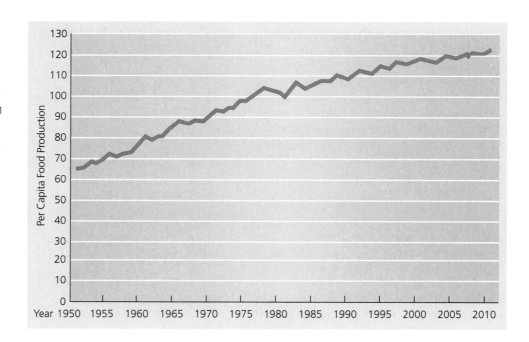

increase yields by planting more than one variety of a grain (Yoon 2000). Chemists have even discovered how to split nitrogen molecules. Since the earth's atmosphere is 78 percent nitrogen, we may be able to produce chemical compounds—including fertilizers—out of thin air (Naj 1995).

Then why do people die of hunger? From Figure 20.4, we can conclude that starvation does not occur because the earth produces too little food, but because particular places lack food. Some countries produce more food than their people can consume, others less than they need for survival. At the same time as famine ravishes West Africa, the U.S. government pays farmers to *reduce* their crops. The United States' problem is too much food, West Africa's is too little.

The New Malthusians counter with the argument that the world's population is still growing and that we do not know how long the earth will continue to produce enough food. They remind us of the penny doubling each day. It is only a matter of time, they say, until the earth no longer produces enough food—not "if," but "when."

Both the New Malthusians and the Anti-Malthusians have contributed significant ideas, but theories will not eliminate famines. Starving children are going to continue to peer out at us from our televisions and magazines, their tiny, shriveled bodies and bloated stomachs nagging at our conscience and calling for us to do something. Regardless of the underlying cause of this human misery, it can be alleviated by transferring food from nations that have a surplus.

These pictures of starving Africans leave the impression that Africa is overpopulated. Why else would all those people be starving? The truth, however, is far different. Africa has 22 percent of the earth's land, but only 13 percent of the earth's population (Nsamenang 1992; Haub and Cornelius 2001). The reason for famines in Africa, then, *cannot* be too many people living on too little land. On the contrary, Africa contains vast areas of fertile land that have not yet been farmed. Rather, these famines are due to three primary causes: drought, inefficient farming, and wars that disrupt harvests and food distribution.

Population Growth

Even if famines are due to a maldistribution of food rather than to world overpopulation, the fact remains that the Least Industrialized Nations are growing *fifteen times faster* than the Most Industrialized Nations—1.7 percent a year compared with 0.1 percent. (This looks like seventeen times faster because of rounding.) At these rates, it will take 800 years for the average Most Industrialized Nation to double its population, but just 42 years for the average Least Industrialized Nation to do so (Haub and Cornelius 2001). Figure 20.5 puts the matter in stark perspective. Why do the nations that can least afford it have so many children?

■ Why Do the Least Industrialized Nations Have So Many Children?

To understand why the population is growing so much faster in the Least Industrialized Nations, let's figure out why Celia is so happy about having her thirteenth child. To do this, we need to apply the symbolic interactionist perspective. We need to take the role of the other so we can understand the world of Celia and Angel as *they* see it. As our culture does for us, their culture provides a perspective on life that guides their choices. Celia's and Angel's culture tells them that

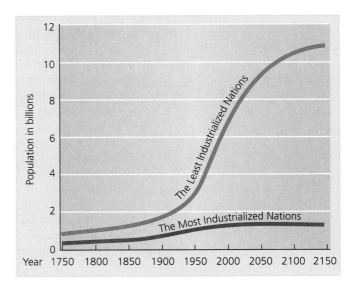

Figure 20.5

World Population Growth, 1750–2150

Source: "The World of the Child 6 Billion," 2000.

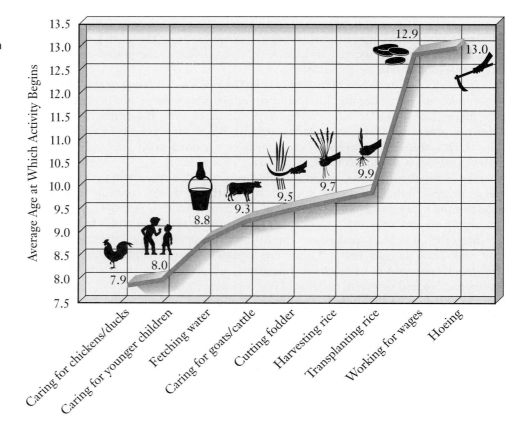

Figure 20.6

Why the Poor Need Children
Surviving children are an economic asset in the Least Industrialized Nations. Based on a survey in Indonesia, this figure shows that boys and girls can be net income earners for their families by the age of 9 or 10.

Source: U.N. Fund for Population Activities.

twelve children are *not* enough, that they ought to have a thirteenth—as well as a fourteenth and fifteenth. How can this be? Let's consider three reasons why bearing many children plays a central role in their lives—and in the lives of millions upon millions of poor people around the world.

First is the status of parenthood. In the Least Industrialized Nations, motherhood is the most prized status a woman can achieve. The more children a woman bears, the more she is thought to have achieved the purpose for which she was born. Similarly, a man proves his manhood by fathering children. The more children he fathers, especially sons, the better—for through them his name lives on.

Second, the community supports this view. Celia and those like her live in *Gemeinschaft* communities, where people share values and closely identify with one another. In their community, children are viewed as a sign of God's blessing. Accordingly, a couple should have many children. By producing children, people reflect the values of their community and achieve status. The barren woman, not the woman with a dozen children, is to be pitied.

These factors certainly provide strong motivations for bearing many children. Yet, there is a third incentive. For poor people in the Least Industrialized Nations, children are economic assets. These people have no Social Security or medical and unemployment insurance. This motivates them to bear *more* children, not fewer, for when parents become sick or too old to work—or when no work is to be found— they rely on their families to take care of them. The more children they have, the broader their base of support. Moreover, like the eldest son of Celia and Angel, children begin contributing to the family income at a young age. See Figure 20.6.

To those of us who live in the Most Industrialized Nations, it seems irrational to have many children. And *for us it would be.* Understanding life from the framework of people who are living it, however—the essence of the symbolic interactionist perspective—reveals how it makes perfect sense to have many children. For example, consider the following incident, reported by a government worker in India:

Thaman Singh (a very poor man, a water carrier) . . . welcomed me inside his home, gave me a cup of tea (with milk and "market" sugar, as he proudly pointed out later), and said: "You were trying to convince me that I shouldn't have any more sons. Now, you see, I have six sons and two daughters and I sit at home in leisure. They are grown up and they bring me money. One even works outside the village as a laborer. *You told me I was a poor man and couldn't support a large family. Now, you see, because of my large family I am a rich man.*" (Mamdani 1973, italics added)

Conflict theorists offer a different view of why women in the poor nations bear so many children. They would argue that Celia has internalized values that support male dominance. In Latin America, *machismo*—an emphasis on male virility and dominance—is common. To father many children, especially sons, demonstrates virility, giving a man valued status in the community. From a conflict perspective, then, the reason poor people have so many children is that men control women's reproductive choices.

■ Implications of Different Rates of Growth

The result of Celia's and Angel's desire for many children—and of the many millions of Celias and Angels like them—is that Mexico's population will double in thirty-seven years. In contrast, Spain's population is growing so slowly that it will take 6,931 years to double (Haub and Cornelius 2001). To illustrate population dynamics, demographers use **population pyramids.** These depict a country's population by age and sex. Figure 20.7 compares the population pyramids of the United States, Mexico, and the world.

You can see how important age structure is. If by some miracle Mexico were transformed overnight into a nation as industrialized as the United States and the average number of children per woman dropped to 2.0, the same as in the United States, the population of Mexico would continue to soar. Mexico has *population momentum* because a much higher percentage of Mexican women are in their childbearing years.

The implications of a doubling population are mind-boggling. *Just to stay even,* within thirty-seven years Mexico must double its jobs, food production, and factories; hospitals and schools; transportation, communication, water, gas, sewer, and electrical systems; housing, churches, civic buildings, theaters, stores, and parks. If Mexico fails to double them, its already meager standard of living will drop even further.

Conflict theorists point out that a declining standard of living poses the threat of political instability—protests, riots, even revolution, and, in response, repression by

population pyramid
a graphic representation of a population, divided into age and sex

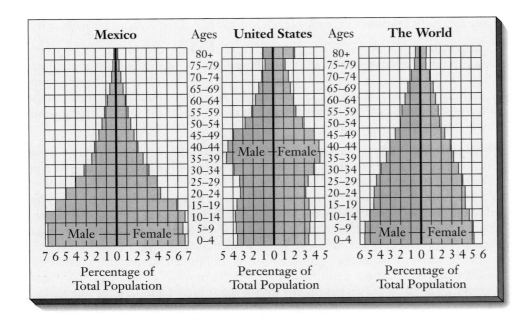

Figure 20.7

Three Population Pyramids
Source: Population Today, 26, 9, September 1998:4, 5.

the government. Political instability in one country can spill over into others, threatening an entire region's balance of power. Fearing this, leaders of the Most Industrialized Nations are using the United Nations to direct a campaign of worldwide birth control. With one hand they give agricultural aid, IUDs, and condoms to the masses in the Least Industrialized Nations—while, with the other, they sell weapons to the elites in these countries. Both actions, say conflict theorists, serve the same purpose of promoting political stability and the dominance of the Most Industrialized Nations in global stratification.

■ The Three Demographic Variables

How many people will live in the United States fifty years from now? What will the world's population be then? These are important questions. Educators want to know how many schools to build. Manufacturers want to anticipate changes in demand for their products. The government needs to know how many doctors, engineers, and executives to train. Politicians want to know how many people will be paying taxes—and how many young people will be available to fight a war.

To project the future of populations, demographers use three **demographic variables:** fertility, mortality, and migration. Let's look at each.

Fertility The **fertility rate** is the number of children the average woman bears. A term sometimes confused with fertility is **fecundity,** the number of children women are *capable* of bearing. The fecundity of women around the world is about twenty children each. Their fertility rate, however (the actual number of children they bear), is much lower. The world's overall fertility rate is 2.9, which means that the average woman in the world bears 2.9 children during her lifetime. At 2.0, the fertility rate of U.S. women is considerably less.

The region of the world that has the highest fertility rate is sub-Saharan Africa, where the average woman gives birth to 5.8 children; the lowest is Europe, where the average woman bears 1.4 children. As you can see from Table 20.1 on page 601, Bulgaria and the Czech Republic tie for the world's lowest fertility rate. There, the average woman gives birth to only 1.1 children. Niger in West Africa holds the record for the world's highest rate. There, the average woman gives birth to 7.5 children, *seven* times as many children as the average woman in Bulgaria or the Czech Republic.

To compute the fertility rate of a country, demographers analyze the government's records of births. From these, they figure the country's **crude birth rate,** the annual number of live births per 1,000 population. There may be considerable slippage here, of course. The birth records in many of the Least Industrialized Nations are haphazard.

Mortality The second demographic variable, **crude death rate,** refers to the annual number of deaths per 1,000 population. It, too, varies widely around the world. The highest death rate is 24, a record held by Niger in West Africa, the country that also has the world's highest birth rate. At 2, three oil-rich countries in the Mideast—Kuwait, Qatar, and United Arab Emirates—tie for the world's lowest death rate (Haub and Cornelius 2001).

Migration The third major demographic variable is *migration,* the movement of people from one area to another. There are two types of migration. The first type is illustrated by the Social Map, people moving from one region to another within the same country. Although there is two-way movement among U.S. regions, at the end of the year each region has a net loss or gain. As you can see from this map, people are moving to the South and the West, while the Northeast and the Midwest are losing people. The South is in the midst of tremendous growth and has a net gain from everywhere. Part of the South's gain is from African Americans who are returning to the South. During and after World War II, in what is known as "The Great Migration," millions of African Americans moved from the South to the North. In a historical shift, millions are returning to the South to participate in its growing economy, to enjoy its warmer climate, and to renew ties with ancestral roots (Frey 2001).

demographic variables
the three factors that influence population growth: fertility, mortality, and net migration

fertility rate
the number of children that the average woman bears

fecundity
the number of children that women are capable of bearing

crude birth rate
the annual number of live births per 1,000 population

crude death rate
the annual number of deaths per 1,000 population

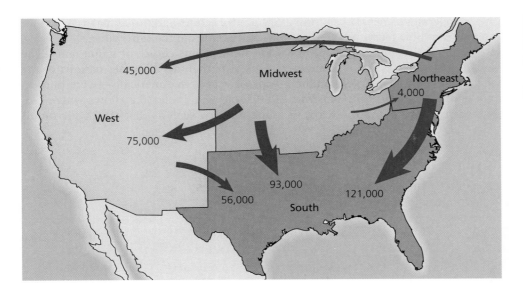

Figure 20.8

Social Map: Net Migration Flows Between Regions, 1999–2000

Source: Statistical Abstract 2000: Table 27.

The second type of migration is people moving from one country to another. Demographers use the term **net migration rate** to refer to the difference between the number of *immigrants* (people moving in) and *emigrants* (people moving out) per 1,000 population. Unlike fertility and mortality rates, migration does not affect the global population, for people are simply shifting their residence from one country or region to another.

As you know, immigrants are seeking a better life. They are willing to give up the security of their family and friends to move to a country with a strange language and unfamiliar customs. What motivates people to embark on such a venture? To understand migration, we need to look at both push and pull factors. The *push* factors are what people want to escape—poverty, the lack of religious and political freedoms, political persecution. The *pull* factors are the magnets that draw people to a new land, such as a chance for higher wages and better jobs.

Around the world, the flow of migration is from the Least Industrialized Nations to the industrialized countries. After "migrant paths" are established, immigration

net migration rate
the difference between the number of immigrants and emigrants per 1,000 population

■ *Between 1892 and 1954, New York's Ellis Island was the port of entry for most immigrants to the United States. The photo on the left shows the inspection that customs officials gave to immigrants in order to weed out those who had obvious medical problems. Current immigration shows greater diversity of origin, as illustrated by the photo on the right. These contemporary immigrants are Sikhs, members of a religion centered in Punjab, India.*

often accelerates as networks of kin and friends become additional magnets that at-tract more people from the same nation—and even from the same villages.

By far, the United States is the world's number one choice of immigrants. The United States admits more immigrants each year than all the other nations of the world combined. Twenty-six million—one of every ten Americans—were born in another country (*Statistical Abstract* 2000:Table 47). Table 20.2 shows where U.S. immigrants were born. To escape grinding poverty, such as that which surrounds

TABLE 20.2 Place of Birth of Immigrants to the United States, by Region and Country, 1981–1998

North America	6,426,000				
Mexico	3,583,000	Lebanon	78,000	Europe	1,792,000
Dominican Republic	557,000	Bangladesh	68,000	Former Soviet Union	500,000
Jamaica	357,000	Jordan	65,000	Great Britain	257,000
Cuba	305,000	Israel	63,000	Poland	246,000
Haiti	283,000	Iraq	52,000	Germany	125,000
Canada	232,000	Afghanistan	42,000	Ireland	90,000
Trinidad and Tobago	92,000	Syria	42,000	Romania	84,000
		Turkey	42,000	Yugoslavia	70,000
				Portugal	60,000
Asia	5,244,000	Central and South America	1,779,000	Italy	51,000
Philippines	927,000	El Salvador	395,000	France	45,000
Vietnam	775,000	Colombia	231,000	Greece	41,000
China	736,000	Guatemala	174,000		
India	573,000	Guyana	160,000	Africa	494,000
Korea	480,000	Peru	152,000	Nigeria	88,000
Iran	309,000	Ecuador	116,000	Egypt	69,000
Laos	188,000	Honduras	106,000	Ethiopia	68,000
Pakistan	158,000	Nicaragua	104,000	Ghana	43,000
Cambodia	132,000	Brazil	65,000	South Africa	34,000
Hong Kong	127,000	Panama	50,000		
Thailand	107,000	Argentina	46,000		
Japan	93,000	Venezuela	41,000		
Taiwan	90,000	Chile	37,000		

Note: Because only the countries with the largest emigration are listed, the total for an entire region is larger than the total of the countries from that region..
Source: Statistical Abstract 2000:Table 7.

Celia and Angel, people also enter the United States illegally. The U.S. government puts their number at 5 million. Most have come from Central and South America, especially Mexico (*Statistical Abstract* 1999:Table 10).

Experts cannot agree whether immigrants are a net contributor to the U.S. economy or a drain on it. Economist Julian Simon (1986, 1993) claimed that they benefit the economy. After subtracting what immigrants collect in welfare and adding what they produce in jobs and taxes, he concluded that immigrants produce more than they cost. Other economists such as Donald Huddle (1993) use figures showing that immigrants are a drain on taxpayers. The fairest conclusion seems to be that the more educated immigrants produce more than they cost, while the less educated cost more than they produce.

Problems in Forecasting Population Growth

The total of the three demographic variables—fertility, mortality, and net migration—gives us a country's **growth rate,** the net change after people have been added to and subtracted from a population. What demographers call the **basic demographic equation** is quite simple:

$$\text{Growth rate} = \text{births} - \text{deaths} + \text{net migration}$$

If population increase depended only on biology, the demographer's job would be simple. But social factors—wars, economic booms and busts, plagues, and famines—push rates of birth and death and migration up or down. As shown in the Cultural Diversity below, even infanticide can affect population growth. Government

growth rate
the net change in a population after adding births, subtracting deaths, and either adding or subtracting net migration

basic demographic equation
growth rate = births – deaths + net migration

cultural **d·i·v·e·r·s·i·t·y**

——— Around the World

Killing Little Girls: An Ancient and Thriving Practice

"The Mysterious Case of the Missing Girls" could have been the title of this box. Around the globe, for every 100 girls born, about 105 boys are born. In China, however, for every 100 baby girls, there are 111 baby boys. Given China's huge population, this means China has about 400,000 fewer baby girls than it should have. Why?

The answer is *female infanticide,* the killing of baby girls. When a Chinese woman goes into labor, village midwives sometimes grab a bucket of water. If the newborn is a girl, she is plunged into the water before she can draw her first breath.

At the root of China's sexist infanticide is economics. The people are poor, and they have no pensions. When parents can no longer work, sons support them. In contrast, a daughter must be married off, at great expense, and at that point her obligations transfer to her husband and his family.

In the past few years, the percentage of boy babies has grown. The reason, again, is economics, but this time it has a new twist. As China opened the door to capitalism, travel and trade opened up—but primarily to men, for it is not thought appropriate for women to travel alone. Thus men find themselves in a better position to bring profits home to the family—giving parents one more reason to desire male children.

Female infanticide is also common in India. Many Indian women use ultrasound to learn the sex of their child, and then abort the fetus if it is a girl. Doctors take portable ultrasound machines from village to village, charging $11 for the test and $44 for the abortion. Although the use of ultrasound for this purpose is illegal, this practice accounts for the abortion of about 3 million girls a year.

One test for sex selection led to a public outcry in India. The outrage was not about female infanticide, however, nor was it due to an antiabortion movement. Rather, the public became incensed when a physician mistakenly gave the parents wrong information and aborted a *male* baby!

It is likely that the preference for boys, and the resulting female infanticide, will not disappear until the social structures that perpetuate sexism are dismantled. This will not take place until women hold as much power as men, a development that, should it ever occur, apparently lies far in the future.

Sources: Lagaipa 1990; McGowan 1991; Polumbaum 1992; Renteln 1992; Greenhalgh and Li 1995; Jordan 2000; Dugger 2001.

■ *Due to the Chinese government's policy of "one couple, one child," the birth rate of China has dropped sharply. As discussed in the text, this policy is carried out ruthlessly, including forcing abortions on protesting women.*

programs also complicate projections. Some governments take steps to persuade women to bear more children. When Hitler decided that Germany needed more "Aryans," the German government outlawed abortion and offered cash bonuses to women who gave birth. The population increased.

Other countries take steps to reduce the number of children. None has been so draconian as China. As you read these details, recall the Big Brother vignette that opened Chapter 15. What occurs in China goes beyond even Orwell's fertile imagination. China's "One couple, one child" national policy is well known, but few know how ruthlessly it is carried out. Steven Mosher, an anthropologist who did fieldwork in China, revealed that—whether she wants it or not—after the birth of her first child, each woman is fitted with an IUD (intrauterine device). If a woman has a second child, she is sterilized. If a woman gets pregnant without government permission (yes, you read that right), she is aborted. If she does not consent to an abortion, one is performed on her anyway—even if she is nine months pregnant (Erik 1982). The government even has its agents check sanitary napkins to make sure that women are having their menstrual periods and are not pregnant.

Letting such policies pass without comment, we can see that a government's efforts to change a country's growth rate complicate the demographer's task of projecting future populations.

The primary factor that influences a country's growth rate is industrialization. *In every country that industrializes, the growth rate declines*. Not only does industrialization open up economic opportunities, but also it makes children more expensive. They require more education and remain dependent longer. Significantly, the basis for conferring status also changes—from having children to attaining education and displaying material wealth. People like Celia and Angel begin to see life differently, and their motivation to have many children drops sharply. Not knowing how rapidly industrialization will progress or how quickly changes in values and reproductive behavior will follow adds to the difficulty of making accurate projections.

Because of these many complications, demographers play it safe by making several projections of population growth. For example, what will the U.S. population be in the year 2050? Will there be **zero population growth,** with every 1,000 women giving birth to 2,100 children? (The extra 100 children make up for those who do not survive or reproduce.) Will a larger proportion of women go to college? (The

zero population growth
a demographic condition in which women bear only enough children to reproduce the population

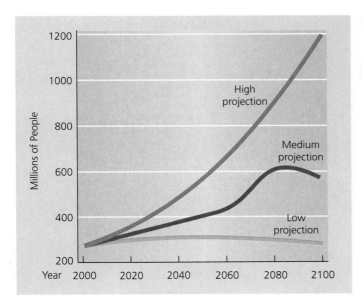

Figure 20.9

Looking toward the Future

Note: The projections are based on different assumptions of fertility, mortality, and, especially, immigration.

Source: Statistical Abstract 2000:Table 3.

more education women have, the fewer children they bear.) How will immigration change during the coming years? Will AIDS rage out of control? Will some other devastating disease appear? What will happen to the new global economy? With such huge variables, it is easy to see why demographers make the three projections of the U.S. population shown in Figure 20.9.

Let's look at a different aspect of population, where people live. Since the world is rapidly becoming urban, we shall concentrate on urban trends and urban life.

URBANIZATION

As I was climbing a steep hill in Medellin, Colombia, in a district called El Tiro, my informant, Jaro, said, "This used to be a garbage heap." I stopped to peer through the vegetation alongside the path we were on, and sure enough, I could still see bits of refuse sticking out of the dirt. The "town" had been built on top of garbage.

This was just the first of my many revelations that day. The second was that El Tiro was so dangerous that the Medellin police refused to enter it. I shuddered for a moment, but I had good reason to trust Jaro. He had been a pastor in El Tiro for several years, and he knew the people well. I knew that if I stayed close to him I would be safe.

Actually, the town had become much safer in recent years. A group of men had banded together to make it so, Jaro told me. A sort of frontier justice prevailed. This group told the prostitutes and drug dealers that there would be no prostitution or drug dealing in town, and to "take it elsewhere." They killed anyone who robbed or killed someone. And they even made families safer—they would beat up any man who got drunk and beat "his" woman. With the threat of instant justice, the area had become much safer.

Jaro then added that each household had to pay the group a monthly fee, which turned out to be less than a dollar in U.S. money. Each business had to pay a little more. For this, they received security.

As we wandered the streets of El Tiro, it did look safe—but I did stick close to Jaro. And I wondered about this group of young men who had made the area safe. What kept them from turning on the residents? Jaro had no answer. When Jaro pointed to two young men, whom he said were part of the ruling group, I asked if I could take their picture. They refused. I did not try to snap one on the sly.

My final revelation was El Tiro itself, shown on the next two pages.

This is the "richer" area below El Tiro. As you can see, some of the residents own cars.

The road to El Tiro. On the left, going up the hill, is a board walk. To the right is a meat market (carniceria). Note the structure above the meat market, where the family that runs the store lives.

a walk through El Tiro in

Medellin, Colombia

Almost at the top of the garbage heap, I saw this boy in front of his house. His mother hung out the family's wash to dry.

El Tiro has home delivery.

An infrastructure has developed to serve El Tiro. This woman is waiting in line to use the only public telephone.

It doesn't take much skill to build your own house in El Tiro. A hammer and saw, some nails and used lumber will provide most of what you need. This man is building his house on top of another house. You can see why so many people are killed in earth tremors in the Least Industrialized Nations.

▼

What do the people do to make a living in El Tiro? Anything they can. This man is sharpening a saw in front of his home. The child looks quite secure behind the barricade the father built.

▲

"What does an El Tiro home look like inside?," I kept wondering. Then Jaro, my guide at the left, took me inside the home of one of his parishioners. Amelia keeps a neat house, with everything highly organized.

▼

◀ This is one of my favorite photos. The woman is happy that she has a home—and proud of what she has done with it. What I find remarkable is the flower garden she so carefully tends and has taken great effort to protect from children and dogs. I can see the care she would take of a little suburban home.

Kids are kids the world over. These children don't know they are poor. They are having a great time playing on a pile of dirt in the street. ▶

In this final part of the chapter, I will try to lay the context for understanding urban life—and El Tiro. Let's begin by first finding out how the city itself came about.

■ ■ ■ ■ ■

The Development of Cities

Cities are not new to the world scene. Perhaps as early as seven to ten thousand years ago people built small cities with massive defensive walls, such as biblically famous Jericho (Homblin 1973). Cities on a larger scale originated about 3500 B.C., about the same time that writing was invented (Chandler and Fox 1974; Hawley 1981). At that time, cities appeared in several parts of the world—first in Mesopotamia (Iran) and later in the Nile, Indus, and Yellow River valleys, in West Africa, around the Mediterranean, in Central America, and in the Andes (Fischer 1976; Flanagan 1990). In the Americas, the first city was Caral, in what is now Peru (Fountain 2001).

The key to the origin of cities is the development of more efficient agriculture (Lenski and Lenski 1987). Only when farming produces a surplus can some people stop being food producers and gather in cities to spend time in other pursuits. A **city,** in fact, can be defined as a place in which a large number of people are permanently based and do not produce their own food. The invention of the plow between five and six thousand years ago created widespread agricultural surpluses, stimulating the development of towns and cities (Curwin and Hart 1961).

Most early cities were tiny in comparison with those of today, merely a collection of a few thousand people in agricultural centers or on major trade routes. The most notable exceptions are two cities that reached 1 million for a brief period of time before they declined—Changan in China about A.D. 800 and Baghdad in Persia about A.D. 900 (Chandler and Fox 1974). Even Athens at the peak of its power in the fifth century B.C. had less than 200,000 inhabitants. Rome, at its peak, may have had a million or more (Flanagan 1990).

Even 200 years ago, the only city in the world that had a population of more than a million was Peking (now Beijing), China (Chandler and Fox 1974). Then in just 100

city
a place in which a large number of people are permanently based and do not produce their own food

■ Early cities were small economic centers surrounded by walls designed to keep out enemies. These cities, built like fortresses, were constantly threatened by armed, roving tribesmen and by the leaders of nearby city-states who raised armies in an effort to enlarge their domain and enrich their coffers by sacking neighboring cities. Pictured here is Carcasonne, a restored medieval city in southern France.

years, by 1900, the number of such cities jumped to sixteen. The reason was the Industrial Revolution, which drew people to cities by providing work. The Industrial Revolution also stimulated rapid transportation and communication, and allowed people, resources, and products to be moved efficiently—all essential factors (called *infrastructure*) on which large cities depend. Today about 300 cities have a million or more people, and, as Figure 20.10 shows, this number is continuing to grow (Brockerhoff 2000).

■ The Process of Urbanization

Although cities are not new to the world scene, urbanization is. **Urbanization** refers to masses of people moving to cities, and these cities having a growing influence on society. Urbanization is worldwide. In 1800, only 3 percent of the world's population lived in cities (Hauser and Schnore 1965). Today 45 percent of the world's population lives in cities: 75 percent of people in the industrialized world and 38 percent of those who live in the Least Industrialized Nations (Haub and Cornelius 2001). By the year 2020, most people will live in cities. Without the Industrial Revolution this remarkable growth could not have taken place, for an extensive infrastructure is needed to support hundreds of thousands and even millions of people in a relatively small area.

To understand the city's attraction, we need to consider the "pulls" of urban life. Due to its exquisite division of labor, the city offers incredible variety—music ranging from rock and nortec to country and classic, diets for vegetarians and diabetics as well as imported delicacies from around the world for everyone else. Cities also offer anonymity, which so many find refreshing in light of the tighter controls of village and small-town life. And, of course, the city offers work.

Some cities have grown so large and have so much influence over a region that the term *city* is no longer adequate to describe them. The term **metropolis** is used instead. This term refers to a central city surrounded by smaller cities and their suburbs. They are linked by transportation and communication and connected economically, and sometimes politically, through county boards and regional governing bodies.

St. Louis is an example. Although this name, St. Louis, properly refers to a city of fewer than 400,000 people in Missouri, it also refers to another 2 million people who live in more than a hundred separate towns in both Missouri and Illinois. Altogether, the region is known as the "St. Louis or Bi-State Area." Although these towns are independent politically, they form an economic unit. They are linked by work (many people in the smaller towns work in St. Louis, or are served by industries from St. Louis), by communications (they share the same area newspaper and radio and television stations), and by transportation (they use the same interstate highways, "Bi-State Bus" system, and international airport). As symbolic interactionists would note, the residents' shared symbols (the Arch, the Mississippi River, Busch Brewery, the Cardinals, the Rams, the Blues—both the hockey team and the music) provide a common identity. Most of the towns run into one another, and if you were to drive through this metropolis you would not know you were leaving one town and entering another—unless you had lived there for some time and were aware of the fierce small-town identifications and rivalries that coexist within this larger identity.

Some metropolises have grown so large and influential that the term **megalopolis** is used to describe them. This term refers to an overlapping area consisting of at least two metropolises and their many suburbs. Of the twenty or so megalopolises in the United States, the three largest are the Eastern seaboard running from Maine to Virginia, the area in Florida between Miami, Orlando, and Tampa, and California's coastal area between San Francisco and San Diego. This California megalopolis extends into Mexico and includes Tijuana and its southern suburbs.

Figure 20.10
The Growth of Cities over 1 Million Residents
Source: Chandler and Fox 1974; Brockerhoff 2000.

urbanization
the process by which an increasing proportion of a population lives in cities

metropolis
a central city surrounded by smaller cities and their suburbs

megalopolis
an urban area consisting of at least two metropolises and their many suburbs

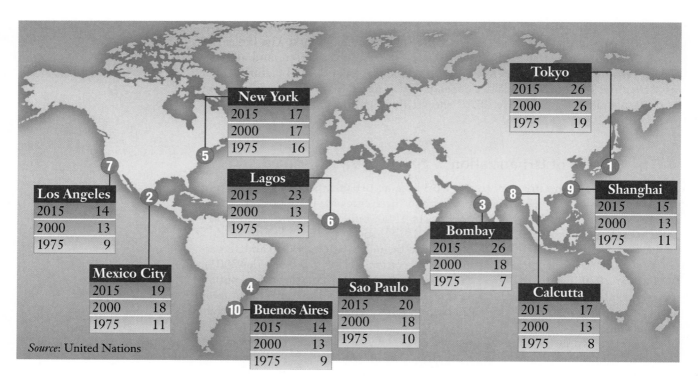

F igure 20.11

Social Map: The Urban Giants: The Population of the World's Ten Largest Megacities, in Millions
Source: United Nations, 2000.

This process of urban areas turning into a metropolis, and a metropolis developing into a megalopolis occurs worldwide. Figure 20.11 shows the ten largest megacities in the world. A **megacity** is a city of 10 million or more residents. Note that most megacities are located in the Least Industrialized Nations.

■ U.S. Urban Patterns

In its early years, the United States was almost exclusively rural. In 1790, only about 5 percent of Americans lived in cities. By 1920, this figure had jumped to 50 percent. Urbanization has continued without letup, and today 75 percent of Americans live in cities. As you can see from the Social Map on the next page, like our other social patterns, urbanization is uneven across the United States.

The U.S. Census Bureau has divided the country into 274 **metropolitan statistical areas (MSAs).** Each MSA consists of a central city of at least 50,000 people and the urbanized areas linked to it. About three of every five Americans live in just fifty or so MSAs.

As Americans migrate in search of work and better lifestyles, some cities gain population while others shrink. Table 20.3 on the next page compares the fastest growing U.S. cities with those that are shrinking. As you can see, seven of the ten fastest growing cities are in the West, and three are in the South. Of the ten declining cities, nine are in the Northeast, while one is in the Midwest.

As Americans migrate, **edge cities** have developed to meet their needs. This term refers to clusters of shopping malls, hotels, office parks, and residential areas that are located near the intersection of major highways. Although these clusters may overlap the boundaries of several cities or towns, they provide a sense of place to those who live, work, or shop there.

Another major U.S. urban pattern is **gentrification,** the movement of middle-class people into rundown areas of a city. They are attracted by the low prices for quality housing that, though deteriorated, can be renovated. One consequence is an

megacity
a city of 10 million or more residents

metropolitan statistical area (MSA)
a central city and the urbanized counties adjacent to it

edge city
a large clustering of service facilities and residential areas near highway intersections that provides a sense of place to people who live, shop, and work there

gentrification
the displacement of the poor by the relatively affluent, who purchase and renovate the former's homes

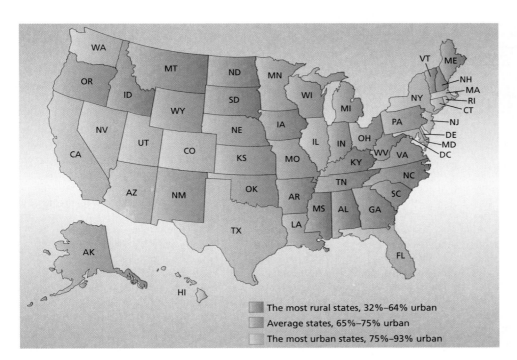

Figure 20.12

Social Map: How Urban Is Your State? The Rural-Urban Makeup of the United States

Note: The most rural state is Vermont, where 2 of 3 residents (68 percent) live in rural areas. The most urban state is California, where 13 of 14 residents (93 percent) live in cities.

Source: Statistical Abstract 2000: Table 37.

The most rural states, 32%–64% urban

Average states, 65%–75% urban

The most urban states, 75%–93% urban

improvement in the appearance of some urban neighborhoods—freshly painted buildings, well-groomed lawns, and the absence of boarded-up windows. Another consequence is that the poor residents are displaced as the more well-to-do newcomers move in and drive up prices. Tension often arises between these groups (Anderson 1990, 1999).

TABLE 20.3 The Fastest-Growing and Fastest-Shrinking U.S. Cities

The Fastest-Growing Cities	The Fastest-Shrinking Cities
1. 55.0% Las Vegas, NV	1. −6.9% Utica-Rome, NY
2. 36.2% McAllen-Edinburg-Mission, TX	2. −3.6% Scranton-Wilkes Barre, PA
3. 33.8% Boise City, ID	3. −3.1% Buffalo-Niagara Falls, NY
4. 30.9% Phoenix-Mesa, AZ	4. −2.9% New London-Norwich, CT
5. 30.7% Austin-San Marcos, TX	5. −2.4% Springfield MA
6. 29.3% Fayetteville-Springdale-Rogers, AR	6. −2.0% Pittsburgh, PA
7. 27.3% Provo-Orem, UT	7. −1.5% Youngstown, OH
8. 26.6% Atlanta, GA	8. −1.4% New Haven-Meriden, CT
9. 25.8% Raleigh-Durham-Chapel Hill, NC	9. −1.2% Hartford, CT
10. 25.5% Brownsville-Harlingen-San Benito, TX	10. −1.0% Providence, RI

Note: The totals indicate the percentage of population change from 1990–1998. A minus sign indicates a loss of population. Providence, Rhode Island, and Syracuse, New York, tied for number 10 in the loss column.

Source: Statistical Abstract 2000:Table 34.

---

down-to-earth
s o c i o l o g y

■ ■ ■ ■ ■ ■

Reclaiming Harlem: "It Feeds My Soul"

The story is well known. The inner city is filled with crack, crime, and corruption. It stinks from foul, festering garbage strewn on the streets and piled up around burned-out buildings. Only those who have no choice live in this desolate, despairing environment where danger lurks around every corner.

What is not so well known is that affluent African Americans are reclaiming some of these areas.

Howard Sanders was living the American Dream. After earning a degree from Harvard Business School, he took a position with a Manhattan investment firm. He lived in an exclusive apartment on Central Park West, but he missed Harlem, where he had grown up. He moved back, along with his wife and daughter.

African American lawyers, doctors, professors, and bankers are doing the same.

What's the attraction? The first is nostalgia, a cultural identification with the Harlem of legend and folklore. It was here that black writers and artists lived in the 1920s, here that the blues and jazz attracted young and accomplished musicians.

The second reason is a more practical one. Harlem offers housing value. Five bedroom homes with 6,000 square feet are available. Some feature Honduran mahogany. Some brownstones are only shells and have to be renovated; others are in perfect condition.

What is happening is the rebuilding of a community. Some people who "made" it want to be role models. They want children in the community to see them going to and returning from work.

When the middle class moved out of Harlem, so did its amenities. Now that

young professionals are moving back in, the amenities are returning, too. There were no coffee shops, restaurants, jazz clubs, florists, copy centers, dentist and optometrist offices, or art galleries—the types of things urbanites take for granted. Now there are.

The same thing is happening on Chicago's West Side and in other U.S. cities.

The drive to find community—to make a connection with others and with one's roots—is strong. As an investment banker who migrated to Harlem said, "It feeds my soul."

Source: Based on Cose 1999; McCormick 1999, Waldman 2000; Scott 2001.

■ ■ ■ ■ ■

A common pattern is for the gentrifiers to be whites and the displaced to be minorities. As discussed in the Down-to-Earth Sociology box above, in Harlem, New York, both the gentrifiers and the displaced are African Americans. As middle-class and professional African Americans reclaim this and other urban areas, an infrastructure—which includes everything from Starbucks coffee houses to dentists—follows. So do soaring real estate prices.

■ ■ ■ ■ ■

Models of Urban Growth

As I mentioned, in the 1920s sociologists at the University of Chicago studied the contrasting ways of urban life. One of these sociologists, Robert Park, coined the term **human ecology** to describe how people adapt to their environment (Park and Burgess 1921; Park 1936). (This concept is also known as *urban ecology*.) The process of urban growth is of special interest to human ecologists. Let's look at the four main models they developed.

■ The Concentric Zone Model

human ecology
Robert Park's term for the relationship between people and their environment (natural resources such as land)

To explain how cities expand, sociologist Ernest Burgess (1925) proposed a *concentric-zone model.* As shown in part A of Figure 20.13, Burgess noted that a city

Concentric zones
A

Sectors
B

Multiple nuclei
C

District
1. Central business district
2. Wholesale light manufacturing
3. Low-class residential
4. Medium-class residential
5. High-class residential
6. Heavy manufacturing
7. Outlying business district
8. Residential suburb
9. Industrial suburb
10. Commuters' zone

Peripheral model
D

District
1. Central city
2. Suburban residential areas
3. Circumferential highway
4. Radial highway
5. Shopping mall
6. Industrial district
7. Office park
8. Service center
9. Airport complex
10. Combined employment and shopping center

F igure 20.13

How Cities Develop: Models of Urban Growth

Source: Cousins and Nagpaul 1970; Harris 1997.

expands outward from its center. Zone 1 is the central business district. Zone 2, which encircles the downtown area, is in transition. It contains rooming houses and deteriorating housing, which Burgess said breed poverty, disease, and vice. Zone 3 is the area to which thrifty workers have moved in order to escape the zone in transition and yet maintain easy access to their work. Zone 4 contains more expensive apartments, residential hotels, single-family homes, and exclusive areas where the wealthy live. Commuters live in Zone 5, which consists of suburbs or satellite cities that have grown up around transit routes.

Burgess intended this model to represent "the tendencies of any town or city to expand radially from its central business district." He noted, however, that no "city fits perfectly this ideal scheme." Some cities have physical obstacles such as a lake, river, or railroad, which cause their expansion to depart from the model. Burgess also noted that businesses had begun to deviate from the model by locating in outlying zones. This was in 1925, and Burgess was seeing the first stage of a major shift that led businesses away from downtown areas to suburban shopping malls. Today, these malls account for most of the country's retail sales.

■ The Sector Model

Sociologist Homer Hoyt (1939, 1971) noted that a city's concentric zones do not form a complete circle, and he modified Burgess' model of urban growth. As shown in part B of Figure 20.13, a concentric zone can contain several sectors—one of working-class housing, another of expensive homes, a third of businesses, and so on—all competing for the same land.

What sociologists call an **invasion-succession cycle** is an example of this dynamic competition. When poor immigrants or rural migrants enter a city, they settle in the lowest-rent area they can find. As their numbers swell, they spill over into adjacent areas. Upset by their presence, the middle class moves out, which expands the sector of low-cost housing. The invasion-succession cycle is never complete, for later another group will replace this earlier one. The cycle, in fact, can go full circle, for with gentrification, the "invaders" can be the middle and upper middle classes.

■ The Multiple-Nuclei Model

Geographers Chauncey Harris and Edward Ullman noted that some cities have several centers or nuclei (Harris and Ullman 1945; Ullman and Harris 1970). As shown in part C of Figure 20.13, each nucleus contains some specialized activity. A familiar example is the clustering of fast-food restaurants in one area and automobile dealerships in another. Sometimes similar activities are grouped together because they profit from cohesion; retail districts, for example, draw more customers if there are more stores. Other clustering occurs because some types of land use, such as factories and expensive homes, are incompatible with one another. One result is that services are not spread evenly throughout the city.

■ The Peripheral Model

Chauncey Harris (1997) also developed the peripheral model shown in part D of Figure 20.13. This model portrays the impact of radial highways on the movement of people and services away from the central city to the city's periphery, or outskirts. It also shows the development of industrial and office parks.

■ Critique of the Models

These models tell only part of the story. They are time bound, for medieval cities didn't follow these patterns (see the photo on page 614). They also are geography bound. England, for example, has planning laws that preserve green belts (trees and farmlands) around the city. This prevents urban sprawl: Wal-Mart cannot buy land outside the city and put up a store; instead, it must locate in the downtown area with the other stores. Norwich has 250,000 people—yet the city ends abruptly, and on its green belt pheasants skitter across plowed fields while sheep graze in verdant meadows (Milbank 1995). The models, then, do not account for urban planning policies.

The models also fall short when it comes to the cities of the Least Industrialized Nations. U.S. visitors are surprised when they visit one of these cities. The wealthy often claim the inner city, where fine restaurants and other services are readily accessible. There, tucked behind tall walls and protected from public scrutiny, they enjoy luxurious homes and gardens. The poor, in contrast, especially rural migrants, settle in areas outside the city—or, as in the case of El Tiro, on top of garbage heaps in what used to be the outskirts of a city. This topic is discussed in the Cultural Diversity box on the facing page.

invasion-succession cycle the process of one group of people displacing a group whose racial-ethnic or social class characteristics differ from their own

The World

Around the World

Why City Slums Are Better than the Country: Urbanization in the Least Industrialized Nations

In the Least Industrialized Nations, rural people have flocked to the cities in such numbers that, as we saw in Figure 20.11 (page 616), these nations now contain most of the world's largest cities. Each year, the cities of the Least Industrialized Nations swell by about 50 million people (Brockerhoff 2000). That's more than all the Spaniards who live in Spain. During the next six years, this is equivalent to the entire population of the United States.

When rural migrants and immigrants move to U.S. cities, they usually settle in areas of deteriorating housing near the city's center. In the Least Industrialized Nations, the wealthy live near the downtown area, and migrants establish squatter settlements outside the city. This is the typical pattern, but as we saw with El Tiro (pages 612–613), they move to any area available, even garbage dumps. As you saw from the photos, there they build shacks from scrap boards and bits of corrugated metal. In some areas, even flattened tin cans are scavenged for building material. At first, the squatters enjoy no city facilities—roads, transportation lines, water, sewers, or garbage pickup. After a while, officials acknowledge the squatters' right to live there by adding bus service and

■ *The Least Industrialized Nations are facing massive upheaval as they rapidly urbanize, resulting in disparities such as those depicted here. Lacking the infrastructure to support their many newcomers, cities in the Least Industrialized Nations, already steeped in poverty, face the daunting task of developing jobs, housing, sewage and electrical systems, roads, schools, and so on. This photo was taken in Bombay, India.*

minimal electric and water lines. Hundreds of people may use a single spigot

Why this vast rush to live in the city under such conditions? First, there are "push" factors. The rural way of life is breaking down. The second leg of the demographic transition has kicked in—death rates are dropping while birth rates remain high—and rural populations are multiplying. No longer is there enough land to

divide up among descendants. There also are "pull" factors that draw people to the city—jobs, schools, housing, and even a more stimulating life.

This vast migration is up against a major problem, the lack of industrialization. Up to now, as cities developed, industrialization generally preceded urbanization. Now, in contrast, *urbanization is preceding industrialization*. The limited technology of the Least Industrialized Nations makes it difficult to support their mushrooming populations.

Will the Least Industrialized Nations adjust to this vast, unwanted migration? They have no choice. Authorities in Brazil, Guatemala, Venezuela, and other countries have sent in the police, even the army, to evict the settlers. It doesn't work. This just leads to violence—and the settlers keep streaming in anyway. The adjustment will be painful. The infrastructure (roads, water, sewers, electricity, and so on) must be built, but these poor countries don't have the resources to build them. As the desperate continue to flock to the cities, the problems will worsen.

for your consideration

What solutions do you see to the vast migration to the cities of the Least Industrialized Nations?

City Life: Alienation and Community

Just as cities provide opportunities, they also create problems. We humans are complex beings. Certainly we have needs of food, shelter, and safety, and satisfying them is important. But this is only part of who we are. We also have a deep need for **community,** a feeling that we belong—the sense that others care what happens to us and that we can depend on the people around us. Some people find this

community
a place people identify with, where they sense that they belong and that others care what happens to them

sense of community in the city; others find its opposite, **alienation,** a sense of not belonging and a feeling that no one cares what happens to you:

> Twenty-eight-year-old Catherine Genovese, who was called Kitty by almost everyone in her Queens neighborhood, was returning home from work. After she had parked her car, a man grabbed her. She screamed, "Oh, my God, he stabbed me! Please help me! Please help me!"
>
> For more than half an hour, thirty-eight respectable, law-abiding citizens looked out their windows and watched as the killer stalked and stabbed Kitty in three separate attacks. Twice the sudden glow from their bedroom lights interrupted him and frightened him off. Each time he returned, sought her out, and stabbed her again. Not one person telephoned the police during the assault. (*New York Times*, March 26, 1964)

When the police interviewed them, some witnesses said, "I didn't want to get involved." Others said, "We thought it was a lovers' quarrel." Some simply said, "I don't know." People throughout the country were shocked. It was as though Americans awoke one morning to discover that the country had changed overnight. They took this event as a sign that people could no longer trust one another, that the city was a cold, lonely place.

Why should the city be alienating? In a classic essay, "Urbanism as a Way of Life," sociologist Louis Wirth (1938) argued that the city undermines kinship and neighborhood, which are the traditional sources of social control and social solidarity. Urban dwellers live in anonymity. As they go from one superficial encounter with strangers to another, they grow aloof from one another and indifferent to other people's problems—as did the neighbors of Kitty Genovese. In short, the personal freedom that the city provides comes at the cost of alienation.

Wirth built on ideas discussed in Chapter 4. As a society industrializes, *Gemeinschaft*, the sense of community that comes from everyone knowing everyone else, is ripped apart. What emerges is a new society based on *Gesellschaft*, secondary, impersonal relationships. Lacking identification with one another, people develop the attitude "It's simply none of *my* business." The end result can be alienation so deep that people can sit by while someone else is being murdered.

The city, however, is more than a mosaic of strangers who feel disconnected and distrustful of one another. It also consists of a series of smaller worlds, within which people find community. People become familiar with the smaller areas of the city where they live, work, shop, and play. Even slums, which to outsiders seem so threatening, can provide a sense of belonging. In a classic study, sociologist Herbert Gans (1962:12) noted,

> After a few weeks of living in the West End (of Boston), my observations—and my perceptions of the area—changed drastically. The search for an apartment quickly indicated that the individual units were usually in much better condition than the outside or the hallways of the buildings. Subsequently, in wandering through the West End, and in using it as a resident, I developed a kind of selective perception, in which my eye focused only on those parts of the area that were actually being used by people. Vacant buildings and boarded-up stores were no longer so visible, and the totally deserted alleys or streets were outside the set of paths normally traversed, either by myself or by the West Enders . . .
>
> Since much of the area's life took place on the street, faces became familiar very quickly. I met my neighbors on the stairs and in front of my building. And, once a shopping pattern developed, I saw the same storekeepers frequently, as well as the area's "characters" who wandered through the streets every day on a fairly regular route and schedule. In short, the exotic quality of the stores and the residents also wore off as I became used to seeing them.

As he lived in the West End, Gans gradually gained an insider's perspective of the area. Despite the narrow streets, substandard buildings, and even piled-up garbage, most West Enders had chosen to live there: *To them the West End was a low-rent district, not a slum.* Within the deteriorated area was a community, people who visited

alienation
a sense of not belonging

■ *The city dwellers whom Gans identified as ethnic villagers find community in the city. Living in tightly knit neighborhoods, they know many other residents. Some first-generation immigrants have even come from the same village in the "old country." Shown here is San Francisco's Chinatown.*

back and forth with relatives and were involved in networks of friendships and acquaintances. Gans therefore titled his book *The Urban Villagers* (1962).

Then came well-intentioned urban planners, who drew up plans to get rid of the "slum." The residents of the West End were upset when they heard about the coming urban renewal, and distrustful that the improvements would benefit them. Their distrust proved well founded, for the urban renewal brought with it another invasion-succession cycle. Along with the gleaming new buildings came people with more money who took over the area. The former residents were dispossessed, their intimate patterns destroyed.

■ Who Lives in the City?

Whether you find alienation or community in the city depends on many factors, but consider the five types of urban dwellers that Gans (1962, 1968, 1991a) identified. Which type are you? How does this affect your chances of finding alienation or community?

The first three types live in the city by choice; they find a sense of community.

The Cosmopolites The cosmopolites are the city's students, intellectuals, professionals, musicians, artists, and entertainers. They have been drawn to the city because of its conveniences and cultural benefits.

The Singles Young, unmarried people come to the city seeking jobs and entertainment. Businesses and services such as singles bars, singles apartment complexes, and computer dating companies cater to their needs. Their stay in the city is often temporary, for most move to the suburbs after they marry and have children.

The Ethnic Villagers United by race-ethnicity and social class, these people live in tightly knit neighborhoods that resemble villages and small towns. Moving within a close circle of family and friends, the ethnic villagers try to isolate themselves from what they view as the harmful effects of city life.

The next two groups, the deprived and the trapped, have little choice about where they live. As alienated outcasts of industrial society, they are always skirting the edge of disaster.

■ *Men like this one, who has drunk himself into a stupor, are not an unfamiliar sight in some parts of U.S. cities. The text describes several types of urban dwellers. What type is this man?*

The Deprived   The deprived live in blighted neighborhoods that are more like urban jungles than urban villages. Consisting of the very poor and the emotionally disturbed, the deprived represent the bottom of society in terms of income, education, social status, and work skills. Some of them stalk their jungle in search of prey, their victims usually deprived people like themselves. Their future holds little chance for anything better in life.

The Trapped   The trapped can find no escape either. Some could not afford to move when their neighborhood was "invaded" by another ethnic group. Others in this group are the elderly who are not wanted elsewhere, alcoholics and other drug addicts, and the downwardly mobile. Like the deprived, the trapped also suffer high rates of assault, mugging, robbery, and rape.

■ Urban Sentiment: Finding a Familiar World

Sociologists note that *the city is divided into little worlds* that people come to know down to their smallest details. City people create a sense of intimacy by *personalizing* their shopping (Stone 1954; Gans 1970). They shop in the same stores, and after a period of time, customers and clerks greet each other by name. Certain bars, restaurants, and shops are more than just buildings in which they make purchases. They become places where neighborhood residents build social relationships with one another and share informal news about the community.

Spectator sports also help urban dwellers find a familiar world (Hudson 1991). When Mark McGwire of the Cardinals hit the 61st home run that broke Roger Maris' longstanding record, fans around the country celebrated, but in the St. Louis area the celebration was special: It was for "our" man on "our" team—even though fewer than one in seven of the area's 2.5 million people live in the city. Sociologists David Karp and William Yoels (1990) note that such identification is so intense that long after moving to other parts of the country, many people maintain an emotional allegiance to the sports teams of the city in which they grew up.

■ The Norm of Noninvolvement and the Diffusion of Responsibility

Urban dwellers try to avoid intrusions from strangers. As they go about their everyday lives in the city, they follow a *norm of noninvolvement.*

> To do this, we sometimes use props such as newspapers to shield ourselves from others and to indicate our inaccessibility for interaction. In effect, we learn to "tune others out." In this regard, we might see the Walkman as the quintessential urban prop in that it allows us to be tuned in and tuned out at the same time. It is a device that allows us to enter our own private world and thereby effectively to close off encounters with others. The use of such devices protects our "personal space," along with our body demeanor and facial expression (the passive "mask" or even scowl that persons adopt on subways). (Karp et al. 1991)

Recall Kitty Genovese, whose story was recounted on page 622. Her story troubled social psychologists John Darley and Bibb Latané (1968), who ran the series of experiments featured in Chapter 6, pages 175–176. Darley and Latané uncovered a *diffusion of responsibility.* They found that the more bystanders there are, the less likely people are to help. As a group grows, people's sense of responsibility becomes diffused, with each person assuming that *another* will do the responsible thing. "With these other people here, it is not *my* responsibility," they reason.

The diffusion of responsibility, along with the norm of noninvolvement, helps explain the response to Kitty Genovese's murder. The bystanders at her death were *not* uncaring people. They *did* care that a woman was being attacked. They simply were abiding by an urban norm, one that is helpful for getting them through everyday city life but, unfortunately, dysfunctional in some crucial situations. This norm, combined with killings, carjackings, muggings, and the generalized fear that the city engenders in many Americans, underlies the desire many have to retreat to a safe haven. This topic is discussed in the Down-to-Earth Sociology box.

---

down-to-earth sociology

Urban Fear and the Gated Fortress

Gated neighborhoods— where wrought-iron gates open and close to allow or prevent access to a neighborhood—are not new. They always have been available to the rich. What is new is the upper middle class's rush to towns where they pay high taxes to keep all of the town's facilities, including its streets, private.

Towns cannot discriminate on the basis of religion or race-ethnicity, but they can—and do—discriminate on the basis of social class. Klahanie, Washington, is an excellent example. Begun in 1985, it was supposed to take twenty years to develop. With its safe streets and 300 acres of open space—and with its ban on satellite dishes, flagpoles, and even basketball hoops on garages—demand for the $300,000-plus homes nestled by a lake in this private community exceeded supply (Egan 1995).

The future will bring many more such private towns as the upper middle class flees urban areas and attempts to build a bucolic dream. A strong sign of the future is Celebration, a town of 20,000 people planned and built by the Walt Disney Company just five minutes

from Disney World. Celebration, which won't be completed until 2014, boasts the usual school, hospital, and golf course, but in addition, it offers paths for walking and bicycling, a hotel with a lighthouse tower and bird sanctuary, and a health and fitness center with a rock climbing wall. The median price of homes is $300,000 (Wilkening 2000, Snyder 2001). With our new technology, the residents of private communities such as these will be able to communicate with the outside world while remaining securely locked within their sanctuaries.

▨ *The U.S. economic system has proven highly beneficial to most citizens, but it also has left many in poverty. To protect themselves, primarily from the poor, the upper middle class increasingly seeks sanctuary behind gated residential enclaves.*

for your consideration

Community involves a sense of togetherness, a sense of identity with one another. Can you explain how this concept also contains the idea of separateness from others (not just in the example of gated communities)? What will our future be if we become a nation of gated communities, where middle-class homeowners withdraw into private domains, separating themselves from the rest of the nation?

■ ■ ■ ■ ■

Urban Problems and Social Policy

The primary problems of urban life today are poverty, decay, and a general decline of U.S. cities. Let's examine underlying reasons for these conditions and consider how to develop social policy to solve urban problems.

■ Suburbanization

suburbanization
the movement from the city to the suburbs

suburb
the communities adjacent to the political boundaries of a city

redlining
the officers of a financial institution deciding not to make loans in a particular area

disinvestment
the withdrawal of investments by financial institutions, which seals the fate of an urban area

deindustrialization
industries moving out of a country or region

Suburbanization, which refers to people moving from cities to **suburbs,** the communities located just outside a city, is not new. Archaeologists have recently found that the Mayan city of Caracol in what is today Belize had suburbs, perhaps even with specialized subcenters, the equivalent of today's strip malls (Wilford 2000). The extent to which people have left U.S. cities in search of a better life is remarkable. Fifty years ago, about 20 percent of Americans lived in the suburbs (Karp et al. 1991). Today, over half of all Americans live in them (Rybczynski 1999).

The automobile was a major impetus for suburbanization. Beginning about one hundred years ago, whites began to move to small towns near the cities in which they worked. Suburbanization picked up pace after the racial integration of U.S. schools in the 1950s and 1960s, as whites fled the cities. Minorities began to suburbanize about 1970. In some of today's suburbs, minorities are the majority.

A new development is bands of suburbs becoming so thick they merge into one another. In some places, suburbs have so merged that they form their own large cities (Firestone 2001). In the area from Atlanta, Georgia, to Raleigh, North Carolina, this filling in is so great that unbroken chains of suburbs stretch for hundreds of miles. This development is so new that we don't yet have a name for it.

The U.S. city has been the loser in this transition. As people moved out of the city, businesses and jobs followed. Now about two-thirds of people who live in the suburbs also work there (Gans 1991b). As the city's tax base shrank, it left a budget squeeze that affected not only parks, zoos, libraries, and museums, but also the city's basic services—its schools, streets, sewer and water systems, and police and fire departments.

This shift in population and resources left behind people who had no choice but to stay in the city. The net result, observes sociologist William Julius Wilson (1987), was to transform the inner city into a ghetto. Left behind were families and individuals who, lacking training and skills, were trapped by poverty, unemployment, and welfare dependency—along with people who prey on others through street crime. The term *ghetto,* says Wilson, "suggests that a fundamental social transformation has taken place . . . that groups represented by this term are collectively different from and much more socially isolated from those that lived in these communities in earlier years" (quoted in Karp et al. 1991).

■ *A fundamental drama being played out in various areas of the United States and throughout the world is the struggle between the haves and the have-nots. As much as possible, the haves segregate themselves from the have-nots. These homeless men sleeping in front of this upscale shop in New York City are unlikely to be allowed here when the shop is open.*

City Versus Suburb Having made the move out of the city—or having been born in a suburb and preferring to live there—suburbanites want the city to keep its problems to itself. They reject proposals to share suburbia's revenues with the city and oppose measures that would allow urban and suburban governments joint control over what has become a contiguous mass of people and businesses. Suburban leaders generally believe it is in their best interests to remain politically, economically, and socially separate from their nearby city. They do not mind going to the city to work, or venturing there on weekends for the diversions it offers, but they do not want to help shoulder the city's burdens.

It is likely that the mounting bill will come due ultimately, however, and that suburbanites will have to pay for their uncaring attitude toward the urban disadvantaged. Karp et al. (1991) put it this way:

> It may be that suburbs can insulate themselves from the problems of central cities, at least for the time being. In the long run, though, there will be a steep price to pay for the failure of those better off to care compassionately for those at the bottom of society.

Our occasional urban riots may be part of that bill—perhaps just the down payment.

Suburban Flight   In some places, the bill is coming due quickly. As they age, some suburbs are becoming a mirror image of the city their residents so despise, with rising crime, flight of the middle class, a shrinking tax base, and eroding services. This, in turn, creates a spiraling sense of insecurity, more middle-class flight, and a further reduction of property values. Figure 20.14 illustrates this process, which is new to the urban-suburban scene.

■ Disinvestment and Deindustrialization

As the cities' tax base shrank and their services declined, neighborhoods deteriorated, and banks began **redlining**: Afraid of loans going bad, bankers drew a line on a map around a problem area and refused to make loans for housing or businesses there. The **disinvestment** (withdrawal of investment) pushed these areas into further decline. Youth gangs, murders, and muggings are high in these areas, while educational attainment, employment opportunities, and income are low—factors that are not unconnected to this process of disinvestment.

The globalization of capitalism has also left a heavy mark on U.S. cities. As sociologist Victor Rodríguez (1994) points out, to compete in the global market, many U.S. industries abandoned local communities and moved their factories to countries where labor costs are lower. This process, called **deindustrialization**, made U.S. industries more competitive, but it eliminated millions of U.S. manufacturing jobs. Lacking training in the new information technologies, many poor people are locked out of the benefits of the postindustrial economy that is engulfing the United States. Left behind in the inner cities, many live in despair.

50 years ago

At first, the city and surrounding villages grew independently.

25 years ago

As city dwellers fled urban decay, they created a ring of suburbs.

Now

As middle-class flight continues outward, urban problems are arriving in the outer rings.

Figure 20.14

Urban Growth and Urban Flight

■ *Suburbs were once unplanned, taking irregular shapes as people moved from the city in search of bucolic dreams. Some are still unplanned as population spills over from the city. Others, however, as this photo of Sun City, Arizona, a surburb of Phoenix, shows, are precisely planned even before the first resident moves in.*

■ The Rural Rebound

The United States is now undergoing a trend that is without precedent in its history. In the 1970s, people began to move from cities and suburbs to rural areas. During the 1990s, seven of every ten U.S. rural counties grew in population. The only losses occurred in the Great Plains and the Mississippi Delta (Johnson 1999). Little farming towns are making a comeback, their boarded-up stores and schools once again open for business and learning.

The "push" factors for this fundamental shift are fears of urban crime and violence. The "pull" factors are safety, lower cost of living, recreation, and more space. Facilitating this movement are improvements in transportation and communication. Interstate highways make airports—and the city itself—accessible from longer distances. With satellite communications, cell phones, fax machines, and the Internet, people can be connected with people in the city—and around the world—even though they live in what just a short time ago were remote areas.

Listen to the wife of a former student of mine describe why she and her husband moved to a rural area, three hours from the international airport that they fly out of each week:

> I work for a Canadian company. Paul works for a French company, with headquarters in Paris. He flies around the country doing computer consulting. I give motivational seminars to businesses. When we can, we drive to the airport together, but we often leave on different days. I try to go with my husband to Paris once a year.
>
> We almost always are home together on the weekends. We often arrange three- and four-day weekends, because I can plan seminars at home, and Paul does some of his consulting from here.
>
> Sometimes shopping is inconvenient, but we don't have to lock our car doors when we drive, and the new Wal-Mart superstore has most of what we need. E-commerce is a big part of it. I just type in www—whatever, and they ship it right to my door. I get make-up and books online. I even bought a part for my stove.
>
> Why do we live here? Look at the lake. It's beautiful. We enjoy boating and swimming. We love to walk in this park-like setting. We see deer and wild turkeys. We love the sunsets over the lake. (author's files)

She added, "I think we're ahead of the learning curve," referring to the idea that their lifestyle is a wave of the future.

■ The Potential of Urban Revitalization

Social policy usually takes one of two forms. The first is to tear down and rebuild—something that is fancifully termed **urban renewal**. The result is the renewal of an area—but *not* for the benefit of its inhabitants. Stadiums, high-rise condos, luxury hotels, and expensive shops replace run-down, cheap housing. Outpriced, the area's inhabitants are displaced into adjacent areas.

The second is some sort of **enterprise zone**, a designated area of the city that offers economic incentives, such as reduced taxes, to businesses that move into it. Although the intention is good, failure is usually the result. Most businesses refuse to locate in high-crime areas. Those that do pay a high price for security and losses from crime, which can run higher than the tax savings. If workers are hired from within the problem area, and the jobs pay a decent wage, which most do not, the workers move to better neighborhoods—which doesn't help the area (Lemann 1994). After all, who chooses to live with the fear of violence?

Although urban renewal and enterprise zones have failed to solve the problems facing U.S. cities, a "nothing works" mentality will solve nothing. U.S. cities can be revitalized and made into safe and decent places to live. There is nothing in the nature of cities that turns them into dangerous, deteriorating slums. Most European cities, for example, are both safe and pleasant. If U.S. cities are to change, they need to become top agenda items of the U.S. government. Adequate resources in terms of money and human talents must be focused on overcoming urban woes.

urban renewal
the rehabilitation of a rundown area, which usually results in the displacement of the poor who are living in that area

enterprise zone
the use of economic incentives in a designated area with the intention of encouraging investment there

■ *Like the phoenix, luxury hotels and apartments, along with exclusive restaurants and shops, have arisen from the ashes of urban decay.* Urban renewal, *a benefit for the privileged, displaces the poor, often shoving them into adjacent areas every bit as deprived as those in which they previously lived.*

Given the deplorable condition of many U.S. cities and the flight of the middle classes—both whites and minorities—to greener pastures, an *urban Manhattan Project* seems in order. During World War II, the United States and the Allies faced a triumphant Hitler in Europe and a victorious Tojo in Asia. The United States gathered its top scientific minds and challenged them to produce the atomic bomb. "Manhattan Project" was the code name for that effort. It involved 37 installations across the country, at least 37 university laboratories, and more than 100,000 people, including several Nobel prize-winning physicists. Today, similar resources may be required to triumph over urban ills.

Sociologist William Flanagan (1990) suggests three guiding principles for working out the solutions to our pressing urban problems:

Scale. Regional and national planning is necessary. Local jurisdictions, with their many rivalries, competing goals, and limited resources, tend to implement a hodgepodge of mostly unworkable solutions. A positive example of regional planning is Portland, Oregon, where a regional government prohibits urban sprawl and ensures a greenbelt.

Livability. Cities must be appealing and meet human needs, especially the need of community we discussed earlier. This will attract the middle classes into the city and increase its tax base. In turn, this will help finance the services that make the city more livable.

Social justice. In the final analysis, social policy must be evaluated by how it affects people. "Urban renewal" programs that displace the poor for the benefit of the middle class and wealthy do not pass this standard. The same would apply to solutions that create "livability" for select groups but neglect the poor and the homeless.

Unless we address the *root* causes of urban problems—poverty, housing, education, and jobs—any solutions we come up with will be, at best, only Band-Aids that cover up problems. Such fixes will be window dressings for politicians who want to *appear* as though they are doing something constructive about the problems that affect our quality of life.

■ ▢ ■ ▢

Summary and Review

A Planet with No Space for Enjoying Life?

■ **What debate did Thomas Malthus initiate?**

In 1798, Thomas Malthus analyzed the surge in Europe's population. His conclusion, called the **Malthus theorem,** was that because the population grows geometrically but the food supply increases only arithmetically, the world's population will outstrip its food supply. The debate between today's New Malthusians and those who disagree, the Anti-Malthusians, continues. Pp. 598–602.

■ **Why are people starving?**

Starvation is not due to a lack of food in the world, for there is now more food for each person in the entire world than there was fifty years ago. Starvation, rather, is due to a maldistribution of food, which is primarily due to drought and civil war. Pp. 602–603.

Population Growth

■ **Why do the poor nations have so many children?**

In the Least Industrialized Nations, children often are viewed as gifts from God, they cost little to rear, they contribute to the family income at an early age, and they represent the parents' social security. Consequently, people are motivated to have large families. Pp. 603–606.

■ **What are the three demographic variables?**

To compute population growth, demographers use *fertility, mortality,* and *migration.* The **basic demographic equation** is births minus deaths plus net migration equals growth rate. Pp. 606–609.

■ **Why is forecasting population difficult?**

A nation's growth rate is affected by unanticipated variables—from economic cycles, wars, and famines to industrialization and government policies. Pp. 609–611.

Urbanization

■ **What is the relationship of cities to farming and the Industrial Revolution?**

Cities can develop only if there is a large agricultural surplus, which frees people from food production. The primary impetus to the development of cities was the invention of the plow about five or six thousand years ago. Almost without exception, throughout history, cities have been small. After the Industrial Revolution

stimulated rapid transportation and communication, cities grew quickly and became much larger. Today **urbanization** is so extensive that some cities have become **metropolises,** dominating the area adjacent to them. The areas of influence of some metropolises have merged, forming a **megalopolis.** Pp. 611–618.

Models of Urban Growth

■ **What models of urban growth have been proposed?**

The primary models are concentric zone, sector, multiple-nuclei, and peripheral. These models fail to account for medieval cities, many European cities, and those in the Least Industrialized Nations. Pp. 618–621.

City Life: Alienation and Community

■ **Is the city inherently alienating?**

Although some people experience **alienation** in the city, others find **community** in it. Five types of people who live in cities are cosmopolites, singles, ethnic villagers, the deprived, and the trapped. Pp. 621–625.

Urban Problems and Social Policy

■ **Why have U.S. cities declined?**

Three primary reasons for their decline are **suburbanization** (as people moved to the suburbs, the tax base of cities eroded and services deteriorated), **disinvestment** (banks withdrawing their financing), and **deindustrialization** (which caused a loss of jobs). Pp. 626–627.

■ **What is the rural rebound?**

As people flee cities and suburbs, the population of most U.S. rural counties is growing. This is a fundamental departure from a trend that had been in place for a couple of hundred years. P. 628.

■ **What social policy can salvage U.S. cities?**

A Manhattan Project on Urban Problems could likely produce workable solutions. Three guiding principles for developing urban social policy are scale, livability, and social justice. Pp. 628–629.

■ *Where can I read more on this topic?*

Suggested Readings for this chapter are at the back of this book.

Additional Online Resources for This Chapter
www.ablongman.com/henslin6e

- *Content Select* Research Database for Sociology, with suggested key terms and annotated references
- Link to 2000 Census, with activities
- Flashcards of key terms and concepts

- Practice Tests
- Weblinks
- Interactive Maps

using . . .
ContentSelect

Research Database for Sociology

city life	infanticide	suburbanization	zero population
gentrification	mortality	urbanization	growth
ghetto	rural		

21

COLLECTIVE BEHAVIOR

Early Explanations:
The Transformation
of the Individual

Charles Mackay, Gustave
LeBon, and Robert Park:
How the Crowd Transforms
the Individual

Herbert Blumer:
The Acting Crowd

The Contemporary View:
The Rationality of the
Crowd

Richard Berk: The Minimax
Strategy

Ralph Turner and
Lewis Killian:

Emergent Norms

Forms of Collective
Behavior

Riots

Panics

Moral Panics

Rumors

Fads and Fashions

Urban Legends

SOCIAL MOVEMENTS

Types and Tactics of
Social Movements

Types of Social Movements

Tactics of Social
Movements

Propaganda and the
Mass Media

Why People Join Social
Movements

Mass Society Theory

Deprivation Theory

Moral Issues and
Ideological Commitment

A Special Case: The Agent
Provocateur

On the Success and
Failure of Social
Movements

The Stages of Social
Movements

The Rocky Road to Success

Summary and Review

Collective Behavior and Social Movements

he news spread like wildfire. A police officer had been killed. In just twenty minutes, the white population was armed and heading for the cabin. Men and mere boys, some not more than 12 years old, carried rifles, shotguns, and pistols.

> One of the men poured oil over him. Another lit a match.

The mob, now about four hundred, surrounded the log cabin. Tying a rope around the man's neck, they dragged him to the center of town. While the men argued about the best way to kill him, the women and children shouted their advice—some to hang him, others to burn him alive.

Someone pulled a large wooden box out of a store and placed it in the center of the street. Others filled it with straw. Then they lifted the man, the rope still around his neck, and shoved him head first into the box. One of the men poured oil over him. Another lit a match.

As the flames shot upward, the man managed to lift himself out of the box, his body a mass of flames. Trying to shield his face and eyes from the fire, he ran the length of the rope, about twenty feet, when someone yelled, "Shoot!" In an instant, dozens of shots rang out. Men and boys walked to the lifeless body and emptied their guns into it.

They dragged the man's body back to the burning box, then piled on more boxes from the stores, and poured oil over them. Each time someone threw more oil onto the flames, the crowd roared shouts of approval.

Standing about seventy-five feet away, I could smell the poor man's burning flesh. No one tried to hide their identity. I could clearly see town officials help in the burning. The inquest, dutifully held by the coroner, concluded that the man met death "at the hands of an enraged mob unknown to the jury." What else could he conclude? Any jury from this town would include men who had participated in the man's death.

They dug a little hole at the edge of the street, and dumped in it the man's ashes and what was left of his body.

The man's name was Sam Pettie, known by everybody to be quiet and inoffensive. I can't mention my name. If I did, I would be committing suicide.

(Based on a May 1914 letter to *The Crisis*)

collective behavior
extraordinary activities carried out by groups of people; includes lynchings, rumors, panics, urban legends, and fads and fashions

■ *U.S. race relations have gone through many stages, some of them very tense. They sometimes have exploded into violence, as with the lynchings in the 1920s and 1930s. This gruesome photo was taken July 15, 1935, in Lowndes County, Mississippi. The victims, Dooley Morton and Bert Moore, were accused of the attempted rape of a white woman.*

COLLECTIVE BEHAVIOR

Why did the people in this little town "go mad"? These men—and the women who watched in agreement—were ordinary, law-abiding citizens. Even some of the "pillars of the community" joined in the vicious killing of Sam Pettie, who may have been innocent.

Lynching is a form of **collective behavior,** actions by a group of people who bypass the usual norms governing their behavior and do something unusual (Turner and Killian 1987; Lofland 1993). Collective behavior is a broad term. It includes not only such violent acts as lynchings and riots, but also panics, rumors, fads, and fashions. Before examining its specific forms, let's look at theories that seek to explain collective behavior.

Early Explanations: The Transformation of the Individual

When people can't figure something out, they often resort to using "madness" as an explanation. People may say, "She went 'off her rocker'—that's why she drove her car off the bridge." "He must have 'gone nuts,' or he wouldn't have shot into the crowd." Early explanations of collective behavior were tied in to such assumptions. Let's look at how these ideas developed.

■ Charles Mackay, Gustave LeBon, and Robert Park: How the Crowd Transforms the Individual

The field of collective behavior began when Charles Mackay (1814–1889), a British journalist, noticed that "country folks," who ordinarily are reasonable sorts of people, sometimes "went mad" and did "disgraceful and violent things" when they formed a crowd. The best explanation Mackay (1852) could come up with was that people had a "herd mentality"—they were like a herd of cows that suddenly stampede.

About fifty years later, Gustave LeBon (1841–1931), a French psychologist, built on this initial idea. In an 1895 book, LeBon stressed how people feel anonymous in crowds, less accountable for what they do. Some even develop feelings of invincibility and come to think that they can do virtually anything. A **collective mind** develops, he said, and people are swept up by almost any suggestion. Then contagion, something like mass hypnosis, takes over, releasing the destructive instincts that society had so carefully repressed.

Robert Park (1864–1944), a U.S. sociologist who studied in Germany and wrote a 1904 dissertation on the crowd, was influenced by LeBon (McPhail 1991). After Park joined the faculty at the University of Chicago, he added the ideas of social unrest and circular reaction. He said,

> Social unrest . . . is transmitted from one individual to another . . . so that the manifestations of discontent in A [are] communicated to B, and from B reflected back to A. (Park and Burgess 1921)

Park used the term **circular reaction** to refer to this back-and-forth communication. Circular reaction, he said, creates a "collective impulse" that comes to "dominate all members of the crowd." If "collective impulse" sounds just like LeBon's "collective mind," that's because it really is. As noted, Park was influenced by LeBon, and his slightly different term did not change the basic idea at all.

collective mind
Gustave LeBon's term for the tendency of people in a crowd to feel, think, and act in extraordinary ways

circular reaction
Robert Park's term for a back-and-forth communication between the members of a crowd whereby a "collective impulse" is transmitted

■ Herbert Blumer: The Acting Crowd

Herbert Blumer (1900–1987), who studied under Park, synthesized LeBon's and Park's ideas. As you can see from Figure 21.1, Blumer (1939) identified five stages that precede what he called an **acting crowd,** an excited group that moves toward a

Figure 21.1

Blumer's Model of How an Acting Crowd Develops
Source: Based on McPhail 1991:11.

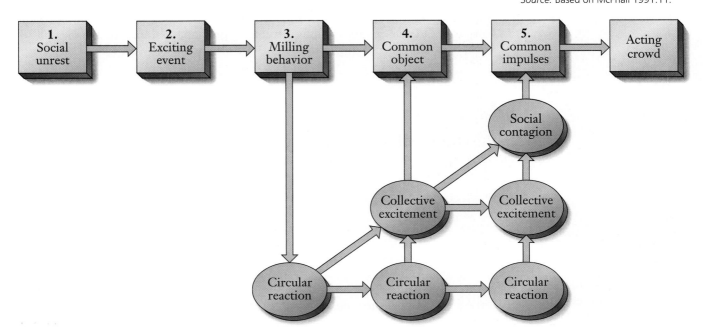

goal. This model still dominates today's police manuals on crowd behavior (McPhail 1989). Let's apply it to the lynching of Sam Pettie.

1. *Tension or unrest.* At the root of collective behavior is a background condition of tension or unrest. Disturbed about some condition of society, people are apprehensive. This makes them vulnerable to rumors and suggestions. Sam Pettie was lynched during the early 1900s. At this time, traditional southern life was in upheaval. Due to industrialization, millions of Americans were moving from farm to city in search of jobs, and from South to North. Left behind were many poor, rural southerners, white and black, who faced a bleak future. In addition, African Americans were questioning the legitimacy of their low status and deprivation.

2. *Exciting event.* An exciting event occurs, one so startling that people become preoccupied with it. In this instance, that event was the killing of a police officer.

3. *Milling.* Next comes **milling,** people standing or walking around, talking about the exciting event. A circular reaction then sets in. As people pick up cues as to the "right" way of thinking and feeling, they reinforce them in one another. During the short period in which Sam Pettie's lynch mob milled, the white residents of this small town became increasingly agitated as they discussed the officer's death.

4. *A common object of attention.* In this stage, people's attention becomes riveted on some aspect of the event. They get caught up in the collective excitement. In this case, people's attention turned to Sam Pettie. Someone may have said that he had been talking to the officer or that they had been arguing.

5. *Common impulses.* A sense of collective agreement about what should be done emerges. These common impulses are stimulated by *social contagion,* a sense of excitement that is passed from one person to another. In this instance, people concluded that only an immediate, public death of the killer would be adequate vengeance—as well as a powerful warning for other African Americans who might even think about getting "out of line."

Acting crowds aren't always negative or destructive, as this one was. Some involve spontaneous demonstrations directed against oppression. Nor are they all serious, for students engaging in food fights are also acting crowds.

■ ■ ■ ■ ■

The Contemporary View: The Rationality of the Crowd

I f we were to see a lynching—or a screaming mob or a prison riot—most of us might agree with LeBon that some sort of "madness" had swept over the crowd. Sociologists today, however, point out that beneath this chaotic surface, crowds are actually quite rational (Yamaguchi 2000). They point out that crowds take deliberate steps to reach some goal. As sociologist Clark McPhail (1991) says, even a lynch mob is cooperative—someone gets the rope while others hold the victim, some tie the knot, and others hoist the body. This is exactly what you saw in Pettie's execution—the men working together: the rope, the boxes, the straw, and the oil.

acting crowd
Herbert Blumer's term for an excited group that collectively moves toward a goal

milling
a crowd standing or walking around as they talk excitedly about some event

◼ Richard Berk: The Minimax Strategy

A general principle of human behavior is that we try to minimize our costs and maximize our rewards. Sociologist Richard Berk (1974) called this a **minimax strategy.** The fewer costs and the more rewards we anticipate from something, the more likely we are to do it. For example, if we believe that others will approve an act, the likelihood increases that we will do it. Whether yelling for the referee's blood after a bad call in a football game, or shouting for real blood as a member of a lynch mob, this principle applies. In short, whether people are playing cards with a few friends or are part of a mob, the principles of human behavior remain the same.

◼ Ralph Turner and Lewis Killian: Emergent Norms

Since collective behavior is unusual behavior, however, could it also involve unusual norms? Sociologists Ralph Turner and Lewis Killian (1987) use the term **emergent norms** to express this idea. They point out that life usually goes much as we expect, and our usual norms are adequate. If some unusual event disrupts our usual ways of doing things, however, our ordinary norms may not cover the new situation. People then may develop *new* norms to deal with the new situation. Sometimes they even produce new definitions of right and wrong that *under the new circumstances* justify actions that they would otherwise consider wrong.

To understand how new norms emerge, we need to keep in mind that not everyone in a crowd shares the same point of view (Snow et al. 1993; Rodríguez

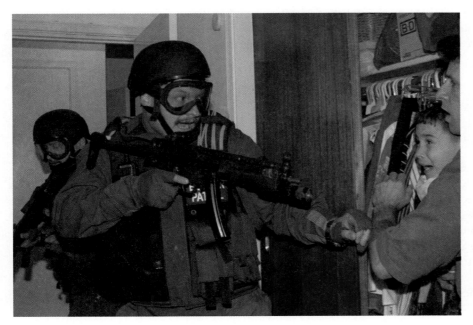

■ *Elián Gonzalez, whose mother died as she fled from Cuba, became a political pawn. Staunch anti-Castro members of the Cuban exile community garnered publicity and rallied anti-Castro supporters, while Castro held his own rallies in Cuba. Invectives flew in both directions—all, supposedly, for "the boy's sake." Elián's uncle's home in the Little Havana section of Miami became a center of protest. The home was surrounded by crowds day and night, even at 5 A.M., when agents of the Immigration and Naturalization Service seized Elián at gunpoint.*

minimax strategy
Richard Berk's term for the effort people make to minimize their costs and maximize their rewards

emergent norms
Ralph Turner's and Lewis Killian's term for the development of new norms to cope with a new situation, especially among crowds

1994). As Turner and Killian (1987) point out, there are at least five kinds of crowd participants:

1. The *ego-involved* feel a personal stake in the unusual event.

2. The *concerned* also have a personal interest in the event, but less so than the ego-involved.

3. The *insecure* care little about the matter, but they join the crowd because it gives them a sense of power, security, or feeling of belonging.

4. The *curious spectators* also care little about the issue, but they are inquisitive about what is going on.

5. The *exploiters* don't care about the event, but they use it for their own purposes, such as hawking food or T-shirts. For them, a rock concert would serve just as well.

You can see how these participants would have different points of view—and how their contrasting attitudes, emotions, and motives would help to set the crowd on a particular course of action. The most important role goes to the "ego-involved." Some of them make suggestions about what should be done; others simply take action. As the "concerned" join in, they, too, influence the crowd. If things get heated up, the "insecure" and the "curious spectators" may also join in. Although the "exploiters" are unlikely to participate, they do lend the crowd passive support. A common mood completes the stage for new norms to emerge: Activities that are "not OK" in everyday life now may seem "OK"—whether they involve throwing bottles at the cops or shouting obscenities at the college president.

This analysis of emergent norms helps us see that collective behavior is *rational*. The crowd, for example, does not consider all suggestions made by the ego-involved to be equal: To be acceptable, suggestions must match predispositions that the crowd already has. This analysis, then, is a far cry from earlier interpretations that people were so transformed by a crowd that they went out of their minds.

Forms of Collective Behavior

Sociologists analyze collective behavior the same way they do other forms of behavior (Turner and Killian 1987; Lofland 1993; Turner 1993). They view collective behavior as the actions of ordinary people who are responding to extraordinary situations (Rodríguez 1994). They ask their usual questions about interaction, such as, How do people influence one another? What is the significance of the participants' age, gender, race-ethnicity, and social class? What were their preexisting attitudes? How did they perceive the situation? How did their perceptions get translated into action?

In addition to lynchings, collective behavior includes riots, panics, moral panics, rumors, fads, fashions, and urban legends. Let's look at each.

Riots

The nation watched in horror. White Los Angeles police officers had been caught on videotape beating an African American traffic violator with their nightsticks. The videotape showed the officers savagely bringing their nightsticks down on a man prostrate at their feet. Television stations around the United States—and the world—broadcast the pictures to stunned audiences.

When the officers went on trial for beating the man identified as Rodney King, how could the verdict be anything but guilty? Yet a jury consisting of eleven whites and one Asian American found the officers innocent of using excessive force. The result was a **riot**—violent crowd behavior aimed against people and property. Within minutes of the verdict, angry crowds began to gather in Los Angeles. That night, mobs set fire to businesses, and looting and arson began in earnest. The rioting spread to other cities, including Atlanta, Tampa, Las Vegas, and even Madison, Wisconsin. Whites and Koreans were favorite targets of violence.

Americans sat transfixed before their television sets as they saw parts of Los Angeles go up in flames and looters carrying television sets and lugging sofas in full view of the Los Angeles Police Department, which took no steps to stop them. Seared into the public's collective consciousness was the sight of Reginald Denny, a 36-year-old white truck driver who had been yanked from his truck. As he sat dazed in the street, Damian Williams, laughing, broke Denny's skull with a piece of concrete.

On the third night, after 4,000 fires had been set and more than 30 people killed, President George Bush announced on national television that the U.S. Justice Department had appointed prosecutors to pursue federal charges against the police officers. The president stated that he had ordered the Seventh Infantry, SWAT teams, and the FBI into Los Angeles. He also federalized the California National Guard and placed it under the command of Gen. Colin Powell, the chairman of the Joint Chiefs of Staff. Rodney King went on television and tearfully pleaded for peace.

The Los Angeles riot was the bloodiest since the Civil War. Before it was over, 54 people lost their lives, 2,328 people were treated in hospital emergency rooms, thousands of businesses were burned, and about $1 billion of property was destroyed. Two of the police officers were later sentenced to 2 years in prison on federal charges, and King was awarded several million dollars in damages. (Rose 1992; Stevens and Lubman 1992; Holden and Rose 1993; Cannon 1998)

The *background conditions* of urban riots are frustration and anger brought on by feelings of deprivation. Frustration and anger simmer in people who are kept out of mainstream society—limited to a meager education and denied jobs and justice. Then a *precipitating event* brings those pent-up feelings to a boiling point, and they erupt in collective violence. All these conditions existed in the Los Angeles riot, with the jury's verdict being the precipitating event.

Sociologists have found that it is not only the deprived who participate in riots. After the assassination of Dr. Martin Luther King, Jr., in 1968, when many U.S. cities erupted in riots, even people with good jobs participated (McPhail 1991). In the L.A. riots, the first outbursts didn't come from the poorest neighborhoods but from the most stable neighborhoods. Why would middle-class people participate in riots? The answer, says sociologist Victor Rodríguez (1994), is the same: frustration and anger. Even though they are gainfully employed and living stable lives, middle-class minorities resent being treated as second-class citizens.

The event that precipitates a riot is less important than the riot's general context. The precipitating event is only the match that lights the fuel. The fuel is the background of tension and unrest—feelings that there is no justice, or that officials condone or encourage unfairness. Beneath what may seem a placid surface lies seething rage. To erupt, it takes but a match, such as the Rodney King verdict. Because these feelings are felt not only by the poor but also by those who are materially better off, both groups become involved. Also participating in the riots are opportunists—people who feel neither rage at their general condition nor outrage at the precipitating event. The riot simply provides an opportunity for looting.

The photo essay on the next two pages illustrates an unusual event. On the day that Timothy McVeigh, the Oklahoma bomber, was to be executed, the authorities anticipated a riot between groups that favored and opposed the execution. They even thought some underground militia were planning to storm the prison where McVeigh was held. I found this irresistible, and I decided that I had to be there to see it first hand.

riot
violent crowd behavior aimed against people and property

The Riot That Never Was

The Execution of Timothy McVeigh

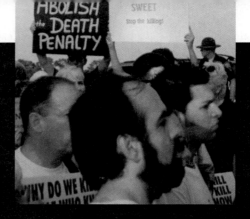

There is so much sociology to do, and so little time to do it! Some events seem irresistible, however.

The execution of Timothy McVeigh, the Oklahoma bomber who claimed more victims than any single individual in U.S. history, was one such event. The media highlighted the possibility of protests and riots at this first federal execution in 38 years. I knew that I could never get inside the prison to do research. Yet, there would be all those public activities, so readily accessible.

When I arrived in Terre Haute, Indiana, I found that the city had been turned into an armed camp. The federal, state, and local authorities had prepared for an attack on the prison, and who knows what else. The local police had been trained in riot control. The state had sent in its Emergency Management Agency. And the federal government had been active, too. Military sharpshooters were present, ready to act in case any group tried to prevent the execution.

The anti-execution people showed up in full force. As you can see from these photos, so few pro-execution protesters appeared that I was able to interview them all.

Here is a pictorial report on "the riot that never was."

Sequestered on one side of town, in a small park, were the pro-execution demonstrators. As is evident from this photo, they were not a large, organized group. These demonstrators had simply used a marking pen to print messages on cardboard,

The pro-execution demonstrators placed their focus on the victims. Some told me that a lethal injection was too good for McVeigh, that he should be made to suffer before he died. The demonstrators in this photo are expressing their feelings that McVeigh's death is not adequate payment for 168 victims.

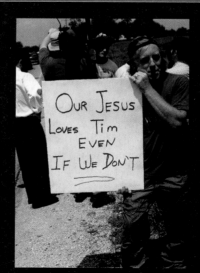

Demonstrators also gathered outside the prison where McVeigh was to be executed. They were kept on the opposite side of the road, where they were constantly scrutinized by armed personnel on the prison side of the road. I was told that inside the prison were hundreds of armed troops—in case anyone tried to rescue McVeigh or otherwise interfere with his execution.

Notice that some of the demonstrators expressed a religious orientation.

Demonstrators often use attention-getting devices. This individual carried a cross to the federal prison. He said that he was convinced that God wanted him to be at the scene. His attention-getting device was effective, as you can see from the individual who is interviewing him.

The anti-execution demonstrators expressed mixed motives for their position. These two, isolated from the organized anti-execution crowd—both physically and in their point of view—were not against the death penalty. They felt that McVeigh should not be executed because he had been railroaded by the government in an unfair trial. For them, McVeigh had become a type of folk hero.

The anti-execution demonstrators displayed professionally made signs that they take from one protest site to another. They were hosted by a local Roman Catholic church. After a rally there, they marched as a group to the prison where the execution took place.

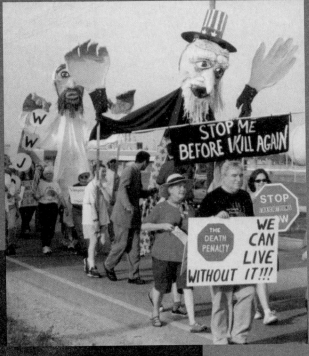

The anti-execution demonstrators—anti-death penalty to the extreme— were so well organized that they sent busloads of people to protest McVeigh's execution.

The huge puppets of the anti-execution demonstrators were an effective attention-getting device. If you look closely, you can see media reporters interviewing the demonstrators.

Panics

> In 1938, on the night before Halloween, a radio program of dance music was interrupted by a report that explosions had been observed on the surface of Mars. The announcer breathlessly added that a cylinder of unknown origin had been discovered embedded in the ground on a farm in New Jersey. The radio station then switched to the farm, where a breathless reporter gave details of horrible-looking Martians coming out of the cylinder. Their death-ray weapons had destructive powers unknown to humans. An astronomer then confirmed that Martians had invaded the Earth.

Perhaps six million Americans heard this broadcast. About one million were frightened by it. Thousands panicked, grabbed their weapons, and hid in their basements or ran into the streets. Hundreds bundled up their families and jumped into their cars, jamming the roads as they headed to who knows where.

Of course, there was no invasion. This was simply a dramatization of H. G. Wells' *War of the Worlds*, starring Orson Welles. There had been an announcement at the beginning of the program and somewhere in the middle that the account was fictional, but apparently many people missed it. Although the panic reactions to this radio program may appear humorous to us, to anyone who is in a panic, the situation is far from humorous. **Panic** occurs when people become so fearful that they cannot function normally, and may even flee.

Why did people panic in this instance? Psychologist Hadley Cantril (1941) attributed the reaction to widespread anxiety about world conditions. The Nazis were marching in Europe, and millions of Americans (correctly, as it turned out) were afraid that the United States would get involved. War jitters, he said, created fertile ground for the broadcast to touch off a panic.

Contemporary analysts, however, question whether there even was a panic. Sociologist William Bainbridge (1989) acknowledges that some people did become frightened, and that a few actually did get in their cars and drive like maniacs. But he says that most of this famous panic was an invention of the news media. Reporters found a good story, and they milked it, exaggerating as they went along.

Bainbridge points to a 1973 event in Sweden. To dramatize the dangers of atomic power, Swedish Radio broadcast a play about an accident at a nuclear power plant. Knowing about the 1938 broadcast in the United States, Swedish sociologists were waiting to see what would happen. Might some people fail to realize that it was a dramatization and panic at the threat of ruptured reactors spewing out radioactivity? The sociologists found no panic. A few people did become frightened. Some telephoned family members and the police; others shut windows to keep out the radioactivity—reasonable responses, considering what they thought had occurred.

The Swedish media, however, reported a panic! Apparently, a reporter had telephoned two police departments and learned that each had received calls from concerned citizens. With a deadline hanging over his head, the reporter decided to gamble. He reported that police and fire stations were jammed with citizens, that people were flocking to the shelters, and that others were fleeing south (Bainbridge 1989).

Panics do occur, of course.

> On December 31, 1999, a rumor spread through Bissau, the capital of Guinea-Bissau, that the "black death" was going to hit at midnight, when the world entered the new millennium. Bissau's 250,000 residents fled ("Fears of . . . " 2000).

panic
the condition of being so fearful that one cannot function normally, and may even flee

Nobody has the right to shout "Fire!" in a public building when no such danger exists. If people fear immediate death, they will lunge toward the nearest exit in a frantic effort to escape. Such a panic occurred on Memorial Day weekend in 1977 at the Beverly Hills Supper Club in Southgate, Kentucky.

About half of the Club's 2,500 patrons were crowded into the Cabaret Room. A fire, which began in a small banquet room near the front of the building, burned undetected until it was beyond control. When employees discovered the fire, they warned patrons. People began to exit in orderly fashion, but when flames rushed in, they trampled one another in a furious attempt to reach the exits. The exits were blocked by masses of screaming people trying to push their way through all at once. The writhing bodies at the exits created further panic among the remainder, who pushed even harder to force their way through the bottlenecks. One hundred sixty-five people died. All but two were within thirty feet of two exits in the Cabaret Room.

Sociologists who studied this panic found what other researchers have discovered in analyzing other disasters. *Not everyone panics.* In disturbances, many people continue to act responsibly. Especially important are primary group bonds. Parents help their children, for example (Morrow 1995). Gender roles also persist, and more men help women than women help men (Johnson 1993). Even work roles continue to guide some behavior. Sociologists Drue Johnston and Norris Johnson (1989) found that only 29 percent of the employees of the Beverly Hills Supper Club left when they learned of the fire. As noted in Table 21.1, most of the workers helped customers, fought the fire, or searched for friends and relatives.

Sociologists use the term **role extension** to describe the actions of most of these employees. By this, they mean that the workers incorporated other activities into their occupational roles. For example, servers extended their role to include helping people to safety. How do we know that giving help was an extension of the occupational role, not simply a general act of helping? Johnston and Johnson found that servers who were away from their assigned stations returned to them in order to help *their* customers. For a fascinating and related type of collective behavior, see the Down-to-Earth Sociology box on the next page.

TABLE 21.1

Employees' First Action After Learning of the Fire

Action	Percentage
Left	29%
Helped others to leave	41%
Fought or reported the fire	17%
Continued routine activities	7%
Other (e.g., looked for a friend or relative)	5%

Note: These figures are based on interviews with 95 of the 160 employees present at the time of the fire: 48 males and 47 females, ranging in age from 15 to 59.

Source: Based on Johnston and Johnson 1989.

■ *Natural disasters often provide examples of collective behavior. A primary finding of disaster research is that people act rationally. Emergency personnel remain on the job. Others first check on the safety of their loved ones, then organize to overcome the effects of the disaster. Although this woman in Georgia is dazed as she stares at what remains of her home, she likely will participate in neighborhood and community-wide efforts to recover from the tornado.*

role extension
the incorporation of additional activities into a role

Mass Hysteria

Let's look at five events.

Several hundred years ago, a strange thing happened near Naples, Italy. When people were bitten by tarantulas, not only did they feel breathless and have fast-beating hearts, but also they felt unusual sexual urges. As though that weren't enough, they also felt an irresistible urge to dance—and to keep dancing to the point of exhaustion.

The disease was contagious. Even people who hadn't been bitten came down with the same symptoms. The situation got so bad that whole villages would dance in a frenzy instead of gathering the summer harvest.

A lot of remedies were tried, but nothing seemed to work except music. Bands of musicians traveled from village to village, providing relief to the victims of *tarantism by* playing special "tarantula" music (Bynum 2001).

• • •

In the year 2001, in New Delhi, the capital of India, a "monkey-man" stalked people who were sleeping on rooftops during the blistering summer heat. He clawed and bit a hundred victims. Fear struck the capital. People would wake up screaming that the monkey-man was after them. To escape this phantom, some people jumped off two-story buildings. One man was killed when he jumped off the roof of his house during one of the monkey-man's many attacks ("'Monkey' . . ." 2001).

There was, of course, no ape-like killer.

• • •

At the United Arab Emirates University in Al-Ain, twenty-three female students rushed to the hospital emergency room after escaping from a fire in their dormitory. As you might expect, they were screaming, weeping, shaking, and fainting (Amin et al. 1997).

There was no fire. A student had been burning incense in her room, a normal event in that culture. The fumes of the burning incense had been mistaken for the smell of a fire.

• • •

People across France and Belgium became sick from drinking Coca-Cola. A quick investigation was held, and the experts diagnosed the problem as "bad carbon dioxide and a fungicide." Coke recalled 15 million cases of its soft drink ("Coke . . ." 1999).

Later investigations revealed that there was nothing wrong with the drink.

• • •

In McMinville, Tennessee, a teacher smelled a "funny odor." Students and teachers began complaining of headaches, nausea, and a shortness of breath. The school was evacuated, and doctors treated more than 100 people at the local hospital. Authorities found nothing.

A few days later, a second wave of illness struck. This time, the Tennessee Department of Health closed the high school down for two weeks. They dug holes in the foundation and walls and

ran snake cameras through the ventilation and heating ducts. They even tested the victims' blood (Adams 2000).

Nothing unusual was found.

• • •

"It's all in their heads," we might say. In one sense, we would be right. There was no external, objective cause of the illnesses from tarantism or Coca-Cola. There was no "monkey-man," no fire, nor any chemical contaminant at the school.

In another sense, however, we would be wrong to say that it is "all in their heads." The symptoms these people experienced were real. They had real headaches and stomach aches. They did vomit and faint. And they did experience unusual sexual urges and the desire to dance until they could no longer stand.

There is no explanation for **mass hysteria**—an imagined threat that causes physical symptoms among a large group of people—except suggestibility. Experts might use fancy words to try to explain mass hysteria, but once you cut through their terms, you find that they are really simply saying, "It happens."

Perhaps one day we will know more about the causes of mass hysteria, but for now we have to be content with not knowing the specifics. We do know that such events occur in many cultures. This would indicate that mass hysteria follows basic principles of human behavior. Someday, we will understand these principles.

▪ ▪ ▪ ▪ ▪

In some life-threatening situations in which we might expect panic, we find, instead, that a sense of order prevails. This seems to be the case during the attack on the World Trade Center when, at peril to their own lives, people helped injured friends and even strangers escape down many floors. These people, it would seem, were highly socialized into the collective good, and had a highly developed sense of empathy.

▪ Moral Panics

Moral panics occur when large numbers of people become concerned, even fearful, about some behavior that they believe threatens morality, and when the fear is out of proportion to any supposed danger (Cauthen and Jasper 1994; Goode and Ben-Yehuda 1994; Jenkins 1998; Jenness 2001). The threat is perceived as enormous, and hostility builds toward those deemed responsible. The most famous moral panic was

mass hysteria
an imagined threat that causes physical symptoms among a large number of people

moral panic
a fear that grips large numbers of people that some evil group or behavior threatens the well-being of society, followed by intense hostility, sometimes violence, toward those thought responsible

the fear of witches in Europe between 1400 and 1650. It resulted in the Inquisition—investigations, torture, and burning at the stake of people accused of witchcraft.

We still have moral panics today. They are fueled by the mass media. During the 1980s, the fear that children were being sexually abused in day care centers spread across the United States. The media reported bizarre rituals with devil worshippers and naked priests and weird sex. The situation grew so bad that almost every day care worker became suspect in someone's eyes. Only fearfully did parents leave their children in day care centers. Although sexual abuse at day care centers has occurred, despite intensive investigation, the stories of children subjected to bizarre sexual rituals were never substantiated.

Like other panics, moral panics center around a sense of danger. The supposed thousands of U.S. children who are snatched by strangers from playgrounds, city streets, and their own backyards are part of a moral panic. Parents are fearful, and others are perplexed, at how U.S. society could have gone to hell in a handbasket. This moral panic is destined to meet the same fate as others. The fear and hysteria will subside, and people will feel less danger as they drop children off at school or let them play outside. The actual number of stranger kidnappings in the United States per year is between 200 and 300 (Bromely 1991).

Moral panics are fed by **rumor,** information for which there is no discernible source and which is usually unfounded. In the 1990s, a rumor swept the country that some of these supposedly thousands of missing children were being sold to Satanists who abused them sexually and then ritually murdered them. This rumor was fueled by people who claimed to have been involved in such sacrifices. The police investigated, but uncovered no evidence to substantiate the rumors.

Moral panics thrive on uncertainty and anxiety. Changes in the nature of the family give rise to a great deal of anxiety. Concerns that children are receiving inadequate care because so many mothers have joined the work force have become linked with thoughts that dangers to children are lurking almost everywhere.

■ Rumors

In *Aladdin,* the handsome young title character murmurs, "All good children, take off your clothes." In *The Lion King,* Simba, the cuddly lion star, stirs up a cloud of dust that, floating off the screen, spells S-E-X. Then there is the bishop in *The Little Mermaid,* who, presiding over a wedding, becomes noticeably aroused.

Ann Runge, a mother of eight who owned stacks of animated Disney films, said she felt betrayed when she heard that the Magic Kingdom was sending obscene, subliminal messages. "I felt as though I had entrusted my kids to pedophiles," she said. (Bannon 1995)

Thriving on conditions of ambiguity, rumors function to fill in missing information (Turner 1964; Shibutani 1966; Noymer 2001). In response to the rumor, Disney reported that Aladdin really says "Scat, good tiger, take off and go." The line is hard to understand, however, leaving enough ambiguity for others to hear what they want to hear, and even to insist that the line is an invitation to a teenage orgy. Similar ambiguity remains with Simba's dust and the aroused bishop.

Most rumors are short-lived. They arise in a situation of ambiguity, only to dissipate when they are replaced by factual information—or by another rumor. Occasionally, however, a rumor has a long life.

In the eighteenth and nineteenth centuries, for no known reason, healthy people would grow weak and slowly waste away. No one understood the cause and people said they had *consumption* (now

rumor
unfounded information spread among people

■ Rumors *have swirled around the Magic Kingdom's supposed plots to undermine the morality of youth. Could Mickey Mouse be a dark force, and these children his victims? As humorous as this may be, some have taken these rumors seriously.*

called tuberculosis). People were terrified as they saw their loved ones wither into shells of their former selves. With no one knowing when the disease would strike, or who its next victim would be, the rumor began that some of the dead had turned into vampire-like beings. At night, they were coming back from the grave and draining the life out of the living. The evidence was irrefutable—loved ones who wasted away before people's very eyes.

To kill these ghoulish "undead," people began to sneak into graveyards. They would dig up a grave, remove the leg bones and place them on the skeleton's chest, then lay the skull at the feet, forming a skull and crossbones. Having thus killed the "undead," they would rebury the remains. These rumors and the resulting mutilations of the dead continued off and on in New England until the 1890s (Associated Press, November 30, 1993).

Why do people believe rumors? Three main factors have been identified. Rumors deal with a subject that is important to an individual, and they replace ambiguity with some form of certainty. They also are attributed to a credible source. An office rumor may be preceded by "Jane has it on good authority that . . . " or "Bill overheard the boss say that . . . "

Ambiguity or uncertainty help give life to rumors. Surrounded by unexplained illnesses and deaths, the New Englanders speculated about why people wasted away. Their rather bizarre conclusions gave them certainty in the face of bewildering events. The uncertainty that sparked the Disney rumor may have been feelings among some that the moral fabric of modern society is decaying. If one believes this, perhaps it is not too far a stretch to believe that a conspiracy may underlie the decay. Perhaps even the Magic Kingdom . . .

■ Fads and Fashions

A **fad** is a novel form of behavior that briefly catches people's attention. The new behavior appears suddenly and spreads by imitation and identification with people who are already involved in the fad. Reports by the mass media help to spread the fad. After a short life, the fad fades into oblivion, although it may reappear from time to time (Aguirre et al. 1993).

Fads come in many forms. Even the administrators of businesses, colleges, and universities get caught up in them. For about ten years, quality circles were a fad, supposedly the best way to get workers and management to cooperate and to develop innovative techniques to increase production. This administrative fad peaked in 1983, then quickly dropped from sight (Strang and Macy 2001). Fads affect child rearing—permissive versus directive, spanking versus non-spanking. Our food is also subject to fads: tofu, power drinks, and organic this and that. Fads in diets also come and go, with so many people seeking the perfect one, and practically all leaving the fad diet disillusioned.

Some fads are like a mist, very short-lived. "Streaking" (running naked in a public place) lasted only a couple of months in 1974. Some fads involve millions of people but still die out quickly. In the 1950s, the Hula Hoop was so popular that stores couldn't keep them in stock. Children cried and pleaded for these brightly colored plastic hoops. Across the nation, children—and even adults—held contests to see who could keep the hoops up the longest or who could rotate the most hoops at one time. Then, in a matter of months it was over, and parents wondered what to do with these items, which seemed useless for any other purpose.

When a fad lasts, it is called a **fashion.** Some fashions, as with clothing and furniture, are the result of a coordinated international marketing system that includes designers, manufacturers, advertisers, and retailers. By manipulating the tastes of the public, they sell billions of dollars of products. Fashion, however, also refers to hairstyles, and

fad
a temporary pattern of behavior that catches people's attention

fashion
a pattern of behavior that catches people's attention and lasts longer than a fad

■ Fads *are one of the fascinating aspects of social life that sociologists study. Body piercing, whose origins reach back into antiquity, has become popular in the Western world. It is unlikely, however, that body piercing will enter the mainstream culture. Certainly its extremes won't.*

even to the design and colors of buildings. Sociologist John Lofland (1985) pointed out that fashion also applies to language, as demonstrated by these roughly comparable terms: "Neat!" in the 1950s, "Right on!" in the 1960s, "Really!" in the 1970s, "Awesome!" in the 1980s, "Bad!" in the 1990s, "Sweet" in the early 2000s, and, recurringly, "Cool."

■ Urban Legends

Did you hear about Katie and Paul? They were parked at Regatta Bay, listening to the radio, when the music was interrupted by an announcement that a rapist-killer had escaped from prison. Instead of a right hand, he had a hook. Katie said they should leave, but Paul laughed and said there wasn't any reason to go. When they heard a strange noise, Paul agreed to take her home. When Katie opened the door, she heard something clink. It was a hook hanging on the door handle!

For decades, some version of "The Hook" has circulated among Americans. It has appeared as a "genuine" letter in "Dear Abby," and some of my students heard it in grade school. **Urban legends** are stories with an ironic twist that sound realistic but are false. Although untrue, they usually are told by people who believe that they happened.

Here is a newer one:

A horrible thing happened. This girl in St. Louis kept smelling something bad. The smell wouldn't leave even when she took showers. She finally went to the doctor, and it turned out that her insides were rotting. She had gone to the tanning salon too many times, and her insides were cooked.

The Internet is helping to spread urban legends at a quick pace. I received this note from an acquaintance on the Net:

This is very scary and is not a joke. It definitely is a serious threat to our lives and health. This is an alert about a virus in the original sense of the word—one that affects your body—not your hard drive. There have been 23 confirmed cases of people attacked by the Klingeman Virus, a virus that arrives in your real mailbox, not in your e-mail inbox.

Someone has been mailing large blue envelopes seemingly at random, to people in the U.S. and Canada. On the front of the envelope in bold black letters is printed "A Gift For You From The Klingeman Foundation." When the envelopes are opened, there is a small sponge sealed in plastic. This sponge carries what has come to be known as the Klingeman Virus and public health officials state this is a strain of virus they have not previously encountered.

Those who have come in contact with the Klingeman Virus have been hospitalized with severe dysentery. So far seven of the twenty-three victims have died. There is no legitimate Klingeman Foundation mailing unsolicited gifts.

If you receive an oversized blue envelope in the mail marked "A Gift For You From The Klingeman Foundation," do not open it!!! Place it in a strong plastic bag or container and call the police immediately. The "gift" is one you definitely do not want to open.

PLEASE PASS THIS ON TO EVERYONE THAT YOU CARE ABOUT.

Folklorist Jan Brunvand (1981, 1984, 1986, 1999) reports that urban legends are passed on by people who often think that the event happened just one or two people down the line of transmission, sometimes to a "friend of a friend." The stories have strong appeal and gain credibility from naming specific people or events. Note the details of where Katie and Paul were, or the details about the warning on the envelope. Brunvand views urban legends as "modern morality stories"; each one teaches a moral lesson about life.

If we apply Brunvand's analysis to these three urban legends, several major points emerge. First, these stories serve as warnings. "The Hook" warns young people that they should be careful about where they go, with whom they go, and what they do when they get there. The tanning salon story warns people about new technology. The "Klingeman Virus" contains a different moral: Do you *really* know what is in

urban legend
a story with an ironic twist that sounds realistic but is false

your mail? We live in an uncertain world, terrorists lurk about, and most of us watched the news as the real anthrax scare unfolded.

Second, each story is related to social change: "The Hook" to changing sexual morality, the tanning salon to changing technology, and the "Klingeman Virus" to changing threats of disease, even to changes in international relationships, especially in the Middle East. Third, each is calculated to instill fear: We should all be afraid, for dangers abound. They lurk in the dark countryside, at the tanning salon, and even inside our mail.

These principles can be applied to an urban legend that made the rounds in the late 1980s. I heard several versions of this one; each narrator swore that it had just happened to a friend of a friend.

> Jerry (or whoever) went to a nightclub last weekend. He met a good-looking woman, and they hit it off. They spent the night in a motel. When he got up the next morning, the woman was gone. When he went into the bathroom, he saw a message scrawled on the mirror in lipstick: "Welcome to the wonderful world of AIDS."

SOCIAL MOVEMENTS

When the Nazis, a small group of malcontents in Bavaria, first appeared on the scene in the 1920s, the world found their ideas laughable. This small group believed that the Germans were a race of supermen (*Übermenschen*) and that they would launch a Third Reich (reign or nation) that would control the world for a thousand years. Their race destined them for greatness; lesser races were meant for their service and exploitation.

The Nazis started as a little band of comic characters who looked as though they had stepped out of a grade B movie (see the photo on page 345.) From this inauspicious start, the Nazis gained such power that they threatened the existence of Western civilization. How could a little man with a grotesque moustache, surrounded by a few sycophants in brown shirts, ever come to threaten the world? Such things don't happen in real life—only in novels or movies. They are the deranged nightmare of some imaginative author. Only this was real life. The Nazis' appearance on the human scene caused the deaths of millions of people and changed the course of world history.

social movement
a large group of people who are organized to promote or resist social change

proactive social movement
a social movement that promotes some social change

reactive social movement
a social movement that resists some social change

Social movements, the second major topic of this chapter, hold the answer to Hitler's rise to power. **Social movements** consist of large numbers of people who organize to promote or resist social change. Members of social movements hold strong ideas about what is wrong with the world—or some part of it—and how to make things right. Examples include the abolitionist (anti-slavery) crusade, the civil rights movement, the white supremacist movement, the women's movement, the animal rights movement, the nuclear freeze movement, and the environmental movement.

At the heart of social movements lies a sense of injustice (Klandermans 1997). Some find a particular condition of society intolerable, and their goal is to *promote* social change. Theirs is called a **proactive social movement.** Others, in contrast, feel threatened because some condition of society is changing, and they organize to *resist* that change. Theirs is a **reactive social movement.**

To further their goals, people develop **social movement organizations.** Those whose goal is to promote social change develop such organizations as the National Association for the Advancement of Colored People (NAACP). In contrast, those who are trying to resist these particular changes form the Ku Klux Klan. To recruit followers and publicize their grievances, leaders of social movements use attention-getting devices, from marches and protest rallies to sit-ins and boycotts. Some stage "media events," sometimes quite effectively, such as the one featured in the Cultural Diversity box below.

Social movements are like a rolling sea, observes sociologist Mayer Zald (1992). During one period, few social movements may appear, but shortly afterward, a wave of them rolls in, each competing for the public's attention. Zald suggests that a *cultural crisis* can give birth to a wave of social movements. By this, he means that there are times when a society's institutions fail to keep up with social change. Then when many people's needs go unfulfilled, massive unrest follows, and social movements spring into action to bridge this gap.

social movement organization
an organization developed to further the goals of a social movement

cultural diversity

—————— in the United States

The Million-Man March:
Another Step in an Unfinished Social Movement

The civil rights movement of the 1950s and 1960s brought huge gains: integrated public facilities, schools, voting booths, housing, and workplaces. Or, rather, the movement affirmed that all Americans have the *right* to such aspects of social life, for many of the gains have been elusive, somehow disappearing just when they seemed on the verge of being realized. The inner city, with all of its ills, from unemployment to violent crime, has become the single most powerful symbol indicating that this social movement is unfinished.

The Million-Man March—which consisted of several hundred thousand African American men and boys from all over the country who gathered on the Mall in Washington, D.C., in the fall of 1995—picked up where this movement stalled. It had two essential features. The first was directed outward: protest at continued obstacles; insistence that the walls of racism come down; voter registration drives; a sense of optimism and determination that good can be accomplished. This first feature is a direct reflection of the old civil rights movement.

The second feature, an inward turning, is a redirecting of the civil rights movement. It is a conservative, proactive stance by African Americans who want to make changes in the African American community. As the organizers of the march stressed, this feature underscores the need to build greater respect between men and women, to reduce spouse abuse, and to assume the obligations of fatherhood—including marriage, nurturing and supporting one's children, and giving them a positive role model of responsible masculinity (Whetstone 1996).

This desire for inward change that is to be manifested in personal relationships reflects the religious orientation of the march's organizers. The emphases are on repentance, atonement, and changed behavior. Although the civil rights movement has always had a religious orientation—a dedication to religious principles motivated by moral outrage over grievous wrongs—this focus on inner change is new.

The Million-Man March did not begin with a march to Washington, nor did it end with the departure of the buses.

There may be other marches, but the specifics are not what is relevant. The march is but one facet of an ongoing social movement, a movement destined to stay with us, for grievances remain and goals have been only partially reached.

for your consideration

What are these marches intended to accomplish? What do you think they accomplish? What other techniques might be more effective? What symbols did the organizers use? What messages are these marches intended to communicate? Who are the intended audiences? Look at Figure 21.2 on page 650; is this an alternative, redemptive, reformative, or transformative social movement? Look at Figure 21.3 on page 651; identify the three memberships and three publics involved in these demonstrations.

■ ■ ■ ■ ■

Types and Tactics of Social Movements

L et's see what types of social movements there are and then examine their tactics.

Types of Social Movements

alterative social movement
a social movement that seeks to alter only particular aspects of people

redemptive social movement
a social movement that seeks to change people totally

reformative social movement
a social movement that seeks to change only particular aspects of society

transformative social movement
a social movement that seeks to change society totally

millenarian movement
a social movement based on the prophecy of coming social upheaval

cargo cult
a social movement in which South Pacific islanders destroyed their possessions in the anticipation that their ancestors would send items by ship

Since social change is their goal, we can classify social movements according to their *target* and the *amount of change* they seek. Figure 21.2 summarizes the classification developed by sociologist David Aberle (1966). If you read across, you will see that the target of the first two types of social movements is *individuals*. **Alterative social movements** seek only to *alter* some specific behavior. An example is the Women's Christian Temperance Union, a powerful social movement of the early 1900s. Its goal was to get people to stop drinking alcohol. Its members were convinced that if they could shut down the saloons such problems as poverty and wife abuse would go away. **Redemptive social movements** also target individuals, but here the aim is for *total* change. An example is a religious social movement that stresses conversion. In fundamentalist Christianity, for example, when someone converts to Christ, the entire person is supposed to change, not just some specific behavior. Self-centered acts are to be replaced by loving behaviors toward others as the convert becomes, in their terms, a "new creation."

The target of the next two types of social movements is *society*. **Reformative social movements** seek to *reform* some specific aspect of society. The environmental movement, for example, seeks to reform the ways society treats the environment, from its disposal of garbage and nuclear wastes to its use of land and water. **Transformative social movements,** in contrast, seek to *transform* the social order itself. Its members want to replace it with their version of the good society. Revolutions, such as those in the American colonies, France, Russia, and Cuba, are examples.

One of the more interesting examples of transformative social movements is **millenarian movements,** which are based on prophecies of coming calamity. Of particular interest is a type of millenarian movement called a **cargo cult** (Worsley 1957).

About one hundred years ago, Europeans colonized the Melanesian Islands of the South Pacific. Ships from the home countries of the colonizers arrived one after another, each loaded with items the Melanesians had never seen. As the Melanesians watched the cargo being unloaded, they expected some of it to go to them. Instead, it all went to the Europeans. Melanesian prophets then revealed the secret of this exotic merchandise. Their own ancestors were manufacturing and sending the cargos to them, but the colonists were intercepting the merchandise. Since the colonists were too strong to fight, and too selfish to share the cargo, there was little the Melanesians could do.

Then came a remarkable self-fulfilling prophecy. Melanesian prophets revealed that if the people would destroy their crops and food and build harbors, their ancestors would see their sincerity and send the cargo directly to them. The Melanesians did so. When the colonial administrators of the island saw that the natives had destroyed their crops and were just sitting in the hills waiting for the cargo ships to arrive, they informed the home government. The prospect of

F igure 21.2

Types of Social Movements

Sources: The first four types are from Aberle 1966; the last two are from the author.

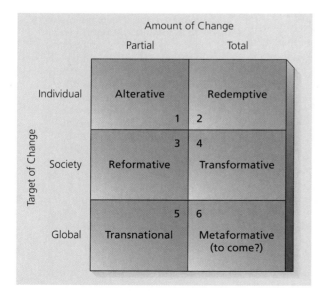

thousands of islanders patiently starving to death was too horrifying to allow. The British government fulfilled the prophecy by sending ships to the islands with cargo earmarked for the Melanesians.

As Figure 21.2 indicates, some social movements have developed a global orientation. As with many aspects of life today, numerous issues that bother people know no national boundaries. Participants of **transnational social movements** (also called *new social movements*) have a goal to change some condition not just in their society, but throughout the world. These social movements often center on improving the quality of life (Melucci 1989). Examples are the women's movement, labor movement, environmental movement, and animal rights movement (McAdam et al. 1988; Smith et al. 1997).

As you can see from Figure 21.2, transnational social movements still focus on some particular condition, even though that condition is global. Cell number 6 in Figure 21.2 is empty. Such metaformative social movements have not yet appeared on the world scene. If they do, the goal will be to change the entire social order around the world. This could lead to a reformulation of race, class, gender, and government. Since this Cell is logical, but nothing yet fits into it, we may be peering into the future. If this type of social movement does appear, it could be one that ushers in a New World Order.

■ Social movements *involve large numbers of people who, upset about some condition in society, organize to do something about it. Shown here is Carrie Nation, a temperance leader who in 1900 began to break up saloons with a hatchet. Her social movement eventually became so popular that it resulted in Prohibition.*

■ Tactics of Social Movements

The leaders of a social movement can choose from a variety of tactics. Should they peacefully boycott, march, or hold an all-night candlelight vigil? Or should they bomb a building, burn down a research lab, or assassinate a key figure? To understand why the leaders of social movements choose their tactics, we need to examine a group's levels of membership, the publics it addresses, and its relationship to authorities.

Levels of Membership Figure 21.3 shows the composition of social movements. Beginning at the center and moving outward are three levels of membership. At the center is the inner core, those most committed to the movement. The inner core sets the group's goals, timetables, and strategies. People at the second level are also committed to the movement, but somewhat less so than the inner core. They can be counted on to show up for demonstrations and to do the grunt work—help with mailings, pass out petitions and leaflets, make telephone calls. The third level consists

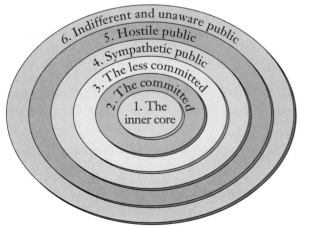

Figure 21.3

The Membership and Publics of Social Movements

6. Indifferent and unaware public
5. Hostile public
4. Sympathetic public
3. The less committed
2. The committed
1. The inner core

transnational social movement
social movements with a new emphasis on some condition in the world, instead of on a condition in a specific country; also known as *new social movements*

▪ *Activists in social movements become committed to "the cause." The social movement around abortion, currently one of the most dynamic in the United States, has split Americans, is highly visible, and has articulate spokespeople on both sides.*

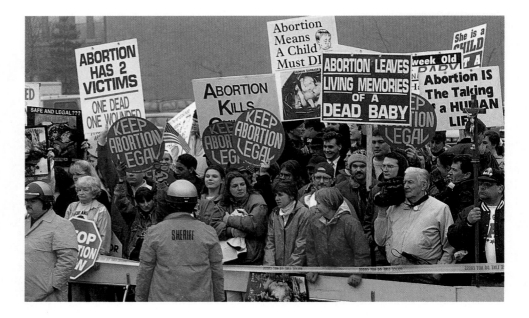

of a wider circle of people who are less committed and less dependable. Their participation depends on convenience—if an activity doesn't interfere with something else they want to do, they participate.

The tactics chosen largely depend on the predispositions and backgrounds of the inner core. Because of their differing backgrounds, some members of the inner core may be predisposed to use peaceful means. Others may be more confrontational, while still others prefer violence. Tactics also depend on the number of committed members. Different tactics are called for depending on whether the inner core can count on seven hundred—or only seven—committed members to show up.

The Publics   Outside the group's membership is the **public,** a dispersed group of people who may have an interest in the issue. As you can see from Figure 21.3 on page 651, there are three types of publics. Just outside the third circle of members, and blending into it, is the sympathetic public. Although their sympathies lie with the movement, these people have no commitment to it. Their sympathies with the movement's goals, however, make them fertile ground for recruitment. The second public is hostile. The movement's values go against its own, and it wants to stop the social movement. The third public consists of disinterested people. They are either unaware of the social movement or, if aware, indifferent to it.

In selecting tactics, the leadership pays attention to these publics. The sympathetic public is especially significant, because it is the source of new members and support at the ballot box. Leaders avoid tactics that they think might alienate the sympathetic public. They look for methods that will create even more sympathy from this group. To make themselves appear a victim—a group whose rights are being trampled on—leaders may even force a confrontation with the hostile public. Tactics directed toward the indifferent or unaware public are designed to neutralize their indifference and increase their awareness.

public
a dispersed group of people who usually have an interest in the issue on which a social movement focuses; the sympathetic and hostile publics have such an interest, but a third public is either unaware of the issue or indifferent to it

Relationship to Authorities   In determining tactics, the movement's relationship to authorities is also significant. This is especially so when it comes to choosing between peaceful and violent tactics. If a social movement is *institutionalized,* accepted by authorities, violence will not be directed against the authorities, for they are on the movement's side. This, however, does not rule out violence directed against the opposition. If authorities are hostile to a social movement, aggressive or even violent tactics may be directed against them. For example, because the goal of a transformative (revolutionary) social movement is to replace the government, the movement and the government are clearly on a collision course.

■ Although the road to the globalization of captialism appears to be a paved highway that leads to an inevitable destination, it does not come without some bumps. Shown here is part of the organized protest against the World Trade Organization when they met in Seattle, Washington in 1999. After these protests, the WTO beefed up the security at its annual meetings, placing a buffer of thousands of riot police between itself and protesters.

Other Factors   Sociologist Ellen Scott (1993), who studied the movement to stop rape, discovered that friendship, race-ethnicity, and even size of town are important in determining tactics. Women in Santa Cruz, California, chose to directly confront accused rapists, to publicly humiliate them. In a town of 41,000, the tactic worked. In Washington, D.C., women rejected confrontation as ineffective because of the anonymity that comes with a city of 640,000. Another factor was race. Both groups of women were white, but in Santa Cruz, it was white women confronting white men, while in Washington, D.C., it would have been white women confronting black men.

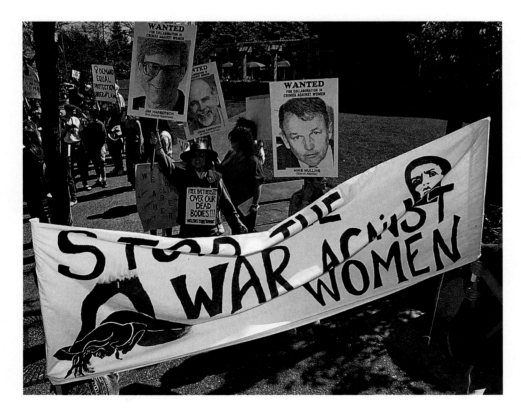

■ The social movement to stop violence against women has had a major impact on our thinking about gender relations, laws, and law enforcement. Discussed in the text are social factors that underlie the choice of tactics used by women's centers. Shown here are the Purple Berets in Santa Rosa, California, who are protesting against county officials for wanting to treat spouse abuse with counseling instead of in the courts.

Friendships were also important. Public confrontations require a closely working team of people who will back each other up. In Santa Cruz, the women had lived together for years, while the group in Washington, D.C., was a more formal organization.

No matter how carefully the leaders choose their tactics, they may backfire. Women from the Santa Cruz center hung pictures of a man accused of rape all around town. He sued. The long litigation that followed sapped the women's energy, and the Santa Cruz center folded.

■ Propaganda and the Mass Media

The leaders of social movements try to manipulate the mass media in order to influence **public opinion,** how people think about some issue. The right kind of publicity enables them to arouse the sympathetic public and to lay the groundwork for recruiting more members. Pictures of bloodied, dead baby seals, for example, go a long way toward getting a group's message across.

A key to understanding social movements, then, is **propaganda.** Although this word often evokes negative images, it actually is a neutral term. Propaganda is simply the presentation of information in the attempt to influence people. Its original meaning was positive. *Propaganda* referred to a committee of cardinals of the Roman Catholic church whose assignment was the care of foreign missions. (They were to *propagate* the faith.) The term has traveled a long way since then, however, and today it usually refers to a one-sided presentation of information that distorts reality.

Propaganda, in the sense of organized attempts to influence public opinion, is a regular part of everyday life. Advertisements, for example, are a form of propaganda, for they present a one-sided version of reality. Underlying effective propaganda are seven basic techniques, discussed in the Down-to-Earth Sociology box on the next page. Perhaps by understanding these techniques, you will be able to resist one-sided appeals—whether they come from social movements or from hawkers of jeans, running shoes, or perfumes.

public opinion
how people think about some issue

propaganda
in its broad sense, the presentation of information in the attempt to influence people; in its narrow sense, one-sided information used to try to influence people

■ *The use of* propaganda *is popular among those committed to the goals of a social movement. They can see only one side to the social issue about which they are so upset. Do you think there is another side to this social issue?*

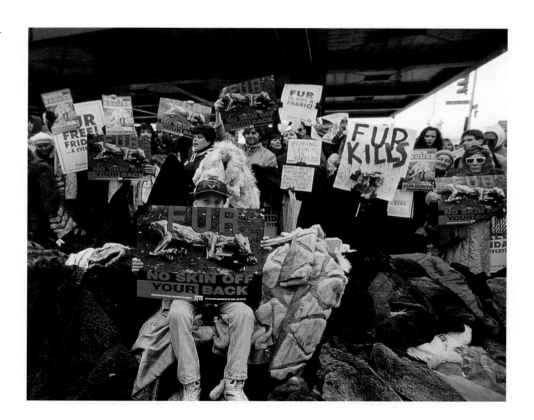

"Tricks of the Trade"—The Fine Art of Propaganda

Sociologists Alfred and Elizabeth Lee (1939) found that propaganda relies on seven basic techniques, which they termed "tricks of the trade." To be effective, the techniques should be subtle, with the audience unaware that their minds and emotions are being manipulated. If propaganda is effective, people will not know *why* they support something, but they'll fervently defend it.

- *Name calling.* This technique aims to arouse opposition to the competing product, candidate, or policy by associating it with a negative image. By comparison, one's own product, candidate, or policy is attractive. Political candidates who call an opponent "soft on crime" or "insensitive to the poor" are using this technique.

- *Glittering generality.* Essentially the opposite of the first technique, this one surrounds the product, candidate, or policy with images that arouse positive feelings. "She's a real Democrat" has little meaning, but it makes the audience feel that something substantive has been said. "He stands for individualism" is so general that it is meaningless, yet the audience thinks that it has heard a specific message about the candidate.

- *Transfer.* In its positive form, this technique associates the product, candidate, or policy with something the public

respects or approves. You might not be able to get by with saying "Coors is patriotic," but surround a beer with images of the country's flag, and beer drinkers will get the idea that it is more patriotic to drink this brand of beer than to drink any other kind. In its negative form, this technique associates the product, candidate, or policy with something the public disapproves.

- *Testimonials.* Famous individuals endorse a product, candidate, or policy. Michael Jordan lends his name to cologne, Nike products, and even underwear, while Britney Spears espouses the merits of Pepsi. Candidates for political office solicit the endorsement of movie stars who may know next to nothing about the candidate or even about politics. In the negative form of this technique, a despised person is associated with the competing product. If propagandists (called "spin doctors" in politics) could get by with it, they would show Saddam Hussein or Osama bin Laden announcing support for an opposing candidate.

- *Plain folks.* Sometimes it pays to associate the product, candidate, or policy with "just plain folks." "If Mary or John Q. Public likes it, you will, too." A political candidate who kisses babies, puts on a hard

hat, and has lunch at McDonald's while photographers "catch him (or her) in the act" is using the "plain folks" strategy. "I'm just a regular person" is the message of the presidential candidate who poses for photographers in jeans and work shirt—while making certain that the chauffeur-driven Mercedes does not show up in the background.

- *Card stacking.* The aim of this technique is to present only positive information about what you support, and only negative information about what you oppose. The intent is to make it sound as though there is only one conclusion a rational person can draw. Falsehoods, distortions, and illogical statements are often used.

- *Bandwagon.* "Everyone is doing it" is the idea behind this technique. Emphasizing how many others buy the product or support the candidate or policy conveys the message that anyone who doesn't join in is on the wrong track.

The Lees (1939) added, "Once we know that a speaker or writer is using one of these propaganda devices in an attempt to convince us of an idea, we can separate the device from the idea and see what the idea amounts to on its own merits."

The mass media play such a crucial role that we can say they are the gatekeepers to social movements. If those who control and work in the mass media—from owners to reporters—are sympathetic to some particular "cause," you can be sure that it will receive sympathetic treatment. If the social movement goes against their own views, it will be ignored or will receive unfavorable treatment. If you ever get the impression that the media are trying to manipulate your opinions and attitudes—even your feelings—on some particular issue or social movement, you probably are right. Far from doing unbiased reporting, the media are under the control and influence of people who have an agenda to get across. To the materials in the Down-to-Earth

Sociology box on propaganda, then, we need to add the biases of the media establishment—the issues it chooses to give publicity, those it chooses to ignore, and its favorable and unfavorable treatment of issues and movements.

Sociology can be a liberating discipline (Berger 1963/2001). Sociology sensitizes us to *multiple realities;* that is, for any single point of view on some topic, there are competing points of view. Each represents reality as people see it, but their different experiences lead them to different perceptions. Consequently, different people find each point of view equally as compelling. Although the committed members of a social movement are sincere—and perhaps even make sacrifices for "the cause"—theirs is but one view of the world. If other sides were presented, the issue would look quite different.

Why People Join Social Movements

As we have seen, social movements are fed by a sense of injustice. They stem from widespread, deeply felt discontent, the conviction that some condition of society is no longer tolerable. However, not everyone who feels dissatisfied with an issue joins a social movement. Why some, and not others? Sociologists have suggested several explanations. One consistent finding is that recruitment generally follows channels of social networks. That is, people most commonly join a social movement because they have friends and acquaintances already in it (McCarthy and Wolfson 1992; Snow et al. 1993). Some explanations are contradictory. For example, some sociologists suggest that social movements attract people with lower self-esteem, while others suggest that people with higher self-esteem are more likely to join them (Stryker et al. 2000). We don't yet have the answer to self-identity and participation in social movements.

Let's look at three explanations.

Mass Society Theory

To explain why people are attracted to social movements, sociologist William Kornhauser (1959) proposed **mass society theory.** Kornhauser argued that **mass society**—an impersonal, industrialized, highly bureaucratized society—makes many people feel isolated. Social movements fill this void by offering a sense of belonging. In areas where social ties are supposedly weaker, such as the western United States, one would expect to find more social movements than in areas where ties are supposedly stronger, such as in the Midwest and South.

This theory seems to match commonsense observations. Certainly, social movements proliferate on the West Coast. But when sociologist Doug McAdam (1988) interviewed people who had risked their lives in the civil rights movement, he found that these people were firmly rooted in families and communities. Their strong desire to right wrongs and to overcome injustices, not their isolation, had motivated their participation. Even the Nazis attracted many people who were firmly rooted in their communities (Oberschall 1973). Finally, those most isolated of all, the homeless, generally do not join anything—except food lines.

Deprivation Theory

A second explanation to account for why people join social movements is *deprivation theory.* According to this theory, people who feel deprived—whether it be of money, justice, status, or privilege—join social movements with the hope of redressing their grievances. This theory may seem so obvious as to need no evidence.

mass society theory
an explanation for why people participate in a social movement based on the assumption that the movement offers them a sense of belonging

mass society
industrialized, highly bureaucratized, impersonal society

Don't the thousands of African Americans who participated in the civil rights movement of the 1950s and the World War I soldiers who marched on Washington after Congress refused to pay their promised bonuses provide ample evidence that the theory is true?

Deprivation theory does provide a starting point. But there is more to the matter than this. Almost 150 years ago, Alexis de Tocqueville (1856/1955) made a telling observation. The peasants of Germany and the peasants of France both were living under deprived conditions. According to deprivation theory, we would expect the German peasants to rebel and overthrow their king. Revolution, however, occurred in France, not Germany. The reason, said de Tocqueville, is *relative* deprivation. The living conditions of the French peasants had been improving, and they could foresee even better circumstances ahead. German peasants, in contrast, had never experienced anything but depressed conditions, and they had no comparative basis for feeling deprived.

According to **relative deprivation theory,** then, it is not people's actual deprivation that matters. Rather, the key to participation in social movements is *relative* deprivation—what people *think* they should have relative to what others have, or relative to their own past or even their perceived future. Relative deprivation theory, which has provided insight into revolutions, holds a surprise. Because improving conditions fuel human desire for even better conditions, *improving* conditions can spark revolutions. As Figure 21.4 shows, this occurs when people's expectations outstrip the actual change they experience.

Relative deprivation also explains an interesting aspect of the civil rights movement. Relatively well-off African Americans—college students and church leaders—were at the center of the sit-ins, marches, and boycotts in the South during the 1950s and 1960s. They went to restaurants and lunch counters that were reserved for whites. When refused service, they sat peacefully while curses and food were heaped on them (Morris 1993). Why did they subject themselves to such treatment? Remember that according to relative deprivation theory, what is significant is not what we have or don't have, but with whom we compare ourselves. Compared with whites of similar status, the African American demonstrators saw themselves as deprived.

How about the white, middle-class college students and church leaders from the North? They, too, risked their lives when they joined the Southern protesters. They weren't comparing themselves with people whose situation was better than their own. Nor was their own personal welfare at stake. Relative deprivation theory doesn't help us here. We need to look at the *moral* reasons for their involvement (McAdam 1988; Fendrich and Lovoy 1993). Let's consider that motivation in social movements.

The growing gap between expectations and conditions

Rising expectations

Actual conditions

Time 1   Time 2

Figure 21.4

Relative Deprivation Theory

■ Moral Issues and Ideological Commitment

As sociologists James Jaspar and Dorothy Nelkin (1992) point out, we would miss the *basic* reason for many people's involvement in social movements if we overlooked the moral issue. Some people join because of *moral shock*—a sense of outrage at finding out what is "really" going on (Jaspar and Poulsen 1995). For people who see a social movement in moral terms, great issues hang in the balance. They feel they must choose sides and do what they can to make a difference. As sociologists put it, they join because of *ideological commitment* to the movement.

Many members on *both* sides of the abortion issue, for example, see their involvement in such terms. Similarly, activists in the animal rights movement are convinced that there can be no justification for making animals suffer in order to make safer products for humans. Activists in the peace movement, the environmental movement, and those who protest against global capitalism see nuclear weapons, pollution, and power in similar moral terms. It is for moral reasons that they risk

relative deprivation theory in this context, the belief that people join social movements based on their evaluations of what they think they should have compared with what others have

■ *Militias—citizens who arm themselves and form paramilitary organizations—have sprung up across the United States. Although all the theories discussed in the text may apply to members of these militias, those that deal with moral issues and ideological commitment are especially relevant. These two are members of the Michigan Militia, the country's largest militia.*

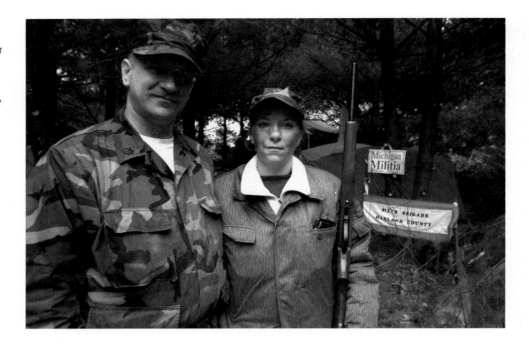

arrest and ridicule for their demonstrations. For them, to *not* act would be an inexcusable betrayal of future generations. The *moral* component of a social movement, then, is a primary reason for many people's involvement.

■ A Special Case: The Agent Provocateur

Agent provocateurs are a unique type of participant in social movements. These are agents of the government or even of the opposing sides of the social movement whose job is to spy on the leadership and perhaps to sabotage its activities. Some are recruited from the membership itself, people who are willing to betray their friends in the organization for a few Judas dollars. Others are police or members of a rival group who go underground and join the movement.

The radical social change advocated by some social movements poses a threat to the power elite. In such cases, the use of agent provocateurs is not surprising. What may be surprising, however, is that some agents convert to the social movement on which they are spying. Sociologist Gary Marx (1993) explains that to be credible, agents must share at least some of the class, age, gender, racial-ethnic, or religious characteristics of the group. This background makes the agents more likely to sympathize with the movement's goals and to become disenchanted with trying to harm the group. Also, to be effective, agents must work their way into the center of the group. This requires that they spend time with the group's committed members. A basic sociological principle is that the more we interact with people, the more we tend to like them. In addition, as these agents build trust, they often are cut off from their own group. The point of view they represent can start to recede, being replaced with concerns about betraying and deceiving people who now trust them as friends.

What also may be surprising is how far some agents go. During the 1960s, when a wave of militant social movements rolled across the United States, the FBI recruited agent provocateurs to sabotage groups. These agents provoked illegal activities that otherwise would not have occurred: They set the leadership up for arrest and, in some instances, set them up for death. Two examples will let us see how agent provocateurs operate (Marx 1993). One of the four men involved in a plot to blow up the

agent provocateur
someone who joins a group in order to spy on it and to sabotage it by provoking its members to commit illegal acts

Statue of Liberty by a group called the Black Liberation Front was an undercover agent. It was he who drew up the plans and even provided funds to pay for the dynamite and rent the car. In another instance, the FBI paid $36,500 to two members of the White Knights of the Ku Klux Klan to arrange for other Klansmen to bomb a Jewish businessman's home. A trap was set in which one Klansman was killed and another was arrested in the unsuccessful attempt.

IN SUM ■ ■ ■ ■

People most commonly join a social movement because they have friends and acquaintances already in it. Motivations are mixed. Some join because of moral convictions, others to further their own careers. Still others join because they find a valued identity, or even because it is fun. Some participate even though they *don't want to.* The Cuban government, for example, compels people to turn out for mass demonstrations to show support of the Communist regime (Aguirre 1993). As we just saw, police agents may join social movements in order to spy on them and sabotage their activities. In no social movement, then, is there a single cause for people joining. As in all other activities in life, people remain a complex bundle of motivations—and this provides a challenge for sociologists to unravel.

■ ■ ■ ■ ■

On the Success and Failure of Social Movements

Social movements have brought us extensive change. The women's movement, for example, has led to not only new legislation but also a different way of thinking about gender relations. Most social movements, however, are not successful. Let's look at the reasons for their success or failure.

■ The Stages of Social Movements

Sociologists have identified five stages in the growth and maturity of social movements (Lang and Lang 1961; Mauss 1975; Spector and Kitsuse 1977; Tilly 1978; Jaspar 1991). They are

1. *Initial unrest and agitation.* During this first stage, people are upset about some condition in society and want to change it. Leaders emerge who verbalize people's feelings and crystallize issues. Most social movements fail at this stage. Unable to gain enough support, after a brief flurry of activity, they quietly die.

2. *Resource mobilization.* A crucial factor that enables social movements to make it past the first stage is **resource mobilization.** By this term, sociologists mean the mobilization of resources—time, money, people's skills, and the ability to get the attention of the mass media. Technology and mailing lists are key resources: direct mailing, faxing, and e-mailing. In some cases, an indigenous leadership arises to mobilize resources. Other groups, lacking capable leadership, turn to "guns for hire," outside specialists who sell their services. As sociologists John McCarthy and Mayer Zald (1977; Zald and McCarthy 1987) point out, even though large numbers of people may be upset over some condition of society, without resource mobilization they are only upset people, perhaps even agitators, but they do not constitute a social movement.

resource mobilization
a theory that social movements succeed or fail based on their ability to mobilize resources such as time, money, and people's skills

3. *Organization.* A division of labor is set up. The leadership makes policy decisions, and the rank and file carry out the daily tasks necessary to keep the movement going. There is still much collective excitement about the issue, the movement's focal point of concern.

4. *Institutionalization.* At this stage, the movement has developed a bureaucracy, the type of formal hierarchy described in Chapter 7. Control lies in the hands of career officers, who may care more about their own position in the organization than the movement for which the organization's initial leaders made sacrifices. The collective excitement diminishes.

5. *Organizational decline and possible resurgence.* During this phase, managing the day-to-day affairs of the organization dominates the leadership. A change in public sentiment may even have occurred, and there may no longer be a group of committed people who share a common cause. The movement is likely to wither away.

■ The Rocky Road to Success

These stages, especially resource mobilization and institutionalization, help us understand why social movements seldom solve social problems. To mobilize resources, a movement must appeal to a broad constituency. This means that the group must focus on things that a lot of people are concerned about. For example, if workers at one particular plant are upset about their working conditions, their discontent is not adequate for recruiting the broad support necessary for a social movement. At best, it will result in local agitation. Unsafe working conditions of millions of workers, however, have a chance of becoming the focal point of a social movement.

Broad problems, however, are deeply embedded in society. This, of course, means that minor tinkering will never be adequate. Just as the problem touches many interrelated components of society, so the solutions must be all-encompassing. With no quick fix available, the social movement must stay around. But longevity brings its own danger of failure. As social movements become institutionalized, they tend to turn inward, to focus their energies on running the organization.

Many social movements, however, do vitally affect society. Some, such as the civil rights and the women's movement, become powerful forces for social change. They highlight problems and turn the society on a path that leads toward solutions. Others become powerful forces for resisting the social change that their members—and the public they are able to mobilize—consider undesirable. In either case, social movements are highly significant for contemporary society, and we can anticipate that new ones will be a regular feature of our social landscape.

As we saw, the fifth and final stage of social movement is decline. However, decline is not inevitable. More idealistic and committed leaders may emerge and reinvigorate the movement. Or, as in the case of abortion, conflict between groups on opposite sides of the issue may continuously invigorate each side and prevent the movement's decline. Let's close this chapter by contrasting the opposing groups in regard to abortion.

thinking
CRITICALLY

Which Side of the Barricades?
Prochoice and Prolife as a Social Movement

No issue so divides Americans as abortion. Although most Americans take a more moderate view, on one side are some who feel that abortion should be permitted under any circumstance, even during the last month of pregnancy. They are matched by some on the other side who are convinced that abortion should never be allowed for any circumstances, not even during the first month of pregnancy. This polarization constantly breathes new life into the movement.

When the U.S. Supreme Court made its 1973 decision, *Roe* v. *Wade,* that states could not restrict abortion, the prochoice side relaxed. Victory was theirs, and they thought their opponents would quietly disappear. Instead, large numbers of Americans were disturbed by what they saw as the legal right to murder unborn children.

The views of the two sides could not be more incompatible. Those who favor choice view the 1.4 million abortions performed annually in the United States as examples of women exercising their basic reproductive rights. Those who gather under the prolife banner see these acts as legalized murder. To the prochoice side, those who oppose abortion are blocking women's rights—they would force women to continue pregnancies they want to terminate. To the prolife side, those who advocate choice are seen as condoning murder—they would put their own desires for school, career, or convenience ahead of the lives of their unborn children.

There is no way to reconcile these contrary views. Each sees the other as unreasonable and extremist. And each uses propaganda by focusing on worst-case scenarios: prochoice images of young women raped at gunpoint, forced to bear the children of rapists; prolife images of women who are eight months pregnant killing their babies instead of nurturing them.

With no middle ground, these views remain in perpetual conflict. As each side fights for what it considers basic rights, it reinvigorates the other. When in 1989 the U.S. Supreme Court decided in *Webster* v. *Reproductive Services* that states could restrict abortion, one side mourned it as a defeat and the other hailed it as a victory. Seeing the political battle going against them, the prochoice side regrouped for a determined struggle. The prolife side, sensing judicial victory within its grasp, gathered forces for a push to complete the overthrow of *Roe* v. *Wade.*

This goal of the prolife side almost became reality in *Casey* v. *Planned Parenthood.* On June 30, 1992, in a 6-to-3 decision the Supreme Court upheld the right of states to require women to wait 24 hours between the confirmation of pregnancy and abortion, to require girls under 18 to obtain the consent of one parent, and to require that women be informed about alternatives to abortion and that they be given materials that describe the fetus. In the same case, by a 5-to-4 decision, the Court ruled that a wife does not have to inform her husband if she intends to have an abortion.

Because the two sides do not see the same reality, this social movement cannot end unless the vast majority of Americans commit to one side or the other. Otherwise, every legislative and judicial outcome—including the extremes of a constitutional amendment that declares abortion to be either murder or a woman's right—is a victory to one and a defeat to the other. To committed activists, then, no battle is ever complete. Rather, each action is only one small part of a hard-fought, bitter, moral struggle.

■ ■ ■ ■ ■

for your consideration . . .

Typically, the last stage of a social movement is decline. Why hasn't this social movement declined? Under what conditions will it decline?

The longer the duration of the pregnancy in question, the fewer the Americans who approve abortion. How do you feel about abortion during the second month versus the eighth month? Or partial-birth abortion? What do you think about abortion in cases of rape and incest? Can you identify some of the social reasons that underlie your opinions?

Sources: Neikirk and Elsasser 1992; McKenna 1995; Williams 1995; *Statistical Abstract* 1999:Table 124; Henslin 2000.

■ ■ ■ ■
Summary and Review

Early Explanations: The Transformation of the Individual

■ **How did early theorists explain how crowds affected people?**

Early theorists of **collective behavior** argued that crowds transform people. Charles Mackay used the term *herd mentality* to explain why people did wild things when they were in crowds. Gustave LeBon said that a **collective mind** develops, and people are swept away by suggestions. Robert Park said that collective unrest develops, which, fed by a **circular reaction**, leads to collective impulses. Pp. 634–635.

■ **What are the five stages of crowd behavior?**

Herbert Blumer identified five stages that crowds go through before they become an **acting crowd**: social unrest, an exciting event, **milling**, a common object of attention, and common impulses. Pp. 635–636.

The Contemporary View: The Rationality of the Crowd

■ **What is the current view of crowd behavior?**

Current theorists view crowds as rational. Richard Berk suggested a **minimax strategy**; that is, people try to minimize their costs and maximize their rewards, regardless of whether they are in crowds. In **emergent norm theory**, Ralph Turner and Lewis Killian analyze how new norms emerge that allow people to do things in crowds that they otherwise would not do. Pp. 636–638.

Forms of Collective Behavior

■ **What forms of collective behavior are there?**

Forms of collective behavior include **lynchings, riots, panics, moral panics, mass hysteria, rumors, fads, fashions,** and **urban legends.** Conditions of discontent or uncertainty provide fertile ground for collective behavior, and each form provides a way of dealing with these conditions. Pp. 638–648.

Types and Tactics of Social Movements

■ **What types of social movements are there?**

Social movements consist of large numbers of people who organize to promote or resist social change. Depending on their target (individuals or society) and the amount of social change desired (partial or complete), social movements can be classified as **alterative, redemptive, reformative, transformative,** and

transnational. A sixth type, **metaformative,** is logical, but it has not yet appeared. Pp. 648–651.

■ **How do social movement leaders select their tactics?**

Leaders choose tactics on the basis of a group's levels of membership, its **publics,** and its relationship to authorities. The three levels of membership are *the inner core, the committed,* and *the less committed.* The predispositions of the inner core are crucial in choosing tactics, but so is the public they wish to address. If relationships with authorities are bad, the chances of aggressive or violent tactics increase. Friendship, size of city, and the race-ethnicity of movement participants and their targets may also be significant. Pp. 651–654.

■ **How are the mass media related to social movements?**

The mass media are gatekeepers for social movements. Because the media's favorable or unfavorable coverage affects **public opinion,** leaders choose tactics with the media in mind. Social movements also make use of **propaganda** to further their causes. Pp. 654–656.

Why People Join Social Movements

■ **Why do people join social movements?**

A primary reason people join social movements is they know others in the movement. According to **mass society theory,** social movements relieve feelings of isolation created by an impersonal, bureaucratized society. According to **relative deprivation theory,** people join movements to address their grievances. A sense of justice, morality, values, and ideological commitment also motivates people to join social movements. The **agent provocateur** illustrates that even people who oppose a cause may participate in it. Pp. 656–659.

On the Success and Failure of Social Movements

■ **Why do social movements succeed or fail?**

Social movements go through several stages—initial unrest and agitation, mobilization, organization, institutionalization, and, finally, decline. Resurgence is also possible. Groups that appeal to few people cannot succeed. To appeal broadly in order to accomplish **resource mobilization,** the movement must focus on broad concerns. These concerns are embedded deeply in society, which makes success difficult. Pp. 659–661.

■ *Where can I read more on this topic?*

Suggested Readings for this chapter are at the back of this book.

Additional Online Resources for This Chapter
www.ablongman.com/henslin6e

- *Content Select* Research Database for Sociology, with suggested key terms and annotated references
- Link to 2000 Census, with activities
- Flashcards of key terms and concepts

- Practice Tests
- Weblinks
- Interactive Maps

using . . .

ContentSelect

Research Database for Sociology

collective behavior	urban legend	propaganda	rumor
fad and fashion	moral panic	public opinion polls	social movement

Jose Ortega, *People with Globe and Computer*, 1998

22

Social Change and
the Environment

How Social Change
Transforms Social Life

The Four Social
Revolutions

From *Gemeinschaft*
to *Gesellschaft*

Capitalism, Modernization,
and Industrialization

Social Movements

Geopolitics and Ethnic
Conflicts

Theories and Processes
of Social Change

Cultural Evolution

Natural Cycles

Conflict Over Power

Ogburn's Theory

How Technology
Changes Society

The Extent of the
Transformation

The Cutting Edge
of Change

Cyberspace and Social
Inequality

The Growth Machine
Versus the Earth

Environmental Problems
in the Most Industrialized
Nations

Environmental Problems
in the Industrializing
and Least Industrialized
Nations

The Environmental
Movement

Environmental Sociology

Summary and Review

T he morning of January 28, 1986, dawned clear but near freezing—strange weather for subtropical Florida. At the Kennedy Space Center, icicles 6 to 12 inches long hung like stalactites from launch pad 39B. Shortly after 8 A.M., the crew entered the crew module. By 8:36 A.M., the seven members of the crew were strapped in their seats. They were understandably disappointed when liftoff, scheduled for 9:38 A.M., was delayed because of the ice.

> In seconds, the glow blossomed into a gigantic fireball.

Due to a strong public relations campaign, public interest in the flight ran high. Attention focused on Christa McAuliffe, a 37-year-old high school teacher from Concord, New Hampshire, the first private citizen to fly aboard a space shuttle. Mrs. McAuliffe had been selected from thousands of applicants (including the author of this text). She was to give a televised lesson during the flight about life aboard a spacecraft, and across the nation, schoolchildren watched with anticipation.

Eagerly awaiting the launch at the viewing site were the families and friends of the crew, as well as thousands of spectators. After two hours of delays, they were delighted to see *Challenger*'s two solid-fuel boosters ignite, and they broke into cheers as this product of technical innovation thundered majestically into space. The time was 11:38 A.M.

Seventy-three seconds later, the *Challenger* was 7 miles from the launch site, racing skyward at 2,900 feet per second. Suddenly a brilliant glow appeared on one side of the external tank. In seconds, the glow blossomed into a gigantic fireball. Screams of horror arose from the crowd as the *Challenger,* now 19 miles away, exploded, and bits of debris began to fall from the sky.

In classrooms across the country, children burst into tears. Adults stared at their televisions in stunned disbelief.

Sources: Based on Broad 1986; Magnuson 1986; Lewis 1988; Maier 1993.

I f any characteristic describes social life today, it is rapid social change. As we shall see in this chapter, technology, such as that which made the *Challenger* first a reality and then a disaster, is a driving force behind this change. To understand social change is to better understand today's society—and our own lives.

How Social Change Transforms Social Life

■ The Four Social Revolutions

The rapid, far-reaching social change that the world is currently experiencing did not "just happen." Rather, it is the result of forces that were set in motion thousands of years ago, beginning with the domestication of plants and animals. This first social revolution allowed hunting and gathering societies to develop into horticultural and pastoral societies (see pages 158–160). The plow brought about the second social revolution, from which agricultural societies emerged. Then the invention of the steam engine ushered in the Industrial Revolution, and now we are in the midst of the fourth social revolution, stimulated by the invention of the microchip. The process of change has speeded up so greatly that we may also be seeing the beginning of the bioeconomy, brought about by the mapping of the human genome system.

■ From *Gemeinschaft* to *Gesellschaft*

Although so many aspects of our lives have already changed, we have seen only the tip of the iceberg. By the time this fourth—and perhaps fifth—social revolution is full-blown, little of our way of life will be left untouched. We can assume this because that is how it was with the earlier social revolutions. For example, the change from agricultural to industrial society meant not only that people moved from villages to cities but also that many intimate, lifelong relationships were replaced by impersonal, short-term associations. Paid work, contracts, and money replaced the reciprocal obligations (such as helping one another) essential to kinship, social status, and friendship. As reviewed on pages 108–110, sociologists use the terms *Gemeinschaft* and *Gesellschaft* to indicate this fundamental shift in society.

Traditional, or *Gemeinschaft*, societies are small, rural, and slow-changing. They are dominated by men, and have firm divisions between the sexes. People look to the past for guidelines on how to deal with the present. They live in extended families, have little formal education, and treat most illnesses at home. People tend to see life and morals in absolute terms. Modern, or *Gesellschaft*, societies, in contrast, are large,

■ *The Protestant Reformation ushered in not only religious change but also, as Max Weber analyzed, fundamental social-economic change. This painting by Hans Holbein, the Younger, shows the new prosperity of the merchant class. Previously, only the nobility and higher clergy could afford such possessions.*

more urbanized, and fast changing. Divisions between the sexes are more fluid. People stress formal education, and are more future-oriented. In the third stage of the demographic transition, they have smaller families and low rates of infant mortality. They live longer lives, have higher incomes, and enjoy vastly more material possessions.

■ Capitalism, Modernization, and Industrialization

Just why did societies change from *Gemeinschaft* to *Gesellschaft*— Karl Marx pointed to a social invention called *capitalism*. He analyzed how the breakup of feudal society threw people off the land, creating a surplus of labor. These masses moved to cities, where they were exploited by the owners of the means of production (factories, machinery, tools). This set in motion antagonistic relationships between capitalists and workers that remain today.

Max Weber traced capitalism to the Protestant Reformation (see pages 188–189). He noted that the Reformation stripped Protestants of the assurance that church membership saved them. As they agonized over heaven and hell, they concluded that God did not want the elect to live in uncertainty. God would surely give a sign to assure them that they were predestined to heaven. That sign, they decided, was prosperity. An unexpected consequence of the Reformation, then, was to make Protestants work hard and be thrifty. This created an economic surplus, which stimulated capitalism. In this way, Protestantism laid the groundwork for the Industrial Revolution that transformed the world.

TABLE 22.1 Comparing Traditional and Modern Societies

Characteristics	Traditional Societies	Modern Societies	Characteristics	Traditional Societies	Modern Societies
General Characteristics			*Social Relationships*		
Social change	Slow	Rapid	Basic organization	*Gemeinschaft*	*Gesellschaft*
Size of group	Small	Large	Families	Extended	Nuclear
Religious orientation	More	Less	Respect for elders	More	Less
Formal education	No	Yes	Social stratification	Rigid	More open
Place of residence	Rural	Urban	Statuses	More ascribed	More achieved
Demographic transition	First stage	Third stage (or Fourth)	Gender equality	Less	More
Family size	Larger	Smaller	*Norms*		
Infant mortality	High	Low	View of reality, life, and morals	Absolute	Relativistic
Life expectancy	Short	Long			
Health care	Home	Hospital	Social control	Informal	Formal
Temporal orientation	Past	Future	Tolerance of differences	Less	More
Material Relations					
Industrialized	No	Yes			
Technology	Simple	Complex			
Division of labor	Simple	Complex			
Income	Low	High			
Material possessions	Few	Many			

The sweeping changes ushered in by the Industrial Revolution are called **modernization.** Table 22.1 reviews these changes. The features listed on this table are *ideal types* in Weber's sense of the term, for no society exemplifies to the maximum degree all the traits listed here. In addition, our new technology has created unevenness around the world. The elite in Uganda, for example, have computers. Thus the characteristics shown in Table 22.1 should be interpreted as "more" or "less" rather than "either-or."

■ *Social change comes in many forms. Shown here is a Chinese peasant in 1911, whose pigtail is being cut off by the revolutionary army. To retain the custom of never cutting one's hair was considered a sign of allegiance to warlords and of resistance to the new regime.*

modernization
the process by which a *Gemeinschaft* society is transformed into a *Gesellschaft* society

When technology changes, societies change. Consider how technology from the industrialized world is transforming traditional societies. When modern medicine was exported to the Least Industrialized Nations, for example, death rates dropped while birth rates remained high. As a result, the population exploded. This second stage of the demographic transition upset traditional balances of family, property, and inheritance. It brought hunger and led to mass migration to cities that have little industrialization to support the masses of people moving into them. The photo essay on pages 612–613 and the Cultural Diversity box on page 621 discuss some of these problems.

■ Social Movements

Social movements reveal the cutting edge of change in society. People band together to express their feelings about something that upsets them. They organize to demand change, or to resist some change they don't like. Because social movements form around issues that bother large numbers of people, they indicate areas of society in which there is the greatest pressure for change. With globalization, these issues increasingly cut across international boundaries, indicating areas of discontent and sweeping change that affect millions of people in different cultures (see pages 648–661).

■ Geopolitics and Ethnic Conflicts

With all the changes surrounding us, it is impossible to pinpoint the most significant one. Among the contenders, however, would be one that often lies below our vision—the arrangement of power among nations. By the sixteenth century, today's global divisions had begun to emerge. Those nations that had the most advanced technology (at that time, the swiftest ships and the most powerful canons) became wealthy by conquering other nations and exploiting their resources. Then, as capitalism emerged, some nations industrialized. The newly industrialized nations exploited the resources of those that had not industrialized. According to *dependency theory*, this made the nonindustrialized nations dependent and unable to develop their own resources (see pages 266–267).

Today's information revolution, including the new bioeconomics, will also have far-reaching consequences for global stratification. Those nations that make the fastest, most significant advances in these areas are destined to dominate in the coming generation. Obviously, this will be a continuation of the dominance of the Most Industrialized Nations.

Since World War II, a realignment of the world's powers (called *geopolitics*) has resulted in a triadic division of the globe: a Japan-centered East, a Germany-centered Europe, and a United States-centered western hemisphere. These three powers, along with four lesser ones—Canada, France, Great Britain, and Italy—dominate the globe today. Known as G7 (meaning *the* "Group of 7"), these industrial giants hold annual meetings at which they decide how to divide up the world's markets and regulate global economic policy, such as interest rates, tariffs, and currency exchanges. Their goal is to perpetuate their global dominance, which includes keeping prices down on the raw materials they buy from the Least Industrialized Nations. Cheap oil is essential for this goal, which requires that they dominate the Middle East— whether that be accomplished through peaceful means or by a joint war effort of the United Nations.

Because of Russia's nuclear arsenal, the G7 has courted Russia—giving Russia observer status at its annual summits and providing loans and expertise to help Russia make the transition to capitalism. The breakup of the Soviet Union has been a central consideration in G7's plans for a

■ *The* Rulers of the World *could be the caption of this photo. These ordinary looking men are heads of G7, the seven most powerful nations of the world. They are shown here in Genoa, Italy, at their annual summit, at which they evaluate their progress in ruling the world. As explained in the text, because others are fearful of its nuclear arsenal, Russia is an honorary member of this exclusive group.*

■ *Despite the globe's vast social change, people all over the world continue to make race a fundamental distinction. Shown here is a Ukrainian being measured to see if he is really "full lipped" enough to be called a Tartar.*

new world order. Events in Russia and in its former satellite nations will help determine the shape of future global stratification.

Threatening the global divisions so carefully constructed by G7 is the resurgence of ethnic conflicts. The breakup of the Soviet empire unleashed the centuries-old hatreds and frustrated nationalistic ambitions of many ethnic groups. With the Soviet military and the KGB in disarray, these groups turned violently on one another. In Africa, similar seething hatreds brought warfare to groups that had been lumped together in arbitrary political boundaries. In Europe, the former Yugoslavia split apart, with ethnic groups turning violently against one another. Ethnic conflicts threaten to erupt in Germany, France, Italy, the United States, and Mexico. At what point these resentments and hatreds will play themselves out, if ever, is unknown.

Another threat to G7 is the growing wealth and power of China. As China expands its domain of influence, it will increasingly infringe on the interests of G7. The most likely scenario is limited conflict and, as G7 accomodates to changing reality, the incorporation of China into this exclusive club.

For the most part, the Most Industrialized Nations care little if the entire continent of Africa self-destructs in ethnic slaughter, but they cannot tolerate interethnic warfare in their own back yard. For example, to let interethnic warfare in Bosnia and Kosovo go unchecked would be to tolerate conflict that could spread and engulf Europe. For global control, G7 must be able to depend on political and economic stability in its own neighborhood, as well as in those countries that provide the raw materials essential for its industrial machine.

Theories and Processes of Social Change

S ocial change has fascinated theorists. We shall consider just four of the many explanations of why societies change: cultural evolution, cycles, conflict theory, and the pioneering views of sociologist William Ogburn.

■ Cultural Evolution

Unilinear and multilinear theories are two views of how societies developed. *Unilinear* theories assume that all societies follow the same path. Each society evolves from simpler to more complex forms, and each goes through uniform sequences (Barnes 1935). Of the many versions of this theory, the one proposed by Lewis Morgan (1877) once dominated Western thought. Morgan said that all societies go through three stages: savagery, barbarism, and civilization. In Morgan's eyes, England, his own society, was the epitome of civilization. All others were destined to follow it.

Multilinear views of evolution replaced unilinear theories. Instead of assuming that all societies follow the same sequence, multilinear theorists proposed that different routes lead to the same stage of development. Although the path leads to industrialization, societies need not pass through the same sequence of stages on this journey (Sahlins and Service 1960; Lenski and Lenski 1987).

Central to evolutionary theories, whether unilinear or multilinear, is the assumption of *cultural progress*. Tribal societies are assumed to have a primitive form of human culture. As they evolve, they will reach a higher state—the supposedly advanced and superior form that characterizes modern societies. Growing appreciation of the rich diversity—and complexity—of tribal cultures has discredited this idea. In addition, Western culture is now in crisis (poverty, racism, discrimination, war, terrorism, alienation, sexual assaults, unsafe streets) and is no longer regarded as the apex of human culture. Consequently, the idea of cultural progress has been cast aside, and evolutionary theories have been rejected (Eder 1990; Smart 1990).

Natural Cycles

Cyclical theories attempt to account for the rise of entire civilizations. Why, for example, did Egypt, Greece, and Rome wield such power and influence, only to crest and fall into a decline? Cyclical theories assume that civilizations are like organisms: They are born, see an exuberant youth, come to maturity, then decline as they reach old age, and finally die (Hughes 1962).

Why do civilizations go through this cycle? Historian Arnold Toynbee (1946) said that each civilization faces challenges to its existence. The solutions to these challenges are not total, and oppositional forces remain. The ruling elite manages to keep these forces under control, but at a civilization's peak, when it has become an empire, the ruling elite loses its capacity to keep the masses in line "by charm rather than by force." The fabric of society is eventually ripped apart. Force may hold the empire together for hundreds of years, but the civilization is doomed.

In a book that provoked widespread controversy, *The Decline of the West* (1926–1928), Oswald Spengler, a high school teacher in Germany, proposed that Western civilization had passed its peak and was in decline. Although the West succeeded in overcoming the crises provoked by Hitler and Mussolini, as Toynbee noted, civilizations don't end in sudden collapse. Because the decline can last hundreds of years, perhaps the crisis in Western civilization mentioned earlier (poverty, rape, murder, and so on) indicates that Spengler was right, and we are now in decline.

Conflict Over Power

Long before Toynbee, Karl Marx identified a recurring process in human history. He said that each *thesis* (a current arrangement of power) contains its own *antithesis* (contradiction or opposition). A struggle develops between the thesis and its antithesis, leading to a *synthesis* (a new arrangement of power). This new social order, in turn, becomes a thesis that will be challenged by its own antithesis, and so on. Figure 22.1 gives a visual summary of this process.

According to Marx's view (called a **dialectical process** of history), each ruling group sows the seeds of its own destruction. Consider capitalism. Marx said that capitalism (the thesis) is built on the exploitation of workers (an antithesis, or built-in opposition). With workers and owners on a collision course, the dialectical process will not stop until workers establish a classless state (the synthesis).

The analysis of G7 in the previous section follows conflict theory. G7's current division of the globe's resources and markets is a thesis. Resentment on the part of have-not nations is an antithesis. If one of the Least Industrialized Nations gains in military power, that nation will press for a redistribution of resources. China, India, and Pakistan, with their nuclear weapons, fit this scenario. So do the efforts of Saddam Hussein and Osama bin Laden to change the balance of power in the Mideast. Any new arrangement, or synthesis, will contain its own antitheses. These may be ethnic hostilities, or leaders feeling that their country has been denied its fair share of resources. These antitheses will haunt the arrangement of power and must at some point be resolved into a synthesis. The process repeats itself.

Ogburn's Theory

Sociologist William Ogburn (1922, 1961, 1964) proposed a view of social change that is based on technology. Technology, he said, changes society by three processes: invention, discovery, and diffusion. Let's consider each.

Invention   Ogburn defined **invention** as a combining of existing elements and materials to form new ones. We usually think of inventions as being only material, such as computers, but there also are *social inventions*. We have considered three social inventions in this text: capitalism (pages 188–189, 415–417), bureaucracy (pages 189–196), and the corporation (pages 200–208, 422–428). As we saw in these instances,

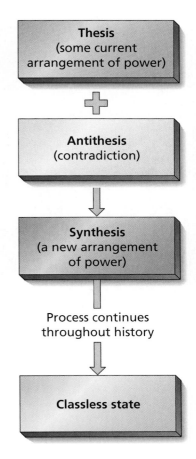

Figure 22.1
Marx's Model of Historical Change

dialectical process
each arrangement, or thesis, contains contradictions, or antitheses, which must be resolved; the new arrangement, or synthesis, contains its own contradictions, and so on

invention
the combination of existing elements and materials to form new ones; identified by William Ogburn as the first of three processes of social change

■ *Culture contact is the source of* diffusion, *the spread of an invention or discovery from one area to another. Shown here are two children of the Huli tribe in Papua New Guinea. They are amused by a Polaroid photo of themselves.*

social inventions can have far-reaching consequences on society and people's relationship to one another. In this chapter, we will examine how two other inventions, the automobile and the computer, have transformed society.

Discovery   Ogburn identified **discovery**, a new way of seeing reality, as a second process of change. The reality is already present, but people now see it for the first time. An example is Columbus' "discovery" of North America, which had consequences so huge that they altered the course of human history. This example also illustrates another principle: A discovery brings extensive change only when it comes at the right time. Other groups, such as the Vikings, had already "discovered" North America in the sense of learning that a new land existed—obviously no discovery to the Native Americans already living in it. Viking settlements disappeared into history, however, and Norse culture was untouched by the discovery.

Diffusion   Ogburn stressed how **diffusion**, the spread of an invention or discovery from one area to another, can have extensive effects on people's lives. Consider a simple object such as the axe. When missionaries introduced steel axes to the Aborigines of Australia, it upset their whole society. Before this, the men controlled axe-making. They used a special stone, available only in a remote region, and they passed axe-making skills from father to son. Women had to request permission to use the axe. When steel axes became common, women also possessed them, and the men lost both status and power (Sharp 1995).

Diffusion also includes the spread of ideas. As we saw in Chapter 11, the idea of citizenship changed political structure around the world; it removed monarchs as an unquestioned source of authority. The concept of gender equality is now circling the globe. Although taken for granted in a few parts of the world, the idea that it is wrong to withhold rights on the basis of someone's sex is revolutionary. Like citizenship, this idea is destined to transform basic human relationships and entire societies.

Cultural Lag   Ogburn coined the term **cultural lag** to refer to how some elements of a culture lag behind the changes that come from invention, discovery, and diffusion. Technology, he suggested, usually changes first, with culture lagging behind. In other words, we play catch-up with changing technology, adapting our customs and ways of life to meet its needs.

Evaluation of Ogburn's Theory   Some find Ogburn's analysis too one-directional, saying that it makes technology the cause of almost all social change. They point out that the way people adapt to technology is only one part of the story. The other part consists of the way people take control over technology. People develop the technology they need, and they selectively use it. Some groups, such as the Amish (see page 110), even reject technologies they perceive as threatening to their culture. Other resistance to technology is discussed in the Sociology and the New Technology box on the next page.

Technology and social change actually form a two-way street: Just as technology leads to social change, so social change leads to technology. For example, a major social change is the growing number of elderly in our society. Their needs have stimu-

discovery
a new way of seeing reality; identified by William Ogburn as the second of three processes of social change

diffusion
the spread of an invention or a discovery from one area to another; identified by William Ogburn as the final of three processes of social change

cultural lag
Ogburn's term for human behavior lagging behind technological innovations

From the Luddites to the Unabomber:
Opposition to Technology

In the early 1800s in Great Britain, a machine was invented that could make stockings. The owners of the stocking-making factories were delighted. The workers were not. Seeing their livelihood, such as it was, jerked from beneath them, they picked up axes and hammers and smashed the machines to bits. The local police were ineffective against this uprising, and the government called out twelve thousand army troops to restore order. Some of the workers were executed. Others were shipped off to Australia.

One of the apprentice stocking makers who destroyed his machine was Ned Ludlum. Since this time, people who oppose new technology have been called *Luddites*. (Volti 1995)

New technology always poses threats and creates fears. Because every new technology replaces some existing technology, it always threatens someone. Opposition to new technology, then, is common. Antagonism is usually directed at a specific new technology, but it sometimes becomes a protest against technology in general.

Jacques Ellul (1965), a French sociologist, became upset at technological change. He warned that technology was destroying traditional values. He said that humans were becoming "a single

■ *Ted Kaczynski after his arrest in Helena, Montana.*

tightly integrated and articulated component" of technology. He feared that technology would produce a monolithic world culture in which "variety is mere appearance." Ellul's message, and that of others, such as Neil Postman (1992), garnered the attention of only a few intellectuals who discussed the matter in faculty seminars and wrote obscure papers on the subject.

In the 1980s, the Unabomber sent a message that was far from subdued. His warning signals came thundering into

the public's consciousness, not in the form of books and articles, but of air-mail explosives that maimed and killed their unsuspecting recipients. For seventeen years, the man sent bombs to addresses in Michigan, Utah, and California. There was no apparent message behind his seemingly random attacks. Then unexpectedly, in 1995, the Unabomber delivered a verbal message. He promised to stop his terror if his 35,000-word essay against technology were published. The *New York Times* and the *Washington Post* duly printed it. His message, in its essence, was similar to Ellul's: Technology is destroying us. A recluse in the mountains of Montana was eventually identified as the Unabomber. Ted Kaczynski, who had an undergraduate degree from Harvard and a Ph.D. from the University of Michigan, was arrested and found guilty.

for your consideration

What do the Luddites, Jacques Ellul, and the Unabomber have in common? Use concepts presented in this and earlier chapters to analyze the effects of technology on society. Given your conclusions, should we fear new technologies?

lated new medical technologies, such as those used to treat Alzheimer's disease. Another example is our changing ideas about the role that people with disabilities should play in society. This has stimulated the development of new types of wheelchairs that allow people who cannot move their legs to play basketball, participate in the Special Olympics, and enter downhill races.

In fairness to Ogburn, we must note that he never said technology is the only force for social change. He did not assert that people are passive pawns in the face of overwhelming technological forces. He did stress, though, that the material culture (technology) usually changes first, and the symbolic culture (people's ideas and ways of life) follows. This direction still holds, as you can see with the many changes that are following on the heels of the development of computers.

Let's consider, then, how technology changes society.

■ ■ ■ ■ ■

How Technology Changes Society

As you may recall from Chapter 2, **technology** has a double meaning. It refers both to *tools*, the items used to accomplish tasks, and to the skills or procedures needed to make and use those tools. Technology refers to tools as simple as a comb and as complicated as a computer. Technology's second meaning—the skills or procedures needed to make and use tools—refers in this case not only to the procedures used to manufacture combs and computers but also to those required to "produce" an acceptable hairdo or to gain access to the Internet. Apart from its particulars, technology always refers to *artificial means of extending human abilities*.

All human groups make and use technology, but the chief characteristic of post-industrial societies (also called **postmodern societies**) is technology that greatly extends our abilities to analyze information, communicate, and travel. These *new technologies*, as they are called, allow us to do what had never been done in history: to probe space; to communicate almost instantaneously anywhere on the globe; to travel greater distances faster; and to store, retrieve, and analyze vast amounts of information.

Change is rapid. We are seeing desktop computers give way to laptops—and some laptops being replaced by handheld devices. And this is just the beginning. In our coming bioeconomic society, we may "wear" computers. Our own proteins (bacteriorhodopsin) will store data on holograms, with 10 gigabytes (enough for several encyclopedias) stored in the size of a sugar cube (Ferraro 2001).

■ The Extent of the Transformation

Although we might be impressed with technology, it is really superficial. Of much greater sociological significance is a deeper issue: how technology changes our way of life. When a technology is introduced into a society, it forces other parts of society to give way. In fact, *a new technology can reshape society*. Let's look at four ways that technology does this.

Changes in Social Organization Technology changes how people organize themselves. In Chapter 6, we discussed how prior to machine technology, most workers labored at home but that the new power-driven machinery required them to be in one place at the same time to do their work. In the first factories, each worker still made an entire item. Then it was discovered that workers could produce more if each person did a specialized task. One worker would hammer on a single part, or turn so many bolts, and then someone else would take the item and do some other repetitive task before a third person took over, and so on. Henry Ford built on this innovation by developing the assembly line: Instead of workers moving to the parts, machines moved the parts to the workers. In addition, the parts were made interchangeable and easy to attach (Womack et al. 1991).

Changes in Ideology Technology also spurs ideology. Karl Marx noted that when workers did repetitive tasks on just a small part of a product, they did not feel connected to the finished product. No longer did they think of the product as "theirs." Workers had become

technology
often defined as the applications of science, but can be conceptualized as tools, items used to accomplish tasks, along with the skills or procedures necessary to make and use those tools

postmodern society
another term for postindustrial society; its chief characteristic is the use of tools that extend human abilities to gather and analyze information, to communicate, and to travel

■ Technology, *which drives much social change, is at the forefront of our information revolution. This revolution, based on the computer chip, allows reality to cross with fantasy, a merging that sometimes makes it difficult to tell where one ends and the other begins. Shown here is Liquid Metal Man morphing into a human in* Terminator 2.

■ In the photo on the left, Henry Ford proudly displays his 1905 car, the latest in automobile technology. As is apparent, especially, from the spokes on the car's wheels, new technology builds on existing technology. At the time this photo was taken, who could have imagined that this vehicle would transform society?

The photo on the right illustrates today's latest automobile technology. This experimental car, built at the University of Missouri at Rolla, runs by solar power.

alienated from the product of their labor. Marx stressed how this **alienation** bred dissatisfaction and unrest.

Marx also noted that workers had become like machines and tools—just another replaceable part. Before factories came on the scene, workers owned their tools and were independent. If they didn't like something, they could pack up their hammers and saws and leave. Someone else would hire them to build a wagon or make a harness. The factory was a great contrast, for there the capitalists owned the tools and machinery. With this ownership came power, which the capitalists used to extract every ounce of sweat and blood they could. The workers had to submit. If they left, other workers took their place. Marx said this exploitation could not continue, that a workers' revolution would follow. Marx believed that when workers realized the common basis of their exploitation, they would unite, violently take over the means of production, and establish a workers' state.

Note how the new technology of power-driven machines stimulated new ideologies. As they built factories, capitalists developed an ideology to support the principle of maximizing profits. Then followers of Marx built theories of socialism to attack capitalism. As we shall see shortly, just as changes in technology stimulated the development of communism, changes in technology have been crucial in bringing about its end.

Changes in Values   Just as ideology follows technology, so do values. If technology is limited to clubbing animals, then strength and cunning are valued. So are animal skins. No doubt primitive men and women who wore the skins of some especially unusual or dangerous animal walked with their heads held high—while their neighbors, wearing the same old sheepskins, looked on in envy. Today's technology, in contrast, produces an abundance of synthetic fabrics. Americans brag about cars, boats, hot tubs, and second homes—and make certain that their jeans have the right labels prominently displayed. In short, while envy and pride may be basic to human nature, the particular emphasis on materialism depends on the state of technology.

alienation
Marx's term for workers' lack of connection to the product of their labor; caused by their being assigned repetitive tasks on a small part of a product

Changes in Social Relationships Technology also changes how people relate to one another. When men left home to work in factories, they grew isolated from many of the day-to-day affairs of the family. One consequence of becoming relative strangers to their wives and children was more divorce. Later changes in technology drew more women from the home to offices and factories. This has had similar consequences—greater isolation from husbands and children, and one more impetus toward fragile marriages. A counter-trend is now in force, as further changes in new technology are allowing millions of workers to do their work at home. One consequence may be a strengthening of families.

To get a better idea of how technology shapes our way of life, let's consider some current changes.

◼ The Cutting Edge of Change

The ominous wail seemed too close for comfort. Sally looked in her rear-view mirror and realized that the flashing lights and screaming siren might be for her. She felt confused. "I'm just on my way to Soc," she thought. "I'm not speeding or anything." After she pulled over, an angry voice over a loudspeaker ordered her out of the car.

As she got out, someone barked the command, "Back up with your hands in the air!" Bewildered, Sally stood frozen for a moment. "Put 'em up now! Right now!" She did as she was told.

The officer crouched behind his open door, his gun drawn. When Sally reached the police car—still backing up—the officer grabbed her, threw her to the ground, and handcuffed her hands behind her back. She heard words she would never forget, "You are under arrest for murder. You have the right to remain silent. Anything you say can and will be used against you in a court of law. You have the right to an attorney. If you cannot afford one, one will be provided for you."

◼ *Most of us take computers for granted, but they are new to the world scene—as are their effects on our lives. This photo captures a significant change in the evolution of computers. The laptop held by the superimposed model has more power than the room-size ENIAC of 1946.*

Traces of alarm still flicker across Sally's face when she recalls her arrest. She had never even had a traffic ticket, much less been arrested for anything. Sally's nightmare was due to a "computer error." With the inversion of two numbers, her car's license number had been entered into the police databank instead of the number belonging to a woman wanted for a brutal killing earlier that day.

None of us is untouched by the computer, but it is unlikely that many of us have felt its power as directly and dramatically as Sally did. For most of us, the computer's control lies quietly behind the scenes. Although the computer has intruded into our daily lives, most of us never think about it. Our grades are computerized, and our paychecks probably are as well. When we buy groceries, a computer scans our purchases and presents a printout of the name, price, and quantity of each item.

Many people rejoice over the computer's capacity to improve their quality of life. They are pleased with the higher quality of manufactured goods and the reduction of drudgery. With e-mail, we can type just one letter, and with the press of a button that letter will be delivered in seconds to everyone in our address book.

Some people, however, have serious reservations about our computerized society. They worry about errors that can creep into computerized records, fearing that something similar to Sally's misfortune could happen to them. Others are concerned that computerized data will allow Orwell's Big Brother to achieve total control. Many are apprehensive about "identity theft." These are legitimate concerns, but space does not permit us to pursue them.

At this point, let's consider how the computer is changing education, the workplace, and war. We'll then consider its likely effects on social inequality.

Computers in Education   Almost every grade school in the United States introduces its students to the computer. Children learn how to type on it, as well as how to use mathematics and science software. Successful educational programs use a gamelike format that makes students forget they are "studying." With classrooms wired to the Internet, students in schools that have no teachers knowledgeable in foreign languages are able to take courses in Russian, German, and Spanish. Even though they have no sociology instructors, they can take courses in the sociology of gender, race, or even sports.

The unequal funding we discussed in Chapter 17 is significant in this context. Schools that can afford the latest technology are able to better prepare their students for the future. That advantage, of course, goes to students of private schools and to the richest public school districts, thus helping to perpetuate the social inequalities that arise from the chance of birth. At one point in our history, some schools could not afford textbooks. It is likely that education's digital divide will also become a distant memory.

The computer will transform the college of the future. Each office and dormitory room and off-campus residence will be connected by fiber-optic cable. Professors will be able to transmit entire books directly from their office to a student's room, or back the other way, in *less* time than it took you to read this sentence. To help students and professors do research or prepare reports, computers will search millions of pages of text. Digital textbooks will replace printed versions such as this one. You will be able to key in the terms *social interaction* and *gender,* select your preference of historical period, geographical area, age, and ethnic group—and the computer will spew out text, maps, moving images, and sounds. You will be able to do the same with any topic: riots and Los Angeles, sexual discrimination in the military, or even the price of marijuana and cocaine. If you wish, the computer will give you a test—geared to the level of difficulty you choose—so you can check your mastery of the material.

Computers in the Workplace The computer is also transforming the workplace. At the simplest level, it affects how we do work. For example, I wrote the first two editions of this book on a computer, which commanded a printer to produce a copy of the manuscript. Even in this electronic age, a series of archaic, precomputer processes followed: I sent the printed copy via the postal service to an editor, who physically handled the manuscript and sent it to others who did the same. The manuscript, marked up in red pencil, was then returned to me, and I mailed back a corrected copy. The process was primitive, much the same as would have occurred during Benjamin Franklin's day.

Practice is finally catching up with potential. My editors and I now zap text back and forth electronically. I may be in the United States or in Spain, while they are in Oregon and Massachusetts. It makes no difference. I print nothing, and send no papers. Although the distances are greater, the time lapse has shrunk. For me, the process is marvelous testimony of our changing world—and, perhaps, unsettling confirmation of our steady steps into a brave new world.

The computer is also bringing changes on a deeper level, for it alters social relationships. I used to bring my manuscript to a university secretary, wait several days for her to type it, and then retrieve it. Now, by making corrections directly at the computer and transmitting a revised electronic copy, the secretary is bypassed entirely. In this instance, the computer enhanced social relationships, for I made fewer demands on the department secretary. This also eliminated the necessity of her making excuses when a manuscript was not ready on time—and the tensions that this brought to our relationship.

For some, including myself, the computer has also reversed the change in work location that industrialization ushered in. As discussed earlier, due to industrialization, work shifted from home to factory and office. Several million workers now remain at home while computers and modems connect them with their bosses and fellow workers at locations around the country—or even on the other side of the globe. We could be seeing the beginning of another historical shift, one that may bring families closer together.

On the negative side are increased surveillance of workers and depersonalization. As a telephone information operator said,

> The computer knows everything. It records the minute I punch in, it knows how long I take for each call. . . . I am supposed to average under eighteen seconds per call. . . . Everything I do is reported to my supervisor on his computer, and if I've missed my numbers I get a written warning. I rarely see the guy. . . . It's intense. It's me and the computer all day. I'm telling you, at the end of the day I'm wiped out. *Working with computers is the coal mining of the nineties.* (Mander 1992:57, italics added)

Computers in Business and Finance Not long ago, the advanced technology of businesses consisted of cash registers and adding machines. Connection to the outside world was by telephone. Today, those same businesses are electronically "wired" to suppliers, salespeople, and clients around the country—and around the world. Computers record changes in inventory and set in motion the process of reordering and restocking. They produce detailed reports of sales that alert managers to changes in their customers' tastes or preferences.

National borders have become meaningless as computers instantaneously transfer billions of dollars from one country to another. No "cash" changes hands in these transactions. The money consists of digits in computer memory banks. In the same day, this digitized money can be transferred from the United States to Switzerland, from there to the Grand Cayman Islands, and then to the Isle of Mann. Its zigzag, instantaneous path leaves few traces for sleuths to follow. "Where's my share?" governments around the world are moaning, as they consider how to control—and tax—this new technology.

Changes in War   The Gulf War was a prelude. Americans watched at home as guided missiles hit targets with precision. Only a handful of U.S. soldiers was lost. Then the war in Afghanistan let us know that we were truly involved in a new type of warfare.

The Predator, an unmanned plane, flies thousands of feet above enemy lines, beaming continuous video back to the base. At the bottom of every image it relays, GPS sensors report the Predator's precise latitude and longitude. When operators at the base see a target they want to hit, they press a button, and the Predator beams a laser onto the target. They then launch guided bombs, striking the precise target (Barry 2001).

Enemy ground troops don't know what hits them. They don't see the Predator, they are unaware of the laser, but, perhaps just before they are blown to bits, they do hear the sound of an incoming bomb.

There are still ground troops, but many of them have become high-tech, too. Special Forces wear goggles that let them see at night. They use lasers to measure a target's exact distance and to transmit the coordinates to the base. Again, satellite-guided weapons destroy the target.

On its way is a uniform that hides soldiers. Containing bacteriorhodopsin proteins, at the molecular level it will let troops appear as plants. Painted on tanks, these proteins will do the same (Ferraro 2001).

On its way also is long-distance surgery. In what is known as *telemedicine*, surgeons in San Francisco or Boston will use sensors to operate on wounded soldiers in Afghanistan—or wherever the next battlefield might be.

These technological marvels make wars "cleaner"—reducing *our* casualties. They also bring us a surrealistic world in which we watch war from the comfort of our living rooms as though the battles and bombings were a video game. It is one thing, however, to wage war with an enemy that still rides horseback, as they do in Afghanistan—but quite another if we face an enemy that possesses similar technology. If so, no longer will our technology make war seem like a bloodless game.

▪ Cyberspace and Social Inequality

The term *information superhighway* conveys the idea of information traveling at a high rate of speed among homes and businesses. Just as a highway allows physical travel from one place to another, so computers and satellite transmissions connect homes and businesses with the rapid flow of information. Already 200 to 300 million people around the world communicate on the Internet. Servers such as America Online, Compuserve, and Prodigy allow electronic access to libraries of information. Programs sift, sort, and transmit images, sound, and video. We use e-mail to zap messages to people on the other side of the world. This is the future, a world linked by almost instantaneous communications, with information readily accessible around the globe and few places that can still be called "remote."

The implications of this new technology for national and global stratification are severe. On the national level, as discussed in the box on the digital divide (page 293), this technology may perpetuate present inequalities. We could end up with information have-nots, primarily inner-city residents. On the global level, the question is: Who will control this new technology? The answer, of course, is obvious, for it is the Most Industrialized Nations that are developing this communications system. This leads to one of the more profound issues of this century: Will such control destine the Least Industrialized Nations to a perpetual pauper status? Or will their access to this new technology be their passport to affluence?

■ **Sumatran Tiger**
Fewer than 400, Indonesia

■ **Gaur**
About 36,000, Southeast Asia

■ **Texas Ocelot**
*Fewer than 250, southern
United States, northern Mexico*

■ **Mountain Bongo**
About 50, Kenya

IN SUM ■ ■ ■ ■

Technology is changing our society and our everyday lives. A change in technology inevitably leads to a change in culture. Technological change always threatens some, for, inevitably, established ways of doing things give way. Consequently, while some welcome new technology, others resist it. Apart from the uprootings that technology brings, there are two other issues: Will the technology that is transforming the face of war come back to haunt us? And will the new technology perpetuate or alleviate social inequalities on both the national and global levels?

■ ■ ■ ■ ■

The Growth Machine Versus the Earth

O f all the changes swirling around us, perhaps those that affect the natural environment hold the most serious implications for human life.

Underlying today's environmental decay is the globalization of capitalism, which I have stressed throughout this text. To maintain their dominance and increase their wealth, the Most Industrialized Nations, spurred by multinational corporations, continue to push for economic growth. At the same time, the Industrializing Nations, playing catch-up, are striving to develop their economies. Meanwhile, the Least Industrialized Nations are anxious to enter the race: Because they start from even farther behind, they have to push for even faster growth.

Many are convinced that the earth cannot withstand such an onslaught. Global economic production creates extensive pollution, and faster-paced production means faster-paced destruction of our environment. The photos to the left illustrate just the tip of the iceberg in this relentless pursuit of economic development. If the goal is a **sustainable environment,** a world system in which we use our physical environment to meet our needs without destroying humanity's future, we cannot continue to trash the earth. In short, the ecological message is incompatible with an economic message that it is OK to rape the environment for the sake of profits.

Before looking at the social movement that has grown around this issue, let's examine major environmental problems. We'll begin with pollution in the Most Industrialized Nations.

Environmental Problems in the Most Industrialized Nations

Although even tribal groups produced pollution, the frontal assault on the natural environment did not begin in earnest until nations industrialized. The more extensive its industrialization, the better it was considered for a nation's welfare. For the Most Industrialized Nations, the slogan has been "Growth at any cost."

Industrial growth did come, but at a high cost to the natural environment. Today, for example, formerly pristine streams are polluted sewers, and the water supply of many cities is unfit to drink. When Los Angeles announces "smog days" on radio and television, schoolchildren are kept inside during recess and everyone is warned to stay indoors. The accumulation of hazardous wastes is a special problem. Despite the danger to people and the environment, in many cases the waste has simply been dumped. The Social Map on the next page shows how the worst hazardous waste

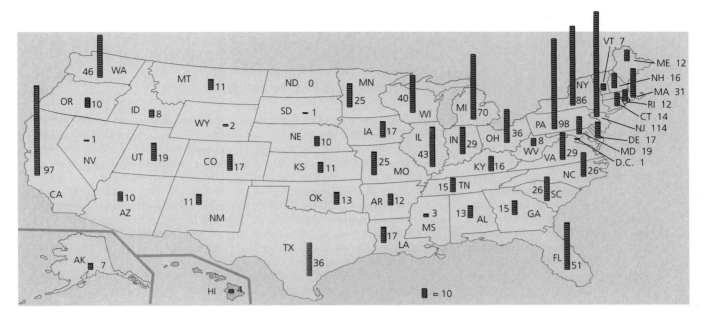

Figure 22.2

Social Map: How Does Your State Rank?
The Location of the Worst Hazardous Waste Sites
Source: Statistical Abstract 2000:Table 402.

sites are distributed throughout the United States. The Down-to-Earth Sociology box on the next page discusses how **corporate welfare** contributes to pollution.

The major polluters of the earth are the Most Industrialized Nations. Our follies include harming the ozone layer in order to have the convenience of spray bottles and air conditioners. With limited space to address this issue, I would like to focus on an overarching aspect of our environment, the burning of fossil fuels.

Fossil Fuels and the Environment   Burning fossil fuels for factories, motorized vehicles, and power plants has been especially harmful. Fish can no longer survive in some lakes in Canada and the northeastern United States because of **acid rain:** The burning of fossil fuels releases sulfur dioxide and nitrogen oxide, which react with moisture in the air to become sulfuric and nitric acids (Luoma 1989; Hao et al. 2001). See Figure 22.3 on the next page.

An invisible but infinitely more serious consequence is the **greenhouse effect.** Like the glass of a greenhouse, the gases emitted from burning fossil fuels allow sunlight to enter the earth's atmosphere freely, but inhibit the release of heat. It is as though the gases have closed the atmospheric window through which our planet breathes. Scientists are increasingly convinced that we face **global warming.** They warn us that polar ice caps may melt and inundate the world's shorelines, the climate boundaries may move north about four hundred miles, and many animal and plant species may become extinct (Weisskopf 1992; Begley 1997). They disagree, however, on whether the warming is due to natural or human causes (McFarling 2000). In 1997, 160 nations approved an environmental treaty to reduce "greenhouse gases."

The Energy Shortage and Multinational Corporations   If you ever read about an energy shortage, you can be sure that what you read is false. There is no energy shortage, nor can there ever be. We can produce unlimited low-cost power, which can

sustainable environment
a world system that takes into account the limits of the environment, produces enough material goods for everyone's needs, and leaves a heritage of a sound environment for the next generation

corporate welfare
the gifts or financial incentives (tax breaks, subsidies, and even land and stadiums) given to corporations in order to attract them to an area or induce them to remain

acid rain
rain containing sulfuric and nitric acids (burning fossil fuels releases sulfur dioxide and nitrogen oxide which becomes sulfuric and nitric acids when they react with moisture in the air)

greenhouse effect
the buildup of carbon dioxide in the earth's atmosphere that allows light to enter but inhibits the release of heat; believed to cause global warming

global warming
an increase in the earth's temperature due to the greenhouse effect

Corporations and Big Welfare Bucks: How to Get Paid to Pollute

Welfare is one of the most controversial topics in the United States. It arouses the ire of many wealthy and middle-class Americans, who view the poor who collect welfare as parasites. But have you heard about *corporate welfare*?

Corporate welfare refers to handouts given to corporations. A state may offer a company tax breaks if it will locate within the state, or remain in the state if it has threatened to leave. A state may even provide land and factories at bargain prices. The reason: jobs.

Corporate welfare even goes to companies that foul the land, water, and air. Borden Chemicals in Louisiana has buried hazardous wastes without a permit and released hazardous chemicals so thick that to protect drivers the police have sometimes had to shut down the highway that runs near the plant. Borden even contaminated the groundwater beneath its plant, threatening the

aquifer that provides drinking water for residents of Louisiana and Texas.

Borden's pollution has cost the company dearly: $3.6 million in fines, $3 million to clean up the groundwater, and $400,000 for local emergency response units. That's a hefty $7 million. But if we add corporate welfare, the company didn't make out so badly. With $15 million in reduced and cancelled property taxes, Borden has enjoyed a net gain of $8 million (Bartlett and Steele 1998). And that's not counting the savings the company racked up by not having to properly dispose of its toxic wastes in the first place.

Louisiana has added a novel twist to corporate welfare. It offers an incentive to help start-up companies. This itself isn't novel; the owners of that little "mom and pop" grocery store on your corner may have gotten some benefits when they first opened. Louisiana's twist is what it counts as a start-up operation.

One of these little start-up companies is called Exxon Corp. Although Exxon opened for business about 125 years ago, it had $213 million in property taxes canceled under this program. Another little company that the state figured could use a nudge to help it get started was Shell Oil Co., which had $140 million slashed from its taxes (Bartlett and Steele 1998). Then there were International Paper, Dow Chemical, Union Carbide, Boise Cascade, Georgia Pacific, and another tiny one called Procter & Gamble.

for your consideration

Apply the functionalist, symbolic interactionist, and conflict perspectives to corporate welfare. Which do you think provides the best interpretation of corporate welfare? Why?

---

environmental racism
the greater impact of pollution on the poor and racial–ethnic minorities

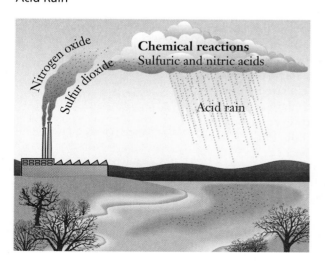

Figure 22.3
Acid Rain

help raise the living standards of humans across the globe. The sun, for example, produces more energy than humanity could ever use. Boundless energy is also available from the tides and the winds. In some cases, we need better technology to harness these sources of energy; in others, we need only to apply the technology we already have.

Burning fossil fuels in internal combustion engines is the main source of pollution in the Most Industrialized Nations. With vast sources of alternative energy available to us, why don't we develop the technology to use them? From a conflict perspective, these abundant sources of energy present a threat to the multinational oil companies. It is in their interest to keep the gasoline-powered engine dominant. Competition is on the way, however, as gas-electric hybrid cars have appeared on the market. The hybrid is a bridge until cars powered by fuel cells become practical (Mateja 2001). Fuel cells convert hydrogen into electricity, and water, instead of carbon monoxide, will come out of a car's exhaust pipe.

Environmental Racism Conflict and unequal power have led to what sociologists call **environmental racism**—minorities being the ones who suffer the most from the effects of pollution (Fitzpatrick and LaGory 2000; Hines 2001). Polluting industries locate where land is cheaper, which is *not* where the wealthy live. Nor will the rich allow factories to spew pollution near their homes. As a result, low-income communities, which are often inhabited by minorities, are exposed to more pollution. Sociologists have studied, formed, and joined environmental justice groups that fight to close polluting plants and to block construction of polluting industries.

◼ Environmental Problems in the Industrializing and Least Industrialized Nations

Severe consequences of industrialization, such as ozone depletion, the greenhouse effect, and global warming, cannot be laid solely at the feet of the Most Industrialized Nations. With their rush to be contenders in the global competition, along with a lack of funds to pay for pollution controls, and few anti-pollution laws, the Industrializing Nations have made enormous contributions to this problem. The air of Mexico City, for example, is so bad that the lungs of *most* children living there have been harmed ("Study . . . " 2001).

The former Soviet Union is a special case. Until this empire broke up, pollution had been treated as a state secret. Scientists and journalists were forbidden to mention pollution in public. Even peaceful demonstrations to call attention to pollution could net participants two years in prison (Feshbach 1992). With protest stifled and no environmental protection laws, pollution was rampant: Almost half of Russia's arable land has been made unsuitable for farming, about a third of Russians live in cities where air pollution is more than ten times greater than permissible levels in the United States, and half of Russia's tap water is unfit to drink. Pollution is so severe that it may be partially responsible for the drop in the life expectancy of Russians. If so, it is a lesson that should not be lost on the rest of us as we make decisions on how to treat our environment.

With their greater poverty and swelling populations, the Least Industrialized Nations have an even greater incentive to industrialize at any cost. These pressures, combined with almost nonexistent environmental regulations, destine the Least Industrialized Nations to become the earth's major source of pollution.

Their lack of environmental protection laws has not gone unnoticed by opportunists in the Most Industrialized Nations, who use these countries as garbage dumps for hazardous wastes and for producing chemicals that their own people will no longer tolerate (Smith 1995; Englund and Cohn 1997). Alarmed at the growing environmental destruction, the World Bank, the monetary arm of G7, has pressured the Least Industrialized Nations to reduce pollution and soil erosion (Lachica 1992). Understandably, the basic concern of these nations is to produce food and housing first, and to worry about the environment later.

Although the rain forests cover just 7 percent of the earth's land area, they are home to *one-third to one-half* of all plant and animal species. Despite our knowledge that the rain forests are essential for humanity's welfare, we seem bent on destroying them. For the sake of timber and farms, we clear the rain forests at a rate of 2,500 acres *each hour* (McCuen 1993). In the process, we extinguish thousands of plant and animal species. Some estimate that we destroy 10,000 species each year—about 1 *per hour* (Durning 1990). Others say that this number is conservative, that we extinguish 100 plant and animal species a day, *4 per hour* (Wolfensohn and Fuller 1998). Whatever the number, as biologists remind us, a species once lost is gone forever.

As the rain forests are destroyed, so are the Indian tribes who live in them. With their extinction goes their knowledge of the environment, the topic of the Cultural Diversity box on the next page. Like Esau who exchanged his birthright for a bowl of porridge, we exchange our future for some lumber, farms, and pastures.

◼ The Environmental Movement

Concern about environmental problems has produced a worldwide social movement. One result is *green parties,* political parties whose central issue is the

cultural d i v e r s i t y

Brazil ———— Around the World

The Rain Forests: Lost Tribes, Lost Knowledge

Since 1900, 90 of Brazil's 270 Indian tribes have disappeared. Other tribes have moved to villages as settlers have taken over their lands. With village life comes a loss of tribal knowledge.

Tribal groups are not just "wild" people who barely survive despite their ignorance. On the contrary, they have intricate forms of social organization and possess knowledge that has accumulated over thousands of years. The 2,500 Kayapo Indians, for example, belong to one of the Amazon's endangered tribes. The Kayapo use 250 types of wild fruit and hundreds of nut and tuber species. They cultivate thirteen types of bananas, eleven kinds of manioc (cassava), sixteen strains of sweet potato, and seventeen kinds of yams. Many of these varieties are unknown to non-Indians. The Kayapo also use thousands of medicinal plants, one of which contains a drug that is effective against intestinal parasites.

Until recently, Western scientists dismissed tribal knowledge as superstitious and worthless. Now, however, some have come to realize that to lose tribes is to lose valuable knowledge. In the Central African Republic, a man whose chest was being eaten away by an amoeboid infection lay dying because he did not respond to drugs. Out of desperation, the Catholic nuns who were treating him sought the advice of a native doctor. He applied

■ Along Sega is the headman of the Penan tribe of the Sarawak rain forests in Malaysia. With their way of life threatened, the Penan are among the last rain forest nomads in the world.

crushed termites to the open wounds. To the amazement of the nuns, the man made a remarkable recovery.

The disappearance of the rain forests means the destruction of plant species that may hold healing properties. Some of the discoveries from the rain forests have been astounding. The needles from a Himalayan tree in India contain taxol, a drug that is effective against ovarian cancer. A flower from Madagascar is used in the treatment of leukemia; a frog in Peru produces a painkiller more powerful, but less addictive, than morphine (Wolfensohn and Fuller 1998).

On average, one tribe of Amazonian Indians has been lost each year for the past century—because of violence, greed for their lands, and exposure to infectious diseases against which they have little resistance. Ethnocentrism underlies much of this assault. Perhaps the extreme is represented by the cattle ranchers in Colombia who killed eighteen Cueva Indians. The cattle ranchers were perplexed when they were put on trial for murder. They asked why they should be charged with a crime, since everyone knew that the Cuevas were animals, not people. They pointed out that there was even a verb in Colombian Spanish, *cuevar*, which means "to hunt Cueva Indians." So what was their crime, they asked? The jury found them innocent because of "cultural ignorance."

Sources: Durning 1990; Gorman 1991; Linden 1991; Stipp 1992; Simons 1995; Nabhan 1998.

---

environment. In some European countries, these parties are politically successful. In Germany, for example, the Green Party has won seats in the national legislature. Green parties have had little success in the United States, but in the 2000 election, a green party headed by Ralph Nader tipped the balance and gave the presidential election to George W. Bush.

Activists in the environmental movement generally seek solutions in politics, education, and legislation. Despairing that pollution continues, that the rain forests are still being cleared, and that species are becoming extinct, some activists are convinced that the planet is doomed unless immediate steps are taken. Choosing a more radical course, they use extreme tactics to try to arouse indignation among the public and thus force the government to act. Convinced that they stand for true morality, many are willing to break the law and go to jail for their actions. Such activists are featured in the following Thinking Critically section.

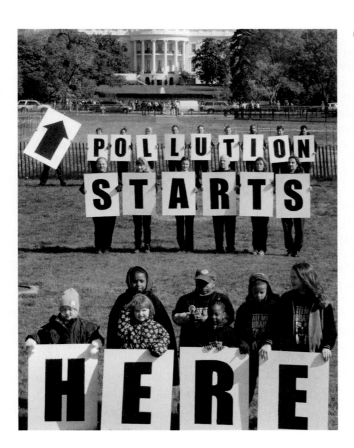

■ *As concern about the environment has grown, a social movement to try to change the course of events has developed. Protest groups have rallied around several issues, including whales, dolphins, seal pups, and the redwood forests. Another concern is the destructive effects of pollution on the planet.*

thinking
CRITICALLY

Ecosabotage

Chaining oneself to a giant Douglas fir slated for cutting; pouring sand down the gas tank of a bulldozer; tearing down power lines and ripping up survey stakes; driving spikes into redwood trees, and sinking whaling vessels—are these the acts of dangerous punks who are intent on vandalizing and who have little understanding of the needs of modern society? Or are they the acts of brave men and women who are willing to put their freedom, and even their lives, on the line on behalf of the earth itself?

To understand why **ecosabotage**—actions taken to sabotage the efforts of people thought to be legally harming the environment—is taking place, consider the Medicine Tree, a 3,000-year-old redwood in the Sally Bell Grove near the northern California coast. Georgia Pacific, a lumber company, was determined to cut down the Medicine Tree, the oldest and largest of the region's redwoods, which rests on a sacred site of the Sinkyone Indians. Members of Earth First! chained themselves to the tree. After they were arrested, the sawing began. Other protesters jumped over the police-lined barricade and planted themselves in front of the axes and chain saws. A logger swung an axe and missed a demonstrator. At that moment, the sheriff radioed a restraining order, and the cutting stopped.

Twenty-four-year-old David Chain's dedication cost him his life. The federal government and the state of California made a deal to purchase 10,000 acres of pristine redwoods for half a billion dollars. As last-minute negotiations dragged on, loggers from the Pacific Lumber Company kept felling trees, and Earth First! activists kept trying to stop them. David Chain died of a crushed skull when a felled tree struck him.

ecosabotage
actions taken to sabotage the efforts of people thought to be legally harming the environment

How many 3,000-year-old trees remain on this planet? Do fences and picnic tables for backyard barbecues justify cutting them down? Questions like these—as well as the slaughter of seals, the destruction of the rain forests, and the drowning of dolphins in mile-long drift nets—spawned Earth First! and other organizations devoted to preserving the environment, such as Greenpeace, Sea Shepherds, and the Ruckus Society.

"We feel like there are insane people who are consciously destroying our environment, and we are compelled to fight back," explains a member of one of the militant groups. "No compromise in defense of Mother Earth!" says another. "With famine and death approaching, we're in the early stages of World War III," adds another.

Radical environmentalists represent a broad range of activities and purposes. They are united neither on tactics nor goals. Most espouse a simpler lifestyle that will consume less energy and reduce pressure on the earth's resources. Some want to stop a specific action, such as the killing of whales. Others want to destroy all nuclear weapons and dismantle nuclear power plants. Some want everyone to become vegetarians. Still others want the earth's population to drop to one billion, roughly what it was in 1800. Some even want humans to return to hunting and gathering societies. These groups are so splintered that the founder of Earth First!, Dave Foreman, quit his own organization when it became too confrontational for his tastes.

Radical groups have had some successes. They have brought a halt to the killing of dolphins off Japan's Iki Island, achieved a ban on whaling, established trash recycling programs in many communities, and saved hundreds of thousands of acres of trees, including, of course, the Medicine Tree.

▪ ▪ ▪ ▪ ▪
for your consideration . . .

Should we applaud ecosaboteurs or jail them? As symbolic interactionists stress, it all depends on how you view their actions. And as conflict theorists emphasize, your view likely depends on your location in the economic structure. That is, if you own a lumber company you will see ecosaboteurs differently from the way a camping enthusiast will. How does your own view of ecosaboteurs depend on your life situation? What effective alternatives to ecosabotage are there for people who are convinced that we are destroying the very life support system of our planet?

Sources: Carpenter 1990; Eder 1990; Foote 1990; Parfit 1990; Reed and Benet 1990; Courtney 1995; Satchell 1998; Skow 1998; Nieves 1999.

Environmental Sociology

About 1970, a subdiscipline of sociology emerged called **environmental sociology.** Its focus is the relationship between human societies and the environment (Dunlap and Catton 1979, 1983; Buttel 1987; Freudenburg and Gramling 1989; Laska 1993; Redclift and Woodgate 1997). Its main assumptions are:

1. The physical environment is a significant variable in sociological investigation.
2. Human beings are but one species among many that depend on the natural environment.
3. Because of intricate feedback to nature, human actions have many unintended consequences.
4. The world is finite, so there are potential physical limits to economic growth.
5. Economic expansion requires increased extraction of resources from the environment.
6. Increased extraction of resources leads to ecological problems.

environmental sociology
a subdiscipline of sociology that examines how human activities affect the physical environment and how the physical environment affects human activities

7. These ecological problems place restrictions on economic expansion.

8. Governments create environmental problems by trying to create conditions for the accumulation of capital.

The goal of environmental sociology is not to stop pollution or nuclear power but, rather, to study how humans (their cultures, values, and behavior) affect the physical environment and how the physical environment affects human activities. Environmental sociologists, however, generally are also environmental activists, and the Section on Environment and Technology of the American Sociological Association tries to influence governmental policies (American Sociological Association n.d.).

Technology and the Environment: The Goal of Harmony It is inevitable that humans will continue to develop new technologies. But the abuse of our environment by those technologies is not inevitable. To understate the matter, the destruction of our planet is an unwise choice.

If we are to live in a world that is worth passing on to coming generations, we must seek harmony between technology and the natural environment. This will not be easy. At one extreme are people who claim that to protect the environment we must eliminate industrialization and go back to some sort of a tribal way of life. At the other extreme are people who are blind to the harm being done to the natural environment, who want the entire world to industrialize at full speed. Somewhere, there must be a middle ground, one that recognizes not only that industrialization is here to stay but also that we *can* control it, for it is our creation. Industrialization, controlled, can enhance our quality of life; uncontrolled, it will destroy us.

As a parallel to the development of technologies, then, we must develop systems to reduce or eliminate their harm to the environment. This includes mechanisms to monitor the production, use, and disposal of technology. The question, of course, is whether we have the resolve to take the steps to preserve the environment for future generations. What is at stake is nothing less than the welfare of the entire planet. Surely that is enough to motivate us to make wise choices.

■ ■ ■ ■ ■

Summary and Review

How Social Change Transforms Society

■ **What major trends have transformed the course of human history?**

The primary changes in human history are the four social revolutions (domestication, agriculture, industrialization, and information); the change from *Gemeinschaft* to *Gesellschaft* societies; capitalism and industrialization; **modernization;** and global stratification. Social movements indicate cutting edges of social change. Ethnic conflicts threaten the global divisions G7 is working out. We may also be on the cutting edge of a new bioeconomy. Pp. 666–670.

Theories and Processes of Social Change

■ **Besides technology, capitalism, modernization, and so on, what other theories of social change are there?**

Evolutionary theories presuppose that societies move from the same starting point to some similar ending point. *Unilinear* theories, which assume the same path for everyone, were replaced with *multilinear* theories, which assume that different paths lead to the same stage of development. In *cyclical* theories, civilizations are viewed as going through a process of birth, youth, maturity, decline, and death. Conflict theorists view social change as inevitable, for each *thesis* (basically an arrangement of power) contains an *antithesis* (contradictions). A new *synthesis* develops to resolve these contradictions, but it, too, contains contradictions that must be resolved, and so on. This is called a **dialectical process.** Pp. 670–671.

■ **What is Ogburn's theory of social change?**

Ogburn identified technology as the basic cause of social change, which comes through three processes: **invention, discovery,** and **diffusion.** The term **cultural lag** refers to symbolic culture lagging behind changes in technology. Pp. 671–673.

How Technology Changes Society

■ How does new technology affect society?

Because **technology** is an organizing force of social life, changes in technology can have profound effects. The computer was used as an extended example. It is changing the way we learn, work, do business, and fight wars. The information superhighway is likely to perpetuate social inequalities on both a national and a global level. Pp. 674–679.

The Growth Machine Versus the Earth

■ What are the environmental problems of the Most Industrialized Nations?

The environmental problems of the Most Industrialized Nations range from smog and **acid rain** to the **greenhouse effect**. The greenhouse effect may cause **global warming** that will fundamentally affect our lives. Burning fossil fuels in internal combustion engines lies at the root of many environmental problems. It is in the interest of the oil companies to keep the internal combustion engine dominant, but alternatives are on the way. Due to the location of factories and hazardous waste sites, environmental problems have a greater impact on minorities and the poor. Pp. 680–683.

■ What are the environmental problems of the Industrializing and Least Industrialized Nations?

The worst environmental problems are found in the former Soviet Union, a legacy of the unrestrained exploitation of resources by the Communist party. The rush of the Least Industrialized Nations to industrialize is adding to our environmental decay. The world is facing a conflict between the lust for profits through the exploitation of the earth's resources and the need to produce a **sustainable environment**. P. 683.

■ What is the environmental movement?

The environmental movement is an attempt to restore a healthy environment for the world's people. This global movement takes many forms, from peaceful attempts to influence the political process to **ecosabotage**. Pp. 683–686.

■ What is environmental sociology?

Environmental sociology is not an attempt to change the environment, but a study of the relationship between humans and the environment. Environmental sociologists are generally also environmental activists. Pp. 686–687.

■ *Where can I read more on this topic?*

Suggested Readings for this chapter are at the back of this book.

Additional Online Resources for This Chapter
www.ablongman.com/henslin6e

- *Content Select* Research Database for Sociology, with suggested key terms and annotated references
- Link to 2000 Census, with activities
- Flashcards of key terms and concepts

- Practice Tests
- Weblinks
- Interactive Maps

using . . .

ContentSelect

Research Database for Sociology

environmental problems	geopolitics	pollution	the environmental movement
environmental sociology	global warming	social revolution	
	greenhouse effect	technology and transformation	

Glossary

acculturation the transmission of culture from one generation to the next

achieved statuses positions that are earned, accomplished, or involve at least some effort or activity on the individual's part

acid rain rain containing sulfuric and nitric acids (burning fossil fuels releases sulfur dioxide and nitrogen oxide which becomes sulfuric and nitric acids when they react with moisture in the air)

acting crowd Herbert Blumer's term for an excited group that collectively moves toward a goal

activity theory the view that satisfaction during old age is related to a person's amount and quality of activity

age cohort people born at roughly the same time who pass through the life course together

ageism prejudice, discrimination, and hostility directed against people because of their age; can be directed against any age group, including youth

agent provocateur someone who joins a group in order to spy on it and to sabotage it by provoking its members to commit illegal acts

agent of socialization people or groups that affect our self-concept, attitudes, behaviors, or other orientations toward life

aggregate individuals who temporarily share the same physical space but do not see themselves as belonging together

agricultural revolution the second social revolution, based on the invention of the plow, which led to agricultural society

agricultural society a society based on large-scale agriculture, dependent on plows drawn by animals

alienation Marx's term for workers' lack of connection to the product of their labor; caused by their being assigned repetitive tasks on a small part of a product: this leads to a sense of powerlessness and normlessness; also used in the general sense of not feeling a part of something

alterative social movement a social movement that seeks to alter only particular aspects of people

anarchy a condition of lawlessness or political disorder caused by the absence or collapse of governmental authority

animism the belief that all objects in the world have spirits, some of which are dangerous and must be outwitted

anomie Durkheim's term for a condition of society in which people become detached from the norms that usually guide their behavior

anticipatory socialization because one anticipates a future role, one learns parts of it now

anti-Semitism prejudice, discrimination, and persecution directed against Jews

apartheid the separation of races as was practiced in South Africa

applied sociology the use of sociology to solve problems—from the micro level of family relationships to the macro level of crime and pollution

ascribed statuses positions an individual either inherits at birth or receives involuntarily later in life

assimilation the process of being absorbed into the mainstream culture

authoritarian leader a leader who leads by giving orders

authoritarian personality Theodor Adorno's term for people who are prejudiced and rank high on scales of conformity, intolerance, insecurity, respect for authority, and submissiveness to superiors

authority power that people consider legitimate, as rightly exercised over them; also called *legitimate power*

back stage where people rest from their performances, discuss their presentations, and plan future performances

background assumptions deeply embedded common understandings, or basic rules, concerning our view of the world and of how people ought to act

barter the direct exchange of one item for another

basic demographic equation growth rate = births − deaths + net migration

bilateral (system of descent) a system of reckoning descent that counts both the mother's and the father's side

bioeconomic society an economy that centers around the application of genetic structures, especially in medicine and food production

blended family a family whose members were once part of other families

born again a term describing Christians who have undergone a life-transforming religious experience so radical that they feel they have become new persons

bourgeosie Karl Marx's term for capitalists, those who own the means to produce wealth

bureaucracy a formal organization with a hierarchy of authority; a clear division of labor; emphasis on written rules, communications, and records; and impersonality of positions

capital punishment the death penalty

capitalism an economic system characterized by the private ownership of the means of production, the pursuit of profit, and market competition

capitalist class the wealthy who own the means of production and buy the labor of the working class

cargo cult a social movement in which South Pacific islanders destroyed their possessions in the anticipation that their ancestors would send them items by ship

caste system a form of social stratification in which one's status is determined by birth and is lifelong

category people who have similar characteristics

centrist party a political party that represents the center of political opinion

charisma literally, an extraordinary gift from God; more commonly, an outstanding, "magnetic" personality

charismatic authority authority based on an individual's outstanding traits, which attract followers

charismatic leader literally, someone to whom God has given a gift; more commonly, someone who exerts extraordinary appeal to a group of followers

charter schools schools that, although financed by taxes, are owned and run by private groups

checks and balances the separation of powers among the three branches of U.S. government—legislative, executive, and judicial—so that each is able to nullify the actions of the other two, thus preventing the domination of any single branch

church according to Durkheim, one of the three essential elements of religion—a moral community of believers; a second definition is the type of religious organization described on page 549, a large, highly organized group with formal, sedate worship services and little emphasis on personal conversion

circular reaction Robert Park's term for a back-and-forth communication between the members of a crowd whereby a "collective impulse" is transmitted

citizenship the concept that birth (and residence) in a country impart basic rights

city a place in which a large number of people are permanently based and do not produce their own food

city-state an independent city whose power radiates outward, bringing the adjacent area under its rule

civil religion Robert Bellah's term for religion that is such an established feature of a country's life that its history and social institutions become sanctified by being associated with God

class see social class

class conflict Marx's term for the struggle between capitalists and workers

class consciousness Karl Marx's term for awareness of a common identity based on one's position in the means of production

class system a form of social stratification based primarily on the possession of money or material possessions

clique a cluster of people within a larger group who choose to interact with one another; an internal faction

closed-ended questions questions that are followed by a list of possible answers to be selected by the respondent

coalition the alignment of some members of a group against others

coalition government a government in which a country's largest party aligns itself with one or more smaller parties

coercion power that people do not accept as rightly exercised over them; also called *illegitimate power*

cohabitation unmarried couples living together in a sexual relationship

collective behavior extraordinary activities carried out by groups of people; includes lynchings, rumors, panics, urban legends, and fads and fashions

collective mind Gustave LeBon's term for the tendency of people in a crowd to feel, think, and act in extraordinary ways

colonialism the process by which one nation takes over another nation, usually for the purpose of exploiting its labor and natural resources

common sense those things that "everyone knows" are true

community a place people identify with, where they sense that they belong and that others care what happens to them

compartmentalize to separate acts from feelings or attitudes

conflict theory a theoretical framework in which society is viewed as composed of groups competing for scarce resources

conspicuous consumption Thorstein Veblen's term for a change from the Protestant ethic to an eagerness to show off wealth by the elaborate consumption of goods

contradictory class location Erik Wright's term for a position in the class structure that generates contradictory interests

control group the group of subjects not exposed to the independent variable

control theory the idea that two control systems—inner controls and outer controls—work against our tendencies to deviate

convergence theory the view that as capitalist and socialist economic systems each adopt features of the other, a hybrid (or mixed) economic system will emerge

corporate capitalism the domination of the economic system by giant corporations

corporate welfare the gifts or financial incentives (tax breaks, subsidies, and even land and stadiums) given to corporations in order to attract them to an area or induce them to remain

corporation the joint ownership of a business enterprise, whose liabilities and obligations are separate from those of its owners

correspondence principle the sociological principle that schools correspond to (or reflect) the social structure of society

cosmology teachings or ideas that provide a unified picture of the world

counterculture a group whose values, beliefs, and related behaviors place its members in opposition to the broader culture

credential society the use of diplomas and degrees to determine who is eligible for jobs, even though the diploma or degree may be irrelevant to the actual work

credit card a device that allows its owner to purchase goods and to be billed later

crime the violation of norms that are written into law

criminal justice system the system of police, courts, and prisons set up to deal with people who are accused of having committed a crime

crude birth rate the annual number of live births per 1,000 population

crude death rate the annual number of deaths per 1,000 population

cult a new religion with few followers, whose teachings and practices put it at odds with the dominant culture and religion

cultural diffusion the spread of cultural characteristics from one group to another

cultural goals the legitimate objectives held out to the members of a society

cultural lag Ogburn's term for human behavior lagging behind technological innovations

cultural leveling the process by which cultures become similar to one another, and especially by which Western industrial culture is imported and diffused into industrializing nations

cultural relativism not judging a culture, but trying to understand it on its own terms

cultural transmission in reference to education, the ways in which schools transmit a society's culture, especially its core values

cultural universal a value, norm, or other cultural trait that is found in every group

culture the language, beliefs, values, norms, behaviors, and even material objects that are passed from one generation to the next

culture of poverty the assumption that the values and behaviors of the poor make them fundamentally different from other people, that these factors are largely responsible for their poverty, and that parents perpetuate poverty across generations by passing these characteristics to their children

culture shock the disorientation that people experience when they come in contact with a fundamentally different culture and can no longer depend on their taken-for-granted assumptions about life

currency paper money

debit card a device that allows its owner to charge purchases against his or her bank account

defensive medicine medical practices done not for the patient's benefit but in order to protect a physician from malpractice suits

deferred gratification forgoing something in the present in the hope of achieving greater gains in the future

degradation ceremonies rituals designed to strip an individual of his or her identity as a group member; for example, a court martial or the defrocking of a priest

degradation ceremony a term coined by Harold Garfinkel to describe an attempt to remake the self by stripping away an individual's self-identity and stamping a new identity in its place

dehumanization the act or process of reducing people to objects that do not deserve the treatment accorded humans

deindustrialization industries moving out of a country or region

deinstitutionalization the release of patients from mental hospitals into the community, supposedly while receiving treatment within a network of outpatient services

democracy a system of government in which authority derives from the people; the term comes from two Greek words that translate literally as "power to the people"

democratic leader a leader who leads by trying to reach a consensus

democratic socialism a hybrid economic system in which capitalism is mixed with state ownership

demographic transition a three-stage historical process of population growth: first, high birth rates and high death rates; second, high birth rates and low death rates; and third, low birth rates and low death rates; a fourth stage has begun to appear in the Most Industrialized Nations, as depicted in Figure 20.3, p. 600

demographic variables the three factors that influence population growth: fertility, mortality, and net migration

demography the study of the size, composition, growth, and distribution of human populations

denomination a "brand name" within a major religion, for example, Methodist or Baptist

dependency ratio the number of workers required to support dependent persons—those 65 and older and those 15 and under

dependent variable a factor that is changed by an independent variable

depersonalization dealing with people as though they were objects; in the case of medical care, as though patients were merely cases and diseases, not people

deposit receipts a receipt stating that a certain amount of goods is on deposit in a warehouse or bank; the receipt is used as a form of money

deviance the violation of rules or norms

dialectical process each arrangement, or thesis, contains contradictions, or antitheses, which must be resolved; the new arrangement, or synthesis, contains its own contradictions, and so on

dictatorship a form of government in which power is seized by an individual

differential association Edwin Sutherland's term to indicate that associating with some groups results in learning an "excess of definitions" of deviance, and, by extension, in a greater likelihood that one will become deviant

diffusion the spread of an invention or a discovery from one area to another; identified by William Ogburn as the final of three processes of social change

direct democracy a form of democracy in which the eligible voters meet together to discuss issues and make their decisions

disabling environment an environment that is harmful to health

discovery a new way of seeing reality; identified by William Ogburn as the second of three processes of social change

discrimination an *act* of unfair treatment directed against an individual or a group

disengagement theory the view that society prevents disruption by having the elderly vacate (or disengage from) their positions of responsibility so the younger generation can step into their shoes

disinvestment the withdrawal of investments by financial institutions, which seals the fate of an urban area

divest to sell off

divine right of kings the idea that the king's authority comes directly from God

division of labor the splitting of a group's or a society's tasks into specialties

documents in its narrow sense, written sources that provide data; in its extended sense, archival material of any sort, including photographs, movies, and so on

domestication revolution the first social revolution, based on the domestication of plants and animals, which led to pastoral and horticultural societies

dominant group the group with the most power, greatest privileges, and highest social status

downward social mobility movement down the social class ladder

dramaturgy an approach, pioneered by Erving Goffman, in which social life is analyzed in terms of drama or the stage; also called *dramaturgical analysis*

dumping the practice of sending unprofitable patients to public hospitals

dyad the smallest possible group, consisting of two people

e–cash digital money that is stored on computers

ecclesia a religious group so integrated into the dominant culture that it is difficult to tell where the one begins and the other leaves off; also called a *state religion*

economy a system of distribution of goods and services

ecosabotage actions taken to sabotage the efforts of people who are thought to be legally harming the environment

edge city a large clustering of service facilities and residential areas near highway intersections that provides a sense of place to people who live, shop, and work there

education a formal system of teaching knowledge, values, and skills

egalitarian authority more or less equally divided between people or groups, in this instance between husband and wife

ego Freud's term for a balancing force between the id and the demands of society

electronic community individuals who regularly interact with one another on the Internet and who think of themselves as belonging together

emergent norms Ralph Turner's and Lewis Killian's term for the development of new norms to cope with a new situation, especially among crowds

empty nest a married couple's domestic situation after the last child has left home

endogamy the practice of marrying within one's own group

enterprise zone the use of economic incentives in a designated area with the intention of encouraging investment there

environmental racism the greater impact of pollution on the poor and racial–ethnic minorities

environmental sociology a subdiscipline of sociology that examines how human activities affect the physical environment and how the physical environment affects human activities

epidemiology the study of disease and disability patterns in a population

estate stratification system the stratification system of medieval Europe, consisting of three groups or estates: the nobility, clergy, and commoners

ethnic (and **ethnicity**) having distinctive cultural characteristics

ethnic cleansing a policy to eliminate an ethnic group; includes forcible expulsion and genocide. The term emerged in 1992 among the Serbians during their policy of expelling Croats and Muslims from territories claimed by them during the Yugoslav wars

ethnic work activities designed to discover, enhance, or maintain ethnic and racial identification

ethnocentrism the use of one's own culture as a yardstick for judging the ways of other individuals or societies, generally leading to a negative evaluation of their values, norms, and behaviors

ethnomethodology the study of how people use background assumptions to make sense out of life

euthanasia mercy killing

evangelism an attempt to win converts

exchange mobility about the same numbers of people moving up and down the social class ladder, such that, on balance, the social class system shows little change

exogamy the practice of marrying outside one's group

experiment the use of control groups and experimental groups and dependent and independent variables to test causation

experimental group the group of subjects exposed to the independent variable

exponential growth curve a pattern of growth in which numbers double during approximately equal intervals, thus accelerating in the latter stages

expressive leader an individual who increases harmony and minimizes conflict in a group; also known as a socioemotional leader

extended family a nuclear family plus other relatives, such as grandparents, uncles and aunts, who live together

face-saving behavior techniques used to salvage a performance that is going sour

fad a temporary pattern of behavior that catches people's attention

false consciousness Karl Marx's term to refer to workers identifying with the interests of capitalists

family two or more people who consider themselves related by blood, marriage, or adoption

family of orientation the family in which a person grows up

family of procreation the family formed when a couple's first child is born

fashion a pattern of behavior that catches people's attention and lasts longer than a fad

fecundity the number of children that women are capable of bearing

fee-for-service payment to a physician to diagnose and treat a patient's medical problems

feminism the philosophy that men and women should be politically, economically, and socially equal; an organized activity on behalf of this principle

feminization of poverty a trend in U.S. poverty whereby most poor families are headed by women

feral children children assumed to have been raised by animals, in the wilderness, isolated from other humans

fertility rate the number of children that the average woman bears

fiat money currency issued by a government that is not backed by stored value

folkways norms that are not strictly enforced

formal organization a secondary group designed to achieve explicit objectives

front stage where performances are given

functional analysis a theoretical framework in which society is viewed as composed of various parts, each with a function that, when fulfilled, contributes to society's equilibrium; also known as functionalism and structural functionalism

functional equivalent in this context, a substitute that serves the same functions (or meets the same needs) as religion, for example, psychotherapy

functional illiterate a high school graduate who has difficulty with basic reading and math

functional requisites the major tasks that a society must fulfill if it is to survive

fundamentalism the belief that true religion is threatened by modernism and its values and that the faith as it was originally practiced should be restored

gatekeeping the process by which education opens and closes doors of opportunity; another term for the social placement function of education

Gemeinschaft a type of society in which life is intimate; a community in which everyone knows everyone else and people share a sense of togetherness

gender the social characteristics that a society considers proper for its males and females; masculinity or femininity

gender age the relative values of men's and women's ages in a particular culture

gender role the behaviors and attitudes considered appropriate because one is a female or a male

gender socialization the ways in which society sets children onto different courses in life *because* they are male or female

gender stratification males' and females' unequal access to power, prestige, and property on the basis of their sex

generalizability the extent to which the findings from one group (or sample) can be generalized or applied to other groups (or populations)

generalization a statement that goes beyond the individual case and is applied to a broader group or situation

generalized other the norms, values, attitudes, and expectations of people "in general"; the child's ability to take the role of the generalized other is a significant step in the development of a self

genetic predispositions inborn tendencies, in this context, to commit deviant acts

genocide the systematic annihilation or attempted annihilation of a people based on their presumed race or ethnicity

genomics the study of genes and how they relate to health and illness

gentrification the displacement of the poor by the relatively affluent, who purchase and renovate the former's homes

gerontocracy a society (or some other group) run by the elderly

Gesellschaft a type of society dominated by impersonal relationships, individual accomplishments, and self-interest

gestures the ways in which people use their bodies to communicate with one another

global warming an increase in the earth's temperature due to the greenhouse effect

globalization the extensive movement of capital and ideas among nations due to the expansion of capitalism

globalization of capitalism capitalism (investing to make profits within a rational system) becoming the globe's dominant economic system

goal displacement a goal displaced by another goal; in this context, the adoption of new goals by an organization; also known as *goal replacement*

gold standard paper money backed by gold

grade inflation higher grades given for the same work; a general rise in student grades without a corresponding increase in learning or test scores

graying of America a term that refers to the rising proportion of older people as a percentage of the U.S. population

greenhouse effect the buildup of carbon dioxide in the earth's atmosphere that allows light to enter but inhibits the release of heat; believed to cause global warming

gross domestic product (GDP) the amount of goods and services produced by a nation

group people who have something in common and who believe that what they have in common is significant; also called a social group

group dynamics the ways in which individuals affect groups and the ways in which groups influence individuals

groupthink Irving Janis' term for a narrowing of thought by a group of people, leading to the perception that there is only one correct answer, in which to even suggest alternatives becomes a sign of disloyalty

growth rate the net change in a population after adding births, subtracting deaths, and either adding or subtracting net migration

hate crime crimes to which more severe penalties are attached because they are motivated by hatred (dislike, animosity) of someone's race-ethnicity, religion, sexual orientation, disability, or national origin

health a human condition measured by four components: physical, mental, social, and spiritual

health maintenance organization (HMO) a health care organization that provides medical treatment to its members for a fixed annual cost

hidden curriculum the unwritten goals of schools, such as teaching obedience to authority and conformity to cultural norms

homogamy the tendency of people with similar characteristics to marry one another

Horatio Alger myth the belief that due to limitless possibilities anyone can get ahead if he or she tries hard enough

horticultural society a society based on cultivating plants by the use of hand tools

hospice a place, or services brought into someone's home, for the purpose of bringing comfort and dignity to a dying person

household people who occupy the same housing unit

human ecology Robert Park's term for the relationship between people and their environment (natural resources such as land)

humanizing a work setting organizing a workplace in such a way that it develops rather than impedes human potential

hunting and gathering society a human group dependent on hunting and gathering for its survival

hypothesis a statement of the expected relationship between variables according to predictions from a theory

id Freud's term for our inborn basic drives

ideal culture the ideal values and norms of a people, the goals held out for them (as opposed to real culture)

ideal type a composite of characteristics based on many specific examples ("ideal" in this case means a description of the abstracted characteristics, not what one desires to exist)

ideology beliefs about the way things ought to be that justify social arrangements

illegitimate opportunity structures opportunities for crimes that are woven into the texture of life

impression management the term used by Erving Goffman to describe people's efforts to control the impressions that others receive of them

in-groups groups toward which one feels loyalty

incest sexual relations between specified relatives, such as brothers and sisters or parents and children

incest taboo the rule that prohibits sex and marriage among designated relatives

indentured service a contractual system in which someone sells his or her body (services) for a specified period of time in an arrangement very close to slavery, except that it is voluntarily entered into

independent variable a factor that causes a change in another variable, called the dependent variable

individual discrimination the negative treatment of one person by another on the basis of that person's perceived characteristics

Industrial Revolution the third social revolution, occurring when machines powered by fuels replaced most animal and human power

industrial society a society based on the harnessing of machines powered by fuels

inflation an increase in prices

institutional discrimination negative treatment of a minority group that is built into a society's institutions; also called *systemic discrimination*

institutionalized means approved ways of reaching cultural goals

instrumental leader an individual who tries to keep the group moving toward its goals; also known as a task-oriented leader

intergenerational mobility the change that family members make in social class from one generation to the next

interlocking directorates the same people serving on the board of directors of several companies

internal colonialism the policy of economically exploiting minority groups

interview direct questioning of respondents

interviewer bias effects that interviewers have on respondents that lead to biased answers

invasion-succession cycle the process of one group of people displacing a group whose racial-ethnic or social class characteristics differ from their own

invention the combination of existing elements and materials to form new ones; identified by William Ogburn as the first of three processes of social change

involuntary memberships (or involuntary associations) groups in which people are assigned membership rather than choosing to join

labeling theory the view, developed by symbolic interactionists, that the labels people are given affect their own and others' perceptions of them, thus channeling their behavior either into deviance or into conformity

laissez-faire capitalism unrestrained manufacture and trade (literally, "hands off" capitalism)

laissez-faire leader an individual who leads by being highly permissive

language a system of symbols that can be combined in an infinite number of ways and can represent not only objects but also abstract thought

latent functions unintended beneficial consequences of people's actions

leader someone who influences other people

leadership styles ways in which people express their leadership

leisure time not taken up by work or required activities

life course the stages of our life as we go from birth to death

life expectancy the number of years that an average newborn can expect to live

life span the maximum length of life of a species

living will a statement people sign that expresses their desires concerning being kept alive on artificial life support systems

lobbyists people who influence legislation on behalf of their clients

looking-glass self a term coined by Charles Horton Cooley to refer to the process by which our self develops through internalizing others' reactions to us

macro-level analysis an examination of large-scale patterns of society

macropolitics the exercise of large-scale power, the government being the most common example

macrosociology analysis of social life focusing on broad features of society, such as social class and the relationships of groups to one another; an approach usually used by functionalists and conflict theorists

mainstreaming helping people to become part of the mainstream of society

Malthus theorem an observation by Thomas Malthus that although the food supply increases only arithmetically (from 1 to 2 to 3 to 4 and so on), population grows geometrically (from 2 to 4 to 8 to 16 and so forth)

mandatory education laws laws that require all children to attend school until a specified age or until they complete a minimum grade in school

manifest functions intended beneficial consequences of people's actions

marginal working class the most desperate members of the working class, who have few skills, little job security, and are often unemployed

market any process of buying and selling; on a more formal level, the mechanism that establishes values for the exchange of goods and services

market competition the exchange of items between willing buyers and sellers

market forces the law of supply and demand

market restraints laws and regulations that limit the capacity to manufacture and sell products

marriage a group's approved mating arrangements, usually marked by a ritual of some sort

marriage squeeze the difficulty a group of men or women have in finding marriage partners, due to an imbalanced sex ratio

mass hysteria an imagined threat that causes physical symptoms among a large number of people

mass media forms of communication, such as radio, newspapers, and television, that are directed to mass audiences

mass society industrialized, highly bureaucratized, impersonal society

mass society theory an explanation for why people participate in a social movement based on the assumption that the movement offers them a sense of belonging

master status a status that cuts across the other statuses that an individual occupies

material culture the material objects that distinguish a group of people, such as their art, buildings, weapons, utensils, machines, hairstyles, clothing, and jewelry

matriarchy a society in which women as a group dominate men as a group

matrilineal (system of descent) a system of reckoning descent that counts only the mother's side

means of production the tools, factories, land, and investment capital used to produce wealth

mechanical solidarity Durkheim's term for the unity that people feel as a result of performing the same or similar tasks; a shared consciousness

medicalization of deviance to make deviance a medical matter, a symptom of some underlying illness that needs to be treated by physicians

medicalization the transformation of something into a matter to be treated by physicians

medicine one of the major social institutions that sociologists study; a society's organized ways of dealing with sickness and injury

medium of exchange the means by which people value goods and services in order to make an exchange, for example, currency, gold, and silver

megacity a city of 10 million or more residents

megalopolis an urban area consisting of at least two metropolises and their many suburbs

melting pot the view that Americans of various backgrounds would blend into a sort of ethnic stew

meritocracy a form of social stratification in which all positions are awarded on the basis of merit

metropolis a central city surrounded by smaller cities and their suburbs

metropolitan statistical area (MSA) a central city and the urbanized counties adjacent to it

micro-level analysis an examination of small-scale patterns of society

micropolitics the exercise of power in everyday life, such as deciding who is going to do the housework or control the remote

microsociology analysis of social life focusing on social interaction; an approach usually used by symbolic interactionists

millenarian movement a social movement based on the prophecy of coming social upheaval

milling a crowd standing or walking around as they talk excitedly about some event

minimax strategy Richard Berk's term for the effort people make to minimize their costs and maximize their rewards

minority group people who are singled out for unequal treatment, and who regard themselves as objects of collective discrimination

modernization the transformation of traditional societies into industrial societies

monarchy a form of government headed by a king or queen

money any item (from seashells to gold) that serves as a medium of exchange; today, currency is the most common form

monopoly the control of an entire industry by a single company

monotheism the belief that there is only one God

moral panic a fear that grips large numbers of people that some evil threatens the well-being of society, followed by intense hostility, sometimes violence, toward those thought responsible

mores (more-rays) norms that are strictly enforced because they are thought essential to core values

multiculturalism (also called **pluralism**) a philosophy or political policy that permits or encourages ethnic difference

multinational corporations companies that operate across many national boundaries; also called transnational corporations

multinational corporations Corporations that have manufacturing, service, distribution systems in several countries.

nationalism a strong identity with a nation, accompanied by the desire for that nation to be dominant

natural sciences the intellectual and academic disciplines designed to comprehend, explain, and predict events in our natural environment

negative sanction a punishment or negative reaction for disapproved behavior, for deviance

negative sanction an expression of disapproval for breaking a norm, ranging from a mild, informal reaction such as a frown to a formal prison sentence or an execution

neocolonialism the economic and political dominance of the Least Industrialized Nations by the Most Industrialized Nations

net migration rate the difference between the number of immigrants and emigrants per 1,000 population

networking using one's social networks for some gain

new technology the emerging technologies of an era that have a significant impact on social life

noncentrist party a political party that represents marginal ideas

nonmaterial culture a group's ways of thinking (including its beliefs, values, and other assumptions about the world) and doing (its common patterns of behavior, including language and other forms of interaction)

nonverbal interaction communication without words through gestures, space, silence, and so on

norms the expectations, or rules of behavior, that develop to reflect and enforce values

nuclear family a family consisting of a husband, wife, and child(ren)

objectivity total neutrality

oligarchy a form of government in which power is held by a small group of individuals; the rule of the many by the few

oligopoly the control of an entire industry by several large companies

open-ended questions questions that respondents are able to answer in their own words

operational definition the way in which a variable in a hypothesis is measured

organic solidarity solidarity based on the interdependence that results from the division of labor; people needing others to fulfill their jobs

out-groups groups toward which one feels antagonisms

pan-Indianism a movement that focuses on common elements in Native-American culture in order to develop a cross-tribal self-identity and to work toward the welfare of all Native Americans

panic the condition of being so fearful that one cannot function normally, and may even flee

participant observation (or **fieldwork**) research in which the researcher participates in a research setting while observing what is happening in that setting

pastoral society a society based on the pasturing of animals

patriarchy a society or group in which men dominate women, authority is vested in males

patrilineal (system of descent) a system of reckoning descent that counts only the father's side

patterns recurring characteristics or events

peer group a group of individuals of roughly the same age who are linked by common interests

personality disorders the view that a personality disturbance of some sort causes an individual to violate social norms

Peter principle a bureaucratic "law" according to which the members of an organization are promoted for good work until they reach their level of incompetence, the level at which they can no longer do good work

pluralism the diffusion of power among many interest groups which prevents any single group from gaining control of the government

pluralistic society a society made up of many different groups

police discretion the practice of the police, in the normal course of their duties, to arrest someone for an offense or to overlook the matter

political action committee (PAC) an organization formed by one or more special-interest groups to solicit and spend funds for the purpose of influencing legislation

polyandry a form of marriage in which women have more than one husband

polygyny a form of marriage in which men have more than one wife

polytheism the belief that there are many gods

population the target group to be studied

population pyramid a graphic representation of a population, divided into age and sex

population shrinkage the process by which a country's population becomes smaller because its birth rate and immigration are too low to replace those who die and emigrate

population transfer forcing a minority group to move

positive sanction a reward given for following norms, ranging from a smile to a prize

positive sanction a reward or positive reaction for approved behavior, for conformity

positivism the application of the scientific approach to the social world

postindustrial (information) society a society based on information, services, and high technology, rather than on raw materials and manufacturing

postmodern society another term for postindustrial society; its chief characteristic is the use of tools that extend human abilities to gather and analyze information, to communicate, and to travel

poverty lacking resources to meet your basic needs

poverty line the official measure of poverty; calculated to include those whose incomes are less than three times a low-cost food budget

power the ability to carry out your will, even over the resistance of others

power elite C. Wright Mills' term for the top people in U.S. corporations, military, and politics who make the nation's major decisions

prejudice an *attitude* or prejudging, usually in a negative way

prestige respect or regard

primary group a group characterized by intimate, long-term, face-to-face association and cooperation

private ownership of the means of production the ownership of machines and factories by individuals, who decide what shall be produced

proactive social movement a social movement that promotes some social change

profane Durkheim's term for the common elements of everyday life

professionalization of medicine the development of medicine into a field in which education becomes rigorous, and in which physicians claim a theoretical understanding of illness, regulate themselves, claim to be doing a service to society (rather than just following self-interest), and take authority over clients

proletariat Marx's term for the exploited class, the mass of workers who do not own the means of production

propaganda in its broad sense, the presentation of information in the attempt to influence people; in its narrow sense, one-sided information used to try to influence people

proportional representation an electoral system in which seats in a legislature are divided according to the proportion of votes each political party receives

Protestant ethic Weber's term to describe the ideal of a self-denying, highly moral life, accompanied by hard work and frugality

public a dispersed group of people who usually have an interest in the issue on which a social movement focuses; the sympathetic and hostile publics have such an interest, but a third public is either unaware of the issue or indifferent to it

public opinion how people think about some issue

pure or **basic sociology** sociological research whose purpose is to make discoveries about life in human groups, not to make changes in those groups

qualitative research methods research in which the emphasis is placed on observing, describing, and interpreting people's behavior

quantitative research methods research in which the emphasis is placed on precise measurement, the use of statistics and numbers

questionnaires a list of questions to be asked

race inherited physical characteristics that distinguish one group from another

racism prejudice and discrimination on the basis of race

random sample a sample in which everyone in the target population has the same chance of being included in the study

rapport a feeling of trust between researchers and subjects

rational-legal authority authority based on law or written rules and regulations; also called *bureaucratic authority*

rationality the acceptance of rules, efficiency, and practical results as the right way to approach human affairs

rationalization of society a widespread acceptance of rationality and a social organization largely built around this idea

reactive social movement a social movement that resists some social change

real culture the norms and values that people actually follow (as opposed to ideal culture)

recidivism rate the proportion of people who are rearrested

redemptive social movement a social movement that seeks to change people totally

redlining the officers of a financial institution deciding not to make loans in a particular area

reference groups Herbert Hyman's term for the groups we use as standards to evaluate ourselves

reformative social movement a social movement that seeks to change only particular aspects of society

reincarnation in Hinduism and Buddhism, the return of the self after death in a different form

relative deprivation theory in this context, the belief that people join social movements based on their evaluations of what they think they should have compared with what others have

reliability the extent to which research produces consistent results

religion according to Durkheim, beliefs and practices that separate the profane from the sacred and unite its adherents into a moral community

religious experience a sudden awareness of the supernatural or a feeling of coming in contact with God

replication repeating a study in order to test its findings

representative democracy a form of democracy in which voters elect representatives to govern and make decisions on their behalf

research method (or **research design**) one of six procedures sociologists use to collect data: surveys, participant observation, secondary analysis, documents, unobtrusive measures, and experiments

reserve labor force the unemployed; unemployed workers are thought of as being "in reserve"—capitalists take them "out of reserve" (put them back to work) during times of high production and then lay them off (put them back in reserve) when they are no longer needed

resocialization the process of learning new norms, values, attitudes, and behaviors

resource mobilization a theory that social movements succeed or fail based on their ability to mobilize resources such as time, money, and people's skills

revolution armed resistance designed to overthrow a government

riot violent crowd behavior aimed against people and property

rising expectations the sense that better conditions are soon to follow, which, if unfulfilled, increase frustration

rituals ceremonies or repetitive practices; in this context, religious observances or rites, often intended to evoke a sense of awe of the sacred

role the behaviors, obligations, and privileges attached to a status

role conflict conflicts that someone feels *between* roles because the expectations attached to one role are incompatible with the expectations of another role

role extension the incorporation of additional activities into a role

role performance the ways in which someone performs a role within the limits that the role provides; showing a particular "style" or "personality"

role strain conflicts that someone feels *within* a role

romantic love feelings of erotic attraction accompanied by an idealization of the other

routinization of charisma the transfer of authority from a charismatic figure to either a traditional or a rational-legal form of authority

ruling class another term for the power elite

rumor unfounded information spread among people

sacred Durkheim's term for things set apart or forbidden, that inspire fear, awe, reverence, or deep respect

sample the individuals intended to represent the population to be studied

sanctions expressions of approval or disapproval given to people for upholding or violating norms

Sapir-Whorf hypothesis Edward Sapir's and Benjamin Whorf's hypothesis that language creates ways of thinking and perceiving

scapegoat an individual or group unfairly blamed for someone else's troubles

science the application of systematic methods to obtain knowledge and the knowledge obtained by those methods

secondary analysis the analysis of data already collected by other researchers

secondary group compared with a primary group, a larger, relatively temporary, more anonymous, formal, and impersonal group based on some interest or activity, whose members are likely to interact on the basis of specific roles

sect a group larger than a cult that still feels substantial hostility from and toward society

secular belonging to the world and its affairs

secularization the process by which spiritual concerns are replaced by worldly concerns

secularization of culture the process by which a culture becomes less influenced by religion

secularization of religion the replacement of a religion's spiritual or "otherworldly" concerns with concerns about "this world"

segregation the policy of keeping racial or ethnic groups apart

selective perception seeing certain features of an object or situation, but remaining blind to others

self the unique human capacity of being able to see ourselves "from the outside"; the picture we gain of how others see us

self-administered questionnaires questionnaires filled out by respondents

self-fulfilling prophecy Robert Merton's term for an originally false assertion that becomes true simply because it was predicted

serial fatherhood a pattern of parenting in which a father, after divorce, reduces contact with his own children, serves as a father to the children of the woman he marries or lives with, then ignores them after moving in with or marrying another woman; this pattern repeats

sex biological characteristics that distinguish females and males, consisting of primary and secondary sex characteristics

sex typing the association of behaviors with one sex or the other

sexual harassment the abuse of one's position of authority to force unwanted sexual demands on someone

shaman the healing specialist of tribal groups who attempts to control the spirits thought to cause a disease or injury; commonly called a witch doctor

sick role a social role that excuses people from normal obligations because they are sick or injured, while at the same time expecting them to seek competent help and cooperate in getting well

sign-vehicles the term used by Goffman to refer to how people use social setting, appearance, and manner to communicate information about the self

significant other an individual who significantly influences someone else's life

slavery a form of social stratification in which some people own other people

small group a group small enough for everyone to interact directly with all the other members

social class according to Weber, a large group of people who rank close to one another in wealth, power, and prestige; according to Marx, one of two groups: capitalists who own the means of production or workers who sell their labor

social cohesion the degree to which members of a group or a society feel united by shared values and other social bonds

social control a group's formal and informal means of enforcing its norms

social environment the entire human environment, including direct contact with others

social facts Durkheim's term for a group's patterns of behavior

social inequality a social condition in which privileges and obligations are given to some but denied to others

social institutions the organized, usual, or standard ways by which society meets its basic needs

social integration the degree to which people feel a part of social groups

social interaction what people do when they are in one another's presence

social location the group memberships that people have because of their location in history and society

social mobility movement up or down the social class ladder

social movement a large group of people who are organized to promote or resist some social change

social movement organization an organization developed to further the goals of a social movement

social network the social ties radiating outward from the self that link people together

social order a group's usual and customary social arrangements, on which its members depend and on which they base their lives

social placement a function of education that funnels people into a society's various positions

social promotion passing students to the next grade even though they have not mastered basic materials

social sciences the intellectual and academic disciplines designed to understand the social world objectively by means of controlled and repeated observations

social stratification the division of large numbers of people into layers according to their relative power, property, and prestige: applies to both nations and to people within a nation, society, or other group

social structure the framework that surrounds us, consisting of the relationships of people and groups to one another, which give direction to and set limits on behavior

socialism an economic system characterized by the public ownership of the means of production, central planning, and the distribution of goods without a profit motive

socialization the process by which people learn the characteristics of their group—the knowledge, skills, attitudes, values, and actions thought appropriate for them

society people who share a culture and a territory

sociobiology a framework of thought that views human behavior as the result of natural selection and considers biological factors to be the fundamental cause of human behavior

sociological perspective understanding human behavior by placing it within its broader social context

sociology the scientific study of society and human behavior

special-interest group a group of people who have a particular issue in common who can be mobilized for political action

spirit of capitalism Weber's term for the desire to accumulate capital as a duty—not to spend it, but as an end in itself—and to constantly reinvest it

split-labor market workers split along racial, ethnic, gender, age, or any other lines; this split is exploited by owners to weaken the bargaining power of workers

state a political entity that claims monopoly on the use of violence in some particular territory; commonly known as a country

state religion a government-sponsored religion; also called ecclesia

status social ranking; the position that someone occupies in society or a social group

status consistency ranking high or low on all three dimensions of social class

status inconsistency (or **status discrepancy**) ranking high on some dimensions of social class and low on others

status set all the statuses or positions that an individual occupies

status symbols items used to identify a status

stereotype assumptions of what people are like, whether true or false

stigma "blemishes" that discredit a person's claim to a "normal" identity

stockholders' revolt the refusal of a corporation's stockholders to rubber-stamp decisions made by its managers

stored value the backing of a currency by goods that are stored and held in reserve

strain theory Robert Merton's term for the strain engendered when a society socializes large numbers of people to desire a cultural goal (such as success) but withholds from many the approved means to reach that goal; one adaptation to the strain is crime, the choice of an innovative means (one outside the approved system) to attain the cultural goal

stratified random sample a sample of specific subgroups of the target population in which everyone in the subgroups has an equal chance of being included in the study

street crime crimes such as mugging, rape, and burglary

structural mobility movement up or down the social class ladder that is attributable to changes in the structure of society, not to individual efforts

structured interviews interviews that use closed-ended questions

subculture the values and related behaviors of a group that distinguish its members from the larger culture; a world within a world

subjective meanings the meanings that people give their own behavior

subsistence economy a type of economy in which human groups live off the land with little or no surplus

suburb the communities adjacent to the political boundaries of a city

suburbanization the movement from the city to the suburbs

superego Freud's term for the conscience, the internalized norms and values of our social groups

survey the collection of data by having people answer a series of questions

sustainable environment a world system that takes into account the limits of the environment, produces enough material goods for everyone's needs, and leaves a heritage of a sound environment for the next generation

symbol something to which people attach meanings and then use to communicate with others

symbolic culture another term for nonmaterial culture

symbolic interactionism a theoretical perspective in which society is viewed as composed of symbols that people use to establish meaning, develop their views of the world, and communicate with one another

system of descent how kinship is traced over the generations

taboo a norm so strong that it brings revulsion if violated

taking the role of the other putting oneself in someone else's shoes; understanding how someone else feels and thinks and thus anticipating how that person will act

teamwork the collaboration of two or more people to manage impressions jointly

techniques of neutralization ways of thinking or rationalizing that help people deflect society's norms

technology in its narrow sense, tools; its broader sense includes the skills or procedures necessary to make and use those tools

the iron law of oligarchy Robert Michels' phrase for the tendency of formal organizations to be dominated by a small, self-perpetuating elite

the McDonaldization of society the process by which ordinary aspects of life are rationalized and efficiency comes to rule such things as food preparation

the quiet revolution the fundamental changes in society that occur as a result of vast numbers of women entering the work force

the scientific method the use of objective, systematic observations to test theories

the social construction of reality the process by which people use their background assumptions and life experiences to define what is real for them

theory a general statement about how some parts of the world fit together and how they work; an explanation of how two or more facts are related to one another

Thomas theorem William I. and Dorothy S. Thomas' classic formulation of the definition of the situation: "If people define situations as real, they are real in their consequences."

total institution a place in which people are cut off from the rest of society and are almost totally controlled by the officials who run the place

totalitarianism a form of government that exerts almost total control over people

tracking the sorting of students into different educational programs on the basis of real or perceived abilities

traditional authority authority based on custom

traditional orientation the idea, characteristic of tribal, peasant, and feudal societies, that the past is the best guide for the present

transformative social movement a social movement that seeks to change society totally

transnational social movement social movements with a new emphasis on some condition in the world, instead of on a condition in a specific country; also known as *new social movements*

triad a group of three people

underclass a group of people for whom poverty persists year after year and across generations

underemployment the condition of having to work at a job beneath one's level of training and abilities, or of being able to find only part-time work

underground economy exchanges of goods and services that are not reported to the government and thereby escape taxation

universal citizenship the idea that everyone has the same basic rights by virtue of being born in a country (or by immigrating and becoming a naturalized citizen)

unobtrusive measures various ways of observing people who do not know they are being studied

unstructured interviews interviews that use open-ended questions

upward social mobility movement up the social class ladder

urban legend a story with an ironic twist that sounds realistic but is false

urban renewal the rehabilitation of a rundown area, which usually results in the displacement of the poor who are living in that area

urbanization the process by which an increasing proportion of a population lives in cities

validity the extent to which an operational definition measures what it was intended to measure

value cluster a series of interrelated values that together form a larger whole

value contradiction values that contradict one another; to follow the one means to come into conflict with the other

value free the view that a sociologist's personal values should not influence social research

values the standards by which people define what is desirable or undesirable, good or bad, beautiful or ugly

variable a factor thought to be significant for human behavior, which varies from one case to another

Verstehen a German word used by Weber that is perhaps best understood as "to have insight into someone's situation"

voluntary association a group made up of people who have voluntarily organized on the basis of some mutual interest; also known as voluntary memberships

voter apathy indifference and inaction on the part of individuals or groups with respect to the political process

war armed conflict between nations or politically distinct groups

WASP a White Anglo-Saxon Protestant; narrowly, an American of English descent; broadly, an American of western European ancestry

wealth property and income

welfare (state) capitalism an economic system in which individuals own the means of production, but the state regulates many economic activities for the welfare of the population

white ethnics white immigrants to the United States whose culture differs from that of WASPs

white-collar crime Edwin Sutherland's term for crimes committed by people of respectable and high social status in the course of their occupations; for example, bribery of public officials, securities violations, embezzlement, false advertising, and price fixing

working class those who sell their labor to the capitalist class

world system theory economic and political connections that tie the world's countries together

zero population growth a demographic condition in which women bear only enough children to reproduce the population

Suggested Readings

CHAPTER 1 The Sociological Perspective

Berger, Peter L. *Invitation to Sociology: A Humanistic Perspective*. New York: Doubleday, 1972. This delightful analysis of how sociology applies to everyday life is highly recommended.

Charon, Joel M. *Symbolic Interactionism: An Introduction, an Interpretation, an Integration*, 7th ed. Englewood Cliffs, N.J.: Prentice Hall, 2001. As it lays out the main points of symbolic interactionism, this book provides an understanding of why symbolic interactionism is important in sociology.

Deutscher, Irwin. *Making a Difference: The Practice of Sociology*. New Brunswick, N.J.: Transaction Publishers, 1999. An evaluation of how sociology can be used to solve social problems.

Henslin, James M., ed. *Down to Earth Sociology: Introductory Readings*, 11th ed. New York: Free Press, 2001. This collection of readings about everyday life is designed to broaden the reader's understanding of society, and of the individual's place within it.

Johnson, Allan G. *The Forest and the Trees: Sociology as Life, Practice, and Promise*. Philadelphia: Temple University Press, 1997. The author illustrates some of the surprising implications of the sociological perspective.

Mills, C. Wright. *The Sociological Imagination*. New York: Oxford University Press, 2000. This classic work provides an overview of sociology from the framework of conflict theory.

Ruane, Janet M., and Karen A. Cerulo. *Second Thoughts: Seeing Conventional Wisdom Through the Sociological Eye*, 2nd ed. Thousand Oaks, Calif.: Pine Forge Press, 2000. If you want to see how enjoyable sociology can be—and have a few common stereotypes and myths exploded at the same time—read this book.

Steele, Stephen F., Anne Marie Scarisbrick-Hauser, and William J. Hauser. *Solution-Centered Sociology: Addressing Problems Through Applied Sociology*. Thousand Oaks, Calif.: Sage, 1999. This overview of applied sociology includes a case study in each chapter.

Journals

Applied Behavioral Science Review, Clinical Sociology, Clinical Sociology Review, International Clinical Sociology, Journal of Applied Sociology, The Practicing Sociologist, and *Sociological Practice Review* report the experiences of sociologists who work in a variety of applied settings, from peer group counseling and suicide prevention to recommending changes to school boards.

Humanity & Society, the official journal of the Association for Humanist Sociology, publishes articles that "serve to advance the quality of life of the world's people."

About a Career in Sociology

What can you do with sociology? You like the subject and would like to major in it, but. . . . The American Sociological Association (ASA) offers three pamphlets free of charge. You can obtain them from the ASA at 1307 New York Avenue NW, Suite 700, Washington, D.C. 20005–4701. Tel. (202) 383–9005. Fax (202) 638–0882. E-mail: ASA_Executive_Office@MCImail.com

The pamphlets are *Careers in Sociology, Majoring in Sociology: A Guide for Students,* and *The Sociology Major as Preparation for Careers in Business and Organizations.* The ASA also sells *Embarking Upon a Career with an Undergraduate Degree in Sociology* and *Mastering the Job Market with a Graduate Degree in Sociology.*

Ferris, Abbott L. *How to Join the Federal Workforce and Advance Your Sociological Career.* American Sociological Association. This pamphlet gives tips on how to find employment in the federal government, including information on how to prepare a job application.

Hess, Beth B. *Individual Voices, Collective Visions: Fifty Years of Women in Sociology.* Philadelphia: Temple University Press, 1995. During the past fifty years, women have played an increasingly larger role in sociology, which, like the other sciences, has been dominated by men. The author examines this change.

Huber, Bettina J. *Embarking Upon a Career in Sociology with an Undergraduate Sociology Major.* American Sociological Association. Designed for undergraduate sociology majors who are seeking employment, this brochure discusses how to identify interests and skills, pinpoint suitable jobs, prepare a resumé, and survive an employment interview.

Miller, Delbert C. *The Sociology Major as Preparation for Careers in Business.* American Sociological Association. What careers can a sociology major pursue in business or industry? This brochure includes sections on job prospects, graduate education, and how to practice sociology in business careers.

Steele, Stephen F., Annemarie Scarisbrick-Hauser, and William J. Hauser. *Solution-Centered Sociology: Addressing Problems Through Applied Sociology.* Beverly Hills, Calif.: Sage, 1999. From this book, you can gain not only a better idea of what applied sociology is but also of what careers are available in sociology.

Stephens, W. Richard. *Careers in Sociology,* 3rd ed. Boston: Allyn and Bacon, 1998. How can you make a living with a major in sociology? The author explores careers in sociology, from business and government to health care and the law.

CHAPTER 2 Culture

Chagnon, Napoleon A. *Yanomamo: The Fierce People,* 5th ed. New York: Harcourt, Brace, Jovanovich, 1997. This fascinating account of a preliterate people whose customs are extraordinarily different from ours will help you to see the arbitrariness of choices that underlie human culture.

Cohen, Mark Nathan. *Culture of Intolerance: Chauvinism, Class, and Racism in the United States.* New Haven: Yale University Press, 2000. The author analyzes how ideas of race, intelligence, and competence permeate U.S. culture.

Cross, Gary S. *An All-Consuming Century: Why Commercialism Won in Modern America.* New York: Columbia University Press, 2001. An analysis of how consumerism (the desire and drive to consume material goods) came about and reshaped U.S. culture.

Edgerton, Robert B. *Sick Societies: Challenging the Myth of Primitive Harmony.* New York: Free Press, 1992. The author's thesis is that cultural relativism is misinformed, that we have the obligation to judge cultures that harm its members as inferior to those that do not.

Fouts, Roger, and Stephen Tukel Mills. *Next of Kin: My Conversations with Chimpanzees.* New York: Daniel M. Barber, 1999. As Fouts recounts his experiences with Washoe, he explains not only the complexities of reasoning by chimpanzees but also why he concludes that it is immoral to lock chimpanzees in cages.

Gitlin, Todd. *The Twilight of Common Dreams: Why America Is Wracked by Culture Wars.* New York: Metropolitan Books, 1997. "Culture wars" refers to fundamental disagreements about the way life should be lived, and to the way certain groups push their own agendas and disparage those of others. The author expresses hope that we can build "cultural bridges" so we once again can dream "common dreams."

Lieberson, Stanley. *A Matter of Taste: How Names, Fashions, and Culture Change.* New Haven: Yale University Press, 2000. It is difficult to imagine a more thorough analysis of how patterns change in the naming of children.

Rogers, Mary F. *Barbie Culture.* Beverly Hills, Calif.: Sage, 1999. As the author examines Barbie's gender, racial, sexual, and class identities, she explains how Barbie has been adapted to diverse cultures and subcultures.

Smith, Shawn Michelle. *American Archives: Gender, Race, and Class in Visual Culture.* Princeton, N.J.: Princeton University Press, 2000. The photos in this book show how gender, race, and class have been conveyed in U.S. history in order to maintain white dominance.

Zellner, William W. *Countercultures: A Sociological Analysis.* New York: St. Martin's, Press, 1995. The author's analysis of skinheads, the Ku Klux Klan, survivalists, satanism, the Church of Scientology, and the Unification Church (Moonies) helps us understand why people join countercultures.

Journals

Qualitative Sociology, Urban Life, Sociological Perspectives, and *Visual Sociology Review* focus on qualitative research on social life.

CHAPTER 3 Socialization

Ariès, Philippe. *Centuries of Childhood: A Social History of Family Life.* New York: Vintage Books, 1972. This path-breaking study of childhood in Europe during the Middle Ages provides a sharp contrast to child-rearing patterns in modern society.

Cohen, Mark. *Lara Croft: The Art of Virtual Seduction.* New York: Prime Publishing, 2000. Interviews with the creators of Lara Croft and her programmers provide insight into Lara's popularity and the "cult" phenomenon centering around this virtual person.

Duncan, Greg J., and Jeanne Brooks-Gunn, eds. *Consequences of Growing Up Poor.* New York: Russell Sage, 2000. Examines how neighborhoods and families influence children's intellectual development and adolescent behavior.

Epstein, Jonathan S., ed. *Youth Culture: Identity in a Postmodern World.* Oxford, U.K.: Blackwell, 1998. Analysis of how youth find their identity in sexuality, music, politics, education, interaction, goals, and frustrations.

Mead, George Herbert. *Mind, Self and Society from the Standpoint of a Social Behaviorist,* Charles W. Morris, ed. Chicago: University of Chicago Press, 1989. First published in 1934. Put together from notes taken by Mead's students, this book presents Mead's analysis of how mind and self are products of society.

Mead, George Herbert. (Mary Jo Deegan, ed.) *Play, School, and Society.* New York: Peter Lang Publishing, 2000. The editor reorganizes notes taken by Mead's students, placing the focus on play as a central component in the formation of the human mind.

Messner, Steven F., and Richard Rosenfeld. *Crime and the American Dream,* 3rd ed. Belmont, Calif.: Wadsworth, 2001. Explains how the "American Dream" produces a strong desire to make money but fails to instill adequate desires to play by the rules. Supports Merton's strain theory featured in this chapter.

Rymer, Russ. *Genie: A Scientific Tragedy.* New York: Harper-Perennial Library, 1994. This moving account of Genie includes the battles over Genie among linguists, psychologists, and social workers, all of whom claimed to have Genie's best interests at heart.

Sociological Studies of Child Development: A Research Annual. Greenwich, Conn.: JAI Press, published annually. Along with theoretical articles, this publication reports on sociological research on the socialization of children.

Van Hoorn, Judith, Elzbieta Suchar, Akos Komlosi, and Doreen A. Samuelson, eds. *Adolescent Development and Rapid Social Change: Perspectives from Eastern Europe.* Albany: State University of New York Press, 2000. Based on the premise that when society changes, we change, this book examines the effects of social change on adolescents in eastern Europe.

CHAPTER 4 Social Structure and Social Interaction

Goffman, Erving. *The Presentation of Self in Everyday Life.* New York: Peter Smith, Publisher, 1999. First published in 1959. This classic statement of dramaturgical analysis provides a different way of looking at everyday life. As a student, this was one of the best books I read.

Helmreich, William B. *The Things They Say Behind Your Back: Stereotypes and the Myths Behind Them.* New Brunswick, N.J.: Transaction Books, 1984. Spiced with anecdotes and jokes, yet sensitively written, the book explores the historical roots of stereotypes. The author also illustrates how stereotypes help produce behaviors that reinforce the stereotypes.

Lennon, Sharron J., and Kim K. Johnson, eds. *Appearance and Power.* Oxford, England: Berg Publishers, Ltd., 2000. The authors of these articles analyze how significant appearance, especially clothing, is for what happens to us in social life.

Schellenberg, James A. *Exploring Social Behavior: Investigations in Social Psychology.* Boston: Allyn and Bacon, 1993. The author takes the reader on an intellectual journey, exploring such "mysteries" as identity, conscience, intelligence, attraction, and aggression.

Sobal, Jeffery, and Donna Maurer, eds. *Interpreting Weight: The Social Management of Fatness and Thinness.* New York: Aldine de Gruyter, 1999. The authors of these articles examine the strategies people use to give meaning to their weight, including how they interpret fatness and thinness and how they become involved in weight-related organizations.

Tönnies, Ferdinand. *Community and Society (Gemeinschaft und Gesellschaft).* New Brunswick, N.J.: Transaction Books, 1988. Originally published in 1887, this classic work, focusing on social change, provides insight into how society influences personality. Rather challenging reading.

Vinitzky-Seroussi, Vered. *After Pomp and Circumstance: High School Reunions as an Autobiographical Occasion.* Chicago: University of Chicago Press, 1998. In this analysis of high school reunions, the author examines the relationships between the self and the past and future.

Whyte, William Foote. *Street Corner Society: The Social Structure of an Italian Slum*, 4th ed. Chicago: University of Chicago Press, 1993. Originally published in 1943. The author's analysis of interaction in a U.S. Italian slum demonstrates how social structure affects personal relationships.

Journals

Qualitative Sociology, Symbolic Interaction, and *Urban Life* feature articles on symbolic interactionism and analyses of everyday life.

CHAPTER 5 How Sociologists Do Research

Becker, Howard S. *Tricks of the Trade: How to Think about Your Research While You're Doing It.* Chicago: University of Chicago Press, 1998. Based on his extensive experience as a participant observer, the author shares insights into how to do research.

Kelley, D. Lynn. *Measurement Made Accessible: A Research Approach Using Qualitative, Quantitative, and Quality Improvement Methods.* Walnut Creek, Calif.: Altamira Press, 2000. In this analysis of both quantitative and qualitative methods for gathering data, the author explains how to develop questionnaires, improve reliability and validity.

Klein, Ethel, Jacquelyn Campbell, and Esther Soler, eds. *Ending Domestic Violence: Changing Public Perceptions.* Beverly Hills, Calif.: Sage, 1998. A solution-oriented overview of domestic violence, with an emphasis on its relationship to gender, ethnicity, and social class.

Lee, Raymond M. *Unobtrusive Methods in Social Research.* Philadelphia: Open University Press, 2000. This clear overview of unobtrusive ways of doing social research summarizes many interesting studies.

May, Tim. *Social Research: Issues, Methods, and Process.* Philadelphia: Open University Press, 2001. An introduction to the ways sociologists do research.

Neuman, W. Lawrence. *Social Research Methods: Qualitative and Quantitative Approaches,* 4th ed. Boston: Allyn and Bacon, 2000. This "how-to" book of sociological research describes how sociologists gather data and the logic that underlies each of their methods.

Scully, Diana. *Understanding Sexual Violence: A Study of Convicted Rapists.* New York: Routledge, 1994. The author's examination of how rapists rationalize their acts helps us to understand why some men rape.

Taylor, Stephen J., and Robert Bogdan. *Introduction to Qualitative Research Methods: A Guidebook and Resource,* 3rd ed. New York: John Wiley, 1998. This introduction to participant observation and in-depth interviewing contains many examples of qualitative research done by sociologists.

Whyte, William Foote. *Creative Problem Solving in the Field: Reflections on a Career.* Lanham, Md: AltaMira Press, 1997. Focusing on his extensive field experiences, the author provides insight into the crucial effects of the researcher in participant observation.

Writing Papers for Sociology

The Sociology Writing Group. *A Guide to Writing Sociology Papers,* 4th ed. New York: St. Martin's Press, 1998. The guide walks students through the steps in writing a sociology paper, from choosing the initial assignment to doing the research and turning in a finished paper. Also explains how to manage your time and correctly cite sources.

Cuba, Lee J. *A Short Guide to Writing about Social Science,* 3rd ed. Glenview, Ill.: Scott, Foresman, 1997. The author summarizes the various types of social science literature, presents guidelines on how to organize and write a research paper, and explains how to prepare an oral presentation.

Journal

Visual Sociology Review. A specialized journal in qualitative sociology that focuses on the analysis of social life through visual means such as photos, movies, and videos.

CHAPTER 6 Societies to Social Networks

Forschi, Martha, and Edward J. Lawler, eds. *Group Processes: Sociological Analysis.* New York: Nelson-Hall, 1994. How do your associates, friends, family—and even strangers—influence you? Among other topics, these authors explore such influences.

Fleisher, Mark S. *Beggars and Thieves: Lives of Urban Street Criminals.* Madison: University of Wisconsin Press, 1995. Based on years of participant observation, the author presents an inside view of thieves, gangs, addicts, and lifelong criminals.

Homans, George C. *The Human Group.* New Brunswick, N.J.: Transaction Publishers, 2001. First published in 1950. In this classic work, Homans develops the idea that all human groups share common activities, interactions, and sentiments; he examines various types of social groups from this point of view.

Janis, Irving L. *Groupthink: Psychological Studies of Policy Decisions and Fiascoes,* 2nd ed. 1982. New York: Houghton Mifflin. Janis analyzes how groups can become cut off from alternatives, interpret evidence in light of their preconceptions, and embark on courses of action that they should have seen as obviously incorrect.

Kephart, William M., and William W. Zellner. *Extraordinary Groups: An Examination of Unconventional Lifestyles,* 6th ed. New York: Worth, 1998. This sketch of the history and characteristics of eight groups (the Old Order Amish, Oneida Community, Gypsies, Shakers, Hasidim, Father Divine Movement, Mormons, and Jehovah's Witnesses) illustrates how groups can maintain unconventional beliefs and practices.

Wilson, Gerald L. *Groups in Context: Leadership and Participation in Small Groups,* 5th ed. New York: McGraw-Hill, 1998. An overview of principles and processes of interaction in small groups, with an emphasis on how to exercise leadership.

CHAPTER 7 Bureaucracy and Formal Organizations

Drucker, Peter F. *The Frontiers of Management: Where Tomorrow's Decisions Are Being Shaped Today.* New York: Penguin, 1999. An analysis of global trends and management practices in business, including hostile takeovers and career gridlocks.

Dupuy, Francois. *The Customer's Victory: From Corporation to Co-Operation.* Bloomington: Indiana University Press, 1999. Written to help managers better understand the organizations they manage.

Freidson, Eliot. *Professionalism: The 3rd Logic.* Chicago: University of Chicago Press, 2001. The author distinguishes between professions, technical occupations, and crafts, analyzing how they differ by knowledge, education, career, organization, and ideology.

Parkinson, C. Northcote. *Parkinson's Law.* Boston: Bucaneer Books, 1997. Although this exposé of the inner workings of bureaucracies is delightfully satirical, if what Parkinson analyzes were generally true, bureaucracies would always fail.

Ritzer, George. *The McDonaldization of Society: An Investigation into the Changing Character of Contemporary Life,* 3rd ed. Thousand Oaks, Calif.: Pine Forge Press, 2000. The author examines how Durkheim's predictions about the rationalization of society are coming true in everyday life.

Wilson, Gerald L. *Groups in Context: Leadership and Participation in Small Groups,* 6th ed. New York: McGraw-Hill, 2001. An overview of principles and processes of interaction in small groups, with an emphasis on how to exercise leadership.

Wilson, James Q. *Bureaucracy: What Government Agencies Do and Why They Do It.* New York: Basic Books, 2001. How bureaucracies develop an organizational culture, and how this sometimes leads to irrational behavior.

Yiannis, Gabriel, Stephen Fineman, and David Sims. *Organizing and Organizations: An Introduction.* Newbury Park, Calif.: Sage, 2nd ed., 2000. The authors draw on many first-hand accounts to help make the study of formal organizations come alive.

CHAPTER 8 Deviance and Social Control

Curra, John. *The Relativity of Deviance.* Beverly Hills, Calif.: Sage, 1999. The author uses provocative examples to illustrate the relativity of deviance, how it varies from place to place, time to time, and situation to situation.

Field, Barry C. *Bad Kids: Race and the Transformation of the Juvenile Court.* New York: Oxford University Press, 1999. In this overview of the juvenile court system, the author analyzes the trend to remove serious offenders from the juvenile system.

Fleisher, Mark. S. *Dead End Kids: Gang Girls and the Boys They Know.* Madison: University of Wisconsin Press, 2000. This fascinating participant observation study provides an insider's perspective on gang life.

Girshick, Lori B. *No Safe Haven: Stories of Women in Prison.* Boston: Northeastern University Press, 1999. Do women occupy a special status in the criminal justice system? The author analyzes the life stories of forty imprisoned women to help find the answer.

Goffman, Erving. *Stigma: Notes on the Management of Spoiled Identity.* New York: Simon & Schuster, 1986. A reprint of a 1968 classic that outlines the social and personal reactions to "spoiled identity," appearances that—due to disability, weight, ethnicity, birth marks, and so on—do not match dominant expectations.

Goode, Erich. *Deviance in Everyday Life: Personal Accounts of Unconventional Lives.* Prospect Heights, IL.: Waveland Press, 2002. These accounts provide insight into the process of becoming deviant and an understanding of how people justify their norm violations.

Jankowski, Martín Sánchez. *Islands in the Street: Gangs and American Urban Society.* Berkeley: University of California Press, 1992. The author's extensive participant observation of street gangs makes a fascinating and insightful introduction to this topic.

Kleinknecht, William. *The New Ethnic Mobs: The Changing Face of Organized Crime in America.* New York: Free Press, 1996. Like ethnic groups before them, the predators among the new immigrants victimize both outsiders and their own groups.

Lott, John R., Jr. *More Guns, Less Crime.* Chicago: University of Chicago Press, 2000. After reviewing state data on crime and right-to-carry gun laws, the author comes to the surprising conclusion that more guns means less crime.

Mann, Coramae Richey, and Marjorie S. Zatz, eds. *Images of Color, Images of Crime.* Los Angeles: Roxbury, 1998. This collection of twenty-two articles examines the relationship between racial stereotypes and crime.

Rafter, Nicole Hahn. *Creating Born Criminals.* Champaign: University of Illinois Press, 1998. Documents how our thinking about the cause of criminality has changed, with an emphasis on "born" criminals and the eugenics movement.

Reinarman, Craig, and Harry G. Levine, eds. *Crack in America: Demon Drugs and Social Justice.* Berkeley: University of California Press, 1998. Examines the consequences of a repressive drug policy and explores constructive alternatives.

Scott, Kody (Sanyika Shakur). *Monster: The Autobiography of an L.A. Gang Member.* New York: Addison Wesley, 1998. This intriguing insider's view of gang life provides a rare glimpse of the power of countercultural norms.

Journals

Criminal Justice Review: Issues in Criminal, Social, and Restorative Justice, and *Journal of Law and Society* examine the social forces that shape law and justice.

CHAPTER 9 Global Stratification

Burawoy, Michael, Joseph A. Blum, Sheba George, Zsuzsa Gille, Teresa Gowan, Lynne Haney, Maren Klawiter, Steve H. Lopez, Sean Riain, and Millie Thayer. *Global Ethnography: Forces, Connections, and Imaginations in a Postmodern World.* Berkeley, Calif.: University of California Press, 2001. The authors illustrate how our emerging global society affects the everyday lives of people around the world—from nurses in Kerala to homeless recyclers in the United States and feminists in Brazil.

Carpenter, Ted Galen, ed. *NATO's Empty Victory.* Cato Institute, 2000. The author analyzes why NATO invaded Kosovo, although no NATO country had been attacked and the U.N. Security Council was divided on the issue.

Cotton, Samuel. *Silent Terror: A Journey into Contemporary African Slavery.* New York: Writers and Research, 1998. A vivid account of slavery in Mauritania, based on the author's observations.

Deliege, Robert. *The Untouchables of India.* Oxford, U.K.: Berg, 2001. An overview of India's caste system, with an emphasis on the *Dalits,* or untouchables.

Hajnal, Peter I., and Sian Meikle. *The G7/G8 System: Evolution, Role, and Documentation.* Burlington, Vermont: Ashgate Publishing, 1999. An analysis of the development of G7 and its role in world affairs.

Kempadoo, Mamala, ed. *Sun, Sex, and God: Tourism and Sex Work in the Caribbean.* Lanham, Md.: Rowman and Littlefield, 2000. The authors analyze connections between the global economy and the women, men, and children who sell sex; contains suggestions for changing the situation.

Miles, Rosalind. *The Woman's History of the World.* New York: HarperCollins, 1990. The author examines the importance of gender in human history.

United Nations. *World Economic & Social Survey 1999.* New York: United Nations Publications, 1999. This survey of the economic characteristics of the world's nations provides a detailed contrast of the rich and poor nations.

Wilkins, David E. *American Indian Sovereignty and the U.S. Supreme Court: The Making of Justice.* Austin: University of Texas Press, 1998. The author traces the relationship of Native Americans and the U.S. government by analyzing fifteen rulings of the U.S. Supreme Court.

Zakarta, Farred. *From Wealth to Power: The Unusual Origins of America's World.* Princeton, N.J.: Princeton University Press, 2000. The author analyzes how growing wealth and the passing of power from the states to the federal government allowed the United States to become a world power.

CHAPTER 10 Social Class in the United States

Brooks, David. *Bobos in Paradise: The New Upper Class and How They Got There.* New York: Touchstone Books, 2001. A light-hearted analysis of bourgeois bohemians (bobos), a new class orientation that combines both affluent success and a rebellious spirit.

Dent, David J. *In Search of Black America: Discovering the African-American Dream.* New York: Simon and Schuster, 2000. The author, a journalist, examines the life of middle-class African Americans, who live in what is largely a segregated world.

Ehrenreich, Barbara. *Nickel and Dimed: On (Not) Getting By in America.* New York: Metropolitan Books, 2001. The author, a sociologist, takes a series of unskilled, minimum-wage jobs—and tries to live on her earnings.

Gatewood, Willard B. *Aristocrats of Color: The Black Elite, 1880–1920.* Fayetteville: University of Arkansas Press, 2000. Analyzing the rise and decline of the African American upper class that developed after the Civil War, the author focuses on marriage, occupations, education, religion, clubs, and relationships with whites and with African Americans of lower classes.

Kushnick, Louis, and James Jennings, eds. *A New Introduction to Poverty: The Role of Race, Power, and Politics.* New York: New York University Press, 1999. In this analysis of major causes and characteristics of U.S. poverty, the authors also analyze why poverty persists.

Liebow, Elliot. *Tally's Corner: A Study of Negro Streetcorner Men.* Boston: Little, Brown, 1999. This reprint of a 1968 classic of participant observation research of a group of Washington, D.C., African American men provides insight into the dynamics of decision making and relationships.

Newman, Katherine S. *Falling from Grace: Downward Mobility in the Age of Affluence.* Berkeley: University of California Press, 1999. The focus of this analysis of downward social mobility is on what happens to people who lose their jobs and are unable to find decent work.

Oliver, Melvin L., and Thomas M. Shapiro. *Black Wealth/ White Wealth: A New Perspective on Racial Inequality.* New York: Routledge, 1997. This book, which makes the first comparison of the wealth (not income) of African Americans and whites, shows how deep the divide is.

Perucci, Robert, and Earl Wyson. *The New Class Society.* Lanham, Md: Rowman and Littlefield, 1999. An overview of the U.S. social class structure, with the suggestion that there no longer is a middle class.

Richardson, Chad. *Batos, Bolillos, Pochos, & Pelados: Class and Culture on the South Texas Border.* Austin: University of Texas Press, 1999. An analysis of class, conflict, cooperation, and identity among Mexican Americans, Anglos, African Americans, and immigrants in the Valley of South Texas.

Wilson, William Julius. *When Work Disappears: The World of the New Urban Poor.* New York: Knopf, 1997. The author analyzes consequences of the disappearance of unskilled jobs near the inner city: the destruction of inner-city businesses, the flight of the middle class, and the stranding of poor people who have few alternatives.

Journals

Journal of Children and Poverty seeks to provide an understanding of global issues that affect the quality of life of children and families.

Race, Gender, and Class publishes interdisciplinary articles on the topics listed in its title.

CHAPTER 11 Sex and Gender

Amott, Teresa. *Caught in the Crisis: Women and the U.S. Economy,* 2nd ed. New York: Monthly Review Press, 2000. A short, readable overview of women's economic roles from a leftist perspective.

Anderson, Margaret L. *Thinking about Women: Sociological Perspectives on Sex and Gender,* 5th ed. New York: Allyn and Bacon, 1999. An overview of the main issues of sex and gender in contemporary society, ranging from sexism and socialization to work and health.

Beynon, John. *Masculinities and Culture.* Philadelphia: Open University Press, 2002. The author's thesis is that because masculinity is shaped by society and culture, differing from place to place and time to time, the term "masculinities" is more appropriate.

Ferree, Myra Marx, Judith Lorber, and Beth B. Hess, eds. *Revisioning Gender.* Thousand Oaks: Sage, 1999. An analysis of changes occurring in gender roles, with an emphasis on the potential for changing human relations.

Gilman, Charlotte Perkins. *The Man-Made World or, Our Androcentric Culture.* New York: Charlton, 1911. Reprinted in 1971 by Johnson Reprint. This early book on women's liberation provides an excellent view of female–male relations at the beginning of this century.

Goldberg, Steven. *Why Men Rule: A Theory of Male Dominance.* Chicago: Open Court, 1993. A detailed explanation of the author's theory of male dominance featured in this chapter.

Kimmel, Michael S., and Michael A. Messner, eds. *Men's Lives,* 5th ed. Boston: Allyn and Bacon, 2001. These authors examine major issues of sex and gender as they affect men. An excellent companion, and often counterpoint, to the Anderson book.

Lefkowitz, Bernard. *Our Guys: The Glen Ridge Rape and the Secret Life of the Perfect Suburb.* New York: Vintage Books, 1998. This account of a rape that made national news provides insight into how subcultures that center on competitive male athletics can encourage aggression, violence, and rape.

Lorber, Judith. *Gender and the Social Construction of Illness.* Thousand Oaks, Calif.: Sage, 1997. Taking the position that both gender and medicine are social institutions, the author examines their interrelationships.

Madriz, Esther. *Nothing Bad Happens to Good Girls: Fear of Crime in Women's Lives.* Berkeley: University of California Press, 1997. The author uses interviews to explain how women's fear of crime contributes to gender inequalities and the social control of women.

McKay, Jim, Michael A. Messner, and Donald F. Sabo, eds. *Masculinities, Gender Identities, and Sport.* Beverly Hills, Calif.: Sage, 2000. The authors of these articles provide an overview of major topics in gender relations, with a focus on the relationship between sport and gender.

Tannen, Deborah. *The Argument Culture: Stopping America's War of Words.* New York: Ballantine, 1999. In this argument that Americans argue too much (including too much public debate), the author, a psycholinguist, also reviews basic differences in how boys and girls express agreement and aggression.

Wymard, Ellie. *Conversations with Uncommon Women: Insights from Women Who've Risen above Life's Challenges to Achieve Extraordinary Success.* New York: AMACOM, 2000. The author, an English professor, interviewed 100 highly successful women to discover their understanding of how they overcame the obstacles they faced.

Zweigenhaft, Richard L. *Diversity in the Power Elite: Have Women and Minorities Reached the Top?* New Haven: Yale University Press, 2000. The author examines the rise of women and minorities in the power establishment and analyzes the obstacles that prevent them from reaching the top rung of power.

Journals

These journals focus on the role of gender in social life: *Feminist Studies; Gender and Society; Gender, Place and Culture: A Journal of Feminist Geography; Journal of Gender, Culture, and Health; Sex Roles;* and *Signs: Journal of Women in Culture and Society.*

CHAPTER 12 Race and Ethnicity

Allen, James, ed. *Without Sanctuary: Lynching Photography in America.* Santa Fe, N.M.: Twin Palms Publishers, 2000. Apart from its gruesomeness, this collection of nearly 100 postcards and photographs from the late nineteenth and early twentieth centuries provides remarkable insight into the mind set of that period.

Blea, Irene I. *U.S. Chicanas and Latinas within a Global Context.* New York: Praeger, 1998. By examining the global context, the author explains why Chicanas and Latinas sometimes feel more in common with women of the Least Industrialized Nations than with feminists in their own country.

Bobo, Lawrence C., and Melvin L. Oliver, eds. *Prismatic Metropolis: Inequality in Los Angeles.* New York: Russell Sage Foundation, 2000. In addition to residential segregation, salary inequities, and workplace issues, the authors of these selections examine interactions among minority groups and how those who immigrated years ago feel about recent immigrants.

Chin, Ko-Lin, and Douglas S. Massey. *Smuggled Chinese: Clandestine Immigration to the United States.* Philadelphia: Temple University Press, 2000. Based on interviews with illegal immigrants, the authors analyze the conditions that illegal immigrants from China face on their journey and after their arrival; includes information on safe houses.

Du Bois, W.E.B. *Black Reconstruction in America: An Essay Toward a History of the Part Which Black Folk Played in the Attempt to Reconstruct Democracy in America, 1860–1880.* New York: Harcourt, Brace 1935; London: Frank Cass, 1966. This analysis of the role of African Americans in the Civil War and in the years immediately following provides a glimpse into a neglected part of U.S. history.

Klinkner, Philip A., and Roger M. Smith. *The Unsteady March: The Rise and Decline of Racial Equality in America.* Chicago: University of Chicago Press, 2000. Examines the conditions under which racial equality increases and decreases and proposes steps to increase racial equality.

Lytle, Clifford M., and Deloria Vine, Jr. *The Nations Within: The Past and Future of American Indian Sovereignty,* 2nd ed. Austin: University of Texas Press, 1998. Analyzes the relationship between legislation and the self-determination of Native Americans.

Mander, Jerry. *In the Absence of the Sacred: The Failure of Technology and the Survival of the Indian Nations.* New York: Pete Smith, Publisher, 1999. With a focus on the impact of technology, the author analyzes past and present relations of Native Americans and the U.S. government.

Patillo-McCoy, Mary. *Black Picket Fences: Privilege and Peril among the Black Middle Class.* Chicago: University of Chicago Presss, 1999. The author analyzes the obstacles and pressures faced by the black middle class.

Press, Riv-Ellen. *Fighting to Become Americans: Jews, Gender, and the Anxiety of Assimilation.* Boston: Beacon Press, 1999. An analysis of the upward mobility of Jews in the U.S. racial-ethnic structure, and how their stereotypes reflect their aspirations and anxiety.

Reskin, Barbara F. *Realities of Affirmative Action in Employment.* Washington, D.C.: American Sociological Association, 1998. The author analyzes how affirmative action works, including the effects it has on employees and employers.

Smith, Barbara E., ed. *Neither Separate nor Equal: Women, Race, and Class in the South.* Philadelphia: Temple University Press, 1999. A special focus of this anthology is the relationship among racial-ethnic groups and the role of a changing economy in shaping those relationships.

Walker, Samuel, Cassia Spohn, and Miriam Delone. *The Color of Justice: Race, Ethnicity, and Crime in America,* 2nd ed. Belmont, Calif.: Wadsworth, 2000. The authors analyze racial, ethnic, and gender discrimination in the criminal justice system.

Wilson, William Julius. *The Bridge over the Racial Divide: Rising Inequality and Coalition Politics.* Berkeley: University of California Press, 2000. The author analyzes how monetary, trade, and tax policies increase social inequality; includes recommendations to increase multiracial political cooperation.

CHAPTER 13 The Elderly

Blaikie, Andrew. *Ageing and Popular Culture.* Cambridge, England: Cambridge University Press, 1999. Examines how the extended leisure that has come with the growing numbers of elderly is breaking down the distinction between middle and old age.

Dychtwald, Ken. *Age Power: How the 21st Century Will Be Ruled by the New Old.* Los Angeles: J. P. Tarcher, 2000. Speculates on how the growing numbers of elderly will affect society, and suggests how we should prepare for the coming change.

Furman, Frida Kerner. *Facing the Mirror: Older Women and Beauty Shop Culture.* Boston: Routledge, 1997. This ethnography of Julie's, a beauty parlor, illustrates how women come face to face with and adjust to the realities of aging.

Gubrium, Jaber F. *Living and Dying at Murray Manor.* Charlottesville: University of Virginia Press, 1998. In this ethnography of a nursing home, the author analyzes how staff and patients relate to one another, how patients pass time, and how they react to death.

Hatch, Laurie Russell. *Beyond Gender Differences: Adaptation to Aging in Life Course Perspective.* Amityville, N. Y.: Baywood Publishing Company, 2000. The author reviews the research on how men and women adapt to growing old.

Quadagno, Jill S. *Aging and the Life Course: An Introduction to Social Gerontology.* New York: McGraw Hill, 1999. This textbook reviews the major issues in gerontology, and stresses that the quality of life that people experience in old age is the result of earlier choices, opportunities, and constraints.

Roszak, Theodore. *America the Wise: The Longevity Revolution and the True Wealth of Nations.* New York: Houghton Mifflin, 1999. The author's thesis is that as the numbers of elderly grow, they will have more wealth and political power, leading to a more compassionate and wise society.

Rubin, Lillian B. *Tangled Lives: Daughters, Mothers, and the Crucible of Aging.* Boston: Beacon Press, 2001. The author reflects on her own experiences with illness and death to try to come to grips with the meaning of growing old—and of life.

Stoller, Eleanor Palo, and Rose Campbell Gibson. *Worlds of Difference: Inequality in the Aging Experience,* 3rd ed. Thousand Oaks, Calif.: Pine Forge Press, 2000. The authors document extensive inequalities borne by the U.S. elderly and explain the social conditions that create those inequalities.

Journals

The Gerontologist, Journal of Aging and Identity, Journal of Aging and Social Policy, Journal of Aging Studies, Journal of Cross-Cultural Gerontology, Journal of Elder Abuse and Neglect, Journal of Gerontology, and *Journal of Women and Aging* focus on issues of aging, while *Youth and Society* and *Journal of Youth Studies* examine adolescent culture.

CHAPTER 14 The Economy

Amott, Teresa. *Caught in the Crisis: Women and the U.S. Economy Today.* New York: Monthly Review Press, 2000. An analysis of how the transformation of the economy is affecting women.

Bales, Kevin. *Disposable People: New Slavery in the Global Economy.* Berkeley: University of California Press, 1999. The author documents the relationship between the globalization of capitalism and current slavery in Brazil, India, Mauritania, Pakistan, and Thailand.

Bluestone, Barry, Bennett Harrison, and Richard C. Leone. *Growing Prosperity.* New York: Houghton Mifflin, 1999. An emphasis on how we can continue economic growth: also focuses on the need for a more just distribution of our wealth.

Blumenberg, Werner. *Karl Marx.* New York: VideoBooks, 1999. Written by a member of the underground that fought against Hitler, this classic biography of Marx explores both his personal and public life.

Bonilla, Frank, Edwin Melendez, Maria de Los Angeles Torres, and Rebecca Morales, eds. *Borderless Borders: U.S. Latinos, Latin Americans, and the Paradox of Interdependence.* Philadelphia: Temple University Press, 1998. Analyzes how the globalization of capitalism is affecting U.S. Latinos, their identity, and their relationship to their home country.

Drucker, Peter F. *The Frontiers of Management: Where Tomorrow's Decisions Are Being Shaped Today.* New York: Penguin, 1999. An analysis of global trends and management practices in business, including hostile takeovers and career gridlocks.

Harrison, Bennett. *Lean and Mean: Why Large Corporations Will Continue to Dominate the Global Economy.* New York: Guilford Press, 1998. As the author examines the role of the giant corporations in technological innovations and economic growth, he explains why a permanent workforce is threatened by the rise in part-time and temporary jobs.

Katz, Richard. *Japan, the System that Soured: The Rise and Fall of the Japanese Economic Miracle.* New York: M. E. Sharpe, 1998. The author analyzes Japan's stunning recovery following World War II and the factors that brought it economic depression.

Sennett, Richard, and Bob Sennett. *The Corrosion of Character: The Personal Consequences of Work in the New Capitalism.* New York: W. W. Norton, 2000. An examination of how the "new efficiencies" of the multinational corporations affect workers; contains case studies.

CHAPTER 15 Politics

Amnesty International. *Amnesty International Report.* London: Amnesty International Publications, published annually. The reports summarize human rights violations around the world, listing specific instances country by country.

Castro, Fidel. *Capitalism in Crisis: Globalization and World Politics Today.* New York: Ocean Press, 2001. This collection of speeches by one of the few remaining communist rulers provides a conflict perspective on geopolitical change.

Chirot, Daniel. *Modern Tyrants: The Power and Prevalence of Evil in Our Age.* Princeton: Princeton University Press, 1996. From Hitler and Stalin to Trujillo, Mao, and Pol Pot, the author analyzes the political expediency that underlies tyranny.

Domhoff, G. William. *Who Rules America?: Power and Politics in the Year 2000,* 3rd ed. Mountain View, Calif.: Mayfield Publishing Company, 1998. An analysis of how the multinational corporations dominate the U.S. government.

Kerbo, Harold R., and John A. McKinstry. *Who Rules Japan?: The Inner Circles of Economic and Political Power.* Westport, Conn.: Praeger, 1995. An analysis of the "iron triangle" that wields power in Japan—the tightly bound group of corporate, bureaucratic, and political elites.

Mills, C. Wright. *The Power Elite,* 2nd ed. New York: Getty Center for Education in the Arts, 2000. Originally published in 1956. This classic analysis elaborates the conflict thesis summarized in this chapter—that U.S. society is ruled by the nation's top corporate leaders, together with an elite from the military and political institutions.

Osiel, Mark J. *Obeying Orders: Atrocity, Military Discipline, and the Law of War.* New Brunswick, N.J.: Transaction Publishers, 1999. The author examines the social basis of constraint and freedom in the military and how orders can lead to atrocities.

Simes, Dimitri K. *After the Collapse: Russia Seeks Its Place as a Great Power.* New York: Simon and Schuster, 1999. The author, a Russian expatriate, analyzes the political turmoil in Russia and makes recommendations for U.S. policy toward Russia.

Stiglmayer, Alexandra, ed. *Mass Rape: The War Against Women in Bosnia-Herzegovina,* Marion Faber, trans. Lincoln: University of Nebraska Press, 1994. Giving chilling accounts, the authors explain why mass rape sometimes accompanies war, as it did in Bosnia.

Zweigenhaft, Richard L., and G. William Domhoff. *Diversity in the Power Elite: Have Women and Minorities Reached the Top?* New Haven: Yale University Press, 2000. The authors explore the extent to which Jews, women, blacks, Latinos, Asian Americans, and homosexuals have joined the power elite.

Journals

Most sociology journals publish articles on politics. Three that focus on this area of social life are *American Political Science Review, Journal of Political and Military Sociology,* and *Social Policy.*

Research in Political Sociology: A Research Annual. Greenwich, Conn.: JAI Press. This annual publication is not recommended for beginners, as the findings and theories are often difficult and abstract. It does, however, analyze political topics of vital concern to our well-being.

CHAPTER 16 The Family

Coontz, Stephanie, Maya Parson, and Gabrielle Raley, eds. *American Families: A Multicultural Reader.* Boston: Routledge, 1999. The articles in this anthology illustrate the diversity of U.S. family life, underscoring the point in the text that there is no such thing as *the* family.

Goetting, Ann. *Getting Out: Life Stories of Women Who Left Abusive Men.* New York: Columbia University Press, 1999. Why don't women leave when they are abused by their husbands? The author uses women's own statements to explore this question—and to examine the situations of those who got out.

Hackstaff, Karla B. *Marriage in a Culture of Divorce.* Philadelphia: Temple University Press, 2000. Through in-depth interviews with couples who married in the 1950s and 1970s, the author examines how the meaning of marriage and divorce has changed.

Hansen, Karen V., Anita Ilta Garey, and Ronnie J. Steinberg, eds. *Families in the U.S.: Kinship and Domestic Politics.* Philadelphia: Temple University Press, 1998. The authors of the sixty-two articles that make up this anthology cover the definition, structure, and economics of family, community, parenthood, kinship, marriage, divorce, caregiving, violence, and housework.

Hochschild, Arlie Russell. *The Time Bind: When Work Becomes Home and Home Becomes Work.* New York: Metropolitan Books, 1998. Do parents really want to spend more time with their families and less at work? Or do parents flee families, finding work a respite from family pressures? The author presents some surprising answers.

LaRossa, Ralph. *The Modernization of Fatherhood: A Social and Political History.* Chicago: University of Chicago Press, 1997. The author's exploration of how ideas of fatherhood have changed over time and varied from one group to another sheds light on our current ideas of fatherhood.

Rubin, Lillian. *Families on the Faultline: America's Working Class Speaks about the Family, the Economy, Race and Ethnicity.* New York: HarperCollins, 1996. Based on interviews, the author maps primary concerns of the working class, allowing us to better understand the tensions they face.

Staples, Robert, ed. *The Black Family: Essays and Studies,* 6th ed. Belmont Calif.: Wadsworth, 1999. The authors analyze black families—from the times of slavery to postindustrial society—reviewing gender roles, marriage and divorce, family life, parenthood, adolescence, health, violence, sexual relationships, and public policy.

Strasser, Mark. *The Challenge of Same-Sex Marriages: Federalist Principles and Constitutional Protection.* New York: Praeger, 2000. Based on challenges to state laws that limit marriage to people of the opposite sex, the author analyzes same-sex marriages in light of the U.S. Constitution.

Journals

Family Relations, International Journal of Sociology of the Family, Journal of Comparative Family Studies, Journal of Divorce, Journal of Family and Economic Issues, Journal of Family Issues, Journal of Family Violence, Journal of Marriage and the Family, and *Marriage and Family Review* publish articles on almost every aspect of marriage and family life.

CHAPTER 17 Education

Corwin, Miles. *And Still We Rise: The Trials and Triumphs of 12 Gifted Inner City Students.* New York: HarperPerennial Library, 2001. The author, a journalist who spent a year in a South Los Angeles high school, details the lives of twelve students in an advanced placement program.

Garrod, Andrew, and Colleen Larimore, eds. *First Person, First Peoples: Native American College Graduates Tell Their Life Stories.* Ithaca, N.Y.: Cornell University Press, 1997. Written by graduates of Dartmouth College, these essays recount the anguish minority students sometimes feel in a predominantly white college.

Kozol, Jonathan. *Ordinary Resurrections: Children in the Years of Hope.* New York: Crown Publishers, 2000. To listen as these children from a dismal neighborhood in South Bronx talk about life is to become aware of the potential that schools have to reach children in poverty and to transform their lives.

Matthews, Jay. *Class Struggle: What's Wrong (and Right) with America's Best Public High Schools.* New York: Times Books, 1999. As the author, a reporter, analyzes the experiences of students at Mamaroneck High School in New York, one of the best public schools in the nation, he focuses on how students from privileged and impoverished backgrounds are served by the emphasis on advanced classes.

Miller, L. Scott. *An American Imperative: Accelerating Minority Educational Advancement.* New Haven: Yale University Press, 1998. The author proposes a national policy to reduce the economic, social, cultural, and institutional barriers to the educational advancement of minorities.

Padilla, Felix M. *The Struggle of Latino/Latina University Students: In Search of a Liberating Education.* New York: Routledge, 1997. The author draws on his students' journal entries and on his own educational experiences to analyze how Latino/a students construct their education in a white university.

Patterson, James T. *Brown v. Board of Education: A Civil Rights Milestone and Its Troubled Legacy.* Oxford, U.K.: Oxford University Press, 2001. A detailed analysis of the U.S. Supreme Court's 1954 epoch-making decision.

Powell, Arthur G. *Lessons from Privilege: The American Prep School Tradition.* Cambridge, Mass.: Harvard University Press, 1998. The author explains why private schools work so well and suggests how public schools can apply those principles to improve the education of their students.

Schiell, Timothy C. *Campus Hate Speech on Trial.* Lawrence: University of Kansas Press, 2000. An analysis of free speech, which lies at the center of personal freedom, and its limits on the college campus.

Weiler, Jeanne Drysdale. *Codes and Contradictions: Race, Gender Identity, and Schooling.* New York: State University of New York, 2000. After studying girls of African American, Latina, Puerto Rican, and European backgrounds who are at risk of failing in school, the author concludes that schools are able to reorient young women so they see educational success as crucial to their future well-being.

Journals

The following journals contain articles that examine almost every aspect of education: *Education and Urban Society, Harvard Educational Review,* and *Sociology of Education.*

CHAPTER 18 Religion

Berger, Peter L., and Jonathan Sacks, eds. *The Desecularization of the World: Resurgent Religion and World Politics.* New York: William B. Eerdmans, 1999. The authors analyze the continuity or resurgence of religion in world affairs.

Galanter, Marc. *Cults: Faith, Healing, and Coercion,* 2nd ed. New York: Oxford University Press, 1999. What do Alcoholics Anonymous, the Unification Church, and the mass suicide in Jonestown have in common? This book, rich in ethnographic materials on charismatic cults, provides answers: however, the sociological reader will have to wade through some unacceptable psychiatric interpretations.

Helmreich, William B. *The Enduring Community: The Jews of Newark and Metrowest.* New Brunswick, N.J.: Transaction, 1999. An analysis of how their subculture helps Jews maintain their identity in the face of declining religiosity.

Lewis, David C. *After Atheism: Religion and Ethnicity in Russia and Central Asia.* New York: St. Martin's Press, 2000. The author reports on changes in religion since the downfall of communism in Russia.

Mazur, Eric Michael. *The Americanization of Religious Minorities: Confronting the Constitutional Order.* Baltimore: Johns Hopkins University Press, 2000. What happens when religious beliefs conflict with U.S. law? The author analyzes the experiences of Jehovah's Witnesses, Mormons, and Native Americans.

Stark, Rodney, and William Sims Bainbridge. *Religion, Deviance, and Social Control.* New York: Routledge, 1997. Does religion prevent crime, delinquency, suicide, or drug abuse? If so, under what circumstances? The authors answer questions such as these.

Thibodeau, David, and Leon Whiteson. *A Place Called Waco: A Survivor's Story.* New York: PublicAffairs, 2000. A first-person account of life inside the Branch Davidian compound, written by one of only four survivors of the fire who were not sentenced to prison.

Williams, Miriam. *Heaven's Harlots: My Fifteen Years As a Sacred Prostitute in the Children of God Cult.* Deerfield, Mass.: Eagle Brook, 1999. A first-person account of membership in the Children of God, a pseudo Christian group with international membership.

Journals

The following three journals publish articles that focus on the sociology of religion: *Journal for the Scientific Study of Religion, Review of Religious Research,* and *Sociological Analysis: A Journal in the Sociology of Religion.*

CHAPTER 19 Medicine

Cockerham, William C. *Health and Social Change in Russia and Eastern Europe.* New York: Routledge, 1999. The author examines the health crisis in Russia and its former satellites, tracing the social causes that have led to an unprecedented drop in life expectancy.

Eaton, William W. *The Sociology of Mental Disorders,* 3rd ed. New York: Praeger, 2001. From this account of "bizarre" behaviors, including unusual thinking, you will be able to see the differences between sociological and psychological analyses.

Fox, Renee C., and Judith P. Swazey. *The Courage to Fail: A Social View of Organ Transplants and Dialysis.* New Brunswick, N.J.: Transaction Publishers, 2002. The authors examine moral and ethical aspects of organ replacement, a social issue destined to grow in importance as medical technology continues to advance.

Grob, Gerald N. *The Mad Among Us: A History of the Care of America's Mentally Ill.* New York: Free Press, 1995. From colonial to contemporary times, a detailed history of attitudes and approaches toward the mentally ill, some enlightened, most repressive.

Jones, James H. *Bad Blood.* New York: Free Press, 1993. An account of the syphilis experiments conducted by the U.S. Public Health Service at Tuskegee Institute, which were carried out on unwitting African Americans.

Karp, David A. *Speaking of Sickness: Depression, Disconnection, and the Meaning of Illness.* New York: Oxford University Press, 1997. Written by a sociologist who has suffered from depression for many years, this book provides deep insight into people's experience with this illness.

Kolata, Gina Bari. *Flu: The Story of the Great Influenza Pandemic of 1918 and the Search for the Virus That Caused It.* New York: Farrar, Straus, and Giroux, 2000.The author recounts the worst pandemic of the twentieth century, in which perhaps 40 million people died within a year.

Resnik, Susan. *Blood Saga: Hemophilia, Aids, and the Survival of a Community.* Berkeley: University of California Press, 1999. An analysis of how the medical community is implicated in the widespread transmission of AIDS to hemophiliacs.

Journals

Health: An Interdisciplinary Journal for the Social Study of Health, Illness and Medicine, Journal of Health and Social Behavior, Research in the Sociology of Health Care, Social Science and Medicine, and *Sociological Practice: Health Sociology* publish research articles and essays in the field of medical sociology.

CHAPTER 20 Population and Urbanization

Anderson, Elijah. *Code of the Street: Decency, Violence, and the Moral Life of the Inner City.* New York: W. W. Norton & Co., 2000. An insider's perspective of how the need and demand for respect dominates social relationships in the inner city, and how this is related to violence, unemployment, and drugs.

Brown, Lester R., Gary Gardner, and Brian Halweil. *Beyond Malthus: Nineteen Dimensions of the Population Challenge.* New York: W. W. Norton & Co., 1999. The thesis is that Malthus was right, and unless governments take strong steps the world will be unable to feed its growing population.

Department of Agriculture. *Yearbook of Agriculture.* Washington, D.C.: Department of Agriculture, published annually. The yearbook focuses on specific aspects of U.S. agribusiness, especially international economies and trade.

DeRosier, Linda Scott. *Creeker: A Woman's Journey.* Lexington: University Press of Kentucky, 2000. The author recounts her life growing up in the "hollers" of Appalachia; provides a good understanding of community and a way of rural life that is fast disappearing.

Duany, Andres, Elizabeth Plater-Zyberk, and Jeff Speck. *Suburban Nation: The Rise of Sprawl and the Decline of the American Dream.* San Francisco, Calif.: North Point Press, 2001. Lays out a vision of how to plan cities and suburbs so they meet human needs and become inviting places to live.

Duneier, Mitchell. *Sidewalk.* New York: Farrar, Straus, Giroux, 2000. This analysis of city streets provides insight into how the urban mosaic works.

Meller, Helen Elizabeth. *European Cities, 1890–1930s: History, Culture and the Built Environment.* New York: John Wiley, 2002. This background on European urbanization provides principles for improving cities.

Mosher, Steven W. *A Mother's Ordeal: One Woman's Fight Against One-Child China.* New York: HarperCollins, 1994. This book puts a human face on China's coercive family planning policies.

Newman, Katherine S. *No Shame in My Game: The Working Poor in the Inner City.* New York: Knopf, 1999. Another look at the residents of the inner city, this time with a focus on the working poor, those who strive to get ahead but are held back by lack of opportunities and education.

Ross, Andrew. *The Celebration Chronicles: Life, Liberty and the Pursuit of Property Values in Disney's New Town.* New York: Ballantine Books, 2000. An analysis of Disney's planned utopian community in Florida, written by a social scientist who lived in Celebration for a year.

Weeks, John R. *Population: An Introduction to Concepts and Issues,* 7th ed. Belmont, Calif.: Wadsworth, 1999. Focusing on both the United States and the world, the author analyzes major issues in population.

CHAPTER 21 Collective Behavior and Social Movements

Barkan, Steven E., and Lynne L. Snowden. *Collective Violence.* Boston: Allyn and Bacon, 2000. The authors analyze riots, revolutions, terrorism, cults, militia, and hate groups.

Brunvand, Jan Harold. *Too Good to Be True: The Colossal Book of Urban Legends.* New York: W. W. Norton, 2000. In this collection of over 200 urban legends, you'll probably find some that you heard and thought were true.

Buechler, Steven M. *Social Movements in Advanced Capitalism: The Political Economy and Cultural Construction of Social Activism.* New York: Oxford University Press, 2000. An analysis of why our current state of economic and political development produces social movements.

Goode, Erich. *Paranormal Beliefs: A Sociological Introduction.* Bellevue, Wash.: Waveland Press, 2000. An examination of how the acceptance or rejection of belief in paranormal events is related to social structure.

Goode, Erich, and Nachman Ben-Yehuda. *Moral Panics: The Social Construction of Deviance.* New York: Blackwell, 1994. An overview of moral panics, one of the forms of collective behavior discussed in this chapter, with an emphasis on the process by which something is determined to be a moral threat.

Gupta, Dipak K. *Path to Collective Madness: A Study in Social Order and Political Pathology.* New York: Praeger, 2002. The author analyzes the process by which people participate in "collective madness"—such events as parents poisoning their children in Jonestown and the genocide of Rwanda.

Hanagan, Michael P., and Leslie T. Moch, eds. *Challenging Authority: The Historical Study of Contentious Politics (Social Movements, Protest, and Contention).* St. Paul: University of Minnesota Press, 1999. The authors analyze how social movements challenge the political order and lead to social change.

Jasper, James M. *The Art of Moral Protest: Culture, Biography, and Creativity in Social Movements.* Chicago: University of Chicago

Press, 2000. A primary thrust of this book is how protest movements shape moral thinking.

Luker, Kristin. *Abortion and the Politics of Motherhood.* Berkeley: University of California Press, 2000. Based on documents and interviews with pro-choice and pro-life advocates, the author demonstrates how people's moral positions on abortion are related to their views on sexual behavior, the care of children, and family life.

Journal

Social Movement Studies examines the origins, development, organization, context, and impact of social movements.

CHAPTER 22 Social Change and the Environment

Arnold, Ron, and Alan M. Gottlieb. *Trashing the Economy: How Runaway Environmentalism Is Wrecking America.* Bellevue, Wash.: Merrill Press, 1999. Taking the opposite view of the Rensenbrink book, the author advances the thesis that the environmental movement can wreak the natural resource base of the U.S. economy.

Breton, Mary Joy. *Women Pioneers for the Environment.* Boston: Northeastern University Press, 1999. The stories of 40 women who stepped out of their traditional roles to spearhead environmental campaigns.

Brown, Lester R., ed. *State of the World.* New York: Norton, published annually. Experts on environmental issues analyze environmental problems throughout the world; a New Malthusian perspective.

Council on Environmental Quality. *Environmental Quality.* Washington, D.C.: U.S. Government Printing Office, published annu-

ally. Each report evaluates the condition of some aspect of the environment.

Gaard, Greta Claire. *Ecological Politics: Ecofeminists and the Greens.* Philadelphia: Temple University Press, 1998. Examines the ideological connections between feminist theory and social activism in the environmental movement, with a special emphasis on Green politics.

Gates, Bill. *Business @ the Speed of Thought: Using a Digital Nervous System.* New York: Warner Books, 1999. The premise is that the speed of business is increasing and that to keep up businesses must develop a "digital nervous system" to gather, manage, and use information.

Homer-Dixon, Thomas F. *Environment, Scarcity, and Violence.* Princeton: Princeton University Press, 2002. The author argues that the growth in population and production will create environmental scarcities, which, in turn, will lead to insurrections, ethnic clashes, urban unrest, and other forms of violence.

Rensenbrink, John. *Against All Odds: The Green Transformation of American Politics.* Gray, Maine: Leopold Press, 1999. The thesis is that to have a "just and self-renewing society" the United States needs a new political system based on "ecological wisdom."

Veltmeyer, Henry, and James F. Petras. *The Dynamics of Social Change in Latin America.* New York: St. Martin's Press, 2000. Analyzes the interrelationship of the globalization of capitalism, ideology, social class, politics, and the economy of Latin America.

Journals

Earth First! Journal and *Sierra,* magazines published by Earth First! and the Sierra Club respectively, are excellent sources for keeping informed of major developments in the environmental movement.

References

Abeil, Hilary. "Endangering Women's Health for Profit: Health and Safety in Mexico's *Maquiladoras.*" *Development in Practice*, 9, 5, November 1999:595–600.

Aberle, David. *The Peyote Religion Among the Navaho.* Chicago: Aldine, 1966.

Aberle, David F., A. K. Cohen, A. K. David, M. J. Leng, Jr., and F. N. Sutton. "The Functional Prerequisites of a Society." *Ethics*, 60, January 1950:100–111.

Ackernecht, Erwin H. "The Role of Medical History in Medical Education." *Bulletin of the History of Medicine, 21*, 1947:135–145.

Adams, Noah. "All Things Considered." *New England Journal of Medicine* report. January 12, 2000.

Addams, Jane. *Twenty Years at Hull-House.* New York: Signet, 1981. First published in 1910.

Adler, Patricia A., and Peter Adler. *Peer Power: Preadolescent Culture and Identity.* New Brunswick, N.J.: Rutgers University Press, 1998.

Adler, Patricia A., Steven J. Kless, and Peter Adler. "Socialization to Gender Roles: Popularity Among Elementary School Boys and Girls." *Sociology of Education, 65*, July 1992:169–187.

Adorno, Theodor W., Else Frenkel-Brunswick, D. J. Levinson, and R. N. Sanford. *The Authoritarian Personality.* New York: Harper & Row, 1950.

Aeppel, Timothy. "More Amish Women Are Tending to Business." *Wall Street Journal*, February 8, 1996:B1, B2.

Aguirre, Benigno E., E. L. Quarantelli, and Jorge L. Mendoza. "The Collective Behavior of Fads: The Characteristics, Effects, and Career of Streaking." In *Collective Behavior and Social Movements*, Russell L. Curtis, Jr., and Benigno E. Aguirre, eds. Boston: Allyn and Bacon, 1993:168–182.

Ahlburg, Dennis A., and Carol J. De Vita. "New Realities of the American Family." *Population Bulletin, 47*, 2, August 1992:1–44.

Akol, Jacob. "Slavery in Sudan." *New African*, September 1998.

Alarid, Leanne Fiftal, Velmer S. Burton, Jr., and Francis T. Cullen. "Gender and Crime among Felony Offenders: Assessing the Generality of Social Control and Differential Association Theories." *Journal of Research in Crime and Delinquency, 37*, 2, May 2000:171–199.

Albert, Ethel M. "Women of Burundi: A Study of Social Values." In *Women of Tropical Africa*, Denise Paulme, ed. Berkeley: University of California Press, 1963:179–215.

Aldrich, Nelson W., Jr. *Old Money: The Mythology of America's Upper Class.* New York: Vintage Books, 1989.

Allport, Floyd. *Social Psychology.* Boston: Houghton Mifflin, 1954.

Alter, Jonathan. "From the Prison of the 'Isms.'" *Newsweek*, January 1, 2000:31.

Amato, Paul R. "What Children Learn From Divorce." *Population Today, 29*, 1, January 2001:1, 4.

Amenta, Edwin, Drew Halfmann, and Michael P. Young. "The Strategies and Contexts of Social Protest: Political Mediation and the Impact of the Townsend Movement in California." *Mobilization, 4*, 1, April 1999:1–23.

American Federation of Teachers. *Survey and Analysis of Teacher Salary Trends 1998.* Washington, D.C.: American Federation of Teachers, 1998.

American Sociological Association, "Section on Environment and Technology." Pamphlet, no date.

American Sociological Association. "Code of Ethics." Washington, D.C.: American Sociological Association, August 14, 1989; Spring 1997.

"Americans Work More." Associated Press, September 1, 2001.

Amin, Yousreya, Emad Hamdi, et. al. "Mass Hysteria in an Arab Culture." *International Journal of Social Psychiatry, 43*, 4, Winter 1997:303–306.

Andersen, Margaret L. *Thinking About Women: Sociological Perspectives on Sex and Gender.* New York: Macmillan, 1988.

Anderson, Chris. "NORC Study Describes Homeless." *Chronicle*, 1986:5, 9.

Anderson, Elijah. *A Place on the Corner.* Chicago: University of Chicago Press, 1978.

Anderson, Elijah. *Streetwise.* Chicago: University of Chicago Press, 1990.

Anderson, Elijah. "Streetwise." In *Down to Earth Sociology: Introductory Readings*, 10th ed., James M. Henslin, ed. New York: Free Press, 1999:193–202.

Anderson, Elijah. "Selling Crack." In *Down to Earth Sociology: Introductory Readings*, 11th ed., James M. Henslin, ed. New York: The Free Press, 2001:247–256.

Anderson, Nels. *The Hobo.* Chicago: University of Chicago Press, 1923.

Anderson, Nels. *Desert Saints: The Mormon Frontier in Utah.* Chicago: University of Chicago Press, 1966. First published in 1942.

Anderson, Philip. "God and the Swedish Immigrants." *Sweden and America*, Autumn 1995:17–20.

Anderson, Teresa A. "The Best Years of Their Lives." *Newsweek*, January 7, 1985:6.

Angell, Marcia. "Euthanasia in the Netherlands—Good News or Bad?" *New England Journal of Medicine, 335*, 22, November 28, 1996.

Angell, Robert C. "The Sociology of Human Conflict." In *The Nature of Human Conflict*, Elton B. McNeil, ed. Englewood Cliffs, N.J.: Prentice Hall 1965.

Angler, Natalie. "Do Races Differ? Not Really, DNA Shows." *New York Times*, August 22, 2000.

Annin, Peter, and Kendall Hamilton. "Marriage or Rape?" *Newsweek*, December 16, 1996:78.

Ansberry, Clare. "Despite Federal Law, Hospitals Still Reject Sick Who Can't Pay." *Wall Street Journal,* November 29, 1988:A1, A4.

Ansberry, Clare. "Nannies and Mothers Struggle over Roles in Raising Children." *Wall Street Journal,* May 21, 1993:A1, A6.

Antecol, Heather, and Deborah Cobb-Clark. "Men, Women, and Sexual Harassment in the U.S. Military." *Gender Issues, 19,* 1, Winter 2001:3–18.

"Anybody's Son Will Do." National Film Board of Canada, KCTS, and Films, Inc. 1983.

Aptheker, Herbert. "W.E.B. Du Bois: Struggle Not Despair." *Clinical Sociology Review, 8,* 1990:58–68.

Archbold, Ronna, and Mary Harmon. "International Success: Acceptance." Online: The Five O'clock Club, 2001.

Arías, Jesús. "La Junta rehabilita en Grenada casas que deberá tirar por ruina." *El Pais,* January 2, 1993:1.

Ariés, Philippe. *Centuries of Childhood.* R. Baldick, trans. New York: Vintage Books, 1965.

Arlacchi, P. *Peasants and Great Estates: Society in Traditional Calabria.* Cambridge, England: Cambridge University Press, 1980.

Armitage, Richard L. "Red Army Retreat Doesn't Signal End of U.S. Obligation." *Wall Street Journal,* February 7, 1989:A20.

Arndt, William F., and F. Wilbur Gingrich. *A Greek-English Lexicon of the New Testament and Other Early Christian Literature.* Chicago: University of Chicago Press, 1957.

Asch, Solomon. "Effects of Group Pressure Upon the Modification and Distortion of Judgments." In *Readings in Social Psychology,* Guy Swanson, Theodore M. Newcomb, and Eugene L. Hartley, eds. New York: Holt, Rinehart and Winston, 1952.

Ashe, Arthur. "A Zero-Sum Game That Hurts Blacks." *Wall Street Journal,* February 27, 1992:A10.

Ashford, Lori S. "New Perspectives on Population: Lessons from Cairo." *Population Bulletin, 50,* 1, March 1995:1–44.

Ashford, Lori S. "New Population Policies: Advancing Women's Health and Rights." *Population Bulletin, 56,* 1, March 2001:1–44.

Ashley, Richard. *Cocaine: Its History, Uses, and Effects.* New York: St. Martin's, 1975.

Ayittey, George B. N. "Black Africans Are Enraged at Arabs." *Wall Street Journal,* interactive edition, September 4, 1998.

Baca Zinn, Maxine. "Adaptation and Continuity in Mexican-Origin Families." In *Minority Families in the United States: A Multicultural Perspective,* Ronald L. Taylor, ed. Englewood Cliffs, N.J.: Prentice Hall, 1994:64–81.

Badgett, M. V. Lee, and Heidi Hartmann. "The Effectiveness of Equal Employment Opportunity Policies." In *Economic Perspectives in Affirmative Action,* Margaret C. Simms, ed. Washington, D.C.: Joint Center for Political and Economic Studies 1995:55–83.

Bai, Matt. "Anatomy of a Massacre." *Newsweek,* May 3, 1999:25–31.

Bainbridge, William Sims. "Collective Behavior and Social Movements." In *Sociology,* Rodney Stark. Belmont, Calif.: Wadsworth, 1989:608–640.

Bales, Robert F. *Interaction Process Analysis.* Reading, Mass.: Addison-Wesley, 1950.

Bales, Robert F. "The Equilibrium Problem in Small Groups." In *Working Papers in the Theory of Action,* Talcott Parsons et al., eds. New York: Free Press, 1953:111–115.

Baltzell, E. Digby. *Puritan Boston and Quaker Philadelphia.* New York: Free Press, 1979.

Baltzell, E. Digby, and Howard G. Schneiderman. "Social Class in the Oval Office." *Society, 25,* Sept/Oct, 1988:42–49.

Bannon, Lisa. "How a Rumor Spread About Subliminal Sex in Disney's 'Aladdin'." *Wall Street Journal,* October 24, 1995:A1, A6.

Barkun, Michael. "Reflections After Waco: Millenialists and the State." *Christian Century,* June 2–9, 1993:596–600.

Barnes, Fred. "How to Rig a Poll." *Wall Street Journal,* June 14, 1995:A14.

Barnes, Harry Elmer. *The History of Western Civilization,* Vol. 1. New York: Harcourt, Brace, 1935.

Barnes, Helen. "A Comment on Stroud and Pritchard: Child Homicide, Psychiatric Disorder and Dangerousness." *British Journal of Social Work, 31,* 3, June 2001.

Baron, Robert, and Gerald Greenberg. *Behavior in Organizations.* Boston: Allyn and Bacon, 1990.

Baron, Stephen W. "Street Youth: Labour Market Experiences and Crime." *Canadian Review of Sociology and Anthropology, 38,* 2, May 2001:189–215.

Barry, John. "A New Breed of Soldier." *Newsweek,* December 10, 2001:24–31.

Barry, John, and Evan Thomas. "Dropping the Bomb." *Newsweek,* June 25, 2001.

Barry, Paul. "Strong Medicine: A Talk with Former Principal Henry Gradillas." *College Board Review,* Fall 1989:2–13.

Bartlett, Donald L., and James B. Steele. "Paying a Price for Polluters." *Time,* November 23, 1998:72–80.

Baskin, D. R., and I. B. Sommers. *Casualties of Community Disorder: Women's Careers in Violent Crime.* Boulder: Westview Press, 1998.

Bazell, Robert. "Medical Errors a Major Killer." NBC Nightly News, November 29, 1999.

Beals, Ralph L., and Harry Hoijer. *An Introduction to Anthropology,* 3rd ed. New York: Macmillan, 1965.

Beck, Allen J., Susan A. Kline, and Lawrence A. Greenfeld. "Survey of Youth in Custody, 1987." Washington, D.C.: U.S. Department of Justice, September 1988.

Beck, Scott H., and Joe W. Page. "Involvement in Activities and the Psychological Well-Being of Retired Men." *Activities, Adaptation, & Aging, 11,* 1, 1988:31–47.

Becker, Howard S. *Outsiders: Studies in the Sociology of Deviance.* New York: Free Press, 1966.

Beckett, Paul. "Even Piñatas Sold in Mexico Seem to Originate in Hollywood Now." *Wall Street Journal,* September 11, 1996:B1.

Beeghley, Leonard. *The Structure of Social Stratification in the United States,* 3rd ed. Boston: Allyn and Bacon, 2000.

Begley, Sharon. "Twins: Nazi and Jew." *Newsweek, 94,* December 3, 1979:139.

Begley, Sharon. "Odds on the Greenhouse." *Newsweek,* December 1, 1997:72.

Belkin, Lisa. "A Brutal Cure." *New York Times Magazine,* May 30, 1999.

Bell, Daniel. *The Coming of Post-Industrial Society: A Venture in Social Forecasting.* New York: Basic Books, 1973.

Bell, David A. "An American Success Story: The Triumph of Asian-Americans." In *Sociological Footprints: Introductory Readings in Sociology,* 5th ed., Leonard Cargan and Jeanne H. Ballantine, eds. Belmont, Calif.: Wadsworth, 1991:308–316.

Bellah, Robert N. *Beyond Belief.* New York: Harper & Row, 1970.

Belluck, Pam. "First Ever Criminal Conviction Levied in Food Poisoning Case." *New York Times,* July 24, 1998.

Belluck, Pam. "Prosecutors Say Greed Drove Pharmacist to Dilute Drugs." *New York Times,* August 18, 2001.

Benales, Carlos. "70 Days Battling Starvation and Freezing in the Andes: A Chronicle of Man's Unwillingness to Die." *New York Times,* January 1, 1973:3.

Bender, Sue, "Everyday Sacred: A Journey to the Amish." *Utne Reader,* September–October 1990:91–97.

Benet, Sula. "Why They Live to Be 100, or Even Older, in Abkhasia." *New York Times Magazine, 26,* December 1971.

Bergen, Raquel Kennedy. *Wife Rape: Understanding the Response of Survivors and Service Providers.* Newbury Park, Calif.: Sage, 1996.

Berger, Peter L. *Invitation to Sociology: A Humanistic Perspective.* New York: Doubleday, 1963.

Berger, Peter L. *The Capitalist Revolution: Fifty Propositions About Prosperity, Equality, and Liberty.* New York: Basic Books, 1991.

Berger, Peter L. "Invitation to Sociology." In *Down to Earth Sociology: Introductory Readings,* 11th ed. James M. Henslin, ed. New York: Free Press, 2001:3–7.

Bergmann, Barbara R. "The Future of Child Care." Paper presented at the 1995 meetings of the American Sociological Association.

Bergström, Hans. "Pressures Behind the Swedish Health Reforms." *Viewpoint Sweden, 12,* July 1992:1–5.

Berk, Laura E. *Child Development,* 3rd ed. Boston: Allyn and Bacon, 1994.

Berk, Richard A. *Collective Behavior.* Dubuque, Iowa: Brown, 1974.

Berle, Adolf, Jr., and Gardiner C. Means. *The Modern Corporation and Private Property.* New York: Harcourt, Brace and World, 1932. As cited in Useem 1980:44.

Bernard, Jessie. *The Future of Marriage.* New York: Bantam, 1972.

Bernard, Jessie. "The Good-Provider Role." In *Marriage and Family in a Changing Society,* 4th ed., James M. Henslin, ed. New York: Free Press, 1992:275–285.

Bernard, Viola W., Perry Ottenberg, and Fritz Redl. "Dehumanization: A Composite Psychological Defense in Relation to Modern War." In *The Triple Revolution Emerging: Social Problems in Depth,* Robert Perucci and Marc Pilisuk, eds. Boston: Little, Brown, 1971:17–34.

Bernhardt, Eva M., and Frances K. Goldscheider. "Men, Resources, and Family Living: The Determinants of Union and Parental Status in the United States and Sweden." *Journal of Marriage and the Family, 63, 3,* August 2001:793–803.

Bernstein, Nina. "Studies Dispute 2 Assumptions About Welfare Overhaul." *New York Times,* December 12, 2000.

Bernstein, Richard. "Play Penn." *New Republic,* August 2, 1993.

Berreby, David. "Scanning Brains for Insights on Racial Perception." *New York Times,* September 5, 2000.

Beynon, John. *Masculinities and Culture.* Philadelphia: Open University Press, 2002.

Bianchi, Suzanne M., and Lynne M. Casper. "American Families." *Population Bulletin, 55, 4,* December 2000:1–42.

Bianchi, Suzanne M., and Daphne Spain. "Women Work, and Family in America." *Population Bulletin, 51, 3,* December 1996:1–47.

Bianchi, Suzanne M., Melissa A. Milkie, Liana C. Sayer, and John P. Robinson. "Is Anyone Doing the Housework? Trends in the Gender Division of Household Labor." *Social Forces, 79, 1,* September 2000:191–228.

Binyon, Michael. "The Graveyard of Invading Armies." *The Times,* September 14, 2001.

Bird, Chloe E. "Gender Differences in the Social and Economic Burdens of Parenting and Psychological Distress." *Journal of Marriage and the Family, 59,* August 1997:1–16.

Bird, Chloe E., and Patricia P. Rieker. "Gender Matters: An Integrated Model for Understanding Men's and Women's Health." *Social Science and Medicine, 48, 6,* March 1999:745–755.

Bishop, Jerry E. "Study Finds Doctors Tend to Postpone Heart Surgery for Women, Raising Risk." *Wall Street Journal,* April 16, 1990:B4.

Bjerklie, David, Andrea Dorfman, Wendy Cole, Jeanne DeQuine, Helen Gibson, David S. Jackson, Leora Moldofsky, Timothy Roche, Chris Taylor, Cathy Booth Thomas, and Dick Thompson. "Baby, It's You: And You, and You . . . " *Time,* February 19, 2001:47–57.

Blassi, Joseph, and Michael Conte. "Employee Stock Ownership and Corporate Performance Among Public Companies." *Industrial and Labor Relations Review, 50, 1,* October 1996:60–79.

Blau, David M. "The Production of Quality in Child-Care Centers: Another Look." *Applied Developmental Science, 4, 3,* 2000:136–148.

Blau, Francine D., and Lawrence M. Kahn. "The Gender Earnings Gap: Some International Evidence." Working Paper No. 4224, National Bureau of Economic Research, December 1992.

Blau, Peter M., and Otis Dudley Duncan. *The American Occupational Structure.* New York: John Wiley, 1967.

Blauner, Robert. "Death and Social Structure." *Psychiatry, 29,* 1966:378–394.

Blumer, Herbert George. "Collective Behavior." In *Principles of Sociology,* Robert E. Park, ed. New York: Barnes and Noble, 1939:219–288.

Blumer, Herbert. "Sociological Implications of the Thought of George Herbert Mead." *American Journal of Sociology, 71,* 1966:535–544.

Blumer, Herbert. *Industrialization as an Agent of Social Change: A Critical Analysis,* David R. Maines and Thomas J. Morrione, eds. Hawthorne, N.Y.: Aldine de Gruyter, 1990.

Blumstein, Alfred, and Jacqueline Cohen. "Characterizing Criminal Careers." *Science, 237,* August 1987:985–991.

Blumstein, Philip, and Pepper Schwartz. *American Couples: Money, Work, Sex.* New York: Pocket Books, 1985.

Bobo, Lawrence, and James R. Kluegel. "Modern American Prejudice: Stereotypes, Social Distance, and Perceptions of Discrimination Toward Blacks, Hispanics, and Asians." Paper presented at the 1991 annual meetings of the American Sociological Association.

Booth, Alan, and James M. Dabbs, Jr. "Testosterone and Men's Marriages." *Social Forces, 72, 2,* December 1993:463–477.

Bosman, Ciska M., et al. "Business Success and Businesses' Beauty Capital." National Bureau of Economic Research Working Paper: 6083, July 1997.

"The Boss's Pay." *Wall Street Journal,* April 6, 2000:R9.

Boulding, Elise. *The Underside of History.* Boulder, Colo.: Westview Press, 1976.

Bourgois, Philippe. "Crack in Spanish Harlem." In *Haves and Have-Nots: An International Reader on Social Inequality,* James Curtis and Lorne Tepperman, eds. Englewood Cliffs, N.J.: Prentice Hall, 1994:131–136.

Bowles, Samuel. "Unequal Education and the Reproduction of the Social Division of Labor." In *Power and Ideology in Education,* J. Karabel and A. H. Halsely, eds. New York: Oxford University Press, 1977.

Bowles, Samuel, and Herbert Gintis. *Schooling in Capitalist America*. New York: Basic Books, 1976.

Boxer, Sarah. "When Emotion Worms Its Way Into Law." *New York Times,* April 7, 2001.

Bradley, Martin B., Norman M. Green, Jr., Dale E. Jones, Mac Lynn, and Lou McNiel. *Churches and Church Membership in the United States 1990.* Atlanta: Glenmary Research Center, 1992.

Brajuha, Mario, and Lyle Hallowell. "Legal Intrusion and the Politics of Fieldwork: The Impact of the Brajuha Case." *Urban Life, 14,* 4, January 1986:454–478.

Brannon, Linda. *Gender: Psychological Perspectives,* 2nd ed. Boston: Allyn and Bacon, 1999.

Brauchli, Marcus W. "Wary of Education But Needing Brains, China Faces a Dilemma." *Wall Street Journal,* November 15, 1994:A1, A10.

Bray, Rosemary L. "Rosa Parks: A Legendary Moment, a Lifetime of Activism. *Ms., 6,* 3, November–December 1995:45–47.

Brecher, Edward M., and the Editors of Consumer Reports. *Licit and Illicit Drugs.* Boston: Little, Brown, 1972.

Breen, Richard, and Christopher T. Whelan. "Gender and Class Mobility: Evidence from the Republic of Ireland." *Sociology, 29,* 1, February 1995:1–22.

Bretos, Miguel A. "Hispanics Face Institutional Exclusion." *Miami Herald,* May 22, 1994.

Brewer, Loretta. "Gender Socialization and the Cultural Construction of Elder Caregivers." *Journal of Aging Studies, 15,* 3, September 2001:217–235.

Bridgman, Ann. "Report from the Russian Front." *Education Week,* April 6, 1994:22–29.

Bridgwater, William, ed. *The Columbia Viking Desk Encyclopedia.* New York: Viking Press, 1953.

Brines, Julie. "Economic Dependency, Gender, and the Division of Labor at Home." *American Journal of Sociology, 100,* 3, November 1994:652–688.

Brines, Julie, and Kara Joyner. "The Ties That Bind. Principles of Cohesion in Cohabitation and Marriage." *American Sociological Review, 64,* June 1999:333–355.

Brink, Susan. "Elderly Empowerment." *U.S. News & World Report,* April 26, 1993:65–70.

Brinton, Crane. *The Anatomy of Revolution.* New York: Vintage Books, 1965.

Broad, William J. "The Shuttle Explodes." *New York Times,* January 29, 1986, A1, A5.

Broad, William J., and Judith Miller. "Rocky Start for U.S. Plan to Stockpile Vaccines to Fight Germ Warfare." *New York Times,* August 7, 1998.

Broad, William J., and Melody Petersen. "The Biological Threat." *New York Times,* September 23, 2001.

Brockerhoff, Martin P. "An Urbanizing World." *Population Bulletin, 55,* 3, September 2000:1–44.

Bromley, David G. "The Satanic Cult Scare." *Culture and Society,* May–June 1991:55–56.

Bronfenbrenner, Urie. "Principles for the Healthy Growth and Development of Children." In *Marriage and Family in a Changing Society,* 4th ed., James M. Henslin, ed. New York: Free Press, 1992:243–249.

Brooke, James. "Amid U.S. Islam's Growth in the U.S., Muslims Face a Surge in Attacks." *New York Times,* August 28, 1995:A1, B7.

Brooks, Virginia R. "Sex Differences in Student Dominance Behavior in Female and Male Professors' Classrooms." *Sex Roles, 8,* 7, 1982:683–690.

Brooks-Gunn, Jeanne, Greg. J. Duncan, and Lawrence Aber, eds. *Neighborhood Poverty, Volume 1: Context and Consequences for Children.* New York: Russell Sage Foundation, 1997.

Brown, Garrett. "Double Standards." *Multinational Monitor, 21,* 11, November 2000:24–28.

Browne, Beverly A. "Gender Stereotypes in Advertising on Children's Television in the 1990s: A Cross-National Analysis." *Journal of Advertising, 27,* 1, Spring 1998:83–96.

Browning, Christopher R. *Ordinary Men: Reserve Police Battalion 101 and the Final Solution in Poland.* New York: HarperPerennial, 1993.

Brueggemann, John. "The Power and Collapse of Paternalism: The Ford Motor Company and Black Workers, 1937–1941." *Social Problems, 47,* 2, May 2000:220–240.

Brunvand, Jan Harold. *The Vanishing Hitchhiker: American Urban Legends and Their Meanings.* New York: Norton, 1981.

Brunvand, Jan Harold. *The Choking Doberman and Other "New" Urban Legends.* New York: Norton, 1984.

Brunvand, Jan Harold. *The Study of American Folklore.* New York: Norton, 1986.

Brunvand, Jan Harold. "Introduction." *Skeptical Inquirer,* May-June 1999:29.

Bryant, Chalandra M., Rand D. Conger, and Jennifer M. Meehan. "The Influence of In-Laws on Changes in Marital Success." *Journal of Marriage and the Family, 63,* 3, August 2001:614–626.

Bryant, Clifton D. "Cockfighting: America's Invisible Sport." In *Down to Earth Sociology: Introductory Readings,* 7th ed., James M. Henslin, ed. New York: Free Press, 1993.

Brzezinksi, Matthew. "Where Cash Isn't King: Barter Lines Pockets in Ex-Soviet States." *Wall Street Journal,* May 1, 1997:A14.

Bumiller, Elisabeth. "First Comes Marriage—Then, Maybe, Love." In *Marriage and Family in a Changing Society,* 4th ed., James M. Henslin, ed. New York: Free Press, 1992:120–125.

Bumiller, Elisabeth. "Weekend Excursion: In Amish Land, Witnesses to Old and New." *New York Times,* June 26, 1998.

Bumpass, Larry L., James A. Sweet, and Andrew Cherlin. "The Role of Cohabitation in Declining Rates of Marriage." *Journal of Marriage and the Family, 53,* November 1991:913–927.

Bureau of the Census. "Income, Poverty, and Valuation of Noncash Benefits: 1994." *Current Population Reports* P60–189. Washington, D.C.: GPO, 1996.

Bureau of Labor Statistics. "News: U.S. Department of Labor." February 4, 2000.

Burgess, Ernest W. "The Growth of the City: An Introduction to a Research Project." In *The City,* Robert E. Park, Ernest W. Burgess, and Roderick D. McKenzie, eds. Chicago: University of Chicago Press, 1925:47–62.

Burgess, Ernest W., and Harvey J. Locke. *The Family: From Institution to Companionship.* New York: American Book, 1945.

Burnham, Walter Dean. *Democracy in the Making: American Government and Politics.* Englewood Cliffs, N.J.: Prentice Hall, 1983.

Bush, Diane Mitsch, and Robert G. Simmons. "Socialization Processes Over the Life Course." In *Social Psychology: Sociological Perspectives,* eds. Morris Rosenberger and Ralph H. Turner. New Brunswick, N.J.:Transaction, 1990:133–164.

Butler, Robert N. *Why Survive? Being Old in America.* New York: Harper & Row, 1975.

Butler, Robert N. "Ageism: Another Form of Bigotry." *Gerontologist, 9,* Winter 1980:243–246.

Buttel, Frederick H. "New Directions in Environmental Sociology." *Annual Review of Sociology, 13,* W. Richard Scott and James F. Short, Jr., eds. Palo Alto, Calif.: Annual Reviews, 1987:465–488.

Bynum, Bill. "Discarded Diagnoses." *Lancet, 358,* 9294, November 17, 2001:1736.

Callahan, Daniel. *Setting Limits: Medical Goals in an Aging Society.* New York: Simon & Schuster, 1987.

Canavan, Margaret M., Walter J. Meyer, III, and Deborah C. Higgs. "The Female Experience of Sibling Incest." *Journal of Marital and Family Therapy, 18,* 2, 1992:129–142.

Cannon, Lou. *Official Negligence: How Rodney King and the Riots Changed Los Angeles and the LAPD.* New York: Times Books, 1998.

Cantril, Hadley. *The Psychology of Social Movements.* New York: Wiley, 1941.

Caplow, Theodore. "The American Way of Celebrating Christmas." In *Down to Earth Sociology: Introductory Readings,* 6th ed., James M. Henslin, ed. New York: Free Press, 1991:88–97.

Carlson, Lewis H., and George A. Colburn. *In Their Place: White America Defines Her Minorities, 1850–1950.* New York: Wiley, 1972.

Carpenito, Lynda Juall. "The Myths of Acquaintance Rape." *Nursing Forum, 34,* 4, October-December 1999:3.

Carpenter, Betsy. "Redwood Radicals." *U.S. News & World Report, 109,* 11, September 17, 1990:50–51.

Carper, James C. "Pluralism to Establishment to Dissent: The Religious and Educational Context of Home Schooling." *Peabody Journal of Education, 75,* 1/2, 2000:8–19.

Carr, Deborah, Carol D. Ryff, Burton Singer, and William J. Magee. "Bringing the 'Life' Back into Life Course Research: A 'Person-Centered' Approach to Studying the Life Course." Paper presented at the 1995 meetings of the American Sociological Association.

Carrasquillo, Hector. "The Puerto Rican Family." In *Minority Families in the United States: A Multicultural Perspective,* Ronald L. Taylor, ed. Englewood Cliffs, N.J.: Prentice Hall, 1994:82–94.

Carrington, Tim. "Developed Nations Want Poor Countries to Succeed on Trade, But Not Too Much." *Wall Street Journal,* September 20, 1993:A10.

Carron, Albert V., and Lawrence R. Brawley. "Cohesion." *Small Group Research, 31,* 1, February 2000:89–106.

Cartwright, Dorwin, and Alvin Zander, eds. *Group Dynamics,* 3rd ed. Evanston, Ill.: Peterson, 1968.

Casper, Lynne M., and Martin O'Connell, "State Estimates of Organized Child Care Facilities." Annual meetings of the Population Association of America, March 1997, as contained in *Population Today, 25,* 5, May 1997:6.

Casper, Monica J. *The Making of the Unborn Patient: A Social Anatomy of Fetal Surgery.* New Brunswick, N.J.: Rutgers University Press, 1998.

Cassel, Russell N. "Examining the Basic Principles for Effective Leadership." *College Student Journal, 33,* 2, June 1999:288–301.

Cauthen, Nancy K., and James M. Jasper. "Culture, Politics, and Moral Panics." *Sociological Forum, 9,* 3, September 1994: 495–503.

Centers for Disease Control. *HIV/AIDS Surveillance Report, 11,* 1, June 1999.

Centers for Disease Control. *HIV/AIDS Surveillance Report, 12,* 2, June 2001.

Cerulo, Karen A., and Janet M. Ruane. "Death Comes Alive: Technology and the Re-Conception of Death." In *Science as Culture,* 1996.

Cerulo, Karen A., Janet M. Ruane, and Mary Chayko. "Technological Ties That Bind: Media-Generated Primary Groups." *Communication Research, 19,* 1, February 1992:109–129.

Cha, Kwang Y., Daniel P. Wirth, and Rogerio A. Lobo. "Does Prayer Influence the Success of In Vitro Fertilization-Embryo Transfer? Report of a Masked, Randomized Trial." *Journal of Reproductive Medicine, 46,* 9, September 2001:781–787.

Chafetz, Janet Saltzman, and Anthony Gary Dworkin. *Female Revolt: Women's Movements in World and Historical Perspective.* Totowa, N.J.: Rowman & Allanheld, 1986.

Chagnon, Napoleon A. *Yanomamo: The Fierce People,* 2nd ed. New York: Holt, Rinehart and Winston, 1977.

Chalfant, H. Paul. "Stepping to Redemption: Twelve-Step Groups as Implicit Religion." *Free Inquiry in Creative Sociology, 20,* 2, November 1992:115–120.

Chalkley, Kate. "Female Genital Mutilation: New Laws, Programs Try to End Practice." *Population Today, 25,* 10, October 1997:4–5.

Chamberlain, Claudine. "Implicit Association Test." ABCNews Online, September 30, 1998.

Chambliss, Daniel F. "The World of the Hospital." In *Down to Earth Sociology: Introductory Readings,* 11th ed., James M. Henslin, ed. New York: The Free Press, 2001:418–429.

Chambliss, William J. "A Sociological Analysis of the Law of Vagrancy." *Social Problems, 12,* Summer 1964:67–77.

Chambliss, William J. "The Saints and the Roughnecks." In *Down to Earth Sociology: Introductory Readings,* 10th ed., James M. Henslin, ed. New York: Free Press, 1999:260–274. First published in *Society, 11,* 1973.

Chambliss, William J. *Power, Politics, and Crime.* Boulder: Westview Press, 2000.

Chandler, Tertius, and Gerald Fox. *3000 Years of Urban Growth.* New York: Academic Press, 1974.

Chandra, Vibha P. "Fragmented Identities: The Social Construction of Ethnicity, 1885–1947." Unpublished paper, 1993a.

Chandra, Vibha P. "The Present Moment of the Past: The Metamorphosis." Unpublished paper, 1993b.

Chang, Leslie. "Confucius Said: Sons, Care for Your Elders; Elders Say: We Sue." *Wall Street Journal,* April 3, 2000:A1, A15.

Charles, *Social Problems, 47,* 3, August 2000:379–407.

Chen, Edwin. "Twins Reared Apart: A Living Lab." *New York Times Magazine.* December 9, 1979:112.

Chen, I-Chun. "Mexico's *Maquiladoras* Go Way South of the Border." *Global Finance, 15,* 2, February 2001:71–72.

Chen, Kathy. "China's Women Face Obstacles in Workplace." *Wall Street Journal,* August 28, 1995:B1, B5.

Cherlin, Andrew. "Remarriage as an Incomplete Institution." In *Marriage and Family in a Changing Society,* 3rd ed., James M. Henslin, ed. New York: Free Press, 1989:492–501.

Cherlin, Andrew, and Frank F. Furstenberg, Jr. "The American Family in the Year 2000." In *Down to Earth Sociology,* 5th ed., James M. Henslin, ed. New York: Free Press, 1988:325–331.

Chin, Nancy P., Alicia Monroe, and Kevin Fiscella. "Social Determinants of (Un)Healthy Behaviors." *Education for Health: Change in Learning and Practice, 13,* 3, November 2000:317–328.

Chivers, C. J. "Officer Resigns Before Hearing in D.W.I. Case." *New York Times,* August 29, 2001.

Chodorow, Nancy J. "What Is the Relation Between Psychoanalytic Feminism and the Psychoanalytic Psychology of Women?" In *Theoretical Perspectives on Sexual Difference,* Deborah L. Rhode, ed. New Haven, Conn.: Yale University Press, 1990:114–130.

Chu, Henry. "China's Declining Health." *Los Angeles Times,* December 24, 1998.

Chua-Eoan, Howard. "Tripped Up by Lies." *Time,* October 11, 1993:39–40.

Churchill, Ward. *A Little Matter of Genocide: Holocaust and Denial in the Americas, 1492 to the Present.* San Francisco: City Lights Books, 1997.

Clair, Jeffrey Michael., David A. Karp, and William C. Yoels. *Experiencing the Life Cycle: A Social Psychology of Aging,* 2nd ed. Springfield, Ill.: Thomas, 1993.

Clark, Candace. "Sympathy in Everyday Life." In *Down to Earth Sociology: Introductory Readings,* 6th ed., James M. Henslin, ed. New York: Free Press, 1991:193–203.

Clark, Candace. *Misery and Company: Sympathy in Everyday Life.* Chicago: University of Chicago Press, 1997.

Clark, Robert L., and Naohiro Ogawa. "Transition from Career Jobs to Retirement in Japan." *Industrial Relations, 36,* 2, April 1997:255–270.

Clay, Jason W. "What's a Nation?" *Mother Jones,* November–December 1990:28, 30.

Cleeland, Nancy. "Slowdown's Silent Victims." *Los Angeles Times,* October 21, 2001.

Clingempeel, W. Glenn, and N. Dickon Repucci. "Joint Custody After Divorce: Major Issues and Goals for Research." *Psychological Bulletin, 9,* 1982:102–127.

Cloud, John. "For Better or Worse." *Time,* October 26, 1998:43–44.

Cloud, John. "A Kinder, Gentler Death." *Time,* September 18, 2000:61–67.

Cloud, John, Mitch Frank, Viveca Novak, and Elaine Shannon. "General on the March." *Time, 158,* 22, November 19, 2001:63.

Cloward, Richard A., and Lloyd E. Ohlin. *Delinquency and Opportunity: A Theory of Delinquent Gangs.* New York: Free Press, 1960.

Cnaan, Ram A. "Neighborhood-representing Organizations: How Democratic Are They?" *Social Science Review,* December 1991:614–634.

Cockerham, William C. "The Social Determinants of the Decline of Life Expectancy in Russia and Eastern Europe: A Lifestyle Explanation." *Journal of Health and Social Behavior, 38,* June 1997:117–130.

Cohen, Joel E. "How Many People Can the Earth Support?" *Population Today,* January 1996:4–5.

Cohen, Roger. "Europe's Shifting Role Poses Challenge to U.S." *New York Times,* February 11, 2001.

Cohen, Steven M. "Hey NCR—We're the Shareholders, You Work for Us." *Wall Street Journal,* December 19, 1990:A16.

"Coke Adds Life, But It Cannot Always Explain It." *Lancet, 354,* 9174, July 17, 1999:173.

Cole, Jeff, and Sarah Lubman. "Weapons Merchants Are Going Great Guns in Post-Cold War Era." *Wall Street Journal,* January 28, 1994:A1, A4.

Coleman, James S., and Thomas Hoffer. *Public and Private Schools: The Impact of Communities.* New York: Basic Books, 1987.

Coleman, James William. *The Criminal Elite: The Sociology of White Collar Crime.* New York: St. Martin's Press, 1989.

Coleman, James William. "Politics and the Abuse of Power." In *Down to Earth Sociology: Introductory Readings,* 8th ed., James M. Henslin, ed. New York: Free Press, 1995:442–450.

Coleman, Joseph "The Son of North Korean Leader Had a Plan." Associated Press, May 4, 2001.

Coleman, Marilyn, Lawrence Ganong, and Mark Fine. "Reinvestigating Remarriage: Another Decade of Progress." *Journal of Marriage and the Family, 62,* 4, November 2000:1288–1307.

Collins, Huntly. "AIDS Activists Join Gray Panthers Against Drug Company." *Philadelphia Inquirer,* February 15, 2001.

Collins, Randall. *The Credential Society: An Historical Sociology of Education.* New York: Academic Press, 1979.

Collins, Randall. *Theoretical Sociology.* San Diego, Calif.: Harcourt, Brace Jovanovich, 1988.

Collins, Randall, Janet Saltzman Chafetz, Rae Lesser Blumberg, Scott Coltrane, and Jonathan H. Turner. "Toward an Integrated Theory of Gender Stratification." *Sociological Perspectives, 36,* 3, 1993:185–216.

Collins, Randall. "Socially Unrecognized Cumulation." *American Sociologist, 30,* 2, Summer 1999:41–61.

Collymore, Yvette. "Conveying Concerns: Women Report on Gender-Based Violence." Washington, D.C.: Population Reference Bureau, 2000.

"Coming to a Neighborhood Near You." *Economist, 360,* 8220, May 5, 2001:23–24.

Conahan, Frank C. "Human Experimentation: An Overview on Cold War Era Programs." Washington, D.C.: U.S. General Accounting Office, September 28, 1994:1–11.

Conrad, Peter. "Public Eyes and Private Genes: Historical Frames, New Constructions, and Social Problems." *Social Problems, 44,* 2, May 1997:139–154.

Cooley, Charles Horton. *Human Nature and the Social Order.* New York: Scribner's, 1902.

Cooley, Charles Horton. *Social Organization.* New York: Schocken, 1962. First published by Scribner's, 1909.

Coolidge, David Orgon. "At Last, Hawaiians Have Their Say on Gay Marriage." *Wall Street Journal,* April 23, 1997:A19.

Cooper, Helene. "Offering Aerobics, Karate, Aquatics, Hospitals Stress Business of 'Wellness.' " *Wall Street Journal,* August 9, 1993:B1, B3.

Corbett, Thomas. "Welfare Reform in the 104th Congress: Goals, Options, and Tradeoffs." *Focus, 17,* 1, Summer 1995:29–31.

Corbett, Thomas. "Poverty: Improving the Measure After Thirty Years, A Conference." *Focus, 20,* 2, Spring 1999:51–55.

Corbin, Robert K. "The President's Column." *American Rifleman,* December 1993:56.

Cose, Ellis. "The Good News About Black America." *Newsweek,* June 7, 1999:29–40.

Cose, Ellis. "What's White Anyway?" *Newsweek,* September 18, 2000:64–65.

Coser, Lewis A. *Masters of Sociological Thought: Ideas in Historical and Social Context,* 2nd ed. New York: Harcourt Brace Jovanovich, 1977.

Costello, Barbara J., and Paul R. Vowell. "Testing Control Theory and Differential Association: A Reanalysis of the Richmond Youth Project Data." *Criminology, 37,* 4, November 1999:815–842.

Cottin, Lou. *Elders in Rebellion: A Guide to Senior Activism.* Garden City, N.Y.: Anchor Doubleday, 1979.

Couch, Carl J. *Social Processes and Relationships: A Formal Approach.* Dix Hills, N.Y.: General Hall, 1989.

Coughlin, Ellen K. "Studying Homelessness: The Difficulty of Tracking a Transient Population." *Chronicle of Higher Education,* October 19, 1988:A6–A12.

Council on Resident Education & Obstetrics. "Information provided by telephone." September 2000.

Courtney, Kelly. "Two Sides of the Environmental Movement: Radical Earth First! and the Sierra Club." Paper presented at the 1995 meetings of the American Sociological Association.

Cousins, Albert, and Hans Nagpaul. *Urban Man and Society.* New York: McGraw-Hill, 1970.

Cowen, Emory L., Judah Landes, and Donald E. Schaet. "The Effects of Mild Frustration on the Expression of Prejudiced Attitudes." *Journal of Abnormal and Social Psychology.* January 1959:33–38.

Cowgill, Donald. "The Aging of Populations and Societies." *Annals of the American Academy of Political and Social Science, 415,* 1974:1–18.

Cowley, Geoffrey. "Attention: Aging Men." *Newsweek,* November 16, 1996:66–75.

Cowley, Geoffrey. "Sobering Up About AIDS." *Newsweek,* June 26, 1998.

Cowley, Geoffrey, and Anne Underwood. "A Revolution in Medicine." *Newsweek,* April 10, 2000:58–62.

Cowley, Joyce. *Pioneers of Women's Liberation.* New York: Merit, 1969.

Crary, David. "Internet Gives Elderly Link to Life." Associated Press. November 21, 1999.

Croal, N'Gai, and Jane Hughes. "Lara Croft, the Bit Girl." *Newsweek,* November 10, 1997:82, 86.

Croall, Hazel. *Understanding White Collar Crime.* Philadelphia: Open University Press, 2001.

Crosbie, Paul V., ed. *Interaction in Small Groups.* New York: Macmillan, 1975.

Crossen, Cynthia. *Wall Street Journal,* November 14, 1991:A1, A7.

Crossette, Barbara. "U.N. Documents Inequities for Women as World Forum Nears." *New York Times,* August 18, 1995a:A3.

Crossette, Barbara. "Worldwide Study Finds Decline in Election of Women Legislators." *New York Times,* August 27, 1995b.

Crossette, Barbara. "Caste May Be India's Moral Achilles' Heel." *New York Times,* October 20, 1996, electronic version.

Crossman, Donna K. "Global Structural Violence Against Women." Paper presented at the 1995 meetings of the American Sociological Association.

Croudace, T. J., R. Kayne, P. B. Jones, and G. L. Harrison. "Non-Linear Relationship Between an Index of Social Deprivation, Psychiatric Admission Prevalence and the Incidence of Psychosis." *Psychology of Medicine, 30,* 1, January 2000:177–185.

Cumming, Elaine. "Further Thoughts on the Theory of Disengagement." In *Aging in America: Readings in Social Gerontology,* Cary S. Kart and Barbara B. Manard, eds. Sherman Oaks, Calif.: Alfred Publishing, 1976:19–41.

Cumming, Elaine, and William E. Henry. *Growing Old: The Process of Disengagement.* New York: Basic Books, 1961.

Curtin, Sharon. "Nobody Ever Died of Old Age: In Praise of Old People." In *Growing Old in America.* Beth Hess, ed. New Brunswick, N.J.: Transaction, 1976:273–284.

Curwin, E. Cecil, and Gudmond Hart. *Plough and Pasture.* New York: Collier Books, 1961.

Dabbs, James M., Jr., and Robin Morris. "Testosterone, Social Class, and Antisocial Behavior in a Sample of 4,462 Men." *Psychological Science, 1,* 3, May 1990:209–211.

Dabbs, James M., Jr., Timothy S. Carr, Robert L. Frady, and Jasmin K. Riad. "Testosterone, Crime, and Misbehavior Among 692 Male Prison Inmates." *Personality and Individual Differences, 18,* 1995:627–633.

Dabbs, James M., Jr., Marian F. Hargrove, and Colleen Heusel. "Testosterone Differences Among College Fraternities: Well-Behaved vs. Rambunctious." *Personality and Individual Differences, 20,* 1996:157–161.

Dahl, Robert A. *Who Governs?* New Haven, Conn.: Yale University Press, 1961.

Dahl, Robert A. *Dilemmas of Pluralist Democracy: Autonomy vs. Control.* New Haven, Conn.: Yale University Press, 1982.

Dahrendorf, Ralf. *Class and Class Conflict in Industrial Society.* Palo Alto, Calif.: Stanford University Press, 1959.

Danzi, Angela D. "Savaria, The Midwife: Childbirth and Change in the Immigrant Community." In *Contemporary Readings in Sociology,* Judith N. DeSena, ed. Dubuque, Iowa: Kendall/Hunt, 1989:47–56.

Darden, Christoper. *Contempt.* New York: HarperCollins, 1997.

Darley, John M., and Bibb Latané. "Bystander Intervention in Emergencies: Diffusion of Responsibility." *Journal of Personality and Social Psychology, 8,* 4, 1968:377–383.

Darnell, Victor. "Qualitative-Quantitative Content Analysis of Graffiti in the Public Restrooms of St. Louis, Missouri, and Edwardsville, Illinois." Master's thesis, Southern Illinois University, Edwardsville, May 1971.

Darweesh, Suzanne. "Use Your Buying Power to Promote Ethics." *Los Angeles Times,* November 5, 2000.

Darwin, Charles. *The Origin of Species.* Chicago: Conley, 1859.

Dasgupta, Nilanjana, Debbie E. McGhee, Anthony G. Greenwald, and Mahzarin R. Banaji. "Automatic Preference for White Americans: Eliminating the Familiarity Explanation." *Journal of Experimental Social Psychology, 36,* 3, May 2000:316–328.

Davies, Kirk L. "The Imposition of Martial Law in the United States." *Air Force Law Review, 49,* 2000:67–112.

Davis, Ann. "Artificial Reproduction Arrangers Are Ruled Child's Legal Parents." *Wall Street Journal,* March 11, 1998a:B2.

Davis, Ann. "High-Tech Births Spawn Legal Riddles." *Wall Street Journal,* January 26, 1998b:B1.

Davis, Fred. "The Cabdriver and His Fare: Facets of a Fleeting Relationship." *American Journal of Sociology, 65,* September 1959:158–165.

Davis, Kingsley. "Extreme Social Isolation of a Child." *American Journal of Sociology, 45,* 4 Jan. 1940:554–565.

Davis, Kingsley. "Extreme Isolation." In *Down to Earth Sociology: Introductory Readings,* 11th ed., James M. Henslin, ed. New York: Free Press, 2001:133–141.

Davis, Kingsley, and Wilbert E. Moore. "Some Principles of Stratification." *American Sociological Review, 10,* 1945:242–249.

Davis, Kingsley, and Wilbert E. Moore. "Reply to Tumin." *American Sociological Review, 18,* 1953:394–396.

Davis, L. J. "Medscam." In *Deviant Behavior 96/97,* Lawrence M. Salinger, ed. Guilford, Conn.: Dushkin, 1996:93–97.

Davis, Nancy J., and Robert V. Robinson. "Class Identification of Men and Women in the 1970s and 1980s." *American Sociological Review, 53,* February 1988:103–112.

Davis, Nanette J. "Prostitution: Identity, Career, and Legal-Economic Enterprise." In *The Sociology of Sex: An Introductory Reader,* rev. ed., James M. Henslin and Edward Sagarin, eds. New York: Schocken Books, 1978:195–222.

Davis, Stan. *Lessons From the Future: Making Sense of a Blurred World.* New York: Capstone Publishers, 2001.

Davis, Stan, and Christopher Meyer. "What Will Replace the Tech Economy?" *Time,* May 22, 2000.

Deck, Leland P. "Buying Brains by the Inch." *Journal of the College and University Personnel Association, 19,* 1968:33–37.

Deegan, Mary Jo. "W. E. B. Du Bois and the Women of Hull-House, 1895–1899." *American Sociologist,* Winter 1988: 301–311.

De George, Richard T. *The New Marxism: Society and East European Marxism Since 1956.* New York: Pegasus 1968.

Deliege, Robert. *The Untouchables of India.* New York: Berg Publishers, 2001.

DeMause, Lloyd. "Our Forebears Made Childhood a Nightmare." *Psychology Today* 8, 11, April 1975:85–88.

D'Emilio, Frances. "Amato Asked to Lead Italy Coalition." Associated Press, April 22,2000.

"Democracy and Technology." *The Economist,* June 17, 1995: 21–23.

Denney, Nancy W., and David Quadagno. *Human Sexuality,* 2nd ed. St. Louis: Mosby, 1992.

Denzin, Norman K. "The Suicide Machine." *Society,* July–August, 1992:7–10.

DePalma, Anthony. "Rare in Ivy League: Women Who Work as Full Professors." *New York Times,* January 24, 1993:1, 23.

DeParle, Jason. "Report to Clinton Sees Vast Extent of Homelessness." *New York Times,* February 17, 1994:A1, A10.

DeParle, Jason. "Bold Effort Leaves Much Unchanged for the Poor." *New York Times,* December 30, 1999.

Derber, Charles, and William Schwartz. "Toward a Theory of Worker Participation." In *The Transformation of Industrial Organization: Management, Labor, and Society in the United States,* Frank Hearn, ed. Belmont, Calif.: Wadsworth, 1988:217–229.

deYoung, Mary. "The World According to NAMBLA: Accounting for Deviance." *Journal of Sociology and Social Welfare,* 16, 1, March 1989:111–126.

Diamond, Edwin, and Robert A. Silverman. *White House to Your House: Media and Politics in Virtual America.* Cambridge, Mass.: MIT Press, 1995.

Diamond, Milton, and Keith Sigmundson. "Sex Reassignment at Birth: Long-term Review and Clinical Implications." *Archives of Pediatric and Adolescent Medicine, 151,* March 1997:298–304.

Dickey, Christopher. "The Death of Innocents." *Newsweek,* September 2, 1996:51.

Diekmann, Andreas, and Henrietta Engelhardt. "The Social Inheritance of Divorce: Effects of Parent's Family Type in Postwar Germany." *American Sociological Review, 64,* December 1999:783–793.

Dietz, Tracy L. "An Examination of Violence and Gender Role Portrayals in Video Games." *Women and Language, 23,* 2, Fall 2000:64–77.

DiGiulio, Robert C. "Beyond Widowhood." In *Marriage and Family in a Changing Society,* 4th ed., James M. Henslin, ed. New York: Free Press, 1992:457–469.

Dillin, John. "Congress Begins Search for Answers in Waco Tragedy." *Christian Science Monitor,* April 22, 1993:1, 4.

Diver-Stamnes, Ann C., and R. Murray Thomas. *Prevent, Repent, Reform, Revenge: A Study in Adolescent Moral Development.* Westport, CT.: Greenwood Press, 1995.

Dixon, Celvia Stovall, and Kathryn D. Rettig. "An Examination of Income Adequacy for Single Women Two Years After Divorce." *Journal of Divorce and Remarriage,* 22, 1–2, 1994:55–71.

Dobash, Russell P., R. Emerson Dobash, Margo Wilson, and Martin Daly. "The Myth of Sexual Symmetry in Marital Violence." *Social Problems, 39,* 1, February 1992:71–91.

Dobash, Russell P., R. Emerson Dobash, Margo Wilson, and Martin Daly. "Marital Violence Is Not Symmetrical: A Response to Campbell." *SSSP Newsletter, 24,* 3, Fall 1993:26–30.

Dobriner, William M. "The Football Team as Social Structure and Social System." In *Social Structures and Systems: A Sociological Overview.* Pacific Palisades, Calif.: Goodyear, 1969a:116–120.

Dobriner, William M. *Social Structures and Systems.* Pacific Palisades, California: Goodyear, 1969b.

Dobyns, Henry F. *Their Numbers Became Thinned: Native American Population Dynamics in Eastern North America.* Knoxville: University of Tennessee Press, 1983.

"Doctors Misdiagnose Women and Blacks." *Heart Disease Weekly,* May 3, 2000-May 10, 2000:9.

Dollard, John, et al. *Frustration and Aggression.* New Haven, Conn.: Yale University Press, 1939.

Domhoff, G. William. *Who Rules America?* Englewood Cliffs, N.J.: Prentice Hall, 1967.

Domhoff, G. William. *The Powers That Be.* New York: Random House, 1979.

Domhoff, G. William. *The Power Elite and the State: How Policy Is Made in America.* Hawthorne, N.Y.: Aldine de Gruyter, 1990.

Domhoff, G. William. *Who Rules America? Power and Politics in the Year 2000,* 3rd ed. Mountain View, Calif: Mayfield Publishing, 1998.

Domhoff, G. William. "The Bohemian Grove and Other Retreats." In *Down to Earth Sociology: Introductory Readings,* 10th ed., James M. Henslin, ed. New York: Free Press, 1999:391–403.

Domhoff, G. William. "State and Ruling Class in Corporate America (1974): Reflections, Corrections, and New Directions." *Critical Sociology, 25,* 2/3, July 1999:260–265.

Donaldson, Stephen. "A Million Jockers, Punks, and Queens: Sex Among American Male Prisoners and Its Implications for Concepts of Sexual Orientation." February 4, 1993. Online.

Donelson, Samuel. "World News Tonight." Television broadcast. May 25, 1992.

Dottridge, Mike. "Dollars and Sense." *New Internationalist,* 337, August 2001:16–17.

Dove, Adrian. "Soul Folk 'Chitling' Test or the Dove Counterbalance Intelligence Test." no date. (Mimeo)

Drucker, Peter F. "There's More Than One Kind of Team." *Wall Street Journal,* February 11, 1992:A16.

Du Bois, W.E.B. *The Souls of Black Folk: Essays and Sketches.* Chicago: McClurg, 1903.

Du Bois, W.E.B. *Black Reconstruction in America: An Essay Toward a History of the Part Which Black Folk Played in the Attempt to Reconstruct Democracy in America, 1860–1880.* New York: Frank Cass, 1966. First published 1935.

Du Bois, W.E.B. *The Philadelphia Negro: A Social Study.* New York: Schocken Books, 1967. First pubulished in 1899.

Du Bois, W.E.B. *The Autobiography of W. E. B. Du Bois: A Soliloquy on Viewing My Life from the Last Decade of Its First Century.* New York: International, 1968.

Du Bois, W.E.B. *Black Reconstruction in America, 1860–1889.* New York: Atheneum, 1992. First published in 1935.

Dudenhefer, Paul. "Poverty in the Rural United States." *Focus, 15,* 1, Spring 1993:37–46.

Duff, Christina. "Superrich's Share of After-Tax Income Stopped Rising in Early '90s, Data Show." *Wall Street Journal,* November 22, 1995:A2.

Duffy, Michael. "When Lobbyists Become Insiders." *Time,* November 9, 1992:40.

Dugger, Celia W. "Wedding Vows Bind Old World and New." *New York Times,* July 20, 1998.

Dugger, Celia W. "Abortion in India Is Tipping Scales Sharply Against Girls." *New York Times,* April 22, 2001.

Duneier, Mitchell. *Sidewalk.* New York: Farrar, Straus and Giroux, 1999.

Dunlap, Riley E., and William R. Catton, Jr. "Environmental Sociology." *Annual Review of Sociology, 5,* 1979:243–273.

Dunlap, Riley E., and William R. Catton, Jr. "What Environmental Sociologists Have in Common Whether Concerned with 'Built' or 'Natural' Environments." *Sociological Inquiry, 53,* 2/3, 1983:113–135.

Durbin, Stefanie. "Mexico." *Population Today,* July–August, 1995:7.

Durkheim, Emile. *The Division of Labor in Society.* George Simpson, trans. New York: Free Press, 1933. First published in 1893.

Durkheim, Emile. *The Rules of Sociological Method.* Sarah A. Solovay and John H. Mueller, trans. New York: Free Press, 1938, 1958, 1964. First published in 1895.

Durkheim, Emile. *Suicide: A Study in Sociology.* John A. Spaulding and George Simpson, trans. New York: Free Press, 1966. First published in 1897.

Durkheim, Emile. *The Elementary Forms of the Religious Life.* New York: Free Press, 1965. First published in 1912.

Durning, Alan. "Cradles of Life." In *Social Problems 90/91,* LeRoy W. Barnes, ed. Guilford, Conn.: Dushkin, 1990:231–241.

Easterbrook, Gregg. "The Revolution in Modern Medicine." *Newsweek, 109,* Jan. 26, 1987:40–74.

"East Germany Used Nuclear Tags on Dissidents." *New York Times,* January 3, 2001.

Ebaugh, Helen Rose Fuchs. *Becoming an EX: The Process of Role Exit.* Chicago: The University of Chicago Press, 1988.

Ebomoyi, Ehigie. "The Prevalence of Female Circumcision in Two Nigerian Communities." *Sex Roles, 17,* 3/4, 1987:139–151.

Eckholm, Erik. "Workers' Rights Suffering as China Goes Capitalist." *New York Times,* August 22, 2001.

Eder, Donna. *School Talk: Gender and Adolescent Culture.* New Brunswick, N.J.: Rutgers University Press, 1995.

Eder, Klaus. "The Rise of Counter-culture Movements Against Modernity: Nature as a New Field of Class Struggle." *Theory, Culture & Society, 7,* 1990:21–47.

Edgerton, Robert B. *Deviance: A Cross-Cultural Perspective.* Menlo Park, Calif.: Benjamin/Cummings, 1976.

Edgerton, Robert B. *Sick Societies: Challenging the Myth of Primitive Harmony.* New York: Free Press, 1992.

Edwards, Richard. *Contested Terrain: The Transformation of the Workplace in the Twentieth Century.* New York: Basic Books, 1979.

Egan, Timothy. "Many Seek Security in Private Communities." *New York Times,* September 3, 1995:1, 22.

"Egipto prohibir la ablación femenina y adoptar medidas contra infractores." *El Pais,* July 19, 1996:22.

"Egypt." *Population Today,* December 1998:7.

Ehrenreich, Barbara, and Deidre English. *Witches, Midwives, and Nurses: A History of Women Healers.* Old Westbury, N.Y.: Feminist Press, 1973.

Ehrlich, Paul R., and Anne H. Ehrlich. *Population, Resources, and Environment: Issues in Human Ecology,* 2nd ed. San Francisco: Freeman, 1972.

Ehrlich, Paul R., and Anne H. Ehrlich. "Humanity at the Crossroads." *Stanford Magazine,* Spring–Summer 1978:20–23.

Ehrlich, Paul R., and Anne H. Ehrlich. *Betrayal of Science and Reason: How Anti-Environmental Rhetoric Threatens Our Future.* Washington, D.C.: Island Press, 1997.

Eibl-Eibesfeldt, Irenäus. *Ethology: The Biology of Behavior.* New York: Holt, Rinehart, and Winston, 1970.

Eichler, Margrit. *Nonsexist Research Methods: A Practical Guide.* Winchester, Mass.: Unwin Hyman, 1988.

Eisenhart, R. Wayne. "You Can't Hack It, Little Girl: A Discussion of the Covert Psychological Agenda of Modern Combat Training." *Journal of Social Issues, 31,* Fall 1975:13–23.

Eisenstadt, Shmuel Noah. *Paradoxes of Democracy: Fragility, Continuity, and Change.* Washington, D.C.: Woodrow Wilson Center Press, 1999.

Ekman, Paul. *Faces of Man: Universal Expression in a New Guinea Village.* New York: Garland Press, 1980.

Ekman, Paul, Wallace V. Friesen, and John Bear. "The International Language of Gestures." *Psychology Today,* May 1984:64.

Elder, Glen H., Jr. "Age Differentiation and Life Course." *Annual Review of Sociology, 1,* 1975:165–190.

Elder, Glen H., Jr. *Children of the Great Depression: Social Change in Life Experience.* Boulder: Westview Press, 1999.

Elkins, Stanley M. *Slavery: A Problem in American Institutional and Intellectual Life,* 2nd ed. Chicago: University of Chicago Press, 1968.

Ellis, Caroline. "Punish and Be Damned." *New Statesman and Society, 17,* 1991:17.

Ellul, Jacques. *The Technological Society.* New York: Knopf, 1965.

El-Meligi, M. Helmy. "Egypt." In *Handbook of World Education: A Comparative Guide to Higher Education and Educational Systems of the World,* Walter Wickremasinghe, ed. Houston, Texas: American Collegiate Service, 1992:219–228.

Emery, Gene. "Blacks Less Likely to Get Clot-Busting Treatments." Reuters, April 12, 2000.

Engeman, Thomas S. "Religion and Politics the American Way: The Exemplary William Dean Howells." *Review of Politics, 63,* 1, Winter 2001:107–127.

England, Paula. "The Impact of Feminist Thought on Sociology." *Contemporary Sociology: A Journal of Reviews,* 263–267.

Englund, Will, and Gary Cohn. "A Third World Dump for America's Ships." *Baltimore Sun,* December 9, 1997.

Epstein, Cynthia Fuchs. "Inevitabilities of Prejudice." *Society,* September–October 1986:7–15.

Epstein, Cynthia Fuchs. *Deceptive Distinctions: Sex, Gender, and the Social Order.* New Haven, Conn.: Yale University Press, 1988.

Epstein, Cynthia Fuchs. Letter to the author, January 26, 1989.

Erickson, Kristan Glasgow, Robert Crosnoe, and Sanford M. Dornbusch. "A Social Process Model of Adolescent Deviance: Combining Social Control and Differential Association Perspectives." *Journal of Youth and Adolescence, 29,* 4, 2000:395–425.

Erik, John. "China's Policy on Births." *New York Times,* January 3, 1982: IV, 19.

Ernst, Eldon G. "The Baptists." In *Encyclopedia of the American Religious Experience: Studies of Traditions and Movements,* Vol. 1, Charles H. Lippy and Peter W. Williams, eds. New York: Scribners, 1988:555–577.

Escalante, Jaime, and Jack Dirmann. "The Jaime Escalante Math Program." *Journal of Negro Education, 59,* 3, Summer 1990: 407–423.

Evans, Peter, and James E. Rauch. "Bureaucracy and Growth: A Cross-National Analysis of the Effects of 'Weberian' State Structures on Economic Growth." *American Sociological Review, 64,* October 1999:748–765.

"Executive Pay." *Wall Street Journal,* April 12, 2001.

Ezekiel, Raphael S. *The Racist Mind: Portraits of American Neo-Nazis and Klansmen.* New York: Viking, 1995.

"Faddish Justice." *Wall Street Journal,* May 2, 1995:A19.

Fairris, David, and Mark Brenner. "Workplace Transformation and the Rise in Cumulative Trauma Disorders: Is There a Connection?" *Journal of Labor Research,* 22, 1, Winter 2001:15–28.

Famighetti, Robert, ed. *The World Almanac and Book of Facts 1995.* Mahwah, New Jersey, 1994.

Famighetti, Robert, ed. *The World Almanac and Book of Facts.* Mahwah, New Jersey, 1999.

Faris, Robert E. L., and Warren Dunham. *Mental Disorders in Urban Areas.* Chicago: University of Chicago Press, 1939.

Farkas, George. *Human Capital or Cultural Capital?: Ethnicity and Poverty Groups in an Urban School District.* New York: Walter DeGruyter, 1996.

Farkas, George, Robert P. Grobe, Daniel Sheehan, and Yuan Shuan. "Cultural Resources and School Success: Gender, Ethnicity, and Poverty Groups Within an Urban School District." *American Sociological Review, 55,* February 1990a:127–142.

Farkas, George, Daniel Sheehan, and Robert P. Grobe. "Coursework Mastery and School Success: Gender, Ethnicity, and Poverty Groups Within an Urban School District." *American Educational Research Journal, 27,* 4, Winter 1990b:807–827.

Farney, Dennis. "They Hold the Cards, But After All, They Do Own the Casino." *Wall Street Journal,* February 5, 1998: A1, A6.

"Fat Is a Financial Issue." *Economist, 357,* 8198, November 25, 2000:93.

Faunce, William A. *Problems of an Industrial Society,* 2nd ed. New York: McGraw-Hill, 1981.

FBI Uniform Crime Reports. Washington, D.C.: U.S. Government Printing Office, published annually.

Feagin, Joe R., "Death by Discrimination?" *SSSP Newsletter,* Winter 1997:15–16.

Feagin, Joe R. "The Continuing Significance of Race: Antiblack Discrimination in Public Places." In *Majority and Minority: The Dynamics of Race and Ethnicity in American Life,* 6th ed., Norman R. Yetman, ed. Boston: Allyn and Bacon, 1999: 384–399.

"Fears of Millennium 'Black Death' Leaves Bissau a Ghost Town." Associated Press Worldstream, January 1, 2000.

Featherman, David L. "Opportunities Are Expanding." *Society, 13,* 1979:4–11.

Featherman, David L., and Robert M. Hauser. *Opportunity and Change.* New York: Academic Press, 1978.

Federal Trade Commission. *Federal Trade Commission Report to Congress for 1994 Pursuant to the Federal Cigarette Labeling and Advertising Act.* Washington, D.C.: U.S. Government Printing Office, October 9, 1996.

Feinglass, Joe. "Next, the McDRG." *The Progressive, 51,* January 1987:28.

Feldman, Saul D. "The Presentation of Shortness in Everyday Life—Height and Heightism in American Society: Toward a Sociology of Stature." Paper presented at the 1972 meetings of the American Sociological Association.

Felsenthal, Edward. "Maine Limits Liability for Doctors Who Meet Treatment Guidelines." *Wall Street Journal,* May 3, 1993:A1, A9.

Felsenthal, Edward. "Justices' Ruling Further Defines Sex Harassment." *Wall Street Journal,* March 5, 1998:B1, B2.

Felton, Lee Ann, Andrea Gumm, and David J. Pittenger. "The Recipients of Unwanted Sexual Encounters Among College Students." *College Student Journal, 35,* 1, March 2001:135–143.

Fendrich, James Max, and Kenneth L. Lovoy. "Back to the Future: Adult Political Behavior of Former Student Activists." In *Collective Behavior and Social Movements,* Russell L. Curtis, Jr., and Benigno E. Aguirre, eds. Boston: Allyn and Bacon, 1993:429–434.

Ferguson, Trudi, and Joan S. Dunphy. *Answers to the Mommy Track: How Wives and Mothers in Business Reach the Top and Balance Their Lives.* New York: New Horizon Press, 1991.

Ferraro, Susan. "Future Fighters: How Military Technology is Advancing Medical Science." *Daily News,* July 11, 2001.

Feshbach, Murray. "Russia's Farms, Too Poisoned for the Plow." *Wall Street Journal,* May 14, 1992:A14.

Feshbach, Murray, and Alfred Friendly, Jr. *Ecocide in the USSR: Health and Nature Under Siege.* New York: Basic Books, 1992.

Fialka, John J. "Demands on New Orleans's 'Big Charity' Hospital Are Symptomatic of U.S. Health-Care Problem." *Wall Street Journal,* June 22, 1993:A18.

Field, Mark G. "The Health Crisis in the Former Soviet Union: A Report from the 'Post-War' Zone." In *Readings in Medical Sociology,* William C. Cockerham, Michael Glasser, and Linda S. Heuser, eds. Englewood Cliffs, New Jersey: Prentice Hall, 1998:506–519.

"Fighting Illiteracy Is Only Way to Development." Xinhua News Agency, September 8, 2000.

Filkins, Dexter. "61 Slain as Violence Rocks the Caste System in India." *Seattle Times,* December 3, 1997, electronic version.

Fineman, Howard. "Pressing the Flesh Online." *Newsweek,* September 20, 1999:50–53.

Finke, Roger, and Roger Stark. *The Churching of America, 1776–1990: Winners and Losers in Our Religious Economy.* New Brunswick, N.J.: Rutgers University Press, 1992.

Finkelhor, David, and Kersti Yllo. "Marital Rape: The Myth Versus the Reality." In *Marriage and Family in a Changing Society,* 3rd ed., James M. Henslin, ed. New York: Free Press, 1989:382–391.

Finkelhor, David, and Kersti Yllo. *License to Rape: Sexual Abuse of Wives.* New York: Henry Holt, 1985.

Firestone, David. "The New-Look Suburbs: Denser or More Far-Flung?" *New York Times,* April 17, 2001.

Fischer, Claude S. *The Urban Experience.* New York: Harcourt, 1976.

Fish, Jefferson M. "Mixed Blood." *Psychology Today, 28,* 6, November–December 1995:55–58, 60, 61, 76, 80.

Fisher, Ian. "At Site of Massacre, Polish Leader Asks Jews for Forgiveness." *New York Times,* July 11, 2001.

Fisher, Julie. "Is the Iron Law of Oligarchy Rusting Away in the Third World?" *World Development, 22,* 2, February 1994: 129–143.

Fisher, Sue. *In the Patient's Best Interest: Women and the Politics of Medical Decisions.* New Brunswick, N.J.: Rutgers University Press, 1986.

Fitzpatrick, Edward. "Kennedy Criticizes Drug Companies for High Prices." *Providence Journal,* July 23, 2001.

Fitzpatrick, Kevin, and Mark LaGory. *Unhealthy Places: The Ecology of Risk in the Urban Landscape.* New York: Routledge, 2000.

Flanagan, William G. *Urban Sociology: Images and Structure.* Boston: Allyn and Bacon, 1990.

Flavel, J. H., et al. *The Development of Role-Taking and Communication Skills in Children.* New York: Wiley, 1968.

Fleming, Joyce Dudney. "The State of the Apes." *Psychology Today, 7,* 1974:31–38.

Fletcher, June. "Address Envy: Fudging to Get the Best." *Wall Street Journal,* April 25, 1997:B10.

Fletcher, Martin. "Jolie Takes Up Plight of World's Refugees." *The Times*, August 28, 2001.

Flexner, Abraham. *Medical Education in the United States and Canada: A Report to the Carnegie Foundation for the Advancement of Teaching*. Bulletin No. 4. Boston: Merrymount Press, 1910.

Flippen, Annette R. "Understanding Groupthink From a Self-Regulatory Perspective." *Small Group Research, 30*, 2, April 1999:139–165.

Flippen, Chenoa. "Neighborhood Transition and Social Organization: The White to Hispanic Case." *Social Problems, 48*, 3, August 2001:299–321.

Foley, Douglas E. "The Great American Football Ritual." In *Down to Earth Sociology: Introductory Readings*, 10th ed., James M. Henslin, ed. New York: Free Press, 2001:454–467.

Foley, Linda A., Christine Evancic, Karnik Karnik, Janet King, and Angela Parks. "Date Rape: Effects of Race of Assailant and Victim and Gender of Subjects on Perceptions." *Journal of Black Psychology, 21*, 1, February 1995:6–18.

Foote, Donna. "And Baby Makes One." *Newsweek*, February 2, 1998:68–69.

Foote, Jennifer. "Trying to Take Back the Planet." *Newsweek, 115*, 6, February 5, 1990:24–25.

Form, William. "Comparative Industrial Sociology and the Convergence Hypothesis." In *Annual Review of Sociology, 5*, 1, 1979, Alex Inkeles, James Coleman, and Ralph H. Turner, eds.

Foster, J. Todd. "Russian Mafia Too Savvy for Deed." *The Oregonian*, March 21, 1998.

Fountain, Henry. "Archaeological Site in Peru Is Called Oldest City in Americas." *New York Times*, April 27, 2001.

Fox, Elaine, and George E. Arquitt. "The VFW and the 'Iron Law of Oligarchy.' " In *Down to Earth Sociology*, 4th ed., James M. Henslin, ed. New York: Free Press, 1985:147–155.

Franklin, Clyde W., II. "Sex and Class Differences in the Socialization Experiences of African American Youth." *Western Journal of Black Studies, 18*, 2, 1994:104–111.

Fraser, Graham. "Fox Denies Free Trade Exploiting the Poor in Mexico." *Toronto Star*, April 20, 2001.

Freedman, Jane. *Feminism*. Philadelphia: Open University Press, 2001.

Freese, Jeremy, Brian Powell, and Lala Carr Steelman. "Rebel Without a Cause or Effect: Birth Order and Social Attitudes." *American Sociological Review, 64*, April 1999:207–231.

Freudenburg, William R., and Robert Gramling. "The Emergence of Environmental Sociology: Contributions of Riley E. Dunlap and William R. Catton, Jr." *Sociological Inquiry, 59*, 4, November 1989:439–452.

Frey, William H. "Migration to the South Brings U.S. Blacks Full Circle." *Population Today, 29*, 4, May-June 2001:1, 2.

Friedl, Ernestine. "Society and Sex Roles." In *Conformity and Conflict: Readings in Cultural Anthropology*. James P. Spradley and David W. McCurdy, eds. Glenview, Ill.: Scott, Foresman, 1990:229–238.

Fritz, Jan M. "The History of Clinical Sociology." *Sociological Practice, 7*, 1989:72–95.

Froman, Ingmarie. "Sweden for Women." *Current Sweden, 407*, November 1994:1–4.

Frumkin, Robert M. "Early English and American Sex Customs." In *Encyclopedia of Sexual Behavior*, Vol. 1. New York: Hawthorne Books, 1967.

Fuller, Rex, and Richard Schoenberger. "The Gender Salary Gap: Do Academic Achievement, Internship Experience, and College Major Make a Difference?" *Social Science Quarterly, 72*, 4, December 1991:715–726.

Furstenberg, Frank F., Jr., and Kathleen Mullan Harris. "The Disappearing American Father? Divorce and the Waning Significance of Biological Fatherhood." In *The Changing American Family: Sociological and Demographic Perspectives*, Scott J. South and Stewart E. Tolnay, eds. Boulder, Colo.: Westview Press, 1992:197–223.

Galbraith, John Kenneth. *The Nature of Mass Poverty*. Cambridge Mass.: Harvard University Press, 1979.

Galinsky, Ellen, James T. Bond, and Dana E. Friedman. *The Changing Workforce: Highlights of the National Study*. New York: Families and Work Institute, 1993.

Galliher, John F. *Deviant Behavior and Human Rights*. Englewood Cliffs, N.J.: Prentice Hall, 1991.

Gallmeier, Charles P. "Methodological Issues in Qualitative Sport Research: Participant Observation among Hockey Players." *Sociological Spectrum, 8*, 1988:213–235.

Gallup Opinion Index. *Religion in America, 1987*. Report 259, April 1987.

Gallup, George, Jr. *The Gallup Poll: Public Opinion 1989*. Wilmington, Dela.: Scholarly Resources, 1990.

Gallup Poll. "Poll Analyses." November 9, 2000.

Gallup Poll. "Poll Analyses." April 13, 2001.

Gans, Herbert J. *The Urban Villagers*. New York: Free Press, 1962.

Gans, Herbert J. *People and Plans: Essays on Urban Problems and Solutions*. New York: Basic Books, 1968.

Gans, Herbert J. "Urbanism and Suburbanism." In *Urban Man and Society: A Reader in Urban Ecology*, Albert N. Cousins and Hans Nagpaul, eds. New York: Knopf, 1970:157–164.

Gans, Herbert J. *People, Plans, and Policies: Essays on Poverty, Racism, and Other National Urban Problems*. New York: Columbia University Press, 1991a.

Gans, Herbert J. "The Way We'll Live Soon." *Washington Post*, September 1, 1991b:BW3.

Garbarino, Merwin S. *American Indian Heritage*. Boston: Little, Brown, 1976.

Garcia, Leslie. "CEO of AARP Not the Retiring Sort." *Dallas Morning News*, October 16, 2001.

Gardner, R. Allen, and Beatrice T. Gardner. "Teaching Sign Language to a Chimpanzee." *Science, 165*, 1969:664–672.

Gardner, Marilyn. "More Families Take Care of Elders Across the Miles." *Christian Science Monitor, 90*, 103.

Garfinkel, Harold. "Conditions of Successful Degradation Ceremonies." *American Journal of Sociology, 61*, 2, March 1956:420–424.

Garfinkel, Harold. *Studies in Ethnomethodology*. Englewood Cliffs, N.J.: Prentice Hall, 1967.

Garrett, Laurie. "Global Warning." *Los Angeles Times*, March 1, 1999.

Garrett, Michael Tlanusta. "Understanding the 'Medicine' of Native American Traditional Values: An Integrative Review." *Counseling and Values, 43*, 2, January 1999:84–98.

Gatewood, Willard B. *Aristocrats of Color: The Black Elite, 1880–1920*. Bloomington, Ind.: Indiana University Press, 1990.

Gaviak, Dale. "In Sudan, Childhoods of Slavery." *Christian Science Monitor*, August 22, 2000:6.

Geis, Gilbert, Robert F. Meier, and Lawrence M. Salinger. *White-Collar Crime: Classic and Contemporary Views*, 3rd ed. New York: Free Press, 1995.

Gelles, Richard J. "The Myth of Battered Husbands and New Facts about Family Violence." In *Social Problems 80–81*, Robert L. David, ed. Guilford, Conn.: Dushkin, 1980.

Genetski, Robert. "Privatize Social Security." *Wall Street Journal*, May 21, 1993.

Gerhard, Jane. "Revisiting 'The Myth of the Vaginal Orgasm': The Female Orgasm in American Sexual Thought and Second Wave Feminism." *Feminist Studies*, 26, 2, Fall 2000:449–477.

Gershenfeld, Neil A. *When Things Start to Think*. New York: Henry Holt, 1999.

Gerson, Kathleen. *Hard Choices: How Women Decide about Work, Career, and Motherhood*. Berkeley: University of California Press, 1985.

Gerth, H. H., and C. Wright Mills. *From Max Weber: Essays in Sociology*. New York: Galaxy, 1958.

Gibbs, Nancy. "The Littleton Massacre." *Time*, May 3, 1999:25–36.

Giddens, Anthony. *Emile Durkheim*. New York: Penguin Books, 1978.

Giele, Janet Zollinger. *Women and the Future: Changing Sex Roles in Modern America*. New York: Free Press, 1978.

Gilbert, Dennis L. *The American Class Structure: In an Age of Growing Inequality*. Belmont, Calif.: Wadsworth Publishing, 1997.

Gilbert, Dennis, and Joseph A. Kahl. *The American Class Structure: A New Synthesis*. 4th ed. Homewood, Ill.: Dorsey Press, 1993.

Gilham, Steven A. "The Marines Build Men: Resocialization in Recruit Training." In *The Sociological Outlook: A Text with Readings*, 2nd ed., Reid Luhman, ed. San Diego, Calif.: Collegiate Press, 1989:232–244.

Gillborn, David. "Citizenship, 'Race' and the Hidden Curriculum." *International Studies in the Sociology of Education*, 2, 1, 1992:57–73.

Gilligan, Carol. *In a Different Voice: Psychological Theory and Women's Development*. Cambridge, Mass.: Harvard University Press, 1982.

Gilligan, Carol. *Making Connections: The Relational World of Adolescent Girls at Emma Willard School*. Cambridge, Mass.: Harvard University Press, 1990.

Gilman, Charlotte Perkins. *The Man-Made World or, Our Androcentric Culture*. New York: 1971. First published 1911.

Gilmore, David D. *Manhood in the Making: Cultural Concepts of Masculinity*. New Haven, Conn.: Yale University Press, 1990.

Gitlin, Todd. *The Twilight of Common Dreams: Why America Is Wracked by Culture Wars*. New York: Metropolitan Books, 1997.

Glenn, Evelyn Nakano. "Chinese American Families." In *Minority Families in the United States: A Multicultural Perspective*, Ronald L. Taylor, ed. Englewood Cliffs, N.J.: Prentice Hall, 1994:115–145.

Glick, Paul C., and S. Lin. "More Young Adults Are Living with Their Parents: Who Are They?" *Journal of Marriage and Family*, 48, 1986:107–112.

"The Global Giants: U.S. and Tech Firms Gain Ground in Annual Survey." *Wall Street Journal*, September 27, 1999:R29.

Glueck, Sheldon, and Eleanor Glueck. *Physique and Delinquency*. New York: Harper & Row, 1956.

Goble, Paul. "Russia: Analysis from Washington—Organized Crime's Three Faces." Radio Free Europe, November 5, 1996.

Goetting, Ann. *Getting Out: Life Stories of Women Who Left Abusive Men*. New York: Columbia University Press, 2001.

Goffman, Erving. *The Presentation of Self in Everyday Life*. New York: Doubleday, 1959.

Goffman, Erving. "The Presentation of Self in Everyday Life." In *Down to Earth Sociology: Introductory Readings*, 11th ed., James M. Henslin, ed. New York: The Free Press, 2001:113–123. Excerpts from Erving Goffman, *The Presentation of Self in Everyday Life*, New York: Doubleday and Company, 1959.

Goffman, Erving. *Asylums: Essays on the Social Situation of Mental Patients and Other Inmates*. Chicago: Aldine, 1961.

Goffman, Erving. *Stigma: Notes on the Management of Spoiled Identity*. Englewood Cliffs, N.J.: Prentice Hall, 1963.

Gold, Ray. "Janitors Versus Tenants: A Status–Income Dilemma." *American Journal of Sociology*, 58, 1952:486–493.

Goldberg, Carey. "Most Get Work After Welfare, Studies Suggest." *New York Times*, April 17, 1999.

Goldberg, Carey, and Sophia Kishkovsky. "Russia's Doctors Are Beggars at Work, Paupers at Home." *New York Times*, December 16, 2000.

Goldberg, Steven. *The Inevitability of Patriarchy*, rev. ed. New York: Morrow, 1974.

Goldberg, Steven. "Reaffirming the Obvious." *Society*, September–October 1986:4–7.

Goldberg, Steven. *Why Men Rule: A Theory of Male Dominance*. Chicago: Open Court, 1993.

Goldberg, Susan, and Michael Lewis. "Play Behavior in the Year-Old Infant: Early Sex Differences." *Child Development*, 40, March 1969:21–31.

Goldhaber, Dan D. *How Has Teacher Compensation Changed?* Selected Papers in School Finance, 2000–01. Washington, D.C.: Education Policy Center, 2001.

Goldman, Kevin. "Seniors Get Little Respect on Madison Avenue." *Wall Street Journal*, September 20, 1993:B6.

Goldsborough, Margaret. "Cybertimes Education." *New York Times*, February 13, 2001.

Goleman, Daniel. "Spacing of Siblings Strongly Linked to Success in Life." *New York Times*, May 28, 1985:C1, C4.

Goleman, Daniel. "Pollsters Enlist Psychologists in Quest for Unbiased Results." *New York Times*, September 7, 1993:C1, C11.

Gomez, Carlos F. *Regulating Death: Euthanasia and the Case of the Netherlands*. New York: Free Press, 1991.

Goode, Erica. "Study Says 20% of Girls Reported Abuse by a Date." *New York Times*, August 1, 2001.

Goode, Erich. *Drugs in American Society*, 3rd ed. New York: Knopf, 1989.

Goode, Erich. "The Ethics of Deception in Social Research: A Case Study." *Qualitative Sociology*, 19, 1, 1996:11–33.

Goode, Erich, and Nachman Ben-Yehuda. "Moral Panics: Culture, Politics, and Social Construction." *Annual Review of Sociology*, 20, 1994:149–171.

Goode, William J. "Encroachment, Charlatanism, and the Emerging Profession: Psychology, Sociology, and Medicine." *American Sociological Review*, 25, 6, December 1960:902–914.

Goodwin, Glenn A., Irving Louis Horowitz, and Peter M. Nardi. "Laud Humphreys: A Pioneer in the Practice of Social Science" *Sociological Inquiry*, 61, 2, May 1991:139–147.

Gorman, Christine. "The Disease Detective." *Time*, January 6, 1997:56–65.

Gorman, Peter. "A People at Risk: Vanishing Tribes of South America." *The World & I*. December 1991:678–689.

Gotschall, Mary G. "A Marriage Made in Hell." *National Review*, 46, 6, April 4, 1994:57–60.

Gottfredson, Michael R., and Travis Hirschi. *A General Theory of Crime*. Stanford, Calif.: Stanford University Press, 1990.

Gottschalk, Peter, Sara McLanahan, and Gary Sandefur, "The Dynamics and Intergenerational Transmission of Poverty and Welfare Participation." In *Confronting Poverty: Prescriptions for Change*, Sheldon H. Danziger, Gary D. Sandefur, and Daniel H. Weinberg, eds. Cambridge, Mass.: Harvard University Press, 1994.

Gourevitch, Philip. "After the Genocide." *New Yorker*, December 18, 1995:78–94.

Gourevitch, Philip. *We Wish to Inform You That Tomorrow We Will Be Killed with Our Families: Stories from Rwanda*. New York: Farrar, Straus, and Giroux, 1998.

Gracey, Harry L. "Learning the Student Role: Kindergarten as Boot Camp." In *Down to Earth Sociology: Introductory Readings*, 11th ed., James M. Henslin, ed. New York: The Free Press, 2001:364–376.

Graham, Ellen. "Christian Bikers Are Holy Rollers of a Different Kind." *Wall Street Journal*, September 19, 1990:A1, A6.

Greeley, Andrew M. "The Protestant Ethic: Time for a Moratorium." *Sociological Analysis*, 25, Spring 1964:20–33.

Greeley, Andrew. "A Religious Revival in Russia." *Journal for the Scientific Study of Religion, 33,* 3, September 1994:253–272.

Greeley, Andrew M., and Michael Hout. "Americans' Increasing Belief in Life After Death: Religious Competition and Acculturation." *American Sociological Review, 64,* December 1999:813–835.

Greenberg, Brigitte. "One Drink Reduces Stroke Risk." CBS News, November 23, 1999.

Greengard, Samuel. "The High Cost of Cyberslacking." *Workforce, 79,* 12, December 2000:22–23.

Greenhalgh, Susan, and Jiali Li. "Engendering Reproductive Policy and Practice in Peasant China: For a Feminist Demography of Reproduction." *Signs, 20,* 3, Spring 1995:601–640.

Gross, Jan T. *Neighbors*. New Haven: Yale University Press, 2001.

Gross, Jane. "In the Quest for the Perfect Look, More Girls Choose the Scalpel." *New York Times,* November 29, 1998.

Grossman, Lawrence K. *The Electronic Republic: Reshaping Democracy in the Information Age*. New York: Viking, 1995.

Guensburg, Carol. "Bully Factories." *American Journalism Review, 23,* 6, 2001:51–59.

Guernsey, Lisa. "Cyberspace Isn't So Lonely After All." *New York Times,* July 26, 2001:E1, E5.

Guice, Jon. "Sociologists Go to Work in High Technology." *Footnotes*, November 1999:8.

Guidubaldi, John, Joseph D. Perry, and Bonnie K. Nastasi. "Growing Up in a Divorced Family: Initial and Long-Term Perspectives on Children's Adjustment." *Applied Social Psychology Annual, 7,* 1987:202–237.

Gupta, Giri Raj. "Love, Arranged Marriage, and the Indian Social Structure." In *Cross-Cultural Perspectives of Mate Selection and Marriage*, George Kurian, ed. Westport, Conn.: Greenwood Press, 1979.

Haas, Jack. "Binging: Educational Control Among High-Steel Iron Workers." *American Behavioral Scientist, 16,* 1972:27–34.

Haas, Jack and William Shaffir. "The Cloak of Competence." In *Down to Earth Sociology: Introductory Readings*, 7th ed. New York: Free Press, 1993:432–441.

Hacker, Helen Mayer. "Women as a Minority Group." *Social Forces, 30,* October 1951:60–69.

Haddad, Angela, and Robert Newby. "Members Comment on ASA's Publication on Affirmative Action." *Footnotes*, May–June 1999:9.

Hafner, Katie. "In the Next Chapter, Is Technology an Ally?" *New York Times*, September 27, 2001.

Hakansson, Stefan. "New Ways of Financing and Organizing Health Care in Sweden." *International Journal of Health Planning and Management, 9,* 1, January 1994:103–124.

Haldane, David. "The Region." *Los Angeles Times*, September 8, 2001.

Hall, Edward T. *The Silent Language*. New York: Doubleday, 1959.

Hall, Edward T. *The Hidden Dimension*. Garden City, N.Y.: Anchor Books, 1969.

Hall, Edward T., and Mildred R. Hall. "The Sounds of Silence." In *Down to Earth Sociology: Introductory Readings*, 11th ed., James M. Henslin, ed. New York: The Free Press, 2001:95–103.

Hall, G. Stanley. *Adolescence: Its Psychology and Its Relations to Physiology, Anthropology, Sociology, Sex, Crime, Religion, and Education*. New York: Appleton, 1904.

Hall, J. A. *Nonverbal Sex Differences: Communication Accuracy and Expressive Style*. Baltimore: Johns Hopkins University Press, 1984.

Hall, Richard H. "The Concept of Bureaucracy: An Empirical Assessment." *American Journal of Sociology, 69,* July 1963:32–40.

Hamermesh, Daniel S., and Jeff E. Biddle. "Beauty and the Labor Market." *American Economic Review, 84,* 5, December 1994:1174–1195.

Hamilton, Kendall, and Susan Miller. "Internet U—No Ivy, No Walls, No Keg Parties." *Newsweek*, March 10, 1997:12.

Hamilton, Richard F. *The Social Construction of Reality*. New Haven, Conn.: Yale University Press, 1996.

Hammersley, Martyn. *Taking Sides in Social Research: Essays on Partisanship and Bias*. New York: Routledge, 2000.

Hammerstein, J. "Auswirkungen der Defensiven Medizin auf die Kosten." *Arztl Fortbild Qualitatssich, 94,* 10, December 2000:800–804.

Hao, Jiming, Lei Duan, Xuelong Zhou, and Lixin Fu. "Application of a LRT Model to Acid Rain Control in China." *Environmental Science and Technology, 35,* 17, September 1, 2001.

Hardy, Dorcas. *Social Insecurity: The Crisis in America's Social Security and How to Plan Now for Your Own Financial Survival*. New York: Villard Books, 1991.

Hardy, Quentin. "Death at the Club Is Par for the Course in Golf-Crazed Japan." *Wall Street Journal,* June 16, 1993a:A1, A8.

Harlow, Harry F., and Margaret K. Harlow. "Social Deprivation in Monkeys." *Scientific American, 207,* 1962:137–147.

Harlow, Harry F., and Margaret K. Harlow. "The Affectional Systems." In *Behavior of Nonhuman Primates: Modern Research Trends*, Vol. 2, Allan M. Schrier, Harry F. Harlow, and Fred Stollnitz, eds. New York: Academic Press, 1965:287–334.

Harpaz, Beth J. "Report: Drug-Resistant TB Spreads." Associated Press, October 29, 1999.

Harrington, Michael. *The Other America: Poverty in the United States*. New York: Macmillan, 1962.

Harrington, Michael. *The Vast Majority: A Journey to the World's Poor*. New York: Simon & Schuster, 1977.

Harris, Chauncy D. "The Nature of Cities and Urban Geography in the Last Half Century." *Urban Geography, 18,* 1997.

Harris, Chauncey, and Edward Ullman. "The Nature of Cities." *Annals of the American Academy of Political and Social Science, 242,* 1945:7–17.

Harris, Diana K. *The Sociology of Aging*. New York: Harper, 1990.

Harris, Marvin. "Why Men Dominate Women." *New York Times Magazine,* November 13, 1977:46, 115, 117–123.

Harrison, Paul. *Inside the Third World: The Anatomy of Poverty,* 3rd ed. London: Penguin Books, 1993.

Hart, Charles W. M., and Arnold R. Pilling. *The Tiwi of North Australia.* New York: Holt, Rinehart, and Winston, 1970.

Hart, Hornell. "Acceleration in Social Change." In *Technology and Social Change,* Francis R. Allen, Hornell Hart, Delbert C. Miller, William F. Ogburn, and Meyer F. Nimkoff. New York: Appleton, 1957:27–55.

Hart, Paul. "Groupthink, Risk-Taking and Recklessness: Quality of Process and Outcome in Policy Decision Making." *Politics and the Individual, 1,* 1, 1991:67–90.

Hartley, Eugene. *Problems in Prejudice.* New York: King's Crown Press, 1946.

Harwood, John. "For California Senator, Fund Raising Becomes Overwhelming Burden." *Wall Street Journal,* March 2, 1994:A1, A13.

Harwood, John, and Geraldine Brooks. "Other Nations Elect Women to Lead Them, So Why Doesn't U.S.?" *Wall Street Journal,* December 14, 1993:A1, A9.

Haslick, Leonard. *Gerontologist, 14,* 1974:37–45.

Hatch, Laurie Russell. *Beyond Gender Differences: Adaptation to Aging in Life Course Perspective.* Amityville, N. Y.: Baywood Publishing Company, 2000.

Haub, Carl, and Diana Cornelius. "World Population Data Sheet." Washington, D.C.: Population Reference Bureau, 2001.

Haub, Carl, and Nancy Yinger. "The U.N. Long-Range Population Projections: What They Tell Us." Washington, D.C.: Population Reference Bureau, 1994.

Hauser, Philip, and Leo Schnore, eds. *The Study of Urbanization.* New York: Wiley, 1965.

"Haves and Have-Nots." *Economist, 355,* 8176, June 24, 2000:23–25.

Hawkes, Nigel. "Asbestos-Related Diseases Will Rise for 20 Years." *The Times,* September 25, 2001.

Hawley, Amos H. *Urban Society: An Ecological Approach.* New York: Wiley, 1981.

Hayashi, Gina M., and Bonnie R. Strickland. "Long-Term Effects of Parental Divorce on Love Relationships: Divorce as Attachment Disruption." *Journal of Social and Personal Relationships, 15,* 1, February 1998, 23–38.

Hayes, Donald P., and Loreen T. Wolfer. "Have Curriculum Changes Caused SAT Scores to Decline?" Paper presented at the annual meetings of the American Sociological Association, 1993a.

Haynes, Richard M., and Donald M. Chalker. "World Class Schools." *American School Board Journal,* May 1997:20, 22–25.

Haynie, Dana L. "Delinquent Peers Revisited: Does Network Structure Matter?" *American Journal of Sociology, 106,* 4, January 2001:1013–1057.

Hechter, Michael. *Containing Nationalism.* New York: Oxford University Press, 2000.

Heckert, D. Alex, Thomas C. Nowak, and Kay A. Snyder. "The Impact of Husbands' and Wives' Relative Earnings on Marital Dissolution." Paper presented at the 1995 meetings of the American Sociological Association.

Hehir, Grainne. "Female Managers Struggle to Break the Glass Ceiling." *Wall Street Journal,* March 1, 2001.

Heilbrun, Alfred B. "Differentiation of Death-Row Murderers and Life-Sentence Murderers by Antisociality and Intelligence Measures." *Journal of Personality Assessment, 64,* 1990:617–627.

Hellinger, Daniel, and Dennis R. Judd. *The Democratic Facade.* Pacific Grove, Calif.: Brooks/Cole, 1991.

Hendin, Herbert, "Euthanasia and Physician-Assisted Suicide in the Netherlands." *New England Journal of Medicine, 336,* 19, May 8, 1997:1385–1387.

Hendin, Herbert. "Suicide, Assisted Suicide, and Medical Illness." *Harvard Mental Health Letter, 16,* 7: January 2000, 4–7.

Hendrix, Lewellyn. "What Is Sexual Inequality? On the Definition and Range of Variation." *Gender and Society, 28,* 3, August 1994:287–307.

Henley, Nancy, Mykol Hamilton, and Barrie Thorne. "Womanspeak and Manspeak." In *Beyond Sex Roles.* Alice G. Sargent, ed. St. Paul, Minn.: West, 1985.

Henriques, Diana B. "Review of Nissan Car Loans Finds That Blacks Pay More." *New York Times,* July 4, 2001.

Henslin, James M. *The Cab Driver: An Interactional Analysis of an Occupational Culture.* Washington University Ph.D. dissertation, September 1967.

Henslin, James M. *Introducing Sociology: Toward Understanding Life in Society.* New York: Free Press, 1975.

Henslin, James M. "It's Not a Lovely Place to Visit, and I Wouldn't Want to Live There." In *Studies in Qualitative Methodology, A Research Annual: Reflections on Field Experiences,* Robert G. Burgess, ed. Greenwich, Conn: JAI Press, 1990a:51–76.

Henslin, James M. "When Life Seems Hopeless: Suicide in American Society." In *Social Problems Today: Coping with the Challenges of a Changing Society.* Englewood Cliffs, N.J.: Prentice Hall, 1990b:99–107.

Henslin, James M. "Centuries of Childhood." In *Marriage and Family in a Changing Society,* 4th ed., James M. Henslin, ed. New York: Free Press, 1992:214–225.

Henslin, James M. "Trust and Cabbies." In *Down to Earth Sociology: Introductory Readings,* 7th ed., James M. Henslin, ed. New York: Free Press, 1993:183–196.

Henslin, James M. "How Sociologists Do Research." In *Down to Earth Sociology: Introductory Readings,* 11th ed., James M. Henslin, ed. New York: Free Press, 2001:33–44.

Henslin, James M. *Social Problems,* 5th ed. Upper Saddle River, N.J.: Prentice Hall, 2000.

Henslin, James M. "On Becoming Male: Reflections of a Sociologist on Childhood and Early Socialization." In *Down to Earth Sociology: Introductory Readings,* 11th ed., James M. Henslin, ed. New York: The Free Press, 2001c:138–148.

Henslin, James M. "The Survivors of the F-227." In *Down to Earth Sociology: Introductory Readings,* 11th ed., James M. Henslin, ed. New York: The Free Press, 2001:238–246.

Henslin, James M. "What Is Sociology? Comparing Sociology and the Social Sciences." In *Down to Earth Sociology: Introductory Readings,* 11th ed., James M. Henslin, ed. New York: The Free Press, 2001a:8–18.

Henslin, James M., and Mae A. Biggs. "Behavior in Pubic Places: The Sociology of the Vaginal Examination." In *Down to Earth Sociology: Introductory Readings,* 11th ed., James M. Henslin, ed. New York: The Free Press, 2001:193–204. Original version published as "Dramaturgical Desexualization: The Sociology of the Vaginal Examination." In *Studies in the Sociology of Sex,* James M. Henslin, ed. New York: Appleton-Century-Crofts, 1971:243–272.

Hentoff, Nat. "Fifth Grade Freedom Fighters." *Washington Post,* August 1, 1998:A15.

Herring, George C. "Vietnam War." *World Book Encyclopedia, 20.* Chicago: World Book, 1989:389–393.

Hertzler, Joyce O. *A Sociology of Language.* New York: Random House, 1965.

Higginbotham, Elizabeth, and Lynn Weber. "Moving with Kin and Community: Upward Social Mobility for Black and White Women." *Gender and Society, 6, 3,* September 1992:416–440.

Higley, John, Ursula Hoffmann-Lange, Charles Kadushin, and Gwen Moore. "Elite Integration in Stable Democracies: A Reconsideration." *European Sociological Review, 7, 1,* May 1991:35–53.

Hill, Paul T. "Home Schooling and the Future of Public Education." *Peabody Journal of Education, 75, 1/2,* 2000:20–31.

Hilliard, Asa, III. "Do We Have the *Will* to Educate All Children?" *Educational Leadership, 49,* September 1991:31–36.

Hiltz, Starr Roxanne. "Widowhood." In *Marriage and Family in a Changing Society,* 3rd ed., James M. Henslin, ed. New York: Free Press, 1989:521–531.

Hines, Revathi I. "African Americans' Struggle for Environmental Justice and the Case of the Shintech Plant: Lessons Learned from a War Waged." *Journal of Black Studies, 31, 6,* July 2001: 777–789.

Hippler, Fritz. Interview in a television documentary with Bill Moyers in *Propaganda,* in the series "Walk Through the 20th Century," 1987.

Hirschi, Travis. *Causes of Delinquency.* Berkeley: University of California Press, 1969.

Hochschild, Arlie Russell. "The Sociology of Feeling and Emotion: Selected Possibilities." In *Another Voice: Feminist Perspectives on Social Life and Social Science,* Marcia Millman and Rosabeth Moss Kanter, eds. Garden City, N.Y.: Anchor Books, 1975.

Hochschild, Arlie. *The Managed Heart: Commercialization of Human Feeling.* Chicago: University of Chicago Press, 1983.

Hochschild, Arlie. *The Second Shift: Working Parents and the Revolution at Home.* New York: Viking, 1989.

Hochschild, Arlie. "Note to the Author." 1991.

Hochschild, Arlie, and Anne Machung. "Men Who Share 'The Second Shift'." In *Down to Earth Sociology: Introductory Readings,* 11th ed., James M. Henslin, ed. New York: The Free Press, 2001:395–409.

Holden, Benjamin A., and Frederick Rose. "Two Policemen Get 2 1/2-Year Jail Terms on U.S. Charges in Rodney King Case." *Wall Street Journal,* August 5, 1993:B2.

Holland, Gina. "New Cigarette Ad Restrictions Urged." Associated Press, June 11, 2001.

Holtzman, Abraham. *The Townsend Movement: A Political Study.* New York: Bookman, 1963.

Homblin, Dora Jane. *The First Cities.* Boston: Little, Brown, Time-Life Books, 1973.

Honeycutt, Karen. "Disgusting, Pathetic, Bizarrely Beautiful: Representations of Weight in Popular Culture." Paper presented at the 1995 meetings of the American Sociological Association.

Hong, Lawrence. "Marriage in China." In *Til Death Do Us Part: A Multicultural Anthology on Marriage,* Sandra Lee Browning and R. Robin Miller, eds. Stamford, Conn.: JAI Press, 1999.

Horowitz, Ruth. *Honor and the American Dream: Culture and Identity in a Chicano Community.* New Brunswick, N.J.: Rutgers University Press, 1983.

Horowitz, Ruth. "Community Tolerance of Gang Violence." *Social Problems, 34, 5,* December 1987:437–450.

Hostetler, John A. *Amish Society,* 3rd ed. Baltimore: Johns Hopkins University Press, 1980.

Houtman, Dick. "What Exactly Is a 'Social Class'?: On the Economic Liberalism and Cultural Conservatism of the 'Working Class'." Paper presented at the 1995 meetings of the American Sociological Association.

Howard, Nelson F., and Jewell C. Gould. "Teacher Salaries, Expenditures and Federal Resources in School Districts Serving the Nation's Largest Cities, 1990–91 to 2000–01." Washington, D.C.: American Federation of Teachers, October 2001.

Howe, Henry, John Lyne, Alan Gross, Harro VanLente, Aire Rip, Richard Lewontin, Daniel McShea, Greg Myers, Ullica Segerstrale, Herbert W. Simons, and V. B. Smocovitis. "Gene Talk in Sociobiology." *Social Epistemology, 6, 2,* April–June 1992:109–163.

Howells, Lloyd T., and Selwyn W. Becker. "Seating Arrangement and Leadership Emergence." *Journal of Abnormal and Social Psychology, 64,* February 1962:148–150.

Hoyt, Homer. *The Structure and Growth of Residential Neighborhoods in American Cities.* Washington, D.C.: Federal Housing Administration, 1939.

Hoyt, Homer. "Recent Distortions of the Classical Models of Urban Structure." In *Internal Structure of the City: Readings on Space and Environment,* Larry S. Bourne, ed. New York: Oxford University Press, 1971:84–96.

Hsu, Francis L. K. *The Challenge of the American Dream: The Chinese in the United States.* Belmont, Calif.: Wadsworth, 1971.

Huber, Joan. "Micro-Macro Links in Gender Stratification." *American Sociological Review, 55,* February 1990:1–10.

Huber, Joan, and William H. Form. *Income and Ideology.* New York: Free Press, 1973.

Huddle, Donald. "The Net National Cost of Immigration." Washington, D.C.: Carrying Capacity Network, 1993.

Hudson, Christopher G. "The Social Class and Mental Illness Correlation: Implications of the Research for Policy and Practice." *Journal of Sociology and Social Welfare, 15, 1,* March 1988:27–54.

Hudson, James R. "Professional Sports Franchise Locations and City, Metropolitan and Regional Identities." Paper presented at the annual meetings of the American Sociological Association, 1991.

Hudson, Robert B. "The 'Graying' of the Federal Budget and Its Consequences for Old-Age Policy." *Gerontologist, 18,* October 1978:428–440.

Huffstutter, P. J. "God Is Everywhere on the Net." *Los Angeles Times,* December 14, 1998.

Huggins, Martha K. "Lost Childhoods: Assassinations of Youth in Democratizing Brazil." Paper presented at the annual meetings of the American Sociological Association, 1993.

Huggins, Martha K. "Urban Violence and Police Privatization in Brazil: Blended Invisibility." *Social Justice, 27, 2,* 2000:113–134.

Hughes, H. Stuart. *Oswald Spengler: A Critical Estimate,* rev. ed. New York: Scribner's, 1962.

Hughes, Kathleen A. "Even Tiki Torches Don't Guarantee a Perfect Wedding." *Wall Street Journal,* February 20, 1990:A1, A16.

Humphreys, Laud. *Tearoom Trade: Impersonal Sex in Public Places.* Chicago: Aldine, 1970. Enlarged ed. 1975.

Humphreys, Laud. "Impersonal Sex and Perceived Satisfaction." In *Studies in the Sociology of Sex,* James M. Henslin, ed. New York: Appleton-Century-Crofts, 1971:351–374.

Hurtado, Aída, David E. Hayes-Bautista, R. Burciaga Valdez, and Anthony C. R. Hernández. *Redefining California: Latino Social Engagement in a Multicultural Society.* Los Angeles: UCLA Chicano Studies Research Center, 1992.

Huttenbach, Henry R. "The Roman *Porajmos:* The Nazi Genocide of Europe's Gypsies." *Nationalities Papers, 19, 3,* Winter 1991: 373–394.

Iori, Ron. "The Good, the Bad and the Useless." *Wall Street Journal,* June 10, 1988:18R.

Isikoff, Michael. "The Waco Flame-Up." *Newsweek,* September 6, 1999:30.

Itard, Jean Marc Gospard. *The Wild Boy of Aveyron.* Translated by George and Muriel Humphrey. New York: Appleton-Century-Crofts, 1962.

Jacobs, Charles. "Money Talks." *The Boston Globe,* February 19, 1999.

Jacobs, Margaret A. " 'New Girl' Network Is Boon for Women Lawyers." *Wall Street Journal,* March 4, 1997:B1, B7.

Jaggar, Alison M. "Sexual Difference and Sexual Equality." In *Theoretical Perspectives on Sexual Difference,* Deborah L. Rhode, ed. New Haven, Conn.: Yale University Press, 1990:239–254.

James, Daniel. "To Cut Spending, Freeze Immigration." *Wall Street Journal,* June 24, 1993:A13.

Janis, Irving. *Victims of Groupthink.* Boston, Mass.: Houghton Mifflin, 1972.

Janis, Irving. L. *Groupthink: Psychological Studies of Policy Decisions and Fiascoes.* Boston: Houghton Mifflin, 1982.

Jankowiak, William R., and Edward F. Fischer. "A Cross-Cultural Perspective on Romantic Love." *Journal of Ethnology, 31,* 2, April 1992:149–155.

Jankowski, Martín Sánchez. *Islands in the Street: Gangs and American Urban Society.* Berkeley: University of California Press, 1991.

Jarley, Paul, Jack Fiorito, and John T. Delaney. "National Union Governance: An Empirically-Grounded Systems Approach." *Journal of Labor Research, 21,* 2, Spring 2000:227–246.

Jaspar, James M. "Moral Dimensions of Social Movements." Paper presented at the annual meetings of the American Sociological Association, 1991.

Jaspar, James M., and Dorothy Nelkin. *Animal Crusade.* New York: The Free Press, 1993.

Jasper, James M., and Jane D. Poulsen. "Recruiting Strangers and Friends: Moral Shocks and Social Networks in Animal Rights and Anti-Nuclear Protests." *Social Problems, 42,* 4, November 1995:493–512.

Jáuregui, Gurutz. "El poder y la soberana en la aldéa global." *El Pais.* July 19, 1996:11.

Jekielek, Susan M. "Parental Conflict, Marital Disruption, and Children's Emotional Well-Being." *Social Forces, 76,* 3, March 1998:905–936.

Jenkins, Philip. *Changing Concepts of the Child Molester in Modern America.* New Haven: Yale University Press, 1998.

Jenness, Valerie. "Moral Panic." *Social Forces, 79,* 3, March 2001:1208–1212.

Jerrome, Dorothy. *Good Company: An Anthropological Study of Old People in Groups.* Edinburgh, England: Edinburgh University Press, 1992.

Johansson, Perry. "Consuming the Other: The Fetish of the Western Woman in Chinese Advertising and Popular Culture." *Postcolonial Studies, 2,* 3, November 1999.

Johnson, Benton. "On Church and Sect." *American Sociological Review, 28,* 1963:539–549.

Johnson, Cathryn. "The Emergence of the Emotional Self: A Developmental Theory." *Symbolic Interaction, 15,* 2, Summer 1992:183–202.

Johnson, Dirk. "Growth of Gambling on Tribal Land Starts Trek Back Home by Indians." *New York Times,* January 17, 1999.

Johnson, Kenneth M. "The Rural Rebound." *Reports on America, 1,* 3, Population Reference Bureau, September 1999.

Johnson, Norris R. "Panic at 'The Who Concert Stampede': An Empirical Assessment." In *Collective Behavior and Social Movements,* Russell L. Curtis, Jr., and Benigno E. Aguirre, eds. Boston: Allyn and Bacon, 1993:113–122.

Johnson, Paul. *A History of the American People.* New York: HarperCollins, 1998.

Johnston, Drue M., and Norris R. Johnson. "Role Extension in Disaster: Employee Behavior at the Beverly Hills Supper Club Fire." *Sociological Focus, 22,* 1, February 1989:39–51.

Johnston, Lloyd D., Patrick M. O'Malley, and Jerald G. Bachman. *National Survey Results on Drug Use from The Monitoring the Future Study, 1975–1994.* Rockville, Md.: U.S. Department of Health and Human Services, 1995.

Johnston, Lloyd D., Patrick M. O'Malley, and Jerald G. Bachman. *The Monitoring the Future National Results on Adolescent Drug Use .* Bethesda, Md.: U.S. Department of Health and Human Services, 2000.

Johnston, Lloyd D., Patrick M. O'Mallley, and Jerald G. Bachman. *Monitoring the Future: National Survey Results on Drug Use, 1975–2000, Volume 2, College Students and Adults Ages 19–40.* Bethesda, Md.: U.S. Department of Health and Human Services, 2001.

Jones, James H. *Bad Blood: The Tuskegee Syphilis Experiment,* 2nd ed. New York: Free Press, 1993.

Jordan, Miriam. "Among Poor Villagers, Female Infanticide Still Flourishes in India." *Wall Street Journal,* May 9, 2000:A1, A12.

Jordon, Mary. "College Dorms Reflect Trend of Self-Segregation." In *Ourselves and Others,* 2nd ed., The Washington Post Writer's Group, eds. Boston: Allyn and Bacon, 1996:85–87.

Josephson, Matthew. "The Robber Barons." In *John D. Rockefeller: Robber Baron or Industrial Statesman?* Earl Latham, ed. Boston: Heath, 1949:34–48.

Judis, John B. "The Japanese Megaphone." *New Republic, 202,* 4, January 22, 1990:20–25.

Kaebnick, Gregory E. "On the Sanctity of Nature." *Hastings Center Report, 30,* 5, September-October 2000:16–23.

Kaelber, Lutz. "Comment." *Sociological Footnotes, 30,* 4, July 2001:429.

Kagan, Jerome. "The Idea of Emotions in Human Development." In *Emotions, Cognition, and Behavior,* Carroll E. Izard, Jerome Kagan, and Robert B. Zajonc, eds. New York: Cambridge University Press, 1984:38–72.

Kahn, Jeremy. "The World's Largest Corporations." *Fortune, 144,* 2, July 23, 2001.

Kanabayashi, Masayoshi. "Work Week." *Wall Street Journal,* August 20, 1996:A1.

Kanter, Rosabeth Moss. *Men and Women of the Corporation.* New York: Basic Books, 1977.

Kanter, Rosabeth Moss. *The Change Masters: Innovation and Entrepreneurship in the American Corporation.* New York: Simon & Schuster, 1983.

Kanter, Rosabeth Moss. *World Class: Thriving Locally in the Global Economy.* New York: Touchstone Books, 1997b.

Kanter, Rosabeth Moss, Fred Wiersema, and John J. Kao, eds. *Innovation: Breakthrough Thinking at 3M, DuPont, GE, Pfizer, and Rubbermaid.* New York: Harper, 1997.

Kantrowitz, Barbara, and Daniel McGinn. "When Teachers Are Cheaters." *Newsweek,* June 19, 2000.

Karnow, Stanley, and Nancy Yoshihara. *Asian Americans in Transition.* New York: Asia Society, 1992.

Karp, David A., Gregory P. Stone, and William C. Yoels. *Being Urban: A Sociology of City Life,* 2nd ed. New York: Praeger, 1991.

Karp, David A., and William C. Yoels. "Sport and Urban Life." *Journal of Sport and Social Issues,* 14, 2, 1990:77–102.

Kart, Cary S. *The Realities of Aging: An Introduction to Gerontology,* 3rd ed. Boston: Allyn and Bacon, 1990.

Katz, Jack. *How Emotions Work.* Chicago: University of Chicago Press, 1999.

Katz, Sidney. "The Importance of Being Beautiful." In *Down to Earth Sociology: Introductory Readings,* 11th ed., James M. Henslin, ed. New York: The Free Press, 2001:297–303.

Kaufman, Joanne. "Married Maidens and Dilatory Domiciles." *Wall Street Journal,* May 7, 1996:A16.

Kazman, Sam. "Here's to Honesty in Liquor Sales." *Wall Street Journal,* February 18, 1999.

Keith, Jennie. *Old People, New Lives: Community Creation in a Retirement Residence,* 2nd ed. Chicago: University of Chicago Press, 1982.

Kelling, George L., and Catherine M. Coles. *Fixing Broken Windows: Restoring Order and Reducing Crime in Our Communities.* New York: Free Press, 1998.

Kelly, Joan B. "How Adults React to Divorce." In *Marriage and Family in a Changing Society,* 4th ed., James M. Henslin, ed. New York: Free Press, 1992:410–423.

Kemp, Alice Abel. "Estimating Sex Discrimination in Professional Occupations with the *Dictionary of Occupational Titles.*" *Sociological Spectrum,* 10, 3, 1990:387–411.

Keniston, Kenneth. *Youth and Dissent: The Rise of a New Opposition.* New York: Harcourt, Brace, Jovanovich, 1971.

Kennedy, Paul. *Preparing for the Twenty-First Century.* New York: Random House, 1993.

Kent, Mary M., Kelvin M. Pollard, John Haaga, and Mark Mather. "First Glimpses From the 2000 U.S. Census." *Population Bulletin,* 56, 2, June 2001:1–39.

"Kenya: Girls Score Court Victory Against Genital Mutilation." *Women's International Network News,* 27, 2, Spring 2001:64.

Kephart, William M., and William W. Zellner. *Extraordinary Groups: An Examination of Unconventional Life-Styles,* 5th ed. New York: St. Martin's Press, 1994.

Kerr, Clark. *The Future of Industrialized Societies.* Cambridge, Mass.: Harvard University Press, 1983.

Kerr, Clark, et al. *Industrialism and Industrial Man: The Problems of Labor and Management in Economic Growth.* Cambridge, Mass.: Harvard University Press, 1960.

Kershaw, Terry. "The Effects of Educational Tracking on the Social Mobility of African Americans." *Journal of Black Studies,* 23, 1, September 1992:152–169.

Kibria, Nazli. *Family Tightrope: The Changing Lives of Vietnamese Americans.* Princeton, N.J.: Princeton University Press, 1993.

Kifner, John. "Building Modernity on Desert Mirages." *New York Times,* February 7, 1999.

Kilbourne, Jean. "Beauty and the Beast of Advertising." In *Down to Earth Sociology: Introductory Readings,* 11th ed., James M. Henslin, ed. New York: The Free Press, 2001:391–394.

Kinsella, Kevin, and Cynthia M. Taeuber. *An Aging World.* Washington, D.C.: U.S. Bureau of the Census, 1993.

Klandermans, Bert. *The Social Psychology of Protest.* Cambridge, Mass.: Blackwell, 1997.

Klonoff, Elizabeth A., and Hope Landrine. "Sex Roles, Occupational Roles, and Symptom-Reporting: A Test of Competing Hypotheses on Sex Differences." *Journal of Behavioral Medicine,* 15, 4, August 1992:355–364.

Kluegel, James R., and Eliot R. Smith. *Beliefs About Inequality: America's Views of What Is and What Ought to Be.* Hawthorne, N.Y.: Aldine de Gruyter, 1986.

Knaus, William A. *Inside Russian Medicine: An American Doctor's First-Hand Report.* New York: Everest House, 1981.

Kohlberg, Lawrence. *The Psychology of Moral Development: Moral Stages and the Life Cycle.* San Francisco: Harper and Row, 1984.

Kohlberg, Lawrence. "Moral Education for a Society in Moral Transition." *Educational Leadership,* 33, 1975:46–54.

Kohlberg, Lawrence. "A Current Statement on Some Theoretical Issues." In *Lawrence Kohlberg: Consensus and Controversy,* Sohan Modgil and Celia Modgil, eds. Philadelphia: Falmer Press, 1986:485–546.

Kohlberg, Lawrence, and Carol Gilligan. "The Adolescent as a Philosopher: The Discovery of the Self in a Postconventional World." *Daedalus,* 100, 1971:1051–1086.

Kohn, Alfie. "Make Love, Not War." *Psychology Today,* June 1988:35–38.

Kohn, Melvin L. "Social Class and Parental Values." *American Journal of Sociology,* 64, 1959:337–351.

Kohn, Melvin L. "Social Class and Parent–Child Relationships: An Interpretation." *American Journal of Sociology,* 68, 1963:471–480.

Kohn, Melvin L. "Occupational Structure and Alienation." *American Journal of Sociology,* 82, 1976:111–130.

Kohn, Melvin L. *Class and Conformity: A Study in Values,* 2nd ed. Homewood, Ill.: Dorsey Press, 1977.

Kohn, Melvin L., and Carmi Schooler. "Class, Occupation, and Orientation." *American Sociological Review,* 34, 1969:659–678.

Kohn, Melvin L., and Carmi Schooler. *Work and Personality: An Inquiry into the Impact of Social Stratification.* New York: Ablex Press, 1983.

Kohn, Melvin L., Kazimierz M. Slomczynski, and Carrie Schoenbach. "Social Stratification and the Transmission of Values in the Family: A Cross-National Assessment." *Sociological Forum,* 1, 1, 1986:73–102.

Kolata, Gina. "The Genesis of an Epidemic: Humans, Chimps and a Virus." *New York Times,* September 4, 2001.

Korbin, Jill E., Georgia Anetzberger, and J. Kevin Eckert. "Elder Abuse and Child Abuse: A Consideration of Similarities and Differences in Intergenerational Family Violence." In *Perspectives in Social Gerontology,* Robert B. Enright, Jr., ed. Boston: Allyn and Bacon, 1994:165–173.

Korda, Michael. *Male Chauvinism: How It Works.* New York: Random House, 1973.

Kornhauser, William. *The Politics of Mass Society.* New York: Free Press, 1959.

Kotlowitz, Alex. "A Businessman Turns His Skills to Aiding Inner-City Schools." *Wall Street Journal,* February 25, 1992:A1, A6.

Kramer, Josea B. "Serving American Indian Elderly in Cities: An Invisible Minority." *Aging Magazine,* Winter–Spring 1992:48–51.

Krane, Vikki, Julie A. Stiles-Shipley, Jennifer Waldron, and Jennifer Michalenok. "Relationships Among Body Satisfaction, Social Physique Anxiety, and Eating Behaviors in Female Athletes and Exercisers." *Journal of Sport Behavior,* 24, 3, September 2001:247–264.

Kraybill, Donald B. *The Riddle of Amish Culture.* Baltimore: Johns Hopkins University Press, 1989.

Kraybill, Donald B., and Carl F. Bowman. *Old Order Hutterites, Mennonites, Amish, and Brethren.* Baltimore, Md.: Johns Hopkins University Press, 2001.

Krog, Antjie. *Country of My Skull: Guilt, Sorrow, and the Limits of Forgiveness in the New South Africa.* New York: TimesBooks, 1999.

Krueger, Robert F., and Avshalom Caspi. *Journal of Personality,* 68, 6, December 2000:967–998.

Krysan, Maria, and Reynolds Farley. "Racial Stereotypes: Are They Alive and Well? Do They Continue to Influence Race Relations?" Paper presented at the 1993 meeting of the American Sociological Association.

Kübler-Ross, Elisabeth. *On Death and Dying.* New York: Macmillan, 1969.

Kübler-Ross, Elisabeth. *Living with Death and Dying.* New York: Macmillan, 1981.

Kübler-Ross, Elisabeth. *Death: The Final Stage of Growth.* Englewood Cliffs, N.J.: Prentice Hall, 1989.

Kuhn, Margaret E. "The Gray Panthers." In *Social Problems,* 2nd ed., James M. Henslin, Englewood Cliffs, N.J.: Prentice Hall, 1990:56–57.

Kuntz, Phil. "Reno, FBI Orders New Investigation of Use of Flammable Devises in Waco." *Wall Street Journal,* August 27, 1999.

Kurian, George Thomas. *Encyclopedia of the First World,* Vols. 1, 2. New York: Facts on File, 1990.

Kurian, George Thomas. *Encyclopedia of the Second World,* New York: Facts on File, 1991.

Kurian, George Thomas. *Encyclopedia of the Third World,* Vols. 1, 2, 3. New York: Facts on File, 1992.

La Barre, Weston. *The Human Animal.* Chicago: University of Chicago Press, 1954.

Lacayo, Richard. "In the Grip of a Psychopath." *Time,* May 3, 1993b:34–36, 39–43.

Lachica, Eduardo. "Third World Told to Spend More on Environment." *Wall Street Journal,* May 18, 1992:A2.

Lagaipa, Susan J. "Suffer the Little Children: The Ancient Practice of Infanticide as a Modern Moral Dilemma." *Issues in Comprehensive Pediatric Nursing, 13,* 1990:241–251.

Lagnado, Lucette. "Another Peril: Smoking Doubles Risk of Old-Age Blindness, Two Studies Say." *Wall Street Journal,* October 9, 1996:B8.

Lalumiere, Martin L., and Vernon Quinsey. "Good Genes, Mating Effort, and Delinquency." *Behavioral and Brain Sciences, 23,* 4, August 2000:608–609.

Lamb, Michael E. "The Effect of Divorce on Children's Personality Development." *Journal of Divorce, 1,* Winter 1977:163–174.

Lancaster, Hal. "Managing Your Career." *Wall Street Journal,* November 14, 1995:B1.

Landler, Mark. "Hi, I'm in Bangalore (But I Dare Not Tell)." *New York Times,* March 21, 2001.

Landtman, Gunnar. *The Origin of the Inequality of the Social Classes.* New York: Greenwood Press, 1968. First published in 1938.

Lang, Kurt, and Gladys E. Lang. *Collective Dynamics.* New York: Crowell, 1961.

Lannoy, Richard. *The Speaking Tree: A Study of Indian Culture and Society.* New York: Oxford University Press, 1975.

Larson, Jeffry H. "The Marriage Quiz: College Students' Beliefs in Selected Myths About Marriage." *Family Relations,* January 1988:3–11.

Lasch, Christopher. *Haven in a Heartless World: The Family Besieged.* New York: Basic, 1977.

Laska, Shirley Bradway. "Environmental Sociology and the State of the Discipline." *Social Forces, 72,* 1, September 1993:1–17.

Lauer, Jeanette, and Robert Lauer. "Marriages Made to Last." In *Marriage and Family in a Changing Society,* 4th ed., James M. Henslin, ed. New York: Free Press, 1992:481–486.

Lawler, Steph. "'Getting Out and Getting Away': Women's Narratives of Class Mobility." *Feminist Review,* 63, Autumn 1999:3–24.

Lazarsfeld, Paul F., and Jeffrey G. Reitz. "History of Applied Sociology." *Sociological Practice,* 7, 1989:43–52.

LeBon, Gustave. *Psychologie des Foules (The Psychology of the Crowd).* Paris: Alcan, 1895. Various editions in English.

Leacock, Eleanor. *Myths of Male Dominance.* New York: Monthly Review Press, 1981.

Lee, Alfred McClung, and Elizabeth Briant Lee. *The Fine Art of Propaganda: A Study of Father Coughlin's Speeches.* New York: Harcourt Brace, 1939.

Lee, Raymond M. *Unobtrusive Methods in Social Research.* Philadelphia: Open University Press, 2000.

Lee, Sharon M. "Asian Americans: Diverse and Growing." *Population Bulletin, 53,* 2, June 1998:1–39.

Leland, John, and Gregory Beals. "In Living Colors." *Newsweek,* May 5, 1997:58–60.

Lemann, Nicholas. *The Promised Land: The Great Black Migration and How It Changed America.* New York: Random House, 1991.

Lemann, Nicholas, "The Myth of Community Development." *New York Times Magazine,* January 9, 1994, p. 27.

Lemert, Charles. "A Classic from the Other Side of the Veil: Du Bois's *Souls of Black Folk*." *Sociological Quarterly, 35,* 3, 1994:383–396.

Lenski, Gerhard. "Status Crystallization: A Nonvertical Dimension of Social Status." *American Sociological Review, 19,* 1954:405–413.

Lenski, Gerhard. *Power and Privilege: A Theory of Social Stratification.* New York: McGraw-Hill, 1966.

Lenski, Gerhard, and Jean Lenski. *Human Societies: An Introduction to Macrosociology,* 5th ed. New York: McGraw-Hill, 1987.

Leonhardt, David. "If Richer Isn't Happier, What Is?" *New York Times,* May 19, 2001.

Lerner, Gerda. *Black Women in White America: A Documentary History.* New York: Pantheon Books, 1972.

Lerner, Gerda. *The Creation of Patriarchy.* New York: Oxford, 1986.

Lesser, Alexander. "War and the State." In *War: The Anthropology of Armed Conflict and Aggression,* Morton Fried, Marvin Harris, and Robert Murphy, eds. Garden City, N.Y.: Natural History, 1968:92–96.

Lester, David. *Suicide in American Indians.* New York: Nova Science Publishers, 1997.

Levine, John M. "Solomon Asch's Legacy for Group Research." *Personality and Social Psychology Review, 3,* 4, 1999:358–364.

Levinson, D. J. *The Seasons of a Man's Life.* New York: Knopf, 1978.

Levy, Marion J., Jr. "Confucianism and Modernization." *Society,* 24, 4, May–June 1992:15–18.

Lewin, Tamar. "Children's Computer Use Grows, But Gaps Persist, Study Says." *New York Times,* January 22, 2001a.

Lewin, Tamar. "Little Sympathy or Remedy for Inmates Who Are Raped." *New York Times,* April 15, 2001b.

Lewis, Oscar. "The Culture of Poverty." *Scientific American, 115,* October 1966a:19–25.

Lewis, Oscar. *La Vida.* New York: Random House, 1966b.

Lewis, Richard S. *Challenger: The Final Voyage.* New York: Columbia University Press, 1988.

Licata, Jane Massey. "Genetic NonDiscrimination: Implications for Employer Sponsored Heath Care Plans." Testimony before the House Committee on Education and the Workforce, *FDCH Congressional Testimony,* September 6, 2001.

Liebow, Elliot. "Tally's Corner." In *Down to Earth Sociology: Introductory Readings,* 9th ed., James M. Henslin, ed. New York: Free Press, 1997:330–339.

Liebow, Elliott. *Tally's Corner: A Study of Negro Streetcorner Men.* Boston: Little, Brown, 1999. Originally published in 1967.

Light, Donald W. "Perestroika for Russian Health Care?" *Footnotes,* 20, 3, March 1992:7, 9.

Light, Richard J. *Making the Most of College.* Cambridge: Harvard University Press, 2001.

Lightfoot-Klein, A. "Rites of Purification and Their Effects: Some Psychological Aspects of Female Genital Circumcision and Infibulation (Pharaonic Circumcision) in an Afro-Arab Society (Sudan)." *Journal of Psychological Human Sexuality,* 2, 1989:61–78.

Lin, Quiyun. "An Evaluation of Charter School Effectiveness." *Education,* 122, 1, Fall 2001:166–176.

Lind, Michael. *The Next American Nation: The New Nationalism and the Fourth American Revolution.* New York: Free Press, 1995.

Linden, Eugene. "Lost Tribes, Lost Knowledge." *Time,* September 23, 1991:46, 48, 50, 52, 54, 56.

Lines, Patricia M. "Homeschooling Comes of Age." *Public Interest,* Summer 2000:74–85.

Linton, Ralph. *The Study of Man.* New York: Appleton-Century-Crofts, 1936.

Lippitt, Ronald, and Ralph K. White. "An Experimental Study of Leadership and Group Life." In *Readings in Social Psychology,* 3rd ed., Eleanor E. Maccoby, Theodore M. Newcomb, and Eugene L. Hartley, eds. New York: Holt, Rinehart and Winston, 1958: 340–365. (As summarized in Olmsted and Hare 1978:28–31.)

Lipset, Seymour Martin. "Democracy and Working-Class Authoritarianism." *American Sociological Review,* 24, 1959:482–502.

Lipset, Seymour Martin. "The Social Requisites of Democracy Revisited." Presidential address to the American Sociological Association, Boston, Massachusetts, 1993.

Lofland, John F. *Protest: Studies of Collective Behavior and Social Movements.* New Brunswick, New Jersey: Transaction Books, 1985.

Lofland, John. "Collective Behavior: The Elementary Forms." In *Collective Behavior and Social Movements,* Russell L. Curtis, Jr., and Benigno E. Aguirre, eds. Boston: Allyn and Bacon, 1993:70–75.

Logue, John, and Jacquelyn Yates. "Modeling an Employee Ownership Sector." *Peace Review,* 12, 2, June 2000:243–249.

Lombroso, Cesare. *Crime: Its Causes and Remedies,* H. P. Horton, trans. Boston: Little, Brown, 1911.

Longman, Jere. "Getting the Athletic Edge May Mean Altering Genes." *New York Times,* May 11, 201.

Lopez, Julie Amparano. "Study Says Women Face Glass Walls as Well as Ceilings." *Wall Street Journal,* March 3, 1992:B1, B8.

Lorber, Judith. *Paradoxes of Gender.* New Haven, Conn.: Yale University Press, 1994.

Lorch, Donatella. "Out of Africa." *Newsweek,* March 19, 2001: 32–35.

Lublin, Joann S. "Trying to Increase Worker Productivity, More Employers Alter Management Style." *Wall Street Journal,* February 13, 1991:B1, B7.

Lublin, Joann S. "Women at Top Still Are Distant from CEO Jobs." *Wall Street Journal,* February 28, 1996:B1.

Lublin, Joann S. "Living Well." *Wall Street Journal,* April 8, 1999.

Lucas, Samuel Roundfield. *Tracking Inequality: Stratification and Mobility in American High Schools.* New York: Teachers College Press, 1999.

Luke, Timothy W. *Ideology and Soviet Industrialization.* Westport, Conn.: Greenwood Press, 1985.

Lundberg, Olle. "Causal Explanations for Class Inequality in Health—An Empirical Analysis." *Social Science and Medicine, 32,* 4, 1991:385–393.

Lunneborg, Patricia. *Chosen Lives of Childfree Men.* Westport, Conn.: Bergin and Garvey, 1999.

Luoma, Jon R. "Acid Murder No Longer a Mystery." In *Taking Sides: Clashing Views on Controversial Environmental Issues,* 3rd ed., Theodore D. Goldfarb, ed. Guilford, Conn.: Dushkin, 1989:186–192.

Lurie, Nicole, Jonathan Slater, Paul McGovern, Jacqueline Ekstrum, Lois Quam, and Karen Margolis. "Preventive Care for Women: Does the Sex of the Physician Matter?" *New England Journal of Medicine, 329,* August 12, 1993:478–482.

Mabry, Marcus. "The Price Tag on Freedom." *Newsweek,* May 3, 1999:50–51.

MacDonald, Heather. "Law School Humbug." *Wall Street Journal,* November 8, 1995:A23.

MacDonald, William L., and Alfred DeMaris. "Remarriage, Stepchildren, and Marital Conflict: Challenges to the Incomplete Institutionalization Hypothesis." *Journal of Marriage and the Family, 57,* May 1995:387–398.

Mack, Raymond W., and Calvin P. Bradford. *Transforming America: Patterns of Social Change,* 2nd ed. New York: Random House, 1979.

Mackay, Charles. *Memories of Extraordinary Popular Delusions and the Madness of Crowds.* London: Office of the National Illustrated Library, 1852.

Mackey, Richard A., and Bernard A. O'Brien. *Lasting Marriages: Men and Women Growing Together.* Westport, Conn.: 1995.

Magnuson, E. "A Cold Soak, a Plume, a Fireball." *Time,* February 17, 1986:25.

Maher, Sarah. *Salvadorans in Suburbia: Symbiosis and Conflict.* Boston: Allyn and Bacon, 1996.

Mahoney, John S., Jr., and Paul G. Kooistra. "Policing the Races: Structural Factors Enforcing Racial Purity in Virginia (1630–1930)." Paper presented at the 1995 meetings of the American Sociological Association.

Mahoney, Patricia. "High Rape Chronicity and Low Rates of Help-Seeking Among Wife Rape Survivors in a Nonclinical Sample: Implications for Research and Practice." *Violence Against Women, 5,* 9, September 1999:993–1016.

Mahran, M. *Proceedings of the Third International Congress of Medical Sexology.* Littleton, Mass.: PSG Publishing, 1978.

Mahran, M. "Medical Dangers of Female Circumcision." *International Planned Parenthood Federation Medical Bulletin, 2,* 1981:1–2.

Maier, Mark. "Teaching from Tragedy: An Interdisciplinary Module on the Space Shuttle *Challenger.*" *T.H.E. Journal,* September 1993:91–94.

Main, Jackson Turner. *The Social Structure of Revolutionary America.* Princeton, N.J.: Princeton University Press, 1965.

Malinowski, Bronislaw. *Sex and Repression in Savage Society.* Cleveland, Ohio: World, 1927.

Malinowski, Bronislaw. *The Dynamics of Culture Change.* New Haven, Conn.: Yale University Press, 1945.

Malmberg, Bo, and Gerdt Sundström. "Age Care Crisis in Sweden?" *Current Sweden, 412,* January 1996:1–6.

Malson, Lucien. *Wolf Children and the Problem of Human Nature.* New York: Monthly Review Press, 1972.

Malthus, Thomas Robert. *First Essay on Population 1798.* London: Macmillan, 1926. Originally published in 1798.

Mamdani, Mahmood. "The Myth of Population Control: Family, Caste, and Class in an Urban Village." New York: Monthly Review Press, 1973.

Manavalan, Theresa. "Why Science Is Sexy Now." *New Straits Times-Management Times,* June 26, 2001.

Mander, Jerry. *In the Absence of the Sacred: The Failure of Technology and the Survival of the Indian Nations.* San Francisco, Calif.: Sierra Club Books, 1992.

Manno, Bruno V. "The Real Score on the SATs." *Wall Street Journal,* September 13, 1995:A14.

Manno, Bruno V., and Chester E. Finn. *Phi Delta Kappan, 79,* 7, March 1998:489–500.

Mansfield, Harvey C. "Grade Inflation: It's Time to Face the Facts." *Chronicle of Higher Education, 47,* 30, April 6, 2001:824.

Manski, Charles F. "Income and Higher Education." *Focus, 14,* 3, Winter 1992–1993:14–19.

Marable, Manning. "Whites Have an Obligation to Recognize Slavery's Legacy." *Newsweek,* August 27, 2001:22.

Marcus, Amy Dockser. "Mideast Minorities: Kurds Aren't Alone." *Wall Street Journal,* September 5, 1996:A12.

Marger, Martin N. *Elites and Masses: An Introduction to Political Sociology,* 2nd ed. Belmont, Calif.: Wadsworth, 1987.

Markson, Elizabeth W. "Moral Dilemmas." *Society,* July–August, 1992:4–6.

Markusen, Eric. "Genocide in Cambodia." In *Down to Earth Sociology,* 8th ed., James M. Henslin, ed. New York: Free Press, 1995:355–364.

Marolla, Joseph, and Diana Scully. "Attitudes Toward Women, Violence, and Rape: A Comparison of Convicted Rapists and Other Felons." *Deviant Behavior, 7,* 4, 1986:337–355.

Mars, Laura, ed. *Nations of the World: A Political, Economic and Business Handbook, 2000/01.* Lakeville, Conn.: Grey House Publishing, 2000.

Marshall, Gordon. *In Search of the Spirit of Capitalism: An Essay on Max Weber's Protestant Ethic Thesis.* New York: Columbia University Press, 1982.

Marshall, Nancy. "Slavery Still a Fact of Life in Mauritania." *Weekly Edition: The Best of NPR News.* September 1, 2001.

Marshall, Samantha. "It's So Simple: Just Lather Up, Watch the Fat Go Down the Drain." *Wall Street Journal,* November 2, 1995:B1.

Marshall, Samantha. "Vietnamese Women Are Kidnapped and Later Sold in China as Brides." *Wall Street Journal,* August 3, 1999.

Martin, William G., and Mark Beittel. "Toward a Global Sociology: Evaluating Current Conceptions, Methods, and Practices." *Sociological Quarterly, 39,* 1, 1998:139–161.

Martineau, Harriet. *Society in America.* Garden City, N.Y.: Doubleday 1962. First published in 1837.

Marx, Gary T. "The New Surveillance." *Technology Review,* May–June 1985:43–48.

Marx, Gary T. "Monitoring on the Job: How to Protect Privacy as Well as Property." *Technology Review,* November–December 1986:63–72.

Marx, Gary T. "Thoughts On a Neglected Category of Social Movement Participant: The Agent Provocateur and the Informant." In *Collective Behavior and Social Movements,* Russell L. Curtis, Jr., and Benigno E. Aguirre, eds. Boston: Allyn and Bacon, 1993:242–258.

Marx, Gary T. "The Road to the Future." In *Triumph of Discovery: A Chronicle of Great Adventures in Science.* New York: Holt, 1995:63–65.

Marx, Karl. "Contribution to the Critique of Hegel's Philosophy of Right." In *Karl Marx: Early Writings,* T. B. Bottomore, ed. New York: McGraw-Hill, 1964:45. First published in 1844.

Marx, Karl, and Friedrich Engels. *Communist Manifesto.* New York: Pantheon, 1967. First published in 1848.

Masheter, Carol. "Postdivorce Relationships Between Ex-spouses: The Role of Attachment and Interpersonal Conflict." *Journal of Marriage and the Family, 53,* February 1991:103–110.

Massey, Douglas S., and Garvey Lundy. "Use of Black English and Racial Discrimination in Urban Housing Markets: New Methods and Findings." *Urban Affairs Review, 36,* 2001:451–468.

Mateja, Jim. "Toyota Mulls Next Move After Success with Gas/Electric Hybrid Car." *Chicago Tribune,* September 6, 2001.

Mateju, Petr, and Martin Kreidl. "Rebuilding Status Consistency in a Post-Communist Society: The Czech Republic." *Innovation: The European Journal of Social Sciences, 14,* 1, March 2001: 17–34.

Mauss, Armand. *Social Problems as Social Movements.* Philadelphia, Penn.: Lippincott, 1975.

Maybury-Lewis, David. "Tribal Wisdom." In *Sociology 95/96,* Kurt Finsterbusch, ed. Sluice Dock, Conn.: Dushkin, 1995:16–21.

Mayo, Elton. *Human Problems of an Industrial Civilization.* New York: Viking, 1966.

McAdam, Doug, John D. McCarthy, and Mayer N. Zald. "Social Movements." In *Handbook of Sociology,* Neil J. Smelser, ed. Newbury Park, Calif.: Sage, 1988:695–737.

McCabe, J. Terrence, and James E. Ellis. "Pastoralism: Beating the Odds in Arid Africa." In *Conformity and Conflict: Readings in Cultural Anthropology,* James P. Spradley and David W. McCurdy, eds. Glenview, Ill.: Scott, Foresman, 1990:150–156.

McCall, Michael. "Who and Where Are the Artists?" In *Fieldwork Experience: Qualitative Approaches to Social Research,* William B. Shaffir, Robert A. Stebbins, and Allan Turowetz, eds. New York: St. Martin's, 1980:145–158.

McCarthy, John D., and Mark Wolfson. "Consensus Movements, Conflict Movements, and the Cooperation of Civic and State Infrastructures." In *Frontiers in Social Movement Theory,* Aldon D. Morris and Carol McClurg Mueller, eds. New Haven, Conn.: Yale University Press, 1992:273–297.

McCarthy, John D., and Mayer N. Zald. "Resource Mobilization and Social Movements: A Partial Theory." *American Journal of Sociology, 82,* 6, 1977:1212–1241.

McCarthy, Michael J. "James Bond Hits the Supermarket: Stores Snoop on Shoppers' Habits to Boost Sales." *Wall Street Journal,* August 25, 1993:B1, B8.

McCartney, Kathleen, et al. "Teacher-Child Interaction and Child-Care Auspices as Predictors of Social Outcomes in Infants, Toddlers, and Preschoolers." *Merrill-Palmer Quarterly, 41,* 3, July 1997:426–450.

McCartney, Scott. "People Most Needing Transplantable Livers Now Often Miss Out." *Wall Street Journal,* April 1, 1993:A1, A7.

McCormick, John. "Change Has Taken Place." *Newsweek,* June 7, 1999:34.

McCormick, John. "The New School." *Newsweek,* April 24, 2000:60–62.

McCoy, Elin. "Childhood Through the Ages." In *Marriage and Family in a Changing Society*, 2nd ed., James M. Henslin, ed. New York: Free Press, 1985:386–394.

McCuen, Gary E., ed. *Ecocide and Genocide in the Vanishing Forest: The Rainforests and Native People*. Hudson, Wis.: GEM Publications, 1993.

McDonald, Peter. "Low Fertility Not Politically Sustainable." *Population Today*, August-September 2001:3, 8.

McFarling, Usha Lee. "Climate Is Warming at Steep Rate, Study Says." *Los Angeles Times*, February 23, 2000.

McGee, Glenn. "Cloning, Sex, and New Kinds of Families." *Journal of Sex Research*, 37, 3, August 2000:266–272.

McGowan, Jo. "Little Girls Dying: An Ancient & Thriving Practice." *Commonweal*, August 9, 1991:481–482.

McIntyre, Jamie. "Army Rape Case Renews Debate on Coed Training." April 30, 1997: CNN Internet article.

McKenna, George. "On Abortion: A Lincolnian Position." *Atlantic Monthly*, September 1995:51–67.

McKeown, Thomas. *The Modern Rise of Population*. New York: Academic Press, 1977.

McLanahan, Sara, and Gary Sandefur. *Growing Up with a Single Parent: What Hurts, What Helps*. Cambridge, Mass.: Harvard University Press, 1994.

McLemore, S. Dale. *Racial and Ethnic Relations in America*. Boston: Allyn and Bacon, 1994.

McLemore, S. Dale, Harriett D. Romo, and Susan Gonzalez Baker. *Racial and Ethnic Relations in America*, 6th ed. Boston: Allyn and Bacon, 2001.

McLuhan, Marshall. *Understanding Media: The Extensions of Man*. New York: Mentor, 1964.

McNeil, Donald G., Jr. "In Angola's Capital, Life Does Not Yet Imitate Art." *New York Times*, January 25, 1999.

McNeill, William H, "How the Potato Changed the World's History." *Social Research*, 66, 1, Spring 1999:67–83.

McPhail, Clark. "Blumer's Theory of Collective Behavior: The Development of a Non-Symbolic Interaction Explanation." *Sociological Quarterly*, 30, 3, 1989:401–423.

McPhail, Clark. *The Myth of the Madding Crowd*. Hawthorne, N.Y.: Aldine de Gruyter, 1991.

Mead, George Herbert. *Mind, Self and Society*. Chicago: University of Chicago Press, 1934.

Mead, Margaret. *Sex and Temperament in Three Primitive Societies*. New York: New American Library, 1950. First published in 1935.

Medln, Richard G. "Home Schooling and the Question of Socialization." *Peabody Journal of Education*, 75, 1/2, 2000:107–123.

Meek, Anne. "On Creating 'Ganas': A Conversation with Jaime Escalante." *Educational Leadership*, 46, 5, February 1989:46–47.

Meier, Barry. "Health Studies Suggest Asbestos Substitutes Also Pose Cancer Risk." *Wall Street Journal*, May 12, 1987:1, 21.

Melloan, George. "Italy 'Steps into the Tunnel' Toward Change." *Wall Street Journal*, April 26, 1993b:A15.

Meltzer, Bernard N., John W. Petras, and Larry T. Reynolds. *Symbolic Interactionism: Genesis, Varieties, and Criticism*. London: Routledge & Kegan Paul, 1975.

Melucci, Alberto. *Nomads of the Present: Social Movements and Individual Needs in Contemporary Society*. Philadelphia: Temple University Press, 1989.

Menaghan, Elizabeth G., Lori Kowaleski-Jones, and Frank L. Mott. "The Intergenerational Costs of Parental Social Stressors: Academic and Social Difficulties in Early Adolescence for Children of Young Mothers." *Journal of Health and Social Behavior*, 38, March 1997:72–86.

Mendels, Pamela. "Rights Group Develops 'Hate' Filter." *New York Times*, November 11, 1998.

Mendelsohn, Robert, and Balick, Michael J. "Drugs and Tropical Forests." *Economic Botany*, June 1995.

Menzel, Peter. *Material World: A Global Family Portrait*. San Francisco: Sierra Club, 1994.

Mersereau, Adam G. "The Military Should Fight Wars, Not Sexism." *Wall Street Journal*, March 17, 1998:A18.

Merton, Robert K. *Social Theory and Social Structure*. Glencoe, Ill.: Free Press, 1949, Enlarged ed., 1968.

Merton, Robert K. "The Social-Cultural Environment and Anomie." In *New Perspectives for Research on Juvenile Delinquency*, Helen L. Witmer and Ruth Kotinsky, eds. Washington, D.C.: U.S. Department of Health, Education, and Welfare, 1956:24–50.

Merwine, Maynard H. "How Africa Understands Female Circumcision." *New York Times*, November 24, 1993.

Messner, Michael. "Boyhood, Organized Sports, and the Construction of Masculinities." *Journal of Contemporary Ethnography*, 18, 4, January 1990:416–444.

Mezentseva, E. *Russian Social Science Review*, 42, 4, July-August 2001:4–21.

Michael, Robert T. "Measuring Poverty: A New Approach." *Focus*, 17, 1, Summer 1995:2–13.

Michalowski, Raymond J. *Order, Law, and Crime: An Introduction to Criminology*. New York: Random House, 1985.

Michels, Robert. *Political Parties*. Glencoe, Ill.: Free Press, 1949. First published in 1911.

Milbank, Dana. "Working Poor Fear Welfare Cutbacks Aimed at the Idle Will Inevitably Strike Them, Too." *Wall Street Journal*, August 9, 1995b:A10.

Milgram, Stanley. "Behavioral Study of Obedience." *Journal of Abnormal and Social Psychology*, 67, 4, 1963:371–378.

Milgram, Stanley. "Some Conditions of Obedience and Disobedience to Authority." *Human Relations*, 18, February 1965:57–76.

Milgram, Stanley. "The Small World Problem." *Psychology Today*, 1, 1967:61–67.

Milkie, Melissa A. "Social World Approach to Cultural Studies." *Journal of Contemporary Ethnography*, 23, 3, October 1994:354–380.

Miller, Dan E. "Milgram Redux: Obedience and Disobedience in Authority Relations." In *Studies in Symbolic Interaction*, Norman K. Denzin, ed. Greenwich, Conn.: JAI Press, 1986:77–106.

Miller, Judith, and William J. Broad. "Clinton Describes Terrorism Threat for 21st Century." *New York Times*, January 22, 1999.

Miller, Laura L. "Women in the Military." In *Down to Earth Sociology: Introductory Readings*, 11th ed., James M. Henslin, ed. New York: The Free Press, 2001:481–496.

Miller, Lisa. "Son of Elijah Muhammad Preaches Gentler Islam in Tune With the Times." *Wall Street Journal*, July 9, 1999.

Miller, Michael W. "Dark Days: The Staggering Cost of Depression." *Wall Street Journal*, December 2, 1993:B1, B6.

Miller, Michael W. "Survey Sketches New Portrait of the Mentally Ill." *Wall Street Journal*, January 14, 1994: B1, B10.

Miller, Walter B. "Lower Class Culture as a Generating Milieu of Gang Delinquency." *Journal of Social Issues*, 14, 3, 1958:5–19.

Miller-Loessi, Karen. "Toward Gender Integration in the Workplace: Issues at Multiple Levels." *Sociological Perspectives*, 35, 1, 1992:1–15.

Mills, C. Wright. *The Power Elite.* New York: Oxford University Press, 1956.

Mills, C. Wright. *The Sociological Imagination.* New York: Oxford University Press, 1959.

Mills, Karen M., and Thomas J. Palumbo. *A Statistical Portrait of Women in the United States: 1978.* U.S. Bureau of the Census, *Current Population Reports,* Series P-23, no. 100, 1980.

Minchin, Timothy J. *Hiring the Black Worker: The Racial Integration of the Southern Textile Industry, 1960–1980.* Chapel Hill, N. C.: University of North Carolina Press, 1999.

Miner, Horace. "Body Ritual Among the Nacirema." In *Down to Earth Sociology: Introductory Readings,* 11th ed., James M. Henslin, ed. New York: The Free Press, 2001:75–79.

Minkler, Meredith, and Ann Robertson. "The Ideology of 'Age/Race Wars': Deconstructing a Social Problem." *Ageing and Society, 11,* 1, March 1991:1–22.

Mintz, Beth A., and Michael Schwartz. *The Power Structure of American Business.* Chicago: University of Chicago Press, 1985.

Mitchell, G., Stephanie Obradovich, Fred Harring, Chris Tromborg, and Alyson L. Burns. "Reproducing Gender in Public Places: Adults' Attention to Toddlers in Three Public Locales." *Sex Roles, 26,* 7/8, 1992:323–330.

Mizruchi, Mark S., and Thomas Koenig. "Size, Concentration, and Corporate Networks: Determinants of Business Collective Action." *Social Science Quarterly, 72,* 2, June 1991:299–313.

"Moderate Drinking Associated With Lower Risk of Death Following Heart Attack." *Heart Disease Weekly,* May 13, 2001:10–11.

Mohawk, John C. "Indian Economic Development: An Evolving Concept of Sovereignty." *Buffalo Law Review, 39,* 2, Spring 1991:495–503.

Money, John, and Anke A. Ehrhardt. *Man and Woman, Boy and Girl.* Baltimore: Johns Hopkins University Press, 1972.

"'Monkey' Gives Delhi Claws for Alarm." *The Australian,* May 17, 2001.

Monk-Turner, Elizabeth, and Charlie G. Turner. "The Relative Pay of Men and Women in South Korea." *Journal of Asian Economics, 11,* 2, Summer 2000:223–236.

Montagu, Ashley, ed. *Race and IQ: Expanded Edition.* New York: Oxford University Press, 1999.

Montagu, M. F. Ashley. *Introduction to Physical Anthropology,* 3rd ed. Springfield, Ill.: Thomas, 1960.

Montagu, M. F. Ashley. *The Concept of Race.* New York: Free Press, 1964.

Moore, Stephen D., and Ron Winslow. "Health-Care Systems in 12 Countries Near Crisis, Drug Maker Study Says." *Wall Street Journal,* September 15, 1993:B6.

Moravec, Hans P. *Robot: Mere Machine to Transcendent Mind.* New York: Oxford University Press, 1999.

Morgan, Lewis Henry. *Ancient Society.* 1877.

Morin, Monte. "$1.7 Million Awarded in Retirement Home Death." *Los Angeles Times,* October 17, 2001.

Morris, Aldon. "Black Southern Student Sit-In Movement: An Analysis of Internal Organization." In *Collective Behavior and Social Movements,* Russell L. Curtis, Jr., and Benigno E. Aguirre, eds. Boston: Allyn and Bacon, 1993:361–380.

Morris, J. R. "Racial Attitudes of Undergraduates in Greek Housing." *College Student Journal, 25,* 1, March 1991:501–505.

Morrow, Betty Hearn. "Urban Families as Support after Disaster: The Case of Hurricane Andrew." Paper presented at the 1995 meetings of the American Sociological Association.

Moscos, Charles, C., and Sydney Butler. *All That We Can Be: Black Leadership and Racial Integration the Army Way.* New York: Basic Books, 1997.

Mosca, Gaetano. *The Ruling Class.* New York: McGraw-Hill, 1939. First published in 1896.

Mosher, Steven W. "Why Are Baby Girls Being Killed in China?" *Wall Street Journal,* July 25, 1983:9.

Mosher, Steven W. "Too Many People? Not by a Long Shot." *Wall Street Journal,* February 10, 1997:A18.

Mount, Ferdinand. *The Subversive Family: An Alternative History of Love and Marriage.* New York: Free Press, 1992.

Moyers, Bill. "Propaganda." In the series "A Walk Through the 20th Century." 1989. (video)

Moynihan, Daniel Patrick. "Social Justice in the *Next* Century." *America,* September 14, 1991:132–137.

Muehlenhard, Charlene L., and Melaney A. Linton. "Date Rape and Sexual Aggression in Dating Situations: Incidence and Risk Factors." *Journal of Counseling Psychology, 34,* 2, 1987:186–196.

Muir, Donal E. "'White' Fraternity and Sorority Attitudes Toward 'Blacks' on a Deep-South Campus." *Sociological Spectrum, 11,* 1, January–March, 1991:93–103.

Murdock, George Peter. "Comparative Data on the Division of Labor by Sex." *Social Forces, 15,* 4, May 1937:551–553.

Murdock, George Peter. "The Common Denominator of Cultures." In *The Science of Man and the World Crisis,* Ralph Linton, ed. New York: Columbia University Press, 1945.

Murdock, George Peter. *Social Structure.* New York: Macmillan, 1949.

Murphy, Kim. "Last Stand of an Aging Aryan." *Los Angeles Times,* January 10, 1999.

Murray, Charles. "The Coming White Underclass." *Wall Street Journal,* October 29, 1993:A16.

Murray, Charles, and R. J. Herrnstein. "What's Really Behind the SAT-score Decline?" *Public Interest, 106,* Winter 1992:32–56.

Murray, G. W. *Sons of Ishmael.* London: Routledge, 1935.

Nabhan, Gary Paul. *Cultures in Habitat: On Nature, Culture, and Story.* New York: Counterpoint, 1998.

Nachman, Sharon. "Elder Abuse and Neglect Substantiations: What They Tell Us About the Problem." *Journal of Elder Abuse and Neglect, 3,* 3, 1991:19–43.

Nagourney, Eric. "Fertility: A Study Links Prayer and Pregnancy." *New York Times,* October 2, 2001.

Naj, Amal Kumar. "Some Manufacturers Drop Efforts to Adopt Japanese Techniques." *Wall Street Journal,* May 7, 1993:A1, A12.

Naj, Amal Kumar. "MIT Chemists Achieve Goal of Splitting Nitrogen Molecules in the Atmosphere." *Wall Street Journal,* May 12, 1995:B3.

Nakao, Keiko, and Judith Treas. "Occupational Prestige in the United States Revisited: Twenty-Five Years of Stability and Change." Paper presented at the annual meetings of the American Sociological Association, 1990. (As referenced in Kerbo, Harold R. *Social Stratification and Inequality: Class Conflict in Historical and Comparative Perspective.* 2nd ed. New York: McGraw-Hill, 1991:181.)

Narayan, Shoba. "A First in Child Care." *Boston Globe,* December 5, 1994:19–20.

Nash, Gary B. *Red, White, and Black.* Englewood Cliffs, N.J.: Prentice Hall, 1974.

Nathan, John. *Sony: The Private Life.* New York: Houghton Mifflin, 1999.

National Center for Education Statistics. *Digest of Education Statistics.* Washington, D.C.: U.S. Government Printing Office, 1991.

National Institute of Child Health and Human Development. "Child Care and Mother-Child Interaction in the First 3 Years of Life." *Developmental Psychology*, 35, 6, November 1999:1399–1413.

National School Safety Center. "The School Associated Violent Death Report," 2000.

National Women's Political Caucus. "Factsheet on Women's Political Progress." Washington, D.C., June 1998.

National Women's Political Caucus. "News and Opinions; 1998 Election Results." November 5, 1998.

Naughton, Keith. "Cyberslacking." *Newsweek*, November 29, 1999:62–65.

Nauta, André. "That They All May Be One: Can Denominationalism Die?" Paper presented at the annual meetings of the American Sociological Association, 1993.

Neikirk, William, and Glen Elsasser. "Ruling Weakens Abortion Right." *Chicago Tribune*, June 30, 1992:1, 8.

Neugarten, Bernice L. "Middle Age and Aging." In *Growing Old in America*, Beth B. Hess, ed. New Brunswick, N.J.: Transaction, 1976:180–197.

Neugarten, Bernice L. "Personality and Aging." In *Handbook of the Psychology of Aging*, James E. Birren and K. Warren Schaie, eds. New York: Van Nostrand Reinhold, 1977:626–649.

Niebuhr, H. Richard. *The Social Sources of Denominationalism*. New York: Holt, 1929.

Nieves, Evelyn. "Lumber Company Approves U.S. Deal to Save Redwoods." *New York Times*, March 3, 1999.

Noah, Timothy. "White House Forms Panel to Investigate Cold War Radiation Tests on Humans." *Wall Street Journal*, January 4, 1994:A12.

Noymer, Andrew. "The Transmission and Persistence of 'Urban Legends': Sociological Application of Age-Structured Epidemic Models." *Journal of Mathematical Sociology*, 25, 3, 2001:299–323.

Nsamenang, A. Bame. *Human Development in Cultural Context: A Third World Perspective*. Newbury Park, Calif.: Sage, 1992.

Nuland, Sherwin B. "Immortality and Its Discontents." *Wall Street Journal*, July 2, 1999.

Nullis, Clare. "U. N.: Worst of AIDS Epidemic Is Still Ahead." Associated Press, June 28, 2000.

Oberschall, Anthony. *Social Conflict and Social Movements*. Englewood Cliffs, N.J.: Prentice Hall, 1973.

O'Brien, John E. "Violence in Divorce-Prone Families." In *Violence in the Family*, Suzanne K. Steinmetz and Murray A. Straus, eds. New York: Dodd, Mead, 1975:65–75.

O'Connell, Martin. "Where's Papa? Father's Role in Child Care." Population Trends and Public Policy no. 20. Washington, D.C.: Reference Bureau, September 1993.

Offen, Karen. "Feminism and Sexual Difference in Historical Perspective." In *Theoretical Perspectives on Sexual Difference*, Deborah L. Rhode, ed. New Haven, Conn.: Yale University Press, 1990:13–20.

Ogburn, William F. *Social Change with Respect to Culture and Human Nature*. New York: W. B. Huebsch, 1922. (Other editions by Viking in 1927, 1938, and 1950.)

Ogburn, William F. "The Hypothesis of Cultural Lag." In *Theories of Society: Foundations of Modern Sociological Theory*, Vol. 2, Talcott Parsons, Edward Shils, Kaspar D. Naegele, and Jesse R. Pitts, eds. New York: Free Press, 1961:1270–1273.

Ogburn, William F. *On Culture and Social Change: Selected Papers*, Otis Dudley Duncan, ed. Chicago: University of Chicago Press, 1964.

O'Hare, William P. "A New Look at Poverty in America." *Population Bulletin*, 51, 2, September 1996a:1–47.

O'Hare, William P. "U.S. Poverty Myths Explored: Many Poor Work Year-Round, Few Still Poor After Five Years." *Population Today: News, Numbers, and Analysis*, 24, 10, October 1996b:1–2.

O'Hare, Bill. "The Rise—and Fall—of Single-Parent Families." *Population Today*, 29, 5, July 2001:1, 4.

Ohmae, Kenichi. *The End of the Nation State: The Rise of Regional Economies*. New York: Free Press, 1995.

Oliver, Pamela E., and Gerald Marwell. "Mobilizing Technologies for Collective Action." In *Frontiers in Social Movement Theory*, Aldon D. Morris and Carol McClurg Mueller, eds. New Haven, Conn.: Yale University Press, 1992:251–272.

Olmsted, Michael S., and A. Paul Hare. *The Small Group*, 2nd ed. New York: Random House, 1978.

Olneck, Michael R., and David B. Bills. "What Makes Sammy Run? An Empirical Assessment of the Bowles-Gintis Correspondence Theory." *American Journal of Education*, 89, 1980:27–61.

O'Malley, Jeff. "Sex Tourism and Women's Status in Thailand." *Society and Leisure*, 11, 1, Spring 1988:99–114.

O'Neill, Helen. "Strange, Strange Worlds." *Alton Telegraph*, April 6, 1997:A10.

Olshansky, S. Jay, Bruce Carnes, Richard G. Rogers, and Len Smith. "Infectious Diseases—New and Ancient Threats to World Health." *Population Bulletin*, 52, 2, July 1997:1–51.

Ono, Yumiko. "By Dint of Promotion Japanese Entrepreneur Ignites a Soccer Frenzy." *Wall Street Journal*, September 17, 1993:A1, A6.

Ono, Yumiko, and Jacob M. Schlesinger. "With Careful Planning, Japan Sets Out to Be 'Life Style Superpower.' " *Wall Street Journal*, October 10, 1992:A1, A11.

O'Rand, Angela M., and John C. Henretta. *Age and Inequality: Diverse Pathways Through Later Life*. Boulder: Westview Press, 1999.

Orlans, Harold. "Members Comment on ASA's Publication on Affirmative Action." *Footnotes*, May–June 1999:8.

Ortega, Bob. "Portland, Ore., Shows Nation's City Planners How to Guide Growth." *Wall Street Journal*, December 26, 1995:A1, A8.

Ortega, Suzanne T., and Jay Corzine. "Socioeconomic Status and Mental Disorders." *Research in Community and Mental Health*, 6, 1990:149–182.

Orwell, George. *1984*. New York: Harcourt Brace, 1949.

Ostling, Richard N. "Faith May Prevent Drug Abuse." *New York Times*, November 14, 2001.

Ouchi, William. *Theory Z: How American Business Can Meet the Japanese Challenge*. Reading, Mass.: Addison-Wesley, 1981.

Ouchi, William. "Decision-Making in Japanese Organizations." In *Down to Earth Sociology: Introductory Readings*, 7th ed., James M. Henslin, ed. New York: Free Press, 1993:503–507.

Paddock, Richard C. "Russians Bank on Bartering." *Los Angeles Times*, December 28, 1998.

Paddock, Richard C. "Patient Deaths Point to Depth of Russian Crisis." *Los Angeles Times*, March 13, 1999.

Pagelow, Mildred Daley. "Adult Victims of Domestic Violence: Battered Women." *Journal of Interpersonal Violence*, 7, 1, March 1992:87–120.

Pandey, Sanjay K., and Gordon A. Kingsley. "Examining Red Tape in Public and Private Organizations: Alternative Explanations from a Social Psychological Model." *Journal of Public Administration Research and Theory*, 10, 4, October 2000:779–799.

Parfit, Michael, "Earth First!ers Wield a Mean Monkey Wrench." *Smithsonian*, 21, 1, April 1990:184–204.

Park, Robert Ezra. "Human Ecology." *American Journal of Sociology, 42,* 1, July 1936:1–15.

Park, Robert Ezra, and Ernest W. Burgess. *Human Ecology.* Chicago: University of Chicago Press, 1921a.

Parker-Pope, Tara. "Making a Stand." *Wall Street Journal,* April 9, 1998.

Parsons, Talcott. "An Analytic Approach to the Theory of Social Stratification." *American Journal of Sociology, 45,* 1940:841–862.

Parsons, Talcott. *The Social System.* New York: Free Press, 1951.

Parsons, Talcott. "Illness and the Role of the Physician: A Sociological Perspective." In *Personality in Nature, Society, and Culture,* 2nd ed., Clyde Kluckhohn and Henry A. Murray, eds. New York: Knopf, 1953:609–617.

Parsons, Talcott. "The Sick Role and the Role of the Physician Reconsidered." *Milbank Memorial Fund Quarterly/Health and Society, 53,* 3, Summer 1975:257–278.

Partington, Donald H. "The Incidence of the Death Penalty for Rape in Virginia." *Washington and Lee Law Review, 22,* 1965:43–75.

Passell, Peter. "Race, Mortgages and Statistics." *New York Times,* May 10, 1996:D1, D4.

Pasztor, Andy. "U.S., Grumman Reach Accord in Pentagon Case." *Wall Street Journal,* November 23, 1993:A3.

Pattillo-McCoy, Mary. *Black Picket Fences: Privilege and Peril Among the Black Middle Class.* Chicago: University of Chicago Press, 1999.

Paul, Ron. "Congressman Ron Paul." Newsletter issued April 1994.

Pearlin, L. I., and Melvin L. Kohn. "Social Class, Occupation, and Parental Values: A Cross-National Study." *American Sociological Review, 31,* 1966:466–479.

Peart, Karen N. "Converts to the Faith." *Scholastic Update, 126,* 4, October 22, 1993:16–18.

Pennar, Karen, and Christopher Farrell. "Notes from the Underground Economy." *Business Week,* February 15, 1993:98–101.

Perreault, George. "Saving the Neighborhood School: The Hometown Story." *High School Journal, 83,* 4, April-May 2000:40–45.

Perrin, Kathleen. "Rationing Health Care: Should It Be Done?" In *Perspectives in Social Gerontology,* Robert B. Enright, Jr., ed. Boston: Allyn and Bacon, 1994:309–314.

Perrow, Charles. "A Society of Organizations." *Theory and Society, 20,* 6, December 1991:725–762.

Persell, Caroline Hodges, and Peter W. Cookson, Jr. "Where the Power Starts." *Signature,* August 1986:51–57.

Persell, Caroline Hodges, Sophia Catsambis, and Peter W. Cookson, Jr. "Family Background, School Type, and College Attendance: A Conjoint System of Cultural Capital Transmission." *Journal of Research on Adolescence, 2,* 1, 1992:1–23.

Peter, Laurence J., and Raymond Hull. *The Peter Principle: Why Things Always Go Wrong.* New York: Morrow, 1969.

Petersen, Melody. "2 Drug Makers to Pay $875 Million to Settle Fraud Case." *New York Times,* October 4, 2001.

Peterson, James L., and Nicholas Zill. "Marital Disruption, Parent–Child Relationships, and Behavior Problems in Children." *Journal of Marriage and the Family, 48,* 1986:295–307.

Peterson, Janice. "Welfare Reform and Inequality: The TANF and UI Programs." *Journal of Economic Issues, 34,* 2, June 2000:517–526.

Pfann, Gerard A., et al. "Business Success and Businesses' Beauty Capital." *Economics Letters, 67,* 2, May 2000:201–207.

Phillips, Barbara D. "TV: America's Forgotten Plague." *Wall Street Journal,* February 9, 1998:A15.

Phillips, John L., Jr. *The Origins of Intellect: Piaget's Theory.* San Francisco: Freeman, 1969.

Piaget, Jean. *The Psychology of Intelligence.* London: Routledge & Kegan Paul, 1950.

Piaget, Jean. *The Construction of Reality in the Child.* New York: Basic Books, 1954.

Pillemer, Karl, and Beth Hudson. "A Model Abuse Prevention Program for Nursing Assistants." *Gerontologist, 33,* 1, 1993:128–131.

Pillemer, Karl, and J. Jill Suitor. "Violence and Violent Feelings: What Causes Them Among Family Caregivers?" *Journal of Gerontology, 47,* 4, 1992:165–172.

Pillemer, Karl, and Rosalie S. Wolf. *Elder Abuse: Conflict in the Family.* Dover, Mass.: Auburn House, 1987.

Pilling, D., and M. Kellmer Pringle. *Controversial Issues in Child Development.* London: Paul Elek, 1978.

Pines, Maya. "The Civilizing of Genie." *Psychology Today, 15,* September 1981:28–34.

Piotrow, Phylis Tilson. *World Population Crisis: The United States' Response.* New York: Praeger, 1973.

Platt, Tony. " 'Street' Crime—A View from the Left." *Crime and Social Justice: Issues in Criminology, 9,* 1978:26–34.

Pollard, Kelvin M., and William P. O'Hare. "America's Racial and Ethnic Minorities." *Population Bulletin, 54,* 3, September 1999:3–47.

Polsby, Nelson W. "Three Problems in the Analysis of Community Power." *American Sociological Review, 24,* 6, December 1959:796–803.

Polumbaum, Judy. "China: Confucian Tradition Meets the Market Economy." *Ms.,* September–October 1992:12–13.

Pope, Liston. *Millhands and Preachers: A Study of Gastonia.* New Haven, Conn.: Yale University Press, 1942.

Population Reference Bureau. "World Information Data Sheet." Washington, D.C., May 1995.

"Population Today." Washington, D.C.: Population Reference Bureau, *30,* 1, January-February, 2002.

"Population Update." *Population Today, 28,* 1, January 2000.

Portés, Alejandro, and Ruben G. Rumbaut. *Immigrant America.* Berkeley: University of California Press, 1990.

Postman, Neil. *Technopoly: The Surrender of Culture to Technology.* New York: Knopf, 1992.

Powell, Bill. "Yeltsin's Legacy." *Newsweek,* January 4, 1999:72.

Power, Carla. "The New Islam." *Newsweek,* March 16, 1998:34–37.

Presley, Cheryl A., Philip W. Meilman, and Rob Lyerla. *Alcohol and Drugs on American College Campuses.* Carbondale, Ill.: Southern Illinois University, 1993.

Pressley, Sue Anne. "The Curious Continue Waco Siege." *Washington Post,* August 28, 1993:A1, A12.

Prud'Homme, Alex. "Getting a Grip on Power." *Time,* July 29, 1991:15–16.

Rabinovitz, Jonathan. "Working Parents Use Internet to Check on Children in Day Care." *New York Times,* December 9, 1997.

Radelet, Michael L. "Humanizing the Death Penalty." *Social Problems, 48,* 1, February 2001:63–87.

Raney, Rebecca Fairley. "Study Warns of Risks in Internet Voting." *New York Times,* March 8, 1999.

Ray, J. J. "Authoritarianism Is a Dodo: Comment on Scheepers, Felling and Peters." *European Sociological Review, 7,* 1, May 1991:73–75.

Read, Piers Paul. *Alive. The Story of the Andes Survivors.* Philadelphia: Lippincott, 1974.

Reat, Noble Ross. *Buddhism: A History.* Berkeley, Ca: Asian Humanities Press, 1994.

Recer, Paul. "Gene Mutation Doubles Life Span." Associated Press, December 14, 2000.

Reckless, Walter C. *The Crime Problem,* 5th ed. New York: Appleton, 1973.

Redclift, Michael, and Graham Woodgate, eds. *The International Handbook of Environmental Sociology.* Cheltenham, England: Edward Elgar, 1997.

Reed, Susan. "My Sister, My Clone." *Time,* February 19, 2001.

Reed, Susan, and Lorenzo Benet. "Ecowarrior Dave Foreman Will Do Whatever It Takes in His Fight to Save Mother Earth." *People Weekly, 33,* 15, April 16, 1990:113–116.

Reibstein, Larry. "Managing Diversity." *Newsweek,* November 25, 1996:50.

Reich, Michael. "The Economics of Racism." In *The Capitalist System,* Richard C. Edwards, Michael Reich, and Thomas E. Weiskopf, eds. Englewood Cliffs, N.J.: Prentice Hall, 1972:313–321.

Reich, Robert B. *Good for Business: Making Full Use of the Nation's Human Capital, The Environmental Scan.* Washington, D.C.: U.S. Department of Labor, March 1995.

Reiser, Christa. *Reflections on Anger: Women and Men in a Changing Society.* Westport, Conn.: Praeger Publishers, 1999.

Reitman, Valerie, and Oscar Suris. "In a Cultural U-Turn, Mazda's Creditors Put Ford Behind the Wheel." *Wall Street Journal,* November 21, 1994:A1, A4.

Renteln, Alison Dundes. "Sex Selection and Reproductive Freedom." *Women's Studies International Forum, 15,* 3, 1992:405–426.

"Reservations With Casinos Gain Ground on Poverty." *New York Times,* September 3, 2000.

Reskin, Barbara F. *The Realities of Affirmative Action in Employment.* Washington, D.C.: American Sociological Association, 1998.

Resnik, David B. "Financial Interests and Research Bias." *Perspectives on Science, 8,* 3, Fall 2000:255–283.

Reuters. "Fake Tiger Woods Gets 200-Years-To-Life in Prison." April 28, 2001.

Rhone, Nedra. "Widespread Violations Found at Care Homes." *Los Angeles Times,* April 18, 2001.

Rich, Spencer. "Number of Elected Hispanic Officials Doubled in a Decade, Study Shows." *Washington Post,* September 19, 1986:A6.

Richards, Bill. "Doctors Can Diagnose Illnesses Long Distance, to the Dismay of Some." *Wall Street Journal,* January 17, 1996:A1, A8.

Richter, Paul. "CIA Director Warns of Terrorist Threat." *Los Angeles Times,* February 3, 1999.

Ricks, Thomas E. "Pentagon Considers Selling Overseas a Large Part of High-Tech Weaponry." *Wall Street Journal,* February 14, 1994:A16.

Ricks, Thomas E. "'New' Marines Illustrate Growing Gap Between Military and Society." *Wall Street Journal,* July 27, 1995:A1, A4.

Ricks, Thomas E. "Defense Chief Won't Segregate Sexes in Basic Training, Despite Panel's Views." *Wall Street Journal,* March 17, 1998:A20.

Rieker, Patricia P., Chloe E. Bird, Susan Bell, Jenny Ruducha, Rima E. Rudd, and S. M. Miller, "Violence and Women's Health: Toward a Society and Health Perspective." Unpublished paper, 1997.

Riesman, David. *The Lonely Crowd.* New Haven, Conn.: Yale University Press, 1950.

Riessman, Catherine Kohler. "Women and Medicalization: A New Perspective." In *Dominant Issues in Medical Sociology,* 3rd ed., Howard D. Schwartz, ed. New York: McGraw-Hill, 1994: 190–211.

Rifkin, Jeremy. *The End of Work: The Decline of the Global Labor Force and the Dawn of the Post-Market Era.* New York: Putnam, 1995.

Rigdon, Joan E., and Alecia Swasy. "Distractions of Modern Life at Key Ages Are Cited for Drop in Student Literacy." *Wall Street Journal,* October 1, 1990:B1, B3.

Riley, Nancy E. "Gender, Power, and Population Change." *Population Bulletin, 52,* 1, May 1997:1–47.

Rishe, Patrick James. "Gender Gaps and the Presence and Profitability of College Football." *Social Science Quarterly, 80,* 4, December 1999:702–717.

Risman, Barbara H. *Gender Vertigo: American Families in Transition.* New Haven, Conn.: Yale University Press, 1998.

Rist, Ray C. "Student Social Class and Teacher Expectations: The Self-Fulfilling Prophecy in Ghetto Education." *Harvard Educational Review, 40,* 3, August 1970:411–451.

Ritzer, George. *Sociological Theory,* 3rd ed. New York: McGraw-Hill, 1992.

Ritzer, George. *The McDonaldization of Society: An Investigation into the Changing Character of Contemporary Life.* Thousand Oaks, Calif.: Pine Forge Press, 1993.

Ritzer, George. "The McDonaldization of Society." In *Down to Earth Sociology: Introductory Readings,* 11th ed., James M. Henslin, ed. New York: The Free Press, 2001:459–471.

Robertson, Ian. *Sociology,* 3rd ed. New York: Worth, 1987.

Robinson, Arthur B., and Zachary W. Robinson. "Science Has Spoken: Global Warming is a Myth." *Wall Street Journal,* December 4, 1997:A22.

Rodash, Mary Flannery. "The College of Midwifery: A Sociological Study of the Decline of a Profession." Unpublished doctoral dissertation, Southern Illinois University at Carbondale, 1982.

Rodriguez, Richard. "The Education of Richard Rodriguez." *Saturday Review,* February 8, 1975:147–149.

Rodriguez, Richard. *Hunger of Memory: The Education of Richard Rodriguez.* Boston: Godine, 1982.

Rodriguez, Richard. "The Late Victorians: San Francisco, AIDS, and the Homosexual Stereotype." *Harper's Magazine,* October 1990:57–66.

Rodriguez, Richard. "Mixed Blood." *Harper's Magazine, 283,* November 1991:47–56.

Rodriguez, Richard. "Searching for Roots in a Changing Society." In *Down to Earth Sociology: Introductory Readings,* 8th ed., James M. Henslin, ed. New York: Free Press, 1995:486–491.

Rodríguez, Victor M. "Los Angeles, U.S.A. 1992: 'A House Divided Against Itself . . .' " *SSSP Newsletter,* Spring 1994:5–12.

Rodwin, Marc A. *Medicine, Money, and Morals: Physicians' Conflicts of Interest.* New York: Oxford University Press, 1993.

Roethlisberger, Fritz J., and William J. Dickson. *Management and the Worker.* Cambridge, Mass.: Harvard University Press, 1939.

Rogers, Joseph W. *Why Are You Not a Criminal?* Englewood Cliffs, N.J.: Prentice Hall, 1977.

Romero, Simon. "Tribes Seeking Phone Systems as Step to Web." *New York Times,* October 2, 2000.

Rosaldo, Michelle Zimbalist. "Women, Culture and Society: A Theoretical Overview." In *Women, Culture, and Society,* Michelle Zimbalist Rosaldo and Louise Lamphere, eds. Stanford: Stanford University Press, 1974.

Rose, Frederick. "Los Angeles Tallies Losses; Curfew Is Lifted." *Wall Street Journal,* May 5, 1992:A3, A18.

Rose, Steven. "Stalking the Criminal Chromosome." *Nation 242* (20), 1986:732–736.

Rosenbaum, David E. "U.S. Breaks a Ring That Smuggled in Thousands of Workers." *New York Times,* November 21, 1998.

Rosenberg, Charles E. *The Care of Strangers: The Rise of America's Hospital System.* New York: Basic Books, 1987.

Rosenthal, Elisabeth. "China's Chic Waistline: Convex to Concave." *New York Times,* December 9, 1999.

Rosenthal, Elisabeth. "Deadly Shadow of AIDS Darkens Remote Chinese Village." *New York Times,* May 28, 2001c.

Rosenthal, Elisabeth. "For a Fee, Chinese Firm Will Beg Pardon for Anyone." *New York Times,* January 3, 2001a.

Rosenthal, Elisabeth. "Harsh Chinese Reality Feeds a Black Market in Women." *New York Times,* June 25, 2001b.

Rosenthal, Elisabeth. "Without 'Barefoot Doctors,' China's Rural Families Suffer." *New York Times,* March 14, 2001d.

Rosenthal, Robert, and Lenore Jacobson. *Pygmalion in the Classroom: Teacher Expectation and Pupils' Intellectual Development.* New York: Holt, Rinehart, and Winston, 1968.

Ross, Catherine E., and Marieke van Willigen. "Education and the Subjective Quality of Life." *Journal of Health and Social Behavior, 38,* 3, September 1997:275–297.

Ross, Emma. "Social Life Helps Prevent Dementia." Associated Press, April 23, 2000.

Rossi, Alice S. "A Biosocial Perspective on Parenting." *Daedalus, 106,* 1977:1–31.

Rossi, Alice S. "Gender and Parenthood." *American Sociological Review, 49,* 1984:1–18.

Rossi, Peter H. *Down and Out in America: The Origins of Homelessness.* Chicago: University of Chicago Press, 1989.

Rossi, Peter H. "Going Along or Getting It Right?" *Journal of Applied Sociology, 8,* 1991:77–81.

Rossi, Peter H. "Half Truths with Real Consequences: Journalism, Research, and Public Policy." *Contemporary Sociology,* 1999:1–5.

Rossi, Peter H., Gene A. Fisher, and Georgianna Willis. *The Condition of the Homeless of Chicago.* Amherst: University of Massachusetts, September 1986.

Rossi, Peter H., James D. Wright, Gene A. Fisher, and Georgianna Willis. "The Urban Homeless: Estimating Composition and Size." *Science, 235,* March 13, 1987:1136–1140.

Rotello, Gabriel. "The Risk in a 'Cure' for AIDS." *New York Times,* July 14, 1996.

Rothman, Barbara Katz. "Midwives in Transition: The Structure of a Clinical Revolution." In *Dominant Issues in Medical Sociology,* 3rd ed. Howard D. Schwartz, ed. New York: McGraw-Hill, 1994:104–112.

Rothschild, Joyce, and J. Allen Whitt. *The Cooperative Workplace: Potentials and Dilemmas of Organizational Democracy and Participation.* Cambridge, England: Cambridge University Press, 1986.

Rubin, Lillian Breslow. *Worlds of Pain: Life in the Working-Class Family.* New York: Basic Books, 1976.

Rubin, Lillian Breslow. "The Empty Nest." In *Marriage and Family in a Changing Society,* 4th ed., James M. Henslin, ed. New York: Free Press, 1992a:261–270.

Rubin, Lillian Breslow. "Worlds of Pain." In *Marriage and Family in a Changing Society,* 4th ed., James M. Henslin, ed. New York: Free Press, 1992b:44–50.

Rubin, Zick. "The Love Research." In *Marriage and Family in a Changing Society,* 2nd ed., James M. Henslin, ed. New York: Free Press, 1985.

Rudner, Lawrence M. "The Scholastic Achievement of Home School Students." *ERIC/AE Digest.* September 1, 1999.

Ruffenbach, Glenn. "Nursing-Home Care as a Work Benefit." *Wall Street Journal,* June 30, 1988:23.

Ruggles, Patricia. "Short and Long Term Poverty in the United States: Measuring the American 'Underclass.' " Washington, D.C.: Urban Institute, June 1989.

Russell, Diana E. H. "Preliminary Report on Some Findings Relating to the Trauma and Long-Term Effects of Intrafamily Childhood Sexual Abuse." Unpublished paper.

Russell, Diana E. H. *Rape in Marriage.* Bloomington: Indiana University Press, 1990.

Ryan, John, and William M. Wentworth. *Media and Soceity: The Production of Culture in the Mass Media.* Boston: Allyn and Bacon, 1999.

Rybczynski, Witold. "The Virtues of Suburban Sprawl." *Wall Street Journal,* May 25, 1999.

Sahlins, Marshall D. *Stone Age Economics.* Chicago: Aldine, 1972.

Sahlins, Marshall D., and Elman R. Service. *Evolution and Culture.* Ann Arbor: University of Michigan Press, 1960.

Salholz, Eloise. "The Push for Power." *Newsweek,* April 9, 1990:19–20.

Sampat, Jyothi. "My Marriage Was Arranged." *Good Housekeeping, 228,* 2, February 1999:76–77.

Sampson, Catherine. "Corrupt Care." *World Press Review, 39,* 5 May 1992:46.

Sampson, Robert J., Jeffrey D. Morenoff, and Felton Earls. "Beyond Social Capital: Spatial Dynamics of Collective Efficacy for Children." *American Sociological Review, 64,* October 1999:633–660.

Samuelson, Paul Anthony, and William D. Nordhaus. *Economics,* 17th ed. New York: McGraw Hill, 2000.

Samuelson, Robert J. "The Elderly Aren't Needy." *Newsweek,* March 21, 1988:68.

Sanchez, Laura. "Gender, Labor Allocations, and the Psychology of Entitlement Within the Home." *Social Forces, 13,* 2, December 1994:533–553.

Sandefur, Gary D. "Children in Single-Parent Families: The Roles of Time and Money." *Focus, 17,* 1, Summer 1995:44–45.

Sapir, Edward. *Selected Writings of Edward Sapir in Language, Culture, and Personality.* David G. Mandelbaum, ed. Berkeley, Calif.: University of California Press, 1949.

Satchell, Michael. "A Whale of a Protest." *U.S. News Online,* October 5, 1998.

Savells, Jerry. "Social Change Among the Amish." In *Down to Earth Sociology: Introductory Readings,* 11th ed., James M. Henslin, ed. New York: The Free Press, 2001:472–480.

Sayres, William. "What Is a Family Anyway?" In *Marriage and Family in a Changing Society,* 4th ed., James M. Henslin, ed. New York: Free Press, 1992:23–30.

Saxe, G. B. "Candy Selling and Math Learning." *Educational Researcher, 17*(6), 1995:14–21.

Scarr, Sandra, and Marlene Eisenberg. "Child Care Research: Issues, Perspectives, and Results." *Annual Review of Psychology, 44,* 1993:613–644.

Schaefer, Naomi. "Slavery in Africa Is Largely Ignored by U.S. Black Leaders and Major Media." *Massachusetts News,* May 12, 1999.

Schaefer, Richard T. *Racial and Ethnic Groups,* 8th ed. Upper Saddle River, N.J.: Prentice Hall, 2000.

Schatz, Thomas A. "Medicare Fraud: Tales from the Gypped." *Wall Street Journal,* August 25, 1995:A8.

Schellenberg, James A. *Conflict Resolution: Theory, Research, and Practice.* Albany: New York University Press, 1996.

Schlesinger, Jacob M. "For What Ails Japan, Some Think the Cure Is a Good Hot Slogan." *Wall Street Journal,* January 31, 1994:A1, A7.

Schlesinger, Jacob M., and Jathon Sapsford. "Japan, Shaken by Plunging Stocks, Mulls Further Economic Measures." *Wall Street Journal,* December 1, 1993:A14.

Schlossberg, Nancy. *Overwhelmed: Coping with Life's Ups and Downs.* Boston: Lexington Books, 1990.

Schmalleger, Frank. *Criminology Today: An Integrative Introduction.* Upper Saddle River, New Jersey: Prentice Hall, 1999.

Schmemann, Serge. "Russia's Precapitalist Economy: How Can You Have a Bust If You Never Had a Boom?" *New York Times,* December 27, 1998.

Schor, Juliet B. "Americans Work Too Hard." *New York Times,* July 25, 1991:A21.

Schottland, Charles I. *The Social Security Plan in the U.S.* New York: Appleton, 1963.

Schwartz, Felice N. "Management Women and the New Facts of Life." *Harvard Business Review, 89,* 1, January–February 1989:65–76.

Schwartz, John. "Internet Filters Used to Shield Minors Censor Speech, Critics Say." *New York Times,* March 19, 2001.

Schwartz, Mildred A. *A Sociological Perspective on Politics.* Englewood Cliffs, N.J.: Prentice Hall, 1990.

Scott, Ellen Kaye. "How to Stop the Rapists: A Question of Strategy in Two Rape Crisis Centers." *Social Problems, 40,* 3, August 1993:343–361.

Scott, Janny. "White Flight, This Time Toward Harlem." *New York Times,* February 25, 2001.

Scott, Monster Cody. *Monster: The Autobiography of an L. A. Gang Member.* New York: Penguin Books, 1994.

Scully, Diana. *Understanding Sexual Violence: A Study of Convicted Rapists.* Boston: Unwin Hyman, 1990.

Scully, Diana. "Negotiating to Do Surgery." In *Dominant Issues in Medical Sociology,* 3rd ed., Howard D. Schwartz, ed. New York: McGraw-Hill, 1994:146–152.

Scully, Diana, and Joseph Marolla. "Convicted Rapists' Vocabulary of Motive: Excuses and Justifications." *Social Problems, 31,* 5, June 1984:530–544.

Scully, Diana, and Joseph Marolla. " 'Riding the Bull at Gilley's': Convicted Rapists Describe the Rewards of Rape." *Social Problems, 32,* 3, February 1985:251–263.

Seaver, W. J. "Effects of Naturally Induced Teacher Expectancies." *Journal of Personality and Social Psychology, 28,* 1973:333–342.

Seib, Gerald F. *Wall Street Journal,* "Click Here for Democracy." *Wall Street Journal,* January 1, 2000:R45–R46.

Sellers, Sean. "Video Games and Simulation." *Women and Language,* 23, 2, Fall 2000:58–61.

Seltzer, Judith A. "Consequences of Marital Dissolution for Children." *Annual Review of Sociology, 20,* 1994:235–266.

Sengupta, Somini. "In Rural Counties, the Squeeze of Poverty Can Be Stronger." *New York Times,* April 29, 2001.

Sennett, Richard, and Jonathan Cobb. "Some Hidden Injuries of Class." In *Down to Earth Sociology: Introductory Readings,* 5th ed., James M. Henslin ed. New York: Free Press, 1988:278–288. Excerpts from Richard Sennett and Jonathan Cobb. *The Hidden Injuries of Class.* New York: Knopf, 1972.

Shapiro, Joseph P. "Euthanasia's Home." *U.S. News and World Report, 122,* 1, January 13, 1997:24–27.

Sharma, S. S. "Untouchables and Brahmins in an Indian Village." In *Haves and Have-Nots: An International Reader on Social Inequality,* James Curtis and Lorne Tepperman, eds. Englewood Cliffs, N.J.: Prentice Hall, 1994:299–303.

Sharp, Deborah. "Miami's Language Gap Widens." *USA Today,* April 3, 1992:A1, A3.

Sharp, Lauriston. "Steel Axes for Stone-Age Australians." In *Down to Earth Sociology: Introductory Readings,* 8th ed., James M. Henslin, ed. New York: Free Press, 1995:453–462.

Sheldon, William. *Varieties of Delinquent Youth: An Introduction to Constitutional Psychiatry.* New York: Harper, 1949.

Shellenbarger, Sue. "The Aging of America Is Making 'Elder Care' a Big Workplace Issue." *Wall Street Journal,* February 16, 1994a:A1, A8.

Shellenbarger, Sue. "How Some Companies Help with Elder Care." *Wall Street Journal,* February 16, 1994b:A8.

Shellenbarger, Sue. "Work and Family." *Wall Street Journal,* May 3, 1995b:B1.

Shenon, Philip. "Arguments Conclude in Army Sex Hearing." *New York Times,* August 26, 1997.

Sherif, Muzafer, and Carolyn Sherif. *Groups in Harmony and Tension.* New York: Harper & Row, 1953.

Sherkat, Darren E., and John Wilson. "Status, Denomination, and Socialization: Effects on Religious Switching and Apostasy." Presented at the annual meetings of the American Sociological Association, 1991.

Sherman, Spencer. "The Hmong in America." *National Geographic,* October 1988:586–610.

Shibutani, Tamotsu. *Improvised News: A Sociological Study of Rumor.* Indianapolis, Ind.: Bobbs-Merrill, 1966.

Shibutani, Tamotsu. "On the Personification of Adversaries." In *Human Nature and Collective Behavior,* Tamotsu Shibutani, ed. Englewood Cliffs, N.J.: Prentice Hall, 1970.

Shirouzu, Norihiko. "Driven by Necessity, and Ford, Mazda Downsizes, U.S.-Style." *Wall Street Journal,* January 5, 2000.

Shirouzu, Norihiko, and Michael Williams. "Pummeled by Giants, Japan's Small Firms Struggle with Change." *Wall Street Journal,* July 25, 1995:A1, A5.

Shively, JoEllen. "Cultural Compensation: The Popularity of Westerns Among American Indians," Paper presented at the annual meetings of the American Sociological Association, 1991.

Shively, JoEllen. "Cowboys and Indians: Perceptions of Western Films Among American Indians and Anglos." *American Sociological Review, 57,* December 1992:725–734.

Shreve, Herbie. Personal communication, 1991.

Signorielli, Nancy. "Television and Conceptions About Sex Roles: Maintaining Conventionality and the Status Quo." *Sex Roles, 21,* 5/6, 1989:341–360.

Signorielli, Nancy. "Children, Television, and Gender Roles: Messages and Impact." *Journal of Adolescent Heath Care, 11,* 1990:50–58.

Sills, David L. *The Volunteers.* Glencoe, Ill.: Free Press, 1957.

Sills, David L. "Voluntary Associations: Sociological Aspects." In *International Encyclopedia of the Social Sciences, 16,* David L. Sills, ed. New York: Macmillan, 1968:362–379.

Simmel, Georg. *The Sociology of Georg Simmel,* Kurt H. Wolff, ed. and trans. Glencoe, Ill.: Free Press, 1950. First published between 1902 and 1917.

Simmons, Ann M. "Survivors of Rwandan Genocide Fear Guilty Will Get Away With Murder." *Los Angeles Times,* December 26, 1998.

Simon, David R., and D. Stanley Eitzen. *Elite Deviance,* 4th ed. Boston: Allyn and Bacon, 1993.

Simon, Julian L. *The Ultimate Resource.* Princeton, N.J.: Princeton University Press, 1981.

Simon, Julian L. *Theory of Population and Economic Growth.* New York: Blackwell, 1986.

Simon, Julian L. "The Nativists Are Wrong." *Wall Street Journal,* August 4, 1993:A10.

Simons, Marlise. "The Amazon's Savvy Indians." In *Down to Earth Sociology: Introductory Readings,* 8th ed. James M. Henslin, ed. New York: Free Press, 1995:463–470.

Simpson, George Eaton, and J. Milton Yinger. *Racial and Cultural Minorities: An Analysis of Prejudice and Discrimination,* 4th ed. New York: Harper & Row, 1972.

Simpson, Glenn R. "Now Showing on an E-Mail Screen Near You: Your Congressman." *Wall Street Journal,* January 7, 2000.

Skeels, H. M. *Adult Status of Children with Contrasting Early Life Experiences: A Follow-up Study.* Monograph of the Society for Research in Child Development, *31,* 3, 1966.

Skeels, H. M., and H. B. Dye. "A Study of the Effects of Differential Stimulation on Mentally Retarded Children." *Proceedings and Addresses of the American Association on Mental Deficiency, 44,* 1939:114–136.

Skiba, Katherine M. "U.S. Slowdown Affects Glendale, Wis.-Based Employment Firm's Mexico Arm." *Milwaukee Journal Sentinel,* July 23, 2001.

Skow, John. "The Redwoods Weep." *Time,* September 28, 1998:70–72.

Sloan, Allan. "A Lot of Trust, But No Funds." *Newsweek,* July 30, 2001:34.

Small, Albion W. *General Sociology.* Chicago: University of Chicago Press, 1905. As cited in Olmsted and Hare 1978:10.

Smart, Barry. "On the Disorder of Things: Sociology, Postmodernity and the 'End of the Social.' " *Sociology, 24,* 3, August 1990:397–416.

Smith, Beverly A. "An Incest Case in an Early 20th-Century Rural Community." *Deviant Behavior, 13,* 1992:127–153.

Smith, Clark. "Oral History as 'Therapy': Combatants' Account of Vietnam War." In *Strangers at Home: Vietnam Veterans Since the War,* Charles R. Figley and Seymore Leventman, eds. New York: Praeger, 1980:9–34.

Smith, Craig S. "China Becomes Industrial Nations' Most Favored Dump." *Wall Street Journal,* October 9, 1995:B1.

Smith, Daniel Scott, and Michael Hindus. "Premarital Pregnancy in America, 1640–1971: An Overview and Interpretation." *Journal of Interdisciplinary History, 4,* Spring 1975:537–570.

Smith, Douglas A., and Robert Brame. "On the Initiation and Continuation of Delinquency." *Criminology, 32,* 4, 1994:607–629.

Smith, Harold. "A Colossal Cover-Up." *Christianity Today,* December 12, 1986:16–17.

Smith, Jackie, Charles Chatfield, and Ron Pagnucco. *Transnational Social Movements and Global Policy: Solidarity Beyond the State.* Syracuse, N. Y.: Syracuse University Press, 1997.

Smith, Joel B., and Dennis A. Tirpak. *The Potential Effects of Global Climate Change in the United States.* Washington, D.C.: U.S. Environmental Protection Agency, October 1988.

Smith, Kristen F., and Vern L. Bengston. "Positive Consequences of Institutionalization: Solidarity Between Elderly Parents and Their Middle-Aged Children." *Gerontologist, 19,* October 1979:438–447.

Smith, Lee. "The War Between the Generations." *Fortune,* July 20, 1987:78–82.

Smith, Simon C. "The Making of a Neo-Colony? Anglo-Kuwaiti Relations in the Era of Decolonization." *Middle Eastern Studies, 37,* 1, January 2001:159–173.

Smith, Wesley J. "Dependency or Death? Oregonians Make a Chilling Choice." *Wall Street Journal,* February 25, 1999.

Smith-Lovin, Lynn, and Charles Brody. "Interruptions in Group Discussions: The Effects of Gender and Group Composition." *American Sociological Review, 54,* 1989:424–435.

Smock, Pamela J., Wendy D. Manning, and Sanjiv Gupta. "The Effect of Marriage and Divorce on Women's Economic Well-Being." *American Sociological Review, 64,* December 1999:794–812.

Snow, David A., Louis A. Zurcher, Jr., and Sheldon Ekland-Olson. "Social Networks and Social Movements: A Microstructural Approach to Differential Recruitment." In *Collective Behavior and Social Movements,* Russell L. Curtis, Jr., and Benigno E. Aguirre, eds. Boston: Allyn and Bacon, 1993:323–334.

Snow, David A., Louis A. Zurcher, and Robert Peters. "Victory Celebrations as Theater: A Dramaturgical Approach to Crowd Behavior." In *Collective Behavior and Social Movements,* Russell L. Curtis, Jr., and Benigno E. Aguirre, eds. Boston: Allyn and Bacon, 1993:194–208.

Snow, Margaret E., Carol Nagy Jacklin, and Eleanor E. Maccoby. "Birth-Order Differences in Peer Sociability at Thirty-Three Months." *Child Development, 52,* 1981:589–595.

Snyder, Jack. "Disney's Town of Celebration, Fla., Still Suffers Growing Pains." *Orlando Sentinel,* June 18, 2001.

Snyder, Mark. "Self-Fulfilling Stereotypes." In *Down to Earth Sociology: Introductory Readings,* 7th ed., James M. Henslin, ed. New York: Free Press, 1993:153–160.

"Social Darwinism in Sweden." *Report* (Alberta Edition), *28,* 14, July 9, 2001:4.

Solomon, Jolie. "Companies Try Measuring Cost Savings from New Types of Corporate Benefits." *Wall Street Journal,* December 29, 1988:B1.

Sorokin, Pitirim A. *Social and Cultural Dynamics.* 4 vols. New York: American Book Company, 1937–1941.

Sorokin, Pitirim A. *The Crisis of Our Age.* New York: Dutton, 1941.

Soss, Joe. "Lessons of Welfare: Policy Design, Political Learning, and Political Action." *American Political Science Review, 93,* 1999:363–380.

Sourcebook of Criminal Justice Statistics. Washington, D.C.: U.S. Government Printing Office, published annually.

South, Scott J. "Sociodemographic Differentials in Mate Selection Preferences." *Journal of Marriage and the Family, 53,* November 1991:928–940.

"South African Government Lifts Moratorium on Crime Stats." Associated Press, May 31, 2001.

Sowell, Thomas. "Effrontery and Gall, Inc." *Forbes,* September 27, 1993a:52.

Sowell, Thomas. *Inside American Education: The Decline, the Deception, the Dogmas.* New York: Free Press, 1993b.

Soysa, Indra de, and John R. Oneal. "Boon or Bane? Reassessing the Productivity of Foreign Direct Investment." *American Sociological Review, 64,* October 1999:766–782.

Specter, Michael. "Plunging Life Expectancy Puzzles Russians." *New York Times,* August 1, 1995:A1, A6.

Spector, Malcolm, and John Kitsuse. *Constructing Social Problems.* Menlo Park, Calif.: Cummings, 1977.

Spencer, Herbert. *Principles of Sociology.* 3 vols. New York: Appleton, 1884.

Spengler, Oswald. *The Decline of the West,* 2 vols. Charles F. Atkinson, trans. New York: Knopf, 1926–1928. First published in 1919–1922.

Spickard, P. R. S. *Mixed Blood: Intermarriage and Ethnic Identity in Twentieth Century America.* Madison: University of Wisconsin Press, 1989.

Spitz, Renée. "Hospitalism." *Psychoanalytic Study of the Child, 1,* 1945:53–72.

Spitzer, Steven. "Toward a Marxian Theory of Deviance." *Social Problems, 22,* June 1975:608–619.

Spragins, Ellyn E. "To Sue or Not to Sue?" *Newsweek,* December 9, 1996:50.

Sprecher, Susan, and Rachita Chandak. "Attitudes About Arranged Marriages and Dating Among Men and Women from India." *Free Inquiry in Creative Sociology, 20,* 1, May 1992:59–69.

Squeo, Anne Marie, and Daniel Pearl. "How Gulf Sheikdom Landed Its Sweet Deal With Lockheed Martin." *Wall Street Journal,* April 20, 2000:A1, A10.

Srole, Leo, et al. *Mental Health in the Metropolis: The Midtown Manhattan Study.* New York: New York University Press, 1978.

Stack, Carol B. *All Our Kin: Strategies for Survival in a Black Community.* New York: Harper, 1974.

Stampp, Kenneth M. *The Peculiar Institution: Slavery in the Ante-Bellum South.* New York: Vintage Books, 1956.

Stark, Elizabeth. "Friends Through It All." In *Marriage and Family in a Changing Society,* 3rd ed., James M. Henslin, ed. New York: Free Press, 1989:441–449.

Stark, Rodney. *Sociology,* 3rd ed. Belmont, Calif.: Wadsworth, 1989.

Starna, William A., and Ralph Watkins. "Northern Iroquoian Slavery." *Ethnohistory, 38,* 1, Winter 1991:34–57.

Starr, Paul. *The Social Transformation of American Medicine.* New York: Basic Books, 1982.

Starrels, Marjorie. "The Evolution of Workplace Family Policy Research." *Journal of Family Issues, 13,* 3, September 1992:259–278.

State of American Education: A 5-Year Report Card on American Education." U.S. Department of Education, February 22, 2000.

"State of the World's Children 2001." *Reading Today, 18,* 4, February-March 2001:24.

Statham, Anne, Eleanor M. Miller, and Hans O. Mauksch. "The Integration of Work: Second-order Analysis of Qualitative Research." In *The Worth of Women's Work: A Qualitative Synthesis.* Statham, Anne, Eleanor M. Miller, and Hans O. Mauksch, eds. Albany, N.Y.: State University of New York Press, 1988:11–35.

Statistical Abstract of the United States. Washington D.C.: Bureau of the Census, published annually.

Stecklow, Steve. "SAT Scores Rise Strongly after Test Is Overhauled." *Wall Street Journal,* August 24, 1995:B1, B12.

Steele, Shelby. "Reparations Enshrine Victimhood, Dishonoring Our Ancestors." *Newsweek,* August 27, 2001:23.

Steele, Stephen F., AnneMarie Scarisbrick-Hauser, and William J. Hauser. *Solution-Centered Sociology: Addressing Problems through Applied Sociology.* Thousand Oaks, Calif.: Sage Publications, 1999.

Stein, Leonard I. "The Doctor–Nurse Game." In *Down to Earth Sociology: Introductory Readings,* 5th ed., James M. Henslin, ed. New York: Free Press, 1988:102–109.

Steinberg, Jacques. "Academic Standards Eased as a Fear of Failure Spreads." *New York Times,* December 3, 1999.

Steinberg, Jacques. "Student Failure Causes States to Retool Testing Programs." *New York Times,* December 22, 2000.

Steinberg, Laurence, Stanford Dornbusch, and Bradford Brown. *Beyond the Classroom.* New York: Simon & Shuster, 1996.

Steinhauer, Jennifer. "Angry at Managed Care, Doctors Start Fighting Back." *New York Times,* January 10, 1999.

Steinhauer, Jennifer. "So, the Tumor is on the Left, Right?" *New York Times,* April 1, 2001.

Steinhauer, Jennifer, and Ford Fessenden. "Medical Retreads: Doctor Punished by State But Prized at the Hospitals." *New York Times,* March 27, 2001.

Stevens, Amy, and Sarah Lubman. "Deciding Moment of the Trial May Have Been Five Months Ago." *Wall Street Journal,* May 1, 1992:A6.

Stevens, Mitchell L. *Kingdom of Children: Culture and Controversy in the Homeschooling Movement.* Princeton: Princeton University Press, 2001.

Stevenson, David Lee, and David P. Baker. "Shadow Education and Allocation in Formal Schooling in Japan." In *Haves and Have-Nots: An International Reader on Social Inequality,* James Curtis and Lorne Tepperman, eds. Englewood Cliffs, N.J.: Prentice Hall, 1994:352–359.

Stevenson, Richard W. "U.S. Debates Investing in Stock for Social Security." *New York Times,* July 27, 1998.

Stewart, Abigail J., Anne P. Copeland, Nia Lane Chester, Janet E. Malley, and Nicole B. Barenbaum. *Separating Together: How Divorce Transforms Families.* New York: Guilford Press, 1997.

Stinnett, Nicholas. "Strong Families." In *Marriage and Family in a Changing Society,* 4th ed., James M. Henslin, ed. New York: Free Press, 1992:496–507.

Stipp, David. "Einstein Bird Has Scientists Atwitter over Mental Feats." *Wall Street Journal,* May 9, 1990:A1, A4.

Stipp, David. "Himalayan Tree Could Serve as Source of Anti-cancer Drug Taxol, Team Says." *Wall Street Journal,* April 20, 1992:B4.

Stockard, Jean, and Miriam M. Johnson. *Sex Roles: Sex Inequality and Sex Role Development.* Englewood Cliffs, N.J.: Prentice Hall, 1980.

Stockwell, John. "The Dark Side of U.S. Foreign Policy." *Zeta Magazine,* February 1989:36–48.

Stodgill, Ralph M. *Handbook of Leadership: A Survey of Theory and Research.* New York: Free Press, 1974.

Stolberg, Sheryl Gay. "Blacks Found on Short End of Heart Attack Procedure." *New York Times,* May 10, 2001.

Stone, Gregory P. "City Shoppers and Urban Identification: Observations on the Social Psychology of City Life." *American Journal of Sociology, 60,* November 1954:276–284.

Stone, Martin. "Hate Site Case Expected to Set Precedents." *Daily News,* March 9, 1999.

Storfer, Miles D. "Intelligence and Giftedness." In *Window on Society,* 5th ed., John W. Heeren, Marylee Requa, Robert H. Lauer, and Jeanette C. Lauer, eds. Los Angeles: Roxbury Publishing Company, 2000:27–32.

Stouffer, Samuel A., Arthur A. Lumsdaine, Marion Harper Lumsdaine, Robin M. Williams, Jr., M. Brewster Smith, Irving L. Janis, Shirley A. Star, and Leonard S. Cottrell, Jr. *The American Soldier: Combat and Its Aftermath,* Vol. 2. New York: Wiley, 1949.

Strang, David, and Michael W. Macy. "In Search of Excellence: Fads, Success Stories, and Adaptive Emulation." *American Journal of Sociology, 197,* 1, July 2001:147–182.

Straus, Murray A. "Victims and Aggressors in Marital Violence." *American Behavioral Scientist, 23,* May–June 1980:681–704.

Straus, Murray A. "Explaining Family Violence." In *Marriage and Family in a Changing Society,* 4th ed., James M. Henslin, ed. New York: Free Press, 1992:344–356.

Straus, Murray A., and Richard J. Gelles. "Violence in American Families: How Much Is There and Why Does It Occur?" In *Troubled Relationships,* Elam W. Nunnally, Catherine S. Chilman, and Fred M. Cox, eds. Newbury Park, Calif.: Sage, 1988:141–162.

Straus, Murray A., Richard J. Gelles, and Suzanne K. Steinmetz. *Behind Closed Doors: Violence in the American Family.* New York: Anchor/Doubleday, 1980.

Straus, Roger A. "The Sociologist as a Marketing Research Consultant." *Journal of Applied Sociology, 8,* 1991:65–75.

Strauss, Neil. "Critic's Notebook: A Japanese TV Show That Pairs Beauty and Pain." *New York Times,* July 14, 1998.

Stryker, Sheldon. "Symbolic Interactionism: Themes and Variations." In *Social Psychology: Sociological Perspectives,* Morris Rosenberg and Ralph H. Turner, eds. New Brunswick, N.J.: Transaction, 1990.

Stryker, Sheldon, Timothy J. Owens, and Robert W. White, eds. *Self, Identity, and Social Movements.* Minneapolis: University of Minnesota Press, 2000.

"Study Suggests Lungs Damaged in Healthy Kids Exposed to High Levels of Air Pollution." *Canadian Press,* November 28, 2001.

Sullivan, Andrew. "What We Look Up to Now." *New York Times,* November 15, 1998.

Sulloway, Frank J. *Born to Rebel: Birth Order, Family Dynamics, and Creative Lives.* New York: Vintage Books, 1997.

Sumner, William Graham. *Folkways: A Study in the Sociological Importance of Usages, Manners, Customs, Mores, and Morals.* New York: Ginn, 1906.

Sun, Lena H. "China Seeks Ways to Protect Elderly." *Washington Post,* October 23, 1990:A1.

Sutherland, Edwin H. *Criminology.* Philadelphia: Lippincott, 1924.

Sutherland, Edwin H. *Principles of Criminology,* 4th ed. Philadelphia: Lippincott, 1947.

Sutherland, Edwin H. *White Collar Crime.* New York: Dryden Press, 1949.

Sutherland, Edwin H., and Donald Cressey. *Criminology,* 9th ed. Philadelphia: Lippincott, 1974.

Sutherland, Edwin H., Donald R. Cressey, and David F. Luckenbill. *Principles of Criminology,* 11th ed. Dix Hills, N.Y.: General Hall, 1992.

Suzuki, Bob H. "Asian-American Families." In *Marriage and Family in a Changing Society,* 2nd ed., James M. Henslin, ed. New York: Free Press, 1985:104–119.

Swedish Institute, The. "Health and Medical Care in Sweden." July 1990:1–4.

Swedish Institute, The. "Fact Sheets on Sweden." February 1992.

Sweezy, Paul M., and Harry Magdoff. "Globalization—to What End? Part II." *Monthly Review, 43,* 10, March 1992:1–19.

Sykes, Gresham M., and David Matza. "Techniques of Neutralization." In *Down to Earth Sociology: Introductory Readings,* 5th ed., James M. Henslin, ed. New York: Free Press, 1988:225–231. First published in 1957.

Szasz, Thomas S. *The Myth of Mental Illness,* rev. ed. New York: Harper & Row, 1986.

Szasz, Thomas S. "Mental Illness Is Still a Myth." In *Deviant Behavior 96/97,* Lawrence M. Salinger, ed. Guilford, Conn.: Dushkin, 1996:200–205.

Szasz, Thomas S. *Cruel Compassion: Psychiatric Control of Society's Unwanted.* Syracuse: Syracuse University Press, 1998.

Szelenyi, Szonja. "Social Inequality and Party Membership: Patterns of Recruitment in the Hungarian Socialist Workers' Party." *American Sociological Review, 52,* 1987:559–573.

Tannen, Deborah. *You Just Don't Understand: Women and Men in Conversation.* New York: Morrow, 1990.

Tannen, Deborah. "But What Do You Mean? Women and Men in Conversation." In *Down to Earth Sociology: Introductory Readings,* 11th ed., James M. Henslin, ed. New York: The Free Press, 2001:168–173.

Tanouye, Elyse. "Researchers Say Chinese Medicine May Aid in Prevention of Liver Cancer." *Wall Street Journal,* September 6, 1995:B1.

Tanouye, Elyse. "SmithKline to Pay $325 Million to Settle Federal Claims of Lab-Billing Fraud." *Wall Street Journal,* February 25, 1997:B8.

Tapia, Andres. "Churches Wary of Inner-City Islamic Inroads." *Christianity Today, 38,* 1, January 10, 1994:36–38.

Taylor, Chris. "The Man Behind Lara Croft." *Time,* December 6, 1999:78.

Taylor, Howard F. "The Structure of a National Black Leadership Network: Preliminary Findings." Unpublished manuscript, 1992. As cited in Margaret L. Andersen and Howard F. Taylor, *Sociology: Understanding a Diverse Society.* Belmont, Calif.: Wadsworth, 2000.

Taylor, Raymond G., and Alexander I. Mechitov. "Russian Schools and the Legacies of the Soviet Era." *Education, 115,* 2, Winter 1994:260–263.

Taylor, Verta. "Social Movement Continuity: The Women's Movement in Abeyance." In *Social Movements: Readings on Their Emergence, Mobilization, and Dynamics,* Doug McAdam and David A. Snow, eds. Los Angeles: Roxbury Publishing, 1997:409–420.

Teacher's College Record. "Brown Plus Forty." New York: Columbia University Teacher's College, 96, 4, 1995:601–788.

Terry, Don. "Getting Under My Skin." *New York Times,* July 16, 2000.

Thayer, Stephen. "Encounters." *Psychology Today,* March 1988:31–36.

Thelen, Esther. "Grounded in the World: Developmental Origins of the Embodied Mind." *Infancy, 1,* 1, 2000:3–29.

Thomas, Melvin E., and Linda A. Treiber. "Race, Gender, and Status: A Content Analysis of Print Advertisements in Four Popular Magazines." *Sociological Spectrum, 20,* 3, July-September 2000:357–371.

Thomas, Paulette. "EPA Predicts Global Impact from Warming." *Wall Street Journal,* October 21, 1988:B5.

Thomas, Paulette. "U.S. Examiners Will Scrutinize Banks with Poor Minority-Lending Histories." *Wall Street Journal,* October 22, 1991:A2.

Thomas, Paulette. "Boston Fed Finds Racial Discrimination in Mortgage Lending Is Still Widespread." *Wall Street Journal,* October 9, 1992:A3.

Thomas, R. Roosevelt, Jr. "From Affirmative Action to Affirming Diversity." *Harvard Business Review, 90, 2,* March–April, 1990:107–117.

Thomas, W. I., and Dorothy Swaine Thomas. *The Child in America: Behavior Problems and Programs.* New York: Alfred A. Knopf, 1928.

Thompson, Ginger. "Chasing Mexico's Dream into Squalor." *New York Times,* February 11, 2001.

Thompson, William E. "Hanging Tongues: A Sociological Encounter with the Assembly Line." In *Down to Earth Sociology: Introductory Readings,* 9th ed., James M. Henslin, ed. New York: Free Press, 1995:193–202.

Thornburg, David. "Why Wait for Bandwidth? Schools Can Teleconference, Even with Ordinary Phone Lines." *Electronic Learning, 14, 3,* November–December 1994:20.

Thorne, Barrie. "Children and Gender: Constructions of Difference." In *Theoretical Perspectives on Sexual Difference,* Deborah L. Rhode, ed. New Haven, Conn.: Yale University Press, 1990:100–113.

Thorne, Barrie, and Zella Luria. "Sexuality and Gender in Children's Daily Worlds." In *Down to Earth Sociology: Introductory Readings,* 7th ed., James M. Henslin, ed. New York: Free Press, 1993:133–144.

Thornton, Russell. *American Indian Holocaust and Survival: A Population History Since 1492.* Norman: University of Oklahoma Press, 1987.

Thrasher, Frederic M. *The Gang.* Chicago: University of Chicago Press, 1927.

Tilly, Charles. *From Mobilization to Revolution.* Reading, Mass.: Addison-Wesley, 1978.

Timasheff, Nicholas S. *War and Revolution.* Joseph F. Scheuer, ed. New York: Sheed & Ward, 1965.

Timerman, Jacobo. *Prisoner Without a Name, Cell Without a Number.* New York: Knopf, 1981.

Tobias, Andrew. "The 'Don't Be Ridiculous' Law." *Wall Street Journal,* May 31, 1995:A14.

Toby, Jackson. "To Get Rid of Guns in Schools, Get Rid of Some Students." *Wall Street Journal,* March 23, 1992:A12.

Toch, Thomas. "Violence in Schools." *U.S. News & World Report, 115, 18,* November 8, 1993:31–36.

Tocqueville, Alexis de. *The Old Regime and the French Revolution.* Stuart Gilbert, trans. Garden City, N.Y.: Doubleday Anchor, 1955. First published in 1856.

Tocqueville, Alexis de. *Democracy in America,* J. P. Mayer and Max Lerner, eds. New York: Harper & Row, 1966. First published in 1835.

Tolchin, Martin. "Surgeon General Asserts Smoking Is an Addiction." *New York Times,* May 17, 1988:A1, C4.

Tolchin, Martin. "Mildest Possible Penalty Is Imposed on Neil Bush." *New York Times,* April 19, 1991:D2.

Tönnies, Ferdinand. *Community and Society (Gemeinschaft und Gesellschaft),* with a new introduction by John Samples. New Brunswick, N.J.: Transaction, 1988. First published in 1887.

Tordoff, William. "The Impact of Ideology on Development in the Third World." *Journal of International Development, 4, 1,* 1992:41–53.

Toynbee, Arnold. *A Study of History,* D. C. Somervell, abridger and ed. New York: Oxford University Press, 1946.

Treas, Judith. "Older Americans in the 1990s and Beyond." *Population Bulletin, 50, 2,* May 1995:1–46.

Treiman, Donald J. *Occupational Prestige in Comparative Perspective.* New York: Academic Press, 1977.

Trice, Harrison M., and Janice M. Beyer. "Cultural Leadership in Organization." *Organization Science, 2, 2,* May 1991:149–169.

Troeltsch, Ernst. *The Social Teachings of the Christian Churches.* New York: Macmillan, 1931.

Tucker, Belinda M., and Claudia Mitchell-Kernan. "New Trends in Black American Interracial Marriage: The Social Structural Context." *Journal of Marriage and the Family, 52,* 1990:209–218.

Tumin, Melvin M. "Some Principles of Social Stratification: A Critical Analysis." *American Sociological Review 18,* August 1953:394.

Turkle, Sherry. *Life on the Screen: Identity in the Age of the Internet.* New York: Simon and Schuster, 1995

Turnbull, Colin M. "The Mountain People." In *Sociology 95/96,* Kurt Finsterbusch, ed. Sluice Dock, Conn.: Dushkin, 1995:6–15. First published in 1972.

Turner, Bryan S. "Outline of a Theory of Citizenship." *Sociology, 24, 2,* May 1990:189–217.

Turner, Jonathan H. *American Society: Problems of Structure.* New York: Harper & Row, 1972.

Turner, Jonathan H. *The Structure of Sociological Theory.* Homewood, Ill.: Dorsey, 1978.

Turner, Jonathan H. *On the Origins of Human Emotions: A Sociological Inquiry into the Evolution of Human Affect.* Stanford: Stanford University Press, 2000.

Turner, Ralph H. "Collective Behavior." In *Handbook of Modern Sociology,* Robert E. L. Faris, ed. Chicago: Rand McNally, 1964:382–425.

Turner, Ralph H. "Race Riots Past and Present: A Cultural-Collective Behavior Approach." Paper presented at the annual meetings of the American Sociological Association, 1993.

Turner, Ralph H., and Lewis M. Killian. *Collective Behavior,* 2nd ed. Englewood Cliffs, N.J.: Prentice Hall, 1987.

Tye, Larry. "After Waco, the Focus Shifts to Other Cults." *The Boston Globe,* April 30, 1993:1, 22.

Uchitelle, Louis. "How to Define Poverty? Let Us Count the Ways." *New York Times,* May 28, 2001.

Udry, J. Richard. "Biological Limits of Gender Construction." *American Sociological Review, 65,* June 2000:443–457.

Udy, Stanley H., Jr. "Bureaucracy and Rationality in Weber's Organizational Theory: An Empirical Study." *American Sociological Review, 24,* December 1959:791–795.

Ullman, Edward, and Chauncey Harris. "The Nature of Cities." In *Urban Man and Society: A Reader in Urban Ecology,* Albert N. Cousins and Hans Nagpaul, eds. New York: Knopf, 1970:91–100.

Ullman, Sarah E. "Does Offender Violence Escalate When Rape Victims Fight Back?" *Journal of Interpersonal Violence, 13, 2,* April 1998:179–192.

UNESCO: Institute for Statistics, 2000.

UNICEF. *The State of the World's Children.* New York: Oxford University Press, 1995.

Uniform Crime Reports. Washington D.C.: FBI, published annually. United Nations.

United Nations Statistical Yearbook 1985–1986. New York: The United Nations, 1987.

United Nations Statistical Yearbook 1990–1991. New York: The United Nations, 1992.

United Nations Statistical Yearbook 1995–1996. New York: The United Nations, 1997.

United Nations. "World Urbanization Prospects: The 1999 Revision." New York: United Nations, 2000.

U.S. Bureau of the Census. *Statistical Abstract of the United States: The National Data Book.* Washington, D.C.: U.S. Government Printing Office. Published annually.

U.S. Department of Energy, Advisory Committee on Human Radiation Experiments. Final Report, 1995. Available online at http://tis.eh.doe.gov/ohreroadmap/achre/report.html.

U.S. Department of Health and Human Services, Public Health Service. *Healthy People 2000.* Washington, D.C.: U.S. Government Printing Office, 1990.

Usdansky, Margaret L. "English a Problem for Half of Miami." *USA Today,* April 3, 1992:A1, A3, A30.

Useem, Michael. *The Inner Circle: Large Corporations and the Rise of Business Political Activity in the U.S. and U.K.* New York: Oxford University Press, 1984.

Vande Berg, Leah R., and Diane Streckfuss. "Prime-Time Television's Portrayal of Women and the World of Work: A Demographic Profile." *Journal of Broadcasting and Electronic Media,* Spring 1992:195–208.

Van Lawick-Goodall, Jane. *In the Shadow of Man.* Boston: Houghton Mifflin, 1971.

van den Haag, Ernest. *Punishing Criminals: Concerning a Very Old and Painful Question.* New York: Basic Books, 1975.

van Den Haag, Ernest, and John Conrad, eds. *The Death Penalty: A Debate.* New York: Plenum, 1983.

Vasil, Latika, and Hannelore Wass. "Portrayal of the Elderly in the Media: A Literature Review and Implications for Educational Gerontologists." *Educational Gerontology, 19,* 1, January–February 1993:71–85.

Vaughan, Diane. "Uncoupling: The Social Construction of Divorce." In *Marriage and Family in a Changing Society,* 2nd ed., James M. Henslin, ed. New York: Free Press, 1985:429–439.

Veblen, Thorstein. *The Theory of the Leisure Class.* New York: Macmillan, 1912.

Vega, William A. "Hispanic Families in the 1980s: A Decade of Research." *Journal of Marriage and the Family, 52,* November 1990:1015–1024.

Verhovek, Sam Howe. "U.S. Acts to Stop Assisted Suicide." *New York Times,* November 7, 2001.

Vernon, JoEtta A., J. Allen Williams, Jr., Terri Phillips, and Janet Wilson. "Media Stereotyping: A Comparison of the Way Elderly Women and Men Are Portrayed on Prime-Time Television." *Journal of Women and Aging, 2,* 4, 1990:55–58.

Violas, P. C. *The Training of the Urban Working Class: A History of Twentieth Century American Education.* Chicago: Rand McNally, 1978.

Volti, Rudi. *Society and Technological Change,* 3rd ed. New York: St. Martin's Press, 1995.

Von Hoffman, Nicholas. "Sociological Snoopers." *Transaction 7,* May 1970:4, 6.

Waddington, Conrad H. *The Man-Made Future.* New York: St. Martin's, 1978.

Wagley, Charles, and Marvin Harris. *Minorities in the New World.* New York: Columbia University Press, 1958.

Waldholz, Michael. "Computer Brain Outperforms Doctors in Diagnosing Heart Attack Patients." *Wall Street Journal,* December 2, 1991:7B.

Waldholz, Michael. "AIDS Spreading to Teenage Girls in Parts of Africa." *Wall Street Journal,* September 15, 1999:B1, B4.

Waldman, Amy. "Homes and Shops to Rise on Abandoned Harlem Properties." *New York Times,* December 27, 2000.

Waldman, Peter. "Riots in Bahrain Arouse Ire of Feared Monarchy as the U.S. Stands By." *Wall Street Journal,* June 12, 1995:A1, A8.

Walker, Alice, and Pratibha Parmar. *Warrior Marks: Female Genital Mutilation and the Sexual Blinding of Women.* New York: Harcourt Brace, 1993.

Wallace, Anthony F. C. *Religion: An Anthropological View.* New York: Random House, 1966.

Wallerstein, Immanuel. *The Modern World System: Capitalist Agriculture and the Origins of the European World-Economy in the Sixteenth Century.* New York: Academic Press, 1974.

Wallerstein, Immanuel. *The Capitalist World-Economy.* New York: Cambridge University Press, 1979.

Wallerstein, Immanuel. *The Politics of the World-Economy: The States, the Movements, and the Civilizations.* Cambridge, England: Cambridge University Press, 1984.

Wallerstein, Immanuel. "Culture as the Ideological Battleground of the Modern World-system." In *Global Culture: Nationalism, Globalization, and Modernity,* Mike Featherstone, ed. London: Sage, 1990:31–55.

Wallerstein, Judith S., and Joan B. Kelly. "How Children React to Parental Divorce." In *Marriage and Family in a Changing Society,* 4th ed., James M. Henslin, ed. New York: Free Press, 1992:397–409.

Wallerstein, Judith, Julia Lewis, and Sarah Blakeslee. *The Unexpected Legacy of Divorce: A 25 Year Landmark Study.* New York: Hyperion Press, 2000.

Walsh, Catherine. "The Life and Legacy of Lawrence Kohlberg." *Society, 37,* 2, January-February 2000:38–44.

Wang, Hongyu, and Paul R. Amato. "Predictors of Divorce Adjustment: Stressors, Resources, and Definitions." *Journal of Marriage and the Family, 62,* 3, August 2000:655–668.

Wark, Gillian R., and Dennis L. Krebs. "Gender and Dilemma Differences in Real-Life Moral Judgment." *Developmental Psychology, 32,* 1996:220–230.

Warner, W. Lloyd, and Paul S. Hunt. *The Social Life of a Modern Community.* New Haven, Conn.: Yale University Press, 1941.

Warner, W. Lloyd, Paul S. Hunt, Marchia Meeker, and Kenneth Eels. *Social Class in America.* New York: Harper, 1949.

Warr, Mark. "Age, Peers, and Delinquency." *Criminology, 31,* 1, 1993:17–40.

Watson, J. Mark. "Outlaw Motorcyclists." In *Down to Earth Sociology: Introductory Readings,* 5th ed., James M. Henslin, ed. New York: Free Press, 1988:203–213.

Watts, Duncan J. "Networks, Dynamics, and the Small-World Phenomenon." *American Journal of Sociology, 105,* 2, September 1999:493–427.

Wayne, Julie Holliday, Christine M. Riordan, and Kecia M. Thomas. "Is All Sexual Harassment Viewed the Same? Mock Juror Decisions in Same-and Cross-Gender Cases." *Journal of Applied Psychology, 86,* 2, April 2001:179–187.

Wayne, Leslie. "Lucrative Lobbying Jobs Await Many Leaving Government Service." *New York Times,* December 16, 2000.

Webb, Eugene J., Donald T. Campbell, Richard D. Schwartz, and Lee Sechrest. *Unobtrusive Measures: Nonreactive Research in the Social Sciences.* Chicago: Rand McNally, 1966.

Weber, Max. *Economy and Society,* G. Roth and C. Wittich, eds. Berkeley: University of California Press, 1978. First published in 1922.

Weber, Max. *From Max Weber: Essays in Sociology.* Hans Gerth and C. Wright Mills, trans. and ed. New York: Oxford University Press, 1946a.

Weber, Max. *The Theory of Social and Economic Organization,* A. M. Henderson and Talcott Parsons, trans., Talcott Parsons, ed. Glencoe, Ill.: Free Press, 1947. First published in 1913.

Weber, Max. *The Protestant Ethic and the Spirit of Capitalism.* New York: Scribner's, 1958. First published in 1904–1905.

Weber, Max. *Economy and Society.* Ephraim Fischoff, trans. New York: Bedminster Press, 1968. First published in 1922.

Webster, Pamela S., and A. Regula Herzog. "Effects of Parental Divorce and Memories of Family Problems on Relationships Between Adult Children and Their Parents." *Journal of Gerontology, 50B,* 1, 1995:S24-S34.

Weeks, John R. *Population: An Introduction to Concepts and Issues,* 5th ed. Belmont, Calif.: Wadsworth, 1994.

Wei, William. *The Asian American Movement.* Philadelphia: Temple University Press, 1993.

Weiler, Jeanne. "Recent Changes in School Desegregation." *ERIC/CUE Digest,* April 1, 1998.

Weintraub, Richard M. "A Bride in India." *Washington Post,* February 28, 1988.

Weisburd, David, Stanton Wheeler, and Elin Waring. *Crimes of the Middle Classes: White-Collar Offenders in the Federal Courts.* New Haven, Conn.: Yale University Press, 1991.

Weisskopf, Michael. "Scientist Says Greenhouse Effect Is Setting In." In *Ourselves and Others: The Washington Post Sociology Companion,* Washington Post Writers Group, eds. Boston: Allyn and Bacon, 1992:297–298.

Wells, Joseph. "Report to the Nation on Occupational Fraud and Abuse." Associaton of Certified Fraud Examiners.

Wells, Susan J. "Making Telecommuting Work." *HR Magazine, 46,* 10, October 2001:34–45.

Welsh, Stephanie. "A Dangerous Rite of Passage." *Nation,* May 7, 1995.

Wenneker, Mark B., and Arnold M. Epstein. "Racial Inequalities in the Use of Procedures for Patients with Ischemic Heart Disease in Massachusetts." *Journal of the American Medical Association, 261,* 2, January 13, 1989:253–257.

Wertz, Richard W., and Dorothy C. Wertz. "Notes on the Decline of Midwives and the Rise of Medical Obstetricians." In *The Sociology of Health and Illness: Critical Perspectives,* Peter Conrad and Rochelle Kern, eds. New York: St. Martin's Press, 1981:165–183.

Wessel, David. "As Populations Age, Fiscal Woes Deepen." *Wall Street Journal,* September 11, 1995:A1.

West, Candace, and Angela Garcia. "Conversational Shift Work: A Study of Topical Transitions Between Women and Men." *Social Problems, 35,* 1988:551–575.

Western, Bruce. *Wealth in America: Trends in Wealth Inequality.* New York: Cambridge University Press, 2000.

Whetstone, Muriel L. "What Black Men and Women Should Do Now (About Black Men and Women)." *Ebony,* February 1996:135–138, 140.

White, Jack E. "Forgive Us Our Sins." *Time,* July 3, 1995:29.

White, James A. "When Employees Own Big Stake, It's a Buy Signal for Investors." *Wall Street Journal,* February 13, 1991:C1, C19.

White, Joseph B., Stephen Power, and Timothy Aeppel. "Death Count Linked to Failures of Firestone Tires Rises to 203." *Wall Street Journal,* June 19, 2001:A4.

White, Richard D., Jr. "Are Women More Ethical? Recent Findings on the Effects of Gender Upon Moral Development." *Journal of Public Administration Research and Theory, 9,* 3, July 1999:459–471.

Whorf, Benjamin. *Language, Thought, and Reality,* J. B. Carroll, ed. Cambridge, MA: MIT Press, 1956.

Whyte, Martin King. "Choosing Mates—The American Way." *Society,* March–April 1992:71–77.

Whyte, William H. *The City: Rediscovering the Center.* New York: Doubleday, 1989.

Whyte, William Foote. "Street Corner Society." In *Down to Earth Sociology: Introductory Readings,* 11th ed., James M. Henslin, ed. New York: The Free Press, 2001:61–69.

Wilensky, Joe. "Rethinking Policy in a Brave New World." *Human Ecology, 29,* 2, Spring 2001:17–19.

Wilford, John Noble. "In Maya Ruins, Scholars See Evidence of Urban Sprawl." *New York Times,* December 19, 2000.

Wilgoren, Jodi. "U.S. Court Bars Race as a Factor in School Entry." *New York Times,* March 28, 2001.

Wilkening, David. "Celebration Hotel Offers a Quiet Reprieve for Disney Visitors." *Travel Weekly, 59,* 57, July 17, 2000:51.

Will, George F. "AIDS Crushes a Continent." *Newsweek,* January 10, 2000:64.

Will, George F. "July 10, 1941, in Jedwabne." *Newsweek,* July 9, 2001:68.

Willhelm, Sidney M. "Can Marxism Explain America's Racism?" *Social Problems, 28,* December 1980:98–112.

Williams, Christine L. *Still a Man's World: Men Who Do Women's Work.* Berkeley: University of California Press, 1995.

Williams, Robin M., Jr. *American Society: A Sociological Interpretation,* 2nd ed. New York: Knopf, 1965.

Willie, Charles V. "Caste, Class, and Family Life Experiences." *Research in Race and Ethnic Relations, 6,* 1991:65–84.

Wilson, Edward O. *Sociobiology: The New Synthesis.* Cambridge, Mass.: Harvard University Press, 1975.

Wilson, James Q. "Is Incapacitation the Answer to the Crime Problem?" In *Taking Sides: Clashing Views on Controversial Social Issues,* 7th ed., Kurt Finsterbusch and George McKenna, eds. Guilford, Conn.: Dushkin, 1992:318–324.

Wilson, James Q. "Lock 'Em Up and Other Thoughts on Crime." *New York Times Magazine,* March 9, 1975:11, 44–48.

Wilson, James Q., and Richard J. Herrnstein. *Crime and Human Nature.* New York: Simon & Schuster, 1985.

Wilson, William Julius. *The Declining Significance of Race: Blacks and Changing American Institutions.* Chicago: University of Chicago Press, 1978.

Wilson, William Julius. *The Truly Disadvantaged: The Inner City, the Underclass, and Public Policy.* Chicago: University of Chicago Press, 1987.

Wilson, William Julius. *When Work Disappears: The World of the New Urban Poor.* Chicago: University of Chicago Press, 1996.

Wilson, William Julius. *The Bridge over the Racial Divide: Rising Inequality and Coalition Politics.* Berkeley: University of California Press, 2000.

Winslow, Ron. "Study Finds Blacks Get Fewer Bypasses." *Wall Street Journal,* March 18, 1992:B1.

Winslow, Ron. "Smoking Increases Heart-Attack Risk Fivefold for People in Their 30s and 40s." *Wall Street Journal,* August 18, 1995:B5.

Wirth, Louis. "Urbanism as a Way of Life." *American Journal of Sociology, 44,* July 1938:1–24.

Wirth, Louis. "The Problem of Minority Groups." In *The Science of Man in the World Crisis,* Ralph Linton, ed. New York: Columbia University Press, 1945.

Wohl, R. Richard, and Anselm Strauss. "Symbolic Representation and the Urban Milieu." *American Journal of Sociology, 63,* March 1958:523–532.

Wolfensohn, James D., and Kathryn S. Fuller. "Making Common Cause: Seeing the Forest for the Trees." *International Herald Tribune*, May 27, 1998:11.

Wolff, Michael, et al. *Where We Stand: Can America Make It in the Global Race for Wealth and Happiness?* New York: Bantam Books, 1992.

Wolfgang, Marvin E., and Franco Ferracuti. *The Subculture of Violence: Toward an Integrated Theory in Criminology.* London: Tavistock, 1967.

Wolinsky, Frederic D., Timothy E. Stump, and Christopher M. Callahan. "Does Being Placed in a Nursing Home Make You Sicker and More Likely to Die?" In *Societal Mechanisms for Maintaining Competence in Old Age*, Sherry L. Willis, K. Warner Schaie, and Mark Hayward, eds. New York: Springer Publishing Company, 1997:94–130.

Womack, James P., Daniel T. Jones, and Daniel Roos. *The Machine That Changed the World: The Story of Lean Production.* New York: Harper Perrenial, 1991.

Wood, Daniel B., "Latinos Redefine What It Means to Be Manly." *Christian Science Monitor, 93,* 161, July 16, 2001.

Wood, Scott Small. "The Price Professors Pay for Teaching at Public Universities." *Chronicle of Higher Education, 46,* 32, A18-A24.

Woodward, Kenneth L. "Heaven." *Newsweek, 113,* 13, March 27, 1989:52–55.

World Health Organization. *Constitution of the World Health Organization.* New York: World Health Organization Interim Commission, 1946.

"The World of the Child 6 Billion." Population Reference Bureau, 2000.

Worsley, Peter. *The Trumpet Shall Sound.* London: MacGibbon and Kee, 1957.

Wright, Erik Olin. *Class.* London: Verso, 1985.

Wright, Lawrence. "One Drop of Blood." *New Yorker*, July 25, 1994:46–50, 52–55.

Wright, Lawrence. "Double Mystery." *New Yorker*, August 7, 1995:45–62.

Wrong, Dennis H. "The Over-Socialized Conception of Man in Modern Sociology." *American Sociological Review, 26,* April 1961:185–193.

Wyatt, Edward. "City Plans to Let Company Run Some Public Schools in a First." *New York Times,* December 21, 2000.

Yamaguchi, Kazuo. "Subjective Rationality of Initiators and of Threshold-Theoretical Behavior of Followers in Collective Action." *Rationality and Society, 12,* 2, May 2000:185–225.

Yat-ming Sin, Leo, and Hon-ming Yau, Oliver. "Female Role Orientation and Consumption Values: Some Evidence from Mainland China." *Journal of International Consumer Marketing, 13,* 2, 2001:49–75.

Yearbook of American and Canadian Churches. Nashville, Tenn.: Abingdon. Various editions.

Yellowbird, Michael, and C. Matthew Snipp. "American Indian Families." In *Minority Families in the United States: A Multicultural Perspective*, Ronald L. Taylor, ed. Englewood Cliffs, N.J.: Prentice Hall, 1994:179–201.

Yinger, J. Milton. *Toward a Field Theory of Behavior: Personality and Social Structure.* New York: McGraw-Hill, 1965.

Yinger, J. Milton. *The Scientific Study of Religion.* New York: Macmillan, 1970.

Yoon, Carol Kaesuk. "Simple Method Found to Vastly Increase Crop Yields." *New York Times,* August 22, 2000.

Young, Laurie E. "The Overlooked Contributions of Women to the Development of American Sociology: An Examination of AJS Articles from 1895–1926." Paper presented at the 1995 meetings of the American Sociological Association.

Zachary, G. Pascal. "Behind Stocks' Surge Is an Economy in Which Big U.S. Firms Thrive." *Wall Street Journal,* November 22, 1995:A1, A5.

Zald, Mayer N. "Looking Backward to Look Forward: Reflections on the Past and the Future of the Resource Mobilization Research Program." In *Frontiers in Social Movement Theory*, Aldon D. Morris and Carol McClurg Mueller, eds. New Haven, Conn.: Yale University Press, 1992:326–348.

Zald, Mayer N., and John D. McCarthy, eds. *Social Movements in an Organizational Society.* New Brunswick, N.J.: Transaction, 1987.

Zampa, Frederick P., and Albert E. McCormick, Jr. "'Proxy Power' and Corporate Democracy: The Characteristics and Efficacy of Stockholder-Initiated Proxy Issues." *The American Journal of Economics and Sociology, 50,* 1, January 1991:1–16.

Zarakhovich, Yuri. "Closing the Door." *Time Atlantic, 157,* 8, February 26, 2001:25.

Zellner, William W. *Countercultures: A Sociological Analysis.* New York: St. Martin's, 1995.

Zernike, Kate. "The Harvard Guide to Happiness." *New York Times,* April 8, 2001a.

Zernike, Kate. "The Reluctant Feminist." *New York Times,* April 8, 2001b.

Zerubavel, Eviatar. *The Fine Line: Making Distinctions in Everyday Life.* New York: Free Press, 1991.

Zeune, Gary D. "Are You Teaching Your Employees to Steal?" *Business Credit, 103,* 4, April 2001:16.

Zielbauer, Paul. "Study Finds Pequot Businesses Lift Economy." *New York Times,* November 29, 2000.

Zola, Irving K. *Socio-Medical Inquiries.* Philadelphia: Temple University Press, 1983.

Zorbaugh, Harvey W. *The Gold Coast and the Slum.* Chicago: University of Chicago Press, 1929.

Zou, Heng Fu. "'The Spirit of Capitalism' and Long-Run Growth." *European Journal of Political Economy, 10,* 2, July 1994:279–293.

Zuckerman, Laurence. "Management Employee-Ownership Experiment Unravels at United." *New York Times,* March 14, 2001.

Zuger, Abigail. "Fever Pitch: Getting Doctors to Prescribe Is Big Business." *New York Times,* January 11, 1999.

Zuger, Abigail. "Infectious Diseases Rising Again in Russia." *New York Times,* December 5, 2000.

Name Index

Abeil, Hilary, 269
Aberle, David, 650
Aberle, David F., 107
Abraham (of Old Testament), 542, 545
Ackernecht, Erwin H., 564
Addams, Jane, 18, 20
Adler, Patricia, 85
Adler, Peter, 85
Adorno, Theodor W., 352
Aeppel, Timothy, 110
Aguilera, Christine, 285
Aguirre, Benigno, 646
Ahlburg, Dennis A., 495
Akol, Jacob, 248
Alarid, Leanne Fiftal, 218
Albert, Ethel M., 57
Aldrich, Nelson W., Jr., 290
Alger, Horatio, 302–3
Allende, Salvador, 425
Allport, Floyd, 355
Alter, Jonathon, 463
Amato, Paul R., 495
Amenta, Edwin, 392
Amin, Yousreya, 644
Anderson, Chris, 147
Anderson, Elijah, 98, 225, 227, 482, 617
Anderson, Margaret L., 322
Anderson, Nels, 51
Anderson, Philip, 549
Anderson, Teresa A., 393
Angel (Mexican of Colima), 597, 603, 610
Angell, Marcia, 580
Angell, Robert C., 30
Angler, Natalie, 343
Annin, Peter, 215
Ansberry, Clare, 289, 581
Antecol, Heather, 333
Appiah, Kwame Anthony, 343
Aptheker, Floyd, 18
Arc, Joan of, 442–3
Archbold, Ronna, 422
Arías, Jesús, 194
Ariés, Philippe, 25, 90
Arlacchi, P., 218
Armitage, Richard L., 458
Arndt, William F., 443
Aron, Arthur, 476
Arquitt, George E., 198
Asch, Arthur, 516
Asch, Solomon, 178–9, 181, 183
Ashford, Lori S., 315, 316
Ashley, Richard, 416
Ayittey, George B. N., 248

Baca Zinn, Maxine, 484
Badgett, M. V. Lee, 374

Bai, Matt, 504
Bainbridge, William Sims, 642
Balch, Emily Greene, 18
Balderas, Castillo family, 243–4
Bales, Robert F., 177
Baltzell, E. Digby, 281, 290
Banks, Laurie, 22
Bannon, Lisa, 645
Barkun, Michael, 552
Barnes, Fred, 138
Barnes, Harry Elmer, 670
Barnes, Helen, 217
Baron, Robert, 144
Baron, Stephen W., 219
Barry, John, 458, 678
Barry, Paul, 528
Bartlett, Donald L., 682
Baskin, D. R., 218
Bassano, Francesco, 190
Beals, Gregory, 343
Beals, Ralph L., 57
Beck, Allen J., 218
Beck, Scott H., 390
Becker, Howard S., 212
Becker, Selwin, 178
Beckett, Paul, 62
Beeghley, Leonard, 278, 287, 291, 292, 295
Begley, Sharon, 681
Beittel, Mark, 33
Belkin, Lisa, 586
Bell, Daniel, 412
Bell, David A., 371
Bellah, Robert N., 535
Belluck, Pam, 228, 576
Ben-Yehuda, Nachman, 644
Benales, Carlos, 50
Bender, Sue, 110
Benet, Lorenzo, 686
Benet, Sula, 380
Bengston, Vern L., 398
Berger, Peter L., 3, 7, 250, 419, 441, 656
Bergman, Barbara R., 480
Bergström, Hans, 591
Berk, Laura E., 74
Berk, Richard A., 637
Berle, Adolf, Jr., 423
Bernard, Jessie, 158
Bernard, Viola W., 357, 460
Bernhardt, Eva M., 472
Bernstein, Nina, 302
Bernstein, Richard, 350
Berreby, David, 348
Beyer, Janice M., 178
Beynon, John, 308
Bianchi, Suzanne M., 473, 474, 486, 489, 490

Biddle, Jeff E., 119
Biggs, Mae A., 123, 130
Bills, David B., 515, 518
bin Laden, Osama, 458
bin Sultan, Bandar, 425
Binyon, Michael, 458
Bird, Chloe E., 147, 478
Bishop, Jerry E., 322
Bjerklie, David, 163
Blasse, Joseph, 203
Blau, David M., 480
Blau, Peter M., 295
Blauner, Robert, 402
Blumer, Herbert, 48, 161, 635–6
Blumstein, Philip, 488
Bobo, Lawrence, 348, 349
Bonds, Barry, 76
Bonds, Nikolai, 76
Booth, Alan, 313
Bosman, Ciska M., 112
Boulding, Elise, 160
Bourgois, Philippe, 227
Bowles, Samuel, 515, 518
Bowman, Carl F., 110
Boxer, Sarah, 214
Bradford, Calvin P., 107
Brajuha, Mario, 148–9, 152
Brannon, Linda, 74
Brauchli, Marcus W., 508
Brawley, Lawrence R., 156
Bray, Rosemary L., 365
Brecher, Edward M., 588
Breen, Richard, 295
Brenner, Mark, 202
Bretos, Miguel A., 361
Brewer, Loretta, 397
Bridgman, Ann, 508
Bridgwater, William, 189, 442, 449, 537, 546, 547, 550
Brines, Julie, 476, 489
Brinton, Crane, 536
Broad, William J., 461
Brockerhoff, Martin P., 348, 615, 621
Brody, Charles, 326
Brolin, James, 386
Bromely, David G., 645
Bronfenbrenner, Urie, 494
Brooke, James, 545
Brooks, Geraldine, 336
Brooks, Virginia R., 326
Brooks-Gunn, Jeane, 83
Brown, Garrett, 269
Browne, Beverly A., 79
Browning, Christopher R., 357
Brueggemann, John, 355
Brunvand, Jan Harold, 647
Bryant, Chalandra M., 499

Bryant, Clifton D., 42
Brzezinski, Matthew, 420
Bumiller, Elisabeth, 477
Burgess, Ernest W., 18, 21, 25, 618–19, 635
Burkhart, Melvin, 214
Burnham, Walter Dean, 448
Burns, Lucy, 320
Bush, Diane Mitsch, 75
Bush, George, 639
Bush, George W., 119–20, 684
Butler, Richard, 353
Butler, Robert N., 387
Butler, Sydney, 130
Buttel, Frederick H., 686
Buzzanca, Jaycee, 487
Buzzanca, John, 487
Buzzanca, Luanne, 487
Bynum, Bill, 644

Caesar (of New Testament), 543
Callahan, Daniel, 393
Calment, Jeanne Louise, 384, 385
Calvin, John, 188–9
Canavan, Margaret M., 498
Cannon, Lou, 639
Cantril, Hadley, 642
Capela, Stanley, 22
Caplan, Arthur, 163
Caplow, Theodore, 130
Carlson, Lewis H., 370
Carpenito, Lynda Juall, 334
Carpenter, Betsy, 686
Carper, James C., 510, 513
Carr, Deborah, 90
Carrasquillo, Hector, 484
Carrington, Tim, 270
Carron, Albert V., 156
Cartwnght, Dorwin, 177
Casper, Lynne M., 480, 486, 489, 490
Casper, Monica J., 589
Caspi, Avshalom, 217
Cassel, Russell N., 177
Castle, John, 280
Castro, Fidel, 363
Catton, William R., Jr., 686
Cauthen, Nancy K., 644
Celia (Mexican of Colima), 597–8, 603, 610
Cerulo, Karen A., 173, 402
Cha, Kwang Y., 535
Chafetz, Janet Saltzman, 314, 320, 321, 337
Chagnon, Napoleon A., 212
Chain, David, 685
Chalfant, H. Paul, 536
Chalker, Donald M., 8, 507
Chalkley, Kate, 317
Chamberlain, Claudine, 348
Chambliss, Daniel F., 50, 222
Chambliss, William, 124, 161
Chambliss, William J., 230
Chandak, Rachita, 477
Chandler, Tertius, 614, 615
Chandra, Vibha P., 249, 250
Chang, Leslie, 388
Chaplin, Charlie, 161
Charlemagne, 257
Charles VII, King, 442–3

Chen, I-Chun, 269
Chen, Kathy, 318
Cherlin, Andrew, 496, 498
Chin Nancy P., 289
Chivers, C. J., 215
Chodorow, Nancy J., 75
Chu, Henry, 592
Chua-Eoan, Howard, 552
Chunlan, Zhao, 388
Churchill, Ward A., 357
Clair, Jeffry Michael, 387, 388
Clark, Candace, 76
Clark, Edward, 322
Clark, Robert L., 207
Clay, Jason W., 463
Cleeland, Nancy, 431
Clingempeel, W. Glenn, 494
Clinton, Bill, 425
Cloud, John, 201, 404
Cloward, Richard, 224, 226
Cnaan, Ram A., 199
Cobb, Jonathan, 295
Cobb-Clark, Deborah, 333
Cockerham, William C., 592
Cohen, Gary, 683
Cohen, Joel E., 600
Cohen, Roger, 462
Cohen, Steven M., 422
Colburn, George A., 370
Cole, Jeff, 458
Coleman, James William, 230, 425, 524
Coleman, Marilyn, 496
Collins, Huntly, 396
Collins, Randall, 256, 314, 509
Collymore, Yvette, 317
Columbus, Christopher, 672
Comte, Auguste, 9, 27, 34
Conahan, Frank C., 589
Confucius, 547
Conrad, Peter, 58
Conte, Michael, 203
Cookson, Peter W., Jr., 519
Cooley, Charles Horton, 24, 70–1, 74, 94, 164–5
Cooper, Helene, 590
Corbett, Thomas, 485
Corbin, Robert K., 552
Cornelius, Diana, 248, 263, 583, 601, 603, 605, 606, 615
Cose, Ellis, 376, 618
Coser, Lewis A., 11, 12, 31, 71
Costello, Barbara J., 219
Cottin, Lou, 387
Couch, Carl J., 94
Coughlin, Ellen K., 147
Courtney, Kelly, 686
Cowen, Emory L., 352
Cowgill, Donald, 388
Cowley, Geoffrey, 55, 593
Cowley, Joyce, 320
Crary, David, 400
Crick, Francis, 162
Croall, Hazel, 227
Crosbie, Paul V., 178
Crossen, Cynthia, 138
Crossette, Barbara, 250, 316
Croudace, T. J., 573
Cumming, Elaine, 389–90
Curtin, Sharon, 398

Curwin, E. Cecil, 614

Dabbs, James M., Jr., 313
Dahl, Robert A., 454
Dahrendorf, Ralf, 30, 256
Danzi, Angela K., 571
Darden, Christoper, 367–8
Darley, John, 175–6, 624–5
Darnell, Victor, 141
Darweesh, Suzanne, 268
Darwin, Charles, 10, 58
Dasgupta, Nilanjana, 348
Davies, Kirk L., 461
Davis, Ann, 487
Davis, Fred, 51
Davis, Kingsley, 66, 67, 254–5, 272, 511
Davis, Nancy J., 295
Davis, Stan, 162–3
Day, Dorothy, 320
De Klerk, Willem, 444
De Parle, Jason, 147
De Vita, Carol J., 495
Deck, Leland P., 178
Degler, Jeffrey, 115
Deliege, Robert, 250, 348
DeMaris, Alfred, 496
DeMause, Lloyd, 91
D'Emilio, Frances, 449
Denney, Nancy W., 93
Denny, Reginald, 639
Denzin, Norman K., 578
Derber, Charles, 204
Dewey, John, 24
Diamond, Edwin, 446
Diamond, Milton, 313
Dickson, William J., 144
Diekmann, Andreas, 494
Dietz, Tracy L, 79
Dillin, John, 552
Dirmann, Jack, 528
Diver-Stamnes, Ann C., 74
Dixon, Celvia Stoval, 495
Doane, Ashley W., Jr., 347
Dobash, Russell P., 496
Dobriner, William M., 11, 101
Dobyns, Henry, 357
Dodd, Molly, 117
Dollard, John, 352
Domhoff, G. William, 107, 281, 285, 426, 449, 455–6, 462
Donaldson, Stephen, 333
Donelson, Samuel, 592
Dottridge, Mike, 248
Douglas, Michael, 389
Dove, Adrian, 516
Drucker, Peter F., 203
Du Bois, W. E. B., 18–20, 29, 247, 355, 374
Dudenhefer, Paul, 298
Duff, Christina, 286, 393
Duffy, Michael, 454
Dugger, Celia W., 477, 609
Duncan, Otis Dudley, 295
Duneier, Mitchell, 98, 367
Dunham, Warren, 290, 573
Dunlap, Riley E., 686
Durkheim, Emile, 11, 15, 27, 33, 34, 108, 126, 164, 224, 239, 404, 421, 532
Durning, Alan, 683, 684

Dutton, Donald, 476
Dworkin, Anthony Gary, 320
Dye, H. B., 68–9

Easterbrook, Gregg, 581
Eaton, Isabel, 18
Ebaugh, Helen, 116
Ebomoyi, Ehigie, 317
Eckholm, Erik, 20
Eder, Donna, 326
Eder, Klaus, 670, 686
Edgerton, Robert B., 30, 42, 47, 61, 213
Edwards, Richard, 204
Egan, Timothy, 625
Ehrenreich, Barbara, 315
Ehrhardt, Anke A., 312
Ehrlich, Ann H., 601
Ehrlich, Paul R., 601
Eibl-Eibesfeldt, Irrenäus, 44
Einstein, Albert, 11
Eisenberg, Marlene, 83
Eisenhart, R. Wayne, 326
Eisenstadt, Shmuel Noah, 446
Ekman, Paul, 44, 75, 76
Elder, Glen H., Jr., 90
Elkins, Stanley M., 247
Ellis, James E., 3
Ellul, Jacques, 673
Elsasser, Glen, 661
Engelhardt, Henrietta, 494
Engels, Friedrich, 11, 252, 319, 536
Engeman, Thomas S., 454
England, Paula, 321
English, Deidre, 315
Englund, Will, 683
Epstein, Arnold M., 351
Epstein, Cynthia Fuchs, 75, 310
Erickson, Kristan Glasgow, 218
Erik, John, 610
Ernst, Eldon G., 540, 550
Esau (of Old Testament), 683
Escalante, Jaime, 527–8
Evans, Peter, 195
Ezekiel, Raphael S., 355–6

Fairris, David, 202
Falcon, Pedro, 48
Famighetti, Robert, 263
Faris, Robert E. L., 290, 573
Farkas, George, 521
Farney, Dennis, 373
Farrakhan, Louis, 545
Farrell, Christopher, 430, 431
Farris-Luse, Maud, 385
Faunce, William A., 599
Feagin, Joe R., 367
Featherman, David L., 295
Feinglass, Joe, 581
Feldman, Saul D., 178
Felsenthal, Edward, 332, 574
Felton, Lee Ann, 334
Fendrich, James Max, 657
Ferracuti, Franco, 218
Ferraro, Susan, 674, 679
Feshbach, Murray, 683
Fessenden, Ford, 574
Fialka, John J., 290
Field, Mark G., 591
Filkins, Dexter, 250

Fineman, Howard, 446
Finke, Roger, 557
Finkelhor, David, 497
Finn, Chester E., 527
Firestone, David, 626
Fischer, Claude S., 445, 614
Fischer, Edward, 476
Fisher, Ann, 331
Fisher, Ian, 342
Fisher, Julie, 200
Fisher, Sue, 575, 577
Fitzpatrick, Edward, 396
Fitzpatrick, Kevin, 682
Flanagan, William G., 614, 629
Flavel, John H., 71
Fleming, Joyce Dudney, 59
Fletcher, June, 283
Fletcher, Martin, 463
Flexner, Abraham, 569
Flippen, Annette R., 181, 363
Flockhart, Calista, 118
Foley, Douglas E., 326
Foley, Linda A., 151
Foote, Donna, 487
Foote, Jennifer, 686
Ford, Henry, 674, 675
Foreman, Dave, 686
Form, William, 419
Foster, J. Todd, 260
Fountain, Henry, 614
Fox, Elaine, 198
Fox, Gerald, 614, 615
Fox, Vicente, 269
Frank (car repair shop owner), 284–5
Fraser, Graham, 269
Freedman, Jane, 320
Freese, Jeremy, 481
Freud, Sigmund, 11, 74–5, 94, 237
Freudenburg, William R., 686
Frey, William H., 606
Friedl, Ernestine, 318
Fritz, Jan M., 32
Froman, Ingmarie, 472
Frumkin, Robert M., 558
Fuller, Kathryn S., 683, 684
Fuller, Rex, 328–9
Furstenberg, Frank F., Jr., 495, 498

Galbraith, John Kenneth, 270
Galinsky, Ellen, 474
Gallambos, Louis, 421
Galliher, John, 15
Gallmeier, Charles P., 326
Gallup, George, Jr., 559
Gans, Herbert J., 61, 622–3, 624, 626
Garbarino, Merwin, 357
Garcia, Angela, 326
Garcia, Leslie, 397
Gardner, Allen, 59
Gardner, Beatrice, 59
Gardner, Marilyn, 491
Garfinkel, Harold, 88–9, 120–1, 214
Garrett, Laurie, 586
Garrett, Michael Tlanusta, 484
Gates, Bill, 254, 279
Gatewood, Willard B., 481
Gautama, Siddhartha, 546
Gaviak, Dale, 248
Geis, Gilbert, 576

Gelles, Richard J., 496
Genetski, Robert, 395
Genovese, Catherine, 622
Gerassimow, Alexander, 417
Gerhard, Jane, 75
Germain, Sophie, 18
Gerson, Kathleen, 486
Gerth, H. H., 253
Gibbs, Nancy, 504
Giddens, Anthony, 12
Giele, Janet, 337
Gilbert, Dennis, 285, 286–7, 292, 304
Gillborn, David, 515
Gilligan, Carol, 74
Gilman, Charlotte Perkins, 17, 18, 79,
   338
Gilmore, David D., 312
Gingrich, F. Wilbur, 443
Ginsberg, Ruth Bader, 331
Gintis, Herbert, 515
Gitlin, Tod, 11
Glenn, Evelyn Nakano, 484
Glick, Paul C., 495
Goble, Paul, 260
Goering, Hermann, 178
Goetting, Ann, 496, 497
Goffman, Erving, 88, 89, 115, 117–18,
   126, 213
Gold, Ray, 283
Goldberg, Carey, 592
Goldberg, Steven, 311
Goldberg, Susan, 78, 79
Golden, Drew, 525
Goldman, Kevin, 389
Goldsborough, Margaret, 173
Goldscheider, Frances K., 472
Goleman, Daniel, 138, 481
Gomez, Carlos F., 580
Gonzalez, Elian, 637
Goode, Erica, 333
Goode, Erich, 587, 644
Goode, William J., 569
Gorman, Peter, 684
Gotschall, Mary G., 552
Gottfredson, Michael R., 219
Gottschalk, Peter, 296
Gould, Jewell C., 526
Gourevitch, Philip, 342
Gracey, Harry L., 85, 516
Graham, Ellen, 556
Gramling, Robert, 686
Gray, Joseph, 215
Gray, William H., III, 350
Greeley, Andrew, 554
Green, Leslie, 22
Greenberg, Brigitte, 587
Greenberg, Gerald, 144
Greengard, Samuel, 205
Greenhalgh, Susan, 609
Greenwald, Anthony, 348
Gross, Jan T., 342, 357
Gross, Jane, 119
Grossman, Lawrence K., 446, 524
Grosz, Barbara, 324
Guensburg, Carol, 83
Guernsey, Lisa, 173
Guevara, Ché, 536
Guice, Jon, 21, 22
Gupta, Gira Raj, 477

Gutenberg, Johann, 106

Haas, Jack, 51, 576
Hacker, Helen Meyer, 318
Haddad, Angela, 14
Hagar (of Old Testament), 545
Haldane, David, 587
Hall, Edward T., 113
Hall, G. Stanley, 91
Hall, J. A., 326
Hall, Richard H., 193
Hallowell, Lyle, 148
Hamermesh, Daniel, 119
Hamilton, Alice, 18
Hamilton, Kendall, 215
Hamilton, Richard F., 14
Hammerstein, J., 574
Hao, Jiming, 681
Hardy, Dorcas, 395
Hardy, Quentin, 422
Hare, A. Paul, 156, 177
Harlow, Harry, 69–70
Harlow, Margaret, 69–70
Harmon, Mary, 422
Harrington, Michael, 270–1, 271, 300
Harris, Chauncey, 620
Harris, Diana K., 380
Harris, Eric, 503–4
Harris, Kathleen Mullan, 495
Harris, Marvin, 319, 346
Harrison, Paul, 266
Hart, Charles W. M., 379–80, 386
Hart, Gudmond, 614
Hart, Paul, 181
Hartley, Eugene, 352
Hartmann, Heidi, 374
Harwood, John, 336, 453
Haslick, Leonard, 380
Hatch, Laurie Russell, 390, 391
Haub, Carl, 248, 263, 583, 601, 603, 605, 606, 615
Hauser, Philip, 216, 615
Hauser, Robert M., 295
Hawkes, Nigel, 588
Hawley, Amos H., 614
Hawthorne, Nathaniel, 214
Hayakawa, S. I., 362
Hayashi, Gina M., 494
Hayes, Donald P., 523
Haynes, Richard M., 8, 507
Haynie, Dana L., 218
Hechter, Michael, 463
Heckert, D. Alex, 493, 494
Hehir, Grainne, 329
Heilbrun, Alfred B, 217
Hellinger, Daniel, 281, 447, 458, 505–6
Hendin, Herbert, 579
Hendrix, Lewellyn, 314
Henley, Nancy, 8
Henretta, John C., 391
Henriques, Diana B., 351
Henry, William E., 389–90
Henslin, James M., 4, 25, 50, 51, 54, 79, 130, 133, 292, 399, 403, 431, 434, 496, 661
Hentoff, Nat, 248
Herod (of New Testament), 543
Herrera, Victor Manuel, 215
Herring, George C., 458

Herrnstein, Richard J., 216
Hertzler, Joyce O., 48
Herzog, A. Regula, 494
Higgens, Elizabeth, 487
Higginbotham, Elizabeth, 295
Higley, John, 291
Hill, Paul T., 512
Hill, Zettie Mae, 289
Hilliard, Asa, III, 528
Hiltz, Starr Roxanne, 481
Hindus, Michael, 29
Hines, Revathi I, 682
Hippler, Fritz, 354, 447
Hirschi, Travis, 219
Hitler, Adolf, 124, 178, 342, 345, 443, 447
Hochschild, Arlie, 75, 474–5, 476
Hoffer, Thomas, 524
Hoijer, Harry, 57
Holbein, Hans, the Younger, 667
Holden, Benjamin A., 639
Holland, Gina, 588
Holtzman, Abraham, 391
Homblin, Dora Jane, 614
Hon-ming Yao, Oliver, 318
Honeycutt, Karen, 119
Hong, Lawrence, 471
Horowitz, Ruth, 218
Hostetler, John A., 110, 539
Hout, Michael, 554
Houtman, Dick, 292
Howard, Nelson F., 526
Howe, Henry, 58
Howells, Lloyd, 178
Hoyt, Homer, 620
Hsu, Francis L. K., 370
Huber, Joan, 252, 319
Huddle, Donald, 609
Hudo, Buba, 129
Hudo, Cindy, 129
Hudson, Beth, 400
Hudson, Christopher G., 573
Hudson, James R., 624
Hudson, Robert B., 391
Huggins, Martha K., 264–5
Hughes, H. Stuart, 671
Hughes, Kathleen A., 115
Huizenga, Wayne, 280
Hull, Raymond, 195
Humphreys, Laud, 149
Hussein, Saddam, 447
Huttenbach, Henry R., 357

Iori, Ron, 422
Isaac (of Old Testament), 542
Ishmael (of Old Testament), 545
Isikoff, Michael, 552
Itard, Jean Marc Gospard, 66
Iutcovich, Joyce Miller, 22

Jackson, Jesse, 366
Jacob (of Old Testament), 542
Jacobs, Charles, 248
Jacobs, Margaret A., 171
Jacobson, Lenore, 521
Jaggar, Alison M., 338
James, Daniel, 451
James, William, 24
Jamie (homeless woman), 238–9

Janis, Irving, 181
Jankowiak, William, 476
Jankowski, Martín Sánchez, 227
Jarley, Paul, 200
Jaro (Colombian of Medellin), 611
Jarrell, John, 284
Jarrell, Sandy, 284
Jaspar, James M., 657, 659
Jasper, James M., 644
Jáuregui, Gurutz, 463
Jefferson, Thomas, 447, 505
Jenkins, Philip, 644
Jennes, Valerie, 644
Jerrome, Dorothy, 390
Jesus, 543
Jifkin, Jeremy, 432
Johansson, Perry, 318
Johns, Charlie, 93
Johns, Eunice, 93
Johnson, Benton, 547
Johnson, Cathryn, 75
Johnson, Dirk, 628
Johnson, Jimmy, 475
Johnson, Lyndon Baines, 394
Johnson, Miriam, 326
Johnson, Mitch, 525
Johnson, Norris R., 643
Johnson, Paul A., 372
Johnston, Drue M., 643
Johnston, Lloyd D., 586, 587
Jones, Catherine Zetta, 389
Jones, James H., 589
Jordan, Mary, 350
Jordan, Miriam, 609
Joseph (of Old Testament), 542
Josephson, Matthew, 416
Joyner, Kara, 489
Judd, Dennis R., 281, 447, 458, 505–6
Judis, John B., 454

Kaczynski, Ted, 673
Kaebnick, Gregory E., 163
Kagan, Jerome, 73, 76
Kahl, Joseph A., 285, 286–7, 292, 304
Kanabayashi, Masayoshi, 208
Kanter, Rosabeth Moss, 130, 200, 202
Kantrowitz, Barbara, 526
Karp, David A., 624, 626, 627
Kart, Cary S., 387
Katz, Sidney, 112, 178
Kaufman, Joanne, 286
Kazman, Sam, 587
Keith, Jennie, 390
Kelley, Florence, 18
Kelly, Joan B., 494, 495
Kelly family, 244
Kemp, Alice Abel, 328
Keniston, Kenneth, 91
Kennedy, John F., 181, 374, 444, 451
Kennedy, Paul, 426
Kent, Mary M., 343, 375
Kephart, William, 539
Kephart, William M., 110
Kerr, Clark, 419
Kevorkian, Jack, 578, 579
Keyes, Alan, 366
Khomeini, Ayatollah, 444
Kibria, Nazli, 484
Kifner, John, 266

Kilbourne, Jean, 79
Killian, Lewis M., 634, 637–8
King, Martin Luther, Jr., 365, 536, 639
King, Rodney, 639
Kingsley, Gordon A., 194
Kinsella, Kevin, 388
Kishkovsky, Sophia, 592
Kitsuse, John, 659
Klandemans, Bert, 648
Klebold, Dylan, 503–4
Klonoff, Elizabeth, 567
Kluegel, James R., 303, 348, 349
Knaus, William A., 577
Knight, Phil, 409
Koenig, Thomas, 424, 425
Kohlberg, Lawrence, 73, 74
Kohn, Melvin L., 82, 290, 457, 480
Kolata, Gina, 583
Kolhlberg, Lawrence, 94
Kooistra, Paul G., 358
Korbin, Jill E., 400
Korda, Michael, 325
Koresh, David, 531, 550–1
Kornhauser, William, 656
Kotlowitz, Alex, 523
Kramer, Josea B., 386
Krane, Vikki, 119
Kraybill, Donald, 110
Krebs, Dennis L., 74
Kreidl, Martin, 283
Krog, Antjie, 250
Krueger, Robert F., 217
Krysan, Maria, 348
Kübler-Ross, Elisabeth, 403, 404, 406
Kuhn, Margaret E., 396
Kuntz, Phil, 552

La Barre, Weston, 57, 469
Lacayo, Richard, 216, 552
Lachica, Eduardo, 683
Lagaipa, Susan J., 609
Lagnado, Lucette, 587
LaGory, Mark, 682
Lalumiere, Martin L., 216
Lamb, Michael E., 494
Lancaster, Hal, 330
Landler, Mark, 412
Landrine, Hope, 567
Landtman, Gunnar, 246
Lang, Gladys E., 659
Lang, Kurt, 659
Lannoy, Richard, 249
Larson, Gary, 172
Lasch, Christopher, 25, 26
Laska, Shirley Bradway, 686
Latané, Bibb, 175–6, 624–5
Lauer, Jeanette, 498
Lauer, Robert, 498
Lawler, Steph, 295
Lay, Kenneth, 279
Lazarsfeld, Paul F., 32
Leacock, Eleanor, 324
LeBon, Gustave, 635, 636
Lee, Alfred McClung, 655
Lee, Elizabeth Briant, 655
Lee, Lois, 23
Lee, Raymond M., 141
Lee, Sharon M., 371
Lehrer, Joshua, 350

Leland, John, 343
Lemann, Nicholas, 628
Lenin, Vladimir Ilyich, 259, 536
Lenski, Gerhard, 159, 256, 272, 283–4, 614, 670
Lenski, Jean, 159, 614, 670
Leo III, Pope, 257
Leonhardt, David, 291
Lerner, Gerda, 247, 314, 318, 319
Lesser, Alexander, 456
Lester, David, 373
Levine, John M., 179
Levinson, D. J., 90
Lewin, Tamar, 293, 333
Lewis, Michael, 78, 79
Lewis, Nancy, 301
Lewis, Oscar, 270, 300
Lewis, Ted, 301
Li, Jiali, 609
Licata, Jane Massey, 593
Liebow, Elliot, 98, 227, 302
Light, Donald W., 591
Light, Richard J., 514
Lightfoot-Klein, A., 317
Lin, Quiyun, 527
Lin, S., 495
Lincoln, Abraham, 254
Lind, Michael, 372, 449
Linden, Eugene, 684
Lines, Patricia M., 512–13
Linton, Melaney. A, 333
Linton, Ralph, 39, 103, 315
Lippitt, Ronald, 177
Lipset, Seymour Martin, 292, 443
Locke, Gary, 371
Locke, Harvey, 25
Lofland, John, 634, 638, 647
Logue, John, 203
Lombroso, Cesare, 216
Longman, Jere, 87
Lopez, Julie Amparano, 330
Lorber, Judith, 337
Lovoy, Kenneth L., 657
Lublin, Joann S., 203, 280, 330
Lubman, Sarah, 458, 639
Lucas, Samuel Roundfield, 511, 517
Ludlum, Ned, 673
Luke, Timothy W., 536
Lundberg, Olle, 290
Lundy, Garvey, 368
Lunneborg, Patricia, 485
Luoma, Jon R., 681
Lurie, Nicole, 322
Luther, Martin, 543–4

Mabry, Marcus, 248
MacDonald, Heather, 230
MacDonald, William L., 496
Mack, Raymond W., 107
Mackay, Charles, 635
Mackey, Daniel, 115
Mackey, Jennifer, 115
Mackey, Richard A., 481
Macy, Michael W., 646
Maher, Sarah, 359
Mahoney, John S., Jr., 358
Mahoney, Patricia, 497
Mahran, M., 317
Main, Jackson Turner, 247

Malinowski, Bronislaw, 48, 469
Malmberg, Bo, 399
Malson, Lucien, 66
Malthus, Thomas, 598–9
Mamdani, Mahmood, 605
Manavalan, Theresa, 162
Mandela, Nelson, 444
Mander, Jerry, 348, 373, 678
Mann, Horace, 506
Manno, Bruno V., 523, 527
Mansfield, Harvey C., 523
Manski, Charles F., 518
Manson, Charles, 234
Marable, Manning, 369
Marcus, Amy Dockser, 463
Marger, Martin N., 85
Markhusen, Erik, 357, 462
Markson, Elizabeth W., 580
Markstein, Gary, 452
Marolla, Joseph, 147, 150–1
Marshall, Nancy, 248
Marshall, Samantha, 119
Martin, William, 33
Martineau, Harriet, 17, 34
Marx, Gary T., 205, 658
Marx, Karl, 11, 30, 34, 188, 194, 208, 251, 252–3, 259, 272, 276, 284, 303, 419, 536, 540, 667, 671
Masheter, Carol, 495
Massey, Douglas S., 48, 368
Mateja, Jim, 682
Mateju, Petr, 283
Matza, David, 220–1
Mauss, Armand, 659
Maybury-Lewis, David, 77
Mayo, Elton, 144
McAdam, Doug, 651, 656, 657
McAuliffe, Christa, 665
McCabe, J. Terrance, 3
McCall, Michael, 51
McCarthy, John D., 141, 656, 659
McCartney, Scott, 571
McCaughey, Bobby, 487
McCaughey, Kenny, 487
McCormick, Albert E., Jr., 422
McCormick, John, 228, 522, 618
McCuen, Gary E., 683
McDonald, Peter, 601
McFarling, Usha Lee, 681
McGee, Glenn, 163
McGinn, Daniel, 526
McGowan, Jo, 609
McGwire, Mark, 87, 624
McIntire, Jamie, 332
McKenna, George, 661
McKeown, Thomas, 598
McKinney, Gene, 332
McLanahan, Sara, 485
McLemore, S. Dale, 272, 373
McNeil, Donald G., Jr., 265
McNeil, William H., 598
McPhail, Clark, 635–6, 639
McVeigh, Timothy, 639
Mead, George Herbert, 18, 24, 71–2, 74, 94
Mead, Margaret, 57
Means, Gardener C., 423
Mechitov, Alexander I., 508
Meek, Anne, 528

Meier, Barry, 588
Melloan, George, 449
Meltzer, Bernard N., 94
Melucci, Alberto, 651
Menaghan, Elizabeth G., 485
Menzel, Peter, 244
Mersereau, Adam G., 332
Merton, Robert K., 27, 167, 225, 238, 240, 520
Merwine, Maynard H., 317
Messner, Michael, 86
Meyer, Christopher, 162–3
Mezentseva, E, 319
Michaelangelo, 538
Michalowski, Raymond J., 161
Michels, Robert, 199, 209
Milbank, Dana, 620
Milgram, Stanley, 169, 179–81, 181, 183
Milkie, Melissa, 81
Miller, Dan E., 180
Miller, Judith, 461
Miller, Laura L., 326
Miller, Lisa, 545
Miller, Michael W., 290, 572
Miller, Walter B., 218
Miller-Loessi, Karen, 429
Mills, C. Wright, 2, 20–1, 34, 93, 150, 253, 256, 281, 304, 455
Mills, Karen M., 327
Minchin, Timothy J., 355
Miner, Horace, 570
Minkler, Meredith, 395
Mintz, Beth A., 425
Mitchell, G., 82
Mizruchi, Mark S., 424, 425
Mohawk, John C., 373
Money, John, 312
Monk-Turner, Elizabeth, 316
Montagu, M. F. Ashley, 344
Moore, Bert, 634
Moore, Wilbert E., 254, 272, 511
Morgan, Lewis Henry, 670
Morin, Monte, 397
Morita, Akio, 207
Morris, Alden, 657
Morris, J. R., 349
Morris, Robin, 313
Morrow, Betty Hearn, 643
Morton, Dooley, 634
Mosca, Gaetano, 256, 272
Moscos, Charles C., 130
Moseley-Braun, Carol, 337
Moses (of Old Testament), 542
Mosher, Steven W., 419, 601, 610
Mount, Ferdinand, 476
Moyers, Bill, 354
Moynihan, Daniel, 299–300
Muehlenhard, Charlene L., 333
Muhammad, Khalid Abdul, 353
Muhammad (the Prophet), 544
Muir, Donal, 349
Mulleta family, 243
Murdock, George Peter, 57, 314, 338, 469
Murphy, Kim, 353
Murray, G.W., 3

Nabhan, Gary Paul, 684
Nachman, Sharon, 400

Nader, Ralph, 684
Nagourney, Eric, 535
Naj, Amal Kumar, 202, 603
Nakao, Keiko, 282
Narayan, Shoba, 204
Nash, Gary B., 372
Nathan, John, 207
Nation, Carrie, 651
Naughton, Kieth, 205
Nauta, André, 540, 550
Neikirk, William, 661
Nelkin, Dorothy, 657
Neugarten, Bernice L., 92
Newby, Robert, 14
Niebuhr, H. Richard, 557
Nieves, Evelyn, 686
Noah, Timothy, 589
Nordhaus, William D., 278
Norris, Chuck, 118
Nowak, Thomas C., 493, 494
Noymer, Andrew, 645
Nsamenang, A. Bame, 603
Nuland, Sherwin B., 405, 579

Oberschall, Anthony, 656
O'Brien, Bernard A., 481
O'Brien John E., 134
O'Connell, Martin, 479, 480
O'Connor, Sandra Day, 331
Offen, Karen, 338
Ogawa, Naohiro, 207
Ogburn, William F., 25, 60, 670, 671, 687
O'Hare, Bill, 485
O'Hare, William P., 287, 296, 300
Ohlin, Lloyd, 224, 226
Ohmae, Kenichi, 463
Olmsted, Michael S., 156, 177
Olneck, Michael R., 515, 518
Olshansky, S. Jay, 586
Ono, Yumiko, 422
O'Rand, Angela M., 391
Orlans, Harold, 14
Orwell, George, 439
Ostling, Richard N., 533
Ouchi, William, 206–7, 507

Paddock, Richard C., 420, 592
Page, Joe W., 390
Pagelow, Mildred Daley, 496
Palumbo, Thomas J., 327
Pandey, Sanjay, K., 194
Parfit, Michel, 686
Park, Robert Ezra, 18, 21, 618, 635
Parks, Rosa, 365
Parmar, Pratibha, 317
Parsons, Elsie Clews, 18
Parsons, Talcott, 20–1, 511, 566
Partingon, Donald H., 235
Pasztor, Andy, 229
Passell, Peter, 351
Paul, Alice, 18, 320
Paul, Ron, 552
Pearl, Daniel, 271
Pearlin, L. I., 82
Peart, Karen N., 545
Pennar, Karen, 430, 431
Pepperberg, Irene, 59
Perdue, Frank, 422

Perot, Ross, 449
Perreault, George, 527
Perrin, Kathleen, 393
Perrow, Charles, 202
Persell, Caroline Hodges, 285, 519
Peter, Laurence J., 195, 208
Peterson, James L., 494
Peterson, Janice, 302
Peterson, Melody, 461, 576
Peterson, Oscar, 361
Pettie, Sam, 634, 636
Pfann, Gerard A., 112
Phillips, Barbara D., 586
Piaget, Jean, 72–3, 74, 94
Pillemer, Karl, 400
Pilling, Arnold R., 380, 386
Pilling, D, 521
Piotrow, Phylis Tilson, 599
Platt, Tony, 230
Polsby, Nelson W., 454
Polumbaum, Judy, 609
Pontiac (Ottawa chief), 372
Pope, Liston, 547
Portés, Alejandro, 374, 451
Postman, Neil, 673
Poulson, Jane D., 657
Powell, Colin, 253, 254, 639
Power, Carla, 545
Presley, Cheryl A., 587
Pressley, Sue Anne, 552
Pringle, M. Kellmer, 521
Prud'Homme, Alex, 451
Prynne, Hester, 214–15

Quadagno, David, 93
Quinsey, Vernon, 216

Rabinovitz, Jonathan, 480
Radelet, Michael L., 14
Ram, Arun Bharat, 477
Raney, Rebecca Fairley, 446
Rauch, James E., 195
Ray, J. J., 353
Read, Piers Paul, 50
Reagan, Ronald, 254, 399
Reat, Noble Ross, 547
Recer, Paul, 385, 405
Reckless, Walter, 219
Redclift, Michael, 686
Reed, Susan, 686
Reeve, Christopher, 103
Reibstein, Larry, 201
Reich, Robert B., 330
Reiser, Christa, 75, 335
Reitman, Valerie, 208
Reitz, Jeffrey G., 32
Renteln, Alison Dundes, 609
Repucci, N. Dickon, 494
Reskin, Barbara F., 374
Resnik, David B., 138
Rettig, Kathryn D., 495
Reynolds, Farley, 348
Rhone, Nedra, 397
Rich, Spencer, 366
Ricks, Thomas E., 89, 333, 458
Rieker, Patricia P., 147, 496
Riessman, Catherine Kohler, 569
Rifkin, Jeremy, 435
Rigdon, Joan E., 523

Riis, Jacob, 253
Riley, Nancy E., 316
Rimland, Ingrid, 353
Rishe, Patrick James, 323
Risman, Barbara H., 474
Rist, Ray C., 520
Ritzer, George, 193
Robertson, Ann, 395
Robertson, Ian, 50, 259, 536
Robertson, Pat, 555
Robinson, Robert V., 295
Rockefeller, John D., 416
Rodash, Mary Flannery, 569, 571
Rodriguez, Richard, 84, 295, 510
Rodríguez, Victor M., 627, 637, 638, 639
Rodwin, Marc A., 576
Roethlisberger, Fritz J., 144
Rogers, Joseph W., 219
Romero, Simon, 293
Roosevelt, Franklin D., 181
Roosevelt, Theodore, 449
Rosaldo, Michelle Zimbalist, 315
Rose, Fredrick, 639
Rosenbaum, David E., 431
Rosenberg, Charles E., 569
Rosenthal, Elisabeth, 42, 119, 318, 585, 592
Rosenthal, Robert, 521
Ross, Catherine E., 573
Ross, Emma, 400
Rossi, Alice, 312
Rossi, Peter, 145–7
Rotello, Gabriel, 585
Rothman, Barbara Katz, 571
Rothschild, Joyce, 202, 204
Ruane, Janet, 402
Rubin, Lillian Breslow, 478, 481
Rubin, Zick, 476
Rudner, Lawrence M., 513
Ruffenbach, Glenn, 398
Ruggles, Patricia, 296, 300
Rumbaut, Ruben G., 374, 451
Russell, Diana E. H., 497, 498
Ryan, John, 389
Rybczynski, Witold, 626

Sahlins, Marshal D., 670
Salholz, Eloise, 451
Salk, Jonas, 196
Sally (computer error), 676
Sampat, Jyothi, 477
Sampson, Catherine, 592
Sampson, Robert J., 83
Samuelson, Paul, 278
Sanchez, Laura, 474
Sandefur, Gary D., 300, 485
Sanders, Howard, 618
Sapir, Edward, 47, 62
Sapsford, Jathon, 208
Sarah (of Old Testament), 542, 545
Satchell, Michael, 686
Savells, Jerry, 110
Saxe, G. B., 74
Sayres, William, 468
Scarr, Sandra, 83
"Scary Guy," 237
Schaefer, Naomi, 248
Schaefer, Richard T., 357, 362, 365, 371
Schatz, Thomas A., 576

Schellenberg, James, 25
Schlesinger, Jacob M., 208
Schneiderman, Howard G., 281
Schnetz, Jean Victor, 257
Schnore, Leo, 615
Schoenberger, Richard, 328–9
Schooler, Carmi, 82
Schottland, Charles I., 392
Schuller, Robert, 555
Schultz, Charles M., 387, 555
Schwartz, Felice N., 330, 331
Schwartz, John, 223
Schwartz, Michael, 425
Schwartz, Mildred A., 440
Schwartz, Pepper, 488
Schwartz, William, 204
Scott, Cody "Monster," 155–6, 166, 168
Scott, Ellen Kaye, 653
Scott, Janny, 618
Scully, Diana, 147, 150–1, 577
Seaver, W. J., 521
Sega, Along, 684
Seinfeld, Jerry, 384
Sellers, Sean, 79
Seltzer, Judith A., 495
Sengupta, Somini, 302
Sennett, Richard, 295
Service, Elman R., 670
Shaffir, William, 576
Shapiro, Joseph P., 579
Sharp, Deborah, 48
Sharp, Lauriston, 672
Shellenbarger, Sue, 331, 491
Shenon, Philip, 332
Sherif, Carolyn, 354–5
Sherif, Muzafer, 354–5
Sherkat, Darren E., 552
Sherman, Spencer, 216
Shibutani, Tamotsu, 462, 645
Shirouzu, Norihiko, 208, 422
Shively, JoEllen, 53
Shreve, Herbie, 556
Sieb, Gerald F., 446
Sigmundson, Keith, 313
Signorielli, Nancy, 79
Sills, David L., 195, 198
Silverman, Robert A., 446
Simmel, Georg, 173–4
Simmons, Ann M., 357
Simmons, Robert G., 75
Simon, Julian L., 602, 609
Simons, Marlise, 684
Simpson, Alan, 393
Simpson, George Eaton, 355, 358
Sims, JoAnne, 302
Singh, Thaman, 605
Skeels, H.M., 68–9
Skeen family, 245
Skiba, Katherine M., 269
Skow, John, 686
Sloan, Allan, 395
Small, Albion, 18, 32, 156
Smart, Barry, 670
Smith, Beverly, 498
Smith, Clark, 462
Smith, Craig S., 683
Smith, Daniel Scott, 29
Smith, Eliot R., 303
Smith, Harold, 395

Smith, Hyrum, 550
Smith, Jackie, 651
Smith, Joseph, 550
Smith, Kristen F., 398
Smith, Lee, 395
Smith, Simon C., 270
Smith, Wesley J., 580
Smith-Lovin, Lynn, 326
Smock, Pamela J., 495
Snell, Pamela, 487
Snipp, C. Matthew, 484
Snow, David A., 637, 656
Snow, Margaret E., 481
Snyder, Jack, 625
Snyder, Kay A., 493, 494
Snyder, Mark, 111, 112, 521
Soloman, Jolie, 204
Sommers, I. B., 218
Sorokin, Pitrim A., 457
Soss, Joe, 292
South, Scott J., 483
Sowell, Thomas, 522
Spain, Daphne, 474
Spector, Malcolm, 659
Spencer, Herbert, 10, 27, 34
Spengler, Oswald, 671
Spickard, P .R. S., 358
Spitzer, Steven, 230
Spragins, Ellyn E., 580
Sprecher, Susan, 477
Squeo, Anne Marie, 271
Srole, Leo, 290
Stack, Carol B., 482
Stalin, Josef, 447
Stampp, Kenneth M., 247
Stark, Elizabeth, 547
Stark, Roger, 557
Starr, Paul, 569
Starrels, Marjorie, 331
Statham, Anne, 429
Stecklow, Steve, 523
Steele, James B., 682
Steele, Shelby, 369
Steele, Stephen F., 21
Stein, Leonard I., 578
Steinberg, Jacques, 522
Steinberg, Laurence, 524
Steinhauer, Jennifer, 574–5, 580
Steinmetz, Suzanne K., 496
Stevens, Amy, 639
Stevens, Mitchell L., 513
Stevenson, Richard W., 395
Stewart, Abigail J., 493, 494
Stinnett, Nicholas, 499
Stipp, David, 59, 684
Stockard, Jean, 326
Stockwell, John, 460
Stodgill, Ralph M., 178
Stohr, Oskar, 67
Stolberg, Sheryl Gay, 351
Stone, Gregory P., 624
Stone, Martin, 353
Storfer, Miles D., 481
Stouffer, Samuel A., 326
Strang, David, 646
Straus, Murray A., 496
Straus, Roger, 145
Strauss, Neil, 336
Streckfuss, Diane, 79

Streisand, Barbara, 386
Strickland, Bonnie R., 494
Stryker, Sheldon, 24, 656
Suiter, J. Jill, 400
Sullivan, Andrew, 259
Sulloway, Frank J., 481
Sumner, William Graham, 40
Sun, Lena H., 388
Sundström, Gerdt, 399
Suris, Oscar, 208
Sutherland, Edwin, 217–18, 227
Suzuki, Bob H., 371, 484
Swasy, Alecia, 523
Sykes, Gresham, 220–1
Szasz, Thomas, 237–8

Taeuber, Cynthia M., 388
Taft, William Howard, 449
Takewell, Terry, 289
Tannen, Deborah, 326
Tanouye, Elyse, 229, 592
Tapia, Andres, 545
Tate, Sharon, 234
Taylor, Chris, 80
Taylor, Howard F., 171
Taylor, Raymond G., 508
Terry, Don, 350
Thayer, Stephen, 114
Thelen, Esther, 73
Thomas, Dorothy Swaine, 122, 344
Thomas, Evan, 458
Thomas, Melvin E., 79
Thomas, Paulette, 351
Thomas, R. Murray, 74
Thomas, William Isaac, 24, 122, 344
Thompson, Ginger, 268
Thornton, Russell, 357, 372
Tilly, Charles, 659
Timasheff, Nicholas S., 457
Timerman, Jacobo, 257
Tito, Josip Broz, 358
Tobias, Andrew, 194
Toch, Thomas, 524
Tocqueville, Alexis de, 197, 657
Tolchin, Martin, 588
Tönnies, Ferdinand, 108, 110, 126
Townsend, Francis, 391
Toynbee, Arnold, 671
Treas, Judith, 282, 397, 398
Treiber, Linda A, 79
Treiman, Donald J., 282
Trice, Harrison M., 178
Troeltsch, Ernst, 547
Trotsky, Leon, 259
Trudeau, Garry B., 137, 474
Trump, Donald, 286, 417
Tumin, Melvin M., 255, 272
Turkle, Sherry, 173
Turnbull, Colin, 77
Turner, Bryan S., 446
Turner, Charles G., 316
Turner, Jonathan H., 27, 31, 75, 516
Turner, Ralph H., 634, 637–8, 638, 645
Tye, Larry, 552

Uchitelle, Louis, 296
Udry, J. Richard, 312
Udy, Stanley H., Jr., 193
Ullman, Edward, 620

Underwood, Anne, 593
Usdansky, Margaret L., 48
Useem, Michael, 107, 423, 425

van Willigen, Marieke, 573
Vande Berg, Leah R., 79
Vanderbilt, Cornelius, 253
Vanderbilt, Gladys, 253
Vargas, Arturo, 449
Vasil, Latika, 389
Vaughan, Diane, 495
Veblin, Thorstein, 411
Vega, William A., 484
Ventura, Jesse, 446
Verhovek, Sam Howe, 578
Vernon, JoEtta A., 389
Violas, P. C., 510
Volti, Rudi, 4, 109, 189, 196, 434, 574,
    582, 673
Von Hoffman, Nicholas, 149
Vowell, Paul R., 219

Wagley, Charles, 346
Waldholz, Michael, 61
Waldman, Amy, 618
Waldman, Peter, 271
Walker, Alice, 317
Wallace, Anthony F. C., 559
Wallerstein, Immanuel, 267
Wallerstein, Judith S., 494, 495
Walsh, Catherine, 73
Wang, Hongyu, 495
Wark, Gillian R., 74
Warr, Mark, 218
Washington, George, 510
Wass, Hannelore, 389
Watson, J. Mark, 51, 222
Watson, James, 162
Watts, Duncan J., 169
Wayne, John, 53
Wayne, Julie Holliday, 331
Wayne, Leslie, 453
Webb, Eugene J., 141
Weber, Lynn, 295
Weber, Max, 13–14, 15, 33, 34, 188–94,
    202, 208, 252, 253–4, 272, 276,
    303, 304, 411, 432, 440, 441, 443,
    444, 464, 541–2, 667
Webster, Noah, 505
Webster, Pamela S., 494
Weeks, John R., 600
Weiler, Jeanne, 517
Weisburd, David, 227
Weisskopf, Michael, 681
Wells, Orson, 642
Wells, Susan J., 433
Wenneker, Mark B., 351
Wentworth, William M., 389
Wertz, Dorothy C., 571
Wertz, Richard W., 571
Wessel, David, 381
West, Candace, 326
Whelan, Christopher T., 295
White, Jack E., 50, 540
White, James A., 203
White, Joseph B., 228
White, Ralph, 177
White, Richard D., Jr., 74
Whitt, J. Allen, 202, 204

Whorf, Benjamin, 47, 62
Whyte, Martin King, 477, 478, 498
Whyte, William H., 130
Wilder, L. Douglas, 366
Wilensky, Joe, 593
Wilford, John Noble, 625
Wilkening, David, 625
Wilgoren, Jodi, 376
Will, George F., 342, 583
William the Conqueror, 457
Williams, Christine L., 330, 661
Williams, Damian, 639
Williams, Michael, 208
Williams, Robin, 52
Willie, Charles V., 367
Wilson, Edward, 58
Wilson, James Q., 216
Wilson, John, 552
Wilson, William Julius, 83, 130, 367,
    482, 626
Winfrey, Oprah, 277
Winslow, Ron, 351, 587
Wirth, Louis, 346, 622
Wolf, Rosalie S., 400
Wolfensohn, James D., 683, 684
Wolfer, Loreen T., 523
Wolff, Michael, 17
Wolfgang, Marvin E., 218
Wolfson, Mark, 656
Wolinsky, Frederic D., 398
Wood, Scott Small, 324, 484
Woodgate, Graham, 686
Woods, Tiger, 343
Woodward, Kenneth L., 559
Worsley, Peter, 650
Wright, Erik, 285, 304
Wright, Lawrence, 343
Wrong, Dennis H., 94
Wurabuti (Tiwi), 381
Wyatt, Edward, 522

Yamaguchi, Kazuo, 636
Yat-ming Sin, Leo, 318
Yates, Jacquelyn, 203
Yellowbird, Michael, 484
Yinger, J. Milton, 353, 355, 358
Yinger, Nancy, 601
Yllo, Kersti, 497
Yoels, William C., 624
Young, Laurie E., 18
Yufe, Jack, 67

Zachary, G. Pascal, 272, 421
Zald, Mayer N., 649, 659
Zampa, Frederick P., 422
Zander, Alvin, 177
Zarakhovich, Yuri, 260
Zeilbauer, Paul, 373
Zellner, William W., 51, 110, 539
Zernike, Kate, 324, 514
Zerubavel, Eviatar, 47
Zeune, Gary D., 227
Zill, Nicholas, 494
Zuckerman, Laurence, 203
Zuger, Abigail, 576, 586
Zundel, Ernst, 353

Subject Index

AARP, 396–7
Abkhasians, 380–1
Abortions, 609, 610, 660–1
Abuse
  of children, 68–9, 496–7, 498, 501, 645
  of elderly, 400
  of spouses, 129, 130, 334, 496, 497–8
  of spouses (research design example), 131–3, 135–7, 139–43
Acculturation, 504
Achievement, 52, 134
Acid rain, 681
Acting crowds, 635–6
Activity theory, 390–1
Acupuncture, 590
Adaptation, 225
Adolescence, 91
Adulthood, 91–3, 95
Advertising
  and body image, 118–19
  and gender, 79, 118
  in the global village, 422
  impact of, 418
  marketing research, 145
  as propaganda, 654–5
  tobacco industry, 588
Affirmative action, 374–6
Africa. *See also specific countries*
  birth/death rates in, 606
  culture of, 37–8, 39
  ethnic conflicts in, 342, 670
  female circumcision in, 317
  slavery in, 247, 248
  starvation in, 603
African Americans. *See also* Race-
    ethnicity; Slavery
  accents and discrimination, 368
  civil rights movement, 365–6
  civil rights of, 649, 657
  and deprivation theory, 656–7
  economic status of, 364, 366, 367
  and education, 19, 32–3, 364, 365, 366–7, 519, 520
  families, 482–3, 492
  gains/losses of, 366–7
  and Harlem, 618
  and health care, 351
  and homicide, 367
  and housing, 350–1, 364, 368
  interracial marriage, 478
  and Islam, 545
  lynching of, 18, 633–4
  middle class, 366
  Million Man March, 649
  in political office, 366
  population statistics, 360, 366, 375
  race *vs.* class, 367

  and religion, 545, 553
  segregation, 32–3, 358
  in sociology, 18–20
  U.S. race relations, 18–20
  voting rights, 365
Age. *See also* Elderly
  at first marriage, 488–9
  life course socialization, 90–3, 95
  and prejudice, 349
  and religious affiliation, 553
Age cohort, 389
Ageism, 387
Agent provocateur, 658–9
Aggregate, 164
Aggression, 310, 313–14
Agricultural revolution, 159, 160, 161, 428
Agricultural societies, 160, 171, 187, 411, 413, 614
AIDS, 582–5
Al-Ghazaly Islamic School, 545
Aladdin, 645
Alcohol as a drug, 583–7
Alienation
  in bureaucracies, 194–5
  and city life, 621–3
  defined, 194
  humanizing the workplace, 202–4
  in the workplace, 194–5, 675
Alterative social movements, 650
Alternative energy, 682
Alzheimer disease, 399
Amazon, 684
American Dream, 418
American Journal of Sociology, 18
Amish, 110, 169, 539, 550
Anarchy, 454
Animals
  deprived, 69–70
  domestication of, 158, 159, 160
  extinction of, 681, 683, 684
  and language, 59–60, 63
Animism, 542
Anomie, 12, 164, 225
Anthropology, focus of, 5
Anti-Defamation League, 353
Anti-Malthusians, 600–2
Anti-Semitism, 543. *See also* Jews
Anticipatory socialization, 87–8
Antithesis and thesis, 671
Apartheid, 250, 358
Apology specialists, 43
Appearance
  beauty and culture, 41, 309
  fashions, 646–7
  impression management, 117
  and leadership, 178

  and mass media, 118–19
  and social interactions, 111
  and subcultures, 51
Applied sociology
  vs. basic sociology, 21–3, 33
  defined, 21–2
  marketing research, 145
Arabs, 37–8, 167, 425
Aryan Nations, 353
Asian Americans. *See also* Race-ethnicity;
    specific ethnic groups
  assimilation of, 371
  diversity among, 370
  education of, 365, 371, 519
  and families, 371, 483, 484
  in politics, 371
  relocation camps, 371
  statistics on, 360, 364, 370, 371
Assimilation, 201, 358, 371
Atlanta University, 17, 18
Attachments, 219
Australia, 379–80, 381, 672
Authoritarian leaders, 177, 178
Authoritarian personality, 352–3
Authority
  charismatic, 442–4, 464, 547–8
  collapse of, 441
  and conflict theory, 31
  defined, 31, 440, 464
  in the family, 471–2
  as ideal type, 444
  and legitimate violence, 441
  punishment and learning (Milgram experiments), 179–81
  rational-legal, 442, 444, 464
  and social movements, 652–3
  traditional, 442, 464
  transfer of, 444
Automobile industry, 288, 422, 674, 675, 682
Average, measuring, 135

Back stage, 115
Background assumptions, 120–2, 126, 214
Baha'is, 542
Band wagon, 655
Barbie dolls, 62, 423
Barter, 413
Basic demographic equation, 609
Basic needs, 105, 107
Battering. *See* Abuse
Beauty. *See* Appearance
Beverly Hills Supper Club, 642
Bias in research methods, 14, 137, 138
"Big Brother," 439–40
Bikers, 222, 556

Bioeconomic societies, 162–3, 412–13, 593
Biology and culture. *See* Nature *vs.* nurture
Birth order, 480–1
Birth rates, 16–17, 592, 599–601, 606
Births to unmarried women, 485, 491
Body. *See* Appearance
Body building, 51
Bolivia, 212
Boot camp, 89, 516
Borden Chemicals, 682
Born again experience, 539
Bosnia, 342, 670
Boston, 622–3
Bourgeoisie, 11, 30, 252, 284
Brajuha research, 148–9
Branch Davidians, 531, 550–2
Brazil, 211–12, 264–5, 684
Brown v. the Board of Education of Topeka, 33
Buddhism, 542, 546–7, 554
Budget surplus, myth of, 394–5
Buerger's disease, 588
Bullfighting, 41–2
Bureau of Alcohol, Tobacco, and Firearms (ATF), 531, 550–2
Bureaucracies, 185–209. *See also* Corporations
    characteristics of, 190–2
    and corporate culture, 200–1
    dysfunctions of, 194–5, 208
    in formal organizations, 189–90, 208
    and goal displacement, 195–6
    "ideal" *vs.* "real," 193–4
    McDonaldization of society, 193
    perpetuation of, 195–6
    sociological significance of, 196
    structure of universities, 191

Caesarian births, 16–17
Calvinism, 188–9, 541
Campaign funding, 453–4
Capital punishment, 234–5, 441, 639–41
Capitalism
    and Calvinism, 188–9, 541–2
    and class conflict, 11, 253
    corporate, 422
    and cultural leveling, 62
    defined, 188, 415, 436
    features of, 415–17
    free trade, 423
    globalization of (*See* Globalization of capitalism)
    ideology of, 418–19
    laissez-faire, 415
    and modernization, 667–9
    and Protestant ethic, 13–14, 188–9, 541–2, 667
    racial/ethnic strife, 354–5
    and rationality, 187–9, 208
    and religion, 8–9, 188–9, 541–2, 560
    in Russia, 260
    and socialism, 415, 418–21
    spirit of, 14
    and tradition, 187–9
    in the U.S., 415–16, 420–1
    welfare or state, 415–17, 418
"Capitalism, spirit of," 541
Capitalist, defined, 11, 284

Capitalist class
    characterized, 285–6
    controlling production, 252, 253
    exploitation of working class, 11, 253, 256, 675
    and new technology, 292
    power of, 230
    workers thinking of self as, 253
Card stacking, 655
Cargo cult, 650
Casey v. Planned Parenthood, 661
Caste system, 249–50, 477, 546
Category, defined, 164
Catholic Church. *See* Roman Catholic Church
Causation, 142
Census Bureau, U.S., 343
Centrist parties, 449
Challenger space shuttle, 665–6
Change. *See* Social change
Charisma, defined, 547–8
Charismatic authority, 442–4
Charismatic leaders, 442–4, 547
Charter schools, 526
Chechnya, 463
Checks and balances, 454
Child abuse. *See* Abuse
Child labor
    in history, 25, 90, 411
    in India, 411
    in poor families, 604
    slavery, 246
Child rearing
    and birth order, 480–1
    and day care, 83, 203–4, 480
    by married couples, 479–81
    by nannies, 480
    and race-ethnicity, 484
    serial fatherhood, 495
    by single mothers, 299, 479–80, 491
    and social class, 82, 290, 480
Childbirth. *See also* Population growth
    birth rates, 16–17, 592, 599–601, 606
    and marital status, 29, 299, 485, 491
    and medical system, 16–17, 571
    midwifery, 571
    and social class, 478–9
    and technology, 487
Children/Childhood
    Brazilian death squads, 264–5
    and divorce, 493–5
    as economic assets, 598, 604–5
    feral, 66
    gender socialization, 78–81, 95
    historical views of, 25, 90–1
    infanticide, 580, 609
    institutionalized, 68–9
    and the Internet, 293
    isolated, 65–6, 69
    in Least Industrialized Nations, 411, 604
    and life course socialization, 90–2
    and marital satisfaction, 478–9
    morality, 73–4, 94, 568
    and poverty, 83, 264–5, 296, 297, 299–300
    reasoning skills, 72–3, 94
    socialization of, 3, 28, 65–9, 71–5, 81–5, 94, 95

Children of the Night, 23
Chile, 425
China
    aging in, 388
    and arms sales, 458
    cultural leveling in, 62
    economy of, 419–20
    education in, 508
    female infanticide in, 609
    health care in, 592
    marriage, forced, 318
    population policy, 610
    religion in, 539, 542
    social change in, 668
    and technology, 164
    women in, 316, 318
"Chinatowns," 623
Chinese Americans, 360, 364, 370–1
Christian Motorcyclists Association (CMA), 556
Christian Solidarity International, 248
Christianity, 542, 543–4, 555, 650. *See also specific denominations*
Chromosomes: "XYY" theory, 216–17
Church, defined, 532, 549. *See also* Religion
Circular reaction, 635
Circumcision, 312, 317
Cities. *See also* Urbanization
    characteristics of residents, 623–5
    defined, 614
    development of, 614–18
    edge cites, 616
    fastest growing, 617
    and globalization of capitalism, 617
    life in, 615, 621–5
    patterns in U.S., 616–18
    revitalization of, 618, 628–9
    and social policy, 626–9
    suburbs, 626–7
    vs. suburbs, 626–7
    world's largest, 616
Citizenship, 445–7
City-states, 445
Civil Rights Act, 365, 366
Civil rights movement, 365, 366, 649, 657
Class, 243–73, 274–305. *See also* Social stratification
    and African Americans, 367–9
    and the automobile industry, 288
    capitalist (*See* Capitalist class)
    and childrearing, 82, 209, 480
    children and marital satisfaction, 478–9
    and city dwellers, 625
    conflict perspective on, 229–31, 240, 255–7, 455–6
    consequences of, 288–93
    and crime, 226–31, 292
    and criminal justice system, 124–5, 222, 229–30, 231–2, 292
    and death, 289
    defined, 101, 276, 304
    determinants of, 252–4, 272
    and divorce, 290
    and education, 259, 286, 291–2, 515, 518–19, 520
    elite (*See* Power elite)
    and emotions, 76

and families, 82, 286, 288, 290, 295, 478, 480, 482
functionalist perspective on, 254–5, 256
and health, 289–90
and legal system, 222, 230–1
macrosociological perspective on, 101
marginal working, 230
and marriage, 249, 250, 290, 470, 477, 478
Marx on, 11, 252–3, 256, 284–5
and mental health, 290, 573–4
merchant, 667
mobility, 294–5
and politics, 292
and poverty, 287–8, 293, 295–303
and power, 253–4, 280–1, 304
and prestige, 253–4, 281–3
and property, 253–4
and religion, 292, 552
and social mobility, 252
sociological models of, 284–8, 304
and teacher expectations, 520–1
and technology, 292–3
and wealth, 276–80, 304
working (See Working class)
Class conflict, defined, 11
Class consciousness, 252–3
Class system, defined, 251–2
Classless state, 671
Cliques, 169
Cloning, 163
Closed-ended questions, 137, 138
Coalition government, 449
Coalitions, 174
Coca-Cola, 416, 422, 644
Coca leaves, 212
Coercion, 440, 441
Cohabitation, 7, 8, 488, 489–90
Collective behavior, 633–48, 662. See also Social movements
acting crowd, 635–6
fads and fashions, 646–7
forms of, 638–48, 662
moral panics, 644–5
panics, 642–4
rationality of, 636–8, 662
riots, 638–41
rumors, 645–6
transformation of individuals, 634–6
urban legends, 647–8
Collective mind, 635
College. See also Education; Schools
bureaucracies, 185–6, 191, 195
and class, 518–19
and drug abuse, 586–8
graduation statistics, 506
optimizing the experience, 514
and pay gap, 324
and race-ethnicity, 349–50
in U.S., 506
Colonialism, 266–7, 270, 358
Colonialism, internal, 358
Colombia, 611–13
Columbine High School, 503–4
Comfort, material, as core value, 52
Commitments, 219
Common sense
defined, 7

and race, 344
and research, 130, 152
and sociology, 7–8
Communication. See also Internet; Mass media; New Technology
in bureaucracies, 191, 194
and cultural leveling, 61–2
electronic, 171–3, 676–9
emotions in e-mail, 46
gestures in, 43–4
and globalization, 4, 60
language, 44–9, 59–60
Communism, 11, 157, 259, 536
Communist Party, 259, 420
Communities. See also Urbanization
in cities, 621–5
electronic, 171–3
and environmental racism, 682–3
gated, 625
and religion, 539
and social integration, 11–13
Compartmentalization, 357
Competition, and education, 510
Computers. See Internet; New technology
Concentric zone model, 618–19
Concrete operational stage, 73, 94
Conflict perspective on
aging, 391–7, 406
authority, 31
class, 230, 240, 255–7, 455–6
class conflict, 11, 30
crime/deviance, 229–31, 240
defined, 30, 35
divorce, 24, 31
education, 85, 515–19, 528
energy shortage, 682
families, 473–5, 500
family size, 605
global capitalism, 423–8, 437
health care, 567–71, 577, 594
homelessness, 31–2
humanizing a work setting, 204, 209
marriage, 31
mass media, 106
population, 601, 605–6
power, 230, 256
power elite, 21, 230, 455–6
power of G7, 671
prejudice, 354–5
religion, 540, 560
ruling class, 455
social control, 229–31, 240
social institutions, 106–8
social stratification, 255–6
work, 204
Conflict theory, defined, 30
Conformity, 94, 179, 222, 225
Confucianism, 542, 547
Congress and lobbyists/PACs, 452–4
Conspicuous consumption, 411
Contradictory class locations, 285
Control groups, defined, 143
Control theory, 219–20
Convergence theory, 419
Cooperatives, 204
Coors Brewery, 201
Core nations, 267
Corporate capitalism, 422
Corporate culture, 200–1, 202–5, 209

Corporate welfare, 681–2
Corporations. See also Bureaucracies
boards of directors, 425–6
computer use, monitoring, 205, 678
criminal activity by, 228, 229
defined, 422
diversity in, 201
and family care, 491
functions of, 423
government handouts to, 682
income of CEOs, 279
in Japan, 206–7, 208, 209
ownership/management of, 422–3
pollution by, 682
women in management, 330
Corporations, multinational
defined, 423
and energy shortage, 681–2
and global domination, 271–2
and inequality, 433
power of, 271, 424, 425
and social stratification, 271–2
world's largest, 424
Correlation, 142
Correspondence principle, 518
Cosmology, 538
Cosmopolites, 623
Countercultures, 50–1, 63
Courtship, 476–8
Credential societies, 509
Credit cards, 414
Crime. See also Delinquents
and class, 226–8, 229–30, 292
conflict perspective on, 229–31, 240
corporate, 227, 228
defined, 212
functionalist view of, 224–9
and gangs, 155–6, 218, 222, 227, 260
and gender, 228–9
hate crimes, 235–6
illegitimate opportunity and, 226–9
relativity of, 235
street, 216–17, 226–7, 228
symbolic interactionist view of, 217–23
white collar, 227–8
Criminal justice system. See also Law
defined, 229
prisons, 88–9, 231–4, 333
reaction to deviance, 222
and social class, 124–5, 222, 229–30, 231–2, 292
"Three strikes," 232–3
women in, 334–5
Crowds. See Collective behavior
Crude birth rate, 606
Crude death rate, 606
Cubans, 362, 363, 364, 637
Cueva Indians, 684
Cults, 547–8
Cultural diffusion, 61–2, 63
Cultural diversity. See Diversity
Cultural evolution, 670
Cultural goals, 224, 225
Cultural lag, 60, 63, 672
Cultural leveling, 61–2, 63
Cultural relativism, 41–3, 62
Cultural transmission of values, 504, 509–10
Cultural universals, 57, 63

Culture, 37–63
  overview of, 39–40, 100
  beauty standards, 41, 309
  corporate, 200–1, 202–5, 209
  counterculture, 50–1, 63
  defined, 5, 39, 62
  and education, 504–6, 509–10
  and emotions, 76
  endangering people, 42–3
  and gestures, 43–4
  and global capitalism, 422, 433
  health/illness, defining, 564–5
  "ideal" vs. "real," 57, 62
  and immigrants, 84
  internalization of, 40
  and IQ testing, 516–17
  and language, 44–9, 62, 68, 84
  material, 39, 40, 60, 62
  and New Technology, 60–2
  nonmaterial, 39, 40, 60–1, 62
  and religious beliefs, 550–2, 558–9
  secularization of, 558–9
  subcultures, 50–1, 63, 218–19
  symbolic, 43–9
  and taken-for-granted orientations, 39–40
  and values, 49–57, 63, 504, 509–10
Culture of poverty, 270
Culture shock, 40
Culture wars, 56
Currency, 413, 462
Cybercommunication. See Internet; Telecommuting
Cyberslacking, 205
Cybersleuthing, 205, 678

Day care, 83, 203–4, 480, 644–5
Death. See also Suicide
  and AIDS, 582–3
  causes of, 572, 575
  and class, 289
  contemplating, 93
  crude death rate, 606
  in HMOs, 580
  mortality rates, 606
  sociology of, 402–4, 406
  stages of, 403
  and tobacco, 587–8
  from unsafe products, 228
Death penalty, 234, 441, 639–41
Death rates, 592, 601, 606
Debit cards, 414
Deferred gratification, 302
Degradation ceremonies, 88–9, 214–15
Dehumanization, 460–2
Deindustrialization, 574, 626
Delinquents
  and differential association, 218–19
  and power of labels, 222
  and social class, 124–5, 222, 237
  techniques of neutralization, 220–1
  and testosterone levels, 313–14
Democracy
  as core value, 54
  defined, 445
  direct, 445, 446
  in Europe, 449
  as form of government, 448–9
  representative, 445–6

Democratic leaders, 177, 178
Democratic party, 448–9, 452
Democratic socialism, 418
Demographic transition, 600
Demographic variables, 606–9, 630
Demography, defined, 598
Denominations, 550
Dependency ratio, 394
Dependency theory, 669
Dependent variables, 143
Depersonalization, 122–3, 575–6
Deposit receipts, 413
Deprivation theory, 656–7
Deprived animals, 69–70
Descent, system of, 470–1
Deviance, 211–41. See also Social control
  conflict perspective on, 229–31, 240
  as conformity, 222
  control theory of, 219–20
  crime and class, 226–9
  and criminal justice system, 229–31, 240
  defining, 212–13, 239
  and differential association, 217–19
  explanations of, 216–17
  and the family, 218
  and friends/neighborhoods, 218–19
  functionalist perspective on, 224–9
  functions of, 224
  humane approach to, 239
  labeling theory of, 220–3, 240
  medicalization of, 237–9
  and mental illness, 238–9
  and norms, 213–15
  pornography, 223
  reactions to, 231–9, 240
  relativity of, 212–13, 219, 223, 235
  in sexual behavior, 213
  and social change, 224
  sociological perspective on, 217–23
  strain theory of, 224–6
  and subcultures, 218–19
  symbolic interactionist perspective on, 217–23, 240
  types of (paths), 225
Dialectical process, 671
Dictatorship, 447–8
Differential association theory, 217–19
Diffusion
  of culture, 61–2, 63
  of ideas, 672
  of inventions, 672
Diffusion of responsibility, 176, 624–5
Digital divide, 293
Dinkas of Sudan, 248
Disabilities, 103, 511
Disabling environments, 288
Disasters, coping with, 7, 8
Discovery and social change, 672
Discrimination. See also Inequality; Race-ethnicity; Racism; Sexism
  African Americans and class, 367–8
  anti-Semitism, 543
  defined, 348, 376–7
  and gender, 314–16, 318–32
  in health care, 351
  in housing, 350–1, 359, 364, 368
  individual, 350–1
  institutional, 350–1

IQ testing, 516–17
  in lending policy, 350–1, 627
  and prejudice, 347–50
  and social groups, 166–7, 171
  and stereotypes, 355
  in the workplace, 430
Disengagement theory, 389–90
Disinvestment, 626
Disney film rumors, 646
Distance learning, 522, 677
Diversity. See also Race-ethnicity
  in the corporation, 201, 208
  loss of tribal peoples, 684
  in marriage, 469, 470–2
  marriage and family, 482–8, 500
  racial-ethnicity in U.S., 360, 608–9
  and rape, 215–16
  and religious groups, 553–4
  and social groups, 166–7, 169
  in U.S. families, 482–8
Divest, defined, 416
Divine right of kings, 257, 540
Division of labor, 108, 159, 160, 190, 310, 421
Divorce
  and blended families, 486
  children, effects on, 493–5, 501
  and cohabitation, 490
  conflict perspective on, 24
  and ex-spouses, 495
  and fatherhood, 495
  financial impact of, 495
  functionalist perspective on, 24, 28–30
  in industrialized nations, 493
  job satisfaction and violence, 134
  patterns of, 493, 494
  and remarriage, 491–6
  and social class, 290
  statistics on, 26, 490, 491–2, 500–1
  in Sweden, 472
  symbolic interactionist perspective on, 24, 25–7
Documents, 140–1
Dollar (U.S.), value of, 414
Domestication revolution, 158, 159–60
Dominant groups, 346, 356–9
Downsizing, 434
Downward social mobility, 294
Dramaturgy, 115–20
Drug use, 87, 219, 431, 586–8
Dumping (health care), 581
Dupont Circle, 97–8
Dyad, 173–4, 175
Dysfunctions, defined, 28

E-cash, 415
Early middle years, 92
Early older years, 92–3
Earnings. See Income
Earth First!, 685–6
Ecclesia, 549
Economic production, and the family, 604–5
Economic production and the family, 28, 30
Economic systems. See also Capitalism; Socialism
  bioeconomy, 162–3, 412–13, 593
  in China, 419–20

in Russia, 259–60
schools' hidden curriculum, 85
transformation of, 410–15
of the world, 415–21
Economics (field of), 5, 105
Economy, 409–37
bioeconomy, 162–3, 412–13, 593
and computers, 678
defined, 410
and environmental concerns, 56
and immigration, 609
of industrialized societies, 411, 413–14
and information age, 412
of Least Industrialized Nations, 270
mediums of exchange, 412–15
and population growth, 605–6
of postindustrial societies, 412–13, 414–15
of preindustrial societies, 410–11
and racism, 356
subsistence, 410
trends in, 433–6
underground, 430–1, 437
Ecosabotage, 685–6
Edge city, 616
Education, 503–29. See also College; Schools
of African Americans, 19, 32–3, 364, 365, 366–7, 519, 520
of Amish, 110, 169
of Asian Americans, 365, 371, 519
in China and U.S., 508
and class, 259, 286, 291–2, 515, 518–19, 520
and competition, 510
computers in, 293, 677
conflict perspective on, 515–19, 528
as core value, 54
correspondence principle, 518
costs/funding of, 513, 517, 677
credentials/diplomas, 509, 511
defined, 505
discrimination in, 516–17
in Egypt, 508–9
and family functions, 511–12
functionalist perspective on, 509–14, 528
functions of, 509–13, 515–16, 518
gatekeeping in, 511
gender inequality in, 17, 315–16, 322–5
gender pay gap, 327–9
in global perspective, 507–9
hidden curriculum, 85, 515–16
history of, 504–6
home schooling, 512–13
and individualism, 510
in Industrializing Nations, 508
and I.Q. testing, 516–17
in Japan, 507
of Latinos, 363, 364, 365, 519
in Least Industrialized Nations, 315, 508–9
level of, and prejudice, 353
McDonaldization of society, 193
in Most Industrialized Nations, 507, 508
and patriotism, 510
and poverty, 298, 517
problems and solutions, 522–8, 529

and race-ethnicity, 323, 365, 371, 518–19
in Russia, 508
segregation in, 32–3
as a social institution, 105
and social integration, 510–11
and social mobility, 287
and social placement, 511
and social stratification, 259
symbolic interactionist perspective on, 520–2, 529
teachers' expectations, 520–1
tracking in, 511
and transmission of values, 504, 509–10
in U.S., 505–7, 508
and voting patterns, 450, 451
Efficiency as core value, 52
Egalitarian societies, 159, 471
Ego, 75
Egypt, 508–9
Elderly, 379–407
abuse, 400
activity theory of, 390–1
changing sentiment about, 388, 393
conflict perspective on, 391–7, 406
costs of caring for, 381, 392, 393–5
defining "old," 385–7, 389
dependancy of, 397–402
disengagement theory, 389–90
Elder care, 491
functionalist perspective on, 389–91, 406
future of, 405
and gender, 397
global aspects of, 382–3
and health care, 393, 395–6, 397–400
and industrialization, 381, 388
isolation of, 397
and life expectancy, 380–1
in mass media, 388–9
Older years and socialization, 92–3
organizations working for, 396–7
perceptions of, 387–9
and poverty, 297, 298, 393, 400–2
social construction of, 380–1, 406
and Social Security, 381, 391–2, 393–5
and socialization, 92–3
statistics on, 382–5
suicide of, 404
symbolic interactionist perspective on, 385–9, 406
Elections, 365, 445–6, 448–9, 450–2, 453–4
Electronic church, 555–6
Electronic communication, 676–9. See also Internet
Electronic community, 171–3
"Electronic primary group," 173
Elephant analogy, 6
Elites. See Power elite
Emergent norms, 637–8
Emigrants, defined, 607
Emoticons, 46
Emotions, 75–8, 94
Empty nest, 481
Endogamy, 249, 470
Energy shortage, 681–2
England, 258–9
"English only" movement, 362, 363

Enterprise zone, 628
Environment, 680–8
and ecosabotage, 685–6
as emerging value, 56
and Industrializing Nations, 683, 688
and Least Industrialized Nations, 683, 688
and Most Industrialized Nations, 680–3, 688
sustainablity, 680
and technology, 682, 687
Environment, social, 66
Environment vs. heredity. See Nature vs. nurture
Environmental movement, 683–6, 688
Environmental racism, 682–3
Environmental sociology, 686–7, 688
Epidemiology, 572
Equality as core value, 54
Eskimos, 386, 505
Estate stratification system, 250–1
Ethics in research, 148–50, 589
Ethiopia, 243
Ethnic cleansing, 342, 358, 670
Ethnic villagers, 623
Ethnic work, defined, 347, 376
Ethnicity, defined, 345. See also Discrimination; Race-Ethnicity; Racism
Ethnocentrism, 40, 41, 62, 348, 684
Ethnologists, 44
Ethnomethodology, 120–2, 126
Europe, 449
Euthanasia, 578–80
Evangelism, 548, 553, 554
Evolution, cultural, 670
Exchange mobility, 294
Execution, 441
Exogamy, 470, 473
Experimental group, defined, 143
Experiments. See also Research
deprived animals (Harlow), 69–70
design of, 141–3
Hawthorne experiments, 144
on peer pressure (Asch), 178–9
"playing god," 589
on punishment and learning (Milgram), 179–81
on radiation, 589
on sexual attraction, 476–7
Tuskegee syphilis, 589
Exponential growth curve, 599
Expressive leaders, 177
Extinction of species, 681, 683, 684
Exxon Corporation, 682
Eye contact, 7, 8, 38

Face-saving behavior, 118
Fads and fashions, 646–7
False consciousness, 253
Falun Gong, 539
Families, 467–500
abuse in, 334, 496–8
African-American, 482–3
Asian-American, 371, 483
blended, 486
childless, 485–6
and class, 477, 478, 480, 482
common cultural themes, 470–1
conflict perspective on, 473–5

Families *(continued)*
 defined, 468, 469–70, 500
 and deviance, 218
 diversity of, 482–8, 500
 dysfunctions of, 473
 and economic production, 28, 30,
  604–5
 and education, 511–12
 extended, 470
 functionalist perspective on, 29–30,
  107, 472–3
 future of, 499–500
 gay and lesbian, 486, 488
 gender messages, 78–9
 global birthrates, 601, 603
 in global perspective, 472, 477, 493
 Latino, 483
 life cycle of, 476–81
 in Mexico, 597
 Native American, 483
 and new technology, 487
 nuclear, 470, 473
 one-parent, 485
 of orientation, 470
 as primary groups, 164–5
 of procreation, 470
 size of, 603–5, 630
 and social class, 82, 290, 294, 295
 as social institution, 105
 and socialization, 78–9, 81–2, 83, 295
 in Sweden, 472
 symbolic interactionist perspective on,
  25–7
 trends in, 488–91
 universality of, 472–3
 White American, 483
Famines, 602–3
Fashion, 646–7
Fatherhood, 495
Fecundity, 606
Federal Bureau of Investigation (FBI),
 531, 550–2, 658–9
Fee-for-service, 570
Female genital mutilation (FGM), 317
Feminism, rise of, 320–2
Feminist perspective on Freud, 75
Feminization of poverty, 298
Feral children, 66
Fertility, 606
Fertility rate, defined, 606
Fetal surgery, 589
Fiat money, 414
Fieldwork, 139–40
Finance, computers and, 678
Fire, and collective behavior, 642–3
First estate, 250
Fitness, as emerging value, 55
Florida, 48, 384, 637
Flu epidemic of 1918, 586
Folkways, 50, 63
Food production, 602–3
Football, as social structure, 101
Footbinding, 316
Ford Motor Company, 228, 288, 422
Formal operational stage, 73, 94
Formal organizations, 189–90, 208
Fossil fuels, 681
France, 442–3
Free trade, 268, 423

Freedom, as core value, 52, 55
French revolution, 9, 10
Front stages, 115
Functional analysis, defined, 27
Functional requisites, 107
Functionalist perspective on
 aging, 389–91, 406
 class, 254–5, 256
 crime, 226–9
 defined, 27, 35
 deviance, 224–9
 divorce, 24, 28–30
 education, 509–14, 528
 family, 28–30, 107
 family and marriage, 472–3, 500
 global capitalism, 421–3, 436
 homelessness, 31–2
 Horatio Alger myth, 303
 illness and health care, 566–7, 577, 594
 mass media, 106
 power of the state, 454–5, 456
 prejudice, 354
 religion, 533–7, 560
 social control, 224–9, 240
 social institutions, 106–7
 social stratification, 254–5, 256
Functions, defined, 27–8
Functions, latent, 28, 84, 509
Functions, manifest, 28, 84, 509
Fundamentalism, 544–5, 555, 650

G7 (Group of 7), 458, 463, 669–70, 671
Games, 72, 79–80
Gangs
 biker, 222, 556
 Crips initiation, 155–6
 functions of, 227
 mafia, 218–19, 260
 "trenchcoat" mafia, 503–4
Gated communities, 625
Gatekeeping, 511, 567
Gemeinschaft, 108–10, 604, 622, 666
Gender, 306–39
 and advertising, 79, 118
 and aging, 397
 and agricultural revolution, 160
 and AIDS, 584
 and biology, 309–14
 and body images, 118–19
 and crime, 228–9
 and criminal justice system, 334–5
 defined, 308
 and division of labor, 160
 education and, 17, 315–16, 322–5
 and emotions, 75–6
 in estate system, 251
 and eye contact, 7, 8, 114
 and health care discrimination, 322,
  577
 housework and, 7, 8, 473–5, 476
 and inequality, 160, 171, 251, 252,
  311, 314–18, 325–33, 540
 and infanticide, 609
 in mass media, 79–81, 118
 and morality, 74
 and pay gap, 7, 8, 316, 324, 326–30
 and peer groups, 81, 85
 and politics, 336–7
 and poverty, 298, 299, 400–1

 in research, 147–8, 295
 school violence, 525
 and sick role, 567
 socialization into, 78–81, 95
 and sports, 86
 and stereotypes, 78–81
 and stratification, 251, 252
 and teacher expectations, 521
 and touching, 114
 and video games, 79, 80
 and violence (*See under* Abuse;
  Violence)
 and voting patterns, 450, 452
 and work, 160, 310, 314–15, 429
Gender age, defined, 385–6, 389
Gender gap
 in pay, 7, 8, 316, 324, 326–30
 in politics, 452
Gender roles, 78–81
Gender socialization, 78–81
Gender stratification, 306–39
General Motors, 422
Generalizability, 140
Generalization, defined, 6
Generalized other, 71–2
Genes, and human behavior. *See* Nature
 vs. nurture
Genetic engineering and sports, 87
Genetic predispositions, 216–17
Genetic profiling, 593
Genocide
 in Bosnia, 342, 358
 defined, 342
 Holocaust, 167, 341–2, 345, 353
 and intergroup relations, 356–60
 Native Americas, 357
 by ordinary people, 357
 in Rwanda, 342
Genomics, 593
Gentrification, 616–17
Geopolitics, 669–70
Georgia Pacific Lumber, 685
Germany. *See also* Nazis
 "Aryan" birthrates, 610
 charismatic authority in, 443
 creating prejudice, 354
 elderly, caring for, 381
 Holocaust, 167, 341–2, 345, 353
 totalitarianism in, 447
 work week, 432
Gerontocracy, 386
Gesellschaft, 108–10, 666–7
Gestures, 43–4
Glass ceiling, 330
Glass escalator, 330
Glittering generality, 655
Global capitalism. *See* Globalization
 of capitalism
Global interconnections, 4
Global perspectives on
 aging, 382–3
 beauty, 41, 309
 capitalism (*See* Globalization of
  capitalism)
 child development, 74
 cities, 614–16
 corporations, 271–2, 423–5, 433
 education, 507–9
 environment, 680–6

ethnic conflicts, 342, 358, 670
gender inequality, 314–18
and "groupthink," 181–2
health care, 590–3
health/disease, 582–6
infectious disease, 586
love and courtship, 476–8
marriage and family, 472, 477, 493
McDonaldization of society, 62, 193
population growth, 598–602
power/geopolitics, 669–70
of social networking, 170
technology, 60–2
unmarried mothers, 491
Global stratification, 260–72. *See also*
    Social stratification
and development, 260–4
distribution of land, population and
    income, 261–6
and environment, 683
and families, 243–5
and health care, 567–9
in Industrializing Nations, 261–2,
    264–6
in Least Industrialized Nations, 261–3,
    265
maintenance of, 270
in Most Industrialized nations, 261–2
and multinational corporations, 271–2
and population growth, 601
resistance to, 653
and technology, 271–2, 669
theories of, 266–70
and women, 252, 255
Global village, 60–2, 412, 413, 422
Global warming, 681, 683
Globalization, defined, 33
Globalization of capitalism
and cities, 627
conflict perspective on, 423–8, 437
corporations (See Corporations, multi-
    national)
defined, 33, 267
and the environment, 680–3
functionalist perspective on, 421–3,
    436–7
future of, 433–6, 462–3
ownership of businesses, 422–3, 426–8
and power elites, 271, 425
and stratification of nations, 261–3
and war, 463
Goal displacement, 195–6
Gold standard, 413–14
Government. *See also* Politics
allocation of funds, 513, 517
checks and balances, 454
conflict perspective on, 455–6
corporate handouts, 682
defined, 441
divine right of kings, 257, 540
functionalist perspective on, 454–5
"groupthink" in, 181–2
iron law of oligarchy, 199
lobbyists, 452–3, 454
Political Action Committees (PACs),
    453–4
and the "power elite," 21, 281, 425
and religion, 534–5, 549, 554, 558
so-called surpluses, 394–5

and social movements, 658–9
Social Security, 381, 391–2, 393–5
types of, 445–8, 449
"tyranny of the majority," 446
Grade inflation, 523–4
Gray Panthers, 396
"Graying of America," 382–5, 406
Great Britain, 258–9
Greece, 246, 445
Greenbelts, 620
Greenhouse effect, 588, 681, 683
Gross domestic product (GDP), 414
Group dynamics, 172–82, 183
Group of seven (G7), 371, 669–70
Group size
diffusion of responsibility, 176
effects on attitudes and behaviors,
    175–6
in hunting and gathering societies,
    158–9
and relationships, 174
small, 172–3
and stability and intimacy, 174–5
Groups, 155–83. *See also* Collective
    behavior; Leaders; Leadership;
    Minority groups; Race-ethnicity;
    Societies
defined, 104, 156–7, 171, 182
electronic communities, 172–3
in experiments, 143
in- and out-groups, 166–8, 182
involuntary membership in, 104
primary, 164–5, 173, 182
reference, 168–9, 182
religious, 547–50, 552–6
secondary, 165–6, 182
and social institutions, 105
social networks, 169–71, 182–3
subcultures, 51–2, 218–19
voluntary associations, 104, 197–200,
    209
"Groupthink," 181–2, 183
Growth rate, defined, 609
Gynecological examinations, 122–3

Happiness, 291
Harlem, 618
Harlow experiments, 69–70
Harvard, 18
Hate crimes, 235–6
Hatred on the Internet, 353
Hawthorne experiments, 144
Hazardous waste sites, 681
Health care
conflict perspective on, 567–71
costs of, 573, 580–2, 592
discrimination in, 322, 351
for the elderly, 393, 395–6, 397–400
fraud in, 576
gender inequality in, 322
global perspective on, 590–3
global stratification of, 567–9
and new technology, 672–3, 679
rationing of, 581–2
as right or commodity, 573
and social class, 289–90
as a social institution, 105
Health care system
alternatives, 590–3

and childbirth, 16–17
in historical perspective, 569–71, 574
in Industrializing Nations, 591–2
in Least Industrialized Nations, 592
monopoly of, 569–71
in Most Industrialized Nations, 591,
    592
Health/illness. *See also* Health care; Men-
    tal health/illness
and alcohol, 586–7
components of, 566
conflict perspective, 567–71, 577, 594
and culture, 564
defined, 566
disabling environments, 588
and divorce, 493, 494
functional interactionist perspective,
    566–7, 577, 594
and gender, 567
global stratification, 568–9
historical patterns of, 572
infections, global, 586
and pollution, 680, 682, 683
smoking, 587–8
and social class, 289
symbolic interactionist perspective on,
    564–6, 577, 594
values and lifestyles, 590
Health insurance, 580–1
Health Maintenance Organizations
    (HMOs), 580
Heart disease, 322
Hemlock Society, 578
Herd mentality, 635
Heredity *vs.* environment. *See* Nature *vs.*
    nurture
Hidden curriculum, 85, 515–16
Hinduism, 532, 540, 542, 546, 554
History. *See also* Revolutions
and biography, 2–3
and capitalism, 671
child labor in, 25, 90
of cities, 614–17
dialectical process of, 671
of education, 504–6
of families, 25, 90–1
life course throughout, 90–3
Marx's model of change, 671
of medical care, 569–71
natural cycles of civilization, 671
and religion, 537, 558
of religions, 542–7
of slavery, 245, 247
social stratification, 245–7, 249–51,
    257
Hitler Youth, 67
Hmong, the, 216
HMOs, 580
Holland, 579, 580
Hollywood, 433
Holocaust, 167, 341–2, 345, 353. *See also*
    Genocide
Home ownership, 350–1, 364, 627
Home schooling, 512–13
Homelessness
author's experience with, 1–2, 97–8,
    275–6
levels of analysis, 31–2, 98–9
and mental illness, 238–9

Homelessness (continued)
  research on, 145–7
  shelters, 1–2, 146, 275–6
  silence of, 1–2, 15
  underclass, 287–8
Homicide. See Murder
Homogamy, 478
Homosexuals
  genetics vs. social factors, and
    exclusion, 58
  research on, 149
  same sex marriage, 469, 486, 488
Hopi Indians, 47
Horatio Alger myth, 302–3, 304
Hospices, 403–4
Household, defined, 469
Housework, 7, 8, 473–5, 476, 493, 494
Housing, segregation of, 349, 350–1, 359,
    364, 368
Hula Hoops, 646
Hull-House, 18
Human ecology, 618–19
Human nature, 66–70, 94
Humanitarianism, as core value, 52
Humanizing a work setting, defined, 202
Humphreys research, 149
Hunting and gathering societies, 158–9,
    410
Hutus, 342
Hypothesis, 132

Id, 74–5
Ideal type, defined, 193
Ideological commitment, 657–8
Ideology
  of capitalism, 418–19
  of the power elite, 257
  and slavery, 247
  and social stratification, 257–8
  of socialism, 418–19
  and work, 674–5
Ifaluk (of Micronesia), 76
Ik (of Uganda), 77
Illegitimate opportunity structures, 226–9
Illiteracy, functional, 524
Illness. See Health/illness
Immigrants
  Asian, 216, 360, 364, 370–1
  culture and illness, 565
  and culture in U.S., 84, 215–16
  and the economy, 431
  entrepreneurial, 451
  European, 360, 361
  language issues, 48, 362, 363
  Latino, 84, 360, 362–5
  origins of, 360, 362, 370, 451, 608
  as out-groups, 167–8
  politics of, 451
  prejudice against, 359, 370–1
  and religion, 533–4
  sojourners, 451
Immigration
  and cultural diversity, 374
  debate concerning, 374
  and minority status, 346
  and population growth, 606–9, 611
  and U.S. population, 360, 362, 371,
    375
Impersonality, 192

Impression management, 117, 119
In-groups, 166–8, 182
Incest, 57, 498
Incest taboo, 470, 473
Income. See also Wealth
  and appearance, 119
  of CEOs, 279
  defined, 276, 277
  distribution of, 261–3, 278–9, 431,
    432, 435–6
  and divorce, 493, 494
  and education, 256
  and gender, 7, 8, 316, 324
  and race-ethnicity, 364, 366, 367, 371
  and religious affiliation, 553
  and voting patterns, 450
Indentured service, 247
Independent variables, 143
India
  caste system in, 249–50
  child labor in, 411
  democracy in, 445
  female infanticide in, 609
  marriage in, 477
  mass hysteria, 644
  phone banks in, 412
  religion in, 546–7
Indigenous peoples. See also Native
    Americans
  destruction of, 684
  Dinkas of Sudan, 248
  Hmong, the, 216
  Hutus and Tutsis, 342
  Ifaluk, 76
  Ik, 77
  Kayapo Indians, 684
  medical knowledge of, 684
  Penan tribe, 684
  Pokot people of Kenya, 213
  poverty in Ethiopia, 243
  Shamans, 158, 565, 654
  Tiwi, 379–80, 381
  Yanomamö Indians, 3, 211–12
  Zapotec Indians, 213
Individualism
  and anomie, 12
  as core value, 52, 57
  and education, 510
  and extreme poverty, 77
Industrial Revolution
  and children/adolescents, 91
  and cities, 615, 630
  effects of, 8–9, 668–9
  and Protestant ethic, 667
  transformation of society, 158, 160–1,
    668
  and workers, 9, 161
Industrial society, defined, 161
Industrialization. See also Industrializing
    Nations; Least Industrialized
    Nations; Most Industrialized Nations
  and aging, 381, 388
  and capitalism/modernization, 667–9
  and childhood, 91, 264–5
  and development of sociology, 8–9
  and dying, 402–4
  and the economy, 411–15
  and education, 505–6
  effects of, 159–60, 432, 668–9

  and families, 28
  and inequality, 160, 411
  and population growth, 610
  in postindustrial societies, 105, 187
  and rationality, 186–9
  and urbanization, 621
Industrializing Nations
  distribution of land, income, popula-
    tion, 261–2
  education in, 315, 508
  environmental issues, 683, 688
  health care, 591–2
Inequality. See also Discrimination;
    Racism; Social stratification
  and abuse, 333–5
  in agricultural societies, 160
  in economic systems, 419, 433
  and education, 516–17, 518–19
  and gender, 160, 251, 252, 310, 311,
    314–18, 320–32, 672
  in health care, 322, 573–4
  in income distribution, 278–9
  and industrialization, 161, 411
  Internet's effects on, 679
  in marriage, 471
  and plant/animal domestication, 160
  in preindustrial societies, 410
  and religion, 540
  and social networks, 171
  in the U.S., 320–6
Infant mortality, 568, 592
Infanticide, 580, 609
Inflation, 414
Information
  and bioeconomic society, 163, 412–13
  and postindustrial society, 162
  and social stratification, 257–8
Information age, 412
"Information superhighway," 679. See
    also Internet
Inheritance, 250, 471
Innovators, 225
Institutionalized means, 224, 225
Instrumental leaders, 177
Instrumental relationships, 86
Intelligence, 68–9
Intergenerational conflict, 392
Intergenerational mobility, 294
Interlocking directorates, 425–6
International Telephone & Telegraph
    Company (ITT), 425
Internet
  and children, 293
  and cyberslacking, 205
  and digital divide, 293
  distance learning, 522, 677
  and education, 293, 677
  electronic communities, 172–3
  emoticons, 46
  hatred on, 353
  information control, 258
  intimacy, 173
  pornography on, 223
  religion on, 560
  and social inequality, 679
  urban legends, 647
  voting by, 446
Internet cafe, 45
Interviewer bias, 137

Interviews, defined, 137
Intimacy and groups, 173–5
Invasion-succession cycle, 620
Inventions. *See also* New Technology
  computers, 676–9
  defined, 671
  diffusion of, 672
  and four social revolutions, 160–1, 666
  plows, 160, 411, 666
  social, defined, 671–2
  and social change, 106, 411
  steam engines, 160–1
Involvements, 219
IQ testing, 516–17
Iron law of oligarchy, 199, 209
Iroquois Federation, 373
Islam, 109, 542, 544–5, 554
Isolation, 65–70, 397
Italy (mass hysteria), 644

Jains, 542
Japan
  body image in, 119
  corporations in, 206–7, 208, 209
  cultural leveling in, 62
  cultural of, 422
  education in, 507
  lobbying efforts of, 454
  prejudice in, 347–8
  and suicide, 7, 8
  teamwork in, 206
  victimization of women, 336
Japanese Americans, 370–1
Jews
  anti-Semitism, 543
  Ethiopians, 345
  as ethnic group, 345–6
  Holocaust, 167, 341–2, 345, 353
  Nazis creating prejudice against, 354
  religion, 542–3, 553, 554
  as targets of racism, 341–2
Jim Crow laws, 365
Judaism, 542–3

Kayapo Indians, 684
Kennedy Space Center, 665–6
Kentucky (fire panic), 642
Kenya, Pokot people of, 213
Kindergarten, 516
Klahanie, Washington, 625
Koran, 544
Kosovo, 670
Ku Klux Klan, 349, 355, 356, 659

Labeling
  and delinquents, 124-5, 222
  and deviance, 220–3, 240
  and education, 520–1
  and perception, 355
  and prejudice, 355
  and teacher expectations, 520–1
Labeling theory, 220–3, 240
Labor. *See* Work
Laissez-faire capitalism, 415
Laissez-faire leaders, 177, 178
Land, income and population distribution, 261–2
Language, 44–9
  and animals, 59–60, 63

and culture, 44–9, 62, 68
and day care, 83
defined, 44
and development, 68, 69
and discrimination, 48, 368
"English only" movement, 362, 363
functions of, 45–9
in online communications, 46
and perception, 47
racial-ethnic terminology, 47, 343,
  360–1
Spanish in U.S., 48, 84, 362
Latent dysfunctions, 28
Latent functions, 28, 84, 509
Later middle years, 92
Latinos. *See also* Race-ethnicity
  car culture, 54
  defined, 361
  diversity among, 362–3
  and education, 363, 364, 365, 519
  and the family, 483–4, 492
  heritage of, 362
  and housing, 359, 364
  income of, 364
  learning a new culture, 84
  in politics, 363
  and Spanish language, 48, 84, 362
  statistics on, 361–5, 375
Law. *See also* Crime; Criminal justice
  system
  conflict perspective on, 230–1
  and oppression, 230–1
  as social institution, 105
  unintended consequences of, 233
  unusual laws, 235
Leaders
  charismatic, 442–3, 464, 547–8
  controlling groups, 176–8, 356
  of social movements, 651
  transfer of authority, 444
  types of, 176–7, 183
Leadership, 176–8, 183, 198–200
Leadership styles, 177–8, 183
Least Industrialized Nations
  birthrates in, 601
  child labor in, 411, 604
  and debt, 270
  distribution of land, income, popula-
    tion, 261–3, 265, 271
  education in, 315, 508–9
  effect of manufacturing, 271
  elites of, 271
  environmental issues, 683, 688
  and global stratification, 261–3, 265
  health care in, 592
  and New Technology, 679
  population growth in, 603–6
  symbolic interactionist perspective on
    births in, 603–5
  urbanization, 611–13, 615, 621
Leisure, 55, 159, 431–2
Liaison Agency Network, 247
Life course, 90–2
Life expectancy
  of Abkhasians, 381–2
  by country, 567–8
  and pollution in Russia, 683
  in U.S., 382–5
Lion King, The, 645

Literacy, 315
Little Mermaid, The, 645
Living together, 7, 8, 488, 489–90
Living will, 578
Lobbyists, 452–3, 454
Looking-glass self, 70–1, 94
Los Angeles riots, 638–9
Louisiana, 682
Love
  in global perspective, 476–8
  and marriage, 25
  romantic, 54, 476
Lower middle class, 287
Loyalty, 156, 166, 221
Luddites, 673
Lynchings, 18, 633–4

Machismo, 484, 605
Macro-level analysis, defined, 31–2
Macropolitics, 440
Macrosociological perspective on
  culture, 100, 126
  vs. microsociology, 24, 98–9, 124–5
  social class, 101, 126
  social status, 101–3, 126
  social structure, 99–104, 125
Macrosociology, described, 98–9
Mafia
  and deviance, 218–19
  Russian, 260
  "trenchcoat," 503–4
Mainstreaming in education, 511
Malpractice, 574
Malthus theorem, 598–602, 630
Mandatory education laws, 506
Manifest functions, 28, 84, 509
Manner, 117
Maquiladoras, 267–9
March of Dimes, 195–6
Mardi Gras, 49
Marines, 89
Market, defined, 410
Market competition, 415
Market forces, 417
Market restraints, 416
Marriage, 468–78. *See also* Divorce;
  Families
  age at, 93, 488–9
  arranged, 477
  buying brides, 318
  and caste, 249, 250, 477
  changing meanings of, 25, 26
  childless, 485–6
  children, effect of, 478
  and class, 290, 470, 477, 478–9
  conflict perspective on, 473–5
  cultural themes, 469, 470–2, 477
  culture clash, 215–16
  defined, 470
  functionalist perspective on, 472–3
  future of, 499–500
  and incest, 57
  interracial, 349, 371, 478
  intimacy in, 25
  and life cycle, 476–82
  vs. living together, 7, 8
  love as core value, 25, 54
  monogamy and polygamy, 51
  postponing of, 488–9

Marriage (continued)
and rape, 215–16
same sex, 469, 486, 488
satisfaction in, 25
spouse abuse, 129, 130, 334, 496, 497–8
statistics, 488–91, 499
successful, 498–9
symbolic interactionist perspective on, 25–7, 93, 475–6, 499
and testosterone levels, 313
two-paycheck, 473, 474–5
and women in labor force, 429
"Marriage squeeze," 483
Martians, 542
Marxism, Marx on, 11
Mass hysteria, 644
Mass media. See also Advertising
and aging, 388–9
biased reporting, 655–6
and body images, 118–19
conflict perspective on, 106
control of, 106, 257–8
defined, 79
as emerging social institution, 105, 106
functionalist perspective on, 106
and gender messages, 79–81
and Native Americas, 53
and New technology, 60
and panics, 642, 645
and prejudice, 353
and public opinion, 654
and social movements, 655–6, 662
stereotypes in, 389
and violence against women, 336
Mass society, 656
Mass society theory, 656
Master status, 102–3, 213
Mate selection, 470. See also Marriage
Material comfort, as core value, 52
Material culture, 39, 40, 60, 62
Matriarchy, 311, 471
Matrilineal system of descent, 471
McDonaldization of society, 62, 193
McGill University, 18
Mean, defined, 135
Meaning and religion, 533
Means of production, 252–3, 256, 415
Mechanical solidarity, 108, 109, 126, 421
Media. See Mass media
Median, defined, 135
Medicaid, 396, 570
Medical care. See Health care
Medicalization of deviance, 237–9
Medicalization of society, 577
Medicare, 392, 396, 570
Medicine, 563–95. See also Health care system; Health/illness
accidents in, 312–13
authority "game," 578
conflict of interest, 576
defensive, 574, 594
defined, 564
depersonalization of, 575–6
genetic profiling, 593
incompetence in, 574–5
and indigenous peoples, 684
monopoly in, 570–1
preventive, 590

professionalization of, 569
sexism in, 322, 577
as a social institution, 105
socialized, 591
Medicine Tree, 685–6
Mediums of exchange, 412–15, 436
Megacity, 616
Megalopolis, defined, 615
Melanesian Islands, 650–1
Melting pot, 347
Men. See also Gender
dominance of, 311, 318–20
and emotions, 75–6
and Million Man March, 649
and sports, 76, 86
in women's occupations, 330
Mental health/illness
and culture, 565
and deviance, 237–8
historical perspective on, 572
and the homeless, 238–9, 563–4
of rapists, 150–1
and social class, 290, 573–4
Mental retardation, 68
Meritocracy, 255
Metropolis, defined, 615
Metropolitan Statistical Area (MSA), 616
Mexico
American products in, 422
factories in, 267–9
population growth, 597, 605
slavery in, 246
social stratification, 243
Mexico City, 683
Miami, Florida, 48, 637
Mickey Mouse, 62
Micro-level analysis, defined, 31–2
Micronesia, 76
Micropolitics, 440
Microsociological perspective on
background assumptions, 120–2
described, 99
vs. macrosociology, 24, 98–9, 124–5
presentation of self, 114–20
social construction of reality, 122–4, 126
symbolic interaction, 111–14, 126
Microsoft Corporation, 279
Middle class, 286–7
Middle years, 92
Midwifery, 571
Migration, 606–9
Military. See also War
as bureaucracy, 192
and resocialization, 89
sexual harassment, 332–3
as a social institution, 105
VFW as oligarchy, 198–200
Millenarian movements, 650
Milling (crowds), 636
Million-Man March, 649
Mind, as a social product, 72
Minimax strategy, 637
Minority groups. See also Race-ethnicity; specific minority groups
defined, 318, 346
digital divide, 293
distribution in U.S., 348
and dominant groups, 346, 356–9
emergence of, 346

shared characteristics of, 346–7
women as, 310, 311, 318–20
Mobility, social, 252, 294–5, 304
Mode, 135
Modernization, 541, 558, 667–9
Mommy track, 331
Monarchy, 445
Money
currency, 413, 462
digitized, 678
e-cash, 415
history of, 413–15
Monogamy, 51
Monopolies, 416, 570–1
Monotheism, 542
Moral community, 532
Moral holidays, 49–50
Moral issues and ideological committment, 657–8
Moral panics, 644–5
Morality, 73–4, 94, 216, 223, 462
Mores, 50, 62
Mormons, 51, 550, 554
Morocco, 37–8, 122
Mortality, defined, 606
Mortgages, 350–1, 627
Mosques, 545
Most Industrialized Nations
and dependency theory, 669
distribution of land, income, population, 261–2
education, 507, 508
and environmental problems, 680–3, 688
and global stratification, 261
health care, 591, 592
population growth in, 603
Movies, 53, 79
Multiculturalism, 358–9, 376
Multinational corporations. See Corporations, multinational
Multiple-Nuclei Model, 620
Murder. See also Genocide
and abuse, 129
of African Americans, 16, 18, 367, 634–5
and alienation in cities, 621–2
of Brazilian children, 264–5
of Cueva Indians, 684
and gangs, 155–6
infanticide, 580, 609
of Kitty Genovese, 622, 624
by Mafia members, 218–19, 260
rates in South Africa, 250
in schools, 503–4, 525
and women, 334
Muslims, 109, 542, 544–5, 554
Myths. See also Stereotypes
about Japanese corporations, 207–8
about poverty, 296, 302–3
about race, 342–5
of a budget surplus, 394–5
energy shortage, 681–2
and rape, 151
of school shootings, 525

NAFTA (North American Free Trade Association), 268
Name calling, 655
Nannies, 480

Nation of Islam, 545
National Association for the Advancement of Colored People (NAACP), 20
National Women's Party, 320
Nationalism, 462–3, 463
Native Americans. *See also* Race-ethnicity
    and casinos, 373
    democracy among, 445
    diversity among, 371–2
    and education, 365, 372, 373
    and the family, 483, 484
    genocide of, 357, 372
    as invisible minority, 372–4
    and marriage, 469
    and mass media, 53
    and "old age," 386
    and population transfer, 372
    and separatism, 373
    Sinkyone Indians, 685
    statistics on, 360, 364, 372–3
    treaties with, 372
Natural sciences, 4, 34
Natural selection, 58–9
Nature *vs.* nurture
    and deviance, 216–17
    gender and behavior, 309–14
    and human characteristics, 66, 67, 94
    social structure, 100
    sociobiology, 58–9
Nazis
    creating prejudice, 354
    Gestapo, 447
    Hitler Youth, 67
    Holocaust, 167, 341–2, 345, 353
    origins of, 648
Neighborhood, 82–3, 218–19
Neo-Nazis, 355, 356
Neocolonialism, 270
Net migration rate, 607
Networking, defined, 171
Networks, social, 169–71, 182–3
Neutralization, techniques of, 220–1
Nevada, 590
New Malthusians, 599–602
New Orleans, 49, 275
New Technology. *See also* Internet; Mass media; Technology
    and aging, 402–3
    and capitalism, 292
    and college registration, 185–6
    and communication, 60
    computers, effects of, 676–9
    and cyberslacking, 205
    and cybersleuthing, 205, 678
    defined, 60, 674
    and dying, 402–4, 578
    and education, 677
    and electronic communities, 171–3
    and health care, 573, 582
    and Least Industrialized Nations, 669, 679
    and mass media, 60
    and medical care, 672–3
    and politics, 446
    and reproduction, 487
    and social change, 674, 676–9
    and social class, 292–3
    and social inequality, 679
    and work, 204–5, 292–3, 433–6

New World Order, 462–4, 465
Nicotine, 587–8
Nike, 409, 421
Noncentrist parties, 449
Nonmaterial culture, 39, 40, 62
Nonverbal interaction, 31
Norm of noninvolvement, 624–5
Norms. *See also* Deviance
    and culture, 49–50, 57, 63
    defined, 49
    emergent, 637–8
    function of, 213–14
    and peer groups, 86
    and social institutions, 105
    in traditional *vs.* modern societies, 668
Nurses, 578
Nursing homes, 397–400

Objectivity, 14
Occupations. *See* Work
Ogburn's theory, 671–3
Older years, and socialization, 92–3
Oligarchy, 198–200, 209, 447–8
Oligopoly, 425
Open-ended questions, 137, 139
Operational definition, 132
"Opium of the people," 540
Organic solidarity, 108, 109, 126, 421
Organizations. *See* Bureaucracies; Groups
Orphanages, 68–9
Other, take the role of, 71, 94
Out-groups, 166–8, 182
Ozone shield, 588

Pacific Lumber Company, 685–6
Pacific Rim nations, 271
Pakistan, 246
Pan-Indianism, 373–4
Panics, 642–4
Papua New Guinea, 672
Parenthood. *See also* Child rearing
    changing meanings of, 26, 487
    status of, 604
Parris Island, South Carolina, 89
Participant observation, 139–40
Patriarchy, 311, 318–20, 471
Patrilineal system of descent, 471
Patriotism, 510
Patterns, defined, 6
Pay gap, 7, 8, 316, 324, 326–30
Peer groups, 81, 85–6, 524
Peer pressure (Asch experiment on), 178–9
Penan tribe, 684
Perception. *See also* Reality, social construction of
    and culture, 39, 122
    and labels, 355
    and language, 47
    selective, 355
Peripheral model, 620
Periphery, 267
Personal identity kit, 88
Personal space, 112–13
Personality, authoritarian, 352–3
Personality, development of, 74–5, 94
Personality disorders, 217
Peter principle, 195
Pietà, 538

Plain folks, 655
Plant cultivation, 158, 159, 160
Play, 71–2, 78–9
Plessy v. Ferguson, 365
Pluralism, 358–9, 376, 454–5
Pluralistic society, 52
Poland, 341–2
Police discretion, 237
Polio, 195–6
Political Action Committees (PACs), 453–4
Political parties
    Communist Party, 259, 420
    Democrats and Republicans, 448–9
    gender and race, 452
    green parties, 683–4
    third parties, 449
Political science, 5
Political system of U.S., 448–54, 464
Politics, 439–65. *See also* Government
    African Americans in, 366
    Asian Americans in, 371
    authority of the state, 440–4
    campaign funding, 453–4
    and education, 510–11
    environmental parties, 683–4
    and gender discrimination, 316, 336–7
    geopolitics, 669–70
    of immigrants, 451
    Latinos in, 363
    and multinational corporations, 424, 425
    and social class, 250–1, 284, 292
    as social institution, 105
    and war, 456–64
Pollution, 680–3
Polyandry, 469
Polygyny, 51, 469, 545
Polytheism, 542, 546
Population, 599–630
    conflict perspective on, 601, 605–6
    demographic variables affecting, 606–9
    elderly, percentage of, 382–5
    global perspective on, 598–602
    of Most Industrialized Nations, 261–2, 603
    race-ethnicity statistics, 348, 360–9, 375
    in research, 135, 136–7
    and starvation, 602–3
Population growth
    and balance of power, 606
    forecasting, 609–11
    and immigration, 606–9, 611
    and industrialization, 610
    in Least Industrialized Nations, 603–6
    and political instability, 605–6
    projection of, U.S., 610–11
    rates of, 599–602, 603, 605
    reasons for, 598–602, 610
Population momentum, 605
Population pyramids, 605
Population shrinkage, 601
Population transfer, 357–8
Pornography on the Internet, 223
Positivism, 9
Postindustrial (Information) societies, 105, 162, 412, 428, 674

Poverty, 295–303
    and age, 297, 298, 299
    author's experience with, 303
    births and marital status, 299
    characteristics of the poor, 287–8,
        296–301, 304
    and children, 83, 264, 296, 299–300,
        597, 630
    in cities, 611–13, 621, 622–3, 624
    culture of, 270, 300
    defined, 295–6
    deserving/undeserving, 301
    dynamics of, 300–1
    in early U.S., 29
    and education, 298, 517
    and the elderly, 393, 400–2
    and families, 482
    feminization of, 298
    geographical patterns of, 296, 297–8
    and health, 289–90, 303, 573–4
    illegitimate opportunity structures,
        226–7
    and industrialization of nations, 261–3,
        264–5
    myths about, 296, 301–2
    patterns of, 270
    and race-ethnicity, 296, 297, 298, 299,
        302, 364, 366, 367
    and social class, 287–8, 293, 295–302
    and social Darwinism, 10
    and social stratification, 264–5
    and socialization, 77
    and starvation, 602–3
    and welfare reform, 301–2
Poverty line, 296
Power. See also Leaders; Leadership
    and authority, 179–81, 440–4, 464
    and class, 230, 250–1, 253–4, 255–6,
        280–1
    conflict perspective on, 31, 230, 455–6,
        464, 671
    of corporations, 271–2
    defined, 281, 304, 440
    functionalist perspective on, 454
    geopolitics, 669–70
    of "groupthink," 181–2, 183
    male dominance, 311, 318–20
    Mill's model of, 21
    of peer pressure, 178–9
    and rape, 151
    and social stratification, 253–4, 257
    thesis and antithesis, 671
    transfer of, 444, 446
Power elite
    conflict perspective on, 455–6, 464
    defined, 21, 281, 464
    in government, 257, 281, 425
    and ideology, 257
    and multinational corporations, 271,
        425
    stratification, maintaining, 256, 257–8
Prayer, effectiveness of, 534–5
Predator (aircraft), 678–9
Prejudice. See also Racism; Segregation;
        Sexism
    ageism, 387
    defined, 348, 376
    and discrimination, 347–50
    extent of, 348–9

and the Internet, 353
and population transfer, 357–8
theories of, 352–6, 377
on U.S. campuses, 349
Preoperational stage, 73, 94
Prestige
    and class, 281–3
    defined, 281
    and occupations, 281–2, 315
    and social stratification, 253–4
Primary groups, 164–5, 173, 182
Prisoners. See also Criminal justice system
    rape of, 333
    resocialization of, 88–9
    in the U.S., 231–4
Proactive social movements, 648
Production
    means of, 252–3, 256, 415
    in nontraditional societies, 187
    in traditional societies, 187
Profane, defined, 532
Progress, as core value, 52
Proletariat, 11, 30, 252, 284
Propaganda, 654–6
Property. See also Wealth
    defined, 276
    and social stratification, 253–4
Proportional representation, 449
Prostitution, 23, 307–8
Protestant ethic, 13–14, 188–9, 411,
        541–2, 667
Protestant reformation, 543–4, 667
Protestantism, 11–12, 13–14
Psychoanalysis, 74–5
Psychologists, 216, 217
Psychology, focus of, 5
Public, defined, 652
Public opinion, 654–6
Punishment and learning (Milgram
        experiments), 179–81
Purple Berets, 653

Quakers, 549
Qualitative analysis, 133
Qualitative research methods, 144, 145
Quality circles, 202
Quantitative analysis, 133
Quantitative research methods, 144, 145
Questionnaires, 137–9
Questions, formulating for research,
        137–9
Quiet Revolution, 430

Race, 341–77. See also Discrimination;
        Diversity; Minority groups; Racism;
        Segregation
    biological classification, 344
    vs. class, 367
    defined, 342, 344
    vs. ethnicity, 345
    multiracial designations, 343, 344
    myths about, 342–5
    terminology of, 47, 343, 360–1
Race-ethnicity, 341–77. See also specific
        groups
    and aging, 384–5
    and AIDS, 584, 585
    and caste systems, 250
    and city dwellers, 623, 626

and digital divide, 293
dividing workers, 354–5
and divorce, 492
and education, 323, 518–19
and the family, 482–5
and global politics, 669–70
and hate crimes, 235–6
and home ownership, 364
identity construction, 347
immigration, U.S., 608
income, 364, 366, 367
and justice system, 232, 235
and marriage, 478, 492
population statistics, 348, 360–9, 361,
        375
and poverty, 296, 297, 298, 299, 302,
        364, 401
and religion, 545, 553
self-segregation, 350
and social groups, 167–8
and suicide, 7, 8, 13
and teacher expectations, 521
in U.S. population, 360–7
and voting patterns, 450–1, 452
well-being, comparative, 364
Race relations, 18–21
Racism. See also Discrimination;
        Genocide; Prejudice; Race-ethnicity
    civil rights movement, 365, 366, 649,
        657
    as core value, 54, 55
    defined, 348
    environmental, 682–3
    ethnic cleansing, 342, 358
    genocide, 342, 345, 347
    hatred on the Internet, 353
    Los Angeles riots, 638–9
    and lynching, 18, 633–4
    reasons for, 352–6
    relocation camps for Japanese
        Americans, 370–1
    and slavery, 247
    in syphilis experiment, 589
Racist Mind, The (Ezekiel), 356
Rain forests, 683, 684
Random sample, 136, 137
Rape
    culture clash, 215–16
    date, 333
    forcible, 333–4
    marital, 497–8
    in the military, 332
    myths about, 7, 8
    and social movements, 653–4
Rapists, 150–1
Rapport, 139
Rationality, 186–9, 636–8
Rationalization of society, 186–9, 208
Rave party, 220
Reactive social movements, 648
Reality, social construction of
    and aging, 380–1
    behavior as dependent upon, 122–4, 126
    defined, 122
    and germs, 122
    and gynecological examinations, 122–3
    and health, 564–7
    and medicalization of society, 571, 577
    multiple realities, 656

Reasoning skills, development of, 72–3, 94
Rebellion, 225
Recidivism rate, 233–4
Red tape, 194
Redemptive social movements, 650
Redlining, 626
Redwoods, 56, 685–6
Reference groups, 168–9, 182
Reform. *See also* Social change; Social
    movements
    vs. applied sociology, 22–3
    vs. research, 32–3
    role of sociology in, 9, 10, 20–1, 118
    of schools, 524, 526–8
    and voluntary associations, 198
Reform Party, 449
Reformation, Protestant, 543–4, 667
Reformative social movements, 650
Reincarnation, 546
Relative deprivation theory, 657
Reliability, 133
Religion, 531–61. *See also specific*
    religions
    as agent of socialization, 83
    Amish, 110
    and capitalism, 13–14, 188–9, 541–2,
      560
    charismatic leaders, 442–4
    in China, 539, 542
    and class, 292, 552
    conflict perspective on, 540, 560
    culture, conflicting with, 550–2
    and culture of poverty, 270
    defined/elements of, 532, 560
    dysfunctions of, 536–7, 540, 560
    evangelism, 548, 553, 554
    functional equivalents of, 536
    functionalist perspective on, 533–7,
      560
    functions of, 533–7, 539, 540, 560
    future of, 559–60, 561
    and gender, 540
    and government, 257, 534–5, 549, 554,
      558
    and hate crimes, 235–6
    India's caste system, 249–50
    and inequality, 540
    and the Internet, 560
    Islam, 109, 542, 544–5, 554
    and Million Man March, 649
    and persecution, 537
    personal belief in, 558–9
    and political power, 250–1
    prayer, effectiveness of, 534–5
    and printing presses, 172–3
    Protestant ethic, 13–14, 667
    and race-ethnicity, 553
    and science, 559
    secularization of, 557–8, 561
    and social change, 535–6
    and social class, 292
    as social institution, 105
    and suicide, 11–12
    symbolic interactionist perspective on,
      537–9, 560
    in U.S., 552–6
    world's largest, 542
Religion, civil, 535
Religion, state, 534, 549

Religiosity, as core value, 54
Religious experience, 539
Religious groups
    characteristics of, 548, 553–6
    diversity of, 553–4, 557
    member characteristics, 552–3
    membership statistics, 552, 553, 554,
      559
    types of, 547–52, 561
Remarriage, 495–6
Replication, defined, 14, 133
Reproduction, 29, 487
Republican Party, 448–9, 452
Research, 128–53. *See also* Experiments
    aggression and testosterone, 313–14
    analysis of results, 133, 138, 139
    causation and correlation, 142
    and common sense, 130, 152
    ethics in, 141, 148–50, 152
    gender in, 147–8
    on homelessness, 145–7
    levels of analysis, 98–9
    misunderstanding subjects, 138
    on rapists, 150–1
    vs. reform, 32–3
    tables summarizing, 134
    and theory, 150–1, 152
    and values, 14–15, 34
    women in, 295
Research methods
    defined, 132
    documents, study of, 140–1
    experiments, designing, 141–5, 152
    fieldwork, 139–40
    influencing findings, 133, 138, 144
    and misrepresentation, 149
    model (steps), 131–3
    protecting subjects, 148–9
    quantitative and qualitative, 133, 144,
      145
    question design, 137–9
    scientific method, 9
    secondary analysis, 140
    statistical analysis, 135
    surveys, 135–9
    unobtrusive measures, 141
Reserve labor force, 354
Resocialization, 88–9, 95
Resource mobilization, 659
Responsibility, diffusion of, 176, 624–5
Retirement, 390. *See also* Social Security
Retreatism, 225
Revolutions
    agricultural, 159, 160, 161
    bioeconomy, 158, 162–3
    and collapse of authority, 441
    defined, 441
    deprivation theory, 657
    domestication, 158, 159–60
    four social, 158, 159–64, 666
    French, 9, 10
    Industrial (*See* Industrial Revolution)
    information, 158, 163
    Thomas Jefferson on rebellion, 447
    and traditions, 9
Rights, 447. *See also* Civil rights
Riots, 638–41
Rising expectations, defined, 366
Ritualism, 225

Rituals, 538
Roe v. Wade, 661
Role conflict, 116
Role confusion, 115, 473
Role expectations, defined, 101
Role extension, 643
Role performance, 115–16
Role strain, 116
Role taking, 71–2
Roles, defined, 101, 103–4
Roles, in social institutions, 105
Roman Catholic Church
    and capitalism, 13–14
    charismatic leaders, 443–4
    member characteristics, 553, 554, 555
    as political power, 250, 257
    school system of, 524, 526
Romance, 54, 476
Romans, 246
Routinization of charisma, 444
Ruling class, 283. *See also* Power elite
Rumors, 645–6
Rural rebound, 628, 630
Rural-urban makeup of U.S., 617
Russia. *See also* Soviet Union (former)
    capitalism, 260
    crime in, 260
    economy of, 260, 419–20
    education in, 508
    and G7 industrial powers, 669–70
    health care in, 591–2
    and wars, 463
Rwanda, 342

Sacred, defined, 532
"Saints" and "Roughnecks," 124–5, 222
Same sex marriage, 469, 486, 488
Sample types, 135–7, 138
Sanctions, defined, 49
Sanctions, negative, 49, 63, 214
Sanctions, positive, 49, 63, 214
Sandwich generation, 491
Sapir-Whorf Hypothesis, 47, 62
SAT (Scholastic Assessment Test) scores,
    523
Saudi Arabia, 425
Scapegoats, 352, 354
Schools. *See also* College; Education
    as agent of socialization, 84–5
    Catholic schools, 524, 526
    charter schools, 526–7
    correspondence with society, 518
    and cultural lag, 60
    high school dropouts, 507
    segregation, 350, 365
    and social class, 286, 291–2, 515,
      518–19, 520
    violence in, 7, 8, 503–4, 524, 525
Science. *See also* Research
    and core values, 52
    defined, 4, 8, 34
    education and gender, 325
    goals of, 6–7
    and religion, 559
    as a social institution, 105
    social sciences compared, 4–6, 34
Scientific method, 9
Second estate, 250
"Second shift," 474–5

Secondary analysis, 140
Secondary groups, 165–6, 182
Sector model, 620
Sects, 548–9
Secular, defined, 556
Secularization of culture, 558–9, 561
Secularization of religion, 556—-558, 561
Segregation
  on campus, 350
  in education, 32–3, 247
  in housing, 349, 350–1, 359, 364, 368
  intergroup relations, 358
  self-segregation, 350
  in the South, 365
Selective perception, 355
Self
  defined, 70
  development of, 70–5, 94
  as object, 72
  presentation of, 115–20
  and primary groups, 165
  racial-ethnic groups, 47
  social control of, 77–8
  and socialization, 94
  as subject, 72
  as a symbol, 25
  work and self-concept, 88
Self-control, 219
Self-fulfilling prophecies, 200, 355,
  520–1, 650–1
Self-fulfilling stereotypes, 112
Self-fulfillment, as emerging value, 55
Semiperiphery, 267
Senate, U.S., 199, 452–4
Sensorimotor stage, 73, 94
September 11th, 119–20, 458–60, 644
Septuplets, 487
Service industries, 162
Sex, defined, vs. gender, 308
Sex, differences due to. See Gender
Sex change operation, 312–13
Sex typing, defined, 314
Sexism. See also Gender; Women
  in everyday life, 325–6
  infanticide, 609
  in medicine, 322, 577
  in sociology, 17, 34
  and work, 201, 326–33, 430
Sexual attraction, 476–8
Sexual behavior, 29, 57, 213
Sexual harassment, 331–3
Sexual orientation. See Homosexuals
Shamans, 158, 565, 654
Shaming, 214
Shell Oil Company, 682
Shintoists, 542
Sick role, 566–7
Sick Societies (Edgerton), 42–3
Sign vehicles, 117
Significant other, 71
Sing Sing Prison, 441
Single mothers, 199, 479–80, 491
Sinkyone Indians, 685
Slavery
  causes of, 160, 246
  conditions of, 246
  freeing slaves, 248
  history of, 245, 247
  ideology of, 247

internal colonialism, 358
  and religion, 540
  reparations for, 369
  in today's world, 248
Small group, defined, 172–3
Small world phenomenon, 169–70
Smoking, 587–8
Snake handling, 107
Social change, 665–88. See also Reform;
    Social movements
  Amish society, 110
  and automobiles, 674
  and computers, 676–9
  defined, 666
  and deviance, 224
  four social revolutions, 158, 159–64,
    666
  natural cycles of, 671
  processes of, 670–3
  and religion, 13–14, 535–6, 541–2, 667
  and technology, 671–9, 688
  theories of, 670–3, 687
  transforming society, 666–70, 674–9
  and value contradictions, 55
Social class. See Class
Social cohesion, 108–10
Social construction of reality. See Reality,
    social construction of
Social control, 211–41. See also Deviance
  conflict perspective on, 229–31, 240
  and crime, 240
  defined, 214
  functionalist perspective on, 224–9, 240
  and norms, 49–50, 88, 105, 214–15
  and pornography, 223
  reactions to deviance, 231–9
  and religion, functions of, 533
  and the self, 77–8
  symbolic interactionist perspective on,
    217–23, 240
Social Darwinism, 10
Social environment, 66
Social facts, 15–17
Social inequality, 81
Social institutions. See also specific
    institutions
  basic types, characterized, 105
  defined, 104, 125
  and social structure, 104–9
Social integration
  defined, 11
  and education, 510–11
  and suicide, 11–13
  and voting patterns, 451–2
Social interaction. See also Social
    Structure
  defined, 31, 99
  importance of for elderly, 399–400
  and microsociology, 99, 111–24
  roles, 71–2, 101, 103–5, 115–16
Social location, 2, 93, 100
Social mobility. See Mobility, social
Social movement organizations, 649
Social movements, 648–62. See also
    Revolutions
  and abortion, 660–1
  and authorities, 652–3
  defined, 648
  effective social change, 660

and the environment, 683–6
  organizations, 649
  reasons for joining, 656–9, 662
  and social change, 669
  stages of, 659–60
  tactics of, 651–4, 662
  types of, 648, 650–1
Social networks, 169–71, 182–3
Social order, defined, 214
Social placement, 511
Social promotion, 524
Social relationships and technology, 676,
  678
Social research. See Research
Social revolutions, 158, 159–61, 666
Social sciences, defined and compared,
  4–6, 34
Social Security, 381, 391–2, 393–5
Social setting, 117
Social solidarity, 108, 533
Social stratification, 243–73. See also
    Class; Inequality
  caste system, 249–50, 477, 546
  class system, 251–2, 257–8
  conflict perspective on, 255–6
  defined, 245
  and estate system, 250–1
  and gender, 251, 252
  global aspects of (See Global
    stratification)
  in Great Britain, 258–9, 273
  maintenance of, 257–8
  and New Technology, 258, 679
  and slavery, 245–8
  and social mobility, 252
  in South Africa, 250
  in Soviet Union, 259–60, 273
  systems of, 245–52, 272
  universality of, 254–7, 272
  and women, 252
Social structure, 97–127
  components of, 100–4
  defined, 99–100
  Gemeinshaft and Gesellshaft, 108–10,
    604, 622, 666–7
  groups (See Groups)
  macrosociology, 98–104
  microsociology, 99, 111–25
  social institutions, 104–10
  sociological significance of, 99–100
Social work, 18, 23
Socialism
  and capitalism, 415, 418–21, 436
  components of, 417–18
  democratic (welfare), 418
  ideology of, 418–19
  in Russia, 259
Socialization, 65–95
  agents of, 81–8, 95
  anticipatory, 87–8
  and biology, 309–14
  of children, 3, 28, 65–9, 71–5, 81–5,
    94, 95
  defined, 70
  and educational paths, 324
  and emotions, 75–8
  into gender, 78–81, 95
  and individuality, 89
  and peer groups, 85–6

and poverty, extreme, 77
resocialization, 88–9, 95
into the self, mind and emotions, 70–5
and social control, 77–8
through life course, 90–2, 95
Societies, 155–83. *See also* Groups
agricultural, 158, 160, 161, 187, 411, 413
bioeconomic, 162–3, 412–13
defined, 2, 157
horticultural, 158, 159–60, 410–11
hunting and gathering, 158–9, 410
industrial, 105, 187, 411, 413–14
and inequality, 160, 161, 410–11
modern, 666–7, 668
pastoral, 158, 159–60, 410–11
pluralistic, 52
postindustrial (information), 105, 162, 187, 412–13, 414–15, 428, 674
preindustrial, 410–11, 413
rationalization of, 186–9, 208
traditional, 187, 666–7, 668
transformation of, 182, 410–12, 428–33, 541–2 (*See also* Social change)
Sociobiology, 58–9. *See also* Nature *vs.* nurture
Sociological analysis
levels of, 98–9
and macrosociological perspective, 24, 98–104, 124–6, 126
and microsociological perspective, 24, 98–9, 111–25
Sociological perspective, defined, 2, 34
Sociological theory. *See* Conflict perspectives; Functionalist perspectives; Symbolic interactionist perspectives; Theories
Sociology
applied, 21–3, 34
basic/pure, 21, 32, 34
careers in, 22
and common sense, 7–8, 130, 152
defined, 4, 9, 34
environmental, 686–7
focus of, 6
in North America, 17–23, 34
origins/development of, 8–14, 17–21, 32–3, 34
purposes/uses of, 14–15, 32
sexism in, 17, 34
as a social science, 6
trends in, 32–3, 35
Solidarity
mechanical, 108, 109, 126, 421
organic, 108, 109, 126, 421
social, 108
Souls of Black Folks, The (Du Bois), 19
South Africa
apartheid in, 250, 358
genocide in, 357
social stratification in, 250
transfer of authority, 444
Soviet Union (former). *See also* Russia
aging in, 380–1
artists in, 157
economy of, 420
pollution in, 683
social stratification in, 259–60, 273

Space shuttle, 665–6
Spain, 189
Spanish language, 48, 362
Special-interest groups, 453
"Spirit of capitalism," 14
Spiritualists, 542
Split-labor market, 269
Sports
as agent of socialization, 86–7
and cultural relativism, 41–2
and emotions, 76
and gender, 86, 326
and genetic engineering, 87
and sense of community, 624
as social structure, 101
Spurious correlations, 142
St. Louis, Misouri, 615
Stability and groups, 173–5
Standard of living, 495, 605–6
Starvation, 602–3, 630
State, defined, 441, 463, 464
State capitalism, 415–17
Statistics, interpreting, 236–7, 240
Status
achieved, 102
ascribed, 102
defined, 101–2, 283, 304
master, 102–3, 213
Status consistency, 283, 304
Status inconsistency (discrepancy), 103, 283–4, 304
Status set, defined, 102
Status symbols, 102, 283
Stereotypes. *See also* Labeling; Myths
and aging, 387, 389
defined, 111
and discrimination, 355
empty nest, 481
in everyday life, 111–12
and gangs, 227
gender, 79–81
and genocide, 356–7
and mass media, 389
self-fulfilling, 112
symbolic interaction, 111–12
Stigma, 213
Stockholders, 202–3, 423
Stockholders revolt, 423
Stored value, 413
Strain theory, 224–6
Stratification. *See* Global stratification; Social stratification
Stratified random sample, 137
Street corner men, 97–9
Street crime, 216–17, 226–7, 228, 231–2
"Stroller effect," 82
Structural mobility, 294
Structured interview, 137
"Studied Nonobservance," 118
Subcultures, 50–1, 63, 218–19
Subjective meanings, defined, 15
Subsistence economy, 410
Suburban flight, 627
Suburbanization, 626
Suburbs, 626–7
Sudan, 247, 248
Suicide
adolescents, 404
and elderly, 404

in Japan *vs.* U.S., 7, 8
medically assisted, 578–80, 594
methods of committing, 13
and race-ethnicity, 7, 8, 13
and social integration, 11–13
Sun City, Arizona, 627
Superego, 75
Superiority, 166
Supreme Court, 661
Surveys, 135–9
"Survival of the fittest," 10
Survivalists, 51
Sustainable environment, 680
Sweden, 472, 591–2, 642
Symbolic, defined, 43
Symbolic culture, 43–8, 62
Symbolic interactionist perspective on
overview of, 24–7, 35
aging, 385–9, 406
births in Least Industrialized Nations, 603–5
city identity, 615
defined, 24, 35, 62
deviance, 217–23, 240
divorce, 24, 25–7
education, 520–2, 529
eye contact, 114
health and illness, 564–6, 577, 594
homelessness, 31
marriage and family, 25–7, 475–6, 499, 500
medicine, 564–6
personal space, 112–13
prejudice, 355, 356
religion, 537–9, 560
stereotypes, 111–12
touching, 114
Symbols
defined, 24
emotions in e-mail, 46
religious, 537–8
Synthesis, 671

Tables, reading, 134
Taboo, 50
Tact, 118
Tartars, 670
Tasmanians, 357
Taxes, 381, 431, 678, 682
Teacher expectations, 520–1
Teamwork, 117–18, 203, 206, 510
Tearooms, 149
Technological lifespace, 402
Technology. *See also* Industrialization; Inventions; New technology
and alienation, 675
bioeconomic societies, 162, 163
and communication, 60
and control, 204–5, 257–8
and core values, 52
and cultural leveling, 61–2
defined, 60, 674
electronic communities, 171–3
and the environment, 682, 687
genetic engineering, 87
and global domination, 669
global perspective on, 60–2
opposition to, 673
in postmodern society, 674

Technology (continued)
  and social change, 669, 671–9, 688
  and social stratification, 271–2
  and values, 675
  and war, 458, 460
Telecommuting, 432–3, 678
Telemedicine, 679
Television, 79. See also Mass media
Temporal priority, 142
Terminator 2, 674
Terrorism
  and "groupthink," 181
  and religion, 536–7
  types of, 458–61
  World Trade Center destruction,
    119–20, 458–60, 644
Testimonials, 655
Testosterone, 313–14
Theocracy, 544
Theories. See also Conflict perspectives;
    Functionalist perspectives; Symbolic
    interactionist perspectives
  of aging, 389–91
  of cultural evolution, 670
  defined, 23, 34
  main sociological perspectives, 23–4,
    31–2, 35
  and research, 150–1, 152
  on stratification, 252–6, 266–70
  testability of, 8
Thesis and antithesis, 671
Third estate, 251
Thomas theorem, 122
"Three strikes," 232–3
Tiwi, 379–80, 381
Total institutions, 88–9
Totalitarianism, 447–8
Touching and gender, 114
Townsend Plan, 391–2
Tracking, 511
Tradition and revolutions, 9
Traditional orientation, 186–9
Traditional societies, 187, 471, 666–7,
    668
Trail of Tears, 372
Transfer, 655
Transformative social movements, 650
Transnational social movements, 651
Trenchcoat Mafia, 503–4
Triad, 174, 175, 176
Tuberculosis (TB), 586, 646
Tunisia, 307–8
Tuskegee Syphilis Experiment, 589
Tutsis, 342
Twins, 67, 118, 312–13

Unabomber, 673
Underclass, 287–8
Underemployment, 419
Underground economy, 430–1, 437
Unemployment, 354
United Nations, 601, 606
Universal citizenship, 447
Universality, 84
Universals, cultural, 57, 63
University of California at Berkeley, 18
University of Chicago, 18
University of Kansas, 17
Unobtrusive measures, 141

Unstructured interview, 137
Upper middle class, 286–7
Upward social mobility, 294
Urban flight, 626–7
Urban legends, 647–8
Urban renewal, 618, 628
Urban revitalization, 628–9
Urbanization, 611–30. See also Cities
  defined, 615
  in Least Industrialized Nations,
    611–13, 615, 621
  models of growth, 618–21
  problems of, 626–9, 630
  rural-urban makeup of U.S., 617
  slums, 264–5, 611–13, 621, 622–3, 626
  solutions to problems, 628–9
Utah, 590

Validity, 132
Value clusters, 55
Value contradictions, 55
Value free, defined, 14
Values
  arising from society, 77
  as blinders, 57
  core, 51, 52, 54, 57, 63
  corporate, 200
  defined, 14, 49, 62
  and education, 54, 504, 509–10
  emerging, 55–6
  and health, 590
  and movies, 53
  overview of U.S., 52, 54, 55–6, 63
  producing deviance, 224–6
  and social institutions, 105
  and technology, 674–6
  transformation of, 675–6
  universal, 57
Variables, 132, 143
Verstehen, 15, 16–17, 34
Veterans of Foreign Wars (VFW), 198–9
Video games, 79–80
Vietnam, 461, 462
Vietnam veterans study, 313–14
Violence. See also Abuse; Murder; Street
    crime
  authority of states, 441
  in cities, 264–5, 624–5
  family (See Abuse)
  and gangs, 155–6, 218, 227
  and gender socialization, 81
  and husband's achievement, 134
  and mass media, 336
  in schools, 7, 8, 503–4, 524, 525
  against women, 129, 130, 316, 333–5,
    496, 497–8
  by women, 228–9
Voluntary associations, 104, 197–200,
    209
Voter apathy, 452
Voting, 445–6, 448–9, 450–2, 453–4
Voting rights, 365, 447
Voting Rights Act, 365

Walt Disney Company, 625
War, 456–62. See also Genocide
  and arms sales, 458, 463
  costs of, 457–8, 464–5
  defined, 456

  and dehumanization, 460–2
  ethnic conflicts, 669–70
  and new technology, 678–9
  reasons for, 457, 536–7
  universality of, 456
War of the Worlds, 642
Washington, D.C., 97–8
WASPs, defined, 361
Wealth. See also Income
  defined, 276–7, 304
  distribution of, 260–6, 261–4, 277–8
  and happiness, 291
  and lifestyle, 279–80, 285
  and the power elite, 253, 271
  and social class, 285–6
  and status, 102–3
Webster v. Reproductive Health Services,
    661
Weight, body, 118–19
Welfare, 7, 8, 296
Welfare, corporate, 681–2
Welfare capitalism, 415–17
Welfare reform, 301–2
Western Electric Company, 144
White-collar crime, 227–8
White ethnics, defined, 361
Whites. See also Race-ethnicity
  of European ancestry, 360, 361
  families, 483
  WASPs, defined, 361
  well-being compared to other groups,
    364
Widowhood, 481
Wilberforce University, 18
Witch hunts, 537
Women. See also Gender; Sexism
  and abortion, 660–1
  and biased medical treatment, 322, 577
  and birthrates, 486
  in China, 316, 318
  circumcision of, 317
  and crime, 228–9
  in criminal justice system, 334–5
  earnings of, 7, 8
  and estate system, 251
  and eye contact, 7, 8
  feminism, 320–2
  and gynecology, 122–4
  housing discrimination, 368
  image of in mass media, 80, 118–19
  in India, 477
  and inequality, 160, 251, 252, 310,
    311, 314–18, 318–20, 320–32, 672
  labor force participation, 327, 428–30
  in the military, 332–3
  and networking, 171
  in politics, 336–7
  and poverty, 296, 298, 299
  single mothers, 299, 479–80, 491
  and social mobility, 294–5
  in sociology, 17, 18
  violence against (See under Abuse;
    Violence)
Women's Christian Temperance Union,
    650
Women's movement, 320–2
Work
  conflict perspective on, 204
  as core value, 52

division of labor, 108, 159, 160, 190,
    310, 421
and gender, 160, 310, 314–15
humanizing, 202–5, 209
and leisure, 431–2
and pay gap, 7, 8, 316, 324, 326–30
and prestige, 281–2
sexism in, 201, 326–33, 430
technology and, 432–3, 434–6
in U.S. society, 428–33
and women, 160, 428–30
Workers
class conflict, 11, 253
and corporate culture, 200–1, 202–5,
    209
defined, 284
effects of technology on, 674–5, 677–8
exploitation of, 11, 253, 256, 675
and globalization, 268
income of, 431, 432, 435–6 (*See also*
    Pay gap)
and Industrial Revolution, 9, 161

Japan *vs.* U.S., 206–7, 208, 209
leisure time, 431–2
in Mexican factories, 268–9
oppression, by the law, 230–1
in postindustrial societies, 428–33
productivity study of, 144
racial/ethnic strife, 354–5
and social class, 252–3, 254–6, 286,
    287–8
and Spanish language, 48
unemployment, 354
Working class. *See also* Workers
defined, 230, 284–5, 287
marginal, 230
Marx on, 11, 252–3, 256, 284–5
and technology, 293
Working poor, 287
Workplace
alienation/isolation, 194–5, 675–6
and anticipatory socialization, 87–8
computers in, 204–5, 677–8
cyberslacking, 205

cybersleuthing, 205, 678
gender inequality, 326–33
and new technology, 293
racial-ethnic diversity, 201, 354–5
sexual harassment in, 331–3
society's values in, 77
World Bank, 683
World system theory, 267
World Trade Center destruction, 119–20,
    458–60, 644
World Trade Organization, 653

"XYY" theory, 216–17

Yanomamö Indians, 3, 211–12
Young adulthood, 91–2
Youthfulness, as emerging value, 55
Yugoslavia, 670

Zapotec Indians, 213
Zero population growth, 610

Credits